THE
ENCYCLOPEDIA
OF
TWENTIETH CENTURY WARFARE

THE
ENCYCLOPEDIA
OF
TWENTIETH CENTURY WARFARE

General Editor
DR NOBLE FRANKLAND

ORION
BOOKS

Copyright © 1989 Mitchell Beazley Publishers
First published in the United States of America by Crown
Publishers, 225 Park Avenue South, New York, N.Y.10003.

THE ENCYCLOPEDIA OF 20TH CENTURY WARFARE was
edited and designed by Mitchell Beazley International Limited,
Artists House, 14-15 Manette Street, London W1V 5LB

Although all reasonable care has been taken in the preparation of
this book, neither the publishers nor the contributors or editors
can accept any liability for any consequences arising from the use
thereof or from the information contained herein.

Typeset by Bookworm Typesetting, Manchester, England
Typeset in 9/10 point Century Schoolbook medium
Reproduction by J. Film Process, Singapore
Printed and bound by Graficas Estella, S.A., Navarra, Spain

Library of Congress Cataloging-in-Publication Data
The Encyclopedia of twentieth century warfare/general editor,
  Noble Frankland.
      p.   cm.
  Bibliography: p.
  ISBN 0-517-56770-9:
  1. Military art and science—History—20th century.   2.
Military history, Modern—20th century.   I. Frankland, Noble,
1922-xx.   II. Title: Encyclopedia of 20th century warfare.
  U42.E533   1989
  355′.009′04—dc19   89-2976
                                                       CIP

First American edition

ISBN 0-517-567709

Contributors

Contributors to the encyclopedia, together with the
initials used to identify them (where appropriate) are
listed below in alphabetical order by surname. All entries
of 100 words or more are signed.

John Allen, Senior Lecturer, Department of
Communication Studies, Royal Military Academy,
Sandhurst

SLB Suzanne L Bardgett, Special Assistant to the Deputy
Director General, Imperial War Museum

AB Antony Beevor, military historian

Matthew Bennett MA, Department of Communication
Studies, Royal Military Academy, Sandhurst

BB Professor Brian Bond MA, FRHistS, Professor of
Military History, Department of War Studies, King's
College, London

SB Stephen Brooks, Curator, D-Day Museum, Portsmouth

J M Bruce ISO, MA, FRAeS, FRHistS, Former Deputy
Director, Royal Air Force Museum, Hendon
Lindbergh Professor of Aerospace History 1983-84,
National Air and Space Museum, Smithsonian
Institution, Washington DC

DC Diana Condell, Imperial War Museum

CD Caroline Detnon

MF M R D Foot, former Professor of Modern History,
Manchester University

ANF Dr Noble Frankland CB, CBE, DFC, Official
Historian of the Strategic Air Offensive of World War II
and former Director of the Imperial War Museum

SKF Sarah K Frankland BA

EJG Eric J Grove, Associate Director of the Foundation
for International Security, Adderbury, Oxfordshire

MH Colonel Michael Hickey

RH Dr Richard Holmes, Senior Lecturer at the Royal
Military Academy, Sandhurst

WGFJ General Sir William Jackson GBE, KCB, MC,
Official Historian for the Mediterranean and Middle East
Campaigns of World War II

DJL David J Lyon MA, naval and maritime historian and
author, underwater archaeologist

CM Dr Callum MacDonald MA, DPhil, Senior Lecturer,
Department of History, University of Warwick, Coventry

Davina Miller, Senior Lecturer, Department of
International Affairs, Royal Military Academy,
Sandhurst; Consultant to Deakin University, Australia

RO'N Richard O'Neill, military historian, author of
Suicide Squads: Special Attack Weapons of World War II

BHR Dr Brian Holden Reid FRHistS, FRGS, Lecturer in
War Studies, King's College, London; Resident Historian,
Staff College, Camberley

CRS Charles R Shrader

PJS Peter J Simkins, Historian, Research and
Information Office, Imperial War Museum

MS Mark Seaman, Research and Information Office,
Imperial War Museum

Gary Sheffield, Royal Military Academy, Sandhurst

JTS Dr Jon Tetsuro Sumida, Associate Professor of
History, University of Maryland, USA

HT Professor Hugh Tinker, Professor Emeritus,
University of Lancaster

WST William S Turley, Professor of Political Science,
Southern Illinois University, USA

CJW Christopher J Ware, naval historian

Contents

The seven essays listed below are evenly distributed throughout the encyclopedia. A-Z entries are interspersed with the essays, beginning on p.22 and continuing through to p.459.

The encyclopedia is arranged alphabetically according to these rules:

1) The seven colour essays in the book follow their own logical and often chronological sequence rather than an alphabetical one (see Contents on preceding page).

2) Biographies are entered by surname, followed by final rank (where appropriate), then given name(s). The Victoria Cross is the only decoration cited in the entry title itself.

3) Entries with the same headword are listed in the order of people, places and things or chronologically.

4) Entries beginning with numerals are listed with the numeral spelt out and placed in the appropriate alphabetical position e.g. **Eighth Army, One Hundred and First Parachute Division.**

Cross-references These have been kept to a minimum; there are over 3,000 entries in the A-Z section of the encyclopedia and should the reader require further information on any given topic, it is probable that it can be found either as a headword in its own right or as part of a relevant entry. *See also* cross-references are used to identify entries that contain especially useful additional information. Prominent people are mentioned only by their surnames in some entries. In all such cases, separate biographical entries supply their full names, dates and ranks.

Major wars Important conflicts have, in addition to a main entry, many other entries giving details of individual battles, actions, theatres or phases of the war. World War II, for example, is covered in this way by 343 separate entries. A list of significant entries relating to each world war and to the wars in Korea and Vietnam can be found on p. 463.

Acronyms/abbreviations Acronyms and abbreviations which appear in SMALL CAPITALS within the text e.g. FULRO, SLBM are defined in the glossary on pp.460-461.

Codewords Only the most familiar e.g. "Overlord" are used. A list of these and their meanings can also be found in the glossary on pp.460-461.

Measurements Imperial measurements are given first, with the metric equivalent in parentheses. However, in some cases, especially weapon specifications (eg. 7.62mm rotary machine gun, or 12-pounder cannon), a conversion is clearly inappropriate. As the A-Z section is written by many different hands, there are variations between the bases of some measurements such as the tonnage of ships or the performance of aircraft.

Ranks A list of the abbreviations used for ranks is included in the glossary on pp.460-461.

Warfare in the twentieth century has been radically different in scale, method and consequence from anything known in previous periods; it has even changed more in this century by comparison with the last, than it had done in the nineteenth century by comparison with Roman times.

At the turn of the century, submarine navigation was beginning to be established and man had taken to the air in lighter-than-air vehicles; but the stage of development of the first, and the restrictive character of the second, meant that warfare was conducted virtually exclusively on the surface of the land or the sea. The air was no more than the medium through which missiles, fired from the surface, passed on their way between military and naval combatants. Civil populations, although they often suffered from the ravages of war, were not primary targets and most of them were beyond the confines of the battlefields. In relation to what was about to come, war was a very limited business.

Four explosive developments occurred early in the twentieth century which, in the manner of a chain reaction, have produced the terms of warfare with which the world is now confronted as the century approaches its end. The first of these is the participation in the aims of warfare of entire populations and not simply of governments and small elements of society. It was the people who pushed the governments, and not the governments who pushed the people, into war in August 1914. The advent of democracy and universal suffrage enlarged the scope and bitterness of war beyond measure. Second, as a by-product of this, and as a consequence of the improvement of communications and transport and the development of mass-production in the aftermath of the industrial revolution, it was possible to increase the numbers of men in the field from thousands to millions. Third, huge improvements in the range and rate of fire power, and especially the development of machine guns, which had shown their potential in the American Civil War, meant that such forces could be contained and, indeed, for much of World War I, limited to movements of thousands or even hundreds of yards, despite the introduction of tanks. Fourth, the conquest of the air and the development of powered flight in heavier-than-air machines, together with the development of efficient engines to drive submarines, opened up two new dimensions of warfare: the air and beneath the sea. With them, there also came the possibility of new forms of warfare, for aeroplanes, in addition to assisting armies and navies, might also strike directly and independently by strategic bombing at the sources of an enemy's war economy and even at the enemy people themselves. Submarines, in addition to their role in naval engagements, might attack merchant shipping and blockade an enemy, using means which were less expensive and more efficient than surface ships could achieve. All these developments showed themselves with a vengeance in World War I.

In World War II they were greatly elaborated and, although tanks and the auxiliary use of air power did much to restore the mobility of armies, a way around ordinary land battle was also pursued with great vigour, especially by the British and Americans in the form of strategic bombing and by the Germans in that of submarine blockade. Neither of these however, in themselves produced conclusive results. The rate at which the bombers could destroy proved to be slower than that at which the victims could repair and when more effective methods were sought, the casualties inflicted on the bombers proved prohibitive. A similar fate befell the submarines. The decisive influence upon World War II remained the clash between armies and navies, albeit with air assistance.

Nevertheless, as World War II neared its end, three further developments occurred which seemed to open up a viable way around the battles between armies and navies. The German V-2, foreshadowing the intercontinental ballistic missile, showed a vehicle of bombing against which there was no defence and which cost the lives of no aircrews. The American production of the first atomic bombs, portending a range of nuclear weapons of unimaginable power, showed a weapon against which no capacity for repair could avail. The relatively simple German *Schnorkel* device offered submarines a far greater survival prospect and operational efficiency.

The combination of these three developments has led to the armoury of the contemporary nuclear stalemate; but the cost in destruction, and the fact that the destruction would be mutual, has so far deterred the operational use of such weapons since the dropping of the two atomic bombs on Japan in 1945. War, as an extension of policy, or as a means of resolving international dispute, has therefore, since 1945, been by limited means and without the use of nuclear weapons. The superpowers have almost entirely avoided direct military confrontation with each other and have tested the issues in actions against surrogates or between them. At the same time by, so to speak, pricing themselves out of the war market, the larger powers have encountered greater difficulties in controlling wars of an old-fashioned kind between lesser powers, such as those between Arabs and Israelis or Indians and Pakistanis.

The subject of warfare in the twentieth century is extensive and complex and I have therefore thought it especially worthwhile to attempt the production of a means of access to its numerous components in a categorized A-to-Z form; I have also thought it essential to provide the user with a series of explanatory essays on some of the main elements of the subject. No two minds would ever be completely in accord on the matters of what should be included and excluded in a work of this character, but I have endeavoured to relate my own opinion to those of the many expert contributors whose wisdom has been woven into the fabric of this book. In thanking them all, I must especially acknowledge the valuable advice on the construction of the volume given to me by Professor Robert O'Neill, Chichele Professor of the History of War at the University of Oxford, the work of Mr Richard O'Neill in laying the foundations of the headword list, the crucial advice on the development of that list offered by Mr Peter Simkins, the Historian at the Imperial War Museum and the indispensable analytical surveys made by Sarah Frankland. Among all the distinguished and expert contributors, I must specially mention Professor William S Turley of Southern Illinois University at Carbondale and Dr Callum MacDonald of Warwick University who have, respectively, written the entire A-to-Z entries on Vietnam and Korea. I should also like to thank Mr Jack Bruce, formerly Deputy Director of the Royal Air Force Museum, who has contributed nearly all of the lucid descriptions of aircraft.

Noble Frankland

Prelude to modern warfare 1815–1914

Dr Hew Strachan
Fellow and Senior Tutor of Corpus Christi College, Cambridge

In 1815 peace was restored to Europe. At Vienna the great powers endeavoured to create a balance which would ensure stability and which, in the Concert of Europe, would provide a mechanism for resolving their disputes without resort to war. Their objectives, tempered by the realization that after the French Revolution and Napoleon little could ever be the same as before 1789, included a restoration of the old order. They aimed, too, to thwart the military adventurism which had characterized France under Napoleon.

Napoleon Bonaparte (1769–1821), whose brilliant victories provided the inspiration for subsequent commanders.

What the great powers created at Vienna remained intact until the revolutions of 1848 and continued to be a point of reference thereafter: even in July 1914 the British Foreign Secretary, Sir Edward Grey, could invoke the Concert of Europe in his bid to control the crisis that was to lead to the outbreak of World War I.

Napoleon, defeated at Waterloo, died in exile on St Helena in 1821. But in the field of warfare at least he remained the dominant figure of the 19th century, the ideal to which soldiers aspired. Rather than a tyrant who had exhausted Europe through continuous campaigning, he was seen as a general who had achieved victory in quick and decisive campaigns, breaking the shackles of supply and fortification and restoring mobility and man-oeuvre to warfare.

Nor was the fixation with the big battle confined to land operations. At sea, the fact that the Napoleonic Wars had continued for ten years after Trafalgar (1805), during which time maritime operations were characterized by blockade and economic warfare, tended to be forgotten. Nelson's two famous victories by manoeuvre, the Nile (1798) and Trafalgar, involved the effective destruction of an enemy fleet. The annihilation of the enemy's forces through a single major battle became the leading idea of both military and naval strategy.

For it was in the realm of ideas that the impact of the Napoleonic Wars proved innovatory. Before 1789, infantry soldiers fought with smoothbore muzzle-loading muskets of doubtful accuracy and sailors manned three-masted wooden battleships whose movements were subject to wind and tide. By 1815 little had changed: the technology with which Napoleon and Nelson fought their battles would have been recognizable 100 years previously. Nonetheless, the wars of the French Revolu-

Admiral Lord Nelson (1758–1805)

tion and of Napoleon were palpably different in duration and intensity from, say, the War of Spanish Succession. In endeavouring to understand why that was so, military theorists effectively founded modern strategic thought. The ideas which they propagated became the analytical framework within which the phenomenon of war could be comprehended. And what had underpinned the change in warfare was nothing less than a transformation in the power of the state. Revolutionary France had achieved the power (at least in theory) to mobilize all the nation's resources for the purpose of national defence. It was, therefore, in the areas of governmental power and of strategic thought that the influences of the Napoleonic Wars on 19th-century military developments were to be felt.

A nation in arms

In 1789 the National Assembly of France had asserted the obligation of a free citizen to undergo military service, and

in August 1793 France permanently requisitioned all French men and women, regardless of age, until her frontiers were secure. The principle of compulsory military service, the idea that citizens' rights included civic obligations, was thus firmly established. Therefore the corollary of the establishment of political rights in the 19th-century nation state was to be the potential to create mass armies. In practice this power remained under-exploited until after 1871. The French claimed, probably with exaggeration, that their army numbered 1,000,000 men in 1794, but under Napoleon, and even more after 1815, the principle of universality was forfeit to a preference for long-service soldiers, drawn from the less-privileged sectors of society. Conscription might operate in theory, but the better-off could purchase exemption by paying a substitute to serve instead. The relatively small armies required for the maintenance of internal order in the revolutions of 1848 displayed an ethos that was professional and socially distinct, and did not identify themselves with liberalism or with the popular forces of radicalism and socialism. Furthermore, operations in far-flung colonies also required long-service troops.

However, the nation in arms, the mass army of the French Revolution, was dormant, not extinct. The growth in the population of Europe in the 19th century – it more than doubled – provided the manpower. Military service created a means by which governments were able to educate and manipulate their burgeoning peoples. Truly universal service on these terms could militarize society as a whole, and thus remove the threat of domestic disorder. Moreover, as the weaknesses of the Concert of Europe became clearer, and inter-state rivalries within Europe reasserted themselves after 1848, the need to match the military strength of one's neighbours overshadowed domestic or colonial priorities. In two wars, in 1866 and 1870–71, Prussia successively crushed Austria and France and achieved the unification of Germany. A new European balance of power was created, and its agent was an army made up of short-service conscripts and large reserves. Between 1871 and 1914 the Prussian model became standard throughout Europe. States adopted conscription, with a two- or three-year period of regular service followed by a longer time in the reserves, and so created the mass armies and the potential to suffer sustained casualties over a long period which characterized World War I.

Karl von Clausewitz

The theorist who saw most clearly that the changed nature of war between 1792 and 1815 was due to the French Revolution and to the changes it had wrought in the relationship between the individual and the state was

9

Antoine-Henri Jomini (1779–1869).

Alfred Thayer Mahan (1840–1914).

a Prussian general, Karl von Clausewitz. Clausewitz's *On War*, published posthumously in 1832, is – for all its imperfections – the most important single statement ever written on its subject. *On War* constitutes, in part, an attempt by its author to come to terms with his own experiences in the Napoleonic Wars. By the standards of the 18th century, those wars were characterized by the loosening of economic constraints, by greater violence in the conduct of war itself, and by apparently limitless political ambition on the part of their leading figure. Clausewitz therefore posited an ideal – that of absolute war. War, he argued, could never be limited of itself: its nature is violent and battle will reach towards extremes. In practice, however, even the campaigns of Napoleon had not actually attained the total form implied in the concept of absolute war. Two types of limitation operated to restrain war's conduct. The first was the influence of politics. This, the formulation for which Clausewitz is now best remembered, was not a particularly original observation for a man born in an age when the field commander might well also be the head of state (as Frederick the Great and Napoleon had been). But Clausewitz, had he lived to complete his revision of *On War*, had intended to incorporate it at every level of his study. The violence in war, the pursuit of war for its own sake, might usurp the political ends of war. However, war ideally was no more than a means, and the political ends could limit the war and the level of mobilization required. The second restraining influence on war was the difficulty inherent in its conduct. Clausewitz called this "friction", and under this heading he included the difficulties of acquiring accurate intelligence, the problems of supply and communication,

and the fact that an army is composed of thousands of individuals, each with his own hopes and fears.

In a neo-Clausewitzian age, when nuclear weapons have given fresh urgency to the notion of absolute war, when political control is imperative, and when "friction" has been minimized by revolutionary technology, it is easy to exaggerate Clausewitz's influence. During the 19th century he was more often quoted than studied. And when Prussia's victories gave *On War* wider currency, soldiers read it for practical guidance in operational matters rather than for an enhanced understanding of the phenomenon of war itself. The internal debate present in *On War* was sacrificed to nostrums about the centrality of the decisive battle in a campaign and the advantage to morale of taking the offensive: many of its readers contended that war most readily attains the objects of policy by achieving the total defeat of the enemy. But Clausewitz also argued that an attack could pass "the culminating point of victory" – the stage at which it ran out of steam – and that the defence was the stronger form of warfare. However, late-19th-century soldiers bent Clausewitz into a shape that conformed with their idea of Napoleonic war, the strategy of annihilation.

Antoine-Henri Jomini

Far more immediately influential, and in many ways a better candidate for the title of the founder of modern strategy, was Antoine-Henri Jomini, a Swiss who had served on Ney's staff and whose writings were admired by Napoleon himself. Jomini's *Traité des grandes opérations militaires* began to appear in 1804, and his distilled wisdom was contained in the *Précis de l'art de la guerre*

(1838). Jomini's writings were didactic: his aim was to produce system, to reduce Napoleonic warfare to basic principles. In endeavouring to instruct rather than to comprehend, by ignoring the exceptional and so spurning the universal, Jomini set the standard for strategic manuals for the education of budding officers. Unlike Clausewitz, Jomini was read widely, and where he was not studied directly he was paraphrased and imitated. Despite his declared horror of the excesses of Napoleonic warfare, Jomini became the medium through which Napoleon's relevance to the 19th century was perceived.

The fundamental principle of war, according to Jomini, was to concentrate mass on the decisive point. To achieve this, the commander's crucial choices were his base of operations and his lines of communication. By retaining unity between his base and his lines, the commander ensured security and direction in his operations. His aim must be to cut the enemy's lines of communication. Jomini distinguished between operations on interior lines and those on exterior lines. By operating on interior lines, the commander kept his force intact and so could concentrate mass on the decisive point. Operations on exterior lines dispersed an army and so made it vulnerable to defeat in detail. Implicit in Jomini's theory was the preference for the small, long-service armies which were typical before 1871: a force on interior lines, kept concentrated to avoid defeat in detail, would have to be small so as to be supplied and fed. Helmuth von Moltke the elder, the Prussian Chief of Staff in 1866 and 1871, recognized that dispersion to allow more lines of communication, thus enabling the deployment of larger armies, was acceptable provided the armies concentrated on the battlefield. Indeed, such a strategy would enable the enemy to be enveloped by converging formations and was potentially more decisive than Jomini's operations on interior lines.

Mahan and naval strategy

Jomini's influence was not restricted to the strategy of land warfare. A T Mahan, the principal naval strategist of the 19th century, was the son of a Jominian exponent at the United States Military Academy, and aimed, through his analyses of naval history, to emulate Jomini in establishing the principles of naval strategy. Mahan's single most important work, *The influence of sea power upon history, 1660–1783* (1890) provided the theoretical underpinnings for the creation of great battle fleets in the two decades before 1914. Using the history of British naval supremacy in the 18th century and under Nelson, Mahan found the Jominian emphasis on lines of communication and the value of a central position, enabling operations on interior lines, peculiarly appropriate. By lying athwart the main sea lanes into Europe, dominating that continent's links with the rest of the world, Britain had been able to concentrate her naval forces while protecting a wide range of interests. Control of the seas was won through the destruction of the enemy fleet in battle. Therefore battleships, kept concentrated, were the heart of maritime supremacy. Ridding the seas of the enemy's fleet was the path to the domination of maritime commerce: raiding, or *guerre de course*, was weaker and more indecisive. Again, the emphasis on the destruction of the enemy's forces through a major battle was affirmed.

Theorists like Clausewitz, Jomini and Mahan could be influential because the Napoleonic Wars had established the foundations of a professional education for officers. In the 18th century most military academies' primary role was to train engineers and gunners in the technicalities of their specialisms, while the aristocracy's need to buttress its hold on the military profession fostered the growth of schools for the other arms. Early in the 19th century the modern military academies were established: Sandhurst in Britain, 1799; West Point in the United States, 1802; St Cyr in France, 1803. Those powers that did not act during the Napoleonic Wars did so soon afterwards.

Most of this education was imparted to young men before they were commissioned. There was also a growing need for a second, higher level of professional instruction. The creation of large field armies increased the reliance of commanders on staffs. In the 18th century the principal staff officers in most armies were an adjutant general (responsible for personnel and discipline) and a quartermaster general (responsible for the collection of intelligence, and the coordination and deployment of units on the march and on the battlefield). It was the functions of the quartermaster general's department which the expanded armies of the Napoleonic Wars enhanced. In many armies the department became a prototype general staff, responsible for the preparation of plans, with schools created to train officers for staff duties.

In Prussia, the evolution of the quartermaster general's department into a staff recruited by competitive examination, to function as a central planning body and to have a responsibility in operational commands, was not checked by the peace of 1815, as it was in some other countries. Between 1821 and 1825 the general staff was separated from the Prussian ministry of war: it was this distinct constitutional position which allowed the staff in Germany to develop a status independent of political control, culminating in 1883 with its chief being granted the right of direct access to the monarch. In particular, in 1866, Moltke the elder, appointed Chief of the General Staff in 1857, was given the power to communicate directly with field commander's; thus, on the outbreak of war, the general staff transformed itself from a planning body to a command headquarters.

Necessity, as well as battlefield success in 1866 and 1870, hallowed the status of the general staff. The speed with which those campaigns were conducted, the mobilization of reserves and the deployment of large field armies, created a demand for extensive planning in peace and for high technical competence in war. The existence of a general staff therefore demanded the formation of a staff college to produce suitably qualified officers. An additional and possibly even more important role of staff colleges was the formation of doctrine. In 1815 a commander could survey the battlefield: his communications with his subordinate commanders were direct and immediate. Orders might miscarry or be badly phrased (like Raglan's instructions to the Light Brigade at Balaclava) but the tactical as well as the strategic responsibility was that of the commander-in-chief. However, Raglan's command consisted of fewer than 20,000 men; Moltke in 1866 and 1870 had ten times that number. Without a field-portable wireless, he could not retain direct tactical control. Moltke's habit was to issue general directives, leaving flexibility and initiative to his subordinate formations. To prevent his army descending into a chaotic mass of divergent units, he relied on the establishment of a common body of strategic ideas through the war college. Staff officers so trained would act in conformity with each other, even when not in direct communication.

The emulation by other powers of the German general

staff after 1871 was often remarkably slow. Austria-Hungary, having been on the receiving end in 1866, proceeded quickly and reorganized its staff in 1871. But Britain and the United States, neither having a mass conscript army, did not establish a general staff until 1906 and 1903 respectively. In France the fear of a politically over-mighty army meant that – despite the lessons of 1870 – the development of the general staff was hampered: in 1914 the French army still had no clear body of doctrine. Nor were French doubts about the inherent political dangers of an independent and powerful general staff without foundation. Once established, such bureaucracies fostered their own growth. The German general staff in 1891 numbered 154 officers; by 1914 it had 650. Its size, range of responsibilities, its high level of competence, and role in the decisions for peace or war, meant that a body of immense political significance had been created. In Germany the staff's freedom from political control was clear; in other countries, the problem of political subordination had not been satisfactorily resolved.

The principal activity of the German general staff in the two decades before 1914 was its preparation of an operational plan for use in the event of European war: specifically between Germany and a Franco-Russian alliance. The plan's key features – its main author was Schlieffen, Chief of the General Staff 1891–1905 – were (apart from its political unreality, since its provisions included the infringement of Belgian neutrality) its emphasis on speedy mobilization and its bid for decisive victory by placing the German army across the French lines of communication, enveloping and destroying France's army in six weeks. The conception was Napoleonic: the strategy one of annihilation. War in 1914, as in 1815, was to be characterized by short campaigns culminating in a single, major battle. This, in crude terms, was the doctrine which the staff colleges of Europe disseminated. Generals in 1914 aspired to campaigns of manoeuvre leading to decisive battles – and at the Marne and at Tannenberg they achieved them on a scale that dwarfed even Napoleon.

Nor was the position appreciably different at sea. The goal of navies was fleet action. Mahan, despite writing more than 50 years later than Clausewitz and Jomini, had also looked to the Napoleonic Wars and earlier for the establishment of his principles of maritime supremacy. His posture was extraordinary. Clausewitz and Jomini wrote before technology had transformed land warfare, but, by 1890, wooden sailing vessels firing broadsides from smoothbore muzzle-loading guns were totally obsolete. In looking for general principles of unvarying application, strategic theorists and military academies had created a rigid doctrine which failed to acknowledge that technological innovation set the tactical foundations of war in constant movement.

The impact of industrialization

The motors of industrial and technological change in the 19th century were coal and iron. Heavy industry was sufficiently capital intensive to be reliant on state orders for its viability: military procurement in the shape of ironclad battleships and heavy artillery, and military demands for standardized, interchangeable, mass-produced parts were key factors in the pace and direction of industrialization. During the 19th century, Britain's maritime supremacy came to rest as much on its abundant supplies of coal of a quality ideal for maritime fuel and of

iron ore for ship construction as on its geographical position. Germany's military pre-eminence drew on a similar abundance of the appropriate natural resources. Coal and lignite production in Germany quintupled between 1815 and 1850, and multiplied 25 times between 1850 and 1913. The availability of cheap steel, and the possibility, through the Siemens-Martin process, of longer working to manufacture a more uniform product, transformed the characteristics and performance of artillery and armour plate.

The impact of industrialization on war at sea was more immediate and more rapid than in war on land. In the first place the new equipment employed iron in its construction and coal as its motive power: the application was therefore direct. Secondly, the pre-eminent industrial and commercial power in the mid-century, Britain, also saw itself as ruler of the seas. The introduction of new methods of ship construction and ship propulsion was in part stimulated by the merchant marine. But, their efficacy established, the Royal Navy sought the means to apply them to warships. Anglo-French naval rivalry in particular provided the context in which developments could then be rapid: by the early 1860s both powers possessed fleets of iron clad, steam-powered battleships. When, during the American Civil War, two ironclads met each other in combat for the first time in Hampton Roads on March 9 1862, the public awoke to a development long appreciated by the admiralties of Europe.

The first steam warship built by Robert Fulton for the United States in 1814–15, never saw action. The peace of 1815 and the contraction of naval estimates acted as brakes on further trials. Commercial steamships were propelled by paddles, vulnerable to gunfire, and the value of steam engines themselves seemed questionable, espe-

Germany's annual Kaiser manoeuvres (*below*) were more display than serious military training. Nonetheless, the Kaiser was the supreme commander of the army, and here at the manoeuvres of 1909, Wilhelm II (centre) is talking with the CGS, Moltke the younger.

Alexander von Kluck (*above*), who was to command the First Army on the right wing of the German advance in 1914, stands in his car on manoeuvres in 1910. The German army had no permanent peacetime establishment for automobiles, although they proved vital for the maintenance of communications in 1914.

***Monitor* versus *Merrimac*.** The aim of the Confederate navy in the American Civil War was to construct sufficient ironclads to break the blockade imposed by the Northern state. The *Merrimac*, a steam frigate scuttled in April 1861, was raised and converted into an

ironclad, shot-proof steam battery. On March 9 1862 *Merrimac* met *Monitor*, one of three Union ironclads designed for coast defence, in a four-hour clash at Hampton Roads. Although the two vessels actually touched neither sustained casualties nor any serious damage.

HMS *Warrior*. Until June 1858, the British Admiralty's response to ironclads remained conservative. Given the Royal Navy's existing superiority in wooden vessels, it seemed folly to pursue new and as yet unproven technology. But in May, news of France's order for *La Gloire* prompted a change of direction. British insecurity was heightened by increasing French bellicosity, which in its own turn was fostered by the discovery that an attempted assassination of Napoleon III had been plotted in England. Palmerston, who returned as Prime Minister in 1859, although a traditionalist in ship design, accepted the recommendation that at least two ironclads be ordered.

Propeller – bronze, two-bladed and weighing 10 tons. It could be lifted clear of the water manually to reduce drag when the ship was under sail only. The operation required the combined muscle power of some 600 men.

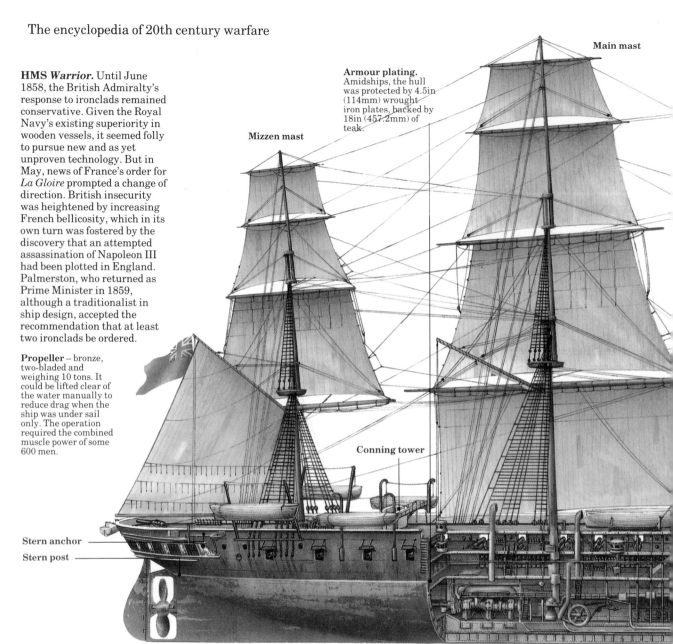

Mizzen mast

Armour plating. Amidships, the hull was protected by 4.5in (114mm) wrought iron plates, backed by 18in (457.2mm) of teak.

Main mast

Conning tower

Stern anchor

Stern post

Double

cially to a global power like Britain. For the range of steam ships was circumscribed by access to bases for fuel. Therefore, whereas Britain's merchant fleet had 680 steamers in 1839, the Royal Navy had only 29 in commission in 1840. The launching in 1842 of the *Great Britain*, a merchant vessel with screw propulsion rather than paddles, marked the possible application of steam to war. By 1845 the Royal Navy had 104 steam vessels. In 1850 the French launched the *Napoléon*, with an engine of 940 horsepower and a possible speed of 12 knots, inaugurating the application of steam specifically to battleships. Thirteen of the 19 British line-of-battle ships dispatched to the Baltic in the Crimean War in March 1854 were steamers. Coal remained the dominant means of ship propulsion until 1914: HMS *Queen Elizabeth*, completed in 1915, was the first battleship to burn oil.

The use of iron in warships had two distinct purposes: construction itself, and protection. It was the latter that prompted the initial development of the ironclad. In 1822 a French officer, Paixhans, argued that naval guns should be bored out to larger calibres so as to be able to fire shells

at flat trajectories. British trials in 1838 demonstrated that shell fire penetrated wooden vessels as effectively as solid shot – and then exploded within the ship, spreading fragments and threatening fire. In 1853 the shell guns of Russian ships shattered the Turkish fleet at Sinope. Thus was an action/reaction cycle established between armour and artillery. The French and British used ironclad floating batteries against Russian fortifications in the Black Sea, and after the Crimean War France suspended all construction of wooden vessels. The French ship, *La Gloire*, launched in 1859, was the world's first ironclad steam battleship, and the application of iron to construction as well as to armour was first achieved in a battleship in HMS *Warrior*, launched in 1861. Wooden ships were restricted in number by the supply of good timber and in size by the natural growth of the tree, and once built they needed constant maintenance. Iron ships were built in cellular, water-tight compartments and were therefore not only more resistant to shot but less vulnerable if their hulls were penetrated. Without iron construction, the carriage of heavier armour protection and the provision of

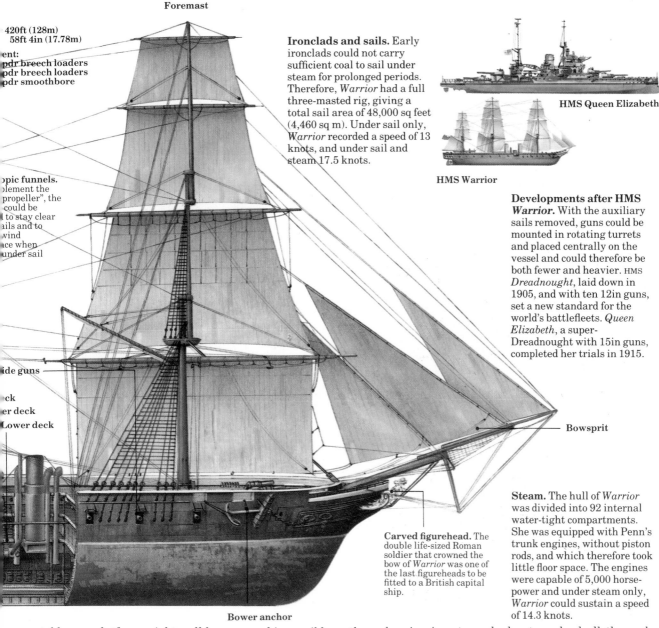

Foremast

420ft (128m)
58ft 4in (17.78m)

ent:
pdr breech loaders
pdr breech loaders
pdr smoothbore

Ironclads and sails. Early ironclads could not carry sufficient coal to sail under steam for prolonged periods. Therefore, *Warrior* had a full three-masted rig, giving a total sail area of 48,000 sq feet (4,460 sq m). Under sail only, *Warrior* recorded a speed of 13 knots, and under sail and steam 17.5 knots.

HMS Queen Elizabeth

HMS Warrior

opic funnels.
lement the
propeller", the
could be
to stay clear
ails and to
wind
ce when
under sail

Developments after HMS Warrior. With the auxiliary sails removed, guns could be mounted in rotating turrets and placed centrally on the vessel and could therefore be both fewer and heavier. HMS *Dreadnought*, laid down in 1905, and with ten 12in guns, set a new standard for the world's battlefleets. *Queen Elizabeth*, a super-Dreadnought with 15in guns, completed her trials in 1915.

ide guns

ck
er deck
Lower deck

Bowsprit

Carved figurehead. The double life-sized Roman soldier that crowned the bow of *Warrior* was one of the last figureheads to be fitted to a British capital ship.

Steam. The hull of *Warrior* was divided into 92 internal water-tight compartments. She was equipped with Penn's trunk engines, without piston rods, and which therefore took little floor space. The engines were capable of 5,000 horse-power and under steam only, *Warrior* could sustain a speed of 14.3 knots.

Bower anchor

a stable gun platform might well have proved impossible. HMS *Inflexible*, completed in 1881, had armour up to 24in (60cm) thick; thereafter the use of compound armour, rather than wrought iron, produced armour half as thick but just as strong. Iron construction, therefore, allowed the big ship to survive the challenge of improved artillery. Indeed the restraints on battleship size were removed: the displacement of *Warrior* was 9,210 tons, while that of HMS *Queen Elizabeth*, was 31,000 tons.

Another key difference between those two vessels lay in their armament. *Warrior* originally had 26 × 68-pounder guns, 10 × 110-pounder Armstrong guns and 4 × 70-pounder Armstrongs; *Queen Elizabeth* had 8 × 15in guns, ranging to 35,000yd (32,000m). The 68-pounder gun of the *Warrior* was the heaviest and longest-ranging of the old muzzle-loading, smoothbore ordnance. The presence of Armstrong guns illustrates the transitional stage of artillery technology: Armstrong's guns were loaded at the breech rather than the muzzle (obviating the need to run the gun in and out each time it was fired) and had rifled barrels, imparting greater accuracy to the projectile

through spin. Armstrong had not resolved all the problems of breech-loading and rifling: slow-burning powders to allow higher muzzle velocities and better steel to produce stronger guns and longer barrels were not widely available until the 1880s. By then, the removal of sail-rigging allowed the guns to be mounted in turrets, centrally placed rather than in broadsides, so they could be both fewer and heavier.

By 1914, therefore, technology had minimized many of the uncertainties that had confronted Nelson's navy. Steam had neutralized the role of the wind. The increased range at which naval battles were to be fought put less premium on the tactical handiness of the small vessel. And, since the cost – as well as the size – of individual ships was now so much greater, fleets in aggregate were smaller. They were therefore less able to mount a continuous close blockade of an enemy coast. For the navies of 1914, the role of blockade was to provoke an enemy into fleet action. Theoretically the big guns promised to make the outcome of that battle more predictable.

Hiram Maxim demonstrates his machine gun. Its mechanism was fully automatic once the first round was fired.

Improvements in firearms

The change in the technology of land warfare was more protracted, and – owing to the relatively greater frequency of land battles – the tactical impact more evolutionary than revolutionary. The application of the principles of rifling and breech-loading to small arms was technically less demanding than in the larger scales required by artillery. It therefore reached a perfected form earlier. In 1815 the rifle was a specialist arm: since it was muzzle-loaded and the bullet had to be rammed down against the grooves of the rifling, its rate of fire was much slower than in the smoothbore musket. The latter, designed for use at ranges of not more than 150yd (137m), emphasized rate of fire over accuracy, and dispatched a massive ball, say 0.70in (18mm) in calibre, to inflict ferocious wounds. Most European powers after 1815, in the search for an efficient rifle, were loath to forfeit the traditional virtues of the musket. By the mid-century they had in the main adopted a compromise developed by a Frenchman, Captain Minié. Minié placed a cup in the base of a conical bullet, so that when the rifle was fired, expansion forced the bullet into the grooves: the bullet could therefore fit more loosely when being loaded. The attractions of the Minié rifle and similar weapons were range – up to 1,000yd (914m) – and reliability. It saw extensive service between the Crimean War and the American Civil War. But, as early as 1840, the Prussians had adopted the Dreyse needle-gun, a breech-loading rifle. Breech-loading allowed the firer to lie prone and made for a faster-firing weapon. But not until the French Chassepot rifle of 1866 was a really reliable breech-loading mechanism devised – using a rubber seal to prevent the escape of gas at the breech. The adoption of metallic cartridges in the 1860s (thus simplifying loading), the development of smokeless powder (thus rendering observation on the battlefield easier, while keeping the rifle cleaner and the firer less exposed), and the appearance of magazine loading in the 1880s all brought the infantryman's rifle to a plateau of perfection whence it underwent few major changes until after 1945.

The armies of 1914 placed great emphasis on magazine rifle-fire. In so doing, they reflected their desire to fuse fire with movement. The rifle was the infantryman's integral weapon: by dispersing he could still move forward, gaining ground, and using his own fire support to effect a successful attack. But the major agents of fire power in 1914–18 proved to be not rifles but machine guns and artillery. The development in both these occurred later in the 19th century, and their tactical roles in 1914 remained both insufficiently developed and often ancillary – rather than integral – to the infantry attack: thus were fire and movement divorced.

Indeed for much of its life before 1914, the machine gun was seen as a form of artillery rather than as an infantry-support weapon. Both the Gatling gun used in the American Civil War and the *mitrailleuse* employed by the French in 1870 were multi-barrelled, heavy weapons. Hiram Maxim's machine gun, developed by 1885, was able to use a single barrel, since the force of the recoil operated the entire extraction, cocking and loading process, and was therefore lighter and fully automatic. But Maxims were still seen primarily as defensive weapons: no army had a clear doctrine regarding use in 1914, and not until a light machine gun was developed would this weapon help to reintegrate fire and movement in the infantry attack.

Artillery

The real change in the balance of combined-arm tactics, and the major challenge to the principles of fire and movement, came from artillery. By 1850 the difficulties of applying rifling and breech-loading to field guns suggested to some that the new arms of the infantry – which now rivalled smoothbore, muzzle-loading ordnance in range and accuracy – might confine artillery to the heavier roles of sieges and coastal defence. However, practicable rifled, breech-loading field guns began to appear in the 1850s, although smoothbores continued to be more reliable and were used in great numbers in the American Civil War. Not until the production of cheaper and better steel in the 1860s was rifled breech-loading artillery put on a firm footing. The Prussians, all but outgunned by the Austrian artillery in 1866, in 1870 brought their steel guns well forward, to prepare their attacks and to suppress the rifle fire of the French. In the 1890s field guns were fitted with a mechanism in which the barrel recoiled on a slide, so that the gun did not have to be relaid after each round. The most famous of the new generation of quick-firing artillery was the French 75mm. Such guns were deployed close to the infantry, giving direct support to the attack.

Selectively examined, military experience between 1850 and 1914 suggested that technological innovation was confirming the conclusions drawn from Napoleonic strategy. The wars of German unification in 1866 and 1870 were settled in matters of weeks and culminated in major decisive battles at Königgrätz and Sedan. On both occasions strategic envelopment, the concentration of forces operating on exterior lines on the battlefield itself, was the vital element in success. Despite Jominian

The French 75mm field gun (*above*) was introduced in 1897 and remained highly successful throughout World War I. Its unusual length was designed to obtain a high velocity and so enable the gun to fire on a flat trajectory, spreading shrapnel widely against dispersed infantry. Not until 1916 was it fully appreciated that the 75mm firing high explosive at long ranges and high angles could also destroy fixed positions. The range of the French 75mm in 1914 – it could fire shrapnel up to 7,300yd (6,700m) and high explosive up to 9,300yd (8,500m), against the German 77mm's 5,800yd (5,300m) and 8,750yd (8,000m) – was partially offset by the German superiority in field howitzers.

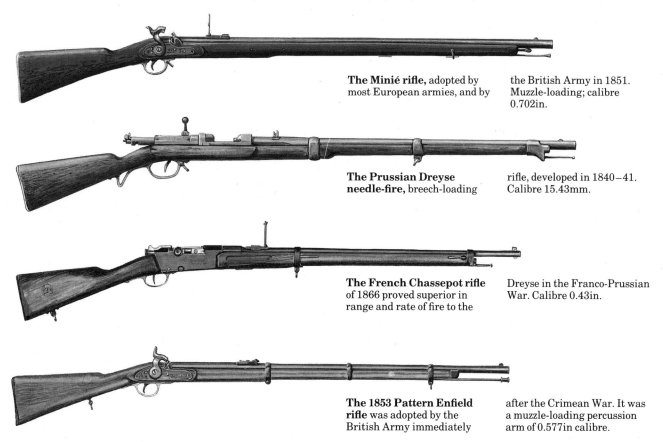

The Minié rifle, adopted by most European armies, and by the British Army in 1851. Muzzle-loading; calibre 0.702in.

The Prussian Dreyse needle-fire, breech-loading rifle, developed in 1840–41. Calibre 15.43mm.

The French Chassepot rifle of 1866 proved superior in range and rate of fire to the Dreyse in the Franco-Prussian War. Calibre 0.43in.

The 1853 Pattern Enfield rifle was adopted by the British Army immediately after the Crimean War. It was a muzzle-loading percussion arm of 0.577in calibre.

preferences for caution and therefore for interior lines, the idea of envelopment from the flank and rear coloured military thought before 1914. But Königgrätz and Sedan were also tactical successes for new technologies: the superior rate of fire of the Dreyse rifle in 1866 and the accuracy and mobility of Krupp field guns in 1870 gave the technical advantage to the Prussians.

Furthermore, most European military experience in this period was garnered not in Europe itself but in the colonial empires. Here the margin of technological superiority granted by industrialization was much more emphatic. Colonial armies were hampered in strategic terms by the problems of climate, terrain, supply and poor intelligence, but once a non-European opponent was committed to the battlefield, magazine rifle-fire and the machine gun usually guaranteed decisive successes. In Britain, France, Russia, Belgium and Italy, military theorists looked to Napoleon or to the Prussian victories for evidence that campaigns were short and decisive, and then confirmed that conclusion with their own experiences in Central Asia, North Africa or India.

With the benefit of hindsight, it is clear that the multiplication of fire power could as easily make for indecisiveness as for crushing victories. Eighteenth-century battles were fought at close range between armies in compact formations; casualties of up to 30 percent in a single day were not uncommon and ensured that battle was infrequent, intense when it occurred, and likely to be significant in its consequences. Increased ranges and rates of fire forced armies to disperse, to use ground and to dig in. The main feature of the Crimean War, although best remembered for epic battles in Napoleonic style, was the opposition of two armies in long trench lines over a period of some ten months. American Civil War generals might have tried to manoeuvre in Jominian fashion, but in the Atlanta campaign Sherman noticed the main characteristic of the 20th-century battlefield – its emptiness. The infantryman, firing his breech-loading rifle from a prone position behind cover, using smokeless powder, and in dispersed formation, was relatively invisible. As a consequence he suffered wounds at a lesser rate than his predecessors: a single day's fighting would not shatter an army as it had done in the age of the muzzle-loader. Furthermore, the dominance of defensive fire suppressed mobility, and above all curbed the traditional arm of decision, the heavy cavalry. The key problem for any soldier by 1900 was how to cross a fire-swept zone in order to come to grips with an entrenched opponent. To break up defensive positions, infantry became increasingly reliant on artillery preparation: in the Russo-Japanese War, howitzers firing high explosive suppressed machine-gun posts. But in doing so the functions of fire, provided by the artillery, and movement, still performed by the infantry, became divided. The cult of the offensive in the decades before World War I was above all an acknowledgment of the difficulty of this phase of battle in modern conditions; the emphasis on morale was an implicit recognition of the failure to find more certain solutions.

Naval actions

War at sea between evenly matched opponents might be equally hard to press to a conclusion. Big, heavily-armoured battleships were difficult to sink. In addition, the ranges at which battles could be fought by 1914, say 20,000yd (18,000m), rendered gunnery a complex art: ships, giving off smoke, using the light or the lack of it,

advancing by rushes—Japanese crossing a field towards
Port Arthur.   Copyright 1905 by Underwood & Underwood

The Battle of Tannenberg
(August 1914) (*left*). Tactically
the Russians learned a fair
amount from their experiences
in Manchuria – including the
value of defensive fire power,
here about to be exploited in
the early days of August 1914.
But the higher command's
operational control was poor.
Successes in Galicia against
the Austrians were offset by a
crushing defeat at German
hands at Tannenberg.

The siege of Port Arthur
(1905) (*above*). Japanese
infantry advance by rushes
two miles behind the line in
the fighting round Port Arthur
during the Russo-Japanese
War in 1905. However, the
tactical precepts of the war –
the use of ground, the dispersal
of infantry into small groups –
were much debated by
European observers and were
not fully confirmed until 1914.

**German reservists depart
for the front.** The Germans
hoped to defeat the French in
six weeks in 1914. Much to the
surprise of their enemies, they
therefore used their reservists
from the outset of the war. To
achieve the mobilization and
concentration of 3.8 million
men, the railways were vital.
In peacetime the German
general staff established close
links with the civilian railway
authorities, and on
mobilization all German
railways passed under
military control. The Belgians
– partly owing to the speed of
the Germans' advance – did
little to impede their progress
by the demolition of railways:
the French were more
thorough.

cruising at speed with their ranges constantly varying,
were hard to hit.

One reason why a clear margin of technological superiority might not in practice prove decisive was that such a margin might deter an opponent from tackling an evidently stronger power. In conception the Crimean War was in large part naval – its aim was to curb Russian seapower in the Black Sea and Mediterranean – but in execution it was largely military. So strong were the combined fleets of Britain and France in 1854 that the Russians did not put to sea to meet them. A more striking illustration of the operation of deterrence was the Anglo-German naval rivalry of the decades before 1914. From 1897, Alfred von Tirpitz set about the creation of a German fleet whose purpose was diplomatic: first, to gain Britain as an ally; then, the first objective having failed, to deter a British attack. The construction of ships at a steady rate of three a year became more important for Tirpitz than the operational efficiency of those ships or their crews. Furthermore the British response – with the construction of Dreadnoughts, battlecruisers and later super-Dreadnoughts – also aimed to deter. Admiral Fisher, the First Sea Lord, asserted that his object in accepting the German challenge was peace: by being ready for war and by stressing its awfulness he would frighten his putative enemy away. In the event, the deterrent effect of the Royal Navy's Grand Fleet operated within the war itself almost as effectively as its predecessor had in the Crimean War.

Deterrence, therefore, was one concept which needed to be more fully recognized in the body of European strategic thought in 1914. Far more significant in operational terms was the idea of attrition. Although the military image of the Napoleonic Wars was of short, decisive campaigns, in aggregate the wars were long and France was defeated because she was drained of her manpower and economically exhausted. Attrition, rather than annihilation, was a perfectly good way of explaining the Allies' eventual triumphs in 1813 and 1815 – and if attrition was appropriate for warfare before the industrialization of Europe, its relevance could only be enhanced thereafter. If tactical trends favoured stalemate on the battlefield, the levelling off of the pace of technological innovation in warfare, which had begun in some areas by the beginning of the 20th century, increased the likelihood of two comparably equipped armies or navies finding themselves evenly balanced and incapable of achieving a swift victory. Superior manpower and greater economic resources would then be decisive. The application of the nation in arms created large reserves of manpower, while the exploitation of economic resources was greatly aided by railways. Mass conscript armies, consuming shells and munitions at ever greater rates, depended on the direct link with their bases which railways provided. Railways meant that the entire nation could become the reserve and base of the army in the field. The army itself, swelled by the tapping of that industrial potential, was therefore tied in its movements to the railways and once removed from them became a beached whale, cut off from its natural environment and floundering under its own weight. Thus railways, which seemed to many before 1914 to be the agents of enhanced mobility, whose conquering of time and distance resulted in hair-trigger reactions to mobilization in 1914, were principal agents in creating a war of immobility to be settled by exhaustion. Their speed was more relevant in giving the enemy time to concentrate against a breakthrough than it was in creating the opportunity for exploitation.

Attrition was therefore a concept which would have repaid attention; another was Clausewitz's idea of "friction". The reliability of the railway, the premium it put on prior planning, encouraged a belief among general staffs before 1914 in the predictability of military operations. Staff preparations and improved technology both served to minimize the impact of "friction". But "friction" was not abolished – and the new conditions of warfare had created a fresh problem in which it was to play a major role. Mass armies, covering fronts of hundreds of miles and drawing on whole nations for their supply, compounded the problems of command and control. Generals became craftsmen, technicians and managers rather than leaders, and yet their own expectations of a commander still assumed that they could play a personal role at the tactical level. Indeed, in the small-scale colonial operations which formed their major military experience before 1914, they were often able to fulfil both roles – and probably a political one (as an imperial proconsul) as well. But in continental war, those who were now responsible for tactical leadership operated at lower levels of command, and at a higher level direct political control over operations was more immediate. The state of signals technology in 1914 enhanced the commander's links with his political masters but not with his tactical units. The subdivision of command required the general to listen to his subordinates' reports of front-line conditions. Only in the navy, whose ships were able to carry the bulky wireless sets of the day, could command be centralized and direct, and this aspect of "friction" thereby minimized.

Doctrine versus technology
A prime consequence of this distancing from the battlefield was a slowness to integrate new technology and its impact on tactics into operational thought. Generals schooled in Napoleonic strategies, seeking victory by manoeuvre and envelopment, were denied the direct experience of the new tactical conditions which industrialized warfare created. New weapons systems suffered one of two fates. If possible they were treated as supplements to existing patterns of warfare. Thus, the aeroplane was appreciated for its contribution to reconnaissance – an already acknowledged operational role, traditionally performed by cavalry – but was not seen as a new weapon in its own right, with its own distinctive capabilities. Tactics were not rethought from the bottom up, and weapons that did not accord with prevailing thinking, or threatened to overthrow it, suffered the second fate – simple neglect. The debates about the continuing role of cavalry on the battlefield and the relatively small distribution of machine guns illustrate the intensity of feeling which might be aroused when new technology refused to undergo this second fate, and yet at the same time would not be pressed into conformity with existing doctrine. The cases, in land warfare, of heavy artillery and, at sea, of the submarine, are noteworthy precisely because so little was said about them in the decade before 1914, and yet in their respective mediums each, arguably, became the dominant weapon of World War I.

If modern fire power enhanced the defence and encouraged the erection of field fortifications, it followed that heavier artillery firing high explosive would be required to destroy an enemy's position if an offensive was to be successful. But in 1914 the number of howitzers capable of high-angle, indirect fire in an infantry division ranged

from a high of 18 (the British) to none (the French, who were trying to decide what calibre to adopt). Munition supplies – which in any case proved inadequate to meet the demands of 1914–15 – were dominated by shrapnel. Shrapnel burst in the air, scattering fragments designed to hit dispersed enemy infantry; it was not intended to break up entrenched positions. No power had adequate supplies of heavy artillery, although in 1914–18 large-calibre guns, previously thought appropriate only for sieges, would be used in battle itself. The purpose of artillery on the battlefield was to support the infantry: it was not, in 1914, seen as a major independent arm, with its own tactics, whose contribution would be a predominant one and therefore should form a central feature of operational planning.

Submarines
Experimental submarines predated the 19th century, but there were institutional biases against their development. The major naval powers had made a considerable investment in capital surface ships, and the shift to ironclad steamers increased the cost per ship. Further, a big-battleship navy confirmed the existing command structure: admirals wanted to hoist their flags in a surface fleet. A submarine, firing a torpedo and operating independently under the command of a junior officer, was therefore doubly destructive of existing naval hierarchies. In 1863 the French completed a practicable submarine, *Le Plongeur*, and by 1906 they had the largest submarine fleet in the world. Their lead was established precisely because they were a second-rank naval power; French submarines were intended for coastal defence against British warships. Nobody in 1914 saw the submarine as revitalizing the *guerre de course*. Germany, the inferior naval power in the arms race with Britain, tried to match

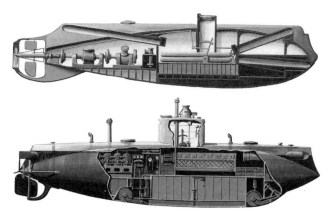

Holland's *Plunger* (*top*). Early French submarines were powered by storage batteries and had only a limited range. J P Holland developed for the US Navy a vessel which used internal combustion engines for surface propulsion and electric motors for submarine cruising. The *Plunger*, contracted for the US Navy in 1893, was never finished. However, in 1900 the US ordered seven "improved Hollands", and, in 1901, the British ordered five.

Lake's *Protector* (*below*). Simon Lake, Holland's rival, believed that the main role, of the submarine would be cutting underwater cables and destroying minefields. He therefore equipped his vessel with wheels, to enable it to move along the seabed, and a diving chamber to allow a crew member to move outside the submarine. Lake's *Protector* had three torpedo tubes to the single tube of *Plunger*, but only the Russians evinced serious interest.

the Royal Navy at its own game by building battleships and had only 28 U-boats in service in August 1914. Here again, prevailing concepts provided their own constraints: submarine blockade, as an instrument of economic war, would of course only be appropriate if the war itself were long and its overall strategy one of attrition.

The popular belief in 1914 that the war would be short was derived from recent history rather than from the state of the art of war. Attitudes, particularly in Germany, were formed by the memories of 1866 and 1870. But some professional soldiers, conversant with technology's impact on fire power, had their doubts. The two opposing commanders in the 1914 campaign in the West, Moltke the younger and Joffre, had both expressed their concern that a future war might not be as brief as statesmen seemed to expect. But their ability to articulate their insights was tragically limited. First, the orthodoxy suggested war could not be long for economic reasons: full-scale mobilization would halt production; unemployment among those not mobilized would soar, and revolution would follow. Second, as generals educated to think in terms of rapid and dazzling victories, they felt it would be rash in career terms to hold out to their political masters the prospect of a long and costly war of attrition. Finally, and perhaps most importantly, military science – since it was based more on history than on informed speculation – could not provide the evidence to add cogency to their case. Lord Kitchener rendered perhaps his greatest service to his country when as Secretary of State for War in August 1914 he told it to prepare for a long war. However, Kitchener's own reputation had been won on colonial battlefields and he was not at all versed in European military thought: his prediction was derived partly from the experience of the American Civil War but rested largely on intuition.

In abstract terms, 20th-century soldiers have to face a major problem in balancing the demands of doctrine with the rapid development of technology. They can abdicate any responsibility for doctrine, professing themselves to be in the hands of science and innovation. According to this argument, doctrine is a straitjacket which prevents the ready acknowledgment of the role of new weapons: before 1914 armies gave more sustained attention to military theory than in any previous (or probably in any subsequent) period, and yet were caught in a historically-derived idea of war that bore little relationship to prevailing tactical conditions. But the armies of 1914 also showed that an army without any doctrine is just as vulnerable as one with a doctrine that is too rigid and narrow. The French army's advocacy of the offensive was in some circles no more than an ill-developed expression of general faith designed to produce a tactical law that was as durable as possible in a time of technological flux. The British army, with its late adoption of a general staff and its lack of a coherent body of experience (given the variety of colonial campaigning), actively resisted the development of doctrine: its component parts were too independent and each of its wars differed too radically from the last. Neither France nor Britain was, as a result, well equipped to cope with the tactical conditions of the Western Front. Doctrine needed to be flexible to be able to make its own demands of science and to be able to see the correct applications of the weapons that science put into its hands. The balance therefore consisted in using doctrine to ask the right questions before attempting any answers. By 1914 the questions posed by new weaponry were so fundamental that they were not pressed to their logical conclusions. The answers that were given were too often either drawn pat from existing doctrine or lacked the doctrinal rigour to be more than vague generalizations.

Doctrine versus technology. Mounted staff officers in full dress uniforms at British manoeuvres shortly before World War I contrast with a BE (Blériot Experimental) 2a aircraft, one of a series developed at the Royal Aircraft Factory at Farnborough between 1911 and 1914. Emphasis was placed on stability, to facilitate observation, rather than on manoeuvrability. The BE 2a was the first British aeroplane to land in France on the war's outbreak, but it was its successor, the BE 2c, which became the principal reconnaissance aircraft ordered in 1914. The French had led the way in the development of aero engines, but in 1914 their army had only 138 aircraft. By contrast, Germany – despite much attention to airships – had 230 aeroplanes attached to its armies.

A-1 Skyraider, Douglas. (US, WWII and after). Single-seat shipboard day attack. Prototype flew March 18 1945; production ordered May 5 1945. An aircraft of exceptional ruggedness and versatility; 28 versions developed, including three-seat night-attack, two-seat/four-seat electronic countermeasures aircraft, airborne early-warning. Much used by US Navy, US Marines: operational Korea, Vietnam. Royal Navy had 36 AEW version; French *Armée de l'Air* used 100 in Algeria. Production 3,180. One 3,050hp Wright R-3350-26WB engine; max. speed 318mph (512kph); four 20mm cannon, up to 5,000lb (2,270kg) bombs and rockets.

Aachen. Situated in southwest Germany, near the Dutch and Belgian borders, Aachen (Aix-la-Chapelle) was the first major German city to fall to the Allies in 1944. The US 1st Infantry and 3rd Armoured divisions, part of the US First Army's VII Corps under Maj Gen Collins, began to penetrate the Siegfried Line southeast of Aachen on September 13 1944. At this stage the city was being evacuated and, unknown to the Americans, Maj Gen Gerhard Graf von Schwerin, commanding the 116th Panzer Division, was willing to give up Aachen without a fight. However, as the American advance stalled in the industrial area around Stolberg in the latter half of September, the Germans rushed reinforcements to Aachen. On October 2, First Army renewed the offensive, this time with the 30th Infantry and 2nd Armoured Divisions of XIX Corps attacking north of the city while VII Corps attempted to break out from the Stolberg corridor. On October 16 the 1st and 30th divisions met on the Ravelsberg, east of the city, thereby completing its encirclement. By now, elements of the 1st Infantry division were already pushing into the city itself but several days of vicious street fighting ensued, with the Germans using the sewer system to mount surprise counterattacks. Finally, on October 21, the surviving defenders, under Col Gerhard Wilck, surrendered. The siege of Aachen had delayed the US First Army for over five weeks and cost it approximately 8,000 casualties *PJS*.

Aarhus. Gestapo HQ at Aarhus in Denmark. Target in a successful RAF low-level precision raid by Mosquito aircraft on October 31 1944.

ABDA Command. American-British-Dutch-Australian joint command formed on January 3 1942 to check Japan's advance in Southeast Asia. It was dissolved seven weeks later (February 25) after continued Allied setbacks.

Abdullah, King of Jordan (1881–1951). Second son of Hussein-ibn-Ali, Emir of Mecca, brother of Feisal I of Syria. As his father's principal political adviser, helped persuade British to assist Arab revolt against Turks, World War I, and in 1928, with British aid, confirmed as ruler of Transjordan. Resolutely supported Allies in World War II, when his Arab Legion served in Syria and Iraq campaigns. Assumed title of King of Jordan, 1949, and annexed Arab areas of Palestine. A moderating influence upon the Arab world until his assassination by an Arab extremist, July 20 1951.

Abe, Vice Adm Hiroaki (1890–1949). Jap. Led bombardment groups at Wake Island and Midway. On November 13–14 1942, his "Tokyo Express" of two battleships, one cruiser and 15 destroyers, tasked with bombardment of Henderson Field, Guadalcanal, was intercepted in Ironbottom Sound by Rear Adm Callaghan's USN task group of four cruisers and eight destroyers. In a short-range night action, two US cruisers and four destroyers were sunk; Abe lost his flagship, *Hiei*, and two destroyers and, with his force severely mauled, failed to fulfil his mission and was removed from command.

Abrams, Gen Creighton Williams (1914–74). US. Commander of the US Army, Vietnam (USARV) and Military Assistance Command, Vietnam (MACV), July 1968–June 1972, succeeding Westmoreland after the Tet offensive, President Johnson's decision to send no more troops to Vietnam, and opening of Paris peace talks. to sustain pressure while reducing US casualties Abrams shifted from large-unit "search and destroy" sweeps to

aggressive patrolling by small units. Believing that such operations furthered "Vietnamization" – the shifting of combat responsibility to the Vietnamese, thus allowing the gradual withdrawal of US troops – he supported the Cambodian "incursion" of 1970 and planned the penetration of southern Laos in Operation "Lam Son 719", February–March 1971. *WST*.

Abrams, M1 (US Main Battle Tank) *see* TANKS.

Absolute war. A war with no objective other than the total destruction of the enemy. In modern terms, an all-out nuclear war in which the scale of destruction would render political objectives meaningless. *See also* LIMITED WAR; TOTAL WAR.

Abwehr. *see* MILITARY INTELLIGENCE ORGANIZATIONS.

Abyssinian campaign (1941) *see* ETHIOPIA, BRITISH CAMPAIGN IN.

Abyssinian War (1935–36). In 1896 Italy's attempt to conquer Abyssinia was rudely halted at the Battle of Adowa when its army was beaten by native forces. The disgrace of this defeat still rankled and although Italy signed a treaty of friendship and non-aggression with Abyssinia in 1928, it still wished to add to its other colonies in the Horn of Africa, Eritrea and Somaliland. Border tension continued and, on December 5 1934, Italian colonial troops fired on Abyssinian soldiers at the oasis of Walwal, some 50 miles (80km) within Abyssinian territory. Further incidents followed and Britain and France put pressure on Mussolini to accept arbitration by the League of Nations. However, a ruling on the Abyssinian problem was not given until September, when Italian plans for an invasion were well advanced. Fascist propaganda promised a quick and easy war with Italy's modern weapons matched against Emperor Haile Selassie's relatively primitive forces.

Substantial colonial forces were collected in Somaliland under Gen Graziani and an even larger Italian army was gathered in Eritrea under Gen de Bono. On October 3 1935, de Bono led 100,000 men across the border and marched on Adowa. He encountered minimal Abyssinian resistance and on October 7 the city fell. But de Bono failed to produce the rapid victory that Mussolini needed to satisfy popular hopes at home and, more significantly, to support his diplomatic position.

International opinion was highly critical of Italy's actions and, if the League of Nations was to add oil sanctions to those imposed on November 18, Mussolini recognized that he might have to accept peace terms. He therefore needed to hold Abyssinian territory as a bargaining counter. On November 26 de Bono was replaced by Gen Badoglio but he too was obliged to adopt a cautious approach in the face of a substantial concentration of Abyssinian forces that attacked in the Tigre region on December 15. Although the Abyssinians were poorly equipped, the mountainous terrain and close-quarter fighting largely offset the Italian monopoly of tanks and aircraft. However, the lamentable communications of the Abyssinian armies and the Italians' use of mustard gas contributed to the ultimate failure of their advances. On February 10 1936 Badoglio launched the first of a series of offensives that shattered Haile Selassie's forces and by mid-March left the Italians in control of northern Abyssinia. The Emperor mustered his troops for one last attack and, at the Battle of Mai Ceu on March 31, he sought to win another Adowa. This time the Italian line held and the Abyssinian armies were forced into retreat, harried by enemy aircraft. On May 2 Haile Selassie left his capital, Addis Ababa, and fled to French Somaliland. Three days later Badoglio's forces entered the city while, in the south, Graziani's troops pushed into the Ogaden and occupied Harar. On May 9 an exultant Mussolini announced the annexation of Abyssinia and, on June 1, all Italy's colonies in the Horn of Africa were amalgamated into a single *Africa Orientale Italiana*. *MS*.

Acheson, Dean G (1893–1971). US Secretary of State at outbreak of Korean War, June 1950: a dedicated anti-communist, convinced of Soviet complicity in the North

Korean attack. He demanded a vast US rearmament programme and increased military commitment to NATO. He discounted the threat of Chinese intervention if UN forces crossed the 38th Parallel, but when the threat materialized was the first to propose a return to the Korean status quo rather than extend the war to the Chinese mainland. This, he believed, would only benefit Russia by diverting US attention from Europe, the vital theatre of resistance to global communism. *CM*.

Adachi, Lt Gen Hatazo (1890–1947). Jap. Following the death of Lt Gen Tomitaro Horii on November 23 1942, Adachi took command of Eighteenth Army in New Guinea. With the Kokoda Trail retreat already begun and the Rabaul base interdicted by US air power, Adachi proved an astute commander in adversity, evacuating *c*14,000 men from the Huon Peninsula early in 1944 by forced marches and coastal barges. Isolated in conditions of great privation at Wewak, Eighteenth Army twice attempted break-outs, notably in a three-week battle at Aitape, July-August 1944. Adachi surrendered on September 13 1945, with only 13,500 men of his original *c*65,000. Sentenced to life imprisonment in 1947 for war crimes, he killed himself. *RO'N*.

Admiral Graf Spee *see* RIVER PLATE, BATTLE OF THE.

Admiralty Islands. Island group on the northwest limit of the Bismarck Sea, captured by US forces February-April 1944.

Adrianople, siege of (1912–13). From the outset of the First Balkan War, the capture of the great stronghold of Adrianople (modern Edirne) in Turkish Thrace was a prime objective of the Bulgarian attack, but when the armistice was signed on December 3 1912, Adrianople was still in Turkish hands. No revictualling was permitted during the weeks of armistice, hostilities were resumed on February 3 1913 and Turkish efforts to break through and relieve Adrianople were beaten back. The Bulgarians, reinforced by the Serbian Second Army and by three divisions from southern

Thrace, began a preliminary bombardment on March 24 and, despite delay caused by Turkish wire, carried the whole position by noon on March 26. *SKF*.

Afghanistan, Soviet intervention in (1979–89). There are two schools of thought concerning the motives underlying the Soviet invasion of Afghanistan in 1979. The first argues that the Soviet Union was tempted to expand southwards as a first step to acquiring a warm-water port on the Persian Gulf. The second asserts that it was a response to an internal Afghan crisis: to support a "fraternal friend" in Kabul. The answer is probably a combination of both; that the latter was justified by the former. At any rate, the Soviet Union greatly underestimated the difficulties of involving herself in the tangled skein of Afghan politics, when she moved at Christmas 1979 to replace Hafizullah Amin with Babrak Karmal as president.

The invasion took the West by

Mujaheddin with captured weapon

surprise. It was mounted by Fortieth Army, employing four motor rifle divisions in a two-pronged thrust. The first was to secure the Salang highway, cross Hindu Kush to Kabul; the second, moving from Kushka through the Hazara mountains, was to seize Herat, Farah and Kandahar. The invasion stirred not only international outrage but opposition from the Afghan middle class, and many valuable citizens – doctors, teachers and civil servants – joined the increasing number of refugees streaming on to the roads to Pakistan. President Carter authorized an increase in CIA covert operations and the dispatch of arms to the scattered and largely rural opposition, the mujaheddin, tacitly

A

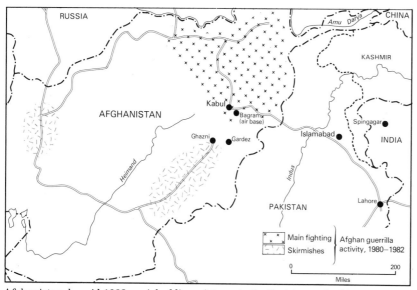

RUSSIA

CHINA

Amu Darya

KASHMIR

AFGHANISTAN

Kabul

Bagram
(air base)

Spinggagar

Ghazni

Gardez

Islamabad

INDIA

Helmand

Indus

PAKISTAN

Lahore

Main fighting

Skirmishes

Afghan guerrilla
activity, 1980–1982

0   200

Miles

Afghanistan: by mid-1982, mujaheddin resistance to the Soviets resulted in stalemate

supplied via Pakistan.

The first stage of the conflict focused largely around Afghan communications, and the need to protect Soviet bases from guerrilla attacks. The first major offensive, in Kuran in March 1980, indicated just how ill-prepared the Soviets were for guerrilla warfare. Neither Soviet training, organization nor doctrine had taken this into account, and the Afghan Army, crippled by desertion, was incapable of offensive effort. Units of Fortieth Army were excessively overcentralized. Guerrilla operations had to be coordinated at regimental level, but all support elements, including artillery, were coordinated at divisional level. From June 1980 to June 1981 the occupying Soviet forces, now entitled the Limited Contingent of Soviet Forces in Afghanistan (LCSFA), underwent a major restructuring.

The effectiveness of the resistance of the mujaheddin was reduced by their internal bickering, especially between the fundamentalist and pro-Western elements. Yet the mujaheddin were tenacious fighters. The Soviets were forced to rethink their all-arms tactics, relying heavily on air power and helicopter-borne forces to land in the rear of the guerrillas and envelop them. In addition, armoured units were employed to attack their villages and destroy their crops, which served only to stiffen resistance.

In May–June 1982, the Soviets mounted the first of a number of major offensives with a broadly similar character, Operation "Panjsher 5", which involved 15,000 men and an intense aerial bombardment lasting a week, in an attempt to regain the length of the valley of the Panjsher Gorge. This had been used by the mujaheddin to attack the Soviet air base at Bagram. Although successful, total casualties numbered 2,000, and the operation had to be repeated the following August.

In April 1983, United Nations peace talks began at Geneva. These had, as yet, little bearing on the war, although the Panjsher cease-fire brought major operations to a temporary halt until 1984.

Increasing mujaheddin raids on the Salang Road provoked Operation "Panjsher 7", involving 10,000 Soviet and 5,000 Afghan troops. The Soviets realized that their earlier offensives had failed because the mujaheddin had slipped away down the side valleys. The area of operations was therefore widened and heliborne forces were used to block this avenue of escape. Tu–16 heavy bombers provided a "rolling barrage" along the valley. Yet no decisive victory was secured.

The second major phase of the war involved Soviet attempts to bring the guerrillas to battle at a disadvantage and to strike at their supply lines in the east. In August 1984 10,000 Soviet and 7,500 Afghan troops swept the Kumar Valley and relieved Ali Khel – but these successes proved transient. In 1985 a policy of "search and destroy" was introduced. The Soviet problem, like that of the Americans in Vietnam, was how to bring their superior fighting power to bear on an elusive enemy. It was calculated that, by moving into what the guerrillas had previously considered "safe areas" and continually harassing their supply lines, the guerrillas could be either trapped or provoked into fighting a set-piece battle which they could not hope to win. But again like the Americans, the Russians discovered, as for example in the relief of Barikot in May 1985, that once their forces moved into an area, the guerrillas moved out; and they returned the day after the Soviets had departed.

Although other major offensives were mounted by the Soviets, notably "Panjsher 9", an attempt to locate and release a number of Afghan prisoners taken by the mujaheddin after the fall of Pechgur in June 1985, the final large-scale operations were launched in the northeast against guerrilla bases and their supply lines. In August 1985 some 20,000 men advanced in a dual thrust, one from Kabul to the Logar Valley, the other to Jalalabad. They were to link up at the "parrot's beak", a large salient along the Pakistani border, which was the nearest point of entry for guerrillas making for Kabul. A large heliborne force was able to cordon off mujaheddin bases, then tighten its grip, moving in a five-day battle on Tani, and then on the principal base, Zhawar. A symbol of guerrilla resistance, Zhawar did not fall. But the struggle for the borderlands continued in 1986, when a second attempt was made to seize Zhawar, this time successfully. The guerrillas stood and fought and were defeated, deluded by the belief that Zhawar was impregnable.

Yet this was a Pyrrhic Soviet victory. The mujaheddin still received large quantities of weapons; their bases simply moved on, their ability to harass Soviet forces largely unimpaired. A Soviet victory seemed as distant as ever. Public opinion was restive. The intervention was a long-running and expensive sore, both at home and abroad, and was a substantial obstacle to improving relations with the United States. In July 1986 the Soviet Union raised the possibility of establishing a timetable for withdrawal. In April 1988 the Geneva Accords were signed, which agreed a timetable so long as outside powers did not interfere in Afghanistan's internal affairs. By August 15 1988 half the Russian forces had departed, the rest by February 15 1989. *BHR*.

Afrika Korps. Rommel's armoured force, shipped to Libya in February 1941; referred to as the DAK (*Deutsches Afrika Korps*).

Agadir crisis *see* MOROCCAN WAR.

Agent Orange *see* CHEMICAL WEAPONS.

Agroville Program. To cope with increased insurgent activity in South Vietnam, President Ngo Dinh Diem launched the Agroville Program in 1959. The program divided the population of insecure areas into loyal and disloyal groups and resettled villages where the government could improve control. However, by attaching a stigma of disloyalty and forcibly resettling people without adequate provision for their welfare, the programme provoked opposition from peasants, Diem's critics, and American aid officials alike. When the programme ended in 1961, only 23 agrovilles had been stablished; these foreshadowed the Strategic Hamlet Program.

AH-1 Cobra. An American attack helicopter derived from the earlier UH-1 Iroquois utility model, which was the workhorse of the US Army during most of the Vietnam War. *See also* HELICOPTER.

Airborne operations. The application of military force, through air-landing or parachute descent, at the point where a decision is required.

Airborne Early Warning and Control System (AWACS). An aircraft carrying a long-range radar and the human and electronic command and control apparatus to allow the management of the air battle. The term is especially associated with the Boeing E-3

Sentry aircraft operated by the USAF, an integrated NATO force and Saudi Arabia. After the failure of its own AWACS version of Nimrod, the UK is purchasing the E-3.

Aircraft. Brief notes on various aircraft types are to be found listed alphabetically throughout this volume. These notes do not constitute an exhaustive or wholly representative list: they are generally typical of their periods. In many cases, designs developed through long series of sub-types; and for practical reasons it is impossible to cover all in every particular. The listed aero-engines are likewise representative rather than comprehensive; details of performance and armament generally represent "best possible" figures and are usually mutually exclusive (for example, the carrying of a specific weapons load over a set distance could impose limitations of speed, range and defensive armament).

Aircraft carrier. A class of warship designed to accommodate aircraft and to provide for their takeoff and landing at sea. Their origin is to be found in the US cruisers *Birmingham* and *Pennsylvania* from and onto which Eugene Ely succeeded respectively in taking off and landing on November 10 1910 and January 18 1911. The French and the British followed suit and several ships, notably HMS *Furious*, were adapted for the purpose. Landing on board, however, continued to be most hazardous until the first completely flat top vessel, HMS *Argus*, came into service in 1918. From her, the first authentic aircraft carrier, the whole class has descended. Naval operations in World War II, and especially those of the US and Japan in the Pacific, indicated that aircraft carriers had superseded battleships as capital ships, but subsequently they were held to have been displaced by nuclear-powered hunter submarines. In recent times, the matter has been put in doubt; although officially they had earlier been abandoned, British aircraft carriers played a decisive role in the Falklands War and the US Navy keeps large carriers in commission. *ANF*.

Air Cushion Vehicle (ACV) *see* HOVERCRAFT.

Airey, Lt Gen Sir Terence. (1900–84). Br. Head of Intelligence at Allied Force Headquarters, who, with Gen Lemnitzer and Allen Dulles, negotiated the German surrender in Italy on May 2 1945.

Air Interception (AI). British airborne radar for detecting enemy aircraft. Introduced 1940.

Air Pressure Strategy and Targeting system. In 1952, the USAF evolved the doctrine of air pressure in an attempt to find a decisive role in the Korean War. The aim was to increase the costs of the war to the communist bloc and produce a breakthrough at the truce talks. This meant bombing North Korean targets of economic value to the Soviet Union and China. It also meant area attacks on cities like Pyongyang to break North Korean morale. The most important air pressure target, the Suiho power station which supplied electricity to both China and the DPRK, was bombed in June 1952. In May 1953 the dams which supplied water for the rice crop were attacked, causing extensive flooding. *CM. See also* "STRANGLE" OPERATION; USAF IN KOREA.

Air Raid Precautions (ARP). British civil defence, i.e. shelters, warning, rescue, evacuation etc.

Air-sea rescue. The organization and employment of specially equipped helicopters and fast vessels for the retrieval of aircrew and other survivors at sea.

Airships. These were basically of two kinds; rigid, i.e. frames with outer skins containing gas bags, and non-rigid, i.e. gas-filled balloons. They were used in World War I for reconnaissance by many belligerents, but their most important roles were developed by the Germans, who, through Count Zeppelin, led the field. By 1914–18, Zeppelin long-range bombers could lift 50 tons, attain 80mph (130kph) and 20,000ft (6,100m). Their large size (2,400,000 cu ft/ 70,000 cu m) limited manoeuvrability, and inflammability made them highly vulnerable to ground and air defences. After heavy losses in 1916, they were used less for strategic bombing than for naval reconnaissance. *ANF*.

A

A

Air supply, clandestine. Became minor war industry in Britain, and was also used by USAAF and Russian air force in early 1940s. Warlike stores could be parachuted, by prearrangement, to moonlit reception committees of resisters: some 16,500 tons were dropped into Yugoslavia; 11,000 tons into France; lesser quantities elsewhere.

Air to Air Missile (AAM). A rocket-propelled missile launched by one aircraft at another. Long- (60 miles/100km plus) and medium-ranged (12–30 miles/20–50km) missiles are usually radar-guided either actively or semi-actively. Shorter-ranged missiles (less than 9 miles/15km) use infrared guidance to home in on the heat of an aircraft's engines. AAMS were first used in World War II, but only became significant from the 1950s onwards when they replaced guns as the main armament of fighter aircraft. This was premature, as earlier air to air missiles lacked reliability, but later versions are now very effective. The trend in AAMS is towards longer ranges, increased agility and wider angles of attack. New medium-range AAMS with inertial guidance systems and fully active radar homing make possible "beyond visual range" (BVR) engagements only limited by the ability to identify friend from foe (IFF). *EJG.*

Air to Surface Missile (ASM). A missile with a guidance system launched from an aircraft to hit a ground or sea target. The term covers guided bombs but is usually used for systems propelled by jets, rockets or ram jets. Ranges vary from less than 3 miles (5km) to over 1,200 miles (2,000km). Long-range missiles require inertial autopilots to keep them on course with active or passive radar, infrared, or other homing systems for the final attack. Shorter-ranged systems used within line of sight of the launch platform usually only require the homing system being locked on before launch. Alternatively, a command guidance system might be used with the missile being guided by an observer in the aircraft. Specialized types of ASM are anti-radiation missiles (ARM) used against radars and anti-ship missiles. *EJG.*

Air to Surface Vessel (ASV). British airborne radar device, similar to H2S, for detecting ships. Introduced 1940.

Armoured car at the Aisne, 1914

Aisne, Battle of the (1914). By September 13 1914, the German First and Second Armies, after retiring from the Marne, had halted in good defensive positions on the heights north of the River Aisne. Because of their somewhat leisurely pursuit, the British missed a golden opportunity to penetrate between the two German armies and, on September 13, the German VII Reserve Corps, freed by the fall of Maubeuge, arrived just in time to fill the gap on the vital Chemin des Dames ridge, having marched 40 miles (64km) in 24 hours. The three corps of the BEF crossed the Aisne that day and, on September 14, attempted to storm the heights. Some units of Haig's I Corps, on the British right, actually succeeded in crossing the Chemin des Dames and looked down into the Ailette valley beyond. Although subsequently driven out of the most advanced positions, I Corps managed to hold on near the crest of the ridge. Elsewhere the II and III Corps made little progress, with the result that, from the Chemin des Dames on the right, the British line ran southwest towards the river at Missy and then west to Crouy, two miles from Soissons. Both sides dug in and, despite German efforts to push the BEF back across the river, the line was virtually unchanged a fortnight later. With the beginnings of the trench warfare deadlock now established on the Aisne, the French took over the BEF's positions in October as the focus shifted to Flanders. *PJS.*

Aisne, Battle of the (1917). By late January 1917, Gen Nivelle, Joffre's successor as French C-in-C, had convinced Allied political leaders that the tactics he had employed so fruitfully at Verdun the previous year would, if applied on a bigger scale, at last produce a decisive breakthrough on the Western Front. In his proposed spring offensive, while the British struck at Arras, the French Reserve and Central Army Groups would respectively attack the Chemin des Dames ridge, north of the Aisne, and the Moronvilliers heights, east of Reims. Although the German withdrawal to the Hindenburg Line freed divisions to reinforce the threatened sectors, and despite the fact that details of the operation were captured, Nivelle did not significantly alter the overall plan. On April 16, following a 14-day bombardment, the French Fifth and Sixth Armies, of the Reserve Army Group, attacked along a 25-mile (40km) front on the Aisne. Because of the new German system of defence-in-depth, their forward positions were only lightly held – largely negating the effects of the preliminary bombardment – and with the main German positions still relatively intact, French gains were limited to a 3-mile (5km) penetration on a narrow front near Juvincourt, in the right centre. The battle continued into May, and footholds were won along the Chemin des Dames, but 187,000 French casualties, and the obvious failure of the offensive after all Nivelle's grandiose promises, kindled mutinies and led to Nivelle's removal on May 15 1917. *PJS.*

Aitape, Battle of *see* HOLLANDIA CAMPAIGN.

Ajax Bay. Settlement on west coast of East Falkland. Site of 45 Commando landing on May 21 1982 and subsequently of British Field Medical unit, housed in a disused meat refrigeration plant, which dealt with battle casualties from both sides throughout the Falklands campaign before their evacuation to ships offshore.

Akagi. Japanese aircraft carrier. Led the attack on Pearl Harbor. Scuttled after being crippled by US aircraft at Midway, June 1942.

Aksai Chin (India-China War, 1959, 1962). The furthermost part of Ladakh on the Tibetan side of the Karakorum mountains. Acquired by India (1947) as part of Kashmir. British political officers had claimed that Aksai Chin was under British suzerainty despite Chinese claims that it was theirs; no agreed border was ever demarcated. After the communist government of China occupied Tibet, a highway was built directly through Aksai Chin linking Sinkiang with western Tibet. The Indian government did not discover the road until 1958. Thereafter, military outposts were set up in Ladakh, despite tenuous communications, either by road or air (because of the altitude). The two sides confronted each other in the Chip Chap valley. When hostilities broke out in October 1962, the Indians (mainly Gurkhas) were reinforced and no serious inroads were made. When China announced a cease-fire all along the front, both sides accepted an arrangement which left the highway in Chinese-occupied territory while Leh and southwest Ladakh remained in Indian hands. *HT*.

Akyab *see* BURMA CAMPAIGN.

Alam Halfa, Battle of (August 30–September 7 1942). Rommel attacked the southern sector of the El Alamein Line with the Afrika Korps (Nehring) in his final attempt to break through to the Suez Canal. Montgomery, anticipating the German plan, strengthened the Alam Halfa ridge in the rear of his position, which Rommel would have to attack once he had broken through the British minefields, with 10th Armoured and 44th Divisions. Rommel did breach the minefields during the night of August 30–31, and, as expected, his panzer divisions swung north to clear Alam Halfa. They were met and decisively beaten by concealed anti-tank guns and tanks that had moved into "hull down" positions as soon as German intentions were clear. By evening Nehring had been wounded; von Bismarck, commanding 21st Panzer Division, had been killed; and von Vaerst of 15th Panzer Division, who had assumed command of the Afrika Korps, had withdrawn to reorganize.

Montgomery resisted the temptation to counterattack with his armour, a tactic which had proved so fatal in past desert battles. Instead, he pounded the Axis forces, stranded for lack of fuel in the low ground between Alam Halfa and the minefields, with intense air and artillery bombardments until Rommel managed to extricate them. At Alam Halfa, Montgomery achieved ascendancy not only over Rommel, but also amongst the officers and men of Eighth Army, who had suffered so many recent defeats. *WGFJ*.

Alamein *see* EL ALAMEIN.

Alamogordo. At 0530 hours on July 16 1945, the first full-scale test of an implosion type atomic fission bomb took place at Alamogordo, New Mexico.

Alanbrooke (*right*) with Montgomery

Alanbrooke, Field Marshal Lord (Sir Alan Brooke) (1883–1963). Br. A former Commandant, School of Artillery, and Director of Military Training, Brooke was a Corps commander in France, 1939–40. Following extrication of the BEF from Dunkirk, he became C-in-C Home Forces, awaiting the apparently imminent German invasion, and, late 1941, Chief of the Imperial General Staff, the professional head of the British army. He was thus Chruchill's principal military adviser, 1942–45. In translating Churchill's often fanciful strategic concepts into military action, he frequently had to run counter to his master's expressed wishes, but performed his tasks with such diplomatic skill and consummate professionalism that he was denied the chance of further field command. His personal diaries, *The Turn of the Tide* and *Triumph in the West* (ed. Bryant),

give a fascinating view of high wartime command. *MH*.

Albania, Italian invasion of (1939). By 1938, Italian economic and political control of Albania was almost total. Its ruler, King Zog, was kept in power largely by Italian subsidies and the Albanian army was mostly staffed by Italian officers. In the spring of 1938 Mussolini and Ciano resolved to annex Albania and tentative plans were laid for the operation to be carried out the following May. Gen Guzzoni, commanding the expeditionary force, was informed of the proposed invasion only a week before it was due to take place. In spite of lamentable planning, intelligence and communications, 22,000 troops made landings at four Albanian ports on April 7 1939. Brief and ineffective resistance was offered by Albanian forces at Durazzo but the major cause of delay in occupying the capital, Tiranë, was Italian disorganization. King Zog fled to Greece and on April 16 King Victor Emmanuel accepted the crown of Albania. However, far from being an economic and political asset, Albania proved to be a financial millstone, and the invasion a diplomatic blunder. Britain and France offered guarantees to Romania and Greece in a clear signal that they wished to limit Italian territorial aspirations. *MS*.

Albatros C III (German, WWI). Two-seat general purpose. Prototype (150hp Benz) flew late 1915; used on Western Front 1916; most numerous of the Albatros two-seaters, served as bomber, reconnaissance and artillery-spotting aircraft; also used in Macedonia, Russia. 160hp Mercedes D III or 150hp Benz Bz III engine; max. speed 87.5mph (140kph); two 7.9mm machine guns, 200lb (90kg) bombs.

Albatros D III (German, WWI). Single-seat fighter. Prototype had flown by October 1916; basic German production orders for 1,340 placed from that month. Also built in Austria in modified, more powerful form; very successful. 160hp Mercedes D IIIa or 200/225hp Austro-Daimler engine; max. speed 108mph (173kph); two 7.9mm machine guns.

A

Albert I, King of the Belgians, (1875–1934). Succeeding his autocratic uncle, Leopold II , in 1909, Albert initiated sensible democratic reforms. Although his attempts to modernize the Belgian army and redeploy it against a perceived German threat were hampered by hidebound generals, he refused the German demand for unopposed passage for their forces through Belgium on August 2 1914, and, becoming c-in-c on the commencement of hostilities, ordered the destruction of bridges and railway tunnels and opposed the advance of 34 German divisions with his small (7 divisions) army. Following the fall of Liège (August 16), he took personal command, making a fighting retreat to Antwerp. Belgium's determined resistance further disrupted the Schlieffen plan, while the reprisals it provoked attracted worldwide sympathy for the Allied cause. Following Antwerp's fall (October 9), Albert withdrew his army to northwest France. In September-November 1918, he commanded an Anglo-Belgian army group in a successful offensive along the Flanders coast. *RO'N.*

Alderson, Lt Gen Sir Edwin (1859–1927). Br. In October 1914, Alderson, an officer with considerable mounted infantry experience, was given command of the 1st Canadian Division, which fought under him in the Second Battle of Ypres and at Festubert and Givenchy in 1915. Later that year, when the 2nd Canadian Division arrived in France, the Canadian Corps was formed, with Alderson at its head. However, he was removed from command in May 1916 following the loss of St Eloi craters near Ypres, and spent the rest of World War I as Inspector General of Canadian Forces in England. *PJS.*

Aleutian Islands campaign (1942–43). Immediately before the Battle of Midway, Yamamoto deployed Northern Area Force (Vice Adm Hoshiro Hosogaya, with two light carriers, transports and escorts) in a diversionary attack on the Aleutian Islands chain, extending *c*1,100 miles (1,760km) southwest from Alaska across the North Pacific. Although forewarned by "Magic", US North Pacific Force (Rear Adm Robert A

"Fuzzy" Theobald; subsequently replaced by Kinkaid) bungled its interception. The US base at Dutch Harbour, Unalaska, eastern Aleutians, was damaged by Japanese carrier aircraft on June 3–4 1942, and on June 7 Japanese troops landed unopposed on the western Aleutian islands of Attu and Kiska.

Although the Japanese made no serious attempt to extend their conquest, air and naval clashes in the fog-shrouded and stormy Aleutians continued through the following year (*see* KOMANDORSKI ISLANDS). From May 11 1943, 12,000 US troops landed on Attu, securing it on June 2 after savage fighting (2,380 Japanese dead and 28 prisoners; 552 US dead and 1,140 wounded). Heavy naval and air bombardments – including the "Battle of the Pips", July 27, when a US battleship task group wasted a prodigious amount of ammunition on radar "ghosts" – preceded an attack on Kiska, but when *c*34,000 US and Canadian troops landed on August 15 it was found that Japanese submarines and warships had evacuated the 5,000-strong garrison during the foggy nights of June–July. *RO'N.*

Alexander, of Tunis, Field Marshal Earl (1891–1969). Br. Came to Churchill's notice when, as Commander 1st Division, he was rearguard commander at Dunkirk

Alexander at Eighth Army HQ, 1942

in 1940. He was sent to save Burma from the Japanese in March 1942, but arrived too late to do more than withdraw the Burma Army back to India.

When Churchill visited Cairo in August 1942, he appointed Alexander to replace Auchinleck as c-in-c, Middle East, and gave him Montgomery as Commander

Eighth Army. They formed a well-balanced team, which won the battles of Alam Halfa and El Alamein, and drove Rommel out of Libya by the end of January 1943.

At the Casablanca Conference, Churchill and Roosevelt agreed that Alexander should become Eisenhower's Deputy Land Force Commander. He commanded First and Eighth Armies (Anderson and Montgomery) from 18th Army Group HQ in the Tunisian campaign, forcing the surrender of all German forces in Africa on May 12 1943; then Seventh US and Eighth British Armies (Patton and Montgomery) from Fifteenth Army HQ in the Sicilian campaign; and invaded Italy with Fifth US Army and Eighth British (Clark and Montgomery) in September 1943.

As Commander, Allied Armies in Italy, he defeated Kesselring in the final battles for Rome in May 1944, and in the battles of the Gothic Line in the autumn of that year. He was promoted Field Marshal with effect from June 4, the day Rome fell. As Supreme Allied Commander, Mediterranean, from December 1944, he crushed the communist rebellion in Greece, and ended the Italian campaign with the German surrender on May 2 1945. Minister of Defence in the last Churchill administration, 1952–54. *WGFJ.*

Alexeiev, Gen Mikhail (1857–1918). Russian. Appointed COS of the Russian South Western Army Group, August 1914, Alexeiev briefly commanded North Western Front, March–September 1915, relinquishing this independent command to become COS to Tsar Nicholas II when the Russian ruler assumed supreme command. In 1916, responding to Allied requests for a major offensive to relieve the Central Powers' heightened pressure on the Western and Italian fronts, Alexeiev approved Brusilov's offensive, but, in failing to give it sufficient support, contributed to its ultimate failure. Involved in the negotiations surrounding the Tsar's abdication in March 1917, Alexeiev was briefly c-in-c under the Provisional Government, but disagreed with Kerensky and was replaced by Brusilov. At the time of his death he was helping to raise an anti-Bolshevik army. *MS.*

A

Algerian campaign (1954–62). The colonization of Algeria, beginning in the 1830s, was regarded as an extension of metropolitan France, and "French" cities grew at Algiers, Oran, Philippeville and Bône. The *colons*, or *pieds-noirs* as they were contemptuously known, made little effort to integrate their culture with that of the Algerian people. At the same time the growth of Arab nationalism was recognized and feared.

The first serious rebellion against French rule occurred in 1945 and was put down ferociously. Algerian nationalism drew its external support mainly from Egypt during the 1950s. On November 1 1954, Cairo Radio announced the formation in Algeria of the *Front de Libération National* or FLN. The French were taken by surprise, but the inexperienced rebels initially achieved only limited local success. The French government now took a hard line. The full weight of its armed forces was directed to Algeria and the rebels resorted to terrorist methods, as did the security forces.

Although the French could defeat the rebels in open battle, using helicopters for the rapid deployment of their infantry, the FLN established lines of supply across the Tunisian border until this was sealed in 1957 by the construction of the Morice Line, an 8ft (2.4m)

used effective propaganda further to erode national confidence in the Army. By 1958 the FLN had established comprehensive military and civilian undergrounds and taken charge of a number of remote areas. Although the French government threw more troops into the struggle, including three divisions actually assigned to NATO, the FLN was now too skilful and elusive to be pinned down, and the ruthlessness of the Paras and Foreign Legion soon became counterproductive. The campaign was actually lost by the French government on the home front, with rising opposition to a costly war. In the summer of 1958, the campaign reached a climax with an all-out security operation against the FLN's sanctuary areas in the Atlas and Kabylian mountains. Thousands of the Muslim civilian population were forcibly resettled and their land devastated in an attempt to destroy the FLN's logistic and political base, but Gen de Gaulle, now back in power, sensed the mood of the French people and was already initiating secret talks with the rebels, offering self-determination.

As the *colons* in Algerian towns and cities realized what was happening, they raised barricades, announced their intention to fight to the end, and obtained military support, principally from the Paras, still smarting from the humi-

began to plot against him, and units of the Army in Algeria mutinied. De Gaulle appealed to the soldiers over the heads of their disaffected officers, confining the trouble to "hard core" elements of the Paras and Foreign Legion. The mutiny collapsed and de Gaulle went ahead to grant Algerian independence, backed by 90 percent of the French electorate who were sickened by the OAS's terrorist tactics. Despite a further OAS revolt, headed by Gen Salan, negotiations with Algerian leaders, headed by Mohammed Ben Bella, were concluded in July 1962. A million settlers left Algeria and the victorious FLN came out of hiding to massacre all Muslims suspected of having helped the French, whilst the OAS persisted for a time with their terrorist campaign. In the longer term, France derived great benefit from the settlement, both economically and politically. The victorious FLN, having slaughtered the collaborators, turned on each other, and Ben Bella's new government soon found itself embroiled in border disputes with its neighbours. *MH.*

Algerian-Moroccan War (1963–64). Before the attainment of Algerian independence in 1962, Morocco had been disputing the alignment of boundaries, never formally demarcated during French colonial rule, mainly in the Colomb-Bechar region, into which Moroccan troops penetrated as early as July 1962. Two months later, there was fighting in the Tindouf area, rich in iron ore deposits. By mid-1963, Moroccan forces were in possession of considerable tracts of territory claimed by Algeria and during October there was sporadic fighting in which the Moroccans tended to get the upper hand. In that month, the Emperor Haile Selassie of Ethiopia visited both Algeria and Morocco in an effort to mediate between the two. As a result, King Hassan of Morocco and President Ben Bella met on neutral ground in Mali and agreed a cease-fire, which came into effect early in November with agreement on the establishment of a demilitarized border zone. Algerian casualties in the fighting came to about 60 dead and 250 wounded. No reliable details of Moroccan losses exist. *MH.*

Algeria, 1954–62: ruthless actions by French forces failed to crush the FLN.

electrified fence with mined approaches. In 1957 the French, refusing demands for Algerian independence, mounted a major offensive against urban guerrillas ("the Battle of Algiers"), a textbook example of ruthlessly executed counterinsurgency action. Reports of its savagery spread throughout France, where the FLN

liations of Indochina and Suez. A terrorist organization, the *Organisation de l'Armée Secrète* (OAS) started a campaign of assassination and terrorism against the FLN in Algeria and metropolitan France in September 1960, but the French electorate backed de Gaulle in the election of January 1961. A number of senior Army officers

"The Bull": Field Marshal Allenby

Allenby, Field Marshal Viscount (1861–1936). Br. A cavalryman whose powerful frame and violent temper earned him the nickname of "the Bull", Allenby was appointed to command the cavalry division which accompanied the BEF to France in August 1914. Later in 1914 he led the newly formed Cavalry Corps at the First Battle of Ypres. In May 1915 he succeeded Plumer at the head of V Corps and in October took over the Third Army. His first major offensive was at Arras on April 9 1917. Although Third Army's attack started well, with a deep penetration north of the Scarpe, the battle deteriorated into another bloody stalemate. Allenby's relations with Haig were never easy and, in June 1917, he was transferred to the command of the Egyptian Expeditionary Force in Palestine. Here he reorganized and revitalized the British and Imperial forces, winning important victories at Beersheba and Gaza prior to the capture of Jerusalem on December 9. Forced to yield troops for the Western Front in the first half of 1918, it was not until September that year that he could launch his final offensive. However, following the breakthrough in the Battle of Megiddo on September 19–21, Allenby's units advanced over 360 miles (580km) in 38 days, taking Damascus and Aleppo and destroying three Turkish armies in the process. Critics argue that these triumphs were achieved in a secondary theatre but, given the right conditions, Allenby's skill in combining all arms in mobile operations cannot be denied. *PJS*.

Allfrey, Lt Gen Sir Charles (1895–1964). Br. Commander V Corps in Tunisia, and in the Italian campaign until August 3 1944.

Allied Forces, Vietnam. The US pressurized its friends in Asia to contribute forces to the war in South Vietnam. The US had to obtain these commitments outside the framework of the Southeast Asia Treaty Organization because key SEATO members were reluctant to become involved. Five countries sent combat troops. These "allies", a term the US used to invoke the spirit of World War II, were formally organized as the Free World Forces or the Many Flags Program. A Free World Military Assistance Policy Council was set up in 1965 to provide staff coordination, but the US commander retained operational control.

Australia was an early and willing participant. In 1962, she sent 30 men to advise the South Vietnamese Army in jungle warfare. The Australian contingent in Vietnam grew to 7,600 by 1968. New Zealand sent about 1,000 infantry and artillery support troops.

Anxious to avoid the appearance of a solely "European" effort, the US avidly sought Asian participation. By far the largest contingent came from South Korea, beginning in mid-1964. By 1968, 50,000 soldiers of the South Korean. Capital Division, 9th Infantry Division and 2nd Marine Brigade were fighting in South Vietnam, mostly in II Corps. South Koreans suffered 4,407 combat deaths. Thailand sent the elite Queen's Cobras and elements of the Black Panther Division to a total of 11,500 by 1969, while the Philippines sent a 2,000-man civic action group. Public support for the dispatch of troops was especially weak in Thailand and the Philippines, and the United States heavily subsidized the contingents of all three countries. Non-US troops began to withdraw along with the reduction of US forces in 1969, and all departed by March 1973.

An offer of troops from the Republic of China (Taiwan) was refused. The US feared that introducing ROC troops would provoke the mainland and arouse the traditional anti-Chinese antipathies of the Vietnamese. However, small teams of ROC political warfare, medical, agricultural and technical advisers were accepted. *WST*.

Alligator *see* LVT *under* AMPHIBIOUS CRAFT AND WEAPONS.

Almond, Maj Gen Edward Mallory (1892–1979). US. When the Korean War broke out, "Ned" Almond was COS at MacArthur's headquarters in Tokyo. He was considered one of MacArthur's favourites and on August 26 1950 was given X Corps which made the amphibious landing at Inchon on September 15 and took Seoul. Almond retained his independent command for the subsequent advance into North Korea and was assigned the mission of clearing the northeast. In November 1950 he shared MacArthur's confidence that China would not intervene and rejected any evidence to the contrary, a performance which nearly brought his troops to grief around the Chosin reservoir. In December 1950, X Corps was evacuated through Hungnam and redeployed below the 38th Parallel where it was subordinated to Eighth Army under Gen Ridgway. Almond returned to the US (July 15 1951) to become commandant of the Army War College. *CM*.

Altmark **incident** (1940). A tender to the German pocket battleship *Admiral Graf Spee*, the tanker *Altmark* (8,053 tons; Capt Heinrich Dau) carried 299 British prisoners from merchant ships sunk in the South Atlantic. On February 14 1940, attempting to evade the British blockade and reach Germany, the *Altmark* entered Norwegian territorial waters. Under International Law, the prisoners should have then been freed, but the Norwegian authorities made only a cursory inspection of the vessel. Tracked by aircraft of Coastal Command, the *Altmark* was intercepted in Jösenfjord on February 16 by the destroyers HMS *Intrepid* and *Cossack*. The *Intrepid*'s approach was blocked by a Norwegian gunboat, but Capt Vian of the *Cossack* sent off a boarding party. In a brief firefight, seven German sailors were killed and 11 wounded: a shout of "The Navy's here!" told the prisoners of their release. The *Altmark* was allowed to proceed to Germany, thus somewhat lessening Norwegian protests at violation of neutrality. *RO'N*.

Ambrosio, Marshal Vittorio (1879–1958). Italian. Chief of Italian Armed Forces from February

4 1943, replacing Cavallero, whom Mussolini thought was too pro-German when first considering defection from the Axis; became Inspector-General in the Badoglio government after the Italian capitulation in September 1943.

American Expeditionary Force (AEF). American armed forces sent overseas, 1917–18, during World War I. Gen Pershing was appointed to command the AEF in May 1917.

American Volunteer Group (**AVG**) *see* "FLYING TIGERS".

Amethyst **incident** (1949). In April 1949, during the Chinese Civil War, communist armies prepared to cross the Yangtze Kiang to assault Nanking. On April 20, the frigate HMS *Amethyst* (Lt Commander J S Kerans), en route to Nanking, crossed the communist front and was subjected to an unprovoked barrage (22 killed; 30 wounded): temporarily disabled, she went aground. The destroyer HMS *Consort*, attempting to aid *Amethyst* from Nanking, came under fire (8 killed; 30 wounded) and was forced to retire; likewise, the cruiser HMS *London* (15 killed; 20 wounded) and frigate *Black Swan*, from Shanghai. *Amethyst* remained trapped until the night of July 30–31, when Lt Commander Kerans daringly broke out, running the gauntlet of communist shore batteries over the 140 miles (225km) to Shanghai at an average speed of more than 22 knots. *RO'N.*

Amiens, Battle of (1918). By August 1918, after months of defensive battles, the Allies were ready to regain the initiative on the Western Front. On August 8, the British Fourth Army, under Gen Rawlinson, and the French First Army, under Gen Debeney, struck the German Second and Eighteenth Armies, east of Amiens. Showing just how far the British had profited from the tactical experience of the previous three years, the Fourth Army's initial assault – following the example of Cambrai – was accompanied by a devastating surprise bombardment by 2,070 guns, using predicted shooting; 414 fighting tanks, supported by supply tanks,

rolled forward through the morning fog, closely cooperating with the infantry; and ground-attack aircraft and wireless sets were also employed to great effect. On the first day, the comparatively fresh Canadian Corps advanced some 8 miles (13km). The Australian Corps, on its left, penetrated about 6 miles (10km) and even the British III Corps, in a sector where the Germans had been more alert, managed to cover 2 miles (3km). Although French progress to the south was generally slower, Rawlinson's formations, on August 8, inflicted losses of 400 guns and 27,000 men – including over 15,000 prisoners – on the Germans, at a cost of 9,000 casualties to themselves. The subsequent advances were less spectacular and, with only six tanks still left in action after five days, Haig persuaded Foch, on August 14, to switch the attack to Third Army's sector farther north. However, Ludendorff recognized the decline in German morale and described August 8 as "the Black Day" of the German Army. *PJS.*

Amphibious craft and weapons. The only purpose-built landing craft of World War I were the British "X-lighters", although the Russians converted a class of dredgers as landing ships. A few experimental craft were built in Britain and the USA in the interwar years, but it was not until 1939 that the RN began to develop the armada of different types of landing craft and ships which were to be built in Britain and America during World War II. There were landing ships for infantry (LSI) and for tanks (LST) – the former mostly conversions, the latter nearly all purpose-built. Medium-sized landing craft for tanks (LCT) and infantry (LCI) were seagoing vessels in their own right. The smaller assault (LCA) and other infantry craft (LCP) with the vehicle-landing vessels (LCM) were designed to be carried by larger craft. The Americans developed amphibious lorries (DUKW) and tracked landing vessels (LVT) – some of the latter fitted as tanks. Landing craft were equipped with guns, rockets and other weapons to provide fire support (LCS) and also as anti-aircraft vessels (LCF). Perhaps the most interesting development

of all was the landing ship which was capable of carrying smaller craft inside a dock within its hull (LSD). This has developed since the war into the assault ship – also capable of operating those new features of amphibious warfare: helicopters and hovercraft. *DJL.*

Anami, Gen Korechika (1887–1945). Jap. As Vice-Minister of War to Tojo in 1940, Anami was influential in his chief's succession to the Prime Minister's office. After various combat commands, he became Minister of War in April 1945 and was the focus of the "fight to the death" faction, who expected him to support their coup against Hirohito's "peace cabinet" in August 1945. Anami's reluctance to oppose the Emperor and his consequent equivocation led to the coup's failure. He committed suicide on August 15, shortly before the Emperor's surrender broadcast.

Anatra DS Anasal (Russian, WWI). Two-seat reconnaissance, development of earlier and more numerous Anatra D. Operational from summer 1917; considered to be quite a successful type. Russian Revolution stopped production, approximately 70 built. 150hp or 160hp Salmson engine; max. speed 89mph (142kph) two rifle-calibre machine guns.

Anaya, Adm Jorge (b.1927). Argentinian. Argentine naval C-in-C in 1982 and most militant member of the three-man ruling junta. He was the chief architect of the Falklands invasion plan and was convinced that Britain would not take up arms to resist such a *fait accompli*, and that the US government would not be as supportive to the British cause as it was. He vigorously turned down all peace proposals, being confident that his navy would obtain mastery of the South Atlantic, but after the *General Belgrano* had been sunk he withdrew all major units to Argentine coastal waters, where they remained for the rest of the war. *MH.*

Ancre, Battle of the. Fought between November 13 and 19 1916, the Battle of the Ancre was the final phase of the British offensive on the Somme in that year.

A

Despite a deterioration in the weather and appalling front-line conditions, the operation proceeded, after repeated postponements, partly because of the favourable effect which a late success might create at the imminent inter-Allied conference at Chantilly. In a scaled-down version of earlier plans, troops of Lt Gen Sir Hubert Gough's Fifth Army attacked astride the River Ancre, north of Thiepval, to reduce the German salient between Serre and the Albert-Bapaume Road. Although the 51st (Highland) Division took Beaumont Hamel and the 63rd (Royal Naval) Division seized Beaucourt – both objectives on July 1 – Serre and Grandcourt still resisted capture when the bad weather brought the offensive to an end on November 19. *PJS*.

Åndalsnes, landings at (April 18– May 2 1940). Maj Gen Paget's force began landing on April 18, led by the lightly equipped, inadequately-trained 148th (Territorial) Brigade, intended to hold Åndalsnes-Dombas as a base from which the regular 15th Infantry Brigade would attack Trondheim from the south. At Gen Ruge's request, the Territorials were rushed south by train to Lillehammer to help the Norwegians stem the German advance up the Gudbrandsdal valley from Oslo. Lacking artillery and AA guns, the Territorials were all but annihilated by German columns with tanks, artillery and close air support in actions at Aasmarka, Balbergkamp and Tretten (April 20–23). German air attacks on Åndalsnes prevented the unloading of heavy equipment, and 15th Infantry Brigade, landing April 24, was also rushed south with only light weapons. Its rearguard actions at Kvam, Kjorem, Otta and Dombas (April 25–30) inflicted considerable loss on the advancing Germans before its evacuation from Åndalsnes by British warships, May 1–2. *WGFJ*.

Anders, Gen Wladyslaw (1892– 1970). Polish. Commander of II Polish Corps during the Italian campaign; took Cassino on May 18 1944, Ancona on July 17, and Pesaro on September 2 before being promoted Acting Commander Polish Armed Forces in February 1945.

Anderson, Gen Sir Kenneth (1891–1959). Br. Commander First Army in the Tunisian campaign.

Anglo-German Naval Treaty (June 18 1935). Under the terms of the Treaty of Versailles, Germany was restricted in the numbers, types and sizes of warships she could have. She could not build or own aircraft carriers or submarines. Hitler repudiated the Versailles arrangements in March 1935. However, both Hitler and the premier European naval power, Britain, felt that their interests were best served by negotiating a naval limitations treaty. Britain was worried about the increasing power of Japan in particular; there was a feeling that Germany had been over-harshly treated at Versailles, and that some degree of recognition and control over Hitler's rearmament was better than none. The agreement that emerged allowed Germany to build up to 35 percent of the Royal Navy's total tonnage. In certain circumstances she would be allowed a submarine fleet equal to the British. France and other powers saw this as appeasement of Hitler, who repudiated the treaty on April 28 1939. *CJW/CD*.

Anglo-Irish War (1916–1921). In 1914 Britain moved towards granting limited independence to Ireland: 26 predominantly Roman Catholic counties desired independence; six predominantly Protestant counties of Ulster fervently opposed it. The Curragh mutiny showed that Home Rule could not be imposed on Ulster by force, and the advent of World War I deferred the issue.

The republican extremists of Sinn Féin and the Irish Republican Brotherhood (IRB) decided to exploit Britain's difficulty. On April 24 1916, *c*1,500 Irish Volunteers under Padraic Pearse of the IRB, and 219 men of the Marxist James Connolly's Citizen Army seized the Dublin General Post Office – where Pearse proclaimed the Irish Republic – and other key points in the city. This "Easter Rising" attracted little popular support and British troops suppressed it within five days, but the subsequent executions of Pearse, Connolly, Sir Roger Casement and 12 other leaders aroused bitter

resentment. Eamonn de Valéra became President of Sinn Féin, with the Irish Republican Army (IRA) as its military branch.

In 1919–21, under Michael Collins, the IRA waged a guerrilla campaign. Collins had no more than 3,000 men under arms, opposed by *c*9,000 men of the Royal Irish Constabulary, strengthened by 1,500 "Auxiliaries" and *c*4,000 "Black and Tans" recruited from

Aftermath of street fighting, Dublin

British ex-servicemen, and some 35,000 regular troops. But the IRA now had popular support: a boycott isolated the British authorities, while the IRA's "Active Service Units" ("flying columns"), supplementing their arms with raids on police barracks, practised ambush and assassination, provoking counter-terror activities that won them further support.

On December 6 1921, the Anglo-Irish Treaty sought to solve the Irish problem by partition, granting dominion status to the 26 "southern" counties (Irish Free State, 1922; Republic of Ireland, 1949) and establishing the six Ulster counties as Northern Ireland. *RO'N*. See also the essay on UNDERGROUND WARFARE.

Anglo-Polish Alliance *see* POLISH GUARANTEE.

An Lao Valley, Battles of. During January-February 1966, the US 1st Cavalry (Airmobile) and South Vietnamese 22nd Divisions pursued three regiments of the 3rd People's Army (PAVN) Division into the An Lao Valley of Binh Dinh province. The operation featured lavish use of artillery and disregarded the needs of refugees this created. Initially codenamed "Masher", the operation was renamed "White Wing" to satisfy President Johnson's concern for public opinion. In the course of the operation one of the first missions of Project "Delta", a programme of long-range reconnaissance deep inside areas under communist control, met disaster in the valley. Project "Delta" was overhauled as a result. A year later, during Operation "Thayer II/Pershing", two Vietnamese Marine battalions drove 5,200 people out of the valley, of whom only 1,886 could be resettled. *WST*.

An Loc, siege of. South Vietnam's Binh Long province northwest of Saigon was one of four "fronts" struck by communist forces during the Easter offensive of 1972. In early April, two tank-led regiments of the People's Liberation Armed Force (PLAF) 5th Division overran the town of Loc Ninh, whose inhabitants fled down highway 13 to An Loc, the province capital. The PLAF 9th Division then laid siege to An Loc, which contained the Army of the Republic (ARVN) 5th Infantry Division and about 10,000 civilians. The People's Army (PAVN) 7th Division blocked the highway. Seven communist regiments eventually took positions around the town and fired thousands of mortar, 155mm howitzer and 122mm rocket rounds into it each day. The communists blunted aerial attack with SAM missiles and anti-aircraft guns and tried three times to breach the town's defences in tank-led assaults. A relief effort by the ARVN 21st Division and Palace Guard bogged down. Credit for breaking the siege on June 18 went to a makeshift defence organized by the province chief and to extremely heavy B-52 and tactical air strikes. The battle marked the first communist use of heavy artillery and armour so near Saigon, and it raised doubts that the ARVN would be able to withstand such assaults without American airpower. *WST*.

Ansaldo SVA-5 (Italian, WWI). Single-seat reconnaissance bomber/fighter. Prototype flew March 3 1917; production started autumn 1917. Operational use on strategic reconnaissance and light bombing began February 1918. Production (several versions) 1917–18 total-

led 1,248; floats fitted to some 50 SVA-5s. 220hp SPA Type 6A or 250hp Isotta-Fraschini engine; max. speed 143mph (229kph); two 7.7mm machine guns.

Anschluss. The term used to describe the integration of Austria into Germany against the wish of the Austrian Chancellor, Schuschnigg, which Hitler achieved on March 13 1938. France, Britain and Italy turned a blind eye.

Anson, Avro 652A (Br, WWII). General reconnaissance/trainer. Prototype flew March 24 1935; first deliveries No. 48 Squadron, RAF, February 1936. Initially undertook coastal reconnaissance; later extensively used as trainer and communications aircraft. Progressive developments through many Marks; total built 11,022. Two 335/395hp Armstrong-Siddeley Cheetah engines; max. speed 188mph (300kph); two 0.303in machine guns, 360lb (162kg) bombs.

Anti-aircraft warfare. During World War I the development of military aircraft led to a requirement for defence against attack from the air. Rifles and machine guns were supplemented by high elevation artillery, while searchlights were increasingly employed to illuminate hostile aeroplanes. Further defence was offered by barrage balloons that forced aircraft to fly high. By World War II, air defence systems had greatly advanced and continued to do so throughout the conflict. The introduction of radar added a new dimension to existing methods of sound and visual detection of aircraft. It was also used increasingly in the fire control systems of improved anti-aircraft artillery. Furthermore, refinements in barrage techniques and the development of the proximity fuse helped to produce even better results. The surface-to-air missile (SAM) now offers ground and naval forces their most effective protection against air attack. *MS*.

Anti-Ballistic Missile Missile (ABM Missile). A missile designed to shoot down an incoming long-range ballistic missile. Crude ABM missiles were developed in the 1960s by both superpowers, but

the problem of hitting a very fast, small target like a ballistic missile re-entry vehicle is such that two complementary missiles with nuclear warheads are required for any chance of success, one designed to engage in space, i.e. exoatmospherically, and the other in the atmosphere, i.e. endoatmospherically. The Americans dismantled their Safeguard system with its Spartan and Sprint missiles in 1976, but the USSR is still deploying 32 exoatmospheric "Galosh" ABM missiles around Moscow and is developing a "Gazelle" endoatmospheric missile. Deployment and further development of ABM missiles is subject to the ABM Treaty (*see below*). The Strategic Defence Initiative includes research into new kinds of non-nuclear ABM missile, including space-based systems. *EJG*.

Anti-Ballistic Missile (ABM) Treaty. The treaty signed in Moscow on May 26 1972 by President Nixon for the United States and General Secretary Brezhnev for the USSR, limiting each superpower to two deployment areas for anti-ballistic missile (ABM) missiles, one defending the national capital and the other a launch complex for intercontinental ballistic missiles (ICBMS). The treaty entered into force on October 3 1972 and was strengthened by a Protocol signed in Moscow on July 3 1974 in which each side agreed to only one ABM missile area, the Soviet one defending Moscow and the American an ICBM complex. Since late 1985, controversy has arisen both within the USA and between the signatories over the treaty's limitation on development of new ABM systems. The Reagan administration argued that its Strategic Defence Initiative was allowed by a "broad interpretation" of the treaty. *EJG*.

Anti-Satellite System (ASAT). Designed to destroy orbiting satellites. The Soviet Union has experimented with ASATS consisting of explosive spacecraft manoeuvred into close proximity to the target spacecraft. This remains operational according to American reports but has not been tested for some time. The Americans have developed an air-launched ASAT missile, but Congressional opposition has led to its abandonment. ASATS are controversial but the importance of space in military surveillance and communications and the possible development of ASAT-capable advanced ABM systems prevents an ASAT ban receiving universal approval. ASATS are discussed at the Defense and Space Talks in Geneva. Other types of system designed to destroy or degrade satellites include ground-based DEWS. *EJG.*

Anti-submarine warfare. This divides into two main problems – location and attack. So far, the most successful method of detecting a submerged submarine has proved to be sound used either passively (hydrophones – used from early in World War I) or actively (SONAR/ASDIC – in service from just after 1918). In certain circumstances, the magnetic signature of the hull can be used by a magnetic anomaly detector, first used in action in 1943. The first effective means of attack – the depth charge fired at a predetermined depth by a pressure-operated fuse – appeared during World War I. At first it was rolled off the stern of a ship, but this was soon supplemented by firing out to the sides by mortars to provide a wider "pattern" of explosions. During World War II, depth charges were adapted to be dropped from aircraft (as were hydrophones in the form of "sonobuoys") and fired ahead of surface ships by mortars ("Squid" and "Limbo"; another multiple mortar device, "Hedgehog", used more, smaller, contact-fused charges). An "intelligent depth charge" appeared in the form of an acoustic-guided torpedo. By the end of the war "snorkels" and new high-speed submarines had shifted the balance, which had been going against the old submersibles, back in favour of what had become true submarines. Since then, detection systems and weapons have been further developed, more use is made of submarines in the anti-submarine role and helicopters are widely used for both detection and attack. *DJL.*

Anti-tank guided weapon (ATGW). Missile guided to its target by remote control through a wire paid out during its flight.

Anti-tank gun. High-velocity, direct-fire gun designed to defeat armoured fighting vehicles, normally using kinetic energy (KE) projectiles. Can be towed or self-propelled.

Anti-tank rifle. An infantry platoon weapon utilizing a high-velocity, armour-piercing cartridge. Germany developed the 13mm Tankgewehr M1918 in World War I; the British army used the 0.55in Boys AT Rifle, 1937–43. The immoderate recoil of such rifles, and the appearance of heavier tank armour, led to the development of anti-tank missile weapons during the course of World War II.

Anti-tank weapons. Anti-tank weapons can penetrate the armour of an enemy armoured fighting vehicle either by crashing through by sheer kinetic energy, by directing the energy of a normal chemical explosion using "shaped charge" techniques or by setting up stresses in the armour by "pancaking" explosive on its surface. Kinetic energy rounds are fired by high velocity guns, often smoothbore. These are large and heavy, usually carried by other tanks, but lighter airborne cannon firing depleted uranium ammunition and modern self-forging fragment bomblets also use kinetic energy to penetrate. Shaped charge or High Explosive Anti-Tank (HEAT) warheads are normal for most anti-tank missiles and infantry anti-tank systems as velocity of impact is not important, but size of charge. Squash head projectiles, (HESH), specially favoured by the British, also do not demand high velocities. The explosive anti-tank techniques are more easily defeated by modern armours. Armour-Piercing Discarding Sabots (APDS) use advanced armour-piercing solid shot with a discarding sabot (DS) of light material to allow a gun to accelerate a sub-calibre projectile to very high velocity. The low-drag projectile maintains its kinetic energy better than a full calibre round. Increasing length and mass requires fin stabilization (FS) as in the APFSDS. Depleted uranium is an excellent material for such rounds, with its high mass and exothermic reaction on impact. *EJG.*

Antonov, Gen Alexei (1896–1962). Russian. COS Southern Army Group and subsequently North Caucasian and Transcaucasian Army Groups 1941–42. In December 1942 he was appointed Chief of Operations of the General Staff and, after April 1943, was also Deputy Chief of the General Staff. Helped plan major Soviet offensives and attended most of the top-level Allied conferences.

ANZAC. Acronym for the Australian and New Zealand Army Corps formed in December 1914. The name was also given to the sector of the Gallipoli peninsula held by that formation in 1915. Later it was often more widely used to describe any member of the Australian and New Zealand forces.

South African AA gunners, Italy, 1944

Anzio, Allied landings (January 22–31 1944). VI US Corps (Lucas) – 1st Armoured, 3rd and 45th US Divisions, 1st British Division and 2nd British Special Service Brigade – was landed on the Italian coast, southwest of Rome, to help II US Corps break through the Gustav Line during the First Battle of Cassino.

There was no German opposition to the landings. It was expected that Lucas would advance rapidly towards Rome, but he chose instead to consolidate his beachhead. By the time he was ready to advance, Kesselring had occupied the high ground around the beachhead and was able to defeat his efforts to break out.

Hitler was determined to teach the Allies a lesson that might deter them from landing in Northwest Europe. He released Fourteenth Army (von Mackensen) from Northern Italy to take charge of operations to destroy the VI US Corps beachhead; and reinforced

Kesselring with an open-handedness not seen since Stalingrad. The preliminary German counterattacks started on February 3. *WGFJ*.

Anzio, German counteroffensives (February 16–19 and February 29-March 3 1944). The first counteroffensive was launched by von Mackensen at Hitler's direction on a very narrow front down the Rome-Anzio road with five divisions under LXXVI Panzer Corps (Herr). It was repulsed after four days' bitter fighting by 45th US and 1st British Divisions, well-supported by heavy naval and air bombardments. To relieve the pressure at Anzio, Alexander opened the Second Battle of Cassino. Lucas was superseded as commander VI US Corps by Truscott from 3rd US Division when the crisis was over.

Hitler did not give up. The second counteroffensive, launched this time on a wider front, again by LXXVI Panzer Corps with five divisions, fell mainly on 3rd US Division, and was again repulsed. The Third Battle of Cassino was launched on March 15 in anticipation of a further German effort at Anzio, but a stalemate was not to be broken until the Allied spring offensive in May. *WGFJ*.

Anzio, Allied breakout from (May 23 1944). VI US Corps (Truscott) broke out on Alexander's orders with instructions to cut off the retreat of the German Tenth Army (von Vietinghoff) at Valmontone. The front of LXXVI Panzer Corps (Herr) collapsed, leaving Valmontone only lightly defended. On May 25, however, II US Corps (Keyes) reached the beachhead from the main front, and enabled the Fifth Army Commander (Clark), in contradiction to Alexander's orders, to turn Truscott's Corps northwards towards Rome instead of eastwards to Valmontone. The German Fourteenth Army fell back through Rome, which was declared an open city, pursued by Truscott. Keyes' Corps was belatedly made responsible for the Valmontone thrust, but was not strong enough and too late to intercept the Tenth Army, which escaped up the east bank of the Tiber. Rome was entered by the Americans on June 4 1944. *WGFJ*.

Aosta, Amadeo, Duke of (1898–1942). Italian Viceroy of Ethiopia and c-in-c East Africa, 1937–1941; surrendered to the British at Amba Alagi on May 16 1941.

Ap Bac, Battle of (1963). The battle near the hamlet of Ap Bac in the Mekong delta signified a turning point in the Vietnam War to strategists on both sides. Up to that time the US had assumed that strengthening and advising Saigon forces would be sufficient to defeat the insurgency, making it unnecessary to send American troops into combat.

In late December 1962, about 2,000 men of the Army of the Republic of Vietnam (ARVN) 7th Division encountered 300–400 People's Liberation Armed Force (PLAF) troops dug in along a canal near Ap Bac. The ARVN brought planes, helicopters, armoured personnel carriers and US advisers to its assistance. Yet when fighting ended on January 2 1963, the ARVN had suffered 165 casualties, while the PLAF had downed five helicopters and escaped with fewer than a dozen dead. The Ap Bac battle forced the US to reassess whether advisory and material assistance alone would be sufficient to guarantee the survival of the Saigon regime. *WST*.

Appeasement. Tolerance of Nazi aggressions, especially Chamberlain's agreement to Sudetenland's seizure in September 1938.

Arab Legion. Major military formation of the Hashemite Kingdom of Jordan (pre-1949, Transjordan); formed 1921 by Lt Col F G Peake and other British officers; owed much of its efficiency to Lt Gen Sir John Glubb, its commandant from 1939 until 1956, when all British officers were dismissed.

Arab Revolt. In June 1916, Sherif Hussein-ibn-Ali declared the Hejaz independent of Turkish rule. His followers seized control of several towns, including Mecca, but suffered heavy losses against Medina. Britain sent material aid and military advisers, amongst whom was Capt T E Lawrence. He helped the Arabs to adopt a strategy of mobile guerrilla warfare that kept the Turks tied to the defence of Medina and the Hejaz

railway, enabling Hussein's forces to advance north and capture Wejh and Aqaba. By the summer of 1917, the revolt had evolved into a nationalist uprising that now reached into Palestine and Syria. Furthermore, in September 1918, the Arab forces were an important feature of the right flank of Gen Allenby's offensive. They captured Deraa and Damascus and were still advancing northwards when halted by the signing, on October 30 1918, of the Allied armistice with Turkey. *MS*.

Arab-Israeli Wars (1948, 1956, 1967 and 1973).

War of Liberation (1948–49). After the defeat of Germany in 1945, Jewish immigration into Palestine, mostly illegal, began in earnest. Arab opposition to the creation of a Zionist state hardened, and the British government made it clear that it wished to abdicate its mandate to govern Palestine as soon as possible. Arab attacks on Jewish settlements increased in 1947 and on the departure of the British in May 1948 the new state of Israel was immediately assailed by its Arab neighbours. The resultant war, lasting into 1949, cost Israel 6,000 killed and ended with the clearing of the Tel Aviv-Jerusalem road and the repulse of the Arab forces, which suffered some 20,000 casualties. Israel now held all the territory granted under the terms of the United Nations' Commission of 1947 and increased its holdings in several areas, notably the Negev, although it failed to regain the old Jewish quarter of Jerusalem now held by the Kingdom of Jordan, which also annexed the West Bank region. Over 700,000 Arab refugees from Israeli-held territory now poured into the West Bank, the Egyptian-held Gaza Strip, Lebanon, Jordan, Syria and Iraq. Thus were laid the foundations of the refugee problem which has bedevilled Arab-Israeli relations ever since.

The 1956 conflict. No Arab state recognized Israel's boundaries, and much of the new state was within artillery range of its hostile neighbours. Prime Minister David Ben-Gurion now created the Israel Defence Force (IDF, or NAHAL) from a number of paramilitary organizations, regularizing what had

A

hitherto been a somewhat anarchic situation. He was assisted by men of remarkable ability like Moshe Dayan, COS of the IDF in 1956 when the Israeli Army attacked the Egyptians in the Sinai on October 26, shortly before the Anglo-French landings at Port Said. Ten IDF brigades outfought their more numerous but ill-coordinated opponents and had little difficulty in reaching the line of the Suez Canal, using paratroops under Col Sharon to seize the strategic Mitla Pass in central Sinai. Israel's southern borders were secured, the Gulf of Aqaba (denied to Israeli shipping by Egypt in 1955) was opened up, and the Gaza Strip passed into Israeli hands, together with its swollen refugee population. The IDF sustained fewer than 200 killed and 1,000 other casualties.

The Six-Day War (1967). Under UN pressure, the IDF withdrew from the Sinai in 1957 and the Arab states, encouraged by President Nasser of Egypt (now also President of the United Arab Republic [UAR]) resumed guerrilla attacks along Israel's borders. On May 14 1967, Cairo Radio called on UAR states to join in a "blow of annihilation" against Israel. Two days later, UN Secretary-General U Thant acceded to Nasser's demand that UN peacekeeping forces withdraw at once from the UAR-Israeli borders. Early on June 5, as 250,000 UAR troops and 2,000 tanks moved towards Israel's borders, the IDF launched a devastating pre-emptive airstrike against the Egyptian Air Force bases, destroying almost 400 aircraft. Whilst this attack was in progress, the IDF's Southern Command attacked the Egyptian Army in the Sinai desert and around Gaza. By June 8 the IDF was back on the line of the Suez Canal, having decisively beaten seven Egyptian divisions equipped with modern Russian tanks and artillery, most of which fell into Israeli hands. On the third day of the war, the IDF retook the old city of Jerusalem and on the fifth and sixth it swept the Syrians off the Golan Heights, capturing the key town of Kuneitra. In the "Six Day War" the Israelis had suffered fewer than 800 dead against more than 20,000 casualties inflicted on the UAR forces, who also lost more than 400 air-

craft and 800 tanks. Israel now held Jerusalem, the Golan Heights, the West Bank, the Gaza Strip and the whole of the Sinai Peninsula.

The war of attrition. Whilst the IDF's application of the classical principles of war drew wide acclaim, the humiliated UAR immediately began to plan revenge. The IDF was now obliged to tie down elite formations in defence of the Suez Canal, and the need to maintain high states of readiness at all times imposed great financial and social strains on Israel. Whilst Egypt was in no state to recommence large-scale military operations, a steady bombardment of the fortified IDF positions on the Canal (the Bar-Lev Line) began in 1968. Israel responded with commando raids against Egyptian military targets. Russian advisers now arrived in Egypt, together with much new equipment. Between 1970 and 1973 Egypt received 600 Russian-built combat aircraft and 2,500 tanks; Syria, 330 aircraft and 2,000 tanks. Both countries were also supplied with large numbers of air defence guns and missiles, which were to prove almost decisive when open war broke out again. Under its energetic COS, the reinvigorated Egyptian Army embarked on an intensive retraining programme. Israel also took delivery of large quantities of military equipment from the West.

Action on the Golan Heights, Oct 1973

The Yom Kippur War (1973). Early in October 1973, Israeli intelligence detected military build-ups along the Syrian border and south of the Suez Canal. After two earlier partial call-outs of IDF reservists that year and the imminence of Yom Kippur, the solemn Day of Atonement, Defence Minister

Moshe Dayan hesitated to order a general mobilization until only a few hours before the attacks were launched on the holiest day of the Jewish calendar. On the Golan Heights near Kuneitra, where the Syrians attacked with five divisions, only two weak IDF brigades were in position; these had to hold and buy time whilst the nation leapt to arms. The IDF no longer enjoyed air mastery as in 1967, for the Syrians had deployed their forward air defences skilfully, shooting down 30 Israeli aircraft on the first day. The attackers made full use of their 5-to-1 superiority on the ground and also seized the vital Israeli electronic monitoring post on top of Mount Hermon, "the eyes and ears of the State of Israel". The IDF narrowly held on, losing 250 tanks, before launching a successful counterattack on October 10 which threw the Syrians back with the loss of 867 tanks. In the south, the battle initially went badly for the IDF. The Egyptians carried out a brilliant assault crossing of the Suez Canal, neutralized the Bar-Lev Line, and set up a line of defence some 6 miles (10km) north of the Canal, carefully siting their newly acquired anti-tank guided missiles. These, courageously served, virtually destroyed an IDF tank brigade when it launched a hasty counterattack without close infantry support. The Egyptians also used self-propelled ZSU-23 quad-barrelled air defence guns and SA-6 missiles with great confidence and skill. The IDF did not regain air superiority until the arrival by air from the USA of sophisticated electronic countermeasures equipment costing $2,200 million.

Having driven off the first Israeli counterattack against their Suez bridgehead, the Egyptians brought armour across the Canal and on October 14 launched a full-scale attack, which was decisively repulsed. The IDF now switched its forces from the Golan Heights to the Sinai, where they counterattacked, drove down to and across the Canal, then swept south towards Suez town, which was entered on October 24. A few hours before the UN Security Council cease-fire took effect, the IDF recaptured the summit of Mount Hermon by helicopter assault.

It had been a close-run affair for the Israelis, who had almost exhausted their ammunition reserves. Their opponents had shown hitherto unsuspected military skills and there had been notable shortcomings in the IDF's performance, leading to much soul-searching and reassessment. Israel lost 2,412 killed in action and more than 5,000 wounded whilst their opponents suffered more than 18,000 dead and 51,000 wounded The financial cost of the war almost bankrupted the state and it was logical that a rapprochement with Egypt took place in 1974 when Premier Begin met President Sadat in Cairo. Agreement was reached whereby Israel withdrew from the line of the Canal and, later, from the strategic passes in Sinai over which so much heavy fighting had taken place in 1967. Egypt's severance of the Moscow connection eased the strategic tensions and the establishment of a de facto border on the Golan took pressure off the Northern Israeli settlements. However, subsequent events in Lebanon, and the relentless enmity of the Arab world have shown that Israel is still beset by implacable foes. *MH.*

Arado Ar 234 Blitz (Lightning) (German, WWII). World's first operational jet-propelled bomber; crew 1. Prototype flew June 15 1943; first production order for Ar 234B series. Deliveries from June 1944; relatively few of 210 completed Ar 234Bs used operationally. Night-fighter and multi-purpose versions existed by war's end. Two 1,980lb (890kg) s.t. Junkers Jumo 004B engines; max. speed 457mph (730kph); 3,308lb (1,500kg) bombs, two rearward firing 20mm cannon.

Aragon offensive (March–July 1938), Spanish Civil War. Following Teruel, the Nationalists' Army of Manoeuvre was rapidly reorganized. A multiphased attack began on March 9 with Yagüe's Moroccan Corps advancing rapidly along the south bank of the Ebro. With massive artillery and air superiority, including the Stuka in action for the first time, the Nationalists shattered the Republican forces, still exhausted and lacking ammunition. Then they advanced

on the sector between Saragossa and Huesca as far as the Segre river. On March 30 the Nationalist forces south of the Ebro pushed the International Brigades back in disorder and reached the sea at Vinaroz on April 15 thus splitting Republican Spain in two. Phase four occupied the Pyrenean border region up to Catalonia. (Franco's German advisers persuaded him not to advance on Barcelona. They feared French intervention and a British reaction following the *Anschluss.*) Phase five in May and June pushed the southern side of the Vinaroz corridor down towards Valencia. But here in the Sierras stretching to the coast north of Viver and Segorbe, the Nationalists were stopped by the defences. There, the Republicans fought their most effective battle of the war, inflicting 20,000 casualties at a cost of only 5,000. *AB.*

Arakan *see* BURMA CAMPAIGN.

Archangel. North Russian port: a supply point for Allied aid to Russia during World War I. Following the Bolshevik Revolution and Russia's withdrawal from the war, a British-French-US force was sent to Archangel (August 2 1918) to retrieve material and to encourage anti-Bolshevik forces establishing a regime that would bring Russia back into the war. Initially 1,500 strong, Allied strength rose to 30,000: still far too few to control such a vast, inhospitable area. The desired White Russian victory failed to materialize and, despite skilful defensive actions, the Allied position became increasingly untenable. Evacuation was ordered, the last units leaving on September 27 1919. *MS.*

Ardennes (1914, 1940, 1944–45). French Third and Fourth Armies lost heavily in a poorly-coordinated offensive against German Fourth and Fifth Armies in the rugged, heavily-forested Ardennes, southeast Belgium August 21–24 1914. The French believed that armoured forces could not swiftly negotiate the region, but in 1940 German panzers did so, reaching the Meuse on May 12.

Germany's surprise Ardennes counteroffensive ("Battle of the Bulge") from December 16 1944, expended irreplaceable men and

equipment in an attempt to bisect the Allied armies and capture Antwerp. Sixth Panzer Army was held at Elsenborn Ridge, but Fifth Panzer Army captured 8,000 US troops in the Schnee Eifel and encircled Bastogne, December 20. By December 24 the panzers were short of fuel; the Allies (c80,000 casualties) reinforced and, with improved weather, increased air operations. Bastogne was relieved, December 26, and German withdrawal began as US First and Third Armies counterattacked. By February 7 1945 the "Bulge" in the Allied line was liquidated. *MS.*

Argus. British aircraft carrier. The first aircraft carrier with a full flight deck, *Argus* was converted from the incomplete hull of the Italian liner *Conte Rosso* in a Scottish shipyard just too late to see service in World War I. Initially used for experiments in aircraft operation, including being fitted with a mock-up "island" superstructure (she was flush-decked). During 1939–45, she was mostly used for training and transport, although also for flying off fighters for Malta and supporting the "Torch" landings.

Arima, Rear Adm Masafumi (1895–1944). Jap. On October 15 1944, Arima, commanding the Manila-based 26th Air Flotilla, led an air strike against US warships off Luzon, reportedly crash-diving his Mitsubishi A6M onto the carrier USS *Franklin*. *Franklin* was not, in fact, damaged by kamikaze that day – but Arima's sacrifice prepared the way for Onishi's "official" initiation of kamikaze tactics four days later.

Arizona. US battleship. Sunk at Pearl Harbor, December 7 1941, with the loss of 1,103 officers and men. Never refloated, she is now a memorial.

Arkansas. US battleship. Served with the British Grand Fleet in 1918. During World War II she escorted Atlantic and Mediterranean troop convoys, 1942–43; provided fire support for the Allied invasions of Normandy and southern France, 1944; and also supported operations on Iwo Jima and Okinawa, 1945. She was sunk in a nuclear test at Bikini Atoll, 1946.

A

Ark Royal. British aircraft carriers. (1) Incomplete freighter hull purchased by the Admiralty (1914) for conversion as a seaplane carrier; served at Dardanelles. (2) Completed 1938, fought off Norway, her aircraft proved vital at Mers-el-Kébir and in the hunting down of *Bismarck*; sunk in 1941 by submarine torpedo and inadequate damage control. (3) 1955-79 core of the British postwar carrier force with sister *Eagle*.

Armed merchant cruiser. A passenger liner or merchant ship refitted as a naval vessel by the addition of guns and other minor modifications. They were extensively used, especially by the British, in both world wars for convoy escort and other cruiser roles. The Germans used them principally as commerce raiders.

Armentières. French town which, after a brief German occupation, was entered by the British in October 1914. It became an important forward base and recreation centre for the BEF until evacuated during the German Lys offensive in April 1918. Armentières was recaptured by Plumer's Second Army on October 2 that year.

Armistice negotiations, German in Italy (October 1944–May 1945). First approaches made by SS Gen Karl Wolff, SS and Police Commander in Italy, to Allen Dulles, American *Chargé d'Affaires* in Switzerland; negotiated secretly by Dulles and Alexander's representatives, Generals Lemnitzer and Airey, in Berne; eventually concluded with the dispatch of a German delegation, headed by Col Viktor von Schweinitz, to Alexander's HQ at Caserta in Italy where the instrument of surrender was signed on April 29, coming into effect on May 2 1945.

Armistice negotiations, Italian (August 4–September 3 1943). Authorized by the Badoglio government, and carried out in secret between Italian Generals Castellano and Zanussi, and Eisenhower's COS, Lt Gen Bedell Smith, and his Head of Intelligence, Brig Kenneth Strong, in Lisbon, Algiers and Sicily. The short unconditional surrender document was signed by Castellano at Alexander's HQ in Sicily on September 3. It was broadcast by Eisenhower and Badoglio on the evening of September 8 as the Allied invasion fleet approached Salerno. The Italian fleet managed to sail for Malta where it surrendered to Adm Cunningham on September 11. The rest of the Italian armed forces were disarmed by the Germans. *WGFJ*.

Armour-piercing ammunition. Solid shot or high explosive shells designed to penetrate armour plating.

Armoured cars. Wheeled fighting vehicles, lightly armoured for surveillance and reconnaissance. Usually armed for self-defence and the defeat of similar vehicles.

Armoured Fighting Vehicles (AFV) *see* TANKS.

Armoured train. Locomotives and rolling stock with ad hoc armour plating, armed with light cannon and machine guns. Now rare.

Armstrong Whitworth FK8 (Br, WWI), Two-seat reconnaissance bomber; crew 3. Prototype (FK7) flew early summer 1916; first production (FK8) delivered August 1916. In production and service until war's end; two VCs (Lt AA McLeod; Capt FMF West, MC) won on FK8s. Total production 1,701. 160hp Beardmore engine; max. speed 98.4mph (157kph) two 0.303in machine guns, 200lb (90kg) bombs.

Army. 1) Lawfully constituted land forces. 2) A number of corps grouped under a single HQ, e.g., Eighth Army 1941–45, Second US Army.

Army Air Corps (AAC) (British Army). The AAC was formed in 1957 to meet increasing demands for light aircraft support for the Army in operations worldwide, and is organized into Regiments, Squadrons and Independent Flights. Lynx helicopters armed with TOW missiles are used for both the anti-tank role and to provide battlefield support for the ground combat arms. The Aérospatiale Gazelle is used for observation and reconnaissance. There is a small fixed-wing element.

Army Group. A number of armies grouped under a single HQ e.g. 21st Army Group (British), Army Group Centre (German, World War II).

Army of Africa, the advance of (August–October 1936), Spanish Civil War. Franco's advance on Madrid began from Seville on August 6 after the first major airlift of troops in history (altogether, 12,000 men were ferried across the Straits of Gibraltar in German and Italian aircraft). Under Col Yagüe, a lorryborne force of around 8,000 Foreign Legionnaires and Moroccan levies known as *regulares*, advanced rapidly north from Andalucia into Estremadura. After an infamous massacre following the capture of Badajoz on August 15, they swung northeast on Madrid. Their reputation and rapid flanking movements created panic amongst the ill-armed Republican militias. At the end of September, having advanced nearly 310 miles (500km) to Talavera de la Reina, Franco deflected his army from the undefended prize of Madrid, to relieve the symbolically important group of defenders in the Alcázar of Toledo. Yagüe, furious that sentiment should take priority, had to be relieved. *AB*.

Army of the Republic of Vietnam (ARVN). Pronounced "arvin", ARVN, or the South Vietnamese army, had its origins in the Vietnam National Army that was created by France in 1950. Vietnamese officers transferred from the French army were sufficient to staff just three battalions, so the large majority of officers were French. Beginning with about 16,000 Vietnamese regulars drawn from French formations in 1950, the National Army grew to 205,000 men by the war's end in 1954. The bulk of the army then regrouped in the South, and Vietnamese were thrust into command positions.

The US took over France's assistance and advisory role in December 1954. The name became Army of the Republic of Vietnam when a republic was proclaimed in October 1955. By autumn 1959 the ARVN had 136,000 regular army soldiers organized into seven divisions, a five-battalion airborne group, eight independent artillery battalions and four armed cavalry squadrons, plus 97,000 regional and popular force troops making a total of 233,000. At its peak in 1972, it had 424,000 regulars organized into eleven infantry divisions, an airborne division and a marine division; plus 532,000 regional and popular forces making a total of 956,000. Main force organization, equipment, training manuals and tactical doctrine were American.

The instability of the Saigon regime invited the officer corps to intervene in politics. Officers overthrew President Ngo Dinh Diem in 1963, and all subsequent heads of state and most province chiefs came from the military. Involvement in politics hindered the ARVN's military effectiveness, however. Competition for political and administrative posts fuelled factional splits within the officer corps. Officers were often appointed to field commands on the basis of political loyalty, not military competence. Frequent rotation, inadequate training, corruption and dependence on the US undermined morale.

Moreover, foot soldiers resented service in an army that sent them far from home to fight for a regime they supported weakly or not at all. In 1964, desertions from all South Vietnamese armed forces numbered 73,000, about 15 percent of the total; in 1970, they numbered over 126,000. Efforts to curb desertions enjoyed only modest success, and desertion remained the largest cause of manpower loss. Desertion was highest, up to 36 percent a year, in frontline combat units. In these respects the ARVN compared unfavourably with the People's Army of Vietnam (PAVN). The ARVN could never match the PAVN's identification with anticolonialism, revolutionary élan, and highly disciplined officer corps.

However, the ARVN was not as uniformly inferior as its detractors sometimes claimed. Where capable officers had good rapport with their men, ARVN units fought well. The 1st Infantry Division, the Marine Division, the Airborne Division and some Ranger battalions distinguished themselves. Officer motivation also improved as the corps became less an elitist club

and more an avenue of upward mobility for young professionals. The common belief that the ARVN shirked combat is contradicted by figures showing that the ARVN suffered heavier casualties than American forces in every year of the war. By 1975, 243,000 ARVN soldiers had died in action and 507,000 had been wounded. *WST*.

Arnauld de la Perière, Vice Adm Lothar von (1886–1941). Ger. Most successful U-boat commander of all time: in *U-35*, November 1915–March 1918, he sank 189 merchant ships (446,708 tons), most with surface gunfire. He headed a "storm battalion" in the civil strife of 1919–20. He rejoined the *Kriegsmarine* in September 1939, holding administrative commands in occupied Europe until killed in an air crash.

Allied paras surrender at Arnhem

Arnhem, Battle of (September, 1944). Montgomery's proposed plan, Operation "Market Garden", was intended to accelerate the progress of the Allied advance into Holland and Germany. He envisaged that a series of airborne assaults would seize crossings over the Maas, Waal and Lower Rhine rivers ("Market"), enabling the British Second Army to make a rapid drive into the Ruhr ("Garden"). While two American airborne divisions were to seize the southern bridges along the route, the 1st British Airborne Division was given the task of capturing the bridges over the Rhine at Arnhem. On September 17 the first of the units landed by parachute and glider but the arrival of vital equipment was delayed and the siting of dropping zones several miles from their objectives resulted in immediate complications. By the time men of 2nd Parachute

Battalion had fought their way to the river, the Germans had destroyed the railway bridge. The road bridge remained intact but although they managed to secure its northern approaches, they were unable to dislodge the Germans from its southern end. The division's commander, Major Gen Urquhart, was plagued by poor wireless communications and adverse weather conditions that hampered the delivery by air of supplies and reinforcements. To make matters worse, German resistance was far greater than anticipated. The two SS Panzer divisions in the vicinity soon began to pin back the lightly armed airborne troops. Not only had the fighting in Arnhem stiffened but the main Allied advance was checked north of Nijmegen. Ill-equipped to carry out an extended defence, the British troops were soon in dire straits. On September 21 the much depleted force at the bridge finally succumbed to German counterattacks and even when the long awaited 1st Polish Parachute Brigade landed to reinforce Urquhart, most were unable to reach the north side of the river. An evershrinking perimeter held out to the west of Arnhem until September 25 when, short of ammunition and knowing that relieving forces were still too far away, the defenders were ordered to break out and try and reach Allied lines. Of more than 10,300 Allied forces engaged at Arnhem, only 2,827 managed to reach safety. *MS*.

Arnim, Col Gen Hans-Jürgen von (1889–1962). Ger. Commander Fifth Panzer Army in Tunisia; promoted to command Army Group Africa in March 1943; surrendered on May 12 1943 after the fall of Tunis.

Arnold, Gen of the Air Force Henry Harley ("Hap") (1886–1950). US. Commanding Gen of the USAAF throughout its participation in World War II. By the outbreak of war Arnold, who had become Chief of the Air Corps in 1938, had demonstrated an outstanding skill as a publicist for the cause of air power and had become one of the most powerful military figures in Washington. Though not of equal rank with Marshall and King, the Chiefs of the United

A

States Army and Navy, he nonetheless achieved an authority and influence which corresponded with theirs, and 1944, with Marshall, MacArthur and Eisenhower, he was promoted to the supreme rank of General of the Army. In 1948, when the air force became an independent service, he became the first General of the Air Force – a remarkable achievement for an officer who never commanded a major formation in battle.

He thus, perhaps, lacked some of the balance and realism which characterized his British opposite number, Portal, and his determination to show that American air power would be guided by independent American ideas and that its importance should be estimated on a scale comparable or, indeed, superior to military and naval power led him at times into error. His determination to develop a day bombing offensive against all the advice of his British colleagues and then to claim, in justification of the idea, that the disastrous attack on Schweinfurt of October 1943 had been a decisive success are evidences of these tendencies. Nevertheless, his radical approach combined with the process of trial and error together with an admixture of luck enabled him to formulate the strategy of victory in the air, both in Europe and the Pacific.

The enormous contribution made by the USAAF to victory over Germany and Japan brought Arnold's ambition to obtain independent status for the service to the point of realization and, within three years it was attained. *ANF*.

Arras, Battle of (1917). The British attack at Arras on April 9 1917 was launched as a diversionary operation in support of Nivelle's offensive on the Aisne, which began a week later. General Allenby's Third Army, at Arras, was to pierce the Hindenburg Line and the older German defences to its north, which were covered in the rear by the Drocourt-Quéant switch; on Allenby's left was the First Army, including the Canadian Corps which was to storm Vimy Ridge; and on his right was the Fifth Army, which would provide flank leverage by attacking the Hindenburg Line at Bullecourt. Haig's GHQ sacrificed sur-

prise by opting for a five-day bombardment by nearly 3,000 guns, while only 60 tanks were available for the assault, yet the opening day of the attack was extremely successful. The Canadian Corps took most of Vimy Ridge and XVII Corps progressed 3.5 miles (5.6km) towards Fampoux – the deepest penetration on the Western Front in one day since 1914. Monchy le Preux fell to the 37th Division on April 11 but an Australian attack, with tanks, at Bullecourt was an expensive failure. Hitherto the German Sixth Army had not properly applied Ludendorff's new flexible defence doctrine, but once the Germans recovered their tactical composure the offensive deteriorated into the familiar mould of bloody attrition. However, to take pressure off the French army, fast degenerating into mutiny after Nivelle's disastrous offensive, Haig prolonged the operations into late May, by which time British casualties were 158,660. *PJS*.

Arras, Battle of (1940). On May 19 1940, during the German drive through France, reconnaissance groups of Rommel's 7th Panzer Division – the spearhead formation on the inner flank of the German westward thrust from the Meuse – brushed against the British defences at Arras. Here, Rommel's armoured units paused for a short time, having pushed too far ahead of their supporting infantry. At this point, Gen Lord Gort, commanding the BEF, initiated a counter-attack against the German armoured column. The attack was made on May 21 by the 4th and 7th Battalions, Royal Tank Regiment, and two infantry battalions from Maj Gen Martel's 50th Division, with some help on their right from the French 3rd Light Mechanized Division. Of the 74 British Matilda tanks available, 58 were armed with machine guns and only 16 with 2-pounder guns. Even so, the British effort surprised the 7th Panzer Division and the SS *Totenkopf* Division, causing some panic in the latter. Rommel too was sufficiently shaken to overestimate the strength of the forces opposing him. The attack was eventually stopped by 88mm guns and by Stuka dive-bombers and the British were forced to withdraw that evening. The counter-

attack, however, exerted a considerable psychological effect upon the German High Command, convincing von Rundstedt and others of the dangers of allowing their armoured spearheads to become overextended. In this respect the Arras counterattack almost certainly influenced the crucial German "halt order" at Dunkirk three days later. *PJS*.

Arromanches *see* NORMANDY, INVASION OF (1944).

Artillery. Generic term describing all forms of indirect fire support, including mortars, guns, missiles and rockets. Greater ranges, developments in ballistics, munitions, control of indirect fire, enhanced target acquisition and improved mobility made artillery the decisive arm in both world wars and likely to retain its preeminence in the missile age.

Arz von Straussenberg Gen Artur (1857–1935). Austrian. Became Austrian Chief of Staff in February 1915; defeated in the twin battles of the Asiago and the Piave in June 1918; and forced by the collapse of his armies in the Battle of Vittorio Veneto in October 1918 to accept the Allies' armistice terms on November 3.

Ascension Island. British dependency in South Atlantic, 3,500 miles (5,600km) north of the Falklands. Its anchorage and American-built airfield ("Wideawake") were indispensable staging posts for shipping and aircraft en route to the South Atlantic during the Falklands War of 1982. The bombing of Stanley airfield by RAF Vulcans was only possible because of in-flight refuelling by Victor tankers from Wideawake Field.

ASDIC (said to stand for Anti-Submarine Detection Investigation Committee) *see* SONAR.

A Shau, Battles of. In March 1966, the People's Army of Vietnam (PAVN) pushed small American and South Vietnamese detachments out of the A Shau Valley, located about 30 miles (50km) southwest of Hue, Vietnam, and transformed it into a major logistical terminus of the Ho Chi Minh Trail. The valley thereby became an important strategic objective for both sides in the Vietnam War. It was two years, however, before US and South Vietnamese forces were able to penetrate the valley in Operation "Delaware" (April 19–May 17 1968).

The US 101st Airborne reinforced by Marine and South Vietnamese units conducted Operation "Apache Snow" in A Shau in May 1969. On the northern edge of the valley atop Hill 937, or Ap Bia Mountain, two deeply entrenched battalions of the 29th PAVN Regiment withstood waves of napalm, high explosive and artillery bombardment while training automatic weapons fire on the attackers below. The Americans suffered high casualties before taking the hill at the fifth attempt, only to abandon it soon after. To American troops, Hill 937 came to be known as "Hamburger Hill".

The battles for the A Shau Valley sparked controversy, for after each operation, US and Army of the Republic of Vietnam (ARVN) forces withdrew and the PAVN returned. Civilian critics asked what point there was in suffering heavy losses if the enemy were not denied use of the valley. Military spokesmen answered that the strategy of attrition required disrupting the communists' logistical effort and inflicting casualties, not occupying territory. US and ARVN forces could not permanently hold many such remote mountain valleys as the A Shau, so long as vast resources were tied down in the defence of the lowlands. *WST*.

Asiago, Battle of (June 15–16 1918). The Austrian offensive of June 1918 was defeated by British and French divisions on the Asiago plateau. *See also* ITALIAN CAMPAIGN, WORLD WAR I.

Asquith, Earl of Oxford and, (1852–1928). Br. As Liberal Prime Minister from April 1908, took Britain into World War I, forming a coalition Cabinet in May 1915, following Adm Fisher's resignation and the Munitions Crisis, and introducing conscription in 1916. His even-handed style of government was not always compatible with the demand of modern, industrialized war, and in December 1916 he was replaced by the more dynamic Lloyd George.

Assault rifle *see* RIFLE.

Atatürk, Gen Mustafa Kemal (1881–1938). Turkish. Mustafa Kemal (later known as Atatürk) saw action in Libya during the war with Italy in 1911–12 and, subsequently, in the Balkan Wars. However, it was not until the Allied attack on the Gallipoli Peninsula in April 1915 that he came to real prominence. As commander of the 19th Division, he appreciated the need to contain the enemy landings instantly and deny them the opportunity to consolidate. Although his command sustained considerable casualties, he personally drove his men forward and restricted the ANZAC forces to a small bridgehead. Four months later, in August, Mustafa Kemal performed a similar feat, frustrating a new Allied offensive. In spite of these victories, his abrasive personality did not win him many supporters and he was sent to lead Turkish forces against the Russians in Eastern Anatolia. He met less success in this theatre of operations but later went on to conduct a skilful campaign in Syria in the closing months of the war. Having always harboured strong political opinions, it was not surprising that Mustafa Kemal should take a hand in determining Turkey's postwar destiny. He played a leading role in the establishment of a Turkish nationalist party and led the resistance to his country's dismemberment by the Allies and Greek attempts at territorial aggrandisement. With the Battle of Sakarya in 1921 he halted the Greek advance and in September the following year completed his victory with the reoccupation of Smyrna (Izmir). His military triumphs certainly helped to persuade the Allied powers to recognize the new regime in Turkey and at the Treaty of Lausanne a new series of frontiers was agreed. On October 29 1923 Mustafa Kemal proclaimed a republic of which he became the first president. He led the new nation into a rapid period of modernization and westernization that was, however, achieved at the expense of his adopting a dictatorial role. *MS*.

Athenia. British 13,581-ton passenger liner sunk by U-boat on September 3 1939 in North Atlantic.

Atlantic, Battle of the (1939-45). The longest battle of World War II was that of the Atlantic seaways – principally those between North America and the British Isles – which lasted from the outbreak of war in 1939 to the surrender of Germany. The chief protagonist on the Axis side was the U-boat force, although long-range bombers (mostly Focke-Wulf Condors), armed merchant raiders (mostly in more distant waters) and occasional sorties by heavy ships played their part. There was also a small contribution by a few Italian submarines.

At first the Germans were handicapped by the small numbers of U-boats available, and by being forced to exit and return by the narrow waters of the North Sea. However the blitzkrieg victories of 1940 brought bases in Norway and on the French Atlantic coast, while isolating Britain and tying down much of her destroyer force on anti-invasion duties. This produced what the U-boat commanders called their "happy time". Using wolf-pack tactics and attacking at night on the surface, the sinkings of merchantmen escalated rapidly. In 1941, however, the increasing number of escorts available from new construction, lend-lease, or freed from anti-invasion duties, began to make a difference. So did the increasing experience of their crews, while the Canadians built up their navy almost from scratch. Radar in some escorts began to lessen the advantages of surface attack at night for the U-boats. In one week of spring 1941, Germany lost three of her greatest U-boat aces (Prien, Schepke and Kretschmer).

For the rest of 1941 the battle was essentially even, although American warships played an increasingly un-neutral role in the Western Atlantic. However the entry of America into the war produced another "happy time" for the U-boats on the coast of America and in the Caribbean. The Americans were unwilling to adopt the tried remedy of convoy, and this cost Allied merchant ships dear; it was not until the middle of 1942 that the situation came back under control, although the failure to obtain the few very long-range aircraft which could cover the "mid-Atlantic air gap" was the cause of a prolonged struggle between the Admiralty and Bomber Command.

The last and worst crisis came early in 1943. In March it began to look as if the wolf packs were gaining the upper hand over the convoy escorts. This triumph proved illusory and the threat disappeared with incredible rapidity. The grossly delayed availability of long-range aircraft; more escorts, some organized in support groups; escort aircraft carriers; the breaking of the U-boat codes; increasing use of new devices (short-wave radar, high-frequency radio direction-finding equipment aboard escorts); and weapons ("hedgehog", the heavy depth charge), all played their part.

Dönitz withdrew his submarines from the North Atlantic and attempted to attack in more distant waters. American escort carrier groups in mid-Atlantic destroyed most of the "milch cow" support submarines and many other U-boats and halted this. Towards the end of 1943, the U-boats began to use acoustic homing torpedoes against escorts. It long remained secret that the Allies were using similar weapons from aircraft. The introduction of snorkels enabled the U-boats to continue to fight the losing battle until the end. Fortunately for the Allies, the new type XXI and XXIII U-boats were only just coming into service at the end of the war. Their high submerged speed and endurance would have been very difficult for the escorts to cope with.

In the end, aircraft sank the most U-boats, although surface escorts were not far behind them. A comparatively small investment in submarines by Germany, plus the skill and bravery of their crews, made the Allies fight a desperate battle, which was vital to their success in the war. Without victory in the Atlantic, nothing else was possible. *DJL.*

Atlantic Conference. Meetings between Churchill and Roosevelt on board USS *Augusta* and HMS *Prince of Wales* between August 9 and 12 1941 in Placentia Bay, Newfoundland. These resulted in the Atlantic Charter, which contained eight clauses to the effect that: neither country should seek territorial aggrandisement; all territorial

changes should be subject to the approval of the local inhabitants; people should have the right to choose their form of government; nations should have equal rights to trade and access to raw materials; improved labour standards, international economic advancement and social security should be sought; after the "final destruction of Nazi tyranny", peace should afford freedom from fear and want; the freedom of the seas should be secured; there should be international agreement to abandon the use of force. Immediately, the Charter drew America, though still neutral, closer to Britain, especially in the Battle of the Atlantic. *ANF.*

Atlantic Conveyor. Cunard container ship of 14,950 tons, requisitioned for use as aircraft and logistics ferry during the Falklands War. Sunk on May 25 1982 off Falklands with the loss of 10 Wessex, 1 Lynx and 3 Chinook helicopters as well as most of the British Task Force's reserves of tentage.

Atlantic wall. While the bulk of Germany's armies were engaged on the Eastern Front, the western extremities of Nazi-occupied Europe were protected by defences that stretched from the North Cape to the Pyrenees. Concrete fortifications, mines, guns and waterline obstacles were arrayed to frustrate any Allied attack.

Atlas missile. America's first intercontinental ballistic missile, first deployed in 1958 and withdrawn for use as a space booster in 1965. Liquid fuelled, later missiles were in semi-hardened installations and silos from which the weapons were elevated before launch. By 1962, 142 Atlases were deployed; range was up to 11,100 miles (18,500km), CEP about 6,600ft (2,000m) and warhead yield 1.4 or 3.75 megatons depending on variant.

Atomic Demolition Munition (ADM). Nuclear explosive charges emplaced as mines or carried as demolition charges. The most recent American ADMs, made in the 1960s, were the 350lb (157.5kg) "Medium ADM" W-45 with a yield of up to 15 kilotons emplaced by 6-man teams using jeeps or helicopters and the 150lb (67.5kg)

0.01-1 kiloton "Special ADM" W-54 emplaced by two men. The latter is still in service.

Atomic bomb. Early name for nuclear weapons. As these use the energy obtained from events concerning the nuclei of atoms, "nuclear" is the more accurate term.

Aubers Ridge. On May 9 1915, in support of the French Artois offensive, the British First Army, under Sir Douglas Haig, attacked either side of Neuve-Chapelle with the object of securing a foothold on Aubers Ridge, 3,000yd (2,700m) to the east. The attack cost the British 11,600 casualties for negligible gains. Complaints about ammunition shortages helped to provoke the "Munitions Crisis" at home and hastened the formation of a coalition Cabinet and the Ministry of Munitions.

Auchinleck, Field Marshal Sir Claude (1884–1981). Br. Commander British forces ashore at Narvik in the Norwegian campaign from May 11 1940 until they were evacuated on June 8; then C-in-C India until Churchill selected him to relieve Wavell as C-in-C Middle East from July 5 1941. He mounted the successful "Crusader" offensive to relieve Tobruk in November 1941 and took personal command of Eighth Army after its

Field Marshal Auchinleck (*left*)

defeat by Rommel at Gazala in June 1942. He succeeded in checking Rommel's advance into Egypt on the El Alamein Line in July, but was dismissed by Churchill in August 1942 and returned to India to take over again as C-in-C when Wavell became Viceroy. Promoted Field Marshal, he handled the partition of the British Indian Army between India and Pakistan in 1947 as Supreme Commander responsible to the two new dominions, but became *persona non grata* to the Indian government and retired at the end of 1947. *WGFJ*.

Augsburg, bombing of April 17 1942. Twelve Lancasters of 5 Group, Bomber Command led by Squadron Leader J D Nettleton were dispatched in daylight on a low-level precision attack upon the U-boat assembly shed within the MAN complex. The objects were to test the capacity of the newly introduced Lancasters for such operations and to contribute to the Battle of the Atlantic. The target was hit, but seven Lancasters were lost and the raid was seen to have been overambitious. Nettleton was awarded the VC.

Austalian Imperial Forces (AIF). Australia made notable contributions in both world wars with the Australian Imperial Forces (AIF). In World War I, the AIF served in the Middle East and with the New Zealand contingent formed the Australian and New Zealand Army Corps (ANZACS) which fought with distinction at Gallipoli. On the Western Front, the Australian corps of five divisions which served in Rawlinson's Fourth Army was reckoned to be an elite formation. Australian troops also served in various minor theatres overseas. Over 59,000 Australians lost their lives on all fronts.

In January 1940, the first units of the 2nd AIF embarked for service in the Middle East, where they played a leading part in Wavell's first successful offensive against Graziani's Italian Army. After service in Greece and in the first siege of Tobruk, where they formed a significant part of the garrison, the Australians were withdrawn to Australia to meet the threat posed by Japanese aggression in the Far East. Thereafter they played a leading part in the Southwest Pacific campaign. A total of 27,073 Australians died in battle, on active service or as POWs in World War II, almost half of them as prisoners of the Japanese. *MH*.

Australian forces in Korea. When the Korean War broke out, Australia had air, sea and ground contingents in Japan serving with the British Commonwealth Occu-

pation Force. On June 29 1950 two destroyers based in Japan were placed at the disposal of Gen MacArthur and later the Australian naval contingent was reinforced by a frigate and an aircraft carrier. On June 30 1950 Australia released No 77 Squadron RAAF based at Iwakuni for action in Korea and also provided an air transport squadron. Although Australia announced the commitment of ground forces on July 14 1950, there was a delay in employing the troops immediately available in Japan, 3rd Battalion, Royal Australian Regiment, because only volunteers could be asked to serve in Korea. The reconstituted battalion, under Lt Col C H Green, finally landed at Pusan on September 28 1950 where it linked up with the British 27th Infantry Brigade which was renamed the 27th British Commonwealth Infantry Brigade. The following year 3rd RAR was incorporated into the 1st Commonwealth Division. In October 1951 Australia agreed to provide a second battalion, 1st RAR, under Lt Col I Hutchison. *CM*.

Autogyro. Autogyros derive lift from an unpowered (autorotating) main rotor system and forward thrust from a conventional propeller. They have a good short take-off and landing capability, but cannot hover or take off vertically.

Auxiliary Territorial Service (ATS). Women's volunteer (and later conscript) force formed in 1938 to provide support services for the British army. From 1949, the force was part of the regular army, known as the Women's Royal Army Corps (WRAC).

Avenger, Grumman TBF-1/TBM-1 (US, WWII). Torpedo-bomber. Prototype flew August 1 1941; entered US Navy service spring 1942; also used by British Fleet Air Arm from early 1943. Operated throughout World War II, Pacific, Atlantic and Mediterranean; used by USMC ground attack and anti-submarine. Production totalled 9,839. One 1,700hp Wright R-2600-8 Cyclone 14 engine; max speed 251mph (400kph); 1,600lb (720kg) bombs or torpedo, two 0.30in and one 0.50in machine guns.

Avon, Earl of (Anthony Eden) (1897–1977). Br. Secretary of State for Foreign Affairs 1935–38, 1940–45, 1951–55, Prime Minister 1955–57. Associated after resigning in 1938 with the anti-appeasement viewpoint, he became one of Churchill's principal lieutenants in the war. In 1956 he was a prime mover in the initiation of the Suez Crisis.

Avranches, Battle of (1944). The American break-out from the Normandy bridgehead – Operation "Cobra" – began on July 25 1944. As German resistance crumbled, the US 4th Armoured Division advanced 25 miles (40km) in 36 hours, and reached Avranches, the gateway to Brittany, at dusk on July 30. The town was cleared next day, and American armour pressed on to take the bridge over the River Sélune at Pontaubault. The US VIII Corps could now break out into Brittany, under the command of Patton's Third Army, which became operational on August 1. However, the narrow American corridor was a tempting target, and Hitler ordered Field Marshal von Kluge to break through to the coast at Avranches. A German counterattack was therefore launched during the night of August 6–7, but it made only small gains around Mortain. The Americans had been forewarned by "Ultra", and the German offensive was soon halted by Allied airpower. *SB*.

Avro 504 (Br, WWI and after). Two-seat reconnaissance-bomber/trainer. Prototype flew September 18 1913; deliveries to RFC began June 12 1914. Three RNAS Avros bombed Friedrichshafen November 21 1914. Limited use RFC in France, RNAS France and Aegean. Majority of later variants used as trainers; in 1918 some 504Ks modified as single-seat night fighters. Production 8,340 to end of war, continued thereafter. One 80hp/130hp rotary engine various types; max. speed 95mph (152kph); 80lb (36kg) bombs, one 0.303in machine gun.

Axis Powers. The alliance between Germany and Japan, forged by the anti-Comintern pact of November 1936. Italy joined the pact in November 1937.

43

B-1. An advanced American swing wing strategic bomber first flown in 1974, cancelled in 1977 but reinstated in 1981. The 100 aircraft ordered have suffered technical problems since entering service in 1986. The B-1B can carry up to 38 free-fall thermonuclear bombs or short-range attack missiles, 22 cruise missiles or 128 500lb (225kg) high-explosive bombs.

B-2 Front. The Vietnamese communists organized the B-2 Front Command in 1963 to coordinate armed struggle in the lower half of South Vietnam. That area comprised two-thirds of the South's population and its capital city. While the B-1, B-3 and B-4 front commands reported directly to Hanoi, B-2 was under the jurisdiction of the Central Office for South Vietnam (COSVN). Distance from Hanoi and the unique combat situations caused the B-2 Command to operate more independently than the others.

B-2 *see* STEALTH.

B-17 Flying Fortress, Boeing (US, WWII). Heavy bomber; crew 10. Prototype flew July 28 1935; first US deliveries July 1939; to RAF from March 1941. Early operational use unsuccessful; modifications and development to later versions for daylight precision bombing to end of war, mostly in Europe and Mediterranean. Defensive armament repeatedly modified/increased. Production total 12,731. Four 1,200hp Wright R-1820-97 engines; max. speed 325mph (520kph); 17,600lb (7,980kg) bombs, up to thirteen 0.5in machine guns.

B-24 Liberator, Consolidated (US, WWII). Heavy bomber; crew 10. Prototype flew December 29 1939; deliveries began 1940. Widely used as transport, maritime reconnaissance bomber and strategic heavy bomber, in Europe, over the Atlantic and Pacific oceans. Production total 18,482 comprised many variants, used by USAAF, USN, USMC, RAF, RAAF, RCAF. Four 1,200hp Pratt and Whitney R-1830-65 engines; max. speed 303mph (485kph); 8,800lb (3,990kg) bombs, up to ten 0.5in machine guns.

B-25 Mitchell, North American (US, WWII). Medium bomber; crew 5. Prototype flew August 19 1940, earliest deliveries February 1941. Noted for the Doolittle raid on Tokyo, April 18 1942. Used by RAF (Mitchell) from September 1942; also flown by US Marine Corps and Dutch units; 870 delivered to Russia; widely used in Europe, Middle East, Far East, Pacific. Production (all variants) 9,816. Two 1,700hp Wright R-2600-13 engines; max. speed 284mph (454kph); 3,000lb (1,360kg) bombs, four 0.5in machine guns.

B-26 Marauder, Martin (US, WWII). Medium bomber; crew 7. Prototype flew November 25 1940; production (total all variants 5,266) until April 18 1945. USAAF use in Pacific, some as torpedo-bombers; later in Europe, North Africa. Over 500 supplied to RAF; use in Middle East, Italy, some by SAAF; six *Groupes* of *Armée de l'Air*. Two Pratt and Whitney R-2800-43 engines; max. speed 298mph (476kph); 3,000lb (1,360kg) bombs or 2,000lb (900kg) torpedo, up to twelve 0.5in machine guns.

B-29 Superfortress (Washington), Boeing (US, WWII). Heavy bomber; crew 11. First flew September 21 1942; first operational mission (from India) June 5 1944; attack on Japan June 15 1944. B-29s *Enola Gay* and *Bock's Car* dropped first atomic bombs on Hiroshima and Nagasaki respectively, August 6 and 9 1945. RAF use as Washington 1950–54. Production 3,905. Four 2,000hp Wright R-3350-23 engines; max. speed 358mph (576kph); 20,000lb (9,070kg) bombs, one 20mm cannon, eight 0.5in machine guns.

B-36. A huge 230ft (70m) wingspan bomber built by Convair which gave Strategic Air Command (SAC) its first means of striking the Soviet Union from the continental USA unrefuelled. Powered by six piston engines, boosted in the more numerous later variants by four jets, the aircraft cruised at 391mph (626kph). It could carry a normal maximum of 72,000lb (32,400kg) of bombs 2,399 miles (3,838km) at 39,900ft (11,970m) and was in service from 1948 to 1959.

B-47. A Boeing jet medium bomber procured in large quantities for Strategic Air Command from 1951 to replace the B-29 Superfortress. Over 2,000 were produced until 1957 when 28 medium bomb wings with 45 aircraft each were in frontline service, plus 300 reconnaissance variants. The B-47 remained in service till 1966–67; it could carry 10,000lb (4,500kg) of bombs just over 2,000 miles (3,200km).

B-52 Stratofortress, Boeing (US). Heavy bomber. Prototype flew October 2 1952; initial deliveries from January 1955. Used exclusively USAF; sequence of variants developed to carry AGM-28 Hound Dog or AGM-86B cruise missiles. On bombing missions Vietnam War carried conventional bombs. Production 744. B-52H – eight 17,000lb (7,710kg) s.t. Pratt and Whitney TF33-P-3 turbofans; max. speed 665mph (1,064kph); two AGM-28 Hound Dog air-to-surface missiles; one multi-barrel 20mm cannon.

Baade, Lt Gen Ernst-Günther (1887–1945). Ger. Commander of the defences of the Strait of Messina during the Sicilian campaign; then Commander of 90th Panzer Grenadier Division during the Italian campaign, successfully holding Cassino in the First and Second Battles. He was Commander of LXXXI Corps in Northwest Europe from March 1945. Killed in action in Germany, April 1945.

Babi Yar. On September 29 and 30 1941, SS *Einsatzgruppen* carried out a two-day massacre of over 33,000 Jews in a ravine at Babi Yar near Kiev in the Ukraine.

Bacon, Adm Sir Reginald (1863–1947). Br. Bacon pioneered the introduction of submarines and was prominent in the planning of HMS *Dreadnought*, which he captained.

Bader, Gp Capt Sir Douglas (1910–82). Br. Outstanding fighter pilot in the battles of France and Britain and "Circus" operations. He played a prominent part in 12 Group's "Big Wing" tactics. POW 1941–45. His brilliance was the more remarkable in that he had lost both legs in a flying accident in 1931.

Badoglio, Marshal Pietro (1871–1956). Italian. COS of Italian Armed Forces 1939–40. He succeeded Mussolini as head of the Italian government on July 26 1943; announced Italy's unconditional surrender on September 8 1943 and then escaped with the King from Rome to Brindisi. His government was accorded "cobelligerent" status by the Allies on October 13 1943.

Baedeker raids *see* BOMBING.

Balbo, Air Marshal Italo (1896–1940). Italian. A lieutenant in the Alpini during World War I, Balbo joined the Italian Fascist Party in 1921 and rapidly became one of Mussolini's closest advisers. As Minister of Aviation (1929–33), his plans for the expansion of the Italian Air Force were not accepted, but he derived some consolation from his personal success as a world-famous aviator. In January 1934 he was sent to Libya as governor and achieved significant success in his administration of the colony. A critic of Italy's close links with Germany, he advocated that his country remain neutral in spite of the Rome-Berlin Axis. Nevertheless, upon Italy's entry into the war in June 1940, he accepted command of the Italian forces in North Africa. He planned to pursue a strategy of "honourable resistance" to the Allied forces in Egypt and Tunisia, but on June 28 1940, his aircraft was shot down over Tobruk by Italian anti-aircraft batteries which mistook him for a British intruder. *MS.*

Balfour declaration. On November 2 1917, A J Balfour, the British foreign secretary, wrote to Lord Rothschild, the Zionist leader, declaring the government's support for the establishment of a Jewish national home in Palestine. Balfour's concern for "the civil and religious rights of existing non-Jewish communities in Palestine" proved well-founded. *MS.*

Balkan Wars (October 1912–May 1913 and June–July 1913). The Balkan Wars followed a pattern that had become familiar in the 19th century. Ambitions for national aggrandisement fired the aggressors, while indignation at reports of maltreatment of Christ-

ians formed the pretext; in labyrinthine negotiations and in conference, the Great Powers presided over the dismemberment of the Ottoman empire and the equipoise of their various spheres of influence. The war was limited, was fought on land and was mobile, with little foreshadowing of the trench warfare that lay so short a time ahead. The dissatisfaction of all parties with the peace settlement, which was still not complete in all details at the time of the outbreak of World War I, heightened international tension and provided the trigger for the general European war which had been apprehended and, by diplomacy, avoided during the Balkan Wars themselves.

The outbreak of the Italo-Turkish War in September 1911 opened the door for the small states that had been formed from Turkey's erstwhile Balkan provinces to enlarge their frontiers, if

Macedonian irregulars, Salonika, 1913

they could far enough surmount their many and bitter differences as to be able to act together. Secretly encouraged by Russia, Bulgaria and Serbia joined hands in March 1912; in May, Bulgaria formed an alliance with Greece and on October 6 1912 with Montenegro. On October 8 Montenegro, protected by her mountains from immediate danger, declared war on Turkey. By October 18 all the four states had declared war and on October 24 an alliance between Montenegro and Serbia completed the Balkan League.

The Great Powers did not expect the League to beat Turkey and on October 10 Russia and Austria, in a joint note, declared they would tolerate no modification of the ter-

ritorial status quo. But Turkey was already at war with Italy, her troops were widely dispersed and outnumbered from the start by their Balkan League adversaries, whose stronger reserves increased the disparity as the war progressed. Moreover, purges intended to reduce the influence of the Young Turks (*see* YOUNG TURKS) carried out in the Turkish army by the War Minister, Nazim Pasha, had weakened the officer corps. The Balkan League swept the Turks before them and, despite a stand at Monastir, by the end of November only isolated pockets of Turkish resistance remained apart from the fortresses of Adrianople, Scutari and Yannina. On December 3 1912, Serbia, Bulgaria and Montenegro concluded an armistice with Turkey; Greece held aloof.

On January 23 1913 a coup d'état in Istanbul brought the Young Turks back to power, Nazim Pasha was murdered and the armistice denounced. Fighting, officially resumed on February 3 by the Balkan League, saw the reduction of Yannina, Adrianople and finally Scutari during March and April and a Collective Note of the Great Powers to Turkey secured a second armistice.

Peace was concluded in London on May 30 1913, but the terms, worked out by the Great Powers and imposed on the belligerents, satisfied no one and left much room for dispute, as no clear frontiers were established. Turkey's Balkan territory was reduced to small areas around Constantinople and Gallipoli and an independent kingdom of Albania was to be set up, which was to include Scutari, to the rage of Montenegro. Bulgaria got the biggest gains, but wanted in addition Salonika, which had been allotted to Greece. Romania, jealous of Bulgarian expansion, demanded compensation. Serbia, denied access to the Adriatic, was also furious with Bulgaria, whom she accused of breaking the terms of their alliance. On June 1 Greece and Serbia signed an alliance aimed at the redivision of Macedonia. Russia summoned Bulgaria and Serbia to accept her arbitration and submit their claims within four days on June 21, but Bulgaria's reply was intransigent and Russia declared she

B

could no longer provide support. Bulgaria's belief that Austria would back her was impossible while Romania was unsatisfied.

On the night of June 29–30 1913 Bulgaria, without declaring war, attacked Greek and Serbian positions. The defenders were dug in, and although in the face of the first surprise assault they gave ground, their counterattacks on July 2 and 3 were successful and a stalemate ensued. This was broken on July 11 when Romania entered the war and began an unopposed march on Sofia; next day the Turks broke out and made for Adrianople, which they reoccupied on July 22. Fighting was over by the end of July and in a series of treaties between the various belligerents signed during August 1913 to March 1914, peace was patched up, although some contentious details remained outstanding.

Serbia, Romania, Greece and Turkey all gained from the new settlement at Bulgaria's expense. Serbia did best from the wars, as her troops had done best in the field. Turkey lost most, but Russia had suffered a rebuff at the hands of an erstwhile protégé and Austria was very seriously alarmed by the increased power of Serbia, whom she feared would foment disturbances among her southern Slav peoples. A full-scale European war had been feared on all sides and Germany and France had both taken steps to increase their armies on a vast scale in anticipation. They had not long to wait before a spark struck in the Balkans ignited the world. *SKF*.

Balkans, German campaign in (1941). The Italian invasion of Greece in October 1940 proved to be a military and diplomatic disaster for the Axis. Not only did Italian forces suffer substantial reverses at the hands of the Greek Army but Great Britain sent military aid and secured a toehold in the Balkans. Furthermore, Anglo-Greek solidarity helped to fortify anti-Axis elements in Yugoslavia, resulting in the renunciation on March 27 1941 of a recent pact with Germany and the overthrow of the government that concluded the agreement. Hitler decided that this unstable and potentially threatening situation in the Balkans could not be allowed to continue.

His concern was all the greater as plans for the invasion of the Soviet Union, were well advanced. In December 1940 he had ordered preparation for Operation "Marita", to secure the southern flank of the Balkans by seizing the north coast of the Aegean Sea. Therefore, with substantial German forces already deployed in Austria, Hungary, Romania and Bulgaria, Hitler amended "Marita" to become the basis for a general conquest of the Balkans. On April 6 1941 Belgrade was subjected to a devastating attack by the Luftwaffe, in which 17,000 of its inhabitants were killed. Meanwhile, in the east, elements of List's German Twelfth Army invaded from Bulgaria, soon to be joined by von Weichs' Second Army attacking from Austria and Hungary. Disorganized and rent by political disaffection, the Yugoslav forces quickly crumbled and, on April 12, Belgrade fell, followed two days later by the capitulation of the army. Stiffer opposition was offered by the Greeks, but with the bulk of the army deployed against the Italians in Albania, it was left to four Greek divisions and 60,000 Australian, New Zealand, British and Polish troops to hold the central and eastern frontiers. However, German attacks from Bulgaria outflanked the Metaxas Line in Thrace and Macedonia and, following an armoured thrust across the Greek-Yugoslav border at the Monastir Gap, the Anglo-Greek forces were obliged to retreat. This southerly withdrawal left Greek forces in the west exposed and, on April 20, the bulk of the army capitulated. Meanwhile attempts to stem the German advance were made at the Aliakmon lines, at Mount Olympus and Thermopylae but it was soon realized that defeat was inevitable. Evacuation offered the only chance of salvation for the British forces and in improvised mass embarkations, by May 1 some 50,000 men had been got away to Crete and Egypt. The relative success of this operation could not disguise Britain's weakened position in the Mediterranean. But the operations in the Balkans had seriously disturbed the schedule for the German invasion of Russia by causing a five-week postponement from May 15 until June 22. *MS*.

Ball, Capt Albert (1896–1917). Br. An individualist who preferred to operate alone, Ball was one of the first RFC fighter pilots to win national fame in World War I, scoring at least 44 victories over the Western Front before he was killed in May 1917. He was awarded a posthumous VC.

Ballistic missile. A missile in which a rocket boosts a payload into a ballistic trajectory. The rocket, usually a multi-stage device, only burns for a very few minutes and acts like a gun propelling an unpowered warhead into the correct trajectory to strike the target. Guidance takes place in the boost phase with an inertial system of gyroscopes and accelerometers sensing the missile's movement and maintaining it on course so that the warhead is in exactly the right place and travelling at the right speed – about 16,000mph (25,600kph) for an intercontinental missile – on burn out. An error of 1ft (0.3m) per second at this point can mean a miss of over a mile (1.6km). The warhead may go hundreds of miles into space before re-entering the Earth's atmosphere. Modern missiles usually carry multiple or multiple independently targetable re-entry vehicles (MIRVs) rather than a single warhead. *EJG*.

Balloons. These were first used in war in the 18th century. In World War I, they were extensively used to spot the fall of artillery fire and in World War II unmanned versions hoisted cables around likely bombing targets or from ships to destroy, or force to higher altitude, attacking aircraft. These were known as barrage balloons.

Ban Me Thuot, Battle of (1975). The People's Army of Vietnam (PAVN) launched the final offensive of the Vietnam War with an attack on Ban Me Thuot, capital of the central highlands' Darlac province and HQ of the Army of the Republic of Vietnam (ARVN) 23rd Division. The PAVN encircled Ban Me Thuot in early March 1975 with its entire 316th Division, one infantry regiment, one sapper regiment, two anti-aircraft regiments, two artillery regiments, two engineering regiments, an armoured regiment, and a communications regiment.

Only one ARVN regiment and three territorial battalions were stationed in the city. Starting at 0200 hours on the 10th, PAVN armour and infantry seized most of the city by late afternoon. The 23rd Division commander, Brig Gen Le Trung Tuong, escaped by helicopter; his deputy and the province chief surrendered early on the 11th. Though the PAVN had the advantages of numbers and surprise, the tendency of ARVN troops with dependants to follow the example of their officers and care first for their families contributed to the rout.

Control of Ban Me Thuot permitted the PAVN to isolate major ARVN garrisons at Pleiku and Kontum. Realizing that these positions had become untenable, President Nguyen Van Thieu ordered the immediate evacuation of the highlands and regroupment on the coast. An ill-planned retreat from Pleiku precipitated a panicky flood of both civilian and military personnel into lowland cities. Uncontested control of the central highlands and chaos in the cities paved the way for the PAVN to seize Hue and Danang, late March. *WST.*

Bangladesh War *see* INDIA-PAKISTAN WAR (1971).

Banzai charge. A final assault, aimed at inflicting the greatest possible damage on the enemy before dying with honour in battle, made by Japanese servicemen when facing certain defeat and possible capture; so called from the battle cry *Tenno heika banzai!* ("Long live the Emperor!"). The largest banzai charge of World War II occurred on Saipan, July 7 1944, when *c*2,000–3,000 Japanese troops died in a dawn assault on strongly-entrenched USMC infantry and artillery. A few hundred walking wounded launched a final banzai charge later that day. Of the *c*25,000-strong garrison of Saipan, fewer than 1,000 Japanese survived. *RO'N.*

Bao Dai, Emperor (b.1913). Vietnamese. Last emperor of the Nguyen Dynasty (1802–1945); the powerless monarch of Annam, the French "protectorate" in central Vietnam. After abdicating in the August Revolution and briefly serving as supreme adviser to the new Democratic Republic, he began negotiating with France on a non-communist alternative that came to be known as the "Bao Dai solution". Urged by non-communist nationalists to hold out for full independence, Bao Dai agreed in March 1949 to the establishment of the State of Vietnam with limited independence in the French Union. During this time Bao Dai spent much time carousing in nightclubs abroad, which raised doubt about the seriousness of his intentions and the goodwill of France. Many Vietnamese regarded the State of Vietnam, with Bao Dai as chief of state, as a collaborationist regime. This was the government seated in Saigon at the war's end. In October 1955 a national referendum organized by Bao Dai's prime minister, Ngo Dinh Diem, called for South Vietnam to become a republic. Bao Dai departed for exile in France. *WST.*

Bapaume. Principal town immediately behind the German Somme front, 1916. Entered by 2nd Australian Division, March 1917, it changed hands again a year later but was retaken by the New Zealand Division, August 1918.

Bär, Lt Col Heinrich (1913–57). Ger. Often called the outstanding German fighter-pilot of World War II, with 124 of his 220 "kills" made in the West. In the defence of Germany, 1944–45, he became the first *Experte* ("ace") jet pilot, with 16 "kills", mostly heavy bombers, in a Messerschmitt Me 262.

Bardia, capture of (January 3–4 1941). After the defeat of the Italian Tenth Army at Sidi Barrani, 6th Australian Division attacked the fortified port of Bardia, garrisoned by 45,000 men with 400 guns. Four days preliminary bombardment by the RAF and Royal Navy preceded the Australian assault. "I" tanks (Matildas) and Australian élan unnerved the defenders, who capitulated on January 4. *See also* WESTERN DESERT CAMPAIGN.

Barents Sea, Battle of (December 31 1942). Convoy JW 51B bound for Murmansk was attacked by *Hipper*, *Lützow* and six large destroyers off North Cape. Sher-brooke's escort of six destroyers gallantly held off the heavy German ships, which were operating independently and badly coordinated, by threatening torpedo attacks with the loss of one of their number and another escort. The British 6in cruisers *Sheffield* and *Jamaica* came dashing out of the Arctic twilight, damaged the bigger *Hipper* and sank one German destroyer. One further uncertain approach by *Lützow* was frightened off by the destroyers of the escort. The convoy had been fought through by a much inferior force with no damage to it. Hitler's restrictions on the use of his heavy ships had been responsible for this German debacle, but he was furious. He ordered the laying up of his major ships and Raeder resigned as head of the *Kriegsmarine*. Dönitz, who replaced him, later persuaded Hitler to withdraw his order. *DJL.*

Bar-Lev Line *see* ARAB-ISRAELI WARS.

Barrage. A controlled concentration of artillery fire for offensive or defensive purposes.

Barrage balloon *see* BALLOONS.

Lysander: vital in Barratt's command

Barratt, Air Chief Marshal Sir Arthur (1891–1966). Br. AOC-in-C British Air Forces in France 1940. Barratt's Command consisted of the Air Component, which initially had five Lysander, four Blenheim and four Hurricane Squadrons for the direct support of the BEF, and the Advanced Air Striking Force with ten squadrons of Battles and Blenheims for longer range tactical and perhaps strategic bombing and two squadrons of Hurricanes. These formations were substantially reinforced when the German attack began, but Barratt never had a chance of realizing the objects of his command. His Battles, Blenheims and Lysanders were outnumbered and comprehensively outclassed by the opposition and his Hurricanes had to operate without the radar direction which Fighter Command enjoyed over England. Nevertheless, Barratt caused some delay to the German advance and contributed to the escape of the BEF from Dunkirk. *ANF.*

Bastico, Marshal Ettore (1876–1972). Italian. C-in-C Italian Armed Forces in North Africa, July 12 1941–February 15 1943.

Bastogne, Battle of *see* ARDENNES OFFENSIVE.

Bataan-Corregidor campaign (1942). Following air bombardment on December 8, the initial Japanese landings in the Philippines were made on December 10 1941. The main invasion force, Fourteenth Army (Homma), landed at Lingayen Gulf, Luzon, December 22. Wainwright's North Luzon Force opposed the Japanese advance while MacArthur drew back to prepared positions on the Bataan Peninsula, west of Manila Bay. By January 7 1942 MacArthur's force, some 80,000-strong, occupied a formidable stronghold, but with little hope of a relief force. The first Japanese assaults, from January 9, were halted by concentrated artillery fire along the main defence line, but ferocious infantry assaults, supported by Japan's total air superiority, steadily drove the US-Philippine forces back down the peninsula. Wainwright assumed overall control when MacArthur was evacuated in March. Food and ammunition shortages forced the defenders of Bataan to surrender on April 9, but resistance continued on the island fortress of Corregidor, off the southern tip of Bataan. After several weeks' relentless bombing and shelling, a Japanese amphibious assault forced the 15,000-strong garrison to surrender on May 6. *MS.*

Battalion. 1) (British Army). Infantry unit organized into Companies, with its own complement of support weapons. Commanded by a Lt Col. 2) In most other armies, all combat arms are organized in battalions.

Battenberg, Prince Louis of *see* MILFORD HAVEN ADM OF THE FLEET.

Battery (British Army). Sub-unit of an artillery regiment. The US equivalent is a company sub-unit of an artillery battalion.

Battle, Fairey (Br, WWII). Light bomber; crew 3. Prototype flew March 10 1936; first deliveries to No. 63 Squadron, RAF, May 1937; by May 1939, 17 Battle squadrons equipped. To France with AASF September 2 1939; two RAF VCs for attack Veldwezelt bridge May 12 1940. Few to SAAF; 366 to Australia; many conversions to trainers/target tugs. Production 2,197. One 1,440hp Rolls-Royce Merlin III engine; max. speed 257mph (414kph); 1,000lb (450kg) bombs, two 0.303in machine guns.

Battlecruiser. The first battlecruisers were developed from armoured cruisers – more lightly armed and armoured, but faster and therefore larger, versions of contemporary battleships. They were intended for the destruction of smaller enemy cruisers, the protection of commerce, and scouting for, but not fighting with, battleships. The British *Invincible*-class battlecruisers were longer than the *Dreadnought*, though with one turret less. Unfortunately there was one basic flaw in the concept in these new ships. Their guns were of the same calibre (12in) as the battleship, ensuring that they would be used in the main battle, but with only cruiser armour. The sensible course would have been to give them smaller calibre guns, which would keep them on the fringes, or to take the alternative which the Germans were to adopt, i.e. to build what were in effect, fast battleships armoured to battleship standards.

British battlecruisers justified themselves in destroying German cruiser forces at the Falklands and the Heligoland Bight but then were trapped in a major battle and met their nemesis at Jutland. It was a controversial and short-lived type. The later French *Dunkerque*,

German *Scharnhorst* and, certainly, the American *Alaska* were really a reversion to the large armoured cruiser concept. *DJL.*

Battleship. The most powerful unit in the surface navy, combining the heaviest possible guns and protection with reasonable speed and endurance, the "capital ship" of the world's navies until supplanted by the aircraft carrier. The word came into use in the 1880s, replacing the earlier "ironclad" and harking back to the old sailing "line-of-battle ship". After the experimental uncertainty of the ironclad period, battleship design had settled down by 1900 to a fairly standard pattern. What were later termed "pre-dreadnoughts" were of about 15,000 tons and 16-18 knots, with two twin heavy gun turrets, one at either end of the superstructure. In between were heavy secondary and tertiary batteries (usually of 6in and 3in calibre). Later examples tended to have fewer but heavier guns in the secondary battery (8-10in). These ships were to give good service in secondary roles during World War I, often seeing more action than their more modern sisters.

However, the real answer was longer-range guns firing in salvoes. The biggest guns had the greatest range and hitting power, so what was needed was the largest possible number of big guns mounted in one ship. Most of the major navies were working towards this solution when the demoniac energy of Adm Fisher, combined with the efficiency of Portsmouth dockyard and the availability of guns and mountings intended for other ships, stole a march on the rest of the world for Britain. The *Dreadnought* was completed in just over a year (a record that still stands) with five twin 12in turrets, no secondary armament, and an unprecedented speed of 21 knots, thanks to the daring step of making her the first large ship fitted with turbines. She was larger than any previous battleship.

Dreadnought set off a chain of developments which made her virtually obsolete within a decade. Probably the already existing naval rivalries made this technical race faster than it would otherwise have been. In any event, gun calibres went up from 12in to 13.5in to 15in. Ships grew correspondingly in size and armour. Interestingly, after the awkward layout of the early dreadnoughts' five turrets, the designs building in 1914 were reverting to something similar to the pre-dreadnought layout of turrets at either end of the superstructure, but now using the superfiring arrangement of the first American dreadnoughts, with two turrets at either end. A further answer to cramming the maximum possible guns into the space available was triple (and later quadruple) mountings.

By the time the Washington Treaty of 1921 put a virtual stop to battleship building for some 15 years, 16in guns had become the latest standard. Apart from the 18in of the monster Japanese *Yamato*-class – the largest battleships ever built, in an attempt to confront American numbers with sheer size – gun size did not increase. However, when construction of the last generation of battleships started on the eve of World War II, size increased further. This was due to the increased threat from under and above the surface – improved torpedo protection, heavy anti-aircraft protection and increased deck armour against bombs. Also the new battleships were given battlecruiser speeds, approaching or even exceeding 30 knots, which meant much greater engine power and therefore size.

Even after the experience of war had shown the vulnerability of battleships to attack from the air and confirmed the danger from underwater attack, there were still occasions at night or in bad weather when only a battleship could match another of the same kind. Today, only the Americans are left with heavily armoured and gunned ships, which gives them a great advantage in that most modern naval weapons are no longer designed to cope with battleships. Not only are the four Iowas useful shore bombardment vessels, they are also very formidable fighting ships. *DJL*.

Bayerlein, Lt Gen Fritz (1899–1970). Ger. Established a brilliant reputation as a staff officer with Guderian's XIX Panzer Corps in France, 1940, and 2nd Panzer Group in the invasion of Russia, 1941. In September 1941 he went to North Africa as COS, Afrika Korps, serving under Rommel and Cruewell. Proving his own command capability by taking temporary control of the Afrika Korps when Nehring was wounded at Alam Halfa, August 1942, he was given a division in Italy, 1943, commanded the noted *Panzer Lehr* division in Normandy, 1944, and headed LIII Corps in the Rhineland and Ruhr, 1945. His postwar writings provide valuable analyses of command decisions. *RO'N*.

Bayonet. Invented in the 17th century, bayonets remain in use even with automatic weapons. Of many types developed, the most enduring have been the spike and knife. In both world wars and even in the Falklands War, the bayonet has featured in infantry close-quarter fighting.

Bazentin le Grand and Bazentin le Petit. Villages in the German second line on the Somme, captured by the British 3rd and 7th Divisions respectively on July 14 1916. Both villages were lost, then retaken, in 1918.

Bazooka. Nickname given to the US 2.36in anti-tank rocket launcher introduced in 1942.

BE 2c, 2d, 2e: Royal Aircraft Factory (Br, WWI). Two-seat reconnaissance - bomber / fighter / trainer. Prototype flew May 30 1914; first BE 2c to RFC in France January 25 1915. Widely subcontracted; employed in many capacities on virtually all fronts. Home Defence fighters usually single-seat conversions. BE 2e most numerous variant. About 3,000 (all versions) were ordered. One 90hp RAF 1a engine; max. speed 90mph (144kph); one 0.303in rifle, carbine or machine gun; 230lb (104kg) bombs.

Beatty, Adm of the Fleet Earl (1871–1936). Br. Commander of the battlecruiser fleet at Jutland, C-in-C Grand Fleet 1916–18, First Sea Lord 1919–27. Beatty's enterprise and daring earned him repeated early promotions so that by 1900 he had reached the rank of captain. Thereafter, he attracted the good opinion of the First Lord of the Admiralty, Churchill. At Jutland, he led his ships straight into action upon sighting the enemy and without waiting for Jellicoe's main fleet to come up. In retrospect, some thought that he had acted too hastily; others that Jellicoe had done so too tardily. None, however, doubted the boldness of Beatty's design and in the aftermath of the battle, when it began to appear that an opportunity of destroying the whole of the German High Seas Fleet had been

Jut-jawed determination: Adm Beatty

lost, Beatty replaced Jellicoe as C-in-C.

Beatty's prestige was an incalculable asset to the navy after the war, both during the years that he was First Sea Lord and when he found it his duty to resist the arguments and claims of Trenchard as Chief of the Air Staff. It may, however, be doubted if the best interests of the two services were served by the contest between them. *ANF*.

Beauchamp-Proctor,   Capt Anthony Wetherby VC (1894–1921). South African. Fighter pilot, credited with 54 victories, including 16 observation balloons, while serving with the RFC and RAF in France in 1918.

Beaufighter, Bristol (Br, WWII). Night fighter/shipping strike; crew 2/3. Prototype flew July 17 1939; to squadrons September 1940. Used in UK, Europe, Mediterranean, Western Desert, Far East. Production (364) in Australia; total production (all Marks) 5,918. Two 1,770hp Bristol Hercules XVII engines; max. speed 303 mph (485kph); 2,127lb (965kg) torpedo, 500lb (225kg) bombs or eight 90lb (40kg) rockets, four 20mm cannon, one 0.303in machine gun.

Beaumont Hamel. Fortified village, northwest of the River Ancre, on the Somme battlefield. The British 29th Division – which included the 1st Battalion, Newfoundland Regiment – suffered 5,240 casualties in its vain attempt to take the village on July 1 1916. Beaumont Hamel finally fell to the 51st Division on November 13 1916.

Beaverbrook, Lord (Max Aitken) (1879–1964). Canadian. Press baron. Served in Lloyd George's government in World War I and Churchill's in World War II. As Minister of Aircraft Production in 1940, he reorganized and expanded the industry dramatically but with the result that fighters were over-, and other types underproduced.

Beck, Gen Ludwig see JULY PLOT.

Beda Fomm, Battle of (February 5–7 1941). After the capture of Tobruk, Gen O'Connor, commanding the Western Desert Force, saw an opportunity to cut off the withdrawal of the Tenth Italian Army (Tellera) from Cyrenaica by launching a surprise and logistically hazardous thrust across the desert via Mechili to the coast road near Beda Fomm, 60 miles (96km) south of Benghazi. On February 5 a small mixed force of armoured cars, artillery, and infantry under the command of Lt Col J F Combe of the 11th Hussars, cut the coast road and managed to hold it until the arrival of 4th Armoured Brigade and the Support Group of 7th Armoured Division. After repeated attempts to break through failed, the remnants of Tenth Army surrendered on February 7. Gen Tellera was mortally wounded, and all his staff and 25,000 men were taken prisoner. *WGFJ.*

Beetham, Marshal of the RAF Sir Michael (b.1923). Br. Chief of Air Staff in 1982, he had some misgivings about sending the Task Force to the Falklands with only the limited air cover provided by the Harriers embarked in the carriers *Invincible* and *Hermes*. However, he accepted that this was essentially a maritime operation and gave Adm Woodward all the help the RAF could provide, chiefly in the form of strategic air transport

to Ascension Island, maritime reconnaissance and a squadron of RAF Harriers. The bombing attacks on Port Stanley airfield by single Vulcan bombers (Operation "Black Buck"), although rightly hailed as extraordinary feats of airmanship, were not effective in denying it to the Argentine Air Force. *MH.*

Belfast. British cruiser; launched 1938; 13,175 tons full load; 12 × 6in guns (triple mounts), 12 × 4in guns (twin mounts) 6 × 21in torpedo tubes. Virtually rebuilt after striking magnetic mine, Firth of Forth, November 1939, rejoining fleet in November 1942. Served in Russian convoys; Battle of North Cape; Normandy bombardment, 1944. Joined Far Eastern Fleet, mid-1945; flagship at time of *Amethyst* incident, 1949. Shore bombardments during Korean War; in reserve 1963. Now preserved in Pool of London.

Defenders of "brave Belgium", 1914

Belgium, invasion of (1914). The German invasion of Belgium – the immediate cause of Britain's entry into World War I – began on August 4 1914. In accordance with the Schlieffen plan, as modified by von Moltke, six brigades from the German Second Army were detailed to capture the Liège forts, which commanded the Meuse gateway into the Belgian plain. This was accomplished, with the help of powerful 30.5 and 42cm howitzers, by August 16, enabling the German right-wing armies to spread out into Belgium more or less on schedule. To adhere to their timetable, and also to avoid having to leave large forces to guard their rear, the Germans deliberately pursued a policy of "Schrecklichkeit" ("Frightfulness"), trying to

cow the population into obedience by means of the execution of civilians and the destruction of property. The Belgians too carried out demolitions in an effort to slow the German advance, but on August 18 the main part of the Belgian Army, having waited in vain behind the Gette for the British and French, withdrew to the fortress of Antwerp. On August 20 the Germans entered Brussels and, the next day, invested Namur, the final fortress obstacle on the Meuse route into France. The city of Namur fell on August 24, the last of its forts capitulating soon afterwards, while Louvain was burned in reprisal for alleged civilian resistance. However, the need to detach units to cover Antwerp and other forts weakened the German right wing, with the heaviest fighting still ahead. British reinforcements, landed at Ostend and Zeebrugge, delayed, but could not prevent the fall of Antwerp on October 10 and the Belgian Army withdrew again, this time to the Nieuport-Dixmude line along the River Yser. Here, in late October, the Belgians stopped an attempted German breakthrough to the Channel ports, compelling the Germans to concentrate their attacks inland, at Ypres, between October 31 and November 11 1914. Following the successful, if costly, defence of Ypres by the British Expeditionary Force, the opposing armies settled into trench lines from the North Sea to the Swiss frontier, leaving only a narrow strip of Belgian territory still free from German occupation. *PJS.*

Belgium, invasion of (1940) see LOW COUNTRIES, INVASION OF.

Ben Bella, Mohammed Ahmed (b.1916). Algerian political activist and anti-colonialist. Founder of FLN. Captured by French, 1956, and interned in metropolitan France. Released by de Gaulle, 1962 prior to cease-fire negotiations. First President of Algeria, 1963. Overthrown by Col Boumédienne (1965) and under arrest until Boumédienne's death (1978) when he was released. *See also* ALGERIAN CAMPAIGN (1954–62) and ALGERIAN-MOROCCAN WAR (1963–64).

Benghazi see WESTERN DESERT CAMPAIGN (1940–43).

Ben-Gurion, David (1886–1973). Israel's first prime minister (1948–53, 1955–63). *See* ARAB-ISRAELI WARS.

Bennett, Air Vice-Marshal Donald Clifford Tyndall (1910–86). Br. Air Officer Commanding Pathfinder Force, Bomber Command 1942–45. Australian by birth, Bennett was one of the greatest experts in and exponents of the art of airmanship. He came into conflict with Cochrane over the latter's belief in low-level visual marking and resolutely adhered to his own in high-level radar-assisted marking. *ANF*.

Bennett, Lt Gen Henry Gordon (1887–1962). Australian. A competent junior commander in World War I, the blustering and belligerent Bennett proved unsuited to high command during World War II. Commanding 8th Australian Division in Malaya, 1941, Bennett was outflanked in Johore by Japanese amphibious operations and retreated to Singapore Island, where his inefficiency contributed largely to the city's fall. Bennett himself escaped, but was given only training commands until his retirement in 1944. In 1946, a military enquiry into his escape found that he was "not justified in handing over his command": a subsequent civilian review stated that his mistakes were attributable to bad judgment, rather than lack of courage or patriotism. *RO'N*.

Berchtesgaden (Berghof). Hitler's private residence in Bavaria, sometimes used as a location for conferences. It was destroyed by Allied bombing in 1945.

Beresford-Peirse, Lt Gen Sir Noel (1887–1953). Br. Commander 4th Indian Division at the Battle of Sidi Barrani in December 1940, and in Eritrea at the battles of Kassala, Agordat and Keren in January–February 1941; Commander Western Desert Force during Operations "Brevity" and "Battleaxe" in May and June 1941.

Beria, Lavrenti Pavlovitch (1899–1953). Russian. Secret policeman in Georgia 1921–38, head of NKVD 1938–53; deputy prime minister 1941; controlled partisans 1941–44; Marshal of the Soviet Union 1945; deposed and arrested shortly after Stalin's death; executed for supposed treason.

Berlin airlift *see* BERLIN, BLOCKADE OF (1948–49).

Devastation by bombing, Berlin, 1945

Berlin, Battle of. The British night bombing of Germany from November 18 1943 until the end of March 1944 when 9,111 bomber sorties were sent against Berlin in 16 major attacks and another 11,113 against other towns throughout Germany to spread the damage and the German air defences. Numerous minor harassing attacks were also made. From the 35 major attacks, 1,047 bombers failed to return (492 of them from attacks on Berlin itself) and another 1,682 were damaged. During this time, the average number of bombers daily available for operations was only 892.

Although terrible damage was done to Berlin, it continued to function as a capital city and Germany as a formidable fighting nation. Bomber Command, although badly mauled, also remained in being and was, in fact, on the eve of much greater successes. The outcome of the battle must therefore be taken as inconclusive.

The principal reason for the disappointment of Harris's hopes was the effectiveness of the German air defences. The very long range of Berlin gave the German night fighter force extra opportunity for interception and the intense flak barrage at the target made it impossible to attain the concentration of bombing needed to cause a catastrophe on the Hamburg or Dresden scale. In addition, the German fire, rescue and repair services worked with remarkable efficiency and resilience. Finally,

apart from one attack in March after their long-range fighters had come into action, the US Eighth Air Force was unable to come in on the battle as Harris had hoped. *ANF*.

Berlin, Battle for (1945). The final battle for Berlin began on April 16 1945 when Marshal Zhukov's 1st Belorussian Front and Marshal Koniev's 1st Ukrainian Front launched a massive offensive. Although their forces amounted to 2,500,000 men, supported by commensurate numbers of tanks, artillery and aircraft, they failed to make an immediate breakthrough. Despite a devastating bombardment carried out by artillery so densely arrayed that there was one gun every 13ft (4m) of the line, the German defenders stubbornly limited the Soviet advance to relatively small bridgeheads. However, the sheer weight of arms of the Red Army, coupled with the inspirational drive of its rival commanders, forced the defenders back from the Oder-Neisse line. On April 25 units of Zhukov's and Koniev's forces linked up to the west of Berlin, completing the city's encirclement. Desultory German attempts were made to re-establish contact with the beleaguered Berlin pocket but they could not break the Soviet stranglehold. The battle thereafter developed into a slow and bloody struggle through the city's battered streets. Elements of Chuikov's Eighth Guards Army had entered the southeastern suburbs on April 21 but it was more than a week before the centre of Berlin fell and the two Fronts met on the Charlottenberg Chaussee. On May 2 Lt Gen Weidling formally surrendered the city together with some 500,000 defenders. Soviet casualties were about 300,000, appreciably less than the estimated 1,000,000 German losses. *MS*.

Berlin, blockade of (1948–49). The Soviet land and water blockade of West Berlin was provoked by the introduction of a new currency in the city on June 23 1948. Stalin claimed that as the Western Allies had abandoned any intention of re-unifying Germany, they should return to their own zones, as Berlin had no role as a future

B

capital of Germany. The West retaliated with a counter-blockade of goods from the Soviet zone. Gen Lucius D Clay, head of the American occupation zone, took a hard line and pressed that American forces fight their way through to the city. President Truman overruled him and decided upon an airlift. He was informed that Berlin needed at least 4,000 tons of food and fuel per day, perhaps 3,500 tons in summer. In fact, aircraft flying two round trips per day averaged 13,000 tons per day, one-third of which was flown by the RAF. At the height of the tension, two groups of possibly nuclear-laden B-29s were dispatched to Britain. But by August 1948 a 25-day reserve of coal and a 30-day reserve of food had been created. On May 12 1949 the Russians lifted their blockade. The counter-blockade had proved effective. And the Soviet action had not prevented the Government of the Federal Republic of Germany taking up its seat at Bonn on May 23 1949. *BHR*.

Berling, Zygmunt (1896–1980). Polish. A major when captured by Russians in 1939, became general commanding six Polish divisions in Red Army 1944; dismissed for trying to help Warsaw rising.

Bernafay wood. Wood facing the extreme British right flank on the Somme, July 1 1916. It was occupied by the 9th (Scottish) Division two days later.

Bernhardt Line. German covering positions in front of the main Gustav Line, held in autumn 1943 to slow Allies' advance on Rome.

Bernhard, Prince of the Netherlands (b.1911). A Prince of Lippe-Biesterfeld in Germany; married 1937 Queen Wilhelmina's daughter Juliana (Queen of the Netherlands 1948–80). Evaded to England with his family, under fire, in May 1940; pilot in RAF 1942–44; commanded Dutch army in exile and Dutch resisters, 1944–45.

Béthouart, Gen Emile (b.1889). Fr. Commander of French forces during Norwegian campaign, 1940.

Betio Island *see* TARAWA CAMPAIGN.

Beurling, Flight Lt George Frederick (1921–1948). Canadian. Generally credited with 31.33 victories, "Buzz" or "Screwball" Beurling, as he was nicknamed, became the top-scoring Canadian fighter pilot of World War II. A "lone wolf", impatient of discipline, he achieved most of his victories flying Spitfires with No.249 Squadron RAF over Malta in 1942.

Bevan, Col John Henry (1894–1978). Br. Controlled, under Churchill, British deception planning, 1942–45.

Biak, Battle of *see* HOLLANDIA CAMPAIGN.

Bien Hoa. Located 20 miles (32km)

People flee from village near Bien Hoa

north of Saigon, South Vietnam, the airfield at Bien Hoa, capital of Bien Hoa province, came under mortar attack on November 1 1964. The attack killed four American servicemen and damaged a large number of aircraft. Occurring shortly after the Tonkin Gulf incident and retaliatory airstrikes against the North, the attack provoked the US Joint Chiefs of Staff to recommend additional airstrikes and the deployment of US Army and Marine units to strengthen base security. Though not immediately accepted, the recommendation intensified pressure on President Lyndon Johnson to increase American involvement.

The Bien Hoa base and adjacent facilities at Long Binh subsequently grew into a giant military base and headquarters connected to Saigon by a four-lane highway. During the 1968 Tet offensive, the complex, which held the command posts of the US 2nd Field Force

and ARVN III Corps, came under rocket and mortar barrage and ground assault by communist forces in regimental strength. *WST*.

"Big Bertha". Nickname given to German World War I 42cm howitzer.

Bigeard, Gen Marcel (b.1916). Fr. A leading paratroop commander of the post-World War II period, Bigeard specialized in deep penetration operations during the Indochina-France War, when he also headed a paradrop at Dien Bien Phu. In 1958–60 he commanded 3rd Colonial Parachute Regiment in the Algerian War of Independence.

"Big Week" (Operation "Argument"). The launching by Spaatz on February 20 1944 from British bases of coordinated American long-range fighter and bomber attacks on the Luftwaffe. The plan exploited the increased range of fighters, especially P-51 Mustangs, and marked the recovery of the US Eighth Air Force from the Schweinfurt disaster of the previous October. "Big Week" led to the gradual achievement of American air ascendancy over the Germans in daylight which was a prerequisite for the day bomber offensive and for "Overlord". *ANF*.

Bikini Atoll (northern Marshall Islands). Site of US nuclear tests. The first (July 1946) was designed to explore the effects of nuclear bombs on naval forces. German and Japanese war trophies were used as targets along with worn-out American vessels. The first explosion of "dry" thermonuclear bomb designs was carried out in 1954. Bikini was also used to test more advanced bomb designs in the "Redwing" Series in 1956 when a weapon was dropped from a B-52, the first air drop of an American thermonuclear bomb, and in the "Hardtack" series in 1958.

Binh Gia, Battle of (1964). Communist forces launched coordinated attacks throughout South Vietnam in December 1964. One of these occurred around the village of Binh Gia, in coastal Phuoc Tuy province 45 miles (70km) southeast of Saigon. Two regiments of

B

the newly formed People's Liberation Armed Force (PLAF) 9th Division, strengthened by the recent infiltration of late model weapons from the North, began probing village defences on the 4th. The probes drew in Army of the Republic (ARVN) reinforcements supported by American helicopter gunships. The PLAF countered with quick movements, lightning strikes, and ambushes. On the 27th it briefly seized the village. By the time it departed, the PLAF had destroyed two ARVN ranger and marine battalions, killed nearly 200 ARVN troops, downed three helicopters, and wounded six American helicopter crewmen. The battle marked the beginning of attacks by PLAF units, with enhanced weaponry, in battalion and regimental strength. American commanders on the scene believed the battle signified a shift in communist strategy and proved the need to introduce US troops. *WST*.

Binh Xuyen. The Binh Xuyen crime syndicate grew out of the banditry that was rife along the Mekong river in Vietnam during the early 1940s. Under the leadership of Le Van Vien, alias Bay Vien, the Binh Xuyen became a significant political and military force following World War II. After briefly cooperating with the communists, Bay Vien switched allegiance to the French, who helped him build an army of 40,000 men. Emperor Bao Dai protected Binh Xuyen rackets in return for money to run his government and gave the syndicate control of the capital police.

South Vietnam's first prime minister, Ngo Dinh Diem, challenged the Binh Xuyen in March 1955, cutting of their sources of finance by closing Saigon's gambling halls, brothels and opium dens. In April he ordered them to remove their armed men from the city. Street fighting between the Binh Xuyen and the National Army left 500 civilians dead and many buildings destroyed. Surprisingly, the National Army stood by Diem, and the Binh Xuyen dispersed to the Mekong delta in late May. A few Binh Xuyen troops sought refuge in areas under communist control, and Bay Vien himself fled to France. *WST*.

Biological weapons. The use of germs, viruses, or other infective agents or the toxins produced by these agents to disable. Biological weapons are unpredictable in their effects and have not found favour, despite the production of such weapons in World War II and afterwards. The Geneva Protocol of 1925 banned first use of "bacteriological methods of warfare" and the stockpiling of such weapons was finally made illegal under the 1972 Biological Weapons Convention which entered into force in 1975. Stockpiles have been destroyed and propaganda allegations of the use or continued possession of these agents have never been substantiated. Research, however, continues and new biotechnologies such as genetic engineering allow the development and easier production of more militarily useful BW agents, both lethal and incapacitating, should any country wish to violate the international ban. *EJG*.

Birch, Capt John (1918–1945). US. A Baptist missionary in China, Birch assisted the Doolittle raid survivors and was recruited by Chennault for intelligence work. On August 25 1945, while on a mission for the Office of Strategic Services, he was murdered by Chinese communists. The anticommunist John Birch Society was founded in 1954.

Field Marshal Lord Birdwood

Birdwood, Field Marshal Lord (1865–1951). Br. A cavalry officer in India during the early part of his career, Birdwood served on Kitchener's staff in the Second Boer War War and by 1914 was Secretary to the Indian Army Department, being heavily involved in the dispatch of Indian units to France and the Middle East on the outbreak of war. He was then

chosen to lead the Australian and New Zealand Army Corps, which he commanded in Gallipoli in 1915. His genuine concern for his troops made him popular with the Australians. He can be criticized for his handling of the unsuccessful advance on Sari Bair between August 6 and 9 when, for once, he seems to have underestimated the effects of sickness upon his men, but his overall leadership caused Gen Sir Ian Hamilton, Allied commander at Gallipoli, to describe him as "the soul of Anzac". When the Australian Imperial Force expanded in 1916, Birdwood was given command of I Anzac Corps, taking it to the Western Front. Despite the losses suffered by the Australians on the Somme and at Bullecourt and Ypres in 1916–17, Birdwood remained loyal to Gough and Haigh, although the latter felt that Birdwood was too tolerant of Australian indiscipline. In November 1917 the Australian divisions on the Western Front were formed into a single Australian Corps under Birdwood and played a vital part in the defence of Amiens in April 1918. From May 1918 until the end of World War I he commanded the re-formed Fifth Army. *PJS*.

Bir El Gubi, Battle of (December 4–7 1941). Rommel's spoiling attack on Eighth Army to cover his withdrawal from Tobruk.

Bir Hacheim, Battle of (1942) *see* GAZALA, BATTLE OF.

Biryuzov, Marshal Sergei (1904–1964). Russian. COS of Second Guards Army during Stalingrad counteroffensive. Held staff posts in the Ukraine and Crimea and commanded Thirty-Seventh Army during its advance into the Balkans.

Bishop, Air Marshal William Avery VC (1894–1956). Canadian. World War I fighter pilot, credited with 72 victories while serving with the RFC and RAF on the Western Front. An individualist who liked to operate alone, "Billy" Bishop won the VC for a single-handed attack on a German airfield on June 2 1917. During World War II he was active in recruiting and in the Empire Air Training Scheme.

Bismarck. German battleship, eight 15in guns and among the most heavily armoured ships of her day.

On May 21 1941, *Bismarck*, sailing in company with the cruiser *Prinz Eugen*, emerged from the Baltic and shaped to break out into the North Atlantic. The British C-in-C, Tovey, on *King George V*, accompanied by *Victorious* and joined by *Repulse* sailed with cruiser and destroyer support to block the break-out. On the evening of May 23, one of his scouting cruisers, *Norfolk*, spotted the German ships on course for the Denmark Strait. *Prince of Wales* and *Hood* altered course to intercept. In a brief action on the 24th, *Hood*

Battleship *Bismarck*, sunk May 1941

was blown up and *Prince of Wales* damaged. *Bismarck* lost about 1,000 tons of fuel, which reduced her range decisively, and heading for the French coast, got south of Tovey's main units. Meanwhile, however, Force H (*Renown*, *Ark Royal* and *Sheffield*) had been called up from the south. On May 26, air patrols spotted *Bismarck* and on that evening she was attacked by Swordfish from *Ark Royal*. One of their torpedoes hit her rudders. Tovey was, therefore, able to come up in *King George V* with *Rodney* in company and, on May 27, they dispatched *Bismarck* with the final assistance of torpedoes from *Dorsetshire*. *ANF.*

Bismarck Sea, Battle of the, (March 2–5 1943). On March 1, a Japanese convoy of eight transports escorted by eight destroyers, carrying *c*7,000 troops from Rabaul to reinforce the garrisons of northeast New Guinea, was sighted by a B-24 Liberator of Gen Kenney's Fifth Air Force. On

March 2, one transport was sunk by B-17 Flying Fortresses: destroyers rescued *c*850 men and delivered them to Lae, but these were the only troops to reach New Guinea. On March 3, in a series of attacks by B-17s, B-24s, B-25 Mitchells, A-20 Havocs and RAAF Beauforts and Beaufighters, with strong fighter escort, six transports and four destroyers were sunk and 25 Japanese fighters shot down. The newly developed technique of low-level "skip bombing" by B-25s carrying 500lb bombs with five-second-delay fuses proved most effective. Japanese survivors in rafts or landing craft were mercilessly strafed. On March 4, USN PT-Boats joined the mopping-up, sinking the one remaining transport and machine-gunning and depth-charging survivors. Some 3,000 Japanese died; *c*2,700 were rescued by the surviving destroyers and two submarines and returned to Rabaul. Only five Allied aircraft were lost. *RO'N.*

Bizerta. Captured by II US Corps (Bradley) on May 7 1943. *See also* TUNISIAN CAMPAIGN.

Black and Tans *see* ANGLO-IRISH WAR.

"Black Day of the German Army", August 8 1918 (so described by Ludendorff). The day on which Haig broke through between Albert and Moreuil.

Blackett, Lord (1897–1974). Br. After naval service in World War I, Blackett became a leading physicist, playing an important part in the development of the radar chain. On the outbreak of war, he went to Anti-Aircraft Command where there was much scope for the application of scientific ideas to the somewhat crude methods of aiming then available. He then went to Coastal Command, where he introduced systems of operational research which were a substantial factor in transforming the force from its relative inefficiency at the beginning of the war to what became by the middle of 1943 a formidable weapon of sea power. Blackett's political views sometimes clouded the objectivity of his assessments and, despite his own naval experience, his opinion was surprisingly theoretical. *ANF.*

Blackhawk, Sikorsky UH-60/S-67. American combat support helicopter replacing the Iroquois.

Blackshirts. Italian fascist supporters whose violent activities helped Mussolini to power.

Blake, George (b.1923). Br. Spy, changed name from Behar; father Egyptian Jewish, mother Dutch Christian; brought up in Cairo by Jewish communist banker; brought out of occupied Holland by SOE; joined Royal Navy, then Foreign Office; vice consul in Seoul, 1950, captured by communists; on release, 1953, joined MI6, having by then become converted to communism; spied for six years for KGB, especially in Berlin. Betrayed, confessed, sentenced to 42 years, 1959; escaped to Russia, 1965.

Blakeslee, Col Donald J M (b.1918). US. Distinguished fighter leader with 15.5 victories in over 1,000 hours of combat flying. As commander of the US 4th Fighter Group in 1944 he helped to pioneer the tactics employed so successfully by P-51 Mustang units on long-range missions over Germany.

Blamey, Field Marshal Sir Thomas Albert (1884–1951). Australian. Distinguishing himself in the Gallipoli evacuation, Blamey ended World War I as a Brigadier; COS to Monash on the Western Front. In 1940 he became commander of the Australian army corps formed for Middle East service. Early in 1941, as Commander, Anzac Corps, he played a major part in planning the Allied evacuation from Greece, but his largely cosmetic appointment (as an Australian "token") as Deputy C-in-C, Middle East, later that year, was marred by clashes with his superior, Auchinleck.

In March 1942, Blamey was recalled to Australia with two divisions of the AIF. He was appointed both C-in-C, Australian Military Forces – a post in which he carried out valuable organizational and training work – and, less happily, C-in-C, Allied Land Forces, Southwest Pacific Area, under MacArthur. Much of the criticism levelled at Blamey and the Australian forces' alleged sluggishness by the autocratic American supremo was unfair: certainly, when ordered to take personal command of Allied land forces in New Guinea, in September 1942, Blamey competently directed the Kokoda Trail offensive that resulted in the recapture of Buna early in 1943. Thereafter, although he retained his appointment, the Australian troops under his command were mainly employed in comparatively minor operations in New Guinea and the Solomons. Retiring in 1946, Blamey was briefly recalled in 1950 in order to be promoted Field Marshal; the first Australian soldier thus distinguished. *RO'N*.

Blanchard, Gen Jean-Georges-Maurice (1877–1954). Fr. As c-in-c, French First Army, May 1940, Blanchard attempted to hold the Gembloux Gap on the Dyle Line against Höpner's XVI Panzer Corps. Succeeding Billotte as Commander, 1st Army Group, May 25, Blanchard – although not fully cooperating with BEF and Belgian commanders – oversaw First Army's rearguard action in the retreat to Dunkirk.

Blaskowitz, Gen Johannes (1883–1948). Ger. Blaskowitz commanded the German Eighth Army in Poland in 1939 and the First Army in France from October 1940 to May 1944. He then became commander of Army Group G, skilfully conducting the German withdrawal from southern France, but was replaced in September 1944. In January 1945 he took over Army Group H, his post being redesignated as c-in-c Netherlands that April. He committed suicide shortly before his trial for minor war crimes.

Blenheim, Bristol (Br, WWII). Medium bomber/long-range fighter; crew 3. First Blenheim I flew June 25 1936, quantity deliveries from early 1937; 18 squadrons by end 1938. Mark IV (long-nose) version in production 1939; built in Canada as Bolingbroke. Many fighter conversions. Unsuccessful Mk V (Bisley) intended to be close-support or high-altitude bomber. Production all Marks 6,355. Two 840/920/950 Bristol Mercury VIII/XV/25 or 30 engines; max. speed 285mph (456kph); up to six 0.303in machine guns, 1,000lb (450kg) bombs.

Blériot XI (French, early WWI). Single-seat/two-seat reconnaissance. Developed from Louis Blériot's 1909 cross-Channel monoplane; existed in several sizes/forms. Used in Italo-Turkish War 1911–12, Balkan Wars, early months World War I; thereafter as trainer. 50hp or 80hp Gnome engine; max. speed 75mph (120kph); makeshift armament of pistols and/or rifle or carbine.

Bletchley Park. British deciphering centre (Government Code and Cipher School) in Buckinghamshire. With indispensable Polish and French help at the start, Bletchley broke most but not all of the German armed forces' "Enigma" machine ciphers, starting with a Luftwaffe cipher in May 1940. By 1943 Hitler's personal orders to his commanders and Dönitz's instructions to U-boats could often be read.

These were priceless insights into the enemy's mind; extra care was taken to ensure he knew nothing of them. Everything from Bletchley was graded "Ultra" – top secret. Churchill himself controlled the short list of those who saw it. Bletchley staff, who came to number several thousand, were a mixture of academics, intellectuals, clerks, and post office engineers; these last developed the world's first electronic computer. Alan Turing, Josh Cooper and Gordon Welchman were the leading brains. Everybody concerned kept the secret for nearly 30 years. *MF*.

Blitz. British slang for German air attack.

Blitzkrieg. "Lightning war". German mechanized and air-supported operations in World War II, notably in Poland in 1939, France in 1940 and Russia in 1941.

Blomberg, Field Marshal Werner von (1878–1946). Ger. After service as a staff officer during World War I, von Blomberg's career progressed steadily in the Reichswehr and on January 1 1933 he was appointed Germany's Minister of Defence. A month later the Nazis came to power but von Blomberg, an admirer of Hitler, retained his post. He showed his loyalty in June 1934 by refraining from interfering in the internecine

"Night of the Long Knives" and by subsequently supporting Hitler's claim to absolute authority after the death of von Hindenburg. Furthermore, his order that the army swear an oath of personal allegiance to the *Führer* greatly diminished the chances of an army opposition to the Nazis. In 1935, he was made c-in-c of the Wehrmacht and, a year later, promoted Field Marshal. However, von Blomberg was regarded with some suspicion and envy within the Nazi party, notably by Himmler and Göring who conspired together to end his career. In January 1938 the widowed von Blomberg judiciously married a young woman with a past that embraced prostitution and pornography. His enemies leaked details of these dubious activities and in the ensuing scandal engineered his resignation in February 1938. Hitler assumed the posts of Minister of Defence and Supreme Commander of the Armed Forces. *MS*.

Bloody April. British name for April 1917 when the RFC and RNAS lost 151 aircraft and 316 aircrew killed or missing over the Western Front.

"Bloody Ridge" ("Edson's Ridge"), Battle of (September 12–14 1942). Late on September 12, Maj Gen Kiyotake Kawaguchi's 3,500-strong 35th Brigade attacked the defensive perimeter along the Lunga river, c1,000yd (914m) south of Henderson Field, Guadalcanal, held by c300 US Marines (Col Edson). In spite of gunfire support from Japanese destroyers in Ironbottom Sound, the attacks were repulsed. Determined infiltration attempts and frontal banzai charges were made on the night of September 13–14. With pre-planned artillery support, the Marines narrowly held their ground (143 killed and wounded). The Japanese withdrew, leaving 600 dead and suffering around 1,500 further losses in retreat. *RO'N*.

Bloody Ridge, Battle of (1951). Bloody Ridge lay in the east/central sector of the Korean front in the area of the Punchbowl. It was attacked by ROK troops in August 1951 to bring pressure to bear on the enemy during the truce talks and to test the ROK army which had been rebuilt by Gen Van Fleet. The feature was tenaciously defended by the NKPA and the ROK assault was repelled. On August 27 American troops were committed. After heavy fighting, the enemy evacuated the feature on September 5. In the fighting, which resembled the trench warfare of World War I, the NKPA suffered 15,000 casualties, the ROK over 1,000 and the Americans 3,000. *CM. See also* HEART-BREAK RIDGE.

Blowpipe missile. A widely exported British-made man-held anti-aircraft missile that is guided onto its target by radio command signals. The missile requires a high level of skill from the operator but it can be very effective: in the Falklands in 1982, British Blowpipes accounted for a Macchi 339 and two Pucaras while an Argentine Blowpipe shot down a Harrier. The automatic command-to-line-of-sight successor system is Javelin, whose launcher can fire the older missile.

Blücher. German cruisers. (1) Armoured cruiser; built because of rumours of the British Invincibles, but, with only an armament of 8.2in guns and less speed, was much inferior. Sacrificed at the Dogger Bank Battle (1915). (2) Heavy cruiser; lost just after completion to shore batteries and torpedoes in Oslo fjord during the invasion of Norway (1940).

Bluff Cove. Settlement on southeast of East Falkland. During the Falklands War of 1982 it was selected, with Fitzroy Settlement, as 5th Brigade's jumping-off base for the capture of Port Stanley, some 20 miles (32km) to the northeast. 2 Para were lifted to Fitzroy by helicopter on June 6 and the Scots and Welsh Guards were shipped around from San Carlos Water. On June 8, half of the Welsh Guards were still aboard the Landing Ship Logistic (LSL) *Sir Galahad* off Port Pleasant, the harbour for Fitzroy, when she was hit and set ablaze by bombs from Argentine fighter-bombers. The Welsh Guards sustained heavy casualties and lost most of their equipment in this attack, in which another LSL, the *Sir Tristram*, was also hit. *MH.*

Blumentritt, Lt Gen (*General der Infanterie*) Günther (1893-1967). Ger. A distinguished staff officer whose career was closely linked to those of Field Marshals von Rundstedt and von Kluge. Blumentritt was Rundstedt's senior operations officer in Poland (Army Group South), 1939, and in the French campaign (Army Group A), 1940, where he was concerned in planning for the invasion of Britain (claiming, postwar, that it was "never contemplated as a serious operation"). From November 1940 he was COS of Kluge's Fourth Army, which formed part of Army Group Centre in the Smolensk-Moscow offensives, 1941-42. In September 1942, following service as head of the operations department of the General Staff, OKH, he became COS to Rundstedt, C-in-C West, the energetic and genial Blumentritt ideally supplementing the elderly, somewhat disillusioned patrician. However, Blumentritt appears to have shared Rundstedt's oversanguine attitude to the Allied invasion threat; while after the Normandy landings his task was made increasingly difficult by Hitler's arbitrary and specific demands. Blumentritt survived Rundstedt's dismissal in July 1944 to serve as COS to his successors Kluge (committed suicide, August 1944) and Model. Replaced by Westphal in September 1944, he was given a series of short-lived combat commands: 12th SS Division; Twenty-fifth Army; and, from March 27 1945, First Parachute Army in the retreat from the Rhine. Finally ordered to hold a Bremen-Hamburg line, he concentrated on orderly retreat rather than resistance, facilitating British capture of Hamburg and Lübeck. *RO'N.*

BMP. The Soviet infantry combat vehicle first developed in the 1960s to give infantry a mobile means of fighting on a nuclear battlefield. It entered service in the Soviet Army in 1967 and has since been widely exported as well as being produced in China and Czechoslovakia. The BMP-1 has a crew of three and carries an infantry section of eight men with firing ports for their weapons. It is armed with a 73mm gun and a Sagger anti-tank missile launcher and has 14mm protection. A new BMP-2 has been developed with capacity for only seven men but improved armament (30mm gun and Spandrel or Spigot missile launchers) and improved protection. *EJG.*

Field Marshal Fedor von Bock

Bock, Field Marshal Fedor von (1880–1945). Ger. The son of a Prussian general, Bock spent the early part of World War I on General Staff duties, but commanded a Foot Guards battalion on the Western Front in 1917–18, winning Imperial Germany's highest gallantry award, the *Pour le Mérite*. Continuing to rise in his profession, he led the German forces which occupied Austria in 1938. Haughty, humourless and ambitious, Bock despised the Nazis but was prepared to support Hitler as long as the Army was strengthened and his own career flourished. He commanded Army Group North in Poland and, in 1940, commanded Army Group B in the west, overrunning the Low Countries and northwestern France. Promoted Field Marshal after the French campaign, he led Army Group Centre in the invasion of Russia in 1941. Normally an industrious rather than an inspired commander, Bock nevertheless encircled and destroyed several Soviet armies at Minsk, Smolensk and Gomel but was robbed of the chance of taking Moscow by Hitler's untimely transfer of panzer units to the north and south in August. When the drive on Moscow resumed, it ground to a halt in the Russian winter and Bock, suffering from ulcers, was relieved of command on December 18. A month later he was given command of Army Group South, only to be removed in July 1942 following strategic disagreements with Hitler. He was killed in an Allied air attack. *PJS.*

Bock's Car. The B-29 flown by Maj Charles W Sweeney from which the second atomic bomb was dropped on Nagasaki on August 9 1945.

"Bodyguard". The need to disguise the time and location of the Allied invasion of Europe was essential to the success of Operation "Overlord". Several stratagems were devised, grouped under the overall title "Bodyguard". Some hinted at an early invasion while others sought to deceive the Germans that the landings might be in Norway, the Balkans or various areas in France. The operation proved so successful that even after the Normandy landings, German commanders were uncertain whether this was the real attack.

Boelcke, Capt Oswald (1891–1916). Ger. Fighter pilot of World War I, with 40 "kills"; most celebrated as a superb tactician and instructor. An advocate of close-range combat (inside 100yd/90m), Boelcke was instrumental in the German Air Force's formation, in mid-1916, of specialized fighter squadrons (*Jagdstaffeln*): the first formed, his own Jasta 2, produced such "aces" as Manfred von Richthofen. His manual of fighter tactics, the *Dikta Boelcke*, was issued to German pilots in both world wars. Boelcke was killed in a collision with one of his own squadron during a dogfight.

Boer War, Second (also called Great Boer War; Second South African War, October 11 1899–May 31 1902). Fearing for the independence of his state, established as a result of the First Boer War, 1880–81, in the face of increasing British imperialist expansion in southern Africa, President Paul Kruger of the South African Republic (Transvaal) moved to war with Britain on October 9–11 1899. His forces were immediately joined by those of the Orange Free State.

The Boers (the word, meaning "farmer", was pejoratively applied by the British to their adversaries, who more often spoke of themselves as Afrikaners, burghers, or Volk, "the people"), had a total military potential of *c*85,000 men, but rarely had more than 35,000 in

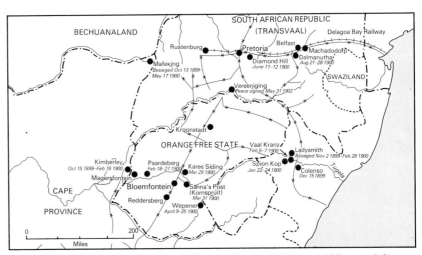

South Africa, 1899–1902: blockhouses and barbed wire finally curbed Boer mobility

the field at any one time. They were well-equipped with small arms, although deficient in artillery, and skilled in fieldcraft. Their looseknit organization into fast-moving mounted columns (commandos) was well-suited to the terrain: the major mistake of such commanders as Cronjé and Commandant-General Pietrus Joubert (1831–1900) was to commit many men to near-static operations at the sieges of Mafeking, Kimberley and Ladysmith.

At first outnumbering the British, who had no more than 25,000 regular troops in South Africa at the outbreak of the war, the Boers achieved notable victories in November–December 1899 at Modder river, Stormberg, Magersfontein and Colenso, where their fluid tactics bemused the more conventional British commanders, Methuen and Buller. From early 1900, however, under the command of Roberts and Kitchener, massive reinforcements of British and Imperial troops were poured in, to a total of *c*450,000 men in the whole course of the war. In February 1900, Kimberley and Ladysmith were relieved and Cronjé was defeated and captured at Paardeberg. The British steamroller moved inexorably onward to the capture of Bloemfontein and annexation of the Orange Free State in May 1900, and the conquest and annexation of the Transvaal in May-September 1900.

Rallying under such charismatic leaders as Botha, De La Rey, De Wet and Smuts, the Boers embarked on an 18-month guerrilla campaign. British countermea-

sures, directed by Kitchener, sought to restrict the mobility of the commandos by sectioning off the country with a chain of about 8,000 blockhouses, linked by some 4,000 miles (6,500km) of barbed wire, along the major communications routes.

Perhaps even more effective were the ruthless measures adopted to break Boer morale. The farms of men on commando duty were burned and their families and others believed to be sympathetic to them were confined in "concentration camps". Some 120,000 Afrikaners and 100,000 non-whites were herded into these camps, where, because of primitive accommodation, inefficient administration and, especially, poor hygiene and lack of medical provision, some 25,000 Afrikaners, the great majority children, died.

The Boers were thus forced into submission. They did, however, achieve what their most realistic leaders, notably Botha and Smuts, saw as the aim of their stalwart resistance: the preservation of their way of life. By the generous Treaty of Vereeniging, May 31 1902, the Transvaal and Orange Free State recognized British sovereignty but were promised eventual self-goverment – speedily achieved in 1907 – and received £3 million compensation for the damaged farms.

Boer military casualties included around 5,000 killed in battle or died of wounds or disease while on campaign. British and Imperial forces suffered 5,774 killed, more than 20,000 dead from disease, 22,829 wounded. *RO'N*.

B

Bofors gun. Widely used, reliable World War II 40mm light anti-aircraft gun.

Bogan, Vice Adm Gerald Francis (b.1894). US. US Navy fleet carrier commander; led carrier support groups in the New Guinea and Marianas campaigns and in the final attacks on Japan. Particularly notable for his handling of Task Group 38.2 at Leyte Gulf, October 1944.

Bogdanov, Marshal Semyon (1894–1960). Russian. A specialist commander of armoured units, Bogdanov distinguished himself during the battles of Moscow, Stalingrad and Kursk. After recovering from serious wounds, he led the Second Guards Tank Army during the advance on Berlin and participated in the city's capture.

Bohusz Szyszko, Maj Gen Z (xxxx–xxxx). Polish. Commander II Polish Corps during the final Allied offensive in Italy in April 1945; entered Bologna before the Americans on April 21.

Bologna, Allied autumn offensives towards (October–December 1944). After breaching the Gothic Line, but failing to break out of the Northern Apennines into the Po Valley in September, Alexander renewed the offensive with both Fifth and Eighth Armies (Clark and McCreery), aiming to take Bologna and Ravenna before winter. Hitler, having refused to authorize the withdrawal to the Alps, demanded a rigorous defence of every Apennine ridge and Romagna river.

In the Fifth Army's offensive, II US and XIII British Corps fought their way forward in the Apennines throughout October in deteriorating weather conditions against a determined defence by I Parachute Corps (Schlemm) and LI Mountain Corps (Feuerstein). Strategic bombers were used on October 12 to blast a way through the German defences covering Bologna, but Schlemm's Corps did not give way. Clark halted his offensive on October 26 only 12 miles (19km) short of Bologna, intending to reopen it when Eighth Army's operations in the Romagna had drawn off some of the German mobile divisions concentrated against him, and provided there was enough fine weather for the strategic bombers to help breach Bologna's defences.

In the Eighth Army's offensive, McCreery adopted the policy of using II Polish Corps (Anders) to turn successive German defence lines based on the Romagna rivers, while V Corps (Keightley) and I Canadian Corps (Burns) attacked frontally. In a series of grinding attritional battles, successive river lines were breached until Eighth Army closed up to the Senio in mid-December when Alexander halted operations for the winter.

Fifth Army's offensive was not resumed because the weather did not improve, and because the Germans opened a spoiling offensive down the Serchio valley on December 26. *WGFJ*.

Bologna, fall of (April 21 1945) *see* PO RIVER, BATTLE OF THE.

Lancaster bomber publicizes war loan

Bomber Command. Created by the reorganization of the RAF in July 1936. This showed the importance which was attached to the prospective strategic air offensive. From 1940 onwards, the headquarters were at High Wycombe. The AOC-in-C during the war were Sir Edgar Ludlow-Hewitt (until April 1940), Sir Charles Portal (until October 1940), Sir Richard Peirse (until January 1942) and Sir Arthur Harris (1942–45). The principal wartime aircraft were Wellingtons, Whitleys, Hampdens and Blenheims, which were progressively replaced by Stirlings, Halifaxes, Lancasters (which derived from Manchesters) and Mosquitoes. In 1968 the Command was merged with others to form Strike Command. *ANF*.

Bombing, types of, to 1945, after which nomenclature changed. *Area*: target was a collection of objects as opposed to an individual one or pinpoint, e.g. built-up area of an industrial town. *"Baedeker"*: British term to describe German attacks on towns of historic interest. *Blind*: bombs or markers aimed from above cloud or in dark on radar indications. *Carpet*: American term for area bombing. *Dive*: bombs aimed by pointing the nose of the aircraft at the target in a steep dive; a speciality of German Stukas. *Incendiary*: use of fire bombs to exploit the self-destructive nature of the target. *Off-Set*: markers deliberately displaced from the target; bombsights then biased so that by aiming at the marker the target would be hit. Done to avoid blowing out of markers by bombing and to deceive enemy into not extinguishing them; a speciality of 5 Group, Bomber Command. *Pinpoint*: target was a discreet object of relatively small size e.g. individual factory or viaduct. *Precision*: literally accurate but by derivation opposite of area bombing, i.e. target was an individual object as opposed to a collection of objects. *Saturation*: object was to swamp ground defences and rescue services. *Selective*: series of attacks aimed at an associated group of targets e.g. oil plants or aircraft factories which were known as "Target Systems". Selective bombing could be attempted either by area or precision attack. *Shuttle*: instead of returning to base the bombers flew on to land beyond the target, e.g. in North Africa or Russia. *Strategic*: attack on the sources, as opposed to the manifestations, of enemy war effort, e.g. production of war materials or morale of industrial population. *Tactical*: attack on the manifestations of enemy armed forces, immediate supply lines or ships at sea. *Terror*: emotive term often used by one belligerent to describe attacks by its enemy or generally by those opposed on principle to bombing. *Visual*: bombs or markers aimed by sighting the target. *ANF*.

Bomdi Lá (India-China War 1962).

Village in North East Frontier Agency, 50 miles (80km) from the Brahmaputra river. Held in November 1962 by 48th Brigade, but the defences were dispersed and easily overwhelmed when the Chinese attacked, November 18.

Bong, Maj Richard I (1920–1945). US. Most successful USAAF fighter pilot of World War II, destroying 40 Japanese aircraft while flying P-38 Lightnings in the Southwest Pacific. Bong owed much to the dedicated support of his wingman, Lt Col Thomas J Lynch (1916–1944), himself with 20 "kills".

Booby trap. A device, usually explosive, designed to inflict casualties on unwary opponents. Frequently used in irregular warfare to redress the tactical balance between guerrilla and regular forces by hampering troop movements and damaging morale.

Boosted fission weapon. This is a halfway house between a fission (see NUCLEAR WEAPON) and fusion (see THERMONUCLEAR WEAPON) device in which a fusion reaction is used to produce extra neutrons which in turn produce more fissions of uranium or plutonium nuclei than would be produced by neutrons from the fission chain reaction alone. The main energy source of the explosion, however, remains the fissile material. The first Soviet "thermonuclear" explosion was such a boosted device and early British "H-bombs" may also have been high-yield boosted fission devices using very large amounts of fissile material to give megaton yields. Half-megaton boosted fission warheads were also used on the first French submarine-launched ballistic missiles. Boosting is carried out by inserting fusion material, e.g. heavy hydrogen gas (deuterium or tritium), into the core of the weapon. Boosting allows the yield of bombs to be varied and the fissile material to be used with maximum efficiency. The first American boosted fission weapon was exploded in 1951 with a yield of 45.5 kilotons; small boosted fission devices have been widely deployed by the US as primaries in lightweight thermonuclear weapons and on their own as efficient low-yield weapons. *EJG*.

Borden, Sir Robert Laird (1854–1937). Canadian. Prime Minister of Canada 1911–20 (Conservative 1911–17, Union 1917–20). Borden was a staunch supporter of Canadian participation in the war and of Imperial unity.

Border War, Vietnam (1950). The supply of Chinese mortars and 130mm artillery to the People's Army of Vietnam (PAVN) following the communist victory in China in 1949 opened a new phase in the Indochina War. With these weapons, the PAVN launched a campaign in the autumn to eject the French from outposts guarding Route Coloniale 4 near Vietnam's border with China. After overrunning the fortress at Dong Khe on September 18, the PAVN attacked outposts around the town of Cao Bang, located 125 miles (200km) north of Hanoi. A botched attempt to evacuate Cao Bang and PAVN ambushes resulted in French losses of 4,000 men. That Khe was quickly surrounded, Lang Son was abandoned. The PAVN killed or captured about 6,000 French troops and seized over 10,000 small arms and 13 pieces of artillery. The campaign eliminated any chance of interference with the free movement of men and supplies across the Chinese border and consolidated the communists' northern base areas into a single liberated zone. *WST. See also* CAO BANG; LANG SON.

Bor-Komorowski, Gen Count Tadeusz (1895–1966). Polish. After Poland's defeat in 1939, Gen Komorowski, a cavalry officer, joined the resistance. In 1943, under the nom de guerre "General Bor", he took command of the Polish Home Army (Armia Krajowa) and led it in the escalating guerrilla campaign against the occupying German forces. On August 1 1944, with the Russians on the outskirts of Warsaw, Bor-Komorowski ordered an uprising to seize control of the Polish capital. Initially successful, the Home Army was faced by unexpectedly fierce German countermeasures and received virtually no Soviet assistance. On October 2, after two months' struggle, Bor-Komorowski and the remnants of his command were forced to surrender. He was sent to Colditz where

he resisted German entreaties to raise a Polish army to fight the Russians. After the war, he settled in London, becoming PM of the Polish Government in exile. *MS*.

Borneo see MALAYSIA-INDONESIA CONFRONTATION.

Borojevic von Bojna, Field Marshal Svetozar (1856–1920). Austrian. Commanded Austrian Third Army in the disastrous first offensive of the Galician campaign, 1914, failing to raise the Russian siege of Przemysl, and in the successful offensive at Gorlice-Tarnow, April–May 1915. In June 1915 he took command of Fifth Army in the critical Isonzo sector of the Italian front, conducting a skilful defence in the series of battles culminating in Caporetto. On the Piave river, June 15–23 1918, where he shared overall Austrian command with Conrad von Hötzendorf, Borojevic's Fifth and Sixth Armies achieved an 8-mile (13km) advance across the lower Piave: floods prevented reinforcement and forced a withdrawal. At Vittorio Veneto, October 24–November 3 1918, Borojevic faced the major Allied assault on the right of the Austrian line around Monte Grappa, stoutly holding his ground for three days before joining the general retreat. *RO'N*.

Bose, Subhas Chandra (1897–1945). Indian. A nationalist extremist, Bose sought Axis help to win India's independence. Imprisoned in 1940, he escaped to Berlin, where he began to recruit an Indian National Army from Indian POWs. In Tokyo from January 1943, he raised three understrength divisions from Indian prisoners of the Japanese (many joined under threat and deserted at the first opportunity) and led them in battle at Kohima and Imphal. The failure of the Japanese invasion of India saw the disintegration of his forces.

Boston/Havoc, Douglas DB-7, A-20, P-70 (US, WWII). Light bomber/night fighter-intruder; crew 3. Prototype flew October 26 1938; first ordered by France but few used before June 25 1940. Taken over by Britain, first deliveries August 1940. Operational Europe, Middle East; Havoc night-fighter conversion full use from April 1941; US counterparts A-20, P-70, latter used in Pacific 1943–44. Production all variants 7,478 (of which 3,600 to Russia). Two 1,600hp Wright R-2600-11 engines; max. speed 350mph (560kph); 2,600lb (1,180kg) bombs, up to 12 machine guns or four 20mm cannon.

Botha: South African Premier

Botha, Commandant-General Louis (1862–1919). South African. Botha joined the Transvaal forces as a junior officer in October 1899. Within two months, as Assistant-General, he had defeated Buller at Colenso and was effectively in command at Ladysmith, where he repulsed relief attempts at Spion Kop and Vaal Kranz. In March 1900 he succeeded Pietrus Joubert as Commandant-General. With instinctive military aptitude, Botha had the charm and strength of personality that enabled him to impose some unity on the independently-minded Boers. Late in 1900, he initiated a guerrilla campaign that tied down vastly superior numbers of British troops for many months. His aim was not the impossible one of victory and independence, but to gain peace terms that would enable the Boers to preserve their way of life.

Botha was the first Prime Minister of the Union of South Africa in 1910–19. In 1914–15, he showed both firmness and magnanimity in suppressing the pro-German insurgency headed by De Wet, Beyers and Maritz; that his military skills extended to modern motorized warfare was shown also in his defeat of German forces in Southwest Africa in March–July 1915. *RO'N*.

Bottomley, Air Chief Marshal Sir Norman (1891–1970). Br. Senior Air Staff Officer, Bomber Command 1938–40, Deputy or Assistant Chief of the Air Staff 1941–45. A key staff officer concerned before the war with the operational appreciation of the Western Air Plans for Bomber Command and, from 1941, with the formulation of air policies and drafting of directives to the AOC-in-C.

Bougainville campaign (1943–44). The capture of Bougainville, the largest of the Solomon Islands, was a vital part of Operation "Cartwheel", the Allied plan to break the Japanese hold on the Bismarck and Solomon seas. The assault on Bougainville was to be carried out by Lt Gen Vandegrift's I Marine Amphibious Corps. At 0722 hours on November 1 1943, elements of the 3rd Marine Division landed at Cape Torokina on the west coast of the island. Light Japanese defences were quickly subdued and efficient air and sea cover protected the beachhead and invasion fleet from strong counter-attacks. A small Japanese force managed to land on the left flank of the bridgehead, but was destroyed on November 8. Slowly the Marines, supported by the 37th Infantry Division, pushed into the interior and at the end of the month they fought a fiercely contested engagement at Piva Forks where more than 1,200 Japanese were killed. The drive inland enabled the construction of the all-important air strips and, by early January 1944, three had been completed. However, Japanese resistance on the island had still not been broken and a major counter-attack was launched against the bridgehead throughout most of March 1944. Its failure led to a withdrawal but, although American forces were now effectively in control of Bougainville, small pockets of enemy resistance were maintained until the end of the war. *MS*.

Bouncing bomb. Designed by Barnes Wallis to attack dams from low level (to avoid breakage on impact) and spinning (to aid the bounce) on water above the dam. It bounced until it reached the dam and sank to the bottom of the lake where it detonated. Thus it shook

the foundations of the dam and fractured the wall. The weight of water above the dam then exploited the fracture. To achieve success and avoid self-destruction, extreme accuracy of aim was essential. The bomb was used only in the Dams raid. *ANF*.

Boxer Rising (1899–1901). In China, 1899–1900, the Society of Righteous Harmonious Fists ("Boxers"), tacitly encouraged by the autocratic Empress-Dowager Tz'u Hsi (1834–1908), began to murder foreign missionaries and their converts and attack Western commercial interests, whose rapacity had long been resented. On June 3 1900, as the Boxers converged on Peking (Beijing), 485 naval troops were sent from Western and Japanese warships at Tientsin (Tianjin) to protect the foreign legations.

On June 10, a 2,100-strong international relief force under British Adm Sir Edward Seymour entrained for Peking, but the Boxers sabotaged the railway and drove Seymour back with *c*300 casualties. On June 15, the landing of further Allied troops at Tientsin was threatened by the batteries of the Taku Forts. In a six-hour night battle on June 17, landing parties (900 men; 172 casualties) from British, French, German, Italian and Russian warships successfully stormed the forts.

In Peking, from July 20, Chinese Imperial troops stood aside as the Boxers conducted a sporadic 55-day siege of the British Legation (where 475 civilians, 450 troops and *c*3,000 Chinese Christians took refuge) and the P'ei Tang Cathedral Compound (40 French and Italian Marines guarding priests, nuns and *c*3,400 Chinese). Casualties totalled 60 military dead and 145 wounded; 16 civilians killed and 23 wounded; *c*450 Chinese Christians killed.

Belated by international rivalries, an 18,700-strong Relief Force (*c*9,000 Japanese, 4,000 Russian, 3,000 British and 2,000 American troops forming the principal contingents) began the 80-mile (128km) march from Tientsin to Peking on August 4. Breaking through fortifications at Peitsang (August 5) and Yangtsun (August 6), it reached Peking on August 13. An immediate assault on the walls by Russian troops was repulsed, but next day Japanese, Russian and American attacks succeeded. The British contingent, entering beneath the walls, via the Water Gate, was first into the beleaguered Legation. The Empress-Dowager fled and the Imperial City was occupied and looted.

The dispersal of the Boxers was completed by punitive expeditions (mostly by German troops) in September 1900–May 1901, while Boxer threats in southern Manchuria were answered by Russian occupation. The Boxer (Peking) Protocol of September 1901 provided for the punishment of pro-Boxer officials and for the payment of massive reparations. *RO'N.*

Boyington, Col Gregory ("Pappy") (1912–87). US. Leading USMC fighter pilot of World War II, with 28 "kills" (including six with the Flying Tigers, 1941–42). From September 1943, Boyington commanded Marine Fighter Squadron 214 (called "Black Sheep", because he could "tame" pilots rejected by other squadrons) in the central Solomons, flying F4U Corsairs. Shot down over Rabaul in January 1944, he became a POW.

A "soldier's general": Omar Bradley

Bradley, General of the Army Omar Nelson (1893–1981). US. Bradley did not see active service during World War I but remained in the United States employed on troop training duties. During the 1930s he continued to specialize in this field, developing a rapport with the men under his command that led to the epithet of "soldiers' general". His qualities were greatly admired by Gen Marshall, the US COS, and in February 1943 Bradley was sent to North Africa

where, in April, he took over the US II Corps. Reliable and conscientious, Bradley lacked flamboyance but not character.

In 1943 he was selected to command the American assault force in Operation "Overlord". He endorsed the addition of a second American landing and insisted on the employment of airborne forces to link the two beaches. On D-Day Bradley was faced with arguably the greatest crisis of the landings when his forces landing on Omaha beach encountered major difficulties. However, he and his subordinates kept their nerve and secured the bridgehead. His initial breakout on July 25 was subsequently exploited by Patton's Third Army.

From August 1 1944, Bradley was in command of US 12th Army Group, in the drive across France. He inevitably suffered in comparison with the high profile personalities of Montgomery and Patton and, in December 1944, following reverses in the Hürtgen Forest and the surprise German offensive in the Ardennes, Bradley's position seemed threatened. He was supported by Marshall, Eisenhower and Patton and his fortunes rallied as his troops crossed the Rhine at Remagen and joined up with Soviet forces in central Germany.

Promoted to full general on March 12 1945, Bradley ended the war in command of some 1,250,000 US troops, more than any other field commander had ever led into battle. In 1950 he was promoted to General of the Army and served as Chairman of the US Joint Chiefs of Staff until his retirement in August 1953. *MS.*

Bramall, Field Marshal Lord (b.1923). Br. Chief of General Staff in 1982. Subsequently Chief of Defence Staff.

Brandenburg Organization. In German army 1939–45, grew from a punishment company eventually to divisional size: composed of desperate men, who were ready to take abnormal risks in the hope – seldom realized – that they would be pardoned and returned to normal units. Brandenburg troops operated, often in Red Army uniforms, on raids and sabotage ventures behind such fixed fighting lines as there were on the eastern

front, sometimes with startling success.

Bratiano, Ion (1864–1927). Romanian. Prime Minister from 1909. In 1916 made secret alliance with Allies which resulted in Romania's entry into the war on their side. Led his country's delegation to the Peace Conference in Paris but resigned after failing to obtain the territorial gains which he felt were due to Romania. *See also* ROMANIAN CAMPAIGN (1916–18).

Brauchitsch, Field Marshal Heinrich Alfred Hermann Walther (1881-1948). Ger. Commissioned into the German army in 1900, Brauchitsch served on the General Staff during World War I. Under Weimar, he became the Reichswehr's Inspector General of Artillery; in 1937 he commanded Fourth Army Group. In February 1938, following the dismissal of von Fritsch for alleged homosexuality as part of Hitler's "purge" of the high command, Brauchitsch became C-in-C, German Army. Hitler would have preferred the openly-dedicated Nazi von Reichenau, but Brauchitsch's appointment was urged by those generals (notably von Rundstedt) who believed that he might support them in opposing the *Führer*'s more precipitately aggressive schemes. However, Brauchitsch's accession marked the beginning of the subjugation of the Army High Command (OKH) to Armed Forces High Command (OKW), dominated by Hitler and headed by his "lackey", Keitel.

Brauchitsch was given a free hand in the planning and execution of *Fall Weiss*, the invasion of Poland, September-October 1939. This success, however, availed him little in early November 1939, when, urged on by Halder, his COS, and Beck he attempted to express OKH's opposition to an immediate invasion in the West. Halder, Beck and others even meditated a coup against Hitler, but were disheartened by Brauchitsch's abject capitulation to the *Führer*'s accusations of "defeatism". Adverse weather caused the postponement of the invasion until May 1940, and when it took place, Brauchitsch's *Fall Gelb* (in essence, a repetition of the Schlieffen plan) was abandoned in favour of

B

von Manstein's plan.

Although Brauchitsch nominally commanded the invasion of Russia, 1941, the command decisions lay with OKW rather than OKH. Brauchitsch saw the taking of Smolensk as opening the way to Moscow; yet failed to oppose Hitler's decision to secure the Ukraine before pressing the attack. In December 1941, with the German offensive stalled within sight of Moscow because of the delay and Zhukov's counterattack imminent, Brauchitsch, suffering the after-effects of a heart attack, recommended withdrawal to defensive positions. Hitler denounced him as a "cowardly wretch" and, forcing his resignation, himself assumed the post of Army C-in-C. Brauchitsch held no further command: arrested by the Allies in 1945, he died while awaiting trial for war crimes. *RO'N*.

Rocket expert von Braun (*right*)

Braun, Wernher von (1912–77). Ger/US. Educated at the Berlin Institute of Technology, von Braun took an early interest in astronomy and space flight. In 1932 he joined the German Army Weapons Department participating in the development of rocket technology and subsequently becoming Technical Director of the rocket weapons establishment at Peenemünde. Throughout the late 1930s he worked on the design of the A-4 rocket that was to be both self-propelled and self-steering and with a range that would give it strategic potential. Research suffered from Hitler's decision to make this type of work a low priority. This situation changed in 1943 when he ordered production of the *Vergeltungswaffe* V-2 rocket, closely based on the A-4. Himmler cast covetous eyes

upon the project and in March 1944 briefly had von Braun arrested on trumped-up charges but he was soon released following the intervention of his superiors and Albert Speer. The weapon went into production and over 1,400 V-2s were launched against Britain. In March 1945 von Braun and many of his research team fled from the advancing Soviet army and surrendered to American forces. After extensive debriefing, von Braun was allowed to continue his research in the United States. He was granted American citizenship and played a vital role in the development of American ballistic missiles. Subsequently he became a leading figure in the US space programme. *MS*.

Braun, Eva (1912–45). Ger. Hitler's mistress and, briefly, his wife before their joint suicide on April 30 1945.

Breguet 14 (French, WWI). Two-seat reconnaissance or bomber. Prototype flew November 21 1916; first ordered March 6 1917. Large-scale production in two forms: 14.A2 reconnaissance, 14.B2 bomber; deliveries from summer 1917. Very successful and widely used in both versions until and after Armistice. Production until 1926: at least 8,000 built. One 300/310hp Renault 12Fcx/Fcy engine (many alternatives also fitted) max. speed 114mph (182kph); three 7.7mm machine guns, 560lb (256kg) bombs.

Bren gun. Reliable British light machine gun in service throughout World War II and later.

Brereton, Lt Gen Lewis Hyde (1890–1967). US. Appointed commander, US Far East Air Forces, in October 1941, Brereton had little time to prepare against a Japanese attack: because of poor communications and warning procedures, most of his force was destroyed on the ground at Clark Field, Manila, December 8 1941. In mid-1942 he took command of USA Middle East Air Forces (from November 1942, Ninth Air Force), contributing substantially to the success of the North African campaign – not least by his insistence on Allied inter-service coordination – and *inter alia* ordering the

controversial low-level Ploesti raids. From late 1943, following Ninth Air Force's re-establishment in the UK, Brereton forged it into a formidable tactical force for the Normandy campaign, its pinpoint attacks on communications routes being particularly effective. On August 2 1944, Brereton became commander, First Allied Airborne Army, responsible for the training, operational planning (including Arnhem), delivery to the combat zone (where they came under ground command), and air supply of all Allied airborne troops. *RO'N*.

Brest. French naval base in Brittany. After German occupation in 1940, it became a major U-boat base. *Scharnhorst* and *Gneisenau* were based there until the Channel Dash of 1942. Heavy bombing by the RAF and USAAF reduced much of the town to rubble, but not the submarine "pens". A German garrison held out until September 1944.

Brest-Litovsk, Treaty of. On December 3 1917 the Bolsheviks and the Central Powers met at Brest-Litovsk to discuss terms for Russia's leaving the war. In the subsequent treaty, signed on March 3 1918, the Russians ceded the Baltic provinces, Ukraine, Finland, Poland, and the Caucasus. However, Germany's defeat later that year nullified the agreement.

Brigade (British Army). Functional grouping of battalions and units of all arms. Commanded by a Brigadier. US Army equivalent: Regimental Combat Team.

Briggs, Gen Sir Harold (1894–1952). Br. Formerly serving in the Indian Army, Briggs came out of retirement to be Director of Operations, Malaya (1950–52). He devised the resettlement plan bearing his name, carried through by Gen Templer. He died from effects of overwork soon after relinquishing his post. *See also* MALAYAN EMERGENCY.

Bristol F.2B Fighter (Br, WWI). Two-seat fighter-reconnaissance. F.2A prototype flew September 9 1916; first deliveries December 1916; first operational use April 5 1917. Very large-scale production

1917–18; Falcon-powered version exceptionally successful. Arab-powered reconnaissance/artillery-spotter version little used. Over 4,400 built to wartime contracts; production continued after Armistice. One 275hp Rolls-Royce Falcon III or 200hp Sunbeam Arab engine; max. speed 119mph (190kph); two or three 0.303in machine guns, up to 300lb (135kg) bombs.

Bristol Scout (Br, WWI). Single-seat fighting scout. Prototype flew February 23 1914; first production delivery February 1915. Widely used RFC and RNAS France, UK, Aegean, Middle East; popular but never effectively armed; never equipped an entire squadron. Pioneered deck flying. Total built 374. One 80hp Gnome, Le Rhône or Clerget, or 100hp Gnome Monosoupape engine; max. speed 94mph (150kph); one, occasionally two, 0.303in machine guns, a few small bombs.

Britain the Battle of (July–September 1940). One of the decisive battles of World War II. The German aim was to engage and destroy the RAF and thus to neutralize the Royal Navy which would have been unable to operate effectively in the face of overwhelming air attack and without any air cover of its own. The German army would then have been able to occupy Britain without undue difficulty. The Germans thought that this could be achieved by fighter-escorted bomber raids on targets which the British would feel compelled to defend. They expected that in the resulting air battles they would quickly gain the upper hand and that within a matter of days the effective fighting strength of their enemy would be destroyed. As they could choose the times and the targets for the attacks and as they had bases all the way from Norway to the French Atlantic coast, the Germans seemed to have the advantage of the element of surprise; they also had an apparently decisive superiority in strength, with about 2,500 aircraft available to take on the 1,200 or so of the RAF. After preliminary skirmishing in July–August, the battle began in earnest on August 13, which, after many postponements, the Germans named *Adlertag*

(Eagle Day). It ended on September 15 by which time the British had inflicted such losses on the Luftwaffe that it was compelled to disengage. A few days later, Hitler cancelled "Sealion", the plan to invade Britain. The issue had been decided in air combat between fighters, the best of which were the British Spitfires and the much more numerous German Messerschmitt Me 109s; these were fighters of comparable performance. The British Hurricanes,

German photograph of Newhaven, 1940

although outclassed by Me 109s, were superior to the longer-range German Me 110s and the German bombers of all types were highly vulnerable to any of the opposing fighters. The apparent German advantage was more than neutralized by two key factors which they had not anticipated. First, the element of surprise was largely negated by the British radar early warning system, assisted to some extent by "Ultra", which enabled the British to put their fighters in the right places at the right moments. Secondly, the German advantage of superior numbers of first-class fighters was qualified by their lack of range. The Me 109s, which had less than half-an-hour of fighting time over England from their nearest bases, were often out of the action before they could bring their potential to bear. There was also the general consideration that German fighter pilots had to attempt to screen their bombers in addition to engaging the British fighters, whereas the latter had free aim at anything hostile they could see. It was also fortunate for Britain that the c-in-c of Fighter Command, Dowding, declined to rule in favour of either of his two principal Group Commanders, Leigh-Mallory and Park, who were

in vigorous dispute as to tactics. Park thought it best to feed his fighters into the attack as and when they arrived on the scene. Leigh-Mallory preferred to assemble an overwhelming force and attack only after this had been achieved. In the event it was the combination of these two ploys which proved the most advantageous.

It may be concluded, although this must for ever be a hypothesis, that the Germans lost the battle because they failed to concentrate the RAF at some point where they could bring their superior strength to bear. Due to the range of their Me 109s, such a point could only have been Kent and East Sussex, and had the Germans made even a limited and, no doubt, a costly military landing there to draw the British defences into the range of their effective air power, the Battle of Britain would probably have had a German name. *ANF*.

Britain, planned invasion of (1940). No real plans had been drawn up for an invasion of the United Kingdom before the summer of 1940, and Hitler harboured hopes of a negotiated peace with Britain. Nevertheless, he issued a directive on July 16 1940 ordering the German army and navy to prepare for a cross-Channel assault on the coast of southeast England, codenamed Operation "Sealion". The British rejection of Hitler's peace terms in July led to increased preparations for invasion but, although the British army was weak, both the Royal Navy and the RAF remained daunting adversaries. The fate of "Sealion" depended upon the outcome of the Battle of Britain and the invasion forces were obliged to postpone and modify their plans throughout most of the summer. The British victory and the onset of adverse seasonal weather in the Channel, combined with Hitler's desire to pursue his ambitions elsewhere, led to the effective abandonment of the venture. *MS*.

British Commonwealth Occupation Force, Japan (BCOF). After the Japanese surrender in 1945, a British Commonwealth Occupation Force consisting of over 40,000 men from Australia, Britain, India and New Zealand was sent to Japan. By 1949, the British, Indian and New Zealand contingents had withdrawn leaving only a token force of 2,630 Australians. This consisted of the 3rd Battalion Royal Australian Regiment, the 77th RAAF interceptor squadron and a naval shore establishment. The BCOF was commanded by an Australian officer, Lt Gen H C H Robertson, who reported to the Supreme Commander Allied Powers in Tokyo, Gen Douglas MacArthur, and to the Chiefs of Staff Committee in Australia, a body which consisted of the Australian Chiefs of Staff with British and New Zealand representatives. The BCOF provided a base and lines of communication organization for Commonwealth forces committed to Korea. In December 1950, this situation was formalized when Robertson became C-in-C British Commonwealth Forces in Korea (BCFK) with administrative responsibility for the contingents engaged there. BCFK expanded during the war to include nearly 100 different headquarters and units in Japan and Korea. *CM.*

British Expeditionary Force (BEF). The British armies dispatched to France in August 1914 and September 1939 under the command of French and Gort respectively.

British forces in Korea. British warships were first ordered into the Korean War on June 28 1950. The British naval contribution eventually consisted of an aircraft carrier, two cruisers, four destroyers and three frigates. Britain was reluctant to send ground troops but under American pressure agreed to commit an infantry brigade on July 26 1950. This force, the 29th British Infantry Brigade under Brig T Brodie, did not arrive in Korea until November 1950. At the beginning of August 1950, when US forces were under heavy pressure on the Pusan perimeter, Britain hastily dispatched the 27th British Infantry Brigade under Brig B A Coad from Hong Kong. This force landed on August 28 1950. It was renamed the 27th Commonwealth Infantry Brigade on October 1 1950 when it was joined by the 3rd Battalion, Royal Australian Regiment. In early 1951 the Brigade

received additional Commonwealth components, the 16th Field Regiment, Royal New Zealand Artillery and the Canadians of the 2nd Battalion, Princess Patricia's Light Infantry. In April 1951 the 27th Commonwealth Infantry Brigade was relieved by the 28th Commonwealth Infantry Brigade. In July 1951, the 28th and 29th Brigades were incorporated into the 1st Commonwealth Division. Britain provided the biggest ground force contingent after the US and the ROK. It also sent two squadrons of Sunderland flying boats and individual British pilots served with US fighter squadrons. *CM. See also* CASSELS, FIELD MARSHAL SIR JAMES; CHONGCHON RIVER, BATTLE OF THE; HOOK, THE BATTLES OF; IMJIN RIVER, BATTLE OF; KAPYONG, BATTLE OF.

Broad front strategy. Gen Eisenhower, the Supreme Commander Allied Expeditionary Force, had a clear strategy for the ultimate defeat of Germany. Once the Normandy landings had been secured and the Allied armies had broken out of the bridgehead, he envisaged a steady advance on a broad front. This would force the Germans to extend their line and expose them to unrelenting, dispersed Allied attacks. He hoped his plan would minimize risks and facilitate the build-up of supplies and communications. However, it was not a strategy favoured by his British allies, Churchill, Brooke and Montgomery. Montgomery agitated for all available logistical support, and the US First Army, to be given to the 21st Army Group which he would lead in a thrust into Germany, crossing the Rhine above the Ruhr. Eisenhower moderated Montgomery's demands and allowed him to proceed with Operation "Market Garden", but the overall broad front strategy was maintained. *MS.*

Broadhurst, Air Marshal Sir Harry (b.1905). Br. Commander Western Desert Air Force, February 1943–April 1944; devised the air plan for the attack at Tebaga during the Battle of Mareth in March 1943; and then Commander No 38 Group RAF in Northwest Europe. After the war, C-in-C 2nd ATAF, 1954–6; C-in-C Bomber Command, 1956–9; C-in-C Allied

Air Forces Central Europe, 1959–61.

Broadmead-Roope, Lt Commander Gerald (1905–40). Br. Captain of the destroyer *Glowworm*, which rammed the German cruiser *Hipper* off Trondheim at the start of the Norwegian campaign in April 1940; he was awarded a posthumous VC.

Broke, British destroyer leaders. (1) In company with Swift, took part in a famous and successful skirmish with a larger force of German destroyers in 1917. (2) Lost during the attack on Algiers in 1942.

Broodseinde. Village, east-northeast of Ypres. Occupied by the British 2nd Division, October 1914, it fell to the Germans in May 1915. Recaptured by 2nd Australian Division, October 4 1917, it was lost again the following April, then finally retaken by Belgian troops, September 28 1918.

Brooke, Gen Sir Alan *see* ALAN-BROOKE, FIELD MARSHAL VISCOUNT.

Brooke-Popham, Air Chief Marshal Sir Robert (1878–1953). Br. Originally an infantryman, he transferred in 1912 to the new Royal Flying Corps after a spell in its precursor, the Air Battalion, Royal Engineers. Joined RAF when it was formed in 1918. Commandant, RAF Staff College 1921–26, then various key staff appointments including command of Air Defence of Great Britain. Retired 1937 to be Governor of Kenya but recalled in 1939; C-in-C Far East 1940. Arriving in Singapore he found that the defence of Malaya, on which security of the Singapore naval base depended, was woefully underequipped, short of trained manpower, and dangerously deficient in modern combat aircraft capable of taking on the latest Japanese fighters and bombers, but his insistent warnings to London went unheeded. When war broke out, all priorities went to the European theatre and Far East Command was starved of aircraft as well as the capital ships for which the Singapore base had been built. As impending Japanese aggression became clear in 1941, the new battleship *Prince of Wales*

Land warfare in the 20th century

General Sir William Jackson GBE, KCB, MC
British Official Historian for the Mediterranean
and Middle East Campaigns of World War II

There are three great differences between naval and air warfare and operations on land. Sailors and airmen fight in homogeneous environments, in which weapon technology can be exploited to the full: soldiers have to contend with the vagaries of topography, which make technological solutions less easy to devise. In economic terms, navies and air forces are capital intensive; armies still depend more upon men than machines.

The second difference is that people inhabit land battle fields, and so political factors tend to impact more on land warfare.

The third difference is the greater vulnerability of armies to logistic factors. A warship at sea can be self-contained for several months; an aircraft returns to its base; but soldiers can only carry a few days supply with them. The easiest way to defeat an army is to cut it off from its source of supply.

Today's cavalry divisions – this armoured personnel carrier is
a typical element – are far removed from the more traditional
mounted units that were still seen as a crucial part of any
fighting force at the outbreak of World War I.

Throughout history, five factors have dictated the mode of land warfare in any particular epoch: first, the balance between fire power, mobility and protection; second, intelligence gathering and target acquisition efficiency; third, means of command and communication; fourth, logistic practicability; and fifth, morale.

In the weapon balance, most armies seek improved fire power. Those armies whose task it is to maintain the status quo – the defenders – tend to place greater emphasis upon protection at the expense of mobility: aggressors prize mobility in their quest for quick and cheap military victories to avoid the cost of long wars.

The pendulum of advantage swings to and fro between attack and defence as new weapons and tactics are evolved; but the decisive factor is morale. Superiority in numbers, weapons, intelligence and logistics, avail an army little if it lacks the will to fight. In the past, Davids have often slain their Goliaths in land warfare and will no doubt continue to do so.

Land warfare is essentially evolutionary. History suggests that major changes are only brought about in its conduct by pressures generated by war itself. It is also noticeable that emergent technologies cast their shadows before them: each major war leaves a legacy of partially exploited techniques to its successor.

Regrettably few military commanders in 1900 foresaw the likely impact of increased fire power of rifle, machine gun and artillery on the balance of advantage between attack and defence. The majority saw it as reinforcing their existing belief that offensive action held the key to military success. Generals still sought to win the initial fire fight, and then to press home the advantage with the cold steel of a bayonet charge. Scant attention was paid to the defensive qualities of the simple pick and shovel. Foch's dictum, *"L'attaque, toujours l'attaque"*, reflected the military consensus of the time in most armies. Cavalry were still seen as the *Arme Blanche*, despite the vulnerability of the horse.

The evolutionary pattern of 20th century warfare was broken dramatically in 1945 when the atomic bombs were dropped on Japan. Fire power was increased by so many orders of magnitude that the military history of the century breaks into two quite separate periods: the pre-nuclear era up to 1945; the nuclear era thereafter. The spectrum of land warfare in the pre-nuclear era had only three bands: war; colonial war; internal security (aid to the police) (see fig 1 *below*).

The Second Boer War (1898-1902)

The 20th century began in the midst of a major colonial war. In the Second Boer War, the British were the first to experience the lethality of the bolt-action, magazine-fed rifle in the hands of determined men who could use field-craft and concealment to inflict severe losses on orthodox military formations. The scarlet tunics, worn by the British since the 17th century, disappeared and were replaced by khaki jackets; extended order became the mode of attack; and controlled and well-aimed fire from concealed and dug-in positions replaced the traditional line and square in defence.

The Boer War was also the forerunner of modern guerrilla war, which was to play a major role in land warfare during the nuclear half of the century. The British army faced all the difficulties of suppressing armed rebellion when the majority of a disaffected population is supporting the rebels and has the will to resist. Kitchener's use of scorched earth, stop-lines, punitive sweeps and concentration camps was to be repeated all too frequently as the colonial powers tried to hold onto their empires after World War II.

A British blockhouse in the Boer War. After their defeat at Paardeberg and the fall of Pretoria in 1900, the Boers fought on, using their highly mobile commandos to wage guerrilla warfare for another two years. The British erected stop-lines of barbed wire along the railways and across the veld in an attempt to trap the commandos. Blockhouses were built at intervals along them to give warning of Boer attempts to break through, so that British mobile columns could be rushed to intercept.

Boer commando riflemen. Armed with bolt-action, magazine-fed rifles, and being born masters of field-craft, the Boers surprised the British. Firing from concealed positions, they could decimate the British infantry, who, at the beginning of the war, were still wearing scarlet tunics, and attacked in close formation, intending to rout their opponents as they had always done in the past with cold steel in a bayonet charge.

fig 1   The spectrum of land warfare at the beginning of the 20th century

| war | colonial war | internal security |

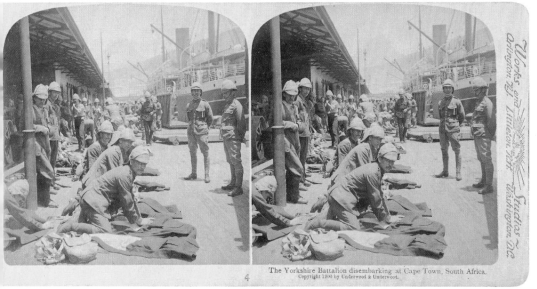

The Yorkshire Battalion disembarking at Cape Town, South Africa.
Copyright 1900 by Underwood & Underwood.

A British infantry battalion landing at Cape Town. This was a familiar sight at colonial ports at the turn of the century, when British imperial activity was at its height and many small colonial wars were being fought. The key to British success in dominating vast areas with so few troops lay in the fighting qualities and discipline of their soldiers, who brought stability to the territories they garrisoned.

Cape Garrison Artillery making it hot for the Boers across Modder River, S. Africa.
Copyright 1900 by Underwood & Underwood.

British field guns in South Africa. Artillery had little more than harassing value to both sides in the Boer War. The Boers had too few guns and their ammunition supply was too limited for them to make effective use of artillery in the sieges of Kimberley and Mafeking. The British, on the other hand, had too few opportunities to make decisive use of their efficient field guns against concealed Boer defensive positions, which were difficult to locate with sufficient accuracy, or against the small, fleeting targets presented by mounted Boer commandos.

In the Orange River Trenches holding back the Boers—South Africa.
Copyright 1900 by Underwood & Underwood.

The British soon replaced scarlet tunics with khaki, and adopted more open formations to reduce vulnerability to rifle-fire when attacking after their disastrous losses in the first major engagements of the Boer War. In defence, they dug in rapidly, as shown here, and developed the accurate and disciplined rifle-fire that was to prove so effective in the early battles of World War I when the Germans thought that they were being opposed by machine-gunners rather than rapid firing riflemen during the Battle of Mons.

Japanese 11in (280mm) howitzer at the siege of Port Arthur (1904). The Russian forts were destroyed by 18 of these guns, used together with 16 5.9s and 28 4.7s. They were the heaviest guns used in land warfare up to that time, and threw a 550lb (250kg) shell to a range of 10,000yd (9,100m). After successive massed infantry assaults had failed, Gen Nogi decided to reduce the fortress by using a combination of bombardment by his siege artillery and mining by his engineers. One-and-a-half million shells were fired, of which 36,000 were 11in. The Russian commander, Gen Stössel, surrendered January 2 1905 after most of his key fortifications had been destroyed.

The Russo-Japanese War (1904-05)

The first European style conflict of the century, the Russo-Japanese War, was just as prescient, although in different ways. For the first time in many centuries an Asiatic people inflicted a decisive defeat upon a European power. Tsarist Russia's military establishment was corrupt and its weapons outdated, making it no match for the ruthless efficiency and high morale of the Japanese. The naval battle in the Strait of Tsushima was the decisive action, but the Russian armies were also humiliated in Manchuria. The destruction wrought by the Japanese siege artillery at Port Arthur pointed to the imminent demise of Vauban-style fortresses.

World War I (1914-18)

The minor Balkan Wars and the colonial conflicts caused by the European partition of Africa were but a prelude to World War I, which, in military terms, began where the Franco-Prussian War had ended. But three things had changed since 1870: the French had learnt some of the lessons of Sedan and were able to oppose mass with mass; the Germans were faced with war on two fronts and had decided to seek a quick decision in the West before turning on the slower-mobilizing Russians in the East; and the machine gun had become a general issue to the infantry of the opposing armies. Small numbers of primitive aircraft were available on both sides; and although most transport was horse-drawn, motor vehicles were being introduced.

There were significant differences in the tactical doctrines. The Germans believed in frontal holding attacks with enveloping thrusts around their opponent's flanks to threaten his communications. In defence, they sought to occupy the best tactical ground, on which they taught their troops to dig in quickly. The French, by contrast, tended to ignore the need for defence, and to rely on offensive tactics. They envisaged an initial fire fight, dominated by their highly successful 75mm quick-firing field gun, followed by a frontal assault, in which they were convinced that the superior intelligence and tactical sense of the French *poilu* (infantryman) would prevail over the Prussian-disciplined automata of the professional German army. In the small British regular army, economy of force was essential: its pride lay in the carefully drilled and disciplined musketry of its infantry, the élan of its cavalry and the accuracy of its artillery.

At the outbreak of war, mobile operations, envisaged in pre-war manuals of all belligerents, lasted only three-and-a-half months in the West, although rather longer on the wider and more open fronts in the East, where the Hindenburg/Ludendorff command team defeated the Russian armies almost as easily as the Japanese had done a decade earlier in Manchuria.

The Russians made the classic error of invading East

Maxim (MG08) 7.92mm (German)

Prussia with their two armies out of supporting distance of each other, on either side of the Masurian Lakes. Rennenkampf's army to the north was held by minimal German forces, while Samsonov's to the southwest was being annihilated by the main body of the German Eighth Army at the Battle of Tannenberg. Countermarching rapidly northwards, the Germans worsted Rennenkampf in the First Battle of the Masurian Lakes and drove him back from East Prussia.

In the West, von Moltke's failure to carry through the Schlieffen Plan led to the German defeat on the Marne, and his own dismissal. Von Falkenhayn's attempts to outflank the Allies' open northern flank led to the "race to the sea". At the First Battle of Ypres, the British regular army – the "Old Contemptibles" – perished, using its splendid musketry to block von Falkenhayn's last major offensive of 1914; while the German officer-producing volunteer corps threw their lives away in vain endeavour to break through the tenuous but unbroken British line.

As winter set in, the Western Front congealed into a continuous front from Channel to Alps. Self-preservation forced the pick and shovel upon both sides. Trench warfare began, in which the combination of machine guns, barbed wire and deep dugouts proved impregnable to the weapons available at that time. The defensive had gained the upper hand. Mobility on the Western Front, and any hope of a short war, were at an end.

The year 1915 was dominated by the quest for ways out of the stalemate. Strategically, the German high command was the more successful. The Austro-German breakthrough at Gorlice-Tarnow on the Eastern Front forced the Russian armies back to their own frontiers and freed German resources for the West. The Western Allies' attempts to use the indirect approach, with diversionary campaigns in the Eastern Mediterranean and Middle East, were costly failures. At Gallipoli in 1915, for instance, the Turks were able to reinforce quicker over land than the Allies could put troops ashore; and the narrow, rugged nature of the peninsula gave every advantage to the Turkish defence. The Allies accepted

defeat by evacuating their troops when winter came.

Tactically, the Germans tried the surprise use of gas at Ypres in April 1915, but it was relatively easily countered by the box respirator. The Allies, for their part, became convinced that the solution lay in heavier guns and more shells to blast a way through the German trenches. The British were encouraged in this belief by near success at Neuve-Chapelle, Festubert and Loos in 1915; and they were not discouraged by the failure of the German artillery to overpower the French defenders of Verdun.

By mid-1916, Kitchener's New Armies were ready for deployment on the continent, and the factories were producing the numbers of guns and quantities of shells deemed necessary for success. The French should have mounted the principal offensive on the Western Front in 1916, but were pinned down in the defence of Verdun. The British government agreed to mount a relieving offensive on the Somme, putting into effect all that had been learnt about the use of artillery in 1915.

The Battle of the Somme was meticulously planned by Haig's staff, but on the false premise that the available artillery resources could obliterate the German defences. It was estimated that some 1,500 guns, firing 200,000 rounds a day for five days, should enable the infantry to overrun the German trenches almost unscathed. Some 60,000 British casualties on the opening day, July 1, and over 400,000 by the time Haig called a halt on November 18, bore witness to the fallacy.

The failure on the Somme stemmed from a number of misjudgments. Stockpiling ammunition and the five-day preliminary bombardment prejudiced surprise: even the heaviest shells rarely penetrated the German dugouts, which had been mined in the solid chalk of the Somme downlands; the barbed wire was only partially cut by shell-fire; enough German machine gunners emerged unscathed when the barrage lifted to decimate the assaulting infantry, often held up by uncut wire; and the cratered ground provided ready-made cover for reinforcing machine gun crews, rushed up from reserve to seal off British penetrations.

Weapons of World War I.
Machine guns (the German version, *opposite)* that favoured defensive action; and quick-firing field guns (the famous French "soixante quinze", *right)*, that gave excellent service against troops in the open.

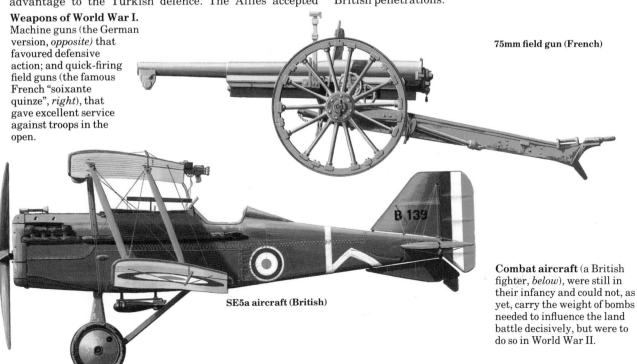

75mm field gun (French)

SE5a aircraft (British)

Combat aircraft (a British fighter, *below)*, were still in their infancy and could not, as yet, carry the weight of bombs needed to influence the land battle decisively, but were to do so in World War II.

Attempts to exploit such successes as were achieved on the Western Front in 1916 and 1917 were aborted by two additional and interconnected factors. The artillery so ploughed up the battlefields that reserves and vital supply vehicles could not be moved forward quickly enough to maintain the momentum of an offensive: in consequence, there was ample time for the defender to move his general reserves by rail to prevent a breakthrough.

Development of the tank
The failure of artillery to restore mobility gave urgency to the quest for other solutions. Colonel E D Swinton suggested armouring track-laying agricultural machines and fitting them with machine guns and light cannon. With Winston Churchill's enthusiastic support from the desk of First Lord of the Admiralty, the concept of the "land ironclad" was born. It was called the "tank" to preserve secrecy.

The earliest mark of tank went into action for the first time in September 1916 in the closing phases of the Somme. Only 49 tanks were committed. They were so mechanically unreliable that only 18 crossed the start line, but 11 of them did manage to crash through the German defences and emerge in their gun lines. There were too few tanks to do more than cause local panic, but their performance had been impressive enough for another 1,000 to be ordered.

Following the Somme action, small numbers of tanks were used at Messines in June 1917 and at Passchendaele that autumn. It was not until November 1917 that enough tanks and trained crews were available for their employment en masse at the Battle of Cambrai, where 375 tanks went into action, supported by six infantry divisions and 1,000 guns. Five cavalry divisions were in reserve. It was decided to dispense with a preliminary bombardment to achieve surprise.

In the event, it was the British who were the most surprised. By noon on the first day, November 20, the first and second German lines had been overrun. The speed of the tanks' advance had been underestimated, and the British reserves were too far back to exploit success quickly enough. Cambrai, however, established the tank as a potential battle-winner – once tactics for its employment were fully worked out and its mechanical reliability had been improved.

In one theatre, mobile operations were still possible. Allenby's campaign against the Turks in Palestine was

Uncut German wire on the Somme. Despite the heaviest artillery bombardment of the war, enough German wire remained uncut to check the assaulting British infantry.

fought over hard ground with the inland flank always open. The cavalry came into their own and were used to out-manoeuvre the Turks in ways that were never possible on the Western Front.

Haig, who had been British c-in-c in France since December 1916, has always been criticized for unimaginative attritional warfare. Much of this criticism is unfair: under his leadership the British army devised the tactics and executed the operations that led to final victory in the West, compensating for the near collapse of the French army, which degenerated into mutiny after Nivelle's disastrous offensive in April 1917.

Nevertheless, it was Ludendorff's tactics that were to make the greatest impact on land warfare in the first half of the 20th century. When he took over as First Quartermaster-General (Chief of the German General Staff) in the autumn of 1916, he brought with him experience of the wider and more open Eastern Front, where he had developed the concept of flexible defence-in-depth: a lightly held front line for observation and early warning, covering the main line of defence half-a-mile or so to the rear, consisting of a series of mutually supporting defended localities rather than a rigid line; and, farther back still, reserve divisions positioned for immediate counter-attacks. Early in 1917, Ludendorff put his theories into practice on the Western Front with his withdrawal to the Hindenburg Line. The highly successful German defence on the Western Front throughout 1917 and 1918 was

American agricultural tractor. Produced by the Holt Corporation and shipped to the UK in 1915 for early experimental work on track-laying vehicles that might be able to cross shell-torn ground and crush barbed wire entanglements.

Killen-Strait experimental armoured vehicle. Although its ditch-crossing capability was poor when driven forwards because the steering tracks in front dropped into obstacles, it was found that the high rear end of its main tracks enabled it to climb out of trenches successfully when it was driven in reverse.

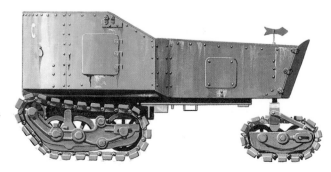

German assault troopers attacking (the Ludendorff offensive, March 1918). Small based upon his flexible defence. lightly armed groups of highly motivated men infiltrated and dislocated the Allies' defences.

But Ludendorff made an even greater contribution to offensive tactics. It was he who inspired the development of infiltration techniques that nearly gave Germany victory in the West in March 1918, and which became standard German tactics in World War II. Instead of the orthodox infantry assault behind a pre-planned rolling artillery barrage, he set up specially trained, lightly armed storm battalions, which were practised in infiltrating and dislocating enemy defences, using small highly motivated groups of *Sturmtruppen* "storm troopers" (a name later purloined by the Nazi party). They were followed by more heavily equipped supporting troops, who dealt with strong points that had been bypassed. And in the rear came the ordinary infantry divisions, to take over the ground won.

Instead of trying to match the British use of tanks, Ludendorff depended on a special "battering train" of artillery that could be moved rapidly from sector to sector to produce surprise concentrations of fire to help the storm battalions through the crust of the enemy defences. At the Somme the British assault had been supported by 1,500 guns, firing a five-day preparatory bombardment; when Ludendorff opened his final offensive in March 1918, the assault was supported by 6,000 guns, firing high explosive, gas and smoke shells for hours rather than days. The British Fifth Army collapsed, but the problems of the maintenance of momentum had not been overcome; these

were to be left for Hitler's generals to solve.

The tank had its greatest successes after the German Army's final effort was spent in June 1918. In the Battle of Amiens on August 8 1918 – Ludendorff's "Black Day of the German Army" – 580 tanks took part; and in the subsequent autumn offensives they proved their worth against failing German resistance. But when the war ended, the tank was still in its infancy and, with aircraft, was bequeathed by World War I to World War II for further development. Both were seen as legacies of uncertain value.

World War II

Between the world wars, it was the Germans and the Japanese who grasped most fully, although in quite different circumstances and ways, the potential of air power used in close support of armoured forces. The Japanese invasion of Manchuria in 1931 and of China in 1937 gave them battle-hardened forces, experienced in handling aircraft and tanks under Far Eastern conditions. Their tanks and infantry worked in close cooperation, but because of communication difficulties their air attacks were aimed at disorientating their opponents rather than supporting their tanks directly.

The Germans were faced with more difficult problems. Under the Treaty of Versailles, their army was restricted to 100,000 men, without military aircraft or tanks, which were proscribed by the treaty. Undeterred, they carried out secret experimental work on both weapons with the cooperation of the Soviet Union in the 1920s. When Hitler repudiated the Versailles Treaty in the 1930s, the re-formed German General Staff already had the data on which to rebuild the army, with dive-bombers and tanks as the principal weapons in their concept of blitzkrieg.

Military conservatism engulfed the victorious powers after World War I. The British had invented the tank, but were more influenced by colonial warfare and clung to the horse for far too long. The RAF sought its own salvation as an independent air force by concentrating upon the strategic use of air power at the expense of tactical support of the army. The French placed their faith in the steel and concrete of the Maginot Line. And the Americans all but disbanded their military establishment as they sank back into isolationism.

The German blitzkrieg that fell on Poland in 1939, on France in 1940 and on Soviet Russia in 1941, was based on fire power, mobility and the psychological unhinging of

"Little Willie" experimental tank. Produced for trials at about the same time as the Killen-Strait. It had the advantage of being steered by braking its tracks, but it could not meet the War Office requirement of being able to cross a 5ft (1.5m) ditch, and so was not put into production.

"Mother" Tank Mk V. A combination of the steering system of "Little Willie" and the Killen-Strait track, led to rhomboid-shaped tanks that met the War Office specification and were put into production. A few went into action for the first time in small numbers on the Somme in September 1916.

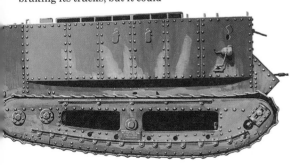

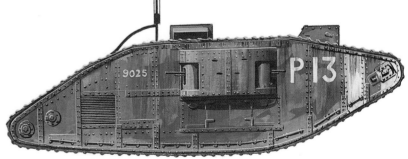

their opponents. The Wehrmacht used the traditional German tactics of frontal holding attack by infantry divisions, coupled with enveloping thrusts on either flank by their new panzer (armoured) divisions. The tanks were closely supported by the Luftwaffe's dive-bombers, and parachute troops and sabotage parties were dropped to spread alarm in rear areas. The encircling thrusts, carried out on narrow fronts and with great ruthlessness, paid handsome dividends. The German panzer divisions and their supporting dive-bombers became the most feared instruments in land warfare. Ludendorff's flexible defence-in-depth and infiltration by storm troopers in attack were retained as standard German practice.

In World War I the decisive land battles had been fought in Western Europe; in World War II they were waged in the East. During the German invasion of Russia in 1941, panzer groups, comprising a number of panzer corps and divisions, were used in the encircling thrusts that broke up the Russian armies and forced their surrender in hundreds of thousands. If Hitler's intuition had not failed him in July 1941, he might have forced Stalin to negotiate. Against the advice of his General Staff, he swung southwards to destroy the southern group of Soviet armies, and to acquire the rich agricultural and industrial potential of the Ukraine, before launching his drive on Moscow. By the time he could swing back, it was too late in the year. Like Napoleon before him, he was stopped initially by the Russian winter, and then by the resilience of the Russian people and their armies.

The pressures of defeat drove Germany's enemies to devise counters to the novel components of the blitzkrieg: the dive-bomber and the tank. The Allied soldiers' immediate reaction was to demand more anti-aircraft weapons and better air cover. The former were provided in growing numbers, but the airmen resisted demands for the latter, believing, quite rightly, that defeating the enemy air forces was the best way to protect their colleagues on the ground.

Counters to the tank lay in the mine, the high velocity gun, and, in the later years of the war, the shoulder-fired missile. The mine was cheap and easy to manufacture in great numbers, and both anti-tank and anti-personnel mines soon replaced the barbed wire entanglements of World War I as the main artificial obstacles in land warfare. This led to the development of mine-clearance techniques, using simple probes, electronic mine detectors and a variety of mine-clearing devices such as flail tanks.

The development of the anti-tank gun led to fierce technological competition to produce not only the most lethal gun, but also the toughest armour plate. The Germans held the advantage in both for most of the war, particularly with their ingenious use of their powerful 88mm anti-aircraft guns as anti-tank weapons.

Two schools of thought on tank tactics arose on the Allied side. Former cavalry officers tended to equate the tank with the horse and advocated the shock action of massed tank attack, similar to the German blitzkrieg. The other school saw tank warfare in naval terms: their aim was to manoeuvre their tanks to within fighting range and to win the battle by superior gunnery. Neither doctrine was successful against the boldly-handled German anti-tank guns and the German tactic of withdrawing their tanks through concealed anti-tank gun screens when faced with adverse odds. The failure of both doctrines was demonstrated by the severity of tank losses inflicted by Rommel's numerically inferior Afrika Korps

on the British Eighth Army in the Western Desert campaigns of 1941 and 1942.

Two decisive battles changed the complexion of armoured warfare. The first was Montgomery's demonstration at the Battle of Alam Halfa, just before El Alamein, of how the German panzer attack could be mastered. When Rommel made his last attempt to break through the El Alamein position at the end of August 1942, Montgomery drew him on to attack the tactically vital Alam Halfa ridge, which he could not risk bypassing. His panzers were stopped by concealed anti-tank guns and tanks waiting for him "hull down". No British tanks moved, and the Afrika Korps was forced to withdraw after suffering severe losses from intense artillery and air bombardment as it lay stranded below the ridge.

The second decisive battle in tank warfare was fought out between the Germans and the Russians in July 1943. Operation "Citadel" was the last and greatest tank battle fought by the Wehrmacht on the original blitzkrieg lines. Hitler decided to forestall the Soviet summer offensive of 1943 with a major counteroffensive of his own to pinch off the large Russian salient around the city of Kursk. While the head of the salient was attacked by infantry divisions, two massive panzer thrusts were launched from either flank by some 2,500 tanks, supported by 2,000 aircraft.

The Russians had anticipated "Citadel", which had been postponed several times through Hitler's vacillation. They had built three concentric rings of anti-tank defences within the salient and had positioned their main reserves behind it. Their defence depended upon mines, large groups of anti-tank guns, 3,500 T-34 tanks, and a massive concentration of artillery and multiple rocket launchers.

Both German thrusts had some initial success, but, as at Alam Halfa, suffered progressive attritional losses from dug-in T-34 tanks and anti-tank guns. The Russians launched their tank counterattacks as the German advance faltered. Tank losses on both sides in the "cauldron" of Kursk were crippling, but the Russians could replace theirs more swiftly than the Germans.

Kursk was not just a battle lost and won; it marked the end of the psychological dominance of blitzkrieg.

The German PzKw III tank
(*right*). Crewed by five men, weighing 20 tons and powered by a 300 bhp engine, it had a speed of 12 mph (19 kph).

It was armed originally with the 37mm general purpose tank gun. In 1941, it was given the 5cm short-barrelled anti-tank gun, which, in 1942, was replaced by the higher velocity long-barrelled version.

Its armour plate was 50mm thick on the front and 30mm elsewhere. Initially, extra face-hardened plates were bolted onto the front for greater protection. Later, the frontal armour was increased to 62mm of face-hardened steel.

The optical sighting and fire control systems were excellent, and, coupled with the long-barrelled 5cm gun, made it the best general purpose armoured "maid of all work" on the battlefield in its day.

Panzerkampfwagen III Ausf M

Length 18.33ft (5.6m)
Width 9.8ft (3m)
Height 8.33ft (2.5m)

The Russian T-34 tank (*left, top*). Simple, robust with low silhouette, and weighing 35 tons, it had few refinements or comfort for its crew of five. Its excellent 85mm gun, 95mm of armour on the turret and 75mm elsewhere, made it a match for all German tanks except the Tiger. It was manufactured in vast quantities. To match the Tiger, the Russians produced the heavy Joseph Stalin in the later phases of the war.

The US Sherman tank (*left, centre*). The principal equipment of American and British armoured divisions from mid-1943. It weighed 32 tons; had a higher silhouette than German and Russian tanks; and caught on fire so often when hit that the Germans nicknamed it the "Ronson". It had a 75mm gun, but a proportion of British Shermans carried 17 pounder anti-tank guns. 50,000 were produced in the USA.

The German Mark VI, Tiger (*left, bottom*). In reality a heavily armoured self-propelled mounting for the famous 88mm gun. It weighed 68 tons with 180mm frontal armour, which in the *Jagdtiger* version was increased to 230mm. *Jagdtiger*s were the most powerful armoured fighting vehicles in World War II, and were being manufactured in increasing numbers by the end of 1944 – too late, however, to stem the tide of Germany's defeat.

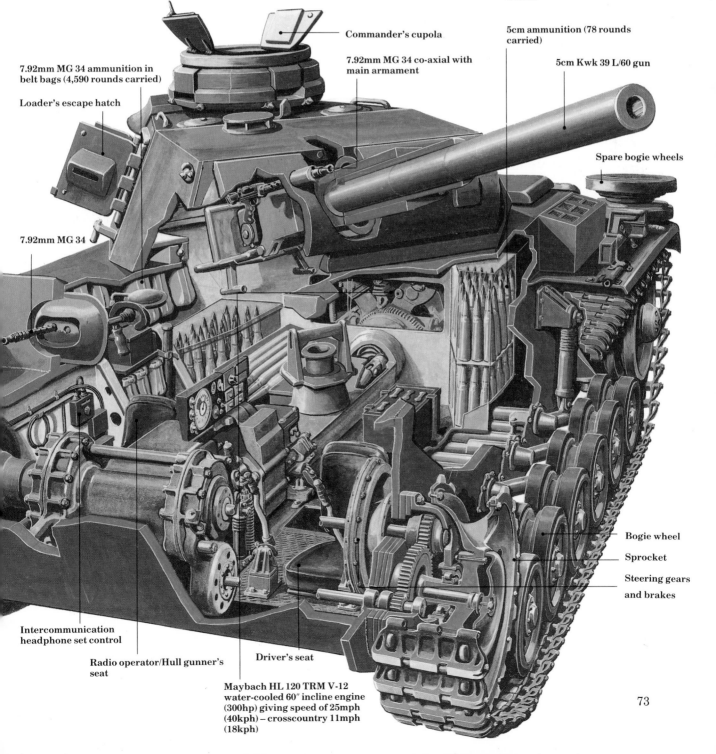

Commander's cupola

7.92mm MG 34 co-axial with main armament

5cm ammunition (78 rounds carried)

5cm Kwk 39 L/60 gun

7.92mm MG 34 ammunition in belt bags (4,590 rounds carried)

Loader's escape hatch

Spare bogie wheels

7.92mm MG 34

Bogie wheel

Sprocket

Steering gears and brakes

Intercommunication headphone set control

Radio operator/Hull gunner's seat

Driver's seat

Maybach HL 120 TRM V-12 water-cooled 60″ incline engine (300hp) giving speed of 25mph (40kph) – crosscountry 11mph (18kph)

Anti-tank guns and mines had begun to swing the advantage back to defence in almost the same way as machine guns and barbed wire had done in 1914. This helped the Germans, who had lost the strategic initiative and were on the defensive. The Allies, on the other hand, had to find effective countermeasures as they went over to the offensive.

The answer was found, through bitter experience, to lie in the close cooperation of tanks, artillery, infantry and engineers in mixed battle groups. The artillery dealt with the hidden but unprotected anti-tank guns; the infantry gave the tanks close protection, particularly at night; and the engineers dealt with the mines.

The composition of the battle groups depended on the conditions on the battlefield at the time. The more cover there was to conceal anti-tank guns, the more infantry were required. In close country, like the Normandy bocage with its small fields and thick hedgerows, the infantry had to clear the way with the tanks in support; but in more open country the tanks would lead with the infantry in support, ready to clear opposition from woods and villages. Towards the end of the war, obsolescent tanks were stripped of their turrets and ammunition bins to provide armoured personnel carriers for the infantry, but these did not become a general issue until after the war.

By 1943, it was already clear to the Allies that the primary requirements for waging an offensive land battle were a favourable air situation over the battlefield and the close cooperation of all arms upon it. It should be noted that the German army fought on in defence without air cover; it was still able to give a good account of itself in 1944 and 1945, under conditions of Allied air supremacy.

In one respect the impact of air power on land operations was disappointing. The use of heavy bombers against fortified defensive positions on land was hardly more successful than the artillery bombardments of World War I: bombing accuracy and weight of bombs carried were inadequate for decisive results. The bombing of Cassino was a failure; "carpet bombing" during the British and American breakout operations in Normandy and Italy was only partially successful; and in the latter phases of the war the battlefields became too fluid for intervention by heavy bombers.

The conflict in the Far East

The land war in the Far East was characterized by the toughness and jungle-awareness of the Japanese. Their equivalent of the German blitzkrieg was the rapid outflanking of their road-bound opponents with enveloping thrusts through the jungle. The psychological effect of encirclement did more to demoralize their enemies than cutting their supply routes. Japanese tactics began to fail as soon as the Allies realized that the antidote was to stand firm even when cut off: the Japanese outflanking forces then had to look to their own supply problems. As soon as re-supply by air became practicable in 1943, the Allied tactics became battle-winners. The battles of Kohima and Imphal, which turned the tide in Burma, were won by British and Indian troops who refused to be frightened out of key strategic positions on the Japanese invasion routes into India. They were sustained by air, while the Japanese forces were starved into retreat.

Amphibious warfare assumed great importance during the American counteroffensive across the Pacific (and in the invasion of Normandy), but it has remained a specialized mode of land warfare. Airborne operations – by

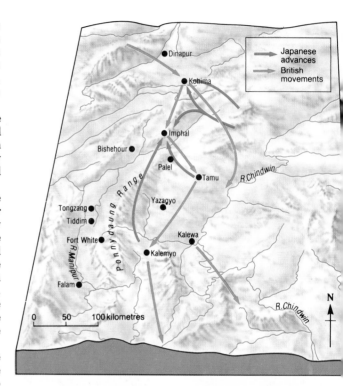

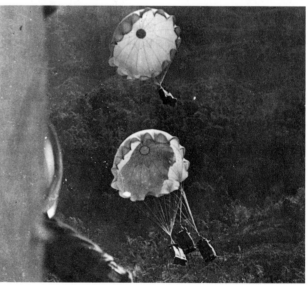

The battles of Imphal and Kohima. In March 1944, the Japanese started their invasion of India, using their previously successful tactic of wide encircling movements to cut British supply lines. This time the British stood fast at Imphal and Kohima, and supplied their besieged troops by air. It was the Japanese who were starved into retreat because they could not capture British supplies as they had done in the past.

Air supply in Burma. Wingate's Chindit operations behind the Japanese lines in 1943–44 were largely dependent upon air supply; and the reconquest of Burma by Slim's Fourteenth Army in 1944–45 could not have been sustained over the poor roads of Northern and Central Burma without the massive air-lift provided by US transport aircraft, flown by British and American air crews. The reconquest took five months, Rangoon falling in May 1945.

Americans landing on Iwo Jima. Amphibious forces were developed to spearhead the US advance from island to island across the Pacific towards Japan.

Landing craft, tank: designed to carry 250–300 tons, and fitted with a strengthened tank deck and a bow unloading ramp for discharging tanks onto beaches.

Landing craft, support (**large**) (*above*): designed to provide close fire support by guns or rockets off the beaches from positions too close inshore for destroyers and frigates.

Landing craft, infantry (**large**) (*below*): specially designed shallow-draft vessels, fitted with landing-ramps either side of the bow and capable of carrying 200 troops at 15 knots.

parachute, glider and air landing – were equally specialized, but of more general application. The Germans' *coup de main* at Fort Eben Emael in 1940 by glider assault, and their costly capture of Crete in 1941 by parachute troops, led to the expansion of the Allies' airborne forces and their successful use in major operations in Sicily (1943), Normandy (1944), and the crossing of the Rhine (1945). They have remained a component of most armies.

Fortunately, neither side deemed it profitable to use chemical or biological weapons, the lethality of which had been greatly increased since World War I by the German discovery of nerve gases. And the war ended before the German "V-weapons" could do decisive damage to Western morale. The V-1 flying bomb and V-2 (A-4) ballistic missile became German bequests to the nuclear era.

The nuclear era
In the aftermath of World War II there were many people who wished to upset the status quo, especially in Afro-Asia. The colonial powers were once more victorious, but their former infallibility had been undermined in nationalist eyes. Two new conflicts set the pattern of land warfare in the immediate postwar period: the Jewish revolt in Palestine showed what could be achieved by terrorism; and Mao Tse-tung's (Mao Zedong's) triumph in the Chinese Civil War demonstrated the potency of his technique of guerrilla war. Neither lesson was lost on the colonial peoples.

The advent of the nuclear weapon, the decay of European colonial power and the evolution of 20th-century terrorism and guerrilla warfare widened the spectrum of land warfare from the original three bands at the beginning of the century to at least six in its latter half (see fig 2 *below*), all of which tend to overlap, and each has a number of gradations of intensity within it.

There were three occasions on which the use of nuclear weapons was threatened: during the Korean War (1950-53), the Suez Crisis (1956), and the Cuban missile crisis (1962). However, eight major wars and the problem of military balance in Europe have so far provided the most significant milestones in the evolution of land warfare in the nuclear era. There have been some 70 lesser conflicts, fought principally for one of two reasons: to win independence from colonial rule; or to settle racial and/or religious rivalries stemming from the days of pre-colonial rule.

Campaigns in Southeast Asia (1946-60)
The first milestone was the attempt by the British, Dutch and French to re-establish their colonial empires in Malaya, Indonesia and Indochina. They were faced with a new type of war, in the "guerrilla war" band of the spectrum. Fire power and tactical mobility seemed to hold the keys to success, but without good intelligence and efficient target acquisition they could not be used decisively. The Dutch and French were blinded by lack of intelligence from the local population, whom they had alienated; and by the cover provided for the guerrillas in the jungle terrain of the Far East. The British, however, found and developed a successful formula for counter-insurgency operations.

After a shaky start, the arrival of General Sir Gerald Templer in Malaya transformed the situation. His concept of winning the battle for the "hearts and minds of the people" was based on four principles: the closest possible cooperation between administration, police, and army;

emphasis on and centralization of all intelligence; the divorce of terrorist gangs from their political supporters and food suppliers; and the methodical destruction of the gangs by operations mounted against specific targets, accurately identified by good intelligence, instead of carrying out blind jungle sweeps.

The British successes in Malaya stemmed largely from breaking the intelligence vicious circle: the flow of information depended on local confidence; local confidence came from security force successes; the security forces, in their turn, required accurate information from local people. It took 12 long years to win the campaign, but in its later phases there was a snowballing effect in intelligence as success led to success and leaders of the terrorist gangs began to defect to the government side.

Another factor was highlighted by the French failure. The Indochina War lost popular support in France. Hanoi was prepared to accept an estimated 200,000 dead; Paris found 75,000 French dead politically unacceptable.

The Korean War (1950-53)
The second milestone was the Korean War, which lay at the most intense end of the "limited war" band of the spectrum. It is, therefore, discussed in detail in the essay entitled *Limited war in the nuclear age* (pp. 261–265). Suffice it to say here that the heaviest weapons in the US non-nuclear armoury, except atomic bombs, were used in an endeavour to neutralize the North Korean and Chinese manpower advantages, but with marked lack of success.

Two major lessons were learnt in waging intense limited war in the nuclear era. Firstly, political and military objectives must be clearly limited, otherwise there is a danger of escalation to nuclear war. MacArthur's advance to the Yalu river breached this principle and caused the Chinese intervention. His demand for the use of nuclear weapons against China was fortunately refused by Washington.

The second lesson was that Asian manpower superiority, when coupled with disregard for human life and dedication to a cause, can neutralize the most advanced conventional weapon systems wielded by the West. The Chinese and North Koreans lost more than 1,500,000 men, compared with the United Nations' loss of just under 500,000. In earlier periods, this would have been deemed a favourable exchange – but the US electorate of the 1950s felt otherwise.

The Algerian War of Independence (1954-62)
The third milestone – the Algerian struggle for independence from France – had echoes of Indochina, but it was a very different type of war. The inspiration was Islamic nationalism rather than communism; it was a civil and racial war between the indigenous Algerians and the French settlers – the *colons* – backed by the French Army; and it was fought in urban areas and in arid mountainous country rather than in lush jungles.

After their defeat in Indochina, the French commanders made a close study of the Maoist doctrine of revolutionary war. They appreciated that they had failed to recognize the political nature of the conflict. They believed that their own objective in Algeria was equally political and must be pursued with the same dedication and ruthlessness. Their policy was *Algérie Française*; and, if the French politicians faltered in its application, they would impose their will upon them.

| nuclear war | conventional war | limited war | guerrilla war | terrorism | internal security |

fig 2   **The spectrum of land warfare in the latter half of the 20th century**

French defeated by Vietnam 1946-54
– beseiged in the Red River delta
from 1951 and finally defeated
at Dieu Bien Phu in 1954

British defeated Indonesian
confrontation in
North Borneo 1962-66

British defeated Communist
terrorists in Malayan jungles
1949-60

Dutch defeated by
Indonesian Nationalists
1946-50

French empire

British empire

Dutch empire

The Algerian nationalists – the FLN – had a weak, divided command, and the supplies that could be sent to them by other Islamic states, like Nasser's Egypt, were inadequate for a war against the experienced French army. Nevertheless, the headline-catching atrocities that they did manage to perpetrate, and the savage reprisals inflicted in return on the innocent Muslim population by the *colons*, brought world opinion onto their side.

The French Army had very considerable successes. The FLN's attempt to set up an urban guerrilla base in the Algiers Casbah was crushed; their efforts to establish a safe haven in Tunisia were frustrated by the construction of an electrified fence, carrying 5,000 volts and protected by anti-personnel mines, along the frontier; and their guerrilla gangs in the mountainous rural areas were all but destroyed by French vertical envelopment operations, in which helicopter-borne troops, supported by armed helicopters, were used for the first time in land warfare.

By 1958, the French Army could justifiably claim that its military successes were being frittered away by vacillation in Paris. Its commanders in Algeria decided to enter French politics, calling for the return of General de Gaulle, whom they believed would consolidate the *Algérie Française* which they had all but won. They were to be disappointed: de Gaulle's sense of history prevented him from trying to reverse its tides in North Africa. Despite colon insurrections and mutinies in the French Army, he would not be deflected from his view that an Algerian Algeria was the only practicable way forward. Islamic nationalism, like Chinese communism, had triumphed, but at an equally heavy cost: more than 1,000,000 Muslims died, compared with some

European operations in Southeast Asia (1946–66). When the Japanese surrendered in 1945, the Dutch, French and British governments attempted to re-establish their former colonial empires in Indonesia, Indochina, and Malaya.

The Dutch failed to unseat the Indonesian Nationalists, who seized power when the Japanese surrendered. They were forced by American pressure and world opinion to withdraw in 1950.

The Communist rebellion against the French in Indochina broke out in November 1946. After seven hard-fought guerrilla campaigns, Gen Giap's communist forces triumphed at Dien Bien Phu in May 1954.

The British were more effective in Malaya. After the first three difficult years of the communist rebellion, which began in 1948, Gen Templer introduced his twin policies of

winning the "hearts and minds" of the Malayan people; and, with their help, of cutting off the terrorists in the jungle from their political support and food supplies in nearby villages and towns.

The British then helped Malaysia to defeat the Indonesian "Confrontation" over the decolonization of the British North Borneo territories in a four-year campaign that ended in 1966.

17,500 French soldiers and 2,800 *colons*. The close linkage between political and military action in 20th century land warfare had again been underscored.

The Suez Crisis (1956)
In the midst of the Algerian conflict came the fourth milestone – Suez – in the "conventional war" band of the spectrum. The British, and to a lesser extent the French, handled the Suez Crisis as if they were opposing a first class power. They assumed that Eastern Bloc volunteers would be manning some of the latest Soviet-supplied tanks, guns and aircraft in Egyptian hands. In consequence, a Normandy-style amphibious operation was planned by the very experienced World War II commanders still serving at the time.

It took two months to prepare the operation, which involved calling up reservists and requisitioning commercial shipping. Despite later criticism of the cumbersome nature of the operation, there was little wrong with the military plan as such, given the assumption of major opposition. The fault lay in the political misjudgments and the cross-purposes of the British, French, Israeli and American governments. But the outcome demonstrated the need for quick, decisive military action in the nuclear era, not so much to reduce the dangers of nuclear retaliation as to pre-empt the crystallization of hostile world opinion.

Vietnam (1959-75) and Malaysia (1962-66)
The United States' effort to curb the spread of communism in Asia by intervention in Vietnam, which was the fifth milestone of the nuclear era, is covered in the *Limited War* essay on pp. 266–271. It should, however, be noted here that during the 12 years in which US combat troops were involved in Vietnam, there were three major technological advances in land warfare.

The first was the massive use of helicopters; some 5,000 were deployed. In the later years of the war, operations tended to be planned almost exclusively around them. There were the usual trade-offs in the balance between fire power, mobility and protection: the superbly mobile helicopter was highly vulnerable to weather and to light shoulder-fired missiles and heavy machine guns.

The second advance was the start made in the application of electronic and computer technologies to target acquisition, communications, and command and control. Pressures generated by the Vietnam War for the detection of targets in jungle country led to the development of a wide range of miniaturized sensors that could be dropped into or placed within potential target areas to give warning of movement within them. The responses from these sensors and inputs from reconnaissance and other intelligence sources were fed to computers for collation and assessment (as in naval and air target acquisition systems), for decisions by commanders as to which targets should be engaged and with what weapons.

The third advance was the application of similar technologies to improve weapon accuracy through in-flight and terminal guidance. The first successful system was the US Air Force's "Smart" bomb, which could home on a laser-illuminated target. For most of the Vietnam War, "carpet bombing" by the heavy B-52 bombers had proved indecisive. When "Smart" bombs were used by laser-equipped F-4 Phantoms in 1972, the picture changed dramatically. After only a few weeks of the last US

bombing offensive against the North, no important bridges were left intact and Hanoi had lost half its electric power supplies. Civilian casualties were surprisingly low because the bombing was so accurate.

Since the Vietnam War ended, the same technologies have been applied to army weapons such as anti-tank missiles; and they are the basis of the "intelligent" sub-munitions or bomblets delivered by various rocket systems that are now being developed. These "emergent technologies" are casting their shadows before them.

Vietnam confirmed the verdicts of Indochina and Korea. The government of North Vietnam accepted more than 1,000,000 dead to achieve its ends. The people of the US, on the other hand, were revolted by the loss of 50,000 men in trying to defeat a political philosophy that they did not see as posing a direct threat to their vital interests.

The American defeat contrasts with the much smaller, but nevertheless significant, British success in defeating the Malaysian "Confrontation" with Indonesia (1962-66), in equally difficult country, but with far greater politico-military finesse.

While these wars had been taking place in the Far East, land warfare in the desert environment of the Middle East was developing in a very different way.

The Arab-Israeli Wars (1948-49; 1956; 1967; 1973)
The four Arab-Israeli Wars constitute the sixth milestone in the nuclear era. Their desert battles were more akin to naval and air operations than land fighting elsewhere. Good visibility out to the horizon, lack of cover, full scope

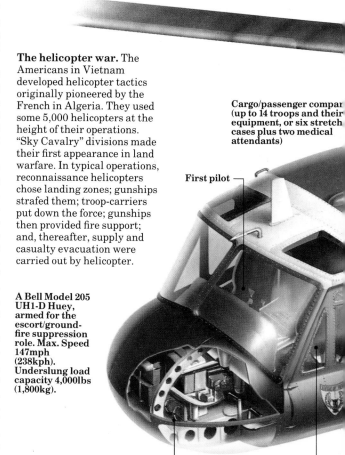

The helicopter war. The Americans in Vietnam developed helicopter tactics originally pioneered by the French in Algeria. They used some 5,000 helicopters at the height of their operations. "Sky Cavalry" divisions made their first appearance in land warfare. In typical operations, reconnaissance helicopters chose landing zones; gunships strafed them; troop-carriers put down the force; gunships then provided fire support; and, thereafter, supply and casualty evacuation were carried out by helicopter.

A Bell Model 205 UH1-D Huey, armed for the escort/ground-fire suppression role. Max. Speed 147mph (238kph). Underslung load capacity 4,000lbs (1,800kg).

Cargo/passenger compartment (up to 14 troops and their equipment, or six stretcher cases plus two medical attendants)

First pilot

Radio and avionics bay

Co-pilot

Skid undercarriage

for cross-country mobility and the absence of civilian populations on the battlefields, all made for the maximum exploitation of weapon performance. Despite this, the dominant factor of morale remained in favour of Israel.

In the first Arab-Israeli War of 1948-49, the beleaguered Jews routed the divided and ill-prepared Arabs. In the second, during the Suez Crisis of 1956, the Egyptians failed, but had the excuse of the Anglo-French landings in their rear.

They had no such excuse in 1967, when they deliberately provoked the Israelis and suffered a devastating defeat in the "Six-Day War". The Israeli Air Force's well-planned pre-emptive strike destroyed most Egyptian aircraft on the ground and gave Israel air supremacy. Deprived of air cover, the Arab armies could not withstand the Israeli armoured forces, operating with close support from their victorious airmen.

The success of their armoured forces led the Israelis to place too great a faith in their tanks and close support aircraft, and to pay too little attention to their probable vulnerability to the anti-tank and anti-aircraft missiles which were being developed by the world's armament manufacturers. A measure of overconfidence crept into Israeli planning before the "Yom Kippur War" burst upon them in 1973.

The Egyptians and their Soviet advisers caught the Israeli forces off guard by attacking during the Jewish Yom Kippur festival. The Israeli airmen were drawn straight into the land battle in support of their hard-pressed soldiers on the Suez Canal. They were met by

"Medivac" by helicopter during the Communist Tet offensive in Vietnam in 1968. Evacuation of casualties in war and peacetime disasters has become a standard role for helicopters. Extracting casualties from forward or isolated positions by helicopter reduces the time taken for casualties to reach hospital, and cuts out long tiring journeys by stretcher and bumping over broken roads in ambulances. It not only saves lives, but is important to troops' morale.

Whip antenna

Anti-torque tail rotor

Counterweight

Main rotor stabilizers

Main rotor gear box

Lycoming T53-L-11 turboshaft engine, 1,100 shp

Honeycomb structure main rotor blade

Tail rotor intermediate gear box

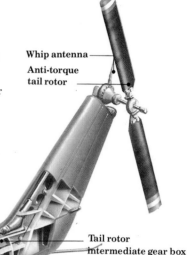

Horizontal stabilizers

Monocoque main fuselage boom

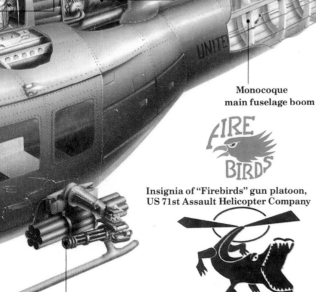

Insignia of "Firebirds" gun platoon, US 71st Assault Helicopter Company

Airlifted into action – Vietnamese soldiers land in a field near Tan Hung in search of their hidden Viet Cong foe (1963).

From UH-1F "Chopper Gator", US 35th Tactical Fighter wing

M-21 armament system

7.62mm XM-134 rotary machine gun (mini-gun)
2.75in XM-158 rocket launcher

barrages of Soviet surface to air missiles (SAMS), which accounted for most of the 60 Israeli aircraft lost in the first week of the war. The Egyptians crossed the Canal successfully and inflicted serious losses on the Israeli tanks, using Soviet Sagger anti-tank missiles.

The Israelis' initial answer to both the anti-aircraft and anti-tank missile threat was saturation tactics. Instead of attacking the missile sites on the Canal with their usual flights of four aircraft, they used squadrons to roll them up with attacks from the flank. In the armoured battles, the Israelis found that suppressive fire by artillery and infantry weapons reduced the effectiveness of Egyptian Sagger crews; thus, they relearned the lesson of all arms cooperation in armoured warfare.

The eventual Israeli victory was helped by the rapid dispatch from the United States of "Smart" bombs to deal with the SAMS; and of TOW anti-tank missiles to match the Saggers. The war was ended not on the battlefield, but by the Arabs' use of the oil embargo, which persuaded the US to bring pressure upon Israel to accept a cease-fire. Nevertheless, an important turning point in land warfare had been reached: the missile age had begun.

The Iraq-Iran Gulf War (1980-88)
The seventh milestone is the very recent Iraq-Iran conflict in the Persian Gulf. It was fought with the full range of conventional weapons, which, because target acquisition is relatively easy in Middle Eastern conditions, gave the Iraqi defence an advantage over the numerically superior but less well-armed, although fanatical, Iranian Revolutionary Guards.

A new factor began to emerge in the fighting. The cost of missiles was so high that operations based upon them could only be carried out in fits and starts as new stocks were acquired. Firing one of the smaller anti-tank guided missiles was financially equivalent to throwing a popular family car at the enemy. The increasing complexity and cost of other major land weapons systems are making armies more capital intensive than they used to be.

Soviet invasion of Afghanistan (1979-89)
The eighth and final milestone so far in the nuclear era is the Soviet invasion of Afghanistan, which straddled the "limited" and "guerrilla war" bands of the spectrum. It showed that the United States is not the only superpower unable to crush an Asian people who have the will to fight and are receiving adequate supplies of weapons from safe havens across their frontiers. In 1988, the Soviets announced their intention to withdraw their military forces from Afghanistan, an operation which was completed in February 1989.

The European Cold War (1945 onwards)
Fortunately, the cataclysmic milestone of unlimited war in Western Europe has not been reached, thanks to the success of the nuclear deterrent. Since 1945, the most heavily armed forces in the world have stood glowering at each other across the Iron Curtain, each modernizing its weapons as technology races onwards, but without any practical experience in their use. Organization, equipment and training on both sides are based upon theoretical projections from the past, simulations of the present and academic debate about the future.

A World War II commander visiting a divisional headquarters on either side in Europe today would find himself in familiar surroundings, because there has been no war to compel major change. He would note the great improvements: in communications and command and control systems; in the obvious increases in range of all weapons and in the computer-based intelligence and target acquisition systems; in the closer integration of army and air staffs; in planning of strikes with tactical nuclear weapons; and in the inventory of weapons, including the "emergent technology" systems. But although the scale of the battlefield has increased, and troops have been given greater armoured and helicopter-borne mobility, the tactics have changed remarkably little and are unlikely to do so until the clash of battle enforces new concepts.

Conclusion
In the nuclear era, the effectiveness of military forces should be judged by their ability to deter war in all the bands of its spectrum. They have been totally successful, so far, in deterring the "nuclear" band; only slightly less so in deterring "conventional war", principally because the risks of such wars escalating into nuclear conflict are so high; much less so in deterring "limited war"; and totally ineffective in the "guerrilla war" band, as the frequency of such wars has shown (see figs 3 and 4 *below*).

Those powers who wish to preserve the status quo and to see the world develop in an evolutionary way have the problem of organizing, equipping and training their military forces so that they can maintain the success achieved in deterring nuclear war, while, at the same time, placing their emphasis on developing techniques for improving their ability to deter or quash attempts to impose revolutionary change by force. On the other hand, those who are bent on revolutionary change will draw the opposite conclusions: the greatest military opportunities in 20th century land warfare have lain in the lower intensity bands of the spectrum, and they seem likely to continue to do so into the 21st century.

The spectrum of war at the end of the 20th century (fig 3). The red curve, representing deterrent effectiveness, has its peak of efficiency over the nuclear band and its trough over the guerrilla war band. Similar notional curves can be plotted for the duration of the different types of war (in blue) and their frequency (in brown). Both show reverse peaks and troughs to the red curve. These conclusions are symbolically summed up in fig 4.

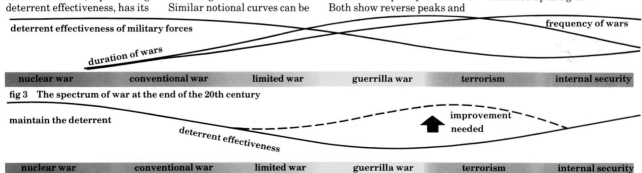

fig 3 The spectrum of war at the end of the 20th century

fig 4 A graphical conclusion

and the elderly battlecruiser *Repulse* were dispatched to Singapore but were sent against the Japanese without air cover and promptly sunk. The disastrous campaign which followed bore out all Brooke-Popham's warnings; as overall commander he bore the inevitable blame and was removed from his post shortly before the fall of Singapore. *MH*.

Gen Browning – witness at Arnhem

Browning, Lt Gen Sir Frederick (1896–1965). Br. In 1941 Browning raised the British Army's first airborne division, moulding his command into an elite whose honours soon included the Bruneval raid and the invasions of North Africa and Sicily. He commanded I Airborne Corps during its successful contribution to the Normandy landings, but his fortunes were to change in September 1944 as Deputy Commander of First Allied Airborne Army in Operation "Market Garden". Having made the prophetic comment "I think we might be going a bridge too far", he witnessed the tragedy of the epic struggle at Arnhem. He was appointed COS to Adm Mountbatten, overseeing the surrender of Japanese forces. *MS*.

Bruchmüller, Col Georg Ger. Bruchmüller was largely unknown until March 1916 when his effective artillery bombardments before German counterattacks in the Vilna-Narotch area on the Eastern Front persuaded Ludendorff to give him wider responsibilites. A specialist in intense surprise bombardments, using predicted shooting and a mixture of gas and high-explosive shells, Bruchmüller orchestrated the German artillery preparations for the attacks on Tarnopol and Riga in 1917 as

well as all the major German offensives on the Western Front in 1918.

Brunei revolt (1962). Indonesian hostility to the impending Malaysian Federation, difficulties over Brunei's inclusion in it under terms acceptable to the Sultan, and the activities of the pro-Indonesian, anti-royalist Peoples' Party (*Partai Ra'ayat Brunei* or PRP) which had recently won an election, led to the revolt. The PRP's militant offshoot, the North Kalimantan National Army or *Tentera Nasional Kalimantan Utara* (TNKU) attacked police stations, the Sultan's palace, the prime minister's house and the main power station on December 8. Britain was still responsible for Brunei's overall security and troops were sent at once from Singapore to restore order. The rebellion spread and the towns of Seria and Limbang quickly fell into rebel hands, to be retaken by British and Gurkha troops within a few days. Of some 4,000 rebels, 40 were killed in action by the security forces and 3,400 captured. The remainder took to the jungle. Elsewhere, British troops were ashore at Kuching by December 14, and it was clear that the TNKU was being supported throughout Sarawak by clandestine Indonesian-backed communist groups. *MH*. For subsequent developments *see* MALAYSIA-INDONESIA CONFRONTATION.

Brunete, Battle of (July 1937), Spanish Civil War. To take pressure off the northern front in a major propaganda exercise, the new Republican government launched an offensive on the left rear of the Nationalist forces facing Madrid. With communists in nearly all key commands, eight divisions supported by 129 tanks broke the Nationalist line, but tiny pockets of Nationalist defence halted the advance long enough for Franco to bring in reinforcements. On the Castilian plain such a force presented a perfect target for the Condor Legion's aircraft. Three-quarters of their tanks were destroyed and, sustaining 25,000 casualties, the ill-supplied Republican infantry was fought back by Carlist and Foreign Legion reinforcements. *AB*.

Bruneval raid (1942). In 1941 a new type of German radar, known as Würzburg, was identified at Bruneval on the French Channel coast. British scientific intelligence requested a raid on the installation. The operation, codenamed "Biting", was entrusted to Combined Operations and, because of the steep cliffs at Bruneval, the raiding force was to land by parachute. On the night of February 27–28 1942, C Company, 2nd Parachute Battalion landed close to the radar site and, after a brief skirmish, captured the Würzburg. An RAF technician examined the set and the more portable pieces were dismantled. With German resistance stiffening, the parachutists fought their way to the beach where Royal Navy vessels evacuated them. The information gathered, supplemented by that gleaned from a captured technician, proved invaluable in developing countermeasures to the Würzburg. Furthermore, the raid epitomized the value of airborne and combined operations. *MS*.

Brusilov, Gen Alexei (1853–1926). Russian. His career started in the corps of Pages at the Imperial Russian court, a recognized "nursery" for the military cadet colleges, and ended in relative obscurity after a spell as Inspector General of Trotsky's cavalry. Brusilov was perhaps the most outstanding Russian general of World War I. In the Galician campaign, he commanded the Eighth Army, and at times was in charge of the entire Carpathian Front. Unlike most of the well-born officers in the Imperial Army, he was a good "soldiers' general" and identified with the front-line troops. He weeded out incompetent staff officers and ran a happy, relaxed and unusually efficient headquarters. In the spring of 1916, he became commander of the central group of armies (Seventh, Eighth and Eleventh) and led them in the most decisive defeat of the Austro-Hungarian army on the Eastern Front. However, this offensive cost the Russians over 1,000,000 casualties and contributed to their collapse. Brusilov threw in his lot with the new communist regime after the revolution, but was never entrusted with a field command. *MH*.

Brusilov's offensives (1916–17). During the winter of 1915–16 the Russians rebuilt their forces yet again in readiness for a decisive campaign. Their government was under constant pressure from the French to initiate large-scale military operations which would divert German armies from the Western Front, especially from Verdun. This led to an ill-conceived Russian attack at Lake Naroch on March 18 resulting in heavy casualties and no gains. By Easter 1916, however, the Russians could deploy 130 divisions against 46 German and 40 Austrian divisions on the Eastern Front, and preparations began for a summer offensive timed to coincide with the Anglo-French attacks on the Somme.

In May, the Austrian commander, Conrad, launched an attack on the Italians in the Trentino which drove the defenders back in chaos. The King of Italy appealed to the Tsar for immediate military action

Russian offensives under Brusilov

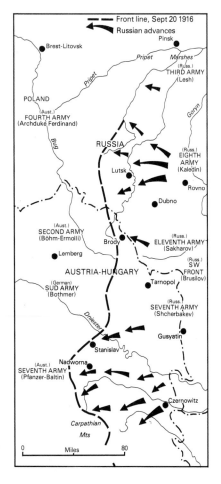

against the Austro-Hungarians and the general Russian offensive planned for June 15 was hurriedly brought forward. The general in charge of the Central Army Group, Evert, was adamant that his thrust towards Vilna could not be advanced, but Brusilov, now commanding the Southern Army Group, was prepared to attack. His plan was to advance simultaneously on a very wide front of more than 200 miles (320km). On June 4 he launched his Third and Eighth Armies against the Austrian Fourth, south of the Pripet Marshes; the Austrians collapsed. Brusilov's southernmost army, the Seventh, thrust deep into Bukovina and within three weeks was amongst the foothills of the Carpathians. Only in the centre, where there was a stiffening of German troops, could the Austrians stem the tide. If Evert's attack in the north, eventually starting on July 2, had been well conducted, it is probable that Austria would have been forced to sue for peace. As it was, the military disasters of 1916 spelt the end of the Austro-Hungarian empire.

It was now that Falkenhayn at last saw the need to transfer troops from the embattled Western Front, if the East was to be saved. Between June 4 and September 15 he moved 15 divisions there by rail. By September 20, when the Russian offensive was finally halted, Brusilov had taken 450,000 prisoners. However, the Russian military machine was nearing breakdown. The summer campaign had cost the Russians about 1,000,000 men, and Brusilov called off the offensive.

Although Russia was now a spent force, Brusilov was to launch one final attack. On March 15 1917, the Tsar abdicated. Kerensky's new government tried to fulfil its obligations to the Western allies by drawing German troops from the Western Front following the French mutinies. On July 1 the now demoralized Austrians broke at the first Russian onslaught; but again the Germans came to the rescue. On September 3 the German Eighth Army, advancing in the North, took Riga. The Russian army was now disintegrating. Lenin seized power in Petrograd and sought an armistice, meeting the Germans at Brest-Litovsk on

December 3. The chief German delegate was Gen Max Hoffmann. When Lenin refused to agree the German armistice terms, Hoffmann ordered a further offensive launched on February 18 1918, capturing Dvinsk and Lutsk before Lenin accepted the terms; even then the advance continued. When a peace treaty was signed on March 3 the Germans occupied Russia's prime agricultural and industrial resources and had rapidly transferred their Eastern armies back to the West for the great offensive of March 1918. *MH*.

Bucharest *see* ROMANIAN CAMPAIGN.

Buckmaster, Col Maurice James (b.1909). Br. Commanded 1942–44 SOE's F (independent French) section, which sent 470 agents to France, 118 of whom were lost.

Buckner, Lt Gen Simon Bolivar, Jr (1886–1945). US. The son of a general in the Confederate States Army, Buckner commanded the Alaska Defense Force from 1940 and served in the Aleutian Islands campaign. In September 1944 he took command of the recently formed Tenth Army, which he led in the invasion of Okinawa, April 1 1945. Although careful and methodical in his command duties, Buckner's inclination was to lead from the front. From May 7 1945, he assumed personal charge of operations against the Japanese stronghold at Shuri, and on June 18, after the fall of Shuri but while fierce Japanese resistance still continued, he was killed by a shellburst in a forward observation post. *RO'N*.

Budapest, Battle for (1944–45). By the autumn of 1944 the Red Army was bearing down upon the Hungarian capital, Budapest. Opposing it was Gen Freissner's sorely depleted Army Group South, supported by generally unreliable units of the Hungarian Army. On October 29 Gen Malinovsky's Second Ukrainian Front launched a headlong attack on the city, but although units reached as far as the suburbs, within a week the Soviet forces had been obliged to disengage. A more systematic approach was then adopted and throughout November Malinovsky's troops, together with Gen Tolbukhin's Third Ukrainian Front, endeavoured to encircle Budapest. Yet again Hitler interfered in his generals' plans and stubbornly refused to contemplate a German withdrawal from the beleaguered city. On December 26 the encirclement was completed but the final attack was delayed and German hopes for a relief operation rose. The first attempts began on January 1 1945 but these were frustrated and, as the Soviet stranglehold on Budapest tightened, Hitler continued to refuse to withdraw. In the face of a renewed Soviet attack Pest was evacuated but the soldiers and civilians who reached the sanctuary of Buda were only postponing the inevitable. On February 11 the German commander at last gave orders for a breakout but by now the Soviet investment was too complete and they were unable to pierce it. On February 13 the shattered remnants of the city fell with 30,000 prisoners joining the 100,000 already captured during the course of the battle. *MS.*

Budenny, Marshal Semyon (1883–1973). Russian. Veteran but unsuccessful Soviet commander during World War II. Budenny was drafted into the Imperial Russian army as a conscript in 1903 and fought in the Russo-Japanese War, 1904–05, and World War I, rising to the rank of cavalry sergeant. Following the Bolshevik Revolution, he joined the Red Army and rapidly rose to senior command during the Civil War. In October 1918 he distinguished himself in defeating Gen Denikin's forces and by 1920 was in command of the First Soviet Cavalry Army. Although he did not acquit himself so well in the war with Poland, Budenny's career continued to prosper. In 1924, he became a member of the Revolutionary Military Council. Aided by Stalin, he emerged at the top of the Red Army hierarchy, a preeminence confirmed in 1935 by his being made one of the first five Marshals of the Soviet Union. On Germany's invasion of Russia, Budenny was appointed c-in-c of the Southwestern Front and ordered to hold the Ukraine. Although he commanded 69 divisions, Budenny was overwhelmed by the speed and daring of his opponents as they began an auda-

cious double encirclement of his forces that soon became trapped in a salient around Kiev. Inhibited by Stalin's orders not to withdraw, Budenny also exhibited a lamentable absence of strategic acumen. He reacted far too slowly to the Germans' advances and before long found himself in a hopeless position. On September 18 he was replaced by Marshal Timoshenko and flown out of Kiev shortly before the city's fall. More than 500,000 of his men were not so fortunate and although he avoided major recriminations, he played no further part in the war. However, his former revolutionary exploits stood him in good stead and, aided by his larger-than-life personality, he remained a popular Soviet hero until his death. *MS.*

Buerat, Battle of (January 15–16 1943). Rommel tried to halt Eighth Army (Montgomery) at Buerat, 200 miles (320km) east of Tripoli, but was outflanked by the New Zealand and 7th Armoured Divisions. The 51st Highland Division broke through on the coast road forcing Rommel to continue his withdrawal on Tripoli.

Bukovina *see* ROMANIAN CAMPAIGN.

Bulge, Battle of the *see* ARDENNES OFFENSIVE.

Bull Ring. Name given to the training grounds in the sand dunes at the British base at Etaples during World War I. The harshness of the training here was a primary cause of the Etaples Mutiny of 1917.

Bullecourt. Village in the Hindenburg Line, southeast of Arras. During the British Arras offensive in 1917, it was attacked by the 4th Australian Division, of Gough's Fifth Army, on April 11 but poor artillery support and the failure of tanks to prepare the way for the infantry led to heavy casualties and further shook Australian faith in British generalship. Another attack, by Australian and British divisions, which began on May 3 and was prolonged to relieve pressure on the mutinous French army, succeeded in clearing Bullecourt by May 17 and, despite its high cost, demonstrated that the Hindenburg Line was not impregnable. *PJS.*

Buller, Gen Sir Redvers Henry (1839–1908). Br. *See* BOER WAR.

Bülow, Field Marshal Karl von (1846–1921). Ger. In August 1914, Bülow commanded the German Second Army, operating to the left of von Kluck's First Army on the right wing of the advance through Belgium, where he was responsible for ordering the destruction of the town of Andenne and the massacre of *c*200 civilians (August 20–21) in reprisal for the alleged activities of *francs-tireurs*. At Charleroi, August 22-23, Bülow, supported by Gen Max von Hausen's Third Army, forced the retreat of Lanrezac's French Fifth Army, thus leaving the BEF exposed to von Kluck's attack at Mons. However, Lanrezac's counterattack at Guise (August 29) delayed Bülow's advance long enough for a gap to open between Second and Third Armies and the fast-moving von Kluck, while at the same time the German right was significantly weakened by Moltke's detachment of two corps to the East Front. This proved Bülow's downfall on the Marne, September 5–10; the French Fifth Army (Franchet d'Esperey) and the BEF moved into the gap between von Kluck and Bülow, while Foch's Ninth Army threatened to open a further gap between Bülow and Hausen, on his left. With his right flank driven in by Fifth Army's night attack on September 8–9, Bülow pressed for a withdrawal: Moltke approved, ordering von Kluck also to retreat and thus signalling the collapse of the Schlieffen plan. In 1915, Bülow retired from active service, handing over Second Army to von der Marwitz. *RO'N.*

Buna, Battle of *see* NEW GUINEA CAMPAIGN.

Bunker, Ellsworth (1894–1984) US. Appointed Ambassador to South Vietnam in 1967, Bunker strongly affirmed the US commitment and trusted the judgment of his most optimistic military advisers. He was an ardent supporter of President Nguyen Van Thieu and effectively countered the arguments of officials in Washington who questioned the viability of Thieu's regime. However, his last important task before stepping

B

down in 1973 was to help Henry Kissinger persuade Thieu to sign the Paris peace agreement.

Burgess, Guy (Francis de Moncy) (1911–1963). Br. Became communist at Cambridge; recruited by Comintern agent as spy; notorious homosexual and heavy drinker, turned both capacities towards helping espionage; dismissed from propaganda section of SOE 1940; became second secretary in Foreign Office; absconded to Russia with Maclean 1951, thus imperilling his friend Philby.

Burke, Vice Adm Arleigh Albert ("Thirty-One Knot") (b.1901). US. Burke's nickname, coined by Halsey, reflected his dashing display as commander of 23 Destroyer Squadron off Bougainville where, often acting independently by night, his squadron fought 22 separate engagements within four months, November 1943-February 1944. He became Mitscher's COS in March 1944. Post-1945, he held destroyer commands in the Atlantic and Mediterranean and commanded a cruiser division during the Korean War. He was Chief of Naval Operations, 1955-61.

Burma campaign (1941–45). The longest continuous operation involving British (and also American) forces. The campaign fell into four main phases: (1) active, December 1941 to May 1942, Japanese victory and occupation of Burma; (2) dormant, the stalemate on both sides; (3) the abortive Japanese advance, March-July 1944; (4) the British offensive into Burma and final Japanese defeat, November 1944 to August 1945. The first and last phases were marked by astonishingly rapid advances over great distances through appalling terrain.

Neither side really desired to make Burma a major theatre of war. For Japan, it offered no important economic resources. The British were humiliated by their abrupt ejection in 1942, but subsequent top-level planning envisaged a largely maritime contest in the East, freeing Burma from the sea. Both sides eventually committed massive forces to the land campaign: Japan fielding nearly 320,000 at peak strength while total Allied forces in the theatre

numbered 650,000 (of whom 340,000 were Indian). The Japanese casualties were much greater than those of their opponents: over 185,000 were killed in Burma, or about three-fifths of those sent there. Most died in the last 15 months of the war.

The initial Japanese objective was to seize the port of Rangoon and thus close the Burma Road into Yunnan: a major supply route for China. The British defenders consisted of two newly raised, half-trained divisions (1st Burma Division and 17th Indian Division). In strength the Japanese were about equal in numbers, but their troops were battle-hardened. British strategy was confused. Wavell, as overall commander, wanted to fight on forward lines; the divisional commanders wanted to withdraw to the Sittang river, conceived as a formidable obstacle. Hutton, in command in Burma, was a staff officer: neither strategy was imposed. In falling back to the Sittang, 1st Burma Division virtually disintegrated and in their retreat across the Sittang, 17th Indian Division endured needlessly heavy casualties. The Japanese advanced from the Sittang to Rangoon in just over one week.

Gen Alexander then succeeded Hutton as field commander with little idea of the situation. Reinforcements were expected, but Churchill diverted the British 18th Division to Singapore (where they marched straight into a prison camp) and the Australian prime minister refused to hand over a Division on its way from the Middle East to Australia. The only effective reinforcement was the 7th Armoured Brigade frrom the Western Desert (actually two regiments only: 7th Hussars and 2nd battalion Royal Tank Regiment). During the following weeks, they prevented the almost certain destruction of the retreating army.

As they fell back northwards the British implemented a scorched earth policy, destroying trains, river steamers, the oilfield at Yenangyaung, and the great Ava bridge over the Irrawaddy. In May, the last elements reached the Indian frontier via Kalewa. Less fortunate were the Indian civilians who followed the retreating army, suffering grievous losses: between 400,000 and 450,000 reached India

but an unknown number (probably between 10,000 and 50,000) died on the way.

Wavell was anxious to boost British morale, and a series of attacks were launched in Arakan with a superiority of five to one. Early gains were followed by crushing defeat (December 1942-March 1943). The first Wingate expedition gave some compensation: this did raise morale. Overall control passed to Mountbatten, appointed Supreme Allied Commander in August 1943.

Japan now endeavoured to break the stalemate. Wingate had demonstrated that long-range penetration across river and jungle could succeed: the Japanese would advance to occupy Assam and East Bengal up to the Brahmaputra as a preliminary to Subhas Chandra Bose stirring up revolt throughout India with his Indian National Army. There was to be a triple thrust. The first prong of Operation *U-Go* advanced through Arakan towards Chittagong. There followed the "Battle of the Admin Box" when, for the first time, the British did not flee but stood firm. They now had air superiority and supplies and reinforcements were flown in. The British were fighting an enemy with one-third their strength. Defeat would have meant disgrace: yet it had happened before. It did not happen again. Then followed the main Japanese offensive aimed at Imphal (capital of Manipur) and Kohima in the Naga hills, key points on the central front. This battle (March-July 1944) was a series of unconnected actions fought at company and battalion level. The battle swung round about April 19, although this was not clear to the desperately struggling British and Indian troops. The fighting continued, even when the Japanese situation was hopeless: those who survived fell back to the Chindwin in July.

Habituated to limited gains, the first British plan, "Capital", envisaged only a push into Upper Burma. The Chindwin river was crossed on December 3. Forces moved through the dry northern plain towards the Irrawaddy. The first major prize was Mandalay, captured after bitter fighting (March 9–21 1945), although Meiktila was taken well ahead (March 3)

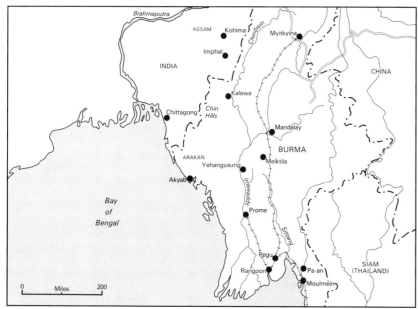

Burma: this vast area saw many Allied operations against the Japanese, 1941–45

opening a thrust down the axis of the north-south railway line. Japanese resistance stiffened, while the British formations had to operate with ever more tenuous lines of communication, impeding supplies to the forward troops. Meanwhile the Irrawaddy was crossed in strength at midstream enabling the two army corps (IV and XXIII) to link up.

The separate operation ("Dracula") by XV Corps was under way. Akyab was captured (January 3–4 1945) and the long advance by land and sea continued, while Fourteenth Army slogged their way down towards Rangoon, fighting on half rations. The seaborne assault from Arakan was finally ready, with a voyage of 480 miles (770km). Rangoon was seized, without resistance, May 3.

A victory parade was held in Rangoon on June 15 although the war was far from over. The Japanese command withdrew to Pa-an, beyond Moulmein, but substantial forces remained within the British lines in the hills of the Pegu Yoma. They endeavoured to break out across the Sittang. The British were aided by Burmese nationalists who fed them intelligence and helped them to set a trap. As scattered Japanese units approached the Sittang, their way was blocked; they still tried to get through, suffering dreadful loss. When the Imperial order to surrender was received the Japanese

were incredulous and recalcitrant. However, Gen Kimura, commander of the Burma Area Army, accepted the terms laid down by Gen Stopford, commanding Twelfth Army (which had taken over from Fourteenth Army). *HT*.

Burma Road *see* LEDO ROAD.

Burns, Lt Gen E L (1897–1985). Canadian. Commander 2nd Canadian Division to January 1944; Commander 5th Canadian Armoured Division in Italy to March 1944; Commander I Canadian Corps, breaching the Hitler Line in May, the Gothic Line in August, and the Rimini Line in September; crossing the Savio in October before handing over the Corps in November 1944. During the Suez Crisis of 1956, commanded the UN Expeditionary Force, 1956–59.

Busch, Field Marshal Ernst (1885–1945). Ger. Busch's service career in World War I was as a front-line infantry officer. His postwar support for the Nazis saw him rewarded by rapid promotion. By the invasion of Poland in September 1939 he commanded VIII Corps, and the next year he was given Sixteenth Army, leading it during the Battle of France. During both Operation "Barbarossa" and the early phases of the war in the east, Busch failed to achieve significant victories. However, Hitler's favour continued and, on

February 1 1943, Busch was promoted Field Marshal. In October, he was given command of Army Group Centre. Facing a resurgent Red Army, and shackled by Hitler's orders of no withdrawal, Busch's commanded was virtually destroyed under the onslaught of the Soviet summer offensive. His loyalty did not save him from dismissal and it was only during the closing months of the war that he was given a new command defending Germany's North Sea coast. In this capacity he was one of the signatories to the German surrender at Lüneburg Heath on May 4 1945. *MS*.

Butte de Warlencourt. Chalk mound near Bapaume, France. The scene of heavy fighting in November 1916, it finally passed into British hands in August 1918.

Byng, Field Marshal Viscount (1862–1935). Br. Byng commanded the South African Light Horse during the Second Boer War. In August 1914 he commanded 3rd Cavalry Division, which he led at the First Battle of Ypres. The following April he took over the Cavalry Corps but was sent to Gallipoli in August 1915 to succeed Stopford at the head of IX Corps. He supported the decision to abandon the peninsula and was the chief architect of the evacuation plan. Byng was given command of the Canadian Corps in May 1916, improving its training and discipline and winning its respect and affection. After leading the Corps on the Somme and in the dazzling capture of Vimy Ridge, he succeeded Allenby as commander Third Army in June 1917. Third Army's attack at Cambrai in November started impressively yet ultimately failed through lack of reserves. Byng can perhaps be accused of unnecessarily delaying the evacuation of the Flesquières salient during the German March 1918 offensive, but Third Army subsequently blunted the German thrust at Arras and, from August 21 onwards, played its full part in the final British drive, crossing the Canal du Nord, the Hindenburg defences and the St Quentin Canal and advancing 60 miles (98km) in 80 days. Byng was created Field Marshal in 1932, an unusual distinction for a retired officer. *PJS*.

C3I. A common abbreviation for "Command, Control, Communications and Intelligence", the means by which military operations are directed. The term implies the close interrelation and synergy of the four factors. Modern systems of automated C3I using computers to handle information, process intelligence and generally aid decision-making are giving commanders unprecedented opportunities to maintain control of complex situations and make maximum use of limited resources. Modern battlefield communications networks such as RITA and Ptarmigan provide a flexible and survivable communications grid. Satellites allow secure ultra high-frequency radio communications on a global basis. Modern systems of surveillance allow intelligence to be provided to the integrated system on a "real time" basis for assessment and action. Electronic warfare (EW) is intended to disrupt the enemy's C3I by jamming and/or deception. *EJG.*

C-47 Dakota, Douglas (US, WWII and after). Transport; crew 3. Prototype (Douglas DST) flew December 17 1935. First ordered as C-47 1941; widely used in every theatre of war by USAAF, USN, USMC and RAF; built in Russia as Lisunov Li-2. Later used Berlin Airlift, Korea, Vietnam; production in Japan. Total production over 12,500. Two 1,200hp Pratt and Whitney R-1830-92 engines; max. speed 229mph (368kph); armament nil (some fitted to Russian Li-2s).

C-130. The Lockheed Hercules transport aircraft first flown in 1954 and delivered to the USAF from the end of 1956. Since then it has been taken into service by the air arms of over 40 countries and has seen active service in most conflicts and crises. It was used by both sides in the Falklands War. The basic transport has been through four major variants and specialized versions have been produced for roles such as gunship, tanker and submarine communications. Over 1,750 C-130s have been built, including C-130Ks with British parts for the UK. The latter have recently been lengthened. The C-130 is powered by four Allison turboprops and has

a maximum speed of 386mph (589kph). *EJG.*

Cadorna, Gen Count Luigi (1850–1928). Italian. Italian COS during the twelve battles of the Isonzo; superseded in November 1917 after Italy's defeat at Caporetto.

Caen, Battle for (1944). Caen, together with its airfield at Carpiquet, were important Allied objectives on D-Day, but the British 3rd Division was forced to halt 3 miles (5km) from the city on encountering strong German positions in Lébisey wood. On June 10 Montgomery planned a double envelopment, with attacks from the bridgehead over the Orne in the northeast and towards Villers-Bocage in the south; but both thrusts met determined opposition. The southern outflanking

Sherman tank at Caen

movement was renewed in Operation "Epsom" on June 25.

On July 8 Montgomery launched I Corps in a direct assault on Caen from the north – Operation "Charnwood". This was preceded by a massive bombardment by 467 aircraft, which devastated Caen and hindered the Allied advance as much as harming the Germans. By July 10, Caen west of the Orne was in Allied hands, including Carpiquet, the scene of a bitter Canadian battle begun on July 4. But the Germans still controlled the suburbs of Vaucelles and Colombelles, where the chimneys of the steelworks provided good observation platforms. To keep up the pressure, Montgomery mounted another major attack – Operation "Goodwood" – on July 18. The armoured divisions of VIII Corps advanced down the eastern flank of the city, while II Canadian

Corps cleared the suburbs. The capture of Caen at an earlier stage would have provided valuable space for the Allied build-up, for airfields and for armoured forces to manoeuvre. But Montgomery's attacks had drawn German armour to the British sector, enabling the Americans to achieve the breakout on July 25. *SB.*

Cairo and Tehran Conferences ("Sextant" and "Cairo Three"). Between November 21–December 7 1943, Churchill and Roosevelt met Chiang Kai-shek in Cairo and Stalin in Tehran. The leaders, their foreign ministers and chiefs of staff reviewed the war situation, especially the development of the Italian campaign, on which Churchill and Roosevelt differed; plans for the Anglo-American invasion of France, on which Stalin needed reassurance; and the future of the war against Japan. Roosevelt was more open than Churchill to the views of Chiang and Stalin.

Russian victories strengthened the force of Stalin's demand for Western support in the form of an invasion of France from both north and south. Churchill's insistence on the capture of Rome and the involvement of Turkey in the war caused Stalin, and to some extent Roosevelt also, to suspect that Britain lacked enthusiasm for the invasion of France, preferring a Mediterranean campaign leading to a thrust into the "soft underbelly" of Europe from the south. Further division arose from Churchill's fears, not fully shared by Roosevelt, for the political freedom of East European countries, especially Poland, if they were "liberated" by the Russians. The rather vague consensus on Japan was that principal operations should be in the Pacific and that the requirements of the campaigns against Germany should have priority.

Strategic divisions were more or less papered over; political ones less so, with adverse results which would became more apparent at Yalta. *ANF.*

Calabria, naval action off (July 9 1940). The first encounter between the British and Italian battle fleets: after Adm Campioni's flagship *Giulio Cesare* had been hit by a salvo from Adm Cunningham's flagship *Warspite*, the Italians disengaged, using smoke and superior speed.

California. US battleship. Completed 1921; 12 × 14in guns and turbo-electric propulsion. Sunk at Pearl Harbor 1941, but raised and rebuilt by 1944. Took part in the Saipan, Leyte, Luzon and Okinawa landings; also the Surigao Strait battle. Decommissioned 1947; was to be a radio-controlled target for anti-ship missiles, but funding not provided.

Calley, Lt William L Jr (b.1943). US. *See* MY LAI MASSACRE.

Cambodia, wars since independence. Cambodia (Kampuchea) became an autonomous state within the French Union in 1949 and achieved full independence in 1953. General elections in 1955 led to the formation of a government under Prince Norodom Sihanouk, the former king. As war spread in neighbouring South Vietnam, Sihanouk allowed the Vietnamese communists to use Cambodian territory in return for their non-support of Khmer communists whom Sihanouk had dubbed the Khmers Rouges. This compromise of Cambodia's neutrality provoked the American "secret" bombing of Vietnamese communist sanctuaries in Cambodia and eventually led to Sihanouk's ousting by anti-communists in his own government on March 18 1970. The new government under Lon Nol launched a campaign to evict the Vietnamese.

In April 1970, a joint US/South Vietnamese task force attacked the sanctuaries on the ground. Retreating Vietnamese communist forces turned over equipment to the Khmers Rouges, and civil war erupted between the Khmers Rouges and the American-backed Lon Nol government. Forbidden by Congress from sending any American military personnel into combat in Cambodia, the US relied on massive airpower to support Lon Nol's army. Further congressional action ended the bombing in August 1973. The corrupt and incompetent Cambodian army proved no match for the implacable Khmers Rouges, who marched into Phnom Penh on April 17 1975.

The Khmers Rouges, however, suspected the Vietnamese of seeking expansion in the guise of a "special relationship" and sought reassurance from China. They also renewed claims to territory in Vietnam's Mekong delta and backed up these claims with commando raids on Vietnamese villages. Hanoi finally launched a full-scale invasion on December 25 1978 to remove the Khmers Rouges regime by force. Up to 200,000 Vietnamese soldiers occupied Cambodia. With the Vietnamese-sponsored People's Republic of Kampuchea ensconced in Phnom Penh and the costs of occupation mounting, Vietnamese troops began slowly to withdraw. In 1988 their number dropped below 100,000, and Hanoi promised to complete the withdrawal by 1990. *WST. See also* KHMERS ROUGES; "MENU" OPERATIONS; SIHANOUK TRAIL.

Cambrai, Battle of. The principal feature of the British offensive at Cambrai on November 20 1917 was that, for the first time, tanks were concentrated for a mass attack instead of being dispersed along the front in "penny packets". The operation was originally planned by the Tank Corps as a large-scale raid but was developed by Gen Sir Julian Byng and Third Army staff into a major offensive against the Hindenburg Line. It was intended to breach the German defences between the Canal de l'Escaut and Canal du Nord;

First major tank commitment: Cambrai.

pass cavalry through to isolate Cambrai and seize the Sensée crossings while infantry and tanks took Bourlon Ridge; and then clear Cambrai and the area between the water obstacles before advancing northeast towards Valenciennes. The problem was that the British

had insufficient reserves for the exploitation phase, and therein lay the germ of ultimate failure. Nevertheless, on November 20, 1,000 guns fired a surprise hurricane bombardment, using "predicted shooting" without previous registration, as 476 tanks – including 378 fighting and 98 support tanks – moved forward to attack with six of Byng's 19 infantry divisions on a 5-mile (8km) front. The initial gains were dramatic, the Hindenburg Line and its Support Line being overrun in most places to a depth of 4–5 miles (6–8km), except at Flesquières, in the left centre, where the 51st Division ignored the prescribed tactics and lagged behind the tanks. Thereafter, direct hits and mechanical breakdowns greatly reduced the number of tanks available and, with the cavalry unable to exploit the breakthrough, the battle became essentially an infantry struggle for possession of Bourlon Ridge, west of Cambrai. For all their efforts, the British infantry never entirely secured Bourlon Wood or village and, on November 30, the Germans delivered a highly effective counterattack in which the hurricane bombardment, low-flying aircraft and infiltration tactics by storm troops were all successfully employed. Although German progress was halted by British reinforcements, Third Army withdrew to a shorter line by December 5, yielding much of the ground won earlier. For both sides, however, the tactics tested during the battle offered an eventual solution to the trench deadlock. *PJS.*

Camel *see* SOPWITH CAMEL.

Camel Corps. The Imperial Camel Corps was formed in Egypt in 1915 from elements of several Australian, New Zealand and British units. It initially operated in the Western Desert and by 1916 had reached brigade strength. A major portion of the force was then switched to the campaigns in Sinai and Palestine.

Cameroons (1914–16). In 1914, the Cameroons, a German protectorate in western equatorial Africa, had an area of *c*200,000 square miles (518,000 sq km), bordered by Nigeria (British), north; French Equatorial Africa, south and east;

C

the Gulf of Guinea, west; Lake Chad, northeast. Although the Cameroons *Schutztruppe* (Col Zimmermann; 200 German officers; c1,600 askaris) and gendarmerie (40 German officers; c1,300 Africans) were outnumbered by Allied troops (the British committed c360 British officers and NCOs and c7,700 African soldiers; the French c11,000 Europeans and Africans), terrain and climate made invasion difficult.

Early in August 1914, French columns achieved limited penetration of the southern and eastern borders; a British assault on the northern mountain fortress of Mora, August 25, was repulsed with heavy losses. (Subsequently besieged, Mora held out in isolation throughout the campaign, surrendering honourably only after German resistance ended elsewhere.) Anglo-French cooperation under British Brigadier-General Sir Charles Dobell was agreed at the end of August, and on September 27, following naval bombardment, a joint expeditionary force drove the Germans from Duala, the major port on the Gulf of Guinea. Zimmermann fell back to Edea and thence to Yaunde.

In April 1915, an additional Anglo-French force (Col Frederick Cunliffe) crossed the northwestern border from Nigeria, taking Garua (July 10) and Ngaundere (July 28) before marching southwest towards Yaunde, on which Dobell, from the west, and two French columns (Gen Aymerich) from the east had been slowly and painfully advancing. The Allies took Yaunde on January 1 1916, although many Germans escaped to the Spanish enclave of Rio Muni. The campaign cost the Allies c4,250 dead (most from disease) and c5,900 wounded. *RO'N*.

Camino Monte, First and Second Battles of (November 5–15 and December 2–10 1943). The key to the German Bernhardt Line defended by 15th Panzer Grenadier Division, which repulsed the 56th British and 3rd US Divisions in the First Battle, but lost the position when 46th British Division reinforced the assault in the Second Battle.

Campbell, Maj Gen John C ("Jock") VC (1894–1942). Br. Originator of the British "Jock" column tactics for harassing operations in desert warfare; Commander 7th Armoured Division's Support Group during Operation "Crusader", winning the VC in the First Battle of Sidi Rezegh; appointed to command 7th Armoured Division, but was killed in a car accident in February 1942.

Campioni, Adm Angelo (1878–1944). Italian. C-in-C Afloat when Italy declared war in 1940. Withdrew in the fleet action off Calabria against Adm Cunningham in July 1940, and again in the fleet action off Cape Spartivento against Adm Somerville in November. He was superseded by Adm Iachino in December.

Cam Ranh Bay. To meet logistical needs that exceeded the capacity of South Vietnam's few ports, the US Army Corps of Engineers began improving the port at Cam Ranh Bay in June 1965. The Americans installed a prefabricated deep draught pier and built roads, warehouses, an airstrip and a fuel storage depot. The base continued to serve as the major port for supplies after the Americans withdrew. South Vietnamese forces abandoned it intact in 1975.

The Soviet Union gained access to Cam Ranh after China invaded Vietnam in spring 1979. The number of Soviet ships operating out of the bay subsequently grew to about 30 in the late 1980s. These ships and Tu–95 Bear D reconnaissance aircraft significantly extended the operational capability of the Soviet Pacific Fleet. *WST*.

Canadian forces in Korea. The first Canadian forces committed to the Korean War were three destroyers deployed to the Far East in July 1950. Canada was reluctant to commit ground forces and it was not until August 1950 that the Canadian government announced it was raising a brigade of volunteers. The unit, under Brig J M Rockingham, moved to Fort Lewis, Washington, where it was designated the 25th Canadian Infantry Brigade. The 2nd Battalion, Princess Patricia's Light Infantry (PPLI), was sent directly to Korea for training. When China intervened, the Canadians resisted any attempt to use their men before they were fully trained. The PPLI first went into action in February 1951 as part of the 27th Commonwealth Brigade. The 25th Canadian Infantry Brigade sailed for Korea in April 1951 where it was rejoined by the 2nd Battalion PPLI and was incorporated into the 1st Commonwealth Division. Canada also provided an air transport squadron to the United Nations command. *CM*.

Canadian Expeditionary Force. A total of 619,636 men and women served in the Canadian Expeditionary Force during World War I, principally on the Western Front, where over 53,000 died.

Canal Defence Light. Covername for World War II battlefield illumination device: tank with powerful searchlight replacing or supplementing turret gun.

Canal du Nord. After breaking through the Drocourt-Quéant Line on September 2 1918, the Canadian Corps, under Lt Gen Currie, approached the Canal du Nord. This canal, under construction in 1914, still had dry stretches and, taking advantage of one of these, Currie extended his corps boundary to the south, proposing to push his troops across on a narrow front, then spread them out beyond the farther bank. When the attack was delivered on September 27, Currie's ambitious plan worked and, although German resistance stiffened for a few days, the Canadian thrust prepared the way for the capture of Cambrai. *PJS*.

Canaris, Adm Wilhelm (1887–1945). Ger. U-boat and intelligence service 1914–18; head of Abwehr 1935–44; loyal German officer, disapproved of Nazism. Protected German forces in action; less successful overseas. Turned a blind eye to July Plot, subsequently arrested; executed in Flossenbürg April 9 1945. *See also* JULY PLOT.

Canberra, English Electric (Br). Bomber/photographic reconnaissance; crew 2. Prototype flew May 13 1949; first delivery (to No. 101 Squadron, RAF) May 25 1951, of PR version 1953. Deliveries to many countries; production in Australia. Modified version built in USA as

Martin B-57. Operational use RAF in Suez Crisis, RAAF and USAF Vietnam, Indian AF Indo-Pakistan War 1971, Argentina Falklands 1982. Two 6,500lb (2,950kg) s.t. Rolls-Royce Avon RA.3 engines; max. speed 570mph (917kph); 6,000lb (2,700kg) bombs.

Canberra. British (P & O) cruise liner of 45,000 tons. Converted in two days into a troopship, with the addition of a helicopter deck, for service in the Falklands War. She sailed from Southampton on April 9 1982 with 2,400 men of 3rd Commando Brigade embarked, landing them on May 21 in San Carlos Water, East Falklands, where she continued to serve as a hospital ship and survived numerous air attacks. Sailed to South Georgia to collect 5th Brigade off the *Queen Elizabeth II* and returned to San Carlos with them. Known affectionately to all ranks in the British Task Force as the "Great White Whale".

Cannon, Lt Gen John K (1892–1955). US. Commander XII US Air Support Command to January 1944; Commander Mediterranean Allied Tactical Air Force and US Twelfth Air Force to March 1945; C-in-C Mediterranean Allied Air Forces to June 1945.

Cannon. Essentially large calibre machine-guns, cannon are used as light, fast-firing armament on aircraft and armoured vehicles and are employed on land and sea for low-level anti-aircraft defence.

Cao Bang. The Vietnamese communists established their first resistance bases in Cao Bang province located on the border with China in 1941–44. Between October 3 and 8 1950, in the Indochina War, they attacked outposts in the province, destroying a French force of almost 4,000 men in ambushes near the province capital. Cao Bang was the scene of heavy fighting again in February and March 1979 when China launched a punitive attack on Vietnam. *See also* BORDER WAR, VIETNAM.

Cao Dai. A religious sect formally organized by Vietnamese civil servants in the Saigon area in 1926. An amalgam of the world's major religions and Vietnamese traditional and folk beliefs, it spread quickly from its urban base to rural areas. By the late 1930s it had 500,000 followers and, with Japanese support during World War II, it became the de facto political authority in large parts of the Mekong delta.

Cao Dai troops fought alongside the communists against the French in 1945–46, but sect-party rivalry allowed France to gain the sect's allegiance. The French helped build a Cao Dai militia of 65,000 men that tied down communist forces in the south, freeing French troops for use elsewhere. At the war's end in 1954, this force dwindled to about 25,000 men, but its officers resisted central government control. Some Cao Dai officers accepted bribes from the American CIA to allow integration into Saigon's army, and in 1956 Saigon forces forcibly occupied Cao Dai HQ in Tay Ninh. A few thousand Cao Dai troops fled to the jungles and about 500 of these wound up in clandestine units controlled by the communists.

Cao Dai remained influential in Tay Ninh province but never regained the autonomy or military power it had enjoyed during the first war. Fragmentation into 12 factions undermined the sect's political clout. The total number of Cao Daists in South Vietnam by the early 1970s was probably not over one million. *WST.*

Cao Van Vien, Gen (b.1921). Republic of Vietnam. The last chairman of the Joint General Staff of the Republic of Vietnam Armed Forces; he held this position for nearly a decade. In 1975 he helped to persuade President Nguyen Van Thieu to shift forces southwards, abandoning territory to the communists in order to retrench around Saigon. Two days before Saigon fell, Vien fled to the US without resigning.

Cape Bon, naval action off (night of December 12–13 1941). Two Italian cruisers, running fuel to Rommel, were surprised and sunk by six British and Dutch destroyers under Commander G H Stokes.

Cape Engaňo, Battle of *see* LEYTE GULF, BATTLE OF (1944).

Cape Esperance, Battle of (October 11–12 1942). The third major naval action of the Guadalcanal campaign, between Rear Adm Norman Scott's USN Task Force 64 (heavy cruisers *San Francisco*, *Salt Lake City*; light cruisers *Boise*, *Helena*; five destroyers) and Rear Adm Aritomo Goto's IJN 6th Cruiser Squadron (heavy cruisers *Aoba*, *Kinugasa*, *Furutaka*; two destroyers). At 2325 hours on October 11, the new surface radar in *Helena* detected the Japanese warships, en route to bombard Henderson Field, from 14 miles (22km), but because of poor intership communications Scott was engaged in a complex reversal manoeuvre when he opened fire from c5,000yd (4,570m) at 2346 hours. Taken by surprise, Goto was mortally wounded early on, when *Aoba* was badly damaged. The Japanese failed to exploit their superior torpedo armament, while two US destroyers were damaged (one later sinking) by fire from both sides. After losing the destroyer *Fubuki*, the Japanese retired; *Furutaka*, having badly damaged *Boise*, was sunk in a chase broken off at 0028. *RO'N.*

Cape Gloucester. Site of landing of the US 1st Marine Division, December 26 1943, during the invasion of New Britain in the Bismarck Archipelago.

Cape Spada, naval action off (July 19 1940). Cruiser HMAS *Sydney* sank one of two Italian cruisers opposing her.

Cape Spartivento, naval action off (November 27 1940). The Italian battle fleet (Campioni) tried to intercept the "Collar" convoy from Gibraltar to Malta and Alexandria, covered by Force H (Somerville). Campioni used his superior speed to avoid a fleet action.

Cape Saint George, Battle of (November 24–25 1943). Classic destroyer night action. Capt Arleigh Burke's five American destroyers intercepted a Japanese force taking troops to Buka. Two escorting destroyers were sunk by surprise torpedo attack. One of the troop-carrying destroyers was then sunk by gunfire; the other two were chased back to their base at Rabaul.

Caporetto, Battle of (October 24–November 3 1917). The German-led Austrian offensive across the Isonzo, which led to the disastrous defeat of Italian Second Army. *See* ITALIAN CAMPAIGN, WORLD WAR I.

Caproni Ca133 (Italian, WWII). Bomber transport; crew 3. In service at time of Abyssinian War, 1935–36, the Ca133 was used in that conflict. By June 1940 14 Italian bomber *squadriglie* in East Africa still equipped with the type, which served on training and general duties in World War II. Ambulance version in use until 1945. Three 460hp Piaggio Stella P.VII C-14 engines; max. speed 165mph (264kph); 1,102lb (500kg) bombs, four 7.7mm machine guns.

Caproni Ca3 (Italian, WWI). Heavy bomber; crew 4. First Caproni trimotor (Ca1) flew October 1914; development with more powerful engines via Ca2 to Ca3 of February 1917. Deliveries from April 1917; also produced in France. Generally successful; remained in service until Armistice and later. Production, 451 Ca3 and Ca3 Mod. Three 150hp Isotta-Fraschini V4B engines; max. speed 87mph (139kph); 1,000lb (450kg) bombs, 2–4 7.7mm machine guns.

Carbine. Light rifle originally designed for mounted troops.

Carl, Maj Gen Marion E (b.1915). US. Marine Corps fighter pilot, credited with 18.5 victories. In August 1942, during the Guadalcanal campaign, he destroyed five Japanese aircraft in three days to become the first USMC "ace" of World War II. After the war he set new world air speed and altitude records, retiring as a major general.

Carlson, Brig Gen Evans Fordyce (1896–1947). US. Having studied Chinese communist guerrilla operations against the Japanese, Carlson advocated the formation of "commando" units in the USMC and in 1942 took command of 2nd Raider Battalion ("Carlson's Raiders"), with the Chinese motto "Gung-ho" ("Work Together"). Landed by submarine on August 17 1942, 220 Raiders wiped out the 83-strong Japanese

garrison of Makin Atoll, Gilbert Islands. In November-December 1942, in a 30-day, 150-mile (240km) patrol on Guadalcanal, the Raiders killed *c*500 Japanese with only 17 US losses. Carlson left the Raiders after Guadalcanal: his elite force aroused antagonism among some senior US officers and existing Raider units were split up in 1944. Wounded on Saipan, he retired on medical grounds in 1946. *RO'N*.

Carne, Col James Power VC (b.1906). Br. Commanded 1st Battalion, Gloucestershire Regiment, during Korean War; awarded VC for his conduct during the Battle of the Imjin, April 22–25 1951, where he was captured, spending remainder of war as POW.

Caroline Islands *see* TRUK CAMPAIGN.

Carpet bombing *see* BOMBING.

Carrier air group. American designation (adopted by British) for complement of aircraft (and their crews) aboard a carrier. Divided into squadrons or flights of fighters, bombers and other aircraft.

Carrier task force. American designation for a naval force centred around an aircraft carrier or carriers; includes surface escorts.

Carrington, Lord (b.1919). Br. Secretary of State for Foreign and Commonwealth Affairs 1979–1982. He resigned after the Argentinian invasion of the Falklands following criticism of his department's handling of the crisis. Subsequently (1984–88) became highly respected Secretary-General of NATO in Brussels.

Carson, Lord (Sir Edward Carson) (1854–1935). Br. Dublin-born Protestant who, as leader of the Ulster Unionist Council from 1911, headed the opposition to Irish Home Rule. He served as Attorney General in Asquith's coalition government, May 1915–October 1916, and as First Lord of Admiralty, under Lloyd George, December 1916–July 1917.

Carton de Wiart, Lt Gen Sir Adrian VC (1880–1963). Br.

Served with the British army before World War I and, in spite of having lost an eye in action, fought on the Western Front. Severely wounded eight times and awarded the VC. In 1939 he headed the British Military Mission in Poland, subsequently serving in Britain and Norway before being sent, in 1941, to establish a Mission in Yuglosavia. His aircraft crashed en route and he was taken prisoner by the Italians. After several attempts to escape, he was released in 1943 to act as an intermediary between the Italian authorities and the Allies. Following the Italian surrender he was appointed Churchill's personal representative to Chiang Kai-shek. *MS*.

Roosevelt and Churchill at Casablanca

Casablanca Conference ("Symbol"). Meetings between Churchill and Roosevelt and the Anglo-American Combined Chiefs of Staff between January 14 and 25 1943. De Gaulle was invited to some meetings and a report of the outcome was sent to Stalin.

The principal matters decided were: the theoretical priorities for the Combined Bomber Offensive; when the conquest of North Africa was complete, Sicily would be invaded; the first steps would be taken to form an army for the invasion of France (Operation "Overlord"); a staff plan for such an invasion would be made under the auspices of a British officer (COSSAC); an offensive against the Japanese in Burma would be coordinated with the Chinese. At a press conference Roosevelt announced, some think inadvertently, that the war in Europe would be ended only by the unconditional surrender of Germany. *ANF*.

Casement, Sir Roger (1864–1916). Br. Irish-born British consular official, hanged for treason in 1916, having negotiated with Germany for aid for Irish insurgents.

Casey, William Joseph (1913–87). US. Head of OSS's SI branch in London 1943–45; campaign manager for Reagan 1979; director, CIA, with seat in cabinet, 1981–86; fell mortally ill during Irangate crisis.

Cassels, Field Marshal Sir James (b.1907). Br. Commanded 1st Commonwealth Division in Korean War, from its activation on July 28 1951 to September 7 1952. He had to integrate his Commonwealth units into an efficient military organization and avoid friction with the US commanders under whom the division served. He was empowered, if orders transmitted to the division were inconsistent with UN aims in Korea or unduly jeopardized Commonwealth troops, to appeal to C-in-C, British Commonwealth Forces in Korea, and if necessary to the Chiefs of Staff Committee, Australia, and the Commonwealth governments. Cassels never invoked this directive, although he complained to the Americans on several occasions about their tactics in the positional warfare of 1951–52. *CM.*

Monte Cassino in ruins after bombing.

Cassino, Battles of (January 24– May 18 1944). There were four battles to take Monte Cassino, the key to the German Gustav Line, dominating the main road to Rome up the Liri Valley.

In the First Battle (January 24– February 11), II US Corps (Keyes) and the French Expeditionary Corps (Juin) attacked two days after the Allied landing at Anzio,

hoping to open up the Liri Valley approach to Rome while the Germans were distracted by the threat to their rear. In three weeks of bitter fighting, XIV Panzer Corps (von Senger) stopped 34th US Division on the "Snakeshead" ridge just short of the monastery, and brought the French to a halt on Monte Belvedere.

In the Second Battle (February 15–18), the temporary New Zealand Corps (Freyberg) attacked the monastery with 4th Indian Division, and the Cassino railway station below with the New Zealand Division, on February 17. This was in order to relieve the German pressure on the Anzio beachhead and to open the road to Rome up the Liri valley. Two days earlier, American bombers had reduced the monastery to rubble. Nevertheless, both divisions were defeated. Credit for the German successes in the First and Second Battles of Cassino must be given to 90th Panzer Grenadier Division (Baade).

With the situation at Anzio still precarious, Alexander ordered a resumption of the New Zealand Corps attack on Cassino (the Third Battle, March 15–25), which was now held by 1st Parachute Division (Heidrich). Bad weather intervened, preventing air support until March 15, when 455 aircraft of the Mediterranean Allied Tactical Air Force (Cannon) destroyed Cassino town. The New Zealand Division attacked the town in the wake of the bombers, but deep bomb craters and rubble stopped their tanks, and the German paratroopers checked their infantry. The 4th Indian Division again attacked the monastery, but this time from below via "Hangman's Hill", which was taken by the Gurkhas, but they could go no farther. After ten days' continuous fighting, Heidrich's paratroopers still held the ruins of both the monastery and the town. Alexander halted operations on March 25 to start preparations for his spring offensive.

In the Fourth Battle (May 11–18 – Alexander's "Diadem" offensive) II Polish Corps (Anders) was given the task of taking the monastery, while XIII Corps (Kirkman) attacked up the Liri valley below. Heidrich's 1st Parachute Division repulsed Anders' first assault on May 11–12 with heavy loss, but

was forced to abandon Monte Cassino when the Poles attacked again on the 17th because XIII Corps' progress up the Liri valley threatened his encirclement. The Polish colours were raised over the monastery on May 18. *WGFJ.*

Cassino, bombing of the monastery (February 15 1944). Although Monte Cassino was not occupied by German troops, there was no means of confirming so when 4th Indian Division (Tuker) was ordered to seize it. Tuker requested the monastery's neutralization. With great reluctance, Alexander authorized its bombing to save Indian lives. A total of 135 Fortresses of the Mediterranean Allied Strategic Air Force (Twining) reduced it to rubble two days before 4th Indian Division could be ready to to attack. This apparent lack of Allied coordination was due to fears that forecasted bad weather would delay bombing. When 4th Indian Division did attack, they found the ruins strongly held by the Germans and they were repulsed. *WGFJ.*

Castellano, Gen Giuseppe (1893– 1977). Italian. Negotiated the Italian Armistice, August 1943.

Castelnau, Gen Noel de (1851– 1944). Fr. Aristocrat and devout Catholic, Castelnau graduated from St Cyr and fought in the Franco-Prussian War of 1870. Despite his removal from the General Staff in 1900 for anti-Dreyfusard views, his career recovered momentum and he became Deputy CGS under Joffre in 1911, exerting an important influence on the French Army's war preparations, including the shaping of Plan XVII.

In August 1914 Castelnau commanded the French Second Army, based on Nancy. Moving into Lorraine towards Morhange, Castelnau's advance was decisively checked on August 20. Although compelled to retreat to the Grand Couronné, his forces, in turn, successfully defended Nancy and the Moselle Line. A believer in large-scale offensives, he was appointed in 1915 to command the French Centre Group of Armies and, in September that year, conducted the major French attack in Champagne which, after initial success, failed to break the German second line. He then returned to his earlier role as Joffre's *sous-chef*. In 1916 his advice was crucial in determining the nature of the French defence of Verdun. Castelnau's influence waned after December 1916 when Nivelle replaced Joffre. Nevertheless, he ended the war in command of the Eastern Group of Armies, directing the final operations in Lorraine. In 1919 he entered politics,

Gen Noel de Castelnau (1851–1944)

serving in the Chamber of Deputies until 1924. His Catholic background militated against his being appointed to the highest military office and, unlike several of his contemporaries, he was never named a Marshal of France. *PJS*.

Castries, Brig Gen Christian Marie Ferdinand de La Croix de (b.1902.) Fr. Chosen by Navarre, who believed that as a cavalry officer he would make effective use of tanks on the valley floor, to command at Dien Bien Phu, spring 1954. Castries failed to anticipate the strength and tactics of the Viet Minh assault (March 13–May 7) and was captured along with 10,000 of his men.

Catalina *see* PBY-5 CATALINA.

Catalonia campaign (December 1938–January 1939). Spanish Civil War. The Battle of the Ebro left the Republic virtually helpless: in Catalonia, there were fewer than 40,000 rifles between 250,000 men. The Nationalist army attacked on December 23: the Italians and Carlists crossed the Segre behind the Ebro front; Yagüe's Moroccan Corps crossed the Ebro on January 3; a further breakthrough was made at Balaguer. The Republicans fell back in

chaos, abandoning Barcelona on January 26. Some 500,000 refugees fled to the border, where the unprepared French authorities interned them in improvised camps where several thousand died in appalling conditions. Two months later, after an anti-communist coup in Madrid, the Republic surrendered. *AB*.

Catapult-Armed Merchant Ship (CAM ship). Allied vessels which launched fighter aircraft to defend convoys, mainly in the Atlantic and generally against German Focke-Wulf Condors. The fighters then ditched.

Caudron G3 (French, WWI). Two-seat reconnaissance, later trainer. In French service at outbreak of World War I as artillery-spotter; some delivered to RFC, RNAS, Belgium, Italy and Russia. Still operational February 1916, but was more widely used as trainer. Some built in Britain and Italy; remained in use until Armistice, some with USAS. One 80hp rotary (various types) or 100hp Anzani radial engine; max. speed 65mph (104kph); armament (light) varied greatly.

Caudron G4 (French, WWI). Two-seat reconnaissance bomber. First appeared March 1915; widely used Western, Italian, Russian fronts and in Aegean. French-built G4s totalled 1,358; type also produced in Britain (for RNAS) and Italy. Good service over Somme 1916. Two 80hp Le Rhône rotary or 100hp Anzani radial engines; max. speed 81mph (130kph); 250lb (113kg) bombs, one 0.303in/7.7mm machine gun.

Caudron R11 (French, late WWI). Three-seat reconnaissance aircraft/escort fighter. The prototype flew in March 1917, but the aircraft's production was retarded by engine problems and operational employment did not begin until February 1918. The Caudron R11 saw more use as an escort fighter than as a reconnaissance aircraft; it was successful and well-liked by pilots, and more powerful developments were designed. Production totalled about 500. Two 215/235hp Hispano-Suiza engines; max. speed 114mph (182kph); five 0.303in/7.7mm machine guns.

Cauldron, Battle of the (1942) *see* GAZALA, BATTLE OF.

Cavallero, Marshal Ugo (1880–1943). Italian. COS of Italian Armed Forces from December 1940; dismissed in February 1943 for being too pro-German when Mussolini was first considering defection from the Axis.

Cavalry. Historically, the mounted arm for shock action, reconnaissance and observation. Former horsed regiments, now part of the Royal Armoured Corps (British Army). In the US army, cavalry units also bear the historical titles (7th Cavalry etc.) and normally function in armoured reconnaissance role.

Cavan, Field Marshal the Earl of (1865–1946). Br. Commander of British troops in Italy and of the British XIV Corps in the Battle of Asiago in June 1918. He then commanded the Italian Tenth Army, which included his XIV Corps, during the Battle of Vittorio Veneto in October 1918. His success in crossing the Piave and scattering the centre of the Austrian line led to the final Allied victory in Italy. He was CIGS 1922–26.

Cavell, Edith (1865–1915). Br. A nurse working in occupied Brussels, Edith Cavell gave assistance to British soldiers evading capture by the Germans. Betrayed with other members of the escape line, she was tried, condemned to death and executed by firing squad on October 11 1915. Allied propagandists fully exploited her "martyrdom".

Caviglia, Gen (1862–1945). Italian. Commanded XXIV Corps during the Battle of Caporetto in 1917; commanded Eighth Army during the Battle of the Piave in June 1918; and coordinated the actions of the Sixth, Eighth, and Tenth Armies during the Battle of Vittorio Veneto in October 1918.

"Cedar Falls" Operation (1967). The Iron Triangle, a communist stronghold 22 miles (35km) northwest of Saigon, was an early target of American "search and destroy" operations during the Vietnam War. The Americans believed the zone held the People's Liberation Armed Force (PLAF) 272nd regiment, two battalions of the PLAF 165th regiment, and communist HQ for the Saigon-Gia Dinh capital region. Operation "Cedar Falls" followed "Attleboro" in attempting to locate and attack these targets. The first corps-sized American operation of the war, "Cedar Falls" led to "Junction City", a thrust into neighbouring War Zone C.

Following four days of B-52 bombardment, "Cedar Falls" deployed 20 battalions from January 8–26 1967 to close the sides of the triangle. Heavy use was made of defoliants and Rome Plow bulldozers to clear jungle. A surprise helicopter assault seized the fortified village of Ben Suc, 6,000 villagers were relocated, searches discovered a vast underground supply complex, and the village and complex were destroyed by bulldozers and explosives. Although the PLAF units eluded the sweep and returned when the operation was over, repetition of such operations eventually forced the communists to relocate much of their support activity in Cambodia. *WST*.

Central Intelligence Agency (CIA). Grew out of the Office of Strategic Services (OSS), founded in 1942. Set up as part of the National Security Act of 1947; authorized to undertake "functions and duties related to intelligence affecting the national security" – covert operations, and received Presidential approval with the issue of NSC directive 4/A in December 1947.

Central Powers. The World War I fighting alliance of Germany, Austria-Hungary, Bulgaria and Turkey.

Ceylon, Battle of (April 5–9 1942). Japanese First Air Fleet (Vice Adm Nagumo: 5 carriers with *c*360 aircraft; 4 battleships; 3 cruisers; 9 destroyers) was sent to strike at the British Eastern Fleet (Adm Somerville: 5 battleships; 3 carriers; 8 cruisers; 15 destroyers). This force, based at Ceylon (Sri Lanka) and Addu Atoll, Maldives, was weaker than it appeared: apart from the refitted *Warspite*, its battleships were old and slow; the carrier *Hermes* carried only 12

Swordfish; the 78 aircraft of the modern carriers *Indomitable* and *Formidable* were inferior in number and effectiveness to the Japanese aircraft.

On April 1, Somerville sent a Fast Squadron (*Warspite*, *Indomitable*, *Formidable*, 4 cruisers and 6 destroyers) – with which, since his aircraft, unlike the Japanese, could operate in darkness, he sought a night action – on a fruitless interception mission. Thus, when Nagumo's carriers struck at Colombo on April 5, Fast Squadron was replenishing at Addu and other units, warned by air reconnaissance, left Colombo before the attack. Nagumo's strike badly damaged installations and destroyed 31 Allied aircraft for only 7 losses, but sank only an auxiliary cruiser and a destroyer. Later that day, however, heavy cruisers *Cornwall* and *Dorsetshire* were intercepted and sunk by Nagumo's dive-bombers.

While Somerville hunted Nagumo, April 5–8, three Japanese raiding squadrons (Vice Adm Ozawa) sank 19 merchant ships totalling *c*92,000 tons. On April 9, Nagumo struck at Trincomalee. Again warned by air reconnaissance, Allied ships fled: Nagumo's raid did considerable damage, but lost 15 aircraft for 9 Allied fighters. Beating off a suicidal attack by nine Blenheims (five lost), Nagumo's carriers located the fleeing ships and sank *Hermes*, a destroyer, a corvette and two tankers. The Japanese withdrew; the British fleet retreated to East Africa. *RO'N*.

Chaco War (1932–1935). Disputes between Paraguay and Bolivia over the 100,000-sq mile (260,000 sq km) wilderness of the Chaco Boreal were exacerbated by oil-strikes in the region. War was narrowly averted in 1928, and both countries began to push forward lines of fortification. Early in 1932 Paraguay invaded and took control of most of the Chaco (but did not declare war until May 10 1933). The Bolivian army, larger (5,000 regulars), better equipped and efficiently trained by its German commander, Gen Hans von Kundt, counterattacked, overwhelming most of Paraguay's outposts. Infantry warfare, often in entrenched World War I style, pre-

vailed in the swampy jungle. In 1934-35, Paraguay, having raised a 60,000-strong army (Bolivia now had *c*50,000) launched a counteroffensive under Col José Felix Estigarribia, reoccupying the Chaco, taking *c*20,000 prisoners and briefly advancing into eastern Bolivia. Overall, Paraguay suffered *c*38,000 killed or wounded; Bolivia *c*75,000. A truce was arranged on June 12 1935: by the Treaty of Buenos Aires, July 21 1938, Paraguay retained *c*75 percent of the Chaco. *RO'N*.

Chaff. US term for radar jamming strips of tin foil similar to the RAF's "Window".

Chain Home. A system of British radar stations installed between 1937 and 1940.

Challenger (British MBT) *see* TANKS.

Chamberlain, (Arthur) Neville (1869-1940). Br. Prime Minister 1937-40. Negotiated the Munich Agreement in 1938. Guaranteed Poland and Romania and introduced conscription in spring 1939. Declared war on Germany September 3 1939. Resigned after defeat in Norway, May 1940. Served in Churchill's government until his death on November 9 1940.

Champagne, First Battle of. In December 1914, with both sides entrenched from the Belgian coast to the Swiss frontier, the French Army launched the first of a series of offensives eastwards from Artois and northwards from Champagne. Determined to drive the Germans out of France, Gen Joffre, the French C-in-C, believed that a succession of "nibbling" attacks would bring that day nearer by gradually weakening German powers of resistance. His immediate aims in the Artois-Champagne offensives were to pinch out the huge German salient between the Aisne and the Somme and to threaten the German lines of communication between Reims and the North Sea. The first attack in Champagne by the French Fourth Army, under Gen de Langle de Cary, started on December 20 1914. Assaulting strong German defences on a 20-mile (32km) front, the French achieved some early

C

successes on the right, where the XVII and the Colonial Corps captured important strongpoints in the German front line, though XII Corps made little headway on the left. The fighting dragged on into January, when worsening weather and the exhaustion of the troops brought the offensive to a temporary halt. After various minor operations, however, the French began the second main phase of the battle on February 16 1915. It raged almost continuously until March 30 but, at an estimated cost of 240,000 casualties, the French won no more than a few hamlets on the forward slopes of the hills, failing to cut the lateral railway communications upon which the German centre depended. *PJS.*

Champagne, Second Battle of.
On September 25 1915, in conjunction with a Franco-British attack in Artois, the French Army launched its second major offensive of the year in Champagne. The objectives of this operation were broadly similar to those of the earlier Artois – Champagne offensives. This time the Champagne attack was to be carried out by the Second Army under Gen Pétain as well as Gen de Langle de Cary's Fourth Army, and would be coordinated by Gen de Castelnau, commander of the French Centre Group of Armies. Thirty-four infantry and eight cavalry divisions were assembled to attack on a front of over 15 miles (24km), but French preparations in the chalk fields of Champagne were obvious to the German Third Army. The preliminary bombardment by 2,500 guns opened on September 22, followed, three days later by the infantry assault which, in some places, was accompanied by bands playing the *Marseillaise.* Despite the strength of the defences, the French at first bit deeply, if unevenly, into the German centre, penetrating up to 3,000yd (2,700m). Next day the German second line was reached on a front of 7.5 miles (12km) but desperate attacks between September 27 and 29 made only a few small breaches in this second position. Renewed assaults on October 6 were equally unsuccessful. When the fighting finally subsided around November 6, the French had suffered some 145,000 casualties and the Ger-

mans approximately 85,000. For Joffre the battle was another strategic failure which further weakened the French Army. *PJS.*

Chanak crisis *see* GRECO-TURKISH WAR.

Chaney, Maj Gen James E (1885–1967). US. One of a group of US officers sent to England in 1940 to observe the Battle of Britain. Chaney reported favourably to Washington on Britain's ability to survive. In May 1941 he returned as head of US Army Specialist Observer Group, to prepare for the eventual establishment of US ground and air forces in Britain, advise on lend-lease equipment and to report to Gen Marshall (and the British Chiefs of Staff Committee) on employment of US forces in Europe. He went to Moscow with the Beaverbrook-Harriman mission, September 1941. Following the initiation of USAAF's bomber offensive in 1942, largely through his efforts, Chaney was briefly Commanding General, US Forces British Isles, but because of policy disagreements with his Washington superiors, notably Gen Arnold, he was recalled and relegated to training posts, ending the war in the position of Island Commander, Iwo Jima *MH.*

German warships in "Channel Dash".

Channel Dash (February 11–13 1942). Popular name for Operation "Cerberus" which returned German warships *Scharnhorst, Gneisenau* and *Prinz Eugen* to Germany from Brest (heavily attacked by the RAF) via the English Channel. Danger to the ships from bombing was the reason. Meticulous preparations were made in minesweeping and air cooperation – for once the Luftwaffe helped the *Kriegsmarine.* A

series of accidents to British patrols enabled Vice Adm Ciliax's ships to sail undetected by night, but they were finally spotted by a roving Spitfire, proceeding up-Channel at 27 knots the next day. Further British confusions and lack of coordination, plus strong and well-organized air and sea escort to the ships prevented attacks by naval and RAF aircraft, destroyers and MTBs having any success. The Dover guns were forbidden to fire until too late. However, mines damaged both battlecruisers. A British humiliation, but not, in the long run, a really satisfactory move for the Germans. *CJW/CD.*

Channel Islands, occupation of. The defeat of France in June 1940 rendered the British Channel Islands indefensible and 29,000 civilians were evacuated before the occupation began on June 30. The British authorities instructed the inhabitants to refrain from acts of resistance and the Islands became rather a backwater until the Germans decided to make them a bastion of the Atlantic Wall. Considerable resources were lavished on the construction of complex fortifications and a substantial garrison manned the concrete fortresses. But the Islands were largely ignored as the Germans were driven out of France for it was felt that an assault would result in needless sacrifice of Allied lives. It was not until May 9 1945, that British forces landed to receive the surrender of the German garrison. *MS.*

Chantilly. Location of French General Headquarters (*Grand Quartier Général*), November 1914–January 1917.

Char B. French heavy tank, introduced in 1931 for close infantry support. 31 tons, 1 × 75mm fixed gun, 1 × 37mm in turret. *See also* TANKS.

Charleroi, Battle of. By August 20 1914 the French Fifth Army, under Gen Lanrezac, had moved up to positions along the Meuse, between Givet and Namur, and the Sambre, between Namur and Charleroi. Advancing through Belgium towards Lanrezac were, from the north, the German Second

Army under von Bülow, and from the east, von Hausen's Third Army. French hopes of launching an offensive to the northeast in accordance with Plan XVII were forestalled on August 21 when Bülow's forces gained footholds across the Sambre. Next day, French counterattacks failed and Bülow, without waiting for Hausen's support, drove the French back some 5 miles (8km) from the Sambre. On August 23 the French I Corps, under Gen Franchet d'Esperey, had to cancel a thrust against Bülow's left to deal instead with Hausen's crossing of the Meuse to the south. That night Lanrezac ordered a withdrawal, thereby saving the French Fifth Army from destruction. *PJS*.

Chemical and Biological Warfare (CBW) *see* CHEMCIAL WEAPONS and BIOLOGICAL WEAPONS.

Chemical weapons. Weapons which use chemically synthesized poisons to kill or disable the enemy or (defoliants) to destroy plants useful to the enemy for food or as cover. The main lethal chemical agents today are nerve gases such as tabun, sarin and the V-agents that attack the central nervous system. Older agents include blood gases such as cyanide that prevent the bloodstream carrying oxygen, blistering agents such as mustard gas that attack all exposed surfaces and choking agents that affect the lungs such as phosgene. Some agents are persistent, others rapidly disappear. They can be released from cylinders, by aircraft sprays, or by shells, rockets, bombs or mines. Chemical weapons were first used in modern times in World War I, first by the Germans on the Eastern and then the Western Fronts and then by the Allies. They achieved some significant local surprise effect, but countermeasures – protective masks and "gas capes" – were soon developed, and chemical weapons had no decisive effect on the outcome of the war. Although less lethal than other types of weapon, the long-lasting effects of chemical weapons spread popular revulsion against this form of war and first use of chemical weapons was banned by the Geneva protocol of 1925, which was only ratified by the USA 50 years later. Chemical weapons were used with some effect against unprotected opponents by Spain in Morocco in 1925, by the Russians in China in 1934, by the Italians in Ethiopia in 1935–36 and by both sides in the Sino-Soviet War of 1937–45, but they were not generally used in World War II, despite fears of widespread strategic bombing with chemical bombs and sprays. Germany, who had a monopoly of the then new nerve agents, feared retaliation and Hitler, who had been gassed in the Great War, disliked chemical warfare. Since World War II, lethal chemical weapons have been used in the Yemen Civil War, and in the Gulf War between Iraq and Iran. Defoliants, notably the infamous "Agent Orange", were used widely by the Americans in Vietnam, causing long-term ecological damage and injury to personnel. Vietnam also saw the use of non-lethal harassing agents ("tear gas") commonly used for riot control. Negotiations progress at Geneva in the United Nations Conference on Disarmament (CD) for a worldwide ban, and an international conference in Paris at the beginning of 1989 reaffirmed the Geneva protocol on no first use. Chemical weapons are stockpiled by the USSR (which possesses the world's most extensive CW infrastructure), the USA and France but not by the UK. The USA is about to replace its older weapons with binary munitions containing two non-lethal toxic chemicals which are mixed to form lethal nerve agent GB2 before impact. Chemical weapons proliferation is an important problem; Syria, Israel, Egypt, Iran, Iraq and Libya all manufacture chemical weapons. Protection against chemical weapons can be provided by special masks and suits, although wearing such equipment itself degrades the combat capability of personnel. A major aim of chemical attack may well be to exploit this effect; for example, to slow down the sortie rate of an enemy airfield. Hallucinogenic drugs such as those based on LSD have also been tested as a means of disorientating an enemy. *EJG*.

Chemin des Dames. This ridge, between the Aisne and Ailette in France, takes its name from the Malmaison-Craonne road built along its crest to allow Louis XV's daughters easier access to the Chateau de la Bove. The summit was reached by the BEF in September 1914 but lost by the French the following winter. A fiercely contested feature, it was a principal objective of the Nivelle offensive in April 1917 and was wholly recovered in November, after Pétain's Malmaison attack. Overrun again in the German "Blücher" offensive of May 1918, it was finally secured for the Allies in October 1918 by the French Fifth and Tenth Armies. *PJS*.

Chengtu. The capital of Szechwan province, China, was selected in 1944 as the main base for B-29 raids against the Japanese home islands. A massive construction programme built four bomber bases in rapid time, but in January 1945 the proximity of Japanese forces led to the abandonment of the airfields.

Chennault, Maj Gen Claire Lee (1898–1958). US. In 1937, forced by deafness to retire as head of US Army Air Corps fighter training, Chennault became military aviation adviser to the Chinese government. Early in 1941, Chinese resources proving insufficient to combat Japanese aggression, he recruited the American Volunteer Group ("Flying Tigers") which he trained – advocating diving attacks in the sturdy P-40 Warhawk against the faster, more agile, but less well-armoured Mitsubishi A6M "Zero" – to become the most effective air unit in the China-Burma-India Theatre in early 1942. Recalled to regular service with the China Air Task Force in mid-1942, from March 1943 he commanded US Fourteenth Air Force. His demands for the limited Allied resources in China to be devoted to air rather than ground power led to repeated clashes with Stilwell, who appeared to be proved right when the Japanese *"Ichi-go"* offensive of 1944–45 resulted in the loss of many Fourteenth Air Force bases. Refusing to preside over the disbanding of the Sino-American wing of the Chinese air service as the Pacific war neared its end, Chennault resigned his command in July 1945. *RO'N*.

Cherbourg, capture of (1944). As the Allies expanded their bridgehead in Normandy after D-Day, the US VII Corps cut the base of the Cotentin peninsula on June 18 1944, isolating the 21,000 Germans defending Cherbourg. VII Corps rapidly fought its way northwards on a front of three divisions – west to east, the 9th, 79th, and 4th. Meanwhile the gale in the Channel destroyed the American Mulberry harbour and disrupted the Allied build-up,

American troops enter Cherbourg, 1944

making the capture of a major port even more urgent. By June 20 the Americans were facing the outlying German defences 5 miles (8km) from Cherbourg. The commander of VII Corps, Maj Gen J Lawton Collins, issued a surrender ultimatum, which expired at 0900 hours on June 22. Soon after midday, hastily-arranged bombing raids by the US Ninth Air Force and ten RAF squadrons, in which 1,100 tons of bombs were dropped in 80 minutes, preceded the American assault.

American troops fought their way into Cherbourg on June 25, as Anglo-American naval forces carried out a bombardment of the defences lasting three hours – twice the planned length. On June 26 the German garrison commander, Gen von Schlieben, surrendered with 800 of his men at the entrance to his underground headquarters. On June 27, 400 Germans defending the Arsenal surrendered in response to loudspeaker warnings by an American psychological warfare unit. All German resistance in the Cotentin peninsula ceased by July 1. The port facilities of Cherbourg had been destroyed and heavily mined, but the first deep-draught supply ships were able to enter the outer harbour on July 16. *SB*.

Chernyakhovsky, Gen Ivan (1906–45). Russian. Chernyakhovsky joined the Red Army in 1924 and on the outbreak of war with Germany was in command of the 2nd Tank Division. He distinguished himself in the fighting around Novgorod but, after a month of heavy fighting, his depleted command had to be reformed into a rifle division. In the summer of 1942 Chernyakhovsky briefly led the XVIII Tank Corps and, in July, took command of the Sixteenth Army, leading it in the recapture of Voronezh and Kursk the following year. Chernyakhovsky's men held the centre of the Kursk salient during the crucial battle of July 1943 and participated in the subsequent Soviet advance into the Ukraine. He was next given command of the Western (later Third Belorussian) Front and was promoted to general, his achievement being all the more remarkable for his relative youth (38 years) and because Chernyakhovsky was one of the few Jews to rise to senior rank. In the summer offensive of 1944 his forces formed the right pincer of an encirclement that resulted in the entrapment of over 100,000 Germans at Minsk. Continuing his advance, he captured Vilnyus on July 14 and then drove on to Kaunas and the borders of East Prussia. A major, new offensive was launched in the New Year when he advanced on Konigsberg and, in spite of fierce German resistance, his forces broke through the defence lines. However, his highly promising career was cut short in February 1945 when he was killed by German artillery fire. *MS*.

Cherwell, Professor Lord (formerly Lindemann) (1886–1957). Br. Scientific adviser to Churchill. Learnt to fly in 1916, when engaged in experimental work at Royal Aircraft Factory, Farnborough, and, it is sometimes claimed, was the first to recover from spinning an aircraft. Supplied Churchill with material to support his rearmament campaign in the 1930s and after 1940, when Churchill replaced Chamberlain as Premier, became the government's *éminence grise*, entering the cabinet as Paymaster General in 1942 and expressing verdicts on a wide range of scientific and strategic issues. In the "Cherwell Minute", March 30 1942, commenting on the deadlocked argument whether Bomber Command should be disbanded or reinforced, he stated that if an expanded Bomber Command could drop even half its load within the built-up areas of Germany's 58 principal cities, the population's will to war would be broken. Although not universally accepted, this proposition settled the issue and the policy of area bombing was endorsed by the government and Air Staff. *ANF*.

Cheshire, Gp Capt Leonard, VC (b.1917). Br. One of the outstanding bomber pilots of World War II, flying more than 100 sorties in Whitleys, Lancasters, Mosquitoes and Mustangs, from the latter two of which he developed a highly accurate but very hazardous system of low-level visual marking.

Chetniks *see* MIHAILOVICH.

Chhamb (India-Pakistan Wars 1965, 1971). Border zone between "Azad Kashmir" (occupied by Pakistan) and the Jammu province of Kashmir and Jammu. In 1965, Pakistani armoured formations crossed the cease-fire line, thrusting towards Akhnur and threatening to sever the vital communication via Pathankot. India responded by an attack over the Punjab border. When the 1965 conflict ended, Pakistan held Chhamb territory but had failed to cut off Kashmir. In 1971, Pakistan repeated this move, but India was prepared and Pakistan sustained losses in men and armour with no significant gains.

Chiang Kai-shek, *Generalissimo* (1887–1975). Chinese. Chiang received his military education in China and Japan, serving in the Japanese army, 1909–11. He returned to China to help Sun Yat-sen build a republican army, visiting Moscow in 1923 to study the Red Army. After Sun's death in 1925, Chiang's military eminence helped him gain control of the Kuomintang. In 1927 he married Soong Mei-ling (b.1898), who became one of his closest advisers, and in 1928 established a Nationalist government at Nan-

Chiang Kai-shek, Chinese nationalist

king. His rule was threatened by dissident elements within the army, communists and, most seriously, the Japanese, who occupied Manchuria in 1931 and attacked Nationalist China in July 1937. Chiang was driven back to Chungking, but recovered with US and British aid from 1941. His relations with the Western powers, particularly with Gen Stilwell, were often strained, however, and post-war he did not receive the assistance he had anticipated against the communists. Driven from the mainland in 1949, he proclaimed himself President of the Republic of China on Formosa (Taiwan), 1950. *MS.*

Chiefs of Staff. The British professional heads of the Navy, Army and Air Force and occasionally of others, e.g. the Chief of Combined Operations, acting together as a group to advise the government.

Chieu Hoi. The "Chieu Hoi" ("Open Arms") program adopted by South Vietnamese President Ngo Dinh Diem in 1963 offered amnesty to soldiers and cadres on the communist side. The program's greatest appeal was the prospect of escape from hardship that it held mainly for low-ranking personnel. Up to 1973 the program attracted nearly 160,000 "returnees" bearing 10,699 individual weapons and 545 crew-served weapons. However, the figures grossly overstated the program's effectiveness. Many ostensible defectors were pro-Saigon civilians who collaborated with officials for a share of the reward, and the communists used the program to provide their cadres with legal cover or to infiltrate Saigon armed forces. The CIA estimated that of 79,000 defectors in 1969–70, only 17,000 were genuine. *WST.*

China-Burma-India Theatre. US command that was largely concerned with the supply, training and transport provided to Nationalist Chinese forces during World War II.

Chindit Operations (Burma campaign, 1941–45). Based on Wingate's concept of the Long Range Penetration Group, and conducted independently of fixed lines of defence. The name derived from the Chindwin river, which had to be negotiated on entry and exit from Japanese-held territory, and from the *Chinthe* (Burmese temple guardian) indentification worn by LRPG columns. His military superiors were unenthusiastic, but Wavell gave his support and Wingate was given a job-lot of troops to prove his ideas. In Operation "Longcloth" (February–May 1943) the columns marched to their objectives, supplied by airdrops. Penetrating 300 miles (480km) into northern Burma, they destroyed railway and other installations and clashed violently with Japanese patrols. One-third of the British infantry became casualties. The material results were disputed, but the operation did much to relieve the dismal spirits of the "forgotten army" in Burma. Churchill was delighted, and Wingate was given forces up to divisional strength for a second operation. For Operation "Thursday", there were gliders to fly in all but one of the six brigades. But soon after it began, in March 1944, Wingate was killed in an air crash and command devolved upon Brig W D Lentaigne, who was out of sympathy with Wingate and his ideas. The Chindits were misused and were expected to go on fighting long after they were at skeleton strength. Placed under the command of Stilwell, they received no proper orders. The surviving Chindits were finally evacuated to India at the end of August 1944. Probably the most important consequence of the Chindit performance was to persuade the Japanese high command to launch a similar attempt at long-range penetration, the ill-fated Kohima-Imphal attack, which broke their reputation for invincibility. *HT.*

Chindwin river *see* BURMA CAMPAIGN (1941–45).

Chinese Civil War (1926-1949). The establishment of a provisional republican government in 1911 brought no unity to China. The authority of Sun Yat-sen's nationalist Kuomintang (KMT) in the south was challenged elsewhere by warlords seeking to establish a new dynasty or to secure independence in their own territories. In 1923, Sun contrived an anti-warlord alliance between the KMT and the Communist Party of China (CPC), but his death in 1925 and the accession to KMT leadership of the anti-communist Chiang Kai-shek increasingly strained the alliance.

The KMT and CPC at first cooperated in the "Northern Expedition" offensives of 1926-28, which by 1927 had curbed the warlords' power south of the Yangtze and in Honan. But the growing political power of the CPC in the "liberated" areas alarmed Chiang: in 1927 he initiated a savage anti-communist purge that resulted, by 1930, in rival regimes: Chiang's KMT-Nationalist government at Nanking, and, farther south, the "Soviet Republic" centring on Nanchang, Kiangsi, headquarters of the People's Liberation Army (PLA) of Chu Teh and Mao Tse-tung.

Japanese activity in Manchuria prevented Chiang's northern advance and he embarked on an anti-communist campaign to the south, launching five "extermination" offensives in 1930-34. With heavy losses on both sides, the PLA was driven south: the fifth KMT offensive, late 1933, with a 700,000-strong German-advised force, a "scorched-earth" campaign including the massacre of the PLA's peasant supporters, ended in 1934 with the epic northern evacuation of the PLA to the mountains of Shensi (*see* LONG MARCH).

In 1937-45 (*see* SINO-JAPANESE WAR) an uneasy truce existed between KMT and PLA forces; the latter gaining popular support by spectacular guerrilla actions against the Japanese. Open warfare recommenced in 1945, as the KMT and PLA fought for control of Manchuria and other areas vacated by the Japanese. At first the KMT, although riddled by corruption and internecine struggle, seemed likely to prevail, with US military aid, but with the failure of Gen Marshall's reconciliation mis-

C

sion, 1946-47, direct US aid decreased.

Meanwhile, the PLA, using Japanese materiel handed over by the Soviet Union, was able to expand its guerrilla operations into full-scale offensives. Late in 1948, the PLA secured Manchuria, where 300,000 Nationalist troops surrendered, and shattered the central KMT forces in the Kaifeng-Suchow area in the Battle of Huai-Hai, November 1948-January 1949. Taking Peking (where the People's Republic of China was proclaimed on October 1 1949) on January 22 1949, the Communist armies crossed the Yangtze in late April, occupying Canton in October and Chungking, the Nationalist capital, in late November. Early in December 1949, Chiang withdrew with the surviving KMT forces to Formosa (Taiwan), where in 1950 he proclaimed the Republic of China. *RO'N.*

Chinese forces in Korea (Army, Air Force). China did not officially participate in the Korean War and its troops were known as the Chinese People's Volunteers. A special standby force was established in September 1950 and the first units crossed the Yalu in mid-October. By December the total number of Chinese troops in Korea was around 200,000. This force reflected its guerrilla origins. It was armed with a mixture of ageing weapons and lacked even a standard calibre of infantry ammunition. There was little artillery, and communications below divisional level were largely by runner and bugle. The supply system was primitive and the soldiers were expected to carry their own supplies of rice and ammunition into battle. The Chinese suffered severely from the cold in the first winter of the war and casualties from frostbite were high. There was also a high incidence of infectious disease. Chinese tactics of ambush and encirclement worked well against a UN army dependent on the roads in November-December 1950, but supply problems meant that successes could not be quickly followed up. Attacking well-prepared troops backed by air power and artillery in early 1951, the Chinese suffered terrible casualties. After June 1951 they went to ground in a network of

deep bunkers and fortifications. By July 1952 there were around 680,000 Chinese in Korea re-equipped with Soviet weapons including tanks and artillery. The Chinese Air Force first became engaged over Korea in November 1950 and by the end of the war around 450 MiGs were based beyond the Yalu. A small number of Ilyushin jet bombers was sent to Manchuria in 1953, but never used in Korea. *CM.*

Chin Peng Chinese. Leader of the Malayan Races' Liberation Army (MRLA). He fought the Japanese in World War II as a member of the Malayan People's Anti-Japanese Army (MPAJA), was decorated by the British government and marched in the Victory Parade, London 1946. He took to the jungle again in 1948. As the MRLA never succeeded in taking over a region of the Malayan Federation and imposing communist rule, the rebellion was doomed, but Chin Peng's resourceful leadership, judicious use of coercion and terror, and the endurance of MRLA members, prolonged the Malayan Emergency until 1960.

Choe Yong Gon (1900–1976). Korean. Served with the Chinese communist Eighth Route Army, 1930s, and as a guerrilla in Manchuria, where he met Kim Il Sung. In Soviet Union from 1941; in September 1945, returned with Kim to Korea, where, as head of Provisional People's Security Bureau from February 1946, he created a Peace Preservation Corps that became the nucleus of the NKPA. Appointed Minister of Defence on the founding of the DPRK, 1948, and became a member of the Military Affairs Committee, created on June 26 1950 to run the Korean War under Kim's chairmanship. Survived postwar purges to become number two in the North Korean hierarchy. *CM.*

Choltitz, Lt Gen Dietrich von (1894-1966). Ger. A regimental commander on the Eastern Front, 1941–43, and commander of a corps severely mauled during the Normandy campaign, June–July 1944, Choltitz was appointed C-in-C, Greater Paris, by Hitler (who, shaken by the July Plot, believed him loyal) on August 7 1944. To

his great credit, Choltitz ignored orders to destroy the city in the face of the Allied advance, while his temporary truce with the Gaullist Resistance (mediated by the Swedish Consul-Gen Raoul Nordling) helped prevent a communist takeover. On August 25, when French and US forces entered Paris, Choltitz surrendered the city with minimal damage. *RO'N.*

Chongchon river, Battle of the, (November 26–30 1950), the Korean War. On November 24, MacArthur launched a two-pronged offensive designed to end the war by Christmas. At first the US Eighth Army under Gen Walker, advancing across the Chongchon river in the northwest, met weak resistance and by November 25 the US 24th Division had reached the outskirts of Chongju. On November 26, however, Walker's command was ambushed by the Chinese People's Volunteers and the NKPA. The ROK divisions on Walker's right flank were routed at Tokchon and the Turkish Brigade, thrown in to plug the gap left by the ROKs, was practically destroyed after heavy fighting at Wawon. On November 28, Walker ordered Eighth Army to retreat. The US 2nd Division, astride the Chongchon river on the east of the front, was threatened by the ROK collapse and fell back on Kunuri, covering the escape across the Chongchon of the divisions to the west. On November 30, trying to withdraw south towards Sunchon, the division was ambushed in a pass near Kunuri. It was practically destroyed, losing over 4,000 men and much of its equipment. The rest of Walker's command, however, was able to break contact with the enemy and fall back through Pyongyang, which was retaken by the NKPA on December 6 1950. American morale was badly shaken and some units "bugged out", retreating without orders. The Battle of the Chongchon showed the effectiveness of Chinese tactics of ambush and encirclement against an army dependent on roads and reversed the verdict of Inchon, forcing the UNC to evacuate North Korea. *CM. See also* CHOSIN RESERVOIR.

Chongju, Battle of (October 1950), the Korean War. Chongju lies in

Churchill, Sir Winston

C

northwest Korea beyond the Taeryong river. On October 25–26 1950 the 27th Commonwealth Infantry Brigade took Pakchon and seized a crossing over the Taeryong. The Brigade then began to advance towards Chongju, defeating a North Korean force in hills south of the town on October 29. Chongju fell the following day. *See also* CHONGCHON RIVER, BATTLE OF THE; PAKCHON, BATTLE OF; UNSAN, BATTLE OF.

Chosin reservoir (Lake Changjin). Lies in the mountains of northeast Korea. In December 1950, the lst US Marine Division and elements of the US 7th Infantry advancing towards the Yalu on either side of the reservoir were ambushed by the Chinese. There was grave concern in Washington that the force would be surrounded and wiped out, but the Marines managed to fight their way back to the sea along narrow mountain roads and were evacuated from Hungnam.

Chou En-lai (1898–1976). Chinese. A close associate of Mao in the development of the Chinese Communist Party, Chou maintained a pragmatic and international perspective on Chinese affairs. He worked closely with the Nationalists during the war against Japan and showed considerable diplomatic skill during the period in which he served as Prime Minister from 1949 to 1976.

Christie. Name given to the revolutionary form of tank suspension developed in the US in 1930s by Col Christie. *See also* TANKS.

Christie, Vice Adm Ralph Waldo (b.1893). US. A pioneer submarine officer and torpedo specialist; commanded submarine *C-1*, 1917–18. After Pearl Harbor, he took a squadron of submarines (No.20, later No.5) to Brisbane, where he became Commander Eastern Australia Submarine Group. Later at Fremantle he became Commander of Submarines, South Pacific in 1943. He initiated a most successful submarine campaign from that base, but at the end of 1944 he was removed from this post at Kinkaid's instigation, and subsequently commanded the naval base at Bremerton, Washington.

Marshal Chuikov plans his campaign

Chuikov, Marshal Vassili (1900–1982). Russian. Chuikov joined the Red Army as a recruit in April 1919 and won command of a regiment during the Civil War. He subsequently graduated from the Frunze Military Academy in 1925 and was sent to China in 1926 where he became a military adviser to Chiang Kai-shek. In 1937 he returned to the Soviet Union and studied mechanized warfare. He participated in the invasion of Poland in September 1939 and gained further combat experience during the war with Finland. In 1941 he returned to China but was recalled in May 1942 to take command of the Sixty-Second Army. The task ahead of him soon proved singularly daunting with the German Sixth Army driving towards Stalingrad. With his headquarters under almost constant enemy bombardment, Chuikov ordered his men to contest every inch of the city. Close-quarter fighting inhibited the Germans' use of aircraft and armour and while their strength was eroded, Chuikov supplied and reinforced his troops from across the Volga. The destruction of the German Sixth Army allowed Chuikov the opportunity to adopt a more offensive role and, now commanding the Eighth Guards Army, he took part in the Red Army's drive into Poland and Germany. His greatest moment came on May 2 1945 when he received the surrender of Berlin from its commander, *Generalleutnant* Weidling. Chuikov later commanded Soviet forces in Germany and in 1972 was senior Inspector General in the Ministry of Defence. MS.

Chu Lai, Battle of (1965) *see* VAN TUONG PENINSULA, BATTLE OF.

Church, Brig Gen John Huston (1892–1953). US. To Korea as head of GHQ Advance Command and Liaison Group, June 27 1950; succeeded Gen Dean as commander, 24th US Infantry Division, July 20 1950.

Churchill, Sir Winston Leonard Spencer (1874–1965). Br. First Lord of the Admiralty 1911–15 and 1939–40. Prime Minister 1940–45 and 1951–55. Churchill's changing political allegiances and his impulsive nature won him both admiration and suspicion. He personally joined in the desperate and unsuccessful defence of Antwerp in 1914. His bold conception of a forcing of the Dardanelles in 1915, which, had it been successful, might well have changed the whole course of the war, ended in a much larger scale of failure and his resignation from the government. After seeing active service on the Western Front, he returned to Lloyd George's government as Minister of Munitions in 1917. Between the wars he was in and out of the government first as a Liberal and then as a Conservative. In the last years of peace, he criticized both Baldwin's and Chamberlain's governments from the Conservative benches, persistently arguing that the rearmament programme was insufficient to meet the threat from Hitler's Germany. On the outbreak of war, he joined Chamberlain's government as First Lord of the Admiralty, but with substantially wider influence than that office alone conferred. He took a major hand in the disastrous Norwegian campaign but the blame was laid, not by him, but by the House of Commons and public opinion, upon Chamberlain. Churchill himself emerged from past controversies as the national leader of a coalition government which succeeded in uniting Britain.

Churchill's speeches galvanized Britain, encouraged resistance in occupied Europe and commanded great attention in the USA. He recognized that Britain's ultimate fate depended on the USA and was quick to see the need to join forces with Russia after June 1941. He constantly harried COSS and c-in-cs; not always realistically, but usually to good effect. He seemed capable of weathering every kind

C

of disaster to British arms, such as the defeats in Greece, Crete and Hong Kong, although had it not been for Montgomery's victory at Alamein he might have fallen at that time. As it was, he survived to draw Britian and the USA into the closest alliance in the history of coalition warfare and achieve at least a partial understanding with Stalin. *ANF*.

Churchill A22. Last British "Infantry" tank and the only one still in front-line service in 1945. Introduced 1941. 38 tons, heavy armour. Early models carried only 2-pounder gun plus a small howitzer, later Marks 75mm. Also used for specialist roles. *See also* TANKS.

Chu Teh, Marshal (1886–1976). Chinese. A supporter of Sun Yatsen in 1911, Chu Teh was converted to communism in Europe in the 1920s. In Kiangsi, 1928-31, with Mao Tse-tung, he formed the original *cadres* of the Chinese Red Army. At the end of the Chinese Civil War 1930-34, he led First Front Army in the Long March. He commanded Eighth Route Army during the Sino-Japanese War 1937-45, and during the Chinese Civil War 1945-49 was C-in-C of the Chinese People's Liberation Army. His political and military power waned in the later 1950s.

Ciano, Count Galeazzo (1903–44). Italian Foreign Minister (1936–43) and Mussolini's son-in-law. Ciano signed the "Pact of Steel" with Germany in May 1939 but subsequently opposed Italy's involvement in the war and dependence on her ally. He participated in Mussolini's overthrow in July 1943 but was forced to flee to German-occupied territory where he was executed in January 1944.

"Cicero". Codename of Elyesa Bazna, the valet of the British ambassador at Ankara, who stole information from the embassy in 1943–44 and sold it to German intelligence.

Circular Error Probability (CEP). The normal index of weapon accuracy, being the radius of a circle around the aiming point in which 50 percent of the projectiles will impact. CEP is of particular importance for long-range missiles where it is the key to their Counter Military Potential (CMP). Early ballistic missiles had CEPs measured in thousands of metres, (although expressed here with imperial measurements first, following the style of the book) – 26,240ft (8,000m) or more in the case of the pioneering German V-2 and 6,560ft (2,000m) for the first-generation intermediate and intercontinental ballistic missiles of the 1950s. Modern ICBMS have CEPs of 656ft (200m) or less; the new American MX/Peacekeeper missile is at about the minimum possible CEP given a wholly inertial guidance system, 328ft (100m). Terminal guidance, possible in relatively slow intermediate missiles like the Pershing 2 can give a CEP of only 130ft (40m). High accuracy requires very precise knowledge of the location of the launch point. Missiles fired from mobile platforms such as submarines therefore have tended to have larger CEPS than fixed land-based systems. Current Western systems such as Trident C-4 have CEPs of 1,476ft (450m), about half the CEP of most modern Soviet SLBMS. Trident D-5 will, however, close the gap with land-based missiles and achieve a CEP of about 394ft (120m). *EJG*.

"Circus" operations. RAF fighter sweeps, often coordinated with bombers, to draw the Luftwaffe into action over the Pas de Calais, which could be reached by superior numbers of Spitfires. Begun in June 1941 and continued as a principal form of attack for about a year, the operations aimed to provoke an air battle which Fighter Command seemed to have the means of winning, and to aid the Russians by forcing the Luftwaffe to reinforce its western strength. It was also hoped that German fighter strength could be pinned to the Pas de Calais, opening a path for daylight attacks on Germany by Bomber Command. These aims were largely frustrated. Because of the Spitfire's limited range, the operations did not reach far enough to force the Germans to respond except when it suited them – as it often did, for they now had many of the advantages enjoyed by the British fighters in the Battle of Britain. Fighter Command claimed more than 400 German fighters destroyed, June–September 1941, for a loss of fewer than 200 British fighters: actual German losses were about 120. Nor did "Circus" operations facilitate daylight bombing away from their immediate area. Bomber Command was confirmed as a virtually exclusively night force, and Fighter Command had to seek other methods of deploying its growing strength. *ANF*.

City bunker complex, Cambodia. Americans in the Vietnam War dubbed the complex of tunnels and bunkers they believed to be headquarters of the communists' Central Office for South Vietnam (COSVN) and National Liberation Front "The City". Located in the "Fishhook", a salient of Cambodia about 50 miles (80km) northwest of Saigon, "The City" was a major target of US and South Vietnamese forces in May 1970. The operation uncovered vast quantities of weapons and supplies and destroyed many bunkers, but failed to turn up concrete evidence of COSVN/NLF headquarters, which in fact were spread over a wide area.

Civilian Irregular Defence Group (CIDG). The CIA began to organize and train CIDGs among Vietnam's ethnic minorities in 1961 to prevent the communists gaining control of the central highlands. US Special Forces took charge of the program in mid–1963 and trained CIDG troops for commando raids and reconnaissance along the Laotian and Cambodian borders. Several battalion and brigade-sized units called Mobile Strike Force Commands were trained and equipped to defend their remote camps against communist main forces, but most CIDG units were suitable only for patrolling, intelligence, and local security. The US turned over command of the CIDG to the South Vietnamese in 1970. Many CIDG units were then converted into border ranger battalions, while ethnic Khmer CIDG troops joined Lon Nol's Khmer republic army. *WST*.

Civil Operations and Rural Development Support (CORDS). The US established CORDS in May 1967 to overcome fragmentation of "pacification" programs during the Vietnam War. CORDS centralized control over the pacification resources of the armed forces, the State Department, the CIA, and other agencies. Unified civilian-military CORDS teams in all of South Vietnam's 44 provinces and 250 districts imposed coordination and discipline on American and South Vietnamese agencies alike. *See also* KOMER, ROBERT W; PACIFICATION PROGRAMS.

French clandestine newspaper, WWII

Clandestine press. The propaganda arm of a resistance movement can play a vital role in sustaining resisters' morale, in keeping alive the hope on which they must rely, in circulating news of the progress of a war or of a political campaign, and in issuing instructions on how to behave in impending emergencies. Clandestine newspapers were often, but not inevitably, run by political parties or splinter groups; some were put out by patriots affronted at their country's recent defeat, who had no particular political axe to grind; many had a moral or religious basis for what they wrote.

The Belgians, with a large, dispersed printing industry, developed an active clandestine press, especially in Brussels, during the German occupation of 1914–18. Clandestine tracts played a small part in the Spanish Civil War. In World War II clandestine newspapers appeared in most occupied countries – typewritten cyclostyled sheets at first, as a rule, passed round from hand to hand; eventually, properly printed newspapers, sometimes

appearing in editions of tens of thousands of copies. The first number of one such sheet came out in the Netherlands on May 15 1940, the day after the Dutch Army surrendered. The Netherlands produced over a thousand clandestine titles; so did the French. In Scandinavia, in eastern and southeast Europe and to a lesser extent in southeast Asia there were others.

This was a field in which academics and other intellectuals, unfitted by temperament for an ordinary line of battle, could find plenty of scope for their talents; if they had the opportunity and the courage. The risks were high: even to possess a clandestine newspaper might incur a prison sentence; to be caught carrying or printing a batch of them certainly meant prison, and might mean death. *MF*.

Clark Field. In December 1941 Philippines-based US Far Eastern AirForce had 35 B-17 bombers and 72 fighters with which to offset US naval weakness and deter Japanese aggression. Following Pearl Harbor, a retaliatory attack on Formosa was planned, but on December 8, as US aircraft were arming and refuelling at Clark Field, Manila, Japanese bombers struck. Two US bomber squadrons and one fighter squadron were effectively destroyed, ensuring invasion. In January 1945, US forces invading Luzon encountered a major Japanese strongpoint at Clark Field: after heavy fighting, XIV Corps secured the area on January 31. *MS*.

Clark, Gen Mark Wayne (1896–1984). US. First attracted attention as Deputy Commander to Eisenhower during the Allied landings in French North Africa in November 1942. He landed clandestinely from the British submarine *Seraph* near Cherchel, 50 miles (80km) west of Algiers, on October 22 1942 to coordinate operations with pro-Allied French officers led by Gen Charles Mast. After the capture of Algiers he provoked a political storm by negotiating a cease-fire with the Vichy Adm Darlan, November 10 1942.

Promoted to command Fifth US Army in January 1943, he planned the Allied invasion of Italy, and commanded the landing at Salerno

on September 9 1943. He captured Naples on October 1, and advanced north towards Rome up the western side of the Apennines until decisively checked at the end of the year by German resistance on the Gustav Line centred on Cassino. His amphibious left-hook to Anzio in January 1944 did not force Kesselring to abandon the Gustav Line, but in May his troops breached the coastal sector of that line and broke out from the Anzio

The "American Eagle": Gen Mark Clark

beachhead. He disobeyed Alexander's instructions to drive eastwards to cut off the German Tenth Army at Valmonte, and turned instead on Rome, which he entered on June 4.

His Fifth Army subsequently breached the centre of the Gothic Line above Florence, but was brought to a halt by German resistance and the onset of winter before he could break through into the Po valley. He took over 15th Army Group from Alexander in December 1944, and succeeded in destroying the German armies south of the Po in April 1945. After the cease-fire on May 2, he personally accepted their surrender two days later. He then became the first US High Commissioner and Commander of the American Occupation Forces in Austria.

In May 1952 he succeeded Gen Ridgway as United Nation's Supreme Commander in Korea, and US c-in-c Far East; and in July 1953 signed the armistice ending the Korean War. He retired that October and was later among the "Hawks" during the Vietnam War. *WGFJ*.

Clay, Lt Gen Lucius Du Bignon (1897–1978). US. A US Army engineer officer from 1918, Clay served in Washington as Deputy

COS for requirements and resources, and then Assistant COS for materiel, from 1942 until October 1944, becoming the linchpin of the US Army's vital procurement system. Transferring to Normandy, he displayed equal logistical genius as base section commander. Following an appointment as Deputy-Director, Office of War Mobilization and Reconversion, he sought a combat command in the Pacific; instead, he was posted to Europe as Deputy Military Governor (under Eisenhower) of the US Zone of Germany. Believing that a prosperous, democratic German state would best serve the West's political and economic interests, he worked tirelessly for economic reconstruction and the restoration of civil government. His uncompromising refusal to make any concessions to the Soviets during their blockade of Berlin, June 1948–May 1949, was fully supported by President Truman. *RO'N.*

Clemenceau visits his troops, 1918

Clemenceau, Georges (1841–1929). Fr. Twice Prime Minister of France, Clemenceau received his political education from the highly charged liberal opposition to the Second Empire, and was an active figure in the Paris Commune and the Third Republic. He was a formidable critic of the conduct of World War I, until in November 1917, aged 76, he took office as Prime Minister. His leadership during the final year of the war earned him the sobriquet *Père la Victoire.* Presiding over the Paris Peace Conference, he was dissatisfied with its outcome, in particular with the failure to secure the Rhine frontier as protection against Germany. This, coupled with his alleged repression of socialists during the war, brought

criticism from Right and Left, and he resigned in January 1920. *SLB.*

Clifford, Clark M (b.1906). US. Succeeded McNamara as US Secretary of Defense, January 1968. As chair of President Johnson's Ad Hoc Task Force on Vietnam, opposed further involvement; convened group of senior statesmen ("the wise men") who advised disengagement. Subsequently took lead in persuading Johnson to end bombing (at first, north of 20th Parallel only) and seek a negotiated peace.

Cluster bomb. A bomb which contains a large number of submunitions which are scattered over the target area, thus compensating for the aiming errors inherent in low-level attack. The submunitions or "bomblets" may be optimized for the anti-personnel or anti-armour role, or be dual-function. The American Rockeye 2 carries 247 dual-function bomblets which it scatters over 51,685 sq ft (4,800 sq m) if released at a height of about 490ft (150m).

Coastwatchers. Solitary observers, mostly Australians and New Zealanders, who transmitted information on Japanese movements from secret locations in the Bismarck and Solomon Islands during World War II.

Coastal Command. Created by the reorganization of the RAF in July 1936. Although an integral part of the RAF, Coastal Command could not be diverted from maritime work without the approval of the Admiralty and, from 1941 onwards, it was placed under the operational control of the Admiralty. At the beginning of the war it was equipped chiefly with Ansons, whose radius of action was limited to about 250 miles (400km). These were gradually replaced by Wellingtons, Sunderlands. Catalinas, Halifaxes, Beaufighters and Very Long Range Liberators. Successive marks of ASV were introduced and, from 1943 onwards, the Command became a highly effective means of dealing with German U-boats. *ANF.*

Cochrane, Air Chief Marshal Sir Ralph (1895–1977). Br. As AOC 5 Group, Bomber Command (1943–

45), he fostered radically new bombing and marking techniques, prime examples of which were the Dams raid, led by Gibson in May 1943, the visual marking of the centre of Munich by Cheshire in April 1944 and off-set bombing which the latter and others directed thereafter. Cochrane's ideas, which depended on low-level visual aiming, were opposed by Bennett.

"Cockade". Allied deception plan feigning an Allied invasion of France in 1943.

Cockerell, Sir Christopher (b.1910). Br. Inventor whose prototype of 1955 made practicable the air cushion vehicle (ACV), since developed for both military and commercial use. *see also* HOVERCRAFT.

Cockcroft, Sir John (1897–1967). Br. From 1925–35, Cockcroft worked under Sir Ernest Rutherford, exploring the physics of atomic nuclei. In 1935 he took over supervision of the Mond Laboratory and increasingly concerned himself with military applications of scientific research. He also successfully enlisted the cooperation of other physicists, especially after Sir Henry Tizard briefed him on work being carried out into RDF. He accompanied Tizard in 1940 on a mission to the US to exchange information on defence-related scientific developments. On his return he was appointed Chief Superintendent of the Air Defence Research and Development Establishment and oversaw major work on radar and proximity fuses. Cockcroft was not intimately involved in the development of an atomic bomb until, in 1944, he went to Canada to take charge of the Montreal Laboratory and the construction of the NRX heavy water reactor. *MS.*

Cogny, Maj Gen René (1904–68). Fr. Appointed Navarre's deputy and commander Tonkin theatre (northern Vietnam), May 1953. Instrumental in "Navarre Plan"; advocated establishment of strong outposts in the enemy's rear. Underestimated Viet Minh capabilities, and must share blame, with Navarre and Castries, for the defeat at Dien Bien Phu.

Colby, William Egan (b.1920). US. Took part in Jedburgh missions to France and Norway 1944–45; director, CIA, 1973–76. *See also* JEDBURGH TEAMS.

Cold War. The term used to describe the condition of extreme ideological hostility, short of war, between the United States and the Soviet Union and their allies. After the Chinese Revolution (1949) it spread to East Asia. Tension sprang from the efforts of the superpowers to reorder the world after 1945. The US sought to establish a world of liberal, capitalist states; the USSR demanded compliant, "friendly" (i.e. communist) neighbours to protect her vulnerable western frontier. The advance of communism in Eastern Europe was interpreted as Soviet aggression. American policy-makers believed, in the words of NSC–68, their central strategy document, that the USSR was "animated by a new fanatic faith antithetical to our own, and seeks to impose its absolute authority over the rest of the world". Ideological competition was extended into all spheres of national life, military, political, technological, cultural and social. After 1960, as tensions were reduced, Cold War strategies became concerned primarily with counterinsurgency. *BHR*.

Colditz. In November 1940, Colditz castle in Saxony was established as Oflag IVC, a special camp for Allied officer POWs. Situated in the heart of Germany, the fortress was an intimidating and supposedly escape-proof prison for some 400 inveterate escapers and special category prisoners of all three British services and members of the armed forces of Poland, Holland, France, Belgium and the US. In spite of all the German precautions, more than 300 escape attempts were made, 30 of which were successful. Colditz was liberated by American forces on April 16 1945.

Collins, Gen Joseph Lawton ("Lightning Joe") (1896–1963). US. COS of the Hawaiian Department in 1941, Collins took command of the Hawaii-organized 25th Infantry Division (nicknamed "Tropic Lightning"; from which his

Gen Collins (*centre*) on Guadalcanal.

own sobriquet derived) in 1942, leading it in the final operations on Guadalcanal, December 1942-February 1943, and New Georgia, July-August 1943. Transferring to the European theatre, he commanded VII Corps in Bradley's US First Army, heading the Utah beach landings in the Normandy invasion, June 6 1944. In the breakout from the beachhead, VII Corps particularly distinguished itself at St-Lô, July 25-31, where, although taking 1,000-plus casualties on the first day, Collins held off German counterattacks on the left while thrusting forward on the right to secure Coutances and Avranches. Collins' hard-driving leadership (although called a "G.I.'s General", he could be ruthless when necessary) here, and subsequently at the Falaise Gap, Aachen and in the Ardennes, won the admiration of Bradley and Montgomery; in April 1945, VII Corps joined hands with the Soviet XXXVI Corps on the Elbe at Dessau. Collins was US Army Chief of Staff, 1949-53, and later was for a time President Eisenhower's personal representative in Saigon, Vietnam. *RO'N*.

Collins, Gen Michael (1890–1922). Irish. A member of the Irish Volunteers from 1909, Collins served six months' imprisonment after the Easter Rising 1916. During the Anglo-Irish War 1916-21, he was a leader in rebuilding the Volunteers as the Irish Republican Army: his own urban guerrilla unit ("The Squad") pursued an effective campaign against British intelligence services, culminating in the assassination of 12 British officers on "Bloody Sunday", November 21 1920. A principal negotiator of the treaty establishing the Irish Free State, he

became its provisional premier in January 1922 and subsequently C-in-C of its army. Regarded by extreme Republicans as a traitor for agreeing to Ireland's partition, he was killed when his armoured car was ambushed during a tour of military inspection in Cork on August 22 1922. *RO'N*. *See also* ANGLO-IRISH WAR; IRISH REPUBLICAN ARMY.

Collishaw, Air Vice Marshal Raymond (1893–1976). Canadian. Collishaw, from British Columbia, scored 60 victories as a fighter pilot with the RNAS and RAF on the Western Front, 1916–18. He later became an Air Vice Marshal and commanded Numbers 202 and 204 Groups of the RAF in the Western Desert, 1940–41.

Colmar Pocket. Although the US 6th Army Group succeeded in reaching Strasbourg by November 23 1944, elements of the German Nineteenth Army clung to a position on the west bank of the Rhine around the town of Colmar in Alsace. The elimination of this bridgehead, the "Colmar Pocket", was essential to Eisenhower's plan to establish a secure line along the Rhine before crossing the river, but the Germans held out for over two months against the overstretched and undermanned 6th Army Group. Indeed, as part of Operation "North Wind", launched late on December 31 1944, German units advanced northwards from the pocket and were within 13 miles (21km) of Strasbourg when halted by French troops. However, towards the end of January 1945, the US Seventh Army and French First Army combined in a two-pronged attack from the north and south and by February 9 the pocket was cleared of German units *PJS*.

Cologne, Thousand-Bomber raid on (May 30–31 1942). A staggering 1,046 British bombers (four from Training Command; the rest from Bomber Command) set course for Cologne in what was substantially the largest air operation ever undertaken to date. The front line strength of Bomber Command at the time was under 500, so that more than 500 of the aircraft and crews came from Operational Training Units. Forty were lost and 116 returned damaged. Six hundred acres of Cologne were devastated. At the risk of the whole of its front line and all its reserves in a single night, Bomber Command secured its first real success against a major German target. *ANF.*

Combined Bomber Offensive (CBO). Air attack on Germany by British Bomber Command and US Eighth (later also US Fifteenth) Air Forces. Decided upon at the Casablanca Conference, January 1943.

Combined Chiefs of Staff. The British Chiefs and the American Joint Chiefs of Staff acting together in meetings or by liaison during World War II to advise the Prime Minister and the President and to authorize directives to commanders-in-chief.

Combined Operations. A British inter-service command later joined by the Americans which emerged in 1940-41 from Churchill's determination to mount commando raids. Its most famous action was the Dieppe raid of August 1942 under Mountbatten's command.

Comintern. The Third (Communist) International, founded by Trotsky 1919, was originally meant to be a world-wide organization, independent of any particular state, for the spread of communist principles. It was based in Moscow; after Trotsky's fall, Stalin made it the tool of Russian foreign policy, and dissolved it formally in 1943. The dissolution was a cosmetic gesture, meant to reassure the governments of the USA and UK that the USSR was not currently pursuing an anti-capitalist policy; meanwhile, such moles as Anthony Blunt and Harry Dexter White remained in place, being run by the KGB or the GRU. *MF.*

Commando. In the Second Boer War (1899–1902), irregular units of mounted Boer riflemen. Since 1940, battalion-sized units of specially-trained dismounted infantry (e.g., Royal Marines Commandos).

Commonwealth Boomerang (Australian, WWII). Single-seat reconnaissance fighter/fighter-bomber. Hurriedly designed early 1942 to counter Japanese threat. Prototype flew May 29 1942; production aircraft into service from October 10 1942. Proved popular, effective and versatile, flying from bases in Australia, New Guinea and New Britain. Total production 250. One Australian-built Pratt and Whitney R-1830 S3C4-G engine; max. speed 305mph (488kph); two 20mm cannon and four 0.303in machine guns.

Commonwealth Division (Korea). The formation of a Commonwealth Division was considered early in the Korean War, but although Britain and Australia agreed in principle, Canada delayed until December 1950. The 1st Commonwealth Division was formally activated under a British commander, Maj Gen A J H Cassels, on July 28 1951. It consisted of Australian, British, Canadian, Indian and New Zealand units. The largest contingent was British and included five battalions of infantry. Canada provided an infantry brigade and Australia two infantry battalions. New Zealand was represented by a regiment of field artillery and a transport platoon. India sent the 60th (Parachute) Field Ambulance. South Africa, which had no ground forces in Korea, later sent a team of officers. The Commonwealth Division served as part of Ist Corps, Eighth Army. *CM. See also* AUSTRALIAN FORCES; BRITISH FORCES; NEW ZEALAND FORCES.

Company (British Army). Sub-unit of infantry battalion, commanded by a major and comprising a small HQ and three rifle platoons. In US and most other armies, "company" is used to describe similarly sized sub-units of any arm or service.

Compiègne. In a forest near this northern French town, the armistice of November 11 1918 was signed in Foch's railway carriage. Hitler used the same scene for the signing of the French armistice on June 22 1940. Subsequently the Germans destroyed the carriage to prevent the full circle of humiliation in it.

Con Thien, Battle of (1967). Con Thien was a forward artillery base established by US Marines just south of the Demilitarized Zone.

As construction began in 1967 on McNamara's Wall, for which Con Thien was to be the western terminus, the North Vietnamese began probing with artillery barrages and ground assaults. The main objective of especially intense North Vietnamese attacks in September was almost certainly to divert attention from plans for the upcoming Tet offensive. The People's Army (PAVN) 324B and 325C Divisions besieged elements of the US 3rd Marine Division. Concentrated strikes by B-52s and tactical air and naval support broke the siege on October 4. *WST. See also* "NEUTRALIZE" OPERATION.

Forced labour in Germany

Concentration camps. Established in Germany shortly after Hitler's assumption of power in 1933. The first camps were opened near Munich and Berlin. Many of the Nazis' political opponents were arrested and placed in "protective custody" in special camps where their "anti-social" tendencies were to be eradicated. Similarly, Jews, gypsies, vagabonds, homosexuals, pacifists, trade unionists, Jehovah's Witnesses and even out-of-favour Nazis were amongst those imprisoned in concentration camps. The outbreak of World War II brought about a radical change in the system. The original six camps in Germany were expanded and new camps were set up throughout Occupied Europe to deal with millions of Soviet prisoners of war and foreign opponents of Nazi domination. The pretence of the concentration camp as an "institute for reform" was effectively stripped away as the Nazis began the systematic extermination of "inferior races" with the implementation of the "Final Solution". Millions of Jews were transported from all over Europe to the death camps of Poland, such as Auschwitz, Treblinka and Maidanek, where they were systematically slaughtered. In addition, some camps were developed by the SS into massive industrial complexes in which the inmates were used as slave labour. The camps varied in size and function but in each there was a common disregard for the humanity, rights and physical well-being of the prisoners who suffered as a result of disease, starvation, neglect, overwork and brutality. *MS*.

Condor Legion. The establishment of the Condor Legion in November 1936 formalized Nazi Germany's support for Franco when it became clear that the Spanish Civil War would be protracted. Its total strength was to vary between 5,000 and 10,000 men. The Luftwaffe contingent played a crucial, sometimes decisive, role in the major battles of the war. Its Junkers 52 bombers and Heinkel 51 biplane fighters, increasing to four squadrons each, began to be replaced by Messerschmitt 109s and Heinkel 111s in 1937. It pioneered the use of napalm; and carpet-bombing, first tried at the siege of Oviedo, was perfected at Guernica. Apart from a general staff advisory role, army elements included heavy machine gun units, artillery, 88mm anti-aircraft guns, and Panzer Mk Is. A naval advisory staff was based on the pocket battleships *Deutschland* and *Admiral Scheer* which were used in several coastal bombardments. *AB*.

Coningham, Air Marshal Sir Arthur "Maori" (1895–1948). Br. From July 1941, Commander 204th Group in Cyrenaica, which became the Western Desert Air Force in October 1941; Commander Allied Tactical Air Forces during the Tunisian, Sicilian, and Italian campaigns until January 1944 when he left Italy to command 2nd Tactical during the Northwest European campaign.

Connolly, James (1868–1916). Irish. Marxist, organized dock and transport workers in Dublin into a small citizen army; led them during the abortive Easter Rising in Dublin in 1916; wounded and executed.

Conqueror. British hunter-killer nuclear-powered submarine of 4,900 tons. Sent to South Atlantic, with others, in April–May 1982, during the Falklands War. On instructions from London, she torpedoed the Argentine cruiser *General Belgrano* on May 2.

Conrad von Hötzendorf, Field Marshal Franz Freiherr (1852–1925). Austrian. As Austria's Chief of General Staff from 1907, Conrad, encouraged by his German counterpart, von Moltke, advocated a war to bind up the crumbling Austro-Hungarian empire. In 1911 he suggested a pre-emptive strike against Italy, then embroiled in Libya, to "rectify" the Italo-Austrian frontier; in June–July 1914, his insistence on a threatening ultimatum to Serbia following the Sarajevo assassination did much to precipitate World War I. Although the Austrian army was poorly-equipped and, because of his own vacillation, slow to mobilize, Conrad launched simultaneous offensives on two fronts. The Galician campaign, which he personally coordinated, ended in disaster; in the Serbian campaign, the Austrians were decisively defeated at the Jadar river. Replaced as CGS by Arz von Straussenberg in 1917, Conrad shared command of the Austrian offensive on the Piave river, June 1918, with Borojevic von Bojna. His Eleventh Army was repulsed with heavy losses early in the battle and failed to support Borojevic's temporary gains. *RO'N*.

Convoys and the convoy system. The organization of merchant ships into groups escorted by warships for protection in time of war goes back at least to the medieval period. It had been a standby of Britain in earlier wars, but was inexplicably abandoned in the late 19th century on the supposition that steam and other technical developments had changed everything. Hard experience in World War I proved this not to be so. Convoy was adopted just in time (1917) to prevent defeat by the U-boat campaign against shipping. World War II merely reinforced the message that the convoy is the best way of destroying enemy raiders, surface and sub-

marine, as well as protecting merchant ships. It may seem to be a defensive measure but this is not so: the convoy forms the bait to attract raiders. In the anti-submarine war, the majority of U-boats were found and sunk in the vicinity of convoys, giving far more successes than the meaningless patrolling favoured by all too many "offensive-minded" naval officers. Convoys also empty the ocean of other targets, then present too many at once.

Atlantic convoy: vital in two world wars

Even in 1914 there were convoys for troopships, and the main fleets with their destroyer escorts were in fact convoys themselves. The British convoyed the Scandinavian trade, vulnerable to German raids. The vital collier trade to France was escorted before the general adoption of convoy, forced on a reluctant Admiralty by Lloyd George. This proved a dramatic and immediate success, and before the end of the war, air escort of convoys had demonstrated its value in preventing ships being sunk.

The sinking of the liner *Athenia* at the beginning of World War II led the British into adopting convoy from the start. The methods of controlling merchant shipping, organizing the ports, and the rest of the infrastructure developed in 1917 were already in place and functioned well, despite an initial lack of escorts. They would be adopted by the Allies and copied by the enemy. Convoys were designated by a numerical code with a two-letter prefix depending on the port of destination or assembly – HX and SC for convoys from Halifax, Nova Scotia to the UK, OG for those from the UK to Gibraltar, PQ and QP for the outward- and homeward-bound Arctic convoys,

C

to be later replaced by JW and RA respectively. They were to cover the world, but probably the best-known are those fought through to revictual Malta against heavy air and sea attack (of which Operation "Pedestal" in August 1942 was the most spectacular) and the grim Arctic convoys to Murmansk and Archangel, which also turned into full-scale engagements (the disaster of PQ17, the fiercely contested success of PQ18 and the heroic defence of JW51B – the Battle of the Barents Sea – all in 1942, are the best known). The fierce actions round the Gibraltar convoy HG76 in which the first escort carrier, *Audacity* proved herself and was then sunk in 1941, involved air and submarine attack. The dramatic battles of March-April 1943 in which the balance of the Battle of the Atlantic swung first one way then the other were of air and surface escorts against submarines. HX229 and SC122 lost 21 ships in return for only one U-boat. However, ONS5 was fought through in April, losing 12 ships but seven U-boats were sunk, and SC130 a month later lost no ships against five U-boats sunk.

The dire results of failing to plan for convoy were illustrated by the great success of American submarines against Japanese commerce in the Pacific, where the Japanese response was too little, too late. Postwar doubt has been expressed at the future of convoy in an atomic age, but there still seems no better answer to the protection of commerce, and we have recently seen it revived during the Persian Gulf War. *DJL*.

Coral Sea, Battle of the (May 4–8 1942). In May 1942, the Japanese moved into the south Pacific with the object of occupying territory that would isolate Australia. Their naval forces were divided into six separate bodies, the main battle group consisting of two fleet carriers, *Shokaku* and *Zuikaku*. Overall command of the Japanese operation was exercised by Vice Adm Shigeyoshi Inouye, the main carrier force being led by Vice Adm Takeo Takagi. The American naval command, alerted by excellent intelligence, dispatched Task Force 17 under the command of Rear Adm Fletcher, which was built up around two fleet carriers,

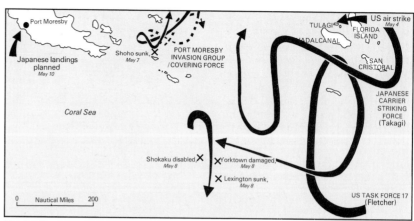

Battle of the Coral Sea, May 4–8 1942: a major Japanese advance was checked

Lexington and *Yorktown*, to the Coral Sea, with orders to thwart Japanese plans to capture Port Moresby in New Guinea and Tulagi in the lower Solomons.

On May 4, planes from *Yorktown* struck Japanese shipping at Tulagi, sinking a destroyer, two patrol boats, and a transport. On May 7, an air strike from both American carriers on the Port Moresby invasion force sank the light carrier *Shoho*. That same day, Japanese aircraft from the main battle group sank an American destroyer and badly damaged a fleet oiler, which later went down, and attempted, unsuccessfully, to attack the American force at night. On the morning of May 8, American air attacks disabled *Shokaku*, while Japanese aircraft damaged *Yorktown*, and made torpedo and bomb hits on *Lexington*, which subsequently resulted in fires and explosions that caused her to be abandoned and scuttled. The battle ended with the withdrawal of the American force.

American warship losses were far more serious than those suffered by the Japanese. Japanese losses in aircraft and personnel, on the other hand, were substantially greater than those suffered by the Americans; the combination of ship damage and air group casualties deprived the Japanese of the use of two fleet carriers that might have turned the tide at Midway a month later, while the Port Moresby operation was cancelled. The Battle of the Coral Sea was both the first time that a major Japanese advance had been turned back, and the first naval battle in which the opposing ships did not come into direct contact. *JTS*.

Cordon and search operations. Sometimes called search and clear operations; employed by American and South Vietnamese forces where enemy troops mingled with the population in confined areas. These operations used high troop densities and combined arms to seal off populated areas. Vietnamese National and Special Branch Police then corralled the population for interrogation in order to identify and remove enemy combatants, with minimum destruction of civilian lives and property. *See also* SEARCH AND DESTROY OPERATIONS.

Corfu, incidents at (1923 and 1946). In August 1923 four Italian members of an international boundary commission were murdered in Greece. Mussolini used this as an excuse to seize the strategically important Greek island of Corfu and, after a brief naval bombardment, the island was occupied. The Greeks appealed to the League of Nations and international pressure secured an Italian withdrawal and the payment of a Greek indemnity. A second incident took place in 1946 when two British destroyers were severely damaged by Albanian mines laid in the Corfu Channel. *MS*.

Cork and Orrery, Adm of the Fleet, the Earl of (1883–1967). Br. Commander of Allied naval forces at Narvik in 1940. *See also* NORWEGIAN CAMPAIGN.

Corlett, Maj Gen Charles H ("Pete") (1889–1971). US. Corlett led the US 7th Infantry Division at Kwajalein Atoll in February 1944

and was then transferred to Europe to command the US XIX Corps, although his experience of Pacific amphibious operations was largely disregarded by his senior American colleagues in the Normandy invasion planning. Tactically competent, if somewhat laborious in method and intense in manner, Corlett, despite illness during the Normandy campaign, commanded XIX Corps up to the assault on the West Wall north of Aachen, but disagreements with the First Army commander, Hodges, hastened his removal on October 18 1944.

Coronel, Battle of (November 1 1914). Commanding North American and West Indies Station at the outbreak of World War I, Rear Adm Sir Christopher Cradock (1862-1914) was tasked with suppressing German commerce-raiders throughout the Atlantic. Warned that von Spee's East Asiatic Squadron was heading across the Pacific and might round Cape Horn to raid the Falklands, he appealed for reinforcement, receiving only the old, slow *Canopus*.

The German light cruiser *Nürnberg*

Cradock took his squadron into the Pacific. A belated order not to engage without *Canopus* had not reached him – and *Canopus* would have slowed the squadron's speed to around 12 knots, making the hunt for von Spee impossible – so Cradock's force comprised the armoured cruisers *Good Hope* (flagship; 14,100 tons; 2 × 9.2in, 16 × 6in) and *Monmouth* (14 × 6in), light cruiser *Glasgow* and armed merchant cruiser *Otranto*. Von Spee's ships – armoured cruisers *Scharnhorst* (flagship) and *Gneisenau* (each 11,600 tons; 8 × 8.2in, 6 × 5.9in) and light cruisers *Leipzig*, *Dresden* and *Nürnberg* – were

newer, faster and better armoured.

When contact was made off Coronel, central Chile, at about 1630 hours on November 1 1914, von Spee manoeuvred skilfully, using his superior speed both to frustrate Cradock's attempts to close the range (in any case, a heavy swell impeded the use of the British ships' secondary armament) and to take advantage of the failing light. Opening from 12,000yd (10,970m) at about 1900 hours, when the British ships were outlined against the sunset, his gunnery was no less effective: *Good Hope* sank with all hands at 1935; *Monmouth*, severely damaged, broke away but was intercepted and sunk by *Nürnberg*. *Glasgow* and *Otranto* had obeyed Cradock's early order to escape. Cradock's defeat provoked immediate British reinforcement in the South Atlantic, leading to von Spee's destruction at the Falklands. *RO'N*.

Corps. 1) Army formation of not less than two divisions, commanded by a Lt Gen, and with its own complement of "corps troops" including combat and logistic units. 2) A functional branch of the Service e.g. Corps of Royal Engineers.

Corregidor, operations (1942; 1945). The heavily-fortified island of Corregidor ("The Rock") off the southern tip of the Bataan Peninsula guarded the entrance to Manila Bay, Luzon, Philippines, and was Gen MacArthur's (and subsequently Gen Wainwright's) HQ during the Bataan campaign. Following the fall of Bataan, April 9 1942, Corregidor was subjected to intensive Japanese air and artillery bombardment: its 15,000 personnel, although protected by a subterranean network centring on the Malinta tunnel, suffered great privation through lack of food and medical supplies. The Japanese amphibious assault began on May 5: Wainright was unable to exploit the attackers' initial weakness and, with the arrial of Japanese tanks and artillery, was forced to surrender on May 6.

The US reconquest of Corregidor began with aerial bombardment from January 22 1945, intensified before amphibious landings by elements of 3rd Infantry Division and an airborne assault by 503rd

Parachute Regimental Combat Team, February 16, The US bridgeheads were quickly secured, but fierce Japanese resistance persisted until the beginning of March. *MS*.

Corsair, Vought F-4U (US, WWII and after). Single-seat shipboard fighter-bomber. Prototype flew May 29 1940; first delivery July 31 1942; first combat mission February 13 1943. Not well regarded as shipboard aircraft but outstandingly effective in action. Widely used USN, USMC, RN, RNZN. Further operational use Korea and Suez (latter with *Aéronavale française*). Production continued until January 31 1953: total 12,571. One 2,250/2,450hp Pratt and Whitney R-2800-8W (-18W) engine; max. speed 425mph (680kph); six 0.5in machine guns, 2,000lb (900kg) bombs or eight 5in rockets.

Corvette. Small warship of about 1,500 tons, usually armed with a 4in gun and depth charges, developed by Britain, primarily for convoy protection, from 1939. Some 150 were laid down in Britain and Canada during World War II and some were transferred to the US Navy. They had much success against the U-boat threat in the Atlantic.

Cos and Leros, Aegean islands. Occupied by British troops after the Italian Armistice in September 1943 and recaptured by German troops in November 1943.

COSSAC (Chief of Staff Supreme Allied Commander). It was decided at the Casablanca Conference in January 1943 to make a plan for the Allied invasion of northern France and this was entrusted to Lt Gen Sir Frederick Morgan, a diplomatically gifted British officer, who, with the title of COSSAC, established an Anglo-American inter-service planning staff. As the appointment of the Supreme Commander (Eisenhower) was delayed until the Cairo Conference in December 1943, COSSAC's position assumed importance. Although radical changes in Morgan's plans were made, his achievement and that of his staff were important elements in the ultimate success of Operation "Overlord". *ANF*.

Cossacks. Granted a degree of semi-autonomy by the Tsars in return for military service, the Cossacks constituted an important element in the Imperial and White Russian armies. During World War II, German offers to restore their pre-revolutionary status induced tens of thousands to serve in the Wehrmacht and SS.

Costa Mendes, Nicanor (b.1922). Argentinian. Foreign Minister, who supported the military junta's decision to invade the Falklands in April 1982. Like Adm Anaya, he miscalculated the British reaction as well as the strength of US support for Mrs Thatcher's government. He saw the invasion in diplomatic rather than military terms, and tendered his resignation when it became clear that the British intended to fight.

COSVN. The Central Office for South Vietnam (COSVN) was the command organ headed by secret members of the Lao Dong (Vietnam Communist) Party Central Committee to supervise the war in the South. Originally established in 1951 during the war against France and disbanded in 1954, COSVN was reconstituted in 1961 on orders of the Central Committee in Hanoi to lead the party's Southern branch in the war for reunification. The two men who headed COSVN from 1964 onward, Nguyen Chi Thanh and Pham Hung, were members of the party Political Bureau.

COSVN was the true locus of decision-making for the National Liberation Front (NLF) and the People's Liberation Armed Force (PLAF). However, its jurisdiction did not cover the People's Army (PAVN) in military regions that reported directly to Hanoi. COSVN's role is accurately indicated by its name in Vietnamese, *Trung uong cuc mien Nam*, which should be translated as Central Committee Directorate for the Southern Region. *WST*.

Cotentin peninsula *see* CHERBOURG, CAPTURE OF (1944).

Counter force. A nuclear strategy which emphasizes attacks on the enemy's armed forces, especially its nuclear forces, rather than attacks on population or economic targets. The latter may suffer collateral damage but the attacker may attempt to keep this as limited as possible by careful targeting. The concept was developed early in US Secretary of Defense Robert McNamara's term of office in order to provide the USA with a nuclear strategy which would give the USSR the greatest possible incentive not to widen a nuclear war to attacks on cities. The threat to Soviet cities posed by America's remaining forces would deter Soviet escalation to counter value exchanges. Counter force in this classical form reflected temporary American superiority in range and accuracy of strategic forces, but as the Soviet Union caught up, the USA did not try to maintain that advantage. Declaratory American strategy moved away from counter force although the SIOP continued to contain various counter-force options and still does. The other side, it is assumed, will have every incentive to show equal restraint in response. The Soviet Union has traditionally emphasized counter-force nuclear operations in its doctrine but in a less sophisticated form, trying to gain military advantage or physically to limit US retaliation as much as possible. *EJG*.

Counterinsurgency. Operations designed to defeat irregular or guerrilla forces. The heyday of counterinsurgency was the three decades after 1945 when the collapse of the old colonial empires caused a number of revolutionary wars, the largest of which was in French Indochina/Vietnam. The classic counterinsurgency success was the defeat of the "Malayan People's Anti-British Army" which led Sir Robert Thompson to develop the main exposition of counterinsurgency theory. This emphasized the importance of political action and victory in the struggle for "hearts and minds" as well as good intelligence and effective military operations at the lowest possible level. British success in Malaya had, however, been helped by full political control, support for the guerrillas being limited to one part of the population and the isolation of the enemy from outside support. The Americans did not share these advantages in Vietnam. *EJG*.

Counter Military Potential (CMP). The relative effectiveness of a nuclear missile system against a hard point target, notably a missile silo. The measure of CMP is the equivalent megatonnage divided by the square of the Circular Error Probability. Improving accuracy thus has a disproportionate effect compared with merely increasing warhead yield. The CMP of the Minuteman 2 with its single warhead of 1.2 megatons and CEP of 1,214ft (370m) is five times less than the new MX/Peacekeeper missile with its 300 kiloton warhead and 328ft (100m) CEP. The Soviet Union, with its historically less accurate missiles, had little alternative but to increase yields to improve the CMP of its intercontinental ballistic missile force, but this only had limited effectiveness. The old SS-9 with a single 25 megaton warhead and a CEP of 4,264ft (1,300m) had marginally less CMP than the original version of Minuteman 3 with its much smaller 170 kiloton warhead but 1,214ft (370m) CEP. The increased accuracy of SLBMs will have considerable effects on their CMP. That of Trident D-5 will be four times that of the current primary Soviet counter-force weapon, the giant SS-18 ICBM. *EJG*.

Countervailing strategy. A deterrent strategy formulated by the Carter administration and promulgated in Presidential Decision 59 (PD59) in 1980. Its essence was a range of nuclear-deterrent capabilities and options that might credibly counter the widest possible range of military actions that could be undertaken by the Soviet Union. The aim was on countering such initiatives for deterrence purposes, not necessarily "prevailing". Nevertheless there was a further shift in American targeting policy to emphasize attacks on hostile military targets both nuclear and conventional, attacks on military and political leadership targets and a reorientation of countervalue targets to those industries that supported the war effort rather than those that contributed to general economic recovery. The Reagan administration extended the logic of Presidential Decision 59 into a prevailing strategy, perhaps in some form of protracted nuclear conflict. *EJG*.

Counter value. Striking with nuclear weapons at an opponent's population and socioeconomic base rather than at its armed forces or military infrastructure. A nation usually adopts a primarily counter-value strategy because it possesses insufficient quantity or quality of forces to engage in Counter Force strikes. Small nuclear forces such as those possessed by Britain and France have such an orientation. The former emphasizes attacks on the opponent's capital, the latter the ability to destroy the opponent's "vital works". All nuclear deterrent strategies, however, rest on the ultimate threat of massive counter-value strikes as the final outcome of an escalation process. Counter-value threats have less credibility than counter-force threats for nuclear first use. Certain weapon systems lend themselves more to counter-value than counter-force purposes, notably SLBMs which in the past have lacked sufficient accuracy and which are still more difficult to control than land-based systems. *EJG.*

Bomb damage in Coventry, 1940

Coventry, bombing of (November 14–15 1940). About 550 German bombers, using beam-assisted navigation, dropped about 500 tons of high-explosive and 30 tons of incendiary bombs on the centre of the town, causing massive damage on a hitherto unknown scale. Sixty-three percent of the activity of the town was knocked out and recovery took 35 days. Due to the beams being detected, the British had advance warning of the attack, but their night-fighter capacity was too primitive to take advantage of this. Coventry became the symbol of this kind of warfare, soon to be known as area bombing.

Coventry. British Type 42 destroyer of 4,100 tons. Sunk on May 25 1982 off West Falkland, by four 1,000lb bombs from Argentine Skyhawk – one of 11 British ships hit by the Argentinians during a six-day period.

Cowan, Adm Sir Walter (1871–1956). Br. Cowan saw action on the west coast of Africa, the Sudan and in the Boer War before 1900. In World War I he commanded a battlecruiser at Jutland and then a light cruiser squadron. His most important role was his independent command (as Rear Adm) in the Baltic in 1919-20, fighting an undeclared war with the Russian Bolsheviks which included a CMB (MTB) attack on the Russian base at Kronstadt. His force played an important part in the survival of the Baltic republics. In World War II he returned from retirement to serve with the Commandos, Indian Army and Yugoslav partisans. *DJL.*

Cowans, Gen Sir John (1862–1921). Br. Cowans became Quartermaster-General of the British Army in 1912, occupying the post until 1919. As Quartermaster-General he was responsible for housing, feeding, clothing and equipping the vastly expanded British Army after 1914 as well as providing it with horses and transporting it to the various theatres of operations. The success with which this brilliant administrator handled such a colossal task may be gauged from the fact that he was the only Military Member of the Army Council to remain in office throughout the whole of World War I. *PJS.*

Crace, Adm Sir John Gregory (1887–1968). Br. Commanded Australian squadron supporting Americans in the Pacific (1942).

Cradock, Rear Adm Sir Christopher (1862-1914) *see* CORONEL, BATTLE OF.

CRDA Cant Z.1007bis Alcione (Kingfisher) (Italian, WWII). Medium bomber; crew 5; prototype first flew March 1937; early production aircraft in service at outbreak of World War II but shortages of materials prevented operational use until Greek campaign.

Thereafter *Alcioni* saw much service, notably in Libya, Algeria, and against Malta. Production totalled more than 560. Three 1,000hp Piaggio P. XIbis RC-40 or 1,175hp Piaggio P. XIX engines; max. speed 283mph; (455kph) 2,645lb (1,200kg) bombs or two torpedoes, two 12.7mm and two 7.7mm machine guns.

Creagh, Maj Gen Sir Michael O'Moore (1892–1970). Br. Commanded British 7th Armoured Division in Western Desert campaign against Italians, 1940–41. Successful in ambush of Italian Tenth Army at Beda Fomm, February 1941, but Division suffered heavily during "Battleaxe" operations against Afrika Korps.

Crerar, Lt Gen Sir Henry Duncan Graham (1888–1965). Canadian. Equally distinguished as staff officer and field commander, Crerar masterminded the expansion and training of Canadian forces, 1935–41, before dropping rank in order to take command of I Canadian Corps in Sicily and Italy, 1943–44. In 1944 he was C-in-C, First Canadian Army, which, as part of Montgomery's 21st Army Group after the Normandy invasion, distinguished itself at Falaise and in the retaking of the Channel ports. In February–March 1945, with much of 21st Army Group added to First Canadian Army, he directed the Rhineland offensive Operation "Veritable": in spite of stiff resistance and adverse weather, his troops broke through the Siegfried Line at Udem (February 27) and captured the last German bridgehead on the Rhine (March 10). *RO'N.*

Cressy. British armoured cruiser. On September 22 1914, while patrolling the southern North Sea with sisters *Aboukir* and *Hogue*, all three were sunk by *U-9*, thus demonstrating submarine menace and the impossibility of close blockade.

Crete, German invasion of (May 20–June 1 1941). After his occupation of Greece in April, Hitler ordered *Luftflotte 4* (Löhr) to capture Crete by airborne assault. *Fliegerkorps XI* (Student) with its Assault Regiment and 7th Air Division provided the air-landing force and 500 transport aircraft; 5th Mountain Division followed up by air and sea. On the island, Freyberg had two of his own New Zealand brigades and one Australian brigade, brought back from Greece with only light weapons, and one British brigade.

Student came close to failure, suffering very high casualties amongst his airborne troops, and the defeat of the seaborne follow-up by the Royal Navy. Nevertheless, the capture of Máleme airfield by the end of the second day enabled him to land the Mountain troops in transport aircraft. The British decision to evacuate the island was taken on May 27, due to

Germans mop up stragglers on Crete.

heavy naval losses suffered from air attacks by *Fliegerkorps X* (Geisler). Evacuation was completed by June 1. Student had lost over 6,000 men; Freyberg about half that number in casualties, but 12,000 of his troops were taken prisoner. The RN lost three cruisers and six destroyers sunk, and 17 warships damaged. Hitler, however, never mounted another major airborne landing. *WGFJ.*

Crimean campaign (1941–44). The rapid German advance on the southern flank of "Barbarossa" and the collapse of Budenny's South-West Front enabled von Manstein's Eleventh Army to advance to the Crimea. On October 28 1941 Soviet defence lines across the Perekop isthmus were breached and German and Romanian forces swept into the Crimean peninsula. Soviet resistance concentrated at the extensively-fortified naval base of Sevastopol, with a 52,000-strong garrison reinforced by units shipped across the Black Sea from Odessa. Manstein's siege of Sevastopol was interrupted in De-

cember, when he moved against Soviet landings at Kerch and Feodosia, frustrating Soviet attempts to enlarge the bridgeheads and, in May 1942, attacking Kerch. Within a fortnight, the Germans shattered Soviet Fortyseventh, Fiftyfirst and Fortyfourth Armies, driving them from the Kerch Peninsula with 176,000 casualties. Now able to concentrate on Sevastopol, Eleventh Army attacked on June 7 after a five-day bombardment, securing the city on July 3.

In April 1944, Tolbukhin's Fourth Ukrainian Front attacked across the Perekop isthmus while Yeremenko's Independent Coastal Army struck in the Kerch Peninsula. The 150,000 German and Romanian defenders of the Crimea were forced to retreat into Sevastopol. Pounded by Soviet artillery and bombers, the defences were quickly stormed: only a few German units escaped by sea before the city fell on May 9. In the Soviet reconquest of the Crimea the German Seventeenth Army was virtually annihilated, sustaining 110,000 casualties. *MS.*

Crittenberger, Lt Gen Willis D (1890–1980). US. Commander IV US Corps during the Italian campaign.

Crockatt, Brig Norman Richard (1894–1956). Br. Fought in France and Palestine, 1914–18; founded and led MI9 1939–45. *See also* ESCAPE.

Crocker, Gen Sir John (1896–1963). Br. Commander IX Corps in Tunisia until April 30 1943; commander, I Corps, Normandy-Germany 1944–45.

Cronjé, Gen Pieter Arnoldus (1835–1911). South African. "The Lion of Potchefstroom" of the First Boer War, 1880-81, acted vigorously in October 1899, immediately commencing operations against Mafeking and Kimberley. However, much of the credit for his successes at the Modder river and Magersfontein in November-December 1899 must go to De La Rey, Cronjé's much-resented "adviser". A patriarchal figure, Cronjé allowed large numbers of women and children in his columns: this contributed to his

downfall at Paardeberg, February 1900, where he surrendered rather than attempt a breakout. So great a blow was this to Boer morale that, on his return from imprisonment on St Helena at the war's end, Cronjé was not forgiven by his countrymen. *RO'N.*

Cruewell, Lt Gen Ludwig (1892-1958). Ger. Commander of the Afrika Korps during Operation "Crusader", and in the early stages of the Battle of Gazala until he was shot down and captured while flying in his Storch reconnaissance aircraft over the battlefield on May 26 1942.

Cruise missile. A missile which carries its warhead to its target using aerodynamic lift rather than throwing it ballistically; effectively a pilotless aircraft. Most tactical missiles are cruise missiles, but the term is usually used for long-range systems. The first cruise missile to be used operationally on a large scale was the German Fi 103 or V-1 used for strategic bombing in 1944-45. Postwar, the USAF first concentrated on cruise missiles rather than ballistic and developed Snark for intercontinental missions and Matador and Mace for intermediate ranges. The US Navy developed the Regulus series for use from surface ships and submarines. The problems with such early systems were vulnerability because of large size and high altitude and guidance inaccuracies due to gyro drift on long missions. The early cruise missiles were therefore overshadowed and superseded by ballistic missiles for strategic missions. Then, in the 1970s, the problems of size and accuracy were solved by the development of small turbofan engines and the development of miniaturized terrain contour matching (TERCOM) guidance systems. The latter allow a very small low-flying missile to compare a radar altimeter picture of the ground over which it is passing with a computer memory and so compensate for drift and other errors. This allows very high accuracy, with CEPs in the 33-98ft (10-30m) category, over ranges of 1,500 miles (2,500km). The USA has developed two types of missile, the air-launched cruise missile (ALCM) and the Tomahawk in both ground (GLCM) and sea (SLCM) variants; GLCMs are being dismantled under the INF Treaty. The Soviet Union is developing similar systems. Tomahawk can also be fitted with supplementary homing devices for use with a conventional warhead. *EJG*.

Cruiser. In the 1880s, the old categories of frigate and corvette were merged in the new type known as "cruiser", or rather the word represented a range of types. There were the large "armoured cruisers", more lightly armed and protected than contemporary battleships but usually faster. Small torpedo cruisers were slowly developed (principally by the Germans) into light cruisers for scouting duties. It was mostly the British, in need of large numbers of trade protection ships, who built an intermediate (second-class cruiser) type. There were also "colonial cruisers", intended for imperial policing duties, which merged (and really belonged) with the sloops and gunboats. Size and fighting power varied.

The decade before World War I saw the armoured cruiser supplanted by the battlecruiser. Both Germans and British evolved sturdy classes of medium-sized cruisers named after towns and cities. By 1914 the latter, by way of the small but fast "scouts", had evolved a new and fast type of "light cruiser" for leading destroyers and scouting in the North Sea. This grew in size to become the 6in armed light cruiser of the interwar years. The limitations set by the 1921 Washington Treaty caused the development of a new type of "heavy cruiser" armed with 8in guns. By 1939, nearly all cruisers could carry catapult float planes.

After 1945, the aircraft capability was removed, although finally to be replaced by helicopters. Cruisers were the first ships to carry anti-aircraft missiles, but also became the last ships to carry big guns (until the Americans revived their battleships). Now, those cruisers that are left are basically larger versions of frigates and guided missile destroyers. *DJL*.

"Cruiser" tanks. Family of fast, but thinly armoured British tanks,

introduced from 1935. *See also* TANKS.

Crutchley, Adm Sir Victor Alexander Charles (b.1893). Br. Awarded the VC in the blocking attempt on Ostend, 1918, he began World War II as Capt of the battleship *Warspite*; became Commodore of Devonport Barracks (1940); and in 1942 took command of the Australian squadron serving with the US Pacific Fleet. His force suffered severely in the Battle of Savo Island, August 1942.

Cuban Missile Crisis (1962). The world moved to the brink of nuclear war in October 1962 when US planes spotted bases under way in Cuba for 42 Soviet IRBMS. On October 22 as a "graduated response" alternative to an air strike, Kennedy announced a naval quarantine to block Soviet shipment of the missiles. While Soviet ships turned away, Kruschev on October 27 offered to remove the bases if the US pledged not to invade Cuba in the future. A call next day for removal of US missiles from Turkey was publicly ignored by the US but privately promised. On the 28th the crisis ended with both sides making concessions for peace – the no-invasion pledge in return for dismantling of the bases. *See also* KENNEDY, JOHN F.

Cumming, Sir Mansfield, Capt (1859–1923). Br. First head of MI6, fostered mystique of clandestine leadership.

Cunningham, Lt Gen Sir Alan (1887–1984). Br. C-in-C East Africa, November 1940; expelled the Italians from Italian Somaliland and Ethiopia in 1940–41; Commander Eighth Army, September 1941; relieved of his command due to ill health in November 1941 during Operation "Crusader"; subsequently became British High Commissioner and C-in-C in Palestine during the Jewish revolt, 1945–48.

Cunningham, Adm of the Fleet Viscount (1883–1963). Br. C-in-C, Mediterranean Fleet 1939–42 and again in 1943. Head of the Naval Delegation in Washington, 1942. Naval C-in-C, North African campaign, 1942. First Sea Lord, 1943–46. The victor of Taranto (1940)

and Matapan (1941), Cunningham is generally regarded as Britain's greatest naval commander in World War II. He was good at selecting subordinates and his offensive spirit and willingness to accept calculated risks enabled him to achieve remarkable successes in the Mediterranean against the Italian Fleet. German intervention and the arrival of powerful forces of dive-bombers exposed the shortcomings of surface sea power within range of shore-based air opposition. Cunningham sustained particularly heavy losses in the Greek and Crete campaigns when he was required to evacuate the British army twice in most adverse conditions. For a time thereafter the British were driven out of the Mediterranean. It may be that Cunningham, who had distinguished himself as a junior officer at the Dardanelles and Zeebrugge, too firmly believed that surface naval strength could avail despite the conditions introduced by air power in World War II. As First Sea Lord, Cunningham's single-minded devotion to the navy did not make him an easy colleague for his fellow chiefs of staff. Nevertheless, he emerged from the war laden with honours. *ANF*.

Cunningham, Adm of the Fleet Sir John (1885–1962). Br. Commanded the British naval force intended to cover the landing of Free French troops in the abortive Dakar operation, September 1940, and then at the Admiralty as Fourth Sea Lord. In late 1942 he became C-in-C Levant, succeeding Adm A B Cunningham as C-in-C Mediterranean when the two commands were merged, October 1943. First Sea Lord (again succeeding A B Cunningham, to whom he was not related), 1946–48, during the Royal Navy's postwar reduction.

Cunningham, Gp Capt John ("Cat's Eyes") (b.1917). Br. Outstanding and much-decorated RAF night-fighter pilot, World War II. With his AI operator, Sergeant C F Rawnsley, played important part in development of radar-assisted night interception. Subsequently a leading test pilot.

Curragh mutiny (1914). On March 20 1914, Brig Hubert Gough, com-

C

manding the British Army's 3rd Cavalry Brigade at the Curragh, near Dublin, and 58 of the Brigade's 71 officers stated that they would resign their commissions if ordered to use force to impose Irish Home Rule on the "loyalist" province of Ulster. Many senior officers, including Sir Henry Wilson, then Director of Military Operations at the War Office, sympathized with the "mutineers", who were swiftly assured that they would not be ordered to Ulster.

Curtin, John (1885–1945). Australian. Curtin, the leader of his country's Labour Party, was Australian Prime Minister from October 1941 until his death in July 1945. He firmly believed in the British Commonwealth but, soon after taking office, publicly acknowledged that Australia was now strategically dependent upon the US.

Cushman, Lt Gen Robert E, Jr (1914–85). US. National security adviser to Vice-President Richard Nixon in 1957; appointed commander of the US 3rd Marine Amphibious Force, Vietnam, June 1967. He was in charge of all Marines and other American forces defending Khe Sanh, Con Thien, the Route 9 outposts, Hue and I Corps during the 1968 Tet offensive. He left Vietnam in 1969 convinced that too much emphasis on static defence had limited the effectiveness of American forces there.

Cuxhaven raid. On December 25 1914, British seaplanes made an unsuccessful attack against the German airship sheds at Cuxhaven. A German airship and seaplanes, in turn, attacked the British seaplane carriers and escorts, making this the first naval action in which aircraft were the principal strike weapons on both sides.

Cyprus (1955–1960). Having been a British Protectorate since 1878, Cyprus became a Crown Colony in 1925. In 1950 it was clear that 95 percent of Greek Cypriots wanted union with Greece ("Enosis") but the British government refused to consider it. The militant wing of the movement (EOKA) gained much popular support. Its leader, Col George Grivas ("Dighenis") was fanatical and uncompromising whereas Archbishop Makarios III,

the political leader, was prepared to accept independence without the corollary of Enosis. Grivas and his followers were fully prepared to use terrorist tactics to attain their aim; Makarios deplored murder but condoned sabotage. EOKA leant heavily on civilian support and the hard-core terrorists moved freely among the population, on whom they relied for safe houses and supplies. By operating against the British garrison's lines of communication in rural areas and through acts of selective assassination in towns, Grivas expected the security forces to overreact, which they sometimes did, thereby providing EOKA with much good propaganda. EOKA also terrorized Greek Cypriots hostile to Enosis. Out of 238 civilians killed by EOKA between April 1955 and March 1959, 203 were ethnic Greeks.

British troops were deployed in large numbers to sweep and clear rural areas of terrorists. From 1955 they were under command of Field Marshal Sir John Harding, who combined the posts of C-in-C and Governor. Makarios was exiled to the Seychelles. As the campaign hardened, recourse was made to detention centres for EOKA suspects, and the security forces tended to use increasingly tough methods. A Turkish paramilitary organization (TMT) was formed; initially for self-defence, it soon became involved in the campaign of murder as EOKA turned on the Turkish population, which tended to support the security forces. Whilst the national governments of Greece and Turkey were reluctant to confront each other over the Cyprus issue, the threat of all-out civil war drove Britain to the negotiating table.

On February 19 1959, an agreement was signed in London creating an independent Republic of Cyprus within the Commonwealth; Britain retained 99 sq miles (256 sq km), to be garrisoned as Sovereign Base Areas (SBAS). On March 1, Makarios returned to Cyprus as president elect and the Republic was formally proclaimed on August 16 1960. Four years later, Grivas returned to the island to resume his campaign for Enosis. He had to wait until 1967, following the "colonels' coup", for a Greek government which would support him openly. In 1974 he

instigated a revolt against President Makarios, who was forced to escape to the SBA, whilst Turkish troops landed at Kyrenia in the north of the island to establish a de facto partition. This has been the status quo ever since, with a UN peacekeeping force to oversee the Greco-Turkish demarcation line. The SBAS continue to give Britain a strategic toehold in the Eastern Mediterranean. *MH*.

Cyrenaica, Rommel's first offensive into (March 1941). After landing at Tripoli on February 12, Rommel decided to probe the British positions on the Cyrenaica frontier, held by the newly formed Cyrenaica Command (Neame) with the inexperienced and inadequately equipped 2nd Armoured Division and 9th Australian Division.

On April 2, with only half his Afrika Korps ashore, he attacked, taking Mersa Brega. In an extraordinary feat of improvisation and personal drive, he threw Neame's forces off balance with a rapid advance across the desert via Mechili, capturing Generals Neame, O'Connor and Gambier-Parry on the way, and arriving at Tobruk just too late to take it before the Australians could settle down in its defence. The rest of Neame's troops fell back to the Egyptian frontier. *WGFJ*.

Cyrenaica, Rommel's second offensive into (January 1942). After his defeat during Operation "Crusader", Rommel's tank losses were quickly replaced by new shipments that reached Tripoli in mid-January. British forces were again depleted, this time by the need to send troops to the Far East, and were logistically overstretched. Rommel struck back on January 21, forcing Eighth Army (Ritchie) to fall back to the Gazala Line, covering Tobruk. A stalemate ensued while both sides prepared for the decisive encounter that was to come in June 1942. *WGFJ*.

Czechoslovak Legion. Formed in Russia to fight the Central Powers, the Legion became enmeshed in the Civil War. From 1918 it controlled the Trans-Siberian Railway and frequently clashed with the Bolsheviks before its withdrawal in February 1920.

Dakar, Free French landing at (September 23–25 1940). Gen de Gaulle, with a largely French force supported by British warships, attempted to oust the Vichy authorities in West Africa. His intentions were leaked by indiscreet talk in London before he sailed. Opposition to him in Dakar was increased by the arrival of French warships from Toulon, which should have been stopped by British forces at Gibraltar. Due to misunderstandings between Whitehall and Adm North at Gibraltar, they were not intercepted. Resistance proved stronger than expected at Dakar, and de Gaulle was forced to withdraw to avoid loss of life through inter-French fighting. Adm North was dismissed on Churchill's orders. *WGFJ.*

Dakota *see* C-47 DAKOTA.

Dak To, Battle of (1967). The effort to halt communist infiltration into South Vietnam's central highlands centred upon the US Army Special Forces camp at Dak To, Kontum province, beginning in June 1967. Elements of the US 173rd Airborne Brigade and 4th Infantry Division reinforced the camp's Special Forces and Montagnard troops to skirmish with the People's Army (PAVN) 24th Regiment. In November a mortar attack on the Dak To airfield hit an ammunition dump, and an American company discovered the PAVN 174th Regiment entrenched on Hill 875, 12 miles (19km) west of the camp. From November 19–23 a reinforced battalion assaulted the hill, attaining the summit after extremely heavy napalm and artillery had forced the PAVN to withdraw. The outcome temporarily blunted the PAVN's ability to stage major highland operations. *WST.*

Daladier, Edouard (1884–1970). Fr. As France's PM and Minister of War before World War II, Daladier led his country's rearmament programme. He resigned in March 1940 but was later tried by the Vichy regime for his responsibility in France's unpreparedness.

D'Albiac, Air Marshal Sir John (1894–1963). Br. Air Commander in Palestine and Transjordan; sent to Greece in November 1940 in command of the RAF contingent

supporting the Greeks during the Italian invasion in the winter of 1940–41; stayed on as Air Commander during the German invasion in April 1941; then sent to Iraq where he helped crush the Rashid Ali rebellion in May 1941, signing the Convention that restored the Iraqi gvernment on June 1. He continued in command in Iraq until March 1942.

Dalmanutha (Bergandal), Battle of (August 21–28 1900), Second Boer War. In a final attempt to preserve the Boers' last rail supply link with the coast, Botha entrenched 5,000 men on a 30-mile (48km) line along the Delagoa Bay Railway between Belfast and Machadodorp (President Kruger's headquarters). Advancing from the west, Roberts divided his 20,000-strong force (losses 500), sending Buller with 8,000 men and 38 guns to attack from the south. Botha, expecting the main attack to be made on his flank, had left his centre weak: Buller's main thrust fell on a sector held by only 74 Zarps (Johannesburg Police). The Boers were forced to evacuate their positions: many, like Kruger, fled to the safety of Portuguese East Africa. *RO'N.*

Dalton, Dr and Lord (Edward) Hugh (John Neale) (1887–1962). Br. As minister of economic warfare, 1940–42, responsible for SOE in its early stages of growth.

Damascus campaign (September–October 1918). By mid-September 1918, Allenby was ready to launch his final offensive against the Turks. His command numbered some 69,000 men (including 12,000 cavalry) and 540 guns. Opposing him, under Liman von Sanders, were three understrength Turkish armies – Fourth (Jemal Pasha); Seventh (Atatürk); Eighth (Jerad Pasha): totalling some 40,000 men (including 4,000 cavalry) and 430 guns. Turkish morale, already low, was further shaken by continual raids by the Arab guerrillas under Col T E Lawrence and Prince Feisal. Allenby also had air superiority, enabling him to carry out thorough reconnaissance while denying it to the Turks.

On September 16–18, while Allenby's aircraft bombed Turkish command centres to disrupt com-

munications and Arab guerrillas struck along the Deraa railway, the major Turkish supply line, Allenby's XX Corps (Lt Gen Sir P Chetwode) advanced towards the Jordan valley. This move, together with false intelligence "leaks", convinced Liman von Sanders that Allenby's major thrust would be made inland, where he concentrated much of the Turkish strength. Instead, early on September 19, following a brief but intense artillery bombardment,

Gen Chauvel's cavalry enter Damascus

XXI Corps (Lt Gen Sir E Bulfin) attacked on the coastal front, towards Megiddo. Within hours, an infantry breakthrough created a gap in the coastal Plain of Sharon through which Allenby hurled three cavalry divisions (Desert Mounted Corps; Lt Gen Sir H Chauvel). While 4th Cavalry Division swung east to trap Fourth Army, in concert with XX Corps' advance inland, 5th Cavalry Division and the Australian Mounted Division drove Seventh and Eighth Armies to the north.

Hotly pursued by the cavalry, and subjected to heavy aerial bombardment and Arab harassment, the Turkish survivors retreated through Damascus (where some 20,000 prisoners were secured by Lawrence's Arabs and 5th Cavalry Division, October 1), Beirut (fell October 2) and Homs (fell October 16) to Aleppo (fell October 26). On October 30, Turkey capitulated.

Allenby's superbly planned and executed offensive had resulted in an advance of some 360 miles (580km) in around 40 days, during which the destruction of three Turkish armies and the capture of some 75,000 prisoners cost about 1,200 killed or missing and 4,500 wounded. *RO'N.*

Dams raid. On May 16–17 1943, 617 Squadron, using bouncing bombs designed by Barnes Wallis, breached the Möhne and Eder dams in the Ruhr valley. The attacks had to be delivered from an altitude of precisely 60ft (18.3m) and an exact accuracy of aim was required. The hazards of the operation were exceptional and, of the 19 Lancasters dispatched, eight were lost and two seriously damaged. This was, perhaps, the most brilliant feat of bombing in World War II. Wing Commander Gibson, who led the attack, was awarded the VC. An enormous flood was caused and the shock to the Germans was profound, but the effect on their war effort proved to be negligible due to the speed with which they succeeded in controlling and then repairing the damage. It was fortunate too for the Germans that the attacks on the associated Sorpe and Schwelme dams failed. The most enduring significance of the raid was the development of bombing and target-marking techniques which followed from it. *ANF.*

Da Nang. South Vietnam's second largest city; headquarters of the Republic of Vietnam I Corps Tactical Zone. The first American combat units landed near Da Nang on March 8 1965. Its jet-capable airfield and major port were developed as a major logistical base for both South Vietnamese and American forces. In spring 1966, troops dispatched from Saigon brutally suppressed massive demonstrations protesting against Premier Nguyen Cao Ky's postponement of elections and dismissal of the popular I Corps commander, Gen Nguyen Chanh Thi. Da Nang's population swelled during the war to half a million, and chaotic conditions created by a huge tide of refugees during the last offensive helped communist forces to seize the city without a fight on March 29 1975. *WST.*

D'Annunzio, Gabriele (1863–1938). Italian. Poet, playwright and novelist – a distinguished Italian Air Force pilot during World War I – who did much to generate the nationalist upsurge within Italy after Caporetto in October 1917.

Danzig *see* POLISH CORRIDOR.

Darby, Brig Gen William Orlando (1911–1945). US. Commander of US Army's first Ranger unit, May 1942. 1st, 3rd and 4th Ranger Battalions were called "Darby's Rangers". Killed in action.

Dardanelles, naval operations in the (1915). The Allied attempt to force the Dardanelles Straits and threaten Constantinople stemmed directly from a Russian request, on January 2 1915, for a demonstration against the Turks in order to induce the latter to withdraw troops from the Caucasus and thus relieve pressure on the Russians in that theatre. In Britain this request led Winston Churchill, the First Lord of the Admiralty, who was among those seeking an alternative to the trench deadlock in France, to revive his earlier proposal for a joint military and naval attack on the Dardanelles. Despite Kitchener's assertion that no troops could be spared for some time, Churchill won approval for a naval expedition "to bombard and take the Gallipoli peninsula with Constantinople as its objective". Before the end of January the French also agreed to cooperate.

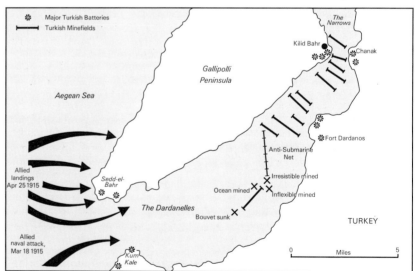

Opening Allied moves in the ill-fated Dardanelles/Gallipoli campaign, spring 1915

From February 19 1915, Allied warships, under Vice Adm Carden, intermittently bombarded the forts at Sedd-el-Bahr and Kum Kale which guarded the entrance to the Straits. Between February 26 and March 3 demolition parties of marines were landed, moving about freely on ground which was fiercely contested two months

later. By mid-March the outer forts had been reduced, but Turkish reinforcements were now arriving and mobile howitzers were seriously hampering the work of Allied minesweepers. The Allies still had to subdue the defences of the Narrows, less than a mile wide and protected by minefields as well as the Kilid Bahr and Chanak forts. The main attack was launched on March 18 by 14 British and 4 French capital ships under Vice Adm de Robeck, who had replaced the ailing Carden. Initially all went well and fire from the batteries at the Narrows began to slacken. However, during the afternoon, the French battleship *Bouvet* blew up. The British battlecruiser *Irresistible* and the battleship *Ocean* were also fatally holed. Both sank, while the French battleships *Gaulois* and *Suffren* and the British battlecruiser *Inflexible* were all disabled. These losses prompted de Roebeck to call off the attack and although, as recent evidence suggests, the Turkish defenders of the Straits had been near collapse, he subsequently refused to resume operations without military aid. *PJS.*

Darfur. In April 1915, Ali Dinar, ruler of Darfur, renounced his allegiance to the Sudanese government. Supported by pro-Turkish elements, he threatened to invade the Sudan in early 1916. An Anglo-Egyptian force defeated his army on May 22 1915 and, in December, Darfur was incorporated as a province of the Sudan.

D

Darlan, Adm Jean François (1881–1942). Fr. c-in-c of the French Navy; refused to order the fleet to British or neutral ports following the French defeat in 1940. He declared his allegiance to Pétain's Vichy regime and was rewarded with the Ministry of Marine. In February 1941 he was appointed Vice-Premier and Foreign Minister and pursued a policy of accommodation with the Germans, seeking to secure a degree of independence for France and her empire. Laval's return to power in April 1942 greatly diminished Darlan's influence. Nevertheless, he returned to prominence when, in November 1942, the Allies invaded French North Africa. Darlan was in Algiers at this time and issued a cease-fire and opened negotiations with the Americans. His actions saved many lives but his tainted reputation and the demands of the Free French affected Allied dealings with him. In December Darlan was assassinated by a French monarchist. *MS.*

Darwin, Battle of (1942). To complete the conquest of the Dutch East Indies, Japan sought to prevent the reinforcement of Java. At dawn on February 19 1942, from the Banda Sea, the four aircraft carriers of Nagumo's striking force launched 71 dive-bombers, 81 torpedo-bombers and 36 fighters (54 medium bombers joined the raid from bases in the Celebes) against Darwin, ABDA Command's major supply base, in Australia's Northern Territory. Although warning was given by Coast Watchers, total surprise was achieved. Darwin's air defences were inadequate, and of the 23 defending fighters, eight were destroyed in the air and the rest on the ground. Five Japanese aircraft were lost. Of 17 ships in the harbour, the destroyer USS *Peary* and seven transports (43,429 tons) were sunk and six large transports damaged. Installations ashore were heavily bombed; the port remained inoperative for several weeks. More than 500 seamen were killed or wounded, and civilian casualties were heavy. *RO'N.*

Davison, Rear Adm Ralph Eugene (1895–1972). US. Graduated from heading escort carrier groups providing air support for Kwajalein and Hollandia landings, early 1944, to command of fast carrier task groups in Third (Halsey) and Fifth (Spruance) Fleets. In October 1944, participated in the massive air assault on Formosa and in the Sibuyan Sea (where his aircraft helped sink super-battleship *Musashi*) and Cape Engaño actions at Leyte Gulf. Took part in first major carrier raids on Japanese home islands, February-March 1945.

Dawley, Maj Gen Ernest J (b. 1886). US. Commander VI US Corps during the Allied landings at Salerno; superseded by Lucas on September 20 1943.

Dayan, Gen Moshe (1915–1981). Israeli soldier and politician. *See* ARAB-ISRAELI WARS.

D-Day *see* NORMANDY, INVASION OF.

Deakin, Col Sir (Frederick) William (Dampier) (b.1913) Br. Research assistant to Churchill 1935, head of first SOE mission to Tito 1943; helped persuade Churchill to support Tito and his Partisans instead of the Chetniks.

Dean, Lt Gen William Frishe (1899–1981). US. In 1947–48 Dean was Military Governor of the US occupation zone in Korea. When the Korean War began, he commanded 24th Infantry Division, the first US ground unit committed to the fighting. Dean's division was defeated by the NKPA at the Battle of Taejon on July 20 1950. Dean lost contact with his command during the breakout from the city and was captured on August 25 1950. He was the highest ranking US officer to fall into enemy hands during the Korean War. *CM.*

Deans, Sergeant James Alexander Graham ("Dixie") (1911–1988). Br. Pilot of RAF Whitley bomber damaged by German AA fire in autumn 1940, which he safely crash-landed. He surrendered, with his crew and was taken prisoner. In several successive prisoner-of-war camps, he achieved an ascendancy over his guards, and dispatched plentiful intelligence to MI9 by coded letters. Deans guided 12,000 fellow-prisoners to safety in 1945.

Deception. Military term derived from feints in sword fighting, an old-established and still current weapon, depends on secrecy for success. It was used by both sides as a minor tactic in the Second Boer War. In the Balkan War of 1912, the Bulgars used it against the Turks: their purely notional victories of Kirk Kilisse and Lule Burgas gave them much credit abroad, and continue to figure in under-informed handbooks of war.

Both sides, again, used it during World War I; especially in feint bombardments, to deceive the enemy about where he was next to be attacked, and persuade him to shift his reserves away from the point that was really threatened. At sea, Hipper's retreat in the first phase of Jutland was a feint, intended to draw Beatty on to Scheer; while Beatty's retreat in the second phase was another, intended to draw Scheer on to Jellicoe. The Royal Navy developed in its Q ships, ostensible tramp steamers, a sound deceptive weapon against attacking U-boats: a party of panic-stricken sailors would leave the steamer; the U-boat would then surface, to deliver the *coup de grâce* by gunfire; and would be sunk by gunners left hidden on the steamer.

Between the great wars, Mussolini and Hitler in turn sought by deceptive propaganda to intimidate and destabilize their enemies. When Franco had four columns advancing on Madrid late in 1936, one of his generals claimed by radio broadcast that there was a fifth column of sympathizers, hidden in the city, waiting to help; the phrase at once became proverbial. Almost all the fifth columnists who were alleged to be supporting Hitler in western Europe in 1940 were notional, not real; the concept was a great help to him all the same.

Deception was used with still greater effect by the Allies. The captain of *Graf Spee* was bluffed by a trick that was old in Nelson's day: the small ships besieging him in the River Plate kept signalling to nonexistent friends over the horizon; he lost his nerve and scuttled his ship.

Wavell appointed Dudley Clarke to run A Force in the Mediterranean; Clarke constantly misled the Germans and Italians about Allied strengths and intentions in North

D

Africa and the Levant. In September and October 1942 a mixture of camouflaged vehicles, dummy pipelines and bogus w/t traffic persuaded Rommel that Montgomery threatened his right flank, before Montgomery attacked his left flank at El Alamein. As the Eighth Army marched westwards, Clarke kept up notional Ninth and Tenth Armies in the Near and Middle East, threatening the Balkans, where many Axis divisions were pinned.

J H Bevan headed the London Controlling Section, a small highly secret staff. They floated a body ashore on the Spanish coast, carrying documents which persuaded the Germans that the Allies' next targets after Tunis would be Sardinia and Greece instead of Sicily (see Ewan Montagu, *The Man Who Never Was*, 1953). With much help from decipher, Bevan supervised Operation "Fortitude". This persuaded Hitler that the Normandy invasion was itself a feint, intended to draw German troops away from the beaches south of Boulogne. On those beaches, which provided the shortest route from England to the Ruhr, the German general staff had always expected the main blow to fall; and Hitler kept his reserves away from Normandy until too late. In addition, he kept over 300,000 troops pinned in Norway to meet a nonexistent threat from Gen Thorne's notional Fourth Army in Scotland.

Since 1945, deception has been used with exceptional skill by Soviet Russia; partly to exaggerate the Soviet Union's prosperity and achievements, partly to sow discord among capitalist states and secret services by spreading rumous about moles. *MF*.

Decipher. Long a vital source of military and political intelligence. The British set up in Room 40, Old Building at the Admiralty in 1914 a staff which, with the help of captured code books, was able for most of the war to read most of the traffic of the High Seas Fleet, and made vital incursions into diplomatic traffic also (see ZIMMERMAN TELEGRAM). Parallel army units flourished on the Western Front, 1914–18, and in north and south Russia, 1919–20. Between the wars, decipher was concentrated in the Government Code

and Cipher School at Bletchley Park from 1939. The operation, renamed Government Communications Headquarters, later moved to Cheltenham, where it forms the main British base of a world network of intercept and decipher stations to which the US, British, Canadian, Australian and New Zealand governments belong.

The Americans first set up a decipher service in 1915; it was disbanded in 1929, and restarted in 1940. Led by William F Friedmann, they broke several important Japanese ciphers, securing some glimpses (although not enough) of the impending attack on Pearl Harbor, reading all the dispatches from the Japanese ambassador in Berlin to Tokyo, and orchestrating several naval victories such as Midway. During the Cold War, they financed the network mentioned above, and now bear the brunt of anti-Soviet interception and decipher.

German decipher enabled Hitler to read most of his putative opponents' diplomatic traffic in the 1930s, and provided useful land and air tactical intelligence. At sea, Dönitz read until June 1943 most British routeing orders to convoys and the Admiralty's daily summary of U-boat activity; thereafter British used unbroken ciphers.

French decipher, active in 1914–18 with good tactical results in France, made a few early inroads into "Enigma" with the help of a spy in the SS, but was then overtaken by France's defeat in 1940. Polish decipher had unravelled "Enigma" as early as 1932. Small teams of Poles were useful at Bletchley Park, and Polish ciphers were so secure that the Poles, alone of the governments in exile in London, were allowed to use their own ciphers in the run-up to Operation "Overlord" in 1944. *MF*.

Decorations. Awards for exceptionally gallant and distinguished service, as opposed to grades of orders of chivalry or merit, campaign medals, or awards for particular skills and proficiencies. The Victoria Cross (vc) (inst. 1856) is Britain's highest decoration. It was augmented in 1940 by the George Cross (gc), awarded for comparable deeds not necessarily in the face of the enemy. Many

nations have to various extents correspondingly exclusive awards, many with long histories; Frederick the Great instituted the *Pour le Mérite* for his Prussian army and this remained the highest German award until 1918. After Hitler's rise to power, the Iron Cross, with progressive grades culminating in the Knight's Cross with Diamonds, became the State's main award for valorous service. The Medal of Honor, awarded by the President of the United States in the name of Congress for "... conduct above and beyond the call of duty" was instituted by President Lincoln in 1861 and remains the highest American award. The highest Soviet award for gallantry is the Gold Star bestowed on "Heroes of the Soviet Union". *MH*.

"Defense and Space" Talks. The American term for the third of the arms control negotiations begun under a common "umbrella" in Geneva in 1985 between the USA and the USSR – for the other two *see* INTERMEDIATE NUCLEAR FORCES and START. The USSR calls this third group the "Space Weapons" talks. The negotiations concern the deployment of weapons in space. The USA wants to obtain Soviet agreement to deployment of a space-based anti-ballistic missile system while the USSR wishes to prevent the deployment of any weapons in outer space. The USSR has made a START agreement conditional on agreement in this area. *EJG*.

Defensively Equipped Merchant Ships (DEMS). In both world wars, merchantmen were armed for defence against raiders, the armament consisting of one medium-size gun on the stern (plus anti-aircraft guns in World War II). DEMS was the British term and organization for this. Gun crews could be either naval or mercantile personnel and, in 1939–45, the Maritime Regiment of the Royal Artillery.

Defiant, Boulton Paul P82 (Br, WWII). Two-seat fighter. Prototype flew August 11 1937; first production aircraft July 30 1939; equipment of first squadron (No. 264) began December 1939; first operation May 12 1940. Unsuccessful as day fighter; transferred to night operations (13 squadrons); briefly on air-sea rescue; finally target-tug and training duties. Production 1,075. One 1,030hp Rolls-Royce Merlin III engine; max. speed 304mph (489kph); four turret-mounted 0.303in machine guns.

De Gaulle, Gen Charles (1890–1970). Fr. During World War I, de Gaulle fought at Verdun, where he was wounded and taken prisoner. After service in 1919–20 with the French Military Mission in Poland he developed a reputation as a theoretician, criticizing postwar French army doctrines in a series of lectures and books. In opposition to the prevailing faith in defensive strategy, he advocated a form of mechanized and armoured warfare that had much in common with the concepts of Guderian, Fuller and Liddell Hart. His outspokenness affected his career prospects and at the outbreak of World War II, de Gaulle was merely commander of the Fifth Army's tank units. During the German invasion, he led the 4th Armoured Division and,

Uneasy allies: de Gaulle and Churchill

although it was far from ready for battle, it performed well. On June 5 1940 he was appointed Under-Secretary of State for National Defence, but the collapse of Reynaud's government and the French request for an armistice persuaded him to continue the fight from Britain. Although at first with few adherents, de Gaulle established the Free French movement in London. His attempt to seize Dakar in September 1940 was an abject failure and support only gradually rallied to him. Fiercely aware of his and France's dignity, de Gaulle was often at odds with the Allies and his own

French political rivals. But, with the liberation of French North Africa and the recognition of his primacy in the French Committee of National Liberation, his position was assured. He returned to France in June 1944 and triumphantly entered Paris on August 26. However, he continued to baulk at his treatment by the Allies and he resented their rejection of his claims to an equal status at the major conferences. In France's immediate postwar political battles, de Gaulle failed to secure sufficient support and resigned in January 1946. He returned to office in 1958 at the height of the Algerian crisis and maintained a personalized and autocratic Presidency until his final resignation in 1969. *MS*.

Degaussing *see* MAGNETIC MINES.

De Guingand, Maj Gen Sir Francis (1900–1979). Br. An infantryman, he became, in 1939, military Assistant to the controversial Secretary of State for War, Leslie Hore-Belisha, gaining invaluable experience of the politico-military interface in Whitehall. Later, as Director of Military Intelligence Middle East, he was selected (1942) by Montgomery to be his COS in Eighth Army. He remained with Montgomery after the North African and Italian campaigns and was COS 21st Army Group, a post he held to the end of the war in Europe. De Guingand was a very different man from his austere teetotal master, but nonetheless they made an ideal pair. Whenever Montgomery upset his American allies (frequently, as it happened) it was de Guingand's diplomacy and evident professional competence which to some extent put things right. *MH*.

De La Rey, Gen Jacobus Hercules ("Koos") (1847–1914). South African. One of the ablest Boer commanders in both conventional and guerrilla operations, De La Rey served first under Cronjé: his advocacy of entrenchment for flat trajectory fire, rather than occupation of the high ground in the traditional Boer manner, was largely responsible for the victories at Modder river and Magersfontein. His guerrilla campaign in the Transvaal reached its climax

at Tweebosch on March 6–7 1902, when, with 1,200 men, he ambushed a column of about equal strength led by Methuen. De La Rey's burghers broke the column with a mounted charge. British losses were 68 killed, 121 wounded and 600 captured, among them the wounded Methuen, whom De La Rey released. Opposing South Africa's participation in World War I, De La Rey was shot dead in a police ambush, allegedly while en route to lead a pro-German revolt in the Transvaal, on September 15 1914. *RO'N*.

De Lattre Line. In spring 1951 the French commander in Indochina, Gen Jean de Lattre de Tassigny, responded to communist offensives along Vietnam's border with China and in the Red River delta by constructing a chain of defensive positions along the delta's outer edge. The "De Lattre" Line was supposed to defend the plain against stronger attacks expected to result from the increase of Chinese supplies to Vietnamese forces. However, the line tied down French resources and failed to halt infiltration of the delta.

Delville wood. Wood in the German second position on the Somme, bitterly contested between July 15 and August 27 1916. The South African Brigade suffered particularly heavy casualties here.

Demilitarized Zone. The Demilitarized Zone was created by the armistice agreement which ended the Korean War to separate the military forces of the belligerents and "prevent the occurrence of incidents which might lead to a resumption of hostilities". It was 2.5 miles (4km) wide, with the line of military contact as the median. The area to the south of this line was to be the responsibility of the UN commander and the area to the north of the supreme commander of the NKPA and the commander of the Chinese People's Volunteers. Supervision of the provisions of the armistice within the zone was to be the responsibility of the Military Armistice Commission and its joint observer teams. *CM. See also* MILITARY ARMISTICE COMMISSION; NEUTRAL NATIONS REPATRIATION COMMISSION; NEUTRAL NATIONS SUPERVISORY COMMISSION.

D

Democratic Republic of Vietnam (DRV). Ho Chi Minh declared independence for the DRV on September 2 1945. Dominated from the beginning by the Lao Dong (Workers' or Vietnam Communist) Party, the DRV, seated in Hanoi, was the de facto if weak and unrecognized central government for all Vietnam until war broke out with France in December 1946. The DRV returned to Hanoi following the Geneva agreement in 1954. In accordance with that agreement, the DRV administered Vietnam north of the 17th Parallel, and so became known as North Vietnam, pending elections on reunification. President Ngo Dinh Diem of the Republic of Vietnam in Saigon refused to hold those elections, so the Lao Dong Party sought reunification by other means. With the accomplishment of that objective in 1975, the DRV was formally superseded by the Socialist Republic of Vietnam (SRV) in 1976. *WST. See also* AUGUST REVOLUTION.

Dempsey, Gen Sir Miles (1896– 1969). Br. As a young officer in the Royal Berkshire Regiment, Dempsey fought on the Western Front from 1916 to 1918 and then participated in the Iraq operations of 1919–20. A thorough professional, with a deep concern for his men, he took his regiment's 1st Battalion to France in 1939 and commanded the 13th Brigade in the counterattack at Arras in May 1940, and also in the battle on the Ypres-Comines Canal which bought extra time for the Dunkirk evacuation. Appointed to command XIII Corps in December 1942, he led it in Sicily and Italy before he was recalled in January 1944, at Montgomery's request, to command the British Second Army, a role which he performed soundly and successfully throughout the campaign in Northwest Europe.. After the war he held senior posts in Southeast Asia and the Middle East, retiring in 1947. *PJS.*

Denikin, Lt Gen Anton Ivanovich (1872–1947). Russian. "White" leader during the Russian Civil War. Denikin defeated the "Reds" in the Caucasus, early 1919, and launched a major Ukrainian offensive, taking Kiev and threatening Moscow. His intransigent nature alienated the Ukrainian and Pol-ish "Whites"; with the Red counteroffensive, his armies crumbled and he went into exile.

Dentz, Gen Henri Fernand (1881– 1945). Fr. Vichy High Commissioner in Syria during the Syrian campaign in 1941.

Depth charge. Cylinder filled with high explosive and set off by an adjustable fuse operated by water pressure. Developed during World War I as an anti-submarine weapon. Usually used in patterns, rolled over the stern and fired from mortars. During World War II, adapted for use from aircraft.

Derby, Earl of (1865–1948). Br. Director-General of Recruiting, October 1915–June 1916, and Secretary of State for War, December 1916–April 1918.

De Robeck, Adm of the Fleet Sir John (1862–1928). Br. Commander of naval forces in the Dardanelles 1915. *See also* DARDANELLES (1915) and GALLIPOLI (1915–16).

Desert campaign . (1940–43) *see* WESTERN DESERT CAMPAIGN.

Desert Rats *see* SEVENTH ARMOURED DIVISION (BRITISH).

Destroyer. A class of warship smaller than cruisers but larger than frigates. Their origin lies in the torpedo boats of the last quarter of the 19th century, but as their role was seen as not only launching torpedoes but also destroying enemy torpedo boats they came to be known as destroyers. They have increased in size from the original 300-400 tons up to about 5,000 tons and their role has been greatly extended from the original function of covering the battle fleet. In both world wars they were extensively used for convoy escort and especially anti-submarine work. Subsequently, the term has been adopted for guided missile ships. *ANF.*

Deterrence. Deterrence is the attempt by one nation or group of nations to prevent another nation or group of nations doing something unacceptable by the threat of the former inflicting unacceptable costs on the latter. Traditionally, deterrence was primarily exerted by the threat of denying the aggressor the possibility of success in its attack – deterrence through denial – with certain elements of punishment in the human and economic costs that fighting would incur and the losses that might ensue in an unfavourable peace settlement. The advent of strategic bombing added a new potency to the direct-punishment aspects of deterrence and these were increased fundamentally by the advent of nuclear and thermonuclear weapons. Deterrence by the threat of nuclear punishment has come to dominate the strategic scene. Deterrence relies on the capability to inflict unacceptable damage on one's opponent, the communication of the threat to do so and the circumstances in which the threat might be carried out, and most of all on the credibility of the threat in the mind of the adversary. The growth of broadly equal invulnerable nuclear capabilites in the hands of both superpowers has created a situation of mutual deterrence, where each side acts with considerable caution in its relations with the other. This, however, has tended to undermine the guarantee of extended deterrence to America's allies that was once relatively easily given. This has required the elaboration of more sophisticated deterrent strategies based on concepts of escalation and limited war that contain some elements of traditional "denial", both nuclear and conventional. Smaller nuclear powers follow policies of minimum deterrence based on a small invulnerable retaliatory force powerful enough to deter nuclear attacks upon their national territories. *EJG.*

De Valéra, Eamonn (1882–1975). Born in New York, Irish revolutionary; column commander in Easter Rising, 1916; escaped from Lincoln prison to fight in Troubles; opposed 1921 Treaty; as Irish prime minister, 1932–48, 1951– 54 and 1957–59, and president, 1959–73, remained irreconcilably anti-English.

Devers, Gen Jacob (1887–1979). US. Chief of Armoured Forces, 1941–43, Commanding General, European Theatre of Operations, 1944. Deputy Allied Supreme commander Mediterranean Theatre 1944 and appointed to command Allied landings in Southern France, August 1944 (Operation "Dragoon"). Despite his lack of combat experience, Devers handled his forces energetically as they advanced north up the Rhône valley to link up with Allied forces striking across from Normandy. He later commanded 6th Army Group (Seventh US Army/First French Army) which, after successfully holding off a German offensive in Alsace, advanced victoriously through southern Germany to Munich, the Alps and Berchtesgaden in 1945. *MH*.

De Wet, Commandant-General Christiaan Rudolph (1854–1922). South African. A veteran of the First Boer War, De Wet became c-in-c of Free State forces early in 1900, following his ambush of a British supply convoy at Waterval Drift on February 15, and Cronjé's debacle at Paardeberg. Although his withdrawal at Driefontein abandoned Bloemfontein to the British, De Wet restored morale with victories at Sanna's Post (Kornspruit) and Reddersberg and proceeded to wage an outstandingly skilful guerrilla campaign. In 1914 he headed the Free State revolt against the pro-Allied Botha, but on November 12, with 6,000 men, was defeated at Mushroom Valley: his subsequent attempt to repeat his guerrilla exploits failed in the face of Botha's expert deployment of mechanized forces. Captured on December 2 1914, De Wet was sentenced to six years' imprisonment, but paroled in 1915. *RO'N*.

Dewoitine D.520 (French, WWII). Single-seat fighter. Prototype flew October 2 1938; first production aircraft November 2 1939; five *Groupes de Chasse* and one naval *Flotille de Chasse* saw some combat before June 25 1940. Production then halted but resumed for Vichy units; some later used by Luftwaffe training units; others to Italy, Bulgaria, Romania. Production 910. One 910hp Hispano-Suiza 12Y-45 engine; max. speed 329mph (530kph); one 20mm cannon, four 7.5mm machine guns.

Deyo, Vice Adm Morton Leyndholm (1887–1973). US. Command-ed destroyer escorts in the Atlantic and bombardment forces for Utah beach, the capture of Cherbourg and (1945) the Okinawa landings.

DFS 230 (German, WWII). Assault transport glider, the first such aircraft to be used in war. Prototype flew late 1937; production started 1939; over 1,500 built. First operation May 10 1940, when 41 DFS 230s transported troops to attack Eben-Emael and strategic bridges. Later used in invasion of Crete 1941 and rescue of Mussolini 1943. Normal towing speed 112mph (179kph); accommodation, pilot and 9 troops; armament, three 7.9mm machine guns.

DFW CV (German, WWI). Two-seat reconnaissance/artillery spotter. Prototype probably flew May 1916. Ordered in large numbers (total at least 4,055); deliveries from August 1916. Efficient, well-liked, and widely used in greater numbers than any other contemporary German two-seater; in service until Armistice. One 200hp Benz Bz IV engine; max. speed 97mph (155kph); two 7.9mm machine guns.

DH 2, de Havilland (Br, WWI). Single-seat fighting scout. Prototype flew June 1 1915; went to France for operational evaluation July 26; shot down, captured, August 9 1915. Production deliveries from November 1915; to RFC, France, from January 1916. Successfully countered Fokker monoplane; remained operational France until June 1917, later in Macedonia and Palestine. Production, over 400. One 100hp Gnome Monosoupape engine; max. speed 93mph (149kph); one 0.303in machine gun; a few had six Le Prieur rockets.

DH 4, de Havilland (Br, WWI and after). Two-seat bomber-reconnaissance. Prototype flew mid-August 1916; production for RFC and RNAS, deliveries starting January 1917. Large orders necessitated use of several types of engine. Eagle VIII version had outstanding performance; widely used France, Macedonia, Mesopotamia, Aegean, Adriatic, Russia. Large-scale production USA; postwar production Belgium (15). Pro-duction: British 1,521, American 4,346. One 250/275/375hp Rolls-Royce Eagle Mks I to VIII, 230hp BHP/Siddeley Puma, 200hp RAF 3a, 260hp Fiat A-12, 400hp Liberty 12 engine; max. speed 136.5mph (220kph); 448lb (202kg) bombs, two/four 0.303in machine guns.

Dhola Post (India-China War 1962). Forwardmost Indian position sited at Che Dong in an area long recognized as Chinese territory: Thag La ridge. Held, September 8 1962 until the Chinese attacked, October 19–20 when all Thag La positions were swept aside.

Diamond Hill, Battle of (June 11–12 1900), Second Boer War. Following the fall of Pretoria, Botha dug in at Diamond Hill some 20 miles (32km) to the southeast, deploying 7,000 men and 23 guns on an extended line along the Delagoa Bay Railway. Roberts advanced with 15,000 men (losses 162) and 70 guns, and after a series of skirmishes Botha, wishing to preserve his men (losses 24), withdrew eastward along the railway.

Armando Diaz: victor at Vittorio Veneto

Diaz, Field Marshal Armando (1861–1928). Italian. Succeeded Gen Cadorna as Italian COS in November 1917 after the Battle of Caporetto. He defeated the Austrians at the Battles of Asiago and the Piave in June 1918, and planned and won the Battle of Vittorio Veneto in October 1918.

Diem, President Ngo Dinh (1901–63). Republic of Vietnam. An anticommunist Catholic nationalist; became premier of South Vietnam in July 1954. In October 1955, he ousted Emperor Bao Dai in a rigged election and proclaimed a Republic with himself as president. Although South Vietnam certainly needed order and stability, Diem's repressive methods and autocratic manner provoked enmity. American officials came to see him more as a liability than an asset. American Ambassador Cabot Lodge encouraged, and President Kennedy approved, the coup by South Vietnamese army officers that overthrew Diem on November 1 1963. An aide to Duong Van Minh, one of the plotters, shot Diem and his brother, Ngo Dinh Nhu. *WST.*

Dien Bien Phu, siege of (1954). French forces seized the valley of Dien Bien Phu in remote northwestern Vietnam on November 20 1953. The objective according to Gen Henri Navarre was to defend northern Laos and penetrate communist-held areas. Some French commanders also hoped to lure communist forces into a "meatgrinder" like the one at Na San. But the French grossly underestimated their adversary.

Napalm from air support, Dien Bien Phu

To attack 10,800 French Union forces supported by 10 tanks and airpower, the People's Army of Vietnam (PAVN) under Gen Vo Nguyen Giap deployed 49,500 combatants and 55,000 support troops equipped with over 140 pieces of 105mm and 75mm artillery. Over 250,000 porters helped to transport the PAVN's supplies and weapons over 600 miles (960km) of rugged trails. PAVN artillerymen entrenched their guns, not on the back sides of the hills as the French expected, but on the sides facing the valley floor. When fighting began in earnest on March 13, the volume and accuracy of PAVN artillery fire took the French by surprise. Three strong-

points quickly fell. The PAVN slowly strangled the remaining positions with trenches in classic siege technique and overran Gen de Castries' command post on May 7. Coming the day before negotiations to end the war were to open at Geneva, the defeat sealed the fate of French Indochina. Altogether in this battle French forces lost about 9,000 killed or wounded at the garrison, over 10,000 in relief efforts, and about 6,500 taken prisoner, while the PAVN was estimated to have lost 23,000 killed or wounded. *WST.*

Dieppe raid (1942). In the spring of 1942 the British Combined Operations Headquarters produced a proposal for an amphibious raid in force against the French port of Dieppe. After an initial cancellation the project was revived on August 12 by the Chiefs of Staff as Operation "Jubilee". The raid was intended to serve several purposes in the preparations for a full, cross-Channel invasion. Enemy coastal defences were to be tested and the difficulties of seizing a major port assessed. New weapons and amphibious landing techniques were to be tried out and Allied troops given vital combat experience. Although this was not to be the Second Front which the Soviet Union wanted, it was anticipated that the raid would at least divert German resources away from the Eastern Front.

In the early hours of August 19 the invasion fleet, comprising 179 landing craft and 73 naval ships, rendezvoused in the Channel and approached the French coast. The first landings took place shortly before dawn to the east and west of Dieppe with Nos. 3 and 4 Commandos detailed to neutralize batteries at Berneval and Varengeville. While No. 4 completed its objectives, No. 3 was confronted by heavy and accurate German fire and was unable to destroy the enemy guns. The main assault force comprised the 2nd Canadian Division with flank landings on either side of the main thrust against Dieppe itself. The South Saskatchewan Regiment and the Queen's Own Cameron Highlanders landed to the west and made reasonable progress but, to the east of the port, the Royal Regiment of Canada suffered dis-

astrously and only a handful of men managed to get off the beach. The main assault was carried out by the Essex Scottish Regiment, the Royal Hamilton Light Infantry Regiment and the 14th Canadian Army Tank Regiment. These units encountered concentrated small arms and artillery fire that poured down on them from the town's defences and emplacements on the heights. The sea wall proved to be a virtually insurmountable barrier both for the infantry and the force's Churchill tanks. Engineers were unable to get close enough to the defensive obstacles to blow a path through them, while the tanks found it difficult to manoeuvre in the shingle and were easy prey to anti-tank guns. Even the commitment of the reserve, the Mont-Royal Fusiliers, failed to improve the situation and, at 1100, the order to withdraw was given.

While it was argued that the lessons learnt in "Jubilee" proved invaluable in preparing "Overlord", much of the disaster was

Canadians in action at Dieppe, 1942

avoidable. Poor intelligence and inadequate naval and air bombardment of the target were crucial flaws in the plans. Furthermore, inadequate communications meant that commanders were unable to assess the extent of the disaster. Allied casualties were high, including 3,374 Canadians, 247 Commandos, 550 naval personnel and 153 men of the RAF while German losses numbered some 600 men. Even the hope of inflicting substantial damage on the Luftwaffe was unrealized with Allied losses of 106 aircraft set against the Germans' 48. *MS.*

Dietl, Gen Eduard (1890–1944). Ger. Commander 3rd Mountain Division at Narvik, April–June 1940, during the Norwegian campaign.

Dietrich, Gen (*Oberstgruppenführer*, SS) Josef (1892–1966). Ger. After service in World War I as a sergeant and a brief period in the Bavarian police, Dietrich joined the Nazi Party and the SS in 1928. He rose rapidly through its ranks and, in 1938, was given command of Hitler's bodyguard. This unit subsequently became the *Liebstandarte SS Adolf Hitler* and Dietrich remained its commander as it expanded from a motorized infantry unit to a full panzer division. He played a leading role in Munich during the "Night of the Long Knives". He led his unit in the invasions of Poland, Holland, France, Yugoslavia, Greece and the Soviet Union. In the process, Dietrich became one of Hitler's favourite generals and was given command of the Sixth Panzer Army in the Ardennes offensive. Far from achieving the miraculous victory Hitler sought, the German attack failed while the atrocities perpetrated by Dietrich's men during the fighting were to have far-reaching consequences. He fought in the concluding campaigns of the war in Hungary and Austria before surrendering to American forces in May 1945. He was tried and convicted of being responsible for the massacre of American prisoners during the Battle of the Bulge and was sentenced to life imprisonment. Released in 1955, he was re-arrested and tried before a German court for his part in the Night of the Long Knives and was sentenced to 18 months' imprisonment. *MS.*

Dill, Field Marshal Sir John (1881–1944). Br. Already a possible candidate for future high command, Dill held a succession of staff posts on the Western Front before he was appointed head of the Operations Branch at British GHQ in France in March 1918. His reputation grew between the wars and, after serving as Commandant of the Staff College and as Director of Military Operations, he became GOC-in-C, Aldershot, from 1937 to 1939. His expected elevation to CIGS did not materialize immediately and, on the outbreak of World War II, he was instead

Dill: British CIGS, 1940–41

given command of I Corps of the Expeditionary Force in France. Recalled in April 1940 to fill the new post of Vice-Chief of the Imperial General Staff, he finally replaced Ironside as CIGS on May 27. His term as CIGS was not a distinguished one, coinciding with a low point in British military fortunes. His desire to avoid risky ventures caused Churchill to regard him as obstructive and unimaginative and, following further British reverses in Greece, Crete and North Africa, Dill was himself succeeded by Brooke in November 1941. Upon America's entry into the war, he went to Washington as Head of the British Joint Staff Mission and senior British member of the Combined Chiefs of Staff Committee. When Dill died in November 1944, President Roosevelt described him as "the most important figure in the remarkable accord which has been developed in the combined operations of our two countries". *PJS.*

Dimitriev, Gen Radko (1859–1919). Bulgarian. Dimitriev graduated from the Military School in Sofia and continued his military education at the General Staff Academy in St Petersburg before returning to Bulgaria in 1885 to take part in the war with Serbia. Deeply involved in political intrigue in Bulgaria, he was obliged to go into exile in Russia, where he joined the army. Dimitriev returned home 10 years later and in 1902 was appointed Chief of the General Staff. He laid plans for a war with Turkey but after a change of government, he was moved to be Inspector-General of the Third Army District. Following the outbreak of the Balkan War (*see* BALKAN WAR), in October

1912 Dimitriev's forces invaded Thrace and in November he led an abortive attempt to force the Chatalja Lines guarding Constantinople (Istanbul).

On the outbreak of World War I, Dimitriev relinquished his post as Bulgaria's minister in St Petersburg and rejoined the Russian Army. He served with distinction in the opening operations of the war, notably at the Battle of Cracow in November 1914. Commanding the Third Army in the spring of 1915 he won a victory on the River Dunajec but was forced to withdraw in the face of the Central Powers' offensive. However his "over confidence" was blamed for the fall of Przemysl and he was relieved of his command. But he returned to service on the Baltic front, blocking German efforts against Riga. Typically, Dimitriev's colourful career ended in controversial circumstances after the Revolution, when he was murdered by the Bolsheviks at Pyatigorsk in 1919. *MS.*

Directed Energy Weapon (DEW). A weapon which uses beams of electromagnetic radiation or atomic particles to inflict damage. These beams travel at very high speeds up to and including the speed of light i.e. reaching the target as soon as they are fired at it. One important group of DEW is lasers which fire coherent beams of electromagnetic radiation. Chemical lasers produce light by the reaction of gases, e.g. hydrogen and fluorine. Free electron lasers pass electrons through a magnetic field that can be varied to alter the wavelength of the radiation. Excimer lasers create pulses of light by the creation and decay of "dimers", molecules of inert and halogen gases. X-ray lasers convert the power of nuclear explosions into a beam, and are sometimes called "third generation nuclear weapons". Particle beam weapons accelerate charged particles, e.g. electrons, to high speeds; in some systems, larger particles are used in neutral beams. DEWS still face many technical problems but low-powered lasers have been deployed in various modes. DEWS are usually thought to have their greates potential in space and in anti-ballistic missile applications. *EJG.*

Dive bombing *see* BOMBING.

Division. Army formation comprising all arms, made up of not less than two brigades, commanded by a major general. Also (British Army) an administrative grouping of infantry regiments, e.g. The King's Division.

Diyala river *see* MESOPOTAMIAN CAMPAIGN (1914–18).

Dneiper, Battle of the (1943). The second longest river in the Soviet Union, the Dneiper formed a natural defence line for the German Army as it struggled to stem the Red Army's drive westwards during 1943. However, the extreme length of the front and the relative weakness of its forces made the German position far from impregnable. On October 10 the Third Ukrainian Front attacked the German bridgehead on the east bank of the river around Zaporozhye. While the German High Command debated an evacuation, two Soviet Corps decided the issue by driving the First Panzer Army back across the Dneiper. Matters were little better for von Kleist's Army Group A to the south where the Fourth Ukrainian Front pushed the German Sixth Army back across the Nogay Steppe to the lower reaches of the Dneiper, isolating the Seventeenth Army in the Crimea. The Soviet pressure was also maintained in the north where, on October 15, Koniev's Second Ukrainian Front launched an attack across the river, striking for Krivoi Rog. A counterattack checked the Soviet advance at the end of the month, but a further assault was now unleashed further north against Kiev. On November 3, Vatutin's First Ukrainian Front broke out of its bridgeheads above the city, shattering the Fourth Panzer Army's front and forced a German evacuation. Although von Mainstein juggled the resources of Army Group South to mount several counterattacks, by the end of the year the defence line on the Dneiper had been destroyed. *MS*.

Dobbie, Lt Gen Sir William (1879–1964). Br. Governor and C-in-C, Malta at the outbreak of war with Italy. A devout and gallant Christian gentleman, he inspired the garrison and people of Malta throughout the worst period of the siege and heaviest bombing from January 1941 to May 1942, when, having reached the point of exhaustion, he was relieved by Field Marshal Lord Gort.

Dobell, Lt Gen Sir Charles (1869–1954). Br. Commanded the Allied forces in the Cameroons, 1914–16. He served in the Egyptian-based campaign of 1916–17 against Turkey and greatly distinguished himself in the attack on Gaza launched on March 26 1917, which he planned and in which he commanded the Palestine Force.

Do Cao Tri, Lt Gen (1929–71). Republic of Vietnam. Widely regarded as the most energetic fighting general of the Army of the Republic of Vietnam (ARVN). Trained in France in 1947–49, Tri became ARVN I Corps commander in 1962; II Corps commander in 1964. Premier Nguyen Cao Ky exiled him to Hong Kong in 1965 for suspected involvement in the Buddhist turbulence. Three years later President Nguyen Van Thieu, short of competent commanders, put him in charge of II Corps. A fearless swashbuckler, Tri swooped down in his helicopter to take over personal command of lagging units, and in spring 1970 he was the ARVN commander of the Cambodia "incursion" by American and Vietnamese forces. He died on February 23 1971 in a helicopter crash. *WST*.

Cruiser *Blücher* sinks at Dogger Bank

Dogger Bank (January 24, 1915), North Sea. On January 24 1915 a German force of three battlecruisers and a large armoured cruiser, supported by light cruisers and destroyers, under the command of Vice Adm von Hipper, steamed to the Dogger Bank in the hope of destroying any British light forces that might be found. The Admiralty, forewarned by decoded radio intercepts, deployed five battlecruisers under Vice Adm Beatty, supported by light cruisers and destroyers, to intercept the Germans.

The opposing forces encountered one another on the morning of January 24. Hipper, recognizing that he was outnumbered and outgunned, fled with the British in hot pursuit. The complete destruction of the German battlecruisers seemed a near certainty, but when Beatty's flagship was disabled, a confusion in flag communication and poor judgment by Beatty's second-in-command resulted in the concentration of the other British battlecruisers against the German armoured cruiser, which had been badly damaged and had fallen away from the main line; this unit was sunk, but the interruption of the chase allowed Hipper's battlecruisers to escape from their pursuers. *JTS*.

Dogger Bank incident (1904). Passing through the North Sea on its long voyage to defeat at Tsushima, the Russian Baltic Fleet under Rozhdestvenski unexpectedly encountered some 40 Hull fishing trawlers off the Dogger Bank on the foggy night of October 21 1904. Believing that Japanese torpedo boats from secret bases in Scandinavia were attacking them, some Russian ships opened fire, sinking one trawler and killing or wounding eight fishermen. War with Britain seemed possible until, in December 1904, Russia apologized and promised full compensation for the error.

Doiran *see* SALONIKA CAMPAIGN.

Donets, Battle of the (1943). By February 1943 the Soviet winter offensive had punched a gap 100 miles (160km) wide in the German line along the River Donets and Kharkov was hastily abandoned. The situation was so grave that Hitler felt it necessary to pay a personal visit to Army Group South's headquarters at Zaporozhye. Consequently von Manstein's forces were reshuffled and reinforced and a major counteroffensive, supported by von Richthofen's Fourth Air Force, was approved. On February 20 Hoth's Fourth Panzer Army pushed out of Dnepropetrovsk and von Mackensen's First Panzer Army closed around the most advanced Soviet formation, Popov's "Mobile Group". By the 24th the exposed Soviet units had been badly mauled and forced to withdraw towards the Donets. Encouraged by this success, von Manstein switched the focus of his attack northwards to Kharkov and the Soviet Voronezh Front. With the thaw threatening to inhibit their operations, the Germans accelerated their advance and, by March 5, First Panzer Army was installed along the Donets. The next objective was the recapture of Kharkov. Ignoring Hoth's orders for a gradual approach, on the 11th, Lt Gen Hausser sent two divisions of his SS Panzer Corps into the city. Three days later Kharkov fell but the offensive was maintained and Hausser's men took Belgorod on March 18. Von Manstein considered continuing the advance but Hoth persuaded him that his troops were exhausted and would need the river line of the Donets as a defence against the next Soviet onslaught. *MS.*

Dong Khe, Battle of *see* BORDER WAR, VIETNAM.

Dönitz, Grand Adm Karl (1891–1980). Ger. Commander of U-boats and later of the German Navy during World War II. In 1914 he was Lt on *Breslau* accompanying *Goeben* in her escape to Turkey. In 1918 he commanded the submarine *U-68* in the Mediterranean and was taken prisoner when she was sunk.

Between the wars, Dönitz helped to develop the "anti-submarine school", clandestinely training submarine crews. Soon after the existence of U-boat arm was officially admitted (1935), Dönitz became its commander. He shaped it in accord with his ideas on "wolf-pack" attacks controlled from shore headquarters, using the cover of darkness to enable U-boats to act as surface torpedo boats. These tactics would provide superb initial results, but would eventually prove vulnerable to allied countermeasures. Central control required much use of radio

Dönitz: German naval chief, 1943–45

by the submarines, which became a fatal weakness in the face of Allied direction-finding and decrypting.

He entered World War II with only 57 operational submarines – far too few for the purpose of sustained attack on British trade. He believed in a protracted struggle, placing a considerable proportion of his resources on training. At first only a few U-boats could be maintained on patrol in the Atlantic. The position was greatly improved by the capture of bases in Norway and France in 1940, and the "happy time" followed, with the available U-boats achieving high scores. A seesaw struggle followed, and in early 1943 it seemed that the convoy system was crumbling under wolf-pack attacks – but by the summer the U-boats were defeated.

Dönitz was now head of the Navy, replacing Raeder in January 1943. He managed to persuade Hitler to rescind his order to get rid of the surface fleet. His main hopes were pinned on the new types of submarine which in the event appeared too late. Dönitz was a fervent Nazi and Hitler bequeathed the headship of the state to him. He was sentenced to 10 years' imprisonment at Nuremberg. *CJW/CD.*

Donovan, Maj Gen William J ("Wild Bill") (1883–1959). US. A much-decorated World War I veteran and a leading lawyer, Donovan was in 1941 appointed head of the Office of Coordinator of Information, renamed the Office of Strategic Services (OSS) in 1942. A wily and efficient organizer, Donovan was a most effective chief of America's premier clandestine warfare organization.

Doodlebug. British slang for German V-1.

Doolittle, Lt Gen James H (b.1896). US. Between the two world wars, Doolittle was a pioneer of instrument flying techniques and a top racing pilot, winning the Schneider Trophy in 1925 and setting a world speed record in 1932. Recalled to active duty from the Air Corps Reserve in 1940, he planned the first American air attack against the Japanese homeland during World War II. Doolittle personally led the 16 B-25s which took off from USS *Hornet* on April 18 1942 to bomb targets in Tokyo, Kobe, Nagoya, Yokohama and Yokosuka. He received the Congressional Medal of Honor for this mission and, in September 1942, was given command of the US Twelfth Air Force, which supported the Allied campaign in North Africa. Early in 1943 Doolittle was, in addition, made head of the Northwest African Strategic Air Forces. Then, after the Allied invasions of Sicily and Italy, he took over the newly activated Fifteenth Air Force in the Mediterranean on November 1 1943. On January 6 1944, Doolittle became commander of the US Eighth Air Force, remaining with it until the

Doolittle aboard USS *Hornet*, April 1942

end of World War II. Eighth Air Force, operating from England until May 1945, made an increasingly weighty contribution to the combined bombing offensive against Germany. Among the policies he encouraged was that of allowing American long-range fighters to seek out and engage enemy aircraft wherever they might be found, a decision which played a significant part in the defeat of the Luftwaffe. *PJS.*

D

Dornberger, Brig Walter (b.1895). Ger. Artillery lieutenant in World War I; in 1930 took charge of the Reichswehr's military rocket programme, where he was joined by von Braun. In 1937 the rocket establishment moved to Peenemünde, where work concentrated on the V-2 (A-4) rocket. Following its first successful flight, October 3 1942, Dornberger told van Braun: "Today the spaceship was born!" Dornberger was under heavy pressure to develop the V-2 as a "decisive weapon". His task was complicated both by Allied bombing and, especially, by a determined bid to take over the programme by Himmler's SS. Speer's support enabled Dornberger to surmount these difficulties and produce the V-2 for operational use from September 1944. In May 1945, Dornberger surrendered to the Allies. His scientific value saved him from a war crimes' trial: in July 1947 he became a missile consultant to the USAF, and in 1950 joined Bell Aircraft Corporation, where his work on a two-stage, winged rocket aircraft contributed to the USAF's Dyna-Soar project of 1958–63 and thus to the development of the Space Shuttle. *RO'N.*

Dornier Do 17/17Z/215 (German, WWII). Medium bomber; crew 3. Prototype flew 1935; first production deliveries late 1936; entered service 1937. Several sent to Spain, operational evaluation in Civil War. Development with engine changes led to Do 17Z and 215. Do 17Z extensively used against Britain, the Balkans and Crete. Total production, all variants, approx. 1,200. Do 17Z-2 had two 1,000hp BMW Bramo Fafnir 323P engines; max. speed 255mph (408kph); 2,205lb (1,000kg) bombs, four (later up to eight) 7.9mm machine guns.

Dornier Do 217 (German, WWII). Heavy bomber/night fighter; crew 4. First prototype flew August 1938; evaluatory service began 1940; first major production (Do 217E) started 1941. Conversion and modification led to Do 217J night fighter, Do 217K bomber and shipping-strike aircraft, Do 217M bomber missile carrier and Do 217N night fighter/intruder. At least 1,730 (all variants) produced.

Do 217M-1 had two 1,750hp Daimler-Benz DB 603A engines; max. speed 348mph (557kph); 8,818lb (4,000kg) bombs, four/six 7.9mm and two 13mm machine guns.

Douaumont *see* FORT DOUAUMONT.

Doughboy. American World-War I slang for a serviceman.

Douglas A-26/B-26 Invader (US, WWII and after). Attack bomber-night fighter; crew 3. Prototype flew July 10 1942. First production A-26 completed September 1942. Earliest operations (spring 1944) in New Guinea adversely assessed; greater success in Europe mid-September 1944, Italy 1945. Used Korean War and Vietnam; by *Armée de l'Air* in Indochina and Algeria. Production 2,450. Two 2,000hp Pratt and Whitney R-2800-79 engines; max. speed 373mph (600kph); 6,000lb (2,720kg) bombs, up to 18 0.5in machine guns.

Douglas, Marshal of the RAF Lord, of Kirtleside (1893–1969). Br. Served as fighter pilot in World War I. After spell as chief pilot for Handley-Page Transport, rejoined RAF, and in 1939 was Assistant Chief of Air Staff. When Air Chief Marshal Dowding was retired from his post as AOC-in-C Fighter Command after the Battle of Britain, Douglas succeeded him and attempted to develop an offensive role for his Command by instituting aggressive fighter sweeps ("Circus" Operations) over occupied northern France. In January 1943 he went to RAF Middle East Command and in 1944 succeeded Air Marshal Joubert at Coastal Command, where he had some of the responsibility for the air protection of the D-Day invasion

Aggressive commander: Douglas

armada. By the end of the war, Douglas's maritime aircraft were operating aggressively against U-boats in their previously safe training areas in the Baltic. *MH.*

Douhet, Gen Giulio (1869–1930). Italian. Douhet believed air power would determine future wars. Like Smuts, he thought other forms of military power would become irrelevant. Self-defending bombers would pulverize the enemy heartland and force surrender. He foresaw no defence against this and thought the side which mounted and maintained the heaviest bombing would win. His writing had little effect upon Italian doctrine, but reflections of his views are clearly visible in the Trenchard doctrine and perhaps in the design of the American B-17. *ANF.*

Doullens Conference. On March 26 1918, during the German spring offensive in Picardy, an inter-Allied conference, held in the Hôtel de Ville of the French town of Doullens, entrusted Gen Ferdinand Foch with the task of coordinating the operations of the Allied Armies on the Western Front. The seeds of a unified command having been sown at Doullens, Foch was named General-in-Chief of the Allied Armies in France on April 14 1918.

Dowding, Air Chief Marshal Lord (1882–1970). Br. AOC-in-C, RAF Fighter Command 1936-40. The victor of the Battle of Britain. As Air Member (of the Air Council) for Research and Development from 1930-36, Dowding was associated with a period of major technical development in the RAF and especially of a new breed of high performance monoplane fighters (Spitfire and Hurricane), a radically improved power unit (Rolls-Royce Merlin) and the coming of radar. This background meant that when he became C-in-C of Fighter Command he was especially alert, perhaps more so than any other senior officer in the RAF, to the changed possibilities of mounting an effective air defence against bombing attack. Although he received much support from the Chief of the Air Staff, Newall, the main credit for the speed, efficiency and radical nature of the development of Fighter Command from its creation in 1936 until 1940 is due to Dowding.

During the Battle of France of May to June 1940, the French naturally pressed their British ally to support them with greater air strength and Churchill was much inclined to accede. Indeed, some reinforcements of the British

Dowding: British fighter supremo

Air Forces in France were sent, but Dowding firmly and courageously resisted the depletion of Fighter Command and thus preserved his force to fight under the conditions for which he had trained and equipped it, that is, within the radar coverage which existed over Britain, but not France.

Dowding's chief work in the Battle of Britain was done before it began. During its course he was already thinking ahead to the development of night fighting tactics, which he rightly foresaw would be the next requirement after victory in daylight. He did, however, show consummate judgment in tolerating the dispute between his two principal Group Commanders, Leigh-Mallory and Park, and allowing them to develop their different tactics.

Dowding was older than most top commanders and would have been replaced in 1940 regardless of whether or not he was *persona grata* with the authorities. That he was not was due, no doubt, to his somewhat crusty manner and advanced views upon spiritual contact with the dead. The way in which he was removed from command in the very hour of victory has, nevertheless, left an enduring impression of ingratitude to the commander who won the last all-British victory in the first, and still the last, decisive air battle in history. *ANF*.

Drapsin, Maj Gen. Yugoslav. Commander Fourth Yugoslav Army during the final offensive up the Dalmatian Coast into Istria in March–April 1945. He led the same unit during the Trieste crisis between Tito and the Western Allies in May 1945.

Dreadnought. The prototype 20th-century battleship which revolutionized the vessels, tactics and strategy of all the major sea powers. (i.e. Britain, Germany, Japan and the US). *Dreadnought's* keel was laid in Portsmouth dockyard on October 2 1905, she was launched by King Edward VII on February 10 1906 and underwent her sea trials in the last three months of the year. Upon the completion of these, every other battleship in the world was shown to be obsolete. "Dreadnought" was adopted internationally as a generic term for up-to-date battleships.

Dreadnought was of 17,900 tons, had a speed of 21 knots (2 knots faster than any other battleship afloat), and was armed with ten 12in guns which could throw a broadside of 6,800lb (1,500lb more than her most powerful predecessors, the "Lord Nelsons"). She was the first turbine-engined big ship in any navy, which meant that she could hold the sea without engine overhaul for much longer than her predecessors. In her first battle practice, *Dreadnought* secured 25 hits from 40 rounds at a range of 8,000yd (7,300m). The concept of a long-range fleet action, which materialized at Jutland, thus became a practicability. By 1916, however, *Dreadnought* was no longer the last word in battleships and, ironically, her main achievement in action seems to have been the ramming and sinking of a German U-boat in 1915. She was scrapped in 1920. *ANF*.

Dresden. German light cruiser. In 1914 joined Von Spee's China Squadron. Fought at the Battles of Coronel and the Falklands, being the only German ship to escape from the latter. Re-entered the Pacific where she was hunted by British cruisers, and finally trapped and shelled into submission by *Kent* and *Glasgow* and the armed merchant cruiser *Orama* at Más Afuera Island, Chile, March 14 1915.

Dresden, bombing of (February 1945). This German city was attacked by 800 aircraft of Bomber Command on the night of February 13–14, by another 400 bombers of the Eighth Air Force on the 14th and by smaller American forces on March 2 and April 17 1945. The city was almost completely destroyed and although the number of people killed is not known, it is likely to have been in the region of 60,000. Much the greatest part of this destruction was caused by the British night attack. The weather conditions were perfect for bombing and the Germans, for unexplained reasons, failed to intercept with night fighters or to engage with AA fire. The result was an unprecedented and unexpected accuracy and concentration of bombing which produced a massive firestorm of the kind which had engulfed Hamburg in July 1943.

Due to the scale of destruction and the late stage of the war, the need for the attack and its morality have been subjects of controversy ever since. The plan for the attack, which lacked this hindsight, was made in January 1945 when the German counteroffensive in the Ardennes, the V-2 attack on England and the deployment of snorkel-equipped U-boats seemed to have re-opened the question of how and when the war would be ended. The attacks on Dresden were part of a plan, known as "Thunderclap", which was intended to convince the Germans that continued resistance would be fruitless. Additional reasons for selecting Dresden were its strategic importance in the rear of the German retreat before the Russian advance (although the Russians seem not to have shared this view) and the possibility that it would be used as an alternative to Berlin as a capital city. The extent of the destruction was not foreseen and similar attacks on other towns in the same area of Germany at the same period were much less effective. *ANF*.

Driefontein, Battle of (March 10 1900), Second Boer War. To face Roberts' advance on Bloemfontein, De Wet deployed c6,000 men along a 7-mile (11km) front. Roberts attacked frontally and on the left flank with 10,000 men (losses 424),

D

the main thrust falling on De La Rey's 1,500-strong force at Abraham's Kraal. The Boers (losses 144) withdrew from their defensive lines. Bloemfontein fell on March 13 and the Orange Free State was annexed on May 24.

Drina river, Battle of the *see* SERBIAN CAMPAIGN.

Drocourt-Quéant Line. This strong defensive position, known to the Germans as the "Wotan" Line, was an outlying spur of the Hindenburg Line, running northward from Quéant, near Bullecourt, and across the Scarpe to Drocourt, 10 miles (16km) northeast of Arras. Supported by 59 tanks, the Canadian Corps – part of the British First Army – stormed the line on September 2 1918 and reached open country beyond. This caused Ludendorff to order a general retirement to the Sensée, Canal du Nord and Hindenburg Line, thus abandoning much of the ground the Germans had won in March and April that year.

DuBose, Rear Adm Laurance Toombs (1893–1967). US. His command, the cruiser *Portland* was torpedoed off Guadalcanal, November 1942. DuBose then became a task force commander, specializing most effectively in shore bombardment in support of landings at Bougainville, the Gilberts, the Marshalls and Leyte Gulf.

"Duisburg" convoy. Seven Axis ships, carrying supplies to Rommel, were sunk by Force K, based on Malta, November 8–9 1941.

Duke of York. British battleship. *King George V* class; completed end 1941. Served, mostly as flagship, with Home Fleet untill 1945. The high point of her career of distant cover to Arctic convoys was the destruction of *Scharnhorst* off North Cape (December 1943). She was the flagship of the British Pacific Fleet in 1945.

Dulles, Allen Welsh (1893–1969). US *Chargé d'Affaire* and representative of the Office of Strategic Services in Switzerland, who carried on negotiations for the surrender of all German forces in Italy during the winter of 1944–45.

Back in the US, he was involved in the setting up of the CIA, and served as its director from 1953–61. *See also* ARMISTICE NEGOTIATIONS, GERMAN.

Dulles, John Foster (1888–1959). US. US Secretary of State from 1953. Dulles attracted much criticism for his "brinkmanship" policies, based on the threat of "massive retaliation", and his formulation, despite his opposition to Anglo-French military action during the Suez Crisis, of the "Eisenhower Doctrine", advocating the use of US forces to "stabilize" the Middle East.

Dunbar-Nasmith, Adm Sir Martin (1884–1965). Br. Won VC commanding the submarine *E-11* during the Dardanelles campaign, 1915. C-in-C Plymouth and Western Approaches (1939), in charge of anti-submarine warfare in the Atlantic. This responsibility was removed to Liverpool in 1941, Dunbar-Nasmith becoming Flag Officer, London.

***Dunkerque*-class.** French battleships; *Dunkerque*, *Strasbourg*; launched 1935–36; 35,500 tons full load; 8 x 13in guns (all forward). Designed against German "pocket battleships". *Dunkerque* damaged by British action at Mers-el-Kébir, still repairing when scuttled at Toulon, 1942, to prevent capture by the Germans.

Dunkirk (1940). By May 20 1940, the German Army had driven an armoured wedge into the Allied armies in Northern France and reached the Channel coast at Abbeville. The BEF, the Belgian Army and the French First Army had been separated from the bulk of the French forces south of the Somme and Aisne rivers. An Allied counterattack at Arras failed on May 21 and, with the Germans pressing in on all sides, evacuation seemed the only salvation. On May 26 the British Cabinet authorized Lord Gort, the commander of the BEF, to withdraw his men to the Channel coast.

Vice Adm Sir Bertram Ramsey, Flag Officer Commanding Dover, had begun making arrangements for an evacuation, codenamed "Dynamo", as early as May 20 and at 1857 hours on the 26th he was

given the order to commence. Warships, ferries, trawlers and a wide variety of civilian craft were pressed into service but their tasks were most carefully coordinated. The capture of Boulogne and Calais ensured that the main evacuation port had to be Dunkirk. The British and French withdrawal to a defended bridgehead around the port was aided by von Rundstedt's decision to halt his exhausted armoured divisions. Meanwhile, overcast skies restricted Luftwaffe attacks and calm

Evacuation from Dunkirk, May 1941

seas aided Ramsey's motley collection of vessels. It was initially predicted that some 45,000 men might be got away in the two days allowed for "Dynamo". This estimate seemed ambitious when, on May 27, the inner harbour became unusable and less than 8,000 men were evacuated. However, ships were berthed alongside the harbour moles and men were ferried from the beaches to the larger ships lying offshore. The number of British and French troops evacuated steadily increased and, on May 31 alone, 68,014 men were lifted. Renewed German attacks forced the bridgehead to contract but the evacuation continued until the morning of June 4 when the rescue fleet was ordered to disperse and the remaining French troops in Dunkirk surrendered. "Dynamo" was a masterpiece of improvised logistics: 338,225 men were evacuated to England, including 140,000 Frenchmen. *MS.*

DUKW *see* AMPHIBIOUS CRAFT AND WEAPONS.

Duong Van ("Big") Minh, Gen (b.1916). Republic of Vietnam. Gained prominence commanding the troops that crushed the religious sects for President Ngo Dinh Diem of South Vietnam in 1955. Resentful of Minh's popularity, Diem assigned him to powerless posts. In revenge, Minh led the coup that overthrew Diem in November 1963 and, it has been alleged, ordered two of his aides to assassinate Diem. Minh himself was deposed in January 1964 and spent the next four years in exile. A rallying point for the putative "third force" or neutralist tendency, Minh returned to power on April 28 1975 when President Thieu's government resigned to let Minh seek an accommodation with rapidly advancing communist forces. The communists ignored Minh's pleas to negotiate, and Minh ordered his troops to surrender on the 30th. *WST.*

Durnford-Slater, Vice Adm D F *see* SUEZ CRISIS.

Dutch East Indies campaign (January–March 1942). While still engaged in Malaya and the Philippines, Japan launched its invasion of the Dutch East Indies (Indonesia), both to secure a vital sector in the defensive perimeter of the Greater East Asia Co-Prosperity Sphere and to acquire control of an area rich in natural resources, including major oilfields. Three invasion fleets were assembled: Western Force, at Camranh Bay, Indochina (with an advance base at Sarawak, northwest Borneo, taken in December 1941); and Central and Eastern Forces, at Davao, Mindanao. Allied ABDA Command hoped to hold the "Malay Barrier" (Sumatra-Java-Sunda Islands-Timor-northern Australia), but although ABDA's garrisons generally outnumbered Japanese invasion troops, Japan had naval and air superiority.

Central and Eastern Forces sailed on January 7 1942. In eastern Borneo, Central Force secured Tarakan by January 13 and the major oil centre of Balikpapan (where three destroyer-transports were sunk by US destroyers of Rear Adm Doorman's Combined Striking Force) by January 24. Eastern Force occupied northeast Celebes on January 11 and moved south to take the air base at Kendari (January 24) and the port of Makassar (February 9). These op-

erations provided "stepping-stones" for the conquests of Amboina (January 30); Bali (February 19), where an ABDA naval attack was repulsed in Lombok Strait; and Timor – within 400 miles (645km) of northern Australia – on February 23. Meanwhile, Western Force landed successfully at Muntok, east Sumatra, on February 14, securing the oil installations at Palembang (aided by airborne invasion), February 16.

On February 27–28 the last Allied counterstroke, aimed at Eastern and Western Forces' converging assault on Java, ended in the destruction of the greater part of Doorman's fleet in the Battle of the Java Sea and the sinking of its survivors in the Battle of the Sunda Straits, February 28–March 1. Initial Japanese landings were made at Banten Bay on February 28, and on March 8 the Dutch command on Java surrendered. *RO'N.*

Dutch-Indonesian War (1962). In January 1962 the 12-year dispute between the Netherlands and Indonesia over West New Guinea degenerated into an undeclared war. Naval forces clashed off Fak Fak, resulting in the loss of an Indonesian torpedo boat. Other engagements occurred near Sorong, Kaimara, and the neighbouring islands of Waigeo and Gag. In February the Dutch released Indonesian prisoners in response to U Thant's appeal that they provide "a humanitarian gesture which might help in easing tension all around". In May the Netherlands accepted the mediation of an American emissary, Ellsworth Bunker. On August 15 the Dutch and Indonesians agreed that the United Nations should administer the territory from October 1 1962 to May 1 1963; Pakistan provided a battalion to police it. Although the Dutch government was angered by the lack of American support during the war, giving up the colony saved their taxpayers $36 million a year. *BHR.*

Dzerzhinsky, Feliks Edmundovitch (1877–1926). Polish aristocrat, joined Russian revolutionaries; as first head of Cheka, from December 1917, helped Bolsheviks to secure state power by policy of terror.

E

Eagle. British aircraft carrier. Laid down in Britain as a battleship for Chile in 1913, she was taken over for conversion in 1917; completed 1923, as the first carrier with an "island" superstructure. Although large (26,880 tons full load; 667.5ft/203m long overall), well-armed (9 × 6in guns) and heavily-protected, she could operate only 21 aircraft. In the Mediterranean during World War II, she was torpedoed and sunk by *U-73* during the "Pedestal" Malta convoy, August 11 1942.

Eaker, Lt Gen Ira C (1896–1987). US. Commanding General US Eighth Air Force 1942–44. Commander Allied Air Forces, Mediterranean 1944. Eaker's selection to command the Eighth Air Force showed the high confidence which Arnold placed in him, for upon the outcome of daylight precision bombing from bases in the UK the whole enterprise of American independent air power seemed to depend. While Eaker's B-17s and B-24s would be supported by strong fighter cover, notably from the large numbers of RAF Spitfires which were available, when they were over the nearer parts of France, this protection could not extend to Germany as no fighters of sufficient range existed. Eaker, however, believed that his heavy bombers with their powerful defensive armament, disciplined formation flying tactics and high ceiling, would be able to defend themselves against German fighters. From August 1942 a series of probing operations over France seemed to suggest that when larger numbers of bombers were available, this might be so. From January 1943 Eaker began to put the theory to the test, but on their longer-range missions the Eighth Air Force suffered severe casualties until, in the disastrous attack on Schweinfurt on October 14 1943, the plan was shown to be impracticable. Eaker, who was guilty of no more than adhering to his directive, was translated to the Mediterranean and the solution of the main problem was left to Spaatz. *ANF.*

East African campaign (1914–18). In August 1914, Col Paul von Lettow-Vorbeck, military commander in German East Africa, deemed it his duty to help the German war effort by posing a threat to the surrounding British and Belgian colonies.

Lettow-Vorbeck decided to mount a guerrilla campaign that would force the British to divert forces from other, more important, theatres. He chose as his target the Uganda railway, upon which the economy of British East Africa depended. His raids were highly successful: in two months, 30 trains were derailed and ten bridges destroyed.

The British reaction was to send troops from India to invade the German colony. The force, 8,000-strong, was landed at Tanga on November 8 1914. There it suffered a humiliating defeat at the hands of only 1,000 men under

Scuttled German cruiser, East Africa

Lettow-Vorbeck, and was forced to withdraw to Mombasa.

The British went onto the defensive until 1916, when the South African government provided fresh troops for an offensive. Lt Gen Jan Smuts was appointed Imperial c-in-c. In March 1916 he crossed the border in the Kilimanjaro area with three divisions, comprised of 27,000 British, South African, Indian and East African troops. At the same time, further British, Belgian and Rhodesian forces invaded the German colony from both the northwest and the southwest.

Lettow-Vorbeck, with a total force of never more than 3,000 Europeans and 11,000 askaris, evaded major engagements unless he had local superiority, and always withdrew before the British

could pin him down. By the end of September 1916, Smuts had taken Dar-es-Salaam and had occupied the northern two-thirds of the German colony, but he had failed to trap the elusive Lettow-Vorbeck. The tse tse fly dismounted Smuts's cavalry, and malaria and other tropical diseases so decimated his British, South African and Indian regiments that most had to be evacuated by the end of 1916.

The remainder of the campaign had to be fought with African troops, who could withstand the climate. In November 1917 Lettow-Vorbeck was nearly cornered in the southeast, but managed to escape into Portuguese East Africa with some 2,000 of his best troops. Still undefeated at the time of the Armistice in Europe, he finally surrendered on November 25 1918. *WGFJ.*

East African campaigns, British (January–November 1941) *see* ERITREA, ITALIAN SOMALILAND and ETHIOPIAN CAMPAIGNS.

Eastern Front (1914–18) *see* BRUSILOV'S OFFENSIVE (1916–17); GALICIAN CAMPAIGN (1914); GORLICE-TARNOW OFFENSIVE (1915); TANNENBERG AND MASURIAN LAKES (1914); WARSAW, BATTLE OF (1914).

Eastern Solomons, Battle of the (August 23-25 1942). Second major naval action of the Guadalcanal campaign, provoked by Japan's urgent need to reinforce Guadalcanal. A Main Force (Vice Adm Kondo: carriers *Shokaku* and *Zuikaku* (Vice Adm Nagumo); seaplane carrier *Chitose*; 3 battleships; 10 cruisers; 21 destroyers) steamed south from Truk, preceded by a Diversion Force (Rear Adm Chuichi Hara: carrier *Ryujo*; 1 cruiser; 2 destroyers), to lure the US carrier groups to battle. Meanwhile, Rear Adm Raizo Tanaka's Landing Force (7 transports; 1 cruiser; 3 destroyers) was to put ashore 1,500 men. Deployed east of the Solomons was US Task Force 61 (Vice Adm Fletcher: carriers *Saratoga*, *Enterprise* and *Wasp*; 1 battleship; 9 cruisers; 18 destroyers).

Early on August 23, Landing Force was sighted by US aircraft, but air strikes from Henderson Field, Guadalcanal, and *Saratoga* failed because of bad weather.

Fletcher, deciding no major action was imminent, detached *Wasp* for refuelling. When Diversion Force was sighted by US aircraft early next day, Fletcher launched strikes from *Saratoga* and *Enterprise* – vainly attempting to divert them when Nagumo's Main Force carriers were spotted. The US aircraft sank *Ryujo*; but counterstrikes from *Shokaku* and *Zuikaku* badly damaged *Enterprise*. A further strike from *Saratoga* damaged *Chitose* but failed to find Nagumo's carriers. The Japanese lost 90 aircraft; the Americans only 20. That night, after a fruitless hunt for Fletcher's force, Kondo withdrew. Early on August 25, Landing Force was attacked by USMC and USAAF aircraft from Guadalcanal and Espiritu Santo: a transport and a destroyer were sunk. The operation was abandoned, and Japanese attempts to reinforce Guadalcanal by day gave way to the "Tokyo Express". *RO'N.*

Easter offensive (1972). Determined to make 1972 the year of "decisive victory", Vietnamese communist forces launched an offensive on four fronts beginning March 30. Three People's Army (PAVN) divisions overran all 12 posts near the demilitarized zone that US Marines had turned over to the Army of the Republic (ARVN) 3rd Division; the PAVN 320th Division attacked ARVN outposts throughout the central highlands: PAVN and People's Liberation Armed Force (PLAF) units besieged the Binh Long province capital; and PAVN units infiltrated from Cambodia to force suspension of "pacification" in the Mekong delta.

The offensive provoked President Nixon to order the mining of harbours and intensified bombing of North Vietnam in May. That pressure combined with high levels of American air support for the ARVN in the South helped to stall the offensive and very likely saved the ARVN from collapse. However, communist forces remained in control of northern Quang Tri province and in a much improved position elsewhere. While the offensive failed to extract the concessions from the US, it revealed the ARVN's continued heavy dependency on American assistance and direct support. *WST. See also* AN LOC, SIEGE OF.

War at sea

John B Hattendorf
Ernest J King Professor of Maritime History
US Naval War College

The main characteristic of navies in the 20th century has been rapid and continual technological change. Between 1588 and 1815, the development of the warship had been relatively slow. There were clear refinements and developments in hull design, ordnance and size of ships, yet they involved adaptations of the same fundamental principles. In the 19th century, the developments were based on entirely new approaches.

Menace from the deep – the submarine remains an undisputable key development in the advance of weapons technology.

The first technological change was in propulsion. In 1814–15, Robert Fulton's catamaran steam frigate, known as both *Demologos* and as *Fulton*, was the first warship powered by steam, but she was not used on active service by the United States Navy. In Britain, the first steam-powered naval vessels were tug-boats acquired in the 1820s. The first steamships were paddlewheel ships, but that form of steam propulsion was too vulnerable in battle. The equipment took up valuable space needed for broadside guns, and it was difficult to manoeuvre a paddlewheel ship in company with sailing vessels. Further progress had to await the development of the propeller, which removed the earlier objections to the sidewheel steamer. Early examples of the screw-propeller frigate demonstrated the advantages of sailing warships with auxiliary steam propulsion using the screw propeller. This change came slowly. The French navy was the first to design a warship along these lines. Laid down in 1848 and launched in 1850, the *Napoléon* started a naval arms race between Britain and France, each seeking to outdo the other in building warships with auxiliary steam power.

In 1854, the British fleet in the Baltic had 10 steam warships out of a total of 14. The next year, the Baltic fleet became the world's first all-steam fighting force. The Crimean War brought home new lessons for the further development of warships. First, it emphasized the uselessness of having sailing warships operate with steam warships in battle. Steam propulsion completely changed the fundamentals of battle tactics. It made a clear distinction between tactical mobility and strategic mobility. The first required speed, while the latter required endurance and range. The introduction of steam led, in the first instance, to tactical mobility. But the shift to steam also meant a new dependence on fuel, which limited strategic mobility, so sails retained an important role.

The development of steam propulsion led to large building programmes in which it was discovered that the new ships to carry the heavy steam machinery required much more wood, for increased strength and size, and thus were much more expensive to build. Second, the Crimean War demonstrated the effectiveness of shell-firing guns. These had been known for some years—a Danish warship had been destroyed by shells in 1849—but it was not until shell-firing Russian warships destroyed the Turkish fleet at the Battle of Sinope in 1853 that most naval officers

realized the effectiveness of shells in destroying wooden ships. This led to further developments. First, there was a revolution in ordnance, changing from round shot to shell guns. Along with this came practical methods of breech-loading, rifled gun barrels, cylindrical shapes for projectiles and powder charges, greater accuracy and increased range.

The ironclad warship

These innovations in offensive capabilities showed the need to develop better forms of defence against them. The most important consideration at this point was armour. The French were the first to react with a new type of ship which took these developments into consideration. This

La Gloire (1860). Designed by Dupuy de Lôme, this French ironclad frigate was the first sea-going armoured warship. The design was an attempt to retain French prestige and outclass Britain's wooden, steam-powered battle fleet, taking into account the new power of rifled artillery.

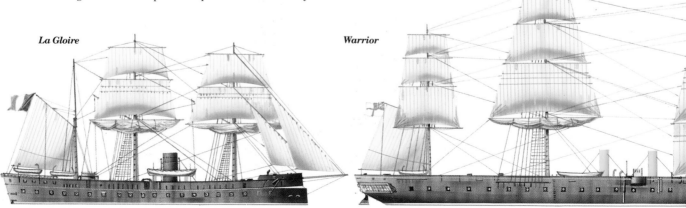

La Gloire

Warrior

A Russian cruiser is struck by a 20cm shell as she lies at anchor in Port Arthur harbour during the Russo-Japanese War, August 1904. The sea battle on August 10 off Port Arthur had forced the Russians back into port, where they were vulnerable to indirect fire from Japanese shore batteries. Three Russian ships were put out of action in this way.

the conventional method of wooden ships with a battery of muzzle-loading guns for broadside firing. Although superior to some of the early breech-loading guns of the day, they were soon to be replaced by heavier and more powerful guns able to penetrate armour plate.

At the same time, guns needed to be handier, in order to operate at quickly changing angles of fire as ships became more manoeuvrable under steam. The answer to this need was the revolving turret gun. An old idea, it had been widely discussed since the early 19th century. During the American Civil War, the Swedish inventor John Ericsson built a turret ship of iron for the US Navy. This ship, called the *Monitor*, demonstrated the value of her turret in a dramatic battle with the Confederate broadside ironclad *Virginia* (formerly *Merrimac*) at Hampton Roads, Virginia, on March 9 1862. Ericsson's design included a number of other innovations, including a forced ventilation system below decks, an armoured pilot house, and a protected anchor housing which allowed the ship to anchor or to weigh anchor without exposing crew members to hostile fire. The battle at Hampton Roads stimulated widespread building of iron warships, and created great interest both in the revolving turret and in new gunnery designs. The battle spurred Austria, Spain, Russia and France in their naval building programmes, while other powers began to give serious consideration to building such ships. During the remainder of the 19th century, there was a wide array of new developments, ranging from the use of electricity on board ship to the invention of the self-propelled, underwater torpedo.

Between 1895 and 1900, a series of technological innovations dramatically improved fighting capabilities. The steam battleship became capable of combat in the open ocean. Improvements in gunpowder and gunnery quadrupled the range of effective naval gunfire. Efficient steam engines and light steel armour gave cruisers an advantage both in terms of protection and in speed to serve as scouts for the battle fleet. Wireless increased the range of communication, allowing collection of information as well as control of distant ships by commanders. In addition, a novel threat to the fleet, the torpedo boat, was neutralized by another innovation: light, quick-firing torpedo defence batteries. This was the first specialized defensive weapon in warships. All of these attributes were brought together for the first time in the Royal Navy's

was *La Gloire*, a wooden warship with iron plate for armour. Up to this point, France had failed to outmatch Britain's wooden, steam-driven battleship fleet, but with *La Gloire*, launched in 1859, she moved to continue the arms race and to match the diplomatic advantages she had gained through the Congress of Paris in 1856. It led shortly to the first seagoing, ironclad fleet.

Britain's response to the challenge was not long in coming. She had already had experience with an even more revolutionary type of ship, Brunel's *Great Britain*, a merchant ship built entirely of iron, with screw propulsion. This led the way to the building of the *Warrior*, the world's first iron warship, in 1859–61. With her came a new age in naval ship construction. She was armed in

Warrior (1861). The British response to the new French ironclads was to create the first iron-hulled warship, designed by Isaac Watts and John Scott Russell. The main guns, boilers and engines were housed in an armoured citadel and the hull had watertight compartments.

Monitor (1862). The Swedish inventor John Ericsson designed the first turreted ironclad warship for the United States, making a complete break with traditional hull design. She fought to a draw with the Confederate ship *Virginia* (ex-USS *Merrimac*) at Hampton Roads on March 9 1862. The battle demonstrated the value of armour and the turret gun.

Terror Laid down in the 1870s, this *Amphitrite*-class warship was the most highly developed of the monitors built for the US Navy. Although she carried such innovations as a pneumatic system for guns and turrets, she was outmoded by the time she was launched in 1896.

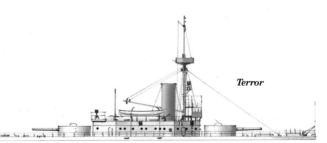

Monitor

Terror

Majestic-class battleships, which established the standard for their type from 1895 to 1906.

The next era began with the completion of HMS *Dreadnought* in 1906. In the years between 1906 and 1914, battle fleets underwent another technological transformation. This involved both the integration of ships within a battle fleet and that of weapons on board a single ship. The integration of the ships in the fleet may be seen in the innovation of the torpedo boat destroyer: this became a specialized vessel, separated from the battle fleet but at the same time an integral part of it. On board ship, the central fire control became the means through which a number of weapons were integrated into a single system. This allowed battleships to shoot with accuracy at twice the range of those without central fire control.

Together, all of these developments created a sense that the traditional ways and methods of a navy were gone forever. The very existence of this vast range of new technology raised questions as to what a navy's role should be and how it should be employed. With it came new connections with industry, new ties to raw materials, scientists, inventors and an entirely different body of technological knowledge. For many naval officers, the wave of the future was to follow technological ingenuity and to apply it in whatever way seemed possible. The new technology created a logic of its own, each new major capability rendering the previous ones obsolete. The very dynamics of technology created competition.

The impact on naval warfare theory

While technological developments fascinated the public as well as professionals, a few thinkers began to examine the nature and character of naval warfare in the context of that change. The pioneers in this group were two brothers, Captain Sir John Colomb, RM, and Rear-Admiral Philip Colomb, along with Professor Sir John Knox Laughton.

Together, they provided the early insights in Britain for discussion of the broad uses of naval power and for examining such issues through ideas gleaned from the study of naval history. This approach was adopted by Rear-Admiral Stephen B Luce of the United States Navy. He combined it with a comparative examination of military thought, focusing on the writings of Jomini and the educational ideas of the Prussian General Staff that were in use in the 1870s and 1880s. In 1884, Luce established the Naval War College at Newport, Rhode Island, as the world's first naval establishment to study the highest aspects of warfare. Many other nations established colleges on this model in the years that followed. The first important product of the College was the work of Captain Alfred Thayer Mahan. In 1890, he published his lectures at the Naval War College, *The influence of sea power upon history, 1660–1783*. Through this book and others that followed it, Mahan established a distinctively Anglo-American concept of sea power which was copied by many other nations in the years to follow. Mahan argued that the lessons of history were still applicable in an age of technological change. By using the example of Britain in the 17th and 18th centuries, Mahan tried to develop parallels between the nature of international relations in that period and those of his own time. Using an interpretation which was compatible with contemporary ideas of empire, race and competition for survival in international relations, Mahan produced a set of ideas which were extremely attractive to the naval leaders of his time. His followers particularly stressed those of his views which emphasized the importance of the capital ship, battle between fleets of capital ships, bases and position along the sea lines of communication and command of the sea. Sir Julian Corbett refined Mahan's ideas and placed them in a new, systematic context of his own, based on deeper investigations of naval history. His

The *Dreadnought*-class of battleships completely altered the appearance of warships, marking the beginning of a new era in naval design. After she entered service, there were two categories of warships in the world; pre-Dreadnoughts and post-Dreadnoughts.

The gun turrets were distributed in a pattern to avoid only one or two shells putting an entire battery out of action. The disposition allowed for eight guns on either broadside or four, possibly six, to be fired ahead or astern. The construction of circular bulkheads carrying roller paths for the mountings was a new and successful innovation.

Magazines. The improved safety of ammunition magazines came through their location on the centre line, rather than along the sides of the ship.

Heavy guns. *Dreadnought* introduced the idea of all-big guns for long-range firing. She carried ten 12-inch, 45-calibre guns.

Funnel ca

Cu

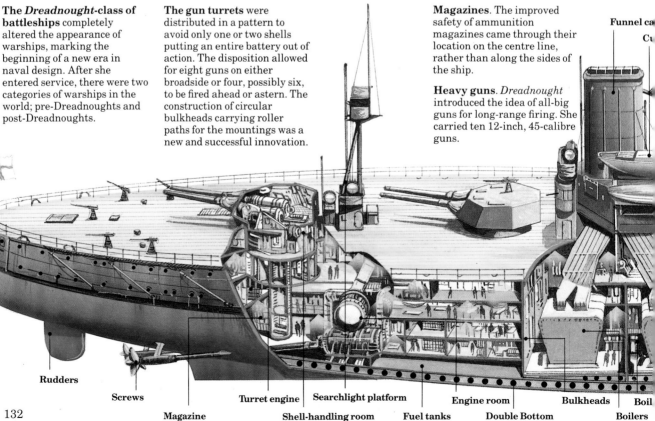

Rudders

Screws

Magazine

Turret engine

Shell-handling room

Searchlight platform

Fuel tanks

Engine room

Double Bottom

Bulkheads

Boilers

Boil

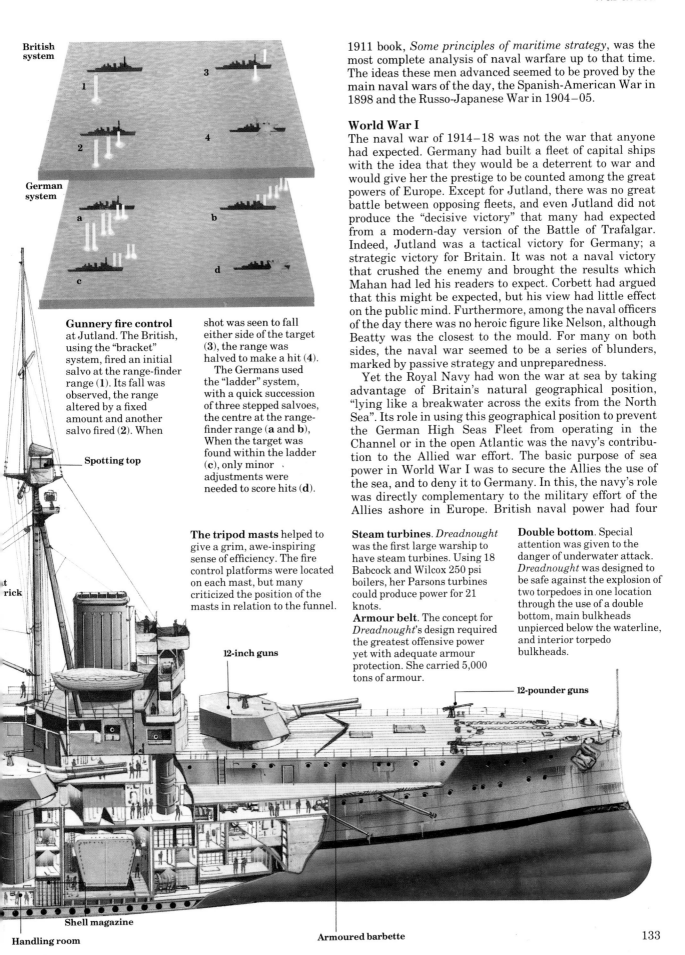

British system

1
2
3
4

German system

a
b
c
d

Gunnery fire control at Jutland. The British, using the "bracket" system, fired an initial salvo at the range-finder range (**1**). Its fall was observed, the range altered by a fixed amount and another salvo fired (**2**). When shot was seen to fall either side of the target (**3**), the range was halved to make a hit (**4**).

The Germans used the "ladder" system, with a quick succession of three stepped salvoes, the centre at the range-finder range (**a** and **b**), When the target was found within the ladder (**c**), only minor adjustments were needed to score hits (**d**).

Spotting top

t rick

The tripod masts helped to give a grim, awe-inspiring sense of efficiency. The fire control platforms were located on each mast, but many criticized the position of the masts in relation to the funnel.

12-inch guns

Steam turbines. *Dreadnought* was the first large warship to have steam turbines. Using 18 Babcock and Wilcox 250 psi boilers, her Parsons turbines could produce power for 21 knots.

Armour belt. The concept for *Dreadnought*'s design required the greatest offensive power yet with adequate armour protection. She carried 5,000 tons of armour.

Double bottom. Special attention was given to the danger of underwater attack. *Dreadnought* was designed to be safe against the explosion of two torpedoes in one location through the use of a double bottom, main bulkheads unpierced below the waterline, and interior torpedo bulkheads.

12-pounder guns

Shell magazine

Handling room

Armoured barbette

1911 book, *Some principles of maritime strategy*, was the most complete analysis of naval warfare up to that time. The ideas these men advanced seemed to be proved by the main naval wars of the day, the Spanish-American War in 1898 and the Russo-Japanese War in 1904–05.

World War I

The naval war of 1914–18 was not the war that anyone had expected. Germany had built a fleet of capital ships with the idea that they would be a deterrent to war and would give her the prestige to be counted among the great powers of Europe. Except for Jutland, there was no great battle between opposing fleets, and even Jutland did not produce the "decisive victory" that many had expected from a modern-day version of the Battle of Trafalgar. Indeed, Jutland was a tactical victory for Germany; a strategic victory for Britain. It was not a naval victory that crushed the enemy and brought the results which Mahan had led his readers to expect. Corbett had argued that this might be expected, but his view had little effect on the public mind. Furthermore, among the naval officers of the day there was no heroic figure like Nelson, although Beatty was the closest to the mould. For many on both sides, the naval war seemed to be a series of blunders, marked by passive strategy and unpreparedness.

Yet the Royal Navy had won the war at sea by taking advantage of Britain's natural geographical position, "lying like a breakwater across the exits from the North Sea". Its role in using this geographical position to prevent the German High Seas Fleet from operating in the Channel or in the open Atlantic was the navy's contribution to the Allied war effort. The basic purpose of sea power in World War I was to secure the Allies the use of the sea, and to deny it to Germany. In this, the navy's role was directly complementary to the military effort of the Allies ashore in Europe. British naval power had four main tasks: first, to protect the sea lines of communication of the Allied armies, particularly those with France where the main offensive lay; second, to halt enemy trade in order to handicap hostile military operations and to exert pressure on the mass of the enemy's people; third, to protect British and Allied trade, which carried the basic source of munitions and supplies for the Allied armies and for the peoples of the Allied nations; and fourth, to resist invasion and raids by sea.

A vital role

In achieving these fundamental goals, the war at sea played a vital and decisive part in the Allies' overall war effort. Germany failed in her attempt to deny the Allies the use of the sea, first through a major fleet battle and then through a submarine war. The Allies' ability to carry out their fundamental objectives at sea were based on four interrelated factors: the strength of the Grand Fleet; its bases; the carrying capacity of Allied merchant shipping; and the ability of the Allied ship-building industry to repair or replace damaged and sunken ships.

The naval war of 1914–18 was an example of the effectiveness of naval power when it is already in control of the sea. In such a position, its tasks normally lack the drama of battle between great ships. At the same time, other kinds of operations at sea were important, particularly those by the vessels that became known as the workhorses of the fleet: cruisers, destroyers, submarines and a wide variety of small craft. The everyday use of the sea is a humdrum affair. It is the story of dowdy merchantmen slowly carrying their cargoes across the wide expanse of water, day after day. It is the story of convoys and patrols, looking, watching and waiting. Boring, perhaps, but it is also a tale of gallantry as men struggle against the elements and the attacks of the enemy. The Grand Fleet had a role to play in all this. If the Grand Fleet had not been as strong as it was, the High Seas Fleet could have raised the blockade, German submarines and surface raiders might have entered the Atlantic more easily than they did and with greater support than they had to sink Allied shipping, cut the communications of the Allies with their armies in Europe and starve Britain into submission. The Grand Fleet may not have lived up to people's expectations for dramatic action, but its presence, ready for battle, was an important element in the balance of naval forces at sea.

The strength of the Grand Fleet had its roots in the technological innovations and ship designs that Admiral of the Fleet Lord Fisher had initiated with the building of HMS *Dreadnought* in 1906. Related to this was the general scientific, technological, economic and industrial base which allowed the shipyards to build ships quickly and efficiently, and which let the navy adapt and use new technology to meet unexpected needs.

The Royal Navy had weaknesses which became apparent during the course of the war. Its projectiles, fuses, mines, torpedoes and submarine defences were deficient. In many ways it had not foreseen the changed conditions of naval warfare which it would face. It lacked destroyers and large dry docks. It had failed to foresee the effects of plunging fire. The officers' fixation with decisive battleship battles left them mentally unprepared to cope with uses of forces which might have proved more productive.

There were mistakes, too: the German battlecruiser *Goeben* was neither stopped in her passage from Messina, Italy, to the Dardanelles in 1914 nor destroyed in 1918;

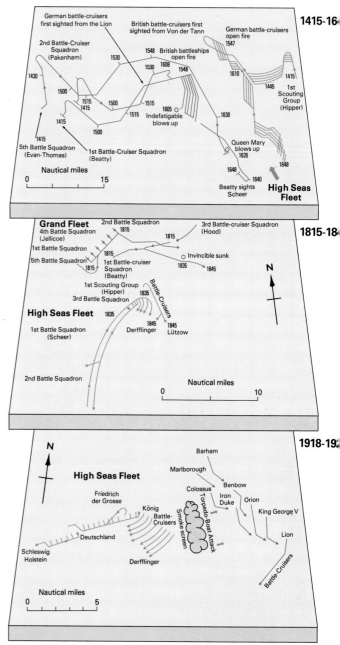

The Battle of Jutland (May 31 1916) began when the British battlecruiser squadron under Vice Adm Sir David Beatty engaged the German battlecruiser squadron under Vice Adm Franz von Hipper (*top*). At 1415 hours that afternoon, the British battle fleet under Adm Sir John Jellicoe was 65 miles (105km) north of Beatty, while at the same time, the German battle fleet under Adm Reinhard Scheer was 60 miles (96km) south of Hipper's position. The opposing battlecruiser squadrons tried to lure one another into range of their own main battle fleet. In the battle that followed, German gunnery outperformed the British, the resulting hits igniting the magazines and sinking two British battlecruisers. At 1645 hours, Beatty turned north, trying to lure Hipper into the range of Jellicoe's guns.

The second stage (*centre*) saw the first clash between the battle fleets (1816 to 1845 hours). At 1800, Beatty joined Jellicoe, and shortly thereafter, at 1815, Jellicoe's battle fleet began deploying into a line ahead in order to cap the German "T", silhouette Scheer's ships against the setting sun and cut off his

retreat to the south. After a heavy gunnery exchange in which one British and four German battlecruisers were sunk, Scheer terminated the action by a brilliant 180 degree battle turn to the south.

The third stage (*bottom*) involved the second clash between the battle fleets (1912 to 1926 hours). At 1912, when Scheer tried to break through the British line, he found that his line of ships was still open to murderous fire from the British broadsides. The Germans replied to this fire, and broke off the action at 1918, when they executed a battle turn away from the British, under cover of a smoke screen laid by their torpedo boats. At 1923, the British turned away to avoid torpedo attack. By sunset the two fleets were running southward on parallel courses trading gunfire with destroyers, the British between the German fleet and Germany. By twilight the next morning, Scheer had silently passed through the British rear and escaped from Jellicoe's grasp.

The wreck of HMS *Invincible* after the Battle of Jutland, May 31 1916.

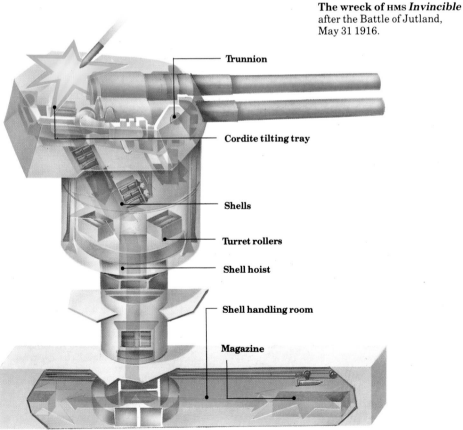

Trunnion

Cordite tilting tray

Shells

Turret rollers

Shell hoist

Shell handling room

Magazine

the response to the German battlecruisers' Scarborough raid in 1914 was poor; the Admiralty too hastily rushed into the Dardanelles campaign in 1915; the Germans were not pursued after the Dogger Bank action also in 1915; until 1917, the anti-submarine warfare campaign was inefficient and failed to use the convoy system effectively; and there were others.

Underlying these weaknesses were two important matters. The Royal Navy lacked a well-organized and competent naval staff and its officer corps was inadequately trained in strategy and tactics. It was hampered by an over-centralized administration in London that paid more attention to details than to broad policy. This weakness was spread to the command of the fleet through the new technology of naval communications. Wireless allowed the Admiralty to give orders to ships and squadrons over the heads of the immediate responsible commanders who were in a better position to judge what actions should be taken. "Yet, in spite of its mistakes," Vice-Admiral C V Usborne wrote, "in gallantry and in fighting efficiency [the Royal Navy] was probably far ahead of its standard at any previous period of its history, and moreover, it most assuredly had achieved its purpose."

The war at sea in 1914–18 laid bare German naval deficiencies, most importantly her deficiency in strategy. The German High Seas Fleet had neither the geographical position, the flexible insight nor the size to secure a strategic victory over Britain. As it grew in size, its strategy became increasingly defensive. It had been built to defend Germany from a British attack no more than 100 miles (160km) from Heligoland. Although technologically superior in a number of ways, when Britain chose to pursue a naval strategy of distant blockade, the German navy found no way to counter it. The German choice to adopt the strategy of the *guerre de course* (commerce

raiding) with submarines had much to recommend it, but the emphasis on building the High Seas Fleet up to 1917 meant there were too few U-boats to destroy Britain's economic and military lifelines quickly. Even so, German submarines were a formidable threat and soon supplanted cruisers as the principal commerce raiders. But they neither supplanted the battle fleet nor drove it from the sea. Although their range and endurance were relatively high, submarines were limited by slow speed and difficulty in finding targets.

All of the major naval powers showed a tendency to be rigid in their thinking and inflexible in changing their focus from battleship actions to other alternatives. The German use of the submarine opened a new dimension in naval warfare. It might have succeeded if the German navy had been equipped with more submarines, but considering how late Germany began the effort, it was still quite an achievement. In the end, Germany's superior military position on land and her submarine campaign at sea were undermined by political, social, industrial and economic weaknesses. In terms of the war at sea, the submarine campaign was thwarted by the ability of the Allies to produce merchant ships and the goods they carried at a rate greater than the U-boats sank them. In order to do this, the Allies had to organize and coordinate their national economies.

Germany faced a strategic dilemma. On the one hand, she had not built a fleet that was superior to the British. On the other hand, Germany's naval expenditures were already too high for her geopolitical position as a pivotal land power between two powerful neighbours, France and Russia. In addition, Germany had built a navy on a misconception and a misreading of Mahan. Admiral Tirpitz thought that his navy was a political tool that would force Britain to accede to Germany's political

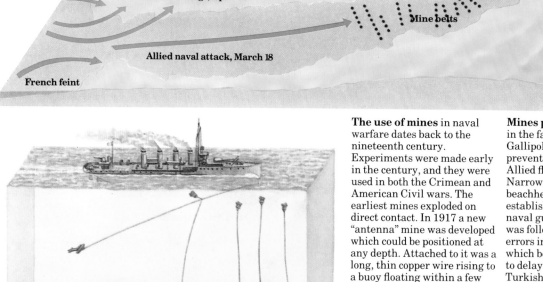

The use of mines in naval warfare dates back to the nineteenth century. Experiments were made early in the century, and they were used in both the Crimean and American Civil wars. The earliest mines exploded on direct contact. In 1917 a new "antenna" mine was developed which could be positioned at any depth. Attached to it was a long, thin copper wire rising to a buoy floating within a few feet of the surface. If a submarine touched any part of the wire, it produced an electric charge which exploded the mine.

Mines played a crucial part in the failure of the landings at Gallipoli in 1915 by preventing the passage of the Allied fleet through the Narrows. Hence the beachheads that were established were deprived of naval gunfire support. This was followed by a series of errors in combined operations which began with the failure to delay naval attack on Turkish forts until an Allied army was available to occupy and hold the Gallipoli peninusla. The entire plan lacked adequate preparation.

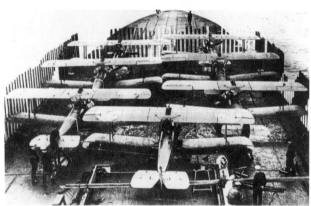

Vice Adm de la Perriére
(*right*), the renowned World-War-I U-boat commander whose *U-35* sank 189 merchant ships. The offensive use of the submarine was one of the most dramatic aspects of the Great War.

Battleships were afforded some protection from submarine attack first through the use of anti-torpedo nets (*left, top*) whilst at anchor – where they would otherwise have been sitting targets – and later through the fitting of anti-torpedo bulges (*left, bottom*), self-contained compartments filled with either water or fuel oil and designed to absorb impact and restrict damage.

The early aircraft carrier, HMS *Furious*, with aeroplanes on deck. In 1914–1918, few people were able to forecast that aircraft could influence naval warfare. This was a period of extensive technical and operational experimentation in the difficulties posed by launch and landing at sea.

desires without war. Tirpitz had planned to achieve this either by forcing Britain into a naval race that she could not sustain in peacetime, or, in wartime, by threatening her in home waters in a manner that would require Britain to withdraw from her global role. In short, Germany's fleet had been inappropriately designed for its strategic position. At the same time, Britain and her allies took advantage of their strategic position. Where a navy was essential to Britain's strategic position, it was a luxury for Germany. Yet German submarines nearly proved to be the weapon that cut Britain's vital arteries.

The interwar period
At the end of World War I, the Royal Navy was the largest navy in the world. For 200 years, it had claimed and exercised supremacy on the high seas. The Allied victory had done very little to bring into question Mahan's basic assumptions about the nature of sea power. Britain's ability to continue as the world's dominant sea power had been clearly demonstrated in the course of the war. The German navy was largely destroyed at Scapa Flow upon its surrender in 1918. In terms of numbers, Britain's naval rivals were now the United States and Japan. They, however, were regional powers. Britain, as the European naval power, remained the world naval power. Yet, within three years, Britain relinquished her naval supremacy.

Britain's main naval competitor was the United States, but not because the United States was a threat. The issue was merely a matter of national prestige. Neither nation expected to go to war with the other. The United States

maintained "War Plan Red" for a war with Britain, but examined projected results in war games at its Naval War College only as a means of measuring the potential effectiveness of the US Navy. The real rivals were Japan and the United States. The United States wanted to increase her naval strength as something necessary for her increasing world importance, and to defend her interests in the Pacific. Japan had become the main power in East Asia and the major threat to American and British interests in the Far East.

In Britain, as in America and Japan, the battleship remained the principal measure of naval strength. Japan and the United States built new battleships to keep pace with one another, and while doing so they outclassed Britain's ageing fleet. Thus, British leaders had a great interest in controlling the naval arms race between those two distant countries. At the same time, Japan was a potential threat to Hong Kong, Malaya and the Straits Settlements (Malaysia), as well as to the sea lanes to Australia and New Zealand. For this reason, in June 1921, British leaders decided to go ahead with plans to build a major fleet base at Singapore.

Until this time, the Anglo-Japanese Alliance of 1902 had been the cornerstone of British defence policy in the Far East and provided the basis for stability. As British statesmen saw at the time, without the treaty Britain could find herself in a difficult position in India and the Far East if confronted by a hostile Japan. Britain's dilemma was that she would need to maintain a naval force in the Far East at least equal in size to Japan's, but she could not afford to maintain large fleets in both Asian and European waters. Britain believed that the only alternative to this situation was to renew the treaty with Japan. It had already been renewed in 1905 and in 1911, and was due for renewal again in July 1921. At the 1921 Imperial Conference, Canada vehemently opposed the renewal, arguing that an Anglo-Japanese alliance would harm relations between Britain and the United States.

As Britain, Japan and the United States moved closer to a naval arms race in the Pacific, a call went out for an international conference on the Pacific security issue. At the same time, the United States convened a conference in Washington. At the first session, Secretary of State Charles Evans Hughes surprised the delegates with his proposal for naval arms limitations. He proposed a ratio of naval strength of 5:5:3 for Britain, America and Japan. After lengthy discussion and modification to the details, the delegates accepted the proposal in 1922. By this treaty, Britain signed away the naval superiority she had demonstrated during the war. Yet, given the economic conditions of the time, she could not sustain that position against the shipbuilding programmes in the United States and Japan. At the same time, all of the powers concerned in the conference won a substantive degree of disarmament. They had prevented a costly arms race. The Washington Treaty both cut the number of battleships drastically and ended battleship building for ten years. Britain had won an opportunity for fiscal economy and a measure of economic relief. Parity in numbers, however, did not mean equality in strength. There was a vast difference in the responsibilities which Britain and the United States had undertaken. While Britain's international role depended upon a routine naval presence in all the oceans of the world, the United States did not have anywhere near the same responsibilities. She could concentrate her force more easily and apply it more readily. Thus, in a sense, parity in numbers conceded naval superiority to the United States.

Effects of the Washington Treaty
Through the Washington Treaty, Britain accepted parity in strength with the United States and a limited margin of superiority over Japan. This became the One Power Standard: a British Fleet equal to the fleet of any other nation, but thus requiring local forces to maintain a situation and prevent irreparable damage pending the arrival of the main fleet. It was a standard which gave no margin of safety should Britain be at war both in Europe and in the Pacific.

The Washington Treaty had another effect. During the interwar period, the rate of technical change was relatively slow, particularly in contrast to the rapid advance in wartime and in the years before 1914. There were few innovations in battleship design. The chief changes were in submarines, cruisers and aircraft carriers. With the limitations on battleship construction, the aircraft carrier provided the best opportunity for naval architects to demonstrate their skills in designing ships of over 10,000 tons. Although this type of construction was also strictly limited by the treaty, it helped to increase the importance of the class, along with new improvements in aircraft. At the same time, the treaty created the heavy cruiser, typically a 10,000-ton ship armed with 8-inch guns and frequently known as the "Washington cruiser", as designers attempted to build the largest warship possible

without being subject to the rules for capital ships. Necessitated by the limitations imposed by the Versailles Treaty of 1919, the German "pocket battleship" design, nominally of 10,000 tons, was another which sought the same ends. Thus, while it limited some types of ships, the Washington Treaty emphasized others.

In 1930, the Treaty of London provided for further limitations in battleships, as well as cruisers, destroyers and submarines. In addition, the major naval powers agreed to continue the ban on building battleships through 1936. While the London Treaty did not aim for the larger disarmament objectives of the Washington Treaty, it was successful in preventing a major arms race in cruisers and in maintaining force levels at about the same as previous years.

There were other consequences of these treaties. The holiday in shipbuilding had a major effect on the shipbuilding industry in both Britain and the United States. Some firms were unable to maintain the capacity for building large ships; others closed down altogether. Among the hardest hit were the firms that produced guns and armour plate.

In the political area, the Washington Treaty failed to give Britain and the United States the margin of superiority over Japan which they had sought in the 5:5:3 ratio. The clause which prevented Britain and the United States from building naval bases within 3,000 miles (4,800km) of Japan served to assure Japanese superiority in East Asia. The treaties signified a major change in the balance of power in the Far East: the decline of Britain in that area and the consolidation of Japanese power, leaving only the United States as a distant counterweight to Japan. Moreover, the ratio offended a large number of Japanese who thought that it relegated Japan to an "inferior status". Some who shared this reaction played an important role in Japanese politics in the 1930s, when that country moved toward more aggressive policies.

The next phase began in June 1935 with the Anglo-German Naval Agreement. In this treaty, Britain recognized Germany's right to build a navy free of the restrictions laid down by the Versailles Peace Treaty. Hitler thought that the day the treaty was signed was "the happiest day" of his life, the day in which Germany escaped from diplomatic isolation and was recognized again as a power. German naval planners saw it as the prelude to a campaign for major German maritime expansion. For the other powers, the period of naval rearmament began with the expiration of both the Washington and London Naval Treaties at the end of 1936. A new Treaty on the Limitation of Naval Armaments had been signed in London in March 1936. However, neither Japan, Italy nor Germany signed the new agreement, so these nations were free to go their own way. Soon Germany's plans were clear. In December 1937, the Germans added six battleships to their shipbuilding programme, as well as two aircraft carriers in addition to the two carriers already under contract. Others followed. The naval rearmament was merely the reflection of similar rearming in other areas and a prelude to new political developments which brought war with Germany in 1939 and with Japan in 1941.

While naval disarmament was the major issue of the 1920s and rearmament the issue of the late 1930s, navies were undergoing a quiet technological evolution. Most importantly, the battle fleet acquired combat capabilities in three mediums. It could now use the air, the surface and the subsurface of the sea for offence, reconnaissance, defence and protection. The shipboard gun remained the dominant weapon, with armour-piercing and high explosive projectiles. The gun became more accurate through the use of gyro-stabilized range finders, data links and analog computers. New short-range anti-aircraft guns complemented the heavy guns and became a new element of defence. In addition, the aerial bomb and torpedo, as well as the submarine torpedo, complemented gunnery. Aircraft added new capabilities for attack and reconnaissance as well as defence. These capabilities were reached through the complementary development of aircraft carriers and of aircraft which could withstand the stress of coming out of a dive after delivering a bomb. By the late 1930s, the Japanese had made a significant innovation by building carrier-based fighter aircraft that were equal to or better than land-based fighters. Despite these innovations, the battleship remained the most powerful and best-protected element of the fleet. In 1939, it was still the centrepiece of the major navies.

World War II

World War II was the largest and most violent naval war in the whole of history. It was a war in two oceans, each illuminating different aspects of sea warfare. In the Atlantic, the naval war was fought as a vital yet subordinate aspect to the land campaigns in the European theatre of operations. Fundamentally, it was about the protection or disruption of shipping which was essential to military operations ashore as well as to national economies. It was a land war, supported by forces at sea and in the air. The war in the Pacific, on the other hand, was essentially a maritime war supported by land and air forces. Its main actions were naval and were characterized by the predominance of naval air power and amphibious operations. Despite the differences between operations in the two oceans, the two theatres shared the fact that the worldwide conflict was a war of logistics: a war of manpower, production, machines, spare parts and supplies. At the same time, both campaigns confirmed anew the necessity for close cooperation and coordination among land, sea and air forces.

The basic challenge which Germany presented at sea to Britain at the outbreak of the war in 1939 remained the essential issue throughout Atlantic operations. Even before war was declared, Germany ordered into the Atlantic every one of its ocean-going submarines fit for sea, while coastal boats patrolled the North Sea and prepared to lay mines. At the same time, the German pocket-battleships *Admiral Graf Spee* and *Deutschland* (renamed *Lützow* in December 1939) took up commerce raiding stations in the Atlantic, while specially-designed German raiders disguised as merchantmen put to sea. Together, they challenged Allied use of the sea.

When the war came, however, the first responsibility of the Royal Navy was to guard the stream of transport and supply ships moving across the Channel. In eight months, 500,000 men and 89,000 vehicles landed safely in France.

The more serious issue was transatlantic shipping. It was important to Britain, not only for food and supplies but for the stream of fighting men that came by sea. Before the end of 1939, the First Canadian Division rapidly crossed the Atlantic, and soon Commonwealth

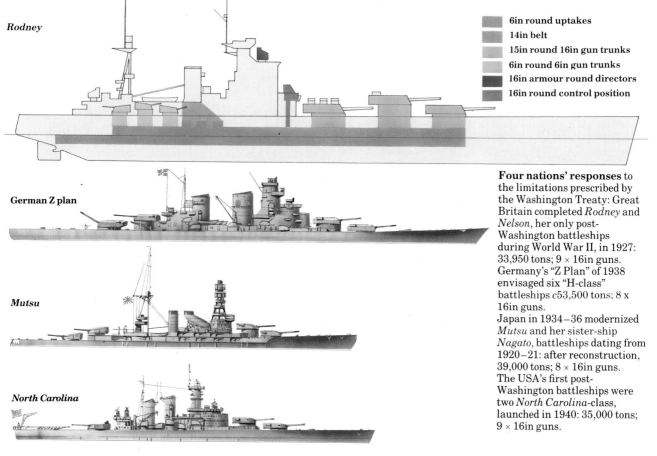

6in round uptakes
14in belt
15in round 16in gun trunks
6in round 6in gun trunks
16in armour round directors
16in round control position

Four nations' responses to the limitations prescribed by the Washington Treaty: Great Britain completed *Rodney* and *Nelson*, her only post-Washington battleships during World War II, in 1927: 33,950 tons; 9 × 16in guns. Germany's "Z Plan" of 1938 envisaged six "H-class" battleships c53,500 tons; 8 x 16in guns. Japan in 1934–36 modernized *Mutsu* and her sister-ship *Nagato*, battleships dating from 1920–21: after reconstruction, 39,000 tons; 8 × 16in guns. The USA's first post-Washington battleships were two *North Carolina*-class, launched in 1940: 35,000 tons; 9 × 16in guns.

troops from the Indian Army, Australia and New Zealand came safely by sea to the Middle East.

It took a great deal of time to convince both the Navy and the shipping companies that the most effective means of protecting shipping and destroying enemy shipping was through convoy. The argument for convoy was hard to make in the early stages of the war, when Britain sank 18 U-boats (more than one-third of Germany's operational force), and sank them faster than Germany could replace them. This early advantage for Britain quickly changed when the German air force began to attack shipping and when the magnetic mine came into use. Many did not accept the advantages of convoy until after the air attacks began. Britain's position became even more difficult in the spring and summer of 1940, when Italy's declaration of war (June 10) along with German successes in north and northwestern Europe changed the strategic picture.

Faced by air and mine challenges in home waters and the submarine challenge in the Atlantic, Britain also needed to replace French naval power in the Mediterranean, keep open the sea lanes in those waters for Allied shipping, safeguard the Suez Canal, and maintain troops in the Middle East. British naval strategy in the Mediterranean was to try to hold the central Mediterranean and to make it impossible for Italy and Germany to supply their land and air forces in North Africa. Despite an unfavourable strategic situation, with Italian naval superiority in the area, the Royal Navy was successful in a surface action off Calabria in July 1940 and an air attack on the Italian fleet at Taranto in November, putting half the Italian fleet out of action.

From the geographical advantage gained by her occupation of Norway and France, Germany increased her attacks on Allied merchant shipping. Following the pocket-battleship *Admiral Scheer's* successful attack on convoy HX84 in November 1940, Germany forced Britain to disperse some of her capital ships to meet this threat by using heavy surface ships for the defence of shipping. The most dramatic event in this aspect of the war was the pursuit and sinking of the *Bismarck* in May 1941.

Until the end of 1941, the Axis powers seemed to gain on all fronts. Despite the victory of British naval forces over the Italian fleet off Cape Matapan in March 1941, the Germans drove back the British in the Mediterranean and in North Africa. By the end of the year, Britain was hard pressed everywhere.

At the same time, Japan threatened war in the Far East. During the 1920s and 1930s, Britain had been able to build a fleet base at Singapore, but because of financial, industrial and other constraints, she could not provide for a Far East fleet to use it permanently. By 1941, with a war in progress in the Atlantic and the Mediterranean, Britain could not afford to send a full fleet to counter the Japanese naval threat. Nevertheless, in October 1941, the new battleship *Prince of Wales* and the old battlecruiser *Repulse* sailed for Singapore as a token deterrent. But in the absence of a fully balanced and efficient fleet, they would be no match for the highly-trained and well-equipped Japanese navy, should it decide to attack.

Japan did attack – not only in southeast Asia, which was her primary source for raw materials. She also attacked the United States in order to pre-empt America's ability to halt her plans for hegemony in southeast Asia. Japan struck at Pearl Harbor, Manila (Philippines), Hong Kong, Malaya and Siam (Thailand) in coordinated attacks on December 7 1941 (west longitude)/December 8 (east

Convoy techniques. Convoy of merchant vessels is an offensive, not a defensive measure. It is designed to ensure the safe transportation of men and material at sea while using them as bait to bring an attacking enemy within range of effective counterattack and into a position where it could be destroyed.

Intelligence of enemy submarine movement as well as safe routeing and secure communications for convoys were essential aspects in convoy technique.

Arranged in columns, the merchant ships were assigned stations, sometimes zigzagging in small convoys or using evasive courses of 20–40 degrees of a base course in larger convoys.

U-boat tactics. At the outset of the war, U-boats attacked individually, submerging before approaching a convoy and attacking at periscope depth in early morning or evening hours when the merchant ships were silhouetted against the sky. In late 1940, a new system, *Die Rudeltaktik* or wolfpack tactic was used. U-boats were sent out in dispersed groups of 8 or 9 boats, their movements closely controlled by radio. When one boat contacted a convoy, the German command ordered the other boats within reach to join in on an attack. The U-boat that made the contact then shadowed the convoy by day at extreme distance, waiting for the others to join. At night, the wolfpack attacked on the surface, where they could not be easily detected by the radar systems then in use. They were also difficult to catch – a surfaced U-boat could outstrip the majority of vessels that made up the bulk of convoy escorts in 1940–41.

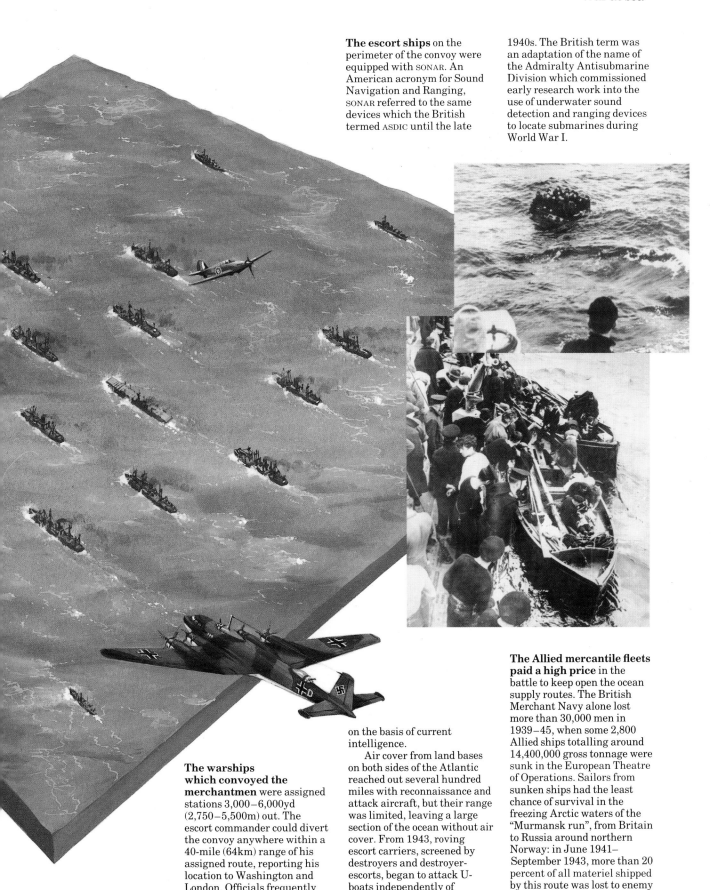

The escort ships on the perimeter of the convoy were equipped with SONAR. An American acronym for Sound Navigation and Ranging, SONAR referred to the same devices which the British termed ASDIC until the late 1940s. The British term was an adaptation of the name of the Admiralty Antisubmarine Division which commissioned early research work into the use of underwater sound detection and ranging devices to locate submarines during World War I.

The warships which convoyed the merchantmen were assigned stations 3,000–6,000yd (2,750–5,500m) out. The escort commander could divert the convoy anywhere within a 40-mile (64km) range of his assigned route, reporting his location to Washington and London. Officials frequently changed pre-established routes on the basis of current intelligence.

Air cover from land bases on both sides of the Atlantic reached out several hundred miles with reconnaissance and attack aircraft, but their range was limited, leaving a large section of the ocean without air cover. From 1943, roving escort carriers, screened by destroyers and destroyer-escorts, began to attack U-boats independently of convoys.

The Allied mercantile fleets paid a high price in the battle to keep open the ocean supply routes. The British Merchant Navy alone lost more than 30,000 men in 1939–45, when some 2,800 Allied ships totalling around 14,400,000 gross tonnage were sunk in the European Theatre of Operations. Sailors from sunken ships had the least chance of survival in the freezing Arctic waters of the "Murmansk run", from Britain to Russia around northern Norway: in June 1941– September 1943, more than 20 percent of all materiel shipped by this route was lost to enemy action.

longitude). Two days later, Japanese aircraft sank *Prince of Wales* and *Repulse*, leaving Japan in undisputed control of the western Pacific and allowing her to move easily into the Dutch East Indies against the remaining light forces of the newly established ABDA (Australian, British, Dutch, American) Command. Japan defeated the ABDA naval forces in the Battle of the Java Sea in February 1942 and moved on into the Indian Ocean and the south and southwest Pacific.

With the United States in the war, Anglo-American planners began to work in very close cooperation, based on earlier links which had been forged with each nation's forces. American leaders saw that the Axis powers in Europe were the most serious threat and that the United States must first support Britain there, and maintain the sea lines of communication across the Atlantic, before turning full attention to the Pacific. The United States quickly trained men and manned ships and aircraft to meet the German challenge. Moving from the defensive to the offensive, American forces were ready to move across the Atlantic by the end of 1942. As the first step, Allied naval forces under Admiral Sir Andrew Cunningham led the way with landings in North Africa during November 1942. Successful there, the Allies established bases from which to make similar landings in Sicily in July 1943, and in Italy in September 1943 and January 1944.

Meanwhile, in the Pacific, American naval forces were on the defensive. With British naval forces fully occupied in the Atlantic and the Mediterranean, the United States Navy operated with assistance from the Royal Australian Navy and the Royal New Zealand Navy. By May 1942, Japanese naval forces began to move southward toward positions from which she could attack Australia. The United States checked this southerly advance at the Battle of the Coral Sea in May 1942. This was the first sea battle in which ships did not fire a shot directly at one another and in which the main battle was carried on by carrier aircraft against ships and other aircraft.

In June 1942, the US Navy halted the Japanese eastward offensive in the Battle of Midway, removing the threat to Hawaii and the Pacific coast of the United States. Except for operations in the Aleutian Islands off Alaska, the Japanese Navy confined itself to the South Pacific. Following Midway, the Allies undertook the first major offensive phase of the war against Japan. This began with the amphibious landings at Guadalcanal and Tulagi in August 1942, initiating a campaign which lasted half a year and included many bitter naval battles. In February 1943, the Japanese abandoned Guadalcanal.

The supremacy of the carrier

The first aircraft carrier battles in the Coral Sea and off Midway Island marked not only a strategic turning point in the war, but also a change in the tactical concept of the fleet. Up to this point, aircraft carriers were regarded only as the advanced striking arm of the main battleship force. Immediately after the Battle of Midway this changed. Japan cancelled all battleship construction and shifted to a new building programme emphasizing carriers, while the United States increased its carrier construction programme and cancelled most of its incomplete battleships. Between 1941 and 1944, the fleet entirely changed its character to one that emphasized aircraft carrier task groups. The key elements in this concept were the use of carrier-based torpedo- and dive-bombers as the primary offensive capability, with fighters for close-in air

defence, and of destroyers for anti-submarine and anti-aircraft defence. This change in weaponry and tactics also brought with it electromagnetic technology for detecting, tracking and targeting an enemy, communications in the command and control of one's own forces, and counter-measures to interfere with enemy systems. By 1942–43, these developments led to the creation of shipboard operations centres where information could be correlated and acted upon by commanders. At the same time the nature of amphibious warfare changed, and its rapid development became the outstanding feature of the war in terms of joint operations.

As these basic changes were taking place in naval warfare, the Allied navies moved towards a new phase in the war. The Allies went on to full-scale offensive operations in which they were able to attack German and Japanese forces at places of their own choice. In the Pacific, Admiral Chester Nimitz's central Pacific campaign laid the first stepping stones across the Pacific with the capture of the Gilbert Islands in late 1943 and the Marshalls and Marianas in 1944. Simultaneously, General Douglas MacArthur took the offensive in the southwestern Pacific along the New Guinea coast, leap-frogging over strong Japanese positions which were not essential to American strategic moves and advancing towards the Philippines. By 1944, these operations had become direct assaults on Japan's defensive perimeter, forcing her into a position whereby she could not defend or use her newly captured territories unless she could defeat the threat of the main fleets. By late 1943, Allied leaders had agreed to concentrate the naval effort on the invasion of France, first at Normandy in June 1944 and then in southern France in August. In the Pacific, they decided to continue to concentrate naval assets in the central and southwestern Pacific, and not to undertake major operations in southeast Asia.

While the Allies planned these broad strategic moves, the campaign under the sea was having a dramatic effect. In the Atlantic, the German attempt to destroy shipping was defeated. Learning how to decode German messages to and from the U-boats at sea, the Allies were able to route their convoys in safe waters and, at the same time, use their air and surface anti-submarine forces to attack U-boats. In the early spring of 1944, the Allied anti-submarine campaign became so successful that 3,360 merchantmen crossed the Atlantic in 105 convoys, losing only three ships in the process. At the same time, Germany lost 29 U-boats. In May 1944, Admiral Dönitz halted German submarine operations in the North Atlantic and Arctic and moved them to less important and less well-guarded waters.

When the German surrender came on May 8 1945, the German High Command ordered all U-boats to surface, radio their position, jettison their ammunition, fly a black flag and proceed to a designated port. Symbolizing the new relationships in naval warfare, the first submarine to comply with this order surrendered to an aircraft on patrol off Land's End, England.

In the Pacific, the United States had been operating its submarines against Japan in much the same way that Germany had done in the Atlantic during the early phase of the war. In contrast to the situation in the Atlantic, the Japanese could not effectively counter the American submarine war, and although it was not planned as a major facet of Allied naval strategy against Japan, it had the most telling direct effect. Immediately after the war,

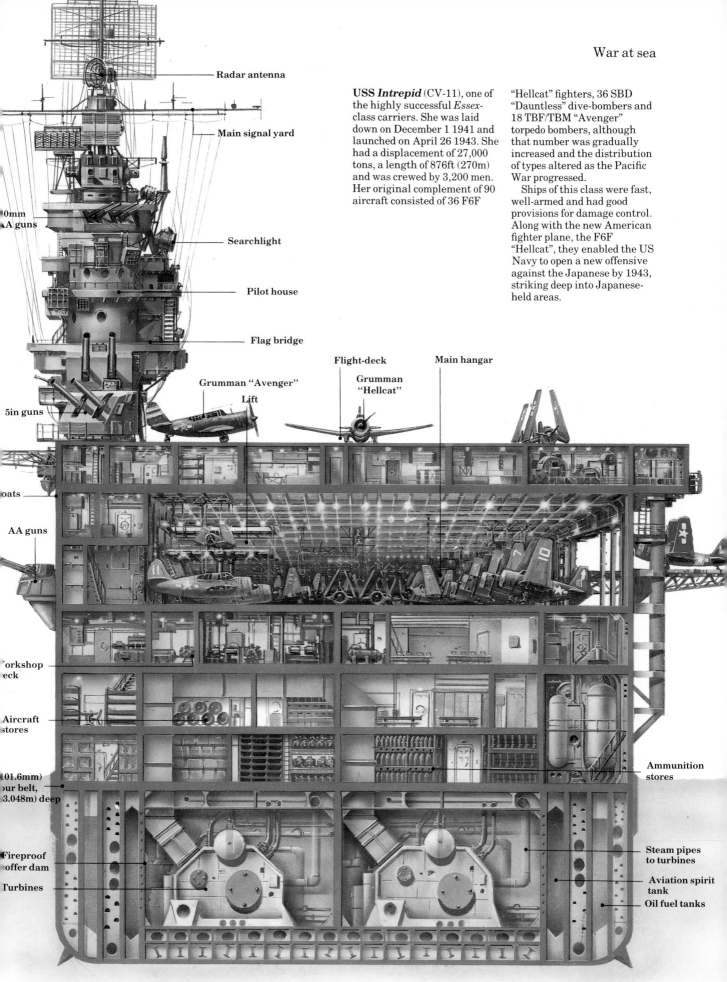

Radar antenna

Main signal yard

0mm
A guns

Searchlight

Pilot house

Flag bridge

Grumman "Avenger"

Lift

Flight-deck

Grumman "Hellcat"

Main hangar

5in guns

oats

AA guns

orkshop
eck

Aircraft
stores

01.6mm)
ur belt,
3.048m) deep

Fireproof
offer dam

Turbines

Ammunition
stores

Steam pipes
to turbines

Aviation spirit
tank

Oil fuel tanks

USS *Intrepid* (CV-11), one of the highly successful *Essex*-class carriers. She was laid down on December 1 1941 and launched on April 26 1943. She had a displacement of 27,000 tons, a length of 876ft (270m) and was crewed by 3,200 men. Her original complement of 90 aircraft consisted of 36 F6F "Hellcat" fighters, 36 SBD "Dauntless" dive-bombers and 18 TBF/TBM "Avenger" torpedo bombers, although that number was gradually increased and the distribution of types altered as the Pacific War progressed.

Ships of this class were fast, well-armed and had good provisions for damage control. Along with the new American fighter plane, the F6F "Hellcat", they enabled the US Navy to open a new offensive against the Japanese by 1943, striking deep into Japanese-held areas.

the Japanese government reported to its people that "the greatest cause of defeat was the loss of shipping". Of the 10,100,000 gross tons available to Japan in the war years, she lost 90 percent: American submarines sank 55 percent of that total, while aircraft accounted for 31 percent.

The major difference in the submarine war in the two oceans was the fact that Japanese merchant ships sailed independently and unarmed in the first year of the war. It was not until November 1943 that Japan began a system of convoying. Even then, Japanese convoy forces were ill-equipped, untrained and uncoordinated. The war in the Atlantic showed that convoy losses were highest in the small convoys and lowest in the large. At the same time, Japan failed to make use of aircraft in the protection of surface shipping, the method that had proved most effective against submarines in the Atlantic.

Defeat for the Japanese
By the end of 1944, the war in Europe became one primarily of armies, while the war in the Pacific was predominantly naval to the end. There, the essential element was the strength of the fleet and its ability to move troops and put them ashore against opposition.

In October 1944, US forces assaulted the east coast of Leyte in the Philippines. Between October 23–30, a series of four nearly simultaneous sea and air engagements took place in the battle for Leyte Gulf. These were the battles of the Sibuyan Sea, Surigao Strait, Samar and Cape Engano. In these actions, American forces damaged Japan's navy so severely that it was never again able to interfere effectively with Allied strategy. By February 1945, US forces had occupied Luzon and returned to Manila.

At the same time, the Allies began the assault on the inner defences of Japan, with direct air raids on Tokyo and amphibious assaults first on Iwo Jima, and then on Okinawa. At this point, the British Pacific Fleet under Admiral Sir Bruce Fraser was able to return to the Pacific to participate in the final phase of the war, along with Australian and New Zealand units which had operated with the United States Navy throughout the war.

As naval forces moved in to assault Japan directly, the Allies continued to blockade Japan's source of supplies. Cut off from overseas trade since the end of 1944, she was still able to obtain access to north Asian ports. By the end of July 1945, a US Army Air Force minelaying campaign in the ports and off the coasts of Japan virtually halted even this traffic.

The first atomic bomb exploded over Hiroshima as the fleet struck airfields on Honshu. The Soviet Union declared war on Japan on August 8 in order to speed the end of the war, undertaking naval operations in the Sea of Japan. British and American naval operations continued until August 14, when Japan accepted the Potsdam declaration. Soviet naval operations continued until Japanese forces surrendered in North Korea, South Sakhalin, the Kurile Islands, and on the Amur, Ussuri and Sungari rivers. The surrender ceremony took place on board USS *Missouri* in Tokyo Bay on September 2 1945.

After the cease-fire, naval forces were engaged in a wide variety of tasks, including the location and repatriation of prisoners of war and the delivery of food and medical supplies, as well as in clearing mines and wrecks to open harbours and waterways to peacetime navigation.

The postwar era
In the years immediately following World War II, there was a worldwide decline in navies, typical in many respects to those which have followed all major wars. Yet in this case, there was also a major difference. The employment of nuclear weapons at the end of World War II changed the context for thinking about future wars. For some leaders of opinion, it also indicated that naval power had a much more limited use. In the late 1940s and 1950s, naval officials had a difficult time in justifying the navy's role to legislative leaders who were more impressed with the ability of aircraft and rockets to deliver nuclear weapons than with the achievements of navies during the war. Naval proponents argued, however, that the experience of the war largely substantiated the ideas of Mahan and Corbett, while also placing new emphasis on naval aviation, submarine blockade and amphibious operations. For some years after World War II there was a basic divergence of opinion between those who thought primarily of nuclear weapons and those who thought first of conventional naval warfare.

The technological advance continues
The link between these two areas of thought came slowly. It began in 1952, with the first tactical nuclear weapon designed for carrier aircraft to use against ships and submarines. In 1957, the development of nuclear weapons for delivery from aircraft carriers was paralleled by the employment of nuclear cruise missiles and, in 1960, ballistic missiles on submarines. It was this last development, the ballistic missile submarine, which brought the navy directly into the realm of long-range nuclear deterrence and the current, central concerns of national defence at the highest levels. This development also moved naval thinking towards refining older ideas about the uses of naval force for political purposes. Together, all of these technological developments helped to link thinking about nuclear and conventional naval warfare.

During the same period, the major naval powers used their navies in regional and local crises. For the United States, the carrier battle force remained the primary means of dissuasion and presence in peacetime. None of the conflicts which erupted in the postwar period involved a contest for use of the sea, but each demonstrated use of it. Prominent among the naval activities connected with the use of the sea were defence of merchant shipping, sea-based air attack, logistics support, and amphibious landing capabilities. These activities were clearly demonstrated by United Nations forces in Korea in 1950–53; by US forces in Lebanon in 1958, Vietnam in 1965–72, Grenada in 1985, Libya in 1986 and in the Persian Gulf in 1987–88; and by British forces in the Falklands in 1982.

The advance of technology has done many things to change the appearance of navies since 1945. Satellite communications and surveillance, electronic sensor systems, guided missiles, new aircraft designs, underwater sound technology and new propulsion systems have revolutionized what navies look like. But naval warfare remains centred on the attrition of an enemy's assets at sea and securing the use of the sea for one's own purposes. Naval battles of the future will no longer be concerned merely with fire power, but with sensor and search effectiveness, the impact of electronic emission control on sensors, and the distances between opposing forces, as well as the ability of commanders to think through the increasingly complex mass of data involved in naval situations which will be fast-moving, destructive and decisive in their outcome.

Easter Rising (1916) *see* ANGLO-IRISH WAR.

East Prussia (1914) *see* TANNENBERG AND MSAURIAN LAKES (1914).

East Prussian offensive (1944–45). During the winter of 1944 Soviet forces halted their operations against East Prussia and prepared for an all-out offensive in the new year. Their opponents, Army Group Centre, remained a potent force of 45 divisions, defending a variety of fortifications. However, the Soviet superiority in men, weapons, aircraft and equipment proved overwhelming. On January 13 Chernyakhovsky's Third Belorussian Front attacked the Third Panzer Army but struggled against resolute German defence. Meanwhile, to the south, Rokossovsky's Second Belorussian Front launched itself against the Second Army. Within a week the German line had been broken and Soviet armoured columns raced along the River Vistula and, on the 24th, reached the Baltic. Army Group Centre, renamed Army Group North, was now isolated. Attempts to break the encirclement failed and the German Fourth Army was pushed back towards Konigsberg. Unrelenting pressure was still being exerted by Chernyakhovsky and Bagramyan's First Baltic Front and the Third Panzer Army, together with hundreds of thousands of refugees, was forced into small pockets of resistance. But the remnants of Army Group North fought with a desperate ferocity and on 20 February even managed to launch a successful counterattack on the Samland Peninsula. However with the main Soviet thrust now directed at Berlin, the German bridgeheads on the Baltic coast were a distraction rather than a threat. But for the Third Belorussian Front, the capture of Konigsberg remained as much a matter of prestige as a strategic necessity and, on April 9, after an attack by four Soviet Armies, the garrison surrendered. *MS.*

Eben Emael Fort, capture of (1940). This vital element in Belgium's eastern frontier defences was audaciously assaulted by German airborne forces on May 10 1940. Landing by glider onto the

Hitler honours his paras, Eben Emael

fort itself, they destroyed emplacements and held the Belgian garrison in check until German support units arrived the next day.

Ebro, Battle of the (July–November 1938), Spanish Civil War. The offensive across the Ebro from Catalonia represented the Republic's last throw to focus international attention on Spain. The stated purpose was to save Valencia, but a very successful defence (*see* ARAGON OFFENSIVE) had already halted the Nationalists who were attacking in Andalucia instead. A Republican army of 80,000 experienced troops, freshly re-equipped with the last batch of Russian material, assembled opposite the convex loop of the Ebro and crossed, achieving complete surprise. But the rapid advance on Gandesa was held by Yagüe long enough for Franco to bring in massive reinforcements. As at Brunete and Teruel, premature propaganda claims trapped the Republican army in a disastrous battle of attrition. Its best formations suffered 70,000 casualties, and by mid-November only an exhausted rump was left to pull back across the river. The sacrifice had been in vain. The Munich agreement emphasized that no help could be expected from Britain and France, and Stalin withdrew from his commitment to Republican Spain to prepare a pact with Germany. *AB.*

Eden, Anthony *see* AVON, EARL OF.

Eder Dam *see* DAMS RAID.

Egypt and Palestine campaign (1914–18). The Suez Canal was arguably Britain's most important strategic asset in 1914. Through this vital waterway passed Britain's communications with India, Australia and New Zealand. The outbreak of the war with Turkey in November 1914 clearly presented a threat to the Canal and the British commander in Egypt, Gen Maxwell, made its defence his major priority. In January 1915 after a long and difficult march across the Sinai Desert, a 20,000-strong Turkish force launched attacks against the Canal. The expedition was too weak to have any real effect, especially as the Canal's defences were supported by British and French warships. Thereafter the British took up a new defence line in the Sinai, to prevent any further Turkish attack from even reaching the Canal. The terrain and climate of the desert presented substantial supply problems but roads, railways and water pipelines were constructed to link the outposts with the main bases on the Canal. The scheme was vindicated when a second Turkish attack was repulsed on August 4 1916 at the Battle of Romani, some 20 miles (32km) from the Canal. Maxwell's successor, Lt Gen Murray, decided to remove the threat once and for all and advanced his forces across the Sinai, pushing the Turks back before them. By December 1916 the British had established a new defence line based on El Arish, nearly 100 miles (160km) from the Canal. In March and April 1917, Murray launched two abortive offensives against Gaza. The arrival of Gen Allenby to succeed Murray in June marked a period of reinforcement and consolidation before, in October, he was ready to attack. He struck first at Beersheba, completing his victory with the capture of Gaza. Jerusalem was the next major objective and, in spite of bad weather and stubborn Turkish resistance, it fell on December 9 1917. While Allenby built up his forces for a fresh offensive, extensive cavalry raids probed at the Turkish lines. Establishing overwhelming superiority in men and equipment, it was Allenby's intention to inflict so comprehensive a defeat that Turkey would be forced to leave the war. On September 19 1918, the British artillery and infantry punched a hole in the Turkish line and the cavalry poured through the gap, trapping two Turkish armies at Megiddo. Meanwhile, on the

145

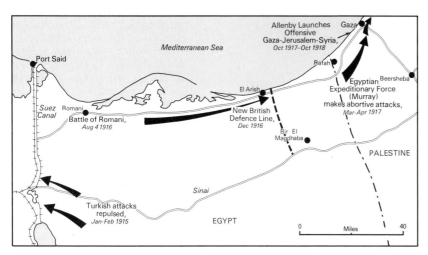

The Allied campaign against the Turks in Egypt and Palestine, 1915–18

right flank, Nazareth was captured on September 20 and the important rail junction of Amman fell on the 25th. The shattered Turkish forces retreated northwards, harried not only by Allenby's troops but by Arab units and aircraft of the RAF. The British advance continued through northern Palestine and Syria and had reached Aleppo and the borders of Anatolia when an armistice ended hostilities on October 31 1918. *MS*.

Egyptian-Libyan War (1977). The deteriorating Egypt-Libyan relationship early in 1977 reflected both policy differences and personal antagonism between their respective leaders, Sadat and Gaddafi. Egypt accused Libya of sabotage; 150,000 Egyptian workers in Libya fled; in April, the Egyptian newspaper *Swat el Arab* advocated Gaddafi's overthrow. Following border clashes, Egypt bombed Libyan airfields and radar installations, July 21; Egyptian troops withdrew next day, but bombing continued until July 24. Although Gaddifi was not overthrown, the confrontation confirmed his isolation in the Arab world – but after Sadat's visit to Israel, November 1977, the isolation was reversed when Gaddafi hosted the "rejectionist front" of Arab states. *BHR*.

Eichelberger, Gen Robert L (1886–1961). US. Arguably one of the finest Allied army commanders in the Pacific during World War II. Eichelberger, at the head of the US I Corps, reorganized and remotivated tired US and Australian troops in New Guinea at the

end of 1942, taking Buna in January 1943. However, it was as commander of the US Eighth Army, after September 1944, that he was best able to demonstrate his audacious and flexible leadership style. In December 1944, during the reconquest of the Philippines, the Eighth Army took over responsibility for the elimination of resistance on Leyte and then, in the last days of January 1945, made two landings on Luzon before advancing towards Manila. Eichelberger's major task from February onwards was the clearance of the southern Philippines, including Mindanao. By the close of the campaign, Eighth Army had carried out 55 amphibious operations in eight months. *PJS*.

Eighth Air Force. The prime US air force in Europe in World War II. By August 1942 it was considered ready to begin operations on a limited and experimental basis. It began its main task of bombing Germany in January 1943 and after the introduction of an effective long-range fighter in March 1944, it began to achieve decisive results. It consisted principally of the Eighth Bomber Command (B-17 and B-24) and the Eighth Fighter Command (P-38, P-47 and P-51). commanded by Eaker until January 1944 and then by Spaatz. *ANF*.

Eighth Army (British). Principal British army formation in the Mediterranean 1941–45. *See* WESTERN DESERT CAMPAIGN; TUNISIAN CAMPAIGN; SICILIAN CAMPAIGN; ITALIAN CAMPAIGN.

Eighth Army (US-Korea). The US occupation force in Japan (under Gen Walton H Walker) when the Korean War began. It consisted of four divisions, the 1st Cavalry and the 7th, 23rd and 24th Infantry, all understrength and poorly trained. The 24th Infantry was committed to the fighting early in July 1950, followed by 1st Cavalry and 23rd Infantry. The 7th Infantry was retained in Japan although milked for reinforcements. It became part of X Corps for the Inchon landings and was reabsorbed into Eighth Army in Korea in January 1951 after the retreat from the north. Eighth Army controlled all UN ground forces, including the ROK army, except in September 1950-January 1951 when X Corps was an independent command. *CM*.

Eighty-Second Airborne Division (US). Formed in August 1942 from the existing 82nd Motorized Division, from which was also formed the 101st Airborne. Motorized battalions were redesignated as gliderborne infantry and a new parachute regiment of three battalions was added to each of the new divisions. 82nd Airborne, with the British 1st Airborne, landed in Sicily and also fought at Salerno before moving to England for "Overlord". Fought with distinction both in Normandy, under Ridgway, and Holland, and played a key role in containing the German offensive in the Ardennes. *MH*.

Eilat *see* SUEZ CRISIS.

Eindhoven. During World War II this Dutch city, situated some 20 miles (32km) north of the Belgian frontier, was the home of the Philips radio and valve works which, as the largest factory of its kind in Europe, supplied around one-third of Germany's radio components. On December 6 1942, the main Philips plant and a smaller factory to the southeast were the target of Operation "Oyster", a daring low-level daylight attack by a force of Mosquitoes, Bostons and Venturas from 2 Group, RAF Bomber Command. Although the main Philips factory was badly damaged, causing delays in production, 15 British aircraft were lost or written off in the operation. Eindhoven became the first city in Holland to be

E

liberated when, on September 18 1944, men of 6th Parachute Regiment of the US 101st Airborne Division and the British Guards Armoured Division linked up here during Operation "Market Garden". *PJS*.

"Ike"; Supreme Commander, Europe

Eisenhower, Gen of the Army Dwight D (1890–1969). US. Eisenhower entered West Point in 1911 and was commissioned in 1915. Although frustrated at not being sent to France, his career nevertheless progressed well with a series of staff and foreign postings. When America entered World War II, Gen Marshall appointed him Deputy Chief of the War Plans Division. Eisenhower's plans for American strategy in Europe met with Marshall's approval and in June 1942 he was sent to Britain as commander of the European Theatre of Operations. He was quickly selected as commander of the Allied invasion of North Africa. Both in this enterprise and throughout the war, Eisenhower displayed a tact and sensitivity in Anglo-American relations that proved almost as important as his military prowess. Under his command, Sicily and mainland Italy were invaded in July and September 1943 respectively and he managed to keep control of his volatile senior commanders, Montgomery and Patton. He was therefore well prepared in January 1944 to take up his position as Supreme Commander, Allied Expeditionary Force for the invasion of Normandy. His personality helped to unite the disparate interests of the Allied politicians and commanders behind his overall strategy. While not afraid to delegate responsibility to his subordinates, the ultimate decision lay with Eisenhower and on June 5

he ordered the invasion in spite of uncertain weather conditions. Eisenhower persisted in the implementation of his "broad front" strategy during the advance from Normandy but, nevertheless, backed Montgomery over the Arnhem operation. Its failure appeared to vindicate Eisenhower's policy and, retaining firm command of the Allied armies until the end of the war, he resisted British demands for amendment of his plans. After a brief period as commander of the American occupying forces in Germany, Eisenhower returned to the US as Chief of Staff of the Army. He retired in 1948 but three years later was appointed Supreme Commander of NATO. In 1952, he resigned to take up the Republican Presidential candidacy; US President, 1952–60. *MS*.

El Agheila, Battle of (December 11–17 1942). Rommel tried to halt Montgomery's pursuit after El Alamein on the Tripolitanian Frontier. XXX Corps (Leese) held him frontally, while the New Zealand Division (Freyberg) turned his desert flank, forcing him to withdraw to Buerat.

El Alamein Line, British withdrawal to (June 21–July 2 1942). After its defeat at Gazala in June, Eighth Army withdrew to the Egyptian frontier, then to Mersa Matruh and finally to the El Alamein Line by the beginning of July. Rommel's pursuit was prog-

ressively weakened by the interception of its fuel supplies at sea, and by the RAF's attacks on his advancing columns. Panzerarmee Afrika reached the El Alamein Line too exhausted to breach it.

El Alamein Line, defence of (July 1942). Rommel attacked first on July 2, but was repulsed, mainly by concentrated artillery fire. Auchinleck then mounted three equally unsuccessful attacks before deciding, towards the end of July, to pause in order to rebuild Eighth Army. *See also* TELL EL EISA; RUWEISAT, BATTLES OF.

El Alamein, Battle of (October 23–November 4 1942). Gen Montgomery's decisive defeat of Rommel's Panzerarmee Afrika at the gateway to the Nile delta. The battle was fought in three phases. In the first phase (the "Break-In" October 24–25), XXX Corps (Leese) assaulted the centre of the Axis position, while XIII Corps (Horrocks) mounted a subsidiary attack in the south: both penetrated the deep minefields, but the armoured divisions of X Corps (Lumsden) failed to complete the breakthrough, and so the second phase had to be fought out within rather than beyond the fortified positions. This took place between October 26–31 (the "Dog-Fight"). Montgomery crumbled away the Axis defences with a series of limited attacks, while fending off Rommel's counterattacks, which were delayed by British air attacks

Battle of El Alamein, October 23- November 4 1942: a turning-point of World War II

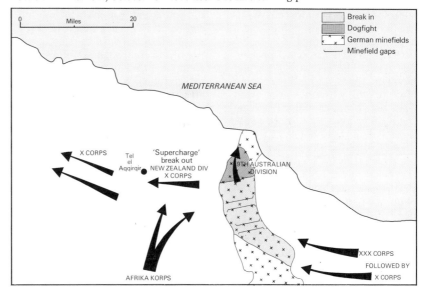

and by shortage of fuel.

In the third phase (the "Break-Out" November 1–4), Montgomery delivered his *coup de grâce* when he judged that the Axis forces were nearing exhaustion. The New Zealand Division, reinforced by one British tank and two infantry brigades, and supported by heavy air and artillery bombardments, punched a hole in the northern half of the Axis defences, through which X Corps broke out of the defensive zone, having repulsed the Afrika Korps' last desperate counterattacks during which its commander, von Thoma, was captured. By November 3, Rommel was making preparations to disengage, but these were countermanded by Hitler. Axis resistance, nevertheless, collapsed; and by the evening of November 4 the remnants of the German and Italian mobile divisions were in full retreat, leaving most of the Italian infantry to surrender. *WGFJ.*

El Alamein, pursuit from (November 5 1942–January 23 1943). Rommel tried to slow down Montgomery's pursuit with a series of rearguard actions until he reached El Agheila on the Tripolitanian frontier. He then fought three unsuccessful defensive battles to halt Eighth Army before it could reach Tripoli. *See also* EL AGHEILA, BATTLE OF; BUERAT, BATTLE OF.

Elands river, Battle of (August 4-15 1900), Second Boer War. Some 500 Imperial Bushmen (Australian and Rhodesian troops) under Col C O Hore, guarding a supply depot at Brakfontein, western Transvaal, took refuge on a kopje when attacked by *c*1,500 Boers under De La Rey. Opposing six Boer guns with nothing heavier than a malfunctioning Maxim and without water other than that brought under fire from the Elands river a half-mile away, the garrison held out for 11 days (losses: 75 killed or wounded), during which time its 3.5-acre position received around 1,800 Boer shells. Boer losses were negligible. On the approach of a relief column, De La Rey withdrew. *RO'N.*

Elba, capture of (June 17 1944). 9th French Colonial Division landed, trapping most of the German garrison.

Electromagnetic Pulse (EMP). One of the effects of a nuclear explosion in which the gamma rays interact with the atmosphere to produce a flow of free electrons radially outwards. These interact with the ions they have left to produce an electrical field. If the field is more or less symmetrical there will be little emission of energy, but if the field is not, considerable pulses of electromagnetic waves result. These can be picked up like normal radio waves, creating strong electric currents and high voltages with potentially catastrophic results. In low air or ground bursts, the net upward electron current creates an EMP that is dangerous out to e.g. 8 miles (13km) for a one megaton burst. A weapon exploded outside the atmosphere creates a net downward current over a large source region in the upper atmosphere. A bomb exploded at 100 miles (160km) altitude would create dangerous EMP effects over a radius of 900 miles (1,440km) from ground zero. Special directed energy "third generation" nuclear weapons designed primarily to produce EMP are under development. Equipment can be hardened to resist EMP. *EJG.*

Electronic Counter Measures (ECM) and **Electronic Counter Countermeasures (ECCM)** *see* ELECTRONIC WARFARE.

Electronic Support Measures (ESM) *see* ELECTRONIC WARFARE.

Electronic Warfare (EW). Electronic command, communication and control systems are at the heart of all modern warfare and both the use of the enemy's electronic emissions to provide intelligence and interference with the opponent's electronics to degrade its capabilities play a central role in all modern military and naval operations. Electronic Support Measures (ESM) cover the devices that listen out for emissions, classifying each radar, radio source, etc. They provide information of a strategic, operational or tactical nature, ranging from the nature of the enemy's dispositions to the presence of an incoming missile. Electronic Countermeasures (ECM) are designed to interfere with the enemy's electronics by jamming or sending misleading or confusing signals. Electronic Counter Countermeasures (ECCM) try to overcome the enemy's ECM in a continuous interactive process. There are specialized EW units, but most large, modern, military platforms like ships or aircraft have some EW capability built in or strapped on. *EJG.*

Eleven Group, RAF Fighter Command. The largest fighter Group in the Battle of Britain, covering London and southeast England, consisting generally of 23 Squadrons directed from seven Sectors. It was commanded by Park, whose headquarters were at Uxbridge. Eleven Group bore the main brunt of the battle, but the supporting roles of 10 Group (southwest), 13 Group (north) and especially 12 Group (Midlands and East Anglia) were crucial.

Eleventh US Air Force. Activated in Alaska in January 1942, the US Eleventh Air Force bombed targets in the Japanese-held Aleutians from the summer of that year. Then, following the American seizure of Attu and Kiska in 1943, Eleventh Air Force B-24s and B-25s waged an increasingly destructive campaign against Japanese ports, airfields and other installations in the Kurile Islands.

El Gamil airfield *see* SUEZ CRISIS.

Elint. Intelligence secured by electronic means. Currently this falls into two main categories: observations made of other powers' radar transmissions, and photographic evidence secured by way of satellite-borne television cameras.

El Kap *see* SUEZ CRISIS.

Elsenborn *see* ARDENNES OFFENSIVE.

Emden. German cruiser, detached from von Spee's East Indies Squadron, 1914, to raid in Indian Ocean. Bombarded Madras, took 23 merchantmen and sank a Russian cruiser and French destroyer before destroyed in action with HMAS *Sydney*, Cocos Island, November 1914.

Endurance. British ice patrol ship of 3,600 tons. Based on the Falklands as permanent British naval presence in South Atlantic and Antarctica. The British Ministry of Defence announcement in June 1981 that she was to be withdrawn without replacement encouraged the Argentine military junta to plan invasion and annexation of the islands.

Enfidaville, Battle of (April 19–21 1943). Montgomery tried to break into the Axis bridgehead around Tunis. X Corps (Horrocks) attacked with 4th Indian and the New Zealand Divisions, but was defeated in the mountainous country, for which his troops were neither equipped nor trained.

Engineers *see* ROYAL ENGINEERS.

Enhanced Radiation Weapon (ERW). Commonly called a "neutron bomb", an ERW is a low-yield fusion weapon designed to provide the same radiation lethality as a higher-yield fission device. The radiation is in the form of high-energy neutrons which have such kinetic energy that they give the same effect as the prompt radiation of a bomb ten times the size. Radiation is the main kill mechanism of all weapons under about ten kilotons and limiting blast and heat effects is of special importance if one is thinking of defensive nuclear use on friendly territory. Enhanced radiation warheads were developed for the Sprint antiballistic missile missile, but the main application has been in battlefield weapons. More than half of the 550 W-79 8in shells built in 1981-86 had a hollow core to allow insertion of tritium gas to provide a fusion component which produced between 50 and 75 percent of the 1-2 kiloton yield. Only 40 ERW shells remained by mid-1987, and conversion of these to fission-only devices was expected. The only ERW to remain in the American inventory is the 1 kiloton (approx) W70 Mod3 warhead for the Lance missile, some 380 of which are stockpiled in the USA. Early misleading hype about the ERW killing people but not destroying buildings backfired and prevented the deployment in Europe of the weapons. *EJG.*

"Enigma". Cipher machine, marketed in 1923, bought out by Ger-mans, who modified it and used it from 1926 for their armed, police and railway services. Poles read it from 1932, French from 1939 and British from 1940. *See also* BLETCHLEY PARK.

Eniwetok, Battle of *see* KWAJA-LEIN-ENIWETOK, BATTLE OF.

Enola Gay. The B-29 flown by Col Paul W Tibbets from which the first atomic bomb was dropped on the Japanese city of Hiroshima on August 6 1945.

Enosis *see* CYPRUS (1955–60).

ENSA (Entertainments National Service Association; nicknamed "Every Night Something Awful"). Provided entertainment for British servicemen, World War II.

Ent, Maj Gen Uzal G (1900–48). US. Despite personal reservations about low-level operations, Ent, as a brigadier general commanding the US IXth Bomber Command, planned and led the American air attack on the oil refineries at Ploesti, Romania, on August 1 1943. Seriously injured in a crash in 1944, he died four years later.

Entente Powers. The World War I fighting alliance of France, Britain, Russia, Serbia, Japan and Italy. These were later joined by Portugal, Romania, Greece and the US, after which time the term "the Allies" was more generally used.

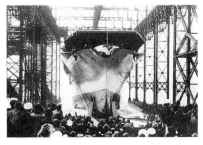

Launching of USS *Enterprise* 1936

Enterprise. (1) US *Yorktown*-class aircraft carrier; launched 1936; 25,500 tons full load; c80 aircraft. Survived most major carrier actions of Pacific War, with heavy damage and much modification. Scrapped 1958. (2) First US nuclear-powered carrier; launched 1960; 89,600 tons full load; 80–100 aircraft; still in service, 1989.

EOKA *see* CYPRUS (1955–60).

Equivalent Megatonnage (EMT). A nuclear explosion acts in a three-dimensional volume so its effects in two dimensions, i.e. on an area, must be calculated by taking the cube root of the yield and then squaring it. This "Y to the two-thirds power" gives the actual effectiveness of one weapon compared with another and is known as the EMT. Thus a 13 kiloton Hiroshima-sized bomb has an EMT of 0.055, a 335 kiloton Minuteman 3 warhead an EMT of 0.48, a 1 megaton bomb an EMT of 1 and a 9 megaton bomb an EMT of 4.3. Simple comparisons of destructive power made from the relative yields of weapons can be most misleading.

Eritrea, British campaign in (January–April 1941). Platt invaded Italian Eritrea with 4th and 5th Indian Divisions, defeated Gen Frusci in the hard-fought, seven-week Battle of Keren in February-March and took Asmara and Massawa on April 1 and 8. By so doing, he had succeeded in opening the Red Sea to British and American shipping.

Erskine, Lt Gen Sir George (1899–1965), Br. Having commanded an infantry brigade in the Western Desert campaign 1941–42, served in a corps headquarters before commanding 7th Armoured Division ("Desert Rats") in Tunisia, Italy and Normandy. From 1945, held various posts demanding acute political sensibility and was COS, Allied Control Commission in Germany. From 1949 to 1952, commanded British troops in Egypt, firmly maintaining order at a difficult time with minimal use of force. In 1953, Erskine became Commander-in-Chief East Africa, where he dealt decisively with the Mau Mau rebellion. *See also* MAU MAU REBELLION.

Escalation. A term popularized in the 1960s to cover an increase of a conflict in intensity or area or both ("compound escalation"). Escalation was traditionally regarded as a tragedy to be avoided, but in 1965 Herman Kahn published an important book, *On Escalation*, that developed a theory of escalation as a strategy to be deliberately adopted in order to demonstrate to an opponent that continuing the conflict is not worth the extra risks now involved. This might involve the escalating party having military superiority at the new level ("escalation dominance") or it might alternatively be a game of bluff to see who is willing to back down first with mutual suicide staring each side in the face. This Kahn compared to the game of "Chicken" played by contemporary American teenagers in which they drove cars towards each other; if one participant swerved he lost, if neither swerved both lost. As a stimulus to thought, Kahn produced an escalation "ladder" with 44 rungs, divided into 7 groups separated by 6 "thresholds", crossing each of which would be especially significant. Over half the "rungs" were above the "no nuclear use" threshold. This has tended to be counterproductive as it has tended to produce an overly mechanistic approach to escalation that calls for each "rung" to be provided. In fact, the basic theory holds with only a few "rungs" and thresholds, with very few rungs necessary above the nuclear threshold. Escalation in its "chicken" form is the theory behind the NATO strategy of Flexible Response adopted in 1967–68. *EJG. See also* FLEXIBLE RESPONSE.

Escape. Like evasion, as old as war. An escaper breaks away from being a prisoner of war, and tries to regain friendly territory; an evader, landed in hostile territory by accident of war, tries to get out of it without having been in enemy hands. Capture used to be thought of as a disgrace, but on the massed battlefields since 1914 it might happen to anybody.

Many chances of escape or evasion offer in the confusion of a battlefield, or soon after being shot down from an aircraft, before the stage of being settled in a prisoner-of-war camp arises. There, the escaper's first problem is how to get out of confinement: over, under, or through whatever obstacles are put round him. Once he has succeeded in this task, often a difficult one, his troubles are only beginning. What is he to wear, where is he to go, how is he to find his way? What is he to eat and drink, where and when dare he

sleep? How will he fare if he is stopped at a control point? How and where will he try to cross out of the enemy's frontier?

Most successful escapers have travelled in pairs; most had clothes, money and food smuggled in to them before they started, either in parcels from their families, or in packages of more official origin after 1939, when MI9 in London (like MIS-X, later, in Washington) undertook the task of communication with POW camps.

There were a few hundred successful escapes during World War I. In World War II, as many as 33,000 British, Commonwealth and American fighting men escaped or evaded with success; in one particular case, a German, shot down over England in 1940 and sent to Canada after an almost successful escape attempt, escaped from there into the neutral US.

Under the Geneva Convention of 1929 escape is legal, and an unsuccessful attempt cannot incur a worse penalty than 30 days' solitary confinement. That did not stop the Gestapo shooting, on Hitler's order, 50 air force officers recaptured after a mass escape by tunnel in 1943 from a camp in Silesia (three got clean away, two through Sweden and one through Spain). The Japanese, though they signed the Convention, never ratified it, and treated any prisoners they took abominably. The Russians never signed it at all, and suffered accordingly. There were a few hundred escapes from Nazi concentration camps; unsuccessful attempts there incurred the death sentence. *MF.*

Espionage. Spying – as old as war – means finding out secretly the strength and intentions of enemies, present or future. If detected, it is universally regarded as a grave offence, liable to severe penalty, even death. The best spies remain permanently undetected. A spy's task is twofold: to secure useful data and to transmit them safely. Like other aspects of conflict, spying becomes more complicated as technology develops. It is often enough, to control a spy or limit damage one can do, simply to control the spy's communications.

The ideal spy is well placed to know the enemy's strategic decisions, or commands an important

post. The Russians, for example, captured in about 1905 the allegiance of Alfred Redl, head of the Austro-Hungarian security service, who betrayed many spies to them. He also passed over the Austro-Hungarian plan of attack on Serbia. This the Russians passed on to the Serbian C-in-C, for his personal information only. At the outbreak of war in 1914 he was taking a cure in Austria, and became a prisoner of war; his plans turned out adequate to defeat the first Austrian attack.

Before 1914, the Germans placed several score of spies in Great Britain: all were rounded up in August 1914, because of a single indiscretion by a visiting German busybody. Both sides on the Western Front used spies for tactical purposes, put in and collected by aircraft.

The British in 1915 broke the main German diplomatic and naval wireless codes, with the help of codebooks captured in Persia and the Baltic. Bad staff coordination between the intelligence and operations branches of the Admiralty prevented these feats from having a decisive effect at the Battle of Jutland, May 31 1916. However, from the broken diplomatic code the British were able to inform the US that Germany was offering Mexico the cession of Texas, New Mexico and Arizona as the price for an alliance; this brought the US into the war.

The Germans had some success in sapping the French will to fight, through the activities of Paul Bolo, a confidence trickster who bore the Egyptian title of Pasha; his friend Louis-Jean Malvy, minister of the interior 1914–1917; and Malvy's friend Joseph Caillaux, an ex-prime minister. All three favoured a negotiated peace with Germany rather than a war *à outrance*; and were arrested at the insistence of Georges Clemenceau. Bolo was executed. Less important, but more sensational, was the case of Marguerite MacLeod, a renowned courtesan of Dutch origin under her *nom de lit* of Mata Hari; she too was executed in Paris, nominally for espionage, really to demonstrate to Clemenceau's supporters that the French security services were not fast asleep.

Propaganda from Lenin in the USSR persuaded many intellectuals outside it that patriotism was an old-fashioned virtue; they transferred their allegiance to world communism, not then understood to be a system of tyranny. Among them were Harry Dexter White, who rose high in the United States Treasury; Donald Maclean, who headed the American desk in the British Foreign Office; and H A R (Kim) Philby who headed the anti-Soviet section of the British secret service before first Maclean and then he defected to Moscow. Maclean's escape was aided by Anthony Blunt, another secret devotee of communism, who spent the 1939–45 war in the British security service before becoming an eminent art historian.

The British security service performed the improbable feat of turning round all the spies the Germans thought they had planted in Great Britain in 1939–45: a double-cross achievement of major import, since it helped to ensure the success of the Normandy landing by making Hitler believe it to be a feint.

Before World War II began, Mussolini had benefited greatly from a spy, a domestic servant in the British embassy in Rome, who kept him fully informed of British policy during the Abyssinian War of 1935–36. Similarly, Hitler studied French, British and Czechoslovak policy in detail during the Munich crisis of 1938, because his research office had broken the French and British ciphers. He did not then know that Frantisek Moravec, head of Czechoslovak intelligence, had bought for half a million dollars the services of Paul Thümmel, a senior German security officer who correctly predicted weeks in advance the dates of the German invasions of Czechoslovakia, France and Russia.

Another spy who predicted correctly the Nazi attack on Russia, Richard Sorge, was another secret communist, a Russian-born German whose cover was that of Nazi war correspondent in Tokyo. He found out, and told Moscow, that the Japanese intended to move southwards against the British and Dutch, not westwards against the Russians: invaluable news. Sorge was executed by the Japanese in 1941 and Thümmel by the Germans later.

A Polish mathematical genius

and a spy hired by the French, combined with the carelessness of German signals operators and the engineering techniques of the British, managed to unravel the workings of the "Enigma" cipher machine the Germans supposed unbreakable. This enabled the British, who soon shared the secret with the Americans, to follow much of what the Germans were saying to each other at every level of command. Similar achievements by a US Army cryptological team led by an American mathematical genius, William F Friedman, enabled the Americans to break many Japanese machine ciphers (*see* MAGIC).

Decipher could do marvels, but it could not do everything. For local detail, and as an insurance against a major change in the German ciphering system, the British and Americans serviced and stimulated numerous networks of spies in German-occupied territory during World War II. The British had had useful experience of such work already during the previous world war. One Belgian at least, Walthère Dewé, organized a widespread information-gathering network in each war; in the end he was shot down by Gestapo agents at a suburban street corner of Brussels in 1944. In France, the young Marie-Madeleine Méric (later Fourcade) took over and led a group of spies that was eventually over 3,000 strong; 438 of them died in German hands.

More modern espionage is divided into elint, from electronic sources; sigint, from decipher and traffic analysis; and humint, from spies. Elint, through satellite photographs, is now said to allow the Kremlin and the Pentagon to review each others' car parking patterns several times a day. Yet spies can still count for a lot: let two cases, one on each side in the Cold War, bear witness. Oleg Penkovsky, a colonel in the Soviet military intelligence service, provided invaluable data about Russian intentions during the Cuban Missile Crisis in 1962. Daulton Lee, to keep himself in drugs, sold to the Russians in the mid-1970s essential data about American secret satellites, collected for him by his friend Christopher Boyce. Penkovsky was executed; Lee and Boyce are in prison. *MF*.

Etaples mutiny. Major series of riots at the British infantry base camp at Etaples, September 9–14 1917. Harsh training and poor accommodation were major grievances. One corporal was executed for his part in the mutiny.

Ethiopia, British campaign in (March–November 1941). After invading Italian Somaliland in February 1942, Cunningham advanced on Addis Ababa with 11th African Division from the southeast via Jijiga and Diredawa, and from the southwest with 12th African Division through Galla-Sidamo, while the "Gideon Force" of Ethiopian patriots led by Col Orde Wingate and accompanied by the Emperor Haile Selassie, invaded the north. The Duke of Aosta, the Italian Viceroy, abandoned Addis Ababa at the beginning of April, and withdrew to the mountain fastness of Amba Alagi, where he was forced to surrender on May 19. It took another six months to enforce the surrender of Gazzera in Galla-Sidamo and Nasi in the Gondar. *WGFJ*.

Etna Line, Sicily, Battles for (July 23–August 6 1943). LXXVI Panzer Corps (Hube) withdrew to this line, which stretched across the northeast corner of Sicily along the southern slopes of Mount Etna, hoping to hold it indefinitely. It was breached by II US Corps (Bradley) on the north coast, and by XXX Corps (Leese) in the centre. Hube gave up its defence after Mussolini had fallen on August 25, and Hitler authorized a deliberate withdrawal to the mainland.

Exocet missile. A widely used French radar homing anti-ship missile first used in action by Iraq in the Gulf War of 1980–88 and famous for its successes in the Falklands War of 1982. Air-launched Exocets sank destroyer *Sheffield* and aviation auxiliary *Atlantic Conveyor*. A land-based Exocet damaged destroyer *Glamorgan*. Exocet exists as the 17ft (5.21m) 25 mile (42km) range ship-launched MM 38, the 15ft (4.7m) 30-42 mile (50-70km) range air-launched AM 39, the 19ft (5.8m) submarine-launched SM 39 and the 18.9ft (5.78m) 42 mile (70km) plus range ship- or ground-launched MM 40. *EJG*.

F-4 Phantom, McDonnell Douglas (US). Two-seat tactical strike/all-weather interceptor fighter; one of the most versatile and successful fighters ever built. Prototype flew May 27 1958; production ordered December 1958, initially for USN; later used by USMC and USAF. Supplied to Britain's RAF and RN, and to nine other nations, including Israel and Iran. Production 5,195 (138 built in Japan), ended May 1981. Two 17,900lb (8,120kg) s.t. General Electric J79-GE-17 or 20,315lb (9,215kg) s.t. Rolls-Royce RB 168-25R Spey engines; max. speed 1,434mph (2,308kph); one 20mm multi-barrel cannon and wide range of external ordnance.

F-105 Thunderchief, Republic (US). Single-seat strike fighter. Prototype flew October 22 1955; production aircraft entered service August 1958; first deliveries to USAFE, Germany, May 1961; to Pacific October 1962. First combat mission North Vietnam August 1964. Two-seat versions (F-105F, F-105G), electronic countermeasure aircraft. Withdrawn from operations October 1970; last flight with Air National Guard May 25 1983. Production 818 F-105Bs, Ds, Fs (60 conversions to F-105G). One 26,400lb (11,970kg) s.t. Pratt and Whitney J75-P-19W engine; max. speed 1,372mph (2,208kph); one 20mm rotary cannon, 12,000lb (5,440kg) external ordnance.

F-86 Sabre, North American (US, Post-WWII). Single-seat fighter/fighter-bomber. Prototype flew October 1 1947; first production aircraft May 20 1948; first deliveries February 1949. Production in Canada; first completed August 1950. Operational Korean War from December 17 1950; successfully contained Chinese MiG-15s. Further successful use by Pakistani Air Force, Indo-Pakistan War 1965. F-86H had one 8,920lb (4,046kg) s.t. General Electric J73-GE-3E engine; max. speed 692mph (1,114kph); four 20mm cannon, six 0.5in machine guns, 1,200lb (540kg) bombs.

F-111/FB-111, General Dynamics (US). Two-seat tactical strike fighter-bomber. First variable-geometry combat aircraft to enter service. First flew December 21 1964; produced in five main fighter versions, one bomber form. Production 520, of which 24 (F-111Cs) went to RAAF. Two 18,500–25,100lb (8,390–11,385kg) s.t. Pratt and Whitney TF30-P-3/TF30-P-100 engines; max. speed (F-111F) 1,453mph (2,338kph); one 20mm rotary cannon, ordnance load 25,000lb (11,340kg).

Fadden, Sir Arthur (1895–1973). Australian. The Acting PM of Australia in 1941 during the controversy over the employment of Australian troops in Greece, and again in 1950 when the decision to send Australian ground forces to Korea was announced.

"Fairfax" Operation. The first large-scale attempt to train South Vietnamese by pairing them with American units. Beginning in late 1966, three US battalions joined with Vietnamese army and territorial units to support "pacification" close to Saigon. The withdrawal of the US 199th Light Infantry Brigade in November 1967, leaving Vietnamese Ranger and province forces in charge, was cited as an early example of "Vietnamization". But training was rushed; these forces failed to screen Saigon during the 1968 Tet Offensive.

Falaise Gap, Battle of (1944). The failure of the German offensive towards Avranches on August 7 1944 gave the Allies the chance of ending the Normandy campaign with a double envelopment of the German army. On August 8 Canadian First Army attacked southwards towards Falaise (Operation "Totalize") while US XV Corps turned north from Le Mans. By August 13, XV Corps had established itself around Argentan, but then Bradley halted it. Whether the Argentan-Falaise gap could have been closed earlier if Patton had been allowed to continue has been much debated, but there was undoubtedly a risk that he might be overwhelmed when the Germans began to retreat, or collide with the Canadians.

On August 14 Canadian First Army mounted a new offensive (Operation "Tractable"), taking Falaise two days later. At last Hitler sanctioned a general withdrawal. Model replaced von Kluge as c-in-c West. The 15-mile (24km) gap between Argentan and Falaise was held open by Fifth Panzer Army facing north and Panzer Group Eberbach facing south, as Seventh Army, pounded by Allied aircraft and artillery, sought to escape from the pocket. First Canadian and First US Armies linked up at Chambois on August 19, the Poles making the first contact with the Americans. Not until August 21, however, was the German route eastwards closed. About 35,000 Germans escaped, but 10,000 were killed and 50,000 captured in the pocket, and some 500 tanks and assault guns were lost. *SB*.

US patrol at Argentan, 1944

Falkenhayn, Lt Gen *(General der Infanterie)* **Erich von** (1861–1922). Ger. Falkenhayn became a line infantry officer in 1880. His service in China and subsequent performance as COS, XVI Army Corps won the Kaiser's approval and in 1913 Falkenhayn was appointed Prussian Minister of War. Von Moltke's loss of nerve on the Marne led to his replacement as CGS by Falkenhayn on September 14 1914. Although the latter believed that the war would be won in the west, he yielded to demands to send reinforcements to the Eastern Front in the late autumn of 1914. In the event, the transfer of troops almost certainly cost him the chance of defeating the BEF at Ypres, while they were too few to be decisive in the east. In April 1915, using poison gas, the Germans broke the Allied lines at Ypres, yet Falkenhayn had not deployed enough reserves to exploit success, having again given in to pressures from the Eastern Front. He also stopped the promising Gorlice-Tarnow offensive in August to concentrate on the defeat of Serbia which, despite securing the land route to Turkey, did not bring overall victory closer. In 1916 his attempt to hurt Britain by bleeding France white at Verdun betrayed a similar confusion of strategic aims and inflicted nearly as many casualties upon the German army as on the French. This, coupled with Romania's declaration of war on the Central Powers, resulted in Falkenhayn's replacement by Hindenburg on August 29 1916. Ironically, as commander of the Ninth Army, he then played an important part in the defeat of Romania by December. In November 1917 he went to Palestine to lead Army Group F. Too late to halt Allenby's thrust at Beersheba, he nevertheless conducted an able defensive battle until succeeded by Liman von Sanders in February 1918. His last post was as commander of the Tenth Army in Lithuania. Throughout World War I, Falkenhayn was prepared to employ ruthless means, such as gas, but he was never sufficiently single-minded in his pursuit of decisive strategic ends. *PJS*.

Falkenhorst, Gen Nikolaus von (1885–1968). Ger. Commanded XXI Corps during the invasion of Poland in September 1939 and led the German invasion of Norway, 1940. Remained in command of German forces in Norway until 1944.

Battlecruiser *Inflexible*, Falklands, 1914

Falkland Islands, Battle of (1914). South Atlantic naval engagement. Early on December 8 1914 a German squadron of two armoured and three light cruisers and three colliers, under Vice Adm von Spee, attempted to raid Port Stanley, Falklands, only to find the harbour occupied by Vice Adm Sturdee's British force, including two battlecruisers, three armoured and two light cruisers and one armed merchant cruiser. Upon sighting the superior British force,

von Spee turned away at top speed. Sturdee's warships pursued, overhauling their quarry after several hours' chase. Battlecruisers *Invincible* and *Inflexible* engaged armoured cruisers *Scharnhorst* and *Gneisenau*, taking several hours to sink them in spite of calm sea and excellent visibility. Von Spee was among those killed. Meanwhile, the five British cruisers pursued the German light cruisers and colliers, sinking two light cruisers and two colliers later in the evening. Only the German light cruiser *Dresden* escaped. *JTS*.

Falklands War (April–June 1982). The Falkland Islands, some 400 miles (640km) off the South American coast, have been in continuous British occupation since 1833. British sovereignty has long been contested by Argentina, where the islands are known as the Malvinas. Anglo-Argentinian negotiations between 1965 and 1982 failed because the islanders insisted on remaining under the British Crown. In 1981 it was announced in London that the ice patrol vessel HMS *Endurance*, the Falklands guardship, would be withdrawn and scrapped without replacement as part of the British government's defence cuts. The Argentine ruling junta headed by Gen Leopoldo Galtieri assumed that the British no longer intended to defend the Falklands and began to plan their campaign. Despite urgent warnings, the British government insisted that the guardship's departure would not trigger an invasion.

Following the illegal landing of "scrap merchants" on South Georgia in March, an Argentine task force appeared off Port Stanley on April 2, and after a short fight against overwhelming odds the resident Royal Marines detachment was ordered to surrender by Governor Hunt. The invasion of South Georgia took place one day later.

On April 8, the Security Council of the United Nations passed Resolution 502, calling for an end to hostilities, a negotiated settlement, and the withdrawal of Argentine troops from the islands. American mediation failed, and President Reagan threw his government's support behind the British, already planning a military

counterstroke to regain the islands.

Successive defence cuts had seriously affected Britain's ability to project military power over a distance of 8,000 miles (13,000km) to the South Atlantic; civilian shipping had to be used, as did the airfield and anchorage at Ascension Island, approximately halfway down the Atlantic.

The task force sailed from Britain on April 5 and 9 amidst remarkable displays of national patriotic fervour; 3rd Commando Brigade, under Brig Julian Thompson, comprised Nos 40, 42 and 45 Royal Marines Commandos, augmented by the 2nd and 3rd battalions of the Parachute Regiment. All were elite non-mechanized troops, hardened by intensive training and capable of remarkable feats of endurance and aggression. The brigade had its own Commando light artillery regiment, engineer squadron and logistics regiment and an experienced air squadron with Scout and Gazelle helicopters. The only combat aircraft were 22 Sea Harriers aboard the flagship HMS *Hermes* and the new light carrier HMS *Invincible*. The force was under command of Rear Adm "Sandy" Woodward. Overall command of the expedition, known as Operation "Corporate", rested with Adm Sir John Fieldhouse, C-in-C Fleet, whose HQ was at Northwood, near London. As the 44 warships and nearly 50 Fleet Auxiliary and merchant ships steamed south, a second formation, 5 Infantry Brigade commanded by Brig Tony Wilson, sailed from Southampton on May 12 in the Cunarder *Queen Elizabeth II*. Its three infantry battalions were the 2nd Scots Guards, 1st Welsh Guards, and the 1/7th Gurkha Rifles.

On April 12, the British declared a 200-mile (320km) Maritime Exclusion Zone (MEZ) around the Falklands, enforced by three nuclear-powered hunter-killer submarines. On April 25 a task force from the main fleet retook South Georgia. A Total Exclusion Zone (TEZ) was now declared. On May 1, the RAF launched Operation "Black Buck I" when a Vulcan bomber, refuelled in flight by a succession of tanker aircraft, flew from Ascension to bomb Stanley airfield. Although one bomb hit the main runway, the airfield remained open to traffic up to the final hours before the Argentine surrender, despite further bombing attacks.

Two Argentine naval groups based around the aircraft carrier *Veinticinco de Mayo* (May 25, ex-HMS *Venerable*) and the old cruiser *General Belgrano* (ex-USS *Phoenix*) were now at sea, threatening Woodward's own carriers away to the east of the Falklands. He therefore recommended to his superiors at Northwood that the *Belgrano* be attacked by one of the nuclear submarines. This was approved, and on May 2 the cruiser was sunk by HMS *Conqueror*. All Argentine surface ships thereupon returned to their own coastal waters and stayed there. Argentine air power, however, remained a very real threat; the destroyer HMS *Sheffield* was lost on May 4.

On May 21, 3 Commando Brigade landed unopposed at San Carlos and Ajax Bay on East Falkland. The Argentine Governor and military commander Gen Menéndez had deployed most of his forces in static defensive positions around Port Stanley, some 50 miles (80km) to the east. Although some elite units were available, many had a high proportion of inexperienced and badly-led conscripts.

Menéndez now called for air strikes against the ships of the British Task Force in San Carlos Water and at sea. During the next six days, 11 ships were hit, including the *Atlantic Conveyor*, lost with its valuable cargo of helicopters and tentage. Although the Argentinian Air Force suffered heavy casualties, these attacks were pressed home with great determination.

On May 27, 3 Commando Brigade moved out of the San Carlos beachhead. Whilst 3 Para and 45 Commando struck out overland for Stanley, 2 Para marched south to take on the Argentine garrison at Goose Green, which was captured after a hard fight.

By the beginning of June, 3 Commando Brigade had reached the hills overlooking Port Stanley and was poised for the final attack; 5 Brigade was ashore and Maj Gen Jeremy Moore assumed command of the British land forces. The Scots and Welsh Guards were ship-

ped round to Fitzroy and Bluff Cove to join 2 Para, who had been helicoptered to Fitzroy on June 6, whilst the Gurkhas patrolled the hills inland. Despite the reverse suffered on June 8 when the LSL *Sir Galahad* was lost at Port Pleasant, the investment of Port Stanley went ahead. On June 11–12 the main Argentine positions in the hills before Port Stanley were taken and on the night of June 13–14 the Scots Guards took Mount Tumbledown whilst 2 Para stormed Wireless Ridge with the support of a 6,000-round barrage. Menéndez surrendered formally to Moore on June 15, as 40 Commando crossed over to West Falkland to take the surrender of its garrison. Moore's troops took more than 11,000 prisoners.

The cost of the war was high. The British lost 255 killed and 777 wounded. The Argentinians

Cease-fire in the Falklands, June 1982

admitted to 652 dead and missing. The British government subsequently announced that Operation "Corporate" had cost £700 million, and that the replacement of ships and aircraft lost would cost a further £900 million. *MH*.

Fallout. When a nuclear or thermonuclear weapon explodes close to the ground, the fireball scours out a crater, the contents of which mix with the radioactive fission products of the weapon. As the fireball rises and cools to form the "mushroom cloud", this radioactive mixture condenses into a dust which falls around ground zero from the cloud and then downwind from ground zero as the cloud is moved by the prevailing winds. The result is a plume of radioactive dust on either side of a special "hot line". This dust emits vari-

ous forms of radiation, the most dangerous of which are gamma rays. The radioactivity decays, but it remains dangerous for some time, depending on the quantity of fallout deposited. Relatively crude shelters can give considerable protection from fallout, but if no measures are taken, a 1 megaton bomb exploded at 200ft (60m) might so contaminate an area of 3,000 sq miles (7,770 sq km) that only a quarter of the population survives. Bombs air burst above a certain height – the height depending on the yield – give more blast and heat effects but little or no immediately dangerous fallout although, as at Hiroshima, radioactive material can be washed out by rain. *EJG.*

Farman F.40 (French, WWI). Two-seat reconnaissance-bomber. Designed late 1915; entered service spring 1916; widely used on Western Front and in Macedonia. Equipped about 50 French *escadrilles*; some to Russia; a few in Belgian service until Armistice. Others used by RNAS; a few to USAS as trainers. One 130/170/220hp Renault engine; max. speed 84mph (134kph); one 7.7mm machine gun, ten Le Prieur rockets, nine 120mm bombs.

Farouk II, King of Egypt (1920–1965). Reigned 1936–52. Deposed by military coup headed by Gen Neguib and died in exile. *See also* SUEZ CANAL.

Fascism. From the Latin *fasces* or parcel of rods around an axe which was the Roman symbol of authority. Adopted by Mussolini as the symbol of his political, hence Fascist, party which governed Italy from 1922 until towards the end of World War II. Since, generally used to describe right-wing authoritarian regimes or advocates.

"Fat Man" *see* NAGASAKI, ATOMIC ATTACK ON.

Fayolle, Marshal of France Marie Emile (1852-1928). Fr. Brought back from retirement in 1914, and regarded as an "intellectual" rather than a "fighting" commander, Fayolle nevertheless achieved a quick though ultimately costly breakthrough when his Sixth Army was opposed to Fritz von Below's Second Army in the Somme offensive, July 1916. He commanded First Army in the disastrous Nivelle offensive (Second Battle of the Aisne, April 1917), and later that year was c-in-c of six French divisions sent to reinforce the Italians after Caporetto. Returning to the Western Front, he commanded French Reserve Army Group (with British Fifth Army temporarily under his command) against the German March offensive, 1918 (Second Battle of the Somme), withstanding Hutier's offensive in the southern sector. *RO'N.*

FE 2b/2d, Royal Aircraft Factory (Br, WWI). Two-seat fighter-reconnaissance/bomber. Prototype (first FE 2a) flew January 26 1915; first FE 2b to France October 20 1915; equipped ten squadrons Western Front, six Home Defence units. Production revived, continued beyond Armistice, to provide night-bomber version (7 squadrons). FE 2d (Rolls-Royce engine) less numerous and shorter-lived. Production: over 2,050 FE 2bs, 265 FE 2ds. One 120/160hp Beardmore/250/275hp Rolls-Royce Eagle engine; max. speed 91/94mph (145/150kph); three 0.303in machine guns, 350lb (157kg) bombs.

Fechteler, Adm William Morrow (1896–1967). US. Commanded amphibious attack groups at Biak (Hollandia), Leyte and elsewhere in Philippines, 1944–45. US Chief of Naval Operations, 1951.

Fegen, Capt Edward Fogarty (1895–1940). Br. Commanding armed merchant cruiser *Jervis Bay*, escorting 37-ship convoy, Fegen engaged German pocket battleship *Admiral Scheer*, November 5 1940, the sacrifice of his ship allowing most of the convoy to escape. Awarded posthumous vc.

Feisal I, King of Iraq (1885–1933). Reigned 1921-33. Son of Hussein-ibn-Ali (1856–1931), Emir of Mecca, who, in 1916, proclaimed himself King of the Hejaz and signalled the beginning of the Arab Revolt. Hussein and Feisal fought with T E Lawrence against the Turks, triumphantly entering Damascus, October 1 1918. In

March 1920, Feisal declared himself King of Syria and Palestine: ousted by the French, he became King of Iraq (formerly Mesopotamia) with British support.

"Felix". German plan to capture Gibraltar in 1940–41; not implemented because Franco would not let German troops cross Spain.

Felixstowe flying-boats (Br, WWI). Maritime-reconnaissance/anti-submarine; crew 4. Hull design developed at Felixstowe by Commander John Porte, RN; principal production types F2A, F3, F5; last-named too late to see wartime use. By 1918 F2As and F3s widely used, mostly over home waters; very effective, even in aerial combat. F2A built in USA as Curtiss H-16. Of 820 ordered (all types) fewer than half delivered. Two 345hp Rolls-Royce Eagle engines; max. speed 95.5mph (154kph); four 0.303in machine guns, 920lb (417kg) bombs.

Festubert, Battle of. Although the British attack at Aubers Ridge failed on May 9 1915, Field Marshal Sir John French, c-in-c of the BEF, remained under pressure to support the French Army's Artois offensive. He therefore agreed that the British First Army, commanded by Sir Douglas Haig, should make a new attack, at Festubert, just north of the La Bassée Canal. Unlike the Aubers Ridge assault, this operation was preceded by a 60-hour bombardment, while Haig's declared intention of gradually wearing down the Germans marked the beginning of a British attrition policy on the Western Front. In the event, the battle, which lasted from May 15 to 27, cost the BEF over 16,000 casualties, as against 5,000 on the German side, but the gain of 1,000yd (910m) on a 3,000yd (2,700m) front raised British hopes and encouraged greater reliance on prolonged artillery bombardments. *PJS.*

Fiat BR 20 Cicogna (Stork) (Italian, WWII). Light bomber; crew 5. Prototype flew February 10 1936; first production aircraft delivered September 1936. Operational Spanish Civil War from November 26 1937. Deliveries to Japan early 1938; used against China. From June 13 1940 Italian *squadriglie*

attacked France; brief unsuccessful operations against Britain end 1940; subsequently Malta, North Africa and Greece. Production 602. Two 1,000hp Fiat A80 RC41 engines; max. speed 267mph (430kph); two 7.7mm, one 12.7mm machine guns, 3,527lb (1,600kg) bombs.

Fiat CR 32 (Italian, pre-WWII). Single-seat fighter biplane. Prototype flew April 28 1933; initial Italian order for 50, but first deliveries made to China. Deliveries to *Regia Aeronautica* from March 1935, others to Hungary and Austria. Use in Spanish Civil War from August 1936; CR 32's exceptional manoeuvrability enabled it to match opposing Russian I-15s and I-16s. Italian production (total 1,211) ended May 1939, but 100 built in Spain 1940–43. Limited use in World War II. One 789hp Fiat A30 RAbis engine; max. speed 221mph (356kph); two 12.7mm machine guns.

Fiat CR 42 Falco (Falcon) (Italian, WWII). Single-seat fighter biplane. Prototype flew early 1939; production deliveries began late 1939; when Italy entered war at least 330 CR 42s had been delivered. Also ordered by Belgium, Hungary, Sweden. Although its biplane configuration imposed limitations, the CR 42 was exceptionally manoeuvrable; it was widely used in North Africa 1940–41 and subsequently as night fighter over Italy. Production 1,781. One 840hp Fiat A74R RC 38 engine; max. speed 274mph (441kph); two 12.7mm machine guns, 441lb (200kg) bombs.

Fiat G 50 Freccia (Arrow) (Italian, WWII). Single-seat fighter monoplane. Prototype flew February 26 1937; of initial order for 45, 12 sent to Spain January 1939 for operational evaluation. Further production ordered; *Regia Aeronautica* had 118 G 50s June 1940. A few flown by Finnish air force against Russians from March 1940; Italian units used in Greece and North Africa. Improved Fiat G 50 bis followed: production 246 G 50s, 421 G 50bis. One 840hp Fiat A74 RC 38 engine; max. speed 293 mph (472kph); two 12.7mm machine guns, 661lb (300kg) bombs.

FIDO. Acronym of "Fog Investigation and Dispersal Operation" by which petrol burners cleared RAF airfields of fog, thereby enabling aircraft to land safely. Also the name given to US homing torpedoes carried by naval patrol aircraft for use against enemy submarines.

Fieldhouse, Adm of the Fleet Sir John (b.1928). Br. In 1982, as Admiral and British C-in-C, Fleet, he commanded the Falklands Task Force from his HQ at Northwood, near London. He was responsible to Chief of Defence Staff, Adm of the Fleet Sir Terence Lewin, for implementing Cabinet instructions for the conduct of Operation "Corporate". He subsequently became Chief of the Naval Staff, then of the Defence Staff.

Fieseler Fi 156 Storch (Stork) (German, WWII). Army co-operation/communications; crew 2. Prototype flew spring 1936; remarkable STOL and slow-flying capabilities made it ideal for army cooperation duties. Luftwaffe received about 2,900 *Störche*; additional use by Bulgaria, Slovakia, Croatia, Finland, Hungary, Romania, Spain, Sweden, Switzerland. Production continued postwar in France and Czechoslovakia; wartime total about 2,900. One 240hp Argus As 10C-3 engine; max. speed 109mph (174kph); one 7.9mm machine gun.

Fifteenth Air Force. US, based in Italy. To extend the range of strategic bombing, it built up to a strength of over 1,000 heavy bomber (B-17 and B-24) and fighter squadrons by June 1944. It was associated with the Eighth Air Force to form the United States Strategic Air Forces in Europe under Spaatz's command.

Fifteenth Army (US). Operational in January 1945, Fifteenth Army, commanded by Lt Gen Gerow, carried out largely back-up tasks in the rear of 12th Army Group's advance across Europe. It administered military government to liberated areas and protected the Rhine's west bank against German counterattack.

Fifth US Air Force. Organized in Australia, 1942, the US Fifth Air Force, commanded by Maj Gen George C Kenney (from August 1942) and Maj Gen Ennis C Whitehead (from June 1944), supported Allied operations in New Guinea and the Philippines, later attacking in the Dutch East Indies, Formosa and Japan.

Fifth Army (World War I). Formerly the "Reserve Army", the British Fifth Army was formed in 1916 under Gen Sir Hubert Gough and fought at Ypres the following year. It bore the brunt of the German March 1918 offensive and was reformed that May under Gen Sir William Birdwood, who commanded it until the end of World War I.

Fifth Army (US). Activated in North Africa on January 5 1943, the Fifth Army was commanded by Lt Gen Mark Clark. It took part in the Salerno and Anzio landings, captured Naples and Rome and fought throughout the Italian campaign until the final surrender of the German forces on April 5 1945.

Fifth column. Spanish Civil War origin: attack on an enemy by clandestine means using spies, saboteurs and internal enemies.

Fifth Fleet (US). Established March 1943, previously Central Pacific Force. Towards the end of the war, the main Pacific Fleet was alternately designated Fifth and Third Fleet, depending on whether Adms Spruance or Halsey were in command. The one not in command would be planning the next operation.

Fighter aircraft. Fighter (American "Pursuit") denotes the class of aircraft specifically designed to engage other aircraft in air combat. Their origin is to be found in the German Fokker Monoplane which made its operational appearance in May 1915 although, before that, there had been improvised air combat.

Fighter Command. Created by the reorganization of the RAF in July 1936. Although discouraging the related employment of fighters and bombers, this favoured the development of a specialized defensive capacity which proved decisive in the Battle of Britain. The AOC-in-Cs during the war were Dowding (until November 1940), Douglas (until November 1942), Leigh-Mallory (until November 1943) and Hill (until May 1945). Fighter Command was known as Air Defence of Great Britain between November 1943 and October 1944. *ANF.*

Fighting French *see* FREE FRENCH.

"Final solution". The Nazis' "Final Solution" (*Die Endlösung*) of the "Jewish problem" was fully embarked upon at the Wannsee Conference, January 20 1942. Senior Nazis approved the evacuation of all Jews to work camps in Eastern Europe and, implicitly, a policy of mass extermination.

Finland, Russian invasion of, (1939–40). In October 1939 the Soviet Union demanded the ceding of Finnish territory that was deemed essential for the defence of Leningrad and Murmansk. The Finns refused, and on November 30 the Red Army invaded. The small but well-organized Finnish Army was short of weapons, ammunition and aircraft but the calibre of the individual soldier was high. Better equipped and vastly superior in numbers, the Red Army fell prey to the Finns' astute use of the terrain and climate.

The major front was on the Karelian isthmus, north of Leningrad, where the Finns had built the Mannerheim Line. Throughout November and December, the Soviet forces were held on the isthmus and were also checked to the north of Lake Ladoga and in the central sector of the front. The Finns also made significant counterattacks, culminating in their comprehensive victory at Suomussalmi (December 27-January 9). But on February 1 the Red Army launched a major offensive in the Karelian isthmus and, employing a massive artillery bombardment and substantial air support, breached the Mannerheim Line. Although Finnish resistance was fierce, they were forced to retreat and, at the beginning of March 1940, the vital town of Vyborg (Viipuri) fell. The Finnish government was obliged to accept the Soviet peace terms and, on March 13, a treaty ending hostilities was signed at Moscow. *MS.*

Finland, War of Independence (1918–1920). Taking advantage of the Russian Revolution and Civil War, the Russian Grand Duchy of Finland declared independence in December 1917. On January 28 1918, Bolshevik-supported Red Guards took control of the capital, Helsinki, and other southern areas. Farther north, the newly appointed Finnish Army commander, Mannerheim, assumed leadership of the anti-Bolshevik "Whites", arming his forces by seizing the Russian garrison at Vaasa and marching south to take Tampere. Blocked by a Red Guard army, Mannerheim was aided by the sudden intervention of a 10,000-strong German force under Gen Count Rüdiger von der Göltz, who landed at Hango on April 3 and marched northeast to take Helsinki, splitting the Red forces. Striking east, Mannerheim secured the Karelian Isthmus, cutting off the Reds from Russia, and on April 29, in alliance with Göltz, decisively defeated them at Vyborg. Sporadic Russo-Finnish combat continued in Karelia until October 14 1920, when the Treaty of Dorpat (Tartu) confirmed Finland's independence. *RO'N.*

Fire Support Base (FSB). In the absence of fixed front lines, American forces in the Vietnam War had to move artillery fire power support of infantry into areas where operations were taking place, often by means of Chinook helicopter. These hastily constructed outposts, often on high-points in insecure areas, were frequently the target of powerful ground assaults and had to be strongly fortified.

Firefly, Fairey (Br, WWII). Two-seat shipboard fighter-reconnaissance. Prototype flew December 22 1941; first production Firefly accepted March 4 1943; first squadron formed October 1 1943; operational from July 1944. Subsequently very widely used and developed through several Marks; remained in service post-war, saw much action Korean War. Production 1,702. One 1,730/ 2,245hp Rolls-Royce Griffon engine; max. speed 316mph (509kph); four 20mm cannon, eight 60lb (27kg) rockets or 2,000lb (900kg) bombs.

First Airborne Division (British). Britain's parachute forces rapidly expanded following their creation in 1940 and, on October 29 1941, the 1st Airborne Division was formed. It served in North Africa, Sicily, Italy and at Arnhem. Subsequently it took part in the liberation of Denmark and Norway before its disbandment on November 15 1945.

First Allied Airborne Army. A centralized, coordinating body for Allied airborne units, the First Allied Airborne Army was formed in August 1944. Under the command of Lt Gen Brereton, it supervised British and American airborne units and their air transportation. It oversaw the operation at Arnhem and the airborne element of the Rhine crossings.

First Army (British). Upon landing at Algiers, the British element of "Torch" became British First Army (Lt Gen Anderson). After the successful Tunisian campaign, it was disbanded in 1943 and its troops absorbed into Allied forces for the invasion of Sicily and Italy.

First Army (Canadian). Formed in Britain in April 1942, elements of the First Army landed in Normandy on D-Day. Under the command of Lt Gen Crerar, it took part in the advance through France, Belgium and Holland. In March 1945, the Canadian II Corps joined it for the final offensive into Germany.

First Army (US). Formed in France in August 1918, the First Army won battle honours at St Mihiel, Meuse-Argonne and Lorraine. It was reactivated in World War II and constituted the American assault force on D-Day before fighting in France, the Ardennes and Germany.

First-strike capability. The ability to strike first with one's nuclear forces and knock out the opponent's means of retaliation, thus allowing one to hold the opponent's population at one's mercy and to prevail in a nuclear war. With the development of invulnerable second-strike forces the term has been refined to mean a strike against those forces on the other side that are capable of a limited strike in kind. The enemy, only being left

with counter value forces whose use is deterred by one's own secure second-strike systems, therefore admits defeat. The latter view became a fashionable fear in the USA in the late 1960s-early 1970s when the Soviet Union developed large counter force missiles. In reality the risks of a first strike are so great that no decision maker is likely to see it as a rational policy option. *EJG.*

First use. The policy of being prepared to use nuclear weapons first as part of an escalation strategy, as in NATO's strategy of flexible response. First use implies not a full-scale first strike with strategic forces but using theatre nuclear weapons in small numbers to show resolve, in the context of the battlefield where conventional forces are failing to cope with the aggression on their own. The aim is to restore deterrence, not win the battle in operational terms. The French call their first use forces (*see* FORCE DE FRAPPE) "pre-strategic".

Fisher; controversial and combative

Fisher, Adm of the Fleet Lord (1841-1920). Br. First Sea Lord 1904-10 and 1914-15. Fisher, more than any other individual, was responsible for converting the Victorian Navy into the force which fought World War I in which it largely outmatched German sea power. In particular, Fisher's radical and vigorous approach led to the development of the *Dreadnought* class of battleships, the introduction of battlecruisers, improvements in submarines and destroyers, higher standards of gunnery and torpedo work, a new deployment of British sea power more relevant to the German threat and an updated system of training for naval

F

cadets. He also introduced a system of partial manning of reserve ships which meant that when the emergency arrived in 1914, the active fleets could be much more rapidly reinforced than the old system would have allowed.

The nature of these changes and the manner of Fisher's advocacy of them affronted conservative opinion in the Navy and, in some important cases, that outside it. By 1910 Fisher had accumulated a formidable volume of dislike and distrust which led to his resignation as First Sea Lord. His reforms had, however, bitten too deeply to be reversed. Most of them produced beneficial results and without some of them Britain could not have survived World War I. The view that the Dreadnoughts were a mistake, because they made Britain's superiority in capital ships obsolete and gave other powers the opportunity of starting level in a new naval race, was misguided because if Britain had not introduced these new ships, the Germans would have done so. The battlecruisers, however, raised a much more controversial issue and in retrospect it can scarcely be doubted that they were an expensive failure.

Upon Prince Louis of Battenberg's resignation as First Sea Lord in October 1914, Churchill brought Fisher back as his successor but this led to a quarrel about the reinforcements which Churchill wished to send to the Dardanelles and to Fisher's departure in high dudgeon. *ANF.*

Fishhook. The American command in the Vietnam War called one of the pieces of Cambodian territory that jutted toward Saigon "the Fishhook". Located 50 miles (80km) northwest of the city, the Fishhook was a sanctuary and supply base for communist forces. The area was a major target of the US-South Vietnamese "incursion" that began on April 29 1970. Though communist forces had withdrawn deeper into Cambodia before the attack, they left behind a sprawling complex of living quarters, mess halls, training sites and storage depots containing a huge stock of material. *WST.*

Fitch, Vice Adm Aubrey Wray- ("Jakey") (1883–1978). US. A naval aviation specialist, Fitch commanded *Saratoga* in the abortive Wake Island relief operation, December 1941. In May 1942 he headed Task Force 11 in the Battle of the Coral Sea, where his flagship, *Lexington*, was sunk. As commander of the land-based Task Force 63 (later of South Pacific Air Forces), he commanded all Allied aircraft in the South Pacific area, 1942–43, during the Solomons campaign, becoming Deputy Chief of Naval Operations (Air) in 1944.

Fitzroy Settlement (Falklands) *see* BLUFF COVE.

Flak. Acronym of the German *Fliegerabwehrkanone* (aviator defence gun), applied to both weapons and barrage.

Flamethrower. Portable weapon that propelled a jet of burning liquid. Used in both world wars; particularly effective against troops manning fortified positions.

"Flaming Dart" Operations I and II. The first routine airstrikes against North Vietnam launched from American aircraft carriers in the Tonkin Gulf. The first "Flaming Dart" strikes were carried out on February 7 1965 in reprisal for a communist mortar attack on a US encampment at Pleiku. "Flaming Dart II" on February 11 was in reprisal for an attack on an American enlisted men's billet in Qui Nhon. In March, when the pretext of retaliation was dropped, "Flaming Dart" was superseded by "Rolling Thunder".

Fleet. The largest unit of naval force. Usually organized on a geographical basis, e.g. the British Home and Mediterranean Fleets or the US Third and Sixth Fleets.

Fleet Air Arm. The air element of the Royal Navy and especially the aircraft which are flown off and onto ships at sea. The origins of the force are to be found in the Naval Wing of the Royal Flying Corps, later named the Royal Naval Air Service, which was created in 1912. In 1918, naval flying was absorbed into the newly created Royal Air Force, but this solution was one which the Navy never approved and in 1937 the Fleet Air Arm became an integral part of the Navy. Partly as a result of the long-running dispute between the two services on this point, partly due to a general lack of air consciousness in the Navy and partly because of other priorities, the Fleet Air Arm was ill-equipped and throughout World War II, its principal aircraft was the Swordfish, essentially an updated version of a World War I vintage. Six of them attacked the *Scharnhorst*, *Gneisenau* and *Prinz Eugen* during their Channel Dash on February 12 1942. All were destroyed and Lt Commander Esmonde, who led the attack, was posthumously awarded the VC. Nevertheless, with nothing better, the Fleet Air Arm had achieved a major success in 1940 when it struck at the Italian fleet in Taranto and it was a Swordfish, flown off *Ark Royal*, which did the vital damage to the *Bismarck* in 1941. In the 1970s, when the Labour government decided to abandon aircraft carriers, it seemed that the Fleet Air Arm had come to the end of its career. However, in the Falklands War the Fleet Air Arm played a decisive role in the Argentinian defeat. *ANF.*

Fleischer, Gen Carl (1883–1942). Norwegian. Commander of Norwegian troops in Narvik area, Norwegian campaign, 1940.

Flers-Courcelette, Battle of. The British attack at Flers-Courcelette on September 15 1916 saw the first use of tanks in warfare. The objectives of the attack, which formed part of the overall British Somme offensive, included the capture, by Rawlinson's Fourth Army, of the German third defence position at Flers and the subsequent seizure of Morval, Lesboeufs and Gueudecourt. On the left the Canadian Corps, in Gough's Reserve Army, was to assault the defences of Courcelette. Of the 49 tanks available to support the infantry, only 32 reached their various starting points on September 15. Causing some alarm among the German defenders, four of the tanks allotted to the 41st Division reached Flers and one entered the main street while the other three engaged strongpoints and machine gun nests on the village's eastern outskirts. Flers was duly captured by XV Corps and the Canadians took Courcelette the same day but, as so often before, the offensive then bogged down. Morval and Lesboeufs remained in German hands for another ten days and Combles and Gueudecourt did not fall until September 26. Sir Douglas Haig, the British c-in-c, has since been accused of committing the tanks prematurely in September 1916 and of deploying them in "penny packets" instead of grouping them together for a decisive breakthrough. However, given their small numbers and mechanical unreliability in 1916, it is difficult to see what alternatives Haig had, for it is doubtful that their existence would have remained secret much longer. *PJS*.

Flesquières. Village southwest of Cambrai, taken by the 51st (Highland) Division on November 21 1917, during the British Cambrai offensive. After the German counterattack of November 30, the British held a salient to the east of the village which was abandoned, somewhat belatedly, on March 23 1918, during the German "Michael" offensive. Flesquières was recaptured by the British 3rd and Guards Divisions on September 27 1918.

Unlucky "Black Jack" Fletcher

Fletcher, Vice Adm Frank Jack (1885–1973). US. A Medal of Honor winner at Vera Cruz, 1914, and a World-War-I veteran, "Black Jack" Fletcher proved a painstaking, but overcautious and unlucky, commander during World War II. He incurred criticism for his refuelling delay during the aborted Wake Island relief operation, December 1941, while his strategic victory in the Coral Sea, May 1942, was marred by the loss of *Lexington* and damage to his flagship, *Yorktown*, at a critical time for the US Navy's carrier

strength. Serious damage to *Yorktown* (ultimately sunk) early at Midway, June 1942, resulted in Spruance assuming tactical command. Fletcher's subsequent reluctance to hazard his carriers was blamed for the US Navy's reverses off Guadalcanal, August 1942: he achieved a tactical victory in the Battle of the Eastern Solomons, but after *Saratoga* was torpedoed, August 31, he was relegated to "commands more commensurate with his abilities" (in the disparaging words of the usn's historian) in the North Pacific. *RO'N*.

Flexible Response. NATO's current strategic compromise concept accepted by the NATO council after years of debate at the end of 1967 and enshrined in Military Committee Document MC14/3 of January 16 1968. The Americans, who had adopted their version of Flexible Response as national strategy from 1961, had wanted NATO to accept that, in an age of nuclear parity, the only credible response to a Soviet conventional attack was a response in kind, a conventional defence. The Europeans, however, wished to maintain the nuclear emphasis in NATO strategy as they doubted the deterrent efficacy of such a limited counter-threat, especially as their national territories would supply the battlefield. They also did not wish to increase defence expenditures unduly, and the 1967 compromise was only accepted on condition that it would not lead to such demands. It placed a new emphasis on conventional forces for crisis management, to defend against limited threats on the flanks and in forcing the Soviets to mount a major attack at a level that would clearly raise nuclear stakes. Various first-use and follow-on-use nuclear escalation options were subsequently worked out in the NATO Nuclear Planning Group. Over the last decade, the attempt has also been made to raise the nuclear threshold and try to defend without necessarily requiring first use. The latter option, however, remains a core element in the overall deterrent effectiveness of the concept, and NATO refuses to predict beforehand precisely how its "triad" of strategic nuclear, theatre nuclear and conventional forces will be used. *EJG*.

Flight. Basic air force unit, usually of about eight aircraft.

Florence, Battle for (July 20–August 4 1944). I Parachute Corps (Schlemm) defended the city on the Paula Line some 10 miles (16km) to the south against the attacks of XIII Corps (Kirkman). The final attack was launched by the New Zealand Division, supported on the right and left by 6th South African Armoured and 8th Indian Divisions. As Schlemm's divisions neared exhaustion, Kesselring authorized his withdrawal to a line through the northern quarters of the city. XIII Corps entered the southern outskirts on August 4 to find all the bridges over the River Arno blown except for the Ponte Vecchio, which was blocked by demolitions and mines at either end. Both sides tried to limit the damage to historic buildings and treasures of the city. *WGFJ*.

Flotilla. Literally a small fleet. A group of ships, more often small ones such as submarines or destroyers, and normally under a single command.

Flush deckers. Nickname for American destroyers built for World War I; unusual for their type in having a continuous ("flush") upper deck from stem to stern. The other nickname was "Four stackers" (after their funnels). Many went to the RN under "lend-lease", others served USN in various guises in World War II.

Flying-boat. A seaplane in which the fuselage serves as the principal buoyancy element; lateral stability on water is maintained by outboard floats or sponsons.

"Flying bomb" *see* V-1 under V-WEAPONS.

Flying Fortress *see* B-17.

"Flying Tigers". Nickname of the American Volunteer Group (AVG): from the "shark's teeth" painted on the noses of its P-40 Warhawks. Some 90 veteran US service pilots and 150 support personnel were recruited by Chennault early in 1941 to serve in China as mercenaries (pilots receiving $600–750 per month, with a $500 bonus for every "kill") against the Japanese.

F

In combat from December 20 1941 until June 1942, they claimed 286 Japanese aircraft for 23 losses. Some AVG personnel subsequently joined Chennault's Fourteenth Air Force, sometimes also referred to as the "Flying Tigers".

Allied supremo in 1918: Marshal Foch

Foch, Marshal Ferdinand (1851–1929). Fr. An artillery officer, Foch was Chief Instructor at the *École Supérieure de Guerre* from 1896 to 1901 and Commandant from 1908 to 1911. As the leading advocate of the offensive, he helped to shape French military doctrine before World War I and must bear much of the blame for the wasteful tactics of 1914–15. In August 1914 he commanded XX Corps in Lorraine and, the following month, led the Ninth Army on the Marne, where his obsessive reliance on offensive tactics proved costly to his own troops. Nevertheless, Joffre was sufficiently impressed to make Foch his deputy in October and put him in command of the Northern Army Group, with the task of coordinating the Allied forces between the Oise and the North Sea. Foch's resolute and energetic leadership during the autumn battles in Flanders was an important factor in enabling the Allies to prevent a German breakthrough and provided him with valuable experience in inter-Allied command. On the other hand, his miserly use of French reserves and his reluctance to withdraw to a more defensible line caused unnecessary problems during the Second Battle of Ypres in 1915. The failures in Artois that year at last persuaded Foch to revise his tactical ideas and place greater emphasis on thorough preparation and artillery superiority in future operations. In 1916 he was pessimistic about the

prospects of the Somme offensive, in which the French played a subordinate role. With Joffre's removal in December, Foch's career too went into temporary eclipse until May 1917, when he was appointed CGS. Then on March 26 1918, at the height of the German offensive in Picardy, Foch was made responsible for coordinating all Allied operations on the Western Front. His powers were extended when he was named General-in-Chief of the Allied Armies on April 14. In this capacity he led the Allies to victory. Although Haig and Pershing continued to exercise a great deal of independence, Foch's overall strategy of keeping the Germans off balance by striking alternate blows at different points on the Western Front certainly contributed to the final Allied success. *PJS*.

Focke-Wulf Fw 189 Uhu (Owl) (German, WWII). Tactical reconnaissance; crew 3. Originally intended as light bomber/ground attack aircraft; prototype flew July 1938; production started 1939; deliveries from late 1940. Much used on reconnaissance/close-support duties Russian front; also in Finland and North Africa. Vulnerable to fighter attack, progressively transferred to liaison and ambulance work. Total production 846. Two 465hp Argus As 410A-1 engines; max. speed 214mph (342kph); four 7.92mm machine guns, 440lb (200kg) bombs.

Focke-Wulf Fw 190/Ta 152 (German, WWII). Single-seat fighter. Prototype first flew June 1 1939; deliveries of evaluation batch early winter 1940, of production aircraft end 1940. With increased armament, later Fw 190s proved to be potent fighters; design developed through numerous subtypes to the Ta 152 series, 1943 and later. Production total over 19,700, all variants. One 1,700hp BMW 801D-2 or 1,750hp Junkers Jumo 213E engine; max. speed 382/472mph (615/760kph); four 20mm cannon and two 7.92mm machine guns/one 30mm and two 20mm cannon.

Focke-Wulf Fw 200 Condor (German, WWII). Long-range maritime reconnaissance bomber; crew 6. Adaptation of civil transport;

first few conversions operating late 1939; attacks on British shipping began 1940. Production Fw 200C-1s came forward that year; deliveries slow, but Condor proved effective until introduction into Allied convoy operations of CAM-ship Hurricanes. Late versions carried guided missiles. Production totalled 276. Four 1,200hp BMW Bramo 323R-2 Fafnir engines; max. speed 224mph (358kph); 4,620lb (2,095kg) bombs, one 20mm and one 15mm cannon, four 13mm and one 7.92mm machine guns; missile-carrying versions, two Hs 293 radio-controlled glider bombs.

Fokker D VII (German, WWI). Single-seat fighter. Prototype (Fokker V11) flew December 1917; won official fighter competition January/February 1918. Production deliveries began February 1918; at least 48 *Jagdstaffeln* equipped, partly or wholly, with D VII. Formidable and successful; best with BMW engine. Front-line strength at August 31 1918, total 828. One 160/175hp Mercedes D III/D IIIa or 185hp BMW IIIa engine; max. speed 125mph (200kph); two 7.9mm machine guns.

Fokker Dr I (German, WWI). Single-seat fighter triplane. Prototypes flew acceptance tests August 16 1917; both to operational units August 21. Production deliveries to *Jagdstaffeln* from October. An aircraft of exceptional manoeuvrability; proved elusive in combat in skilled hands, but had serious limitations. Production 320. One 110hp Oberursel Ur II(Rh) engine; max. speed 115mph (184kph); two 7.9mm machine guns.

Fokker monoplane (German, WWI). Single-seat fighter. Basic design (Fokker M.5K) flew April 1914; experiments with mechanical interrupter gear for fixed machine gun led to Fok. E I, spring 1915. This was a significant new weapon; development led to Fok. E II (July 1915), E III (August 1915) and twin-gun E IV (November 1915). Production about 450. One 80/100/160hp Oberursel engine; max. speed (E IV) 100mph (160kph); one 7.9mm machine gun (two on E IV).

Follow-On Forces Attack (FOFA). A concept developed under the aegis of NATO's SACEUR, Gen Rogers, in the early 1980s as a means of raising the nuclear threshold. It was included as an important mission area in the Conceptual Military Framework endorsed by NATO ministers at the end of 1985. FOFA places emphasis on long-range interdiction to destroy "second-echelon" Warsaw Pact forces so they cannot follow on the front-line attackers to renew pressure on weakened areas of resistance or exploit any breakthroughs already made. Although FOFA missions can be carried out with existing assets, notably aircraft, new "deep strike" surveillance, target acquisition and conventional missile systems were implied by the concept and are under development, e.g. JSTARS. These are controversial, especially as the Soviets claim to find FOFA an aggressive concept providing a cover for the acquisition of systems capable of destroying Warsaw Pact command and control as a prelude to attack. *EJG.*

Fonck, Capt René (1894–1953). Fr. Having joined the French air service in February, 1915, Fonck flew on reconnaissance and bombing sorties for nearly two years before training as a fighter pilot. By November 1918 he had been credited with 75 victories, becoming the leading Allied "ace" of World War I.

Fontainebleau Conference. During 1946, President Ho Chi Minh of the DRV engaged in protracted negotiations with the French over Vietnam's relations with the French empire. These negotiations came to a head at a meeting convened on July 6 at Fontainebleau outside Paris. Rightist pressures on the French government nearly sabotaged the talks, and Ho made concessions that many of his supporters were unwilling to accept. Ho signed a modus vivendi on September 14 that guaranteed France's economic rights in northern Vietnam without securing French agreement to relinquish Cochin China. *WST.*

Forbes, Adm of the Fleet, Sir Charles (1888–1960). Br. C-in-C Home Fleet during the Norwegian campaign of 1940; C-in-C Plymouth from December 1940; helped plan St Nazaire raid of March 1942.

Force de Frappe. The original name for the French nuclear strategic deterrent force, now renamed *Force de Dissuasion*. It became operational in 1964 with Mirage IV bombers. Some of these remain in service, forming a "triad" with 18 SSBS intermediate range ballistic missiles in the Plateau D'Albion and 6 MSBS ballistic missile-firing submarines, 3 of which are normally at sea at one time. This force is under purely national command.

Force H. British naval force created in June 1940, based at Gibraltar to compensate for the collapse of France. Composition varied, but included the carrier *Ark Royal* until her loss. Suppressed French fleet, Mers-el-Kébir; helped sink *Bismarck*; escorted Malta convoys; took part in "Torch", Sicily and Salerno landings.

Force K. Formed October 1941, based at Malta, and comprising British cruisers and destroyers.

Force Z. British squadron sent to Far East, December 1941. Although "Main fleet to Singapore" had featured largely in interwar planning, Force Z comprised only battleship *Prince of Wales*, battlecruiser *Repulse* and a few destroyers. Attempting to intercept invasion convoys and without air cover, both capital ships were sunk by Japanese land-based aircraft, December 10 1941.

Ford, President Gerald R Jr (b.1913). US. Replaced Richard Nixon as President in August 1974. American forces had by then withdrawn from Vietnam, but the ceasefire provided by the Paris Agreement had broken down. Ford requested $300 million in emergency aid for South Vietnamese forces in January 1975. The communist offensive unleashed in March prompted him to make an additional request for $722 million. Congress appropriated $300 million for the evacuation of Americans and "humanitarian purposes", but denied supplementary military assistance for the South Vietnamese army. As Saigon fell, Ford declared that the war was "finished as far as America is concerned". *WST.*

Foreign Legion (French) *see* ALGERIAN CAMPAIGN.

Formidable *see* ILLUSTRIOUS.

Forrestal, James Vincent (1892–1949). US. Administrator. Served in the navy, 1917–18. As Under Secretary of the Navy (1940) he was very successful in administering procurement. In 1944 he became Secretary of the Navy and retained this office under President Truman. Supporting Truman's moves towards unification of the services, he became first Secretary of Defense, 1947. He committed suicide.

Fort Douaumont. Key Verdun fort, captured by Germans February 25 1916, retaken by French October 24.

Fort Vaux. Verdun fort, seized by Germans, June 7 1916, reoccupied by French, November 2.

Forward Based Systems (FBS). The American nuclear capable tactical strike aircraft capable of reaching the Soviet Union and deployed around its periphery in Allied nations and on aircraft carriers. The USSR has persistently wanted to add these to American strategic forces for the purposes of arms control, but the USA has equally persistently refused.

Forward Edge of the Battle Area (FEBA). The limit of the farthest forward area in which main force ground combat units are deployed, excluding areas occupied by covering and screening units. Used as a point of reference in the coordination of fire support, and the manoeuvre and positioning of units.

Forward Line of Own Troops (FLOT). The front line of one's own units, usually formed by covering and reconnaissance forces. It is usually forward of the FEBA.

Foss, Maj Joseph Jacob (b.1915). US. Marine Corps Grumman F4F Wildcat pilot and winner of the Congressional Medal of Honor who destroyed 26 Japanese aircraft in a brief but spectacular combat career while flying with VMF-121 from Henderson Field, Guadalcanal between October 1942 and January 1943. He subsequently became Governor of South Dakota and a brigadier general in the Air National Guard.

F

Fourteen Points. Announced to Congress by President Wilson on January 8 1918, these constituted the American view of the main elements which were to compose the peace settlement. They were: (1) treaties and diplomacy must be open and public; (2) the freedom of the seas must prevail outside territorial waters; (3) trade barriers should be reduced or removed; (4) nations should disarm to provide only for domestic security; (5) colonial claims should be adjusted in accordance with the interests of the indigenous populations; (6) Russia should be welcomed into the international fraternity and her territory evacuated by foreign occupiers; (7) Belgian sovereignty should be restored; (8) France should be restored to her pre-1870 sovereignty; (9) the Italian frontiers should be drawn on the principle of the nationalities concerned; (10) Austro-Hungarian territories should be afforded autonomous development; (11) Romanian, Serbian and Montenegrin sovereignty should be restored and guarantees afforded to the Balkan states generally; (12) Turkish sovereignty over Turks should be guaranteed but non-Turkish Ottoman subjects should be afforded autonomous development, and freedom of navigation in the Dardanelles should be assured; (13) Polish national independence should be guaranteed and (14) an international association of states should be formed to protect the interests of the large and the small nations alike. *ANF*.

Fourteenth Air Force (US). Activated in March 1943 to augment 10th Air Force. Formed in South China from original China Air Task Force of 1942 (Commander Maj Gen Claire Chennault) and adopted the famous "Flying Tiger" badge; 14th Air Force operated over huge area of Southeast Asia, making bombing attacks against targets in Indochina, North Burma, the Formosan Straits and Thailand from its clutch of bases around Kunming. Its training and maintenance bases were in North India.

Fourteenth Army (Burma campaign, 1941–45). Formed October 1943 from what was previously Eastern Army under GHQ India

and placed under the orders of Adm Mountbatten as the major element in South East Asia Command. Fourteenth Army was responsible for a front of 700 miles (1,130km) along the Assam-Burma border. Its commander was Lt Gen Slim, and his main formations were IV Corps (Lt Gen G Scoones, 1943–44, Lt Gen F W Messervy, 1944–45, XV Corps (Lt Gen Sir Philip Christison), XXIII Corps (Lt Gen M G N Stopford). The army fought a prolonged defensive battle in 1944 (*see* KOHIMA). After the successful outcome, Slim and his three Corps commanders were knighted on Imphal plain. The offensive was taken early in 1945 with 14 divisions (9 Indian, 3 African, 2 British). After the thrust down from Mandalay to Rangoon, Twelfth Army took over in Burma from Fourteenth Army (June 1 1945) when Slim and his staff were withdrawn to plan the invasion of Malaya. *HT*.

Fourth Army (US). Primarily concerned with the defence of the Pacific coast and Alaska during World War II. It supplied staff for newly formed armies and helped train and equip other units. Its duties were exclusively performed in the US.

Fractional Orbital Bombardment System (FOBS). A system which puts a nuclear warhead into an orbital trajectory to send it the "long way" round the Earth to approach the target from an unexpected direction behind the radar

early-warning screen or in a very low trajectory under the radar. On approaching the target, retro-rockets fire to bring the warhead down. The Soviet Union tested such a system on an SS-9 missile in the late 1960s but did not develop it. A complete orbit of the Earth would violate the 1966 Outer Space Treaty, prohibiting weapons of mass destruction in orbit.

France, Battle of (1940). Few campaigns between great and approximately equal powers have been decided so swiftly and conclusively as the German conquest of France in May and June 1940. For many years the myth prevailed that France and Britain had been beaten by overwhelming numerical and material odds, but it is now generally accepted that this was not the case.

On May 10 1940 Germany had 136 divisions in the West, of which 10 were armoured (Panzers). France fielded 94 divisions, Britain 10 and Belgium 21. The French had more tanks than their opponent – approximately, 3,250 against 2,500 – and their latest models, such as the Char B, were superior to anything on the German side. However, as events were to prove, the panzer divisions' organization and doctrine gave them a decisive advantage.

Only in the air did the attacker have a clear numerical advantage – German air strength in May 1940 exceeded 3,000 aircraft (including more than 1,000 fighters

End of the first phase of the Battle of France, 1940: Allies fall back to Dunkirk

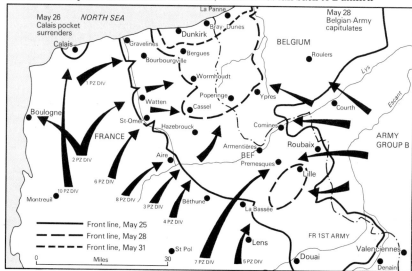

and over 300 Stukas) whereas the French possessed little more than 1,000 modern aircraft. Even allowing for the British contribution, the Germans had the advantage.

In February 1940 Hitler had adopted the Manstein Plan, under which Army Group A, employing seven of the ten panzer divisions, was to penetrate the Ardennes, cross the Meuse, break out as quickly as possible and drive towards the Channel coast. Army Group B, facing the Low Countries, took the supporting role. Manstein convinced Hitler that by cutting off the Allied armies north of this deep armoured thrust, his plan would deal the enemy a crippling blow.

Between May 10 and 12 Army Group A crossed the supposedly impassable Ardennes with minimal opposition on the ground and from the air. The Meuse was reached two days earlier than the French expected and crossings began immediately on May 13. All the bridges had been blown and the defenders fought bravely, yet by the end of the day, four precarious bridgeheads had been established on the west bank.

The German thrust across the Meuse deliberately struck the junction between two weak French armies (Second and Ninth), which reeled back in confusion and panic. By nightfall on May 14 the German bridgehead was already about 30 miles (48km) wide and 15 miles (24km) deep. Heroic Anglo-French air attacks on the pontoon bridge at Sedan failed at a cost of 85 bombers (mostly Blenheims) out of 170. Worse still, by May 15, all three French armoured divisions had been shattered in ill-organized and separate counterattacks.

By May 20 the leading panzer divisions had reached the Channel near Abbeville. The order which halted the panzer forces on the Canal line between May 24 and 27 enabled most of the British (and many Allied) troops to escape at Dunkirk, but when the evacuation ceased on June 4 the first phase had ended with a resounding German victory. France had lost 30 divisions including virtually all her armour.

When the second phase of the German offensive began on June 5 the French situation was desperate, with only 66 weak divisions to defend a Somme line longer than the original front. Although some French units fought heroically in the final days, the end was clearly in sight when Paris fell on June 14, and Reynaud was replaced by the defeatist Pétain two days later. Rommel's 7th Panzer Division swept through to Cherbourg and the 5th to Brest causing a second, chaotic British evacuation. Meanwhile Lyons fell to XVI Corps and XIX Corps reached the Swiss border before swinging northeast to Belfort. France surrendered on June 22. *BB*.

France, capitulation in the Mediterranean (June 24 1940). When the Franco-Italian Armistice was signed, the main units of the French Mediterranean Fleet, away from Toulon, were under Adm Gensoul at Mers-el-Kébir (Oran), and under Adm Godfroy at Alexandria. Godfroy agreed to demilitarize his ships, but Gensoul did not. On July 3 1940, acting under Churchill's direct orders, Adm Somerville's Force H from Gibraltar gave Gensoul an ultimatum. When this was refused, the British ships, with great reluctance, opened fire on their former allies in Mers-el-Kébir harbour. *WGFJ*.

Allied landing in southern France, 1944

France, Southern, Allied invasion of (August 15 1944). Carried out by Hewitt's Allied Naval Task Force and Patch's Seventh US Army with VI US Corps (Truscott) and French Army B (de Lattre de Tassigny), and supported by US XII Tactical Air Command (Saville); opposed by Nineteenth Army (Wiese), which had been seriously weakened by having to send reinforcements to Normandy.

The landings were carried out successfully either side of St Tropez, using overwhelming force. With the Battle of Falaise raging in Normandy, Hitler ordered a methodical withdrawal of all forces from Southern France, starting on August 18. Toulon and Marseilles fell on August 28. An attempt was made to cut off the German retreat up the Rhône Valley at Montélimar, but the American forces were not strong enough to prevent the German divisions breaking through, although the Allied air forces inflicted heavy losses during the battle. *WGFJ*.

Franchet d'Esperey, Marshal Louis Félix (1856–1942). Fr. Known as "Desperate Frankie" to his British allies in World War I, Franchet d'Esperey had seen extensive service outside France before 1914. In the early weeks of the 1914 campaign he commanded I Corps in Lanrezac's Fifth Army, handling his forces superbly in the Battle of Charleroi on August 23 and leading a vital counterattack at Guise six days later. He succeeded Lanrezac at the head of the Fifth Army on September 3, in time to command it in the victory on the Marne. Towards the end of 1914 he advocated an Allied offensive in the Balkans as an alternative to the western trench stalemate, although his idea foundered on the opposition of Joffre and other French generals. Remaining on the Western Front, he was given command of the French Eastern Group of Armies in April 1916 and then, following Foch's removal in December 1916, took over the Northern Army Group. His own career received a temporary setback when he failed to hold the German May 1918 offensive between the Aisne and Marne but, having been transferred to command the Allied Armies of the Orient in Salonika in June 1918, he was better placed to exploit his undoubted strategic flair and attacking instincts. Once his plans had won the belated approval of the Allied governments, he launched an offensive on September 15 which, within two weeks, forced Bulgaria to sue for peace. He was created Marshal in 1922. *PJS*.

Franco y Bahamonde, Gen Francisco (1892–1975). Spanish Nationalist leader; a political general, not a strategist. His ambition and cleverness at playing rivals off against each other won him supreme command of the Nationalists in the Spanish Civil War. Although a former Foreign Legion commander, he was the opposite of a daring leader like Yagüe. Axis diplomats were shocked by Franco's cold-blooded cruelty and German generals exasperated by his complacency and military orthodoxy. Head of state until his death in 1975. *AB*.

Frank, Anne (1929–45). Dutch. A young Jewish victim of the Holocaust, Anne Frank wrote diaries while in hiding in Amsterdam. Published after the war, they received worldwide acclaim.

Franz Ferdinand, Archduke (1863–1914). Austrian. The heir to the Austro-Hungarian throne, assassinated by a Serbian nationalist at Sarajevo in Bosnia, June 28 1914. This provoked an Austrian ultimatum to Serbia which, in turn, called the intricate network of European alliances into play and led to World War I.

Fraser, Adm of the Fleet Lord (1888–1981). Br. c-in-c Home Fleet 1943–44, c-in-c Eastern Fleet 1944–45, c-in-c British Pacific Fleet 1945. In the last months of peace, Fraser served as cos to Pound while the latter was c-in-c Mediterranean Fleet. Upon the outbreak of war he became Third Sea Lord and Controller of the Navy, a post of particular importance due to the rapid and urgent naval expansion. In May 1943 he took command of the Home Fleet. In December, he received intelligence indications that *Scharnhorst* might be about to put to sea. He sailed to engage and thus brought on the Battle of North Cape in which *Scharnhorst*, was sunk.

This was one of the basic steps towards the possibility of reinforcing Anglo-American sea power in the Pacific. Fraser's selection to command the British Pacific Fleet which was able to do this in January 1945 reflected the renown he had achieved. He signed the Japanese instrument of surrender and from 1948–51 was First Sea Lord and Chief of Naval Staff. *ANF*.

Fredendall, Lt Gen Lloyd R (1883–1963). US. As Commander 1st US Division, Fredendall took Oran during the North African landings in November 1942. As Commander II US Corps in Southern Tunisia, he was defeated by Rommel in the Battles of Sidi Bou Zid and Kasserine, and relieved of his command and assigned to training duties in March 1943.

Free French (Fighting French). Broadcasting from London on June 18 1940, de Gaulle proclaimed "Free France", with the Cross of Lorraine as its emblem. The "Free French" opposed Vichy France and formed their own army, navy and air force units to serve the Allied cause. In June 1942, the name was changed to "Fighting France".

Freikorps. The demobilization of Germany's army in December 1918 left the Weimar government vulnerable to internal and external threats. Freikorps (Free Corps) volunteer paramilitary units were formed ostensibly to combat disorder at home and stabilize the chaotic situation on Germany's eastern frontiers but themselves proved a threat to the republic.

French army mutinies. By the spring of 1917, the French army was showing clear signs of exhaustion. Gen Nivelle's offensive was a disaster resulting in over 200,000 casualties. Discipline amongst the troops deteriorated and on April 17 the first case of mutiny occurred when men of the 108th Infantry Regiment abandoned their posts in the face of the enemy. By the end of August, 250 cases of mutiny had been reported, affecting 68 of the French army's 112 divisions. On May 15 Gen Pétain replaced Nivelle and set about suppressing the mutinies with a mixture of sternness and compassion. Some 50 soldiers were executed (out of an estimated 35,000 involved) while many grievances were redressed. *MS*.

French Committee of National Liberation. Le Comité Français de Libération Nationale (CFLN), formed in June 1943 as a coalition of senior elements in the Free French movement, became the provisional government of France in May 1944.

French, Field Marshal Sir John *see* YPRES, FIELD MARSHAL EARL OF.

French forces in Korea. When the Korean War broke out, French forces were already engaged in Indochina but France committed a battalion led by Lt Col Raoul Montclar which was attached to a US infantry unit. France also sent a frigate, withdrawn in November 1950 to serve in Indochina.

French Resistance *see* RESISTANCE MOVEMENTS.

Freya. German early warning radar for detecting aircraft. Introduced summer 1941.

Freyberg, Gen Lord VC (1889-1963). New Zealand. Freyberg fought at Gallipoli, and by 1917 was a brigade commander on the Western Front. He was wounded nine times, and awarded the vc, the dso and two bars, and the cmg during World War I.

Throughout World War II, he

Much-decorated Gen Freyberg

commanded the New Zealand Forces and was Commander 2nd New Zealand Division in the Mediterranean. After the disastrous campaign in Greece, he took command of the Anglo-Greek garrison on Crete. Although forced to evacuate the island, his men inflicted such losses on the Germans that Hitler forbade further major airborne operations.

In the Western Desert and Tunisian campaigns, he fought the Second Battle of Sidi Rezegh, receiving a third bar to his dso; was wounded for the tenth time at Minqar Qaim; led the "Supercharge" break-out at El Alamein; commanded the out-flanking forces during Eighth Army's advance to Tripoli, and at Mareth; but failed to break through at Enfidaville.

In the Italian campaign, he commanded the New Zealand Corps in the Second and Third Battles of Cassino; played a leading role in the advance to and breaching of the Gothic Line, and in the destruction of the German armies south of the Po. He led the final advance on Trieste, which he entered on May 2 1945. *WGFJ*.

Friedrichshaften FF 33 (German, WWI). Two-seat patrol seaplane. First deliveries of FF 33a March 1915. Developed and improved through several variants; widely and effectively used as fighter-reconnaissance and shipping-strike aircraft. At least 725 (all variants) ordered. One 150hp Benz Bz III engine; max. speed 85mph (136kph); two 7.9mm machine guns, small bomb load.

Frigate. A class of warship smaller than destroyers but larger than corvettes. They were extensively used for convoy escort by the British from 1942 and by the Americans from 1943. Since World War II the term has been less precisely used to describe a wide range of small warships from guided missile to anti-submarine ships.

Fritsch, Gen Werner Freiherr von (1880–1939). Ger. A protégé of von Hindenburg, he was appointed Chief of the High Command of the Army in 1934 and in 1935 became c-in-c. With von Blomberg he oversaw the reorganization and expansion of Germany's armed forces, but opposed Hitler's precipitate policy of military aggression. This resulted in a plot to discredit him. Framed on charges of homosexuality and blackmail, Fritsch was forced to resign in February 1938 (at the same time as von Blomberg). Subsequently cleared by a military court, he was killed in action, September 22 1939. *MS*.

FROG rocket. The family of Soviet unguided artillery rockets of the Luna series known in the West as "Free Rocket Over Ground" or FROG. The last model, the 42-mile (70km) range FROG 7, introduced in 1965, was used in a conventional mode by Egypt in the 1973 Arab-Israeli War and by Soviet forces in Afghanistan, but the primary purpose of the series was tactical nuclear delivery.

Fromelles. On July 19 1916 the Australian 5th and British 61st Divisions attacked a German salient near the French village of Fromelles, southeast of Armentières, to pin down German units which might otherwise be used against the British on the Somme. After a preliminary bombardment, which removed all hope of surprise, these inexperienced divisions had to advance across open, waterlogged ground against strong defences. The Australians suffered 5,533 casualties and the British 1,547, but, apart from some temporary gains on the left, this badly planned minor offensive served only to further reduce Australian confidence in the British High Command. *PJS*.

Front de Libération National **(FLN)** *see* ALGERIAN CAMPAIGN.

Frontiers, Battle of the. Between August 14 and 25 1914, as both sides endeavoured to implement their war plans, Allied and German armies clashed in four major engagements extending from Lorraine to Belgium. The main thrust of the French First and Second Armies into Lorraine was checked at Morhange-Sarrebourg on August 20, with the French subsequently thrown back to Nancy. The French Third and Fourth Armies, attacking northeast into the Ardennes, were also repulsed with heavy losses after blundering into the Germans around Virton and Neufchateau on August 22, and the Fifth Army was obliged to withdraw following the action on the Sambre in the Namur-Charleroi area. On August 23, at Mons, the BEF briefly held up the advance of von Kluck's First Army on the German right wing. By then, Plan XVII was in ruins, and the Allies were in retreat, but the Franco-British armies had not been destroyed. *PJS*.

Frusci, Gen. Italian. Commander in Eritrea; took Kassala, July 1940; was defeated by Gen Platt at Keren, March 1941; surrendered with the Duke of Aosta at Amba Alagi, May 1941.

Fuchida, Capt Mitsuo (1902–1976) Jap. Naval aviator who gained important combat experience during the war with China and was appointed Air Group Commander for the attack upon Pearl Harbor, December 1941. Fuchida accompanied his bomber force on the raid and coordinated the attack on the US battleships before returning to the aircraft carrier *Akagi*. He unsuccessfully urged Adm Nagumo to launch a second attack on the remaining American ships and installations. Fuchida was also closely involved at Midway in June 1942 but was struck down by appendicitis. Later held a senior staff post as Air Operations Officer, Combined Fleet. *MS*.

Fuller, Maj Gen J F C (1878–1964). Br. Military writer and proponent of armoured warfare. *See also* TANKS.

Fulmar, Fairey (Br, WWII). Two-seat shipboard fighter-bomber. Prototype flew January 4 1940; first squadron formed July 1940. Extensively used Mediterranean from carriers and, from Malta, as night intruders; a few covered North Russia convoys. Although a sound aircraft, even the more powerful Fulmar II lacked speed to combat later opponents. Production 601. One 1,080/1,300hp Rolls-Royce Merlin engine; max. speed 272mph (438kph); nine 0.303in machine guns, 500lb (225kg) bombs.

FULRO. Resentment of the Saigon government among South Vietnam's ethnic minorities caused the latter to organize an inter-tribal united front in August 1964, called the *Front Unifié pour la Lutte des Races Opprimées*, or FULRO. In September FULRO instigated a rebellion of Montagnard troops in the Ban Me Thuot area of the central highlands. American protection won concessions from Saigon for the Montagnards. *WST*. *See also* MONTAGNARDS.

Fuso-class. Japanese battleships: *Fuso*, *Yamashiro*; launched 1914–15; 35,000 tons full load (following 1930's reconstruction); 12 × 14in guns; first Japanese-built 14in battleships. Both sunk in Surigao Strait, October 25 1944.

Gaba Tepe *see* GALLIPOLI (1915—16).

Gabreski, Col Francis S (b.1919). US. As a member of the US 56th Fighter Group, Gabreski became the top-scoring American fighter pilot in the European Theatre of Operations during World War II, with 28 confirmed victories between August 1943 and July 1944. Later, in Korea, he added 6.5 MiG-15s to his total.

Galician campaign (1914). As the Russians moved into East Prussia, a huge battle was developing farther south, where the Austro-Hungarians faced four Russian armies across the Galician border. In August 1914, the Habsburg empire had mobilized 3,350,000 men of all categories of whom some 1,400,000 could be regarded as front-line combat troops. This huge army consisted of many distinct racial groups: Austro/German, 28 percent; Slavs, 44 percent; Hungarian/Magyar, 18 percent; Italian 8 percent; Romanian, 2 percent. Slavs made up 67 percent of the infantry and their loyalties were inclined to the Russians rather than their German allies. In a war in which infantry were to play a key role, the Austro-Hungarians could field 1,100 battalions, of which 700 were fit for front-line duty. The German and Hungarian-speaking regiments would prove the steadiest, whilst Czechoslovak units surrendered in droves rather than fight their fellow Slavs.

In charge of this heterogeneous army was Field Marshal Baron Conrad von Hötzendorff, its Chief of General Staff. Universally respected, he was an able strategist commanding a tactically defective instrument. His army was short of

Austro-Hungarian officers, Galicia, 1914

modern artillery and standardized small arms, thus adding to logistic problems. The officer corps was competent and conscientious, and with racial differences in mind, close attention was paid to man-management. The common language was a patois known as "Army Slav", in addition to which all recruits, in theory, understood up to 80 German words of instruction and command.

Conrad's staff had estimated that by August 20 there would be 31 Russian divisions on the Galician front, rising to 52 by August 28 when the Russians would have a 4:3 superiority. A pre-emptive Austrian offensive was therefore considered essential. On August 20, Conrad attacked. His two best armies, the First (Dankl) and Fourth (Auffenberg), were on the left, advancing northeast into Poland with Dankl's left flank on the River Vistula, whilst the Third, from its position in front of the fortress of Lemberg, covered the right flank of the Fourth. On the Russian side, Ivanov's South West Army Group (Fourth, Fifth, Third and Eighth Armies) was deploying behind the Russian frontier. The Fourth Army, still not fully mobilized, immediately advanced towards the Austrian First Army and was repulsed at Krasnik on August 23. Ivanov ordered Plehve's Fifth Army to wheel right and take Dankl in the flank, but no sooner had this move been initiated than its own left flank was caught in turn by Auffenberg's Fourth Army. A huge melee ensued, with Conrad drawing troops away from Lemberg to reinforce Fourth Army, giving the Russians local numerical superiority on which they managed to capitalize. On August 27 the Austrians began to break, but the Russian follow-up was slow. However, Brusilov's Eighth Army now attacked decisively in the south and the Austrians fled.

Conrad evacuated Lemberg on September 2 but persisted with Fourth Army's advance on the left, despite the total collapse of his right, and failed to destroy the Russian Fifth Army which had rashly advanced too far. Great gaps, rapidly filling with Russians, were now opening up between the Austrian armies, but Conrad was still issuing brilliantly-conceived

plans which could not be implemented. On September 11, the Austrians intercepted an unciphered Russian signal revealing Ivanov's intentions. This prompted Conrad to order a withdrawal behind the line of the River San.

The Russians, with chaotic lines of communication and exhausted by continual forced marches, failed to pursue. Conrad threw a huge garrison into the fortress of Przemysl and continued his withdrawal to the line of the Dunajec. Galicia had fallen to the Russians and the Austrians had lost 350,000 out of 900,000 men committed to battle. There were bitter recriminations against the Germans who, it was felt, should have hastened south from East Prussia to the rescue. But Hindenburg had other affairs in train. *MH. See also* WARSAW, BATTLE OF (1914).

Galland, Gen Adolf (b.1912). Ger. An outstanding fighter pilot of World War II, having gained combat experience in the Spanish Civil War. He was among the top-scoring German pilots in the Battle of Britain and "Circus" operations, 1940—41; eventually credited with 103 victories. Galland became General of the Fighter Arm in late 1941, with responsibility for the night fighter force also following Kammhuber's departure in 1943. His position did not give him executive command: he had direct access to Göring and, not infrequently, to Hitler, but his situation was fundamentally unsound, for Göring's intrusive impulsiveness and Hitler's failure to understand the fundamentals of air power made the development of systematic policies impossible.

Galliéni, Marshal Joseph (1849— 1916). Fr. Galliéni fought as an infantry officer in the Franco-Prussian War and spent 30 years in colonial service, becoming Governor of Madagascar from 1896 to 1905. In 1911, nearing retirement, he declined the post of Chief of the General Staff, recommending Joffre, a former subordinate in Madagascar, as a candidate. Galliéni was recalled to duty at the start of World War I and nominated as Joffre's successor in case of emergency, but the latter felt he was a potential threat and kept him away from the French General Headquarters. On August 26 1914 Galliéni was appointed Military Governor of Paris. Eight days later, on September 3, he recognized the chance offered by Kluck's wheel west of Paris, directing Maunoury's Sixth Army to prepare to attack the exposed German flank. On September 4 Joffre, who had considered withdrawing farther south, backed Galliéni's proposal. This led to the Allied victory on the Marne, though Galliéni's critics claim that Maunoury's attack was launched prematurely, enabling the Germans to avoid total disaster. Galliéni remained Military Governor of Paris until October 1915, when Briand made him Minister of War. Dissatisfied with the conduct of operations, Galliéni tried to move Joffre aside and give de Castelnau command of the field armies. However, Briand was reluctant to risk the probable political furore which would have resulted and Gallieni himself resigned in March 1916. Already ill, he died in May. He was posthumously created Marshal in 1921. *PJS.*

Gallipoli (1915–16). After the failure of the Anglo-French naval operation to force the Dardanelles, all now rested on a land campaign. In late February 1915 the Turks were in disarray and Allied landing parties went ashore unopposed to demolish batteries left intact by the earlier naval bombardment; but with the appearance in Constantinople of the formidable Gen Liman von Sanders as head of the German military mission, and the timely arrival of Lt Col Mustafa Kemal "Atatürk" as commander of the Turkish Army's Gallipoli garrison, the defence was galvanized into activity.

On March 13 1915, Gen Sir Ian Hamilton, appointed by Lord Kitchener to direct the Gallipoli landings, left London. Four days later he joined the fleet off the Dardanelles, where confusion reigned. The ships carrying the British 29th Division, assigned to lead the operation, had been loaded piecemeal and dispatched to the Eastern Mediterranean without proper plans for disembarkation, and Hamilton had to shift his base to Alexandria, where major logistic reorganization was necessary. The naval commander,

Heavy howitzer in action at Gallipoli

Vice Adm de Robeck, told Hamilton on March 22 that his ships could no longer enter the Narrows because of strengthened coastal batteries and new minefields. Nevertheless, Hamilton devised a sound plan for the landings: to seize the tip of the Gallipoli peninsula prior to a victorious advance on Constantinople. That the defenders were given sufficient time to prepare themselves was not entirely Hamilton's fault. The Allied landings took place on April 25 – a full month after Liman von Sanders' appointment as commander of the Turkish Fifth Army, during which time great progress had been made on the beach defences. Hamilton's plan was for a series of landings under the guns of the fleet. These had been carefully planned, with feints to north and south and diversionary landings by French marines on the southern side of the Straits. However, the Turks were waiting for the 29th Division at Helles and despite the gallantry of the British infantry a narrow lodgement was only secured at terrible cost. The landing of the Australian and New Zealand Corps (ANZACs) at Gaba Tepe was initially unopposed, but Mustafa Kemal's quick reaction to this crisis soon pinned them down.

The expedition was now effectively stranded. The formations ashore were hemmed in, and the Turks fiercely repelled any attempt at a breakout. In an effort to get the campaign going again, Hamilton put two further divisions ashore to the north, at Suvla, on August 6, achieving complete tactical surprise. However, the general in command ashore, Stopford, made no attempt to exploit inland. The Turks quickly contained this second landing and stalemate set

in again. As summer gave way to an unseasonably cold autumn, conditions for both sides became appalling, with disease claiming as many victims as the fighting, in which the ANZAC troops distinguished themselves. In November, no decision having been obtained, Kitchener visited the peninsula to see things for himself and signalled Whitehall that the ANZAC and Suvla beachheads must be evacuated forthwith. Hamilton was superseded as c-in-c by Gen Sir Charles Monro and the energetic Lt Gen Sir William Birdwood (ANZAC commander) took command of all troops ashore. Between them, they prepared a brilliant evacuation plan, executed without the loss of a man on the night of December 19–20. A similar operation took place at Helles on the night of January 8–9 1916.

There were many reasons for the failure of this initially promising campaign. The amphibious landings should have been carried out at the time of the earlier naval operation; as it was, the enemy had four weeks in which to prepare for the obvious. Gross breaches of security by the Allies gave the highly-developed German Intelligence Service ample warning. Hamilton's scratch force of largely under-trained troops was actually outnumbered at the start of the campaign, and subordinate commanders like Stopford and Hunter-Weston (commanding 29th Division) made matters worse by failing to capitalize on the success of many of the initial landings. The sensitive and compassionate Hamilton was reluctant to drive his men or sack their commanders when this would have gained a decision. His plan was imaginative and radical, but the wherewithal for its execution was absent. The Turkish soldier, stoic and courageous, proved a formidable opponent. Amphibious landings demand high standards of training and much rehearsal if they are to succeed, and no amount of heroism could have saved this operation once it was launched. Out of 410,000 British and Empire troops and 70,000 French committed to battle, 252,000 were killed, wounded, missing, prisoners or victims of disease. Turkish casualties were 218,000, of whom 66,000 were killed in action. *MH.*

Galtieri, Lt Gen Leopoldo
(b.1926). President of Argentina
and c-in-c Army in 1982. His
decision to invade the Falklands
was made in December 1981 to
distract public attention from
mounting economic chaos and the
military junta's unsavoury record
of political repression. He also had
political debts to repay, chiefly to
Adm Anaya, naval c-in-c and most
hawkish of the service chiefs forming the junta. Following the invasion, Galtieri visited the garrison,
exhorting them to "fight to the last
man" against impending British
attack. After the Argentine surrender, Galtieri's government fell;
he was subsequently tried by the
new administration of President
Alfonsin and sentenced to 12
years' imprisonment. *MH*.

Gamelin, Gen Maurice (1872–
1958). Fr. An extremely clever and
serious soldier who always seemed
destined to reach the top of his
profession, but whose career ended
disastrously in May 1940. From
September 1939 to May 1940
Gamelin commanded all the
French services and was also Supreme Commander of the Anglo-
French alliance. In the autumn of
1939 he developed and gained
approval for a plan for an Allied
advance into Belgium in the event
of a German attack and a Belgian
appeal for help. This plan, though
risky, had several points in its
favour. But Gamelin added to it a
plan to send some of his best
mechanized units (Giraud's Seventh Army) into the Netherlands,
which in effect sacrificed his reserve in a hopeless cause.

Between January and early May
1940 Gamelin received intelligence from various sources of a
German build-up opposite the
Ardennes facing his own two
weakest armies, Second and
Ninth. Yet he did not reinforce
them or modify his plans for advance. Consequently, once the
German panzer columns crossed
the Meuse on May 13, Gamelin
lost control of the battle. When the
general direction of the German
breakthrough became apparent by
May 15, he tried to coordinate an
Allied counterattack from the
north and south to cut the panzer
corridor, but he never attained full
control over his own commanders,
several of whom panicked and

Gamelin: sacked from command, 1940

broke down. Reynaud sacked
Gamelin on May 18, when he was
at last on the point of issuing
crucial orders. In the confusion
which followed, another 48 hours
were wasted, during which the
leading German divisions reached
the Channel coast. *BB*.

Gandhi, Mrs Indira (1917–84).
The only senior politician to visit
the theatre of war with China in
1962. Prime Minister 1966. As
crisis mounted in 1971 in East
Pakistan (Bangladesh) she urged
world statesmen to check Pakistan's repression. Receiving no response, she gave strong support to
Gen Manekshaw in mounting an
all-out attack (in contrast to the
political indecisiveness shown in
1962 and 1965). The same relentless determination was shown in
the order for the attack on the
Golden Temple at Amritsar which
incurred deep Sikh enmity and led
to her assassination. *HT*.

Gariboldi, Gen. Italian. Acting
Commander of Tenth Army in December 1940; Commander of Tripolitania until February 1941
when he replaced Graziani as Italian c-in-c in Lybia, a command
which he held only until July
1941.

Garigliano, crossing of the (January 17 1944). X Corps (McCreery)
crossed with 5th and 56th Divisions five days before the Anzio
landings to pin down German reserves and to start breaching the
Gustav Line. They were opposed
by 15th Panzer Grenadier and
94th Divisions of XIV Panzer
Corps (von Senger). The crossing
was successful, but no breach was
made in the Gustav Line, which
lay in the hills some miles north.

Garros, *Capitaine* Roland (1888–
1918). Fr. Famous pre-war aviator
who, in April 1915, pioneered the
use of the machine gun firing
forward through the arc of a propeller fitted with deflector plates.
After scoring five victories in 18
days, he was taken prisoner. He
escaped in 1918 only to die in air
combat in October that year.

**Gaza, First, Second and Third
Battles of** (March–November
1917). Having effectively removed
the Turkish threat to the Suez
Canal, in 1916 the Egyptian Expeditionary Force under Lt Gen
Sir Archibald Murray steadily
advanced across the Sinai Desert.
After a period of consolidation,
Murray made plans for a limited
spring offensive against Palestine
and the capture of the strategically
important town of Gaza. Dominating the northern coastal route,
Gaza had long been recognized as
one of the gateways into Palestine
and was heavily defended by Turkish VIII Corps. The British attack
launched on March 26 met with
initial success. The cavalry of Lt
Gen Chetwode's Desert Column
encircled Gaza from the east while
Lt Gen Dobell's infantry divisions
of the Eastern Force made a frontal advance. By nightfall British
troops had entered the outskirts of
Gaza and victory seemed within
their grasp but the commanding
officers underestimated the
strength of their position and
ordered withdrawal. British disappointment was compounded by
orders from London that the offensive was to be renewed. The commander of the Turkish forces, Col
Kress von Kressenstein, used the
respite between battles to strength-
en Gaza's defences and increase its
garrison. The second British offensive began on April 17 but had
none of the subtlety of the first
battle. Neither the British use of
gas nor a few fairly dilapidated
tanks made much impact and, having sustained casualties of 6,500 to
the Turks' 2,000, the attack was
called off. Murray was removed
and replaced on June 28 1917 by
Gen Allenby. Gaza also featured in
his plans for a major offensive but
Allenby took pains to prepare and
strengthen his forces and the
attack was not launched until
October 31. While an initial thrust
was made at Beersheba, a British

advance against Gaza by XXI Corps was intended to divert Turkish attention and draw off their reserves. Making the best use of a sustained bombardment and a force of tanks, the British infantry began the assault on the strongly defended lines of Turkish trenches on November 1. After a week's hard fighting, Gaza was evacuated by its defenders and captured by British units on November 7 1917. *MS*.

Gaza Strip *see* ARAB-ISRAELI WARS.

Gazala, Battle of (May 26–June 17 1942). Both sides in the Western Desert were planning an offensive to break the stalemate on the Gazala Line – the British to drive Rommel back to Tripoli before the Allied landings in French North Africa (planned for the autumn of 1942), and the Germans to implement Hitler's strategic concept for seizing the Middle East.

Rommel struck first in the opening phase of the battle (May 26–29) with an attempt to outmanoeuvre Eighth Army (Ritchie) by driving with his armoured forces around the open desert flank to the south of the Free French positions at Bir Hacheim so that he could attack the heavily mined and fortified positions of XIII Corps (Gott) from the rear. He found himself trapped in the "Cauldron", where XXX Corps (Norrie), commanding the British armoured forces, should have been able to annihilate the Afrika Korps (Cruewell until captured on June 28; then Nehring).

In the next phase (May 30–June 10), the battles of the Cauldron and Bir Hacheim were fought. Rommel set about opening a supp-

British 25-pounder in action , Gazala

ly route through the British minefields by successfully overrunning the 150th Brigade "box", which barred his way to the west, on June 1. Norrie's attacks on the Cauldron mounted by 5th Indian and 7th Armoured Divisions from the north and east on June 5 and 6 were costly failures, leaving Rommel free to clear his rear by attacking Bir Hacheim. The Free French under Koenig resisted stubbornly until June 10, when they were successfully evacuated.

The final phase (June 11–June 17) saw the Battle of Knightsbridge and the investment of Tobruk. The Afrika Korps defeated the British armoured forces in engagements around the Knightsbridge "box", which blocked the direct approach to Tobruk, enabling Rommel to invest the fortress by June 17. Eighth Army abandoned the Gazala Line and fell back to the Egyptian frontier. *WGFJ*.

Gazelle, Aérospatiale/Westland. Light (1.9t) helicopter in service with AAC and in the French Army for reconnaissance and observation. *See also* ARMY AIR CORPS.

Gazzera, Lt Gen Pietro. Italian. Supreme Italian Commander, Ethiopia, from May 1941; surrendered on July 6 1941.

GEE (for Grid). British. Usually classified as, although technically not, radar aid to air navigation. The time differential for pulses from ground transmitters to reach an aircraft was displayed on a cathode-ray tube from which the navigator could plot his latitude and longitude. First used by Bomber Command operationally on August 11 1941 and generally introduced in 1942. Revolutionized the accuracy of navigation but was later effectively jammed over most of Europe by the Germans. *ANF*.

Gehlen, Gen Reinhard (1902–79). Ger. Intelligence officer; 1942 head of foreign armies east, supplying Hitler with data on Red Army; dismissed, April 1945; captured and debriefed by Americans. Returned to West Germany 1946, established Gehlen Organization; 1955 headed federal intelligence service, heavily penetrated by Russians; retired 1968.

Geisler, Lt Gen (*General der Flieger*) Hans-Friedrich (1891–1966). Ger. Commander *Fliegerkorps X* until August 1942. Mounted first air bombardment of Malta in January 1941; then responsible for Luftwaffe maritime operations in the Mediterranean, with HQ in Greece.

Genda, Gen Minoru (b.1904). Jap. A naval pilot (Commander, 1941), Genda advised Rear Adm Onishi on shallow-running torpedo techniques for the Pearl Harbor attack, where he served as Adm Nagumo's air operations officer. With Commander Fuchida, he was Nagumo's chief air adviser at Midway, 1942. Postwar he joined the Japanese Air Self-Defence Force, becoming its C-in-C, 1959–62.

***General Belgrano*.** Argentinian cruiser of 13,600 tons full load. Formerly the USS *Phoenix*, she had escaped from the Japanese attack on Pearl Harbor in December 1941 and had been modernized following her acquisition by Argentina (originally named *Diecisiete de Octubre*) in 1951. In 1982 she was carrying Exocet missiles in addition to her main guns. Adm Woodward, aware that she was at sea with two escorts and threatened his carrier group over to the east of the Falklands, sought and obtained permission from London for her to be sunk. Two out of three torpedoes fired by HMS *Conqueror* struck and *Belgrano* sank with the loss of 368 men. At the time of the attack she was some 40 miles (64km) outside the exclusion zone previously declared in London. *MH*.

Geneva Agreements (1954). The Geneva Conference held May 8–July 21 1954 ended the Indochina-France War which centred upon the conflict in Vietnam. An agreement signed by the high commands of France and the Democratic Republic of Vietnam (DRV) provided an armistice, regroupment of forces, and provisional partition of Vietnam roughly along the 17th parallel. The agreement permitted free movement between North and South for 300 days and established an International Control Commission to oversee implementation. A separate "Final Declaration" stressed that the 17th parallel was a

G

provisional military demarcation line, not a political or territorial boundary, and scheduled elections on reunification for July 1956. None of the nine countries attending the conference signed the Final Declaration, and only four (France, Great Britain, the Soviet Union and China) gave it their unqualified endorsement. The Saigon government denounced it, and the US promised only to refrain from the threat or use of force to disturb it.

Whether the Geneva Agreements bound all parties to a new status quo was subsequently a matter of controversy. Saigon and the US argued that communist violations relieved the South of obligation to discuss the elections on reunification, while the North insisted that the agreements had irrevocably established Vietnam's juridicial unity. *WST.*

Geneva Conference on peace settlement in Korea (1954). The armistice which ended the Korean War called for a political conference within three months. The issue, however, was not discussed until the Geneva Conference of 1954. The negotiations bogged down when the US insisted that elections for a reunified Korea must be held only in North Korea, supervised by the UN, a position unacceptable to the DPRK and China because the UN had been a belligerent in the war. The communists demanded elections in both Koreas under an all-Korea electoral commission supervised by the Neutral Nations Supervisory Commission. The deadlock left the political issues of the war unresolved. *CM.*

Geneva Conventions. From 1864 onward a series of conferences at Geneva attempted to set international standards for the conduct of war. The term "Geneva Conventions" usually refers to that "Relative to the Treatment of Prisoners of War", promulgated July 27 1929, reaffirmed 1949, which enjoins humane treatment monitored by neutral officials.

Genghis Khan Line. German defensive positions based on the Idice and Reno rivers in Northern Italy, covering Bologna and the Po Valley in 1944–45.

Gentile, Capt Don S (1920–51). US. Volunteered for the RAF in 1940 and flew with No. 133 Eagle Squadron before transferring to the USAAF in September 1942. He then served with the US 4th Fighter Group and was ultimately credited with 19.83 aerial victories, over half of them scored in March 1944.

George II, King of the Hellenes (1890–1947). Reigned 1922–24 and 1935–47. After the defeat of his and the British forces in 1941 he maintained a government in exile, first from London and then Cairo. This was challenged by the communists in the civil war after the German collapse, but he was restored by a plebiscite in 1946.

George VI, King of Great Britain, Ireland and the British Dominions (1895–1952). Reigned 1936–52. While recognizing that war might become inevitable, he gave every encouragement to Chamberlain in his attempts to avert it. Although initially doubtful about Churchill as PM, he soon established an excellent relationship with him. Throughout the war he worked selflessly and became completely identified in the nation's mind with the spirit of resistance and the will to victory. *ANF.*

Georges, Gen Alphonse (1875–1951). Fr. In 1918 Georges served on the Western Front as Marshal Foch's operations chief and, after the war, was Pétain's Chief of Staff in North Africa during the Riffian wars. In January 1940 Georges was made commander of the North East Front, facing the brunt of the German attack in May. The sheer speed and power of the advance overwhelmed Georges' forces and after only nine days he was re-

Georges: broke with Pétain after 1940

lieved of his command. He refrained from close association with the Vichy regime and in 1943 joined the Free French forces in North Africa, becoming a member of the French Committee of National Liberation. *MS.*

Georgia, South, Argentine invasion of (1982). In March 1982, a party of Argentine scrap metal dealers, having landed without permission, hoisted their national flag at Leith Harbour on South Georgia, a dependency of the Falklands some 800 miles (1,290km) to the southeast of Port Stanley. Governor Rex Hunt dispatched a party of Royal Marines aboard HMS *Endurance* to investigate and to safeguard the interests of the British Antarctic Survey base. On April 3, the Argentinians invaded South Georgia; the Marines detachment surrendered on Hunt's orders after inflicting casualties on the invaders, but HMS *Endurance* evaded the Argentine force and escaped. On April 23, South Georgia was retaken after preliminary forays by the SAS and Special Boat Squadron and an attack by helicopters on the submarine *Santa Fe*, which was damaged by missiles. *MH.*

German Southwest Africa campaign (August 1914–July 1915). In August 1914, the 318,000-sq mile (824,000-sq km) territory of Southwest Africa (Namibia), a German colony since 1892, with Atlantic ports at Swakopmund, Lüderitz and Walvis Bay (a British enclave occupied by German forces) and rail links from the coast to the borders, offered potential for a German invasion of British Bechuanaland and Southern Rhodesia, assisted by an anti-British rising in South Africa. However, the Caprivi Zipfel (Caprivi Strip), the northeastern invasion corridor, was swiftly secured by Rhodesian forces; Swakopmund was neutralized by British naval bombardment; and South African troops landed at Lüderitz and simultaneously secured the Orange river crossings from Cape Province, on the southern border, in mid-September 1914.

Having suppressed a revolt by Boer irredentists, Premier Louis Botha took personal command of the South African Defence Force's invasion of German Southwest

Africa, his *c*50,000 men being opposed by some 8,000 white *Schutztruppe* under Col Viktor Francke. In February 1915, a two-pronged thrust on the capital, Windhoek, began: Botha's Northern Force moved along the railroad from Swakopmund; Smuts's Southern Force pushed north from Lüderitz and the Orange river. Botha's advance across the Namib desert, making good use of armoured cars, was met by poisoned wells and improvised land mines; the main stand against Smuts' force was made at Gibeon, April 25–26. Some 6,000 *Schutztruppe* made an orderly retreat to Windhoek, but when Botha entered the city on May 12, resistance was minimal. The main German force marched north to the Grootfontein-Otavi area, where they surrendered on July 9, having suffered 1,331 killed. South African and Rhodesian losses in Botha's skilful campaign amounted to 266 dead and 263 wounded. *RO'N.*

Gerow, Lt Gen Leonard Townsend (1888–1972). US. Head of the War Plans Division when the US entered World War II. In February 1942 he took command of the 29th Division, and the following year he became commander of the American field forces in Europe. In July 1943 he took charge of V Corps, which landed on Omaha Beach on D-Day under his command. In January 1945, Gerow became commanding general of the US Fifteenth Army. *SB.*

Gestapo. Acronym of *Ge*heime *Sta*ats *Po*lizei, the German secret police under the Nazis.

G-H. British air to ground to air blind bombing radar system, similar to but the reverse of Oboe. Capable of use by up to 100 aircraft at one time. Introduced October 1943.

Gheluvelt *see* YPRES, FIRST BATTLE OF (1914).

Ghormley, Vice Adm Robert Lee (1883–1958). US. Ghormley was a senior US Navy representative at Anglo-US staff talks in London and Washington, August 1940–January 1941, during which decisions concerning America's role,

should she enter the war, were made. In April 1942 he became Commander, South Pacific Forces and Area, having overall direction of the Solomon Islands campaign until October 1942, when Adm Nimitz, deeming Ghormley insufficiently aggressive in the struggle to establish naval supremacy off Guadalcanal, replaced him with the more charismatic Halsey.

GI (General Issue). Slang for American private soldier (enlisted man).

Giap, Snr Gen Vo Nguyen (b.1912). Democratic Republic of Vietnam. The organizer and chief strategist of Vietnamese communist armed forces in the wars with France and the US. Giap joined the Communist Party in 1933. He had no military training or experience until assigned by Ho Chi Minh in 1941 to construct a revolutionary base area in Cao Bang province. From these beginnings Giap formed in December 1944 a 34-person "Vietnam Propaganda and Liberation Unit", forerunner of the People's Army of Vietnam (PAVN). The PAVN defeated the French at Dien Bien Phu, using a battle plan originally drawn up with the help of Chinese advisers but revised by Giap. At war's end in 1954, Giap was Chief of Staff and Minister of Defence of the Democratic Republic of Vietnam (DRV).

Giap was a proponent of "People's War" but modified this doctrine for Vietnamese circumstances. The absence of a vast hinterland in which to manoeuvre and disastrous experiences attacking fortified French outposts in the lowlands convinced him of the need to use main forces cautiously and in close coordination with political struggle behind enemy lines. During the late 1950s, when Soviet aid became available, Giap embraced conventional warfare, but only as a graft upon "People's War". Though he supported the war for reunification, he was more reluctant than some other leaders to commit Northern resources to combat in the South, and he increasingly had to share authority over strategic planning. Thus it was Gen Van Tien Dung, not Giap, who took charge of the final offensive in 1975. Giap was implicated in the failure to prepare for Chi-

Master of "People's War": Giap

na's cross-border attack in February–March 1979, and in February 1980 Dung replaced him as Minister of National Defence. He subsequently was dropped from the Political Bureau and shunted off into minor appointments, though he remained a vice-chairman of the Council of Ministers. *WST.*

Gibson, Wg Commander Guy, VC (1918–44). Br. Formed and commanded 617 Squadron, Bomber Command, which he led on the Dams raid of May 1943.

Gideon Force. Irregular troops commanded by Orde Wingate in Northern Ethiopia; paved the way for Haile Selassie's return to Addis Ababa, April 1941.

Gilbert Islands *see* TARAWA CAMPAIGN.

Gillars, Mildred (b.1900). American-born woman, nicknamed "Axis Sally", recruited by the Germans to broadcast propaganda to American troops during World War II.

Ginchy *see* SOMME, BATTLE OF THE.

Giraud, Gen Henri Honoré (1879–1949). Fr. Captured as captain of Zouaves during World War I, escaped; captured 1940 as general, escaped 1942 first to France and then Gibraltar; shared leadership of Free French movement with De Gaulle, 1943; resigned in April 1944.

Givenchy. On December 20 1914, in retaliation for Allied operations in Flanders six days earlier, the German VII Corps, having first exploded ten small mines, attacked positions held by the Indian

Corps at Givenchy, north of the La Bassée Canal. Although the 1st Battalion of the Manchester Regiment was eventually forced to evacuate Givenchy, after the Germans had seized the trenches on either side, the village was retaken on December 21 by the British 1st (Guards) Brigade with the help of a French Territorial infantry unit. Another German attack in this sector on January 25 1915 was also driven back. On June 15 and 16 1915, the British 7th and 51st Divisions and the 1st Canadian Division in turn assaulted the German lines east of Givenchy in support of the continuing French Artois offensive. However, while the German front trenches were entered, the British and Canadians were unable to retain their few tiny lodgements. *PJS*.

Gladiator, Gloster (Br, WWII). Single-seat fighter/shipboard fighter biplane. Prototype flew September 12 1934; first production aircraft accepted February 16 1937; eight Gladiator squadrons in September 1939, six more equipped thereafter. Sea Gladiator produced as shipboard fighter, in service 1939–43. Gladiators fought on most fronts, notably in Norway and Mediterranean. Production 649 Gladiators, 98 Sea Gladiators. One 830hp Bristol Mercury VIIIA, VIIIAS or IX engine; max. speed 257mph (414kph); four 0.303in machine guns.

Glamorgan, British *County*-class guided missile destroyer of 6,200 tons full load. Damaged by shore-launched Argentine Exocet missile whilst giving fire support to British troops near Port Stanley, the Falklands, June 12 1982. Although 13 of her crew were killed and fires broke out, her robust construction enabled her crew to continue the action.

Gliders. The value of troop-carrying gliders was appreciated by the German General Staff in the 1930s and successful use was made of them against the Low Countries in May 1940. Following heavy losses in the airborne attack on Crete in 1941, Hitler forbade further large-scale use of gliders by the Wehrmacht. The Allies used them in large numbers for the invasion of Sicily (1943), the Nor-

mandy landings and the invasion of Southern France (1944), Operation "Market Garden" (Holland) later that year, and finally the Rhine crossing in March 1945. They were also used in support of deep penetration operations in Burma. With the subsequent development of light anti-aircraft weapons, their military use had ceased by 1951.

The principal types of glider used by the Allies were the British Horsa carrying up to 30 troops, the slightly smaller American Waco CG-4A or Hadrian, and the Hamilcar, a British heavy glider capable of carrying a light tank or its cargo equivalent. The most successful German glider was the DFS 230, although a powered version of their Me 323 Gigant saw service in some numbers as a troop and vehicle transport. *MH*.

Glowworm. British "G"-class destroyer. Sunk during Norwegian campaign (1940) in one-sided action with German cruiser *Admiral Hipper* which she damaged by ramming.

Godfrey, Maj John T (1922–58). US. Canadian-born but raised in the USA, Godfrey joined the RCAF in 1941, transferring to the USAAF in England in 1943. In the US 4th Fighter Group he became wingman to Don Gentile. Godfrey scored 16.33 aerial combat victories before being shot down and made a POW in August 1944.

Godwin-Austen, Lt Gen Sir Alfred R (1889–1963). Br. Commander 12th African Division in invasion of Italian Somaliland and Ethiopian campaign. Commander XIII Corps during Operation "Crusader" in November 1941, and in the withdrawal to Gazala in January 1942. Gave up his command over a disagreement with Eighth Army's Commander (Ritchie), February 1942.

Goebbels, Doctor Joseph (1897–1945). Ger. Goebbels joined the Nazi Party in 1922. At first on the left-wing of the party, he became a fervent admirer of Hitler and in 1926 was rewarded by being made Gauleiter of Berlin. He made an immediate impact with his powerful oratory and skilful manipulation of propaganda techniques. He

played a leading role in building the Nazis' image and did much to coordinate their political campaigns during the elections of 1932. On March 13 1933 he was appointed Reich Minister for Public Enlightenment and Propaganda. Under his astute control the arts, the media and even sport were subverted to maintain and propagate Nazi policies. With the advent of World War II his ministry concerned itself with raising the morale and war effort of both the civilian population and the armed forces. In July 1944 Goebbels was thrust into a more active role when his quick thinking helped to thwart the army uprising in Berlin following the abortive attempt on Hitler's life. This was followed by his appointment as General Plenipotentiary for Total War but no austerity programme nor husbanding of manpower resources could effectively alter the war's course. He remained at the Berlin *Führerbunker* until Hitler's suicide, whereupon his six children were given poison and he and his wife ordered an SS orderly to shoot them. *MS*.

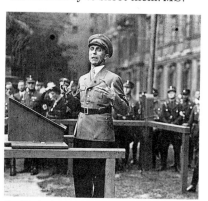

Goebbels: Hitler's propaganda wizard

Goeben and **Breslau, cruise of** (1914). These two German warships, *Goeben*, a battlecruiser with ten 11in guns, and *Breslau*, a light cruiser, shelled the French Algerian ports of Bône and Philippeville on August 4 1914 and then, shadowed by powerful units of the British Mediterranean fleet, which stood off until it was confirmed that war had been declared, succeeded in reaching the neutral Italian port of Messina where they coaled. From there they sailed, not as the British expected into the Adriatic, but towards the Dardanelles. Rear Adm Troubridge commanding a squadron of 4 British cruisers, 4 light cruisers and 16 destroyers, had an opportunity of engaging but did not as he had been ordered not to attack unless he had a superior force. The German ships reached Constantinople inflicting a serious blow to British and French naval prestige and giving encouragement to the pro-German "Young Turks". *ANF*.

Golan Heights *see* ARAB-ISRAELI WARS.

Gold beach *see* NORMANDY, INVASION OF (1944).

Golikov, Col Gen Filip Ivanovich (b.1900). Russian. Following commands in the invasions of Finland and Poland, 1939, Golikov led missions to Washington and London, negotiating Allied aid to Russia, in 1941. He was then head of GRU and was instrumental in the recruitment of Western intellectuals – notably the Rosenbergs in the USA – to the communist cause. He was an army group commander in the Moscow counteroffensive, 1942, and at Stalingrad, 1942-43. A favourite of Kruschev, he was Deputy People's Commissar of Defence and Chief of Personnel, Red Army, 1943-50.

Goltz, Field Marshal Freiherr Colmar von der (1843–1916). Ger. In 1883 Goltz was sent to Constantinople to reorganize the Turkish army along Prussian lines. At the beginning of World War I he was appointed Governor General of Occupied Belgium but in November 1914 returned to Constantinople as the Sultan's "adjutant general". Following Turkey's entry into the war, he was given command of Sixth Army, leading it in a successful campaign against British forces in Mesopotamia. He died in Baghdad on April 29 1916, shortly before the British surrender at Kut. *MS*.

Gommecourt. Fortified village, attacked by the British 46th and 56th Divisions of Allenby's Third Army, at heavy cost, on July 1 1916, as a diversionary operation in support of the main British Somme offensive farther south. The Germans held the village until their withdrawal to the Hindenburg Line in 1917.

Goose Green. Largest settlement, with nearby Darwin, on East Falkland outside Port Stanley; scene of 2 Para's assault, after several postponements, on May 28 1982. The attackers were heavily outnumbered by the reinforced elite Argentine 12th Regiment and surprise was compromised by a BBC World Service broadcast on May 27, prompting Gen Menéndez, the Argentine commander at Port Stanley, to reinforce Goose Green garrison overnight. Before reaching the airstrip at Goose Green, 2 Para had to attack along the narrow isthmus overlooking Darwin settlement, which was defended by well dug-in troops. There was little cover and almost no artillery support, and when it was apparent that one of his forward companies was pinned down, the commanding officer of 2 Para, Lt Col H Jones, personally led an attack in which he lost his life. By dawn on May 29, 2 Para had fought their way to Goose Green and the Argentine garrison surrendered. Displaying a high degree of offensive spirit, the British battalion of fewer than 500 men had defeated three times their number of well-equipped troops in prepared positions, taking more than 1,500 prisoners. *MH*.

Göring *Reichsmarschall* **Hermann** (1893–1946). German. A World-War-I fighter ace, with 21 "kills". Göring was awarded the *Pour le Mérite* and Iron Cross (First Class) and in 1918 commanded the "Flying Circus" squadron made famous by Manfred von Richthofen. His military prestige made him a valuable recruit to the Nazi Party, which he joined soon after meeting Hitler in 1922. He became commander of the SA, but after being seriously wounded in the Munich Putsch, 1923, fled to exile. Returning to Germany in 1927, he was elected to the Reichstag as a Nazi in 1928, securing influential support for the Party through his conservative contacts. Following the Nazis' accession to power in 1933 he received a series of appointments: Prussian Minister of the Interior, Commissioner for Aviation, C-in-C of the Prussian Police and Gestapo.

Often charming, Göring was also ruthless, playing a major part in the Reichstag fire, the establish-

Göring: Luftwaffe supremo, 1935–45

ment of concentration camps and the eradication of Hitler's opponents both within and outside the Party. In March 1935 he became C-in-C of the Luftwaffe, promising to make it the world's most powerful air force. But when war came, success in Poland and France made Göring overconfident. His promise to crush the RAF was never made good; the erosion of the Luftwaffe on the Eastern Front and the Allied strategic bombing offensive dramatically diminished his reputation and his interest in his duties. Hitler's designated successor until 1945, he played little part in strategic or political decisions in the later war years. On trial at Nuremberg in 1946, he conducted a brilliant personal defence: sentenced to death for war crimes, he poisoned himself, October 15 1946 *MS*.

Gorlice-Tarnow offensive (1915). Winter 1914–15 gave both the Russians and Germans a chance to make good their enormous losses. Russia now made an extraordinary effort to fulfil her obligations to her allies. But of the 6,250,000 Russians under arms in January 1915 only 60 percent had rifles. There was still a dearth of field artillery and ammunition was strictly rationed. Despite this, Grand Duke Nicholas, the Russian C-in-C, planned for a renewed spring offensive aiming to secure both his flanks prior to a major drive into Silesia.

January–April, the Russian armies edged forward to the line of the Carpathians. Initially this ponderous offensive was successful; on March 22 Przemysl fell, together with its Austro-Hungarian garrison of over 200,000 and much booty, but the

Russians lost momentum and failed to follow up. In any case, they had been soundly beaten early in February in East Prussia when a sudden German advance in the Masurian Lakes region inflicted 200,000 casualties.

A great Austro-German offensive was now in hand. Conrad had chosen the Gorlice-Tarnow front, where Mackensen was put in charge, with Seeckt as his COS and Eleventh German and Fourth Austro-Hungarian Armies at his disposal. Facing them across the Dunajec was Ivanov's Army Group. On May 2, after a short but devastating barrage supported by ground-attack aircraft, the onslaught was delivered. Surprise was absolute. The Russians collapsed and on May 14 the Austro-Germans had reached the River San, having advanced 80 miles (130km) in 12 days. The Russian high command had been diverted by a German feint attack against the line of the Dvina.

On June 3, Mackensen recaptured Przemysl. Lemberg fell on June 22. Mackensen now wheeled north as Hindenburg attacked south from East Prussia in an attempt to isolate the Russian armies in the Polish salient. Grand Duke Nicholas, however, managed to extricate the bulk of his forces, because Falkenhayn again refused to reinforce Hindenburg from the Western Front. Despite this, the Germans took Warsaw on August 4 and Brest-Litovsk on August 25. The Polish salient had now been eliminated, and with it the threat to Silesia. Tsar Nicholas now assumed Supreme Command with Alexeiev as COS. Ludendorff resumed the attack on September 9, advancing to 130 miles (210km) east of Warsaw.

At the end of September the Austrians launched a major offensive in Galicia; it failed and they tried again, this time with even greater loss. When, early in October, the two sides prepared for the winter, the Austrians had lost a further 230,000 men, and Russia was near military collapse, from which she had been saved only by the diversion of the main Austro-German effort to the successful campaign against Serbia in the autumn of 1915. *MH. See also* EASTERN FRONT (1916–17); BRUSILOV'S OFFENSIVES.

Gorringe, Lt Gen Sir George (1868–1945). Br. Commanded 12th Indian Division, Mesopotamia 1915. Later COS, Tigris Force, then commanded III Indian Corps in attempts to relieve Kut.

Gorshkov, Adm of the Fleet Sergei Georgievich (1910–1988). Russian. As C-in-C, Soviet Navy, 1956-1985, Gorshkov transformed it from a coastal defence force of obsolescent ships to a major world power. He presided over the Soviet development of aircraft carriers, the "Kirov"-class battlecruisers and other major surface units, and nuclear submarines, including the 30,000-ton *Typhoon* SSBNs. His writings, notably *The Sea Power of the State* (1976), established him as an international authority on naval strategy and tactics.

Gort, Field Marshal Viscount ("Jack") VC (1886–1946). Br. Perhaps the most decorated British field officer of World War I. He was promoted Chief of the Imperial General Staff in 1937. On the outbreak of war in 1939 he left the War Office to command the field force in France. Gort was determined to be a loyal ally and too readily agreed to Gamelin's plan for the Anglo-French forces opposite Belgium to advance into that country in the event of a German attack. When this occurred on May 10 1940, Gort had the unenviable responsibility of commanding the British contingent (ten divisions) in the three-week campaign that culminated at Dunkirk. He soon came to believe that the French high command was not functioning and began to think of saving his own forces and on May 25 made the agonizing decision to retreat towards the Channel coast. Next day his act of disobedience was approved and the evacuation from Dunkirk began. To the French, Gort's decision seemed a betrayal and inter-Allied friction increased. He conducted the retreat with skill, but to his lasting regret was ordered home by Churchill when he reached Dunkirk to avoid the risk of his being captured. Gort was not offered another field command, but he was an inspirational Governor of Malta during the siege of the island in 1942–43, and for this was promoted Field Marshal. *BB.*

Gotha bombers, attacks by (1917). Gotha aircraft were the mainstay of German long-range bomber operations in 1917 and 1918. Paris and London were among targets attacked. Two of the attacks on London, June 17 and July 11 1917 (see p.195 in the essay *The emergence of air power*) changed the course of air history. The British response led to the creation in April 1918 of the Royal Air Force, the world's first independent fighting air service, and the development of a doctrine of long-range strategic bombing which formed the basis of the operations of Bomber Command in World War II. *ANF.*

Gotha G IV/G V (German, WWI). Long-range bomber; crew 3. Prototype Go. G II flew March 1916; first production G II completed April 25 1916; G III followed and developed into G IV and G V: these last were the most numerous versions. G IV into operational service March/April 1917, G V in August. Both used in attacks on England 1917–18; about 30 G IVs to Austria. Production (all variants) probably less than 500. G IV had two 260hp Mercedes D IVa engines; max. speed 84mph (134kph); 660lb (300kg) bombs, two/three 7.9mm machine guns.

Gothic Line. The Allied name for the German "Green Line" defences in the Northern Apennines, stretching from Carrara on the west coast along the spine of the range to Pesaro on the east coast. It consisted of two lines of fortified positions – Green I and Green II – about 10 miles (16km) apart.

Gothic Line, breaching of (August 25 –September 27 1944). Alexander adopted his favourite strategy of the two-handed punch, attacking alternately with Eighth Army (Leese) on the Adriatic coast and Fifth Army (Clark) in the central Apennines above Florence. Leese struck on August 25 to draw German reserves away from the Fifth Army sector; Clark opened his offensive three weeks later.

Eighth Army's offensive, which struck the front of Tenth Army (von Vietinghoff), was masked by the advance of II Polish Corps (Anders) on the quiet Adriatic coast. It took the German com-

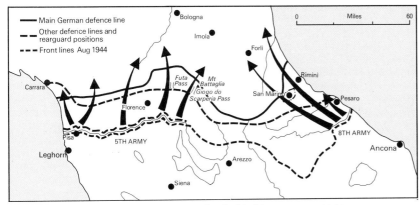

Alexander's "two-handed punch" against the Gothic Line, autumn 1944

mand several days to realize that Eighth Army had crossed the Apennines and was fighting its way through the outpost zone in front of Green I, the first of the Gothic's two defence lines. They did not manage to man the fortifications of Green I fully before I Canadian Corps (Burns) attacked and breached it on August 30–31, supported by V Corps (Keightley) in the hills on the inland flank and the Poles on the coast. By September 3, V Corps and the Canadians were probing Green II after a stubbornly contested advance, during which the first of Kesselring's mobile reserves, 26th Panzer Division, was committed.

Breaking through Green II brought on the First and Second Battles of Coriano. Keightley thought that he saw an opportunity to use 1st Armoured Division to hustle LXXVI Panzer Corps (Herr) out of Green II. The second reserve division released by Kesselring, 29th Panzer Grenadier Division, arrived just in time to check the attempted breakthrough over the Coriano ridge on September 4, inflicting serious tank losses on 2nd Armoured Brigade.

Heavy rain stopped operations until the 12th when the Second Battle of Coriano started with I Canadian and V Corps attacking simultaneously. Kesselring released his third reserve mobile division, 90th Panzer Grenadier, to shore up Tenth Army's front, but after four days' unrelenting British pressure during which the Coriano ridge was cleared, von Vietinghoff fell back to the last practical position for covering the Po Valley – the Rimini Line.

Although Leese had not broken through into the better tank-going

of the Po Valley, he had drawn three of Kesselring's best mobile formations to the Adriatic coast. Alexander, therefore, ordered Clark to start Fifth Army's offensive on September 13.

Clark attacked the Futa and Il Giogo Passes on Green I, held by Fourteenth Army (Lemelson), with the four divisions of II US Corps (Keyes). It took Keyes ten days of the severest fighting before he became master of the two passes, but he was then fortunate to strike down the boundary between I Parachute Corps (Schlemm) and LI Mountain Corps (Feuerstein), forcing them apart, and seizing the key feature of Monte Battaglia, on the shortest route to the Po Valley, September 27. A junction with Eighth Army at Imola seemed imminent when the weather broke and halted operations. The situation was so serious that Kesselring called upon Hitler to authorize the withdrawal of Army Group C across the Po to the Voralpen Line running along the southern foothills of the Alps. Hitler refused and continued to do so throughout the winter.

Eighth Army had resumed its offensive on September 18, forcing von Vietinghoff to abandon the Rimini Line, but, as Eighth Army nosed its way over the Marrechia river into the plain of the Romagna – the southeastern corner of the Po Valley – the rain poured down, turning the supposedly good tank-going into a morass. There was to be no junction with Fifth Army until the spring of 1945. *WGFJ.*

Gott, Lt Gen William Henry Ewart "Strafer" (1897–1942). Br. Commander of 7th Armoured Division's Support Group during

the Battle of Sidi Barrani and Operations "Brevity" and "Battleaxe" (1940–41). Commander 7th Armoured Division from September 1941, including Operation "Crusader"; Commander XIII Corps from February 1943 in the battles of Gazala and Mersa Matruh, and during the withdrawal to El Alamein. Defeated by Nehring's Afrika Korps in the First and Second Battles of Ruweisat. Gott was killed in early August 1942, flying back to take over command of Eighth Army. The command was taken by Montgomery.

Gough, Gen Sir Hubert (1870–1963). Br. Gough's prominent role in the Curragh Incident in March 1914 might have damaged a promising career but, when war came, he took his 3rd Cavalry Brigade to France and, in September 1914, was given command of the 2nd Cavalry Division, which he led at the First Battle of Ypres. The following year he commanded the 7th Division at Festubert and I Corps at Loos. During the British offensive on the Somme in 1916, Gough was commander of the Reserve Army, renamed the Fifth Army in October that year. His troops captured the German strongpoints at Pozières, Thiepval and Beaumont Hamel, suffering fewer casualties than Rawlinson's Fourth Army, yet Gough's tactics were criticized, particularly by the Australians. An ill-conceived and costly operation at Bullecourt in April-May 1917 further reduced Australian faith in his generalship. In the Third Battle of Ypres, starting on July 31 1917, Gough's Fifth Army was initially entrusted with the task of seizing the Passchendaele Ridge, but its failure to secure the vital Gheluvelt plateau on the right persuaded Haig to transfer responsibility for the main attack to Plumer's Second Army. When the German spring offensive struck Fifth Army on March 21 1918, Gough's front was thinly held, partly because of GHQ's miscalculations about the likely direction of attack. Given the circumstances, Gough conducted a skilful defensive battle against great odds. However, he was undeservedly made the principal scapegoat for the British retreat and removed from command on March 27 1918. *PJS.*

Gouraud, Gen Henri (1867–1946). Fr. Gouraud saw extensive active service in Africa before World War I and in 1914 commanded a division in the Argonne. In May 1915 he led the *Corps Expéditionnaire d'Orient*, the French contingent on the Gallipoli Peninsula. Severely wounded by Turkish shell fire, he returned to France and resumed active service on the Western Front. As commander of the Fourth Army, he won praise for his leadership in the Champagne sector during 1918. After the war he served as c-in-c and High Commissioner in Syria and played a major role in maintaining French control of the region. *MS*.

Governments in exile. When Germany overran most of Belgium in 1914, King Albert managed to remain on Belgian soil in the westernmost corner of his country, which was within Allied lines. In 1939–41 German conquests were more complete; most governments evaded into exile. The government of the Polish republic moved to Paris in 1939, and on to London in 1940; quarrelling irretrievably with the USSR in 1943 on account of the bodies found at Katyn, and being replaced eventually in Warsaw by a rival Government in exile run by Polish communists from Lublin. In the spring of 1940 the King of Denmark and his ministers stayed in Copenhagen, nominally neutral until 1943; while the King of Norway and his government got away to London, where Norwegian shipping kept them solvent. A month later, the King of the Belgians stayed to share his subjects' fate in Brussels, but most of his ministers found their way to London, where they set up a government in exile which received such revenues as came from the Belgian Congo. The Queen of the Netherlands, her family and her ministers got away under fire from The Hague to set up a government in exile in London.

Charles de Gaulle's Free French movement, based in London from June 1940 until early 1943 when it moved to Algiers, was not recognized by Britain or the US as a government until October 1944, by which time it was back in France; the Russians had been more forthcoming. The young King of Yugoslavia reached London with a few ministers in 1941, and had the diplomatic apparatus of a government in exile, but was never able to reassert his hold over his kingdom, which was conquered from him in his absence by Tito's partisans. King George II of the Hellenes and his government moved from Athens to Cairo, then to Johannesburg; he went on to London, and eventually returned to Greece behind a screen of British bayonets. *MF*.

Grand Fleet. The British main fleet in World War I, commanded by Jellicoe 1914–16 and then by Beatty until the end of the war. Based upon Scapa Flow, it consisted originally of four battle squadrons and one battlecruiser squadron (21 Dreadnoughts, 8 pre-Dreadnoughts, 4 battlecruisers) and supporting ships including 42 destroyers. Its chief role was to counter the German High Seas Fleet, of which the corresponding strength was 13 Dreadnoughts, 16 pre-Dreadnoughts, 5 battlecruisers, and supporting ships including 88 destroyers.

Grand Slam. Code name for British 22,000lb (10,000kg) penetrating earthquake bomb. First used on March 14 1945. Capable of producing a crater 30ft (9m) deep and 124ft (38m) wide.

Graziani, Marshal Rodolfo, Marquis de Negelli (1882–1955). Italian. Graziani participated in the Italian conquest of Libya before World War I and became Vice-Governor of Libya in 1930. In early 1935 he was appointed Military Governor of Italian Somaliland, where border clashes between Italian and Ethiopian forces presaged Italy's invasion of Ethiopia in October 1935 (*see* ABYSSINIAN WAR 1935–36). As commander of the southern invasion force, Graziani's hesitancy belied his martial appearance, while a reputation for ruthless cruelty gained in Libya was enhanced by his use of mustard gas and his deliberate bombing of field hospitals. Although his forces were far superior to the ill-armed Ethiopians, who were routed at Ganale Doria, January 12–15 1936, his conquest of the Ogaden was not completed until late April 1936. Following Badoglio's brief tenure, Graziani was appointed Governor General and Viceroy of Ethiopia (Honorary Military Governor of Italian East Africa, 1938), administering Mussolini's prescription of "terror and extermination" against Ethiopian irredentists.

During World War II he became Army cos and c-in-c Italian Forces in Libya, 1940. His forces were defeated at Sidi Barrani, Bardia, Tobruk and Beda Fomm, and were forced to evacuate Cyrenaica by the British Western Desert Force under Gen O'Connor in January–February 1941. Graziani became Mussolini's Minister of War in 1943. In 1945 he was sentenced by an Italian court to 20 years' imprisonment for war crimes; released 1950. *WGFJ*.

"Great Marianas Turkey Shoot" *see* PHILIPPINE SEA, BATTLE OF.

Greater East Asia Co-Prosperity Sphere. Japanese scheme, formed in the late 1930s, to substitute its own influence for western imperial interests in Asia and the Pacific.

Grechko, Marshal of the Soviet Union Andrei A (1903–76). Russian. A Civil War veteran who rose from the ranks under the patronage of Shaposhnikov to the command of a cavalry division in 1941 and of the elite First Guards Army by 1945. In 1960–67, Grechko was c-in-c of the Warsaw Pact armies.

Greco-Turkish War (1921–22). In January 1921, attempting to strengthen their hold on western Anatolia and Thrace, claimed by Atatürk's provisional nationalist government, a Greek army advanced on Eskisehir. Following Turkish victories at Inönü in January and March, the Greek victory at Eskisehir on July 17 drove Atatürk back to the Sakarya river, where he defeated King Constantine on August 25–September 16. The Turkish counteroffensive drove the Greeks back to Smyrna (Izmir), which fell on September 11 1922. Atatürk's subsequent advance on Allied-occupied Constantinople (Istanbul) briefly threatened a Turkish-British clash, but this "Chanak Crisis" was resolved by negotiation for the return to Turkey of much of the disputed territory, confirmed by the Treaty of Lausanne, July 1923. *RO'N*.

Greece, first Italian invasion of (October 28 1940). Despite Hitler's opposition, Mussolini authorized Prasca, Italian c-in-c in Albania, to invade Greece, expecting little or no opposition. By November 8, the Italian offensive had collapsed in the face of resolute Greek resistance. The Greek counteroffensive started on November 18. They recovered most of their lost territory and advanced a short distance into Albania before winter set in. A small RAF contingent under D'Albiac was sent from Egypt to support the Greeks.

Greece, second Italian invasion of (March 9–16 1941). Mussolini tried to pre-empt Hitler's invasion of Greece with a further offensive of his own from Albania, mounted with 28 divisions. Fourteen Greek divisions broke the Italian effort, but were exhausted themselves when the Germans struck (April 6).

Greece, German invasion of (April 6 1941). Hitler invaded Yugoslavia and Greece simultaneously to secure his southern flank before his invasion of Russia. Twelfth Army (List), supported by 1,000 aircraft of *Luftflotte 4* (Löhr) attacked Greece. The British Force W (Wilson) – I Australian Corps (Blamey) with 6th Australian and the New Zealand Divisions – was hastily shipped to Greece, and placed under the overall command of Gen Papagos, the Greek Prime Minister and c-in-c, for the defence of the Aliákmon Line. The short campaign was a withdrawal operation in four phases. In the first (April 6–11), the Aliákmon Line was abandoned when the rapid collapse of Yugoslav resistance enabled the Germans to advance through the Monastir Gap. In phase two (April 11–14), the Olympus-Servia Line was abandoned when outflanked by the German advance through the Pindus Mountains. Phase three (April 15–19) saw the withdrawal to Thermopylae due to the collapse of exhausted Greek divisions on the Albanian front and general decline in Greek morale. During the final phase (April 24–30), Force W was evacuated by sea to Crete and Egypt, and the Germans entered Athens on the 27th. All Greek resistance had collapsed by the end of the month. *WGFJ*.

The flag of the Third Reich is hoisted over the Acropolis, Athens, 1941

Greece, liberation of (October 16 1944). III Corps (Scobie) landed at the Piraeus to re-establish the legitimate Greek government as the Germans withdrew from Athens, and to bring supplies to the starving population. On December 3, a communist rebellion broke out in Athens. The Greek Government, the British Embassy and Scobie's HQ were besieged. Reinforcements had to be rushed from Italy to defeat the insurgents in Athens, Salonika and Patras. It took a month of street-fighting to clear the capital. The Communist leaders accepted a negotiated cease-fire on January 15, and a tenuous peace agreement was concluded on February 12 1945. *WGFJ*.

Greek Civil War (1946–49). During the German occupation, Greek resistance was dominated by the Communist Party (KKE) through the National Liberation Front (EAM) and its National People's Army of Liberation (ELAS). Following liberation, a communist uprising, December 1944–February 1945, against the National Unity government was suppressed by British troops (*see* GREECE, LIBERATION OF) and a tenuous peace established by the Varkiza Agreement, February 12 1945.

Tito's Yugoslavia facilitated the training of the communist "Democratic Army of Greece" under Markos Vafiades ("General Markos"), and from mid-1946, following anti-communist measures by the Populist (Royalist) government of Constantine Tsaldaris, Markos commenced guerrilla operations into northern Greece from bases in

Yugoslavia, Albania and Bulgaria. Winning control of the rural north and raiding south, the communists inflicted severe losses on government forces, whose position seemed grave when British aid ended in February 1947. In March, however, the establishment of the Truman Doctrine presaged US economic and military aid.

Several other factors combined to defeat the communists. Their kidnapping ("removal to safety") of children for indoctrination alienated many Greeks; the accession of King Paul in April 1947 rallied royalists; and the insistence of the KKE leader Nikos Zachariades on a "conventional" campaign to seize urban centres weakened Markos's guerrillas, especially after Yugoslav support ended after the Tito-Stalin rift, June 1948.

From July 1948, government offensives drove the communists back to their northern stronghold on Mount Grammos, where, late in August 1949 – now commanded by John Ioannides – they were shattered in a final offensive by Marshal Alexander Papagos (1883-1955). A cease-fire was announced on October 16 1949. *RO'N*.

Green Berets (US Special Forces). The green beret was chosen by President Kennedy as the headgear of US Army Special Forces in 1961. Searching for a response to "wars of national liberation" like the one then beginning in Vietnam, Kennedy embraced "counterinsurgency" and believed the Green Berets were the force to implement it, significantly enlarging the role that US Special Forces had played in South Viet-

G

nam since 1957. Their principal mission was to develop paramilitary forces among the ethnic minorities. Between 1961 and 1965 the Green Berets established over 80 CIDG camps in the central highlands. The Green Berets in Vietnam reached a peak of 3,700 in 1968. *WST. See also* CIVILIAN IRREGULAR DEFENCE GROUPS.

***Greer*.** American destroyer (incident, September 1941). During the period of American "all aid short of war" to Britain in the Atlantic, *Greer* was taking supplies to the US garrison in Iceland when British aircraft reported a U-boat. *Greer* located the submarine, which fired a torpedo after being bombed by the British aircraft. *Greer* dropped depth charges and was missed by another torpedo. Roosevelt called this an unprovoked attack.

Greim, Field Marshal Robert Ritter von (1892–1945). Ger. A World-War-I pilot, later an able Air Corps commander in France, 1940, and on the East Front, Greim was summoned to besieged Berlin by Hitler. Arriving in a light aircraft piloted by Hanna Reitsch on April 24 1945, he was promoted Field Marshal and appointed c-in-c of a non-existent Luftwaffe, succeeding Göring. Captured, Greim committed suicide.

Grenade. Defensive (shrapnel) and offensive (blast) infantry bomb thrown or fired by rifle.

Grey, Viscount, of Falloden (Sir Edward Grey) (1862–1933). Br. A Liberal Imperialist MP who supported Second Boer War, he recognized the threat posed by growing German imperialism and, when the Liberals came to power in 1906, committed himself as Foreign Secretary to forging precautionary alliances, notably the Entente Cordiale with France. Grey secretly sanctioned Anglo-French "Military Conversations" from 1906 which were instrumental in getting the BEF across to France within days of the outbreak of war in August 1914. He made the famous comment, on August 3 1914: "The lamps are going out all over Europe; we shall not see them lit again in our lifetime". *MH*.

Grierson, Lt Gen Sir James (1859–1914). Br. While serving as Director of Military Operations in the reorganized War Office from 1904 to 1906, Grierson was influential in shifting the focus of British military strategy away from India towards possible cooperation with the French Army in the event of a future war with Germany. He was centrally involved in the staff conversations with the French early in 1906 which helped to shape the British Army's role on the Western Front in World War I. In 1914, Grierson went to France as commander of II Corps in the BEF, but collapsed and died suddenly on his way to the front on August 17 1914. *PJS*.

Grivas, Gen George (1898–1974). Greek. Regular officer in Royal Hellenic Army, 1941–53. On retirement, settled in Cyprus, became leader of EOKA throughout its terrorist campaign for Enosis (union between Greece and Cyprus). He was appointed General-in-Command of the Greek Cypriot National Guard, 1960–67, when he went back to Athens. Returned to Cyprus in 1971 to prepare a coup against the Makarios Government. He died there in hiding after failing to seize power. Adopted the nickname of "Dighenis" in 1955.

Gromyko, Andrei (b.1910). Russian. Diplomat who served as ambassador to the US during World War II and as Foreign Minister from 1953 to 1985.

Gröner, Gen Wilhelm (1867–1939). Ger. In October 1918, Gröner (distinguished as the German army's transport supremo in the 1914 mobilization) replaced Ludendorff as Hindenburg's deputy, mediating between the high command and Kaiser Wilhelm in the latter's abdication. Irredentist animosity caused his resignation in 1919. A mainstay of the Weimar Republic, he resigned the ministries of Defence and the Interior in 1932 when Hindenburg failed to support his anti-Nazi policies.

Group of Soviet Forces Germany (GSFG). The Soviet garrison in the German Democratic Republic and the first echelon in any attack on NATO's Central Front. Its HQ is at Zossen-Wunsdorf and it deploys five armies, Third Shock Army (three Guards tank divisions and a motor rifle division) at Magdeburg; Second Guards Tank Army (a Guards tank division, a tank division, a Guards motor rifle division and a motor rifle division) at Fürstenberg; Eighth Guards Tank Army (a Guards tank division and three Guards motor rifle divisions) at Weimar; First Guards Tank Army (two Guards tank divisions, a tank division and a Guards motor rifle division) at Dresden; and Twentieth Guards Army (three Guards motor rifle divisions) at Eberswalde. There is an artillery division, an air assault brigade, two tactical missile brigades, five artillery brigades and five attack helicopter regiments. It has a strength of some 380,000 men and is supported by some 685 combat aircraft of the "Air Forces of the GSFG". *EJG*.

Gruenther, Gen Alfred M (b.1899). US. Commissioned in 1918, Gruenther attracted increasing attention within the US Army as a highly talented staff officer, performing particularly well during the large-scale manoeuvres held in the US in September 1941. Later that year he succeeded Eisenhower as COS Third Army, and in the summer of 1942 went to London as Deputy COS of Allied Force Headquarters, serving under Eisenhower in the planning of Operation "Torch". In January 1943 the US Fifth Army was formed in Algiers, under the command of Lt Gen Mark W Clark, and Gruenther was appointed as its COS, playing a leading part in the planning of the Allied landings

Gen Gruenther: eminent US staff officer

at Salerno, 1943, and Anzio, 1944. When Clark took over from Gen Alexander as commander of 15th Army Group in December 1944, Gruenther remained as his COS until the end of the war. Throughout the Italian campaign, Gruenther worked hard to maintain reasonably smooth relations between the able but sometimes brash Clark and his multinational Allies. Postwar, Gruenther was COS at SHAPE from 1951–53 and Supreme Allied Commander, Europe, 1953–56. *PJS.*

Grytviken. Old whaling station on South Georgia; scene of Argentine landing on April 3 1982 in the Falklands War.

Guadalajara, Battle of (March 1937), Spanish Civil War. In theory, the Jarama and the Guadalajara offensives were to form Franco's pincer attack on Madrid, but the Malaga campaign had delayed the redeployment of Mussolini's 35,000-strong Italian Corps. On March 8, this force of mainly Blackshirt militia, with a Nationalist brigade as flankguard, broke the Republican lines astride the main road to Madrid. Bad weather slowed the advance, giving the Republicans time to rush three divisions forward including the Italian Garibaldi battalion, XII International Brigade). Counterattacking with air and tank support, they put the Blackshirts to flight and recaptured Brihuega. Franco abandoned attacks on Madrid and launched the Vizcaya campaign on German advice. *AB.*

Guadalcanal campaign (1942–43). Following the loss of four carriers at Midway, Japan sought to establish a major air base on Guadalcanal, Solomon Islands. On August 7 1942, therefore, the US implemented Operation "Watchtower": Rear Adm Turner's invasion fleet landed some 12,000 men of 1st Marine Division (Maj Gen Vandegrift) at Lunga Point, Guadalcanal, and a further 7,000 Marines on Tulagi and Gavutu islands on the north of Ironbottom Sound (the strait between Guadalcanal and Florida Island; so-called, from late 1942, because of the many ships sunk there). The Japanese (about 2,200 men) abandoned the Guadalcanal airfield

(named Henderson Field by the Americans), which was quickly secured, but the dispersal of Turner's fleet in the Battle of Savo Island, August 8–9, left the Marines ill-supplied to establish a defensive perimeter under naval and air bombardment. The first Japanese reinforcements from Lt Gen Hyakutake's Seventeenth Army landed at Taivu, east of Henderson Field, on August 18, but their attack was bloodily repulsed on the Tenaru river, August 21.

US aircraft were operational at Henderson Field from August 20, and the Battle of the Eastern Solomons, August 23–25, further strengthened US air-sea power, forcing Japan to rely on "Tokyo Express" night convoys for reinforcement. After the defeat of Maj Gen Kawaguchi's assault at "Bloody Ridge", September 12–14, Hyakutake himself took command; following the naval battle of Cape Esperance, October 11–12, he deployed some 25,000 men around Tenaro, while Vandegrift's force numbered about 23,000. A major attack across the Matanikau river, October 23–26, by some 5,600 Japanese (3,500 killed) under Maj Gen Maruyama was beaten off, while the naval battle of Santa Cruz, October 25–26, further weakened Japan's air arm. Vandegrift repulsed Hyakutake's final attack west of Henderson on November 19–21, while Carlson's Raiders harried the remaining Japanese in the east.

Japan's final large-scale reinforcement attempt was defeated in the naval actions off Guadalcanal, November 12–15, and, despite a naval victory at Tassafaronga, November 30–December 1, they were considering evacuation by mid-December, when XIV Army Corps (Maj Gen Patch) relieved Vandegrift's Marines. Pursued by Patch (who was reinforced following the naval battle of Rennell Island, January 29–30 1943), the Japanese fell back to Cape Esperance, whence some 13,000 survivors were evacuated, January 31–February 7. The Guadalcanal campaign cost the Japanese some 25,000 dead (including around 9,000 killed by disease or starvation in the island's malarial jungles and swamps) and *c*600 aircraft; US losses were *c*1,500 dead and about 4,800 wounded. *RO'N.*

Japanese naval troops on Guadalcanal

Guadalcanal, naval battles off (November 12–15 1942). In November 1942, planning a major offensive on Guadalcanal, Japan stepped up attempts to land reinforcements and to neutralize Henderson Field by bombardment. On the night of November 12–13, Rear Adm Daniel Callaghan (heavy cruisers *San Francisco* (flagship) and *Portland*; three light cruisers; eight destroyers) intercepted Vice Adm Abe's bombardment force (battleships *Hiei* and *Kirishima*; light cruiser *Nagara*; 11 destroyers) in Ironbottom Sound. Although surface radar located Abe at 15 miles' (24km) range, poor communications' discipline lost Callaghan the advantage of surprise. A hectic close-range action resulted in the sinking of light cruisers *Atlanta* and *Juneau* and four destroyers and severe damage to *Portland*. Both Callaghan and Rear Adm Norman Scott were killed. Abe lost *Hiei*, crippled by gunfire and sunk by aircraft from Henderson Field and the newly arrived USS *Enterprise* next day, and two destroyers.

On the night of November 13–14, as a Japanese supply convoy (Rear Adm Tanaka) headed for Tassafaronga, Vice Adm Gunichi Mikawa's heavy cruisers bombarded Henderson Field. Twenty US aircraft were destroyed, but air attacks as Mikawa withdrew at dawn sank *Kinugasa* and damaged *Maya* and *Chokai*. Daylight air strikes sank seven of Tanaka's 11 transports, but he pressed on, hoping for support from Vice Adm Kondo's approaching bombardment force (battleship *Kirishima*; four cruisers; nine destroyers). At around 2300 hours on November 14, Kondo was intercepted in Ironbottom Sound by Rear Adm Lee

G

G

(battleships *Washington* (flagship) and *South Dakota*; four destroyers). Within 15 minutes, "Long Lance" torpedoes and gunfire had crippled the US destroyers (three sunk). *South Dakota* was severely damaged, but *Washington*, in a radar-assisted surprise attack, wrecked *Kirishima* (scuttled next day). Kondo, having also lost a destroyer and with two cruisers badly damaged, withdrew with his mission unfulfilled.

Air attack next morning destroyed Tanaka's remaining transports: only about 4,000 troops and little materiel got ashore. US naval and air superiority off Guadalcanal was now firmly established and, notwithstanding Tanaka's victory at the Battle of Tassafaronga, November 30–December 1, Japan made no further large-scale reinforcement attempts. *RO'N.*

Guards Armoured Division. British Army. Formed 1941 from several Guards brigades; fought throughout the Northwest European Campaign 1944–45. Its armoured regiments were manned by retrained Foot Guards battalions and its armoured car regiment by the Household Cavalry. The division featured in the liberation of Brussels and in the attempt to relieve 1st Airborne Division at Arnhem.

Guards Division. British Army. An elite formation serving on the Western Front in World War I. Its distinctive "Gladeye" divisional badge was taken up by the Guards Armoured Division in World War II.

Gubbins, Sir Colin McVean (1896–1976). Br. Fought as a regular gunner officer in France, Russia and Ireland 1914–21; led independent companies (forerunners of commandos) in Norway 1940; organized civilian stay-behind parties to resist anticipated German invasion of England, 1940; director of operations, SOE from November 1940; became its executive head, September 1943, until it was disbanded January 1946.

Guderian, Gen Heinz (1888–1954). Ger. Guderian served as an infantry and staff officer during World War I but early in his

postwar career he specialized in mechanized warfare. In 1922 he joined the Army Transport Department of the Defence Ministry and by 1934 was Chief of Staff of the Armoured Corps Command. He published his theories of armoured warfare in a book, *Achtung Panzer*, in 1937. His revolutionary tactics of "blitzkrieg" warfare echoed the dynamism and aggression of Nazi ideology and were to provide an ideal tool for Hitler's war plans. Its efficacy was revealed in the German victories of 1939 and 1940 during which Guderian commanded XIX Corps in the invasions of Poland and France. His armoured thrust at Sedan proved crucial to the campaign's success and he pressed on to the Channel coast. Although he enjoyed further good fortune during the invasion of Russia, he clashed once again with the High Command. He criticized their failure to exploit the initial success and, on December 26 1941 was relieved of his command. However, Guderian returned in February 1943 when he was appointed Inspector of Panzer Troops. He continued to oppose Hitler on many issues but was nevertheless made Chief of the General Staff on July 21 1944. However, there was little he could do to alter the *Führer*'s orders and he had little control over the disposition of German forces. On March 28 1945 he argued once too often and was sent on "convalescent leave". He was captured by American forces on May 10 1945. *MS.*

Guernica, destruction of (April 26 1937), Spanish Civil War. Halfway through the Vizcaya campaign, Col von Richthofen, the air operations commander of the Condor Legion, decided to repeat the experiment of Durango, a town at an important crossroads behind the enemy line, which his aircraft had destroyed on March 31. Guernica, the old Basque capital, was selected for similar reasons. On April 26, Guernica's market day, his heavy squadrons (three of Junkers 52 and one of Heinkel 111) carpet-bombed the town in rigid formation, shuttling back to Burgos to reload. Meanwhile Heinkel 51 fighters machinegunned the fleeing civilians. The town was destroyed with bombs

from 1,100lb (500kg) down to small incendiaries. Casualties amounted to about one-third of the population: 1,654 killed and 889 wounded. In the international outcry which followed, the Nationalists claimed that the Basques had set fire to their own ancient capital. *AB.*

Guerrilla. Irregular operations by amateur soldiers, often in plain clothes, against oppressive regimes or foreign occupiers; sometimes near banditry or terrorism. *See also* MAQUIS.

Guevara, Ernesto ("Che") (1928–1967). Argentinian. Guevara experienced guerrilla warfare in Guatemala, 1954, and in 1956-59 was Fidel Castro's chief aide during the Cuban Revolution. His classic *Guerrilla Warfare*, 1960, stressed rural guerrilla activity and promulgated "the revolution in the revolution", stating that guerrilla action could create a successful revolution even where the predispositionary conditions (as defined by orthodox Marxism) did not exist. In 1965 he set out with a small band – the *foco*, "eye of the hurricane", intended to be the nucleus of a guerrilla army – to revolutionize Latin America. In October 1967 he was captured and shot by Bolivian troops.

Guidance systems. Most long-range missiles use inertial systems for mid-course guidance; a gyroscopically stabilized platform mounting accelerometers senses movement and adjusts the missile back to the correct path or trajectory. For long flights, or when the launch point is not very precisely known, some updating of the inertial system from outside sources is necessary. For shorter-range systems, simpler gyroscope autopilots are adequate. For attacking targets that can be tracked optically or by radar, command guidance is used with commands sent to the missile by radio or down a wire; alternatively the missile may fly down a radar beam. To engage moving targets, some homing system is often used. The missile might contain its own radar in an active system illuminating the target and homing on the reflections; or in a semi-active system it homes on the reflected emissions of an external radar source. Other passive homing missiles rely on picking up and homing on the infra-red heat or radar emissions of the target. For precise attack of land targets, scene matching technology can allow CEPs of 33ft (10m). Sometimes missiles use two or three different guidance systems for different parts of their mission, e.g. the US Navy's Standard missile used with the Aegis system which uses a combination of command guidance, autopilot and semi-active homing. *EJG.*

Gulf of Sirte incident (1981). The first combat involving the US Navy's multi-role carrier fighter, the Grumman F-14 Tomcat, began at 0715 hours, August 19 1981. Two F-14s from USS *Nimitz,* exercising in international waters north of Libya, were intercepted over the Gulf of Sirte by two Soviet-built Sukhoi Su-22 ("Fitter") fighters of the Libyan Arab Air Force. In an unprovoked attack, one Su-22 fired an air-to-air missile. Evading the AAM and anticipating further attack, the F-14s retaliated with AIM-9 Sidewinder missiles: one Tomcat shot down the aircraft that had fired; the other destroyed the remaining Su-22, outclassing it in a brief dogfight. In a similar incident off Benghazi, January 4 1989, two F-14s from USS *John F Kennedy* destroyed two Libyan MiG-23s ("Flogger"). *RO'N.*

Gulf War (1980–88). In terms of length, intensity and casualties, the greatest conflict since 1945. The Iraqi President, Saddam Hussein, hoped for a quick and decisive victory, but fanatical Iranian resistance at Khorramshahr turned the war into a slogging match. It may be divided into seven phases: the invasion (September 1980); static war (October 1980–May 1981); first Iranian offensive (May 1981–July 1982); into Iraq (July 1982–March 1984); tanker war (February–December 1984); stalemate again (December 1984–February 1986); transient Iranian success, followed by the return of stalemate (February 1986–summer 1988). Neither side could muster sufficient resources to attain decisive victory. Iran had the advantage in numbers; Iraq

had the advantage in defensive technique and air power. By mid–1984, the war of attrition had taken on economic form. Iraq strove to weaken Iranian counter-offensives by attacking her oil exports, and Iran threatened to close the Straits of Hormuz. Western naval forces were dispatched to ensure that they remained open. With financial aid from other Arab states, Iraq managed to survive the Iranian onslaught (five Iranian offensives were launched in 1983 alone). After the capture of the Faw Peninsula in February 1986, hope of an Iranian victory receded, and by July 1988 Iran had reversed her intransigent attitude and agreed to negotiations. *BHR.*

Gumbinnen, Battle of (1914). On August 15 1914 the Russian First Army advanced into East Prussia and, on the 20th, it was engaged by the German Eighth Army at Gumbinnen. After initial German success, the Russians repulsed the main assault and launched effective counterattacks.

Gunship *see* HELICOPTER.

Gurkha(s). Nepalese hillmen renowned for their loyalty, courage and humour. Recruited by the British and Indian armies since the mid-19th century.

Gurney, Sir Henry (1898–1951). Br. Colonial administrator. *See* MALAYAN EMERGENCY.

Gustav Line. German defensive position running across the Italian Peninsula from the Garigliano in the west, through Cassino in the centre, to the Sangro in the east.

Gustav line, breaching of (May 11–18 1944). This was the first phase of Alexander's "Diadem" offensive to take Rome, in which Fifth Army (Clark) attacked XIV Panzer Corps (von Senger) holding in the coastal sector, while Eighth Army (Leese) breached the central Cassino sector held by LI Mountain Corps (Feuerstein). Both German corps were under Tenth Army (von Vietinghoff).

Alexander deceived Kesselring into keeping his reserve mobile divisions away from the battle until too late by threatening landings on the coast north of Rome.

Fifth Army attacked with two corps: II US Corps (Keyes) with three divisions along the coast, and the French Expeditionary Corps (Juin) with four mountain-trained and equipped North African divisions, including Moroccan Goumiers, inland through the Aurunci Mountains. II US Corps made slow progress, but the French achieved surprise and made unexpectedly rapid progress in the mountains after taking Monte Majo – the southern key to the Gustav Line – on May 12, outflanking the German forces opposing both II US Corps on the coast and Eighth Army in the Liri Valley to the north.

In Eighth Army's attack, II Polish Corps (Anders) was given the task of wresting Monte Cassino from 1st Parachute Division, while XIII Corps (Kirkman) with four divisions forced crossings over the fortified Rapido stream in the Liri Valley below, defended by 44th Division. The Polish attack on May 11–12 failed with heavy losses. After two days of intense fighting, 4th British and 8th Indian Divisions had secured firm enough bridgeheads over the Rapido to allow Leese to destroy the Gustav defences in the Liri Valley, using Kirkman's two reserve divisions – 6th Armoured and 78th – in the northern and I Canadian Corps (Burns) in the southern halves of the valley, while Anders' Poles renewed their attack on Monte Cassino on May 17. Kesselring's mobile reserves arrived too late. Monte Cassino fell to the Poles on May 18, and I Canadian and XIII Corps broke through up the Liri Valley towards the Hitler Line, the next obstacle across Eighth Army's road to Rome. *WGFJ.*

Guynemer, Capt Georges (1894–1917). Fr. Second highest-scoring French fighter pilot of World War I, with 54 "kills", Guynemer flew with the elite *Les Cigognes* (Storks) Escadrille 3. He favoured lone patrols at up to 13,000ft (4,000m), making surprise diving attacks. Disappeared without trace in September 1917.

Guzzoni, Gen Alfredo (1887–1965). Italian. Commander Italian Sixth Army in Sicilian campaign, July–August 1943.

G

H2S (Home Sweet Home). British airborne radar aid to navigation and bomb aiming. Downward transmissions from the aircraft were reflected from the surface beneath and displayed on a cathode ray tube showing the distinctions between land and sea and built-up and open areas. Although the earliest by inception of all such devices, H2S was not introduced to operational service in Bomber Command until January 1943 due to fear of disclosing a system upon which ASV and AI were also based. The H2S picture was often difficult to read and although the system could not be jammed, the bomber using it disclosed its position by transmitting. *ANF.*

H2X. American version of H2S.

Haakon VII, King of Norway (1872–1957). Reigned 1905–57. After the German occupation of Norway, 1940, Haakon established a government of resistance in London.

Hadrian, Waco CG-4A (US, WWII). Transport glider; crew 2. Prototype flew 1942; ordered from 16 assembly lines. First operational use invasion of Sicily, July 1943; later Normandy, southern France, Arnhem, Rhine crossing. Could carry 13 troops, a Jeep, a ¼-ton truck with four-man crew, or a 75mm howitzer and crew. Production 13,912, of which 694 to Britain, lend-lease. Max. towing speed 149mph (240kph); load 3,800lb (1,725kg).

Haganah. Zionist organization founded in Palestine 1936, at first cooperated with British occupying force against Arabs; then, less agreeably to the British, arranged for large illegal immigrations of Jews. During World War II Haganah developed into a citizen army, including almost every able-bodied Jewish man of military age in Palestine; with this army, the Jews defeated the Arabs, securing independence for Israel, 1948–49.

Hague Conventions. Two international conferences at The Hague, in 1899 and in 1907, originated by Tsar Nicholas II, adopted numerous conventions bearing on the laws of war; prohibiting, for instance, acts of undeclared war, the

use of expanding bullets, or the dropping of weapons from the air. All took for granted that only men would act as combatants. Recommendations that disputes should be settled by arbitration rather than by war have usually, like many of the other provisions, been ignored.

Haifa, Battle of (1918). During the British offensive in Palestine in September 1918, the capture of Haifa was entrusted to the 5th Division. On September 23, elements of the 15th Cavalry Brigade, supported by a battery of the Honourable Artillery Company, charged and overwhelmed the strong Turkish defensive positions and advanced on the city.

Haig, Field Marshal Earl (1861–1928). Br. Having attended the Staff College in 1896–1897, Haig served under French on the staff of the Cavalry Division in South Africa. For the rest of his military career, Haig retained a cavalryman's outlook and largely adhered to the concept of war he had learned at the Staff College. As Director of Military Training in 1906–07 he helped Haldane create the BEF and the Territorial Force, and when the BEF went to war in August 1914, Haig commanded I Corps at Mons, the Marne, the Aisne and First Ypres. Elevated to the command of the First Army in December 1914, he misinterpreted the lessons of Neuve-Chapelle the following March, relying upon bigger forces and weightier bombardments rather than tactical flexibility in most battles before 1918. Doubting French's suitability for command of the BEF, Haig was involved in engineering his dismissal over the mishandling of the reserves at Loos, even though faulty arrangements by Haig's own staff were partly responsible for their late arrival. Haig succeeded French on December 19 1915, but his period as C-in-C of the BEF in France and Flanders still remains highly controversial. The evidence indicates that he originally envisaged a breakthrough in his offensives on the Somme in 1916 and at Ypres in 1917 and persisted with them far longer than was desirable, justifying them as battles of attrition when it was clear that decisive strategic advances were

no longer possible. His reluctance to discuss problems fully with his principal subordinates also led to glaring contradictions in the plans for both offensives. Nevertheless, while he underestimated the danger to the Fifth Army's front in March 1918, he displayed great tenacity during the crises in the spring of that year and was quick to acknowledge the value of a unified Allied command under Foch. Moreover, as John Terraine observes, between August 8 1918 and the end of the war, the forces led by Haig defeated the main body of the German army in the greatest succession of victories in the British army's history, a fact all too often obscured by his previous failures. *PJS.*

Haig, Gen Alexander Meigs Jr (b.1924). As US Secretary of State in 1982, embarked on an intensive 12-day session of "shuttle diplomacy" in an attempt to mediate between Britain and Argentina. Having failed to bring about rapprochement, he announced on April 30 that his government would henceforth support Britain.

Haile Selassie, Emperor of Ethiopia (1892–1975). Reigned 1930–74. The Italian invasion and annexation of Ethiopia in 1935–36 drove the emperor into exile in England. Restored in 1941, following the victorious British campaign against the Italians, he was deposed by a left-wing army coup in 1974.

Haiphong. Up to 85 percent of North Vietnam's war supplies during the late 1960s and early 1970s moved through Haiphong, the North's second largest city and major port. The US bombed targets in and around the city 1965–68 but generally stopped short of striking the harbour to avoid hitting Soviet and other ships. President Nixon ordered US planes on May 9 1972 to mine the harbour in response to the communists' Easter offensive. The US Navy helped clear the harbour following the signing of the Paris Agreement, and the port re-opened in July 1973.

Halberstadt CL II (German, WWI). Two-seat escort fighter/infantry support. Prototype passed official tests May 7 1917; production aircraft operational Western Front from August 1917. As protection fighter for reconnaissance aircraft, subsequently on infantry-support duties, was popular and successful. Production at least 900. One 160hp Mercedes D III/185hp BMW IIIa engine; max. speed 103mph (165kph); two/three 7.9mm machine guns; 110lb (50kg) bombs, anti-personnel grenades.

Haldane, Richard Burdon, 1st Viscount Haldane of Cloan (1856–1928). Br. As Secretary of State for War, 1905–12, Haldane vigorously implemented the modernization of the British army in the light of the shortcomings revealed by the Esher Committee's report (1903–04) on the Boer War. His achievements included the creation of an effective General Staff; of a force capable of continental commitment – eventually the BEF of 1914; and of the Territorial Army as a ready reserve.

Halder: half-hearted opponent of Hitler

Halder, Gen Franz (1884–1972). Ger. After service as a staff officer during World War I, Halder continued in the Weimar Republic's Reichswehr. By 1938 he had reached the rank of Gen and held the post of CGS. Like many of his fellow officers, he was torn between dislike for the Nazis and loyalty to the state. He contemplated mounting a coup in 1938 to overthrow Hitler, but the reluctance of his C-in-C, von Brauchitsch, to commit himself to

the cause, and the relaxation of international tension following the Munich Agreement resulted in the abandonment of his plans. Halder opposed Hitler's decision to risk a war with Britain and France, but he played a full part in planning the victories of 1940 and the invasion of the Soviet Union in 1941. Hitler's confidence in his own grasp of strategy led to increased interference in Halder's work and frequent arguments. In September 1942 their stormy relationship ended with Halder's dismissal, following a clash over plans to capture Stalingrad. Halder went into retirement but his reputation as a frequent critic of Hitler led to his arrest following the July Plot of 1944. Innocent of any involvement, Halder was nevertheless imprisoned in a concentration camp until liberated in Austria by US troops in May 1945. *MS.*

Halfaya Pass *see* TOBRUK, BRITISH RECONNAISSANCE IN FORCE TOWARDS.

Halifax, Handley Page HP 57 (Br, WWII). Heavy bomber/anti-submarine patrol; crew 7. Prototype flew October 25 1939, first production aircraft October 11 1940. First operational mission March 10 1941; Coastal Command versions long-range anti-submarine duties from October 1942. Developed through many variants, some as glider tugs and transports. Production 6,179. Four 1,390hp Rolls-Royce Merlin/1,675hp Bristol Hercules engines; max. speed 282mph (454kph); 13,000lb (5,900kg) bombs, nine 0.303in machine guns.

Hall, Adm Sir William Reginald (1870–1943). Br. "Blinker" Hall was perhaps the greatest intelligence officer of his time. Forced from active service by ill health, 1914, he was made Director of Intelligence at the Admiralty (later Director of Naval Intelligence). Unfortunately it was not until 1917 that the extremely successful code-breakers of "Room 40" came under him, for he was the first to use this invaluable resource to full effect. He had already masterminded a number of intelligence coups, including a nearly successful attempt to buy Turkey out of the war. His greatest triumph was

the successful handling of the decoded "Zimmerman Telegram", which helped bring America into the war without disclosing that German codes were being read. Equally successful in espionage and counter-espionage, he was an inspired leader. *DJL.*

Halsey, Fleet Adm William Frederick, Jr (1882–1959). US. A World-War-I destroyer commander, Halsey thereafter devoted himself to naval aviation (qualifying as a carrier pilot at the age of 53), and became one of the pre-eminent carrier admirals of World War II. At sea in *Enterprise* at the time of Pearl Harbor, he was soon launching air strikes against Japanese bases in the Gilberts, Marshalls and at Wake Island, February-March 1942, and commanding the escort force for the Doolittle raid on Tokyo, April 1942.

Illness kept Halsey from Midway, but on October 18 1942, he succeeded Vice Adm Ghormley as Commander, South Pacific Forces, with Kinkaid as commander of carrier forces. Under Halsey's direction, Kinkaid inflicted severe loss on Japan's naval aviation at Santa Cruz and defeated a major bombardment/reinforcement operation off Guadalcanal, November 12–15 1942. Halsey's aggressive and opportunistic leadership also contributed largely to the success of the "leap-frogging" campaign in the Solomons, February 1943–March 1944.

From June 1944, under Nimitz, Halsey (under whom the major US task force was designated Third Fleet) alternated command with Spruance (Fifth Fleet) in the Central Pacific. As a result of his wide-ranging operations in preparation for the reconquest of the Philippines, the invasion of Leyte was advanced by two months, but his impetuosity nearly led to disaster at Leyte Gulf, October 1944, when his pursuit of Ozawa's "decoy" carrier force (which he destroyed) almost allowed Kurita to reach the vulnerable US transports. The overall success of his leadership and his inestimable contribution to morale (such flamboyant signals as "Kill more Japs!" and "Keep the bastards dying!" contributed to the public-relations'-inspired nickname "Bull",

Halsey: "Keep the bastards dying!"

which he detested) saved him from condemnation both after Leyte and when, in December 1944 and June 1945, he was censured for exposing Third Fleet to typhoon damage.

In May-August 1945, Halsey led Third Fleet (with British Pacific Fleet in cooperation) at Okinawa and in devastating strikes against the Japanese home islands. He was promoted Fleet Adm in December 1945, retiring from active duty in 1947. *RO'N.*

Hambro, Air Commodore Sir Charles Jocelyn (1897–1963). Br. Fought in France, 1916–18; head of SOE's Scandinavian section 1941; SOE's second-in-command 1941–42, executive head 1942–43; exchanged atomic secrets with Americans, 1943–45.

Hamburg, Battle of. The term describes the British night bombing of Germany between July 24 and November 18 1943. It began with a sustained and massive series of attacks upon Hamburg itself and then shifted its focus generally eastwards and towards Berlin. The campaign is sometimes called the Battle of the Central Complex; it was the bridge between the battles of the Ruhr and of Berlin.

During this battle, Bomber Command dispatched 17,021 sorties in 33 major attacks on German targets. The cost was heavy – 695 aircraft failed to return, while 1,123 were damaged, sometimes to the point of total loss. The casualty rate was, though, lower than that suffered in the Battle of the Ruhr and substantially so than in the Battle of Berlin, but the damage was much greater. Hamburg was the most successful episode in Bomber Command's general area offensive before D-Day.

By far the greatest amount of the damage done was in Hamburg itself, which, on the nights of July 24–25, 27–28 and 29–30 and August 2–3 1943, sustained four huge night attacks by Bomber Command and some lesser activity by the day bombers of the US Eighth Air Force. The four British attacks involved the dispatch of 3,095 sorties carrying nearly 9,000 tons of bombs, about half of which were incendiaries. In these four nights about 50,000 people were killed and 40,000 injured. Close on 1,000,000 people fled from the city. More than half the houses and half the factories in Hamburg were completely destroyed. Some of the bombing was so highly concentrated that firestorms were generated. Speer concluded at the time that six more such attacks would end the war. These, however, could not be achieved; indeed, in the attacks on Hamburg, Bomber Command had special advantages which were either unique to that city or were temporary. Among the former was the relatively short penetration of enemy territory needed and the amount of water in the target area, which produced an unusually good H2S picture. Among the latter was the surprise element caused by Window, used for the first time in these attacks and which the Germans later, to a considerable extent, circumvented. *ANF.*

"Hamburger Hill" *see* A SHAU, BATTLES OF.

Hamilcar *see* GLIDERS.

Hamilton, Gen Sir Ian (1853–1947). Br. Hamilton was one of the most intellectually gifted officers of his generation, while three recommendations for the VC testified to his courage. When serving in Afghanistan in the early 1880s he became a protégé of Sir Frederick (later Earl) Roberts, and during the Second Boer War he was Kitchener's chief of staff, commanding 17,000 men in the final drive against the Boers. From 1910 to 1914 he held the post of GOC, Mediterranean Command. Soon after the outbreak of war in 1914, Kitchener appointed him to lead the Central Force, with responsibility for home defence in the event of invasion. However, on

March 12 1915, he was given his greatest challenge, being made commander of the Mediterranean Expeditionary Force for the forthcoming military operations in the Dardanelles. His plans for the landings on Gallipoli on April 25 1915 were overambitious for brave but largely inexperienced troops with scant logistical support but, even when any chance of an easy success had clearly evaporated, he was slow to ask for reinforcements. His headquarters at Imbros were too distant and he exercised insufficient control over incompetent subordinates such as Hunter-Weston, who wasted lives in futile frontal assaults at Cape Helles. Dissatisfaction with Hamilton increased after his abortive August offensive at Anzac and Suvla, when he again intervened too late to snatch a fleeting opportunity of victory. He was replaced by Monro in October 1915. Considering his many outstanding gifts, Hamilton's failure at Gallipoli was all the more tragic. *PJS.*

Hamlet Evaluation Survey (HES). Initiated in 1963 to measure the effectiveness of "pacification" in the Vietnam War. The survey depended on monthly reports filed by American district adviser and was used to support the contention that the US was winning the war. Despite overhaul in 1967 to remove optimistic bias, the survey continued to underrate the communists' access to the people and hold on their loyalties. It claimed 93 percent of the people were living under Saigon's influence or control in late 1972, when the Pentagon estimated that communist and front organizations still lived among or had access to 71 percent. *WST.*

Hampden, Handley Page HP 52 (Br, WWII). Medium bomber/torpedo bomber; crew 4. Prototype flew June 21 1936. Deliveries began August 1938; ten squadrons by September 1939. First operational mission September 3 1939. Built in Canada. Five squadrons operated as torpedo-bombers 1942–43. Twenty-three to Russians. Withdrawn end 1943. Production 1,532. Two 965hp Bristol Pegasus engines; max. speed 247mph (397kph); 4,000lb (1,800kg) bombs, four 0.303 in machine guns.

Handley Page 0/100 and 0/400 (Br, WWI). Heavy bomber; crew 3–4. Prototype flew December 17 1915; much corrective experimentation needed before operational use; first mission night March 16–17 1917. Improved design, 0/400, ordered August 1917; first deliveries March 1918; thereafter increasingly used by RAF and Independent Force until Armistice. Production: 0/100, 46; 0/400, 491; plus at least 107 built in US. Two 375hp Rolls-Royce Eagle, 275hp Sunbeam Maori or 350hp Liberty 12-N engines; max. speed 97.5mph (157kph); 2,000lb (900kg) bombs, five 0.303in machine guns.

Handley Page V/1500 (Br, post-WWI). Heavy bomber; crew 9. Prototype flew May 22 1918. Was RAF's first four-engine bomber; intended to bomb Berlin from bases in England. Of the 243 originally ordered at least 44 were completed, but the type was too late to see operational use. One bombed Kabul May 24 1919. Four 375hp Rolls-Royce Eagle, 500hp Galloway Atlantic, or 450hp Napier Lion engines; max. speed 99mph (158kph); 7,500lb (3,402kg) bombs, five 0.303in machine guns.

Hannover CL II/III/IIIa (German, late and post-WWI). Two-seat escort fighter/infantry support. Prototype flew 1917; first production aircraft (CL II) entered service late 1917. Modification and development led to CL III (160hp Mercedes) and CL IIIa of 1918. Compact, sturdy and manoeuvrable, Hannover two-seaters were widely and successfully used; a few operated by Polish air force 1919–20. Production: 439 CL IIs, 80 CL IIIs, 537 CL IIIas. One 180hp Argus As III engine; max. speed 103mph (165kph); two 7.92mm machine guns.

Hanoi. American bombardment of North Vietnam encroached upon Hanoi, the capital, in 1965. US planes hit transportation and fuel facilities on the outskirts and gradually increased the scope of attack to include industrial targets. Most government offices, factories and up to three-quarters of the city's 710,000 people (in 1970) were dispersed to the countryside. In reprisal for the Easter offensive of 1972, President Nixon intensified the bombing, and in December, to break the negotiating deadlock, he sent B-52s to strike targets inside as well as near Hanoi. Two full loads of bombs missed their targets, flattening residential neighbourhoods and killing 2,196 people. Aside from that, the city suffered mild damage compared with the destruction of cities in other modern wars. *WST*.

Hanriot HD-1 (French, WWI). Single-seat fighter. Prototype flew summer 1916. Quantity production for Belgium and Italy; also produced in Italy from November 1916. Used by at least 16 Italian *squadriglie* with considerable success; a few, plus some HD-2s (seaplane version), with French naval units. Production: reported 125 delivered to Belgium, and that 831 were completed in Italy to war's end, 70 more thereafter. One 110/120/130hp Le Rhône engine; max. speed 115mph (184kph); one 7.7mm machine gun.

Hansa-Brandenburg C I (Austro-Hungarian, WWI). Two-seat reconnaissance bomber; German design built in Austria-Hungary. Prototype flew 1915; extensively used January 1916 to war's end. Production, in 19 series with at least seven types of engine 1,258. With 160hp Austro-Daimler engine max. speed 87mph (139kph). Two machine guns, 220lb (100kg) bombs.

Hansa-Brandenburg D I (Austro-Hungarian, WWI). Single-seat fighter; German design, built in two series Austria-Hungary, one in Germany. Prototype flew early 1916; production deliveries that autumn. Although fast had unpleasant flying qualities. One 150/160/185hp Austro-Daimler engine; max. speed 116mph (187kph); one 7.9mm machine gun.

Hansa-Brandenburg W12 (German, WWI). Two-seat fighter seaplane. Prototype tested January 1917. Production deliveries from August 1917; effectively used against Allied ships and aircraft in Channel and North Sea. Production 146. One 150hp Benz Bz.III or 160hp Mercedes D.III engine; max. speed 100mph (160kph); two or three 7.7mm machine guns.

Hanson, First Lt Robert M (1920–44). US. Third-ranked Marine Corps fighter pilot with 25 victories. He shot down 20 Japanese aircraft in January 1944 alone.

Harding, Field Marshal Lord (1896–1989). Br. Governor and C-in-C, Cyprus (1955–57) when he handed over to Sir Hugh Foot (later Lord Caradon) who was responsible for bringing about a negotiated settlement resulting in the creation of the Republic of Cyprus, in which Britain retained Sovereign rights over two tracts containing military cantonments, a strategic airfield, and certain electronic monitoring sites. *See also* CYPRUS (1955–60).

Harkins, Gen Paul D (1904–84). US. Appointed the first Commander of the US Military Assistance Command, Vietnam (COMUSMACV) in February 1962. Opposed the coup against President Ngo Dinh Diem, setting himself against Ambassador Lodge. Harkins' perennial optimism exasperated officials who had a better understanding of the Saigon government's weaknesses, and he was replaced by Gen William Westmoreland as MACV commander in June 1964.

Harmon, Maj Gen Ernest Nason (1894–1979). US. Aggressive commander of armoured formations. Led US 2nd Armored Division in North Africa, 1942–43, and, after commanding 1st Armored Division in Italy, 1943–44, again led 2nd Armored, and finally XXII Corps, in Northwest Europe, 1944–45.

Harmon, Lt Gen Millard F (1888–1945). US. The overall commander of the USAAF in the Pacific Ocean Area, 1944–45.

Harpoon missile. An American medium-range jet-propelled anti-ship missile which can be launched from surface, sub-surface or air platforms. It is fired down a pre-set bearing using a simple but accurate autopilot. It switches on its homing radar at a point chosen considering the characteristics of the target. Range is over 54 miles (90km). Harpoon is operated by 16 countries in addition to the USA, which has used it with success against both Libya and Iran.

H

Harrier/Sea Harrier, British Aerospace (Br). Single-seat close-support/tactical reconnaissance/shipboard fighter. World's first operational fixed-wing VTOL aircraft; conspicuous success Falklands 1982. Prototype (Hawker P.1127) flew (in hover) October 21 1960, (free) November 19 1960. First production Harrier GR Mark I flew December 28 1967; further Marks developed. First Sea Harriers to RN June 18 1979. USMC uses extensively; version built USA. Production 77 GR Mk I, 37 GR Mk 3, 113 AV-8As for USMC and Spain; 57 Sea Harriers, continuing. One 21,500lb (9,752kg) s.t. Bristol-Siddeley Pegasus 103/104 engine; max. speed 720mph (1,159kph; two 30mm cannon, two Sidewinder missiles, 5,000lb (2,250kg) external ordnance.

Harriet, Mount. The heavily mined southern end of the Argentinian defences around Port Stanley during the Falklands War of 1982. It was stormed on the night of June 11 by 42 Commando, who breached the minefield, then captured the position from the rear, taking more than 300 prisoners.

Harris: advocate of area bombing

Harris, Marshal of the RAF Sir Arthur Travers (1892–1984). Br. AOC-in-C, RAF Bomber Command 1942–45. Harris, who had served in the RFC in World War I, was selected to command 5 Group, Bomber Command on the outbreak of World War II. Later he was Deputy Chief of the Air Staff and Head of the RAF delegation in Washington. In February 1942 he was given the prime command in the RAF, that of Bomber Command.
The CAS (Portal) told Harris to attack large German towns at night; other policies were tactically impossible. Harris was also confronted with a lack of confidence in Bomber Command which threatened its existence. He took drastic steps to implement his orders and to restore confidence. At 1205 hours on May 30 1942 he gave the order "Thousand Plan Cologne" and that night 1,046 bombers took off in the largest scale of air operations ever undertaken. The centre of Cologne was devastated, the Germans were given warning of recompense to come and the British changed their sights from survival to victory. To do it, Harris, whose front line strength was barely more than 400 bombers, committed all his reserves and every available crew in his operational training units; seldom can a commander have staked more on his judgement.

Harris's style, for such a commander, was unusual; he seldom emerged from his headquarters and was unknown, even by sight, to the vast majority of his crews, yet his remarkable command over them was sustained throughout all the dark nights which, in the end, cost nearly 50,000 of their lives. Harris stuck resolutely to the policy of massive area bombing, in pursuit of which he waged the battles of the Ruhr, Hamburg and Berlin, and some, including Portal, thought that he did so for too long and after other policies were within his grasp. Eventually he became identified with an outmoded policy and his real achievements were obscured. *ANF*.

Hartlepool, bombardment of (December 16 1914). In an attempt to destroy isolated British squadrons, the High Seas Fleet was kept as a covering force while battlecruisers were sent to bombard Hartlepool and Scarborough on the English east coast to provoke a reaction. Three ships bombarded Hartlepool, causing civilian casualties but little real damage. The local shore battery caused damage to all three before being silenced. The prevailing poor visibility and communications difficulties caused both sides to miss each other in the subsequent manoeuvrings.

Hartmann, Lt Col Erich (b.1922). Ger. Most successful fighter pilot of World War II, with 352 "kills"

(345 Russian, including 11 in one day; 7 American). He flew 1,425 combat missions in Messerschmitt Me 109s, surviving *c*800 dogfights and 18 crash-landings and parachute escapes. Hartmann surrendered to US forces in May 1945, but was handed over to the Russians and served 10 years' imprisonment. He subsequently joined the West German Luftwaffe.

Haruna see KONGO.

Harwich Force. British scouting force of light cruisers and destroyers based at Harwich, World War I, under the efficient and inspiring command of Adm Tyrwhitt. One of its destroyers fired the first shot of the naval war; fought at Heligoland Bight and many later actions.

Harwood: his squadron sank *Graf Spee*

Harwood, Adm Sir Henry (1888–1950). Br. Commanding the British Squadron on the South American Station, December 1939, Harwood was confronted by pocket battleship *Admiral Graf Spee*, whose 11in guns, with a range of 30,000yd (27,000m), outranged his 6in cruisers, *Ajax* and the New Zealand *Achilles*, and 8in cruiser *Exeter*. Nevertheless, in a brilliant manoeuvre on December 13 1939, Harwood brought the German ship to action and forced her to divide her fire. She was severely damaged and put in to Montevideo for repairs. On coming out, her captain, Langsdorff, scuttled the ship and committed suicide. Although *Exeter* was crippled and *Ajax* and *Achilles* were both hit, Harwood won a brilliant victory. Langsdorff believed that Harwood had a much more powerful force than was the case. *ANF*.

Hassan II, King of Morocco (b.1929) *see* ALGERIAN-MOROCCAN WAR.

Hauck, Lt Gen Friedrich-Wilhelm (1897–1979). Ger. Commander 305th Division in the Italian campaign until he became Acting Commander LXXVI Panzer Corps in November 1944, and then Commander LI Mountain Corps in March 1945.

Hausser, Col Gen *(Obergruppenführer, SS)* **Paul** (1880–1972). Ger. A World-War-1 veteran, Hausser retired from the Reichswehr as a Lt Gen in 1932. He soon joined the SS Verfügungstruppe, playing a major part, under Himmler, in its development in 1934–39 into the Waffen SS. He commanded "Das Reich" Division in France, 1940, and II SS Panzer Corps on the Eastern Front, transferring with it to the West following the Normandy invasion. On June 28 1944 he became commander of Seventh Army, bitterly contesting the Allies' Normandy breakout. From early 1945 he commanded Army Group G in its final resistance on the Rhine and in the Ruhr. *RO'N*.

Havoc *see* BOSTON.

Haw-Haw, Lord *see* JOYCE, WILLIAM.

Hawker, Maj Lanoe George VC (1890–1916). Br. A reconnaissance and bomber pilot in 1914-15, Hawker took command of 24 Squadron, the first British unit in France (from February 27 1916) equipped with single-seat fighters (DH 2). He was awarded the VC after vanquishing three German aircraft in single combat on July 25 1915. On November 23 1916, he was shot down and killed by Manfred von Richthofen.

Hawksworth, Lt Gen Sir John "Ginger" (1893–1945). Br. Commander 46th Division in the Italian campaign; promoted to command X Corps in November 1944. Sent to Greece by Alexander in December 1944 to establish "Military Command Athens" with the task of clearing the communist forces from Athens. He died soon after successfully accomplishing his task.

Heartbreak Ridge, Battle of (1951). Heartbreak Ridge lay in the east/central sector of the Korean front, adjacent to Bloody Ridge. On September 13 1951 it was attacked by US infantry and a French battalion. The NKPA resisted fiercely. During the battle, US artillery fired 229,724 supporting rounds and the fighting was often hand to hand. The struggle for Heartbreak Ridge lasted until October 15 when the feature was outflanked and taken. The NKPA suffered 35,000 casualties and the US Army 5,600.

Hébuterne. Village, near Gommecourt, forming the boundary between the British Third and Fourth Armies, July 1 1916.

Hedgehog (anti-submarine weapon). Multiple mortar throwing pattern of contact-fused bombs ahead of ship. In service 1943.

Heidrich, Lt Gen *(General der Fallschirmtruppen)* **Richard** (1896–1947). Ger. Commander 1st Parachute Division during the Italian campaign until November 1944 when he took over I Parachute Corps, and won fame as the defender of Cassino in the Third and Fourth Battles.

Heikoutai, Battle of *see* SANDEPU.

Heinkel He 111 (German, WWII). Bomber; crew 5. Prototype flew February 24 1935; deliveries early production He 111B-1 began winter 1936–37. Initially four sent to Spain for operational evaluation January 1937; others followed for *Condor Legion*. Design developed and revised through many versions; deliveries basic He 111P started spring 1939; by September adoption He 111P/111H virtually complete. Widely used various tasks, latterly as transport and glider tug, until war's end. Production: over 7,300. Two 1,020hp Daimler-Benz DB601Aa/1,350hp Junkers Jumo 211F-2 engines; max. speed 252mph (406kph); 7,165lb (3,250kg) bombs, one 20mm cannon, one 13mm and up to five 7.9mm machine guns.

Heinkel He 177 Greif (Griffin) (German, WWII). Heavy bomber, crew 5, to Luftwaffe specification of mid-1936. Prototype flew November 19 1939; evaluation batch of 35 underwent many modifications, suffered many problems, especially in power installation. Production halted 1942 but resumed; finally terminated October 1944; total built 1,094; about 200 used operationally. Some, with He 293 missiles, used for anti-shipping strikes. Two 2,700hp Daimler-Benz DB606 (double DB601) or 2,950hp DB 610 (double DB605) engines; max. speed 336mph (540kph); 13,230lb (6,000kg) bombs/three torpedoes/two Hs 293 or Fritz X missiles; two 20mm cannon, three 7.9mm and two 13mm machine guns.

Heinkel He 219 Uhu (Owl) (German, WWII). Night fighter; crew 2. Prototype flew November 15 1942; eleven pre-series He 219s delivered by end 1943; further deliveries retarded by engine problems. Although Germany's best night fighter, its production on scale warranted by its quality and capability was frustrated by intrigue. Production 268. Two 1,800hp Daimler-Benz DB 603E engines; max. speed 363mph (584kph); two 30mm and four 20mm cannon.

Heinrici, Col Gen Gotthard (1886–1971). Ger. Came to prominence as an expert defensive tactician on the Eastern Front during World War II. He commanded the German XLIII Corps in 1941 and led the Fourth Army from January 1942 until August 1944, when he was appointed to the First Panzer Army. On March 20 1945 he replaced Himmler as commander of Army Group Vistula, with a key role in the defence of Berlin. Although he conducted a skilful defensive battle, he was removed from command on April 28 for withdrawing without Hitler's authority and refusing to mount hopeless counterattacks. *PJS*.

Hejaz. A region of the Arabian peninsula bordering the Red Sea. In 1916 its ruler, Hussein-ibn-Ali, declared its independence from Turkish rule.

Hejaz railway. Before the outbreak of World War I, Germany extended its influence in the Middle East by assisting the Ottoman empire in building a network of railways. One line stretched into the Hejaz region of Arabia and by 1908 had linked Damascus with Medina although the extensions to Mecca and Aqaba had not been completed by 1914. The railway greatly facilitated Turkish military control of the Hejaz and was therefore a primary target during the Arab Revolt. Arab guerrillas kept substantial Turkish garrisons pinned in the towns along the railway and severely dislocated communications by constantly raiding the line. *MS*.

Helicopter medical evacuation (Korea). This was hastily improvised in the first months of the Korean War, employing the 3rd Air Rescue Squadron of the USAF to carry casualties from the front line to Mobile Army Surgical Hospitals. A shortage of helicopters meant that only the most severely wounded could be evacuated by this method and the USAF always insisted that the primary mission of its helicopter units should be rescue. In the course of the war, the army acquired its own helicopters, which became responsible for transporting casualties within the combat zone. On the UN side, thanks to helicopters, a severely wounded soldier could be undergoing surgery within an hour. Chinese and North Korean wounded took at least a day to reach any kind of hospital, by which time the worst cases had already died. *CM*.

Helicopter. An aircraft normally deriving its lift and thrust from the aerodynamic resultant of horizontally-mounted rotating wings, or rotors. Directional control in most helicopters is obtained by varying the pitch of a tail-mounted rotor, counteracting the torque generated by the main rotor system. Early military helicopters (1940s and 50s) were suitable only for reconnaissance, light cargo and liaison, and the evacuation of casualties from the forward combat zone. However, development of lightweight gas turbine engines led, in the 1960s, to great improvement in performance and extension of helicopter roles. The French army began to arm its helicopters during the Algerian campaign (1954–62), and as the result of lessons learned in Vietnam the US army introduced the purpose-built UH-1 Cobra attack helicopter, de-

Arming an American AH-1G Cobra attack helicopter ("gunship"), Vietnam

signed around various weapon systems, protected by integral armour from the effects of hostile fire, and manned by specially trained crews. An attack helicopter (or "gunship") will normally mount a mixture of anti-tank guided missiles, free-flight rockets, and cannon or machine guns. With the appearance in the Soviet inventory of helicopters clearly designed to attack opposing helicopters in flight, it is becoming necessary to mount air-to-air weapons on many NATO battlefield helicopters.

Armies are increasingly reliant on larger types of helicopter, capable of moving formed bodies of troops and their equipment rapidly to wherever a tactical decision is required. These can be as large as the Boeing-Vertol Chinook, classified as medium-lift, or smaller support helicopters such as the Aérospatiale Puma and the Sikorsky S-67 Blackhawk. Helicopters have been used at sea since the mid-1940s with conspicuous success in anti-submarine, countermine and amphibious assault roles. Advanced-technology rotor blades, the use of titanium, high efficiency power plants, and advanced flight control systems all feature in contemporary designs. Although early machines had only a limited capacity for operations by night and in adverse weather conditions, the need for 24-hour battlefield support and for survival in increasingly hostile combat conditions has resulted in improved navigational aids. Passive and active sensors for target acquisition and surveillance now permit the deployment of helicopters in virtually all conditions as 24-hour battlefield vehicles. *MH*.

Heligoland Bight (August 1914). North Sea naval engagement. On August 28 1914, Commodore Reginald Tyrwhitt's light cruiser and destroyer force moved into the Heligoland area against patrolling German flotilla units. The Admiralty had not informed Tyrwhitt that it had also deployed a light cruiser force (Commodore W R Goodenough) and a battle cruiser squadron (Vice Adm Beatty) in support. A British decoy submarine attracted German light cruisers and destroyers, and in confused daylight engagements the German lost three light cruisers and a destroyer. But Admiralty planning had been seriously defective and the success was largely attributable to good luck and to poor German dispositions. *JTS*.

Hellcat, Grumman F6F-3/5 (US, WWII). Single-seat shipboard fighter. Prototype flew June 26 1942; first production aircraft October 30 1942; first deliveries to US Navy Fleet units January 16 1943. Highly effective until war's end. Royal Navy received 252 F6F-3s (Hellcat I) and 930 F6F-5s (Hellcat II). Production 12,275. One 2,000hp Pratt and Whitney R-2800-10/10W engine; max. speed 386mph (621kph); six 0.5in machine guns, 2,000lb (900kg) bombs or six 5in rockets.

Hell Fire Corner. World War I name for the place, just east of Ypres, where the Menin Road is crossed by the Zillebeke-Potijze Road and the Ypres-Roulers railway. Since German gunners knew its precise range, it became a particularly dangerous spot for British troops in the Ypres salient.

Helles, Cape *see* DARDANELLES, GALLIPOLI.

Henry Farman F20 (French, WWI). Two/three-seat general-purpose/trainer. Prototype flew summer 1912. In service with Belgian, French and Royal Flying Corps units from spring 1913. Early RFC experiments with machine guns from June 1913. Eleven to France with RFC August 1914; operational use brief but long service as trainer thereafter. Production in England, Belgium, Russia. One 80hp Gnome/Le Rhône engine; max. speed 65mph (104kph); improvised armament of rifle, revolvers, some small bombs.

Hercules, Lockheed C-130 (US). Tactical transport/flight-refuelling tanker; crew 4/5. Prototype flew August 23 1954; first production deliveries to US Tactical Air Command December 9 1956. Phenomenally successful: by 1987 had been delivered to 57 nations; production had exceeded 1,800. Many sub-types developed, including special-role variants for USAF, USN Navy, USCM. Four 4,508ehp Allison T56-A-15 engines; max. speed 384mph (618kph); max. payload 92 troops, 64 paratroops or 74 stretchers with two attendants.

Hermes. British aircraft carriers. (1) In 1913, the old cruiser *Hermes* was converted to operate seaplanes – the first British carrier. Sunk by U-boat in 1914. (2) The first aircraft carrier designed and built as such. Sunk by Japanese bombers off Ceylon, 1942. (3) Light fleet carrier, served as Adm Woodward's flagship in the Falklands War (1982); now sold to India as the *Virant*.

Hermon, Mount *see* ARAB-ISRAELI WARS.

Herr, Lt Gen Traugott (1890–1976). Ger. Commander LXXVI Panzer Corps in the Italian campaign until November 1944; then temporary Commander Fourteenth Army before taking over Tenth Army, February 1945.

Hess, Rudolf (1894–1987). Ger. Joined the Nazi Party in 1920; helped Hitler write *Mein Kampf* during their imprisonment at Landsberg after the Munich

Rudolf Hess: Hitler's absconding deputy

Putsch. Hitler's private secretary 1925–32; appointed Deputy Leader, April 21 1933. Thereafter received other senior posts; nominated as Hitler's successor after Göring. On May 10 1941, acting on his own initiative, he flew himself to Scotland, hoping that a casual acquaintanceship with the Duke of Hamilton would enable him to be received by the British government for peace negotiations. Instead, Hess was imprisoned for the rest of the war and at Nuremberg was sentenced to life imprisonment. Held at Spandau prison in Berlin, he committed suicide in 1987. *MS*.

Heusinger, Gen Adolf (b.1897). Ger. Chief of Operations Section, German Army General Staff, 1940–44; Chairman, NATO Military Committee, 1961–1964.

Hewitt, Adm Henry Kent (1887–1972). US. Amphibious warfare expert; directed Atlantic Fleet amphibious training, 1942. Commanded US naval forces in "Torch" landings and Sicily invasion; headed Allied naval forces at Salerno, Anzio and landings in Southern France.

Heydrich, Reinhard (1904–42). Ger. Cashiered from German navy for immoral conduct 1931, thereupon joined Nazi SS; at once made head of security; organized concentration camps from 1933; initiated "Final Solution" of Jewish question; appointed *Reichsprotektor* in Prague 1941; mortally wounded there by two Czechoslovak SOE agents, May 1942.

Hickam Field *see* PEARL HARBOR.

High Wood. Situated on the brow of a rise behind and between Bazentin le Petit and Delville Wood on the Somme battlefield, High Wood was in the rear of the German second main defensive line south of the Albert-Bapaume Road in July 1916. Having wasted an apparent opportunity to gain a foothold in the wood immediately after the successful dawn attack in the sector on July 14 1916, the British were forced to engage in a costly two-month struggle for this important position. The wood was finally cleared by the 47th (London) Division, September 15 1916.

Hill 861 *see* HILL FIGHTS, VIETNAM.

Hill 70. This prominent knoll, overlooking Lens in France, was attacked, though not held, by British troops of the 15th (Scottish) and Guards Divisions during the Battle of Loos, September 1915. It was eventually captured by the Canadian Corps in August 1917.

Hill 875 *see* DAK TO, BATTLE OF.

Hill 881 *see* HILL FIGHTS, VIETNAM.

Hill 937 *see* A SHAU, BATTLES OF.

Hill Fights, Vietnam (1967). In April–May 1967, US Marines and troops of the People's Army of Vietnam (PAVN) battled for control of Hills 861, 881 North and 881 South around Khe Sanh combat base. The Marines triggered the fights by discovering a regiment of the PAVN 325C Division that was preparing to attack Khe Sanh. The Marines needed massive air and artillery support to push the PAVN off the hills, with heavy losses on both sides.

Hill, Vice Adm Harry Wilbur (1890–1971). US. Hill commanded the heavy cruiser *Wichita*, escorting North Atlantic convoys, in 1942. In the Pacific, he led Battleship Division 4 in naval actions at Guadalcanal, 1942, and covered the landings on New Georgia, Solomons, July 1943. Thereafter he commanded amphibious groups at Tarawa, Kwajalein-Eniwetok and supervised the Saipan and the Tinian landings, July–August 1944, and Okinawa, 1945. He directed the occupation of southern Japan, September–October 1945.

H

H

Fighter commander Sir Roderick Hill

Hill, Air Chief Marshal Sir Roderick (1894–1954). Br. Air Marshal Commanding, Air Defence of Great Britain, 1943–44, AOC-in-C, Fighter Command 1944–45. Hill was intellectually gifted and well able to understand the advice of scientists. This was especially relevant because the main threat to Britain while he commanded her air defences came from entirely new developments, namely, the German V-1 and V-2 weapons. There was no means of active defence against the latter, but Hill's skilful deployment of his fighters produced very effective results against the former. He recognized the great importance of anti-aircraft guns in any scheme of defence against the V-1s and, earlier than Anti-Aircraft Command itself, he foresaw the need for the forward deployment of the guns as opposed to their concentration around the expected targets. When this was done, the V-1 campaign was virtually defeated. *ANF.*

Hillenkoeter, Rear Adm Roscoe Henry (1897–1982). US. Naval intelligence staff, Pacific, 1942–43; first director of CIA, 1947–50.

Himmelbett. German night fighter control station consisting of a Freya and two Würzburgs, one to plot the fighter and the other the bomber. In 1942 Kammhuber organized them in zones to cover the approaches to Germany.

Himmler, *Reichsführer* Heinrich (1900–1945). Ger. An early member of the Nazi Party, Himmler was given command of the SS in 1929 and built it into a cornerstone of the Third Reich. He organized the persecution and repression of Hitler's enemies both inside and

outside the party and was directly responsible for the implementation of the "Final Solution" and the concentration camp system. Although late in World War II his duties included the Ministry of the Interior and command of Army Group Vistula, he was ill-equipped to carry out his tasks. Arrested by British forces, he committed suicide on May 23 1945. *MS.*

Hindenburg, Field Marshal (later President) Paul von (1847–1934). Ger. Hindenburg was decorated for bravery at Königgrätz in 1866 and in the war against France in 1870–71. He retired in 1911 after commanding the IV Army Corps, but was recalled in August 1914 to replace von Prittwitz following the Battle of Gumbinnen and took over the German Eighth Army in East Prussia on August 22, with Ludendorff as his COS. While the victories at Tannenberg in August and the Masurian Lakes in September 1914 undoubtedly owed more to the planning of Ludendorff and Hoffmann, or even to Russian blunders, than to any contribution of Hindenburg, he carried the ultimate responsibility and then and subsequently acted as a steadying influence upon Ludendorff, who was prone to fits of doubt and apprehension. A national idol as a result of Tannenberg, Hindenburg was appointed C-in-C of the German armies on the Eastern Front on November 1 1914, with Ludendorff and Hoffmann still at his side. Hindenburg shared Ludendorff's illusion that the Eastern Front was the decisive theatre, a belief which caused repeated disputes with Falkenhayn. When Falkenhayn fell from grace, Hindenburg succeeded him as CGS on August 29 1916, Ludendorff becoming his "First Quartermaster-General". Hindenburg's legendary reputation, added to the swift defeat of Romania and the ending of the costly struggle at Verdun, served initially to reassure the German people but, for the remainder of the war, he allowed Ludendorff to dominate him almost completely and lent his authority to many of the latter's more extreme war aims. Even as a figurehead, therefore, Hindenburg played his part in the strategic and political mistakes which determined the extent of Germany's

defeat in 1918. Elected President of the Weimar Republic in 1925, he was re-elected in 1932, although his increasing senility enabled von Papen and others, including his own son Oskar, to persuade him to appoint Hitler as Chancellor in January 1933. *PJS.*

Hindenburg Line. To economize on manpower and to replace the costly linear defence tactics of previous years, the Germans, from September 1916 onwards, not only began to evolve a new doctrine of flexible and mobile defence-in-depth but also initiated the construction of fresh positions behind the existing Western Front. The most important section of this new fortified belt ran from Arras, through St Quentin, to a point east of Soissons and, although called the *Siegfried Stellung* by the Germans, was known to the British as the Hindenburg Line. By withdrawing to the Hindenburg Line between February and April 1917 – implementing a "scorched earth" policy as they did so – the Germans abandoned the huge Noyon salient and shortened their front by 25 miles (40km), freeing up to 14 divisions. The *Siegfried Stellung* was not merely a "line" but rather a series of defensive zones. The "outpost zone", some 600yd (550m) deep, was manned by small squads in shallow concrete dugouts. Behind this was the main "battle zone", up to 2,500yd (2,300m) deep and containing the first and second trench lines as well as a network of skilfully-sited concrete machine gun emplacements. The trenches were protected by thick belts of wire, laid out in a zig-zag pattern to enable machine guns to sweep the angles. A "rear zone" and then a fourth zone were subsequently added, bringing the Hindenburg Line to a depth of 6,000–8,000yd (5,500–7,300m). Despite their formidable nature, the main Hindenburg defences were decisively breached in the British offensive operations of September-October 1918. *PJS.*

Hipper, Adm Franz Ritter von (1863–1932). Ger. Commander of the German Scouting Force at Jutland. C-in-C, the High Seas Fleet August–November 1918. Hipper, who was often the direct opponent of Beatty, several times had the better of the exchange. He led the naval attacks on the British east coast in 1914, in which he proved to be too elusive for the defenders, but in the action at Dogger Bank in January 1915, he suffered a reverse when Beatty caught him with a superior force. He lost the cruiser *Blücher* and very nearly his flagship, *Seydlitz*. At Jutland, in the initial battlecruiser confrontation, the outcome was much more in Hipper's favour. Although in a five to six inferiority, he sank two of Beatty's battlecruisers, *Indefatigable* and *Queen Mary*, without loss to himself. As the battle developed and the battlecruiser scouting forces became absorbed into the main action, Hipper's flagship, *Lützow*, was sunk and he had to transfer for a time to a destroyer. Although Hipper, like Beatty, was doubtful of the wisdom of some of his c-in-c's orders, there has probably been less controversy about the brilliance of his leadership than has been the case, perhaps, with any other admiral at Jutland.

After Jutland, the High Seas Fleet never again effectively came out. The morale of its men declined and when Hipper became c-in-c, it was nearly a spent force. In October 1918 mutinies broke out but Hipper had no real responsibility for the collapse. *ANF.*

Hirohito: obscure wartime role

Hirohito, Emperor of Japan (1901–1989). The 124th god-emperor in a line descended from the sun goddess Amaterasu, Hirohito acceded in 1926. Himself scholarly and withdrawn, he presided over a period of extreme militarism in which his personal role was, and will likely remain, obscure. He may have approved (if only by not opposing) the aggressive policies culminating in World War II, and certainly evoked the suicidal devotion of Japanese servicemen. In 1945 – at some personal risk, and realizing that the Imperial status would be forever changed – he supported the peace faction, personally announcing Japan's surrender over the radio on August 16. Although China, Australia and New Zealand pressed for his trial as a war criminal, MacArthur recognized Hirohito's value as a focus of political stability in the reconstruction of Japan. Renouncing his divinity, he became a constitutional monarch. *RO'N.*

Hiroshima, atomic attack on. Hiroshima, a major military base and naval port, Japan's seventh largest city, was chosen as the primary target of the first atomic bomb. At 0245 hours on August 6 1945, the B-29 Superfortress *"Enola Gay"* took off from North Field, Tinian, Mariana Islands, on "General Bombing Mission 13". The aircraft, from USAAF's 509th Composite Group, was seven tons overweight and, with a crew of nine, four scientists and its "Little Boy" atomic bomb struggled to clear the runway. It was accompanied by two observer B-29s. As a safety precaution the bomb was armed in flight and, with favourable weather conditions over the target, the pilot, Col Paul Tibbets, began his bombing run at 0811. The bomb was released by bomb-aimer Maj Thomas Ferebee shortly after 0815 hours from a height of six miles. "Enola Gay" made a sharp turn and less than one minute later the bomb exploded at a height of 1,850 feet. The city's air-raid warning system had not reacted to "Enola Gay" and the inhabitants were therefore denied even the scant protection of conventional shelters. The fireball generated a ground temperature of 6,000 degrees C.; thermal radiation vaporized thousands of people and buildings and burnt and scorched everything within a radius of two miles. A shock wave of tremendous force increased the destruction, flattening nearly everything in its path. People still on the streets were prey to flying debris caught in the fierce winds generated by the explosion, while these same winds fanned raging fires. Apart from the dead and wounded, thousands more soon succumbed to the effects of radiation. Figures for casualties vary enormously, both because of the total chaos occasioned by the bomb and because of the ultimately incalculable after-effects of radiation. However, figures of approximately 70,000 killed and 70,000 wounded are generally accepted, with the numbers eventually dying of radiation poisoning amounting to some 200,000. *MS.*

Hiryu. Japanese aircraft carrier. Slightly modified version of *Soryu* with greater tonnage (21,900 tons full load) and (unusually) the "island" superstructure on the port side of the flight deck. Completed 1939. With her sister in the Pearl Harbor attack and subsequent raids on Darwin, Ceylon etc. Sank after dive-bombing, Midway (1941).

Hitler, Adolf (1889–1945). Ger. Born in Braunau am Inn in Austria, Hitler's character and many of his political and social attitudes were formed during a frustrating period spent as an unsuccessful artist in Vienna. On the outbreak of World War I, he joined the German Army, becoming a dispatch runner in the 16th Bavarian Infantry Regiment. Serving on the Western Front, Hitler was wounded and gassed and, although he failed to rise above the rank of lance-corporal, he was awarded the Iron Cross. After the war he acted as a political agent for the army in Munich, investigating the activities of the German Workers' Party. But observation changed to participation and, by July 1921, Hitler had become its chairman, changing its name to the National Socialist German Workers' Party (NSDAP). Steadily the characteristics of the Nazi Party began to develop; the swastika, stormtroopers, vehement anti-semitism and violent recriminations against the Treaty of Versailles and the Weimar politicians who had negotiated it. Still politically naive, in November 1923, he mounted an ill-fated putsch in Munich. Convicted for this foolhar-

Chancellor Adolf Hitler with President von Hindenburg, 1933

dy effort, he emerged from Landesberg prison with a more considered political approach. Although he maintained his use of strong-arm tactics, he simultaneously courted powerful conservative elements in society who sought to use him as a tool against the communist threat. The Nazis' votes increased throughout the early 1930s and on January 30 1933 Hitler was appointed Chancellor (although his triumph came at a time when the Nazis' performance at the polls began to slip). Having secured power by "legal" means, he exploited his position to eliminate all opposition to his regime, including, on the "Night of the Long Knives", those within his own party. Domestically, he took action to alleviate the effects of the depression while focusing popular discontent upon the communists and Jews. He also won support from large sections of the armed forces by adopting a policy of rearmament. Hitler's foreign policy mesmerized his countrymen and foreign diplomats alike with a series of spectacular coups, notably the annexation of the Saar, Rhineland, Austria, Sudetenland and Memel. Finally, with the invasion of Poland in September 1939, he achieved a stunning victory but involved Germany in a world war for which its armed forces were ill-prepared. In the opening campaigns, Hitler's intuitive grasp of blitzkrieg tactics surprised his adversaries and many of his own generals. But success brought over-confidence and resulted in his taking command of Germany's armies in December 1941. He proved unequal to the task, especially as sycophants protected him from adverse reports, compounding his own failure to appreciate the realities of strategic and tactical problems. He interfered in his generals' conduct of operations and developed a questionable faith in the salvation offered by forlorn offensives and secret weapons. He committed suicide in Berlin on April 30 1945. *MS.*

Hitler Line. Constructed across the Liri Valley north of Cassino as a reserve position behind the Gustav Line. It was breached by I Canadian Corps (Burns) on May 23 1944 during Alexander's "Diadem" offensive to take Rome.

Hitler Youth. Compulsory Nazi organization for boys (*Hitler Jugend*) and girls (*Bund Deutscher Mädel*).

Hiyo. Japanese aircraft carrier. *Junyo* class; converted while building from liner; completed 1942. In action at Guadalcanal, and at Philippine Sea where she was sunk by aircraft torpedoes (1944).

Hoa Binh, Battle of (1951–52). French forces occupied the town of Hoa Binh, 47 miles (75km) west of Hanoi, in November 1951 for the purpose of blocking a vital communist supply line and influencing debate in Paris. Though direct attacks by the People's Army (PAVN) failed to dislodge the French, attacks on access routes and the spreading of insecurity in the Red River delta forced the French to abandon Hoa Binh on February 24 1952. The battle revealed the greatly improved ability of communist forces to operate on a sustained basis and declining French offensive capability.

Hoa Hao. A religious sect, a variant of Theravada Buddhism; founded in 1939 in the Mekong delta of southern Vietnam. By the late 1940s the sect had one million followers (1.5 milion in 1970) and rivalled the communists for influence on the peasantry. Like the Cao Dai, the Hoa Hao had their own armed forces and considerable autonomy in areas where they were concentrated. The sect cooperated with the communists against the French but switched allegiance in 1947.

In 1955, Ngo Dinh Diem dispersed the Hoa Hao army along with the Cao Dai and Binh Xuyen, but the sect remained influential. Though declining zeal and sectarian disunity let the communists make inroads into Hoa Hao areas, sect villages generally resisted communist control; armed Hoa Hao bands continued to fight after Saigon's fall in 1975. *WST.*

Hoang Xuan Lam, Lt Gen (b.1928). Republic of Vietnam. Commander of the Army of the Republic of Vietnam (ARVN) I Corps; responsible for the recapture of Hue in the 1968 Tet offensive and for organizing the South Vietnamese force that was sent into Laos during Operation "Lam Son 719" in 1971. President Thieu replaced Lam with the more dynamic Ngo Quang Truong following the North Vietnamese attack on Quang Tri in spring 1972.

Hobart. Australian guided missile destroyer that relieved a US destroyer off the coast of central Vietnam near Chu Lai on March 31 1967. Thus Australia became the first American ally to make a tri-service (land, sea, air) contribution to the war. Under Australian command but US Navy operational control, *Hobart* engaged in shore bombardment, picket duties for carriers and coastal patrolling.

H

The emergence of air power

Dr Noble Frankland CB, CBE, DFC
Official historian of the Strategic Air Offensive of World War II and former Director of the Imperial War Museum

Within 42 years of man's first heavier-than-air powered flight, two aircraft were enough to destroy two major cities in two attacks. The Wright brothers achieved their first flight on December 17 1903; two B-29 aircraft dropped the first two atomic bombs on Hiroshima and Nagasaki on August 6 and 9 1945.

Air power brought destruction on the scale of the battlefield to the hearts of belligerent nations. Germany and Japan were the principal victims of this development. The ultimate in piston-driven heavy bombers was the aircraft shown here, the American B-29.

The origins of of this extraordinary development may be traced to the discovery of hydrogen gas by Cavendish in 1760, for this provided man with the capacity to take off from the Earth's previously constraining surface. In January 1785, a Frenchman, Blanchard and an American, Jeffries, crossed the English Channel in a gas-filled balloon. Within another ten years, balloons began to play a part in warfare. At the Battle of Fleurus in 1794, the French General Jourdan used them to reconnoitre the Austrian lines. Balloons appeared over the battlefields of Italy in 1859 and America during the Civil War, while during the siege of Paris of 1870-71, Gambetta himself left the capital by air to join a relieving army in the south of France. Meanwhile, on September 24 1852, Giffard had made a powered flight from Paris in an elongated balloon carrying a steam engine to drive the propeller. In 1883, the brothers Tissandier flew with an electrically-driven propeller, and in 1900 Count Zeppelin ascended in an aluminium airship of 420ft (128m) in length driven by four propellers powered by two 16-horsepower Daimler engines. This was the forerunner of the Zeppelins, the first long-range bombers with which the Germans were to attack England from the early stages of World War I. However, the Wright brothers' flight was a much more portentous event. Although the general and naval staffs of the great powers were not in a hurry to recognize the fact, the apparatus of a revolution in warfare now existed. Within Orville Wright's lifetime (1871-1948), its effects could be measured.

Early developments

War is a great accelerator of invention and the exploitation of it. If peace had generally prevailed in the first half of the 20th century, as it more or less had done for most of the 19th, the ingredients provided by Count Zeppelin and the Wright brothers would, no doubt, have been slow to mature and the ways in which they did develop might well have proved irrelevant to the needs of warfare. The great passenger liners of the North Atlantic route, which had been developed in the era of peace, had war roles, it is true, but they were never of decisive war-like significance. Even the Dreadnought battleships, which had been designed for war but built in peacetime, played a much less important part than their creators had expected. War itself, much more than the prospect of it, generates the most important advances in the machines and weapons which make it increasingly ruinous. Airships and aeroplanes were seized by the compelling appetite of war when they were scarcely beyond their early infancy.

The chief thing, it seemed, which the new flying machines could do in war was to survey the enemy, as the French balloons had done in 1794, but the difference between that beginning and the situation in 1914 was that aeroplanes and dirigible airships had the potential of fighting each other. As intelligence of enemy movements obtained from the air was valuable (in fact, it played a useful part in the opening battles in France in 1914), it paid an opponent to try to prevent its collection. The result was that pilots and observers soon began to arm themselves with revolvers, rifles and even duck guns with which to shoot at each other, and designers began to think of aircraft, not simply as vehicles of observation, but as fighting machines. These began to appear in 1915 when machine guns, which had already made such an impact on land, took to the air and the first "fighter" aircraft began to do battle with each other. The British adapted their

original machines for the purpose; the Germans took the lead by introducing one tailor-made for the job. This was the Fokker monoplane fitted with an interrupter gear to make it possible to fire through the propeller circumference and thus to aim the aircraft at its target. A fundamental principle of air power emerged. The ulterior object, observation of the enemy army in this case, could only be achieved if enemy aeroplanes could be prevented from interfering unduly or if air superiority, as it was later called, could be won. The appearance of the Fokker monoplane in May 1915 placed a new meaning on this.

In another respect, too, the Germans led the way. If aircraft could fly over the enemy lines and look at them, could they not also drop explosives and could they not fly beyond the lines and bomb targets behind them? Both sides soon began to attempt such things, but the results were restricted by the limited ranges of the aeroplanes and their small weight-lifting capacity. The German Zeppelins, however, were a different matter; they could cruise for hours on end and carry much greater loads than any contemporary heavier-than-air flying machine. The Germans, who had already bombarded some coastal towns in England with naval gunfire, now decided upon a Zeppelin bombing offensive against England. The first target was Yarmouth on the night of January 19-20 1915. Thereafter the attack was developed until, on the night of May 31-June 1 1915, 14 airships dropped nearly a ton of bombs on London. This caused shock and outrage out of all proportion to the actual damage done, because the island British, used to comparative immunity from the effects of war, had not expected any such intrusion. There also seemed to be no means of defence against the attacks. Indeed, there were 51 such air raids during the war, in which nearly 200 tons of bombs were dropped and some 557 people were killed. Nevertheless, as fighter aircraft and anti-aircraft guns were brought to bear against the large, slow moving and highly inflammable Zeppelins, they suffered growing casualties and, in the course of 1916, it became apparent that something much faster and more manoeuvrable than an airship was needed if that sort of attack was to be maintained and increased.

The German determination to find a solution to the Zeppelin debacle produced a chain reaction which governed the nature of air power until the arrival of guided missiles and nuclear weapons. An understanding of this provides the key to air warfare from 1917 to 1945. It is amazing that it could have occurred so early in the history of heavier-than-air flight, and that is one of the reasons

Unequal combat. The German Fokker Monoplane began to operate over the Western Front in May 1915. It was specially designed and equipped for combat with opposing aircraft and was the first "fighter" or "pursuit" aircraft in history. One of the many advantages it enjoyed over its general purpose predecessors was its ability to fire "through" the propeller, the blades of which were protected by an interrupter gear. This enabled the pilot to bring his opponent into his gunsight by aiming his machine at the target. This proved far superior to the more limited manoeuvre available to the BE2c with its free gun rotated on a ring by the observer. The Fokker Monoplane was designed around its gun; the BE2c was an observation aeroplane to which armament had been added as an afterthought. The combat between the two demonstrated the inevitability of specialization in the design of military aircraft and resulted in a design race and fluctuating air ascendancy. In the spring of 1915, the Fokker Monoplane reigned supreme.

195

why it was so imperfectly understood by those who caused it and by others who followed to try to exploit its characteristics for the purposes of the war aims of their various countries in both world wars and other conflicts. We must, therefore, now master the narrative of these events and consider the meaning of each development.

The advent of the Gotha

Early in 1917 the Germans brought a new breed of aircraft into service. This was the twin-engined Gotha, the first authentic long-range heavy bomber in the history of aviation. It could fly 80mph (129kph) and reach 15,000ft (4,600m) with a 660lb (300kg) bomb load. In April, flying from captured Belgian bases, the first Gotha squadrons began probing attacks on southeast England. These were gradually extended until, on June 13 1917, a formation of 14 Gothas appeared over the centre of London in broad daylight. They dropped 118 bombs, secured a direct hit on

Liverpool Street Station and killed 160 people (including 25 women and 43 children). Nearly 100 British fighters went up to engage the German bombers, but all returned safely to their Belgian bases. There was a public outcry far outdoing that which had followed the Zeppelin raids; it amounted virtually to a panic and this quickly spread to the Government. The Prime Minister, Lloyd George, bent to the wind at once and an immediate military consequence followed. Two squadrons of fighters were withdrawn from France to reinforce the defences of London and the Government ordered an inquiry into what was to be done about this seemingly unanswerable threat.

To deal with it, their choice fell upon General Smuts. They needed someone whose words would carry weight, not simply with the military, but also with the public, for this was a matter which the 14 Gothas had carried beyond the headquarters of generals and the committee rooms of ministers to the arena of democracy. The point was

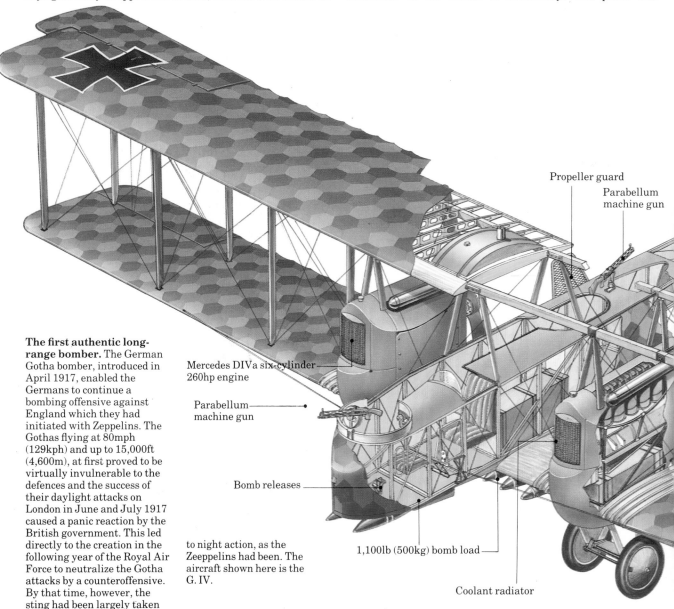

The first authentic long-range bomber. The German Gotha bomber, introduced in April 1917, enabled the Germans to continue a bombing offensive against England which they had initiated with Zeppelins. The Gothas flying at 80mph (129kph) and up to 15,000ft (4,600m), at first proved to be virtually invulnerable to the defences and the success of their daylight attacks on London in June and July 1917 caused a panic reaction by the British government. This led directly to the creation in the following year of the Royal Air Force to neutralize the Gotha attacks by a counteroffensive. By that time, however, the sting had been largely taken out of the Gothas by fighter defences and they were driven

to night action, as the Zeeppelins had been. The aircraft shown here is the G. IV.

Mercedes DIVa six-cylinder 260hp engine

Parabellum machine gun

Bomb releases

1,100lb (500kg) bomb load

Coolant radiator

Propeller guard

Parabellum machine gun

underlined, for at the very time at which the Cabinet met on July 11 to decide upon Smuts' appointment, the Gothas appeared again over central London.

Smuts' report was finished within five weeks and was placed before the Cabinet on August 17 1917. For those who were full of anxiety, it was gratifyingly radical. It recommended the creation of an entirely new fighting service to deal with the war in the air, which would be independent of the Navy and the Army. The idea behind this extraordinary proposal was that, although some improvements could be made to the defence of the country, and particularly of London, from air attack, there was no prospect of an effective defence. In other words, the advantage was seen as lying with the offensive bombers. The fundamental solution, therefore, lay not in air defence, but in counter-air offence. Britain must mount a bomber offensive against Germany which would dwarf, and therefore presumably eventually deter, German bombing of Britain. Nor was this by any means all. General Smuts concluded that this bombing would be so effective that it would become the principal way of waging war, rendering the existing forms of land and sea warfare secondary and subordinate. If this was so, the control and direction of a bombing offensive would be a specialized business of the greatest importance meriting a specialized staff and command which would be independent of traditional naval and military control. This was why Smuts recommended that the Royal Flying Corps and the Royal Naval Air Service should be amalgamated, removed from their naval and military overlords, formed into a new fighting service and placed under the control of an air ministry and an air staff. Even more remarkable than

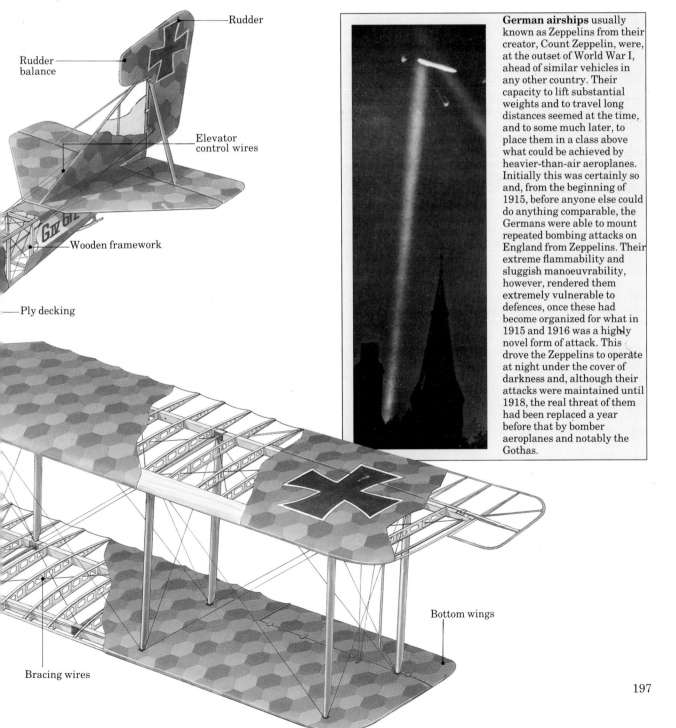

Rudder

Rudder balance

Elevator control wires

Wooden framework

Ply decking

Bracing wires

Bottom wings

German airships usually known as Zeppelins from their creator, Count Zeppelin, were, at the outset of World War I, ahead of similar vehicles in any other country. Their capacity to lift substantial weights and to travel long distances seemed at the time, and to some much later, to place them in a class above what could be achieved by heavier-than-air aeroplanes. Initially this was certainly so and, from the beginning of 1915, before anyone else could do anything comparable, the Germans were able to mount repeated bombing attacks on England from Zeppelins. Their extreme flammability and sluggish manoeuvrability, however, rendered them extremely vulnerable to defences, once these had become organized for what in 1915 and 1916 was a highly novel form of attack. This drove the Zeppelins to operate at night under the cover of darkness and, although their attacks were maintained until 1918, the real threat of them had been replaced a year before that by bomber aeroplanes and notably the Gothas.

these proposals was their immediate acceptance by the government and their rapid translation into action.

The new service, the Royal Air Force, came into being on April 1 1918. Even before that, steps had been taken to start a sustained bombing offensive against Germany. The irony was that by this time the Gothas had been defeated by the British air defences. It was not only the performance of bombers which had taken a leap forward; so had that of fighters. The immunity which the Gothas had originally enjoyed was short-lived. Higher perform-ance fighters made life too dangerous in daylight: the Gothas sought the cover of darkness by changing to night attack, but this too had its hazards. Of the 60 bombers which the Germans lost in their attacks on Britain in 1917 and 1918, 36 were destroyed in crashes on returning to their Belgian bases. Nor was the achievement of the offensive, apart from its effect upon the British govern-ment, of any great consequence. It killed 835 people and injured another 1,972. By comparison with what was happening in the apparently about-to-be-outmoded land battles, and even the naval actions, this was chicken-feed. These facts, the defeat of the Gotha offensive by the defences and the relatively minor consequences of them, seemed to go unnoticed; at any rate the government held to its course of implementing the Smuts report, which was founded on such very different assumptions.

The Independent Force

Meanwhile, the main activity of British air power con-tinued, as it had begun, to be the support of the army in the field, but efforts were now made to form an element specifically devoted to the task of bombing Germany. This began as the 41st Wing, developed into VIII Brigade and, on June 6 1918, it became the Independent Force. The choice of the term "Independent" signalized the principle that these bomber aircraft were reserved for the attack upon Germany and were not available for absorption in the land battle in France, where the tasks were spotting artillery fire, bombing enemy supply dumps, carrying out reconnaissance and fighting for superiority over German air strength in the immediate vicinity of the front. The device more or less succeeded and, in the five months which remained of the war, the Independent Force carried out 239 raids, nearly all of which were on industrial complexes, transportation targets and aerodromes in the nearer parts of Germany. These attacks, which involved the dropping of 543 tons of bombs, had only a marginal effect upon the war, which was dominated by the great land battles which followed the failure of the German offensives in March and April 1918.

The operations of the Independent Force in 1918 were, however, expected to be no more than the prelude to something altogether on a much larger scale. The RAF was developing a new heavy bomber, the four-engined Hand-ley Page V/1500. It was to have the range to fly to Berlin and back from bases in Norfolk and the capacity to lift a 3,300lb bomb. Although 225 of these aircraft were ordered, only three had been delivered at the time of the armistice. The impact upon the war of the Independent Force remained, therefore, as an aspiration which had been overtaken by the victory of conventional forces before it could be realized. It was not to be until 1936 that Bomber Command, directly descended from the Indepen-dent Force, was created and a specification issued for an updated version of the V/1500, which eventually produced the Stirling, Halifax and Lancaster.

The interwar debate

The trial by ordeal of the conclusions reached in the Smuts report was postponed but, in the 20 years of interlude, the matters were hotly contested in theoretical debate. Those claiming that long-range bombing would always meet its Waterloo when the opposing air defences got organized could cite the examples of the Zeppelins and the Gothas, but they could not prove that the V/1500s or some later super-bomber would not break the cycle. Those observing that the effects of strategic bombing in the whole of World War I had produced only insignificant results could not prove that larger and more efficient forces might not realize the expectations of the Smuts report. Indeed, the opposite of these arguments tended to be the easier to win, because the first flush of wonder at the conquest of the air was still far from exhausted and there was a natural inclination to wonder, if 14 bombers could kill 160 people, how many 225 could kill, and so on. Indeed, in the interval between the two world wars, apprehension of the second one centred to a large extent upon the fear of bombing, especially in Britain, the only country which had an

Trenchard. Chief of the British Air Staff until 1929. He was the driving force behind the early Royal Air Force and its doctrine of defence against bombing attack by heavier counterattack.

independent air force and a professional plan for a strategic bombing offensive.

General Trenchard, the Commander of the Royal Flying Corps in France during the war, had been strongly opposed to the proposal to establish the Royal Air Force, of which he was later regarded, rather to his own irritation, as the Father. He had thought that the result would be a diminution of the air resources necessary to sustain the army, which he regarded as a much more important commitment than any plan for the bombing of Germany. After the war, when he was no longer bound by the ties of loyalty to his former Commander-in-Chief, Haig, he adopted the opposite point of view. As Chief of the Air Staff he remained at the helm for ten years, much longer than any of his successors, and developed a theory of air power, often referred to as the Trenchard doctrine, which became the governing factor in the British conduct of air warfare, and to a great extent of the American too. The principles of air power, according to the Trenchard doctrine, were that the heart of the matter was direct strategic bombing of the enemy heartland, that the moral effect of this in proportion to the physical would be twenty to one and that there could be no effective defence against such attack. If one route to the target could be blocked, another would be taken. If one ruse to deceive the enemy as to the route the bombers were taking failed, another would be available. Defensive fighter aircraft were a waste of effort and could be dispensed with except in so far as they were necessary as a sop to politicians and civil clamour. Naval and military operations, as Smuts had forecast, were subordinate and largely irrelevant; the air force could proceed over the lines, over the ships, directly to the sources of the enemy's war strength. Victory would be won by the side which maintained the heaviest bombing offensive for the longest.

While this doctrine was being hatched between 1919 and 1929, there was not much prospect of it being put to

"Air control" of the Northwest frontier of India.

the test. There was, at one time or another, talk of war with Turkey and then with France and, in the latter case, there was even some thought given to how a bombing offensive might be directed. It was obvious all the same that nothing much would happen, since the aircraft and crews to carry out such plans did not exist, nor in the political climate of the times was there much prospect of their being provided. Moreover, there were many who thought that the bombing of targets away from the battle zones was immoral and ought to be outlawed. Such a possibility was discussed internationally and Ramsay MacDonald's government seemed inclined to subscribe to a convention to that effect. Nothing, however, had been settled when Hitler arrived on the scene. The Trenchard doctrine was, so to speak, still on the books and the Royal Air Force still existed as an independent fighting service,

a fact which it owed, however, not so much to the Trenchard doctrine as to the economy with which it was considered that it could maintain order in difficult areas of British control, such as the Middle East and the North-west Frontier. This was done by punitive bombing raids, which proved to be much cheaper and at least as effective as military expeditions. This system, known as air control, convinced successive governments that it paid to retain the Royal Air Force. Otherwise, despite Trenchard's arguments, it would probably have been abolished and its remnants returned to the Army and Navy. Such was another of the ironies which punctuated the development of events from the Smuts report to the bombing of Germany in World War II. Another and a greater one was now at hand.

World war looms again

The German renunciation of the Versailles Treaty and subsequent rearmament programme quickly put Hitler not merely into a threatening position, but a commanding one. By 1936 the combination of his finesse and rumours of his military strength, which in truth was not yet very great, enabled him to embark upon a series of diplomatic triumphs, starting with the reoccupation of the Rhineland in 1936 and ending with the annexation of Sudetenland in 1938. One of his trump cards was the revived Luftwaffe which, through skilful propaganda, created an impression of devastating power. The British Air Staff now had to turn its attention not just to the bombing offensive which might be needed against Germany, but also, and even more urgently, to that of how to survive the Luftwaffe offensive, the "knockout blow" as they called it. In 1936, both thoughts were in mind when the air force was reorganized and multi-purpose regional forces were filtered into functional commands, which included Bomber Command to take the offensive and Fighter Command to defend the homeland. Three other steps of critical importance were also taken. First, specifications for high-performance monoplane interceptor fighters were brought forward, which led, with the usual deviations, to the Hurricane and the Spitfire. Second, a search began for some means of providing early warning of the approach of enemy bombers with sufficient precision and time-gap to enable defending fighters to engage them. This, through Tizard's Air Defence Committee, produced the radar chain. Third, a specification was issued for a very heavy long-range bomber to succeed the twin-engined Wellington, Whitley and Hampden, which were at that time coming into service. This led to the Stirling, the Halifax and, through the Manchester, to the Lancaster.

Despite their apparently overwhelming superiority, the Germans, in fact, matched only one of these measures: the production of a short-range, high-performance interceptor fighter which presently appeared as the Messerschmitt 109 – not a very useful machine for a knockout blow against Britain. They did begin to introduce radar systems, but these lacked most of the features which made Tizard's scheme so practicable and therefore effective. As to bombers, they seemed content with what was in the squadrons or the pipeline. These were broadly of the Wellington and Whitley vintage. No equivalent of the Lancaster was put in hand. General Wever, the chief advocate of German long-range bombing, had been killed in a flying accident at Dresden in 1936 and German aspirations for a four-engined heavy bomber curiously perished with him. There is some reason to suppose that

Hitler assumed that victory would be won before such a project could be got from the drawing board to the runway.

All the same, the British Air Staff was now in a very awkward position. The view that the bombing offensive would be the decisive element in air warfare and would far outweigh the value of any direct support which the Air Force might give to the Army and the Navy, looked fallible in the context of their own plans for Fighter Command vis-à-vis the German bombing offensive. Such an issue, however, largely eluded the newspapers and the House of Commons, where the fashion was to shout at each other about what they called air parity, or how the numbers of aircraft in the Luftwaffe compared with those in the Royal Air Force. Such arguments took little account of what types of aircraft were being counted or mis-counted. They nevertheless accounted for another, and perhaps the greatest, irony in the succession of develop-ments from the Smuts report. By 1938 the Government's pledge to maintain parity with the Luftwaffe seemed to have worn very thin. As far as aircraft production was concerned, numbers of units turned out became much more politically attractive than any consideration of what the units might be. The Government also wished to save its face at the minimum cost. The Air Staff, imbued with the principles of the Trenchard doctrine, wished priority in production to be given to bombers, but when the Minister for the Coordination of Defence, Sir Thomas Inskip, examined their programme, he inquired about the speeds of production and the unit costs of bombers as opposed to fighters. He had to be told that fighters could be built much faster than bombers. As fighters therefore amounted to cost-effective numbers, which was the consid-eration in air parity, Sir Thomas Inskip took the historic decision to reverse the Air Staff priority; he gave it to fighter production. Although the Air Staff considered that this was tantamount to losing the war before it had begun, and circulated memoranda within the Service to that effect, the decision turned out to be providential. It resulted in Fighter Command receiving enough aircraft, although no more than just enough of them, to fight the Battle of Britain two years later. Nor, in the long run, did it make much difference to Bomber Command, whose malaise was due to other reasons. Seldom in the realm of the political management of military affairs can such an ill-informed decision have had such a beneficial effect.

The impact of war

When war came the Air Staff could scarcely be blamed for taking the view that salvation lay in inaction. The strategic air offensive was deferred; Bomber Command was ordered to strike only at military and naval targets which could not possibly be taken to be anything else. The object was to avoid provocation which might unleash upon Britain the potentially more terrible offensive of the Luftwaffe. The Germans, however, proved to be unin-terested in strategic bombing, to which, since Wever's death, they had devoted little attention. They had concen-trated upon the development of aircraft and tactics which would support the advance of the army. Their school of thought was that aircraft, like tanks, were a means of producing the breakthrough, disorientation and defeat of the enemy army. The Spanish Civil War gave them the opportunity to test these ideas so that, before the blitz-krieg was attempted, they had gained some practical experience of their doctrines. The attack on Poland showed the effectiveness of the idea and gave the Germans

a further chance of perfecting their techniques before turning to destroy the French and British armies.

In the interval between the Polish and Norwegian campaigns, the British too made some revisions of their air doctrine in the light of the experience gained by Bomber Command in the so-called "phoney war". The main lesson was that heavy bombers could not survive in daylight, even in attacks of slight penetration. At night, however, the casualties suffered on very long-range flights were surprisingly low. Wellingtons attacking the German fleet by day were decimated, but Whitleys, ranging at night all over Germany as far as Berlin to drop leaflets, mostly came home. Fifty percent of the Wellingtons were shot down; hardly any of the Whitleys were battle casualties. Plans for a day offensive were virtually scrapped and the decision made that when the bombing offensive began it would be carried out at night. It was not, however, thought necessary to revise the targets which would be the objects of this offensive.

Although German bombing of Warsaw during their invasion of Poland was held to have removed any moral restraint upon Bomber Command retaliating in kind, the decision was that this would not be done until the Germans carried out such attacks nearer home or until the general war situation became so serious that heavy bombers must be used to redress it. When either of these eventualities arose, then Bomber Command would go into action under the pre-war plans, known as the Western Air Plans. These envisaged a range of targets, such as key points in the transportation system, oil plants, factories nourishing the enemy war effort and the like. Although these were of various sizes, all were essentially pinpoint targets. No one inquired how the crews would sight them at night. Radar in Bomber Command was still a thing of the future, nor had any systematic training in the basic skills of air navigation yet been instituted. The Whitleys, indeed, on their night missions had been all over the place, often far removed from the areas which they were theoretically saturating with propaganda leaflets. As far as their respective air doctrines were concerned, the Germans had made better use of the breathing space of the "phoney war" than the British; the French had done nothing at all.

Within a few days of the German attack on the West in May 1940, the grave situation which merited the opening of the British bombing offensive was judged to have arrived. After several anxious meetings, the War Cabinet authorized this and, on the night of May 15 1940, 99 aircraft of Bomber Command were dispatched to attack rail and oil targets in the Ruhr. As cameras were not carried, it was possible to take an optimistic view of the results achieved, but, as was gradually discovered in the course of the next 12 months, they were, in fact, negligi-ble. The success of the German air tactics, on the other hand, was evident for all to behold, as the troops who returned from Dunkirk were usually ready to explain.

Nevertheless, British faith in the value of a strategic air offensive was reinforced rather than diminished by these discouraging beginnings. This was partly due to the ignorance which prevailed about the real results of the bombing which had so far been attempted by Bomber Command; but more important than this was the lack of alternatives available to the Chiefs of Staff and the government. The British Army had been driven from the continent and, although a military campaign was begun in the Middle East and an attempt was made to re-open a

In the Battle of Britain, the German advantage lay in the superior numbers of Messerschmitt 109 high performance fighters which they possessed and the bases in Northwest France, which they had captured. The British advantage lay in her radar system which enabled her to plot the approach of enemy aircraft, (in the case of those from Northwest France, almost from take-off), and her possession of a small force of Spitfires, whose performance matched the Messerschmitt 109s, and a larger one of Hurricanes, which outmatched the Messerschmitt 110s and all types of German bombers.

Thus the Germans could win only if they could draw a decisive part of the British defences into action within Messerschmitt 109 range (southwest of the red line on the map) and destroy them. The short range of the Messerschmitt 109s, the need to protect the German bombers and the British radar advantage prevented them from doing so.

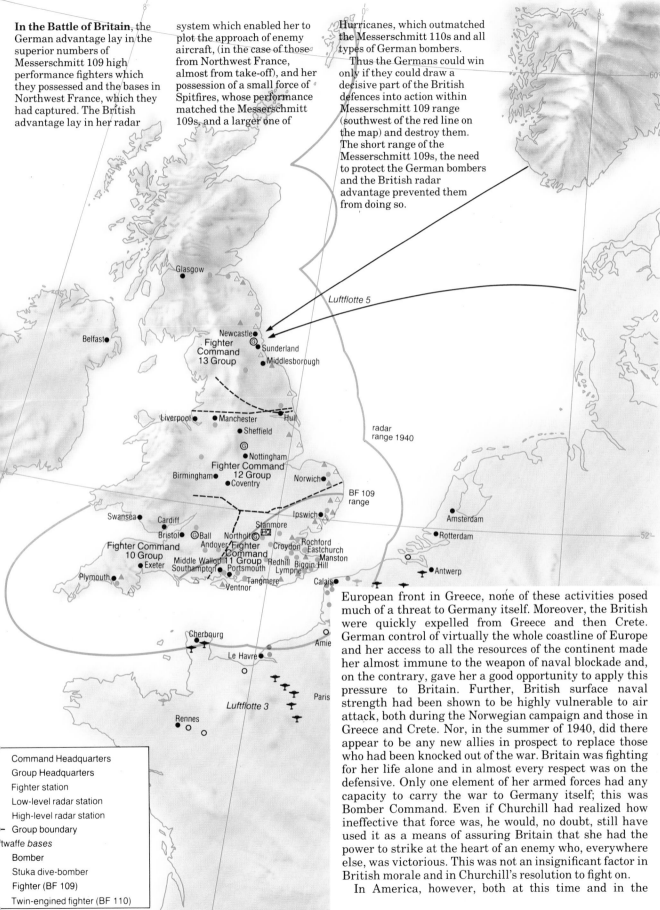

Legend
Command Headquarters
Group Headquarters
Fighter station
Low-level radar station
High-level radar station
Group boundary
Luftwaffe *bases*
Bomber
Stuka dive-bomber
Fighter (BF 109)
Twin-engined fighter (BF 110)

European front in Greece, none of these activities posed much of a threat to Germany itself. Moreover, the British were quickly expelled from Greece and then Crete. German control of virtually the whole coastline of Europe and her access to all the resources of the continent made her almost immune to the weapon of naval blockade and, on the contrary, gave her a good opportunity to apply this pressure to Britain. Further, British surface naval strength had been shown to be highly vulnerable to air attack, both during the Norwegian campaign and those in Greece and Crete. Nor, in the summer of 1940, did there appear to be any new allies in prospect to replace those who had been knocked out of the war. Britain was fighting for her life alone and in almost every respect was on the defensive. Only one element of her armed forces had any capacity to carry the war to Germany itself; this was Bomber Command. Even if Churchill had realized how ineffective that force was, he would, no doubt, still have used it as a means of assuring Britain that she had the power to strike at the heart of an enemy who, everywhere else, was victorious. This was not an insignificant factor in British morale and in Churchill's resolution to fight on.

In America, however, both at this time and in the

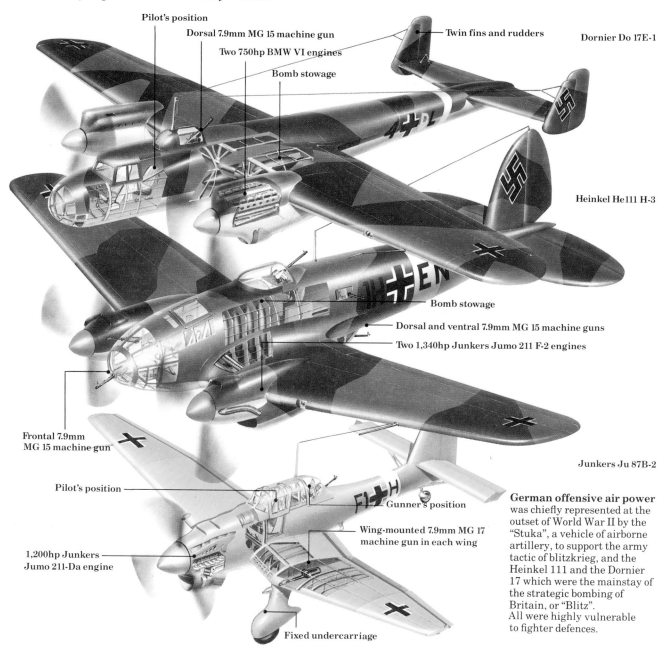

Pilot's position

Dorsal 7.9mm MG 15 machine gun

Two 750hp BMW VI engines

Bomb stowage

Twin fins and rudders

Dornier Do 17E-1

Heinkel He111 H-3

Bomb stowage

Dorsal and ventral 7.9mm MG 15 machine guns

Two 1,340hp Junkers Jumo 211 F-2 engines

Frontal 7.9mm
MG 15 machine gun

Junkers Ju 87B-2

Pilot's position

Gunner's position

Wing-mounted 7.9mm MG 17
machine gun in each wing

1,200hp Junkers
Jumo 211-Da engine

Fixed undercarriage

German offensive air power
was chiefly represented at the
outset of World War II by the
"Stuka", a vehicle of airborne
artillery, to support the army
tactic of blitzkrieg, and the
Heinkel 111 and the Dornier
17 which were the mainstay of
the strategic bombing of
Britain, or "Blitz".
All were highly vulnerable
to fighter defences.

following months, some of the shortcomings of British
night bombing had been perceived. The United States was
still a neutral power and continued to have diplomatic and
business representatives in Germany. They provided
first-hand information on the British raids which showed
them to be largely ineffective. This confirmed the American air planners in their conviction that effective bombing could only be achieved in daylight. The belief was that
the so-called "stratosphere" bomber, which was under
development and presently emerged as the B-17, would be
able to fly above the defences and hit pinpoint targets in
daylight. The fact that the weather in Texas was generally clearer than that over Europe was neglected, but the
American belief in day bombing, although doomed in the
short term, was ultimately to be of cardinal importance.

Meanwhile, disappointed in the expectation that Britain would sue for peace, Hitler ordered the invasion of the
country and directed the Luftwaffe to clear a straight path
for it. This resulted in the first major test of air power, in
which the issue, as it turned out, determined not simply

which side would gain the advantage for the time being,
but the outcome of the war. Had the Luftwaffe been able to
knock out Fighter Command, or even to gain a marked
advantage over it, then the German army could have
occupied Britain to the same extent that it already had
done or was about to do in the rest of Europe.

The general principle of the German air attack was
sound and anticipated many of the lessons which the rest
of the war taught. German bombers were used not so
much for the actual destruction of targets which they
hoped to achieve, as to pose the threat which would compel
Fighter Command to respond and therefore, the Germans
hoped, come under the guns of superior numbers of their
own fighters. Success in such a battle would have
neutralized the surviving elements of British air power
and also the operations in the immediate area of Britain's
surface naval strength. The clear path for invasion and
occupation would thus have been opened. The survivors of
Dunkirk and the Home Guard could scarcely have
maintained soldier-to-soldier and tank-to-tank defence.

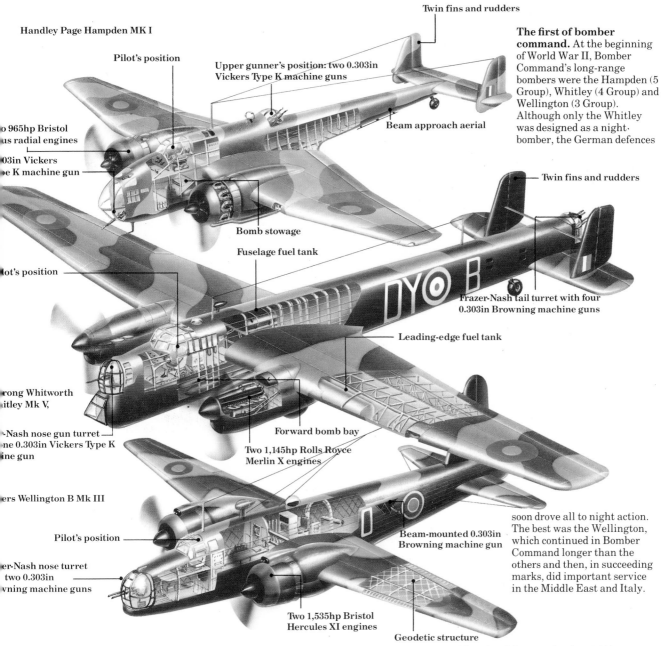

Twin fins and rudders

Handley Page Hampden MK I

Pilot's position

Upper gunner's position: two 0.303in Vickers Type K machine guns

Beam approach aerial

o 965hp Bristol
us radial engines

03in Vickers
e K machine gun

Bomb stowage

Fuselage fuel tank

The first of bomber command. At the beginning of World War II, Bomber Command's long-range bombers were the Hampden (5 Group), Whitley (4 Group) and Wellington (3 Group). Although only the Whitley was designed as a night-bomber, the German defences

Twin fins and rudders

lot's position

Frazer-Nash tail turret with four 0.303in Browning machine guns

Leading-edge fuel tank

rong Whitworth
itley Mk V,

-Nash nose gun turret
ne 0.303in Vickers Type K
ine gun

Forward bomb bay

Two 1,145hp Rolls Royce Merlin X engines

soon drove all to night action. The best was the Wellington, which continued in Bomber Command longer than the others and then, in succeeding marks, did important service in the Middle East and Italy.

ers Wellington B Mk III

Pilot's position

Beam-mounted 0.303in Browning machine gun

er-Nash nose turret
two 0.303in
vning machine guns

Two 1,535hp Bristol Hercules XI engines

Geodetic structure

Conditions would have been similar to those which had arisen in Norway, where, due to the distance from Britain and the fear of depleting the home air defence, Fighter Command could only make a marginal intervention, thus reproducing the situation which would have arisen if it had been defeated at the outset.

The correctness of the German strategic aim was not, however, matched by the tactics they adopted nor the equipment which they had available. As there were no means of fighting major battles between opposing fighters at night, the operations, if they were to lead to the destruction of the British fighter force, had to be carried out in daylight. The German bombers were lightly armed and lacked power-operated gun turrets, with the result that they became sitting ducks for the British fighters. This drew the German fighters into the main role of trying to defend their bombers as opposed to seeking and engaging the British fighters. Moreover, the best German fighters, the Messerschmitt 109s, lacked the range to stay long enough to exploit their potential, while their long-

range fighters, notably the Messerschmitt 110s, were seriously out-performed by the short-range interceptors of Fighter Command, the Hurricanes and Spitfires. Finally, the Germans chose to spread their attacks over much of southern England in an attempt to exploit the element of surprise. This meant they were often fighting at long range unnecessarily; nor did it create surprise, since it played into the very net which had been spread by the British radar chain. Thus, the Germans attacked not only at Britain's strongest point, but at the only point in which effectively she was dominant. The result of the first major air battle in history was a decisive victory for the defending force; it was a complete reversal of the expectations set out in the Smuts report and of those which had been incorporated into the Trenchard doctrine.

This, however, was not the way in which it was viewed at the time by either side, both of which drew the same conclusions. The Battle of Britain was not taken to mean that bombing could not be successful; it was read simply as a sign that it would have to be carried out at night, a tactic which the British had already adopted and to which the Germans now turned. Nor did the Battle of Britain suggest to either side that the main challenge of the future was to find the means of defeating the air defence of their opponent. Such an aim would depend upon the production of a fighter with the range of a bomber, yet with the performance to engage the defending fighters; that is, to do the very thing which the Messerschmitt 110s had failed to do. Greater range seemed to mean greater weight, and greater weight seemed to mean lower performance. A long-range fighter, it therefore seemed, would always be out-classed by a short-range interceptor. The solution, both sides concluded, lay in evading, not confronting, the opposing air defences; thus, the conversion of bomber forces to night action was brought about.

Night bombing

As was so often the case, the Germans took the lead and their night "Blitz" of the winter of 1940-41 was much more effective than the British attack on Germany. London, Birmingham, Bristol, Liverpool, Glasgow, Manchester and Coventry and many other towns felt the weight of war much more heavily than their equivalents in Germany. All the same they did not feel it heavily enough to produce any decisive effect upon the outcome of the war. Industries, such as those in Coventry, were broken up into smaller units and dispersed throughout remote parts of the country and, in addition to that, the means of intercepting the night bombers began to improve with the introduction of AI (Air Interception) and the development of specialized night fighting tactics.

The test of how the night bombing offensive would develop from these beginnings was left largely to the British for, in April 1941, the Germans turned away from Britain and towards the Balkans and Russia. Bomber Command, on the other hand, encouraged by the effectiveness of the German night bombing, by a force which, in comparison to what they were hoping to build up, was very weak, began to step up their campaign and the expectation of its outcome. There was the prospect of better machines to come and substantial reinforcement from the Commonwealth. Indeed, Australia, New Zealand and Rhodesia were to provide several first class squadrons and Canada an entire Bomber Group.

Two main lessons seemed to have emerged. First, the aim of hitting individual pinpoint targets, such as specific factories, was unprofitable. Aiming at night was not accurate enough and, as the factories usually lay on the edges of towns, most of the bombs meant for them tended to fall in open country. If, however, the bombs were aimed at the centres of the industrial towns, many of them would fall on factories and other important objectives. The rest would dislocate the town generally and demoralize, dehouse or kill the workers. The second lesson learnt from the Germans was that incendiary bombs were far more effective than previously thought. By starting fires which then spread of their own accord, incendiary bombs exploited the self-destructive nature of targets more than did high explosives.

The absorption of these lessons took a long time and it was not until the beginning of 1942 that the policy of night "area bombing" with a high proportion of incendiaries aimed at the centres of the main German industrial towns was explicitly laid down in the form of instructions from the Air Staff to the C-in-C, Bomber Command. Only in March, after the Cherwell minute had

been issued, was the plan approved by the Cabinet. Meanwhile, the Germans had turned away from strategic bombing and were once more concerned with the application of air power to the blitzkrieg. Although this brought them further successes, notably in the opening stages of the invasion of Russia, they were eventually to pay a heavy cost for leaving aside something which they themselves had been the first to exploit, namely, the strategic uses of air power. Nor, for geographical reasons among others, did the Japanese develop the idea. Their prowess lay in the application of carrier-borne air power, of which the attack on Pearl Harbor was a classic demonstration. Subsequent events showed, however, that these tactics depended more upon the traditional principles of sea power than any independent concepts of the air and, as far as the use of the new styles of fleet actions were concerned, the Americans proved to be convincingly superior. Thus it was left to the British to carry forward the concept of independent or strategic air power.

The night area offensive, which absorbed the greater part of the Bomber Command effort, although not its entirety, produced massive devastation throughout Germany and at times seemed to portend the downfall of her war economy. After the opening of the Battle of Hamburg in July and August 1943, for example, Speer told Hitler that six more attacks on that scale would finish the war. Six more attacks of such strength and effectiveness proved, however, to be beyond the capacity of Bomber Command, and Speer soon recovered his confidence. There was, indeed, a fatal flaw in Bomber Command's strategy.

In combat, the British night bombers could be no match for German interceptor fighters. The former, which had to carry maximum bomb loads to make their sorties worthwhile, had significantly less speed, manoeuvrability and armament than the latter. It was a lucky Lancaster which survived a well-established contact with a Junkers 88. The success of the bomber operations, indeed the ability to continue them at all, depended, therefore, upon the avoidance to the greatest possible extent of such contacts. Sustained bomber operations, in fact, depended upon the restriction of losses per attack to about five percent. Numbers above that which lasted for more than a few weeks would first eat away the efficiency of the force through the introduction of too high a proportion of new inexperienced crews, and then the actual existence of the front line through the loss of those new crews. A second cardinal point was that, in order to find their targets at night, the bombers needed radar assistance. The prime reason for the ineffectiveness of the early attacks was the lack of this. Radar, however, had the general effect of turning night into day; different exploitations of the same radar principles enabled the British night bombers to find and destroy their targets, but they also enabled the German night fighters to find and destroy the bombers.

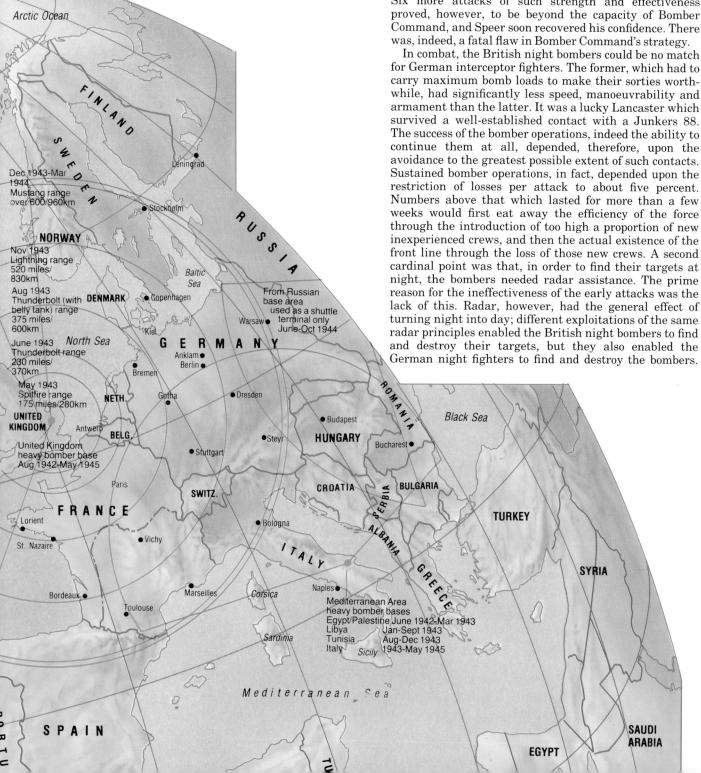

The advantage swung to and fro, as it did between the offence and defence in land warfare, in accordance with the introduction by both sides of new equipments and new ruses, but in this case, the advantage to the bombers was always more short-lived than that to the fighters, as fundamentally was likely, due to the intrinsically higher performance of the latter. Bomber Command, therefore, had to seek to avoid interception not only by technical means, such as "Window", radar jamming and spoof raids; it also had to constrain its style of attack for the same purpose. For example, bombing often could not be concentrated for long enough on the right point because, by showing the purpose, the night fighter force would also be given the opportunity to concentrate. Spreading the defences and, therefore, dispersing the attack, became a harsh necessity which reduced the effectiveness of Bomber Command.

A nation of lesser determination than Hitler's Germany would have succumbed to the British night offensive; many would have done so to a small part of it. The damage done to the German war effort by the area offensive was enormous, but, due to German resilience, the powers of compulsion and reorganization and the resources of slave labour which were available to a totalitarian government, the damage caused was not in itself decisive.

American strategy
Although not for the right reasons, the Americans had expected this. Their view that night bombing was ineffective had led to the development as day bombers of the B-17 and B-24. Although the Americans thus rejected British advice, and although they were not to follow the British in forming an independent air force until 1948, they nevertheless had produced an air doctrine related to, but independent of, British ideas. The centre of this was the determination to mount a bombing offensive in daylight in which the targets would be the same as those the British had sought at the outset, that is, pinpoints. They realized that the British had been defeated in the same purpose, but they believed that their much more heavily armed Flying Fortresses would be able to defend themselves against fighter attack. Operations leading up to,

and, in particular, that at Schweinfurt in October 1943 exploded this idea and showed the Americans that, *mutatis mutandis*, they were as vulnerable as the British had been in 1939. Their reaction, however, was critically different; instead of turning to night attack and the evasion of the enemy fighter force, they resolved to fight it. Arnold was more open to the possibility of a long-range fighter than Portal had been; he now saw the necessity for one. Before the arrival of the P-51 Mustangs, the Germans had been able to hold back their attacks until the American bombers passed beyond the reach of their supporting fighters. From March 1944, Mustangs carried fighter support to the full range of the bombers and, by removing the option of the range at which to engage from the Germans, they not only gained a huge advantage for themselves, but also validated the contribution which could be made by the shorter-range machines. Thus, overwhelming fighting air power was brought to bear upon the defending Luftwaffe, which was worn down and defeated.

This was the key event in the development of strategic applications of air power which stemmed from the Smuts report. The air situation which arose from the introduction of the tactics of long-range air fighting enabled long-range bombers, first by day and later also by night, to carry out attacks of decisive importance, such as, for example, upon German oil production and her transport system. In these conditions, British night bombing proved to be not only much more destructive, but also more accurate than American day bombing. The air superiority which made this possible was, however, primarily due to the long-range air battles resulting from the threat of the American day bombers, which drew up the German fighters, and the defeat of them by the American long-range fighters. Bomber Command played a leading part in the exploitation of this advantage, but a much smaller one in the creation of it.

Conclusions
Although reluctant to concede the greater power and effectiveness of British bombing in Germany, the Americans absorbed the point, and, against Japan, they launched a night area bombing offensive of their own, which, due to the nature of the targets and the greater power of the B-29 bombers, proved to be even more destructive than the blows which had been delivered against Germany by Lancasters. This offensive, important as it was in reducing Japan's capacity to continue the war, added nothing to the principles which had been established at Germany's cost. Air superiority was never complete, bomber losses had to be balanced against concentration of attack, and there continued to be a race between the destruction wrought by the bombers and the repair, dispersal or substitution available to their enemy. The principal restricting factors in the bombing offensives against Germany and Japan were the rate of casualties suffered by the bombers and the shifting balance between the rate and degree of destruction as compared to the extent to which it could be repaired. The achievement of air superiority tipped the scales heavily in favour of the bombers, but they and the bombs they carried were of insufficient power to render other forms of warfare subordinate and irrelevant. Strategic bombing alone was not enough to knock a resolute power out of a war, or so it seemed until almost the end.

The introduction by the Germans of the V-2 (A-4)

Strategic bombing and range. Obviously bomber operations were limited by the range of the bombers. In this, the Germans had an advantage in that London was much nearer their bases than Berlin was to British bases. Nevertheless, at the outbreak of World War II both Britain's and Germany's bomber forces could, in terms of range, reach most worthwhile targets in each other's countries and when, in January 1943, the Americans joined in bombing Germany, they could do the same. What had not been appreciated was that effective bombing and the concomitant of command of the air was not a question only of bomber ranges; it was equally one of fighter ranges. Even after the occupation by the Germans of the Low Countries and Channel coast of France, their effective fighter range into England was insufficient for them to win the Battle of Britain. The American tactic of massing heavily armed bombers in tight mutually supporting formations failed to circumvent the problem. They then recognized that an aircraft with the performance of a fighter and the range of a bomber was needed. The map shows the stages by which the P-38 Lightning, P-47 Thunderbolt and the P-51 Mustang reached outwards over the principal areas of the bomber offensive. Eventually there was scarcely anywhere that the Germans might not encounter a fighter of the Spitfire or Mustang class.

The shape of things to come. German V-2 partially-guided missiles.

partially-guided missile removed, at least for the time being, one of the restrictions, for no means of defence against it existed. The warhead it carried was, however, many times less powerful than the bomb load of a Lancaster and the accuracy of its attack far less precise than that of aimed bombs from manned aircraft. As a means of delivery, the V-2 was, nevertheless, extraordinarily advanced for its time and its appearance presaged a revolution in the terms of warfare comparable to that of the first heavier-than-air flight of the Wright brothers in 1903. The second part of this revolution was completed by the production in America of the atomic bomb. The first two of these were sufficient to destroy two major towns in Japan; in two sorties, two bombers were afforded the capacity to achieve what by previous means would have taken thousands of sorties and, because of the subsequent consequences of an atomic explosion, a great deal more than that. The final stage of the revolution arrived with the marriage of the nuclear bomb to the guided missile, producing, as far as the warhead was concerned, the ultimate in destructive power and, as far as the delivery system went, a vehicle against which no defence could be offered. This at last seemed to realize the expectations of the Smuts report, but whether or not it has, in fact, fortunately remains a speculative matter. The weapon may be too powerful to use and already there are the prospects of a defence against it in the shape of "Star Wars".

Postwar developments
Meanwhile, the employment of heavy long-range aircraft with conventional bombs has continued since the end of

World War II. They have, for example, taken part in the Korean, Vietnamese and Falklands wars, but such operations have not been in the tradition of strategic bombing, for in these wars there have been no strategic targets in the sense of those in Germany and Japan during World War II. Strategic bombing, indeed, is a concomitant of total war, where the object is to destroy the structure of the enemy's war potential which depends upon his industrial production, system of communications and civil morale. In the wars since 1945 the great powers have confronted one another, as in Korea and Vietnam, but the contest has not been extended beyond the realms of the immediate dispute and the fundamental resources upon which those wars have been based have, therefore, remained hors de combat. Air power has been used, not in its independent role, but only as an extension of military and naval operations. The extent to which this is due to the balance of terror created by the possession on both sides of the ultimate expression of strategic air power represented by the nuclear-armed missile is a matter of controversy. It may, however, be noted, as a fact of history, that no nation has yet launched a major strategic air offensive against another which had the power to retaliate in kind. When the Germans attacked London with their Gothas in 1917, they knew that the British could not retaliate against Berlin. When the British wrecked the heart of Germany between 1943 and 1945, they knew that the Germans could not do the same to them. When the Americans dropped atomic bombs on Japan, they knew that they alone possessed weapons with such destructive capabilities.

Hobart, Maj Gen Sir Percy Cleghorn Stanley (1885–1957). Br. Tank pioneer. *See also* TANKS.

Ho Chi Minh (1890–1969). Democratic Republic of Vietnam. Ho embraced Marxist-Leninism in 1920, and after training in Moscow and a stint as an agent of the Communist International in southern China, founded the Vietnam Communist Party in 1930. On March 2 1946 Ho was elected first president of the Democratic Republic (DRV), a post he held until his death on September 3 1969. He was responsible for the party's decision to initiate armed struggle in 1940, the united front strategy that brought the party to power in 1945, the leadership of the DRV during the war with France, the consolidation of communist rule in the North after 1954, and the North's steadfast commitment to reunification with the South. For these accomplishments he must be regarded as the most important figure in modern Vietnamese history. Ho was more an activist, organizer and inspirational leader than a theorist. *WST*.

Ho Chi Minh campaign (1975). Vietnamese communist leaders named the attack that culminated the war for reunification the Ho Chi Minh campaign. This attack on Saigon took place in the last ten days of April 1975, following strikes that had precipitated the collapse of the Army of the Republic of Vietnam (ARVN) in virtually all of South Vietnam except the capital and parts of the Mekong delta. Fifteen communist divisions opened the attack against the five tattered ARVN divisions defending Saigon on April 29. Sweeping aside pleas to negotiate from Gen Duong Van Minh, who had just taken over the presidency, the communists shelled Tan Son Nhut airfield and closed on the city from five directions. A few ARVN units resisted, but most were overwhelmed and surrendered or fled. As Soviet-made tanks approached, Gen Minh ordered remaining ARVN troops to lay down their arms. *WST*.

Ho Chi Minh Trail. In the first Indochina War, the Vietnamese communists developed routes through the mountains dividing Laos and Cambodia from Vietnam in order to have a secure link between North and South. In the late 1950s they began reopening these routes and in May 1959 the Party Central Committee commissioned the 559 Transportation Group of the People's Army (PAVN) to take charge of this task. After American naval action ended supply by sea in 1965, the network of paths and trails, named after the Truong Son Range by the communists and dubbed the Ho Chi Minh Trail by western newsmen, became the main conduit of reinforcements and supplies for the war in the South.

At first, the trail linked camps about a day's march apart. Troops and porters took up to three months to reach base areas straddling the Laotian and Cambodian borders with South Vietnam. As the number of PAVN troops and the sophistication of their weapons in the South increased, the Trail grew in importance. Paths became roads, and in 1966 trucks began replacing porters.

So important a communist lifeline inevitably became the target of American interdiction efforts. However, extremely heavy bombardment managed only to slow the annual increase in the movement of men and supplies. The PAVN adapted by developing alternative routes. By 1972 the total length of roads and paths had grown to 9,375 miles (15,000km). The costly attempt by South Vietnamese forces to cut the Trail on the ground in 1971 had little effect. American withdrawal in 1973 relieved the aerial pressure, and from then until spring 1975 the PAVN consolidated routes into a few main arteries in preparation for the final offensive. *WST. See also* "LAM SON 719" OPERATION.

Hochmuth, Maj Gen Bruno A (1911–1967). US. Took command of the US 3rd Marine Division on March 20 1967. On November 14 1967, he became the first American general to be killed in the Vietnam War when his helicopter exploded.

Hodge, Lt Gen John Reed (1893–1963). US. Commander XXIV Corps on Okinawa when Japan surrendered. In August 1945 he was ordered to occupy Korea south of the 38th Parallel and establish a US Military Government, a task for which he was ill-prepared. Deeply conservative, Hodge opposed the Korean left which he saw as the tool of the Russians and supported the right under Syngman Rhee.

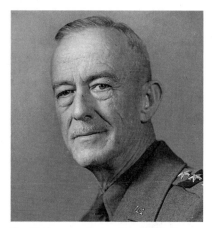

Gen Hodges: modest and methodical

Hodges, Gen Courtney H (1887–1966). US. In March 1944 Hodges was appointed deputy commander of US First Army, under Gen Bradley. He helped to prepare the formation for the Normandy invasion and was given command on August 1 1944, when Bradley moved up to lead US 12th Army Group. Operating on 12th Army Group's left flank, First Army crossed the Seine, liberated Liège and, in the third week of September 1944, breached the Siegfried Line. However, now short of troops and supplies, Hodges became embroiled in the bloody battle of Aachen, which fell on October 21. In December he narrowly avoided disaster when the German offensive in the Ardennes struck First Army's thinly-held front. He was forced to fight a series of delaying actions until, under Montgomery's overall direction, First Army was able to counterattack early in January 1945. In the following months First Army captured the vital bridge across the Rhine at Remagen and participated in the encirclement of the Ruhr before driving east towards the Elbe to link up with the Russians. A self-effacing, methodical man, Hodges seemed colourless alongside figures like Patton, yet he was undoubtedly one of the most skilful Allied commanders in Northwest Europe. *PJS*.

H

Hoffmann: victorious in East Prussia

Hoffmann, Brig Max (1869–1927). Ger. Widely regarded as possessing one of the finest minds on the German General Staff, and an acknowledged expert on Russia, Hoffmann was First General Staff Officer to the Eighth Army in East Prussia in August 1914. Having played a major part in the planning of the great victory at Tannenberg in August, Hoffmann transferred with Hindenburg and Ludendorff to Ninth Army as Chief of Operations, moving with them again on Hindenburg's appointment as c-in-c East in November 1914. However, when Hindenburg and Ludendorff became Chief of the General Staff and First Quartermaster-General respectively in August 1916, Hoffmann stayed on the Eastern Front as Chief of Staff to the new c-in-c, Prince Leopold of Bavaria, although Hoffmann was commander in all but name. He planned the successful offensive at Riga in September 1917 and negotiated the armistice with the Bolsheviks at Brest-Litovsk in December, launching another offensive in February 1918 to force the prevaricating Russians to sign peace terms on March 3. Hoffmann was briefly involved with the *Freikorps* but opposed the emerging Nazi party. *PJS*.

Hoge, Maj Gen William Morris (1894–1979). US. Engineer officer who, on March 7 1945, commanded Combat Command B, US 9th Armored Division, which captured bridge at Remagen, first Allied bridgehead over the Rhine. Ended war in command of US 4th Armored Division.

Holland, invasion of *see* LOW COUNTRIES, INVASION OF.

Hollandia campaign (1944). Following decisions made at the Quebec Conference, August 1943, Gen MacArthur launched a "leapfrogging" coastal campaign in western New Guinea, to secure air bases for the forthcoming assault on the Philippines and to isolate the main body of Japanese Eighteenth Army (Lt Gen Adachi) in northeast New Guinea.

In March–April 1944, sustained assault by B-24 bombers of US Thirteenth Air Force shattered Japan's air power in western New Guinea, destroying some 500 aircraft. On April 22, simultaneous amphibious assaults were made by I US Corps (Maj Gen Eichelberger) of Sixth Army (Lt Gen Krueger) at Aitape and at Hollandia, 120 miles (193km) farther west. Taken by surprise, the Japanese put up only brief resistance; US aircraft were operational from Aitape by April 24 and at Hollandia from April 26. US losses were c550 killed and 3,500 wounded; the Japanese lost c14,000 dead, some 5,000 survivors fleeing inland.

On May 17–18, US forces "leaped" a further 125 miles (200km) west from Hollandia when simultaneous landings secured the airstrips on Wakde Island and around Maffin Bay (US: 455 killed 1,500 wounded; Japanese: c4,000 killed). The main remaining objective was Biak Island, 200 miles (322km) west of Wakde. Discounting "Magic" intelligence, MacArthur believed Biak was held by only 3,000 troops: in fact, Lt Gen Takuzo Numata deployed some 7,000 combat troops and 4,000 men of construction battalions in well-fortified positions inland. The landings of US 41st Infantry Division (Maj Gen Horace Fuller; replaced on June 15, when Eichelberger took personal command, by Brig Gen Jens A Doe) on May 27 were virtually unopposed, but savage resistance was soon encountered. Although three Japanese attempts to reinforce by sea were repulsed (May 31–June 12), Biak's airstrips were not secured until late June and mopping-up continued until July 22. US losses were c470 killed, 2,440 wounded and some 6,000 incapacitated by typhus; more than 6,000 Japanese died.

The Hollandia campaign was completed by the capture of the western islands of Noemfoor (July 2–7) and Sansapor (July 30). MacArthur was poised to begin the reconquest of the Philippines with the invasion of Leyte. *RO'N*.

Hollis, Sir Roger (1905–73). Br. Head of MI5 1956–65; alleged, probably falsely, to be Russian agent.

Holocaust (1933–45). A term now used to signify the Nazis' attempt at a "final solution" (*Endlösung*) of the "Jewish problem". Between March 1933, when Himmler established Dachau concentration camp, and 1945, an estimated 5.1–5.5 million Jews (out of a total pre-war European Jewish population of 8.3 million) died as a result of Nazi policies.

Home Guard. British militia created in July 1940 from the Local Defence Volunteers (LDV) and intended to supplement Britain's defences against invasion.

Homma, Lt Gen Masaharu (1887–1946). Jap. Although he had held no previous combat command, Homma took over Fourteenth Army shortly before the attack on Luzon, Philippines, December 1941. His insistence on taking Manila allowed US and Filipino troops time to withdraw to Bataan-Corregidor, where their prolonged resistance (until April 9 1942), in spite of Homma's great superiority in men and materiel, led to his effective deposition (although he remained nominally in command) in the later stages of the campaign. Held responsible for the "Bataan Death March", he was executed as a war criminal in 1946.

Hong Kong, fall of (1941). Japan's control of the Chinese hinterland in December 1941 posed grave problems for the defence of the British colony and naval base of Hong Kong. Consequently, the garrison and fortifications were hastily strengthened, but air cover was minimal and the defences remained far from adequate. When the Japanese launched their attack on December 8 1941, the British commander, Maj Gen Maltby, was only able to allot three battalions and 16 pieces of

Japanese troops attack Hong Kong island, which fell on December 25 1941

artillery to man the defence lines on the Kowloon Peninsula. The British force managed to hold out for six days until Maltby withdrew them to Hong Kong island. The original six battalions of British, Canadian and Indian troops had been substantially weakened and, although reinforced by a Volunteer Defence Corps, they faced over 20,000 men of the Japanese 38th Division. Calls to surrender were rejected and the city was subjected to heavy bombing and shelling before the Japanese made a landing in the northeast of the island on the 18th. They captured the heights and took control of the island's centre of communications at Wong Nei Chong Gap. The British forces were now exhausted, dispersed and gravely under-strength and, on December 25, Maltby advised the Governor, Sir Mark Young, that further resistance was useless. That evening, he surrendered Hong Kong unconditionally to Lt Gen Sakai, commanding officer Twenty-third Army. *MS*.

Hook, Battles of the (1952–53). The Hook was a position in Korea at the western end of the Jamestown Line held by the lst Commonwealth Division. The first battle occurred on November 17–18 1952 when the Chinese established a foothold in the position but were driven off by a determined counterattack supported by artillery. The second battle occurred on May 28-29 1953 when the Hook was attacked in battalion strength. The defenders withdrew into tunnels calling down artillery fire on their own positions. By dawn the Chinese had been repulsed.

Hopkins, Harry Lloyd (1890–1946). US. Special Adviser to Roosevelt, World War II. Used as an emissary without title. Abroad, especially in Britain, he was recognized as among the most influential Americans.

Hornet. US aircraft carriers. (1) Built to *Yorktown* class design to save time, completed 1941; launched Doolittle's B-25 bombers on the Tokyo raid; fought at Midway; lost October 1942 at Battle of Santa Cruz. (2) *Essex* class, in service November 1943 and served for rest of war in Pacific; modernized, anti-submarine carrier (1958), in reserve (1970).

Horrocks, Lt Gen Sir Brian (1895–1985). Br. An infantry subaltern early in World War I, Horrocks was taken prisoner and spent the duration in German POW camps. His career was closely linked with that of Montgomery, under whom he served in France in 1940 as a battalion commander. After commanding a brigade and a division in Montgomery's corps in England he was summoned to rejoin his erstwhile leader in North Africa and take over the XIII Corps of the Eighth Army. He acquitted himself well in the battles of Alam Halfa and El Alamein and met further success in command of X Corps during the Allied drive westwards. Horrocks completed the campaign with the First Army in Tunisia but was seriously wounded during an air raid shortly before the invasion of Sicily. He was still recuperating in England in August 1944 when Montgomery sent for him to take over XXX Corps in Normandy. Horrocks'

leadership revived the fortunes of his new command and it performed with distinction in British Second Army's rapid advance through France and Belgium. Montgomery entrusted the main ground element in Operation "Market Garden" to Horrocks, but XXX Corps failed to relieve 1st Airborne Division at Arnhem. It was more successful in Operation "Veritable", the clearing of the approaches to the Rhine and the advance into Germany. *MS*.

Horsa, Airspeed AS 51/58 (Br, WWII). Transport glider; crew 2; accommodated 20–25 troops. Prototype flew September 12 1941; first operational use invasion of Sicily July 1943; later extensively and successfully used D-Day, Arnhem. Production 3,799, of which 95 went to USAF. Max. towing speed 150mph (240kph); load 6,630lb (3,007kg).

Horton, Adm Sir Max Kennedy (1883–1951). Br. A pioneer submariner, Horton was appointed to command the Royal Navy's experimental *A.1* in 1905. On September 13 1914, he became the first British submarine commander to destroy an enemy warship, when *E.9* torpedoed the German cruiser *Hela* in Heligoland Bight. The successes of his submarine flotilla operating from Russian bases, 1914–15, caused the Baltic to be nicknamed "Horton's Sea". His openness to innovation was reflected in his command of the experimental submarine *M.1* (mounting a 12in gun), 1917–18; his appointment to the steam-driven "K"-class flotilla, 1922; and his encouragement of the development of midget submarines and manned-torpedoes ("Chariots") during World War II.

In relative obscurity as commander of the Reserve Fleet, 1937–39, and Northern Patrol, 1939, Horton made a triumphant return to his own field as Flag Officer Submarines, January 1940–October 1942, where his organizational and training skills were employed to great effect. As a submariner, he fully realized the value of aircraft in anti-submarine operations and, having refused command of the Home Fleet in October 1940, because he would not have full control of air operations, he put this

H

perception to full use when he succeeded Adm Noble as c-in-c, Western Approaches, November 1942. Under his direction, "support groups" of escort warships and MAC ships (later escort carriers), working closely with long-range aircraft, successfully operated against U-boat packs. *RO'N*.

Hoth, Gen Hermann (1885–1971). Ger. Commanded 3rd Panzer Group in invasion of Russia; from January 1942, led Fourth Panzer Army at Stalingrad and Kursk; dismissed by Hitler, late 1943.

Hovercraft. Used in Vietnam by the Americans as patrol craft in the Mekong delta, and by the British – mainly for logistic support – in Borneo. Other uses are coastal patrol, anti-submarine and counter-mine operations.

Howitzer. An artillery piece that fires shells at a high trajectory.

H

Hube, Gen Hans (1890–1944). Ger. Directed Italo-German defence and evacuation of Sicily, July–August 1944; led XIV Panzer Corps in defence of Italian mainland. Commanded First Panzer Army in Manstein's resistance to Soviet winter offensive, 1944.

Hudson, Lockheed B14L, A-28, A-28A, A-29, A-29A (US, WWII). Maritime reconnaissance-bomber; crew 4/5. Development of Lockheed 14 commercial transport; to squadron May 1939. Extensively used on early photographic-reconnaissance work, clandestine operations, Air-Sea Rescue; RAAF, RNZAF, later by USAF, USN. Production 2,934. Two 1,100hp Wright Cyclone R-1820-G102A engines; max. speed 222mph (355kph); seven 0.303in machine guns, 1,600lb (725kg) bombs.

Hue, Battle of (1968). Nowhere during the 1968 Tet offensive did communist forces sustain their attack as long as in Hue, one of the few places where the assault force was composed largely of People's Army of Vietnam (PAVN) regulars. A force of 7,500 men entered the city on January 31, entrenched itself behind the walls of the old citadel, and held out until February 24. Constrained at first by orders not to destroy the imperial

palace, the counterattack began slowly, but air and artillery strikes and house-to-house fighting later inflicted heavy damage. The fighting left over 100,000 people homeless; 2,800 bodies were found in mass graves and another 2,000 were missing, victims of communist assassinations, political vendettas and crossfires. Despite heavy losses, the communists demolished the credibility of claims that the cities were safe from attack. *WST*.

Huj, Battle of (November 8 1917). Immediately after the fall of Gaza, 60th (London) division (Maj Gen Shea) pursued the Turks. On November 8 1917, a Turkish column was sighted near Huj. Shea called on three squadrons of Desert Mounted Corps: 12 officers and 158 troopers under Lt Col Gray-Cheape. The cavalry charged sword in hand, dispersing the infantry and twice charging flanking batteries. Eleven guns, four machine guns and 70 prisoners were taken; all three British squadron commanders, 26 troopers and 100 horses were killed.

Hull, Field Marshal Sir Richard (b.1907). Br. Commander 1st Armoured Division in the First and Second Battles of Coriano in September 1944; CGS, 1961; Chief of Defence Staff, 1965.

Humint. Intelligence secured by human observation.

"Hump, The" *see* STILWELL, GEN JOSEPH; LEDO ROAD.

Hunter, Hawker P1067/P1099 (Br). Single-seat fighter/ground attack. Prototype flew July 20 1951; first deliveries to RAF July 1954. Extensively used by RAF and foreign air forces; produced in Belgium (255) and Netherlands (189). India acquired 160 Hunters Mk 56 and 53 FGA56As. Production: approximately 2,000. Hunter F6 had one 10,000lb (4,500kg) s.t. Rolls-Royce Avon 203 engine; max. speed 715mph (1,150kph); four 30mm cannon, 2,000lb (900kg) bombs, 24 3in rockets or two pods 24 or 37 FFAR missiles.

Hurricane, Hawker (Br, WWII). Single-seat fighter/ground attack, an aircraft of exceptional versatility. Prototype flew November 6

1935; first deliveries December 1937. Eighteen squadrons by outbreak of war; four to France with AASF. Much modification and development, particularly in armament. Sea Hurricane conversions to RN 1941–43. Production 14,232. One 1.030–1,300hp Rolls-Royce Merlin engine; max. speed 340mph (544kph); eight/twelve 0.303in mchine guns, four 20mm cannon, or two 40mm cannon with 2 machine guns- eight rockets.

Hürtgen Forest, Battle of (1944). In September 1944, US 9th Infantry Division attempted to clear Germans from dense Hürtgen Forest, southeast of Aachen. Opposed by units of German Seventh Army, they took substantial casualties for little territorial gain. A fresh attack was launched on November 2 by US 28th Infantry Division, but in a German counterattack on the 4th the 116th Panzer Division forced an American retreat. The forest was cleared in mid-December. More than 120,000 US troops were engaged, of whom 33,000 became casualties. *MS*.

Hutier, Lt Gen Oskar von (1857–1934). Ger. Commanding Eighth Army on the Eastern Front in 1917, Hutier, with the assistance of his artillery commander, Col Georg Bruchmüller, was largely reponsible for the development of assault tactics designed to overcome Hindenburg-Line-type defence-in-depth. "Hutier tactics" proved successful in their originator's capture of Riga, September 3 1917, and a little later at Caporetto. Hutier was brought to the Western Front to command Eighteenth Army, achieving spectacular advances at the Somme, March 1918, where he shattered Gough's Fifth Army, and at the Aisne, May–June 1918, but taking severe casualties at Amiens, August 8 1918. *RO'N*.

Hyakutake, Lt Gen Harukichi (1888–1947). Jap. Commanded Seventeenth Army in the attempted reconquest of Guadalcanal. In 1944–45 he fought another fiercely attritional campaign on Bougainville.

Hydrogen Bomb (H-Bomb) *see* THERMONUCLEAR WEAPON.

Ia Drang river, Battle of the (1965). The first major engagement between American and North Vietnamese regular army units occurred in the valley of the Ia Drang river, which flows out of South Vietnam's Pleiku province into Cambodia. Following an attack by the People's Army (PAVN) 32nd and 33rd Regiments on the Plei Me Special Forces camp in October 1965, elements of the US 1st Cavalry Division (Airmobile) pursued these regiments into the valley where bloody fighting ensued November 14–18. The PAVN disengaged when confronted by superior American fire power and the first direct support of ground combat by B-52s in the war. The battle marked not only the beginning of the PAVN's "big unit" warfare but also the introduction of new airmobile tactics by the Americans. *WST*.

Iachino, Adm Angelo (1889–1976). Italian. Italian Fleet Commander, succeeding Adm Campioni, December 1940–September 1943. In command at the Battle of Cape Matapan, March 1941, and First and Second Battles of Sirte, December 1941 and March 1942. A generally ineffective commander; partly because constantly adjured not to hazard Italy's capital ships.

Ichi-go *see* SINO-JAPANESE WAR.

Identification Friend or Foe (IFF). A system whereby a sensor contact can be automatically interrogated by electronic means to identify its status as a friend or foe. A transponder (transmitter/receiver) responds to a complex coded signal from another transponder and sends back a different coded signal that identifies the contact as friendly. As engagement ranges increase in all forms of warfare, NATO is trying, with some difficulty, to develop a comprehensive IFF system including a laser/radar unit for battlefield operations.

Iida, Lt Gen Shojiro (b.1888). Jap. Commander Fifteenth Army, later Burma Area Army. Announced formation of New Era Burma Government, August 1 1942; General Defence Commander, 1943.

***Illustrious*-class.** British aircraft carriers: (Group 1) *Illustrious, formidable, Victorious*; launched 1939; 28,600 tons full load; 36 aircraft; pioneered armoured box hangar. *Illustrious* launched Taranto strike; pioneered radar-controlled interception from carriers; served Madagascar; Salerno landings; Indian and Pacific Oceans, 1944–45; used post-war for jet aircraft trials; scrapped 1955. *Formidable* at Matapan; Indian Ocean, 1942; kamikaze damage (like others of class) with British Pacific Fleet, 1945; scrapped 1955. *Victorious* participated *Bismarck* hunt; "Pedestal" Malta convoy; "Torch" landings, North Africa; with US forces in Pacific, 1943; *Tirpitz* strike, 1944; British Pacific Fleet, 1944–45; major conversion, 1950s; scrapped 1969. (Group 2) *Indomitable*; launched 1940; 29,700 tons full load; 48 aircraft; modified with extra hangar deck (as in Group 3), increasing aircraft capacity. Served Madagascar; bomb damage in "Pedestal" convoy; torpedoed Sicily; British Pacific Fleet, 1944–45; scrapped 1953. (Group 3) *Implacable, Indefatigable*; launched 1942; 32–33,000 tons full load; 54 aircraft. *RO'N*.

Ilyushin DB-3/Il-4 (USSR, WWII). Long-range bomber; crew 3. Prototype flew spring 1936; DB-3s into service 1938. Progressively modified; final version (DB-3F) was redesignated Il-4. Mainstay of Soviet Air Force's long-range bombing strength throughout war; also served as torpedo-bomber, transport and glider tug. Production about 6,800. Two 1,100hp Tumansky M-88B engines; max. speed 267mph (430kph); 5,952lb (2,700kg) bombs, three 7.62mm or 12.7mm machine guns.

Ilyushin Il-2M3 Shturmovik (USSR, WWII). Two-seat armoured ground-attack aircraft; entered service mid-1941 as single-seater; later modified to two-seater. Despite poor performance and handling qualities proved to be formidable tank destroyer, but no match for German fighters. Designed for ease of mass production: some 36,150 Il-2s (several sub-types) built. One 1,720hp Mikulin AM-38F engine; max. speed 255mph (410kph); two 23mm or 37mm cannon, three machine guns; 1,102lb (500kg) bombs or alternative loads of rockets or anti-armour (hollow-charge) bombs.

Imamura, Lt Gen Hitoshi (1886–1968). Jap. One of Japan's most able generals, Imamura was Vice-COS, Kwantung Army, 1936–37. Early in 1942, he led Sixteenth Army in the occupation of Java, where his comparatively benevolent occupation measures won considerable support for the Greater East Asia Co-prosperity Sphere from Indonesian nationalists. As Commander, Eighth Area Army, from November 1942, with his HQ at Rabaul, Imamura was ordered to re-secure the Solomon Islands (Seventeenth Army; Hyakutake) and New Guinea (Eighteenth Army; Adachi), but despite determined efforts to reinforce Guadalcanal and other islands his forces were either evacuated or isolated by late 1943-early 1944. Imprisoned for "war crimes" in 1946 – like a number of senior Japanese commanders, the scapegoat for the excesses of junior officers – Imamura was paroled in 1954. *RO'N*.

UN forces on the Imjin river, Korea

Imjin river, Battle of the (1951). Occurred during the Korean War 35 miles (56km) north of Seoul. On April 22–25 1951, during the first phase of their spring offensive, the Chinese attacked the 29th British Infantry Brigade which was holding a 12,000yd (11,000m) front along the Imjin river. The Brigade was deployed with 1st Battalion the Gloucestershire Regiment to the left and 1st Battalion the Royal Northumberland Fusiliers to the right. The 1st Battalion the Royal Ulster Rifles was in reserve. An attached Belgian battalion was holding a position north of the river. The Chinese attack began on the night of April 22. The following day the enemy established a road block behind the Gloucesters and repulsed two attempts by tanks to relieve the battalion. By April 24, the Gloucesters had concentrated on Hill 235 (Gloucester Hill) where they repulsed a series of Chinese attacks. On the night of April 24–25, the Brigade was ordered by I Corps to withdraw to new positions. The next morning the Gloucesters attempted to fight their way out by companies but only 39 men reached the UN lines. The 29th Brigade suffered 25% casualties but inflicted such losses on the Chinese Sixty-third Army that it was withdrawn from the fighting. For their part in the battle, the Gloucesters were awarded a US presidential citation. *CM. See also* CARNE, LT COL JAMES POWER VC.

Immelmann, Lt Max (1890-1916). Ger. Along with Boelcke, the most influential German fighter pilot of early World War I. He gave his name to the "Immelmann Turn", in which a diving attack from the rear was followed by a steep half-loop culminating in a stall-turn, thus regaining height advantage for a further attack. The "Eagle of Lille" gained most of his 15 victories in a Fokker "Eindecker"; he was killed when his Fokker E.III broke up in the air.

Incendiary bomb. Fire-raising bombs were most destructive agents in area attacks on towns by Germans against Britain (1940-41), British against Germany (1940-45), and Americans against Japan (1944-45).

US Marines land at Inchon, Korea, 1950

Inchon landings (1950), the Korean War. On July 23 1950, with his forces struggling to avoid defeat, Gen MacArthur produced a

plan to exploit his control of the sea and win the war. Codenamed "Chromite", it called for a landing by two US divisions at Inchon to cut enemy supply lines, recapture Seoul and envelop the NKPA in conjunction with a counteroffensive by Eighth Army from the Pusan perimeter in the south. The Joint Chiefs of Staff had grave misgivings regarding Inchon as an unsuitable spot for an amphibious landing. MacArthur won the argument, emphasizing the element of surprise. On August 26 he appointed Gen E M Almond to command the landing force, X Corps, consisting of the US lst Marine Division, the US 7th Infantry Division and a force of ROK marines. Inchon was secured on September 15–16 1950, changing the course of the Korean War and giving MacArthur one of his greatest victories. It was the last amphibious operation on the scale of World War II. *CM.*

Independence. US aircraft carrier. Name ship of class of light carriers, built on *Cleveland* class cruiser hulls; 14,750 tons full load; 30 aircraft; successful but cramped. Completed in 1943 and served with fast carrier task force in Pacific. A target at the Bikini Atoll atomic tests.

Independent Force. The British long-range bombing force designated for the strategic attack of German targets in World War I, commanded independently of the land battle. It was formed on French bases from VIII Brigade and became effective on June 6 1918. It was the precursor of Bomber Command in World War II.

India-China War (1959, 1962). The India-China War is more important in relation to international diplomacy than to warfare, in which it features only as a series of skirmishes. Its origins lie in British policy in the 19th century, but only after China occupied Tibet in 1959 did the issues raised assume urgent importance. In order to consolidate their control, the Chinese constructed an east-west highway across Aksai Chin which India claimed as a dependency of Kashmir. The remoteness of this mountainous area was such that an Indian army patrol only

bumped into the Chinese after the road was built. Thereafter, Nehru played down the scale of the dispute because of his policy of cooperation with China. However, India began to establish posts in areas previously unexplored. Attention shifted to the border tracts north of Assam – the North East Frontier Agency (NEFA). With this new "forward policy", claim was made to the strip of territory abutting on Bhutan which provided a north-south trade route via the great Buddhist monastery Towang up to the Himalayan mountain divide.

In 1960, 4th Division was moved up to NEFA; its effectiveness was limited by poor communications, including a total absence of lateral roads. The army still had weapons of World War II vintage and had no equipment for mountain warfare. Operational control was impaired by an absence of detailed maps. The crucial decision was the order to occupy Thag La, an area firmly claimed by China, during summer 1962. In response, Chinese formations in superior strength concentrated opposite.

Indian GHQ appointed Gen B M Kaul, CGS, to head a new IV Corps and to direct operations: Kaul had no previous experience of command. His hasty appreciation that the Chinese would not fight conflicted with all the reports he was getting. When the Indian attempt to take over Thag La ridge was repulsed, Kaul flew to Delhi, where the order to throw the Chinese back was reiterated. The night of October 19–20 1962 witnessed a major Chinese assault. The long Indian retreat began. The order was given for a stand at Se La pass, about 30 miles (48km) below Thag La ridge and 4th Division concentrated in a defensive arc. During November 17 the Chinese bypassed the Indian defences. Although the troops were firmly in position, Kaul ordered a withdrawal of 40 miles (64km) to Bomdi La. This was the junction of a two-prong Chinese advance: the Indian defence at brigade strength was rapidly overrun and the remnants of 48th Brigade fell back, receiving contradictory orders about making a further stand. By November 20 all Indian troops were out of NEFA. Senior cabinet ministers predicted that Assam and maybe north Bengal would fall. Appeals for help were addressed to the US and Britain.

Unexpectedly, on November 21, China announced a unilateral cease-fire and their withdrawal behind what they termed "the line of actual control", meaning the border they had claimed in earlier negotiations with Nehru. India was warned to keep 12 miles (20km) back on their side, leaving a demilitarized zone of 25 miles (40km). This included the Aksai Chin sector. Defeat did have positive consequences. There was a shakeup at the senior levels of command and the "political" generals departed. The army embarked on a massive re-equipment and re-armament programme. In two years, defence expenditure more than doubled. Six special mountain divisions (later increased to ten) were formed. When next India went to war it was a very different story. *HT.*

India-Pakistan Wars (1965, 1971). These conflicts have more in common with 1914-18 than with other recent Asian wars. The 1965 affair ended in stalemate; that in 1971 in the decisive defeat of Pakistan. In 1965 all operations took place along the Punjab border; the second war saw inconclusive fighting on the same lines but the decisive clash was in East Pakistan (subsequently Bangladesh).

The first conflict arose out of Pakistan's frustration at the denial of Kashmir, a largely Muslim territory which they saw as their rightful possession. An attempt to foment a guerrilla rising totally failed, and Pakistan sought to isolate Indian forces in Kashmir by advancing through the neck of territory north of Jammu (the Chhamb salient). This armoured thrust went well and India responded by a counteroffensive across the Punjab border towards Sialkot. This involved crossing a recognized international frontier (September 6) and the Pakistan Air Force responded with a pre-emptive strike which knocked out most of the Indian fighters on the ground. The attempt to repeat this success by launching the armoured division "The Shield of Pakistan" against Indian tanks was a disaster: most of the Pattons were knocked out. Thereafter hostilities

were limited to a series of slugging actions by the infantry. One Indian battalion penetrated to the outskirts of Lahore, but the overcautious divisional commander failed to reinforce them. Both sides were reluctant to throw in everything: they did not intend to destroy their military strength for no clear objective. India was satisfied to have frustrated the attempt to gain advantage in Kashmir; after the initial failure of surprise, Pakistan could not hope to obtain its goal; and the US had frozen military aid on which they relied. There was a cease-fire on September 22 and subsequent negotiations at Tashkent confirmed the status quo: both sides pulled back.

The 1971 conflict followed the political demand for complete autonomy by East Pakistan. The Bengali agitation was forcibly suppressed and massive military and paramilitary forces were ferried around, via Ceylon, to East Pakistan from the West. Ten million refugees fled into India; Mrs Gandhi appealed to the international community without response. Military action seemed to be the only remedy. Pakistan had the active support of the US and China (in 1965, China had organized a hostile demonstration on the Himalayan border). Military intervention would have to be quick and decisive. Mrs Gandhi gave resolute support to the armed forces, placing Gen Manekshaw in overall command. The field commander was Lt Gen J S Aurora.

His forces consisted of three army corps, along with the Mukti Bahini, the underground army of Bangladesh, said to number 100,000. The Pakistan defences were commanded by Lt Gen A A K Niazi and included three infantry divisions, a Border Security Force of 39 battalions, and the Razakars, paramilitary forces raised from the East Pakistan population.

All these forces were waiting on the eastern front, but the first action came on the western front when on December 3 1971 the Pakistan Air Force launched another pre-emptive strike, aimed at the airfields of Srinagar, Avantipur, Pathankot, Jodhpur, Ambala and Agra. This time the Indians were ready for them. On the eastern front, India had overwhelming air superiority. Niazi's plan was to hold the frontiers without giving up ground. Aurora planned to move rapidly: for political rather than military reasons. There was the danger that Pakistan's friends would protest at the UN against an invasion of a neighbouring country. Making a massive single-pronged attack, the Indian army reached the outskirts of Dacca by December 16 1971 and Niazi signed an instrument of surrender. In the path of the invasion, 1,293 Pakistani defenders were wiped out and 2,539 wounded (according to their own estimates). Over 90,000 Pakistani officers and men passed into Indian captivity, and it would be a whole year before they were repatriated. *HT*

India-Pakistan War, 1971: India's victory saw the establishment of Bangladesh

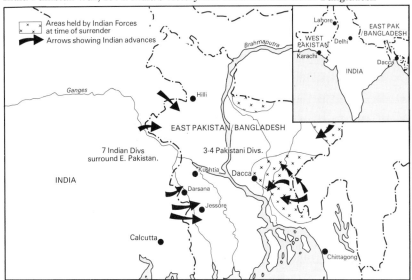

Indian Army. In the reforms of 1858–60, the old East India Company was disbanded and a new Indian Army created from those of the former Presidencies. Recruited during the British Raj from the martial races of the subcontinent and mainly British-officered, its roles were internal security, frontier operations (at which it excelled) and imperial policing. Enormously expanded for service on many fronts in both world wars. On the Partition of India in 1947, it was divided to form the new Indian and Pakistani armies.

Indian Army in Korea. India did not commit combat troops to Korea but sent the Indian 60th (Parachute) Field Ambulance. As part of the cease-fire agreement, India also provided a custodial force to guard POWs on behalf of the Neutral Nations Repatriation Commission.

Indian National Army *see* BOSE, SUBHAS CHANDRA.

Indiana. US battleship. *South Dakota*-class. 9 × 16in guns, 44,500 tons full load. Completed in 1942 and went into action at the Solomons landings: bombarding Gilberts and Tarawa (1943); Marshalls landings, collision with *Washington*, bombardment of Saipan, Leyte invasion (1944); and Okinawa operations then bombardments of Japanese mainland (1945). She was scrapped in 1963.

Indianapolis, sinking of. On July 28 1945, the heavy cruiser USS *Indianapolis* (9 × 8in; *c*9,950 tons), having just delivered atomic bomb components from the US to Tinian, sailed from Guam for Leyte Gulf. Although unescorted, Capt Charles B McVay did not zig-zag and did not have his ship fully secured. At 2332 hours on July 29, *Indianapolis* was struck by two torpedoes from the Japanese submarine *I-58* (Lt Commander Mochitsura Hashimoto). Immediate electrical failure meant that no SOS was sent; *Indianapolis* sank within 12 minutes, taking *c*350 men with her. The signal giving the cruiser's ETA at Leyte on July 31 had been garbled by weather conditions, and Hashimoto's signal claiming "an *Idaho*-class battleship" was at first discounted by US codebreakers. Thus, three days elapsed before rescue aircraft and ships were dispatched: the total death roll from a complement of 1,199 reached 883. Postwar, Capt McVay was court-martialled for hazarding his ship: he was found guilty but sentence was remitted. *RO'N.*

Indochina, French reoccupation of. The effort of France to re-establish its authority in Indochina after World War II was greatly complicated by the agreement at Potsdam providing for the surrender of Japanese troops to the Chinese in the north and the British in the south. Blocked by the Chinese, the French Expeditionary Corps entered Saigon on October 5 1945 with the aid of 20th Indian Division under British Maj Gen Douglas Gracey. Subsequent negotiations with the Chinese led to the entry of French ships into Haiphong on March 6 1946. On that date Ho Chi Minh also agreed to allow 15,000 French troops to be stationed in the north for five years, while France recognized the Democratic Republic of Vietnam as a "free state" in the French Union. Further negotiations were inconclusive, and violent incidents occurred repeatedly. On November 20 the French commander in Haiphong seized control of the city, and firing by the French heavy cruiser *Suffren* caused the deaths of 6,000 civilians. Anticipating war, the Vietnamese struck French posts and garrisons on December 19. In counterattack the French took two months to subdue Hanoi, and 47 days to break a siege at Hue. Reinforcements brought the total of French troops in Vietnam to 94,000 by March 1947. *WST.*

Indochina-France War (1946–54). The First Indochina War centred upon the conflict between Vietnam's communist-led anti-colonial movement and the French empire. Seizing the opportunity presented by World War II, during which Japan invaded and occupied Indochina, the communists decided in 1940 to prepare for an armed struggle. In two base areas near the Chinese border they set up the Viet Minh front and began organizing guerrilla forces. From the latter they formed a mobile force that numbered about 1,000 troops by spring 1945 and these, in combination with a rural militia and dextrous manipulation of mass demonstrations, were sufficient for them to seize power in the August Revolution. For the next 15 months the communists exercised real if unsteady power over a united Vietnam. But they were unable by means of tactical concessions, such as Ho Chi Minh made at the Fontainebleau Conference, to deter France from attempting to reoccupy all of Indochina. The French returned to Saigon in October 1945, gradually extended control to the Mekong delta, and seized Haiphong in November 1946. Open warfare broke out on December 19.

The lightly armed People's Army of Vietnam (PAVN), commonly referred to as the Viet Minh, were at first no match for French regulars. But they compensated for their material deficiencies with superior motivation, popular support and guerrilla tactics. They were most numerous in Tonkin, where the communists enjoyed their strongest popular support, but communist political organizations and guerrilla forces were active in all regions of the country. In 1947 the French attempted to surround and seize the entire communist leadership in the mountains of Cao Bang province and to seal off northeastern Vietnam from China. But the communists eluded them, and the French fell back on the lowlands to begin a frustrating search for a big set-piece battle in which their mobility and fire power should give them an advantage.

Meanwhile, the United States pressured the French to mobilize Vietnamese support by making an unequivocal commitment to independence for Vietnam. Although, since 1945, the US had permitted France to redirect US-supplied war materials from Europe to Indochina and had provided ships for the transport of French troops, it made expanded direct aid contingent on the creation of a Vietnamese national government. This led to negotiations between France and Emperor Bao Dai, which culminated in 1949 in the establishment of the State of Vietnam as an Associated State of the French Union. The French also set up a Vietnamese National Army, forerunner of the Army of the Republic of Vietnam (ARVN). American contributions to the French war effort rose from 33 percent of the total cost in 1953 to 78 percent in 1954, one-third of the global US foreign aid programme.

The Vietnamese communists also sought assistance abroad. But the decisive break came with the conclusion of the Civil War in China in 1949. The occupation of the border area by Chinese communist forces in December that year opened China as a source of arms, training and sanctuary. From then on China annually provided training for 10,000–20,000 PAVN officers and men, and material aid that grew from 10–20 tons per month in 1951 to 1,500 tons per month in early 1954. Over the course of the war, however, the tonnage of foreign military assistance that reached the PAVN was just one-tenth of what the US gave to the French. Only by coordinating guerrilla action with conventional offensives, and political struggle with armed struggle in a "people's war", were the communists able to offset the French advantage in material resources.

In 1950 the PAVN organized its first main force division and overran a string of French strongpoints along the northern border. With control of the mountains and unimpeded access to China, PAVN commander Vo Nguyen Giap believed the war was about to enter the stage of "general counteroffensive" and planned main force thrusts into the lowlands. In assaults on fortified French positions from January to June 1951 in the Red River delta, the PAVN failed to achieve its objectives and suffered extremely high casualties. After this setback the communists chose targets more carefully, partially dispersed their forces, and placed greater emphasis on political agitation and guerrilla warfare to bring lowland population and territory under their control. Main force units slipped through the De Lattre Line, a chain of defences around the northern delta, to hit more vulnerable positions.

Proof that the communists' setback was only tactical came in late 1951 at Hoa Binh. The French easily penetrated the area but were unable to halt infiltration of the Red River delta or sustain offensive action. The French held the major roads but were too dependent on them to operate on a large scale for long in remote areas. The largest French operation of the war, a thrust in late 1952 against PAVN supply and communications lines up the Red River, placed enormous strain on French resources, without lasting results. Even as that operation was in progress the PAVN swept small French outposts out of the northwestern hills and then, in spring 1953, struck into Laos. Vietnamese support of communist movements in Laos and Cambodia also helped to keep French resources dispersed.

By 1953 communist forces operated freely outside the major towns and cities, areas inhabited by anti-communist religious sects such as the Hoa Hao and Cao Dai in the south, and the mountain redoubts of a few pro-French ethnic minorities. Hoping only to restore stalemate, French commander Navarre then made the fateful decision to implant a "hedgehog" strongpoint in the valley of Dien Bien Phu, 190 miles (300km) west of Hanoi. The PAVN lay siege to Dien Bien Phu in March 1954, finally giving the French the big set-piece battle they had so avidly sought. However, the French had limited resources with which to support so remote an outpost, totally dependent on resupply by air. As the siege dragged on, the United States considered intervening but demurred after weighing the impact on its global obligations and the objections of the British. The French government, wracked by dissension at home, agreed to negotiate. Dien Bien Phu fell on May 7, the day before negotiations began at Geneva. The Geneva Agreements, signed on July 20 1954, permitted the French to withdraw and left the communists in indisputable control of the northern half of the country. Separate agreements were also concluded for Laos and Cambodia. *WST. See also* AUGUST REVOLUTION; BORDER WAR; DE LATTRE LINE; DIEN BIEN PHU, BATTLE OF; FONTAINEBLEAU CONFERENCE; GENEVA AGREEMENTS; HOA BINH, BATTLE OF; INDOCHINA, FRENCH REOCCUPATION OF; "LEA" OPERATION; "LORRAINE" OPERATION; NA SAN, BATTLE OF.

Indochina, Japanese invasion of. Japan exploited France's defeat by Germany in June 1940 to pressure the colonial administration of Indochina into giving Japan access to the peninsula. After Japanese attacks on French border posts in September, the French agreed. Japanese forces gained transit rights and airfields in northern Indochina and stationed troops at Haiphong. In July 1941 they occupied southern Vietnam as well. Leaving the French in charge of administration, the Japanese garrisoned Indochina with about 50,000 men and used it as a staging area for operations in China and Southeast Asia.

Indomitable *see* ILLUSTRIOUS.

Indonesia-Malaysia Confrontation *see* MALAYSIA-INDONESIA CONFRONTATION.

Indonesian War of Independence (1945–1950). The first phase of this disjointed conflict was between the Indonesian Nationalists and British-Indian forces dispatched to Java under the terms of MacArthur's last-minute orders to Mountbatten to take the surrender of the Japanese and liberate Dutch and other prisoners. On August 17 1945, Sukarno had proclaimed Indonesian independence with himself as president. Aided by Japanese collaborators, the young men who had formed the Japanese-trained military force *Peta*, were rearmed and deployed. Not until October 2 did advance elements of 23rd Indian Division disembark at the port for Jakarta (Batavia). Desultory street fighting ensued. Ordered to move only into key areas for the rescue of the POWs, 23rd Division deployed a brigade in Bandung, an improvised brigade in Semarang, and a brigade in Surabaya (together with a force in Jakarta). The senior British officer, Maj Gen D C Hawthorne, persuaded Sukarno to fly to Surabaya, and an agreement was patched up. The same day, October 29, the local British commander, Brig A W Mallaby was killed. Three days later 5th Indian Division landed. When negotiations broke down, heavy fighting followed, with naval and artillery bombardments and bombing by Thunderbolts and

Mosquitoes. Fighting continued for three weeks and British casualties numbered about 1,000. The Indonesians lost many more. The government of India informed Mountbatten that no more Indian troops would be sent to Java. Public opinion was highly critical, and out of 30 battalions all but four were Indian.

Mountbatten wanted to recognize the Nationalists as a legitimate force, as he had done in Burma, but Bevin as Foreign Secretary called for punitive action against these "terrorists". The British now had to reckon with an Indonesian army, *Tentara Keamann Raykat*, and despite their doubts about the Dutch military forces, implacably opposed to the Nationalists and all too ready to shoot, a force equivalent to two divisions arrived. They doubled the area of occupation: control was slipping from British hands. The Dutch and Indonesians laboriously reached agreement: the authority of the Republic was recognized in Java and Sumatra; elsewhere Dutch-sponsored administrations would join in a federal union. This agreement enabled the British to leave: the last units departed before November 30 1946.

After further desultory negotiations, the Dutch launched what they called a "police action" in Java, thrusting deep into Republican territory. The UN intervened and the parties agreed to accept the "Van Mook Line" in Java which yielded further gains to the Dutch. There was a large communist component within the Indonesian army and the 4th (Senapati) Division raised the Red Flag. Inter-unit fighting followed, but the crack Siliwangsi Division suppressed the revolt. The Dutch seized the opportunity to kidnap Sukarno, intending to liquidate the Republic.

International opinion, especially in Asia and Australia, was outraged. The US suspended part of their aid to the Netherlands. Negotiations were resumed and the Dutch agreed that sovereignty would be transferred to a United States of Indonesia before December 30 1949. This was not quite the end of the fighting as a Dutch officer, "Turk" Westerling, raised a mercenary force which swiftly captured Bandung (January 22 1950).

Disavowed by his government, he hastily departed.

The Dutch did not include New Guinea within the territory transferred and this remained in dispute, subject to ineffective Indonesian invasion attempts until, in 1962, the Dutch abandoned the attempt to form a separate semi-colonial state. After brief UN control, Indonesia moved in. Sukarno's doctrine of "continuous revolution" then led to "confrontation" with newly constituted Malaysia and jungle fighting in Borneo. This ended only when Sukarno was ousted by the army, 1965–67. *HT*.

INF Treaty *see* INTERMEDIATE NUCLEAR FORCES TREATY.

Infrared. That portion of the electromagnetic spectrum between 1,000Ghz and visible light. Hot objects emit infrared radiation which can be detected at low frequencies by thermal sights that can thus "see" in darkness. Guided weapons can also home on higher-frequency infrared emissions while optical sights can also see into higher infrared frequencies. Lasers used for range-finding and guidance purposes also operate in the infrared band.

Ingenohl, Adm Friedrich von (1857–1933). Ger. A protégé of Tirpitz, Ingenohl became C-in-C, High Seas Fleet, in 1913. Over-cautious, he failed to exploit his near-parity in battleships with Jellicoe in 1914: the numerical difference became increasingly unfavourable to Germany as the war progressed. Following von Spee's defeat at the Falklands, Ingenohl finally took the initiative. He sent battlecruisers to bombard the British east coat, hoping to lure out British squadrons to be destroyed by his supporting main fleet. But poor visibility, bad luck – and Ingenohl's caution – resulted in the withdrawal of the High Seas Fleet with the bombardments accomplished but the trap unsprung. His failure to support Hipper at the Dogger Bank led to his replacement by the equally cautious von Pohl. *CJW/CD*.

Ingersoll, Adm Royal Eason (1883–1976). US. Commanded US Atlantic Fleet from 1942, with responsibilities that included anti-

U-boat campaign until formation of specialized Tenth Fleet, May 1943. Participated in Operation "Torch", November 1942; commanded Western Sea Frontier from November 1944.

Intercontinental Ballistic Missile (ICBM). A land-based ballistic missile with a range of over 3,300 miles (5,500km). ICBMS may be launched from fixed sites, usually protected silos, or from road or rail mobile launchers.

Intermediate Nuclear Forces (INF). Nuclear forces with a range of 300 to 3,300 miles (500-5,500km), subdivided into short-range INF (SRINF), 300-600 miles (500-1,000km) and long-range INF (LRINF), 600-3,300 miles (1,000-5,500km). Land-based LRINF include the Soviet SS-20 IRBM and SSC-X-4 cruise missile, and the American Tomahawk ground-launched cruise missile and Pershing 2 IRBM. SRINF include the Soviet SS-12 and 23 missiles and the American Pershing 1 missile operated by the West German Air Force. All these systems are being destroyed under the INF Treaty and associated understandings. Both sides will retain nuclear-capable aircraft of intermediate range. Intermediate nuclear forces are seen as especially appropriate for nuclear first use.

Intermediate Nuclear Forces Treaty. The Treaty signed by the USA and USSR in Washington in December 1987 and ratified in Moscow at the end of May 1988; it came into force on June 1 1988. The treaty covers the destruction over three years of all land-based intermediate range cruise and ballistic missiles, both long-range and "shorter range", the latter within 18 months. Protocols to the treaty lay down detailed elimination procedures for the missiles and on-site inspection arrangements to monitor the process. The treaty is a bilateral US-Soviet accord, but the European nations with INF missile bases have formally acceded to inspectors having rights of access to their territory. Negotiations on INF began at Geneva in November 1981, but were broken off two years later when the first missiles arrived in Western Europe. They began again as part of the "Defense and Space Talks" in 1985. The INF Treaty is of great significance as the first arms control treaty to ban a particular category of nuclear weapon, the first to make major reductions of forces, as a precedent for on-site inspection arrangements and as a major step in improved East-West relations. *EJG.*

Intermediate Range Ballistic Missile (IRBM). A land-based ballistic missile with a range of around 1,500-3,300 miles (2,500-5,500km). In the late 1950s Thor and Jupiter IRBMs were rapidly developed in the USA and these were briefly forward-deployed in Turkey, Italy and the UK in the early 1960s. The Soviet Union maintained a large IRBM force into the 1980s until the INF Treaty.

Britons in an International Brigade

International Brigades, Spanish Civil War. In the autumn of 1936 during the Nationalist advance on Madrid, the Comintern, through the Communist Parties of Europe, called for volunteers for Spain. In theory non-partisan, the Brigades were entirely under Party control. Although some 35,000 foreigners served in the Brigades, the maximum was 18,000 at any one time, and by 1938, their ranks largely consisted of Spanish soldiers. The French contingent of over 9,000 was the largest although they became quickly disillusioned and left. Poles and German speakers represented some 5,000 each, Italians 3,000, the US provided slightly less and Britain about 2,000. In all there were volunteers from 53 countries. The first and reputedly best was XI International Brigade which fought in the defence of Madrid. Although their role has been exaggerated both by Communists and Nationalists, the Brigades greatly boosted Republi-

can morale. After Brunete, resentment at the waste of lives sometimes flared into mutiny. Many returned to their countries horrified by Stalinist witch-hunts for "Trotskyist-Fascist spies". The Comintern organizer of the Brigades, André Marty, admitted to executing about 500 Brigaders, nearly one-tenth of their casualties in the war. After their sacrifice on the Ebro, the International Brigades were withdrawn by the Republican government in a vain gesture to the Non-Intervention Committee. *AB.*

Intrepid. US aircraft carrier. *Essex* class; completed 1943. Marshalls; Truk raid (1944); Palau; Leyte Gulf; damaged by kamikaze at Okinawa but back in service by end of war. Subsequently full Hancock-type modernization with steam catapults, angled deck etc. In 1962 an anti-submarine carrier. Established as museum ship in New York Harbor (1982).

Invincible. British anti-submarine warfare carrier of 19,800 tons. In 1982, her sale to Australia had recently been announced as part of the defence cuts which included the proposal to scrap HMS *Endurance.* Her embarked Sea Harriers, with those from HMS *Hermes,* were an essential part of the British Task Force's air defence and close air support for troops ashore during the Falklands War.

Iowa. US battleship. Name ship of class; largest and fastest American battleships and the only surviving battleships; 57,540 tons full load, 32 knots; 9 × 16in guns. Completed in 1943, *Iowa* took Roosevelt to the Teheran conference, then joined Pacific Fleet. Screened landings at Marshalls, Marianas, Palaus, Philippines, Iwo Jima and Okinawa. In reserve for many years but recommissioned recently with guns supplemented by missiles.

Iran-Iraq War *see* GULF WAR.

Iraq, Rashid Ali rebellion (April 3–May 31 1941). Rashid Ali seized power in Baghdad on April 3. By late April the Iraqi Army was besieging the RAF training air base at Habbaniya, where Air Vice-Marshal Smart used training air-

craft as improvised bombers. He was reinforced with 300 troops flown in from Basra under Col Ouvry Roberts, who organized the ground defences. On May 18, "Habforce", an improvised relief column from 1st Cavalry Division in Palestine, reached Habbaniya, and went on to re-establish the Iraqi government in Baghdad.

Irish Republican Army (IRA). Terrorist organization dedicated to a united Ireland. With its immediate origins in the Irish Republican Brotherhood (Fenians; founded 1858), and the Irish Volunteers of 1916, the IRA was organized in 1919 by Michael Collins as the military branch of de Valéra's Sinn Féin. Refusing to accept the 26-county Free State after the Anglo-Irish War, the IRA turned against both Collins (assassinated) and de Valéra and waged civil war, 1922-23. Its continuing terrorism against Free State and British authorities culminated in a bombing campaign in Britain, 1939-40. From c1967, it has pursued an escalating campaign of violence aimed at ending British rule in Ulster, in which the "Official" IRA has been overshadowed by the more extreme "Provisional" IRA ("Provos") and the Marxist Irish National Liberation Army (INLA). *RO'N. See also* the essay UNDERGROUND WARFARE pp.322-324.

Irish War of Independence *see* ANGLO-IRISH WAR.

Irgun Zvai Leumi (IZL). Zionist extremist organization, founded 1931; from 1936 aided Jewish illegal immigrants to Palestine; developed systematic terrorist attacks on Arabs and British; killed Lord Moyne, British high commissioner in Egypt, 1944; wiped out Arab village, 1948; then disbanded.

Iron Curtain. The ideological barriers between the West and Soviet bloc.

Ironbottom Sound *see* GUADALCANAL.

Ironside Field Marshal Lord (Sir Edmund Ironside) (1880–1959). "Tiny" (he was massively built) Ironside's exploits as a spy in German Southwest Africa, following service in the Second Boer War, inspired John Buchan's "Richard Hannay" character. After serving on the Western Front throughout World War I, he commanded the Allied intervention force in Northern Russia, 1919; the British Military Mission to Hungary, 1920; and the Allied contingents in Turkey and Persia (Iran), 1921.

In 1939 Ironside was C-in-C (Designate) of the BEF, but on the outbreak of war Lord Gort took this command and Ironside replaced Gort as CIGS. He was ill-suited to the appointment. He shouldered the blame for the disasters in Norway and France before stepping down after Dunkirk to organize Britain's anti-invasion defences. Differences with Churchill led to his retirement in July 1940. *WGFJ*

Iron Triangle. The nickname of a communist stronghold in the Vietnam War located 22 miles (35km) northwest of Saigon. Bounded on two sides by rivers and on another by a forest reserve, heavily forested and thinly populated except for the village of Ben Suc, this area of about 116 sq miles (300 sq km) was headquarters of the communists' Military Region IV and the base of political and military operations in the capital region. *See also* "CEDAR FALLS" OPERATION.

Irrawaddy river *see* BURMA CAMPAIGN (1941–45).

Ise. Japanese battleship. Name ship of class, 12 × 14in guns. Launched 1917, rebuilt 1935–37. Midway operations (1942); converted to carrier/battleship with flight deck replacing after turrets (1943). Lack of pilots and planes made this expedient useless. Laid up and sunk by air attack (July 1945).

Ismay, Gen Lord Hastings ("Pug") (1887–1965). Br. Chief staff officer to the prime minister and a member of the Chiefs of Staff Committee from May 1940 to 1945. Completely trusted by Churchill, he was an invaluable link between the civil and military sections of the government and, later, between the British and American service leaders. He accompanied Churchill to nearly all the major Allied conferences. Ismay's chief personal task was to

supervise and promote deception measures. He enjoyed a spectacular and subsequently famous success with Operation "Mincemeat", which distracted German attention from Allied preparations to invade Sicily. *BB*.

Isolationism. American policy of non-intervention in foreign affairs, especially those of Europe.

Battles of the Isonzo

			Losses	
First:	June 29–July 7 1915:		Italian	14,947
			Austrian	9,958
Second:	July 18–August 3 1915:		Italian	41,866
			Austrian	46,640
Third:	October 18–November 4 1915:		Italian	67,008
Fourth:	November 10–December 2 1915:		Italian	48,967
	Austrian losses for 3rd and 4th Battles			71,691
Fifth:	March 11–15 1916:		Italian	1,882
			Austrian	1,985
Sixth:	August 6–17 1916:		Italian	51,232
			Austrian	41,835
Seventh:	September 14–17 1916:	}	Italian	75,500
Eighth:	October 10–12 1916:		Austrian	63,000
Ninth:	November 1–4 1916:	}		
Tenth:	June 10–29 1917:		Italian	22,950
			Austrian	8,828
Eleventh:	August 18–29 1917:		Italian	166,000
			Austrian	85,000
Twelfth:	October 24–November 3 1917:		Italian	305,000
	Austrian losses are not recorded			

Isonzo, Battles of the (1915–1917). There were twelve battles on the Isonzo river in northeast Italy, of which the first eleven were abortive Italian offensives, and the twelfth was an Austrian offensive that led to the Italian disaster at Caporetto.

Israeli Defence Force (IDF or NAHAL) *see* ARAB-ISRAELI WARS.

Italian armistice negotiations 1943 *see* ARMISTICE NEGOTIATIONS, ITALIAN.

Italian campaign, (May 3 1915–November 4 1918). Although Italy had been a member of the Triple Alliance with Germany and Austro-Hungary since 1882, she remained neutral when Germany attacked France in 1914. After hard political bargaining, she entered the war on the side of the Entente in May 1915.

Due to the Alpine nature of the Austro-Italian frontier, the cam-

paign was fought on two widely separated fronts. In the west, the great salient of the Austrian-held Trentino presented a constant threat to the cities of Lombardy, which the Italians could not ignore, although major offensive operations there were restricted by the mountains. In the east, the last 50 miles (80km) of the frontier ran across the Venetian plain just west of the Julian Alps and the Istrian peninsula where the city of Trieste was the coveted Italian objective. Most of the major operations took place on the rivers of the Venetian plain: from east to west, the Isonzo, the Tagliamento and the Piave.

The Italian army had gained recent operational experience in Libya, but its logistic resources and artillery were inadequate by European standards. However, it had the advantage of operating on interior lines. Its reserves could be switched between fronts using the extensive Italian railway network, more quickly than the Austrians could move theirs through the Alps. The Austrians were better equipped and trained, but the bulk of their army was deployed in central Europe, facing the Russians.

Initially, Conrad von Hötzendorf, the Austrian COS, adopted a defensive strategy towards Italy. The Italians, on the other hand, wishing to expand their frontiers eastwards, mounted 11 offensives across the Isonzo towards Trieste between June 1915 and August 1917 (*see* ISONZO, BATTLES OF). Such marginal successes as they achieved were bought at the debilitating cost of over 1,000,000 casualties.

The Austrians made one attempt in 1916 to exploit their possession of the Trentino salient. On May 14 the Archduke Eugene attacked there on a 21-mile (34km) front east of the Adige valley, but had little more success than the Italians on the Isonzo. Operations were halted on June 3 when the opening of Brusilov's offensive on the Eastern Front forced Conrad to rush troops eastwards. The Austrian Emperor Franz Joseph died in November 1916. His successor, Karl, replaced Conrad as Austrian COS with Gen Arz von Straussenberg in February 1917. Conrad was sent to command the Trentino Front.

Gen Cadorna, the Italian COS, was preparing to mount the Twelfth Battle of the Isonzo when the Russian collapse on the Eastern Front in July 1917 freed German and Austrian troops for counteroffensives in the West. Ludendorff, by then Chief of German General Staff, sent Arz a force under Gen Otto von Below of six experienced infantry divisions and a new *Jäeger* division of storm battalions to spearhead an offensive on the Isonzo. Allied intelligence warned Cadorna in time to go onto the defensive before the Austrians attacked.

The Twelfth Battle of the Isonzo, called the Battle of Caporetto, started on October 24 1917. Von Below's German troops broke through the Italian front near Caporetto with an early version of the infiltration tactics, using specially trained and motivated stormtroopers, which were to prove so successful on the Western Front in March 1918. The Italian Second Army collapsed in a rout, and Cadorna was forced to withdraw over the Tagliamento to form a new front on the Piave.

When the enormity of the disaster – 265,000 Italians taken prisoner and 40,000 battle casualties – became known, there was a spontaneous upsurge of Italian nationalism. The poet Gabriele D'Annunzio, and the journalist Be-

nito Mussolini were prominent in sounding the clarion calls and every city, town and village sent its contingent to help replace the Army's losses. The Western Allies responded too by rushing six French and five British divisions to Italy. The front was stabilized on the Piave; and Cadorna was superseded by Gen Armando Diaz as Italian COS.

The Peace of Brest-Litovsk in March 1918 freed still more Austrian troops for the Italian front, but growing racial disharmony within the multi-racial Austro-Hungarian empire was beginning to cause concern in Vienna. Victory in Italy was seen as essential to the continued survival of the Dual Monarchy, but Ludendorff could spare no German troops to help the Austrians.

The Austrian plan for the offensive was an unfortunate compromise. The principal Austrian Army Group Commanders – Conrad in the Trentino and Borojevic on the Piave – both demanded operational priority. Arz weakly divided resources between them and gave neither the principal role. When the offensive opened on June 15 1918, Conrad was defeated in the Battle of Asiago by the British and French divisions holding the Asiago plateau; and Borojevic failed against the Italians in the Battle of the Piave.

Despite pressure from the Allies' Supreme War Council, Diaz refused to mount a counteroffensive to profit from the Austrian failure. He was not convinced that the Germans could no longer reinforce their failing ally. The subsequent Allied victories on the Western Front changed the Italian view. If they did not strike quickly, they would have few cards to play at the peace conference. Nevertheless, it was not until the beginning of October that Diaz decided to risk an offensive.

In the Italian plan for the final battle in Italy – Vittorio Veneto – the Italian Eighth Army under Gen Luigi Caviglia was to breach the centre of the Austrian front on the Piave and wheel northwards to cut their communications with the Trentino at Vittorio Veneto. The Tenth Army (Lord Cavan), including the British XIV Corps, was to support Eighth Army's right flank. While Diaz was making his pre-

parations, the political situation in Austro-Hungary worsened. On October 16 the Emperor Karl granted autonomy to the principal nationalities within his empire, declaring the Dual Monarchy to be a Federal State. Instead of strengthening the Austrian war effort, the decree led to the Hungarian, Czech, Croat and Slav contingents in the army demanding repatriation to defend their new states.

The Battle of Vittorio Veneto opened on October 24 1918 in pouring rain. Only the British XIV Corps managed to establish an exploitable bridgehead over the Piave. Lord Cavan thrust his Tenth Army forward and scattered the Austrian divisions opposing him. His success enabled the rest of the Italian armies to cross the swollen river by October 28. The Austrian forces rapidly disintegrated as many units mutinied and made for home.

In the Trentino, there was a similar collapse of Austrian resistance when the British and French divisions advanced on the Asiago plateau and entered Trent on November 3. Austro-Hungary accepted the Allies' armistice terms that day; the cease-fire came at 1500 hours, November 4. *WGFJ.*

Italian campaign (September 1943–May 1945). The Allies had three strategic objectives in invading Italy: to drive Italy out of the war; to draw as many German troops and aircraft as possible into the Mediterranean before the landings in Normandy (which would be made in June 1944); and then to hold them there so that they could not be used to reinforce the Eastern or Western fronts. Each provided the basis for one of the three phases of the campaign; and all three were made easier to achieve by Hitler's obsession with his "no withdrawal" policy.

Phase one involved the landings and the advance to the Gustav Line (September-November 1943). Eighth Army (Montgomery) crossed the Straits of Messina on September 3, meeting little opposition, but was delayed advancing up the toe of Italy by German rearguards and their demolition of the poor Calabrian roads.

Marshal Badoglio and Gen Eisenhower broadcast their an-

I

nouncements of Italy's unconditional surrender as the landing ships carrying Fifth Army (Clark) were nearing the Bay of Salerno on the evening of September 8. The 82nd US Airborne Division (Ridgway) was to have landed on Rome's airfields to seize the capital, but the operation was cancelled at the last moment because too many German troops had reached the Rome area.

Fifth Army with VI US Corps (Dawley) and X British Corps (McCreery) landed at Salerno early on September 9. Although beachheads were successfully established and linked up, the Germans could reinforce more quickly over land than the Allies by sea. Had it not been for the weight of Allied bombing and naval gunfire, Fifth Army might have been defeated before Montgomery's Eighth Army could reach Salerno. The crisis ended with the junction of the two Allied armies on September 16.

Simultaneously with the landings at Salerno, the British 1st Airborne Division was landed from warships at Taranto, almost unopposed. It advanced northwards on September 11, taking Bari and Brindisi before the Germans could organize forces for their defence.

Hitler's intention at the beginning of the Allied invasion was for Kesselring to withdraw Tenth Army (von Vietinghoff) slowly northwards to allow Army Group B (Rommel) time to fortify the Pisa-Rimini Line (later known as the Gothic Line) in the Northern Apennines. The apparent slowness of the Allied advance north from Naples, which fell on October 1, led him to agree to Kesselring's proposal that he should attempt to check them on a winter line, running from the Garigliano river in the west, through Cassino and over the Apennines to the Sangro river in the east.

Fifth Army advanced on the western side of the Apennines, crossing the Volturno by October 15 and reaching the Garigliano on November 2. Eighth Army fought its way up the east coast, taking the strategically important Foggia airfield complex at the end of September, crossing the Trigno on November 2, and reaching the Sangro on the 8th. Both armies experienced steadily increasing

German resistance as they fought their way through a series of delaying positions in front of Kesselring's proposed winter line.

Hitler did not attempt to hold either Sardinia or Corsica, which were evacuated by October 3. On the Italian mainland, Kesselring's success in slowing the Allied advance resulted in Hitler making the final decision to hold them well south of Rome on the winter line, later renamed the Gustav Line. From then onwards, he would allow no further voluntary withdrawals in Italy. The campaign became a grim attritional struggle in terrain and weather that favoured the defenders.

Phase two included the three offensives to take Rome, staged between November 1943 and May 1944. Hitler's decision to hold south of Rome gave Alexander a strategic target, the defence of which drew more and more German forces into Italy. He made three major efforts to take the city.

From November 29 1943 to January 21 1944, Fifth Army was to continue thrusting northwards while Eighth Army made the main effort, crossing the Sangro, breaching the Gustav Line on the Adriatic coast, and advancing on Rome from the east. Clark's Fifth Army closed up to the Gustav Line, fighting the First and Second Battles of Monte Camino (November 5–December 10), and crossing the Garigliano on January 17. Defeat came, however in the First Battle of Cassino, which started on the 20th.

Due to bad weather, Montgomery did not cross the Sangro until December 1, and was then defeated in the battles of Orsogna and Ortona, December 4-28. He handed over command of Eighth Army on the 30th to Gen Leese before returning to England to prepare for Operation "Overlord". Alexander's first effort was spent.

The second effort to take the city occurred between January 22 and May 10 1944. Under pressure from Churchill, and with some misgivings, Alexander tried to manoeuvre Kesselring out of the Gustav Line by delivering an amphibious right hook to Anzio on the coast just west of Rome, while at the same time making a further attempt to break through at Cassino. VI US Corps (Lucas; later

Truscott) landed at Anzio on January 22, but Kesselring did not abandon the Gustav Line. On the contrary, Hitler was determined to teach the Allies a lesson by destroying their Anzio beachhead. Fourteenth Army (von Mackensen) was rushed down from Northern Italy to surround the beachhead, and five of Hitler's best divisions were sent from Germany for a counteroffensive.

The two major German attempts to destroy the Anzio beachhead started on February 16 and 29. Both were defeated, but in order to relieve the pressure on Anzio, Alexander was forced to mount the costly Second, Third and Fourth Battles of Cassino, where he had no more success than Kesselring did at Anzio. At the end of March, stalemate was accepted by both sides, and preparations were begun for the decisive battle for Rome when the weather improved in May.

The final attempt to take the city took place between May 11 and June 4. Alexander launched his "Diadem" offensive on May 11. Eighth Army, which had been moved secretly across the Apennines, breached the Gustav Line at Cassino; Fifth Army, attacking along the coast, linked up with the Anzio beachhead, from which VI US Corps (Truscott) broke out on Alexander's orders, to cut off the German Tenth Army (von Vietinghoff) as it withdrew northwards in front of Eighth Army. Clark unfortunately disobeyed Alexander's orders and turned VI US Corps' thrust northwards towards Rome. The city fell on June 4, but the Tenth Army escaped. Alexander had drawn 23 German divisions into Italy by the time Eisenhower's forces landed in Normandy two days later.

The last phase of the Italian campaign saw the holding and destroying of German forces in Italy. After the fall of Rome, the Allies were in strategic disagreement: Alexander, fully supported by Churchill, wished to exploit his "Diadem" victory with an all-out offensive to breach the Gothic Line in the Northern Apennines, and to advance through the Po Valley into Austria; the American Chiefs of Staff, with Roosevelt's agreement, insisted on invading Southern France and on withdrawing the necessary troops (including Juin's mountain-trained French Expeditionary Corps) from Italy to do so. The planned invasion was launched on August 15 and achieved little of strategic value, but it seriously weakened Alexander's forces in Italy.

Fifth and Eighth Armies pursued the German Fourteenth and Tenth Armies to the Gothic Line, fighting the battles of Lake Trasimeno and Florence, and seizing the island of Elba during June and July. Alexander hoped to attack the centre of the Gothic Line in early August, but Leese, commanding Eighth Army, persuaded him that it would be sounder to move Eighth Army secretly back across the Apennines to attack up the East coast where he thought the country was better for tanks. Highly efficient staff work and air superiority enabled Eighth Army to re-cross the Apennines undetected, but in doing so lost three weeks precious summer weather.

Eighth Army gained surprise when it opened its attack on the Gothic Line on August 30, but, by the time it reached the Po Valley, the weather had broken. In front of it stretched the waterlogged plain of the Romagna.

Fifth Army attacked the centre of the Gothic Line above Florence a fortnight later, taking the Il Giogo and Futa passes, and surprising the German defenders of Monte Battapaglia, but bad weather and Kesselring's ability to shift his hard hitting mobile divisions quickly between the American and British fronts prevented a breakthrough by either Allied army.

Alexander continued to attack in order to prevent Hitler withdrawing troops to shore up his Eastern and Western fronts. Eighth Army, now commanded by McCreery, attacked across the succession of Romagna rivers throughout the autumn, taking Ravenna on December 4 and reaching the Senio. The weather never cleared sufficiently for Clark to launch his final offensive in the Apennines to take Bologna. At the end of December, Alexander halted operations so that both Armies could rest and retrain for his spring offensive.

For the final spring offensive, Alexander proposed to carry out an envelopment of Trieste. Eighth

Army was to land in Yugoslavia, and advance with Tito's forces up the Dalmatian coast, while Fifth Army thrust its way north eastwards across the Po Valley, both armies meeting at Trieste before mounting a decisive thrust towards Vienna. When Churchill and Roosevelt met at the Yalta conference in January 1945, it was decided that seven divisions would be sent from the Mediterranean to strengthen Eisenhower's final offensive in Northwest Europe. Alexander was to confine his operations to pinning down German forces in Italy.

Alexander did more: in his final offensive, launched on April 9, he destroyed Army Group C south of the bridgeless River Po, and in the pursuit north of the river forced von Vietinghoff to surrender on May 2. The Allies' three strategic objectives for the Italian campaign had been fulfilled. *WGFJ.*

Italy, German occupation of (July 27–September 10 1943). Originally planned in May 1943 after the fall of Tunis, in which Rommel would occupy northern Italy with his Army Group B should Italy try to defect. During June and July, German divisions were infiltrated through the Brenner Pass. On July 27, two days after Mussolini's fall, Hitler ordered preparatory measures to be taken to implement a new plan for the occupation and disarmament of Italy. On August 8, Tenth Army (von Vietinghoff) took over command of all German troops in southern Italy, and ten days later Rommel did the same in the north. The infiltration of German troops accelerated, and when, on September 8, Badoglio announced Italy's unconditional surrender, the Germans had little difficulty in disarming Italy's armed forces except for the Fleet, which sailed to Malta and surrendered to Adm Cunningham on September 11. *WGFJ.*

Ito, Vice Adm Seiichi (1890–1945). Jap. Influential Japanese staff officer. As Vice-Chief, Naval General Staff, an architect of the Pearl Harbor attack 1941, and in 1944 a major advocate of the kamikaze effort. On April 6–7 1945, he commanded the "suicide sortie" of the *Yamato* task force and went down with the super-battleship.

Iwabuchi, Vice Adm Sanji (1893–1945). Jap. Commanded battleship *Kirishima* until sunk at Savo Island. In February 1945, commanding 15,000-strong 31st Naval Base Force and 4,000 Army personnel garrisoning Manila, Luzon, disregarded Yamashita's order to retire north and fought a street-by-street battle until March 3 1945. Iwabuchi and 16,000 Japanese died, along with *c*100,000 Filipino civilians.

Iwo Jima, Battle of (1945). Situated north of the Marianas chain, the small, volcanic island of Iwo Jima was a vital Japanese air base and a major US objective. The Japanese by the end of 1944 had

Flames of battle on Iwo Jima, 1945

turned the island into a fortress, garrisoned by 23,000 men. Following weeks of air raids and a three-day naval bombardment, US V Amphibious Corps began landing on February 19 1945. The assault troops of 4th and 5th Marine Divisions experienced severe difficulties with the surface of thick, volcanic ash that inhibited the movement of men and vehicles, while fierce fire was directed at the beaches by Japanese strong-points that had survived the American bombardments. But the Marines edged steadily inland, supported by tanks and flamethrowers, and by nightfall 30,000 men were ashore. In the south, the Japanese clung tenaciously to the extinct volcano, Mount Suribachi, eventually capured on the 23rd. The drive northwards, now including 3rd Marine Division, was hard-fought, but on March 26, Iwo Jima was declared secure. The Americans sustained nearly 25,000 casualties, while the Japanese garrison was all but wiped out with over 20,000 killed. *MS.*

Jackson, Adm of the Fleet Sir Henry Bradwardine (1855–1929). Br. Pioneer of radio, second in importance only to Marconi, with whom he collaborated from 1896. Responsible for the Royal Navy's early lead (first sets purchased in 1900) in this field. Much less successful as the First Sea Lord between Fisher and Jellicoe (May 1915–December 1916).

Jadar river, Battle of the *see* SERBIAN CAMPAIGN.

Jamestown Line. This was a defensive position established by UN forces during the Korean War. It ran from just beyond the Imjin river in the west to the north of Chorwon in the centre. It was seized in October 1951 as part of a series of operations launched by Eighth Army to improve its military position and maintain pressure on the enemy.

Japan bases for UN Command and forces. Japan served as a privileged sanctuary for UN forces during the Korean War, playing the same role as Manchuria on the communist side. The US maintained an extensive system of army, naval and air bases in Japan which it retained under a mutual security pact ratified along with the Japanese Peace Treaty of September 1951. Without this network it would have been impossible to fight the war.

Japan, logistic support by. After the Korean War broke out, Japan provided logistical support for American forces engaged there through the US Special Procurements Program. American war orders created an economic boom which provided the basis for postwar Japanese prosperity.

Japan, plan to invade (1945). The fanatical resistance displayed by the Japanese defenders of the Pacific islands had given clear indications of the difficulties inherent in an Allied invasion of the home islands. It was therefore hoped that the attritional effect of the Allied strategic air offensive and naval blockade would undermine the Japanese economy to such an extent that they would sue for peace. But contingency plans for an amphibious assault were

still required, and in April 1945 Gen MacArthur and Adm Nimitz instructed their staffs to draw up studies for the invasion. They produced a scheme for a two-stage operation beginning with a landing on the island of Kyushu on November 1 1945, followed, on March 1 1946, by an assault on the main island of Honshu. The first attack, codenamed "Olympic", was to be carried out by Gen Krueger's veteran Sixth US Army, numbering some 650,000 men, supported by the 3rd and 5th Fleets under Admirals Spruance and Halsey. Suicide attacks by Japanese aircraft and naval vessels were anticipated, while it was clear that the second assault, Operation "Coronet", would be confronted by the entire Japanese nation in arms. For this invasion, two American armies, the First and Eighth, would land on the Kanto Plain on the east coast of Honshu, backed up by a rapidly escalating reinforcement programme. Japan surrendered before the attacks were due to be launched. *MS.*

Jarama, Battle of (February 1937), Spanish Civil War. Franco's offensive south of Madrid to cut the Valencia road began on February 5. His force of 25,000 men backed by Col von Thoma's Panzer Mk Is and 88mm guns about to be battle-tested for the first time, attacked westwards from the Madrid-Aranjuez road. The Pindoque bridge over the Jarama was taken in a surprise attack six days later, and the Nationalist forces were soon attacking the International Brigades' hurriedly prepared positions in olive groves on the east bank. The ensuing battles of attack and counterattack caused heavy casualties, up to 20,000 killed and wounded on both sides. The Nationalist side nevertheless developed their inter-arm cooperation with effective close-support bombing by the Condor Legion's Junkers 52 and the skilful use of Fiat fighters by Nationalist pilots. *AB.*

Java Sea, Battle of (February 27 1942). Japanese naval victory off Indonesia against an ABDA fleet. Both forces consisted of cruisers and destroyers with no heavier ships present, although the Japanese had air superiority. The

Japanese commander, Takagi, had the most powerful ships, the heavy cruisers *Nachi* and *Haguro*; the Allies' heaviest cruiser, USS *Houston* had one 8in turret out of action and HMS *Exeter* was less powerful. However the Allies had three lighter cruisers (the Dutch *De Ruyter* and *Java* plus HMAS *Perth*) against the Japanese two. Fourteen Japanese destroyers were matched against a mixed bag of US (4), British (3) and Dutch (2) destroyers. The weary Allied force under the Dutch Rear Adm Doorman was handicapped by lack of experience in operating together plus inevitable communications difficulties. The well-trained and coordinated Japanese force won an extra advantage from their use of spotter planes.

The Japanese force was protecting an invasion convoy approaching Java. Battle began in mid-afternoon with a long-range exchange of fire. As the forces closed, *Exeter* was badly hit and had to retire. Then one Dutch and one British destroyer were lost. *Houston* received some damage, but the Allied force otherwise managed to survive the intermittent exchange of gunfire and torpedoes until dusk. A British destroyer then sank on a Dutch mine and, on relocating the intact enemy, both Dutch cruisers were torpedoed and sunk. Doorman was lost, but had already ordered the dispersal of his remaining ships. The loss of all three remaining cruisers followed rapidly in the Battle of the Sunda Straits. *CJW/CD.*

Jean Bart. French battleship. *Richelieu* class. Only 77 percent complete when the Germans over-ran France in 1940; escaped under her own power to Casablanca. Badly damaged by American bombardment in the 1942 landings. Not completed until 1949, scrapped 1970.

Jedburgh teams. SOE/OSS joint ventures. Three highly trained men – one British, one American, one local – took part in each of 93 ventures, parachuting into France, Belgium, Holland or Norway to provide training, leadership, advice and arms drops for resistance groups during the Allied landings in Normandy in June 1944.

Jeep: all-purpose workhorse

Jeep. Quarter-ton, 4-wheel-drive "command and reconnaissance car", developed by Willys for the US Army from 1940: name comes from *General Purpose* vehicle. Total wartime production: *c*640,000.

Jellicoe, Adm of the Fleet Earl (1859–1935). Br. c-in-c, Grand Fleet at Jutland, First Sea Lord 1916–19. A commander charged with a duty which afforded him the opportunity of a famous victory, which might not much have changed the subsequent course of the war, and also the risk of a defeat, which would have done so. On his own admission, he missed one of the greatest opportunities a man ever had: victory at Jutland on the scale of Nelson's at Trafalgar. But Jellicoe's real task was to ensure that, whatever actions might occur, the Grand Fleet would remain superior to the High Seas Fleet, for if that balance was lost, Britain, an inferior military power, was also lost. As Churchill put it, Jellicoe was the man who had the opportunity of losing the war in a day.

Jellicoe had made meticulous plans for the action with the German High Seas Fleet. He had anticipated that his freedom of action would be restricted by the threat of torpedoes and mines and he had rehearsed the means by which, notwithstanding, he believed that the German main fleet could be brought to action and destroyed. In the event, two factors weighed against his preparations; low visibility which made Scheer's movements obscure, and abysmal communications, which meant that Jellicoe's intelligence of them, once spotted, was late and inaccurate.

In the final reckoning Jellicoe's calculated caution was justified by the facts that the German fleet did not come out again and that his apparently more daring successor,

Beatty, when saddled with Jellicoe's responsibilities, followed a distinctly similar policy of caution. *ANF.*

Jerusalem, capture of (1917). Following the British capture of Gaza, Gen Allenby, aspiring to take the Holy City of Jerusalem by Christmas, ordered yet another offensive. The advance began on November 18 1917 in cold, wet weather. The fighting ebbed and flowed over the Judean hills with the 75th Division capturing the strategically important village of Nabi Samweil on the 21st. Counterattacks frequently forced the advance to halt, but only at the expense of heavy Turkish casualties. At last Gen Chetwode's XX Corps came up against the Turkish Seventh Army's defensive ring around Jerusalem. At dawn on December 8 the British forces attacked, making sufficient headway against the Turkish strongpoints to force a withdrawal. This evacuation remained largely unnoticed and it was left to two infantry sergeants to discover on the morning of the 9th that the city was undefended. British casualties in men and animals had been high but the Turks had also suffered badly and lost valuable reserves that they had planned to employ in a counterattack in Mesopotamia. Above all, the capture of Jerusalem offered an important boost to morale at a time when the Allies had encountered major setbacks on other fronts. *MS.*

Jervis Bay *see* FEGEN, CAPT EDWARD FOGARTY.

Jeschonnek, Gen Hans (1899–1943). Ger. Originally an infantry officer in the Imperial German Army, Jeschonnek transferred to flying duties in 1917, serving with Erhard Milch as a fighter pilot in *Jagdstaffel* 40. Between the wars he was directly involved in the formation and expansion of the Luftwaffe, and he became its cos, in succession to Stumpff, in 1939. Like Hitler, whose views he rarely questioned, Jeschonnek saw aircraft primarily as an offensive weapon and championed the dive-bomber and close air support for ground troops, but he allowed development and production, particularly of fighter air-

craft, to stagnate until late 1942 – a failure which subsequently placed the Luftwaffe at a severe disadvantage. Unaccustomed to defensive operations, he came under increasing criticism from Hitler and Göring as the Allied bombing offensive against Germany grew in scale and intensity. He shot himself on August 18 1943, immediately after the major Allied attacks on Schweinfurt, Regensburg and Peenemünde. *PJS.*

Jodl: hanged, then exonerated

Jodl, Gen Alfred (1890–1946). Ger. After service as a frontline artillery officer in World War I, Jodl became a member of the Reichswehr's General Staff. He was an early admirer of Hitler. In April 1939 he was appointed Chief of Wehrmacht Operations Staff (*Wehrmachtführungstab*), thus playing a major role in the direction of Germany's strategy during World War II. He was Hitler's closest military adviser, although the enduring relationship owed more to his powers as a courtier that his strategic insight. Like Keitel, Jodl rarely argued against Hitler's plans and contented himself with implementing his superior's orders. Inevitably Jodl became distanced from the realities of the war and, rather than listen to the advice of frontline commanders, followed Hitler's often fanciful interpretation of the strategic situation. During the Ardennes offensive of 1944–45, Jodl conspicuously failed to correct Hitler's faulty assessment of the material needed. Ironically, one of Jodl's few active roles in the war was to sign the surrender at Reims on May 7 1945 when he represented Adm Dönitz. Convicted of war crimes at Nuremberg, he was hanged on October 16 1946, but in 1953 was exonerated by a German de-Nazification court. *MS.*

J

The imperturbable "Papa" Joffre

Joffre, Marshal Joseph (1852–1931). Fr. The son of a cooper, Joffre served with distinction as an engineer officer in France's colonies before being nominated as a member of the *Conseil Supérieur de Guerre* in 1910. Regarded as a methodical soldier with no embarrassing political connections, he was appointed CGS the following year, also becoming C-in-C designate in the event of war. Plan XVII, with which France went to war in 1914, reflected Joffre's belief in the superiority of the offensive but underestimated the German strength and use of reservists. However, in contrast to the mercurial Sir John French and the nervous Moltke, Joffre remained calm during the crisis of August 1914 and, even as Plan XVII collapsed, cleverly transferred troops from his right wing to help form fresh armies on the threatened left. It has been argued that the Allied victory on the Marne owed more to Galliéni's vision than to Joffre's tactical judgement, yet it was Joffre who bore the awesome responsibility of potential failure. After the Marne his reputation was at its zenith and his position seemingly impregnable. Known as "Papa" Joffre, his bulky figure and imperturbable demeanour reassured compatriots and Allies alike. Nevertheless, with the advent of the trench deadlock, his lack of tactical imagination became more apparent and, considering that he was an engineer, he was slow to adapt his methods to what were essentially siege warfare conditions. His offensives in Champagne and Artois achieved little and weakened the French army, while at Loos in September 1915 and on the Somme in 1916 he imposed an unsuitable choice of ground for attack upon his British

allies. Disenchantment with him grew, and although he survived an attempt by Galliéni to dilute his power, he was blamed for the neglect of Verdun's defences. Ironically, during the defensive phase of the 1916 battle at Verdun, Joffre again acted as a steadying influence, deploying his reserves with skill, but in the end Nivelle and Pétain emerged with the lion's share of the credit. Joffre was finally replaced by Nivelle in December 1916 and took no further part in the war. *PJS*.

Johnson, Air Vice-Marshal James Edgar ("Johnnie") (b.1915). Br. The officially accredited top-scoring British fighter pilot of World War II with 38 kills. He also served in the Korean War.

Johnson, President Lyndon Baines (1908–73). US. Succeeded Kennedy upon the latter's assassination in November 1963. Guided by advisers retained from the Kennedy Administration, Johnson committed the United States to war in Vietnam by obtaining the Tonkin Gulf Resolution from Congress, ordering retaliatory strikes on North Vietnam, and approving the deployment of over half a million American ground forces for offensive action. He was reluctant to mobilize further for fear of impact on domestic programmes. When the 1968 Tet offensive discredited claims of imminent victory, Johnson turned for advice to advocates of compromise, announced a unilateral halt to the bombing of North Vietnam, accepted negotiations, and declared his intention not to run for re-election. *WST*.

Johnson, Lt Col Robert S (b.1920). US. Having joined the USAAF in November 1941, he flew P-47s from the UK with the US 56th Fighter Group, April 1943–May 1944, completing 100 missions and scoring 27 confirmed victories. Johnson was a test pilot with Republic Aviation after World War II.

Joint Chiefs of Staff. The American professional heads of the Navy, Army and, after they became separate services, the Air Force and Marines, acting together to advise the government.

Joint Surveillance and Target Attack Radar System (JSTARS). An American airborne radar system that can survey the situation on the ground deep into hostile territory, detecting, locating and classifying slow-moving targets such as tanks in order to give warning of attack and to target various deep-strike systems. Such surveillance capability is a prerequisite for FOFA (Follow On Forces Attack). The system is carried on a variant of the Boeing 707, the EC-18c, and combines synthetic aperture radar technology with advanced computer processing. Targeting information is passed digitally to army and air force commanders. JSTARS promises a major breakthrough in the ability to see behind enemy lines on a "real-time" basis.

Joint Tactical Information Distribution System (JTIDS). An American joint service information system under development that will allow automatic interchange of coded digital data between surveillance and combat platforms, both in the air and on the ground. The system fires information in short bursts with rapid changes of frequency and is virtually invulnerable to hostile ECM. JTIDS will give e.g. combat pilots a complete "real time" picture of the developing operational environment and their own location in relation to both friendly and hostile forces.

Jones, Lt Col H, VC, (1939–82). Br. Officer commanding 2nd Battalion the Parachute Regiment (2 Para) during the Falklands War of 1982. Killed in action near Goose Green. Before going into battle, he threatened to sue the Secretary of State for Defence, John Nott, if any of his men died in the engagement; this was due to the announcement, probably originating from the Ministry of Defence and broadcast on BBC World Service on May 27, that 2 Para was within 5 miles (8km) of Darwin Settlement. Posthumously awarded the VC.

Jones, Professor R V (b.1911). Br. Of all the scientists employed to aid the British war effort in World War II, Jones was one of the most brilliant. He was unusual, and perhaps unique, in retaining the complete confidence of Tizard and Cherwell and he was able to bring the fruit of his brilliant deduction to bear directly upon Churchill himself. Among his most important divinations was the German system of beam navigation used in the attack on Coventry.

Joubert de la Ferté, Air Chief Marshal Sir Philip (1887–1965). Br. Joined the Royal Flying Corps in 1913 and served throughout World War I, transferring to the RAF in 1918. Subsequently Commandant of the RAF Staff College, 1930–34. In 1939 made Assistant Chief of the Air Staff, with particular responsibility for radar and maritime air warfare – hitherto a neglected area. In 1941 he was appointed to Coastal Command, where he created a highly effective anti-submarine force which eventually played a decisive role in the Battle of the Atlantic. Retiring in 1943, he was immediately re-employed on Mountbatten's staff in Southeast Asia Command as Deputy Chief of Staff with responsibility for Information and Civil Affairs. *MH.*

Joy, Vice Adm Charles Turner (1895–1956). US. Commander, US Naval Forces Far East, when the Korean War began. Joy was nominated by Gen Ridgway to head the UN Command armistice delegation in July 1951, an experience he often found frustrating. He asked to be relieved, April 1952, and was replaced by Lt Gen Harrison.

Joyce, William ("Lord Haw-Haw") (1906–1946). Born in the USA of Anglo-Irish parentage, Joyce spent World War II in Germany, becoming notorious for anti-British propaganda broadcasts in a pretentiously genteel accent. Charged with treason against Britain in 1945, he claimed US citizenship, but the fact that he had held a British passport – albeit obtained by a false declaration – from 1933 until July 1940 was sufficient to send him to the gallows.

Juin, Marshal Alphonse (1888–1967). Fr. Graduated with distinction from the St Cyr Military Academy in 1912 and received early combat experience with a colonial unit in Morocco. Served on the Western Front for much of World War I; wounded and decorated for bravery. In October 1919 entered staff college, then returned to North Africa, where he took part in the Rif War. During the 1920s and '30s held various staff appointments in France and Africa. With the outbreak of World War II, returned to active command, leading the 15th Motorized Infantry Division with conspicuous success during the Battle of France. However, he and his men were amongst the force obliged to surrender at Lille on May 30 1940. Released from captivity to command the Vichy forces in Morocco and, after Weygand's dismissal, all French army units in North Africa. Never an adherent of the Vichy regime, he helped to engineer the largely peaceful response to the Allied landings of November 1942. He soon took an active role in fighting German units in Tunisia, and in September 1943 formed the French Expeditionary Corps. This force, largely made up of North African units, fought well in Italy and participated in the capture of Rome. When the French divisions were switched to the invasion of Southern France, Juin was appointed Chief of Staff of National Defence. He continued to serve in the postwar French army and held several senior posts in NATO. *MS.*

July Plot (1944). Gestapo distinguished among Hitler's opponents a group of senior staff officers and diplomats who disapproved of both his morality and his methods. Their leading figure was Gen Ludwig Beck (1880–1944), Chief of Army Staff 1935–38; backed by Ulrich von Hassell, former ambassador in Rome; K F Goerdeler, former mayor of Leipzig; H B Gisevius, vice-consul in Zürich; and Hans Oster, deputy to Adm Canaris. A group of younger officers centred on Count Helmuth von Moltke. Col Count Claus Schenk Stauffenberg (1907–44) emerged as architect of a detailed planned attempt on Hitler's life, and overrode his colleagues' objections that they had sworn an oath of fealty to Hitler on their regimental colours. He had been severely wounded in Tunisia, so was an unlikely suspect. He managed to plant a bomb containing a kilogram of SOE's plastic explosive (provided by Oster) in a briefcase close to Hitler's ankle at a conference at Rastenburg on July 20 1944; he made an excuse to leave the room and saw the bomb explode. He concluded, wrongly, that Hitler was dead, flew to Berlin, and initiated operation "Walküre"; but Hitler was only debagged and shaken. The *Führer* and Himmler exacted a fierce revenge: Beck and Stauffenberg were dead before the night was out, and most of their colleagues died after torture in the next few months. Hitler seized the chance to rid himself of the core of the Prussian officer class. *MF.*

"Junction City" Operation (1967). Led by American forces in the Vietnam War to search for and destroy the Central Office of South Vietnam (COSVN) and other communist installations located in War Zone C. Lasting from February 22 to May 14 1967, "Junction City", the largest operation of the war to that date, involved 22 US and South Vietnamese battalions. The operation mauled the 9th Division of the People's Liberation Armed Force (PLAF) and destroyed large stocks of weapons and supplies, but it failed to uncover COSVN and had no more lasting effect than to make the 9th Division shift its base across the border into Cambodia.

Junkers Ju 52/3m (German, WWII). Bomber/transport/glider tug; crew 3/4. First flew in commercial form 1932; military version produced for Luftwaffe 1934; 450 supplied 1934–35. Extensively used in Spanish Civil War as bomber. With Luftwaffe very widely used throughout World War II as transport, paratroop carrier, glider tug, ambulance and minesweeper. Production 1934–44 totalled 4,845; continued postwar in France and Spain. Three BMW 132T engines; max. speed 165mph (264kph); 1,102lb (500kg) bombs, one 13mm and two 7.9mm machine guns.

Junkers Ju 87 (German, WWII). Two-seat dive-bomber/ground attack. Prototype flew spring 1935; earliest production aircraft entered service summer 1937; three sent to Spain December 1937, more in 1939. Devastatingly employed against Poland, autumn 1939, but no match for effective fighters. Later used in Russia, Italy, eastern Mediterranean and North Africa; Ju 87G anti-tank version in service to end of war. One 1,800hp Junkers Jumo 211J-1 engine; max. speed 255mph (408kph); 3,968lb (1,800kg) bombs, three 7.9mm machine guns; Ju 87G, two 37mm cannon.

Junkers Ju 88 (German, WWII). Dive-bomber/night fighter; crew 4. One of the most versatile and successful aircraft of its war, in many sub-types. Originally designed to 1935 specification for high-speed bomber; prototype flew December 21 1936; orders for 1,060 Ju 88s had been placed by spring 1938; first operational sortie September 26 1939. Progressively modified and developed: torpedo, ground-attack, shipping-strike and night-fighter versions followed. Production, about 15,000 (all variants). Two 1,340/1,725hp Junkers Jumo or 1,730hp BMW 801G-2 engines; max. speed (Ju 88S-1) 379mph (610kph); 7,935lb (3,600kg) bombs, up to 16 machine guns in ground-attack form or single 50mm anti-tank cannon.

Junkers Ju 188 Rächer (Avenger) (German, WWII). Medium bomber developed from Ju 88; crew 4. Prototype flew September 1941; first production deliveries March 1943; photographic-reconnaissance version used Russian front; high-altitude variants with pressure cabin developed 1944. Production, total 1,076, apparently ended 1944. Two 1,677hp BMW 801C-2 engines; max. speed 338mph (544kph); 6,614lb (3,000kg) bombs, one 20mm cannon, two 13mm and twin 7.9mm machine guns.

Juno beach see NORMANDY, INVASION OF (1944).

Jutland, Battle of (May 31 1916). North Sea naval engagement. On the evening of May 30 1916 the British Grand Fleet steamed from its bases upon receiving word that the German High Seas Fleet was about to move into the North Sea. Adm Jellicoe exercised overall command and direction of the main body, which consisted of 24

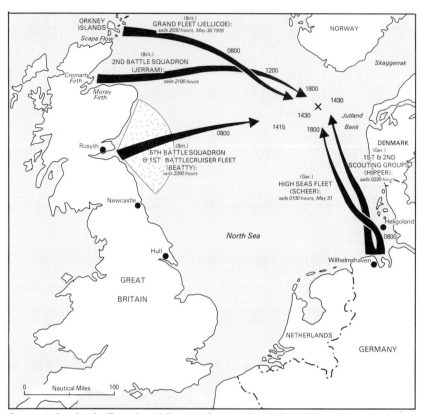

Courses taken by the British and German fleets to the clash at Jutland, May 1916

dreadnought battleships and three battlecruisers, while Vice Adm Beatty led the Battlecruiser Fleet, which contained six battlecruisers and four fast battleships. Adm Scheer commanded the German fleet as a whole and the main body directly, which included 16 dreadnought and six pre-dreadnought battleships, while Vice Adm Hipper led the scouting force, with five battlecruisers. Both sides deployed cruiser scouts and many screening cruisers and destroyers.

In the late afternoon of May 31, the battlecruiser forces of both sides – positioned ahead of their respective main bodies – encountered one another, the Germans turning to retire towards their advancing battleships. During the British pursuit (the "Run to the South"), which involved heavy action, two British battlecruisers were sunk. The British reversed course upon sighting the German main body, retreating in the direction of their own main body (the "Run to the North"), drawing the German forces into contact with Jellicoe's battleships and battlecruisers in the early evening. Just before the main forces engaged, German fire sank one of Jellicoe's

scouting armoured cruisers and battered another, which would later sink, while Jellicoe's battlecruisers smashed a light cruiser. Severe damage was inflicted on the German fleet in the ensuing fighting but skilful retreats and Jellicoe's unwillingness to pursue given the risk of losses to torpedo attack enabled Scheer and Hipper to exploit poor visibility conditions and disengage; during this period, a third British battlecruiser was sunk, and a German battlecruiser damaged fatally. Intermittent exchanges of fire occurred at dusk, and in brief encounters during the night the British lost a third armoured cruiser, while the Germans lost a pre-dreadnought battleship and three light cruisers. Good fortune, failures to communicate vital information to Jellicoe, and British misjudgments enabled the German fleet to escape. Over the course of the battle, the British lost eight destroyers, the Germans five. The failure to achieve a decisive victory, concern over material defects and heavy losses left the British deeply dissatisfied; the Royal Navy's dominance of the North Sea, however, remained undiminished. *JTS*.

Kaesong. Chosen by the communists as the site of the Korean War armistice negotiations in July 1951. In October 1951, at the insistence of the UN Command, the talks were transferred to the village of Panmunjom to the south.

Kaga. Japanese aircraft carrier. Launched as a battleship; cancelled under the Washington Treaty. Completed as carrier 1928; reconstructed 1934–35; 43,650 tons full load, 90 aircraft. Took part in Pearl Harbor, Java and Darwin attacks. Sunk by dive-bombers at Midway (1942).

Kaiser, Henry John (1882–1967). US. Industrialist who developed the assembly-line techniques – including prefabrication and simplified welding – that made possible the *Liberty/Victory* ship programmes of World War II.

Kaiserschlacht *see* MARCH OFFENSIVE, GERMAN (1918).

Kaiten. Japanese suicide weapon: a "Long Lance" torpedo lengthened to incorporate a one-man cockpit. Launched from a submarine or surface warship to steer a ramming course: maximum range 85,300yd (78,000m) at 12 knots; 3,418lb (1,550kg) impact-fuzed warhead. Some 150 *kaiten* were launched, 1944-45, sinking a destroyer-escort and a fleet oiler and damaging at least five other ships.

Kalabakan *see* MALAYSIA-INDONESIA CONFRONTATION.

Kaltenbrunner, Lt Gen (SS-Obergruppenführer) Dr Ernst (1903–46). Austrian. A former leader of the Austrian SS; became head of *Reichssicherheitshauptamt* (RSHA), the Reich Central Security Office, January 30 1943. His office controlled most of the Nazi organs of persecution and repression. He was executed for war crimes.

Kamikaze. The term most often used in the West to describe Japanese suicidal operations and weapons, principally aircraft, of World War II. *Kamikaze* ("divine wind") refers to the typhoon that saved Japan from invasion in the 13th century by destroying a Mongol fleet. Japanese prefer the term *shimpu*: the Imperial Navy's suicide squadrons were known as *Shimpu Tokubetsu Kogekitai* ("Divine Wind Special Attack Force"), and *toku* or *tokko* ("special") was frequently used as a euphemism for suicidal operations.

Kamikaze acts by individuals and up to unit level occurred throughout the war, but "official" kamikaze air units, formed by Vice Adm Onishi, were not sent into action until October 25 1944, at Leyte Gulf. The major commitment was at Okinawa, March-August 1945: 10 *kikusui* ("floating crysanthemum") mass kamikaze attacks and many smaller sorties sank 20 Allied ships (including 9 destroyers) and damaged 217, while conventional air attacks sank only 6 and damaged 45. According to a Japanese estimate, 2,409 naval and 2,206 army pilots died as kamikaze.

Other weapons used in kamikaze operations included the *ohka* piloted bomb; several types of midget submarine; the *kaiten* manned-torpedo; and the *shinyo* (IJN) and *maru-ni* (IJA) explosive motor-boats. By August 1945, suicidal weapons of all kinds – including c5,300 kamikaze aircraft and *ohka*, c520 midget submarines and *kaiten* and c4,000 explosive motor-boats were deployed in the Japanese home islands to meet the expected Allied invasion. *RO'N.*

Kammhuber, Gen Josef (1896–1987). Ger. Commander of the German night fighter force 1940–43.

Kammhuber Line. Linear system of German night air defence devised by Kammhuber in 1940. Consisted of a series of "boxes" each containing a Himmelbett, night fighter and searchlight support, extending across the likely Bomber Command approaches. By 1943, the Line reached from Jutland to the Mediterranean.

Kampuchea *see* CAMBODIA, WARS SINCE INDEPENDENCE.

Kangaroo. Armoured Personnel Carrier based on RAM chassis. *See also* TANKS.

Kansas Line. UN defence line during the Korean War, running beyond the 38th Parallel from the Imjin river in the west to just beyond Kansong in the east. It was gained in April 1951 after a series of counteroffensives had driven the enemy from South Korea and recaptured Seoul. The Chinese spring offensives forced the Eighth Army back on No-Name-Line just north of Seoul, but by June it had regained the Kansas Line and moved on in the central sector to the Wyoming Line which controlled the base of the Iron Triangle (Chorwon, Kumhwa, Pyonggang), an area important for east-west communications. The military position was further improved by a series of local offensives in the early autumn of 1951, which created the battleline on which the armistice was later concluded.

Kapyong river, Battle of the (1951). Occurred 40 miles (64km) northeast of Seoul during the Korean War. The 27th Commonwealth Infantry Brigade, in a defensive position astride a bend in the river, north of Chongchon-Ni, was attacked by the Chinese on April 23–25 1951 during the first phase of the communist spring offensive. After heavy fighting, in which the Brigade was supported by US tanks, the enemy withdrew on April 25. The battle was the last fought by the Brigade, which was relieved by the 28th Commonwealth Infantry Brigade. *CM.*

Karch, Brig Gen Frederick J (b. 1917). US. Commanded first integral US ground combat unit in Vietnam, 9th Marine Expeditionary Brigade, which landed at Da Nang on March 8 1965 to provide security for Da Nang air base.

Karee Siding, Battle of (March 29 1900), Second Boer War. Some 3,500 Boers under De La Rey occupied high ground commanding the Central Railway about 18 miles (29km) north of Bloemfontein. Attacked by 9,000 British troops (losses 182), the Boers were forced from their positions and the way was cleared for Roberts' advance up the railway to Kroonstadt, new capital of the Orange Free State, and thence to Pretoria. De La Rey lost only 34 men. *RO'N.*

Karelian Isthmus *see* FINLAND, RUSSIAN INVASION OF.

Kashmir *see* INDIA-PAKISTAN WARS.

Casualty of battle at Kasserine

Kasserine, Battle of (February 18–22 1943). Rommel launched his spoiling offensive against II US Corps (Fredendall) immediately after von Arnim had driven 1st US Armoured Division out of Sidi Bou Zid on February 14. He attacked the Kasserine Pass on the 19th with the Afrika Korps' Assault Group, and routed the inexperienced American troops sent to defend it, spreading alarm amongst the Allies, whose rear areas were exposed. Having cleared the American threat to his own rear, he broke off the offensive on the 22nd, and drove back south to attack Montgomery at Medenine.

Katyn Wood massacre. Mass murder of 4,253 Polish POWs by the NKVD. The corpses were discovered by the Germans in 1943.

Katyusha. Mobile Soviet multiple rocket projector used for area bombardment. Introduced during World War II; variants remain in service in the 1980s.

Kawabe, Lt Gen Masakazu (1886–1965). Jap. COS to China Expeditionary Force, then Commander Burma Area Army, 1943. Proclaimed Burma's "independence", August 1 1943. Commander, Central District Army, 1944.

Kawabe, Lt Gen Torashiro (1890–1960). Jap. A long-serving staff officer, brother of Masakazu Kawabe; appointed Army Vice-COS in April 1945. On August 19–21 1945, he flew to Manila as plenipotentiary to MacArthur, receiving the US commander's instructions regarding the surrender ceremony, the demobilization of Japanese forces, and the initial stages of the occupation.

Kawanishi Type 2 Flying Boat (H8K2) "Emily" (Japanese, WWII). Long-range maritime reconnaissance-bomber; crew 10. Prototype flew December 30 1940; officially adopted June 26 1943. Exceptionally long range and heavy armament made it formidable and effective in the Pacific. Production 175. Four 1,850hp Mitsubishi MK4Q Kasei engines; max. speed 282mph (454kph); 3,528lb (1,600kg) bombs, or two 1,764lb (800kg) or 2,204lb (1,000kg) torpedoes; three 20mm cannon, three 7.7mm machine guns.

Kawanishi N1K2-J *Shiden-Kai* **(Violet Lightning) "George"** (Japanese, WWII). Single-seat fighter derived from *Kyofu* seaplane fighter; prototype *Shiden* flew December 27 1942. Production aircraft coming forward late 1943; engine and undercarriage problems delayed general use for some months. More than a match for contemporary American fighters 1944; development *Shiden-Kai* better still, but production severely hampered by American strategic bombing. Production 1,007 *Shiden*, 428 *Shiden-Kai*. One 1,990hp Nakajima NK9H Homare 21 engine; max. speed 370mph (595kph); four 20mm Type 99 cannon, up to 1,102lb (500kg) bombs.

Kawasaki Ki 61 Hien (Swallow), "Tony" (Japanese, WWII). Single-seat high-altitude interceptor fighter; prototype flew December 1941. First production delivery August 1942; operational use began April 1943. Heavier armament fitted to some aircraft; extensive modifications made to the design. Combat qualities excellent but use impaired by serious engine defects. American bombing virtually stopped engine production; adoption (late 1944) of 1,500hp Mitsubishi Ha 112-II engine created the very successful Ki 100. Production 3,078. One 1,175hp Kawasaki Ha 40/1,500hp Kawasaki Ha 140 engine; max. speed 379mph (610kph); two 20mm cannon, two 12.7mm machine guns, 1,102lb (500kg) bombs.

Kearby, Col Neel E (1911–44). US. Commander of the US 348th Fighter Group in the Pacific, 1943–44, Kearby won the Congressional Medal of Honor for des-

troying six Japanese aircraft in a single mission near Wewak, New Guinea, on October 11 1943. Having scored 22 victories, he was killed in action on March 5 1944.

Keightley, Gen Sir Charles (1901–1974). Br. Commander 6th Armoured Division during the Tunisian campaign. He took over 78th Division in Italy in February 1944, was promoted to command V Corps in August, and remained in its command for the rest of the Italian campaign. Subsequently he was C-in-C BAOR, 1948–51: C-in-C Far East Land Forces, 1951–3; C-in-C Middle East, 1953–7, commanding the Anglo-French forces in the Suez Crisis of 1956 before becoming Governor of Gibraltar, 1958–62.

"Hitler's lackey": Field Marshal Keitel

Keitel, Field Marshal Wilhelm (1882–1946). German. Served in the artillery and then held various staff posts, Western Front, World War I; with the Freikorps on the Polish border, 1919. Keitel, exploited his personal contacts to gain a succession of staff and command posts. In 1935 he became chief of the Armed Forces Office (*Wehrmachtamt*) of the Defence Ministry, but was soon dismissed as inadequate by von Blomberg. But Keitel's pliancy appealed to Hitler, who in February 1938 appointed him Chief of the High Command of the Armed Forces (OKW), where his major role was slavishly to endorse Hitler's strategic decisions. He acquiesced in the worst features of Nazi oppression, *inter alia* issuing the infamous *Nacht und Nebel* ("Night and Fog") decree. Keitel signed the final ratification of surrender at Berlin, May 8 1945. Convicted at the Nuremberg trials of war crimes, he was hanged on October 16 1946. *MS*.

Kennedy, John Fitzgerald (1917–63). US. Lieutenant, US Navy (commander PT–109 torpedo boat), 1941–45. 35th President of the United States, 1961–63, when the US reached the apogee of its military power and international influence. The "finest hour" of his Administration was the resolution of the Cuban Missile Crisis (1962). Favoured counter-insurgency strategy in Cold War, especially in East Asia; inaugurated the space race. Assassinated Dallas, Texas, November 22 1963. *BHR.*

Kenney, Gen George C (1889–1977). US. A man of immense drive and ability, Kenney joined the Aviation Section of the US Signal Corps in 1917 and served as an officer in France with the US 91st Aero Squadron, shooting down two German aircraft before the Armistice in November 1918. Although still only a lieutenant colonel in January 1941, he rose rapidly to the rank of major general by February 1942. In July that year he was appointed Commanding Gen of the Allied Air Forces in the Southwest Pacific, thus becoming Gen MacArthur's senior air officer. In September 1942 he also took command of the US Fifth Air Force. His units provided invaluable support for Allied ground and naval forces in the New Guinea campaign and the Battle of the Bismarck Sea and later helped to neutralize the Japanese base at Rabaul on New Britain. The use of parachute fragmentation bombs, the supply by air of troops in the jungle and the development of skip-bombing and low-altitude attacks against Japanese shipping were all techniques which Kenney fostered. From the summer of 1944 he commanded the Far East Air Forces and led this formation throughout the reconquest of the Philippines and until the end of the war, by which time his bombers were operating from Okinawa against targets in Japan. From 1946 to 1948 he was Commanding Gen of the US Strategic Air Command. He retired in 1951. *PJS.*

Kerch Peninsula, Battle of (1941–42). By the winter of 1941 the Germans were in control of the entire Crimean peninsula with the exception of Sevastopol. The Soviet High Command therefore decided to land forces on the Kerch Peninsula, the easternmost point of the Crimea, and attack the rear of von Manstein's Eleventh Army. On December 26, in appalling weather conditions, Soviet Fiftyfirst Army began landing near Kerch but failed immediately to secure its objective. Meanwhile, over 40,000 men of Fortyfourth Army went ashore near Feodosia and captured the port. The presence of these substantial forces in his rear forced Manstein to break off his attack against Sevastopol. On January 15 1942 he drove the Soviet forces out of Feodosia. Nevertheless, Gen Kozlov, the commander of the Crimean Front, and Commissar Mekhlis, Stalin's representative, determined to launch an offensive. Their attack began on February 27 but made little headway; on May 8, Manstein counterattacked. The Soviet units were poorly positioned and lacked adequate command and soon all three of their armies were in headlong retreat. By May 14 the Germans had entered Kerch. Kozlov frantically attempted the evacuation of his forces to the mainland, with little success. The Kerch enterprise was another disaster for the Red Army with the loss of 176,000 men, 350 tanks and 3,500 guns. Manstein returned to the reduction of the Sevastopol defences. *MS.*

Keren, Battle of (February–March 1941). In hard fighting from February 3–10, 4th Indian Division failed to manoeuvre Frusci's forces out of the strong natural defensive position at Keren. Platt brought up 5th Indian Division and launched a two divisional offensive on March 15. Italian resistance did not collapse for another ten days. Keren fell on March 27, Asmara on April 1, and Massawa on the 8th.

Kerensky, Alexander (1881–1970). Russian. A Socialist politician who played a leading part in the overthrow of the Tsar in March 1917. He became Minister of Justice in Prince Lvov's provisional government and in the succeeding coalition of Socialists and Mensheviks he was Minister of War. He believed he could maintain the Russian war effort and his brilliance as an orator created the illusion, shared among others by Lloyd George, that this might be so. In July 1917, he became Prime Minister. He escaped into exile when the Bolsheviks seized power in November 1917. Russia then made a virtually unconditional surrender to Germany. *ANF.*

Kesselring, Field Marshal Albert (1885–1960). Ger. COS of the Luftwaffe in 1936; Commander *Luftflotte 1* in the Polish campaign of 1939; Commander *Luftflotte 2* in the invasion of France and the Battle of Britain in 1940, and in the invasion of Russia in 1941. When Hitler decided to intervene again in the Mediterranean in the autumn of 1941, *Luftflotte 2* was redeployed to Italy, and Kesselring was appointed C-in-C South with the task of establishing Axis naval and air superiority over supply routes to North Africa. His responsibilities were progressively widened and he became all but C-in-C of Axis forces in the Mediterranean, which were nominally under Italian command.

After the fall of Mussolini and the Allied invasion of Italy, he proposed defending Italy as far south as possible, contrary to Rommel, who advocated withdrawal to the Pisa-Rimini Line in the Northern Apennines. Hitler sided with Rommel initially, but changed his mind when Kesselring managed to slow the Allies' advance north from Naples, and authorized him to stand on the Gustav Line.

Kesselring defeated Alexander at Anzio and Cassino early in 1944, but was decisively defeated by Alexander in the "Diadem" offensive in May, and was forced to abandon Rome and withdraw to the Gothic Line. When that line was breached by the Allies in the autumn, he advocated withdrawing to the Alps, but Hitler refused. Nevertheless, he managed to hold the Allies in the Northern Apennines until spring of 1945. On March 10 1945, Hitler made him C-in-C West with the impossible task of preventing the Anglo-American forces overrunning the Reich from the West. After the war, he was found guilty by the War Crimes Tribunal in Venice of atrocities against Italian partisans. The death sentence was commuted to life imprisonment. He was released in 1952. *WGFJ.*

Keyes, Adm of the Fleet Lord, Roger John Brownlow (1872–1945). Br. As a destroyer commander during the Boxer Rebellion, captured four Chinese destroyers by boarding at Taku (1900). In 1914 he was in command of the British submarine force and present at the Heligoland Bight battle. As COS to Adm Carden at the Dardanelles (1915), he did his best to push the naval attack to a successful conclusion and personally organized minesweeping operations in the Straits. He took over the command of the Dover Patrol from the unsatisfactory Bacon at the beginning of 1918 after a period as Director of Plans at the Admiralty and achieved much greater success in preventing U-boats from passing through the Straits of Dover. He was responsible for the spectacular but ultimately unsuccessful Zeebrugge and Ostend attacks in 1918. Perhaps fortunately, he failed to succeed Beatty as First Sea Lord in 1927. In 1940 he was retired, but was an envoy to the King of the Belgians during the German attack. Then appointed to the post of Director of Combined Operations where his immense seniority, enthusiasm for the offensive at all costs and lack of tact were probably counterproductive and his retirement in 1941 probably for the best. However, he can claim some of the credit for the formation of the Commandos. *DJL.*

Keyes, Lt Col Geoffrey VC (1917–41). Br. Son of Adm Sir Roger Keyes; led an audacious but poorly planned raid on what was erroneously believed to be Rommel's HQ in Libya. Mortally wounded during this attack on November 17–18; posthumously awarded the VC for his valour. *MS.*

Keyes, Lt Gen Geoffrey (1888–1967). US. Deputy Commander to Patton during Seventh US Army landings in Sicily; Commander of US Provisional Corps for rest of Sicilian campaign. Commander II US Corps throughout the Italian campaign, 1943–45.

KGB. Russian committee of state security, since 1953 name of the secret police of the USSR: supposed to have over 250,000 employees, frontier guards, interrogators, and spies at home and abroad. One head of KGB, Yuri Andropov (1914–84), rose to be head of state.

Khaki (derived from the Persian for "dust-coloured"). Shade adopted by British Army for field service uniform from 1840s in India. In more general use from 1880s.

Khalkhin Gol *see* NOMONHAN INCIDENT.

Kharkov, Battles of (1942 and 1943). In spring of 1942 both the Soviet and German High Commands laid plans for offensives on the southern flank of the line around Kharkov. Marshal Timoshenko's Southwest Front hoped to carry out a pincer movement against the German Sixth Army and seize Kharkov while Army Group South's Operation "Fridericus" was intended to reduce the Soviet salient around Izyum. The Red Army struck first on May 12 and opened large gaps in the German line, pressing to within 11 miles (18 km) of Kharkov itself on the first day. It only remained for Timoshenko to throw in his armoured reserves in order to complete the encirclement of von Paulus' Sixth Army. But the Southwest Front commander failed to act and Field Marshal von Bock was able to launch "Fridericus" as a counteroffensive. Belatedly, on the 17th, Timoshenko committed his follow-up forces but they were confronted by von Bock's offensive, which was strengthened by substantial air support. Although the Soviet forces endeavoured to resume their advance, German resistance had stiffened and a powerful attack from the III Panzer Corps and the Seventeenth Army made substantial inroads into the Southwest Front's south flank. Too late Timoshenko realized the threat to his rear and, on the 19th, ordered a halt to his offensive and a redeployment of his forces. But the Germans completed their encirclement on the 22nd. For the next six days they completed their destruction of Timoshenko's command, taking nearly a quarter of a million prisoners. Kharkov finally fell to the Red Army in February 1943 but was retaken the next month during Army Group South's counteroffensive. However, on August 3 an overwhelming Soviet attack was launched by the Voronezh, Steppe and Southwest Fronts. Recommendations that Kharkov be evacuated were refused by Hitler but by the 20th even he had to concede that the city might have to be relinquished. With their ammunition exhausted and threatened with encirclement, the German Eighth Army withdrew from the city and, on August 23 1943, Kharkov changed hands for the last time. *MS.*

Khe Sanh, siege of (1968). For much of 1967, the People's Army of Vietnam (PAVN) probed US Marine outposts along Route 9 just below the demilitarized zone. In response, the Americans and South Vietnamese increased the force at Khe Sanh near the Laotian border from a US Marine rifle company to 6,000 men. The PAVN laid siege to Khe Sanh beginning January 21 1968, maintaining pressure with massive artillery barrages and ground assaults for 77 days.

Many observers, including President Johnson, believed that the PAVN objective was to create "another Dien Bien Phu". North Vietnamese strategists, however, realized that overrunning Khe Sanh was impossible as long as the Americans were determined to hold it. The PAVN's main purpose was to draw American forces away from cities slated for attack on January 31. In this they succeeded, as the US Command dispatched 15,000 troops to reinforce other Route 9 outposts and used 50,000 troops to support Khe Sanh. For days after the attacks on the cities began, both Gen William Westmoreland and President Nguyen Van Thieu maintained that the "real" target of the Tet offensive was Khe Sanh. *WST.*

Khmers Rouges. The Indochinese Communist Party divided into three national parties for Vietnam, Laos and Cambodia in 1951. Dubbed by Prince Norodom Sihanouk the "Khmers Rouges", or "Red Cambodians", the Cambodian communists became increasingly radical and xenophobic after the election of Pol Pot as secretary general in 1963. During the Civil War (1970–75), the Khmers Rouges turned peasant youths from Cambodia's poorest regions into tough, disciplined and ruthless troops. Yet, suspicious of their Vietnamese allies, obsessed with ethnic purity and riven by factionalism, they exterminated cadres suspected of pro-Hanoi sympathies, depopulated the cities, and imposed a reign of terror on that part of the population that had not lived in "liberated areas" before 1975. Up to one million Cambodians died in the terror before the Vietnamese invaded in December 1978. The Khmers Rouges survived, with Chinese and Thai support, as a guerrilla movement based in refugee camps along the Thai border. They were militarily the most effective of the three components of the Coalition Government of Democratic Kampuchea resisting the Vietnamese occupation. *WST*.

Khomeini, Ayatollah Ruholla (1900–89). Iranian. Religious leader and prophet of the Iranian Revolution. He led riots against the Shah's land reforms in 1963; exiled 1964–79; returned to Iran in February 1979 as Mahdi Bazargar, or religious leader.

Kiel mutiny (1918). On October 28 1918, the German High Seas Fleet was ordered to sortie from Kiel on a supposed "death ride" against the British Grand Fleet. War-weary and aroused by socialist agitators, the crews of several of the 19 battleships and 5 battlecruisers mutinied. By November 3, Kiel was controlled by a "Sailors' Soviet" and the High Seas Fleet had ceased to be a fighting force.

Kiev, Battle of (1941). Four weeks into the invasion of Russia, the German army had achieved some stunning successes but some doubt existed as to its main objectives. Hitler ordered von Rundstedt's Army Group South to destroy the Soviet forces occupying a substantial salient around Kiev in the Ukraine. While the capture of Leningrad also remained a vital priority, the advance on Moscow was halted. Although most of his commanders expressed their reservations at this new strategic turn, Hitler's directives were implemented. Three German infantry armies, the Second, Sixth and Seventeenth were to attack around

Kiev while Guderian and von Kleist's panzer groups at the north and south of the salient were to execute a great pincer movement to prevent any Russian withdrawal. The German plan was greatly assisted by the ineptitude of the Soviet commander, Marshal Budenny, and Stalin's insistence that there be no retreat. By September 11 even Budenny had grasped what was happening as the Germans closed in around Kiev. Meanwhile the pànzers continued their advance and, on September 16, the northern and southern columns met at Lokhivitsa. Belatedly the Soviet High Command authorized a withdrawal but it was now impossible for the defenders to escape. On September 19 Kiev fell and by the end of the month more than half-a-million Soviet prisoners had been taken. Although the Germans had accomplished a majestic tactical achievement and the Red Army had suffered grievous losses, Soviet military power remained unbroken and Moscow and Leningrad were still in Russian hands. *MS*.

Kiloton (KT). A release of energy equivalent to 1,000 tons of TNT. Purely fission nuclear weapons are always in the kiloton range and most fusion weapons nowadays are also "only" a few hundred kilotons in yield rather than up in the megaton range. This is sufficient yield for most purposes.

Kimberley, siege and relief of (October 15 1899–February 16 1900), Second Boer War. Kimberley, Cape Province, was invested by Orange Free State forces (maximum strength $c10,000$) commanded first by Gen C J Wessels and then by Cronjé. The garrison consisted of 500 regulars and 3,500 militia under Col Robert Kekewich; the town's 50,000 civilians included 13,000 Europeans, among them Cecil Rhodes, whose bombastic appeals for action contributed to the unfortunate relief attempts by Methuen, repulsed at the Modder river and Magersfontein.

Boer bombardment was heavy but ineffective; only 21 persons were killed by an estimated 8,500 shells; total military casualties amounted to 134. Disease and starvation were largely limited to the non-white population, of whom

$c1,500$ died. Arriving on the Modder river in February 1900, Roberts flung forward 5,000 cavalry under Maj Gen Sir John French. Sweeping aside weak Boer resistance with a massive cavalry charge at Klip Drift on February 15, French entered Kimberley next day. The retreating Cronjé was trapped at Paardeberg. *RO'N*.

Kim Il Sung (b.1912). Korean. The North Korean leader during the Korean War. He was born when Korea was a Japanese colony and his father was jailed for nationalist activities in 1919. Kim joined the Chinese Communist Party in Manchuria, and after Japan's seizure of Manchuria, 1931, spent ten years as a partisan on the Korean/Manchurian border, retreating into Russia in 1940. He returned to Korea in September 1945 after its liberation by the Red Army and in February 1946 became chairman of the North Korean Interim People's Committee which emerged as a separate administration in the Soviet occupation zone. In November 1948, he became premier of the Democratic People's Republic of Korea (DPRK) and in 1949 Chairman of the Korean Workers Party, formed by a fusion of the northern and southern wings of the communist movement. In 1949 he decided to reunite Korea by force, a plan launched in June 1950. Despite his failure to achieve this goal during the Korean War, Kim remained in power. *CM*.

Kimmel, Adm Husband E (1882–1968). US. *See* PEARL HARBOR.

Kimura, Lt Gen Heitaro, (b.1888). Jap. Vice Minister of War, 1941–43 Commander, Burma Area Army, 1944–45.

King, Fleet Adm Ernest Joseph (1878–1956). US. In December 1940, King assumed command of the Atlantic Squadron (from February 1941, the Atlantic Fleet), taking charge of forces that by autumn were engaged in hostilities with German submarines. Following Pearl Harbor, King's reputation as a man of action led to his appointment as c-in-c of the United States Fleet, and in March 1942, he also became Chief of Naval Operations, the holding of both positions giving him control

K

of operations, planning, logistics, shipbuilding, and appointments. With the formation of the Anglo-American Combined Chiefs of Staff, which called into being the American Joint Chiefs of Staff, in January 1942, King became part of bodies that were charged with the overall coordination of the British and American war effort, thus being able to influence the making of strategy at the highest level.

King overcame British objections to the diversion of resources from the Europe to the Pacific, and built up superior forces that were able to take the offensive against the Japanese earlier than planned. In the European theatre, King obtained a commitment to build escorts in large numbers, supervised their production, and centralized the American anti-submarine command. King's selection of highly capable subordinate commanders, and delegation to them of considerable autonomy were also major contributions to the US naval success.

King's intelligence, courage and determination made him a great war leader. He was also parochial, petty, tactless, and hot-tempered, and as a consequence a poor diplomat. A strict disciplinarian, he was never a popular officer. His effective service life ended shortly after the war. *JTS.*

King, W L Mackenzie (1874–1950). Canadian. As Canadian Prime Minister throughout World War II, he hosted two Allied conferences and eventually ushered in conscription.

King George V-class. British battleships: *King George V, Prince of Wales, Duke of York, Anson, Howe*; launched 1939–40; 42,000 tons full load; 10 × 14 in guns. Well-protected and powerful; not significantly handicapped by Treaty imposal of smaller armament than contemporaries. *King George V* flagship, Home Fleet, during *Bismarck* action, 1941; Sicily, 1943; first flagship, British Pacific Fleet, 1944; bombarded Japan, 1945. *Prince of Wales* badly damaged in *Bismarck* action; carried Churchill to Atlantic Conference; sunk by Japanese aircraft off Malaya, December 10 1941. *Duke of York* served Home Fleet, mostly as

flagship, 1942–45, covering Arctic convoys and participating in Battle of North Cape; flagship, British Pacific Fleet, 1945. Survivors scrapped, 1957. *DJL.*

Kinkaid, Adm Thomas Cassin (1888–1972). US. One of the ablest US Navy commanders of World War II. Kinkaid commanded a cruiser force in the Battle of the Coral Sea, May 1942, when his handling of rescue operations for the survivors of USS *Lexington* was highly acclaimed. After heading carrier task forces off Guadalcanal, notably at Santa Cruz, Kinkaid relieved Rear Adm Robert Theobald (1884–1957) at the head of North Pacific Forces, successfully concluding the Aleutian Islands campaign. In November 1943 he succeeded Vice Adm Arthur Carpender (1884–1960) in command of Seventh Fleet in Gen MacArthur's Southwest Pacific Area. At Leyte Gulf, October 1944, division of command between Kinkaid's Seventh and Halsey's Third Fleet led to near-catastrophe: Seventh Fleet's escort carriers fought desperately off Samar Island to keep Japanese heavy units from the US transports, while a peremptory radio message from Kinkaid recalled Halsey from his pursuit of Ozawa's "decoy" force. Kinkaid commanded Seventh Fleet during the Leyte and Luzon campaigns. *RO'N.*

Kirishima see KONGO.

Kirk, Adm Alan Goodrich (1888–1963). US. Naval Attaché, London 1939-41 and 1942. Director of Naval Intelligence March-October 1941. He commanded the Atlantic Fleet Amphibious Force in the invasions of Sicily and Normandy (1943-44), then US Naval Forces in France. One of the great practitioners of amphibious war.

Kirk Kilisse see DECEPTION.

Kissinger, Henry A (b.1923). US. As special assistant for national security affairs to President Nixon, Kissinger sought to end US involvement in the Vietnam War on terms that would not undermine American credibility. He supported "Vietnamization" while secretly approaching Moscow and Peking (Beijing) to put pressure

on Hanoi to compromise. It was Kissinger's belief, however, that the trend in American public opinion favouring disengagement weakened Hanoi's incentive to make concessions. Secret talks between Kissinger and his North Vietnamese counterpart, Le Duc Tho, resulted in the Paris Agreement to end the war, signed on January 27 1973, for which both men were awarded the Nobel Peace Prize. *WST.*

Kitchener's "New Armies" in training

Kitchener, Field Marshal Earl (1850–1916). Br. Born in County Kerry, Kitchener was commissioned into the Royal Engineers in 1871 and by 1892 had become Sirdar of the Egyptian Army, reconquering the Sudan and defeating the Khalifa at Omdurman in 1898. He succeeded Roberts as c-in-c in South Africa in November 1900. His introduction of concentration camps aroused widespread criticism, although his attrition policy eventually wore down Boer resistance and he performed a conciliatory role in the 1902 peace settlement. As c-in-c in India from 1902 to 1909 he instituted overdue reforms, including the organization of standardized divisions and the modernization of training. In 1911 he went to Egypt as British Agent but, on August 5 1914, Asquith persuaded him to accept the post of Secretary of State for War. Virtually alone among Britain's military and political leaders in predicting that the war against the Central Powers would be long and costly, his greatest contribution to the war effort lay in convincing the government and people that they must prepare for a protracted struggle.

Kitchener quickly began the task of mobilizing Britain's resources and, in response to his appeals, nearly 2,500,000 men enlisted voluntarily before 1916, enabling him to expand the British Army to 70 divisions. He was fiercely attacked in May 1915 for the shell shortages experienced by the BEF in France yet he had, in fact, done much to build the foundations for the huge increases in munitions production for which Lloyd George later claimed the credit. However, being accustomed to making his own decisions, and distrusting politicians, he was ill-at-ease in the Cabinet system of government, while his reluctance to delegate authority temporarily weakened the Army Council and General Staff. Kitchener himself did not take the lead in initiating alternative strategic ventures and showed irresolution throughout the Dardanelles campaign. Indeed, although he was still popular with the public, his power and influence within the Cabinet and Army declined perceptibly during 1915. He was drowned on June 5 1916 when the cruiser HMS *Hampshire*, which was taking him on a military mission to Russia, struck a mine off the Orkneys. *PJS*.

Kitchener's Army. Although frequently used as a collective term for the 2,466,719 men who volunteered for the British Army between August 1914 and December 1915, the name "Kitchener's Army" is more accurately applied to 30 new divisions – numbered 9th to 26th and 30th to 41st – which were raised during the first 18 months of Lord Kitchener's term of office as Secretary of State for War. The infantry battalions of these formations were called "Service" battalions to distinguish them from corresponding Regular and Territorial Force units. Nearly 40 percent of the "Service" and reserve battalions formed at this time were raised by local authorities, and many were known as "Pals" battalions, consisting as they did of recruits who lived in a particular city or district or who shared a common social and occupational background. "Kitchener's Army" played a major role in the Battle of the Somme in 1916, where it suffered heavy casualties. *PJS*.

Kitson, Gen Sir Frank (b.1926) Br. An authority on irregular warfare and counterinsurgency operations, having acquired practical experience in Kenya, Malaya, Cyprus and Northern Ireland. When in Kenya 1953–55, served in a special unit formed to penetrate Mau Mau, using surrendered and captured terrorists in "pseudo-gangs" led by British officers disguised as native Kikuyu. As commander of an infantry brigade in Northern Ireland, achieved notable successes against Republican activists. Kitson subsequently became Commandant of the Staff College, Camberley, after commanding a division in the British Army of the Rhine, and was later c-in-c UK Land Forces. His *Low Intensity Operations* is in worldwide use as a textbook. *MH*.

Kiu-Lien-Cheng, Battle of (Battle of the Yalu, April 30–May 1 1904), Russo-Japanese War. A Japanese force of 40,000 (losses 1,100) under Kuroki forced a crossing of the Yalu river and drove the 7,000-strong (losses 3,500) Russian garrison from Kiu-Lien-Cheng.

Klopper, Gen Hendrik Balzazer (b.1902). South African. Commander 2nd South African Division; responsible for the defence of Tobruk during the Battle of Gazala in June 1942; failed to defeat Rommel's assault on June 20 and was forced to surrender the fortress.

Kluck, Col Gen Alexander von (1846–1934). Ger. In 1914 Kluck, already 68, commanded German First Army, with the key role on the extreme right wing in the proposed sweep through Belgium and the wheel west of Paris. On August 17, in a belated attempt to ensure the coordination of the right wing armies, von Moltke, temporarily placed First Army under the more cautious von Bülow, the Second Army commander, a step which Kluck resented. Bülow's desire to keep First Army within supporting distance prevented Kluck from outflanking the Allied left and brought him up against the BEF at Mons on August 23. However, three days later, after Le Cateau, Kluck lost contact with the BEF, mistakenly believing that it was retreating to the west, not southwards. He was released

from Bülow's direct control on August 27 but, tempted by the possibility of rolling up the French left wing, swung First Army inwards, east of Paris, thus exposing his own right to a counterattack from the direction of the French capital. During the ensuing Battle of the Marne between September 5 and 9, Kluck very skilfully reversed three of his corps and pivoted to the west to face the French Sixth Army on the Ourcq, yet in doing so he opened the gap between himself and Bülow which prompted Moltke's representative, Lt Col Hentsch, to order a withdrawal to the Aisne. Severely wounded in March 1915, Kluck retired the following year. *PJS*.

Kluge, Field Marshal Guenther Hans von (1882–1944). Having started as an artillery officer, Kluge held both staff posts and field commands on the Western Front in World War I. He did not become a convinced Nazi but saw benefits in cooperating with Hitler and commanded the German Fourth Army in the Polish and French campaigns, being promoted to Field Marshal in July 1940. During the advance towards Moscow in 1941 he was criticised by panzer leaders for over-cautious tactics, yet he retained Hitler's support and replaced von Brock as commander of Army Group Centre on December 18. Nicknamed "Der Kluge Hans" (Clever Hans), he fought mainly defensive battles in 1942–43 and, though forced back to the Dnieper and beyond in the latter half of 1943, kept his forces and front relatively intact until a motor accident in October 1943. On July 2 1944 he succeeded von Rundstedt as c-in-c West. Kluge could not stop the Allied breakout from Normandy and was blamed for the failure of the Mortain counterattack early in August. While never fully committed to the anti-Hitler plot, his involvement was sufficient to render his position extremely precarious and his temporary disappearance on August 15, during the Falaise battle, caused Hitler to suspect him of negotiating with the Allies. He was replaced by Model two days later. On August 19, fearing disgrace and retribution, Kluge poisoned himself on his way back to Germany. *MS*.

K

Knickebein. German system of beam navigation used for bombing England in 1940. It was discovered by the British, to a considerable extent due to the intuition and insight of R V Jones. Methods of jamming Knickebein were then devised. Somewhat similar to the later British system Oboe.

Knightsbridge, Battle of *see* GAZALA, BATTLE OF (1942).

Koeltz, Gen Louis Marie (1884–1970). Fr. Commander of XIX Corps throughout Tunisian campaign; commanded French sector of Allied front at Pont du Fahs in the final offensive, late April 1943.

Koenig, Marshal of France Marie-Pierre (1898–1970). Fr. Free French defender of Bir Hacheim during the Battle of Gazala, June 1942.

Koga, Vice Adm Mineichi (1885–1944). Jap. A former Vice-Chief, Naval General Staff, Koga became c-in-c, Combined Fleet, on the death of Yamamoto, April 18 1943. A conservative and unimaginative commander, he adhered to Yamamoto's concept of a "decisive battle": his "Plan Z", finalized on March 8 1944, envisaged the employment of Hollandia, New Guinea, as the major base from which US forces would first be devastated by air attack and then given the *coup de grâce* by surface forces. The concentrated US air assaults on Rabaul, beginning in October 1943, the loss of the Gilbert Islands, November 1943, and the near-neutralization by air assault of Truk, from February 1944, all partly ascribable to Koga's over-caution, militated against "Plan Z". Koga himself died in an air crash on March 31 1944, to be succeeded by Toyoda. "Plan Z" finally became inoperative when full details were captured by US forces on the fall of Hollandia, April 26 1944. *RO'N.*

Kohima, the struggle for (April–June 1944, the Burma campaign). Situated on a ridge, meeting point of three mountain spines, Kohima offered no space for manoeuvre: the main fighting took place across a tennis court. In the opening phase, the Japanese 31st Division surrounded the miscellaneous gar-

rison which fell back into an ever smaller perimeter, short of rations, without water and unable to move the wounded. By April 13, "Black Thirteenth", the British situation appeared hopeless. However, relief was on its way. XXXIII Corps, hastily summoned from central India, advanced up the road from the Dimapur base with 2nd Division leading. On April 18 the garrison saw British infantry and tanks advancing up the road. The Japanese still held most of Kohima, persisting in their attacks. But the British were steadily reinforced: the Japanese were not, and their 31st Division wasted away until, exhausted and starving, they received the order to retire. The vital road link with Imphal was reopened on June 22. British-Indian casualties in the defence and relief of Kohima were over 4,000 (three brigade commanders were killed). Japanese losses were higher: approximately 6,000, although many more died in the retreat to the Chindwin. *HT.*

Koje Island. Koje became the main holding centre for Chinese and North Korean POWs during the Korean War. The camp was poorly run and the compounds were the scene of a political struggle between communist and anticommunist POWs. When POW repatriation became an issue at the armistice talks, the communists scored a propaganda point by kidnapping the camp commander, Brig Gen Francis Dodd, in May 1952. As the price of his release, they secured a statement that the Americans had been terrorizing POWs. The mutiny was only put down when combat troops broke up the communist compounds. *CM.*

Kolchak, Adm Aleksandr (1874–1920). Russian. Achieved distinction as a naval officer in the Russo-Japanese War and as an Arctic explorer. In World War I he was a conspicuous success first in the Baltic and then in command of the Black Sea Fleet. Motivated by a desire to keep Russia in the war against Germany, Kolchak was respected by the Allies, who assisted his joining the White Russian forces at Omsk. In November 1918, a coup gave Kolchak command and the title of "Supreme Ruler". However, chaotic organiza-

tion and the multiplicity of sectional interests made effective control all but impossible. In addition, his qualities as a naval commander were not matched by his generalship and his 1918–19 offensive was first checked and then routed by the Bolsheviks. All but abandoned by his erstwhile allies, Kolchak resigned and was arrested by Bolshevik authorities in Irkutsk. He was tried for atrocities carried out by his forces and executed on February 7 1920. *MS.*

Koller, Lt General der Flieger Karl (1898–1951). Ger. Koller, a Bavarian, entered the Imperial German Army in 1914, transferring to the Air Service in 1917 and undergoing pilot training. Between the two world wars he served in the Bavarian police but joined the new Luftwaffe in 1935 and was made head of the operations staff of *Luftwaffengruppe 3* in 1938, this command being redesignated as *Luftflotte 3* the following year. An excellent administrator, Koller became *Luftflotte 3*'s cos in 1941 and, in September 1943, was appointed head of the Luftwaffe Operations Staff. In this capacity he grew increasingly critical not only of OKW's neglect of the Luftwaffe in the overall armaments programme but also of Göring's readiness to take advice from inexperienced young officers rather than his senior staff. Even so, on November 12 1944, he accepted the vacant post of CGS of the Luftwaffe and held it until the end of the war. Although a master of detailed staff work, Koller lacked the personality needed to achieve meaningful changes in Luftwaffe policy or the allocation of resources during the last months of the war. *PJS.*

Kolombangara, Battle of (July 12–13 1943). Night action fought one week after Kula Gulf: a further Japanese success in almost the same location. Rear Adm Ainsworth's Task Group 36.1 (three light cruisers, including HMNZ *Leander*; 10 destroyers) intercepted Rear Adm Shunji Izaki's "Tokyo Express" (four destroyer-transports, escorted by light cruiser *Jintsu* and five destroyers) carrying reinforcements to Kolombangara. Tracking the Japanese approach by radar, Ainsworth deployed for a surprise torpedo attack, but the Japanese, warned by radar detector equipment, launched torpedoes first. *Leander* was badly damaged; and although radar-controlled fire from US cruisers destroyed *Jintsu*, five US destroyers lost radar contact and left the action. Four Japanese destroyers retired under cover of a squall, reloaded their torpedo tubes and attacked once more. Ainsworth, fearing the approaching ships were his errant destroyers, held fire: the Japanese salvoes damaged cruisers *St Louis* and *Honolulu* and sank destroyer *Gwin*. The transports unloaded safely at Kolombangara. *RO'N.*

Kolubara river, Battle of the *see* SERBIAN CAMPAIGN.

Komandorksi Islands, Battle of the (March 26 1943). Notable as the only "traditional" daylight gunnery action (aircraft and submarines playing no part) of the Pacific War. Having made radar contact west of Attu, Aleutians, a US force (heavy cruiser *Salt Lake City*; one light cruiser and four destroyers) under Rear Adm Charles H McMorris intercepted at 0800 hours Vice Adm Hoshiro Hosagaya's superior force of two heavy cruisers, two light cruisers and four destroyers, escorting two large transports to reinforce Attu. In a gun duel opening at 20,000yd (18,300m), both *Salt Lake City* and the Japanese heavy cruiser *Nachi* were severely damaged. Failing with long-range torpedo attacks, Hosagaya attempted to close the range; McMorris, taking high-speed evasive action, ordered three destroyers to threaten a suicidal "charge". Thus harassed, low on ammunition, and fearing the intervention of US land-based aircraft, Hosagaya retreated with his mission unaccomplished. *RO'N.*

Komer, Robert W (b.1922). US. In May 1967 President Johnson appointed Komer civilian deputy to the commander of the US Military Assistance Command, Vietnam, in charge of pacification. Komer organized the Civil Operations and Revolutionary Development Support (CORDS) programme. He strongly advocated giving greater emphasis to political and economic development programmes

in the belief that the war was essentially a contest for the loyalty of the South Vietnamese people, which had to be won mainly by non-military means. He also inaugurated the Accelerated Pacification and Phoenix programmes.

Komorowski *see* BOR-KOMOROWSKI.

Komura, Rear Adm Keizo (b.1896). Jap. Commanded heavy cruiser *Chikuma* at Pearl Harbor, Midway and Santa Cruz. Ozawa's COS at Battle of Philippine Sea, June 1944, and led 1st Carrier Division at Leyte Gulf, October 1944. In April 1945, commanding Destroyer Squadron 2, survived sinking of his flagship, light cruiser *Yahagi*, when escorting "death-ride" of battleship *Yamato*.

Kondo, Adm Nobutake (1886–1953). Jap. Commanded 2nd Fleet 1941–43, covering invasions of Malaya, Philippines and Dutch East Indies, and attempted taking of Midway. Kondo commanded Forces at the battles of the Eastern Solomons, Santa Cruz and Guadalcanal. In 1945, he was appointed to the Supreme War Council.

Kongo-**class**. Japanese battlecruiser (reclassed fast battleships following reconstructions, 1929–30s): *Kongo, Haruna, Hiei, Kirishima*; launched 1912–13, 32,000 tons standard (reconstructed); 8 × 14in guns. *Kongo* last Japanese capital ship build abroad (Britain); participated Malaya operations, Midway, Guadalcanal operations, Phillippine Sea, Leyte Gulf; sunk by US submarine off Formosa, November 21 1944. *Haruna's* service mainly as *Kongo*; sunk by US aircraft while moored at Kure, July 27 1945. *Kirishima* participated Pearl Harbor, Darwin, Midway; scuttled after severe damage off Guadalcanal (*Hiei* sunk in same battle), November 1942.

Koniev, Marshal Ivan (1897–1973). Russian. Koniev was conscripted into the Imperial Russian Army in 1916 and saw active service in Galicia. An early convert to communism, he acted as a military commissar during the Civil War and participated in the suppression of the Kronstadt naval mutiny of 1921. In 1924 the politic-

al side of Koniev's career diminished and he transferred to the regular officer corps. By 1937 he was in command of a corps. His role at Nomonhan, 1939, was overshadowed by Zhukov's triumphs, but he survived Stalin's purges to take command of the North Caucasus Military District in January 1941. By July he was leading Nineteenth Army in the fighting around Smolensk and in September was rewarded with command of the Western Front. But his failure to check the German advance led

Koniev survived Stalin's pre-war purges

to his being replaced by Zhukov on October 10 and a transfer to the newly created Kalinin Front. Although he performed well in the defence of Moscow, his operations against the German salient around Rzhev were unrewarding. Nevertheless, in summer 1943 he was given command of the Steppe (later 2nd Ukrainian) Front. Thereafter, Koniev played a major role in most of the Red Army's victories. After the war he held many senior positions with Soviet and Warsaw Pact forces. *MS.*

Kontum. Kontum province in South Vietnam's central highlands was one of four "fronts" attacked by communist forces during the Easter offensive of 1972. On April 24 the People's Army of Vietnam (PAVN) 320th and 2nd Divisions overran Dak To, threatening Kontum city, the province capital of about 35,000 people. The Army of the Republic (ARVN) 22nd and 23rd Divisions, supported by American tactical aircraft and B-52 strikes, withstood the PAVN's assault in late May. The ARVN abandoned Kontum in March 1975 as part of the general retreat from the highlands ordered by President Nguyen Van Thieu.

Korea, Democratic People's Republic of State and Government (North Korea). The DPRK was founded on September 9 1948 by Kim Il Sung in the former Soviet occupation zone north of the 38th Parallel. It was dominated by the Korean Workers or Communist Party and claimed to represent all of Korea. Soviet troops were withdrawn at the end of 1948 although military advisers remained with the NKPA and economic relations were close. Despite the Russian connection, the regime was never simply a Soviet puppet and there was a strong emphasis on reunification. *CM.*

Korea, Republic of State and Government (South Korea). The ROK was founded on August 15 1948 in the former US occupation zone south of the 38th Parallel after elections observed by UNTCOK. The government was dominated by the Korean right under Syngman Rhee and claimed to represent all Korea. US troops withdrew in 1949 leaving a military mission with the ROK Army. The US also provided economic assistance. Despite American influence, the regime was never simply a puppet and there was a strong emphasis on reunification. *CM.*

Korean War (1950–1953). Korea, annexed by Japan in 1910, occupies a key strategic position in Northeast Asia. When Japan surrendered in 1945 the US proposed and the Soviet Union accepted the 38th Parallel as the demarcation line between the occupation zones in Korea. At the Moscow Foreign Ministers' Conference in December 1945, Byrnes and Molotov agreed on the creation of a provisional national government, followed by a period of international trusteeship in Korea. The Moscow Accords, however, were never implemented. Separate administrations, already emerging in each occupation zone, were encouraged by the development of the Cold War. The Russians supported the Korean communists and backed Kim Il Sung, a prominent anti-Japanese guerrilla. The US Military Government, under Gen Hodge, suppressed the left and backed the right led by Syngman Rhee, an ageing nationalist. In

Holding the UN line in Korea, 1950–53

1947 Washington proposed elections under UN supervision to create a national government. The General Assembly responded by creating the UN Temporary Commission on Korea (UNTCOK). Refused entry into the north, UNTCOK observed separate elections in the south in May 1948. In December the UN recognized the Republic of Korea (ROK) under Syngman Rhee. In the north Kim Il Sung founded the Democratic People's Republic of Korea (DPRK). Both regimes claimed to represent all Korea.

Except for a group of advisers, Soviet forces left the DPRK in December 1948. The North Korean People's Army (NKPA) founded by Choe Yong Gun was equipped with Soviet tanks and artillery. The last US troops left the south in July 1949. Washington trained and supplied the ROK Army but denied it heavy weapons. In 1949 there were clashes along the 38th Parallel and guerrilla warfare in the south. The decision to attack the ROK was taken by Kim Il Sung in 1949 and approved by Stalin. Kim wanted to unify Korea while the military balance favoured the north and believed that the Americans would not intervene. On June 25 1950 the NKPA crossed the 38th Parallel, capturing the ROK capital Seoul. Although taken by surprise, Washington reacted swiftly. President Truman and his Secretary of State, Acheson, regarded the attack as a Soviet move and believed that further acts of aggression would follow unless they responded firmly. At American prompting and in the absence of the Russian delegate, Malik, the UN Security Council condemned the DPRK, called on UN members to assist the ROK and established a Unified Command (UNC), under Gen MacArthur. Sixteen nations eventually sent contingents. The

main ground forces were the US Eighth Army under Gen Walker and ROK troops. The US provided most of the air and sea power. This military effort was supported from US bases in Japan which were allowed to remain by the Japanese peace treaty of 1951. Japan also provided UN forces with logistical assistance.

Initially the Americans were unable to halt the NKPA. The first US troops, Task Force Smith, were defeated at Osan on July 5 1950. On July 20 the US 24th Division was driven from Taejon. The Americans were soon clinging to a narrow perimeter around Pusan. In September 1950, however, MacArthur transformed the situation by landing a force under Gen Almond at Inchon, cutting off the NKPA in the south. In October UN forces entered North Korea and the General Assembly passed a resolution calling for reunification. While Eighth Army advanced towards Pyongyang, X Corps was landed at Wonsan in the east. These developments alarmed China which feared US troops on its borders. When warnings conveyed through Panikkar, the Indian ambassador to Peking (Beijing), were ignored, Chinese "volunteers" under Gen Peng Dehuai crossed the Yalu river. MacArthur pressed ahead despite the first clash with the Chinese at Unsan. At the end of November his final offensive was defeated at the Chongchon river and the Chosin reservoir and he fell back across the 38th Parallel. Washington now had to decide whether to limit the fighting or to retaliate directly against China. MacArthur argued that he could not hold in Korea without attacking Manchuria. Truman, however, regarded war with China as a Soviet trap which would divert American strength from more vital areas. The best solution was to limit the war and force the enemy to accept a ceasefire. This outcome became possible when the new commander of the Eighth Army, Gen Ridgway, not only held on in Korea but pushed the Chinese back across the 38th Parallel in March 1951. When MacArthur continued to press for a wider war and publicly objected to Truman's policy, he was fired on April 11 1951.

In April-May 1951 the Chinese

launched a final massive offensive. During the first phase the Gloucesters were overrun at the Imjin river. By June, Eighth Army, under Gen Van Fleet, had repulsed the attack and reached the Kansas/Wyoming Line. In July truce talks began at Kaesong, later moving to Panmunjom. The UNC delegation was headed first by Adm Joy and later by Gen Harrison. The chief communist delegate was Gen Nam Il. The war entered a static phase. The UNC restricted ground operations after battles around the Punchbowl like Heartbreak Ridge and Bloody Ridge in the autumn of 1951, relying on air pressure to wear down the enemy. The communists used local attacks against outposts like the Hook and Pork Chop Hill to influence the truce talks. In 1952 negotiations bogged down on the POW issue. While the communists insisted on automatic repatriation under the Geneva Convention, the Americans proposed non-forcible repatriation to protect anti-communist POWS in their hands. In an effort to embarrass Washington, communist POWS on Koje Island mutinied. The US was also accused of launching germ warfare attacks. In 1953 the new Eisenhower administration moved to end the deadlock, threatening to use atomic weapons, a solution favoured by the UNC commander, Gen Clark. In June 1953, however, a compromise was reached on POWS. The armistice was finally signed on July 27 1953 despite an attempt at sabotage by Rhee. It established a Demilitarized Zone centred on the battleline and a Military Armistice Commission to monitor the truce. A Neutral Nations Supervisory Commission was to prevent reinforcement by either side. Non-repatriate POWS were handed over to a Neutral Nations Repatriation Commission. However, at the Geneva peace conference in 1954, no agreement on reunification proved possible. *CM*.

Kornilov, Gen Lavr (1870–1918). Russian. At the outbreak of World War I Kornilov was a brigade commander in Brusilov's Eighth Army. In May 1915 he was taken prisoner by the Austrians while leading the 48th Infantry Division in the Carpathians. He escaped in the summer of 1916 and, on his

return to Russia, Kornilov was given command of a corps. Drawn into Russia's political upheavals, he reluctantly supported Kerensky. Kornilov's forces performed well in the otherwise unsuccessful July 1917 offensive and he was given command of the South Front. In August he was elevated to C-in-C because it was felt that he could hold the crumbling armies together. Once again he clashed with Kerensky and, in September, he sought to mount a coup in Petrograd. This was frustrated by the indecision of his subordinates and the strengthening of Kerensky's position by left-wing support. Kornilov was arrested but, following the Bolshevik Revolution, he was allowed to escape. He joined with other generals in the Don region to form the Volunteer Army and, in January 1918, became its C-in-C. While trying to capture the Bolshevik town of Ekaternodar, Kornilov was killed by shell fire on April 13 1918. *MS*.

Kornspruit, Battle of *see* SANNA'S POST.

Korten, Gen Günther (1898–1944). Ger. An Imperial German Army officer in World War I, Korten transferred to the Luftwaffe in 1934. He served as COS of *Luftflotte 4* in Poland (1939) and the Balkans (1941) as well as during the initial phases of the attack on Russia. He was given command of *Luftflotte 1* in Russia in June 1943. After Jeschonnek's suicide in August that year, Korten became CGS of the Luftwaffe, although his relations with Göring soon deteriorated. Before he could resign, however, he was fatally wounded in the attempt to assassinate Hitler on July 20 1944. *PJS*.

Kosciuszko division. Formed, trained and equipped in the Soviet Union, the 1st Polish Infantry (Kosciuszko) Division had, by July 1943, reached a strength of nearly 16,000 men. It first went into action on October 14 near Lenino in Belorussia and subsequently took part in the liberation of Poland and in the Battle of Berlin.

Kozhedub, Maj Gen Ivan N (b.1920). Russian. Top-scoring Soviet fighter pilot of World War II, credited with 62 "kills" in 120

air combats. In February 1945, in a Lavochkin LA-7, he became the only Soviet fighter pilot to shoot down a jet-propelled Messerschmitt Me 262.

Krebs, Lt Gen Hans (1898–1945). Ger. COS Ninth Army from January 1942 to September 1944; then similar duties with Army Groups Centre and B. A loyal Nazi, he was recalled to Berlin early in 1945 to become Chief of Staff to Guderian, Chief of the OKW. Following an argument with the *Führer*, Guderian was replaced by Krebs. After Hitler's death, he began peace negotiations with the Soviet forces but committed suicide before they matured.

Kretschmer, Capt Otto (b.1912). Ger. U-boat "ace", sinking 44 merchantmen (*c*267,000 tons) and destroyer HMS *Daring* in *U-23* (September 1939–March 1940) and *U-99*. "Silent Otto" often penetrated convoy escort screens on the surface by night, attacking from close range with a single torpedo. *U-99* was sunk by destroyers HMS *Walker* and *Havoc*, March 27 1941; as a POW in Britain and Canada, Kretschmer established a clandestine intelligence service that gained him promotion to Captain. Postwar he held flag rank in the Federal German Navy's submarine branch.

Kronstadt, action at (August 18 1919). Kronstadt was the heavily defended Russian naval base near Leningrad. British naval forces under Adm Cowan had clashed with Bolshevik warships and, in June 1919, the motor torpedo boat CMB 4 had sunk the Russian cruiser *Oleg*. Seven larger CMBs then arrived at the RN's secret base in Finland and were used in a brilliant night raid on Kronstadt. Guided in by CMB 4 and under cover of an air raid by the RAF, they lost three of their number, but sank the battleships *Petropavlovsk* and *Andrei Pervozvanni* and the depot ship *Pamyat Azova*. The threat from the Bolshevik navy was greatly reduced by this daring stroke, which was, however, little to the taste of the British Cabinet, who had not intended anything so drastic. It played its part in enabling Finland and Estonia to gain their independence. *DJL*.

K

Krueger, Lt Gen Walter (1881– 1967). US. Born in Germany but largely raised in America, Krueger was commissioned as a second lieutenant in the US Army in 1901 and served in France in World War I. By mid-1941 he was a lieutenant general commanding the US Third Army, with Dwight D Eisenhower as his cos. Early in 1943 he took over the US Sixth Army, becoming Gen MacArthur's main ground force commander in the Southwest Pacific. From June 1943, Sixth Army units participated in offensive operations in northern New Guinea and on the islands of New Britain, the Admiralties, Biak, Noemfoor and Morotai, gradually working their way towards the Philippines. Krueger's forces landed on Leyte on October 20 1944, although they had to battle hard in mountain and jungle terrain before the port of Ormoc was taken, with the help of an amphibious assault, on December 10. In January 1945 Sixth Army came ashore at Lingayen Gulf on Luzon, subsequently having to engage in a month of fierce street fighting for Manila, which was cleared by March 4. Krueger had secured most of Luzon by July and, when the war ended, he was preparing for the invasion of Japan. The differing conditions and tasks which he faced in 1944–45 gave him ample opportunity to reveal his considerable range of tactical skills yet, like Hodges in Northwest Europe, he avoided the spotlight and his thorough but unspectacular command style was insufficiently colourful to win him wider public recognition. *PJS*.

Kruschev, Nikita Sergeyevich (1894–1971). Russian. Served in the Red Army during the Civil War. Member of Politburo; 1941– 42 directed guerrilla warfare; party representative on southern front at Stalingrad; conducted purge of collaborators in Ukraine. In 1953 first secretary of the Communist Party; in 1956 at 20th Party Congress denounced Stalin's crimes; 1958 appointed chairman of the Council of Ministers. Launched policy of "peaceful coexistence" designed to reduce military expenditure and boost consumer spending. Rash conduct of policy, culminating in the Cuban Missile Crisis (1962), undercut his politic-

al position. Removed from office, October 15 1964, on grounds of "ill-health". *BHR*.

Krylov, Marshal Nikolai (1903– 1972). Russian. During World War II Krylov was a staff officer in the Ukraine, the Crimea and at Stalingrad and commanded Fifth Army during the Soviet advance in East Prussia. In August 1945 he led Fifth Army in Manchuria against Japan.

Kuala Lumpur *see* MALAYSIA-INDONESIA CONFRONTATION.

Kuching *see* BRUNEI REVOLT; MALAYSIA-INDONESIA CONFRONTATION.

Küchler, Field Marshal Georg von (1881–1969). Ger. Commanded the German Third Army in Poland (1939), then the Eighteenth Army in Holland and France (1940) and Russia (1941). He replaced von Leeb as commander of Army Group North in January 1942 but, like his predecessor, was unable to take Leningrad. He was relieved of command, following a retreat, in January 1944.

Kula Gulf, Battle of (July 5-6 1943). A "Tokyo Express" of seven destroyer-transports, escorted by destroyers *Niizuki* (Rear Adm Hiseo Akiyama), *Suzukaze* and *Tanikaze*, attempted to reinforce the garrison at Vila, Kolombangara, Solomons. Forewarned by "Magic", Rear Adm Walden Ainsworth's Task Group 36.1 (three light cruisers, four destroyers) was deployed to intercept. Both sides made radar contact at *c*0118 hours, July 6. Three destroyer-transports were then already unloading at Vila; the remaining Japanese destroyers were redeployed for torpedo action. Although US radar-controlled gunfire sank *Niizuki*, killing Akiyama (total Japanese losses: 300 men), Long Lance torpedoes from the two remaining escorts sank the light cruiser USS *Helena* (168 dead). Using their superior night-fighting techniques, the Japanese avoided further combat and successfully unloaded all seven transports at Vila. Thus, although the destroyer-transport *Nagatsuki* was destroyed, the engagement must be adjudged a Japanese victory. *RO'N*.

Kum Kale *see* DARDANELLES (1915).

Kuneitra *see* ARAB-ISRAELI WARS.

Kuomintang. Chinese Nationalist Party that initially promoted broadly based social democratic principles. Led by Chiang Kai-shek in the 1930s; defeated by communists in Civil War, 1949.

Kuribayashi, Lt Gen Tadamichi (1885-1945). Jap. Commanding 109th Division in May 1944, Kuribayashi conducted the *defence à outrance* of Iwo Jima, exploiting natural features in the construction of bunkers to withstand prolonged pre-invasion naval and air bombardments. He committed suicide on March 23 1945, two days before Iwo Jima fell.

Kuroki, Gen Count Tamesada (1844-1923). Jap. Commanding First Army during the Russo-Japanese War, Kuroki conducted the initial landings at Chemulpo (Inchon, Korea), February 17 1904, and began a rapid northward advance to the Yalu river, Manchuria. Here, diligent intelligence-gathering and well-contrived surprise (a major bridge was constructed under fire, shielding the fact that the main thrust was to be made across a number of smaller bridges) enabled him to force a crossing and rout an inferior Russian force commanded by Lt Gen M I Zasulich. Thus Kuroki was the first "eastern" commander to defeat a "western power" by the use of "western" weapons and techniques. *RO'N*.

Kuropatkin, Gen Alexei Nikolaievich (1848-1921). Russian. Minister of War from 1898, Kuropatkin was appointed c-in-c Far East on the outbreak of the Russo-Japanese War. An able enough commander in defence, he tended to be over-cautious – as at the Shaho river, where a sustained assault might have turned the 12-day battle in Russia's favour – and was handicapped also by the demands of Viceroy Alexeiev and by jealous subordinates. Although he succeeded in extricating the bulk of his forces from the defeat at Mukden, he was subsequently reduced to an army command. In 1916, Kuropatkin was briefly c-in-c on the Northern Front. *RO'N*.

K

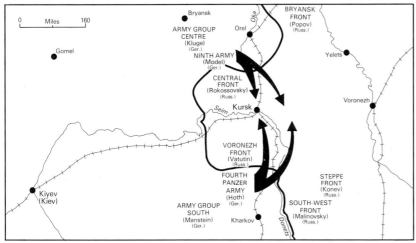

Battle of Kursk, July 1943: the German pincers failed to close on the Soviets

Kursk, Battle of (1943). In spring 1943, the German High Command planned a massive offensive against the Soviet salient around Kursk on the central front. Yet again they sought to execute a giant pincer movement, with two strong attacks at the base of the salient to encircle the Soviet forces. Codenamed Operation "Citadel" (*Zitadelle*), the attack was to avenge the disaster at Stalingrad and also act as the springboard for the destruction of the Soviet Union's southern flank. The Germans painstakingly mustered a force of 900,000 men, 2,700 tanks and assault guns, 10,000 artillery pieces and 2,000 aircraft. Meanwhile, Soviet intelligence and the perspicacity of the Red Army commanders provided clear indications of the German plan. Zhukov therefore was able to make exhaustive preparations for a defensive battle that he would then transform into a counterattack against his weakened foe. German delays in launching the offensive allowed Zhukov to accumulate even greater resources than his opponents. So astute was the Soviet anticipation of events that, on July 4, in the north of the salient, Rokossovsky's Central Front opened a four-hour artillery barrage before the beginning of the offensive by Model's German Ninth Army. Stubborn Soviet defence in strong prepared positions restricted Model's advance to 5 miles (8km) on the first day. Progress was more rapid in the south where Hoth's Fourth Panzer Army made a substantial penetration of Vatutin's Voronezh Front. But

there seemed to be no end to the Soviet minefields and their apparently limitless reserves of men and tanks frustrated the increasingly exhausted German forces. By July 12, Hoth's armour had lost some 50 percent of its equipment and in the north of the salient a Soviet counterattack quickly drove the Germans back to their start line. Even Hitler realized "Citadel" was doomed to fail and, on July 13, he issued the first orders that marked the termination of the offensive. Now it was the turn of the Red Army to launch its own offensive and Zhukov's reserve, the Steppe Front, had recaptured Kharkov by the end of August. Kursk left the German army irrevocably weakened and marked the beginning of the Soviet Union's irreversible dominance of the Eastern Front. *MS.*

Kusaka, Vice Adm Ryunosuke (1893–1971). Jap. Aircraft carrier specialist. As cos to Adm Nagumo, played a large part in formulating plans for the Pearl Harbor and Midway attacks. In 1944 again cos to the commander of the Combined Fleet, Adm Toyoda.

Kut-al-Amara campaign (1915–17) *see* MESOPOTAMIAN CAMPAIGN.

Kuznetsov Adm Nikolai G (1902–74). Russian. Became Chief of Naval Forces in 1939 in the aftermath of Stalin's purges. Thanks to Kuznetsov, the Russian navy was alert to the German attack in 1941, although its role in the war was minor. He persuaded Stalin to permit the navy an air arm.

Kwajalein-Eniwetok campaign (1944). Following the conquest of the Gilberts (*see* TARAWA CAMPAIGN), the next move in the US amphibious campaign in the Central Pacific was the subjection of the Marshall Islands. Nimitz determined on the capture of Kwajalein and Eniwetok atolls in the western Marshalls, where the establishment of US bases would neutralize Japanese strongholds (Maloelap and Wotje) in the eastern Marshalls. Nimitz deployed Fifth Fleet (Vice Adm Spruance), Fifth Amphibious Force (Vice Adm Turner) and V Amphibious Corps (Maj Gen H M Smith). Japanese air power in the area was successfully suppressed by the carriers of Task Force 58 (Rear Adm Mitscher) and a logistics base was secured by unopposed landings on Majuro atoll, about 250 miles (400km) southeast of Kwajalein, January 30, 1944.

On February 1, in Operation "Flintlock", 4th Marine Division (Maj Gen Harry Schmidt) assaulted Roi-Namur, on the north of Kwajalein lagoon, while 7th Infantry Division (Maj Gen Charles H Corlett) landed on Kwajalein Island, 40 miles (64km) to the south. Both operations were preceded by heavy air and naval bombardment and supported from artillery positions established on smaller islands seized the day before. Kwajalein atoll's 87 islands were secured by February 6, when 41,000 US troops (490 dead; 1,300 wounded) had landed. Only a handful of the 8,400-strong Japanese garrison (Rear Adm M Akiyama) survived.

Massive pre-invasion bombardment and the initial establishment of artillery positions again minimized US casualties in Operation "Catchpole", February 17, when Amphibious Group 2 (Rear Adm Harry Hill) landed Marines of Tactical Group 1 (Brig Gen Thomas Watson) on Engebi Island, Eniwetok atoll. Eniwetok Island was secured by 7th Infantry Division, landing February 19, and the conquest was completed by the Marines' seizure of Parry Island, February 22. Of the 3,500 Japanese defenders (Maj Gen Yoshima Nishida), only a few hundred Korean labour troops survived; US losses were some 350 killed and 870 wounded. *RO'N.*

K

La Boisselle. Fortified village on the Somme which was the objective of the British 34th Division's costly but unsuccessful attack on July 1 1916.

Labuan *see* MALAYSIA-INDONESIA CONFRONTATION.

Ladoga, Lake *see* FINLAND, RUSSIAN INVASION OF.

Ladysmith, siege and relief of (November 2 1899-February 28 1900), Second Boer War. Some 10,000 Boers under Commandant-General Petrus Joubert (with Gens Botha and Lukas Meyer) invested Ladysmith, Natal, garrisoned by 12,000 men under Gen Sir George White. Buller's relief attempts were repulsed at Colenso, December 15 1899, Spion Kop and Vaal Kranz. The failure of their attempt to breach the defences of Ladysmith at Waggon Hill-Caesar's Camp on January 6 cost the Boers *c*800 casualties (about half the overall British military casualties of 894 were caused in this action). Thereafter, they confined themselves to bombardment from the surrounding hills, which was largely ineffective because its "timetable" was so regular that the besieged were usually able to take shelter in advance. Only about 60 deaths were caused by shelling but more than 400 by disease.

On February 19, poor troop dispositions by Lukas Meyer allowed Buller, whose relief force now numbered *c*25,000 men (losses February 19-28: 1,896 killed or wounded), to seize the commanding height of Hlangwane and secure crossings on the Tugela. Opposed by some 5,000 Boers under Botha, Buller at first fumbled his attempts to clear the hills, but a 24-hour armistice from the morning of Sunday February 25, readily agreed to by the Sabbatarian Boers, allowed him to regroup for a coordinated assault. On February 27, attacking along a 3-mile (5 km) front with support from 76 guns, British infantry secured the vital hills, entering Ladysmith next day. The losses of the retreating Boers might have been severe if Buller, ever-solicitous of his men and disregarding the urgings of his subordinates, had not decided against pursuit. *RO'N*.

Lafayette Escadrille. Formed in April 1916 under the official designation of Escadrille N124, and also known as the *Escadrille Américaine*, this fighter squadron of the French Air Service was composed of American volunteers. The unit was transferred to the US Air Service in February 1918.

Laird, Melvin R (b.1922). US. US Secretary of Defense (1969–72); took positions on the Vietnam War that reflected intense concern to maintain Congressional support. He coined the term "Vietnamization" for the policy of turning responsibility over to the South Vietnamese and advocated phased withdrawal of American troops to placate the growing impatience in Congress and public to end US involvement. He also urged President Nixon to respond with restraint to the communists' Easter offensive of 1972.

Lami Dozo, Brig Gen Basilio. Argentinian. Air Force commander and junior member of the military junta which assumed power in December 1981.

Lammerding, Brig (*Brigadeführer*, SS) Heinz (1905–71). Ger. Commander of the *Das Reich* Division during the Oradour massacre. He was later COS, Army Group Vistula.

"Lam Son 719" Operation (1971). With US forces providing only logistical support, the Army of the Republic of Vietnam (ARVN) undertook in 1971 to cut the Ho Chi Minh Trail by stabbing across the border into Laos. A force of 5,000 men, eventually increased to 21,000, set out on February 8 and pushed slowly to Tchepone, Laos, on March 6. The People's Army (PAVN) counterattacked on the ARVN's extended flanks, turning the retreat into a rout. The operation stalled communist plans for an offensive that year, but the ARVN's poor discipline and high casualties fuelled doubts that it was ready to face the PAVN alone in conventional combat.

Lancaster, Avro 683 (Br, WWII). Heavy bomber; crew 7. Developed from Avro 679 Manchester. Prototype flew January 9 1941; first operation March 3 1942. War-long

Avro Lancaster of Bomber Command

use as heavy bomber mostly operating by night. Operations included No. 617 Squadron's dam-breaching attacks, 1943, and use of 22,000lb (9,980kg) *Grand Slam* deep-penetration bombs. Production 7,378 (430 in Canada). Four 1,280–1,750hp Rolls-Royce Merlin, or four 1,650hp Bristol Hercules engines; max. speed 287mph (462kph); eight 0.303in machine guns, up to 22,000lb (9,990kg) bombs.

Landing craft and ships *see* AMPHIBIOUS CRAFT AND WEAPONS.

Land reform, Vietnam. In their wars with France and, later, for reunification, the Vietnamese communists capitalized on land issues to win popular support. In the first war they attracted poor peasants by reducing rents, lowering taxes and redistributing the lands of pro-French landlords. A more radical programme to equalize land holdings began in 1953. Where two-thirds of the rural population were tenants and nearly 50 percent owned no land at all, this programme had much appeal.

Saigon government reforms passed during the 1950s were unattractive by comparison because they tended to confirm existing arrangements. Belatedly, in March 1970, the government of Nguyen Van Thieu promulgated a Land-to-the-Tiller Law to compete with the communists for rural support. Under this law 400,000 landless peasants received a total of 1.5 million acres and tenancy virtually disappeared, leaving the land about equally distributed among peasant freeholders. While the law came too late to make a difference to the war's outcome, it did alleviate one cause of peasant grievance against the government. *WST*.

Langemarck *see* YPRES, FIRST AND SECOND BATTLES OF (1914, 1915).

Langle De Cary, Gen Fernand Louis Armand Marie de (1849-1927). Fr. Commanded Fourth Army in battles of Ardennes, August 1914, withdrawing after suffering heavy losses, and Marne, September 1914, making a determined stand at Vitry-le-François. Commanded jointly with Pétain in the costly offensive of Second Champagne, September-November 1915; in December 1915 was promoted to command Centre Group of Armies. In March 1916, after being briefly engaged at Verdun, he was retired as over-age.

Langley. America's first aircraft carrier, converted from the fleet collier *Jupiter* in 1922. Converted to seaplane tender in 1937 and sunk by Japanese bombers off Java, early 1942. Name revived for *Independence*-class carrier which fought at Philippine Sea and Leyte Gulf.

Lang Son. French armed forces abandoned Lang Son, the capital of Vietnam's Lang Son province located 9 miles (14km) from the Chinese border, on October 18 1950. In near panic the French left behind 1,300 tons of ammunition, food, equipment and artillery for capture by the Vietnamese communists. Lang Son was also a major target of China's "punitive strike" against Vietnam during February-March 1979. The Chinese Army held the city for several days in early March and dynamited many buildings. *See also* BORDER WAR, VIETNAM.

Lanphier, Maj Thomas G (b.1915). US. USAAF P-38 pilot widely credited with having destroyed the Japanese "Betty" bomber in which Adm Isoroku Yamamoto died near Kahili, Bougainville, on April 18 1943. Some evidence suggests, however, that Lt Rex T Barber, rather than Lanphier, may have shot down Yamamoto's aircraft.

Lanrezac, Gen Charles Louis Marie (1852–1925). Fr. In August 1914, Lanrezac, commanding the French Fifth Army, was one of the very few Allied commanders to apprehend the full implications of the German dispositions. Fearing envelopment by an advance through Belgium, he persuaded Joffre to allow him to deploy in the Sambre-Meuse angle rather than attack into the Ardennes. On August 22–23, while the BEF, on his left, were engaged at Mons, he met the German Second and Third Armies at Charleroi. Unfortunately, Lanrezac's tactical skills did not match his strategic percipience: Fifth Army was severely mauled and its withdrawal left the BEF unsupported. Lanrezac earned Joffre's disfavour both for his hasty retreat and for his poor cooperation with the BEF: the sharp-tongued Lanrezac and the mercurial British commander, French, were here equally at fault. Lanrezac temporarily checked the Germans at Guise on August 29, but the major credit went to his flamboyant I Corps' commander, Franchet d'Esperey, in whose favour he relinquished Fifth Army on September 3. *RO'N.*

Lansdale, Maj Gen Edward G (b.1908). US. His involvement in Vietnam began in 1954–56, when President Eisenhower assigned him to Saigon to help consolidate the regime of Ngo Dinh Diem. To coup-minded army officers and leaders of religious sects alike, Lansdale offered bribes in return for acceptance of the Diem regime. He also coordinated the CIA's psychological and sabotage campaign against North Vietnam. Lansdale returned to Vietnam in 1965–68 as special assistant to the US ambassador. His taste for clandestine activities and his role in designing unconventional counter-insurgency programmes made him a controversial figure. *WST.*

Laos, wars since independence. Mountainous, sparsely populated (3.6 million in 1983) and landlocked, Laos is inevitably embroiled in the wars of Vietnam. During the first Indochina War (1946–54) the French treated Laos along with Cambodia and Vietnam as one part of a single unit. The Vietnamese communists, who needed secure bases in the mountains anyway, responded by operating in Laotian territory and organizing the Laotian communist Party. Commonly known as the Pathet Lao, the Laotian communists joined a coalition Royal Lao Government in 1957, but a US-supported rightist coup and intervention by Thai troops ended that experiment. From September 1960, when Pathet Lao troops and Vietnamese "volunteers" evicted the Royal Lao Army from Sam Neua province until 1975, except for another brief coalition government in 1962, Laos was at war.

The Pathet Lao were solidly backed by the North Vietnamese, who began building the Ho Chi Minh Trail through Laotian territory in 1959. The Royal Lao Government enjoyed the support of the United States. The CIA separately supplied an army of 25,000 men composed largely of the H'mong minority to fight the Pathet Lao and harass the North Vietnamese. The US began providing aerial support to the Royal Lao Army (Operation "Barrel Roll") in December 1963. Sustained bombing of the Trail began in April 1965 (Operation "Steel Tiger") and ended with the signing of a peace agreement on February 21 1973. In that bombing, US planes dropped 2,092,000 tons of bombs, two-thirds of a ton for every Lao citizen. A coalition government established on April 5 1974 in accordance with the peace agreement came apart as the Pathet Lao staged demonstrations and seized government offices following the communist victory in Vietnam. On December 3 1975, the Pathet Lao abolished the monarchy and proclaimed a People's Democratic Republic. *WST.*

La Pallice. Port near La Rochelle, west coast of France. Used by the Germans as a U-boat base from 1940–44.

Laser-guided weapons. Weapons which home on the reflected infra-red radiation of a laser designator shone on to the target by a ground observer or aircraft. The bomb, missile or shell has only to be dropped into the "basket" of reflected energy and it then homes automatically with great precision on to the target as long as the designator remains locked on. The best known laser-guided weapons are the American Paveway family of bombs which proved very effective in the Vietnam War during the 1970s.

Laser weapons *see* DIRECTED ENERGY WEAPONS (DEW).

Veteran de Lattre de Tassigny

Lattre de Tassigny, Marshal Jean de (1889-1952). Fr. Graduating de Lattre fought as a junior cavalry officer in the early part of that conflict. By the end of the war, during which he was wounded four times, he had transferred to the infantry and was commanding a battalion of the 93rd Infantry Regiment. Between 1921 and 1926 he saw further action in Morocco and was again wounded. Steady promotion continued throughout the 1920s and 1930s. On the eve of World War II he was appointed COS of the French Fifth Army and in 1940 was given command of the 14th Division, which performed well at Rethel against Guderian's panzer units and held together during the subsequent retreat. Following the armistice with Germany, de Lattre served for a while under the Vichy regime but, in November 1942, he resisted the German movement into the previously unoccupied area of France. Although captured and imprisoned, he escaped and, towards the end of 1943, reached North Africa where he took over *Armée B*, later renamed as the French First Army. He led this formation in the invasion of Southern France on August 15 1944 and in the ensuing advance to Alsace and the German frontier. The determination and drive of the tough and flamboyant de Lattre, who did not suffer fools gladly, compensated in some respects for his army's lack of battle experience at this stage of the campaign. In 1945, the French First Army helped to eliminate the Colmar Pocket and crossed the Rhine into southern Germany, reaching the Swiss border. On May 8 1945, in Berlin, de Lattre received and signed, on behalf of France, the final capitulation of Germany. In the years immediately after World War II he held the combined post of Inspector General and COS of the French Army. He was C-in-C of the Land Forces of the Western European Union from 1948 to 1950. His last appointment was as High Commissioner and C-in-C in Indochina until illness compelled him to retire shortly before his death in January 1952. He was posthumously created Marshal the same year. *PJS.*

Laval, Pierre (1883–1945). Fr. Held several senior governmental posts during the 1930s, when twice prime minister. He was strongly criticized for his appeasement of Italian aggression towards Abyssinia and dropped out of politics until his appointment in June 1940 as deputy head of state and foreign minister in the Vichy government. Dismissed by Pétain later that year, he was recalled in April 1942. Although he sometimes obstructed German policy, Laval generally pursued a programme of collaboration. In 1945 he was convicted of treason and executed. *MS.*

Lavarack, Lt Gen Sir John (1885–1957). Australian. Commander 7th Australian Division in the Western Desert and in the Syrian campaign until promoted to command I Australian Corps in June 1941. Commander First Australian Army in the Pacific 1942–45.

Lavochkin LA-5 (USSR, WWII). Single-seat fighter, wooden construction; passed official acceptance trials May 1942; in production until war ended. Enough available November 1942 to participate effectively in Stalingrad fighting. Well thought of, LA-5 saw wide use on bomber-escort, ground-attack and general combat duties. Also used by 1st Czechoslovak Mixed Air Division; some saw operational use Korean War with North Korean air force. Production: about 10,000. One 1,850hp Shvetsov Ash-82FN engine; max. speed 403mph (649kph); two 23mm or 20mm cannon, 662lb (300kg) bombs or rockets.

Lawrence, Lt Col Thomas Edward (1888–1935). Br. Carried out archaeological work in the Middle East before 1914; this experience led to his employment in the Arab Bureau in Cairo. Sent in 1916 to the Hejaz to assist the Arab Revolt. Developed an empathy with Emir Feisal and a realization of the potential of the Arab form of guerrilla warfare. Organized and led hit-and-run raids on the Hejaz railway that tied down substantial Turkish forces. Gen Allenby supported his actions and the Arab irregulars became a flexible extension of the British right flank during the advance into Palestine. After the Arab entry into Damascus in October 1918 Lawrence concerned himself with the postwar fate of the Middle East and served as a political adviser to the Colonial Office. Following several conspicuously unsuccessful attempts to achieve the anonymity of enlisted service life, "Lawrence of Arabia" died in a motorcycle accident in May 1935. *MS.*

Laycock, Maj Gen Sir Robert (1907–1968). Br. Having raised one of the first commando units in mid-1940, Laycock formed the Special Service "Layforce" in the Middle East; in April 1941 led a raid on Bardia, Libya, which, while unsuccessful, taught many useful lessons for subsequent operations. In November 1941, Laycock was one of only two survivors of the raid on Rommel's supposed HQ (*see* KEYES, GEOFFREY). After commanding Special Services Brigade, organizing and training all commandos in Britain, 1942–43, he succeeded Mountbatten as Chief of Combined Operations (October 1943–47), overseeing special forces' operations in the Normandy invasion and elsewhere. *RO'N.*

Leaflet raids. Principally the night sorties by Whitleys of 4 Group, Bomber Command September 1939 to May 1940, when only propaganda leaflets were dropped. The restriction was due to Britain's reluctance to provoke a bombing exchange while the Luftwaffe had the upper hand or until a decisive threat was posed to Britain.

League of Nations. Founded in 1919 as an international organization to preserve peace and arbitrate in disputes between nations. Powerless to intervene in the major crises of the interwar years, it was increasingly ignored by the great powers. In 1946 its activities were incorporated in the United Nations Organization.

Leahy, Fleet Adm William Daniel (1875–1959). US. After a long and distinguished naval career, extending from service in the Spanish-American War, 1898, to appointment as Chief of Naval Operations, 1937–1939, Leahy retired. He was entrusted with the politically sensitive post of Ambassador to Vichy France, 1940, and in 1941 became President Roosevelt's personal COS. Restored to active service in 1942, he also chaired the meetings of the US Joint Chiefs of Staff and was a member of the Anglo-US Combined Chiefs of Staff. His major function, performed with great tact and skill, was that of Roosevelt's military "interpreter" and, with Harry Hopkins, indispensable adviser. The five-star rank of Fleet Admiral was created for Leahy in December 1944. He was President Truman's COS until 1949. *RO'N.*

"Lea" Operation (1947). French forces in Indochina attempted during autumn 1947 to end the war at a stroke by parachuting troops into communist headquarters while enveloping enemy units in a classic pincer manoeuvre. Operation "Lea" just missed capturing Ho Chi Minh and other senior communist leaders at their camp near the Chinese border, and the attempt to encircle communist forces in so vast an area of mountains and jungle proved futile. "Lea" was aborted on November 8, one month after it had begun.

Lebanon-Jordan intervention (1958). Following the abortive Anglo-French Suez expedition of 1956 and the resounding defeat of the Egyptian Army by the Israelis in the Sinai which preceded it, there was a steady rise in the activities of pro-Nasser factions throughout the Middle East. This took several forms: political instability in Lebanon, and anti-royalist activity in Jordan and Iraq, where the coup of July 1958 resulted in the murder of the royal family. King Hussein of Jordan appealed for British military support and the 16th Parachute Bri-

gade was sent by air to Amman. At the same time President Eisenhower authorized US Marines embarked with the Sixth Fleet, reinforced by parachute units from US forces in Germany, to land at Beirut to restore order in Lebanon. By October, the situation in Jordan and Lebanon was under control. This was, however, the first step towards the Lebanon's political disintegration. *MH.*

Le Cateau, Battle of (August 26 1914). During the retreat of the BEF from Mons, its two corps became separated by the Forest of Mormal. Although under orders from the C-in-C, Sir John French, to continue the retirement, Gen Sir Horace Smith-Dorrien – commanding II Corps – judged that the Germans were too close for him to disengage without another battle and he therefore resolved to fight a holding action north and west of Le Cateau. The German First Army, under von Kluck, attacked the British positions from 0600 hours onwards but the assaults were repeatedly halted by the superb musketry of the BEF's infantry and the close support of the Royal Artillery, while British cavalry units helped to ensure that the flanks of II Corps were not enveloped. By the evening, Smith-Dorrien's troops resumed their withdrawal in reasonably good order, despite suffering 7,812 casualties and losing 38 guns. The resistance encountered by the Germans at Le Cateau led von Kluck to overestimate British strength and greatly eased the pressure on the BEF, allowing it to retreat virtually unmolested for five more days. Smith-Dorrien's decision to stand at Le Cateau was undoubtedly vindicated by later events, but strained his relations with Sir John French and thus contributed to his own removal from command in May 1915. *PJS.*

Leckwitz. On April 25 1945, elements of the US 273rd Infantry Regiment entered the village of Leckwitz, Saxony, near the River Elbe and made contact with Soviet forces, the first meeting of the American and Soviet combat forces in Europe. The location was incorrectly reported and Torgau was erroneously cited as the first meeting point.

Leclerc, Marshal Jacques (1902–1947). French. Philippe, Vicomte de Hautecloque, was twice captured by the Germans and twice escaped during the battle for France in 1940. He made his way to England where he enlisted in the Free French forces and, fearing German reprisals against his family, assumed the *nom de guerre* Leclerc. He was sent to Africa as Military Governor of Chad and Cameroon before being appointed General Officer Commanding French Equatorial Africa. After meticulous planning, in December 1942 he led a column 1,500 miles (2,400km) across the Sahara from Fort Lamy in Chad to a union with the British Eighth Army in Libya in January 1943. The prestige of the Free French soared and Leclerc became an obvious choice to lead the French 2nd Armoured Division forming in Britain for the invasion of France and soon in action in the breakout from Normandy. Leclerc accepted the surrender of Paris in the name of the Provisional Government and thereafter his division played a prominent part in the advance through France and southern Germany. He was sent to Indochina in June 1945 but his uncompromising policies towards the nationalists led to his recall in 1946. A year later, while serving as Inspector-General of French troops in North Africa, Leclerc was killed in an aircrash. Posthumously made a Marshal of France. *MS.*

Ledo Road (Stilwell Road). By mid-1942 the Japanese conquest of Burma had cut the Burma Road, the 717-mile (1,154km) supply route from Lashio, Burma, to Kunming, China, thus forcing the Allies to supply China by air, over the Himalayas ("the Hump"). From late 1942, therefore, US Army engineers under Lt Gen Raymond Wheeler, urged on by Stilwell, constructed a highway from Ledo, Assam, India, across the formidable Naga Hills, to join the eastern, Chinese-held sector of the Burma Road near Wanting, Burma. Following the capture of Myitkyina (August 1944) and Wanting (January 1945) by Chinese troops, the link was completed and the first Ledo-Burma Road convoy entered China on January 28 1945. *RO'N.*

L

Le Duan (1907–86). Democratic Republic of Vietnam. Vietnamese communist leader most closely identified with the war for reunification. He served as secretary of the party committee for South Vietnam during the war against France and remained in the South until 1957. Duan contended that the North had an obligation to help the South achieve "liberation". The Third Party Congress elected him first secretary in 1960 at the same time that it ratified plans for an armed struggle. In 1973 he predicted that the US, having withdrawn, would not return, and approved plans to resume open warfare. *WST*.

Le Duc Tho (b.1910). Democratic Republic of Vietnam. Deputy secretary to Le Duan in the party committee for the South in 1951–54, the fifth-ranked member of the Lao Dong (Vietnam) Communist Party Political Bureau, Le Duc Tho began secret negotiations with Henry Kissinger in February 1970 to end the Vietnam War. These negotiations paralleled the Paris talks and resulted in the Paris Agreements of January 1973. Awarded the Nobel Peace Prize along with Kissinger, Tho declined on the grounds that the Agreements produced no lasting peace.

Lee, Rear Adm Willis Augustus, Jr ("Ching") (1888–1945). US. Commanding battleship group (*Washington, South Dakota*) during Naval Battles off Guadalcanal, November 14–15 1942, engaged Vice Adm Kondo's bombardment group. Lee's destroyers were put out of action and *South Dakota* crippled, but *Washington*, skilfully handled, sank Japanese battleship *Kirishima*. Co-director with Mitscher of Truk and Carolines attacks, 1944; later 2-i-c Third Fleet (Halsey). Died while researching anti-kamikaze measures.

Leeb, Field Marshal Wilhelm Ritter von (1876–1956). Ger. An austere Bavarian aristocrat, von Leeb served as a staff officer on both the Western and Eastern Fronts in World War I. He stayed in the German army after 1918, becoming an acknowledged authority on defensive warfare. A Catholic, Leeb had little love for the Nazis, yet he commanded

Ritter von Leeb: an austere aristocrat

Army Group 2 at Kassel from 1934 until 1938, when he was removed during the Blomberg-Fritsch crisis. He was recalled by Hitler in 1939 to command Army Group C, entrusted with defending the Reich against France. Leeb's units played a subordinate role in the invasion of France in May 1940 but later, in June, they encircled four French armies in the Epinal-Belfort area. Promoted to Field Marshal in July 1940, he commanded Army Group North in Russia in 1941, his task being to cut off and eliminate the Soviet forces in the Baltic states, then advance on Leningrad. He was not at his best directing large armoured formations and his panzer commanders criticized him for being too cautious. Even so, he was on the verge of capturing Leningrad when, in September 1941, Hitler ordered him to starve the city into surrender rather than storm it. His relations with Hitler worsened the following January with the *Führer's* refusal to allow him to withdraw and shorten his line in the face of a Soviet offensive. Leeb was relieved of command on January 17 1942 and saw no further active service. *PJS*.

Leefe Robinson, Capt William (1895–1918). Br. An RFC pilot, Leefe Robinson won the Victoria Cross for destroying the German airship SL 11 at Cuffley, Hertfordshire, on September 3 1916. Himself brought down in France in 1917, he remained a POW until shortly before his death from influenza on December 31 1918.

Leese, Gen Sir Oliver (1894–1978). Br. Commander XXX Corps in Eighth Army from El Alamein

in August 1942 to the Sangro river in November 1943; responsible at El Alamein for the initial "break-in" in the northern sector on October 23–24 1942, and for the "break-out" at the end of the battle on November 1–2. He led Eighth Army's advance along the coast road from Benghazi to Tripoli and launched the main frontal assaults on the Mareth Line and Wadi Akarit. He captured the western beachhead in Eighth Army's landing in Sicily.

He took over from Montgomery on the Sangro in December 1943, and moved Eighth Army secretly across the Apennines for Alexander's "Diadem" offensive, in which he attacked in the Cassino sector, taking the monastery, breaching the Gustav and Hitler Lines, and pursuing von Vietinghoff's Tenth Army to the Gothic Line.

Dissatisfied with Alexander's plan to assault the centre of the Gothic Line because he had too few mountain-trained troops, he persuaded him to switch Eighth Army back to the Adriatic coast where he assumed that he would find better tank country. This was a superb feat of staff work, but it lost three weeks of summer weather.

He achieved surprise when he opened his offensive on August 25 1944, successfully breaching the Gothic Line, but his subsequent advance was fiercely contested by von Vietinghoff. The weather had broken by the time he had managed to fight his way out of the hills into the plain of the Romagna. He handed over Eighth Army on October 1 1944 on leaving to command Allied Land Forces Southeast Asia in the reconquest of Burma. Clashes of personality led to his dismissal by Mountbatten in May 1945. *WGFJ*.

Legentilhomme, Gen Paul (1884–1975). Fr. Commander Free French forces during the Syrian campaign of 1941.

Leigh light. Airborne searchlight used in RAF Coastal Command to illuminate ASV contacts. First operational use, June 1942.

Leigh-Mallory, Air Chief Marshal Sir Trafford (1892–1944). Br. AOC, 12 Group, 1937–40, 11 Group 1940–42, AOC-in-C, Fighter Command 1942, Air C-in-C Allied

Expeditionary Air Force 1943–44, Allied Air c-in-c, Southeast Asia 1944. Leigh-Mallory's main task in the Battle of Britain, during which he commanded 12 Group, was less to prevent German bombing, a task which fell to Park in command of 11 Group, than to penalize the Germans as heavily as possible for having carried it out. This gave him the opportunity to mass his fighters in what were known as "Big Wing" formations and only to attack when he had a marked superiority. These tactics proved to be highly successful, contributing significantly to the defeat of the Luftwaffe. Park, however, felt that Leigh-Mallory was too reluctant to reinforce the efforts of his own more hard-pressed 11 Group and this contributed to bad feeling between the two commanders.

By the time Leigh-Mallory became c-in-c, Fighter Command, the crisis had passed and his most important subsequent command was of the Allied Expeditionary Air Force, an Anglo-American combination, which was designed to assist the preparation and provide the air support of Operation "Overlord" Leigh-Mallory played an important part in planning this, but his contribution was seriously diminished by his failure to get on with American colleagues. Moreover, he had little chance of gaining the cooperation of the heavy bombers as he was on especially bad terms with both Harris and Spaatz. Much of his intended role was, therefore, discharged by the Deputy Supreme Commander, Tedder, who was more statesmanlike. Even so, much credit is due to Leigh-Mallory for the brilliant work done by the tactical air forces before and during the invasion of Normandy and the subsequent break-out. He was subsequently selected for the important Air Command in Southeast Asia but, flying out to take up the appointment, was killed in an air crash. *ANF*.

Leith Harbour. Old whaling station on South Georgia; scene of illegal landing by Argentinian scrap merchants in March 1982 which triggered the Falklands War. The British Antarctic Survey team on Grytviken requested them to leave but were ignored.

Leman, Lt Gen Comte Gérard Mathieu (1851–1920). Belgian. On August 5-16 1914, commanding Belgian 3rd Division, Leman held Liège against Ludendorff's 14th Brigade of Gen Otto von Emmich's Second Army. Although the forts were reduced severally by 420mm ("Big Bertha") and 305mm howitzers, Leman refused to surrender: when the last, Fort Loncin, fell, he was captured unconscious in its ruins.

LeMay, Gen Curtis E (b.1906). US. Originally a fighter pilot, LeMay distinguished himself as a navigator on long-range flights in prototype B-17 and B-24 bombers, 1938–40. In November 1942, he took command of 305th Bombardment Group in the UK, which later joined the daylight bombing offensive against Germany. In training B-17 crews, he developed the necessary flying skills to make possible bombing in rigidly-preserved formations directed by "lead" crews. Promoted Brig Gen, he took command of 4th Bombardment Wing (later 3rd Bombardment Division), July 1943–June 1944, personally leading a number of major operations, and evolving the "combat box", in which bomber formations flew at staggered heights for mutual protection.

In September 1944, LeMay, succeeded Brig Gen LaVerne Saunders in command of XX Bomber Command in the China-Burma-India theatre. In spite of teething troubles with the newly operational B-29 Superfortresses, he carried out successful raids on targets in Formosa and Manchuria. The strategic bombing offensive against Japan itself had begun from XXI Bomber Command's bases in the Marianas Islands in November 1944: disappointed with the results achieved by Brig Gen Haywood Hansell's high-level precision raids, Gen Arnold in January 1945 gave LeMay command of XXI BC, ordering an area fire-bombing offensive. High-level raids proved relatively ineffective, so LeMay stripped his B-29s of defensive armament (permitting greater speed and increased bomb-load) and began low-level – 5,000–8,000ft (1,525–2,440m) – saturation night attacks. In the first major fire raid, March 9–10, 325 B-29s devastated Tokyo. Equally

destructive attacks on other cities followed (*see* STRATEGIC BOMBING OFFENSIVE, JAPAN).

LeMay briefly commanded Twentieth Air Force, July–August 1945, before becoming Spaatz's cos in US Army Strategic Air Forces, Pacific. He was c-in-c, US Air Forces Europe, 1947–48; c-in-c, Strategic Air Command, 1948–57, at the time of the Korean War and sac's rapid expansion; and Vice cos, 1957–61, and then cos, USAF, from 1961 until his retirement in 1965. *RO'N.*

Lemelsen, Lt Gen (*General der Panzertruppen*) Joachim (1888–1954). Ger. Commander Fourteenth Army in the Italian campaign from June 7 1944.

Lemnitzer, Gen Lyman (1899–1988) US. In 1942 Lemnitzer was selected by Eisenhower as Assistant cos at Allied Force Headquarters in London, where he helped to plan Operation "Torch". In October 1942 he accompanied Gen Clark on a clandestine mission to Algeria to negotiate with the Vichy authorities. He later returned to North Africa as Deputy cos of the US Fifth Army and subsequently commanded 34th Anti-Aircraft Brigade in the Tunisian campaign. Lemnitzer reverted once again to staff duties with the Fifteenth Army Group in Sicily and Italy and, in 1944, became Deputy cos Supreme Allied Command Mediterranean. He took part in discussions regarding Italy's capitulation in 1943 and the surrender of German forces in Italy in May 1945. His expertise in military and diplomatic affairs came to the fore in his postwar role developing US military aid to Europe. He returned to active service in the Korean War commanding an infantry division. He subsequently held senior staff posts in the Far East before returning to Washington, where he was Chairman of the Joint Chiefs of Staff, 1960–62. Although tainted by the Bay of Pigs fiasco, he became SACEUR, 1963–69. *MS.*

Lend-lease. Scheme devised by President Roosevelt by which the US supplied Britain and the Allies with war materiel and other goods. The Lend-Lease Act was passed by Congress on March 11 1941.

L

Lenin, Vladimir Ilyich (Ulyanov) (1870–1924). Russian leader of the Boshevik revolution of 1917; then Chairman of the Soviet government. Lenin's fundamental belief was in the use of violence to achieve political aims at which he proved to be adept. On gaining power, he made peace with Germany through the Treaty of Brest-Litovsk in March 1918 and thus afforded Germany a chance of decisive attack upon France and Britain before the Americans had arrived in strength. From a long and bloody civil war in Russia, Lenin eventually emerged as the unchallenged dictator, albeit of a country now deprived of much of the territory which the Tsars had won. He was succeeded by Stalin. *ANF*.

Soviets advance to relieve Leningrad

Leningrad, siege of (1941–44). By the beginning of September 1941 the German Army Group North had reached the outskirts of Leningrad. Finnish troops occupied the Karelian Isthmus and German units reached the shores of Lake Ladoga on the 8th, surrounding the city. But the German advance had slowed, enabling substantial fortifications to be constructed around Leningrad; on September 13, Zhukov arrived to coordinate the defences. By the end of the month the Germans had given up hope of carrying the city by assault and settled for a siege. The incessant German bombing and shelling, together with food shortages and the severity of the Russian winter took a dreadful toll on the inhabitants. A tenuous supply line was established across the frozen Lake Ladoga and hundreds of thousands of civilians were evacuated to safety across the ice. But the main sources of relief were the sporadic Soviet offensives

that drew German resources away from the siege. Finally, on January 12 1943, the Soviet forces launched Operation "Iskra", with the Leningrad garrison striking south along the lake to link up on the 18th with elements of the Volkhov Front. German artillery fire still limited the flow of supplies and reinforcements into the city but the first breach had been made in the envelopment. However, the final victory had to wait another full year until, in January 1944, an offensive forced the German lines away from Leningrad. On the 27th, Stalin formally announced the end of the siege. Some 633,000 civilians had died from starvation and a further 200,000 from enemy action. *MS*.

Lens. Important French coal-mining town, north of Arras, occupied by the Germans in 1914. The Allies failed to retake it during the Artois operations in September 1915 and, although the Canadian Corps secured nearby Hill 70 in August 1917, Lens was not recaptured until October 3 1918.

Lent, Col Helmut (1918–44). Ger. Having claimed eight day-victories in 1939–40, Lent later became Germany's second highest-scoring night-fighter pilot, flying Messerschmitt Bf 110s and registering a further 102 kills in over 300 night actions. An exceptional leader and marksman, he died landing at Paderborn.

Lentaigne, Brig Walter *see* CHINDIT OPERATIONS.

Leopard I. West German Main Battle Tank, introduced 1965. *See also* TANKS.

Leopold III, King of the Belgians (1901–83). Reigned 1934–50. The German invasion of the Low Countries on May 10 1940 rapidly placed Leopold, who assumed command of his army in the field, in a hopeless position which the British and French were unable to relieve. The King surrendered and remained to face the music. In France and Britain and by some in Belgium, he was unjustly held to have betrayed the cause. Controversy made his situation impossible and he eventually abdicated in 1950. *ANF*.

Lettow-Vorbeck, Gen Paul von (1870–1964). Ger. Commander of German Forces in East Africa in World War I. An expert on colonial affairs on the German General Staff, having fought in China, 1900–01, and in Southwest Africa, 1904. His guerrilla campaign in East Africa successfully diverted British Imperial resources from more important theatres.

Lewin, Adm of the Fleet Lord (b.1920). Br. Chief of the Defence Staff in 1982. As the Prime Minister's principal adviser on the conduct of the Falklands campaign, he proved extremely skilful in briefing the War Cabinet, especially when confronted by sensitive issues such as the decision to torpedo the *General Belgrano*.

Lexington (1) US aircraft carrier. Converted from a battlecruiser design and completed in 1927, she was sunk after being severely damaged by Japanese carrier-borne aircraft at the Battle of the Coral Sea, May 8 1942. (2) The later *Essex*-class carrier of the same name, commissioned in 1943, supported the Tarawa, Iwo Jima and Okinawa landings as well as seeing action in the Battle of the Philippine Sea and at Leyte Gulf.

Leyte campaign (1944–45). The successful Hollandia campaign and the weakening of Japanese air power by US carrier operations allowed MacArthur to advance the initial step in the reconquest of the Philippines, the invasion of Leyte Island, from October to December 1944. On October 20, following a two-day bombardment by Rear Adm Oldendorf's support group, a 700-ship armada of Vice Adm Kinkaid's Seventh Fleet landed Lt Gen Krueger's Sixth Army on the east coast of Leyte. Some 132,000 men and 200,000 tons of materiel were ashore by nightfall.

At first encountering only light resistance from the 15,000-strong Leyte garrison (Thirty-fifth Army; Lt Gen Sosaku Suzuki), US X Corps (Maj Gen Franklin Sibert) advanced north and west from its beachheads south of Tacloban, while XXIV Corps (Maj Gen John Hodge) moved south and west from around Dulag, quickly securing the airfields in both areas. The invasion force's supply lines were

L

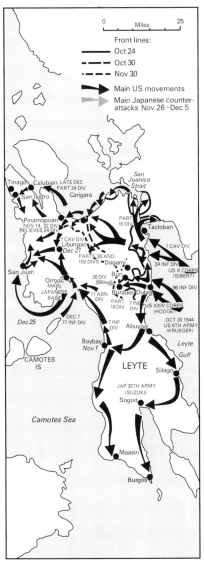

US operations to recapture Leyte, 1944–45

secured by the Battle of Leyte Gulf, October 23–26, but ashore the US advance was slowed by torrential rains, which hampered operations from the captured airstrips, and by increasing resistance as some 45,000 Japanese reinforcements landed at Ormoc on the west coast, October-December.

Japanese counterattacks, including suicidal raids by paratroopers against the central Buri and Burauen airfields were defeated, November 26–December 5, and Krueger's two-pronged offensive, skilfully blending land and amphibious operations, outflanked Suzuki to the south, where Ormoc was taken on December 10, and north, where the last Japanese port fell on December 25 (when Lt Gen

Eichelberger's Eighth Army relieved Sixth Army), isolating some 27,000 Japanese in the central highlands. Mopping-up continued into April 1945. The conquest of Leyte cost US ground forces around 4,000 dead and 12,000 wounded; only some 400 Japanese prisoners were taken. *RO'N. See also* LUZON CAMPAIGN.

Leyte Gulf, Battle of (Oct 23–26 1944). The American invasion of the Philippines from October 1944 prompted the Japanese to activate a variant of the *Sho-go* defence plan which called for the destruction of the landings by naval forces supported by land-based aircraft. The Japanese operation, directed by Adm Toyodo, involved four groups of warships approaching from three different directions. The American invasion was directly covered by warships of Vice Adm Kinkaid's Seventh Fleet and supported by Vice Adm Halsey's Third Fleet, containing four fast carrier task groups.

On October 23 the main force of Japanese surface ships, under Vice Adm Takeo Kurita, suffered serious losses from submarine attacks; on October 24 air strikes from Third Fleet carriers in the Battle of the Sibuyan Sea sank additional major units and caused the Japanese to retreat temporarily. That same day, Japanese land-based aircraft attacked Third Fleet, fatally damaging a light carrier. Early on October 25, surface units of the Seventh Fleet under Rear Adm Oldendorf annihilated a force of Japanese surface ships commanded by Vice Adm Kiyohide Nishimura and routed a supporting group under Vice Adm Kiyohide Shima in the Battle of Surigao Strait. A Japanese carrier group under Vice Adm Ozawa had advanced from the north in order to draw the main American carrier forces. Halsey moved north in pursuit as the Japanese intended, launching air strikes on the morning of October 25 that sank or heavily damaged all four Japanese carriers in the battle off Cape Engaño. Kurita, meanwhile, had altered course the previous day and, with Halsey away to the north and the Seventh Fleet capital ships preoccupied in the south, on the morning of October 25 moved towards the landings

opposed only by Rear Adm Clifton Sprague's force of escort carriers and their destroyer and destroyer escort screens, and aircraft from two other escort carrier groups. A determined advance by the Japanese could have succeeded, but fierce resistance put up by the American light forces and naval aircraft in the battle off Samar, which inflicted substantial losses, confused Kurita and caused him to order a withdrawal. On October 25, land-based Japanese aircraft launched the first successful kamikaze operations against US warships, badly damaging four and sinking one escort carrier. On October 25–26, retreating Japanese warships suffered further losses.

The Japanese deployed forces that were both quantitatively and qualitatively much inferior to those possessed by the Americans, but the clever use of Ozawa's carriers as a decoy, and the failure of the senior American naval commanders to coordinate their actions, nearly enabled Kurita to disrupt seriously if not destroy the invasion. As it was, the Japanese navy failed in attack on the landings, and suffered catastrophic losses. *JTS.*

Liaoyang, Battle of (August 25–September 3 1904), Russo-Japanese War. In an engagement 40 miles (64km) southwest of Mukden, Manchuria, 125,000 Japanese (losses 23,000) under Oyama drove 158,000 Russians (losses 19,000) under Kuropatkin from prepared defensive positions.

Liberty ship. War standard merchantman, built to modified version of British design and adapted for welding in American shipyards. 7,126 tons gross, 11 knots. 2,710 built, including troop transport and hospital ship versions. Over 200 lost during World War II, but played a vital part in ensuring that Allies had sufficient shipping.

Libya, Italian conquest of (Italo-Turkish War) (1911–12). From *c*1880, determined to become a North African colonial power, Italy poured immigrants into Libya (the Ottoman provinces of Tripolitania and Cyrenaica). On September 28 1911, claiming that her settlers were endangered by un-

L

L

rest among the native Muslims, fomented in Constantinople, Italy demanded Ottoman recognition of an Italian protectorate, declaring war next day.

Italian warships shelled and blockaded Turkey's eastern Mediterranean ports, while other squadrons bombarded the Libyan ports and, with naval landing parties, secured Tobruk (October 4), the capital, Tripoli (October 5), Homs, Derna and Benghazi (October 17–21), meeting little resistance. The main Italian expeditionary force, 50,000-strong, landed at Tripoli on October 10. It included nine aircraft. On October 23, Capt Piazza in a Nieuport NG made the first reconnaissance flight in a military aircraft. On October 26, two aircraft directed ground and naval artillery contributing to the Turkish defeat at Sciara-Sciat. On November 1, Lt Giulio Gavotti flew in an Etrich Taube monoplane from Tripoli on history's first bombing mission, dropping (by hand) four 4.5lb (2kg) bombs on Turkish positions *c*30 miles (48km) inland. The first "leaflet raids" and photographic reconnaissance flights followed.

The Turks and their Senussi allies retreated to the interior; the Italians held their coastal enclaves and maintained a close blockade. Elsewhere, Italian warships bombarded Beirut and Smyrna (January–February 1912), forced a temporary closure of the Dardanelles by shelling the forts (April), and in May landed occupation forces on Rhodes, Kos and other Dodecanese islands. In July, Italy launched an offensive into the Libyan interior. Threatened by the approach of the First Balkan War, Turkey sought peace. By the Treaty of Ouchy, October 15 1912, Libya and the Dodecanese Islands were ceded to Italy. *RO'N.*

Lichtenstein. German airborne radar to intercept night bombers. First used August 1941.

Liddell Hart, Capt (Sir) Basil (1895–1970). Br. Military thinker and author. *See also* TANKS.

Lidice. Czechoslovakian village razed by German troops, June 9 1942, and its *c*390 inhabitants shot as reprisal for assassination of Heydrich.

Lie, Trygve Halvdan (1896–1968). Norwegian. The first Secretary General of the UN and a strong supporter of UN involvement in the Korean War. He lobbied the Security Council to vote for the American resolutions of June 25 and 27 1950 condemning the DPRK and calling on UN members to assist the ROK.

Liège, Battle of (1914). Von Moltke's modifications to the Schlieffen plan meant that, in August 1914, the Germans had to ensure the immediate capture of the 12 forts around Liège in Belgium so that their invading armies could pass safely through the corridor between Holland and the Ardennes en route to France. Six brigades from Second Army were assigned to the attack, which began on August 5. Two days later, under the temporary command of Maj Gen Erich Ludendorff – who had largely planned the operation before the war – men of the 14th Infantry Brigade penetrated Liège itself and enabled Ludendorff to demand the surrender of the Citadel. With the surrounding forts still holding out, the Germans deployed huge 30.5cm and 42cm howitzers. Two forts were taken by infantry assaults but the remainder were battered into submission by the howitzers, the last two falling on August 16. *PJS.*

Lightning *see* P-38 LIGHTNING.

Liman von Sanders, Gen Otto Victor Karl (1855–1929). Ger. Late in 1913, Liman von Sanders was appointed head of the German military mission charged with the reorganization of the Turkish army. When Turkey declared war on the Allies, October 29 1914, he was given titular command of the invasion of the Russian Caucasus, Enver Pasha's vainglorious offensive (which Liman attempted to discourage) ending in defeat at Sarikamis. In March 1915, only a few weeks before the Allied landings, Liman took command at Gallipoli, where his well-prepared fortifications and mobile defence (for which Ataturk must share the credit) repelled the invasion. Succeeding Colmar von der Golz in command of Turkish forces in the Middle East, 1916, Liman was c-in-c at the time of Allenby's

Damascus campaign, September-October 1918. He failed to anticipate Allenby's coastal thrust and his armies, outnumbered and low in morale, were shattered at Megiddo and driven in hectic retreat to Damascus and beyond, capitulating on October 30. *RO'N.*

Limbang *see* BRUNEI REVOLT.

Limited war. A conflict with an aim that may be achieved without accomplishing the total defeat of the enemy and without the use of the ultimate weapons.

Lincoln, Avro 694 (Br, post-WWII). Long-range heavy bomber; crew 7. Prototype flew June 9 1944; initial deliveries September 1945; eventually equipped 20 squadrons of RAF. Bombing operations against terrorists, Negri Sembilan 1950; against Mau Mau, Kenya, 1954. Finally withdrawn 1955. Production 604. Four 1,750hp Rolls-Royce Merlin engines; max. speed 295mph (475kph) two 20mm cannon, five 0.5in machine guns, 14,000lb (6,350kg) bombs.

Lindemann, Professor F A *see* CHERWELL, LORD.

Lindley, Battle of *see* DE WET.

"Linebacker" Operations (1972). US Air Force and Marine aircraft conducted Operation "Linebacker I" in response to the communists' 1972 Easter offensive in South Vietnam. Mine-laying aircraft closed North Vietnam's harbours, while B-52s were used for the first time since 1968 to destroy airfields and supply depots. "Linebacker I" was restricted to the area south of the 20th Parallel when secret talks seemed to produce progress in October.

Operation "Linebacker II" was the 11-day 1972 "Christmas bombing" launched by President Nixon when Hanoi appeared to back away from a tentative agreement. Nixon unleashed all the B-52s stationed in Southeast Asia against previously forbidden targets in Hanoi and Haiphong. The operation, combined with the mining of harbours in "Linebacker I", sharply cut the flow of supplies into North Vietnam and left the North, after the expenditure of nearly all of its SA-2 missiles, virtually defenceless against high-altitude aircraft. However, American losses of 15 B-52s and 92 crewmen also were strategic. The impact of this operation on the negotiations is controversial, for while the North Vietnamese agreed to resume talks as Nixon demanded, they did not make further significant concessions. The operation strengthened opposition in Congress to Nixon's war policies. *WST*.

Lingayen Gulf. Location of the main Japanese landings on Luzon in the northern Philippines in December 1941. The US Sixth Army also landed here on January 9 1945 during the Allied reconquest of the Philippines.

Linton, Commander John VC (1905–43). Br. Commanding submarines HMS *Pandora* (1940–41) and then *Turbulent* in the Mediterranean, Linton had great success against Italian supply convoys to North Africa. *Turbulent* was sunk by Italian MTBS, February 12 1943; Linton received a posthumous VC.

Lioré-et-Olivier LeO 451.B4 (French, WWII). Medium bomber; crew 4. Prototype (LeO 45) flew January 16 1937; first production aircraft March 24 1939. By June 25 1940 at least 452 completed and flown; continued in production and use with Vichy forces; a few used by Italian and German units. Limited postwar French use until September 1957. Production 584. Two 1,140hp Gnome-Rhône 14N 48/49 engines; max. speed 307mph (494kph); one 20mm cannon, two 7.5mm machine guns, 4,410lb (2,000kg) bombs.

Liquid fuel. Ballistic missiles were originally powered by liquid fuel rockets using alcohol or kerosene oxidized by liquid oxygen or nitric acid. Such substances were not only often difficult to handle, but they had to be loaded into the missile just before launch and could not be kept inside the rocket for extended periods. This meant that early rockets were both operationally inflexible and vulnerable. Storable liquid fuels were therefore developed which could be kept in rockets for extended periods. The most common are dimethyl hydrazine (a compound

of hydrogen and nitrogen) oxidized by dinitrogen tetroxide (N_2O_4). These are still more prone to accidents and handling problems than solid fuels, but they give higher thrust per unit weight. The USSR has kept storable liquid fuel missiles longer than the USA, even for submarine-launched missiles, sometimes with tragic results. *EJG*.

Field Marshal List: victor in Greece

List, Field Marshal Siegmund Wilhelm (1880–1971). Ger. One of the 12 generals promoted to Field Marshal after the fall of France in 1940, List, the son of a Württemberg doctor, served as a staff officer with various Bavarian formations on the Western Front during World War I, apart from a tour of duty in the Balkans and with Turkish forces in 1916–17. Between the wars he rose steadily in his profession, gaining a reputation as a cool and methodical soldier. List backed Hitler in the Blomberg-Fritsch crisis in 1938 and, having thereby escaped the subsequent purge, he was chosen, after the *Anschluss*, to establish the new Army Group 5 in Austria. In 1939 he led the Fourteenth Army, on the southern flank of the German forces, during the Polish campaign. The following year he commanded the Twelfth Army in the battle for France and won praise not only for the speed with which his infantry units reinforced the "Panzer Corridor" in the drive towards the Channel but also for his tactful handling of the brilliant but volatile commander of XIX Panzer Corps, Heinz Guderian. His performance in the operations on the Aisne in June 1940 was less distinguished, although his troops ultimately pierced the Weygand Line and outflanked the Maginot fortifications before advancing to

the Swiss frontier.

In 1941 List was sent to the Balkans where, in February, he secured an agreement enabling Germany to attack Greece through Bulgaria. The ensuing campaign in Greece, which started on April 6, was another triumph for the Twelfth Army, with Athens falling to List's forces three weeks later. His last major appointment was as commander of Army Group A in Russia in June 1942. He was directed by Hitler to take Rostov and then to occupy the Black Sea coast and seize the oilfields in the Caucasus, but his supply lines became overextended, slowing the offensive. His failure to achieve all his objectives precipitated his dismissal in September 1942. In 1948 a military tribunal sentenced him to life imprisonment for war crimes in the Balkans. However, he was released at the end of 1952 and lived to the age of 91. *PJS*.

"Little Boy" *see* HIROSHIMA, ATOMIC ATTACK ON.

Little Gibraltar (Hill 355). During the Korean War, Little Gibraltar overlooked the southeastern part of the Imjin salient allowing the Chinese to observe all movement in the area. On October 4 1951, it fell to the 1st Commonwealth Division and became a key position in the defences beyond the Imjin river. *See also* JAMESTOWN LINE.

Littorio. Italian battleship. Completed 1940; damaged at Taranto, November 1940; fought in First and Second Battles of Sirte, 1941–42; renamed *Italia* before internment, 1943.

Lloyd, Air Chief Marshal Sir Hugh (1894–1972). Br. Air Commander during the siege of Malta in 1941–42.

Lloyd George, Earl (1863–1945). Br. Chancellor of the Exchequer 1908–15, Minister of Munitions 1915–16, Secretary of State for War 1916, Prime Minister 1916–22. As a war leader, Lloyd George's reputation was founded upon his response to the Munitions Crisis in 1915. The military requirement for shells far exceded anything envisaged before the war and, indeed, by Kitchener, during it. As Minister of Munitions, Lloyd

L

George swept aside traditional procedures with the result that, in the great battles of 1916, the British army was able to mount the gigantic artillery barrages which were held to be essential prerequisites to the breakthrough. But the breakthrough was not achieved and Lloyd George became convinced that the main war effort should be transferred away from the deadlock of the Western Front to other theatres, such as Salonika. This brought him into conflict with the military authorities. When, however, Kitchener was drowned in 1916, Asquith chose Lloyd George to succeed him as Secretary of State for War. From this vantage point, Lloyd George skilfully marshalled the disquiet about Asquith as a war leader. In December 1916 he displaced Asquith as PM.

In the nation's perception, he was a great war leader but 1917 proved to hold even greater disasters in store than 1916, and Lloyd George failed to exert a decisive grip upon the situation. Haig maintained that the Western Front was the decisive theatre and Lloyd George felt strong enough, not to dismiss him, but only to intrigue against him. Moreover, if the war was to be fought to a conclusion, there was no viable alternative to the western strategy, especially after the collapse of Russia in 1917.

In 1922 Lloyd George resigned and never returned to office. *ANF*.

Local Defence Volunteers (LDV) *see* HOME GUARD.

Local Forces Militia, NLF. The local guerrilla or popular forces of the National Liberation Front of South Vietnam were one of three categories of troops nominally under NLF command during the Vietnam War. The *Dan quan du kich*, or civilian guerrillas, were subdivided into secret, self-defence or combat groups, depending on place and function, and operated under the jurisdiction of village Communist Party organs. Ideally each hamlet had a squad and each village a platoon for use in night raids, intelligence gathering and mobilization into the main forces. Estimates of their number were notoriously unreliable. The capacious definition used by the com-

munists led them to count 320,000 people in guerrilla and local militia forces in the South in 1966, while US estimates in 1967 varied between 156,000 and 244,000. *WST. See also* PEOPLE'S LIBERATION ARMED FORCE.

Local Self-Defence Forces Militia, DRV. The armed forces of the Democratic Republic of Vietnam comprised main, regional and local self-defence categories. The latter, part-time militia, provided local security and labour to support the regular army. At the height of the Vietnam War about 10 per cent of the DRV's 20 million people (1969–70) were enrolled in local self-defence units, although in the area just north of the demilitarized zone this proportion reached as high as 42 percent. Hanoi credited local self-defence forces with snaring American planes in "networks" of small-arms fire, but their contribution to road maintenance and public order probably was more valuable to the war effort. *WST*.

Locarno Pacts. In October 1925 an international conference was convened at Locarno in Switzerland. The delegates negotiated a series of treaties that would remove potential causes of friction between states and promote collective security. Germany, France and Britain were the main initiators while other signatories included Belgium, Italy, Poland and Czechoslovakia.

Lockwood, Vice Adm Charles Andrews, Jr (1890–1967). US. As Commander Submarines Pacific (ComSubPac) at Pearl Harbor from January 1943, Lockwood correctly indentified the mechanical faults in the Mark XIV torpedo that had plagued US submariners and went on to direct the most successful submarine offensive of all time. US submarines sank 174 Japanese warships (*c*494,000 tons) and, 877 transports and merchantmen (*c*3,500,000 tons): more than half the total Japanese tonnage lost. Lockwood's boats also performed vital reconnaissance, raiding and aircrew-rescue missions.

Loc Ninh, Battle of (1967). The town of Loc Ninh, located 81 miles (130km) north of Saigon, South Vietnam, was defended in 1967 by

three Civilian Irregular Defence Group companies and one company of Regional forces. The 9th Division of the People's Liberation Armed Force (PLAF) attacked the town on October 29 but withdrew on November 7 after Army of the Republic (ARVN) and American troops reinforced the defenders. The US Command believed this and similar attacks on isolated outposts marked a shift by the communists to conventional big unit tactics, but the purpose was to draw American and ARVN forces out of the cities in preparation for the Tet offensive. *WST*.

Lodge, Ambassador Henry Cabot (1902–85). US. President Kennedy sought bipartisan support for his Vietnam policy by appointing Republican Lodge Ambassador to South Vietnam in June 1963. Lodge believed President Ngo Dinh Diem was the chief obstacle to successful prosecution of the war and urged Kennedy to support the coup that ended in Diem's assassination. He resigned in May 1964, continued to advise President Johnson on the war, and returned as ambassador in July 1965. During his second tour he intervened in the conflict between Premier Nguyen Cao Ky and anti-government Buddhists and attempted to unify Saigon's squabbling military leaders. Lodge left Vietnam in May 1967, served on Johnson's Senior Advisory Group on the war in March 1968, and accepted appointment as chief negotiator to the Paris peace conference in January 1969. Finding the latter futile, he resigned in October 1969. *WST*.

Loerzer, Gen Bruno (1891–1960). Gen. Loerzer, a close friend of Göring, commanded *Jagdstaffel 26* and *Jagdgeschwader Nr. 3* on the Western Front in 1917–18. Credited with 4 victories, he became Germany's ninth highest-scoring fighter pilot of World War I. After serving as President of the *Deutsche Luftsportverband* (German Air Sports League) and as Reich Air Sport Leader in the 1930s, Loerzer commanded *Fliegerkorps II* in the French campaign and the Battle of Britain in 1940 and subsequently in the Mediterranean. In 1944–45 he was Chief of the Luftwaffe's Personnel Office.

Löhr, Gen Alexander (1885–1947). Austrian. Former head of the Austrian Air Force, Löhr transferred to the Luftwaffe following the 1938 *Anschluss*, leading *Luftflotte 4* in Poland and the Balkans, the airborne invasion of Crete and in southern Russia before taking over from List as C-in-C South-East in mid-1942. In January 1943, he took command of Army Group E, covering Greece and the Aegean. Late in 1944 he saved this formation by conducting a skilful fighting retreat through Yugoslavia. Hanged in 1947 after being found guilty of war crimes by a Yugoslav court. *PJS*.

Lohner flying-boats (Austrian, WWI). Maritime reconnaissance-bomber; crew 2–3. Series progressively developed from Type L. First Type M flew early 1914; first delivery February 1914. Most numerous variants Types T and R, latter with mine-laying capability. A Type L captured by Italy (May 27 1915) was copied and produced as Macchi L1. Production, Lohner types 161; Macchi L1, 140; L2, 10. One 160hp Austro-Daimler, 175hp Rapp or (in Macchi-built version) 150/160hp Isotta-Fraschini engine; max. speed 68mph (109kph); one rifle-calibre machine gun, 440lb (200kg) bombs.

Longdon, Mount. At the northern point of the Argentine positions before Port Stanley during the Falklands War of 1982, and defended by the 7th Regiment, whose Regular element, augmented by commandos, fought stubbornly against the night attack by 3 Para on June 11. This proved the most costly attack in the campaign for the British; 3 Para lost 18 dead and more than 35 wounded. Amongst the casualties was Sergeant McKay (1952–82), subsequently awarded a posthumous VC. More than 50 defenders died, and some 50 were captured.

Long March (1934–35). In October 1934, hard-pressed by the Kuomintang, the Chinese communists retreated from southern Kiangsi, across southwest China, to the mountains of Yenan, northern Shensi. The longest trek, more than 6,000 miles (9,650km) in 13 months, was made by Chu Teh's First Front Army (*c*100,000-

strong, with Mao Tse-tung (Mao Zedong) as political commissar). Shorter routes were taken by Ho Lung's Second Front Army (*c*55,000) and Hsu Hsiang-chien's Fourth Front Army (*c*50,000). All subsequently formed the Eighth Route Army. Of *c*200,000 persons concerned in the Long March, *c*100,000 became casualties (although 50,000 recruits were gained en route), and *c*40,000 fell out to form communist cadres along the line of march. *RO'N*.

Longmore, Air Chief Marshal Sir Arthur (1885–1970). Br. AOC-in-C Middle East from the outbreak of war with Italy to June 1941.

Long Range Desert Group (LRDG). Raised by Maj R A Bagnold with Gen Wavell's encouragement, the LRDG's British/New Zealand motorized units (using specially-adapted 15-cwt and 30-cwt Chevrolet trucks) made armoured reconnaissance and raiding patrols in North Africa, August 1940–late 1942, also transporting and recovering Commando and SAS raiding parties. From 1943, a constituent of Raiding Forces Middle East in the Mediterranean and Balkans.

Long Range Penetration Group *see* CHINDIT OPERATIONS.

Lon Nol, Gen (b.1913). Cambodian. Variously Minister of National Defence and Prime Minister of Cambodia since 1954; engineered the overthrow of Prince Norodom Sihanouk on March 18 1970 while Sihanouk was out of the country. Along with other conservative leaders, Lon Nol had grown exasperated with Vietnamese communist use of Cambodian territory as sanctuary for the war in South Vietnam and held Sihanouk responsible. His coup and subsequent attacks on the sanctuaries brought the Phnom Penh government into the war on the US and Saigon side, provoked the Vietnamese communists to increase support for the Khmers Rouges, precipitated a civil war, and invited the devastating bombardment of Cambodia by American air forces. The Khmers Rouges swept aside Lon Nol's corrupt and incompetent government on April 17 1975. *WST*.

British troops move up at Loos, 1915

Loos, Battle of. The British part in the Allied offensive in Artois on September 25 1915 was to attack over unfavourable ground between Lens and the La Bassée Canal, a mining area containing fortified villages and slag-heaps. Both Sir John French and Sir Douglas Haig, whose First Army was to carry out the attack, were forced to comply with the French plan to relieve pressure on Russia. Poison gas, now to be used by the British for the first time, appeared to compensate for the shortage of artillery ammunition. The gas was released an hour before the main assault by Gough's I Corps and Rawlinson's IV Corps but it was a failure in the centre and on the left, drifting back over the British trenches in some places. Even so, the 15th (Scottish) Division took Loos village while farther north the 9th (Scottish) Division captured the Hohenzollern Redoubt and Fosse 8. French kept the general reserve too far back. When he belatedly placed the inexperienced 21st and 24th Divisions under Haig's control, congestion in the rear delayed their arrival, compelling them to march at night, across the debris-strewn battlefield, for an attack against the uncut wire of the strong German second position between Lens and Hulluch the next morning. Not surprisingly their attack ended in a disorganized retirement and German counterattacks recaptured most of the earlier British gains, including the Hohenzollern Redoubt. Another attack on that strongpoint on October 13 only secured its western face. French's poor handling of the reserves at Loos helped to precipitate his replacement by Haig as C-in-C of the BEF in December 1915. *PJS*.

L

253

Lopatin, Gen Anton (1897–1965). Russian. Commanding a corps of the Twentysixth Army during the German invasion of 1941, Lopatin was fortunate to escape the massive encirclement of the Southwestern Front. In November he led the Thirtyseventh Army in the fighting for Rostov and, in August, received command of the Sixtysecond Army. His forces took the brunt of the German offensive in the summer of 1942 and retreated to Stalingrad. During the course of the withdrawal the bulk of Lopatin's forces were lost at Kalach and this reverse, together with his pessimistic appreciation of the defence of Stalingrad, led to his replacement by Chuikov. *MS.*

LORAN. Acronym of *Long Range Navigation*, an American radio navigational system first used by the US Navy during World War II.

Lorenz beam. Radio system to direct pilots in blind landing.

Lorient. French Atlantic port; German U-boat base and operational HQ from 1940. Heavily bombed by Allies. German garrison held out until end of war.

Lorraine, Battle of (1914). On August 14 1914, in accordance with Plan XVII, the French First Army, (Dubail) and Second Army (de Castelnau) attacked areas of Lorraine, ceded to Germany in 1871. The Schlieffen plan envisaged that the German Sixth Army, under Crown Prince Rupprecht of Bavaria, and Seventh Army, under von Heeringen, would give ground and draw the French on, but on August 17 Rupprecht obtained Moltke's permission to counterattack. At the resultant actions of Morhange and Sarrebourg on August 20, the French were decisively checked and forced back to their frontier fortifications. However, in changing a vital element in the Schlieffen plan, the Germans had merely inflicted a reverse on the French instead of letting them advance far enough to be trapped. Once behind the frontier, the French regained cohesion and strength. *PJS.*

Los Alamos, New Mexico, USA. Selected November 1942 as centralized, secure and expansion-capable laboratory for develop-

ment of atomic bomb. Operational from March 1943.

Lossberg, Gen Fritz von (1868–1943). Ger. From early 1915, Lossberg was deployed by Falkenhayn as a peripatetic COS on the Western Front, becoming the German army's chief defensive expert. He evolved the Hindenburg Line system, replacing rigid linear defence with a defensive zone some 2,000yd (1,800m) in depth, peppered with strongpoints and machine gun nests. Infantry were entrenched on the reverse slopes and *Eingreif* (counterattack) formations were deployed farther back in readiness to aid threatened sectors.

Louvain. Between August 25 and 30 1914 the Germans, claiming that the rearguard of Kluck's First Army had been fired upon by civilians, burned the Belgian city of Louvain by way of reprisal. Louvain's famous library, with its unique collection of medieval manuscripts, was destroyed, civilians were killed and looting was widespread.

Low Countries, invasion of the (1940). Holland and Belgium were the earliest victims of the German offensive in the West in May 1940, the former capitulating after 5 days and the latter after 18. Rotterdam and The Hague were attacked by bombers and airborne forces in the early hours of May 10; simultaneous attacks were made on the frontier defences 100 miles (160km) to the east. The German attacking forces were much smaller than those opposing them. Only one panzer division (the 9th) was available, and its line of advance was intersected by canals and rivers that should have been easy to defend. All depended on the vital bridges such as those at Rotterdam, Dordrecht and Moerdijk, but these and other crossing points were seized in a brilliant airborne operation which employed 4,000 out of Germany's 4,500 trained parachutists. The remaining 500 parachutists were employed in the capture of the supposedly impregnable Belgian fortress of Eben Emael and two vital bridges over the Albert Canal. The westward thrust of German Army Group B, which followed its parachutists

Congested German advance, Belgium

into Belgium, was deliberately constrained in the first week or so of hostilities. The aim was to lure the British Army and First French Army away from the main French forces to the south, and drive them relentlessly northwards to the Channel coast. This the Germans achieved.

Belgium put 21 divisions into the field under the personal command of King Leopold. Although virtually devoid of tanks and air cover, the Belgian forces, especially the seven divisions of regular troops, generally gave a good account of themselves in what became a demoralizing retreat that abandoned most of their country to the invader by May 21. After giving several warnings to his allies, the King asked for a cease-fire on the evening of May 27. This action, which briefly exposed the retreat route to Dunkirk, caused Leopold to be unjustly castigated. *BB. See also* FRANCE, BATTLE OF (1940).

Low, Vice Adm Francis Stuart ("Frog") (1894–1964). US. As Adm King's Operations Officer, Low was an originator of the plan for the Doolittle raid on Tokyo, April 1942, and as COS, US Tenth Fleet, 1943–45, he played an important part in the Atlantic anti-U-boat campaign. Transferring to the Pacific, he commanded bombardment groups at Okinawa, June–August 1945.

Lübeck, bombing of. On the night of March 28 1942, 234 aircraft of RAF Bomber Command were dispatched to the German Baltic port of Lübeck. For the first time in such an attack, they had the advantage of the newly introduced Gee system, although its range only extended part of the way. Also for the first time, the bombers, like

L

the Germans in 1940–41, carried a high proportion of incendiaries and the German plan of sending a flare-equipped force ahead to illuminate the target was copied. These tactics succeeded and about 200 acres of the town, which contained much woodwork, was devastated, mainly by fire. This was the greatest success which Bomber Command had achieved to date and it had a formative influence upon subsequent tactics, including the introduction of the Pathfinder Force. *ANF.*

Lucas, Maj Gen John Porter (1890–1949). US. Commander VI US Corps from September 1943; carried out Anzio landings in January 1944; superseded by Truscott on February 22 1944 after failing to break out.

Ludendorff bridge *see* RHINE CROSSING (1945).

Ludendorff, Lt Gen *(General der Infanterie)* Erich von (1865–1937). Ger. By 1908, Ludendorff had joined the General Staff and was head of the key mobilization and deployment section, responsible for the detailed blueprint for the invasion of Belgium and France. His uncompromising advocacy of the need for additional regimental duties but in August 1914 he was temporarily attached to the German forces assigned to capture the Liège forts, an operation which he had planned. His initiative and leadership in taking

Ludendorff: master planner of WWI

the Liège Citadel earned him national fame and also the post of COS of the German Eighth Army under Hindenburg, thus beginning a close partnership which lasted

over four years. With Hoffmann, Ludendorff masterminded the victories at Tannenberg and the Masurian Lakes and he remained as Hindenburg's COS on the latter's appointment as C-in-C East. Germany's successes against the Russians made the arrogant Ludendorff ever more obsessive about the importance of the Eastern Front and contributed to mounting animosity in his relations with Falkenhayn. When Hindenburg replaced Falkenhayn on August 29 1916, Ludendorff refused the title "Second Chief of the General Staff" and insisted on being called "First Quartermaster-General" besides being given joint responsibility for all decisions. With Hindenburg acquiescent, Ludendorff now assumed almost dictatorial powers, wielding enormous influence over the German economy, political life and foreign affairs as well as military operations, yet, for all his tactical brilliance, he lacked strategic objectivity. By supporting the unrestricted submarine campaign, he helped to bring America into the war while his annexationist war aims rendered it increasingly unlikely that Germany could secure an acceptable negotiated peace. The failure of his 1918 offensives and the Allied advances in August led him to seek an armistice, but his subsequent rejection of the terms offered resulted in his dismissal on October 26 1918. After the war, as his mental instability grew more pronounced, he took part in Hitler's abortive Munich Putsch of 1923, although even the Nazis eventually broke with him. *PJS.*

Ludlow-Hewitt, Air Chief Marshal Sir Edgar (1882–1973). Br. AOC-in-C, Bomber Command 1937–40. The plans made for Bomber Command before the war proved to be impracticable. In daylight, the bombers could not survive in the face of the German defending fighters and at night the crews could not find, let alone hit, pinpoint targets such as oil plants or even railway marshalling yards. Against criticism of Ludlow-Hewitt, it must be recognized that no-one else in the RAF appreciated the true position and that, as to scientific aids, Fighter Command absorbed a consuming priority from 1938 onwards.

Luftwaffe. The German Air Force was prohibited under the terms of the Treaty of Versailles, but from 1933 the Nazis made its build-up a major priority. By 1939 it was the most powerful in the world.

Lule Burgas *see* DECEPTION.

Lumsden, Lt Gen Herbert (1897–1945). Br. Commander 1st Armoured Division in Battle of Mersa Matruh, in June 1942; promoted to command X Corps for El Alamein in August 1942; failed to break through in first phase of the battle, but broke out successfully at the end and led pursuit of Rommel as far as El Agheila where he was relieved of his command by Montgomery, December 1942.

Lüneberg Heath. By the beginning of May 1945, the Tactical HQ of Montgomery's 21st Army Group was situated on Lüneberg Heath, 25 miles (40km) southeast of Hamburg. There, on May 4, a German delegation led by Adm von Friedeburg signed the surrender of all German armed forces in Northwest Germany, Holland and Denmark.

***Lusitania*.** A Cunarder of about 31,000 tons, sunk on May 7 1915 by a German U-boat as she was nearing the end of her homeward voyage from New York. She sank very quickly and over 1,000 people lost their lives, including more than 100 American citizens. German warnings that they would attack the ship had been ignored and in Britain and America it was held that the sinking of an unarmed merchant ship without inspection to see what she was carrying was contrary to international law. *ANF.*

Lütjens, Adm Günther (1889–1941). Ger. Flag Officer, Torpedo Craft, 1937–39; C-in-C, Reconnaissance Forces, 1939. Commanded battlecruiser *Gneisenau* (flag) and *Scharnhorst* in invasion of Norway, sinking carrier HMS *Glorious* and escorting destroyers, 1940, and in Atlantic raiding cruise in which 22 unescorted Allied ships were sunk or captured, January–March 1941. In May 1941, commanded a similar sortie by battleship *Bismarck*, accompanied by cruiser *Prinz*

L

Adm Lütjens: lost with *Bismarck*, 1941

Eugen. Bismarck sank battlecruiser HMS *Hood* and damaged Battleship *Prince of Wales*, but was hunted down and sunk; Lütjens and most of his men were lost. *CJW/CD.*

Lützow. (1) German *Derfflinger*-class battlecruiser sunk at Jutland, 1916. (2) In 1940, the pocket battleship *Deutschland* was renamed *Lützow*. In action off Norway (1940) and in the Barents Sea (1942). Damaged in air raids and scuttled in 1945.

Luzon campaign (1945). Following the Leyte campaign, Gen MacArthur's next step in the reconquest of the Philippines was the invasion of Luzon Island. Air bases to support the invasion were gained, December 15–20 1944, by unopposed amphibious landings on lightly-garrisoned Mindoro Island. In spite of US air superiority, Rear Adm Oldendorf's bombardment force suffered heavy kamikaze air attack, January 4-7 1945, en route from Leyte to Luzon.

On January 9 1945, some 68,000 men of I Corps (Maj Gen Innis Swift) and XIV Corps (Maj Gen Oscar Griswold), the vanguard of Lt Gen Krueger's Sixth Army, were landed at Lingayen Gulf, western Luzon. Although Gen Yamashita deployed some 260,000 men of Fourteenth Area Army in defence of Luzon, he was ill-supplied and had few aircraft. He therefore did not oppose the landings, but deployed in three groups – Shobu Group, 152,000-strong, under Yamashita himself, in northern Luzon; Kembu Group (30,000 men; Maj Gen Rikichi Tsu-

kada) defending the west-central airfields; Shimbu Group (80,000 men; Lt Gen Shizuo Yokoyama), northeast of Manila – hoping by prolonged resistance to delay the invasion of Japan.

By early February, aided by secondary landings by US Eighth Army (Lt Gen Eichelberger) on the southwest coast, US forces had secured the western airfields, driving the survivors of Kembu Group into the central highlands, isolated the Bataan Peninsula and were advancing on Manila from north and southwest. Yamashita's order that Manila should not be defended was disobeyed by Iwabuchi, whose 19,000 troops waged a savage house-to-house battle, laying the city in ruins and killing some 100,000 civilians, until March 3, when they were wiped out.

In March–May a US offensive north of Manila virtually des-

US troops advance on Luzon, Philippines

troyed Shimbu Group and secured central Luzon, while to the south the Bicol Peninsula was cleared, April 1–14. Yamashita, with some 65,000 men, withdrew from his HQ at Baguio (fell April 27) into the northern mountains, where his determined resistance tied up a considerable part of US Sixth Army until the war's end. US losses on Luzon were around 8,000 killed and 33,000 wounded; Japanese dead exceeded 190,000. *RO'N.*

LVG CV (German, WWI). Two-seat reconnaissance. Prototype flew December 1916; by August 31 1917, 98 were with operational units. In service proved dependable and popular; progressively superseded by LVG C VI from June 1918. A few LVG C Vs used operationally by Polish units 1919–20. Production: total ordered 1,250, some de-

livered as C VIs. One 200/220hp Benz Bz IV/IVU engine; max. speed 103mph (166kph); two 7.92mm machine guns, 250lb (112kg) bombs.

Lyautey, Marshal Louis Hubert Gonzalve (1854–1934). Fr. Lyautey served in Algeria, Indochina and Madagascar (1880–1902). Sent as Resident-General to Morocco on its annexation in 1912, Lyautey successfully applied a policy of quadrillage: the pacification of a chosen zone, followed by outward extension (the *tache d'huile*, "oil stain") of the pacified area, introducing economic and social reforms but respecting local institutions and customs. During World War I, he kept the peace in Morocco with minimum force, but his last proconsular years were shadowed by the Riffian War, 1921–26. Disliking Pétain's draconic measures against Abd el-Krim's nationalists, he resigned in September 1925. *RO'N.*

Lynch, Lt Col Thomas J (1916–44). US. One of the leading USAAF fighter pilots in the Southwest Pacific, Lynch flew with the US 35th Fighter Group, scoring 20 victories before he was shot down off New Guinea in March 1944.

Lynx. Westland/Aérospatiale. General-purpose helicopter in service with AAC as Lynx AH1. Fitted with eight TOW missiles in the anti-tank role, it can also be used as a battlefield troop lifter and general combat support aircraft. *See also* ARMY AIR CORPS.

Lys, Battle of the *see* MARCH OFFENSIVE, GERMAN (1918).

Lysander, Westland P8 (Br, WWII). Two-seat army-cooperation/special duties. Prototype flew June 15 1936; first deliveries to squadron June 1938. Fully slotted and flapped for slow flying and STOL; 174 Lysanders went to France September 1939-May 1940. Some air-sea rescue work 1940–41, then supply and agent-dropping missions Occupied France. Production 1,652. One 870/890hp Bristol Mercury or 905hp Bristol Perseus engine; max. speed 230mph (368kph); three/four 0.303in machine guns, 500lb (225kg) bombs.

L

Limited war in the nuclear age

Robert O'Neill
Chichele Professor of the History of War
All Souls College, Oxford

Nuclear weapons may have made the prospect of war between the superpowers unthinkable as an act of deliberate policy, but their development certainly has not discouraged other forms of conflict. This essay examines how, through the ordeals of limited engagements of force, the process of competition between East and West gradually came to be disciplined and the Cold War gave way, in uneven stages, to the more restrained form of competition symbolized by the round of summit meetings that President Reagan and President Gorbachev have held in the late 1980s.

A US machine-gun team in the Tet offensive of January 1968. The long drawn-out conflict in Vietnam still represents, perhaps, the clearest demonstration of the nature of limited war in the nuclear age.

It would be shallow thinking to attribute the essential causation of what we have come to call limited wars to superpower rivalry and the existence of nuclear weapons. Most of these conflicts also had local causes, and frequently these were more important than external influences in initiating and sustaining the bloodshed. Yet they have nearly all touched superpower interests and the superpowers' presence has been evident, hovering above the battlefield if not directly engaged in some way. At the very least, the superpowers' clear interest has imposed some upper limit on the nature of the operations conducted, or each has inhibited the other from intervention in some way. The bipolar structure of military power which nuclear weapons have sustained has changed the nature of international conflict fundamentally.

The Malayan Emergency

The first two major conflicts involving Western powers and communist insurgents outside Europe occurred in the British and French empires. It is interesting that they should both have occurred in Southeast Asia, but no mere coincidence. Both Malaya and Indochina had experienced a degree of liberation through the Japanese occupation and the following brief power vacuum.

Malay nationalism had been fostered by the Japanese during their occupation, partly with an eye to their own long-term interests as hegemon of East Asia and the Pacific. They gave the Malays a greater degree of administrative responsibility than the British had done. They treated the substantial Chinese minority harshly, and many Chinese fled into the jungle where they formed the Malayan People's Anti-Japanese Army (MPAJA). This organization maintained its cohesion and infrastructure after the Japanese surrender and worked closely with the Malayan Communist Party (MCP). In 1948 the MCP launched a major campaign of violence against the British and those who worked for them, striking particularly at remote planters and their families. Through a determined and well-organized series of operations, the communist guerrillas soon had the colonial administration on the defensive. The British government in London had to decide whether to mount a major and expensive military counteroffensive. Despite grave economic problems at home and rising demands for force commitments in Europe as Stalin mounted the Berlin blockade, the Attlee government accepted the challenge, motivated not only by Cold War considerations and reasons of national prestige but also by a keen sense of the economic benefits that Malaya's exports of rubber and tin brought Britain.

The key element in British strategy during the Malayan Emergency was a realization that the campaign could not succeed without the political support of the Malayan people, both Malay and Chinese. The challenge was to devise a more attractive political strategy than that of the MCP. Clearly, security was an important short-term benefit that Britain could help to confer, but of far greater significance in the long term was the prospect of independence. By 1952 the British authorities under Templer were working closely with the leader of the United Malay National Organization (UMNO), Tunku Abdul Rahman, towards delegation of responsibility.

A political approach alone could not defeat the communists. Their military power had to be contained and then destroyed before they were able to cause sufficient damage to the political and economic fabric of British Malaya to prevent an orderly transition to independence as a viable

During the Malayan Emergency, 1948–60, most of the insurgents were Chinese. Under a policy initiated by Lt Gen Sir Harold Briggs, Director of Operations of the British security forces, 1950–51, and continued by Gen Sir Gerald Templer, rural Chinese from all parts of Malaya were "resettled" in "New Villages", where they were kept fenced in, by barriers like that shown here, during curfew periods and under strict supervision but also provided with good health and educational facilities in an attempt to "win hearts and minds". This system helped to sever the jungle-based insurgents from their sources of food and information among the people.

non-communist state. British military strategy was governed by a highly selective and sensitive approach. Considerable restriction had to be placed on civil liberties, but it was recognized that this had to be done in such a way that popular support for the government's plan was maintained. Fairness in application of the restrictions, demonstrable effectiveness, and a flow of side benefits such as improved housing, health programmes and public education, were major elements in the approach.

Gradually, through re-settlements, a wall of separation was built between the more densely populated areas and the guerrilla bases, facilitated by the fact that the insurgents were almost wholly Chinese. They lost access to their sources of support among the people – food, recruits and, above all, intelligence on which to plan effective operations. A particularly noteworthy feature of the campaign was the predominance of the civil authorities over the army in the planning and coordination of operations. The role of the army was to work with the police, recognizing that the problem of insurgency was primarily a political and civil one. Of course, it had its military aspects. The guerrillas were too deeply based in the jungle to be rooted out without the help of the army, with mobility increased by air support. Some insurgent bands were equipped with automatic weapons and could mount powerful ambushes which required military countermeasures. Many were expert at booby-trapping, which again called for a specialized military response. But the elements of the security forces which had closest contact with the people were the police, and their steadfast conduct did much to ensure the growth of community support for the British strategy, particularly as embodied in the Briggs plan of 1950–51.

The United Malay National Organization joined with the Malayan Chinese Association in 1952 to form a powerful political bloc, the Alliance, led by Tunku Abdul Rahman. In the 1955 general elections, the Alliance won 51 out of 52 seats. The British government recognized that time was nearly ripe for the granting of independence, and in 1957 it handed power over to the Alliance. The Emergency was declared formally as ended in 1960, although some few insurgents continued to operate in the Thai-Malayan border area for many years. The British counterinsurgency strategy has served as a paradigm ever since. There were, however, special elements of the Emergency which made a powerful difference to the ease of application of control measures. Above all, the insurgents were principally Chinese, enabling the number of suspects to be reduced substantially and complicating their task in building a nationwide revolt against British rule. The effectiveness of the civil infrastructure, the strength of the nationalist movement and the relatively good state of transport and communications all played important roles in easing the task of the security forces.

The French Indochina War
The French experience in Indochina was almost a total contrast. Their task was, admittedly, far more difficult than that of the British in Malaya. A strong, communist-led nationalist movement had arisen in the 1930s. In the brief interval between the Japanese capitulation and the French return to Indochina, the Viet Minh nationalists had installed a government led by Ho Chi Minh and had proclaimed the People's Republic of Vietnam. An interim British and French force ejected its southern section from office in Saigon in September 1945 and the French then proceeded to negotiate with the main northern element in Hanoi. These negotiations made little progress and broke down in late 1946. The French Commissioner-General, Admiral Thierry d'Argenlieu, ordered a naval bombardment of the northern port of Haiphong. The Viet Minh response was to attack French troops in Hanoi on December 19. Ho then offered to discuss a cease-fire, but the French proceeded to evict the Viet Minh from Hanoi.

Thus the French made their choice. Political compromise was ruled out and a military solution was to be sought. Despite the formidable military power of France, it was not well-suited to a military struggle for the three states of Indochina – Vietnam, Cambodia and Laos – against a numerically strong and well-led Viet Minh force commanded by Vo Nguyen Giap. He had foreseen that the French

Battlegrounds and deaths since 1945 (estimates where figures available)

- States in which more than 1,000,000 people have died in war
- States in which 100,000 – 1,000,000 people have died in war
- States in which 10,000 – 100,000 people have died in war
- Other states where war has occurred
- Other states

A full-scale global war in which nuclear weapons would wreak almost unimaginable destruction is a nightmare which has since 1945 deterred the greatest powers from direct action against each other and their allies. Nevertheless, as the map indicates, the Soviet Union, United States, France, Britain and China have all been major participants – "liberators", "peace-keepers" or "oppressors", depending upon the ideology or nationality of the adjudicator – in conflicts that have claimed millions of lives during almost a half-century of uneasy peace.

might try to subdue the nationalists by force and had prepared a network of bases in the rugged country south of the Chinese border. By mid-1946 he had assembled a main force of 31,000 men. To the French, faced with a need to maintain a large army in Europe, North Africa and Indochina, as well as being impoverished by the effects of World War II, this Viet Minh force should have appeared a much more formidable obstacle than it did. An even greater obstacle was the nationalistic spirit of the Vietnamese people, with which the French failed utterly to come to terms.

The early stages of the French campaign proved deceptive. The Viet Minh had to be cautious while they were gathering their strength in the far north, and the French were able to re-establish a far-flung network of posts, giving the appearance of a successful re-assertion of authority. In reality it over-extended the French forces and made them all the more vulnerable to the Viet Minh counteroffensive. The first major blow fell on September 16-17 1950, when the Viet Minh, supported logistically by the Chinese Communists, overran the key border fort of Dong Khe and isolated a 1,500-strong garrison farther inland. Within a month the Viet Minh had ousted a French force of over 10,000 from the Chinese border region, inflicting 6,000 casualties and capturing sufficient weapons to equip an entire Viet Minh division.

Forced back upon the Red River delta, the French under General de Lattre prepared a strong defensive perimeter against which Giap unwisely hurled his forces for four months in early 1951. Then it was the French turn to be imprudent: in 1952 they lost heavily in making major forays into the Red and Black River valleys and the highlands between. Giap now had the initiative and, having learned from his reverses of 1951, he conducted a war of mobility which threatened French authority throughout the northern highlands and Laos, thereby compelling the French to respond or cede these important areas. Cession being too much to contemplate, the French cast about for an appropriate military counter-blow. This took the form of the Navarre plan of 1953. General Henri Navarre, Commander-in-Chief in Indochina from May 1953, ordered a number of containment and reinforcing operations in the Red River delta and southern Annam as a preliminary to a bold attempt to smash Giap's main force by bringing it to battle on ground of French choice.

As a result of woeful confusion of directives, Navarre ordered this operation just when the French government had decided to seek a negotiated settlement and strictly limit its military commitment to Indochina. Giap had exploited the uncertainty in French strategy in October 1953 like a good chess player, sliding one of his divisions diagonally across the board of northern Vietnam to threaten the French hold on Luang Prabang, Laos. Navarre took the bait and sent an airborne division into the remote mountain valley of Dien Bien Phu to cut Giap's lines of supply and force him either to give the decisive battle that the French sought or to withdraw from Laos. However, it was the French who were humiliated in a desperate six-month struggle. Giap had concentrated around Dien Bien Phu a far bigger force than the French had anticipated, well supported by artillery.

Defeat for the French

French airpower was inadequate to sustain the garrison and the United States and its allies offered no assistance. Having just concluded three years of war in Korea, they did not relish the prospect of a wider engagement, particularly when it would be the West that would be seen in the eyes of the world as the escalating side in the struggle. Had the Chinese intervened directly then the situation would have been different, but they did not need to. The French had got themselves into an impossible position and in the view of their allies they had to live with the outcome. A limited engagement had to remain limited. The Americans, having blundered into one war with China, did not want to face another without very good reason. After 57 days of continuous Viet Minh assaults, the Dien Bien Phu garrison was forced to surrender early in May 1954. French losses, although not catastrophic in terms of the overall size of the French force in Indochina, were sufficient to destroy the last vestiges of popular support for the war in France. Having no real strategy other than a military one, the only way for the French to go thereafter was out of Indochina.

The Malayan Emergency and the French Indochina conflict served to sensitize Western opinion to the existence of a connection between East-West rivalry in Europe and insurgency in Southeast Asia. Stalin's lifting of the Berlin blockade seemed to reinforce the lessons of the late 1930s that it was foolish to give way in the face of intransigence or aggression. The USSR or its clients had to be met with firmness wherever they caused trouble.

French paratroops jump to reinforce the garrison at beleaguered Dien Bien Phu, early 1954. The base was established late in 1953 to interdict the Viet Minh's Laotian supply lines and thus force them to a decisive battle. French airpower was unable to sustain the garrison against the overwhelming forces concentrated by the Viet Minh commander, Vo Nguyen Giap, from March 13 1954, and after 57 days of continuous Vietnamese assaults the French surrendered.

Indochina, 1945–54. Laos, Cambodia and Vietnam became "independent" states while still under French authority in 1946–49. Cochin China, governed from Saigon, was under close French control, but in Tonkin, northern Vietnam, Ho Chi Minh established a communist regime whose military force, the Viet Minh, retained important areas under their own control. By late 1950 the Viet Minh had driven the French from the far north, but in 1951 they incurred heavy losses in attacks on the "de Lattre Line", the defensive cordon around the Red River delta. French attempts to reassert control beyond the delta area were generally unsuccessful, and late in 1952 the Viet Minh seized the strategic initiative with an offensive towards Luang Prabang, Laos. The fall of Dien Bien Phu, May 1954, destroyed French political support for the colonial war. Under the Geneva Agreements, July 1954, Vietnam was partitioned along the 17th Parallel. French military withdrawal was completed in April 1956.

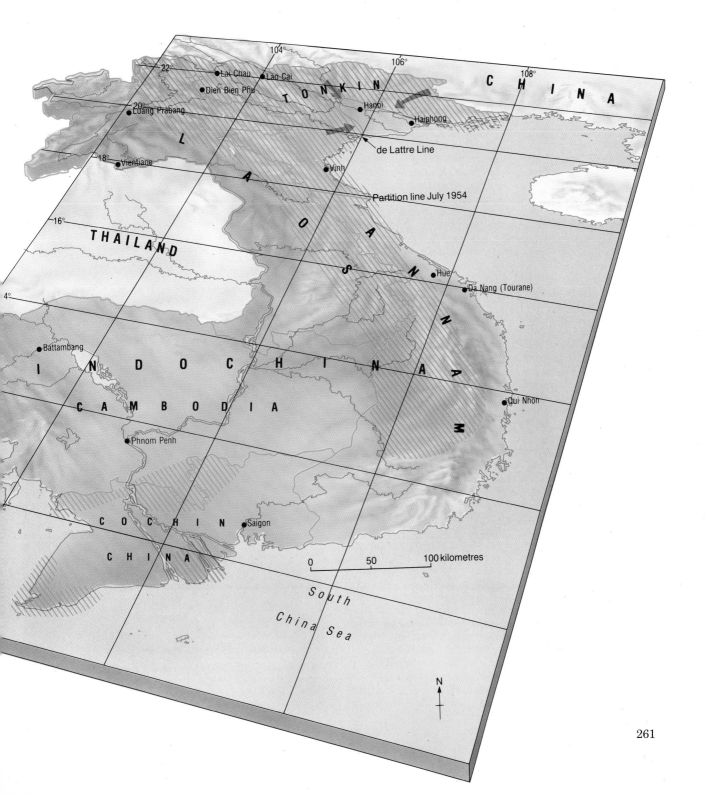

The Korean War

Consequently it is not difficult to understand the immediate American response to the North Korean invasion of South Korea on June 25 1950. A global, Cold War interpretation was placed on a conflict which also had important local origins. Its global nature derived from the postwar division of the peninsula agreed between Truman and Stalin to permit the rapid demobilization and disarmament of the Japanese armed forces there. Failure to agree on procedures and policies for reunifying Korea led to the entrenchment of separate regimes deeply hostile to each other and openly calling for the use of force to bring about re-unification. Yet the interests and prestige of each superpower were threatened by any violation of the 38th parallel. The situation was made fragile by the existence of several differences between the two halves of Korea. The most important was that the North Koreans, armed by the Soviets, had a formidable offensive capability. The South Koreans had been denied tanks, heavy artillery and combat aircraft to eliminate the possibility of President Syngman Rhee's ordering a march to the north. Second, the proximity of North Korea to China and the Soviet Union made it virtually inevitable both that its government was communist and that there would be close consultation, even mutual support, between all three over regional security issues. South Korea was remote from its protector – indeed, it was far from clear that the United States would provide protection should it be required. Third, although the South was far from being a liberal democracy, the North's communism was of the harshest kind which, once its nature was widely known, would strengthen support for the less totalitarian South.

Although reasonably close relations existed between the leaders of the Soviet Union, China and North Korea, and Mao Tse-tung (Mao Zedong) and Stalin almost certainly had approved Kim Il-Sung's plan to invade the South, Soviet and Chinese forces did not directly assist in the operation. Indeed, Stalin withdrew Soviet military advisers from North Korean front-line divisions as soon as he heard that the invasion had commenced. The Americans, taken by surprise, hastened to the aid of the South, even though they were not well situated to do so. They had available only four understrength occupation divisions in Japan and relatively few long-range fighters and bombers that could fly missions over Korea from bases in Japan and the Philippines. The US Pacific Fleet was able to provide powerful assistance, augmented by the British Pacific Fleet, to give gunfire support, ferry supplies, evacuate threatened South Korean units and deny the North Koreans the use of the sea. This form of assistance became even more important in the long term as the strength of the United States and its allies was brought to bear. Troops could be transported to Korea without hindrance and naval aircraft could attack the North Korean forces and their logistics systems. The farther south the North Koreans came, the longer were the flanks they exposed to constant attack from the sea.

President Truman was not content merely to provide military assistance: he set about aligning the United Nations to support the commitment and make South Korea's cause its own. Stupidly, the Soviets aided him by continuing a boycott of the Security Council that they had initiated in protest at the failure of the People's Republic of China to be given the permanent seat occupied by Chiang Kai-shek's Taiwan government. The Security Council's formal espousal of the need to repel the North Koreans and the consequent formation of the United Nations Command under American leadership gave the West a very useful political, and to some extent moral, ascendancy in the eyes of international opinion.

It could not be taken for granted, even at the outset, that the Korean War would prove to be limited in character. Part of the American motivation for involvement was the possibility that the North Korean invasion might have been a feint to divert Western attention from more vital theatres such as Europe or the Middle East. Until, and even after, the Soviet Union proposed armistice negotiations in mid-1951, Western military leaders were on the alert for trouble elsewhere and Western governments undertook extensive rearmament programmes. Another related concern was the possibility of the conflict in the Korean Peninsula itself escalating to the point at which one or the other of North Korea's major supporters was drawn in. A third possibility for escalation lay in the use of nuclear weapons. Not a great deal could be done to eliminate the first possibility except to try to deter it by showing firmness in Korea and offering no direct provocation to the Soviets elsewhere.

A UN propaganda poster dating from the time of the Korean War, 1950–53, shows Koreans passing into slavery under the threatening shadow of a communist soldier.

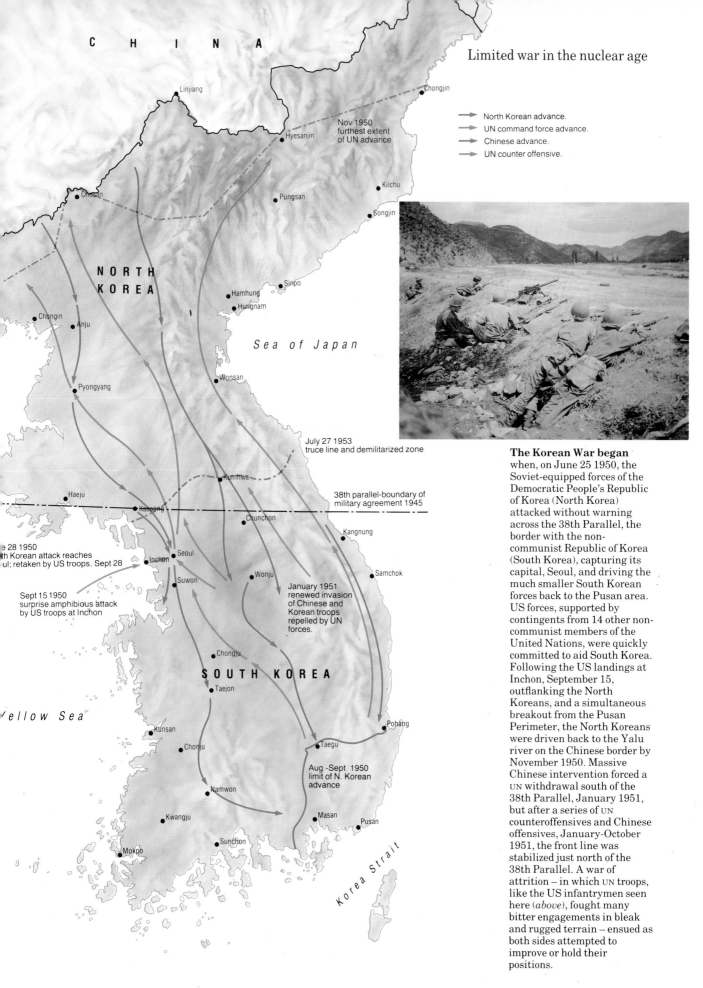

C H I N A

Linjiang

Chongjin

Hyesanjin

Nov 1950
furthest extent
of UN advance

Kilchu

Pungsan

Songjin

Chosan

NORTH KOREA

Sinpo

Chongin

Hamhung

Anju

Hungnam

Sea of Japan

Pyongyang

Wonsan

July 27 1953
truce line and demilitarized zone

Haeju

Kumhwa

38th parallel-boundary of
military agreement 1945

Kaesong

Chunchon

Kangnung

...e 28 1950
...h Korean attack reaches
...ul; retaken by US troops, Sept 28

Inchon Seoul

Suwon

Wonju

Samchok

Sept 15 1950
surprise amphibious attack
by US troops at Inchon

January 1951
renewed invasion
of Chinese and
Korean troops
repelled by UN
forces.

Chongju

SOUTH KOREA

Taejon

Yellow Sea

Kunsan

Pohang

Chonju

Taegu

Aug -Sept 1950
limit of N. Korean
advance

Namwon

Masan

Kwangju

Pusan

Sunchon

Mokpo

Korea Strait

Limited war in the nuclear age

→ North Korean advance.
→ UN command force advance.
→ Chinese advance.
→ UN counter offensive.

The Korean War began
when, on June 25 1950, the
Soviet-equipped forces of the
Democratic People's Republic
of Korea (North Korea)
attacked without warning
across the 38th Parallel, the
border with the non-
communist Republic of Korea
(South Korea), capturing its
capital, Seoul, and driving the
much smaller South Korean
forces back to the Pusan area.
US forces, supported by
contingents from 14 other non-
communist members of the
United Nations, were quickly
committed to aid South Korea.
Following the US landings at
Inchon, September 15,
outflanking the North
Koreans, and a simultaneous
breakout from the Pusan
Perimeter, the North Koreans
were driven back to the Yalu
river on the Chinese border by
November 1950. Massive
Chinese intervention forced a
UN withdrawal south of the
38th Parallel, January 1951,
but after a series of UN
counteroffensives and Chinese
offensives, January-October
1951, the front line was
stabilized just north of the
38th Parallel. A war of
attrition – in which UN troops,
like the US infantrymen seen
here (*above*), fought many
bitter engagements in bleak
and rugged terrain – ensued as
both sides attempted to
improve or hold their
positions.

The second danger, regional escalation, was not so expeditiously handled. After General MacArthur's brilliant amphibious flank attack at Inchon in mid-September 1950 had routed the North Koreans, he naturally pursued them into their own territory. However, this act changed the nature of the war. In effect, the UN Command's aim widened from that of repelling aggression to the reunification of Korea under a government of which the West approved. This prospect was intolerable to the Chinese, who issued dire warnings before MacArthur's forces crossed the 38th parallel. These monitions were dismissed as bluff and the result was that, in late November 1950, UN Command forces walked into the biggest ambush in military history. They were routed by the Chinese People's Volunteers and sent reeling southward. The conflict had now escalated to a war between the United States and China – still limited to the Korean Peninsula but clearly more important to contain than had been the case before the advance to the Yalu river.

MacArthur's cries of despair soon raised the question as to whether the third type of escalation should be employed. President Truman's overly firm indication at a press conference that the use of nuclear weapons was under active consideration in late November 1950 precipitated a crisis in alliance relationships. While Truman was not able to give British Prime Minister Attlee any veto over nuclear weapon employment, an important point had been made by Attlee's urgent mission to Washington in early December. The United States could not expect to carry its allies with it unless it maintained close consulta-

US Army M4A3E8 Sherman tanks in Korea (*top*). The Sherman medium tank proved more manouevrable in the often swampy Korean terrain than more modern, more heavily-armoured and -gunned tanks such as the Centurion. The main armament of these Shermans is a high-velocity 76mm gun; a 0.50in machine gun is mounted on the turret roof.

B-26 Invader tactical bombers (*above*) of the US Far East Air Forces drop napalm on a communist barracks area, Korea, February 1951. Along with B-29 Superfortresses of the US Fifth Air Force, based in Japan, B-26s were employed in Operation "Strangle", the bombing campaign against communist communication and supply routes in North Korea from June 1951.

tion with them on all major strategic policy issues, including the use of nuclear weapons.

Having established a political framework of limitation, at the cost of the dismissal of MacArthur and some public criticism of the administration by conservative spokesmen later in 1951 and 1952, Truman had to confront the question as to what the strategic aim of his forces was. The lessons of the policy debacles of late 1950 were clear, if frustrating. The UN Command's objective in the war now had to be essentially the restoration of the status quo, albeit on the basis of a demarcation line which was more defensible than the 38th parallel. Generals Ridgway and Clark, successors to MacArthur, were permitted to undertake some initiatives to this end, achieving a considerable improvement in the line which had to be held after the armistice. Those gains, however, were not the sole mission of the UN Command forces between mid-1951 and mid-1953. Their other responsibility was to maintain effective

military pressure on the communist forces by offensive action designed, like the great offensives of World War I, to wear the enemy down without seeking to change the relative positions of the front lines to any great extent, thereby compelling them to accept a truce on UN Command terms.

Sustaining this pressure was an exacting and frustrating task, which placed severe stresses on military morale. Allied service personnel had to accept that they were placing themselves more or less continuously at risk but could not strike at their enemies with the full force at their disposal. Offensive operations were conducted by land, sea and air, perhaps the most spectacular, and certainly the most controversial, being the bombing offensive directed against North Korea. In its earlier phase in 1951, Operation "Strangle", the results obtained represented poor value in terms of the cost in aircraft losses and ordnance expended. In 1952 a new approach, the Air Pressure Strategy, was used. The essential criterion of this method was to maximize the ratio of enemy losses inflicted to allied costs suffered in its implementation. Although it was an improvement on Operation "Strangle", the Chinese and North Koreans were able, through concealment and night movement of men and supplies, to frustrate much of the bombing effort. Their front-line armies were capable of significant offensive action right up until the cease-fire.

The strategy of attrition applied after the major UN Command offensives of 1951 had high political costs for the Truman administration and led to accusations that the President was conducting a war without end. This had considerable impact on the 1952 presidential elections. The Democrats lost support through being unable or unwilling to offer any immediate prospect of a successful conclusion. The Republicans' popularity increased when their candidate, General Eisenhower, promised to go to Korea to examine ways of ending the conflict. How this might change the situation was far from clear, but to an electorate bored or exasperated by the war, this mattered less than that Eisenhower had proclaimed a personal commitment to bringing the war to an honourable end.

While Eisenhower wanted to liquidate the war as an American responsibility, his visit if anything hardened his resolve to stick to the principles for which the Truman administration had fought, particularly its refusal to send back to North Korea and the People's Republic of China those prisoners in allied hands who did not wish to return to their native countries. He let it be known that if the armistice negotiations did not yield fruit in the coming spring, then the United States would not feel itself as restricted as in the past with regard to the use of force against the communists. What he had in mind was the possible use of nuclear weapons against China. In the event, the Chinese and North Koreans accepted a truce which permitted voluntary repatriation of prisoners – although Stalin's death in the preceding month may have had more to do with the change in communist policy than the not-altogether credible threat of nuclear bombing. Detailed negotiations in the following three months led to a cease-fire on July 27 1953.

A crudely-drawn propaganda poster shows a UN soldier dying in Korea to swell the money-bags of an American "bloated capitalist". Other communist psychological-warfare techniques were more subtle – and more effective. Captured UN personnel were treated with barbaric cruelty by the North Koreans (of around 7,200 American and 1,100 British personnel taken

prisoner by the communists, some 3,000 died in captivity) and somewhat better by the Chinese. Prisoners were offered relief from their privations if they responded to "re-education" in communist ideology. Having been brought to acknowledge the virtues of communism and their own "sin" in opposing it, "brain-washed" prisoners were often required to participate in anti-UN propaganda.

The Suez Crisis

While world attention was on East Asia, tensions had been rising in the Middle East, particularly in Egypt, leading to King Farouk's overthrow in 1952. The new government, led by General Mohammed Neguib and

Colonel Gamal Abdel Nasser, reached agreement with Britain in 1954 that she should withdraw from the great military base in the Canal Zone, subject to the proviso that occupancy could be resumed in time of crisis. The Suez Canal was still seen as an extremely important strategic asset and there was concern in Washington, London and Paris lest it fall under Soviet influence.

Nasser, President from June 1956, soon began to raise apprehensions in the West. Some were concerned that his nationalism and Egypt's poverty would lead him into the arms of the Kremlin. These fears seemed to be confirmed when he began obtaining arms from Czechoslovakia and the Soviet Union. Sir Anthony Eden, British Prime Minister, thought he was another Hitler who needed to be put down firmly before he did real damage. Nasser infuriated the French government by supplying arms to the Algerian nationalists. While not initially pro-Soviet, he became increasingly alienated from the West. He saw Britain's formation of the Baghdad Pact as a device to contain Egypt. His economic plans for Egypt were jeopardized when the West refused to fund the projected Aswan High Dam, and on July 26 1956, by way of compensation, he nationalized the Suez Canal.

This action set Britain and France working together, with Israeli collusion, to humble him. They ordered the commencement of military preparations soon after Nasser's announcement, while applying pressure politically through the formation of the Suez Canal Users Association. Tension built up rapidly as negotiations failed and Nasser also increased military pressure on Israel. When a joint Egyptian-Jordanian-Syrian army command was announced in mid-October, Israel prepared for war and attacked in the Sinai on October 29.

The Israelis quickly defeated the Egyptians, in effect removing the pretext that Britain and France had manufactured for their own intended invasion of the Canal Zone. The Egyptians had blocked the Canal, making a Franco-British invasion even more pointless. Nevertheless, the invasion began on November 5. The US government was appalled, and President Eisenhower threatened severe economic sanctions unless Britain and France withdrew their forces.

The Suez operation was one of the worst conceived limited engagements of the post-1945 period and resulted in a crop of disasters. Eden fell from power. Nasser's status was greatly increased throughout the Arab world and the Afro-Asian states. The Russians gained influence in the Middle East. Transatlantic and Commonwealth relations were severely strained. Oil supplies to Western Europe were reduced. It was an object lesson in the dangers of overreaction and failure to consult allies.

The Vietnam War

After the French withdrawal from Indochina and the failure to conduct the elections for which the Vietnamese communists had hoped, guerrilla action began to become a significant problem in the South. Escalation led to increasing demands by the Saigon government of Ngo Dinh Diem for American support. Although the Eisenhower administration provided logistic support and a small advisory mission, it did not commit American resources to any appreciable extent. During the early 1960s the situation facing the Diem government began to deteriorate as popular support declined and insurgent activity became more intense.

The Kennedy administration, not wanting to be seen as responsible for "losing" Vietnam and conscious of Vietnam's important strategic position, chose to intensify support for Diem. The number of advisers provided rose from 335 in 1954 to 3,150 in 1962. The support was not decisive – in fact it was counterproductive in some ways, encouraging greater communist effort in the South, assisted by the Northern government. Increasing disunity undermined Diem's regime, finally leading to his assassination by the military who saw him as an obstacle to effective counterinsurgency. The absence of any strong political alternative to Diem was very much the fruit of the French attitude of intolerance towards independent figures in the early 1950s.

After Kennedy's assassination, the Johnson administration faced a steadily worsening situation in Vietnam, demanding more than the mere provision of advisers and supplies. Escalation, at first gradual, increased considerably after the Gulf of Tonkin incident, in August 1964, when Congress voted the President authority to take whatever measures he deemed necessary to repel armed attack against American forces in Southeast Asia and to prevent further aggression. Johnson, fearing for the future of his "Great Society" programme, did not wish to mobilize the American people. He did not ask Congress for a declaration of war, which he would almost certainly have been given then. Congress, in passing the Tonkin Gulf resolution, did not see it as a blank cheque to conduct a war in Southeast Asia. Consequently, there were different understandings on the parts of both the executive and the legislative branches of the government about the aims of the Vietnam commitment. This confusion was to plague the conduct of the war and bedevil relations between Congress and the administration in later years.

The Suez Crisis (July-December 1956). President Nasser of Egypt had alarmed Britain by his increasingly pro-Soviet stance, antagonized France by his support for Algerian nationalism, and was the leader of Israel's major enemy. His nationalization of the Suez Canal (closed to Israeli shipping from 1950) brought all three countries into collusion to oppose him. Israel's intention to invade the Sinai was known to Britain and France: following it, Israel acceded to Anglo-French demands for a cease-fire and withdrawal; Egypt, as expected, did not, thus providing a pretext for Anglo-French military intervention. Worldwide condemnation of the ill-considered operation and especially the US threat of severe economic sanctions, forced the cessation of Anglo-French operations and the withdrawal of their forces. The Canal, blocked by Egypt at the time of the invasion remained closed until March 1957.

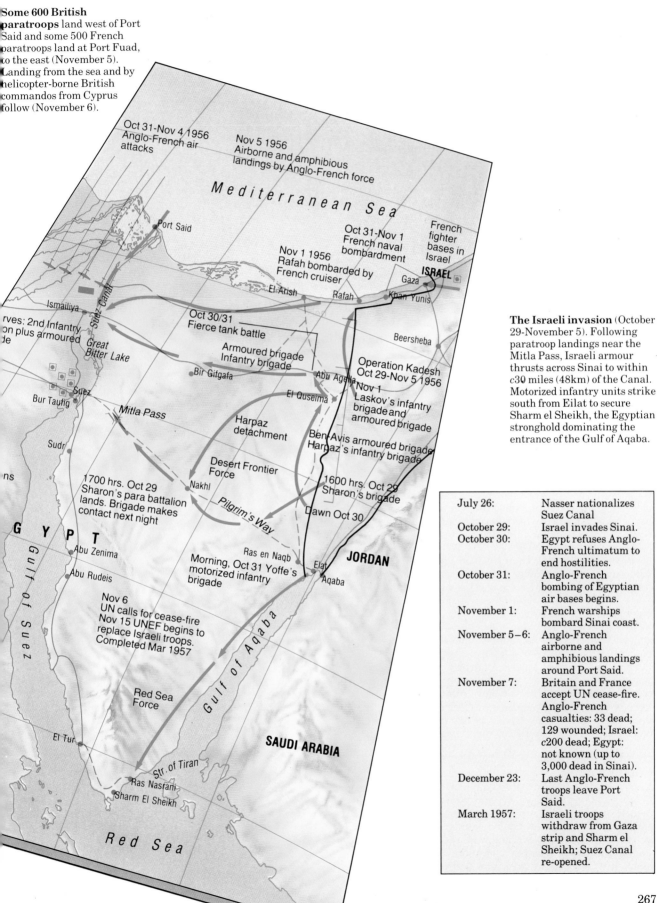

Some 600 British paratroops land west of Port Said and some 500 French paratroops land at Port Fuad, to the east (November 5). Landing from the sea and by helicopter-borne British commandos from Cyprus follow (November 6).

Oct 31–Nov 4 1956 Anglo-French air attacks

Nov 5 1956 Airborne and amphibious landings by Anglo-French force

Mediterranean Sea

Port Said

Oct 31–Nov 1 French naval bombardment

Nov 1 1956 Rafah bombarded by French cruiser

French fighter bases in Israel

ISRAEL

Gaza

Ismailiya

rves: 2nd Infantry on plus armoured de

El Arish

Rafah

Khan Yunis

Suez Canal

Oct 30/31 Fierce tank battle

Great Bitter Lake

Armoured brigade Infantry brigade

Beersheba

Bir Gifgafa

Abu Agella

Operation Kadesh Oct 29–Nov 5 1956

Suez

El Quseima

Nov 1 Laskov's infantry brigade and armoured brigade

Bur Taufiq

Mitla Pass

Harpaz detachment

Ben-Avis armoured brigade Harpaz's infantry brigade

Sudr

Desert Frontier Force

1700 hrs. Oct 29 Sharon's para battalion lands. Brigade makes contact next night

Nakhl

Pilgrim's Way

1600 hrs. Oct 29 Sharon's brigade

Dawn Oct 30

E G Y P T

Abu Zenima

Ras en Naqb

Morning, Oct 31 Yoffe's motorized infantry brigade

Elat

JORDAN

Abu Rudeis

Aqaba

Gulf of Suez

Nov 6 UN calls for cease-fire Nov 15 UNEF begins to replace Israeli troops. Completed Mar 1957

Red Sea Force

Gulf of Aqaba

El Tur

SAUDI ARABIA

Str. of Tiran Ras Nasrani Sharm El Sheikh

Red Sea

The Israeli invasion (October 29–November 5). Following paratroop landings near the Mitla Pass, Israeli armour thrusts across Sinai to within c30 miles (48km) of the Canal. Motorized infantry units strike south from Eilat to secure Sharm el Sheikh, the Egyptian stronghold dominating the entrance of the Gulf of Aqaba.

July 26:	Nasser nationalizes Suez Canal
October 29:	Israel invades Sinai.
October 30:	Egypt refuses Anglo-French ultimatum to end hostilities.
October 31:	Anglo-French bombing of Egyptian air bases begins.
November 1:	French warships bombard Sinai coast.
November 5–6:	Anglo-French airborne and amphibious landings around Port Said.
November 7:	Britain and France accept UN cease-fire. Anglo-French casualties: 33 dead; 129 wounded; Israel: c200 dead; Egypt: not known (up to 3,000 dead in Sinai).
December 23:	Last Anglo-French troops leave Port Said.
March 1957:	Israeli troops withdraw from Gaza strip and Sharm el Sheikh; Suez Canal re-opened.

In using his new authority Johnson and his advisers were ever-conscious of the shadow of China looming over North Vietnam. If he escalated too sharply for China's tolerance, he would be faced with the same predicament that had confronted Truman in Korea. Punitive action was taken therefore against the southern part of North Vietnam, leaving the strategically vital area of Hanoi and the Red River delta unscathed. Similarly, the land and sea supply lines from China and the Soviet Union were not attacked, even inside Vietnamese territory. Although the Johnson administration saw North Vietnam as a Chinese proxy, it had no wish to engage in a fight to the finish with China. America's European allies placed a much less direct interpretation on China's support for Vietnam, seeing North Vietnam as a more autonomous actor. The Europeans were concerned from 1965 onwards that the Americans were becoming too heavily committed to the war in Vietnam, leaving other more important areas too thinly covered.

US forces move in

The initial commitment of US ground forces to combat in Vietnam was to protect air bases and major logistic centres. These roles were chosen with an eye to escalation control, in the hope that they would deter the North Vietnamese from direct action without being unduly provocative. This approach did not work and the North Vietnamese increased their pressure. The US Marines were then given the task of securing the northern provinces of South Vietnam and began mobile operations. The South Vietnamese armed forces were clearly having difficulty in controlling the countryside and ensuring the security of the major towns and roads, and although some South Vietnamese units fought with great distinction, these were the exception rather than the rule. The indigenous guerrilla forces, the Viet Cong, were able to increase their strength and conduct operations up to regimental level. As the North Vietnamese continued to increase their commitment to the war, so the burden was borne increasingly by the Americans and their allies from South Korea, Australia and New Zealand.

American strategy from 1964 to 1968 concentrated on giving military rather than political support to the South Vietnamese government. Even American civilians concerned with policy for Vietnam tended to see the commitment largely in military terms. Most of them scarcely knew where to begin in building a politically cohesive society in South Vietnam and saw no alternative to the generals who ruled the country. Indeed, there were few South Vietnamese of real governmental potential.

As a result the American armed forces tended to conduct their operations as if they were involved in a war set in a firm political context. This is understandable: they were military professionals, not politicians, and they saw their essential aim as being the defeat of the enemy's main force. But without a firm political foundation, operational successes were simply a structure built on sand. To experts who understood this kind of conflict, the struggle was set to last many years, requiring a continuous and heavy American commitment if any positive result was to be achieved. General Westmoreland seemed to believe that victory would be possible within a few years, and there was all too little understanding at senior levels of the Johnson administration of the need to build strong political foundations in the US for the commitment. It was not like the Korean War, which was over in

three years and where serious armistice negotiations were underway after the first year of fighting.

An unpopular war

The Tonkin Gulf resolution sufficed to carry Johnson through his expansion of the commitment in 1964 and 1965, but by 1967 it was beginning to wear thin. He declared that he did not need the resolution to permit him to conduct the war: his powers as commander-in-chief were adequate. In a sense they were, but the running battle he and his successor Richard Nixon had to wage with Congress over Vietnam policy, and Congress's final refusal to provide the aid that the Saigon government needed to continue to hold back the North Vietnamese, showed ultimately that Johnson was wrong. The lack of national consensus in the United States on the need to be in Vietnam posed clear dangers to a policy which required large contributions from the public purse and the sending of hundreds of thousands of draftees to the war. Viewed from the North Vietnamese side, the weak point in their

1. Bunkers for infantry and night observation equipment

2. Howitzer emplacements

3. Fire Support Coordination Centre

4. Command post

5. Mortar emplacements

6. "Huey" gunship

7. Observation tower

8. Communications centre

9. Barbed wire perimeter

Fire Support Bases (FSBs) (*above*) were located for mutual support. Here, FSB 3 is under attack and receives supporting fire from FSBs 1 and 2. A typical US Fire Support Base in Vietnam (*left*). It is a self-contained stronghold, housing a battery of six M102 105mm howitzers and garrisoned by an infantry company, with specialized medical and communications personnel. Supplied by transport helicopters, and given extra fire power at need by rocket-firing helicopter gunships, it provides instantly responsive support for infantry patrols into the surrounding area. Triple-dannert barbed wire surrounds the FSB in a circle of some 250ft (76m) radius from its centre; bunkers for infantrymen with rifles and squad weapons (including recoilless rifles and grenade launchers), supported by four 81mm mortar emplacements, extend in a circle of about 135ft (41m) radius. FSBs were sometimes deliberately established at locations where Viet Cong/North Vietnamese forces would be tempted to concentrate against them and thus become vulnerable to counterattack.

US soldiers help a wounded comrade at Hue, a major objective of the Tet offensive (map; *below*).

opponent's stance was not his military capability in Vietnam but his political base at home. To a communist leadership which had already won one war against a Western power, in which public opinion had played a significant role, this knowledge must have been both reassuring and useful in shaping their own strategy.

In military terms the strategies of the two sides were very different. The communists sought to avoid pitched battles and relied for their effectiveness on simply keeping the costs of the war high for the Americans, occasionally humiliating the South Vietnamese armed forces and constantly undermining the capacity of the South Vietnamese government to govern. They did not try to eject the Americans, but chose to rely on American public opinion becoming impatient with the prolonged and indecisive nature of the struggle and on a collapse of morale in the South Vietnamese armed forces.

The Americans sought to make the elusive enemy main force stand and fight, and often accepted serious risks to their own security in order to draw it into battle. When the Americans caught their quarry they usually fought bravely and well. But the North Vietnamese and Viet Cong were also doughty fighters and often inflicted losses on the Americans which, while in no way decisive in a military sense, carried accumulating political consequences in Washington, on the college campuses and on the streets of American cities. To most American generals the notion that the correct military strategy for the war was to keep casualties low, exclude the North Vietnamese from the more densely populated areas but not pursue

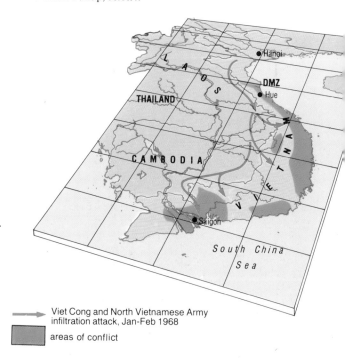

→ Viet Cong and North Vietnamese Army infiltration attack, Jan-Feb 1968

▉ areas of conflict

them onto ground of their own choosing, and try to help build an efficient Vietnamese state, seemed wrong. Yet their preferred alternative, of trying to destroy the North Vietnamese main force, could not be achieved within the framework of a limited war. They could not go into North Vietnam and challenge the enemy in his own base for fear of widening the war beyond the limits that Johnson wished to maintain.

The major turning point of the war was the Tet offensive of January 31 1968. This was such a military disaster for the Viet Cong that it is hard to believe that their aim was of a military nature. Perhaps the guerrillas thought that the South Vietnamese people would rally and rise against their own government and armed forces. If so, the Viet Cong were cruelly disillusioned. The people did not rise and the South Vietnamese forces fought back well. But in political terms, Tet was a triumph for Hanoi. The coordinated wave of violence that erupted over Vietnam showed that there was no basis to the claims of the US administration and General Westmoreland that victory was not too far away. It was a major blow to the credibility of President Johnson and his policy, and he saw it as such. On March 31 he announced that he would not seek a second term of office. Eight days earlier he had announced that General Westmoreland was to return to Washington to become Army Chief of Staff.

The beginning of the end

It is impossible to say with any certainty that the principal aim of those who had masterminded the offensive was to strike a blow at the weak political foundations of the American effort. These men were no novices and

US Marine at Hue.

they had seen the politically debilitating effect of the French defeat at Dien Bien Phu. It is thus not beyond the bounds of possibility that they knowingly hurled the Viet Cong against the South Vietnamese essentially to lay bare the disparity between what the American military strategy in Vietnam could achieve and what was required in a political sense for an American victory, namely a different strategy and a very long commitment to the struggle. This is certainly what they achieved. The American people looked at the price they would have to pay, assessed the continuing uncertainties and difficulties, and turned away.

President Nixon played for time. He saw that he had to get America out of the war but he also saw that it had to be extricated carefully or else its position as Western leader and ultimate guarantor of the freedom of other states would be jeopardized. His strategy was not one of desertion of the South Vietnamese, but "Vietnamization", a strategy which should have been Johnson's ultimate goal but which required far more time than Nixon (or Johnson) had available to be feasible. During the early 1970s the South Vietnamese armed forces were developed considerably. Their improvement bothered the North Vietnamese, who in March 1972 launched a twelve-division offensive designed to crush them before they became too powerful. The South Vietnamese Army, supported strongly by American air power, saw them off with heavy losses. The North Vietnamese bided their time for a more favourable opportunity. It came in 1975, after Nixon had fallen to the Watergate crisis and Congress had become increasingly restrictive in authorizing the supply of assistance to South Vietnam. In March, the North Vietnamese launched a seventeen-division blitzkrieg which swept through to take Saigon in just over seven weeks. It was all over: except for the prison camps, the "Boat People", the continuing economic poverty of North Vietnam and the agony of the Cambodian people, which had only just entered a new phase under Pol Pot. But the war, as a war, was over. Vietnam was reunited and the United States had been defeated.

The consequences of that defeat have been less drastic than many would have predicted. There was, inevitably, a period when the United States recoiled from any new military commitments. It continued, however, to hold fast to its existing alliance obligations, encouraging its partners, as ever, to make greater efforts for their own security. But the Ford and Carter administrations did not retreat into impotence or abdicate Western leadership. The Reagan administration, judging from its rhetoric, seemed all too willing to buy a fight with communists around the world. The reality was somewhat more moderate. Vietnam has cast a long shadow over those who would like to see the US Marines fighting in Central America. The United States invaded Grenada and sustained an expensive, short commitment of a peace-keeping force in Lebanon, 1983-84. It has seen further action in the Gulf and maintains a significant intervention capability in the Western Pacific, with reinforcement of Korea particularly in mind. The Vietnam debacle did not seriously undermine America's power or real influence in the world. It did, however, teach a little wisdom – although at too high a price, and not necessarily the right wisdom. But out of the Vietnam experience the United States has drawn a clearer understanding both of what it can and cannot do and of the nature of conflict in developing countries.

Afghanistan

This getting of wisdom could have been a dangerous thing if it had been an entirely one-sided process. Had the Soviet Union, with its formidable panoply of power projection capabilities, striven to intervene in troubled regions around the world while the United States was more quiescent, a wider crisis would eventually have developed. But the Soviets have generally (although not always, as experience in Cuba, Egypt and Somalia has shown) had a more realistic view of their capabilities in distant regions than the United States. Despite the rhetoric of Lenin, their specific objectives have been pursued with a keen sense of service of their own national interests. They have been cautious in accepting risk and have used their armed forces more on their allies in Eastern Europe than anywhere else. But perhaps we credit them with more understanding of the realities of the international power struggle than they deserve, for suddenly, in December 1979, the Soviet leadership overthrew this pattern of behaviour and invaded Afghanistan.

The specific objectives of the invasion were clear: to bring order out of chaos in a neighbouring state and to install a government which would be more amenable to Soviet interests than others which might arise without Soviet military intervention. But these objectives proved to be much more expensive than the Soviet leadership expected. Unlike the Americans in Vietnam, the Soviets had a comprehensive political strategy for Afghanistan – but it did not work. It was rejected by almost all the Afghan people.

The Soviet military strategy worked to a degree, enabling them to control the major cities and highways by day, and to deny fixed bases in the countryside to the insurgents. But this neither kept the war out of the media nor broke the spirit of the resistance. The determination and independence of the Afghan people, fighting in extremely rugged terrain, often with few supplies and in appalling weather, provided a foundation on which others, notably the United States and the Islamic nations, have been very willing to build. The realities of limited war prevented the Soviets from striking at either the bases or the backers of the mujaheddin, in Pakistan, Iran and farther afield. The political cost of the continued commitment, both in the Soviet Union and abroad, was much higher than the authors of the invasion had imagined. The opportunity of a new General Secretary and a fresh group of advisers enabled the Soviet Union in 1988 to begin the process of extrication rather earlier than otherwise would have been the case, but clearly extricate it had to. It is to be hoped that the experience was profitable for Soviet strategists in terms of learning or re-learning the lessons of feasibility in limited war in the late 20th century.

The Falklands

By comparison with the conflicts discussed above, the Falklands War seems barely worth mentioning. It was of brief duration, in a very remote part of the world from a strategic point of view, and of significance largely to Britain and Argentina alone. But it is unusual in offering an example of successful counter-intervention, over great distances, in a difficult political context. The British government did not have to worry about lack of public support in the operation. Rather it was placed somewhat on the defensive towards public opinion by having allowed the Argentinians to achieve surprise. The Foreign Secret-

ary, Lord Carrington, resigned, but Prime Minister Thatcher soon showed the instincts that the British people were expecting: the promptly-dispatched Task Force sailed with the national will strongly behind it.

Once the Task Force was underway, the national fortunes were very much in its hands. It was impossible to reinforce substantially, because of shortage of suitable ships and aircraft. The Argentinians soon found that their force on the islands was in the same position, once British control of the surrounding sea was established, but at least they were on dry land, not on vulnerable ships. The final approach to the islands and the landings were the most dangerous parts of the operation. Had the Argentinians been able to use their submarines to sink one or more of the main British troopships, an effective landing could have been frustrated. But the force was placed ashore largely intact and in good order. The protracted overland approach to Port Stanley also carried risks. Not only was it a hard slog for the troops, but also conditions at sea were extremely testing for a force which had been hastily assembled and dispatched. Ships overdue for maintenance became unserviceable and there was a danger that the Royal Navy would not be able to sustain the support which the Army needed to take Port Stanley. In the event, Stanley fell before the Task Force ran out of destroyers and frigates, and Britain celebrated a victory with little knowledge of how close to disaster it had been.

The Thatcher government was fortunate to have carried off the operation so successfully and was well rewarded at the polls in 1983. More to the point, it was fortunate that it had just enough ships available, particularly aircraft carriers, to enable the operation to have taken place at all. The war decided nothing save the fate of the Galtieri regime. If anything, it has produced greater intransigence on both sides, and the Falklands/Malvinas issue seems likely long to obstruct British-Argentinian relations.

Conclusion

Limited warfare over the past 40 years has been shown to be a very difficult art to practise. While as a strategy it has had some successes, as in Korea, it is clearly a demanding and frustrating framework in which to conduct a war. The Americans brought the Chinese in on top of them in Korea and had to change the basic objective for which they were fighting. Both they and the French in Indochina had to leave China as a sanctuary and support base for their enemies and pay a heavy price on the battlefield. American strategic power was of little avail except for occasional use as a threat, and even here it was a declining asset because it lacked credibility. The Americans in Vietnam had to deny themselves the kind of operations that they could best conduct, namely to pursue the North Vietnamese Army into its home territory and destroy it as a major fighting force. In Afghanistan the USSR had to live with the insurgents' use of Pakistan as a support area.

All that one can say after examining the conduct of these wars is that the successes achieved in limited war come at very high cost and the probability of obtaining a successful outcome is low. Fortunately the superpowers have succeeded in groping their way towards a system of regulation of these conflicts, while becoming increasingly reluctant to commit their own forces to combat in regional issues. But there is no sign of an end to such conflicts and the dilemma of how far to intervene in them will remain a challenge for East and West for many years to come.

Maastricht. The Dutch city of Maastricht and its bridges over the River Maas were important, early objectives in the German invasion of the Low Countries in May 1940. Maastricht was finally liberated on September 14 1944 by units of XIX Corps of the First US Army.

MacArthur: the "American Caesar"

MacArthur, General of the Army Douglas (1880–1964). US. Served in France during World War I, commanding the 42nd Division with distinction and ending the war as the US army's youngest divisional commander. Later Superintendent of West Point and from 1930–35, Army cos. Sent to assist in the creation of a Philippine army. After retirement in 1937, remained in the islands, and in the summer of 1941 was recalled to the active list and appointed commander of the American and Philippine forces.

Although MacArthur's forces stubbornly resisted the Japanese invasion of December 1941, the Philippines fell and MacArthur was evacuated to Australia. Vowing "I shall return", he was appointed Supreme Allied Commander, Southwest Pacific. He had already disagreed with many of his superiors regarding their "Europe first" policy; now he also clashed with his fellow Pacific commanders over his strongly expressed opinions on strategy. However, his plans and tactics proved effective and, in a series of island-hopping operations, his forces advanced from New Guinea to the Philippines and were preparing for the invasion of Japan when the war ended. Fittingly, MacArthur was granted the honour of accepting the formal Japanese surrender onboard uss *Missouri* in Tokyo Bay on September 2 1945.

MacArthur served as a conscientious and subtle commander of the occupying forces in Japan before the outbreak of the Korean War thrust him back into the spotlight when, on July 7 1950, he was named c-in-c, United Nations Command. He showed characteristic flair and boldness with the landings at Inchon, but his desire to broaden the conflict led him openly to contradict President Truman's prescribed policy. His outspokenness resulted in his dismissal, and although at first it appeared that this would generate a major political crisis, MacArthur slipped into retirement. *MS.*

McAuliffe, Maj Gen Anthony C (1898–1975). US. As a brigadier general, McAuliffe was in temporary command of the US 101st Airborne Division when it was encircled at Bastogne in December 1944, during the German Ardennes offensive. When asked to surrender, his reply – "Nuts!" – won him lasting fame. Mid-1950s, commanded US Army in Europe.

McCain, Vice Adm John Sidney ("Slew") (1884–1945). US. An early naval pilot, McCain commanded South Pacific Air Forces during the Guadalcanal operations, 1942. From August 1943 to May 1945, he commanded carrier task forces, finally succeeding Mitscher in command of Fast Carrier Force (Task Force 38/Task Force 58). Completing the Okinawa campaign, he launched the final strikes against Japanese home islands, July–August 1945.

McCain, Adm John S, Jr (1911–81). US. As c-in-c US Pacific Command, July 1968 to September 1972, McCain was theatre commander of all American forces in the Vietnam War. He supported the policy of "Vietnamization" and presided over the reduction of US armed forces in the region. He also urged President Nixon to respond to the 1972 Easter offensive with extreme force and advocated the bombing and mining of Haiphong harbour to wring negotiating concessions from Hanoi.

Macchi C202 Folgore (Thunderbolt) (Italian, WWII). Single-seat fighter; development of Macchi C200 with 1,175hp Alfa-Romeo RA

1000 RC41-I *Monsone* engine (Daimler-Benz DB601 licence-built). Operational service began November 1941. Production (several variants) about 1,100. Developed, with 1,475hp Fiat RA1050 RC58 (licence-built DB605A), into Macchi C205 *Veltro* (Greyhound); 265 built. Max. speed 373mph (600kph) (*Folgore*); 399mph (638kph) (*Veltro*). Two 12.7mm and two 7.7mm machine guns, latter replaced in *Veltro* by two 20mm cannon; 705lb (320kg) bombs.

McClusky, Lt Commander Clarence Wade, Jr (1902–76). US. Leader of the uss *Enterprise* air group at Midway, June 4 1942. His dive-bombers located the enemy and eliminated three out of four Japanese carriers.

McCreery, Lt Gen Sir Richard (1898–1967). Br. In August 1942, following a brief and unhappy period as armoured warfare adviser to Auchinleck, McCreery was appointed cos to Alexander, c-in-c, Middle East. Alexander described his plan for the breakout stage of El Alamein – adopted by Montgomery only at the last moment – as a "key decision": postwar (1959) controversy arose when McCreery published a critical account of Montgomery's conduct of the battle. Taking command of X Corps at Salerno, September 1943, McCreery led it at Monte Cassino and across the Garigliano. In November 1944 he succeeded Leese as commander, Eighth Army, for the final Italian offensive, April–May 1945. *RO'N.*

McCudden, Maj James Thomas Byford, VC (1895–1918). Br. The fourth highest-scoring British fighter pilot of World War I, with 57 "kills", McCudden went to France in 1914 as a mechanic and rose from the ranks to command a squadron. He was killed when his engine cut out on take-off.

McCutcheon, Lt Gen Keith B (1915–71). US. To Vietnam, 1965, as commander 1st Marine Aircraft Wing. Commander, 3rd Marine Amphibious Force, February–March 1966, March–December 1970. Notable for securing helicopters for usmc and developing combat tactics for light helicopters.

M

Machine Gun Corps. Formed in October 1915 to enable Vickers guns to be concentrated for better tactical handling, and to make training more systematic, the Machine Gun Corps initially consisted of infantry machine gun companies, cavalry machine gun squadrons and motor machine gun batteries. The Heavy Branch, formed in November 1916, became the Tank Corps in July 1917. In 1918 machine gun battalions were organized by grouping together three or four companies of 16 Vickers guns each. The Corps was disbanded in 1922.

Mackay, Maj Gen Sir Iven (1882–1966). Australian. As Commander 6th Australian Division, 1940–41, took Bardia, Tobruk and Benghazi during the first British Western Desert offensive, and then took part in the Greek campaign; Commander Home Forces, Australia, 1941–42; Commander Australian forces in New Guinea, 1943.

Mackensen, Field Marshal August von (1849–1945). Ger. Mackensen served in the 2nd Life Hussar Regiment during the war of 1870–71, was assigned to the General Staff in 1880 and was later appointed as an *aide de camp* to Kaiser William II. In 1908 he took over the German XVII Corps, which he was still commanding at the outbreak of war in 1914. Fighting on the Eastern Front, XVII Corps engaged the Russian III Corps at Gumbinnen on August 20, being forced to retire with heavy casualties, but recovered to play an important role at Tannenberg, where Mackensen delivered a telling blow against the right of the Russian Second Army. In September, XVII Corps was in action against Rennenkampf's First Army at the Battle of the Masurian Lakes, then switched to Silesia to take part in the drive on Warsaw. When this was checked and the German command on the Eastern Front was reorganized, Mackensen was appointed, in November, to lead the Ninth Army, with which he recaptured Lodz on December 6. In the spring of 1915 he was placed at the head of the Eleventh Army which, as the spearhead of the Austro-German offensive in Galicia, won a major victory at Gorlice-Tarnow

Field Marshal August von Mackensen

on May 2–3 and took Przemysl and Lemberg in June, during the subsequent pursuit. These triumphs earned Mackensen promotion to Field Marshal and, in July 1915, he was given command of an Army Group. He captured Brest-Litovsk on August 26 but, soon afterwards, was made commander of another new Army Group – containing German, Austrian and Bulgarian formations – for the offensive which overran Serbia in October and November. The following year Mackensen led the combined southern Army Group which helped inflict the crushing defeat on Romania and, on December 7 1916, he entered Bucharest. Mackensen commanded the army of occupation here until the end of the war. *PJS*.

Mackensen, Gen Eberhard von (1889–1969). Ger. The son of August von Mackensen, he commanded III Panzer Corps, spearheading the attack on Rostov, November 1941. In autumn 1943, he handed over First Panzer Army to Hube and transferred from the East Front to Italy. Following the Allied landings at Anzio, January 1944, he took command of Fourteenth Army, hastily improvised to contain the beachhead. Taking advantage of Lucas's initial tardiness in advancing, he launched fierce counteroffensives in February and succeeded in preventing an Allied breakout until late May. Postwar, he received a life sentence for having hostages shot, but was freed in 1952. *RO'N*.

Maclean, Donald Duart (1913–83). Br. Became communist at Cambridge; joined diplomatic service; spied for Comintern until 1951, when fled to Moscow.

Maclean, Brig Fitzroy (b.1911). Br. Parachuted into occupied Yugoslavia in September 1943 as head of a military mission to Tito. Advised that British support be devoted to the partisans rather than to Mihailovich's Chetniks.

McMahon Line. British demarcation of Burma/China frontier, 1913, repudiated by China. Scene of constant fighting. Superseded by Burma-China treaty, 1960.

McNamara, Robert S (b.1916). US. Secretary of Defense from 1961, McNamara became President Kennedy's most influential adviser on the Vietnam War. In August 1964 he persuaded Congress to approve the Tonkin Gulf Resolution. He subsequently lobbied Congress to support the bombing of North Vietnam and the build-up of US ground forces in the South. Continuing as Secretary of Defense under Lyndon Johnson, McNamara came to doubt the war could be won at acceptable cost. He also questioned the effectiveness of the bombing, was appalled at the killing of civilians, and found himself opposed to the Joint Chiefs of Staff. In November 1967 he urged Johnson to cease the bombing, freeze US troop levels and turn over responsibility for ground combat to the South Vietnamese. Rebuffed, he resigned. *WST*.

"McNamara's Wall". The 25-mile (40km) barrier to block infiltration from North into South Vietnam advocated by US Secretary of Defense McNamara, successively codenamed Project Practice Nine, Project Illinois City and Project Dye Marker, was popularly known as "McNamara's Wall". After bitter fighting to clear a path in spring 1967, US Marines constructed test lengths studded with electronic sensors, infrared devices, barbed wire and land mines. However, the professional military were sceptical and the Marine Corps opposed it. Excessive cost, redeployments during the Tet offensive, and the loss of western Route 9 following the abandonment of Khe Sanh ended the project in 1968. *WST*.

MAC Ship (Merchant Aircraft Carrier Ship). Improvised from merchant ships with long deck

M

capacities, e.g. oil tankers, in World War II.

Madagascar, British invasion of (May 5–November 6 1942). To pre-empt Japanese use of the island, which was held by the Vichy French, a British landing force, consisting of Adm Syfret's Force H from Gibraltar and 5th Division from England, was assembled at Durban in April. The landings on May 5 were opposed, but Diégo Suarez, the northern naval base required for operations against the Japanese, fell on May 7. The rest of the island was not occupied until early November due to continued Vichy resistance.

Madras, bombardment of (September 22 1914). Night raid by German light cruiser *Emden*, which closed to within 2,500yd (2,250m) of the Indian port, illuminated it with searchlights, and fired 125 4.1in shells into its oil storage tanks.

Madrid, defence of (November 1936–January 1937), Spanish Civil War. Franco's colonial troops reached the western edge of Madrid on November 7. The attack of November 8 was fought off in an action psychologically vital to Republican morale. Although numerically superior (40,000 to 20,000) it was a considerable feat for untrained and badly armed volunteers. That afternoon, XI International Brigade arrived, and with Russian fighters overhead, the *madrileños* believed international solidarity would triumph. They endured a renewed attack via the university, the first intensive bombing of a capital and then a semi-siege which lasted to the end of the war. Franco, overconfident of victory, launched one offensive after another around Madrid. In December 1936 and January 1937 he attacked the Corunna road, then tried to surround the city from the east at the Jarama and Guadalajara. *AB*.

Mafeking, siege and relief of (October 13 1899–May 17 1900), Second Boer War. Mafeking, Cape Province, was besieged by 5,000 Boers under Cronjé (reduced to 2,000 men under Assistant Commandant-General Snyman from November 18), and defended by

c1,100 colonial troops, militia and armed Bantu under Col Robert Baden-Powell. The latter had been ordered to raise mounted infantry to patrol the Bechuanaland border: his unthinking creation of a garrison was the main reason for the investment of a town of little military significance.

The half-hearted siege was interrupted by frequent truces. The only determined assault was made on the night of May 11–12 by 300 burghers under Commandant Sarel Eloff: the Boers penetrated the defences but were forced to withdraw (74 captured) when Snyman failed to support them. Total Boer casualties during the 217-day siege were around 800; the defenders had 273 casualties, and of the population of 1,074 Europeans and 7,500 Bantu, 4 Europeans and 329 Bantu were killed. Largely because of Baden-Powell's flair for publicity, the siege captured the avid attention of the British public. Near-hysterical celebrations followed the news of Mafeking's relief by a cavalry column under Col Bryan Mahon. *RO'N*.

"MAGIC". American intelligence operation based on the decryption of Japanese codes before and during World War II. Col William Friedman (1891–1969) led a US Army team that broke the Imperial Japanese Navy's "Purple" code, used up to the highest diplomatic levels, in September 1940. Although the intercepts of 1941 failed, for various reasons, to warn of the Pearl Harbor attack, "Magic" made a vital contribution to the US victories at Midway and elsewhere in the Pacific.

A magazine within the Maginot Line

Maginot Line. The subject of much unjust vilification. It was never intended to provide France with an impregnable barrier from Switzerland to the sea, but more modestly to deter Germany from attacking

across the Rhine or through Lorraine. The Franco-German frontier comprised two sectors standing almost at right angles: the first running along the Rhine between Basel and Lauterbourg (110 miles/176km); the second from Lauterbourg to Longwy on the Belgium-Luxembourg frontier (115 miles/184km). It was in Lorraine that the formidable Maginot defences were most fully developed. This left more than 200 miles (320km) of France's eastern border from Dunkirk, along the Franco-Belgian frontier to the Rhine, largely unfortified. It was intended to tempt Germany into a trap to repeat her mistake of 1914.

By 1936 some seven billion francs had been invested in building the Maginot Line: more than 15,000 labourers and engineers were employed in moving 15,700,000 cu yd (12,000,000 cu m) of earth and replacing it with 2,616,000 cu yd (2,000,000 cu m) of cement and 50,000 tons of steel plate. Beneath the virtually impregnable crust there lay a subterranean world of galleries protected alike from poison gas and the leak of fumes from the gun chambers. Communications with the outside world were secured by telephone lines embedded in concrete linked with exchanges 150ft (45m) below ground. Above ground there were dense anti-tank obstacles and fire zones.

Was this whole remarkable feat of military engineering a colossal waste of money and materials? The answer must be negative: though costly, it fulfilled its main purpose of forcing the enemy to funnel his offensive through Holland and Belgium. Moreover, the Maginot Line *did* prove impregnable to frontal attack and was only taken from the rear in the last days of French resistance. *BB*.

Magnetic mine. Operated by metallic ship's hull, causing changes in local magnetic field. The British used a magnetic mine in 1918; the Germans produced one in 1939. The answer was to "degauss" or "wipe" a ship to reduce the magnetic signature and to sweep mines by electrical pulses. The battle between increasingly sensitive mines and sophisticated countermeasures has continued.

M

Mahurin, Lt Col Walker M "Bud"
(b.1918). US. Fighter pilot with
24.75 victories. Most were scored
while flying P-47s with the 56th
Fighter Group in the European
Theatre of Operations, 1943–44,
but he also destroyed a Japanese
bomber in the Southwest Pacific
and 3.5 MiG-15s in Korea – a
unique combination of victories
among leading American "aces".

Majo, Monte, Battle for (May 11–
13 1944). The key to the German
Gustav Line defences in the south
Liri valley, Monte Majo was taken
by the French Expeditionary
Corps (Juin) at the outset of Alexander's "Diadem" offensive.

**Makarios III, Archbishop
Michael Mouskos** (1913–77).
Cypriot. Founding President of Re-
public of Cyprus 1960–77. *See also*
CYPRUS (1955–60).

Makarov, Adm Stepan Osipovich
(1848–1904). Russian. During the
Russo-Turkish War of 1877–78,
Makarov had pioneered the use of
torpedoes: his subsequent book on
naval tactics was much admired by
Togo, who ordered it translated for
the use of Japanese officer cadets.
He was both a scientist – designing
a successful ice-breaker and a
floating dock – and a fighting
admiral: as commander of the
Pacific Fleet at Port Arthur from
March 1904, he personally led
several sorties against the blockading Japanese. Returning from
one such expedition on April 13
1904, his flagship *Petropavlovsk*
struck a mine and sank with all
hands, depriving Russia of her
ablest commander. *RO'N*.

Makassar Straits, Battle of. In the
early hours of January 24 1942,
four American destroyers attacked
Japanese shipping at anchor in the
Makassar Straits, off Balikpapan,
Borneo. Four transports, one cargo
ship and a patrol vessel were sunk
without American loss; but the
Japanese invasion of the Dutch
East Indies continued.

Makhno, Nestor Ivanovitch
(1889–1935). Ukrainian. Ran
anarchist army which defeated Denikin and nearly defeated Trotsky
during Russian Revolution.

Makin *see* TARAWA CAMPAIGN.

**Malan, Group Capt Adolph Gys-
bert ("Sailor")** (1910–63). South
African. Malan, an ex-merchant
seaman, was one of the RAF's foremost fighter tacticians of World
War II. He commanded No. 74
Squadron during the Battle of Britain and led fighter wings in 1941
and 1944. He is usually credited
with 35 victories.

Malaya and Singapore (1941–42).
Within hours of the attack at Pearl
Harbor, the Japanese struck at the
Philippines and Malaya in their
drive for the strategic oilfields of
Borneo and Sumatra. Malaya was
also valued for its rubber and tin,
and Singapore for its naval base
and refineries. On December 8
1941, Twentyfifth Army (Yamashita) landed unopposed in Southern Thailand and rapidly marched
for the Malayan frontier, whilst
"Takumi Force", at brigade/
regimental strength, landed at
Kota Bharu.
　British empire forces in Malaya/
Singapore consisted of III Corps of
two weak divisions in North and
Central Malaya and 8th Australian Division in the South. "Singapore Fortress" had a small garrison but relied mainly on its heavy
coastal batteries to deter attack
from the sea. Reinforcements were
on the way from England and
Australia. Although there were
sufficient military airfields, the
aircraft operating from them were
inadequate in numbers and performance, despite the insistent
pleas of the c-in-c, Brooke-
Popham, for modern interceptors
and torpedo-bombers. Two capital
ships, *Prince of Wales* and *Repulse*,
arrived six days before the
Japanese attack, but without the
support of an aircraft carrier.
　Brooke-Popham's staff had correctly assessed the Japanese
attack as coming overland and
plans had been made for a pre-
emptive advance ("Matador") into
Thailand up the Kroh-Pattani
road, but this was not sanctioned
by Whitehall until too late. The
highly professional Japanese set
about the undertrained (mostly Indian) troops opposing them, whose
units had lost their best men as
reinforcements for the Western
Desert campaign. Within three
days the defenders were in full
flight and their attackers gave
them no respite until they had

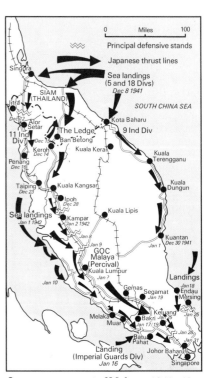

Japanese conquest of Malaya, 1941–42

been driven off the Malayan
Peninsula and onto Singapore Island. The British land forces commander, Lt Gen Percival, was outflanked every time he attempted to
make a stand on the west side of
the central mountain range, with a
series of seaborne landings by the
elite Imperial Guards Division. Inland, Japanese infantry showed
considerable resource when moving off the roads to which the
defenders were tied.
　Morale had been affected at the
outset by the loss, on December 10,
of the two British capital ships. The
southernmost Malay state of
Johore, where Percival had planned to make a stand, was lost at
the end of January when 9th Indian Division was routed and its
commander killed, and the Australian 8th Division dispersed after a
gallant fight at Muar and Bakri.
　Percival now withdrew to Singapore Island which, despite its swollen garrison, was short of water
and actually indefensible on the
landward side. The Japanese
started to land in strength on the
northwest coast on the night of
February 8–9 and, although many
of Percival's units fought stubbornly, some newly arrived reinforcements broke at the first
assault and the defence collapsed.
To avert further bloodshed, Perci-

val surrendered on February 15.

This was the most disastrous reverse ever inflicted on a British army. The Japanese had planned for a 100-day campaign, but had taken Singapore in 70. A total of 130,000 British and empire soldiers were captured, including the entire British 18th Division which had only arrived at the end of January and barely took part in the fighting. Vast stocks of all types of military equipment were seized intact. Japanese battle casualties throughout the entire campaign totalled 9,824. *MH.*

Malayan Communist Party (MCP) *see* MALAYAN EMERGENCY.

Malayan Emergency (1948–1960). Many members of the pre-war Malayan Communist Party (MCP) served in the Malayan People's Anti-Japanese Army (MPAJA) which offered the only active guerrilla opposition during most of the Japanese military occupation (1941–45). After the war, the MCP soon fell foul of the reinstated colonial government and in 1948 a number of its leaders went underground to initiate a war of liberation on Maoist lines.

Calling themselves the Malayan Races' Liberation Army (MRLA), the communists, almost all ethnic Chinese, enlisted the support of many Chinese "squatters" as a support organization (Min Yuen) whose purpose was to pass food and other supplies to the MRLA and act as a low-level intelligence-gathering agency.

The ensuing campaign reached its high-water mark for the MRLA in 1952 with the assassination of the High Commissioner, Sir Henry Gurney. In his place, doubling as Director of Operations, the British government appointed Gen Sir Gerald Templer, who immediately injected a new sense of purpose into the Security Forces and transformed their morale. The Squatter population was resettled into "New Villages" surrounded by barbed wire; rigorous food control was imposed. This plan had been prepared by Gen Sir Harold Briggs, Director of Operations (1950–51). Chin Peng, the MRLA leader, emerged briefly under amnesty from the jungle in 1955 for inconclusive talks with the government and the campaign dragged on until 1960 when virtually all terrorist activity had ceased.

The MRLA failed because the Briggs plan cut the guerrillas' supply line, isolated them from their supporters and drove them into deep jungle where they could be hunted down. The Security Forces won through good intelligence, constant aerial surveillance of the jungle, painstaking jungle patrolling, and the winning of the hearts and minds of the majority of the civil population. All operations were planned and executed on a joint basis by the civil administration, military, and police, whether at national, state, district or village level. The campaign demanded a disproportionate effort from the British government; 40,000 Commonwealth troops, 60,000 police and more than 250,000 local Home Guards were involved at its height, against never more than 3,000 guerrillas. It remains, however, the only true complete victory over communist insurgency won by a former colonial power and a newly emergent nation since 1945. *MH.*

Malayan People's Anti-Japanese Army (MPAJA) *see* MALAYAN EMERGENCY.

Malayan Races' Liberation Army (MRLA) *see* MALAYAN EMERGENCY.

Malayan Scouts *see* SAS.

Malaysia-Indonesia confrontation (1963–66). After the 1962 Brunei revolt, many of the rebels found sanctuary across the Indonesian border, from where they continued to operate, helped by elements of the Indonesian army.

In answer to this threat, and as the Indonesian government was now actively backing the communists in Seria, harbouring TNKU rebels and fomenting dissension throughout what was soon to be East Malaysia, Maj Gen Walter Walker was appointed Commander British Forces Borneo. Experienced in the earlier Malayan Emergency, he immediately stressed the need for the security forces to dominate the jungle. By April 1963 Walker had set up his headquarters in Labuan, with brigade HQS at Kuching and Brunei. The theatre of operations was huge, the border with Indonesia being 900 miles (1,450km) long and, because of the wild terrain, very easy to infiltrate. Walker saw the need for air mobility and the campaign hinged on the use of helicopters. Helicopter pads were hacked out of the jungle every few miles and well-protected patrol bases, often with field artillery, were located some miles inside the border.

With the creation of the Malaysian Federation in September 1963, supreme control of military operations passed from British hands, to be vested in the Malaysian National Operations Committee in Kuala Lumpur, of which the British C-in-C, Far East Command, was a member, passing instructions down to Walker as Director of Operations on the ground. Prior to Federation Day, the Indonesian Ambassador had been recalled from Kuala Lumpur and President Sukarno, who laid claim to Borneo, Sarawak and Brunei, promised what he termed a "terrible confrontation". Within days the Indonesian Army launched an attack on the Malaysian military base at Long Jawi which was repulsed with the aid of "stops" placed on the Indonesian border by helicopter to intercept the attackers' retreat. In December, the Indonesians surprised a Malaysian battalion at Kalabakan, inflicting the most serious reverse of the campaign. Walker's answer was to strengthen the jungle patrol bases and increase pressure on Indonesian infiltrators and their supporters. A highly successful campaign was mounted to "win the hearts and minds" of the indigenous population and enlist their aid in providing accurate intelligence of Indonesian activity.

The year 1964 saw the climax of the campaign, with an abortive Indonesian parachute incursion into West Malaysia and many border incidents in Borneo and Sabah. The security forces now adopted a policy of "hot pursuit", chasing Indonesian patrols back across their own frontier. Intelligence sources identified a plan for an all-out Indonesian offensive directed against Kuching, accompanied by a nationwide campaign of civil disturbance and sabotage. At this time, Walker had 10,000 combat troops available. Reinforcements airlifted from the UK

M

brought these up to some 14,000, with five batteries of artillery, two squadrons of armoured cars and four engineer squadrons, plus logistic troops (including a trials hovercraft unit which proved invaluable on the many rivers flowing down from the interior). For all these troops there were never more than 60 support helicopters for trooplift and resupply.

The initiative swung firmly in favour of the security forces in 1965 and by the middle of the year virtually all contacts with hostile forces took place on the Indonesian side of the border. In September, following an unsuccessful communist coup in Jakarta, Indonesian military activity began to fall off. In March 1966, Gurkha units raided Indonesian bases in Kalimantan and it was clear that the military in Jakarta were tiring of the campaign. They seized power later that month, Sukarno being ousted by Gen Suharto, and in August 1966 the confrontation came to an end. Losses to Commonwealth forces totalled 114 killed and 181 wounded, whilst Indonesian casualties, officially given as some 600 killed, were substantially higher.

Despite the peculiar political constraints under which Gen Walker was obliged to operate, success stemmed from the fact that the population was friendly and supportive; had it not been for the helicopter, however, it is doubtful that the security forces could have managed to keep the Indonesians and their supporters under control in such a huge theatre, equal in area to England and Scotland and virtually without roads. *MH.*

Malaysian National Operations Committee *see* MALAYSIA-INDONESIA CONFRONTATION.

Malik, Jacob Alexandrovich (b.1906). Russian. When the Korean War began, Malik was Soviet representative on the UN Security Council, but was not present, because of Soviet boycott, to veto the resolutions which involved the UN in the fighting. He returned in August 1950, paralysing the Security Council as an instrument of US policy. On June 23 1951 Malik called for an armistice in Korea, opening the way to the truce talks which began the following month. His speech had been preceded by secret talks on Korea with George Kennan of the US State Department. *CM.*

Malinovsky: defeated Kwantung Army

Malinovsky, Marshal Rodion (1898–1967). Russian. Malinovsky was drafted into the Imperial Russian Army in 1916 and, the next year, was sent to France as a member of the Russian Expeditionary Force. He was arrested by the French authorities for inciting his fellow soldiers to support a Russian withdrawal from the war and was removed to North Africa. Malinovsky returned to Russia in 1918 and joined the Red Army, rising to regimental command during the Civil War. He completed his officer training in 1930 and served as a military adviser to the Republican forces during the Spanish Civil War. Following the German invasion of the Soviet Union in June 1941 Malinovsky held various commands during the defence of the Ukraine before taking over the Southern Army Group early in 1942. His forces were badly mauled in the German spring offensive and he was switched to the Don Group until, when his command was disbanded, he led the Sixtysixth Army in the defence of Stalingrad. By the end of the year he had been given command of the recently formed and extremely powerful Second Guards Army, leading it in the encirclement of von Paulus' Sixth Army. Malinovsky's success led to a string of appointments variously to command the Southern, Southwestern, Third and Second Ukrainian Fronts. Often working in concert with Gen Tolbukhin's forces he drove his armies through the Ukraine and Romania and launched an invasion of Hungary, capturing Budapest in April 1945. He continued his offensive through central Europe by advancing into Austria and Czechoslovakia and completed his participation in the war in Europe with the capture of Prague. However, the Soviet Union still had need of Malinovsky's talents and he was sent to Mongolia where he took command of the Trans-Baikal Front during the Soviet invasion of Japanese-held Manchuria. His strong and battle-hardened armoured and mechanized divisions quickly broke through the Japanese defences and constituted the main thrust that brought about a rapid Soviet victory. Malinovsky held a prominent place in the Soviet military hierarchy after the war and served as Minister of Defence from 1957 until his death in 1967. *MS.*

Malmédy massacre. On December 17 1944, SS troops executed over 70 American prisoners near Malmédy, Belgium.

Malta convoys. Ten major operations were mounted to fight convoys through to Malta (January 1941–October 1942):
1) "Excess" from Gibraltar (January 6–10 1941). Opposed by *Fliegerkorps X* (Geisler); all ships arrived, but one cruiser was lost, and the aircraft carrier *Illustrious* and a destroyer were badly damaged.
2) "Substance" from Gibraltar (July 20–24 1941). All ships arrived at the price of one destroyer sunk and a cruiser and destroyer damaged.
3) "Style" from Gibraltar (July 31–August 2 1941). No losses.
4) "Halberd" from Gibraltar (September 24–28 1941). Battleship *Nelson* damaged by aerial torpedo and one store ship lost.
5) "March" (MG1) from Alexandria (March 20–23 1942). Led to the Second Battle of Sirte; three out of four ships reached Malta, but were sunk after arrival by bombing.
6) "Harpoon" from Gibraltar (June 12–15 1942). Strongly opposed by Italian cruisers and by Axis submarines and aircraft. Only two out of six ships reached Malta. Two destroyers of the escort were sunk.
7) "Vigorous" from Alexandria (June 14–16 1942). Turned back by heavy bombing in "Bomb Alley", south of Crete, and by the intervention of the Italian battle fleet (Iachino). The Italian battle-

M

ship *Littorio* was damaged and one cruiser sunk, but the British lost one cruiser, three destroyers and four of the eleven merchantmen.

8) "Pedestal" from Gibraltar (August 10–15 1942). The last strongly opposed convoy. Only five out of fourteen merchantmen, including the British-crewed US tanker *Ohio*, reached Malta at a cost of the aircraft carrier *Eagle* torpedoed by *U-73*, two cruisers and a destroyer sunk.

9) "Stonehenge" from Alexandria (November 16–20 1942). Opposed only by Axis aircraft; one cruiser was damaged, but all merchant ships arrived safely.

10) "Portcullis" from Alexandria (December 1–5 1942). Unopposed, signalling end of siege. *WGFJ.*

Malta, siege of (January 1941–October 1942). British naval and air forces on Malta posed a major threat to Axis communications with Libya. Although plans were made to invade the island, Hitler chose to neutralize it by air attack from Sicily, when resources could be spared from Russia, and by naval and air interdiction of British re-supply convoys.

The siege went through five phases. The initial phase (January to May 1941) saw intense bombing by *Fliegerkorps X* (Geisler) while Rommel's Afrika Korps was being shipped to Libya. The attack reached a crescendo in April and then died away as aircraft were redeployed for the invasion of Greece. During the same period, British forces based on Malta sank nine German ships and damaged another nine, sailing to and from Tripoli.

Phase two (June 1941 to January 1942) involved supplying Malta by convoys from Gibraltar and Alexandria in the face of air attacks from Sardinia, Sicily, Crete and other Aegean islands; and reinforcing its air defences with fighters flown off Force H carriers. By early 1942 the people of Malta were being severely rationed for food and fuel.

The third phase (February to April 1942) saw the second and most intense period of bombing carried out by *Luftflotte 2* (Kesselring) in preparation for Rommel's offensive to seize the Suez Canal. By the end of April Kesselring could justifiably claim that Malta's

sting had been drawn.

In the next phase (May to September 1942), the Axis planned to invade Malta with a specially trained airborne and amphibious force to support Rommel's offensive; it was not carried out because all Axis resources were concentrated on exploiting Rommel's victories at Gazala. Malta was kept under air attack.

In the final phase (October to December 1942), Malta remained a threat to Axis communications with Libya. British air and naval forces operating from the island took a significant toll of Rommel's supply ships prior to and during El Alamein. The siege was raised at the beginning of December 1942 with the arrival of the "Stonehenge" and "Portcullis" convoys, almost unopposed. *WGFJ.*

Malvinas. The Hispanic-speaking world's name for the Falklands, derived from the name *Iles Malouines* originally given to them *c*1700 by French seal fishers from St Malo.

Manchester, Avro 679 (Br, WWII). Heavy bomber, crew 7. Prototype flew July 25 1939; production deliveries began August 5 1940; first to squadron November 10 1940. First operational mission February 24 1941. Equipped 13 squadrons, but phased out June 1942 after many serious difficulties, mostly with engines. Production 202. Two 1,760hp Rolls-Royce Vulture engines; max. speed 265mph (426kph); eight 0.303in machine guns, 10,350lb (4,695kg) bombs.

Manchurian campaign (1945). Throughout 1944 the Soviet Union built up its forces on the Manchurian border, moving battle-hardened armies to the Far East after the defeat of Germany. On August 8 1945, war was declared against Japan and 1,500,000 Soviet troops and an awesome array of tanks, guns and aircraft were launched against the Kwangtung Army. The Trans-Baikal Front plunged southwards from Mongolia while the First and Second Far East Fronts attacked from the east and north. The Japanese forces were everywhere quickly overwhelmed and final victory was announced by the Soviets on August 23. *MS.*

Manchuria, Japanese occupation of, (1931–45) *see* SINO-JAPANESE WAR.

Mandalay *see* BURMA CAMPAIGN (1941–45).

Manekshaw, Field Marshal H J F (b.1914). Appointed to command IV Corps, Assam, after 1962 debacle. Appointed Chief of Army Staff (India), 1969. Given overall command of the three services in 1971 and gave vigorous leadership in India-Pakistan War. Promoted Field Marshal (the first and only one since independence).

Mangin, Gen Charles (1866–1925). Fr. Known to French troops in World War I as "the butcher" or "eater of men" because of his predilection for vigorous attacks regardless of cost, Mangin led a division, then a corps, at Verdun, recapturing Fort Douaumont in October 1916. As Nivelle's protégé he was given command of the French Sixth Army but was removed after its bloody failure in Nivelle's 1917 offensive on the Aisne. His fortunes revived under Foch in 1918 and, as commander of the French Tenth Army, he delivered the crushing counterstroke on the Marne on July 18 which effectively killed Germany's remaining hopes. *PJS.*

Manila *see* LUZON CAMPAIGN.

Mannerheim, Marshal Baron Karl von (1867–1951). Finn. Born in the Russian Grand-duchy of Finland, Mannerheim served as a cavalry officer in the Imperial Russian Army during the Russo-Japanese War and commanded a corps in World War I. Following the Bolshevik Revolution, Finland declared independence, resulting in civil war between "Reds" and "Whites" from January 1918. Mannerheim raised and led the "White" forces, breaking "Reds" resistance at Tampere in April, while a German expeditionary force took Helsinki. Appointed Regent, December 1918, he retired on the creation of the Finnish Republic, July 1919. From 1931, as Chairman of the Defence Council, he supervised the build-up of Finland's defences, notably the "Mannerheim Line" on the Karelian Isthmus, separating Finland from

M

the Soviet Union. During the Soviet invasion, beginning November 30 1939, the defences held and Mannerheim's forces mounted effective counterattacks until overwhelmed by weight of numbers, March 1940. In 1941, led by Mannerheim, Finland joined Germany's attack on the Soviet Union, recovering most of the territory lost in 1939–40 and, to Germany's displeasure, refusing to exceed this limited objective. In June 1944, Soviet forces under Marshal Leonid Govorov (1896–1955) broke through the Mannerheim Line. Mannerheim, appointed President in August, conducted negotiations that resulted in armistice on September 19. He retired in 1946. *MS*.

Mannerheim Line campaign *see* FINLAND, RUSSIAN INVASION OF.

Mannheim, bombing of (December 16 1940). This night attack, on which 134 bombers were dispatched, marked an important turning point in British bombing policy. Before this, Bomber Command, wherever its bombs actually fell, intended them for precise targets such as oil plants, railway stations or factories. For the Mannheim attack, the aiming point was the centre of the city; it was the first deliberate British area attack. The German attack on Coventry was thought to justify it.

Mannock, Maj Edward ("Mick"), VC (1887–1918). Br. The highest-scoring British fighter pilot of World War I, with 73 "kills" between May 1917–July 1918. An advocate of formation flying, Mannock's tactical doctrine was "always above; seldom on the same level; never underneath". A ruthless fighter, he was known to strafe the crews of aircraft he had forced down. He died when his aircraft was downed by rifle fire.

Manoeuvring Re-entry Vehicle (MARV). A ballistic missile re-entry vehicle which can change its trajectory once it strikes the atmosphere in order to confuse ABM defences or to achieve pinpoint accuracy. No strategic MARV system has yet been deployed, as inertial guidance system improvements have increased the accuracy achieved by more conventional

and simpler means, and ABM defences have been constrained by treaty. One problem is the difficulty of fitting a homing system to a very fast moving re-entry vehicle, and the only application to date has been in the Pershing 2 IRBM warhead which re-enters at slower velocity than an ICBM.

Manstein, Field Marshal Fritz Erich von (1887-1973). Ger. Eminent strategist and field commander of World War II. He was von Rundstedt's COS in Poland, September 1939, transferring with his chief to the Western Front in October. Opposing OKH's plan for the invasion of France, "Case Yellow", he proposed instead a

Von Manstein: master of mobile warfare

sudden armoured thrust through the Ardennes followed by a drive to the Channel to divide the Allied armies. Although this plan was adopted by Hitler, Manstein himself, having aroused the ire of OKH, was relegated to command of XXXVIII Corps. His brilliant handling of LVI Panzer Corps in "Barbarossa" – advancing 200 miles (322km) in four days, June 22–26 1941 – brought him command of Eleventh Army in its successful Crimean campaign, September 1941–July 1942, culminating in the capture of Sevastopol after a 250-day siege. As C-in-C, Army Group Don, November–December 1942, he failed to relieve Stalingrad – hampered by Hitler's interference and Paulus's vacillation – but preserved sufficient forces on the German right to launch Army Group South's counteroffensive of February–March 1942, recapturing Kharkov against massive odds and temporarily stabilizing the front along the Donets. Hitler's refusal to

allow an early assault on the Kursk salient, however, allowed the Russians to establish numerical superiority there: Manstein's penetration of July 5–10 1943 was achieved at high cost and he was driven back.

Manstein's mastery of mobile warfare was now manifested in his fighting retreat across the Dnieper and into the Ukraine. But although his "mobile defence" – giving ground in order to build up for counterattacks – inflicted severe losses on the advancing Russians, it conflicted with Hitler's insistence on holding all territory *à outrance*, and on March 30 1944 Manstein was permanently removed from command. Postwar, he underwent four years' imprisonment for "war crimes". *RO'N*.

Manteuffel, Lt Gen (*General der Panzertruppen*) Hasso-Eccard von (b.1897). Ger. The effectiveness of this Panzer general's hard-driving leadership and tactical ability was reflected in his rapid promotion: from Lt Col in 1939 to Lt Gen in 1944. Briefly a divisional commander in Tunisia, Manteuffel from mid-1943 commanded 7th Panzer Division in Russia, stemming the Soviet advance at Berdichev and briefly recapturing Zhitomir (November 19 1943) during Manstein's southern counteroffensive. In late 1944, after leading *Grossdeutschland* Panzer Division in Romania and East Prussia, he took command of Fifth Panzer Army in the Ardennes offensive, December 1944–January 1945. Advancing on the northern flank of Dietrich's Sixth SS Panzer Army, Manteuffel forced the surrender of US 106th Infantry Division in the Schnee Eifel (December 19) and captured Saint-Vith (December 22), but the determined defence of Bastogne and shortage of fuel slowed his thrust towards the Meuse. Early in March 1945, he was rushed to take over Third Panzer Army in Army Group Vistula (Heinrici), facing the northern Soviet advance on Berlin. With what he called "a ghost army" – most tanks had gone to meet Zhukov's southern offensive – Manteuffel staunchly contested Rokossovsky's advance until late April. Then he retreated swiftly, surrendering to US 8th Infantry Division on May 3. *RO'N*.

"Man who never was" *see* DECEPTION.

Mao Tse Tung (1893–1976). Chinese. Born in the Hunan province of central China, Mao came from a peasant background but achieved an education at Changsa and Peking (Beijing), where he worked in the university library. During this period he was introduced to Marxism and, in 1921, became a co-founder of the Chinese Communist Party. His influence steadily increased and, with his associates, Chou En-lai and Chu Teh, he endeavoured to establish a Soviet republic in Kiangsi province. But Nationalist opposition ensured its failure and forced a mass migration of the communists. Known as "The Long March", the 8,000 mile (12,900km) trek to the north west reaches of China was completed in October 1935 by only 30 percent of the 100,000 who had embarked upon it a year earlier. Subsequently Mao accepted a truce with Chiang Kai-shek during the early phases of the war against Japan, their common enemy. Mao's forces favoured guerrilla warfare. Punitive Japanese measures helped reinforce peasant support for the communists. The truce with the Nationalists was regularly broken and open conflict was resumed in 1945. The communists gradually won control of the country and, as their strength grew, they switched from guerrilla tactics to set-piece battles. By the beginning of 1949 victory was in their grasp and in January Peking was captured, followed in the spring by the fall of Nanking and Shanghai. On October 1 1949, the People's Republic of China was proclaimed and Mao was appointed Chairman of its Central Administrative Council. While concentrating on economic, industrial and ideological matters, Mao steered a difficult path in international affairs, notably over Korea and China's uneasy relationship with the Soviet Union. In April 1959 he relinquished his position as head of state but retained the party chairmanship. During the "cultural revolution" in the 1960s, his theories of agrarian communism were adopted by the Red Guards and a cult of Maoism proliferated. He died in relative obscurity in 1976. *MS*.

Maquis. Corsican for "brushwood", used of Frenchmen who fled to the hills instead of undertaking forced labour in Germany, 1942–44. Often underfed, underarmed and ill-disciplined, but in midsummer 1944 distracted large bodies of German troops from Normandy with SOE and SAS help. Two notable massacres of the Maquis, in the Vercors near Grenoble and at Montmouchet in the Auvergne, were offset by successes in Brittany, Burgundy and near Carcassonne.

Marauder *see* B-26 MARAUDER.

March offensive, German (1918). Their unrestricted submarine campaign having failed, but with troops freed from the Eastern Front following the Russian Revolution, the German High Command decided to seek a decisive victory in the west in 1918 before American manpower made its presence felt. Ludendorff therefore planned a *Kaiserschlacht* ("Kaiser's Battle") aimed at causing the collapse of the Allied armies on the Western Front. Operation "Michael", the first of a series of major offensives, was launched on March 21 1918 by the German Second, Seventeenth and Eighteenth Armies against the front held by the British Third and Fifth Armies between Arras and La Fère, on either side of St Quentin. Attacking after a five-hour hurricane bombardment devised by Col Bruchmüller, and using storm troops trained in infiltration tactics, the Germans hoped to drive a wedge between the French and British forces and wheel to the north to roll up the BEF and press it back to the sea. On March 21 British Fifth Army under Gough – starved of men and inadequately trained in a new elastic defence system – quickly gave way, compelling Byng's Third Army, on its left, to retire in turn. However, while Fifth Army continued to retreat, Byng was more successful in limiting German gains on his front. Thus, what was originally intended as a subsidiary advance by von Hutier's Eighteenth Army on the German left had become the main area of German progress. On March 23 Ludendorff was tempted into altering his plan in order to exploit this situation, now directing Second and Eighteenth Armies west and southwest towards Amiens and Paris. Albert was evacuated on March 26 and, the same day, with Pétain seemingly reluctant to support the British, Gen Foch was appointed to coordinate Allied operations. Operation "Mars", a German attack at Arras on March 28, was repulsed with heavy losses. Although, by this time, Gough had been removed from the command of the British Fifth Army, the German offensive had already lost its momentum and, when the German drive towards the key communications centre of Amiens was halted by the Australians at Villers Bretonneux on April 4–5, Ludendorff called off "Michael". Despite having advanced 40 miles (64km) and taken some 70,000 British prisoners, the Germans had fallen far short of their principal strategic objectives.

Ludendorff's next offensive, "Georgette", which was smaller in scale, opened on April 9 against the British front on both sides of the River Lys, between Armentières and the La Bassée Canal. The Germans brushed aside a Portuguese division near Neuve-Chapelle and advanced 3.5 miles (5.5km) on the first day. Armentières was abandoned on April 10 and as the Germans neared the vital rail junction of Hazebrouck, Haig issued a "backs to the wall" order on April 11, appealing to his soldiers to hold their positions at all costs. The German attack spread to the British Second Army's sector south of Ypres, and much of the ground won by the British in 1917 was given up, with Plumer withdrawing to a shorter line just east of Ypres itself. French troops, having arrived as reinforcements, lost Mount Kemmel on April 25 but this was "Georgette's" last success. By April 30 Ludendorff had realized that all hope of achieving a decisive breakthrough had disappeared for the time being: he ordered operations in Flanders to cease.

Still intent on launching a further offensive in Flanders, Ludendorff endeavoured to lure French reserves away from that region by means of Operation "Blücher", an attack along the Chemin des Dames on May 27 1918. Within a few hours the Germans had cros-

M

sed the Aisne and by the evening of May 29 they were beyond Soissons. German Seventh Army reached the Marne near Chateau Thierry, 56 miles (90km) from Paris, but, significantly, US 2nd and 3rd Divisions helped to block the advance at this point, with 2nd Division counterattacking at Belleau Wood on June 6. To expand the shoulders of the salient which had been formed, a fourth German offensive was improvised against French Third Army, between Noyon and Montdidier, on June 9. Once more the Germans were initially successful, progressing 6 miles (9km) on the first day, yet by June 11 this attack too had ground to a halt. Ludendorff's final offensive was unleashed east and west of Reims on July 15. Its failure, and the Allied counterstroke between the Aisne and Marne on July 18, persuaded Ludendorff to yield the strategic initiative to the Allies. *PJS.*

Marco Polo Bridge incident (1937) *see* SINO-JAPANESE WAR.

Mareth Line, Battle of (March 19–28 1943). Montgomery's Eighth Army defeated Messe's First Italo-German Army (*Panzerarmee Afrika*, renamed after Rommel relinquished command), which held the pre-war French fortifications of the Mareth Line on the Tunisian frontier.

In the first phase (March 19–22) Montgomery attempted to breach the Line's coastal sector with a frontal assault by XXX Corps (Leese), while threatening to turn the position with a wide left hook through the desert by a specially-formed New Zealand Corps (Freyberg). Leese's attack failed badly; Freyberg's outflanking manoeuvre therefore became the main effort.

In the second phase (March 22–28) Montgomery sent Horrocks with X Corps HQ and 1st Armoured Division to reinforce Freyberg and break through the Tebaga Gap in the Matmata Hills to Messe's coastal supply road. The Gap was breached on March 26–27 by divisions advancing behind a curtain of air attacks and artillery fire, a tactic devised by Desert Air Force (Broadhurst). Messe had to abandon the Mareth Line to avoid encirclement. *WGFJ.*

Margate, German destroyer raid on (February 25–26 1917). In 1917, the British Dover Straits anti-submarine patrol was vulnerable to German destroyers based in Flanders. On this night, two forces of five destroyers each attacked. One fought an indecisive action with one British destroyer, the other bombarded Margate.

US field gun team in the Marianas, 1944

Marianas Islands campaign (1944). The primary strategic importance of the Marianas lay in their potential as bases from which B-29 Superfortresses could strike at targets in the Philippines and the Japanese home islands. The main objectives were the large, strongly garrisoned southern islands of Saipan, Tinian and Guam. Adm Nimitz created two separate task forces for the assaults: the Northern, of 71,000 men, was to attack Saipan and Tinian; the Southern, with 56,000 troops, was to seize Guam. Landings on Saipan began on June 15 1944 and were characterized by fierce fighting and a fanatical determination shown by both Japanese troops and civilians not to surrender. On July 9 with over 20,000 of the defenders having fought to the death, the island came under US control. Tinian, three miles to the south, was the next objective and proved to be a simpler task. The assault was preceded by a massive bombardment by warships and Saipan-based aircraft. A feint landing on the south of the island confused the Japanese commander and the real attack in the north was largely unopposed, allowing the Marines quickly to secure a large bridgehead. Sufficient troops and artillery had been landed to repulse a Japanese counterattack the following day and, by August 1 when all substantial Japanese re-

sistance was at end, American losses totalled some 300 killed while their opponents lost 5,000. This left only Guam, which was to have been invaded on June 13, but the difficulties encountered on Saipan forced a postponement. The delay was partially offset by the opportunity it offered to carry out a 13-day bombardment prior to the landings. However, sufficient Japanese defences remained intact to cause serious problems. US Marines suffered heavy casualties in establishing their bridgeheads but managed gradually to force their way into the island's interior. By August 10 Japanese resistance had effectively been eradicated. The victory in the Marianas concluded amphibious operations in the Central Pacific. *MS.*

Maricourt. Village just behind the British front line, and at the junction of the British and French forces on the Somme, July 1 1916.

Mark I. The earliest pattern of British tank to see action in 1916. Armed with 2 x 6 pounder guns and 4 x 8mm machine guns (male) or 4 x 7.7 mm and 1 x 8 mm machine guns (female). Crew of 8. 105hp Daimler petrol engine. Max road speed 4mph (6kph), cross-country 2mph (3kph). Weight 27.5 tons. Radius of action 15 miles (24km). Superseded by Mks IV and V. Plans existed in 1918 for a Mk VIII "Liberty" tank to go into mass production in 1919.

"Market Time" Operation. Stemmed from the discovery in February 1965 of a camouflaged trawler offloading military supplies in Vung Ro Bay off South Vietnam. Beginning March 11 1965, US and South Vietnamese navy coastal patrols coordinated efforts to interdict seaborne infiltration of arms and supplies from North Vietnam into the South. "Market Time" forced the communists to accelerate development of the Ho Chi Minh Trail for infiltrating supplies. *WST.*

Marne, Battles of the (1914, 1918). The check to the German Second Army at Guise on August 29 1914 led its commander, von Bülow, to call upon von Kluck's First Army, on his right, for support. Kluck, who had discounted the BEF since

M

Le Cateau, began to wheel inwards to the southeast, seduced by the prospect of rolling up what he thought was the Allied left flank. This manoeuvre caused Kluck to pass northeast of Paris, not west as in the original plan, and rendered his own right flank vulnerable to counterattack by the French Sixth Army, under Maunoury, which was concentrating north of Paris. On September 4, with Kluck already across the Marne and some way ahead of Bülow, the Military Governor of Paris, Galliéni, persuaded Joffre to halt the Allied retreat and order a general counterattack. Maunoury's pressure on the German First Army's sensitive flank, September 5–7, induced Kluck to reverse three of his corps and change front to the west. Although reinforced by troops sent from Paris in taxicabs, Maunoury was being driven back from the Ourcq by September 9, but Kluck's westward movement had widened the existing gap between himself and Bülow. As the BEF advanced towards this gap, Bülow, now also under attack from the French Fifth Army and part of Foch's new Ninth Army, decided to retreat. Kluck too was therefore compelled to retire northward, ending German hopes of a swift victory in the west in 1914.

At the end of May 1918, the Germans again reached the Marne, following Ludendorff's *Blücher* offensive on the Aisne. Planning eventually to defeat the British in Flanders, Ludendorff attempted to draw off Allied reserves by attacking either side of Reims on July 15. German Seventh Army crossed the Marne east of Chateau Thierry and, despite stubborn resistance by US 3rd Division, established a bridgehead. On July 18, in a counterstroke prepared by its commander, Gen Mangin, French Tenth Army – with Sixth Army on its right – attacked the western side of the German salient between the Aisne and Marne. US 1st and 2nd Divisions were in the spearhead of Tenth Army's surprise assault, which was supported by over 200 tanks, and within two days Mangin had advanced some 6 miles (10km). By August 6 1918, the Germans, after losing 168,000 men, including 29,000 prisoners, and 793 guns, had withdrawn and

Ludendorff abandoned any illusions of German victory. *PJS*.

Marseille, Hauptmann Hans-Joachim (1919–1942). Ger. Having earlier seen action in the Battle of Britain, Marseille became the Luftwaffe's leading fighter pilot in North Africa before he died in a crash in September 1942. Credited with 158 victories, he destroyed more British aircraft than any other German pilot this century.

Marshall, General of the Army George (1880–1959). US. Served with the AEF in France during World War I as Chief of Operations, 1st Division and, later, of First US Army. He held varied staff and training posts in the inter-war period before being appointed Army COS on September 1 1939. He ensured that in his first year as COS, the strength of the army almost doubled and it was to rise from less than 200,000 in 1939 to over 8,000,000 in 1945. From the outset, Marshall advocated the formation of unified Allied commands and upheld the decision made at the Washington Conference of December 1941 that the defeat of Germany be the major Allied priority. However, in the Combined Chiefs of Staff he opposed British tendencies to favour the indirect approach in the Balkans and the Mediterranean and pressed them to retain their commitment to a cross-Channel assault on France. Marshall was a strong candidate to lead this invasion, but President Roosevelt deemed his presence in Washington indispensable and Marshall's protégé, Eisenhower, was appointed Supreme Commander, Allied Expeditionary Force. Shortly after the end of the war, Marshall retired as COS, but in December 1945 he was sent to China as President Truman's special envoy to try to mediate between the Nationalists and Communists. His failure to secure peace in China did not prevent his appointment as Secretary of State in January 1947. Once again Marshall's organizational skills came to the fore and he instigated and promoted the "Marshall Plan", the regeneration of the economy of Europe through a massive programme of American aid. *MS*.

Marshall Islands campaign *see* KWAJALEIN-ENIWETOK.

Martel, Lt Gen Sir Gifford Le Quesne (1889–1958). Br. Involved in training the first tank crews, 1916, Martel became an important advocate of armoured warfare (Guderian acknowledged his influence). He designed the first "tankette", 1925–26. After commanding a division in the Battle of France, 1940, he was Commander, Royal Armoured Corps, 1940–42.

Martin, Ambassador Graham A (b.1912). US. A firm supporter of American objectives in the Vietnam War and of President Nguyen Van Thieu; replaced Ellsworth Bunker as US Ambassador to Saigon in June 1973. Taking this post after the US withdrawal, it was Martin's task to reassure the South Vietnamese that the US remained committed to their defence. Martin delayed the evacuation of endangered personnel, and hoped for a political solution almost until the day of his own evacuation from the rooftop of the American Embassy, April 30 1975. *WST*.

Martin, Air Marshal Sir Harold ("Micky") (b.1918). Australian. Served in the RAF and was one of the greatest of Bomber Command's pilots in World War II. Played a prominent part in the Dams raid and in many other low-level precision attacks. Also flew as a long-range night fighter pilot.

Martinsyde G100/G102 Elephant (Br, WWI). Single-seat scout/bomber-reconnaissance. Prototype flew summer 1915; production deliveries from early February 1916; used by 13 RFC squadrons but only No. 27 Squadron wholly equipped. Not successful as fighter but usefully employed as bomber-reconnaissance April 1916 to November 1917, France; until August 1919 in Middle East. Production 251. One 120/160hp Beardmore engine; max. speed 108mph (173kph); two 0.303in machine guns, 336lb (151kg) bombs.

Massy, Lt Gen Hugh Royds Stokes (1884–1965). Br. Commander Allied Land Forces, Central Norway, during the Norwegian campaign in 1940.

M

Massive Retaliation. American strategic policy 1954–60, associated with the Eisenhower Administration's "New Look" and articulated by Secretary of State John Foster Dulles. The policy emphasized the threat of retaliation "at times and places of our own choosing" to communist attack anywhere and this was generally held to mean a full-scale strategic nuclear offensive against the Soviet Union and China. Conventional and limited war forces were de-emphasized but recently released documents clearly show that Dulles still saw a role for conventional resistance as a deterrent to some limited contingencies, e.g. a wholly East German attack on the Federal Republic. Nevertheless American, and after 1957 NATO forces became highly dependent on nuclear weapons at all levels both for the "shield" to keep back Soviet armies on the battlefield and for the "sword" that would destroy the Soviet heartland itself. Massive Retaliation was a reflection of frustration with the Korean War and the economic problems created by the attempt at large-scale rearmament in the early 1950s. The British played a significant role in formulating the idea and were always willing to go further in emphasizing the "tripwire" nature of the strategy than the Americans. Massive Retaliation was undermined by the Soviet acquisition of missile capabilities that could strike directly at the USA. The Kennedy administration abandoned the concept in 1961, but NATO clung on until the end of 1967 when agreement was reached to replace it with Flexible Response. *EJG.*

Mast, Gen Charles-Emmanuel (1889–1977). Fr. COS XIX Corps in Algiers; organized anti-Vichy factions to assist Allied landings in French North Africa, November 1942.

Mata Hari. Stage name of Marguerite Gertrud MacLeod, *née* Zelle (1876–1917), Dutchwoman who became dancer and courtesan. Recruited by German intelligence 1916; arrested by French, before she had done much; shot. *MF.*

Matapan, Battle of (March 28 1941). The Germans having asked the Italian Navy to strike against British troop convoys to Greece, a cruiser force covered by the battleship *Vittorio Veneto* and commanded by Adm Iachino was sent to sweep south of Crete. British signals intelligence revealed this move and Adm Cunningham with the battleships *Warspite, Valiant, Barham* and the carrier *Formidable* moved to intercept. Adm Pridham-Wippell with four cruisers was already in the area, and he was the first to make contact. Out-ranged by the heavier guns of the Italian cruisers, as well as the battleship, he withdrew at speed. After a fruitless chase, Iachino decided he was getting too close to British air bases and started for home. *Formidable* launched a number of air strikes, one of which obtained a torpedo hit which reduced *Vittorio Veneto*'s speed, while the last of the day immobilized the cruiser *Pola*. Iachino, not realizing how close Cunningham now was, left two other cruisers in support. That night Cunningham's light forces, which he had sent on ahead to make torpedo attacks (his battleships were old and not very fast), failed to make contact with the fleeing Iachino. But thanks to radar (which the Italians did not have) he obtained total surprise with his battleships, sinking the *Zara* and *Fiume* at point-blank range. *Pola* was also sunk. This victory removed any danger of Italian naval interference in the evacuations from Greece and Crete, at the expense of one plane lost. *DJL.*

Matilda. British "Infantry" tank Mk II. Introduced 1939. Served in France 1940 and Libya 1940-42. *See also* TANKS.

Mau Mau rebellion (1952–60). From around 1948, resentment among native Africans regarding the possession of prosperous farms in Kenya's "White Highlands", the prime agricultural area north of Nairobi, by European settlers, found expression through the "secret society" called Mau Mau. Drawing most of its members from the dominant Kikuyu tribe, Mau Mau enforced solidarity with primitive and obscene "oathing" rituals and, from strongholds in the forests of the Aberdare Mountains and Mount Kenya, launched

Kikuyu auxiliaries hunt down Mau Mau

a guerrilla campaign against the settlers and their employees.

On October 20 1952, the Governor of Kenya, Sir Evelyn Baring, declared a state of emergency. British troops strengthened the existing security forces; some 180 suspected Mau Mau leaders, including the Kikuyu leader and later Kenyan Premier and President Jomo Kenyatta (1897–1978), were arrested; a "Home Guard" was raised from loyal Kikuyu. Nevertheless, the Mau Mau campaign escalated, the most serious incidents occurring on March 26 1953, when Mau Mau gangs sacked a police post at Naivasha and massacred *c*80 Kikuyu at Lari.

In May 1953, Gen Sir George Erskine took command of all security forces, amounting, at maximum, to *c*10,000 troops (five British and six African battalions) with air and artillery support, 21,000 police and 25,000 Kikuyu Home Guards. Mau Mau was estimated to have up to 15,000 warriors – with few conventional arms – and some 30,000 "passive" supporters. To destroy their urban support, Erskine in April 1954 launched Operation "Anvil": the African area of Nairobi was surrounded by troops and police moved in to "screen" suspects: of *c*30,000 Africans questioned, *c*16,500 were detained. Alleged brutality in the "concentration camps" for detainees (*c*50,000 in 1952–60) caused controversy.

Conventional military operations against Mau Mau's mountain strongholds dispersed but failed to extirpate them. In 1955, Erskine's successor, Lt Gen Gerald Lathbury, expanded the use of "pseudo-gangs": loyal Africans, including ex-Mau Mau, led by British officers and NCOs, who posed as insurgents in order to locate and ambush the Mau Mau bands. These operations, with which Gen Sir Frank (then Maj) Kitson is particularly associated, were successful. Following the killing of Mau Mau's "Field Marshal" Dedan Kimathi in October 1956, army units were withdrawn, although the emergency remained in force until January 1960.

Operations in 1952–60 cost the British and Kenyan governments an estimated £55,000,000. Some 10,500 Mau Mau were killed; the security forces had 600 killed (including 63 Europeans) and 579 wounded; the British army lost 12 killed and 69 wounded; civilian casualties were 1,888 killed (32 Europeans) and 980 wounded (26 Europeans). *RO'N.*

Maunoury, Marshal Michel (1847–1923). Fr. Commander of the newly-formed French Sixth Army in September 1914. It was Maunoury's pressure against the exposed German right flank east of Paris, between September 5 and 7, that threw the German advance off balance and facilitated the Allied victory on the Marne.

Maurice Farman S7 Longhorn (French, WWI). Two-seat reconnaissance/trainer. Prototype flew 1911; in French military service 1912; with RFC from August 1912. By outbreak of war was used almost exclusively as trainer, but RFC in France had a few late 1914, one or two in Mesopotamia 1915. Produced in England for RFC and RNAS, and widely used as elementary trainer. One 80hp Renault or 75hp Rolls-Royce Hawk engine; max. speed 65mph (104kph); no formal armament.

Maurice Farman S11 Shorthorn (French, WWI). Two-seat reconnaissance/trainer. Prototype flew 1913; type into French service 1913; first delivery to RFC March 1914. Operational with RFC France until November 1915, later in Mesopotamia. Produced in Britain and Italy (as Fiat 5B) in large numbers and several variants. As trainer in RFC and RAF served on well into 1918. One 80hp Renault/100hp Fiat A-10 engine; max. speed 72mph (115kph); one 0.303in machine gun, or rifles/pistols.

Max of Baden, Prince (1867–1929). Ger. The heir presumptive to the Grand Duchy of Baden, Prince Max, a known advocate of peace, became Imperial German Chancellor on October 3 1918. With Hindenburg and Ludendorff already favouring an armistice, it fell to Prince Max to try to negotiate an honourable peace for Germany. He resigned after announcing the abdication. *PJS.*

Me 323 "Gigant" *see* GLIDERS.

Médenine, Battle of (March 6 1943). After routing the Americans at Kasserine, Rommel rushed back southwards to check Montgomery's advance into Tunisia. The latter, warned by Allied intelligence, immediately reinforced his advanced troops at Médenine, held by XXX Corps (Leese) with 7th Armoured and the New Zealand Divisions. Rommel tried to envelop the British position by moving through the hills on the desert flank and attacking from the west. Montgomery stood fast and allowed the Afrika Korps with 10th, 15th and 21st Panzer and 90th Light Divisions to run into his concealed tanks and anti-tank guns. Rommel withdrew after serious tank losses. It was his last battle in Africa. *WGFJ.*

Mediterranean campaigns (1939–45). Mussolini ordered "offensive at all points" when he declared war on Britain and France on June 10 1940.

The Italians invaded the Sudan and Kenya in July, British Somaliland in August, Egypt in September and Greece in October. Their only success was in British Somaliland, which was evacuated by British troops on August 19 1940. Early in 1941, British counteroffensives led to the destruction of the Italian forces in Cyrenaica, Ethiopia, Eritrea and Somaliland; and the Greeks brought the Italian invasion of their country to an ignominious halt.

Hitler decided that he must aid his ally in order to secure his southern flank before he attacked Russia. The German invasion of Yugoslavia and Greece in April 1941 drew British forces from Egypt in a vain attempt to help the Greeks, enabling Rommel's Afrika Korps, which landed at Tripoli in February 1941, to drive the British out of Cyrenaica except for Tobruk, to which Rommel laid siege. British forces were further dissipated in defeating the Rashid Ali rebellion in Iraq (April) and the Vichy French in Syria (June–July).

While Hitler was fully engaged in Russia during the summer and autumn of 1941, the British attempted to relieve Tobruk and finally succeeded in December. Rommel withdrew to Tripolitania to await reinforcements.

Hitler's plan for 1942 envisaged seizing the whole of the Middle East with a grandiose pincer movement, his forces in southern Russia thrusting through the Caucasus from the north, while Rommel advanced on the Suez Canal from the West. In June 1942 Rommel defeated the British at Gazala and drove them back to El Alamein, but Hitler's thrust through the Caucasus failed.

By autumn 1942, America's entry into the war had enabled the Allies to take the offensive: Rommel was defeated by Montgomery at El Alamein in October and driven back to Tunisia; the Allied landings in French North Africa, November 1942 led to the surrender of all Axis forces in Tunisia, May 1943.

Allied strategy was to attack "the soft under-belly of Europe" as a means of drawing Axis forces southwards and away from the invasion beaches of Northwest Europe. The invasions of Sicily and Italy led to the collapse of Mussolini's Italy in September 1943, and the bitter fighting at Cassino and Anzio forced Hitler to feed the Italian front with many of his best divisions. Rome fell to Alexander's Allied Armies in Italy on June 4 1944, two days before the Normandy landings.

Thereafter it was Alexander's task to hold as many German divisions in Italy as possible. He hoped to break into the Po Valley and to advance on Vienna in the summer of 1944, but the Americans insisted on diverting almost one-third of his forces to the landings in Southern France. His troops were stalled for the winter in the Northern Apennines, but destroyed their opponents in the final battles south of the Po in May 1945. *WGFJ.*

M

Mediterranean Expeditionary Force. Formed consequent to the British decision in March 1915 to land troops on the Gallipoli Peninsula. It landed in April and was finally evacuated in December. The remaining elements were amalgamated with forces in Egypt in March 1916 and renamed the Egyptian Expeditionary Force.

Mediterranean, the war in the air (June 1940–May 1945). Until Allied strategic bombers were established on the Foggia airfields in Italy in the autumn of 1943 and could therefore reach targets in Germany and central Europe, air operations in the Mediterranean were essentially tactical, in support of the war at sea and on land. Mediterranean air commanders on both sides did not have first call on national air resources, and could only fight for local air superiority with what was available at the time. From 1940 until the end of 1942, when the Allies landed in French North Africa, the Axis were able to reinforce more quickly across the Mediterranean than the British, who had to ship aircraft to Takoradi on the Gold Coast and fly them across Africa to Egypt, or fly them off carriers in the Western Mediterranean.

Until the beginning of 1941, neither the RAF Middle East (Longmore) nor the Italian Air Force (Pricolo) had the power decisively to influence naval or land operations, with the notable exception of the Fleet Air Arm's raid on Taranto, November 1940, which crippled half the Italian battle fleet. The situation changed radically in January 1941 when Hitler decided to intervene in the Mediterranean. Thereafter there were three major phases in the air war. The first (January 1941– October 1942) was a period of Axis air superiority. The arrival of *Fliegerkorps X* (Geisler) in Sicily in January 1941 jeopardized British naval operations in the central Mediterranean and brought Malta under siege. The deployment of *Luftflotte 4* (Löhr) in March 1941 with *Fliegerkorps VIII*, *X* and *XI* for the invasion of Greece and the capture of Crete gave the Luftwaffe domination of the Eastern Mediterranean as well. When *Luftflotte 4* departed for the invasion of Russia in June 1941, *Fliegerkorps*

X was left to dispute the passage of British convoys through the Mediterranean from airfields in Sicily and the Greek islands, and to support Rommel's Afrika Korps in the Western Desert with a detachment under *Fliegerführer Afrika* (Fröhlich).

Fröhlich's resources were modest because Africa in 1941 had little strategic importance to Hitler. Its priority increased in late 1941 with the dispatch of *Luftflotte 2* (Kesselring) from Russia with *Fliegerkorps II* (Loerzer) during the winter lull to support Rommel's offensive towards the Suez Canal and the capture of Malta in 1942. The demands of the Russian front in the summer and autumn reduced Kesselring's resources and enabled RAF Middle East (Tedder) to maintain a tolerable air situation in the Western Desert, although not at sea where convoys had to be fought through to Malta at high cost.

In the second phase (October 1942–February 1944), the flow of American air reinforcements to the UK and Egypt, and the attrition of German air resources in Russia, turned the tide in the Allies' favour. The Western Desert Air Force (Coningham) contributed to Montgomery's victory at El Alamein in October 1942 both through direct air support to Eighth Army, and by the sinking of Rommel's supply ships. The Allied landings in French North Africa further reduced the Luftwaffe's numerical and reinforcement advantages, but Allied air superiority could never be taken for granted and still had to be fought for in all the Allies' offensive operations in the Tunisian and Sicilian campaigns, and until spring 1944, in the Italian campaign. The critical factor in the amphibious landings in Sicily, at Salerno and at Anzio was the Allies' success in providing air cover over the beaches.

During the final phase (March 1944–May 1945), Allied air supremacy was firmly established. By the spring of 1944, the Luftwaffe had been forced onto the defensive by the Combined Bomber Offensive against Germany, to which the Mediterranean Allied Strategic Air Force (Twinning) contributed from its bases in Italy, and by preparatory air operations

for Operation "Overlord" in Northwest Europe. The tasks of the Mediterranean Allied Air Forces (Eaker) were threefold: first to convert air superiority into air supremacy; second to disrupt Army Group C's communications and supply; and third to support land operations, using, when conditions were favourable, massed bomber effort against fortified lines. Specific air operations of note were:

1) the bombing of the monastery of Monte Cassino and Cassino town, February and March 1944.
2) the disruption of the Italian railway system before the "Diadem" offensive (March 19–31 1944).
3) the successful destruction of all bridges over the Po river (July 12–27 1944).
4) assistance to Fifth Army in breaching the Gothic Line (September 9–11 1944).
5) assistance to Fifth Army attacking the Bologna defences (October 12 1944).
6) destruction of electric power supplies to the Brenner Pass railway (November 6 1944). *WGFJ*.

Mediterranean, the war at sea (June 1939–November 1943). The British and Italian navies had a common task: ensuring the safe passage of reinforcements and supplies across the Mediterranean. Malta lay at the crossroads of their lines of communication. The island was an important strategic asset to the British as an advanced base from which light naval forces and submarines could attack Axis shipping; but it was also a liability in that it was isolated and vulnerable to air attack and invasion from Sicily. The constant need to fly in fighter reinforcements and to fight through supply convoys to the island proved a major drain.

The Italians had three major advantages: their geographic position, dominating the Central Mediterranean Basin; air superiority with air bases in Sardinia, Sicily, and, later, on the Greek islands; and faster, although less heavily armed and armoured, warships that could use their speed to escape engagement if the odds were unfavourable.

With the loss of French naval support in June 1940, the British had to reinforce Adm Cunningham's Mediterranean Fleet, based

M

at Alexandria, to control the Eastern Basin and the Aegean Sea; and to assemble a new force at Gibraltar – Adm Somerville's Force H – to control the Western Basin. The war at sea was largely shaped by the air situation and, in particular, by the priorities accorded by Hitler to Luftwaffe operations in the Mediterranean. There were five main phases.

In June–December 1940, the British won naval superiority over the Italians in several actions after destroying the French fleet on July 3. On November 11, at Taranto, the Fleet Air Arm attacked the Italian battle fleet in harbour, putting half of it out of action for many months.

The second phase (January to May 1941) saw the first intervention by the Luftwaffe. *Fliegerkorps X* (Gen Geisler), which specialized in anti-shipping operations, was sent from Norway to Sicily in January for operations with the Italian Navy; and in April *Luftflotte 4* (Löhr) arrived in the Balkans to support the German invasion of Yugoslavia and Greece. On January 10, the Luftwaffe divebombed and badly damaged the carrier *Illustrious.* She became the target of intense attacks in the Malta dockyard until she slipped away to Alexandria, January 23.

On February 9, Force H bombarded and badly damaged Genoa. On March 28, the two battle fleets met southwest of Crete at Matapan. The Italians lost three heavy cruisers and two large destroyers. There followed the British bombardment of Tripoli (April 21) to reduce supplies to Rommel, the evacuation of 50,000 men from

At action stations in the Mediterranean

Greece (April 24–May 1) at the cost of two destroyers and four transports, and the successful passage of the "Tiger" Convoy (May 2–18) with urgently needed tanks for the Western Desert. May 20–June 1 saw the defence and evacuation of Crete at the heavy price of nine warships sunk and seventeen damaged in air attacks.

During the third phase (July to December 1941), *Luftflotte 4* was withdrawn for the invasion of Russia, but German submarines entered the Mediterranean in September. An Italian human torpedo attack on September 20 in the Bay of Gibraltar, sank one merchant ship and damaged two others. On November 8, Force K destroyed the Tripoli bound "Duisburg" convoy. November 13 and 25 saw the loss of *Ark Royal* and *Barham* to *U-81* and *U-331*. This was followed by the sinking off Cape Bon on December 12, of two Italian cruisers. The First Battle of Sirte (December 16–18) led to Force K sustaining heavy losses in a minefield off Tripoli. On December 18–19, another Italian human torpedo attack, at Alexandria, crippled the battleships *Valiant* and *Queen Elizabeth.*

The fourth phase (January to October 1942) saw the second intervention by the Luftwaffe; the withdrawal of British capital ships to meet the Japanese threat in the Indian Ocean; the British loss of forward airfields in the Western Desert from which air cover could be provided in the Eastern Basin; and Axis attempts to dominate the Central Basin to keep Rommel supplied.

Intense bombing of Malta was resumed by the Luftwaffe on March 1. The Second Battle of Sirte (March 22) followed, fought to protect the passage of the "March" convoy from Alexandria to Malta. October 11–29 saw the launching of the last Axis blitz to help protect fuel shipments to Rommel before the Battle of El Alamein. And, from June 12–December 5, five convoys fought their way through to Malta. The island was at last relieved.

For the last phase (December 1942), Montgomery's advance to Tripoli, and the Allied landings in North Africa cleared the southern Mediterranean of Axis ports and air bases. The war at sea, thereafter, became an integral part of Allied operations aimed at Europe's "soft underbelly". *WGFJ*.

Medium Range Ballistic Missile (MRBM). A land-based ballistic missile with a range of about 600-1,500 miles (1,000-2,500km). The Soviet Union deployed large numbers of MRBMs, first SS-3s and then SS-4s covering Eurasian targets from the late 1950s to the late 1980s when the last sites were dismantled under the INF Treaty.

Megaton. An explosive yield equivalent to a million tons of TNT, normally only attainable by thermonuclear weapons. The largest operational American bomb is a 9 megaton weapon but Soviet bombs up to 25 megatons have been reported. The USSR has tested a 57 megaton device.

Megiddo, Battle of *see* DAMASCUS CAMPAIGN (1918).

Meiktila-Mandalay campaign (1945) *see* BURMA CAMPAIGN (1941–45).

Mekong river. From its source in Tibet, the Mekong river flows 2,800 miles (4,500km) through China, Burma, Laos, Thailand, Cambodia and Vietnam to the South China Sea. Its delta totalling 26,000 sq miles (67,340 sq km) in area is the rice basket and population centre of southern Vietnam. During the Vietnam War, the Army of the Republic of Vietnam (ARVN) IV Corps embraced the delta, as did the communists' military regions 8 and 9. The U Minh Forest, a mangrove swamp in the southwest, had been a communist base area since the war against France.

Menéndez, Brig Gen Mario (b.1930). Argentinian. Military governor and C-in-C of Falklands from April 3 1982 until his surrender on June 14.

Menin Gate. The present Menin Gate at Ypres in Belgium was designed by Sir Reginald Blomfield and unveiled in 1927. It bears the names of 54,896 men who fell in the Ypres Salient between 1914 and August 15 1917, but who have no known grave. The Last Post is still sounded here every evening.

Menin Road. As the main axis of advance for both sides in the Ypres

M

Salient, the road running in a southeasterly direction from Ypres through Gheluvelt to Menin figured prominently in most of the major operations in Flanders during World War I. In the Battle of the Menin Road Ridge from September 20–25 1917 – part of the British offensive at Ypres – Plumer's Second Army secured much of the vital Gheluvelt plateau, although Gheluvelt itself remained in German hands until taken by British II Corps in September 1918. Earlier, in April 1918, the Germans had reached Hell Fire Corner on the Menin Road, the closest they came to Ypres that year. *PJS.*

"Menu" operations. At the behest of the American Command in Vietnam, which had long wished to attack the Cambodian sanctuaries of Vietnamese communist forces, President Nixon approved bombing operations, collectively known as "Menu" to begin March 18, 1969, which eventually struck 13 out of the communists' 15 base areas in Cambodia. Though tacitly approved by Sihanouk they were kept secret. "Menu's" disclosure by the *New York Times* in May 1970 provoked the effort to plug leaks that led to the Watergate scandal. When US and South Vietnamese forces attacked the sanctuaries on the ground that same month, "Menu" was renamed "Freedom Deal" and expanded to other targets. The US Congress ended the bombing by cutting off funds, effective Agusut 15 1973, by which time US planes had dropped 383,851 tons of bombs on Cambodia. *WST.*

Menzies, Sir Robert Gordon (1894–1978). Australian Prime Minister 1939–41 and 1949–66. He involved Australia in the Korean and Vietnamese wars and attempted to assist Britain's position in the Suez Crisis by leading a delegation to Nasser.

Menzies, Maj Gen Sir Stewart Graham (1890–1968). Br. Fought at First Ypres; on GHQ intelligence staff 1915–18; as deputy head of MI6 responsible for Venlo incident, 1939; as head of MI6, 1939–53, took responsibility for Bletchley Park's results; dismissed after Maclean's defection.

Merkava. Israeli Main Battle Tank. Introduced 1978. *See also* TANKS.

Merrill, Maj Gen Frank (1903–55). US. Assistant Military Attaché to Japan 1938–41; following America's entry into the war, joined Gen Stilwell's staff in Burma. In January 1944 he was given command of the recently formed 5307th Composite Unit (Provisional), soon known as "Merrill's Marauders". Emulating the Chindits, this specialist long-range penetration force embarked upon its first operation in February 1944. Merrill participated in three raids but twice had to be evacuated after suffering heart attacks. He subsequently served in various staff posts until his retirement in 1947. *MS.*

Mersa Matruh, Battle of (June 26–27 1942). Fought to gain time for the preparation of the El Alamein Line. X Corps (Holmes) from Syria with 10th Indian and 50th Divisions held the coastal sector, while XIII Corps (Gott) with 5th Indian, New Zealand and 1st Armoured Divisions covered the open desert flank. The Afrika Korps (Nehring) attacked and penetrated the centre of the British position during the night of June 26–27. Failing to re-establish his line during the 27th, Auchinleck, who had personally taken command of Eighth Army from Ritchie on June 25, continued the withdrawal to El Alamein. XIII Corps disengaged successfully, but due to poor communications X Corps was delayed and lost heavily breaking out from Matruh. *WGFJ.*

Mers-El-Kébir, bombardment of (July 3 1940). French naval base near Oran. With the fall of France, the British government feared a German takeover of the powerful French fleet. Adm Somerville was sent with *Hood*, *Resolution*, *Valiant*, *Ark Royal*, 2 cruisers and 11 destroyers to present Adm Gensoul at Mers-el-Kébir with the alternatives of joining him, going to the West Indies, or scuttling his ships. Failing acceptance of one of these within six hours, force would be used. Gensoul, understandably, proved difficult; initially refusing to speak to the envoy, he failed to

present the alternatives to scuttling to his Admiralty, and inevitably tragedy followed. The British mined the harbour entrance to prevent escape, and finally opened fire some time after the original ultimatum expired, on the news that the French were preparing to go to sea. *Bretagne* blew up, *Dunkerque* and *Provence* and several smaller ships were badly damaged; *Strasbourg* escaped. French loss of life was heavy. Controversy will continue about the handling of this incident, and the responsibility of Churchill, and the local commanders. Both sides were probably too inflexible, and not enough time was allowed by the ultimatum. *DJL.*

Mesopotamian campaign (1914–18). In August 1914 Britain had considerable interests in the oilfields at the head of the Persian Gulf. Secretary of State for India (Lord Crewe) foresaw the threat posed if Turkey was to join the war on the side of the Central Powers. Without consulting Kitchener, (Secretary of State for War), Crewe ordered the Viceroy of India to dispatch a division to Abadan. The resultant campaign was thus simultaneously managed from London and New Delhi. Britain and France declared war on Turkey on November 5 1914. British and Indian troops had already arrived at Bahrein and on November 22 captured Basra. Reinforced from India, the force, now a corps of two infantry divisions and a cavalry brigade, was placed under command of Gen Sir John Nixon, an Indian Army officer who directed Maj Gen Charles Townshend to advance up the Tigris whilst Maj Gen Gorringe's smaller force moved up the Euphrates. On June 3 1915, Townshend took Amara; Gorringe captured Nasiriya on July 25. Both columns were now extended on long lines of communication, depending largely on river boats for logistic support. Against stubborn Turkish resistance, Townshend took Kut on September 28, but instead of consolidating, he rushed impetuously towards Baghdad. On October 5 he reached El Aziziya, but then the river fell and his supply line began to collapse. After a bloody repulse at Ctesiphon (November 22) Townshend evacuated his sick and

M

wounded, then fell back on a strong defensive position in a loop of the Tigris at Kut. With two months' supplies, he was confident that he would be relieved, but the Turks, now led by the outstanding German Gen von der Goltz, fought off successive attempts by Aylmer and Gorringe to relieve Kut, where conditions became appalling.

Despite resupply by air – the first instance of this on any significant scale – Townshend was authorized by Kitchener to negotiate a surrender and the garrison of 10,000 marched into captivity on April 29 1916. The Turks' treatment of the British and Indian prisoners was abominable, and some 6,000 died in captivity.

In August 1916 Gen Sir Frederick Maude (1864–1917) was appointed as new British commander. He was allocated five divisions, four in two corps on the Tigris and one on the Euphrates; a total of 340,000 men of whom 160,000 were combat troops. His force comprised 107,000 Indian and 59,000 British soldiers. Against them were 42,000 Turks.

On December 13 1916, Maude's revitalized force advanced, recaptured Kut on February 25 1917 and moved on to the next Turkish line of defence behind the Diyala river, 10 miles (16km) from Baghdad. Backed by river gunboats, artillery and close air support, Maude entered Baghdad on March 11 as the Turks, now under the resolute Halil Pasha, retired further up river. Eight months later, Maude died of cholera. His victory was due to good man-management as much as sound logistics and availability of military resources. His successor, Lt Gen Sir William Marshall (1865–1939), immediately had to lose two of his best divisions to Palestine but in any case, with the collapse of Russia and the imminent fall of the Ottoman empire, the urgency had gone from the campaign. In October 1918, the Turks were ready to negotiate a separate peace.

British/Indian casualties in Mesopotamia amounted to over 92,500, of whom more than 19,000 were killed in battle or died of disease. Despite the greater glamour attached to the Palestine campaign, it was in Mesopotamia that the Turkish main armies were held down and defeated. *MH.*

Desert march in Mesopotamia, 1917

Messe, Marshal Giovanni (1883–1968). Italian. Led Italian contingent in Russia from 1941. Assumed command of First Italo-German Army (Panzerarmee Afrika, renamed on Rommel's departure) in southern Tunisia, March 20 1943. Defeated by Montgomery at Mareth and Wadi Akarit in March and April; surrendered on May 13 after the fall of Tunis.

Messerschmitt Bf 109 (German, WWII). Single-seat fighter. Prototype flew May 28 1935; first of pre-production series completed February 1937; 112 of first batch to Condor Legion March 1937. Production Bf 109Cs and 109Es followed and were very successful. By September 1 1939 Luftwaffe had 850 Bf 109Es and 235 Bf 109Ds. Development led to further subtypes, notably Bf 109F and 109G, widely and effectively used. Total German production about 30,500. Bf 109G-6 had one 1,800hp Daimler-Benz DB 605 AM engine; max. speed 386mph (621kph); one 30mm or 20mm cannon, two 13mm machine guns.

Messerschmitt Bf 110 (German, WWII). Strategic fighter/night fighter. Prototype flew May 12 1936; production deliveries from July 1938; by August 1939 Luftwaffe had accepted 159. Although unsuccessful in fighter-to-fighter combat, especially during Battle of Britain, Bf 110 proved effective as defensive fighter. Fighter-bomber and photographic-reconnaissance versions 1940; by 1944 night-fighter version still highly effective. Production, about 6,000. Bf 110G-4c had two 1,475hp Daimler-Benz DB 605B-1 engines; max. speed 342mph (550kph); two 30mm and two 20mm cannon, one 7.9mm machine gun.

Messerschmitt Me 262 (German, WWII). Interceptor fighter/fighter-bomber. First flight with jet engines July 18 1942. Hitler decreed that Me 262 be employed as bomber, but pre-production batch (March-April 1944) were fighters: bomber, ground-attack and photographic-reconnaissance versions followed. First operational fighter use September/October 1944; bomber unit established late 1944. Extensively used to end of war against Allied day-bombing formations. Production continued in Czechoslovakia after end of war. Total German production at least 1,380 (of which only a small proportion was operationally deployed). Two 1,980lb (900kg) s.t. Junkers Jumbo 109-004B-1 engines; max. speed 542mph (872kph); four 30mm cannon, up to 24 × 55mm R4M rockets.

Messerschmitt Me 410 (German, WWII). Heavy fighter/fighter-bomber developed from unsuccessful Me 210 twin-engined fighter (production of which was abandoned early in 1942). Prototype flew autumn 1942; Luftwaffe acceptance of production Me 410 began January 1943. Many used as defensive fighters against Allied bomber formations 1943–44; weapon installations varied; final production version (Me 410B-3) was photographic-reconnaissance fighter. Production (ceased September 1944), 1,160. Two 1,750hp Daimler-Benz DB 603A engines; max. speed 388 mph (624kph); four 20mm cannon, two 7.9mm and two 13mm machine guns.

Messervy, Gen Sir Frank Walter (1895–1974). Br. Commander 9th Infantry Brigade at Keren, Ethiopian campaign, 1941. Commander 4th Indian Division during the second and third offensives to relieve Tobruk in 1941, and Commander 7th Armoured Division in the Battle of Gazala in 1942. He returned to India to command 43rd Indian Armoured Division in 1943, and was Commander 7th Indian Division in the Arakan and at Kohima in 1944. Commander IV Corps during reconquest of Burma, 1944–45, and c-in-c Northern Command in India 1946–47, then c-in-c Pakistan Army after partition of India 1947–48.

M

Messina, crossings of the Straits of. From August 11–17 1943, XIV Panzer Corps (Hube) withdrew over the Straits with minimal loss despite Allied naval and air superiority, thanks to the concentrations of anti-aircraft guns under Col Baade, and of naval manned ferries under Capt von Liebenstein. On September 3 1943, XIII Corps (Dempsey) of Eighth Army (Montgomery) crossed the Straits, covered by a heavy naval and air bombardment. The landings were unopposed because LXXVI Panzer Corps (Herr) had been ordered to withdraw gradually from Calabria, using rearguards and demolitions to delay Montgomery's advance northwards. *WGFJ.*

Messines, Battle of (1917). The capture of the Messines-Wytschaete Ridge, south of Ypres, was regarded as a vital preliminary to the main British 1917 offensive in Flanders. This operation, intended to secure the flank of the subsequent advance against the Passchendaele-Staden Ridge, was entrusted to the Second Army, under Gen Sir Herbert Plumer. Of Plumer's three attacking corps, II Anzac Corps, on the right, was to capture the southern shoulder of Messines Ridge and Messines village itself, IX Corps was to seize the central sector and Wytschaete village, while X Corps was to secure the northern portion. The meticulous preparations included a systematic barrage and counter-battery programme and the completion of a number of huge mines, some of which had been started over a year before. At 0310 hours on June 7 1917, 19 of these mines – containing nearly 1,000,000lbs of high-explosive – were detonated, and nine infantry divisions went forward, supported by over 2,000 guns. Quickly overwhelming stunned German defenders, Second Army was established along the crest of the Ridge by 0900 hours, at relatively light cost compared with the usual standards of the Western Front. Casualties later increased, partly because of overcrowding on the Ridge and confusion in the II ANZAC Corps sector during the advance down the eastern slope between June 7 and 14. Nevertheless, in overall planning and execution, the Messines attack was a model of its kind. *PJS.*

Metaxas, Gen Joannis (1871–1941). Greek. Pro-German adviser to King Constantine during World War I; went into exile in 1917 but returned to Greece in 1936 to mount a coup that left him dictator. He led the successful resistance to the Italian invasion of October 1940.

Meteor, Gloster (Br, WWII and after). Single-seat fighter/two-seat night fighter. Prototype flew March 5 1943; first deliveries to No. 616 Squadron July 12 1944. Notably successful against V-1s from August 1944. Development through long line of variants. Meteor F8 operational Korean War with RAAF. Prototype NF11 night-fighter flew May 31 1950; Marks NF12-14 followed. Production, 3,545. Two 3,500/3,800lb (1,590/1,725kg) s.t. Rolls-Royce Derwent engines; max. speed 598mph (962kph); four 20mm cannon, up to 24 rockets or 4,000lb (1,800kg) bombs.

Methuen, Field Marshal Lord *see* BOER WAR.

Metz, Battle of (1944). Lying at the junction of the Moselle and Seille rivers, Metz controlled one of the major routes to the Rhine. It was surrounded by more than 20 forts which, although antiquated, still constituted a substantial defensive ring. In September 1944 Metz stood in the path of Gen Patton's Third US Army as it made its rapid advance to the Rhine. Plagued by fuel and ammunition shortages, the Americans' advance had slowed and although elements of 5th Infantry and 7th Armoured Divisions crossed the River Moselle on September 7, they were unable to enlarge their bridgeheads. The 14,000-strong German garrison of Metz put up a spirited fight from the old fortifications which offered good protection from artillery and air bombardment. Attempts by US XX Corps to breach the defences at the beginning of October met with little success and although elements of 5th Division managed to enter the key bastion of Fort Driant, a German counterattack forced them to retire on the 16th. On November 18, 5th, 90th and 95th Divisions completed an encirclement of Metz. German units trying to escape were cut off and, by the 20th, American units were in the outskirts of the city. On November 22 all resistance ceased in Metz but the fighting continued in the outlying forts and the last, Fort Jeanne d'Arc, did not capitulate until December 12. *MS.*

Meuse-Argonne offensive (1918). After the successful attack at St Mihiel on September 12 1918, some 400,000 American and French troops were swiftly transferred to the Meuse-Argonne region so that they could participate in the general Allied offensive scheduled to begin during the last week of September. This rapid movement of men and materiel owed much to the organizing ability of George C Marshall – future US COS and Secretary of State – then a colonel in US First Army's Operations Section. The Germans were taken by surprise when the joint offensive, involving the US First Army and French Fourth Army, opened on September 26 and the Americans advanced up to 3 miles (5km) on the first day. German resistance then became more stubborn, their formidable defences adding to the natural obstacles presented by the steep, densely-wooded country between the River Meuse and the Argonne Forest. Severe logistical problems in this terrain and the tactical inexperience of the American troops also hampered progress. Although the attacks were pressed with great courage, it took US First Army until November 1 to break through the last main German defence line. Once in the open the Americans cut the vital Lille-Metz rail link on November 3 and reached the outskirts of Sedan three days later, although the honour of entering Sedan itself was left to the French. In 47 days of hard fighting the Americans suffered some 117,000 casualties. *PJS.*

Mexican punitive expedition (1916–17). Angered by US support for President Venustiano Carranza (1859–1920), the Mexican bandit-revolutionary Francisco ("Pancho") Villa (1877–1923) led some 500 riders across the Mexican-US border to raid Columbus, New Mexico, March 8-9 1916, clashing with 13th US Cavalry Regiment (24 US military and civilian casualties; *c*100 Villista casualties). On March 15, Maj Gen Pershing was appointed to head a US Army punitive expedition (*c*6,000 cavalry, with artillery support and reconnaissance aircraft) against Villa. Penetrating some 400 miles (640km) into Mexico, Pershing's columns dispersed Villa's guerrilla army but failed to capture him. Increasing Mexican resentment of the incursion and clashes with Carranza's regular army – notably at Carrizal, June 21 (US: 12 dead, 33 prisoners; 33 Mexican casualties) – contributed to US withdrawal on February 5 1917. *RO'N*.

Meyer, Gen John C (1919–75). US. Fighter pilot credited with 24 aerial combat victories while flying with the 352nd Fighter Group in the European Theatre of Operations, 1943–45. He also destroyed two MiG-15s in Korea. Later reached rank of General and served as USAAF's Vice COS.

MI5, MI6, MI9. British security, intelligence and escape services. *See also* MILITARY INTELLIGENCE ORGANIZATIONS.

MICV (Mechanized Infantry Combat Vehicle). An armoured vehicle from which infantry can fight rather than a mere armoured personnel carrier (APC) or "battle taxi" that transports infantry to dismount and fight on foot. The Germans pioneered the concept with armoured half tracks in World War II, and postwar the Soviet Union has developed it furthest with the BMP series. This has led to Western MICVs, notably the West German Marder and the American M2 Bradley, which are equipped with both vehicle-mounted weapons (20–25mm guns and anti-tank missiles) and fire ports for the infantry to use their own small arms on the move. The British decided to produce an armed APC rather than a true MICV in their new Warrior vehicle. This is intended to give fire support to dismounted troops. *EJG*.

Middle East campaign (1916–18). By 1916 the primary British objectives of safeguarding the Suez Canal and the Arabian Gulf against Turkey had been achieved. In Egypt Gen Murray drove the Turks back across the Sinai, re-

pulsing a counterattack at Romani on August 3. In Mesopotamia though, the Turks' siege of Kut-al-Amara remained unbroken and, on April 29, Gen Townshend was obliged to surrender. It was not until the end of the year that a fresh offensive was launched under Gen Maude. On December 13 Anglo-Indian forces began their advance up the River Tigris. Kut was recaptured on February 23 1917 and Baghdad fell on March 11. The summer brought a temporary halt to Maude's offensive but soon after its resumption in September he threatened to seize control of the Mosul oilfields. However, with the general's death on November 18 the campaign's impetus was lost.

In Palestine, Murray suffered two reverses against Gaza, on March 26 and April 17–19. He was replaced by Allenby, who brought about a British revival. On October 31 British forces won the Third Battle of Gaza and pressing north, took Jerusalem on December 9.

In autumn 1918, the British made their final push for victory in Palestine and Mesopotamia. On September 18 Allenby smashed two Turkish armies at Megiddo and advanced rapidly to Aleppo and the borders of Turkish Anatolia. Meanwhile, on October 23 British forces in Mesopotamia moved to seize control of the Mosul oilfields before the impending Turkish collapse. Lt Gen Cobbe failed to secure these objectives before the signing of the Armistice with Turkey on October 30 but pressed on to occupy Mosul on November 14. *MS*.

Midway, Battle of (June 3–6, 1942). In June 1942, the major elements of the Japanese navy, including four fleet carriers, advanced against the Midway Island group, which served as an outpost for the defence of Hawaii, with the objective of drawing out and destroying the main American carrier forces. The Japanese armada was divided into three parts, and substantial other naval forces, in addition, were dispatched north to the Aleutians to act as a diversion. Overall command of the operation was exercised by Adm Yamamoto, while the carrier strike force was led by Vice Adm Nagumo. Adm Nimitz, commander US Pacific Fleet, deployed his forces on the basis of detailed knowledge of the Japanese plans provided by "Magic" and other intelligence. The Midway garrison was reinforced, and three fleet carriers under Rear Adm Spruance were sent to intercept the Japanese fleet. Only a small force was detached to the Aleutians.

The Japanese transport force was discovered and attacked ineffectually by aircraft from Midway on June 3. On June 4, Japanese aircraft heavily bombed shore installations and suffered only light losses, while half of Midway's strike aircraft were shot down in unsuccessful attempts to inflict damage on the Japanese carriers; American carrier-based torpedo-bombers were practically annihilated in attacks against the Japanese carriers, which failed completely, but American dive-bombers struck three Japanese carriers (*Akagi, Kaga,* and *Soryu*)

Midway, June 1942: Japan's unfortunate attempt to provoke a "decisive battle"

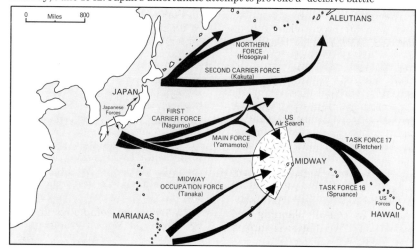

M

while their decks were filled with fuelled and armed aircraft. This resulted in catastrophic explosions and fires; and although the surviving carrier *Hiryu* launched strikes that heavily damaged the carrier *Yorktown*, she was smashed in turn by aircraft from carriers *Hornet* and *Enterprise*. By the morning of June 5, all four Japanese carriers had been abandoned and sunk, and a retreat ordered by Yamamoto. On June 6, American carrier dive-bombers sank one Japanese heavy cruiser and severely mauled another. American attempts to salvage *Yorktown* failed on June 7, when the Japanese submarine *I–168* torpedoed the carrier and an accompanying destroyer, sinking both.

In spite of enjoying what should have been an overwhelming superiority in numbers, the Japanese effort was compromised by faulty strategy, poor intelligence, tactical error, and misfortune on the one hand and the excellence of American intelligence, naval air organization, tactical command, and luck on the other. Japan's heavy losses equalized the naval balance of power in the Pacific. *JTS.*

MiG 15/15bis, "Fagot" (USSR, post-WWII). Single-seat high-altitude interceptor fighter. Prototype flew December 30 1947; deliveries began 1948, with production extended to Czechoslovakia and Poland. Extensive use, flown by Chinese pilots in Korean War. Several thousands built; in production until late 1951. One 5,005lb (2,270kg) s.t. Klimov RD-45F/5,952lb (2,700kg) s.t. Klimov VK-1 engine; max. speed 692mph (1,114kph); two 23mm and one 37mm cannon.

MiG-17 "Fresco" (USSR). Single-seat fighter. Prototype flew January 13 1950; early production aircraft entered service late 1952. MiG-17F with more powerful engine produced from 1953, together with MiG-17PF all-weather fighter; these produced in Poland (as LIM-5 and LIM-5M) and China (as Jian-5 and Jian-5A); several thousands built. MiG-17F had one 7,452lb (3,380kg) s.t. Klimov VK-1F engine; max. speed 711mph (1,144kph); one 37mm and two 23mm cannon (MiG-17PFU, four K-5 beam-riding missiles).

MiG-21 "Fishbed" (USSR). Single-seat interceptor fighter. Prototype (Ye-6) flew late 1957; production as MiG-21 began 1958; improved development MiG-21F entered service late 1959. Licence-built Czechoslovakia; copy manufactured China as Jian-7 (with developments Jian-7B and 7C). Supplied to most Russian satellite countries and to Cuba, Egypt, Finland, India, Indonesia, Iraq. Developed through several sub-types to MiG-21bis "Fishbed-N" with 19,840lb (9,000kg) s.t. R-25 engine. MiG-21F had one 12,675lb (5,750kg) s.t. Tumansky R-11F-300 engine; max. speed 1,320mph (2,124kph); one 30mm cannon, two K-13 missiles.

MiG Alley. The area of most intense enemy air activity during the Korean War. It ran in a curve from the Chinese border at the Suiho reservoir in the east over Huichon to end on the Korean coast at Sinanju in the west. It first emerged at the end of 1950 when MiGs based across the Yalu in Manchuria challenged UN control of the air. Normal counter-air attacks on this airfield complex were ruled out for fear of expanding the war and causing unacceptable attrition to UN air power. Instead the MiG threat was contained by two wings of Sabres which flew patrols in the alley to prevent interference with interdiction operations. *CM.*

"MiG" Operation. Mounted in July 1951 during the Korean War. Its objective was to seize a MiG which had crashed on a coastal sandbar in northwest Korea and return it to the US for intelligence evaluation. The aircraft was successfully raised by a US naval task force.

Mihailovich, Gen Draza (1893–1946). Yugoslavian. A staff officer in the Yugoslavian Army at the time of the German invasion of 1941. Formed a Serbian-based guerrilla organization, the Chetniks, largely made up of elements from the old royalist army. He was initially supported by the Allies and in June 1942 was appointed war minister by the Yugoslavian government in exile. However, his opposition to the Germans was matched by his anti-communism

and his Chetniks frequently clashed with Tito's partisans. Pursuing this internecine conflict led to cooperation with the German and Italian occupying forces and he thereby alienated himself from the Allies. In May 1944 Britain withdrew support for Mihailovich and gave Tito full backing. Following the partisans' victory, Mihailovich went into hiding but was captured in March 1946. He was subsequently executed for having collaborated with the enemy. *MS.*

Milan missile. A Franco-German wire-guided anti-tank missile. The system automatically commands the missile to fly down the operator's line of sight tracking the missile by infra-red means. Milan, widely exported, is also produced in India, Italy and the UK. It has been used with success against the Libyans in Chad, in the Falklands (against strongpoints) and by Iran and Iraq in the Gulf War. A larger, more powerful Milan 2 is under development.

Milch: major architect of the Luftwaffe

Milch, Field Marshal Erhard (1892–1972). Ger. Transferred from the artillery to train as an aircraft observer, July 1915, Milch, although not a pilot, commanded a fighter squadron, October 1918. After commanding a police air squadron, 1919–21, he began a successful career in civil aviation with Junkers and by 1929 was chief executive of the German national airline, *Deutsche Lufthansa*. A close associate of Göring, he became State Secretary, Reich Air Ministry, when the Nazis came to power in 1933.

Although Göring was its figurehead, Milch was the true architect of the Luftwaffe, his knowledge of the civil aircraft industry proving invaluable in its rapid expansion.

In 1939 he took his only operational command, successfully leading *Luftflotte 5* in Norway. He was promoted Field Marshal in 1940, and, following Udet's suicide in 1941, became Director of Air Armament. Production and maintenance much improved under his control, but he became increasingly estranged from Göring, who refused to credit his realistic estimates of Allied aircraft production and failed to support him in controversy with Hitler over new aircraft types (notably the Messeschmitt Me 262 jet). He was sentenced to life imprisonment at Nuremberg but released in 1955. *MS.*

Milford Haven, Adm of the Fleet Lord (1843–1921). Br. As Prince Louis of Battenberg, he was First Sea Lord on the outbreak of war in 1914. Due to his decision, taken in the absence of the First Lord (Churchill), the Fleet was ready for action when war was declared. Prejudice against him due to his German birth led to his resignation soon afterwards. His second son became Adm of the Fleet Lord Mountbatten of Burma.

Military Armistice Commission. Established "to supervise the implementation" of the armistice agreement which ended the Korean War. It was to be composed of five senior officers from either side and to meet "in the vicinity of Panmunjom". Ten joint observer teams were to be established to assist the commission in supervising the provisions of the armistice "pertaining to the Demilitarized Zone and to the Han River Estuary". Outside this area, the Military Armistice Commission could call upon the Neutral Nations Supervisory Commission to investigate violations. It could also "make recommendations to the Commanders of the opposing sides with respect to amendments or additions" to the armistice agreement. The Military Armistice Commission has continued to meet at Panmunjom but in an atmosphere of mutual hostility and there have been many unresolved incidents in the Demilitarized Zone. *CM.*

Military Assistance Command, Vietnam (MACV). Established in Saigon on February 8 1962 to provide a joint headquarters for the growing American advisory and support presence authorized by President Kennedy. In May 1964 it absorbed Military Assistance Advisory Group (MAAG), which had operated in Vietnam since 1950. A "subordinate unified command" reporting to C-in-C, Pacific (CINCPAC), MACV combined the functions of a field army headquarters, an advisory mission to the South Vietnamese government, and a military assistance team to the Army of the Republic of Vietnam (ARVN). Its commanders were Gen Paul D Harkins (February 1962-June 1964), Gen William Westmoreland (June 1964-July 1968), Gen Creighton Abrams (July 1968-June 1972), and Gen Frederick Weyand (June 1972-March 1973). MACV formally departed Vietnam on March 29 1973. *WST.*

Military intelligence organizations. Security services are of long standing. Fouché and Metternich elaborated those of France and Austria early in the 19th century. So are decipher staffs, established by most European powers before 1900; likewise staffs to collect intelligence about warmaking capabilities. These collectors need to know the size, location and capacities of the navies, armies, air and missile forces, fixed defences, and armament industries of actual and potential enemies. To know an enemy's order of battle is the ambition of every intelligence officer, for from it much can be deduced.

Every combatant unit and formation includes an intelligence element, varying from a junior officer and a few other ranks at battalion level to a score or more officers, with clerks and draughtsmen to support them, at GHQ. Service directorates of intelligence arrange for their training and keep them supplied with data about enemy forces and equipment. Good commanders take care to consult their intelligence officers in good time, but not to be commanded by them. *MF.*

Military Service Acts (1916-18). In 1914 the British Army was manned by volunteers; Kitchener's appeal for more men to furnish the "New Armies" was answered by hundreds of thousands. By mid-1915, however, increasing political pressures led Asquith's government to pass the first Military Service Act (Jan 1916), calling up all unmarried men in age groups 18-41, and setting up tribunals to vet applications for exemption by "conscientious objectors". In May, a second Act extended conscription to married men; the third Act, in 1918, raised the upper age limit to 50. Conscription probably destroyed the old Liberal Party; it exposed one-third of the adult male population to military service and, by driving women into war work, was instrumental in their enfranchisement. *MH.*

Milne, Field Marshal Lord (1866–1948). Br. A gunner since 1885, Milne commanded the artillery of the 4th Division in France and Flanders in 1914 and was appointed as the Second Army's chief of staff the following February. He was then given the 27th Division in July 1915, taking it to Salonika where he became commander of XVI Corps in January 1916 and of the British Salonika Army as a whole in May that year. Milne experienced many difficulties in Salonika. His units, starved of reinforcements and wasted by disease, faced formidable Bulgarian defences on the Doiran front while Milne himself had to deal with a host of political problems arising from the multinational character of the Allied forces in the theatre. Nevertheless, as a result of the September 1918 offensive, the Bulgarians collapsed and Milne's army marched on Turkey and occupied Constantinople. CIGS 1926 to 1933. *PJS.*

Milner, Viscount Alfred (1854–1925). Br. A lifelong believer in the need for British Imperial unity, Milner was High Commissioner in South Africa from 1897 to 1905. He became a member of Lloyd George's War Cabinet in December 1916. He played a central role in the removal of Robertson from the post of CIGS in February 1918 and in March was the senior British representative at the Doullens Conference, when Foch was given the task of coordinating Allied operations on the Western Front. Milner was Secretary of State for War, April–December 1918. *PJS.*

M

293

Mindanao. The most southerly and second largest of the Philippine islands, Mindanao was invaded by Japanese forces on December 20 1941. Landing at Davao on the southeast coast, they were resisted by Philippine units under the command of Brig Gen Sharp. They were unable to stem the Japanese advance and withdrew to the interior of the island where they prepared to continue the struggle as a guerrilla force. However, on May 6 1942, Lt Gen Wainwright ordered the surrender of all American and Philippine troops on the islands. Mindanao remained under Japanese occupation, albeit with strong guerrilla resistance, until the spring of 1945 when the Eighth US Army launched an invasion. On April 17 the 24th and 31st Divisions of Maj Gen Sibert's XX Corps landed at Illana Bay on the west of the island and pushing eastwards, on May 2 captured the vital town of Davao. This split the bottom half of Mindanao in two and offered an ideal base from which to continue the campaign. But the Japanese Thirty-fifth Army resolutely maintained its resistance and fresh landings in the north, south and east were needed. But by the end of July, remaining Japanese units could be dealt with by Philippine guerrillas or local US forces. *MS*.

Mindoro *see* LUZON CAMPAIGN.

Minelayer. Vessel built or converted to lay mines. Many cruisers and destroyers could be converted for the purpose. Special mines could be laid from submarine torpedo tubes; there were also purpose-built submarine minelayers and aircraft were sometimes used as minelayers.

Mines, land. Defensive weapons, often hidden, designed to blow up tanks, vehicles or personnel.

Mines (sea). Underwater explosive devices, moored, bottom-laid or drifting. Divided into "contact" or "influence" (magnetic, acoustic, pressure) mines according to method of causing explosion.

Minesweeper. Vessel used to clear passage through minefields; it may be a converted fishing craft or tug or purpose-built, using cutting sweep or special electrical or acoustic gear to break mines from moorings or set them off. The "Minehunter" was developed after 1945 to locate bottom mines with sonar, then destroy them using divers or remote-control devices. Magnetic mines caused development of non-magnetic (wooden or fibreglass) sweepers for inshore work.

Minsk. The capital of Soviet Belorussia, Minsk lay directly in the path of German Army Group Centre's advance on Moscow during Operation "Barbarossa". Soviet commander, Col Gen Pavlov, stood little chance with shortages of weapons, ammunition and equipment. On June 26 1941 a German artillery bombardment added to the destruction already meted out by the Luftwaffe. On the 28th Guderian and Hoth's panzers completed the encirclement of the city, trapping over 287,000 prisoners who constituted the remnants of four Soviet armies. Minsk remained in German hands until July 1944 when the Red Army made a rapid and comprehensive encirclement of the city. The recently appointed German commander, Model, was unable to extricate most of his Fourth Army and, on July 3, Chernyakovsky's Third Belorussian Front advanced into the city from the north while elements of the First Belorussian Front entered from the south. Over 100,000 German troops were trapped in a pocket to the east of Minsk, where more than 40,000 were killed trying to break out. Whole areas of Minsk had been blown up by the retreating German forces and under Nazi rule the civilian population had decreased by 25% in three years. *MS*.

Minuteman missile. America's most numerous ICBM deployed in three versions since 1962; 1,000 were in service by 1967. Minuteman is a solid-fuel missile deployed in silos. Minuteman 1 and 2 carried single warheads each of 1-2 megatons; 450 Minuteman 2s remain in service. Minuteman 3, introduced in 1970, has MIRVed warheads, either three 170 kiloton or, from 1980, three 335 kiloton; 227 of the former and 300 of the latter are currently on alert.

Min Yuen *see* MALAYAN EMERGENCY.

Mirage III, Dassault (French). Single-seat all-weather interceptor fighter/strike aircraft. Prototype flew November 18 1956; first production Mirage IIIC, October 9 1960; Mirage IIIE multi-role development, April 5 1961. Israel acquired 72 Mirage IIICs; Pakistan air force operated Mirage IIIEPs and IIIRPs against India, December 1971. Australia bought 100 Mirage IIIOs, South Africa 16 Mirage IIICZ. Mirage IIIC has one 9,370lb (4,250kg) s.t. SNECMA Atar 9B3 engine; max. speed 1,386mph (2,230kph); two 30mm cannon.

Mississippi. US battleship. *New Mexico* class. Completed 1918. Moved from Atlantic to Pacific after Pearl Harbor; took part in most of the landings and fought at Surigao Strait. After the war, a weapons trial ship, the first to fire anti-aircraft missiles (1952).

Missouri. US battleship. *Iowa* class. Last American battleship completed (1944) – bombarded Iwo Jima and Okinawa. Japanese surrender signed on board. Now back in active service.

Mitchell *see* B-25 MITCHELL.

Mitchell, Maj-Gen William ("Billy") (1879–1936). US. A professional soldier who learnt to fly in 1915 and in 1918 commanded substantial air forces in France. He became convinced of the future importance of air power and advocated the creation of an independent air force in the US. He organized demonstrations of how warships could be sunk by air attack and popularized his views in a series of sensational publicity campaigns. In 1925 he was court-martialled for insubordination and resigned his commission. *ANF*.

Mitla Pass. One of several defiles on the routes across the Sinai Desert where fierce fighting took place in 1967 and 1973. *See also* ARAB-ISRAELI WARS.

Mitscher, Adm Marc Andrew (1887–1947). US. One of the first US naval officers to qualify as a pilot, following graduation from

M

the Naval Academy in 1910. Mitscher was one of the pre-eminent carrier admirals of World War II. Flying his flag in USS *Hornet*, he commanded task groups in the Doolittle raid on Tokyo, April 1942, and at Midway, June 1942. As Air Commander, Solomons, his successes included direction of the operations resulting in the aerial "ambush" of Adm Yamamoto, April 18 1943. In January 1944 he took command of Carrier Division 3 which, as 1st Carrier Task Force and then Task Force 58, he headed until July 1945.

As commander of the major carrier force, Mitscher ideally complemented Adm Spruance, C-in-C Fifth Fleet, who relied heavily on his advice in all air operations. Although lacking Spruance's depth of intellect, Mitscher leavened his senior's instinctive caution with an intuitive tactical sense based on his vast experience in and knowledge of naval air power. Their partnership proved superbly effective in the battles of the Philippine Sea, Leyte Gulf and Okinawa; Mitscher's contribution was also vital to success in the Marshall Islands, Hollandia, Truk and Iwo Jima campaigns. Deputy Chief of Naval Operations, July 1945–March 1946, Mitscher refused appointment as Chief in order to return to sea in command of Eighth Fleet. He died as C-in-C, Atlantic Fleet, February 1947. *RO'N*.

Mitsubishi A6M2 Reisen (Zero Fighter), "Zeke" (Japanese, WWII). Single-seat shipboard fighter. Prototype flew April 1 1939. Designed to have two 20mm cannon and two machine guns, the A6M2 had a powerful impact when it first fought Allied aircraft 1941–42. Centre-float seaplane version (A6M2-N) also built; later, more-powerful sub-types of the basic design followed. Production, over 11,280 *Reisen* (all types). One 950hp Nakajima NK1C Sakae 12 engine; max. speed 332mph (534kph); two 20mm cannon, two 7.7mm machine guns, 264lb (120kg) bombs.

Mitsubishi G4M1/2, 1-Rikko, "Betty" (Japanese, WWII). Long-range medium bomber; crew 7. Prototype flew October 23 1938; first production aircraft completed

April 1940; by December 7 1941 about 150 on Japanese Navy's strength. With progressive modifications and improvements served in bomber units until 1945; a good aircraft, but vulnerable to fighter attack. Production, 2,446. Two 1,825hp Mitsubishi MK4T Kasei engines; max. speed 272mph (438kph) one 1,764lb (800kg) torpedo or up to 2,205lb (1,000kg) bombs, one 20mm cannon and four 7.7mm machine guns.

MLRS (Multiple Launch Rocket System). An American battlefield support system: a tracked launcher for 12 x 227mm rockets with a range of 19 miles (32km). Each rocket carries 644 0.5lb (0.225kg) shaped charge/fragmentation dual-purpose sub-munitions. A production line in Europe will supply the British, French, Italian and West German armies. The Germans are developing a mine-laying rocket for MLRS that will allow a vehicle to lay 336 anti-tank mines in an area of 2 sq miles (5 sq km) in one minute at a range of 24 miles (40km) and an international consortium is developing a 27-mile (45km) range rocket with radar homing anti-tank sub-munitions. The Americans are also developing a 144-mile (240km) range ballistic missile, ATACMS (Army Tactical Missile), which can be substituted for six of the smaller rockets on the launcher. *EJG*.

Model on the Eastern Front

Model, Field Marshal Walther (1891–1945). Ger. Served during World War I on the Western Front and on the General Staff. A staff officer early in World War II; not until the invasion of the Soviet Union was he fully able to display his talents as a brave, energetic and tactically astute commander,

leading 3rd Panzer Division to major successes at Bialystok, Minsk, Smolensk and Kiev. This resulted in a meteoric rise to command of the Ninth Army in January 1942. A loyal servant of Hitler, Model was nevertheless prepared to back his own judgement against the *Führer's* interference. Unusually, this attitude was respected, especially as he continued to achieve success early in 1942 with the Battle of Rzhev. His failure in Operation "Citadel", the German offensive at Kursk, summer 1943, was to a great extent offset by the need for his defensive qualities in meeting the Soviet counterattack.

In January 1944 Model was appointed C-in-C Army Group North to check the seemingly inexorable advance of the Red Army and instituted a policy of *Schild und Schwert* "Shield and Sword", consisting of systematic withdrawal followed by counterattack. His reputation as a troubleshooter earned him the nickname of "The *Führer's* Fireman", and by the end of June he had been given command of Army Groups South and Centre. Having stabilized the Eastern Front, albeit on the East Prussian border, Model was next sent to France. As C-in-C of Army Group B and OB West, Model could do little but try to extricate his troops; in September he was replaced as OB West by von Rundstedt. Model achieved one more victory against the Allied airborne forces at Arnhem, but his participation in the Ardennes offensive of December 1944 and the defence of the Ruhr in the spring of 1945 were, by his standards, failures. Finally, with defeat inevitable, Model committed suicide on April 21 1945. *MS*.

Moehne Dam *see* DAMS RAID.

Mölders, Col Werner (1913–41). Ger. Top-scoring fighter pilot of the Condor Legion in Spanish Civil War (14 "kills"), Mölders was instrumental in the Luftwaffe's adoption of the *Schwarm* tactical formation – four fighters in close (c200yd/180m apart) line abreast – adopted by the RAF as the "Finger Four". He commanded *Jagdgeschwader* 51 in France, 1940 (c20 "kills") and the Battle of Britain (c20 "kills"). Raising his total to

M

115 victories on the Eastern Front, he was promoted to Inspector General of Fighters, but died in an air accident.

Molotov, Vyacheslav (1890–1986). Russian. Major role in the Bolshevik Revolution; joined Politburo; Soviet PM, 1930–41. A close associate of Stalin; appointed Foreign Minister in May 1939 and remained in office throughout World War II and into Cold War.

Molotov, Vyacheslav (1890–1986).

Molotov Cocktail (Breadbasket). This name for an improvised hand grenade – typically a petrol-filled bottle with a rag wick – dates from its use against the Red Army during the invasion of Finland, 1940, when the incendiary-bomb clusters dropped by the Soviet Air Force were called "Molotov Breadbaskets", after the Soviet Commissar for Foreign Affairs.

Moltke, Gen Helmuth Graf von (1848–1916). Ger. Nephew of the Prussian hero of 1866 and 1870, Moltke succeeded von Schlieffen as Chief of the German General Staff in 1906. He advocated an early war against the Entente powers but significantly altered Schlieffen's war plan by strengthening the German left wing at the expense of the right and abandoning the proposed wheel through Holland. In August 1914, alarmed by Russia's surprisingly swift deployment, he further weakened the German right wing in the west to provide reinforcements for the Eastern Front. Inadequate communications, a remote headquarters and his own loss of nerve all contributed to his failure to give proper direction to his right wing armies between September 4 and 9 and led to the German retreat from the Marne. Falkenhayn took over on September 14. *PJS*.

Momyer, Gen William W (b.1916). US. Commander of US Seventh Air Force and Deputy Commander of Military Assistance Command, Vietnam (MACV) from July 1966. He was in charge of the planning and conduct of Air Force operations over Indochina, instituting the SLAM approach (seek, locate, annihilate and monitor) to breaking up enemy troop concentrations. From March to August 1968, when he departed, Momyer took control of all US tactical air resources in South Vietnam in order to coordinate the US air response to the Tet offensive. *See also* SLAM.

Monash, Gen Sir John (1864–1931). Australian. Born in Melbourne, of Jewish parentage, Monash was a noted civil engineer before World War I, combining his profession with enthusiastic membership of Australia's Citizen Forces. Soon after the outbreak of war in 1914 he was given command of the Australian 4th Infantry Brigade and led it throughout the Gallipoli campaign in 1915. In July 1916 he took over the 3rd Australian Division, which distinguished itself at Messines Ridge and in the Third Battle of Ypres during 1917 and also at Villers-Bretonneux in March-April 1918. He succeeded Birdwood as commander of the Australian Corps in May 1918. Under Monash, the Australian Corps became a spearhead formation of the BEF in the successful offensive at Amiens on August 8, and again played an important role in the subsequent capture of Mont St Quentin and Peronne and in the breaking of the Hindenburg Line. Monash, whose great strengths were his planning and attention to detail, was undoubtedly one of the BEF's outstanding corps commanders, but Lloyd George's later claim that he was a possible replacement for Haig appears unrealistic. *PJS*.

Monastir, Battle of (1912). At the beginning of the First Balkan War, Monastir (now Bitolj, Yugoslavia) was in Turkish Macedonia. Turkish troops, falling back before the Serbian armies attacking from the north and east and from the Greek forces pushing up from Elasson in the south, concentrated at Monastir and on November 2 and 3 1912, detachments sent from

there defeated the Greeks at Banitsa and Kastoria. The Serbs, who had advanced to Prilep on November 5, mustered there, planning a decisive defeat of the Turks, who had taken up a strong position north of Monastir. Prince Alexander, commanding the Serbs, planned a frontal assault on November 18, combined with attacks on both enemy flanks, but the division detailed to operate against the Turkish left launched a premature night attack on November 15 and was hard put to hold off determined counterattacks until the main Serbian thrust was launched on November 18. Turkish resistance then collapsed and the battle proved a decisive victory for the Serbs, who killed, wounded or captured half the defenders. *SKF*.

Monitor. A class of naval vessels designed to mount heavy guns for shore bombardment. Named from the first such ship USS *Monitor* of 1862.

Monro, General Sir Charles (1860–1929). Br. As Chief Instructor and, later, Commandant of the School of Musketry at Hythe between 1901 and 1907, Monro instigated important changes in British musketry training and tactics before World War I. He commanded the BEF's 2nd Division in 1914 and took over I Corps that December, leading it at Aubers Ridge, Festubert and Givenchy in 1915. He became commander of the Third Army in July 1915 but in October he replaced Sir Ian Hamilton at the head of the Mediterranean Expeditionary Force. It was Monro who advocated the evacuation of Gallipoli, a recommendation subsequently endorsed by Kitchener. Monro returned to France, commanding the First Army from January to August 1916, then, in October, he was appointed Commander-in-Chief in India. Under Monro, recruiting was reorganized and the Indian Army considerably expanded, enabling it to play a major role in the victories in Mesopotamia and Palestine. *PJS*.

Montagnards. The French word for mountain dweller; commonly applied to the ethnic minorities inhabiting the mountains dividing Vietnam, Laos and Cambodia.

Vietnam alone has 60 distinct groups that account for 16 percent of the total population. The highland H'mong, T'ai and Lao-Theung comprise 40–50 percent of the population of Laos.

The Vietnamese communists cemented relations with a number of these groups during the war with France. In the late 1950s they used Montagnards to scout the Ho Chi Minh Trail, and one of the first incidents of the Vietnam War, the Tra Bong uprising of March 1959, involved minorities in South Vietnam's Quang Ngai province. The communists also cultivated the minorities in Laos because so much of the Trail passed through mountains inhabited by them. Meanwhile, the government of Ngo Dinh Diem alienated the hill people by encouraging ethnic Vietnamese to settle in highland areas. Montagnard rebellions against the Saigon government 1964–65 were ended by American mediation, and US Special Forces and aid officials acted as patrons of the Montagnards for much of the war. As the Americans withdrew, turning over their responsibilities to the South Vietnamese, relations between the Montagnards and Saigon deteriorated. Some Montagnards shifted support to the communists; others continued an armed opposition to the communists in Lam Dong province after Saigon fell. Out of South Vietnam's approximately 1,000,000 ethnic minority citizens, about 200,000 died in the war. *WST. See also* CIVILIAN IRREGULAR DEFENCE GROUP; FULRO.

"Monty" with Eighth Army, 1943

Montgomery of Alamein, Field Marshal the Viscount (1887–1976). Br. First came to public attention as Commander 3rd Divi-

sion and then II Corps in the retreat to Dunkirk in May 1940.

In August 1942, he was selected by Churchill to command the defeated Eighth Army at El Alamein. He restored its confidence, and gained ascendancy over Rommel and over his own subordinate commanders through the professionalism with which he won the Battles of Alam Halfa and El Alamein. His success was based on meticulous planning; fighting divisions as divisions and not in *ad hoc* groupings as had so often happened in previous Western Desert battles; maintaining balance at all times so that he could react to the unforeseen and never court disaster; and, above all, ensuring that every man knew what was intended and what part he was to play. His pursuit of Rommel into Tunisia may have seemed ponderous, but he was determined not to be defeated as Wavell and Auchinleck had been due to logistic overstretch. Eighth Army remained victorious throughout the Tunisian, Sicilian and Italian campaigns until he returned to England in December 1943 to prepare for the invasion of Northwest Europe as Commander, 21st Army Group.

The campaign in Normandy was a triumph for his strategy of drawing the German panzer formations towards the British-held eastern sector of the beachhead, enabling the Americans to break out in the west. His handling of subsequent disagreements with Eisenhower did him little credit. Right though he may have been to advocate a concentrated thrust by his 21st Army Group into northern Germany, he was wrong not to appreciate that such a policy was politically impossible for Eisenhower. The failure of his thrust to Arnhem in September, and his tactlessness during the Ardennes crisis in December 1944, almost led to his dismissal. Nevertheless, his crossing of the Rhine in March, and his advance to Lüneburg Heath where he accepted the surrender of all German forces in the Northwest on May 4 1945, crowned his war-time career.

After the war, he fought to establish a sound structure for Western European defence, retiring in 1958 as Deputy Supreme Allied Commander, Europe. *WGFJ.*

Montreuil. Home of the GHQ of the BEF in France, 1916–19.

"Moolah" Operation. Mounted in 1953 towards the end of the Korean War. The objective was to persuade a pilot to defect with a MiG by offering a large reward. The word was spread by leaflet and radio in Korean, Chinese and Russian without immediate results. After the armistice a North Korean MiG arrived at Kimpo airfield, but the defecting pilot knew nothing about the reward.

Moore, Maj Gen Sir (John) Jeremy (b.1928). Br. Royal Marines officer commanding Land Forces, Operation "Corporate" (Falklands War 1982). Moore landed in the Falklands with 5th Infantry Brigade and was responsible thereafter for all operational and logistic matters ashore. He took the surrender on June 14.

Morane-Saulnier MS 406 C 1 (French, WWII). Single-seat fighter. Prototype (MS 405) flew August 8 1935; initial production batch April 1937; deliveries from December 1938. At outbreak of war *Armée de l'Air* had 573 MS 406s on charge, 24 *escadrilles* equipped, but type was inferior to Messerschmitt Bf 109. Thirty to Finland 1939; 15 fitted with captured Klimov M-105P engines, designated Mörkö Moraani, in service until 1952. One 860hp Hispano-Suiza 12Y31 engine; max. speed 289mph (465kph); one 20mm cannon, two 7.5mm machine guns.

Morane-Saulnier Parasol monoplanes (French, WWI). Two-seat reconnaissance. Prototype flew August 1913; first production version, Type L, supplied to French *Aviation militaire*, RFC, RNAS, Russia, 1914–15. Flown as single-seat fighter by Roland Garros, with forward-firing machine gun, April 1915. Developed via refined Type LA to 110hp Type P of 1916. Operational use in RFC ceased January 1917. On Type L No. 3253 of No. 1 Wing, RNAS, Flt Sub-Lt R A J Warneford's VC action June 7 1915. One 80hp (in Type P, 110hp) Le Rhône engine; max. speed 77/100mph (123/160kph); one/two 0.303in machine guns, small load bombs.

Moravec, Frantisek (1895–1966). Czech. Deserted from Austro-Hungarian army to Russians in 1916. Head of Czechoslovak intelligence, 1937–45, escaping from Prague to London in March 1939; escaped again 1948, to work with US intelligence.

Morgan, Lt Gen Sir Frederick. Br. *See* COSSAC.

Morice Line *see* ALGERIAN CAMPAIGN.

Moroccan War (1907–12). The "special interests" in Morocco of France and Spain were recognized by other North African colonial powers at the Algeciras Conference, 1906. Moroccan resentment led in 1907 to riots in Casablanca: French troops occupied the city following a naval bombardment on July 20. Following the unpopular Sultan's request for further Franco-Spanish support, Rif (Muslim Berber) tribesmen attacked Spanish forces in northern Morocco and, in April 1911, moved on Fez, which the French occupied. Germany, claiming that French expansion threatened her own North African interests, dispatched the gunboat *Panther* to Agadir, July 1 1911. Britain strongly supported France, and a European war seemed possible until, in November, Germany recognized France's Moroccan claims in return for the cession of French territory in the Congo. On March 30 1912, the Treaty of Fez established Morocco as a French protectorate (Spain subsequently gaining suzerainty over northern enclaves) and Lyautey became France's Resident-General. *RO'N*.

Morrison shelter. British steel indoor table shelter, 1941–45, named after Herbert Morrison, Home Secretary and Minister of Home Security.

Morshead, Lt Gen Sir Leslie James (1889–1959). Australian. A much-decorated battalion commander on the Western Front, 1916-18, Morshead became commander of the newly raised 9th Australian Division in February 1941. Only part-trained, but sustained by his hard-driving leadership (he was nicknamed "Ming the Merciless"), 9th Division bore the brunt of the siege of Tobruk

from April 1941 until relieved in October. Appointed GOC, AIF, Middle East, Morshead led 9th Division at Alamein before transferring with it to Southwest Pacific Area, where, as GOC, New Guinea Force, and then GOC, I Australian Corps, he ably directed the amphibious operations resulting in the securing of Borneo, May–August 1945. *RO'N*.

Mort Homme *see* VERDUN (1916).

Mortain (Brittany) *see* AVRANCHES, BATTLE OF (1944).

Anti-tank gun teams outside Moscow

Moscow, Battle of (1941). Hitler's indecision regarding the primary strategic objectives to be pursued in the invasion of the Soviet Union led, on August 21 1941, to his ordering Army Group Centre to halt its advance on Moscow. Resources were diverted to assist in operations in the Ukraine and it was not until the end of September that Field Marshal von Bock's forces were able to renew their attack. Throughout October they made rapid progress and the threat to Moscow was so strong that the Soviet administration prepared to evacuate the city and, on October 20, a state of siege was declared. But the German advance was beginning to slow down in the face of deteriorating weather conditions and stubborn resistance by the Red Army. But on November 15, with muddy roads firmed by frost, von Bock's armour struck from the north and south of the city, reaching its outer suburbs by the end of the month. However, the cold grew increasingly severe with the temperature dropping to -30 degrees centigrade and heavy falls of snow hampered movement so greatly that, on December 5, the German attack ground to a halt. That same day the Soviet commander, Gen Zhukov, unleashed his

counterattack. Reinforced by fresh, seasoned troops from Siberia and Mongolia, the Kalinin, Western and South Western Fronts took the Germans by surprise and forced them to retreat. Although Zhukov's plan for a concentrated thrust was adulterated by Stalin's intervention, by the end of the year the threatened German encirclement of Moscow had been removed. *MS*.

Moscow Conference. Meetings between Stalin and Churchill and their military advisers in Moscow on August 12–16 1942. Churchill's principal task was to assure Stalin of Anglo-American support, but also to convince him of the impracticability of an invasion of Northern France in 1942. To some limited extent he succeeded and the two leaders gained a certain degree of mutual respect.

Mosley, Sir Oswald Ernald (1896–1980). Br. Leader of British Union of Fascists (1932–40); detained in 1940–43 under the terms of Defence Regulation 18B.

Mosquito, de Havilland DH 98 (Br, WWII). Two-seat bomber/photographic reconnaissance/fighter/shipping strike. Prototype flew November 25 1940; effective bomber deliveries April 1942; first bombing mission May 31 1942. Fighter prototype flew May 15 1941; first squadron formed December 1941. Mosquito's exceptional performance and versatility led to many variants, extensive development, and widespread use. Production (continued until 1950): 6,411 in Britain, 1,134 Canada, 212 Australia. Mosquito B XVI had two 1,680hp Rolls-Royce Merlin engines; max. speed 415mph (668kph); 4,000lb (1,800kg) bombs. Fighter versions had four 20mm cannon and four 0.303in machine guns.

Motor Gun Boat (MGB). A class of naval vessels displacing about 100 tons, capable of up to 40 knots and armed with light guns.

Motor Torpedo Boat (MTB). A class of naval vessels displacing about 100 tons, capable of up to 40 knots and armed with torpedoes. MTBS were extensively used in World War II.

M

Mountbatten at Japanese surrender

Mountbatten Adm of the Fleet Earl (1900–1979). Br. Related to the Royal Family, the son of a previous First Sea Lord, a prominent socialite, Mountbatten was, and remains, a controversial figure. In 1939 he took command of 5th Destroyer Flotilla led by the *Kelly*. His leadership was outstanding, his tactical skill perhaps less so. In 1941, *Kelly* was sunk off Crete. Mountbatten was to have become captain of *Illustrious*, but Churchill instead appointed him as head of Combined Operations, where he contrived to produce a lively and inventive organization to which much credit for subsequent amphibious successes is due. In October 1943 he became Supreme Allied Commander in Southeast Asia where he had to cope not only with inter-service problems but also delicate problems of inter-allied relations. With the sudden surrender of the Japanese the problems became, if anything, worse. The complexities of dealing with Japanese and nationalist forces and the desperate need to reconstruct wrecked communications and industries – all were somehow dealt with. In 1947–1948 Mountbatten became the last Viceroy of India with the task of granting independence. He then returned to the Navy, and in 1955 became First Sea Lord (always an ambition after his father was driven from the post by anti-German agitation and tiredness in 1914). He opposed the Suez Crisis (1956) and ensured that the Navy began to build guided-missile ships. In 1959 he became Chief of the Defence Staff, organizing the merging of the three service ministries into a greatly strengthened Ministry of Defence. He was killed in a bomb attack by Irish terrorists. *DJL*.

Mujib-ur-Rahman, Sheikh, (1920–75). Formulated so-called Six Point Demand for virtual separation from Pakistan. Arrested, 1971, and sentenced to death but reprieved by rapid Indian victory. Prime Minister then President of Bangladesh. Assassinated August 1975.

Mujaheddin *see* AFGHANISTAN, SOVIET INTERVENTION IN (1979–89).

Mukden, Battle of (February 21–March 10 1905). In the last major land battle of the Russo-Japanese War, 300,000 Japanese (losses 84,000) under Oyama forced 310,000 Russians (losses 100,000) under Kuropatkin to retreat from entrenchments along a 47-mile (75 km) front, taking Mukden but failing to encircle and destroy the Russian force.

Mukden incident (1931) *see* SINO-JAPANESE WAR.

Mukti Bahini (or Mukti Fauj). The underground army which harassed the Pakistani troops in East Pakistan (Bangladesh) up to the Indian invasion, December 1971, in the India-Pakistan War. Said to number 100,000, its principal purpose was to provide legitimacy for Indian intervention.

Mulberry harbour. Code name for the two artificial harbours created for the D-Day invasion of Normandy, 1944. The Dieppe raid had shown how difficult it was to capture a port, and the Germans were known to be prepared for massive demolitions, so to keep the Allied army supplied, it was necessary to transport a harbour with the invasion fleet. Concrete breakwaters and pontoon jetties were towed over, floating roadways installed and old ships ("gooseberries") sunk as breakwaters to provide sheltered anchorages. Bad weather soon after the invasion destroyed the harbour in the American sector off Omaha beach and supplies continued to be landed over the beaches there, but the one in the British sector at Arromanches was of use for several months. *DJL*.

Mullhouse, Battle of. On August 8, 1914. Gen Bonneau's VII Corps, covering the extreme right flank of the French armies, entered Mul-

house in Alsace. Within 24 hours the irresolute Bonneau lost the city to the German Seventh Army, forcing Joffre to reorganize the French right wing.

Multiple Independently Targetable Re-entry Vehicle (MIRV). Most modern ballistic missiles have the facility to engage a number of different targets with individual warheads. They carry post-boost vehicles (PBVs) which manoeuvre in space into a number of different trajectories into each of which they inject a warhead. Large missiles can carry large numbers of large warheads and enough fuel in the PBV to give a large "footprint" i.e. area in which a single missile's warheads can fall. The Soviet SS-18 has been pictured in American sources distributing ten 500-750 kiloton MIRVs between the East Coast of the United States and the Rocky Mountains. Smaller missiles, like the American Poseidon SLBM, can carry 10-14 warheads but these are small, only 50 kilotons, and targets have to be found in a "footprint" that is reportedly about 150 miles (240km) long and 90 miles (144km) wide. MIRVs were first developed by the Americans in the late 1960s and first deployed in 1970-71 in the belief that the USSR would take a long time to catch up, but within a few years the Soviets had done so. Given the counter-force potential of MIRVs, there is now a tendency on grounds of stability to revert to single-warhead missiles. *EJG*.

Multiple Re-entry Vehicle (MRV). Instead of a single warhead, a ballistic missile might deliver a cluster of warheads. This increases the destructive effect against soft area targets and lessens the likelihood of the attack being disabled by an ABM missile. The warheads are, however, all directed at the same target area and bear a fixed relationship to the original trajectory of the rocket. Polaris A3 had such an MRV system with three 200 kiloton re-entry vehicles landing about 1,640ft (500m) apart. Soviet missiles have also deployed MRVs e.g. the SS-11 ICBM with three 100-300 kiloton warheads and the SS-N-6 SLBM with two 500 kiloton MRVs. The old SS-9 ICBM was tested with

M

an MRV pattern similar to that of Minuteman silos. The current British Polaris missile "front end" is officially described as an MRV as its two warheads are targeted on the same general area, but it seems to possess a post-boost vehicle and is hard to distinguish technically from a MIRV. *EJG*.

Munich Agreement. The Agreement between Hitler, Mussolini, Chamberlain and Daladier was signed on September 30 1938. Under its terms the Germanic parts, and in the event several other parts, of Czechoslovakia were ceded to Germany. This averted war, which had been imminent, until September 1939. Chamberlain announced it as bringing "peace in our time".

Munich Putsch (1923). On November 8 1923, at a political meeting held in a Munich beer hall, Hitler launched a national uprising. Although supported by Gen Ludendorff, Hitler's plans were inept. The next day, state police fired on the Nazi demonstrators, killing 16. With the subsequent arrest of Hitler and the ringleaders, the coup was at an end.

Munitions Crisis. Towards the end of 1914 and in the opening months of 1915, the C-in-C of the BEF, French, repeatedly complained of a shortage of shells. He communicated his discontent to the military correspondent of *The Times*, Col Repington, who gave it sensationalized publicity. This led to a reduction in Kitchener's powers, to the establishment of a Ministry of Munitions under Lloyd George and to the formation of a coalition government between Liberals and Conservatives.

"Musketeer" Operation. Anglo-French operation against Egypt, 1956. *See also* SUEZ CRISIS (1956).

Mussolini, Benito (1883–1945). Italian. A schoolteacher turned political journalist, Mussolini split from the Socialists over Italy's participation in World War I, in which he saw active service. His miltaristic, nationalistic *Fasci di Combattimento* (fascist) party, formed in March 1919, rose to power in the postwar political chaos: Mussolini formed a government in October 1922 and assumed dictatorial powers in November. *"Il Duce"* ("The Leader") planned domination of the Mediterranean and the creation of an Italian empire in Africa, but his Abyssinian conquest, 1936, alienated Britain and France, while intervention in the Spanish Civil War proved both economically and diplomatically costly. He had entered into alliance with Germany by the "Axis" agreement of October 1936 and "Pact of Steel" of May 1939. Expecting to share the spoils of a German victory, Mussolini declared war on Britain and France on June 10 1940.

Many Italians lacked enthusiasm for the conflict, and Italian forces fared badly, especially in North Africa and Greece, increasingly reducing Italy to a client state of Germany. Yet Mussolini, his grip on reality clearly weakening, declared war on Russia and the US. On July 25 1943 he was ousted by the Grand Fascist Council, supported by King Victor Emmanuel III, and imprisoned. Spectacularly rescued by Skorzeny's German commandos, he was established as head of the puppet Salò Republic in German-occupied northern Italy. As German forces in Italy collapsed, Mussolini and his mistress, Clara Petacci (1912–45) were captured by Italian partisans, April 27 1945, shot next day, and their bodies degradingly put on public display. *MS*.

Mustang *see* P-51 MUSTANG.

Mutually Assured Destruction (MAD). A formula for strategic stability in which each side has enough secure second-strike forces to be able in all circumstances to inflict unacceptable damage on the other, defined by the Americans in the 1960s as between a quarter to a third of the other side's population and about two-thirds of its industrial capacity. Although the Americans never abandoned more flexible targeting policies, maintaining an assured destruction capability became the major criterion for strategic force sizing in the late 1960s once the Soviets had acquired secure second strike capabilities to match those of the US. The maintenance of stable mutually assured destruction was the aim of the Strategic Arms Limitation Talks. The USSR, however, still tended to emphasize the war-fighting role of nuclear forces if deterrence failed, and maintained counter-force capabilities that encouraged the Americans to move away from assured destruction as public strategic rhetoric after the signature of the SALT-1 treaty. Mutually Assured Destruction however still remains the ultimate fact of the nuclear age. *EJG*.

MX missile. The latest American ICBM, dubbed "Peacekeeper" by President Reagan, originally intended for mobile deployment in some form. The first 50 were actually deployed in modified Minuteman silos in 1986-88. MX carries ten 300 kiloton MIRVed warheads with great accuracy (328ft/100m CEP) over 6,600 miles (11,000km).

My Lai massacre (1968). On March 16 1968, a company of the newly created US Americal Division entered My Lai hamlet of Son My village, Quang Ngai province, South Vietnam. Told to expect resistance and to destroy the hamlet, the platoon led by Lt William Calley Jr herded 70–150 civilians into a ditch and shot them. An orgy of slaughter, rape and pillage brought the number of noncombatant women, children and old men killed by the company to a conservatively estimated 175–200 and possibly as high as 350. Still more were killed by other units in the area. Ambiguous orders, inadequate training, permissive leadership, low morale, lack of previous combat experience and a pervasive perception that residents of the village were communists or sympathizers were among the factors blamed. Americal Division commanders ignored or concealed the incident until it was disclosed a year later in a letter from an ex-soldier, Ron Ridenhour, to Pentagon and Congressional leaders. Following an inquiry headed by Lt Gen W R Peers, 25 officers and enlisted men were charged, but only six were actually tried and only Calley was convicted, specifically for the murder of 22 civilians. In 1971 President Nixon reduced Calley's sentence to 20 years, and on March 19 1974 he was paroled. *WST*.

M

N

Nagano, Adm Osami (1880–1947). Jap. Navy Minister, 1936; c-in-c Combined Fleet, 1937; Chief of Naval General Staff, April 1941–February 1944. Like Yamamoto, originally opposed attacking USA but then supported Pearl Harbor operation.

Nagasaki, atomic attack on. Following the atomic raid on Hiroshima (August 6 1945), President Truman threatened Japan with "a rain of ruin from the air, the like of which has never been seen on this earth". However, this failed to elicit a Japanese surrender and the use of a second atomic bomb was agreed. Kolura, a city boasting a major arsenal, was selected as the primary target with the port of Nagasaki as the alternative.

Shortly before 0400 hours August 9 1945 the B-29 bomber *Bock's Car* and its "Fat Man" bomb took off from Tinian. The pilot, Maj Charles Sweeney, was soon beset by problems; cloud over Kokura resulted in a switch to Nagasaki but a faulty fuel pump limited the aircraft's flying time and only one bombing run was possible. The weather over Nagasaki was not good either and radar had to be used for the bomb run. Finally, a gap in the clouds appeared and, at 1058, from a height of 28,900ft (8,800m), "Fat Man" was released. This bomb, using the implosion method, was more efficient than "Little Boy" and possessed a greater blast effect. However, the fairly mountainous terrain, the irregularity of the city plan and the incidence of stretches of water helped to limit the devastation. Nevertheless, an area of almost 2 sq miles (5 sq km) was laid waste and substantial damage was sustained to buildings for a further mile from the epicentre of the explosion. As with Hiroshima, casualty statistics for Nagasaki vary greatly but a figure of 40,000 killed with a similar number wounded is generally accepted. The final total of those afflicted by the after-effects of radiation is also uncertain. *MS*.

Nagato. Japanese battleship. Name ship of class; with sister ship *Mutsu*, first Japanese 16in gun ships. Flagship of Combined Fleet until replaced by *Yamato*. Sunk at Bikini atomic tests (1946).

Nagumo, Vice Adm Chuichi (1887–1944). Jap. A cruiser admiral specializing in torpedoes, Nagumo somewhat reluctantly took command of First Air Fleet,

Nagumo: commander at Pearl Harbor

Japan's major carrier force, for the attack on Pearl Harbor, December 1941. Although he achieved complete surprise, his failure to launch a follow-up air strike – as Yamamoto had probably expected, but had not ordered, him to do – resulted in the base's infrastructure remaining virtually intact. There followed five months' unbroken success, as First Air Fleet covered the conquest of the Dutch East Indies and launched devastating raids on Darwin and Ceylon.

The limitations of Nagumo's painstaking, conventional style of command were seen at Midway, June 1942. Ordered to destroy both the island's defences and the US carriers – twin tasks made more difficult by Yamamoto's overcautious deployments and Nagumo's own failure to ensure adequate reconnaissance – he hesitated at the crucial moment and lost all four of his fleet carriers. His almost complete loss of confidence thereafter was manifested in his failure to exploit initial advantages at Eastern Solomons, August 1942, and Santa Cruz, October 1942. Handing over the main carrier force to Ozawa, November 1942, Nagumo was relegated to the minor Central Pacific Fleet. As senior officer in the Marianas, 1944, he jointly commanded the defence of Saipan with Lt Gen Yoshitsugo Saito. On July 6 1944, having ordered the garrison's c3,000 surviving troops to make a *banzai* charge, Saito and Nagumo committed suicide. *RO'N*.

Nakajima Ki 43 Hayabusa (Peregrine Falcon), "Oscar" (Japanese, WWII). Single-seat fighter, Japanese Army Air Service specification. In action from December 7 1941. Production, 5,919. One 990hp Nakajima Ha-25 or 1,150hp Ha-115 engine; max. speed 329mph (530kph); two 12.7mm machine guns, 1,102lb (500kg) bombs.

Naktong river *see* PUSAN PERIMETER CAMPAIGN.

Nam Dong, Battle of (1964). In July 1964, Nam Dong was a Civilian Irregular Defence Group (CIDG) camp in north central Thua Thien province, South Vietnam. Early on July 6, a communist battalion struck behind a mortar barrage, killing 58 CIDG troops, two US Special Forces and one Australian adviser. The camp escaped being overrun (but only narrowly) partly because, having once been a French outpost, it had two defence perimeters around a central strongpoint. This design was later incorporated into all US Special Forces compounds.

Nam Il, Gen (1914–82). Korean. COS of the NKPA during the Korean War and chief communist delegate at the truce talks in July 1951.

Namsi, Battle of (1951). Korean War. One of a series of clashes over northwest Korea in October 1951 involving B-29 Superfortresses and communist MiGs. On October 23 Superfortresses attacking Namsi airfield were engaged by a large force of MiGs which swamped escorting fighters, destroyed three of the bombers and seriously damaged five. On October 24 another Superfortress was claimed by MiGs over Sunchon. On October 27 during a raid on Sinanju a Superfortress was seriously damaged. As a result, daylight bombing by Superfortresses ceased and a second wing of Sabres was rushed to Korea to preserve air supremacy in MiG Alley. *CM*.

Namsos, landings at (April 16–May 3 1940). The force commanded by Maj Gen Carton de Wiart started landing on April 16, led by the lightly equipped and inadequately trained 146th (Territorial) Brigade, followed three days later

301

by the French 5th Demi-Brigade of *Chasseurs Alpins*. Two disasters occurred due to local German air and naval superiority: on April 20, the Luftwaffe started heavy air attacks on Namsos, which stopped the landing of artillery and anti-aircraft guns, and made the supply of the Allied forces precarious; on April 21, the ice which had been blocking the fjord flanking the route south to Trondheim thawed, enabling German destroyers to land troops behind the advanced positions of the Territorial Brigade at Verdalsora, and to drive it back to Steinkjer before the French were ready to intervene. The Steinkjer area was held until Carton de Wiart's force was evacuated by sea on May 2–3. *WGFJ.*

Namur, siege of. The Belgian city of Namur, at the confluence of the Sambre and Meuse, was, like Liège, ringed by forts. In 1914, after the capture of Liège, the German Second Army advanced on Namur, investing it on August 21. The defenders, although reinforced by the Belgian 4th Division and three French battalions, were outnumbered and subjected to a bombardment by the huge German 42 and 30.5cm howitzers used previously at Liège. On August 23, with the loss of three of its northern forts, Namur was evacuated by its defenders and fell next day.

Naking, siege of (1937) *see* SINO-JAPANESE WAR.

Nanshan Hill, Battle of (May 25 1904), Russo-Japanese War. In an all-out assault, 30,000 Japanese (losses 4,500) overwhelmed a Russian garrison of 3,000 (losses 1,500) to capture a dominant feature of the Port Arthur defences.

Napalm. An incendiary bomb with spectacular area effect based on petrol (gasolene) which is made into a "jelly" in order to increase its destructive potential both in terms of burning and asphyxiation. First developed in World War II by the Americans it was used both in the close air support role and as a counter-city incendiary weapon. It has been widely used in the former role by many nations since 1945.

Narvik, Battles for (April 9–June 8 1940). The first naval battle took place on April 10. Captain Warburton-Lee, with five destroyers, surprised ten larger and more modern German destroyers refuelling after landing the leading elements of 3rd Mountain Division (Dietl) at Narvik. He sank two, disabled three others, and sank seven store ships for the loss of two British destroyers.

In the second naval battle three days later, Vice Adm W J Whitworth in *Warspite*, with a strong destroyer escort and supported by the aircraft carrier *Furious*, destroyed the rest of the German destroyers at Narvik, but there was no landing force immediately available to take the town. An unsuccessful attempt to induce the surrender of the Narvik garrison by naval bombardment, rather than direct assault by land forces being assembled under Maj Gen Mackesy at Harstad some 60 miles (96km) away, took place on April 24.

Narvik was gradually brought under siege between April 28 and May 22 by Mackesy's land forces: British 24th Guards Brigade, the French 27th Demi-Brigade *Chasseurs Alpines*, 13th Demi-Brigade Foreign Legion under Gen Béthouart, the Polish Brigade (*Chasseurs du Nord*) under Gen Bohusz-Szyszko, and local Norwegian units under Gen Fleischer. A tolerable air situation was achieved by the establishment of RAF Gladiator fighters on the airfield at Bardufoss, 50 miles (80km) north of Narvik, and air cover provided by carriers.

The German garrison was reinforced by air and by clandestine use of the railway from Sweden. To stop further help reaching them, 24th Guards Brigade was moved south to Bodo to help a force of independent companies (later renamed Commandos) under Brig Gubbins that delayed the advance of 2nd Mountain Division (Feuerstein) northwards from Trondheim. The final assault of May 27–28 was mounted by Lt Gen Auchinleck with French, Polish and Norwegian troops, supported by British naval gunfire. The 3rd Mountain Division evacuated Narvik and withdrew towards the Swedish frontier, but was able to reoccupy the port when it was evacuated by the Allies on June 8. *WGFJ.*

Na San, Battle of (1952). From November 23–30 1952, nine French battalions held off assaults by two regiments of the People's Army of Vietnam (PAVN) at Na San, a fortified strongpoint 125 miles (200km) west of Hanoi. With air support, five batteries of 105mm howitzers and control of the high ground, the French inflicted 6–7,000 casualties. For both sides the battle was a dress rehearsal for Dien Bien Phu: it encouraged the French to set up a post deep in enemy territory to lure the PAVN to destruction, while PAVN commanders drew lessons on how to avoid that outcome. *WST.*

Nasi, Lt Gen Guglielmo. Italian. Commander of the Gondar district, Ethiopia. Invaded southern Sudan, July 1940; organized resistance to patriot forces in northern Ethiopia, 1941; last senior Italian commander to surrender, November 1941.

Nasser, Col Gamal Abd Al-Nasir (1918–70). Egyptian. Army officer and politician. *See also* ARAB-ISRAELI WARS; SUEZ CRISIS 1956.

National Liberation Front of South Vietnam (NLF). Needing an overt leadership organ for the revolutionary movement it had already initiated in South Vietnam, the Lao Dong (Workers', or Vietnam Communist) Party, at its 3rd National Congress in September 1960, authorized the establishment of the National Liberation Front. The NLF had its public unveiling at a Congress of People's Representatives held in a "liberated area" of South Vietnam on December 20 1960. The front chose a dissident Saigon lawyer, Nguyen Huu Tho, as chairman, and held its first formal congress in February–March 1962. The purpose of the front was to attract non-communist support; however, while non-communists joined, Communist Party members held the key posts. Through overlapping membership, the Party maintained control of the front at all levels. The real locus of authority and planning on the revolutionary side throughout the Vietnam War was in organs of the Party, such as the Central Office for South Vietnam (COSVN) and the Political Bureau in Hanoi. *WST.*

NATO *see* NORTH ATLANTIC TREATY ORGANIZATION.

Navarre, Gen Henri E (1898–1983). Fr. Picked to command the French Expeditionary Corps in Indochina in May 1953. It was hoped that, as a counter-guerrilla expert with experience in Morocco, he would bring a fresh perspective. Along with his deputy, Maj Gen René Cogny, Navarre requested nine additional French battalions in order to launch a major offensive, break up the communists' main forces, and turn over the mopping-up to a strengthened Vietnamese National Army. The proposal came to be known as the Navarre Plan. Striving to seize the initiative, Navarre also authorized the reoccupation and reinforcement of Dien Bien Phu. Implicated in the defeat, he was relieved in June 1954 and retired. *WST*.

Nazi. Acronym formed from *Nationalsozialistische Deutsche Arbeiterpartei* (National Socialist German Workers' Party).

Nazi-Soviet Pact. Non-aggression pact signed in Moscow by foreign ministers von Ribbentrop and Molotov, August 23 1939. Germany and Russia agreed on their respective expansionist plans in Poland and the Baltic states.

Neame, Lt Gen Sir Philip, VC (1888–1978). Br. Commander Cyrenaica Command during Rommel's first offensive. Captured with Gen O'Connor by a German reconnaissance patrol, April 7 1941.

Negev *see* ARAB-ISRAELI WARS.

Neguib, Gen Mohammed (b.1901). Egyptian. Soldier and leader of coup establishing Egyptian Republic, of which he was the first President in 1952. *See also* SUEZ CANAL.

Nehring, Lt Gen Walther (1892–1983). Ger. Commanded Afrika Korps after capture of Cruewell, at Gazala, Tobruk and Mersa Matruh in June 1942, and fighting on El Alamein Line until wounded at Alam Halfa in August. Commander XC Corps in Tunisian campaign to December 1942, Commander XXIV Panzer Corps, 1943–44, Commander First Panzer Army, March 1945.

Nehru, Jawaharlal (1889–1964). Indian. India's first prime minister after its independence in 1947.

Nelson. British battleship. Name ship of class; 9 x 16in guns, all forward of the bridge. Best protected battleships of their day. Completed 1927. Served with Home Fleet till 1942, then in Mediterranean, Normandy landings and Far East.

Nerve gas. War gases that attack the central nervous system of the victims. *See also* CHEMICAL WEAPONS.

Néry, Battle of. Just after dawn on September 1 1914, during the retreat from Mons, "L" Battery of the Royal Horse Artillery was surprised by the advancing German 4th Calvalry Division at Néry, south of Compiègne, France. In the desperate rearguard action which followed, "L" Battery won three VCs. The gun has been preserved by the Imperial War Museum.

"Neutralize" Operation (1967). Intensification of North Vietnamese pressure on the US Marine base at Con Thien, just south of Vietnam's demilitarized zone, provoked an American relief effort, September 11 to October 31 1967, Operation "Neutralize". A combined air, army and navy operation, "Neutralize" dropped 40,000 tons of bombs on an area the size of Manhattan, the first application of the SLAM approach.

Neutral Nations Repatriation Commission (NNRC). Established by the armistice which ended the Korean War to take custody in the Demilitarized Zone of those POWs who 60 days after the armistice had refused repatriation to their own side. It was composed of five nations, Sweden, Switzerland, Poland, Czechoslovakia and India. The NNRC was to hold the POWs for 90 days to allow the nations to which they belonged an opportunity to provide "explanations" which might persuade them to return home. The ultimate disposition of those who refused repatriation at the end of this period was to be decided within 30 days by the political conference to be held under article four of the armistice agreement. The NNRC was to de-clare the release to civilian status of any POW who had not opted for repatriation or whose disposition had not been agreed by the political conference within 120 days of assuming custody. The POWS were to be guarded by Indian troops. This clumsy mechanism reflected the bitter controversy which had developed over the POW issue and delayed the armistice for over a year. *CM*.

Neutral Nations Supervisory Commission (NNSC). Established by the armistice which ended the Korean War to police the paragraphs of the cease-fire agreement prohibiting the introduction of military reinforcements by either side. It consisted of four senior officers, two nominated by the UN command and two nominated by the communists. It was to establish inspection teams at five ports of entry on either side and could also conduct "special observations and inspections" at places outside the Demilitarized Zone where violations were reported to have occurred. The NNSC was to report to the Military Armistice Commission. The NNSC never worked effectively. *CM*.

Neutron bomb *see* ENHANCED RADIATION WEAPON (ERW).

Neuve-Chapelle, Battle of. The first major British set-piece attack of the 1914–18 War was made by Haig's First Army at Neuve-Chapelle, south of Armentières, on March 10 1915. Originally conceived as part of a combined offensive, it was decided to proceed independently when French commitments in Champagne precluded their cooperation. Meticulously planned by the First Army staff, the attack, on a narrow 2,000yd (1,800m) front, was intended to eliminate the troublesome salient around Neuve-Chapelle, gain a foothold on Aubers Ridge and threaten Lille, a key railway junction in the region. The artillery was issued with 100,000 rounds, or one-sixth of the BEF's total shell stocks, for its various tasks. On March 10, after a 35-minute hurricane bombardment, the assaulting brigades of IV Corps and the Indian Corps seized the German front trenches, while the artillery provided a curtain of shells to impede the arrival of German reinforcements. However, delays on the flanks caused congestion in the British centre, robbing the attack of its impetus, and German strongpoints also held up the advance. Although the British won possession of Neuve-Chapelle village and flattened the salient, they were unable to exploit their initial success by the time the battle ended on March 13. The British incurred nearly 13,000 casualties, the Germans about 12,000. Neuve-Chapelle furnished the BEF with a preliminary grammar of trench warfare assaults, but many of its lessons – particularly the value of hurricane bombardments – were ignored over the next two years. *PJS*.

Nevada . US battleship. Name ship of class; 10 x 14in guns; first dreadnoughts with "all or nothing" protection. At Scapa Flow 1918. Reconstructed after damage at Pearl Harbor; took part in invasion of France, then Iwo Jima and Okinawa. Target at Bikini; sunk 1948.

Newall, Marshal of the RAF Lord (1886–1963). Br. Chief of the Air Staff 1937–40. During Newall's tenure as CAS it became apparent that the German air force had outstripped the British in numbers and capacity. This resulted in the view that it would be imprudent to provoke German air attack until the imbalance had been corrected. Newall endorsed the policy of restricted bombing which the British followed in the opening months of the war but he believed that the main function of the RAF would be strategic bombing against the heart of Germany, and in the last year of peace he was seriously disquieted by the priority given, at political insistence, to Fighter Command at the expense of Bomber Command. Nevertheless, he deserves credit for the technical and tactical development of Fighter Command which enabled it to win the Battle of Britain. *ANF*.

New Armies. Name given to new military formations – other than those of the Regular Army and Territorial Force – raised in Britain by voluntary enlistment in 1914–15. Like the original BEF, each New Army contained six in-

fantry divisions. The first three New Armies (9th to 26th Divisions) were recruited directly by the War Office, while the Fourth and Fifth New Armies (30th to 41st Divisions) were largely composed of units raised by cities, towns and private committees. The title "New Army" was only used for administrative and training purposes and the individual divisions did not necessarily fight alongside each other on active service. *PJS*.

Newfoundland Regiment. Granted the prefix "Royal" in 1917, the regiment provided an active service battalion which fought on Gallipoli and the Western Front with the British 29th Division and, later, the 9th Division, 1915–18. Only one British battalion suffered heavier losses on July 1 1916.

New Guinea campaign (1942–44). In April 1942, the Japanese offensive was at the flood. The Philippines, Malaya, Singapore, Burma, Dutch East Indies, most of New Guinea and numerous British Pacific islands were in their hands and they had attained the outward limits of expansion previously set by their strategic planners. The ease with which they had gained these prizes now tempted them to extend further the bounds of the "Greater East Asia Co-Prosperity Sphere". The first step was to go for the underbelly of Papua and take Port Moresby with a sea landing launched from Rabaul in New Britain. However, the Japanese radio codes had been broken. Through intercepted signals, the Port Moresby invasion force was caught

off Misima Island on May 7 by carrier-borne aircraft from Adm Fletcher's Task Force 17 in the Coral Sea. After losing a carrier, the Japanese were forced to abandon the Port Moresby plan. Instead, Maj Gen Horii landed with 11,000 troops at Gona on July 21 1942, took Buna and marched south across the Owen Stanley Range, using the Kokoda trail. By September 26 Horii was only 30 miles (48km) from Port Moresby despite vigorous Australian resistance. A landing at Milne Bay at the eastern tip of Papua was successfully repulsed by the Australian garrison in August, and early in October the Australians began to force the Japanese back over the Owen Stanleys.

Heartened by their success at Milne Bay – the first resounding defeat inflicted on Japanese land forces in the war – the Australians invested Buna and Gona by late November. Gona fell on December 19 and Buna early in January 1943. Allied sea and air power were now in the ascendant and through 1943 a series of amphibious landings, brilliantly executed by the US 32nd Division, steadily forced the Japanese back along the coast of northeast New Guinea. Inland, a bold parachute descent, personally overseen by Gen MacArthur, was made at Nadzab on September 5. It was synchronized with the sea landing of the Australian 9th Infantry Division, backed by US Army combat engineers, near Lae. The Australian 7th Division was then flown in to Nadzab. Salamaua was taken on September 12 and Lae four days

Operations on New Guinea-Papua, 1942–44: Japan's Rabaul-based invasion thwarted

later. By now, the Allies were getting highly effective air support from Gen Kenney's 3rd US Air Force and the irresistible drive continued under the energetic Allied commander, Gen Blamey. The 7th Division now drove up the Markham valley whilst the Americans continued their sea landings in support of the Australian 9th Division as it advanced around the coastline of the Huon Peninsula. Finschhafen was captured on October 2 and in April 1944 the jaws of the pincer met at Bogadjim. Madang fell on April 24.

During the period December 1943-March 1944, the US Marines had regained New Britain and the Solomons. Remaining Japanese naval and air bases on New Britain and New Ireland (Rabaul and Kavieng), were now isolated. Between April and July 1944 a series of US landings along the coast of New Guinea eliminated the last Japanese resistance. Although it owed much to air power, the fighting qualities of the incomparable Australian infantry and their American partners showed that the Japanese were not unbeatable supermen. *MH*.

New Jersey. American World War II battleship. Brought out of mothballs to support shore operations during Korean War, and again in Vietnam following the bombing halt in 1968. Her nine 16in guns had much greater power and range than the 8 and 5in guns of the cruisers and destroyers that made up the Navy's shore bombardment force, Task Group 70.8. From September 1968 to March 1969, *New Jersey* mainly supported 3rd Marine Division operations along the demilitarized zone. She also bombarded targets in the North.

New Mexico. US battleship. Name ship of class; 12 x 14in guns. Completed 1918. Major part in Pacific landings, 1943–45.

"New Villages" *see* MALAYAN EMERGENCY.

New York US battleship. Name ship of class; 10 x 14in guns. Completed 1914. Flagship of US squadron with Grand Fleet 1917–18. Atlantic service 1941–43 included "Torch" landings; later at Iwo Jima, Okinawa.

New Zealand Expeditionary Forces. New Zealand troops served overseas in both world wars. In World War I, when 16,654 New Zealanders lost their lives, they usually fought alongside the Australians as part of ANZAC formations. In World War II, the 1st NZ Division served in Greece, Crete, North Africa and Italy. The 2nd Division also fought in Italy where it joined the 1st NZ Division and the 4th Indian Division to form the New Zealand Corps under command of Lt Gen Freyberg. A third NZ division served in the Southwest Pacific theatre (Fiji, New Guinea, Solomons) until 1944 when it was disbanded and used as a reinforcement pool for the 2nd NZ Division in Italy. New Zealand dead in World War II totalled 11,671. *MH*.

New Zealand forces in Korea. The first New Zealand forces to fight in the Korean War were two frigates committed on August 1 1950. They were followed in January 1951 by the 16th Field Artillery Regiment. *See also* BRITISH FORCES IN KOREA; COMMONWEALTH DIVISION.

Ngaundere *see* CAMEROONS (1914–16).

Nghia Lo Ridge campaign (1952). The struggle between Vietnamese and French forces for control of the T'ai hill country west of Hanoi came to a climax in October 1952. The 308th, 312th and 316th Divisions of the People's Army (PAVN) swept over the small French outposts surrounding Nghia Lo and then seized the town on the 18th. That victory immediately placed all other French posts to the north and west in jeopardy. Airheads hastily established by the French at Lai Chau and Na San could be nothing more than isolated strongpoints. The deteriorating situation in this region led the French to mount Operation "Lorraine".

Ngo Dinh Diem *see* DIEM, PRESIDENT NGO DINH.

Ngo Quang Truong, Lt Gen (b.1929). Republic of Vietnam. Commanded the Army of the Republic of Vietnam (ARVN) 1st Division in Hue during the 1968 Tet offensive. Elements of his division were the first to counterattack. In April 1972, as Quang Tri province fell to the communists, Truong took over as I Corps commander and organized a defence line on the south bank of the My Chanh river that saved Hue from capture. Still I Corps commander in 1975, Truong was ordered on March 25 to evacuate Hue and Chu Lai and regroup in Da Nang. However, the rapidity of the communist advance, delays and general chaos prevented his mounting a defence of the latter. On March 28 he ordered his remaining troops to leave Da Nang by sea. *WST*.

Nguyen Cao Ky, Air Vice-Marshal (b.1930). Republic of Vietnam. Received flight training under French auspices and rose to lieutenant in the Vietnam National Army. As a lieutenant colonel in the South Vietnamese Air Force in 1963, Ky participated in the coup against Ngo Dinh Diem. The subsequent jockeying for power subsided in July 1965, when Ky accepted the post of premier in a government headed by Gen Nguyen Van Thieu. Imperious as he was impetuous, Ky alienated support by crushing Buddhist dissidence with force. Under pressure from the US and senior South Vietnamese officers, he agreed in 1967 to run for vice-president on Thieu's ticket. He gradually slipped from view, and Thieu disqualified his candidacy for the presidency in 1971. Ky's flamboyant, martial personality gave him a certain appeal among his fellow-countrymen, but Americans tended to perceive him as brash and irresponsible. *WST*.

Nguyen Chanh Thi, Gen (b.1923). Republic of Vietnam. Commander of I Corps, Army of the Republic of Vietnam (ARVN) when demonstrators led by the militant Buddhist monk Tri Quang rose to protest against Premier Nguyen Cao Ky's postponement of elections in 1966. Ky dismissed Thi, a political ally of Quang's, in March, thinking this would quell the disturbance. But Thi's troops joined the demonstrators and helped them take over the cities of Hue and Da Nang. Fearing regional secession, Ky dispatched loyalist troops to suppress the rebellion and sent Nguyen Chanh Thi into exile.

Nguyen Chi Thanh, Senior General (1914–67). Democratic Republic of Vietnam. On becoming a senior general in 1959, Nguyen Chi Thanh attained a rank in the People's Army of Vietnam (PAVN) held by only one other person, Vo Nguyen Giap. That date also marked the beginning of his assignment, as a member of the Lao Dong (Workers', or Vietnam Communist) Party Political Bureau, to supervise preparations for armed struggle in South Vietnam. In 1961 he relinquished his post as chief of the PAVN General Political Directorate to take over as secretary of the Central Office for South Vietnam (COSVN). A proponent of main force offensives, Thanh opposed reverting to guerrilla warfare, as some advocated when the United States intervened. In June 1967 he travelled to Hanoi to present the draft plan for attacks on the cities that became the Tet offensive and died there of a heart attack on July 6. *WST.*

Nguyen Van Thieu *see* THIEU, GEN NGUYEN VAN.

Nicholas, Gen Grand Duke (1856–1929). Russian. Grand Duke Nicholas' prominence in Russian military affairs was by no means solely a result of his position in the royal family. He studied at the General Staff Academy, served in the Russo-Turkish War, 1877–78, and in 1895–1905 introduced valuable reforms as Inspector General of Cavalry. After the Russo-Japanese War, 1904–05, he became president of the Imperial Committee of National Defence, established to attempt to correct some of the shortcomings of Russian arms revealed in that conflict.

On August 2 1914, Tsar Nicholas II, the Grand Duke's distant cousin, appointed him C-in-C of the Russian armies; this was a position that he neither expected nor desired. Although a physically imposing figure, he was unable to exert close control over the various fronts and was frequently at variance with Sukhomlinov, the Minister of War. Encouraged by French entreaties for help in relieving German pressure in the west, Nicholas' general strategy consisted of little more than launching his armies in a series of offensives that lasted from August

to November. The casualty lists grew without any significant advantage to show for them and the situation did not improve in 1915 with the checking of Gen Ivanov's spring offensive and the Central Powers' counter thrust. A year of reverses inevitably resulted in criticism of the Grand Duke's strategy while, at the same time, the Tsar's unpopularity resulted in his being spoken of as a possible successor. The Tsar's answer to these problems was to take personal control of his armies and the Grand Duke was appointed Governor General of the Caucasus. He nevertheless remained an important figure in Russian political events. In November 1916 he tried to convince the Tsar of the need for constitutional reform in order to prevent the impending catastrophe. Six months later he telegraphed a message to the Tsar adding his voice to the others calling upon him to abdicate. Nicholas wished to re-appoint the Grand Duke as C-in-C but the Provisional Government felt that public feeling would no longer tolerate a Romanov in the post. Instead, he retired to the Crimea and in March 1919 went into exile, spending the remaining years of his life in France and Italy. He thenceforth eschewed any close involvement in the "White Russian" cause. *MS.*

Nicholas II, last Tsar of Russia, in 1915

Nicholas II, Tsar of Russia (1868–1918). Reigned 1894–1917. Defeat in the Russo-Japanese War and the deprivations of 1914–16 damaged his prestige. He assumed the supreme command of his armies in September 1915. He abdicated in March 1917 and was murdered by the Bolsheviks in July 1918.

Nieuport IVG/VIM (French, pre-WWI). Two-seat reconnaissance monoplane. First flew 1911; Type IVM won French military aeroplane competition, 1911. In addition to French military use, several Type IVG supplied to RFC and to Italian *Battaglione Specialisti*, which took three to Libya October 1911: one made the first wartime aerial reconnaissance, October 23, Italo-Turkish War 1911–12. In RFC no Nieuport monoplane actively survived the so-called Monoplane Ban of 1912. Some, including later but similar Type VIM, acquired by many other nations before 1914. One 50hp, 70hp or 100hp Gnome engine; speed 55mph (88kph); armament nil.

Nieuport Scouts 11 to 27 (French, WWI). Single-seat fighting scout. Prototype Nie 11 flew summer 1915; first delivery to operational *escadrille* January 5 1916. Successfully countered Fokker monoplanes; developed via 110hp Type 16 to Types 17, 17bis, 21, 23, and to more refined Types 24, 24bis and 27. Outclassed by autumn 1917; Type 27 in use with RFC/RAF until April 1918. Widely used by Allied air services; various types built Britain, Italy, Russia and (postwar) Japan. One 80–130hp rotary engine, normally Le Rhône or Clerget; max. speed (Nie 27) 107mph (171kph); one (rarely two) 0.303in machine gun.

"Night of the Long Knives". Hitler's purge of the SA, carried out on June 30 1934.

Nijmegen. The bridges across the Waal river at Nijimegen, about 10 miles (16km) south of Arnhem, and across the Maas at Grave, some 7 miles (11km) south of Nijmegen, formed the central objectives of "Market Garden", the airborne operation to open a corridor to the Lower Rhine. In a daylight landing on September 17 1944 – when British 1st Airborne Division landed at Arnhem to the north and US 101st Airborne Division at Eindhoven to the south – Maj Gen James Gavin's US 82nd Airborne Division paratroopers dropped at Grave, where 504th Parachute Infantry quickly secured the bridge. Reinforced by glider-borne troops, 82nd Airborne advanced on Nijmegen against stiff resistance (about 1,400 casualties, September 17–19). British XXX Corps advanced from Eindhoven to link with 82nd Airborne early on September 19. Later that day, British Guards Armoured Division and 82nd Airborne secured Nijmegen bridge – but the delay had serious consequences at Arnhen. *RO'N*.

Nimitz, US Navy c-in-c, Pacific

Nimitz, Fleet Adm Chester William (1885–1966). US. c-in-c US Pacific Fleet 1941–45. On assuming command after Pearl Harbor, Nimitz faced an alarming preponderance of Japanese naval strength and badly damaged morale in the surviving portions of his own. He met the situation with strategic insight unsurpassed by any other naval commander of the time and an unerring judgment of his subordinate commanders. A delicately balanced combination of patience and daring resulted in the crucial victory at Midway in June 1942, severely reducing the Japanese numerical superiority in carriers. A series of brilliant victories followed until, in October 1944, the Battle of Leyte Gulf resulted in an overwhelming victory for Nimitz's fleets, the Seventh under Kinkaid and the Third under Halsey. Japanese losses included four aircraft carriers, three battleships, ten cruisers and eleven destroyers. The Americans lost no heavy ships and only two destroyers, one light carrier and two escort carriers and some auxiliary vessels. With overwhelming naval superiority in the Pacific, Nimitz was able to strengthen the blockade which ensured Japan's ultimate defeat (although not the date of it, as other actions did). Unlike most of his predecessors and many of his contempor-

aries, Nimitz commanded from ashore but the glamour which he thus sacrificed was more than amply compensated for by the results he achieved. *ANF*.

Nimrod, British Aerospace (Br). Maritime reconnaissance; crew 12. Prototype flew May 23 1967; first deliveries from October 2 1969; first squadron formed mid-1970. Thirty-two aircraft converted to Nimrod MR Mark 2 from 1981. Several operated from Ascension Island during Falklands War, 1982: about 150 sorties, some up to 19 hours' duration. Four 12,140lb (5,507kg) s.t. Rolls-Royce Spey 250 engines; max. speed 575mph (925kph); war load wide range sonobuoys, Stingray torpedo, AGM-84 Harpoon, mines, depth charges, bombs, air-surface missiles.

Ninth Air Force (US). Formed in 1942 for operations in North Africa, flying alongside 12th US Air Force and British Desert Air Force in the Tunisian campaign and against Axis shipping in the Mediterranean. Moved to Britain for "Overlord" and, with 8th USAAF, constituted the greatest instrument for total support of land operations ever seen, operating from the front line to targets deep within the Third Reich.

Ninth Army (US). Fought under command of Lt Gen William H Simpson in Northwest European campaign, 1944–45. After the Normandy landings, deployed in Brittany. In November, was advancing up to German border. When Germans attacked in Ardennes, December 1944, Ninth Army was placed under command of Montgomery's 21st Army Group and after crossing the Rhine, March 1945, formed left wing of pincer which cut off the Ruhr. Pushing aside the collapsing German Army Group H, the Ninth advanced to the Elbe and met the Red Army on April 25 1945.

Nishizawa, Chief Warrant Officer Hiroyoshi (1920–44). "Devil" Nishizawa, a naval Mitsubishi A6M Zero pilot, was Japan's leading ace in World War II, variously credited with 74-200 "kills" (104 seems the nearest correct figure).

Nivelle, Gen Robert (1856–1924). Fr. Commanded an artillery regiment in 1914 and distinguished himself at the Battle of the Marne, where he deployed his guns swiftly and skilfully to engage the Germans at close range. Thereafter his rise was meteoric. A firm believer in the offensive, he was promoted brigadier in October 1914, given a division early in 1915 and by December that year was in command of III Corps. In late March 1916 he was transferred to the Verdun sector, where Pétain considered his tactics too costly, but Joffre was impressed by him and, on April 19, when Pétain was elevated to command the Central Army Group, Nivelle took over the Second Army. In the French counterstrokes at Verdun from October to December, Nivelle's use of the "creeping barrage", behind which the infantry advanced, was outstandingly successful. Now a national hero, he replaced Joffre as French c-in-c in December 1916. Allied political leaders were persuaded by Nivelle's eloquence and self-confidence that his tactical formula of saturation bombardment, followed by the creeping barrage and violent infantry assaults, would achieve the long-promised decisive breakthrough in his proposed spring offensive. At the Calais Conference in February 1917, Lloyd George even tried to make Haig permanently subordinate to Nivelle. However, the disastrous failure of his April offensive on the Aisne and in Champagne provoked widespread mutinies in the French Army and Nivelle was succeeded by Pétain on May 15 1917. He never again held high command. *PJS*.

Nixon, Gen Sir John (1857–1921). Br. Indian Army officer (Cavalry); commanded Expeditionary Force in Mesopotamia, 1915–16.

Nixon, President Richard M (b.1913). US. Elected President of the United States partly on the strength of popular expectations that he would end American involvement in the Vietnam War. In fact, Nixon had previously defended the war on the grounds that it contained China and bought time for "free" Asian nations to develop. Upon taking office in

N

January 1969, however, his main aim was simply to extricate the US in circumstances that would not be construed as defeat. The strategy gradually worked out by Nixon and his national security adviser, Henry Kissinger, had two main components: improvement of relations with the Soviet Union and China in return for their help in extracting compromise from Hanoi and "Vietnamization".

Nixon also exceeded previous tacit limits on the use of armed force. He authorized the secret "Menu" bombings of communist base areas in Cambodia beginning March 1969; he approved the "incursion" into Cambodia in 1970; and he supported the South Vietnamese penetration of southern Laos (Operation "Lam Son 719") in 1971. When Hanoi refused to make concessions and launched the Easter offensive in March 1972, Nixon retaliated with the most devastating bombardment of the war and mined the North's harbours.

The hope that spasms of force combined with his reputation for anti-communist zeal would induce Hanoi to compromise constituted Nixon's "madman theory of war". However, Nixon undermined the credibility of his own threat by withdrawing troops in order to maintain domestic support. Those withdrawals brought the number of US troops in South Vietnam down to 47,000 by June 1972, leaving airpower as Nixon's only military option. His order for B-52s to bomb Hanoi and Haiphong in December 1972 (Operation "Linebacker II") brought Hanoi back to the negotiating table but did not result in substantive change of the draft agreement. That bombing also turned opinion in Congress decisively against Nixon's conduct of the war, and once the Paris Agreement was signed Congress began to legislate restrictions on the use of American forces, beginning with an August 15 deadline for the cessation of bombing in Cambodia. In April 1974, with renewed fighting in Vietnam, the House of Representatives rejected Nixon's request for a $474 million increase in military aid to Saigon. The Watergate scandal then overwhelmed his administration, and on August 9 Nixon resigned, to be replaced by Gerald R Ford. *WST*.

NKVD. Acronym from *Narodnyi Kommissariat Vniutrennikh Del* (People's Commissariat of Internal Affairs), a Soviet organization with a wide range of security, intelligence and special operations tasks.

Noble, Adm Sir Percy Lockhart Harnam (1880–1955). Br. A cruiser officer during World War I, Noble commanded on the China Station, 1937–40, and in February 1941 succeeded Adm Dunbar-Nasmith as c-in-c, Western Approaches. His training and organizational skills laid the basis for the successful anti-submarine campaign pursued by his successor, Adm Horton, from November 1942. As head of the British Admiralty delegation in Washington, 1943, he was notable for his diplomatic handling of Anglo-US naval cooperation.

Nogi: embodiment of Samurai virtues

Nogi, Gen Count Maresuke (1849–1912). Jap. In Japan, Nogi was long regarded as the embodiment of all the traditional *bushido* virtues of the samurai, and the suicidal gallantry displayed by Japanese servicemen in World War II owed much to his example. He proved outstandingly successful in transmitting the values of absolute loyalty and unquestioning self-sacrifice to the men under his command during the Russo-Japanese War. Commanding Third Army, Nogi conducted the siege of Port Arthur (which he himself had taken from the Chinese in 1894) with utter ruthlessness, flinging his men in human waves against field fortifications strengthened by barbed wire, well-sited machine guns and supporting artillery. In an unsuccess-

ful frontal attack on August 19–24 1904, Nogi lost 15,000 men to the Russian's 3,000; in the decisive assault on 203 Metre Hill, November 27–December 5 1904, some 11,000 Japanese were killed. Both of Nogi's sons fell. Nogi, who believed himself permanently dishonoured after losing an imperial standard during the Satsuma Rebellion of 1877, manifested a strong death-wish: immediately after the war he asked, and was refused, Emperor Meiji's permission to commit suicide. In 1912, on the death of Meiji, Nogi and his wife committed suicide. *RO'N*.

Nomonhan incident (Khalkhin Gol), (May–August 1939). On May 11 1939, claiming territory along the Khalkhin Gol (Khalkha river), Outer Mongolia, for their puppet state of Manchukuo (Manchuria), the Japanese Kwantung Army attacked border forces of the Mongolian Republic, which invoked Soviet aid. By early August, Japanese Sixth Army deployed c75,000 men, 500 guns, 200 tanks and 500 aircraft; opposed was a combined Soviet-Mongolian force under Zhukov, with c100,000 men, 1,000 guns, 700 tanks and armoured cars and 500 aircraft. On August 20, Zhukov launched a massive attack at Nomonhan. Japanese forward positions were plastered by Soviet bombers; the main advance was spearheaded by flame-throwing tanks; tanks, armoured cars and Mongolian horsed cavalry supported infantry in a frontal attack, while an independent tank force circled to strike at the Japanese rear. In a ten-day blitzkrieg, Zhukov drove back the Japanese into Manchuria. The Japanese admitted to 18,000 casualties; the Soviets to 9,800. The outcome of the major air battles of the campaign remains obscure: the Japanese claimed 1,260 victories for 168 losses; the Soviets claimed 660 victories and admitted 207 losses. *RO'N*.

Nomura, Adm Kichisaburo (1877–1964). Japanese Foreign Minister, 1939; Ambassador to US, 1940. Attempted to improve relations, but on December 7 1941 was ordered to deliver declaration of war in Washington: circumstances resulted in delivery shortly *after* Pearl Harbor attack.

Non Proliferation Treaty (NPT).
In 1969 the USA, USSR, UK and most nations of the world signed a treaty to prevent the transfer of nuclear weapons from a nuclear weapons state to a non-nuclear weapons state and the making of nuclear weapons by non-nuclear weapons states. The treaty entered into force in 1970. Non-nuclear weapons states must submit all their nuclear facilities to a system of safeguards run by the International Atomic Energy Authority. These monitor that no fissile material is being diverted for illicit purposes. Not all nations have signed the NPT. Of the nuclear weapon states, France and China refused to sign, although they state unilaterally that they will not transfer nuclear weapons. A number of near-nuclear states are also non-signatories, notably India (which has exploded a nuclear device), Israel (which has not openly tested), Pakistan and South Africa. NPT cannot prevent these states or others acquiring nuclear weapons, but it does create an international consensus against proliferation and reassures many states that their neighbours do not harbour nuclear ambitions. The treaty is reviewed at five-yearly intervals. *EJG.*

Normandy, invasion of (1944).
Planning for the opening of the long-awaited Second Front in western Europe began in earnest in April 1943 with the appointment of Lt Gen Sir Frederick Morgan as COS to the Supreme Allied Commander, as yet unnamed. Normandy was chosen for the invasion in preference to the Pas de Calais, where the beaches were more heavily defended and German fighters in the Low Countries much nearer. Elaborate deception plans (codenamed "Fortitude") were devised to convince the Germans that the Pas de Calais, even Scandinavia, were the real targets. In preparing for the assault, valuable lessons were learnt from the failure of the Dieppe raid in 1942. New landing craft were developed, together with a "siege-train" of armoured vehicles – nicknamed "Funnies" – adapted for specialized tasks, such as mine-clearing, bridge-laying and flame-throwing. Eisenhower was appointed Supreme Commander for the invasion – Operation "Overlord" – in December 1943, with Gen Montgomery as ground forces commander in the opening phase.

On D-Day, June 6 1944, the invasion began with airborne landings to protect the flanks – the US 1st and 82nd Airborne Divisions to the west and the British 6th Airborne Division to the east. Bad weather had delayed D-Day for 24 hours, but it also put the Germans off their guard. Heavy air and naval bombardments preceded the amphibious landings. Some 7,000 vessels were available for naval operations, codenamed "Neptune". From 0630 hours the Allied assault divisions landed on five beaches – west to east, the US 4th Division (Utah beach), US 1st Division (Omaha), British 50th Division (Gold), Canadian 3rd Division (Juno) and British 3rd Division (Sword). Allied aircraft dominated the skies, flying over 14,000 sorties on June 6. The Americans on Omaha suffered the heaviest casualties, but the Allies had put 156,000 troops ashore.

The Allies had established a solid lodgement area 50 miles (80km) wide by June 12, and were rapidly building up their forces. Two artificial harbours – Mulberries – were constructed at Arromanches and off Omaha beach. But a storm in the Channel (June 19–22) wrecked the latter, and badly delayed Allied operations. Progress was slow, as the thick hedgerows of the bocage favoured the German defenders, although they were never able to wrest the initiative from the Allies, who had mastery of the air. The British and Canadians had a bitter struggle to capture Caen, but this achieved Montgomery's aim of drawing the Germans to the British sector, easing the way for the Americans in the west. St Lô fell to the Americans on July 18, and their breakout – Operation "Cobra" – began on July 25. Armoured forces raced into Brittany and turned east towards Le Mans. Hitler ordered a counterattack to cut them off at Avranches on August 7. It failed, leaving the Seventh Army trapped in a pocket as the Canadians took Falaise on August 16 and the Americans swung north to Argentan. When the pocket was finally closed on August 21, the Battle of Normandy was over. *SB.*

D-Day, June 6, 1944: the Normandy landings mark the beginning of Operation "Overlord"

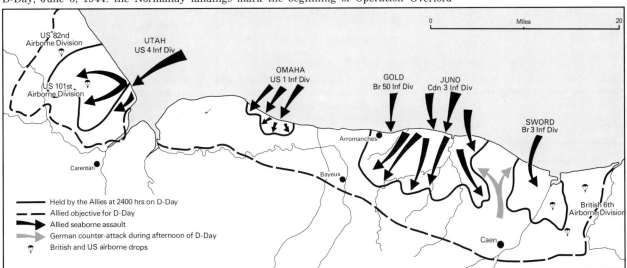

309

Norrie, Lt Gen Lord (1893–1977). Br. Commander XXX Corps in Operation "Crusader", at Gazala, and during withdrawal to El Alamein, 1941–42.

Norstad, Gen Lauris (1907–88). US. Beginning his military career as a cavalry officer, Norstad transferred to the US Army Air Corps in 1931 and, by February 1942 was a lieutenant colonel on Gen Arnold's staff in Washington. In August he was appointed Assistant Chief of Staff for Operations first with the Twelfth Air Force and, from February 1943, with the Northwest African Air Forces. After service in Italy, he was recalled to Washington in August 1944 to become Chief of Staff of the Twentieth Air Force. In addition, Norstad was called upon to act as Deputy Chief of Air Staff at Army Air Force Headquarters. After the war his career continued to flourish with appointments as Director of Plans and Operations at the War Department (1947) and Commander-in-Chief of the US Air Force in Europe (1950). From November 1953 he served as Supreme Allied Commander (SHAPE) and Commander-in-Chief of US European Command. He retired in 1963. *MS*.

NORTHAG. NATO's Northern Army Group which occupies the northern half of the Central Front in West Germany. Commanded by a British general, subordinate to the NATO C-in-C Central Europe, NORTHAG consists, north to south, of I Dutch Corps, I German Corps, I British Corps and I Belgian Corps; III American Corps would form the Army Group reserve on mobilization. NORTHAG's commanders in the early 1980s developed an innovative concept of more mobile and fluid conventional defence designed to raise the nuclear threshold.

North, Adm Sir Dudley (1881–1961). Br. Commander North Atlantic Station at Gibraltar during the destruction of the French Fleet at Mers-el-Kébir in July 1940; somewhat unfairly dismissed by Churchill for not intercepting the French cruisers that ran the Straits of Gibraltar in September 1940 on their way to Dakar in French West Africa.

North African landings, Anglo-American (Operation "Torch", November 7–10 1942) under Supreme Allied Command of Eisenhower. The landings were divided between three main areas. *Western Task Force* was sent to Morocco: three US divisions under Patton landed at Safi, Fedala and Port Lyautey against sporadic French resistance, and advanced on Casablanca, which was entered on November 10 after considerable naval and land-forces resistance was overcome. *Central Task Force* landed at Oran, where 1st US Division (Fredendall) met stiff French resistance. US parachute landings to capture the airfields failed. The garrison of Oran resisted until a direct assault was launched, supported by naval and air bombardments, on November 10. *Eastern Task Force* deployed at Algiers: the landing of 34th US Division with one brigade of 78th British Division was helped by anti-Vichy French officers organized by Gen Mast, COS of the French XIX Corps in Algiers. The fortuitous presence of Adm Darlan led to a negotiated cease-fire at Algiers on November 8, and its extension to the rest of French North Africa on the 10th. *WGFJ*.

North Atlantic Treaty Organization (NATO). The alliance formed in 1949 between the USA, the UK, France, Italy, Belgium, the Netherlands, Luxembourg, Norway, Denmark, Canada, Iceland and Portugal and subsequently joined by Greece, Turkey, West Germany and Spain. The parties to the Atlantic Treaty agree to treat an attack on one as an attack on all. NATO has an integrated military command structure in which all but France, Spain and Iceland (which has no armed forces) participate. The supreme authority in NATO is the North Atlantic Council that meets once a week at ambassadorial level and twice a year at foreign-minister level. When representatives of those countries that do not participate militarily are excluded, the Council becomes the Defence Planning Committee (DPC). NATO's main military authority is the Military Committee that contains representatives of the members' chiefs of staff; the latter meet twice a year. Under the Military Committee come the three regional commands, Europe, Atlantic and Channel. The commands are integrated HQS responsible for planning the defence of their respective areas and holding exercises. The Atlantic and Channel commands have their own small integrated multinational forces under command in peacetime and Allied Command Europe has the ACE Mobile force for rapid dispatch to the flanks of the command. The commands are further subdivided into army groups and air forces or maritime areas and sub-areas. Policy guidance on nuclear strategy and forces is worked out in the Nuclear Planning Group, effectively a subcommittee of the DPC. *EJG*.

North Cape, Battle of. The action off the North Cape of Norway fought on December 26 1943 in which the German battlecruiser *Scharnhorst* was sunk. On the evening of Christmas Day, *Scharnhorst*, supported by five destroyers under Rear Adm Erich Bey sailed from Alten Fjord with orders to attack a convoy of 19 ships escorted by 10 destroyers en route for Russia, but to evade contact with major British units. Intelligence and intuition enabled Fraser, commanding the British Home Fleet, to manoeuvre three cruisers, *Belfast*, *Norfolk* and *Sheffield*, under Vice Adm Burnett, to an interposing position which, on the morning of December 26 brought on an action in which *Scharnhorst*'s radar was damaged. After a second encounter with Burnett's force, Bey broke off the action and proceeded at high speed towards the haven of a Norwegian port. Meanwhile, Fraser had come up with his 14in-gun flagship, *Duke of York*, and, at 1647 hours, he opened fire at 13,000yd (12,000m) range. Although *Scharnhorst* received three direct hits, her speed was greater than *Duke of York*'s and she succeeded by 1900 hours in opening the range to 22,000yd (20,000m). Fraser, however, had worked four destroyers ahead of her and they delivered a torpedo attack which slowed *Scharnhorst* and enabled *Duke of York* to come up again. At least ten more shell hits and further torpedo strikes crippled *Scharnhorst*; she capsized and sank with the loss of all but 36 of her complement of 1,900. *ANF*.

North Kalimantan National Army (TENTERA NASIONAL KALIMANTAN UTARA [TNKU]) *see* BRUNEI REVOLT.

North Korean People's Army (NKPA). Originated in the national security forces created by the North Korean Interim People's Committee in 1946. These forces, organized by Choe Yong Gon, became the nucleus of an army which grew to 100,000 men when the DPRK emerged in 1948 and Soviet troops withdrew. The NKPA was structured on the Soviet model with manpower concentrated in the combat units and was trained by Soviet advisers. Before the Korean War began in June 1950, it was strengthened by 150 Soviet tanks and the return of Korean veterans who had been fighting in the Chinese Civil War. On June 25 1950 the NKPA crossed the 38th Parallel with the main weight of the attack directed towards Seoul. The NKPA was not fully mobilized, deploying 38,000 men in the initial attack, suggesting that either the North Koreans expected a quick victory or that the offensive had been launched earlier than planned. When the US intervened, the NKPA hastily mobilized additional divisions. Although outnumbered and outgunned by August 1950, the NKPA fought with skill and fanaticism, creating a crisis on the Pusan Perimeter as late as September 1950. The Inchon landings dealt the NKPA a heavy blow but many troops continued to fight in the south as guerrillas or escaped into the northern mountains. The NKPA was reorganized with Soviet equipment after China entered the war in December 1950 and fought on the eastern sector of the front. In August–September 1951 it was involved in the heavy fighting around the Punchbowl at Bloody Ridge/Heartbreak Ridge. By the end of the war, total NKPA strength was approximately 257,000. *CM.*

Northrop F-5 (US). Single-seat/two-seat lightweight fighter. Prototype flew July 30 1959; selected by US Department of Defense for supply to favoured nations (over 30) under Military Assistance Program, May 1962; these included Iran, which received 104 F-5As/RF-5As, 23 F-5Bs, 141 F-5Es, 28 F-5Fs; and South Vietnam, 172 F-5As, 8 F-5Bs and about 48 F-5Es. Production 2,610, ended January 1987. Two 4,080/5,000lb (1,851–2,268kg) s.t. General Electric J85-GE-13/-21 engines; max. speed (F-5A) 898mph (1,445kph); two 20mm cannon, 6,200lb (2,812kg) external ordnance.

North Russian Expeditionary Force. The deteriorating situation in North Russia in the spring of 1918 led to the dispatch of British forces to protect Allied supplies and deter any German moves in the area. They became increasingly involved in operations against Bolshevik forces before their final evacuation from Murmansk in October 1919.

North Vietnamese Army *see* PEOPLE'S ARMY OF VIETNAM (PAVN).

Northwest European campaign (1944–45). Although the Allied bridgehead in Normandy was quickly secured, mounting German resistance frustrated attempts at achieving a breakout. The British Second Army's Operation "Goodwood" soon degenerated into an attritional struggle for Caen while the Americans' Operation "Cobra" was slow to develop. However Patton imparted a fresh impetus, attacking on August 1 and striking into Brittany before wheeling eastwards. A German counterattack against the bridgehead was frustrated and 50,000 troops were encircled and captured in the Argentan-Falaise gap. The success of the Allied breakout and the disarray of the German forces led Eisenhower to amend his plans and approve a rapid advance to the River Seine. On August 25 Paris was liberated; meanwhile on the 15th the Allies had landed in the South of France. On September 11 the Allied invasion forces met and Eisenhower had a continuous front from the Mediterranean to the Channel. While wishing to exert pressure along the length of the line, the Supreme Commander supported a thrust by Montgomery's 21st Army Group into northern France and Belgium. On September 3 the British Second Army captured Brussels and the following day took Antwerp. As the Allies approached the German border, enemy resistance grew more resolute. Furthermore the rapidity of the advance had exhausted Allied manpower and resources. These factors helped convince Eisenhower to approve Operation "Market Garden", that envisaged the seizure of the Rhine Crossings and a sweep into the Ruhr. Launched on September 17, the plan failed with ground troops unable to relieve airborne forces at Arnhem. Although the broad front policy was thus vindicated, a measured advance also entailed heavy fighting in the Vosges, the Hürtgen Forest and the Saar. Allied fatigue and complacency proved costly when, on December 16, the Germans launched a counteroffensive in the Ardennes. Although with little chance of success, the strength of the attack surprised and disturbed the Allies. Insufficient men and material forced the Germans to retire and, by the end of January 1945, they had nothing to show for their 100,000 casualties and the loss of irreplaceable reserves of fuel and equipment. Furthermore, Hitler's refusal to allow a retreat to the east bank of the Rhine resulted in additional losses. Ultimately, the Rhine failed to constitute a major defensive barrier, for on March 7, elements of the American 9th Armored Division were able to establish the first Allied bridgehead across the river, securing the Ludendorff bridge at Remagen while German army engineers were in the very act of demolishing it. However, the main Allied effort came on the 23rd with Operation "Plunder", the 21st Army Group's assault across the Rhine. By April 18 the Ruhr "pocket" had been encircled, eliminating 325,000 German troops, and Allied forces streamed into Germany, encountering both fanatical resistance and peaceful capitulation. American, French and British units fanned out into southern Germany, Austria, Czechoslovakia and Italy and on April 25 1945 contact was made with Soviet ground forces. Finally on May 4 Montgomery received the formal surrender of German forces in the north while Gen Devers accepted the capitulation of those in the south. The formal conclusion of hostilities occurred on May 7 1945 with a surrender ceremony concluded at Reims. *MS.*

Norway, German invasion of

(April 2–9 1940). The plan depended on surprise, which was successfully achieved. Equipment carrying merchantmen, disguised as coal ships, left German ports on April 2, followed on the 6th by six naval task forces, transporting the leading elements of the German occupation forces for Oslo, Kristiansand, Egersund, Bergen, Trondheim and Narvik. They were assisted by parachute drops on important Norwegian airfields, and air-landing of reinforcements. Two-thirds of the German submarine fleet was deployed to protect them. The winter weather fortuitously helped – fog and low cloud blinding Allied air reconnaissance, and high seas in the North Sea slowing the British Home Fleet which failed to intercept through faulty intelligence.

All objectives were taken against sporadic Norwegian resistance. German naval losses were significant: cruiser *Blücher* was sunk and pocket battleship *Lützow* damaged by the guns of the Oslo forts; cruiser *Karlsruhe* was sunk by the British submarine *Truant* off Kristiansand; the cruiser *Königsberg* was damaged by fire from the forts at Bergen on April 9, then sunk by Skua dive-bombers next day (usually accepted as the first sinking of a major warship by dive-bombers); cruiser *Hipper* was rammed and damaged by the British destroyer *Glowworm* off Trondheim; battlecruiser *Gneisenau* was hit twice and badly damaged by *Renown* off Narvik; battlecruiser *Scharnhorst* suffered torpedo damage and some ten equipment-carrying merchant ships were sunk. *WGFJ*.

Norwegian campaign

(April 8– June 8 1940). During the winter of 1939–40, both Allied and German High Commands drew up contingency plans to invade Norway. In September 1939, the Allies planned to mine Norwegian territorial waters – the Leads – to stop the flow of Swedish iron ore from Narvik to Germany. By December, the plan included a landing at Narvik, and an advance inland to occupy the iron ore mines in the Kiruna-Gallivare district of northern Sweden, close to the Finnish frontier. Landings at Stavanger, Bergen and Trondheim would fore-

German machine gun team (with Norwegian prisoner) in action near Narvik, 1940

stall German countermeasures.

Occupation of Norway was not included in Germany's original war plans. However, Hitler, advised by Adm Raeder, decided in December 1939 that there would be advantage in occupying Denmark and Norway to secure submarine and air bases from which to outflank the British naval blockade, while protecting supplies of Swedish iron ore, vital to German armament production. Hitler considered engineering a coup d'état led by the pro-Nazi Vidkun Quisling, but, doubting the strength of Quisling's support, opted for a military solution. Gen von Falkenhorst was appointed to plan and command a joint naval, land and air operation, deploying six divisions (including the specially trained and equipped 3rd Mountain Division, commanded by Gen Dietl. The leading elements of the invasion forces were to be transported and covered by the whole German Navy, and supported by over 1,000 aircraft.

Neither side was prepared to infringe Scandinavian neutrality without a good excuse. The Russian invasion of Finland in November 1939 gave the Allies a pretext for intervention, but their plans collapsed when the Finns accepted Russian armistice terms on March 12 1940. The Allies revived their invasion plans on March 28 1940 in order to bring greater economic pressure to bear on Germany. Mining of the Leads was to start on April 5. They made two grave errors of judgment: first, they assumed that the Germans would not risk their fleet in the face of British naval superiority; and, secondly, they underesti-

mated the crippling effects of German air superiority.

Hitler struck first: in a superbly coordinated operation, Copenhagen, Oslo, Kristiansand, Egersund, Stavanger, Bergen, Trondheim and Narvik were all occupied by April 9. German naval losses were heavy, but their troops held all the Allies' proposed objectives.

The Allies' reaction was fumbling and piecemeal. As soon as the German Fleet was known to be at sea, the British Home Fleet (Adm Forbes) disembarked all troops already loaded for the proposed occupation of Stavanger, Bergen and Trondheim, and sailed to intercept, but was too late. Five of six German naval task forces had landed their troops and returned to Germany, but ten destroyers of the sixth were destroyed in the Narvik fjords on April 10–13.

On April 10, the Allies decided to concentrate on the capture of Narvik, placing naval forces under Adm of the Fleet, the Earl of Cork and Orrery, and two British infantry brigades (one regular and one territorial) under Maj Gen Mackesy (1883–1956), Commander 49th Division. The troops started to land on April 14 at Harstad, on an island 60 miles (96km) west of Narvik, which was to be developed as an advanced base for an attack on the port, and an advance to the Swedish iron ore mines. The Admiral wanted to attack at once while the Germans were disorganized after the second naval engagement, but Mackesy deemed it impractical to do so without landing craft, and in the prevailing bad weather. The subsequent naval bombardment on April 24 did not induce a German surrender, but by then Narvik had lost operational priority.

Appeals from the Norwegian government to help re-take Trondheim and to check the German advance north from Oslo, led to an Allied decision to intervene in Central Norway. A direct attack on the city was rejected as too hazardous. Instead, an envelopment was attempted with the landings of British and French troops at Namsos to the north on April 16, and of British troops only at Åndalsnes to the south two days later. Allied operations were under the command of Lt Gen Massy.

Luftwaffe bombing soon made it impossible to unload ships in daylight at either port. With barely four hours of darkness at that latitude, and with only the most primitive port facilities, logistic support of both forces became impracticable. A squadron of RAF Gladiator fighters was landed on a frozen lake near Åndalsnes, but only operated for a day before the ice was broken up by German bombing. Fighter cover from carriers and long-range RAF attacks proved ineffective. A decision to abandon central Norway and to concentrate once more on securing Narvik was taken on April 27. The hazardous evacuations of Åndalsnes and Namsos were completed by May 3.

The collapse of British efforts to re-take Trondheim led to Chamberlain's replacement by Churchill as British Prime Minister. Lt Gen Auchinleck was sent to take command of the British, French, Polish and Norwegian land forces by then besieging Narvik. He arrived on May 11, but again operations at Narvik lost importance because the German invasion of France had started on May 10. Although Narvik fell on May 28, a decision to abandon northern Norway had been made in London on May 24.

The evacuation of Narvik on June 8 was marred by the loss of the carrier *Furious* in a chance encounter with *Gneisenau* and *Scharnhorst*, both of which suffered serious damage, leaving the German fleet without a major unit fit for sea by the end of the campaign. The German occupation of Norway was completed when Gen Ruge, the Norwegian c-in-c, accepted armistice terms on June 9 1940. *WGFJ*.

Notre Dame de Lorette. Commanding spur, northwest of Vimy Ridge, captured by the French Tenth Army, after heavy fighting, in May 1915.

Nowotny, Maj Walter (1920-1944). Austrian. Highest-scoring Austrian (and fifth-highest-scoring Luftwaffe) fighter pilot of World War II. With 255 "kills" over Russia, Nowotny returned to Germany to command *Erprobungs Kommando Nowotny*, first Messerschmitt Me 262 fighter unit, operational October 1944. After scoring three victories, he was killed on November 8 1944.

Noyon-Montdidier, Battle of *see* MARCH OFFENSIVE, GERMAN (1918).

Nuclear weapon. The proper name for weapons that use the energy locked up in the nucleus of the atom, where the strong nuclear force binds together electrostatically repellent protons and neutral neutrons. Certain "fissile" materials, notably uranium-235 and plutonium-239, can be induced to produce explosive nuclear chain reactions in the right or critical masses/densities. A neutron source causes one nucleus to fission, which produces neutrons, which produce more fissions, etc. A robust old form of nuclear weapon was the "gun" type, in which a small piece of uranium-235 was shot into a larger piece, producing criticality. A more efficient form is to implode a sub-critical sphere of fissile material to critical density. Fission nuclear weapons have yields in the kiloton range which can be boosted using thermonuclear material and form the "primaries" of thermonuclear weapons proper. *EJG*.

Nungesser, Capt Charles Eugène Jules Marie (1892-1927). Fr. Third highest-scoring French fighter pilot of World War I, with 45 "kills". Flamboyant and aggressive, Nungesser was seriously injured, in combat or accidents, more than 12 times. He disappeared while attempting a solo east-to-west crossing of the Atlantic.

Nuremberg, bombing of, (March 30–31 1944). RAF Bomber Command's most disastrous major attack: of 795 aircraft dispatched,

Nuremberg after RAF raid, 1944

94 failed to return and 74 were damaged, (12 beyond repair). The German night-fighter force inflicted most casualties. An undeviating route from Charleroi eastward for nearly 250 miles (400km) to near Fulda took the bombers past the known positions of two night-fighter beacons, giving the fighters exceptional opportunities for interception (more than 40 combats on the long leg), and making the eventual target obvious. No diversionary operations were mounted. In the target area, where visibility was unexpectedly good, there were 23 combats. *ANF*.

Nuremberg Rallies. Spectacular Nazi Party celebrations first held in 1923 and increasing in size throughout the 1930s.

Nuremberg: Nazis in the dock

Nuremberg Trials. Military Tribunal convened by Britain, USA, France and Soviet Union following victory in Europe, 1945. In the principal trial, November 20 1945 – September 30 1946, 21 surviving Nazi leaders were charged with various "war crimes": 11 were condemned to death, 7 to long imprisonment and 3 acquitted. Although the charges were based on internationally accepted laws and conventions, doubts have been expressed concerning the ethics of the victors judging the vanquished. *MS*.

O

Oboe. British ground to air to ground blind bombing radar system. Two ground stations ("Cat" and "Mouse") calculated the range and track of the aircraft and directed the pilot by notes resembling woodwind. Introduced December 1942; chiefly used by Pathfinder Force Mosquitoes for target marking. Oboe depended for range upon altitude and could only be used by small numbers of aircraft at one time.

Occupied Europe. The European territories conquered by Germany in World War II, i.e. Poland, Denmark, Norway, France, Belgium, Holland, Yugoslavia, Greece, Western Russia, Lithuania, Latvia and Estonia.

O'Connor, Gen Sir Richard (1889–1988). Br. Commander Western Desert Force to February 1941. Destroyed Italian Tenth Army in Egypt and Cyrenaica during the Battle of Sidi Barrani (December 1940). Captured during Rommel's first offensive into Cyrenaica, April 1941 and imprisoned in Italy, but escaped during the confusion of the Italian capitulation in September 1943. Commanded VIII Corps in Northwest Europe 1944, then Eastern Command in India in 1945 and Western Command in 1946–47 during the partition.

October Revolution *see* RUSSIAN REVOLUTION.

O'Daniel, Lt Gen John Wilson ("Iron Mike") (1894–1975). US. A combat veteran of World War I, O'Daniel was a brigade commander in North Africa, Sicily and at Salerno, 1942–43. In February 1944, he took command of 3rd Infantry Division at Anzio, succeeding Truscott, who had replaced Lucas in overall command, and led it until the war's end, when it occupied Hitler's mountain retreat at Berchtesgaden, southern Bavaria. O'Daniel held a command in the Korean War and in 1954–55 headed the US Military Assistance and Advisory Group (MAAG) in South Vietnam.

Oder-Neisse Line. River line recognized as the boundary between Poland and Germany after World War II.

Oesterreichische-Aviatik (Berg) D I (Austro-Hungarian, WWI). Single-seat fighter. Prototype flew January 24 1917; initial deliveries May/June 1917. Well received, but original armament badly arranged; progressively improved from January 1918. Built by six contractors; weaknesses in wing construction impaired combat effectiveness. Production: of 990 ordered at least 420 were accepted. One 160/185/200/225hp Daimler engine; max. speed 123mph (197kph); two 8mm machine guns.

Office of Strategic Services (OSS). US offensive secret service, developed mid-1942 out of OWI, had three branches: SI to gain intelligence; SO to conduct covert operations; and R&A for research and analysis. It operated over most of the world, with a total strength of about 13,000. It worked in cooperation, and occasional rivalry, with the British MI6 and SOE. In northwest Africa, with Polish help, it secured useful intelligence before Operation "Torch". Its SO branch operated with success into northwest Europe, Italy, Yugoslavia and Greece; and both branches had some successes in China. It was disbanded in October 1945; many of its staff were soon recruited into the CIA. *MF.*

Off-Set bombing *see* BOMBING.

O'Hare, Lt Commander Edward H ("Butch") (1914–43). US. Navy Hellcat pilot awarded the Congressional Medal of Honor for destroying five Japanese aircraft in one engagement near Rabaul on February 20 1942. With 12 victories to his credit, he was killed in November 1943.

Ohka ("Cherry Blossom"). Japanese manned flying bomb designed to attack invading forces. Carried by conventional aircraft to target area, then released and flown by suicide pilot into precise target. Powered by rocket thrust. First used March 1945.

Okamura, Gen Yasuji (1884–1966). Jap. As Vice-COS, Kwantung Army, Okamura helped plan the invasion of Manchuria, 1931–32, and the expansion into Northern China that initiated the Sino-Japanese War, 1937–45. As C-in-C,

North China, from 1941, and from November 1944 (succeeding Field Marshal Shunroku Hata), C-in-C of all Japanese forces in China (China Expeditionary Army), he was the leading figure in planning and executing Operation *Ichi-go*, May–December 1944, the partially successful eastern China offensive against Allied air bases. His final offensive in central China, March-May 1945, was initially successful, but the threats posed farther north by Allied and (potentially) Soviet operations forced him to regroup and withdraw, abandoning *c*100,000 troops in the Canton (Kwangchow) area. On September 9 1945, Okamura surrendered at Nanking to the Nationalist General Ho Ying-chin, subsequently escaping imprisonment for "war crimes" by serving as military adviser to the Nationalist forces, 1946–48. *RO'N.*

O'Kane, Rear Adm Richard Hetherington (b.1911). US. Leading US Navy submarine commander of World War II in terms of ships sunk (24 sinkings in five Pacific patrols in USS *Tang*, January-October 1944); fourth-ranking in total tonnage sunk (93,824 tons). On October 25 1944, *Tang* was sunk by malfunction of her own torpedo: O'Kane and seven survivors became POWS.

Okinawa campaign (1945). The conquest of Okinawa, largest of the Ryukyu Islands and only 330 miles (530km) south of Kyushu, marked the final step in the Allies' "island-hopping" advance on Japan. From mid-March 1945, Allied carrier task forces intensified their attacks on Formosa and other Japanese air bases. Okinawa itself was subjected to intensive air and naval bombardment from March 23, while on March 26-27 US 77th Infantry Division seized the Kerama-Retto islands, 15 miles (24km) west of Okinawa, as a naval support base.

Operation "Iceberg" began on April 1, when Task Force 51 (Vice Adm R K Turner) of Fifth Fleet (Adm Spruance), covered by the carriers of Task Force 58 (Vice Adm Mitscher) and the British Pacific Fleet (Vice Adm Sir Henry Rawlings), landed the initial waves of Lt Gen Buckner's

US landing craft at Okinawa, June 1945

183,000-strong Tenth Army on the Hagushi beaches, southwest Okinawa. Lt Gen Ushijima, commanding Japanese Thirtysecond Army, deployed about 80,000 combat troops, plus some 10,000 naval personnel and 20,000 Okinawan conscripts. Ordered to prolong his defence *à outrance* as long as possible, he made little effort to oppose the landings, concentrating most of his troops in a triple ring of fortifications (the "Shuri Line") around his HQ at Shuri Castle, southern Okinawa.

Immediately after the landings, III Marine Amphibious Corps (Lt Gen Roy Geiger) and XXIV Corps (Maj Gen John Hodge) bisected Okinawa by an eastern thrust. III Marines then swung north, meeting tough opposition from *c*2,000 well-entrenched Japanese at Yae Take, Motobu Peninsula, but subduing all northern Okinawa by April 20. The airfield on Ie Shima, just off the Motobu Peninsula, was secured (April 16-21) by an amphibious operation by 77th Infantry Division. In the south, XXIV Corps faced increasing resistance as it approached the Shuri Line, where the Japanese fought from a network of caves and tunnels in the hilly terrain. US conquest (April 26-May 3) of the Maeda Escarpment, a vantage position north of the Shuri Line, provoked savage counterattacks (May 4-5) costly to both sides. Buckner's offensive, assisted by naval and air bombardments, resulted in a breakthrough, following a week-long battle for Sugar Loaf Hill, on May 21; Ushijima withdrew his *c*30,000 surviving men to the southern highlands around Mabuni and Shuri Castle fell to 1st Marine Division, May 29.

A final offensive (directed by Lt Gen Geiger after Buckner's death in action, June 18) ended in Ushijima's suicide (June 20) and the disintegration of his command. Japanese dead on Okinawa exceeded 100,000; of *c*8,000 prisoners taken, many were Okinawan conscripts. US Army and Marine losses were around 7,600 killed or missing and 32,000 wounded. The US Navy also lost heavily: some 760 aircraft were destroyed and 26 warships were sunk and 262 damaged (*c*4,900 killed; 4,800 wounded) off Okinawa, most in kamikaze attacks in which some 2,000 Japanese aircraft and pilots were expended. *RO'N.*

Oklahoma. US battleship. *Nevada* class. Convoy duties 1917–18. Torpedoed, capsized at Pearl Harbor (1941). Salvaged in 1943 and scrapped in 1946.

Oldendorf, Rear Adm Jesse Barrett (1887–1974). US. In command of the Aruba-Curaçoa area which was under U-boat attack (1942–43). Then saw service in the Pacific (Marshalls, Carolines and Marianas). At the Battle of Leyte Gulf he was in command of the bombardment force of old battleships which annihilated a Japanese force already much battered by air attack in Surigao Strait (*see* LEYTE GULF). Oldendorf later commanded a battle squadron at Lingayen Gulf. *CJW/CD.*

Oldfield, Sir Maurice (1915–81). Br. Security officer 1943–47, entered MI6 1947, head of it 1973–78; security coordinator in Northern Ireland 1978–80.

Omaha beach *see* NORMANDY, INVASION OF (1944).

One Hundred and First Airborne Division (US). Formed in August 1942, the "Screaming Eagles" participated in the invasion of Normandy, Operation "Market Garden", the Battle of the Bulge and the advance into Germany. Deactivated in 1945 and reformed in 1956, it served with distinction during the Vietnam War. In 1974 it was redesignated the 101st Airmobile Division.

Onishi Vice Adm Takijiro (1891-1945). Jap. A pioneer of Japanese paratroop forces, and an air combat veteran of the Sino-Japanese War, Onishi (having initially opposed Yamamoto's concept) worked with Genda in planning the Pearl Harbor attack. An abrasive and arrogant manner caused his temporary eclipse following a triumphant command in the air assault on the Philippines, 1941. On October 17 1944 he took command of 1st Air Fleet in the Philippines, where the "decisive battle" of Japanese naval doctrine was imminent (*see* LEYTE GULF). With only *c*150 effective aircraft to provide cover for Kurita's fleet, Onishi called for the formation of "suicide attack units . . . with each plane to crash-dive into an enemy carrier". Although he presented this as a temporary expedient, the kamikaze units, flying their first missions on October 25, received official sanction and persisted until the war's end. Appointed Vice-Chief, Naval General Staff, May 1945, Onishi bitterly opposed surrender, committing ritual suicide (deliberately prolonging his death agony) on August 16. *RO'N.*

Oppenheimer, J Robert (1904–67). US. Widely respected physicist who worked on the US atomic bomb programme from 1943. As Director of the Scientific Laboratory at Los Alamos he played an important role in uniting the efforts of the scientists and the military.

Oppy Wood. World-War-I German strongpoint some 6 miles (10km) northeast of Arras. Scene of heavy fighting in May 1917 and again in March 1918. Eventually taken by the British 8th Division, October 7 1918.

Oradour-sur-Glane. French village whose inhabitants were brutally massacred by SS troops in July 1944.

Orel, Battle of (1943). Orel's central position made it an important feature of the sector of the German line in the Ukraine held by Army Group Centre. During Operation "Citadel" on July 5 1943 the Ninth Army pushed south from the Orel "bulge" into the Kursk salient. But the failure of the German offensive coincided with a Soviet riposte and, on July 12, units of Popov's Bryansk Front and Sokolovsky's

O

West Front attacked towards Orel. The next day Model, the commander of the Ninth Army, was also given the Second Panzer Army and was instructed to check the substantial Soviet penetrations of the Orel sector. The conclusion of the German offensive against Kursk enabled strong reinforcements to be sent to Popov and Sokolovsky but stubborn German resistance and poor weather slowed their advance. However, Model recognized that his forces could no longer hold the Orel "bulge" and planned a shortening of the line and a retreat to the hastily prepared "Hagen" defence line along the base of the salient. Harassed by partisans, under continuous attack by the Soviet air force and hard pressed by the advancing Red Army, the Germans conducted a skilful withdrawal and fell back to the incomplete line of fortifications. On August 5 Orel fell to the Bryansk Front but on the 14th the first German units reached the relative safety of the "Hagen" position. Model, "Hitler's Fireman", had stabilized the situation and by the 17th the last of the German forces were extracted from the Orel salient. *MS*.

Organisation de L'Armée Secrète (OAS) *see* ALGERIAN CAMPAIGN.

Ormoc, Western Leyte, Philippines (renamed MacArthur, 1950). During the Leyte campaign, the major Japanese supply port, where convoys landed 45,000 men and 10,000 tons of materiel, October–December 1944. Krueger's two-pronged land assault met savage resistance, but on December 7, US 77th Division made an unopposed amphibious landing *c*3 miles (5km) south, taking Ormoc on December 10. In this operation some 1,500 Japanese were killed; US casualties amounted to about 125 killed and 345 wounded or missing.

Orne river. Constituted the eastern flank of the Normandy landings in June 1944. Its bridges were captured by British airborne units in the first assault.

Orsogna, First, Second and Third Battles of (December 3–24 1943). After crossing the Sangro,

XIII Corps (Dempsey) advanced on the inland flank of Eighth Army (Montgomery). On December 3 the New Zealand Division tried to rush the hill town of Orsogna, but LXXVI Panzer Corps (Herr) reinforced it too quickly. Successive divisional attacks on the 8th, 15th and 24th all failed. Orsogna remained in German hands for the winter.

Ortona, Battle of (December 11–28 1943). After crossing the Sangro, V Corps (Allfrey) led the advance of Eighth Army (Montgomery) up the Adriatic coast. It was stopped just south of Ortona by 1st Parachute Division (Heidrich). 1st Canadian Division, leading V Corps, lost over 1,000 men in the preliminary operations between December 11–19. In the fierce street fighting, which started on December 21, Heidrich's paratroopers contested every house. The last of them were not cleared until December 28. By then the Canadians had lost a further 650 men, and Montgomery had halted his offensive for the winter. *WGFJ*.

Osaka, bombing and mining of. Japan's second largest city, a major port, an industrial centre and an arsenal, Osaka was consequently a primary target in the American strategic air offensive against the Japanese homeland. During a raid on March 13 1945 B-29 bombers dropped 2,000 tons of incendiaries on the city, reducing more than 8 sq miles (20 sq km) of it to ashes. Another large raid took place on June 1 when nearly 500 aircraft devastated Osaka. A total of 3,200 tons of bombs razed 3 sq miles (8 sq km) of the city, destroying 136,107 houses and 4,222 factories and killing 4,000 of its inhabitants. In addition to the

bombing raid, the city suffered during Operation "Starvation"; the wholesale mining of Japanese inland waters, carried out by the 313th Wing of the Twentieth Air Force. The sea approaches to Osaka were strewn with mines, curtailing its use as a port to all but the smallest of vessels. *MS*.

Osan, Battle of (July 5 1950). First battle in the Korean War involving US troops. Advance elements of the US 24th Infantry Division, Task Force Smith, occupying a blocking position on the Suwon road 50 miles (80km) south of Seoul, engaged a column of NKPA tanks and infantry. The US artillery had only two armour piercing shells and the infantry bazookas proved useless against tanks. Task Force Smith scattered, losing most of its equipment. Osan began a month of American retreats.

Ostend raid (1918). German submarines and destroyers using Belgian ports threatened British cross-channel communications. Roger Keyes therefore worked out a plan for blocking the narrow entrances to both Ostend and Zeebrugge. He was then placed in charge of the attacks. On the night of April 23-24 1918, as the attack on Zeebrugge began, two old cruisers (*Brilliant* and *Sirius*) went in to block Ostend under cover of smoke. The wind shifted, the smoke moved, and furthermore, the Germans had learned some of the details of the plan a few days before. The ships grounded in the wrong place. On the night of May 8–9 a repeat attempt was made with the battered *Vindictive* (Another blockship broke down on the way). CMBS fired torpedoes at the piers and the attempt was supported by monitors and des-

Ostend, 1918: the British raid failed, but the departing Germans wrecked the dock area

troyers, but the combined effect of mist and German fire prevented the *Vindictive* being put ashore in the intended manner and her hull did not completely block the channel. The raids were therefore a failure, and the amount of German activity from the port probably did not justify mounting them in the first place. However, with Zeebrugge, they did give the British Navy the sense that it was doing something apart from blockading the inactive German fleet, and sharing the losses of the Army. Further, their effect on morale in Britain was considerable; the many individual acts of gallantry at both Ostend and Zeebrugge being prominently reported. *DJL.*

OV-10A Bronco, North American Rockwell (US). Two-seat counter-insurgency aircraft. Prototype flew July 16 1965; first production August 6 1967; first deliveries to USAF and USMC February 23 1968; USN later acquired 18 from USMC. All three services flew OV-10As extensively in Vietnam; first combat sorties July 6 1968. Production 271. Two Garrett-AiResearch T76-G-10 and -12 engines; max. speed 279mph (449kph); four 7.62mm machine guns or one 20mm cannon, external ordnance up to 4,600lb (2,087kg); alternatively it could carry 5 paratroops or 2 stretcher cases.

Owen gun. Sub-machine gun designed and manufactured in Australia during and after World War II. Its unusual top-mounted magazine belied its overall effectiveness and reliability.

Oyama, Field Marshal Iwao (1843–1916). Jap. *See* RUSSO-JAPANESE WAR.

Oyem *see* CAMEROONS (1914–16).

Ozawa, Vice Adm Jisaburo (1886–1966). Jap. An early advocate of the formation of large carrier groups for offensive operations. In 1937–38 he was COS, Combined Fleet; 1941–42 commanded task forces during the conquest of the Dutch East Indies, Malaya and the Philippines. Succeeded Nagumo as C-in-C, Third Fleet November 1942, when Japanese naval aviation had been seriously weakened at Midway

Ozawa: the IJN's last C-in-C

and in the Solomons. It was crushed beyond recovery in the Battle of the Philippine Sea, June 1944, where Ozawa's skilful manoeuvring was negated by the US superiority of 15-to-9 in carriers and 2-to-1 in aircraft. At Leyte Gulf, October 1944, Ozawa's decoy force succeeded brilliantly in luring Halsey from the battle, but to no avail. Appointed Vice-Chief of Naval General Staff in November 1944, he succeeded Adm Toyoda as C-in-C, Combined Fleet – what little remained of it – on May 29 1945. *RO'N.*

P

P-38 Lightning, Lockheed (US, WWII). Single-seat interceptor fighter. Prototype flew January 27 1939; production deliveries from June 1941. Fighter Groups arrived in Britain for use in Europe summer 1942; subsequently P-38s operated North Africa, Sicily, Italy, Pacific. Progressive improvement and development through several sub-types to P-38J and "Droop Snoot" two-seat fighter-bomber. A few reconnaissance versions (F-4A, F-5C, F-5E, F-5G) flown by French *Groupe de Reconnaissance* II/33 from November 1943. Production, 9,393. Two 1,425hp Allison V-1710-89/81 engines; max. speed 414mph (666kph); one 20mm cannon, four 0.5in machine guns, 3,200lb (1,452kg) bombs.

P-40 Tomahawk/Kittyhawk/Warhawk, Curtiss (US, WWII). Single-seat fighter. Prototype flew October 1938; production deliveries began May 1940. Those ordered

by France taken over by RAF as Tomahawks from September 1940, mostly used for training; 100 to China, used by AVG. Use of better Allison V-1710-39(F3R) engine and development led to improved P-40E (RAF Kittyhawk IA) and to Packard-Merlin-powered P-40F (Kittyhawk II). Production 13,740. One 1,150/1,325hp Allison V-1710-33/39/73 engine; max. speed 364mph (586kph); six 0.5in machine guns, 700lb (318kg) bombs.

P-47 Thunderbolt, Republic (US, WWII). Single-seat fighter. Prototype flew May 6 1941; production aircraft March 1942. First deliveries for Eighth Air Force arrived England January 1943; first operation March 10 1943. Production expanded, design progressively modified and improved; eventually P-47s used with great success in virtually every theatre of war. Also used by RAF, Free French, Soviet, Brazilian and Mexican air forces. Production, 15,634. One 2,000hp Pratt and Whitney R-2800-59 Double Wasp engine; max. speed 435mph (700kph); eight 0.5in machine guns, 2,500lb (1,125kg) bombs.

P-51 Mustang (US, WWII and after). North American Inc. produced prototype for the British Purchasing Commission in the US, 1940; production deliveries to RAF began November 1941. First saw significant action in the Dieppe raid, 1942. Replacement of Allison engine with Packard-Merlin in the P-51B led to much improved performance; large orders for this model placed by the USAAF after Schweinfurt disaster of October 1943. Production by the end of WWII approx. 14,000; undoubtedly one of the most important aircraft of that war. Also saw combat in the Korean War. Performance (P-51B); 375mph (600kph) at 5,000ft (1,500m), 455mph (728kph) at 30,000ft (9,000m), 440mph (704kph) at 35,000ft (10,500m). Capacity to carry extra droppable petrol tanks which, at a loss of only about 35mph (56kph), gave it a range of 600 miles (960km). *ANF.*

Paardeberg, Battle of (February 18-27 1900), Second Boer War. Cronjé, his position at Magersfontein threatened by Roberts' advance after the relief of Kimberley, pulled his 5,000 men back to Paardeberg Drift on the Modder river. French's cavalry blocked his further retreat and, although outnumbered, held the Boers until the arrival of the main British force, c20,000 strong. Roberts being indisposed, Kitchener launched a frontal assault costing c1,200 casualties. Reassuming command, Roberts encircled and bombarded the laager: after eight days, Cronjé and 4,100 men surrendered.

Pacification programmes. Americans borrowed the term pacification from the French for programmes designed during the Vietnam War to win popular support by political and economic means and to uproot the communists' political "infrastructure". However, US commanders generally assigned pacification low priority in the belief that the conventional military threat had to be dealt with first. It was uncoordinated and weakly supported until the "new model" programme in mid-1967.

The new programme stressed territorial security, revival of rural administration, rural economic development, provision of social services, and centralized coordination. Still, the programme depended on the shock of the Tet offensive to be fully implemented, and an Accelerated Pacification Campaign opened in November 1968. Village elections and administrative decentralization in 1969 and the Land-to-the-Tiller reform of 1970 were also components of pacification strategy.

Pacification officials took much of the credit for increasing Saigon government influence in rural areas and bringing down the number of people living under exclusive communist control to 7,000 by late 1971. This was an absurdly low estimate, however. Although pacification helped to restore a Saigon government presence in many villages, whatever it accomplished was swept aside in the communist main force offensive of 1975. *WST. See also* AGROVILLE PROGRAM; CHIEU HOI; CIVIL OPERATIONS AND RURAL DEVELOPMENT SUPPORT (CORDS); KOMER, ROBERT W; PHOENIX PROGRAM; REVOLUTIONARY DEVELOPMENT PROGRAM; STRATEGIC HAMLET PROGRAM; TERRITORIAL FORCES MILITIA ARVN.

Paget, Gen Sir Bernard Charles (1887–1961). Br. Commander at Åndalsnes during the Norwegian campaign in 1940. Achieved notable results in the training of troops and maintaining morale while c-in-c, Home Forces, 1942–43; c-in-c, Middle East Land Forces, 1944–46.

Pakchon, Battle of (1950), the Korean War. By the end of October 1950, the Eighth Army advance, spearheaded by the US 24th Division and the 27th Commonwealth Infantry Brigade, had crossed the Chongchon river and was within 62 miles (100km) of the Chinese border. On October 31, however, Gen Walker, concerned about the threat developing on the eastern flank of the advance, ordered a withdrawal to the Chongchon. A bridgehead was preserved on the northern bank around Pakchon by the 27th Commonwealth Infantry Brigade and the 19th US Regimental Combat Team. On November 5-6, the Commonwealth Brigade was heavily engaged by the Chinese and North Koreans and retreated towards the Chongchon. An outflanking movement towards Anju was blocked by the Australians. The enemy did not press the offensive and withdrew northwards on November 6. *CM. See also* UNSAN, BATTLE OF.

Pak Hon Yong (died 1956). Korean. Although he expected to lead the Korean communist movement, Pak was outmanoeuvred by Kim Il Sung. When the DPRK was founded in 1948, Pak became Foreign Minister and Vice Premier. He was also made Vice Chairman of the Korean Workers Party. During the Korean War he was a member of the Military Committee under Kim Il Sung. He accused the ROK of starting the fighting and also launched the communist germ warfare propaganda campaign of 1952. He supposedly opposed the armistice but was made a scapegoat for Kim's failure to liberate the south. In August 1953 leading members of his group were arrested and charged with planning a coup to make Pak leader in collusion with the Americans. Pak himself was secretly arrested and sentenced to death. His successor was Nam Il. *CM. See also* KIM IL SUNG; NAM IL.

Palau Islands campaign (1944) *see* PELELIU.

Panay incident (1937) *see* SINO-JAPANESE WAR.

Panikkar, Kavalam Madhava (1895-1963). Indian. Indian ambassador to China during the Korean War. In September 1950, as UN forces advanced towards the 38th Parallel, the Chinese used Panikkar to send a series of warnings against entering North Korea. These were dismissed in Washington as bluff. The Americans considered Panikkar too sympathetic towards communism.

Panmunjom. The site of the Korean War armistice negotiations in October 1951 at the insistence of the UN commander, Gen Ridgway. In the next three months the main outlines of the armistice agreement were concluded but the talks bogged down on the issue of POWS. In October 1952 the UN command called an indefinite recess which lasted until spring 1953 when a compromise was finally reached on the POW issue. At 1000 hours on July 27 1953 the final text of the armistice was signed by Lt Gen William K Harrison and Gen Nam Il. *CM.*

Pantellaria, Allied capture of (June 6–11 1943). After a five-day naval and air bombardment, during which more than 5,000 tons of bombs were dropped, the garrison capitulated to 1st British Division when it landed on June 11. Nearby Lampedusa fell the next day.

Panzer. German for both armour and tank. Also used to refer to armoured formations during World War II.

Panzergrenadier. Mechanized infantry attached to a German panzer unit during World War II.

Panzerschiff *see* POCKET BATTLESHIP.

Papen, Franz von (1878–1969). Ger. Military attaché, Washington, 1914–16; chancellor of Weimar republic 1932; Hitler's vice-chancellor 1933–34; German ambassador in Vienna 1934–38, and Ankara 1939–44; tried and acquitted at Nuremberg.

Parachuting. Developed by Russians from 1931, by Germans, 1937, by British, 1940 and by Americans, 1941; by that date, had become a normal means of sending agents and light infantry into battle. *See also* AIRBORNE OPERATIONS; AIR SUPPLY, CLANDESTINE.

Paratroops. Troops trained to drop by parachute from aircraft. An elite force in many nations' armies during, and after, World War II.

Paris gun. German 21cm gun, with 82-mile (132km) range, which bombarded Paris, 1918.

French armour returns to Paris, 1944

Paris, liberation of (1944). In August 1944, Gen Eisenhower did not wish to divert men and resources away from the pursuit of the German armies in France to the liberation of Paris. Although SHAEF advocated by-passing the city, other factors forced their way into their plans. The German commander, Maj Gen von Choltitz, had no desire to implement Hitler's orders to make Paris into a new Stalingrad while a premature uprising by various Resistance groups in the city further complicated matters. In this confused state of affairs, Gen de Gaulle pressed Eisenhower that the French 2nd Armoured Division be allowed to liberate Paris. Accordingly, on August 23 the division was permitted to accelerate its advance, supported by the US 4th Infantry Division. On the 25th, Gen Leclerc received the formal surrender of the city from von Choltitz and the next day de Gaulle made his formal entry into the French capital. *MS.*

Paris Peace Talks. Negotiations to end the Vietnam War began after President Johnson halted the bombing over most of North Vietnam and accepted Hanoi's condition that talks begin by discussing a halt to the bombing altogether.

Talks began in Paris on May 12 1968 and soon reached an impasse. The US insisted upon mutual withdrawal of American and North Vietnamese forces, leaving the Saigon government intact, while Hanoi refused to countenance any arrangement that might perpetuate Vietnam's division. To break the deadlock, President Nixon in 1971 authorized his national security adviser, Henry Kissinger, to initiate secret negotiations in Paris with Le Duc Tho, a member of the Communist Party Political Bureau. This eventually led to the Agreement on Ending the War and Restoring Peace in Vietnam, signed in Paris on January 27 1973. That Agreement stipulated the withdrawal of all remaining American troops by March 29 while permitting North Vietnamese troops to stay in the South. It also provided for a cease-fire and consultations among the Vietnamese on the South's political future. However, the cease-fire broke down soon after the Americans left, and the consultations were never held. Open warfare resumed in 1974. *WST.*

Park, Air Chief Marshal Sir Keith (1892–1975). New Zealand. AOC, 11 Group in the Battle of Britain, AOC, RAF Malta, 1942–43, AOC-in-C, Middle East 1944, Allied Air C-in-C, Southeast Asia, 1945–46. Fought at Gallipoli and the Somme in World War I before taking to the air. Went to 11 Group in April 1940 after serving as Senior Air Staff Officer to Dowding at Fighter Command from July 1938. After the fall of France in 1940, Park was quicker than most to appreciate that the possession of French bases would greatly reduce the range of Luftwaffe operations. He therefore demanded substantial reinforcement of 11 Group at the expense of 12 and 10 Groups. As a result, Park had the command of seven Sectors and an average of about 23 Squadrons during the Battle of Britain. He used these to great advantage, particularly aided by his full utilization of resources of information which he knew to be available from Fighter Command Headquarters and the radar system. He was particularly astute in adapting to the changes of tactics which the Luftwaffe adopted. *ANF.*

Parrot's Beak. A piece of Cambodian territory that jutted toward Saigon where Vietnamese communist forces established a base area. Aside from the safety of "neutral" territory, the Parrot's Beak afforded a staging area for operations close to Saigon and in the Mekong delta. B-52s began hitting this and other Cambodian sanctuaries in March 1969 (*see* "MENU" OPERATIONS), and the Army of the Republic of Vietnam (ARVN), with US advisers and air support, staged a major operation there beginning April 28 1970.

Partisans. Irregular troops operating under open or secret communist control behind German lines 1941–45. On the eastern front, strictly controlled by the Soviet Communist Party, they infested the Germans' rear areas, receiving some support by air supply and providing tactical intelligence as well as raiding stores and interrupting traffic. In Yugoslavia, once SOE switched support to them in 1943, they created a peripatetic revolution, and in 1944–45 secured state power. In Italy they cooperated with other parties; in France they were outwitted by the Gaullists. Their rising in Slovakia in August 1944 failed. *MF.*

Partridge, Lt Gen Earle Everard (b.1900). US. Commanded the US Fifth Air Force in the first year of the Korean War.

Passchendaele *see* YPRES, THIRD BATTLE OF (1917).

Patch, Lt Gen Alexander McCarrell, Jr (1889–1945). US. In 1942 he led the Americal Division in New Caledonia and was given command of all US forces on Guadalcanal on December 8 that year, seeing the campaign to a successful conclusion. On August 15 1944 he commanded the US Seventh Army in the invasion of southern France, helping to liberate southern France and, within four weeks, reaching the Vosges. Early in 1945 Patch's troops were involved in the Colmar Pocket battle but crossed the Rhine at Worms on March 26 and drove southeast, taking both Nuremberg and Munich in the latter half of April. Patch died in Texas in November 1945. *PJS.*

Pathet Lao ("Land of Lao"). Common name of communist movement in Laos. The official framework of this movement, the Neo Lao Hak Sat (Lao Patriotic Front), was controlled by the Lao People's Revolutionary Party (LPRP). The Front was established in 1956, while the Party, formally launched in 1955, resulted from the division in 1951 of the Indochinese Communist Party into three separate national parties for Vietnam, Cambodia and Laos.

The North Vietnamese helped the Pathet Lao gain control of Laos's eastern provinces in mid-1959 in order to secure the Ho Chi Minh Trail linking North and South Vietnam. From then onwards the leadership, headquartered in the caves of Sam Neua province, directed an insurgency against the Royal Lao Government and withstood the extraordinary bombardment that the US directed against the Trail complex. The Pathet Lao emerged from that experience a tough, disciplined movement capable of dominating its rivals both politically and militarily after "cease-fire" in 1973. *WST. See also* LAOS, WARS SINCE INDEPENDENCE.

Pathfinder Force. Established August 11 1942 in RAF Bomber Command under the command of Gp Capt D C T Bennett. Tasked with flying ahead of the main force to mark and illuminate the target. First operation was against Flensburg, night of August 18 1942.

Pattle, Squadron Leader Marmaduke T St John ("Pat") (1914-1941). South African. Flying a Gladiator, Pattle destroyed many Italian aircraft during the Western Desert campaign and in Greece, 1940-41. Flying a Hurricane over Athens, April 20 1941, he died in a dogfight after destroying three German planes. With 40-50 victories (detailed records were lost in Greece), he was possibly among the highest-scoring Allied fighter pilots of World War II.

Patton, Gen George Smith, Jr (1885–1945). US. One of the finest field commanders of World War II – and among the most controversial – whose contribution to the art of armoured warfare was as practi-

tioner rather than theorist. Patton was Pershing's aide in the Mexican punitive expedition, 1916–17. In France, 1917–18, he was the first commander of the US Tank School and led 304th Brigade, US Tank Corps, with distinction at St Mihiel and Meuse-Argonne Forest.

In November 1942 Patton commanded Western Task Force in the North African landings. Promoted Lt Gen, he replaced Fredendall in command of II US Corps after its defeat at Kasserine, successfully restoring morale, March–April 1943. Commanding Seventh Army, his triumphant progress during the invasion of Sicily was marked by a much publicized assault on a shell-shocked soldier and he was "sidelined" for months before taking command of Third Army early in 1944.

Patton's overt arrogance and insensitivity – and the rifts in the Allied command caused by his feuds with other generals, notably Montgomery – must be weighed against his performance as commander of Third Army after the Normandy landings. Driven by his ruthless leadership Third Army raced across France to the German border, the speed of its advance (albeit sometimes achieved at the expense of Patton's colleagues) keeping its opponents always off-balance. Taking Metz on December 13, Patton made a bold diversion to strike at the German southern flank in the Ardennes and relieve Bastogne, crossed the Rhine on March 22 and advanced through central Germany to meet the Red Army in Czechoslovakia (from which he withdrew under protest, even suggesting an anti-Soviet advance into Eastern Europe with German aid).

In May 1945, Patton was appointed Military Governor of Bavaria. Openly expressing his disagreement with Allied occupation policies, he was removed, also losing command of Third Army, in October. He died on December 21 1945, following a road accident. *RO'N.*

Paula Line *see* FLORENCE, BATTLE FOR (1944).

Paulus, Field Marshal Friedrich von (1890–1957). Ger. Distinguished himself in the Polish and French campaigns as COS of von

Reichenau's Tenth (later the Sixth) Army. Appointed Deputy Chief of the General Staff, September 1940; ordered to plan the invasion of the Soviet Union. The realization of this work, Operation "Barbarossa", led in January 1942 to his first operational command, the Sixth Army. They performed well, repulsing the Soviet May offensive around Kharkov and, later that summer, spearheading Army Group B's advance on Stalingrad.

Seriously weakened by the diversion of resources to other objectives, the attack was unable to maintain its impetus. The city was entered, but the German forces were unable to wrest complete control from its defenders. Paulus' options were limited by the fatigue of his men, the absence of reinforcements and, most significantly, Hitler's insistence that Stalingrad be captured. The situation continued to worsen, but Hitler refused to allow Paulus to retreat and, on November 19, the Red Army counterattacked and completely encircled Sixth Army.

Paulus' requests to be allowed to break out were denied and his command therefore wasted away under the attritional effects of combat, cold and fatigue. Finally, on January 31 1943, the day after Hitler promoted him Field Marshal, Paulus surrendered. In captivity he was persuaded to collaborate with the Russians, making broadcasts to Germany and joining anti-Nazi movements. He was eventually released in 1953 and settled in East Germany. *MS.*

PBY Catalina, Consolidated (US, WWII). Long-range maritime patrol/bomber flying-boat; crew 7–9. Prototype flew March 21 1935; first production deliveries to US Navy and first squadron formed October 1936; licenced manufacture in USSR began 1939. PBY-5 ordered for RAF as Catalina; deliveries from early 1941; also to Australia and Canada. Built in Canada. Wartime development improved basic design; sub-types included amphibian versions. Production, 3,290. Two 1,200hp Pratt and Whitney R-1830-82/92 engines; max. speed 196mph (314kph); six machine guns, 4,000lb (1,800kg) bombs, two torpedoes, or four depth charges.

Underground warfare

M R D Foot
Former Professor of Modern History
Manchester University

Underground warfare, essentially secret, is as a rule fought by weaker against stronger forces; often, although not always, with success. Its most secret and most deadly form – espionage – is treated separately. Underground warriors make much use of surprise; to help secure this, they often operate in plain clothes, or even in enemy uniform. Although generally far outnumbered by their enemies, they try to secure superior force at their rare chosen points of attack, often by laying ambushes. Women may participate on equal terms with men. Such activity falls outside the usages of "conventional" war. It is not adequately covered by the Hague or Geneva conventions; following a precedent maintained by the Prussian army as recently as 1870–71 in France, those caught taking part in it can expect summary execution without trial. Some of those who practise it enjoy the extra risk of suffering that this entails.

Image of the guerrilla – an Afghan
underground warrior surfaces.

During the Second Boer War of 1899–1902, Boer mounted infantry on the run sometimes disguised themselves as farmhands – easily enough done: they had only to hide the bandoliers which were all that they wore as uniform. Farmers' wives were often glad to help the Boer "commandos". Some 25,000 Boers tied down ten times as many British troops, who at last suppressed them by methodical blockade, the destruction of their sympathizers' farms, and the concentration of non-combatants in camps (where poor administration, and their unhygienic habits, killed many of them). These "methods of barbarism" were denounced by the British leader of opposition at the time, Campbell-Bannerman; but they worked.

At the turn of the century several groups of anarchists were active, who advocated the assassination of monarchs or ministers as the first step towards political salvation. Leon Czolgosz, an anarchist, shot President McKinley dead at Buffalo, New York, in 1901, thus bringing Theodore Roosevelt to the United States presidency, but otherwise leaving American policy intact. In Portugal, King Carlos I and the Crown Prince were assassinated in 1908 and another murder brought in a republic two years later; in Spain, King Alfonso XIII and his bride narrowly escaped assassination on their wedding day in 1906, and the prime minister was shot dead at a bookshop window in Madrid in 1912. In Russia, assassination was an established form of political action, however illegal. Three ministers' violent deaths preceded the failed revolution of 1905, and Stolypin, the prime minister, was killed in 1911, but these acts of terrorism were hardly coordinated enough to count as warfare.

The Macedonian revolutionary organizations, founded in the 1890s, flourished early in the century in secrecy: they were violent, but not anarchist, in their leanings. Their importance was confined to the Balkans, but ripples from disturbances in the Balkans could upset the delicate balance between greater powers. This was shown dramatically at Sarajevo, the chief town of Bosnia, on June 28 1914, when a couple of revolver shots fired by Gavrilo Princip, a Serb student demonstrator in his late teens, killed the heir to the Habsburg throne and precipitated World War I, in which four empires fell and two more were mortally wounded. Ever since, security authorities have looked askance at revolting students. Princip, it turned out, had been acting with half-a-dozen friends who like himself resented Habsburg control of a Serb province: their political motives were strictly nationalistic.

So preoccupied were the British, after their recent experiences in the Sudan and in Somaliland, with the threats which tribal warfare might impose on them, that from 1915 to 1918 they kept 30,000 men to garrison northern Egypt, locked away from the world war's fighting fronts, because they thought the Senussi tribesmen of Libya might attack the then crucial lifeline of the Suez Canal. Afghan rifle thieves continued to trouble the sleep of British units on the Northwest Frontier of India, and of Russian units over the northern borders of Afghanistan: a fact of life in south-central Asia. But the perpetual small campaigns fought by imperial powers against tribesmen who resent inclusion in empires normally count as minor, rather than underground, wars.

The Irish question
One colonial problem in particular beset the English: the Irish question, dating back to 1169 when the English conquest of Ireland had begun. Proposals to grant Ireland

Home Rule – now called devolution – had been defeated in parliament in 1886 and 1893; on the first occasion Lord Salisbury had remarked that what Ireland needed was 20 years of resolute government. Twenty years after he said so, in 1905, a body of disaffected Irish founded a secret society, *Sinn Féin amhain* ("Ourselves alone"), dedicated – like the Irish Republican Brotherhood (IRB), secretly founded as far back as 1858 – to the expulsion of the British from Ireland. Plenty of local tradition in Ireland, as in Iberia or Russia, supported the notion of violent activity by underground means.

Two general elections in 1910 left the Liberal government in London dependent on Irish MPs' votes to retain power; the Irish Nationalist Party in parliament insisted on Home Rule as the price of their support. Under the threat thus raised of being ruled from Dublin instead of from London, Protestant extremists in northeastern Ireland raised a private army of Ulster Volunteers and armed them with 25,000 rifles from Germany smuggled

Irregular warfare is endemic over much of the world. Not all of it is mappable. Great propaganda efforts were made by the British towards the USA between 1914–17 and 1939–41; and towards the rest of the world by the USSR from 1917, by fascist Italy 1922–40, and by Nazi Germany 1933–45.

BELIZE
GUATEMALA
EL SALVADOR
NICARAGUA
Contra campaign 1980–
HONDURAS
COSTA RICA
PANAMA
CUBA
Cuban revolution 1956-59
MEXICO
USA
CANADA
Cuban inspired rural guerrilla movements 1959-68
ECUADOR
COLOMBIA
HAITI
DOMINICAN REPUBLIC
PERU
VENEZUELA
CHILE
GUYANA
BOLIVIA
SURINAM
FRENCH GUIANA
ARGENTINA
PARAGUAY
BRAZIL
Urban guerrillas from late 1960s
URUGUAY
Urban guerrillas from late 1960s
IRA campaign 1957–
IRA National insurgency 1919-21
Basque (ETA) separatist insurgency 1975–
WEST SAHA
SENEGAL
THE GAMBIA
GUINEA-BISSAU
GUINEA
SIERRA-LEON
AUSTRIA
BELGIUM
BULGARIA
BURUNDI
CZECHOSLOVAKIA
DENMARK
Atlant

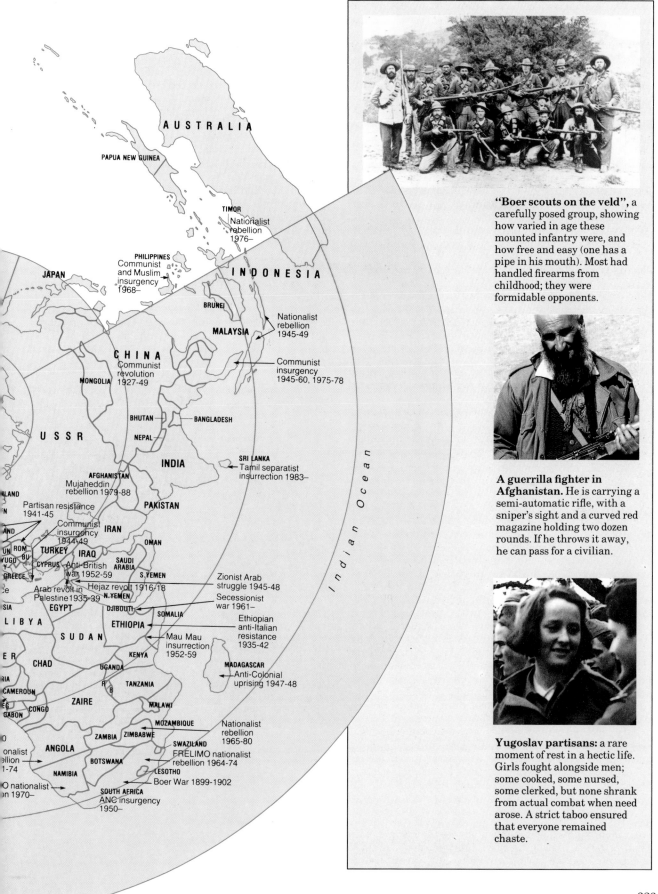

AUSTRALIA

PAPUA NEW GUINEA

TIMOR
Nationalist
rebellion
1976–

PHILIPPINES
Communist
and Muslim
insurgency
1968–

JAPAN

INDONESIA

BRUNEI

MALAYSIA
Nationalist
rebellion
1945-49

Communist
insurgency
1945-60, 1975-78

CHINA
Communist
revolution
1927-49

MONGOLIA

BHUTAN — BANGLADESH

NEPAL

USSR

INDIA

SRI LANKA
Tamil separatist
insurrection 1983–

AFGHANISTAN
Mujaheddin
rebellion 1979-88

PAKISTAN

...LAND
Partisan resistance
1941-45

Communist
insurgency
1944-49

IRAN

OMAN

...UN ROM...
TURKEY   **IRAQ**
...UGO BU   CYPRUS   SAUDI
Y   ARABIA
GREECE   Anti-British   S.YEMEN
              war 1952-59

Arab revolt in   Hejaz revolt 1916-18
Palestine 1935-39   N.YEMEN

...SIA   **EGYPT**   DJIBOUTI
                      SOMALIA

Zionist Arab
struggle 1945-48

Secessionist
war 1961–

LIBYA

SUDAN   **ETHIOPIA**

Mau Mau
insurrection
1952-59

Ethiopian
anti-Italian
resistance
1935-42

...ER   **CHAD**   KENYA
                      UGANDA
...RIA
CAMEROUN   TANZANIA
...EG   CONGO   **ZAIRE**
GABON   MALAWI   MADAGASCAR
                                Anti-Colonial
                                uprising 1947-48

MOZAMBIQUE
Nationalist
rebellion
1965-80

ZAMBIA   ZIMBABWE
ANGOLA   SWAZILAND
...onalist   BOTSWANA   FRELIMO nationalist
ellion   rebellion 1964-74
1-74   NAMIBIA   LESOTHO
...O nationalist   Boer War 1899-1902
on 1970–   SOUTH AFRICA
              ANC insurgency
              1950–

Indian Ocean

a n

"Boer scouts on the veld", a
carefully posed group, showing
how varied in age these
mounted infantry were, and
how free and easy (one has a
pipe in his mouth). Most had
handled firearms from
childhood; they were
formidable opponents.

**A guerrilla fighter in
Afghanistan.** He is carrying a
semi-automatic rifle, with a
sniper's sight and a curved red
magazine holding two dozen
rounds. If he throws it away,
he can pass for a civilian.

Yugoslav partisans: a rare
moment of rest in a hectic life.
Girls fought alongside men;
some cooked, some nursed,
some clerked, but none shrank
from actual combat when need
arose. A strict taboo ensured
that everyone remained
chaste.

ashore at Larne on April 24 1914. Two rival private armies drilled in the rest of Ireland to oppose them: the Irish Volunteers, backed by Sinn Féin and the IRB, and the much smaller Irish Citizen Army, Dublin dockers organized by the Marxist James Connolly. As the third Home Rule Bill neared its final stages in the late summer of 1914, Ireland seemed to be on the verge of civil war; this encouraged German politicians to discount the possibility of English intervention in the impending European war. (The German general staff, with better political sense than the politicians, reckoned on English hostility.)

As a legacy from the great 19th-century peace movement, many liberal and socialist groups inherited a tradition of opposition to war and to spending on armaments. The socialist Second International resolved, at Stuttgart in 1907, that declarations of war might be met by insurrectionary general strikes; a proposal slipped into a composite resolution by a Russian in exile, V I Ulyanov – better known by his pen name of Lenin – and a rising German revolutionary social democrat, Rosa Luxemburg. Nothing came of this resolution seven years later, when World War I broke out, and the working classes of the great powers marched off cheerfully to slaughter each other: partly because the French socialist Jean Jaurès, the Second International's most powerful orator, was shot dead by a nationalist fanatic on July 31 1914; partly because chauvinism had – as it retains – much stronger popular appeal than coordinated international action. The time when pacifist sentiment could be fostered from abroad as a means of weakening a country's will to fight still lay ahead.

During World War I Franz von Papen, later Chancellor of Germany, coordinated, as German military attaché in Washington, a campaign of sabotage against ships carrying American munitions to Europe, with occasional successes. More important underground campaigns were fought in Ireland, in Arabia and in Russia, in parallel with the more formal battles.

"England's difficulty, Ireland's opportunity" is an old Irish saying. The deeper the English government sank in the labours and expenses of a major war, the higher rose the hopes of the most violent Irish. At Easter 1916 some of the Irish Volunteers – the inner core, that was under IRB command – combined with Connolly's few hundred dockers to try to seize power in Dublin. They had hoped for German support. Sir Roger Casement travelled by German submarine to tell them they would get none, beyond 3,000 rifles (which in any case were scuttled when intercepted), and to try to call the rising off; he was arrested and executed after the Easter Rising. This attempt at urban guerrilla attracted little popular support and was put down within a week by a brigade of part-trained young soldiers from England; but the political aftermath was ineptly handled from London. Strong Irish and Irish-American sympathy was aroused for the Rising's captured leaders as they were executed seriatim – except for one of them, who had a foreign name and an American passport and was therefore spared: Éamonn de Valéra. The eventual Irish Republic, of which more later, dates its foundation to Easter Monday 1916. The Rising's impact on the general course of the war was imperceptible, save that, in the year of an American presidential election in which Woodrow Wilson needed the Irish vote, it helped to delay American entry into World War I.

The same could not be said of the Arab revolt. Arabia, the cradle of Islam, had for centuries formed part of the

Ottoman empire, ruled from Constantinople (Istanbul). Many Arab sheikhs, quasi-independent nomads, disliked their nominal Turkish masters, and when Turkey entered World War I late in 1914 on Germany's side, some began minor acts of ambush and sabotage against Turkish troops and trains. The Arab Bureau, staffed by British intelligence experts in Cairo directed by D G Hogarth (keeper in peacetime of the Ashmolean Museum in Oxford), encouraged a more thorough rising. One of them, T E Lawrence, proved to be a clandestine adviser of genius. He encouraged several Arab tribes to combine under the leadership of the Emir Feisal, son of the Sherif of Mecca, and to operate in 1917–18 on the desert flank of the army advancing northwards across Palestine under Allenby. The ballyhoo that has often since attached to the legend of "Lawrence of Arabia" cannot conceal his important strategic achievement in distracting the Turks from their main enemy; and Feisal's men reached Damascus en masse before Allenby's, as Turkish power collapsed.

The Russian revolution

In Russia, the Tsarist regime foundered under the weight of its own incompetence. The liberals and socialists who succeeded to power in March 1917 began to organize Russia's resources sensibly for war. The German general staff arranged for the exiled Lenin to travel – like "a plague bacillus", in Churchill's immortal phrase – from

British troops at a slender street barricade in Dublin during the Easter Rising, 1916. A posed photograph – no one here is under fire, as is shown by the unguarded air of the civilian onlookers in the background, and by the slack set of the shoulders of the infantry section in the foreground. Some men have fixed bayonets on their Lee-Enfield rifles, which will spoil their aim in a fire fight: bayonets are for close quarters only. The platoon commander, fourth from left (holding pistol) looks keen; no one looks worried; probably they have not yet been shot over.

Switzerland back to his native Russia.

Lenin had not loved the established order since he was twelve, when his elder brother had been hanged for a failed attempt to assassinate the Tsar. As a devout communist, he followed the slogan laid down by Marx and Engels as far back as 1848 in the *Communist Manifesto,* which demanded "the forcible overthrow of all existing social conditions". In exile, he had worked out how this could be achieved through a strictly disciplined party – the Bolshevik (that is, Majority) wing of the Russian Social-Democratic Party, of which he had become the leader. He brushed aside the bouquet with which he was greeted on arrival on April 16, and announced the need to press on immediately with revolution.

It took him nearly eight months – April to November – to overthrow the overthrowers of the tsars. A premature Bolshevik rising in July was easily suppressed, but with a few thousand really determined armed followers, and massive trade union support, Lenin and his friend Trotsky succeeded in making Russia's capital, then called Petrograd (now Leningrad), ungovernable except by themselves. They seized state power on November 7 1917 (October 26 in the Julian calendar the Russians were still using, hence the name of "October Revolution"). Within six months, on March 3 1918, the Germans' gamble paid off: Trotsky signed away at the capitulation of Brest-Litovsk one-third of Russia's population and cultivable land, more than half

Ireland during the Troubles. In the shires west of a line from Sligo to Wexford, peasants deserted the shire courts, and went to impromptu IRA courts in the open. With fewer than 3,000 weapons, Michael Collins outfaced some 80,000 British troops and police. After the British agreed to withdraw (December 1921), the Irish fell out among themselves: in a bitter civil war in 1922, Collins was shot near Bandon, but the extreme republicans were defeated. Under the 1922 settlement, the six counties of northeast Ireland remained part of the United Kingdom, which retained naval bases at Queenstown (now Cobh), Berehaven and Lough Swilly until 1938.

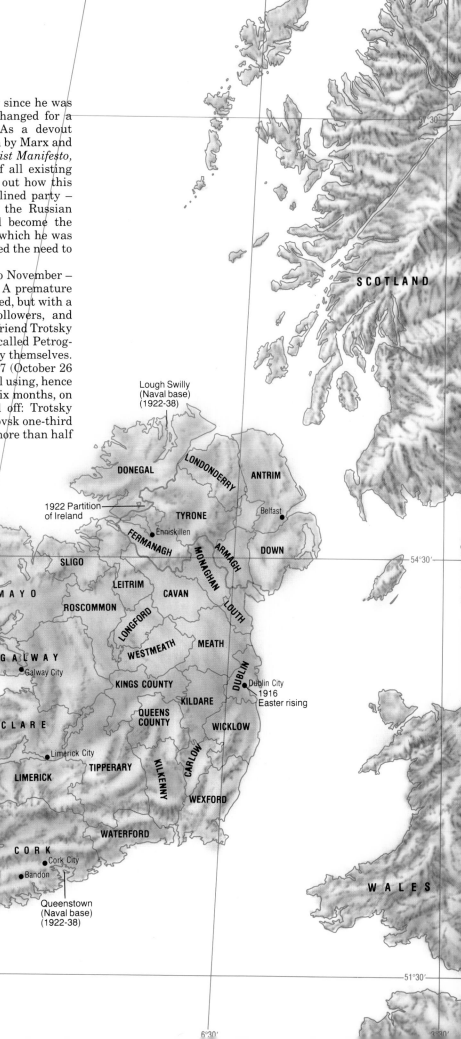

its factories and all but nine-tenths of its coal mines, and took Russia out of World War I.

The Bolsheviks' hold on power in Russia was not at first secure. They had to fight for it, in a many-sided civil war, in which they had to use underground as well as normal methods of warfare in order to survive. Three leaders combined to achieve their victory: Lenin, who handled politics and the trade unions, Trotsky, who commanded the army, and Dzerzhinsky, who ran the secret police.

The Russian officer corps split. Most obeyed orders, and stayed with Trotsky's Red Army. Dzerzhinsky put a political commissar at the elbow of each unit commander, from infantry companies upward, to make sure he kept on the straight and narrow path of Bolshevik salvation; no orders could be issued unless the commissar approved them. The rest of the Tsar's officers went into exile straightaway, or joined the "White Armies" that were trying to overthrow the revolution, under Admiral Kolchak and Generals Wrangel and Denikin. As is usual in civil wars, atrocious behaviour, both by formed bodies of armed men and by marauding bandits, was widespread.

Denikin advanced from a base at Odessa on the Black Sea across most of the Ukraine – which had regained quasi-independence, as a German satellite, at the peace of Brest-Litovsk – but could not control his own rear areas against the depredations of a large body of anarchists inspired by Nestor Makhno. The anarchists drove Denikin's White Army out, and almost succeeded in doing the same to Trotsky's Red Army, which just managed to defeat them by superior discipline and mobility.

One of Dzerzhinsky's most effective weapons for keeping tsarist officers in line was the indication he gave them that their families would be imprisoned, if not killed, if they deserted: an early instance of the system of secret police intimidation by which Russia has been run ever since. Like Kitchener's combination of camps and blockhouses in South Africa, this may have been barbarous, but it worked. The White Armies were defeated, in spite of help provided to them by American, British, French and Japanese forces. These troops had originally gone to Russia in an attempt to keep some sort of eastern front open against Germany, but were inevitably perceived by the revolutionary Russians as counter-revolutionary in intent. Hence much later bitterness; the scars of civil war, intervention and atrocity mark the Russian attitude to the outside world even now. A regime that arose from such turmoil finds it hard to trust its neighbours.

The founding of the Comintern
Trust was not enhanced, either, by an invention of Lenin and Trotsky in March 1919. While they were still struggling to secure their hold on their homeland, they were impressed with stories that reached them from farther west of enthusiasm for their revolutionary principles. In fact, they had missed the tide, which had already started to turn against them (Rosa Luxemburg and her friend Karl Liebknecht, leaders of the Spartacus rising, had been assassinated in the streets of Berlin in January). They founded the Comintern, a body – at first genuinely international – devoted to the spread of communism the world over. By the end of the 1920s, Stalin had transformed it into an extra tool of Russian foreign policy. No one doubts that since its cosmetic dissolution in 1943, it has been continued in divers forms. One of its aims has always been to prepare countries judged ripe for the treatment to be the scene of underground warfare,

communist-inspired, leading to an eventual overthrow of all non-conformist states and the arrival of a Marxist paradise on earth.

It was not only in Russia that many thousands of young men who had got used to the business of killing during World War I, and survived, wanted to go on plying their soldiers' trade. Some 1,500 British ex-officers were recruited into a force of auxiliary police in Ireland, to help the Royal Irish Constabulary contain a further effort by the IRB (or IRA: Irish Republican Army) to seize power. This too developed into full-scale civil war, accompanied by atrocities on both sides. Nearly 6,000 more volunteer policemen, nicknamed the "Black and Tans" after a pack of hounds in Co. Limerick (and from the black caps worn with their khaki uniforms), joined the auxiliaries, the RIC and three divisions of regular troops; with fewer than 3,000 armed men, the IRB (IRA) under a guerrilla leader of genius, Michael Collins, managed to defeat them all. Collins began by securing the allegiance of the Roman Catholic peasantry of the countryside, who were persuaded not only to store arms, hide fugitives and give misleading answers to questions from troops or police, but also to take their grievances against each other to republican courts, and to ignore the panoply of English justice. He then advanced to further experiments in urban guerrilla, in Cork and Dublin. He was greatly helped by an excellent intelligence system, including three spies inside Dublin Castle, the seat of English administration. His plain-clothes gunmen carried out several successful ambushes, and it became clear to the English electorate and prime minister (David Lloyd George) that Collins' movement rested on broad Irish Catholic popular support.

Royal Irish Constabulary auxiliaries at drill: these men were dangerous.

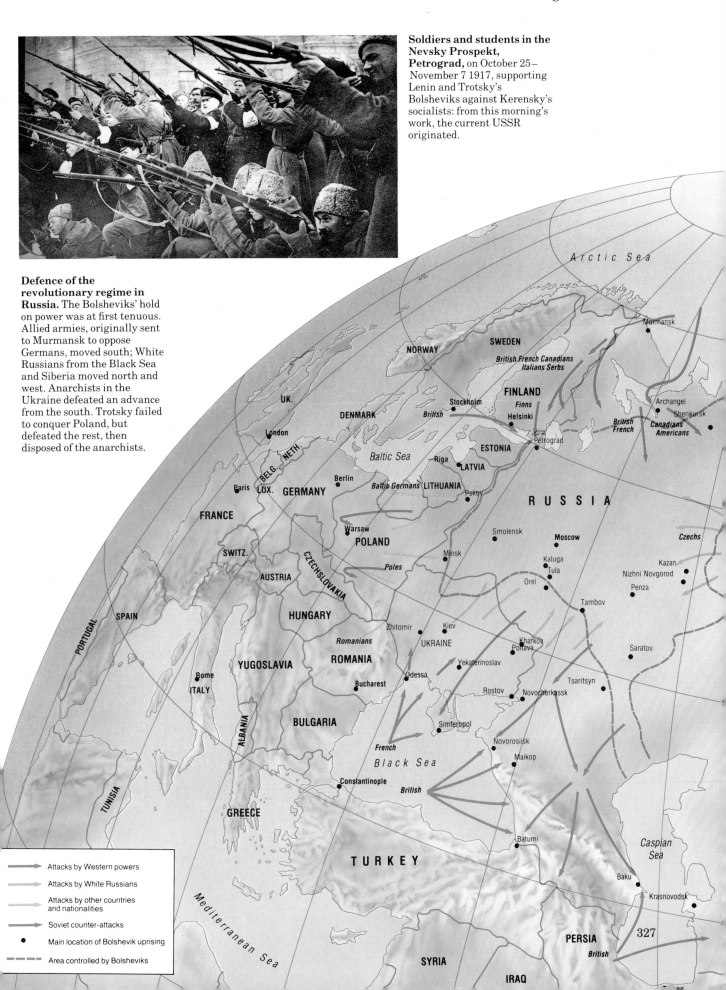

Soldiers and students in the Nevsky Prospekt, Petrograd, on October 25–November 7 1917, supporting Lenin and Trotsky's Bolsheviks against Kerensky's socialists: from this morning's work, the current USSR originated.

Defence of the revolutionary regime in Russia. The Bolsheviks' hold on power was at first tenuous. Allied armies, originally sent to Murmansk to oppose Germans, moved south; White Russians from the Black Sea and Siberia moved north and west. Anarchists in the Ukraine defeated an advance from the south. Trotsky failed to conquer Poland, but defeated the rest, then disposed of the anarchists.

Attacks by Western powers

Attacks by White Russians

Attacks by other countries and nationalities

Soviet counter-attacks

● Main location of Bolshevik uprising

- - - Area controlled by Bolsheviks

327

The English therefore withdrew from 26 of Ireland's 32 counties. Civil war continued through most of 1922 between extreme and less extreme Irish gunmen, led respectively by de Valéra and by Collins. De Valéra's hard core of surviving followers escaped to America; Collins was himself shot dead in a country ambush.

In Italy, many former soldiers found solace of a kind in the combat units (*fasci di combattimento*) assembled and inspired by a renegade socialist, Benito Mussolini, in what was named after them: the original Fascist Party. They had uniforms, ranks, all the paraphernalia of a private army, and repeatedly outfaced their political opponents – socialist, communist or liberal – in street battles. In October 1922, by their "March on Rome" – which Mussolini himself made in the comfort of an overnight sleeping-car – they secured state power and with it an aura of respectability. Mussolini became Italian prime minister, proclaimed himself the *Duce* (Leader) of the nation, and used his private army to stamp out any trace of opposition.

Many German ex-officers, like the auxiliaries and the Black and Tans, had an exciting but politically unrewarding spell in various *Freikorps,* often little more than bodies of roving bandits, rough in their manners and unstructured in their politics. Twice, ex-*Freikorps* members joined in an attempted coup d'état: in Berlin in 1920, the Kapp *Putsch,* which was defeated by an immediate, all-embracing general strike; and in Munich, the capital of semi-independent Bavaria, in November 1923. This latter *Putsch* had as its figurehead General Ludendorff; its mainspring was the leader of the then still obscure National Socialist German Workers' Party (the "Nazis") an art school dropout from Vienna called Adolf Hitler. He was a spellbinding orator; the *Putsch* was his first serious attempt at underground warfare. A single volley from the local police sufficed to put it down; Hitler was arrested and imprisoned. There he worked out a doctrine for seizing power through control of urban streets by disciplined gangs; and wrote his turgid autobiography, *Mein Kampf,* in which he set out in lavish though contradictory detail the ideas that would inspire his foreign policy, if he ever obtained control of a state. The strongest of the ideas that impelled him was a virulent anti-semitism. He could in fact have learned something about underground warfare from the Jews, had he been able to bring himself to do so.

Theodor Herzl's pamphlet *The Jewish State* (1896) revivified the Zionist movement, which strove to re-establish a Jewish presence in Palestine, the traditional land of Israel. On November 2 1917 A J (later Earl) Balfour, then British Foreign Secretary, made a carefully hedged declaration:

> His Majesty's Government view with favour the establishment in Palestine of a national home for the Jewish people, and will use their best endeavours to facilitate the achievement of this object, it being clearly understood that nothing shall be done which may prejudice the civil and religious rights of the existing non-Jewish communities in Palestine or the rights and political status enjoyed by Jews in any other country.

In the peace settlement of 1919–20, the British secured a League of Nations mandate – forerunner of the United Nations trusteeship – for Palestine, and Jewish immigrants began to settle there.

Quarrels between Arabs and Jews, even longer standing in history than quarrels between Irish and English or

Scots, at once flared up again. Arabs soon began applying techniques of underground warfare, including ambushes and assassinations; some of the Jews replied in kind. In the late 1930s, Orde Wingate, then a major in the British army of occupation, organized – with the leave of Wavell, his commander – special night squads of picked men. He picked them, as the biblical Gideon had done (7 Judges 2:7), from the Jews who seemed to him the most independent-minded. The squads helped the Jews to secure their hold on their communities; and when Wingate and Wavell went away to fight in World War II, the Jews developed from the squads the Haganah military force, through which they secured their independent state.

The situation in India
In parallel with their lasting Irish difficulty, the British remained unsure of their hold on the Indian subcontinent. Much time was spent in the early days of the security service in keeping an eye on Indian extremists, mostly Punjabi Sikhs, some of them exiles in Canada. In 1912 a bomb injured the viceroy, Lord Hardinge, at a grand parade in Delhi. During World War I there was no serious trouble, but widespread riots greeted its end. These culminated on April 13 1919 in a fusillade by 50 Indian troops under command of Brigadier-General R E H Dyer, in the enclosure of the Jallianwala Bagh at Amritsar, in which nearly 400 people were killed. (Dyer's chief of staff said later that his general had not known there was no way out at the back of the enclosed area.)

For weeks thereafter, all over the Punjab, not a

A mass rally of SA storm-troopers on the Luitpoldhain at Nuremberg in 1933 after the Nazi seizure of power. The choreography of these occasions was carefully stage-managed to give an overwhelming impression of power. The arena was gradually packed full with squads of men, immaculately aligned, to impress the party faithful in the sloping stands visible at the back. Loudspeakers broadcast Beethoven, then Wagner, then a propaganda speech by Röhm the SA leader or by Hitler.

A party of leading Nazis, before they reached power, at Bad Harzburg, southeast of Hanover, in autumn 1931. The hatless men in the front rank are Bernhard Rust, the local Gauleiter, and Hermann Göring (in the dark shirt). Two to Göring's right, and half a pace in front, is the SA leader Ernst Röhm; next to him (chinstrap), Heinrich Himmler, his rival and the head of the SS.

cockroach stirred: the Raj seemed wholly restored by Dyer's atrocious act. In the longer run, his name has been execrated and the site has become a memorial to race hatred: Indians look back to the Amritsar massacre much as the Irish look back to the Easter Rising.

Mahatma Gandhi, who took over the leadership of the movement to expel the British, insisted on non-violence; not all his followers listened. India was a weakness rather than a strength to British security for the next 20 years.

Reverting to western Europe, it is worth looking briefly at the United Kingdom, where strong trade unions sometimes seemed to endanger national security. In the summer of 1920 the threat of a general strike was enough to alter government policy towards Poland and Russia. In May 1926 a long-running dispute between coal-miners and coal-owners escalated into a nationwide general strike, which was called off after nine days, having achieved nothing. The Communist Party of Great Britain, founded in July 1920, played no important part in the strike; in fact, it has never received substantial popular backing. Its membership before 1941 was hardly greater than that of Sir Oswald Mosley's British Union of Fascists on the opposite wing of politics, founded in 1932.

In France also there was a newly founded Communist party, which sank some roots among the peasantry – always anxious to protect their gains of 1789–93 – as well as in industrial areas, but never threatened the Republic's safety. Nor did various French parties of the far right, founded in imitation of the fascists and the Nazis. On February 6 1934 there was a major confrontation between

left-wing and right-wing rioters in the Place de la Concorde in the centre of Paris, in which several people were killed, but nothing to amount to proper underground war. Rioting stopped on the stroke of midnight, so that rioters of both parties, and the police who had tried to keep them apart, could all cram together into the last Metro trains home, which left at five minutes past.

The French occupation of the Ruhr valley in 1923 gave some early practice to Nazi and communist street gangs, who fought all over Germany for the next decade for control of the pavements: sometimes fighting each other, knuckleduster to knuckleduster, sometimes unofficially cooperating against their two common enemies, the socialists and the police. Early in 1933 the Nazis won. Hitler became chancellor of the Weimar Republic on January 30. He had only two other Nazis in his cabinet at first, but one of them, Göring, was minister of the interior and thus controlled the police. Police and Nazis together were too much for the communists, who were all rounded up, or changed sides, or went into hiding; for 12 years there was no serious communist threat in Germany.

Hitler tried to make sure also that there was no threat to himself from within his own party or the German armed forces. Most of his party's street fighters belonged to the *Sturmabteilungen* (SA), who wore brown shirts as part of their uniform. He expanded his private bodyguard or *Schutzstaffel* (SS), who wore black shirts, under their commander Himmler, to brigade strength, and on June 29–30 1934 (the "Night of the Long Knives") used the SS to arrest the leaders of the SA, most of whom were at once shot. Next year, after Hindenburg died, Hitler became head of state. Every officer in the army, navy and nascent air force had to swear an oath of personal allegiance to him on the unit's colours – the equivalent of an oath on the sacraments to a Roman Catholic – a powerful brake, as it turned out, against any attempts to undermine Hitler by disaffecting his own troops.

Hitler's party, controlling the whole German state, spent the second half of the 1930s softening up Germany's next intended targets: partly by planting spies in them to report on their armed forces and their industry, partly by propaganda to magnify the greatness of Germany and its forthcoming inevitable victory.

The Spanish Civil War, which raged from July 1936 to the end of March 1939, provided chances for undercover activity, a few direct on the ground, more for great powers at rivalry with each other outside. The German and Italian governments joined those of Britain and France on a Non-Intervention Committee, promising to take no part in the war, and instantly broke their words. Italian and German tank units supported Franco's rebel army, and German bomber crews destroyed the centre of the ancient Basque city of Guernica. German air force and tank crews got plenty of hard training in Spain; even if their staff officers sometimes drew wrong conclusions from it. For the other side, the Russians provided both open and secret support. They supplied volunteers, organized and transported by Comintern agents – a Croat called Josip Broz, later world-famous as Marshal Tito, was in charge of the Paris end of an "underground railway" to Barcelona. They also supplied arms, aircraft (although not spares), propaganda backing and a large contingent of secret police.

These devoted themselves to discrediting and demolishing the powerful anarchist party (POUM) in Catalonia. Although George Orwell saw and said this at the time, in *Homage to Catalonia* (1937), it took a generation for the bulk of the left intelligentsia to disillusion itself about the real nature of the Spanish Civil War, which it saw at the time as a clear struggle of good/socialist/freedom-loving forces against bad/fascist/tyrannical ones.

Russia emerged from the propaganda tussle as the only reliably anti-fascist power. That, in fact, the Spanish Civil War coincided with the *Yezhovshchina,* Stalin's great purge which arrested almost every officer in the Soviet Union of major's rank and above, was also for many years a secret. Russia's actual weakness, shortly to be proved in Finland, was concealed by a colossal bluff.

The trust in Russia aroused by Stalin's anti-Franco stance made the shock of the Nazi-Soviet Pact of August 23–24 1939 all the more severe.

Mao's guerrilla

Meanwhile in China Mao Tse-tung (Mao Zedong) wore his Marxism with a difference. In spite of pronouncements to the contrary by Marx and by Stalin, he maintained that society could move directly from a feudal peasant economy to a communist one, without taking in a phase of capitalist industrial production on the way, and set out to prove his point on the ground. He began by intensive propaganda, from village to village, among as many of the peasants as he could reach. He then created a mobile, flexible infantry force, called the Eighth Route Army, armed with field artillery as well as hand weapons, and with it took part in the many-sided war that was already raging in China. In 1934–36 the Eighth Route Army marched right across that vast country, from the southeast, to create a commun-

Sharp edge of combat (*above*): Robert Capa, taking the same risks, snapshoots a Republican rifleman falling dead near Cordoba, September 1936, during the Spanish Civil War.

Young Marxists (*below left*) on their way up to the front early in the war, cheerful because they have not yet been shot over, nor met the muddle and dirt of battle. Meanwhile they provide splendid propaganda to cheer up those they left behind.

An encounter battle (*below right*): field guns had not been supposed to get so far forward since Buller's disaster at Colenso in 1899. One of the loyalist infantrymen with this gun has already fixed his bayonet, and may shortly need it.

SOE and the Underground.
There were many more foci of underground and resistance activity than can be shown here. SOE played a hidden but vital part in encouraging United States newspapers and broadcasters, during the winter of 1940 to 1941, to turn against the Axis. SOE also had a role in smuggling South African diamonds and Swiss luxury watches into China, where it made a vast cash profit; and in the international currency black market, where its accounts also remained in the black. Thousands of individuals, notably in Germany, made private acts of resistance that had no visible impact on the course of the war. Gestapo success in Holland was more than counterbalanced by MI5's success in England, where all supposed German agents worked under British control.

Active resistance forces, enormously varied, fell into two main groups: pro-communist and un-communist. The pro-communist groups were all, directly or indirectly, governed by Moscow, under the guidance of Beria. In France and Italy the pro- and un-communist groups managed an uneasy co-existence, cooperating against the greater danger of German power. In Greece the pro-communists all but crushed their un-communist opponents; in Poland, in Albania (nominally then an Italian province) and in Yugoslavia they did so.

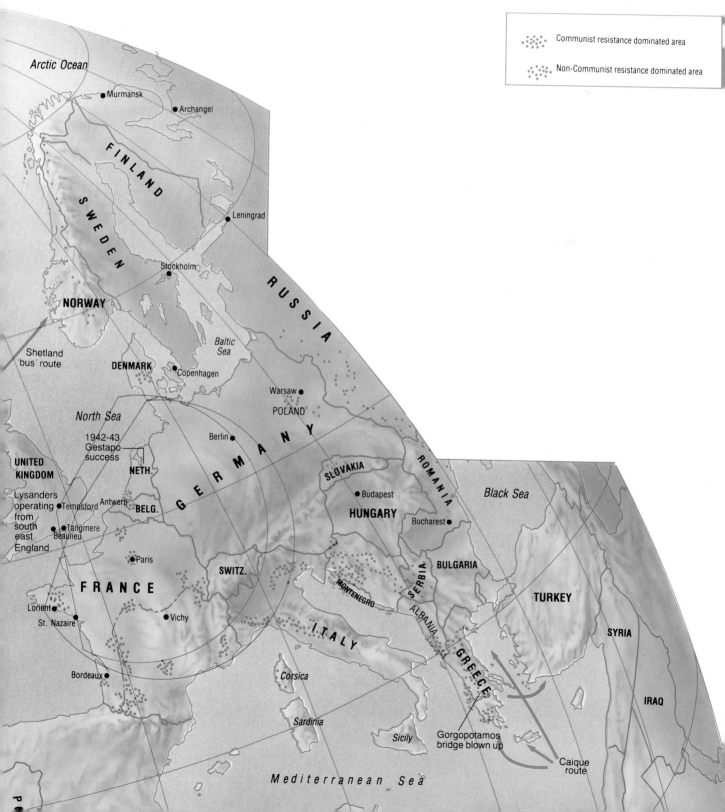

Communist resistance dominated area

Non-Communist resistance dominated area

Arctic Ocean

Murmansk
Archangel

FINLAND
SWEDEN
Leningrad
NORWAY
Stockholm
RUSSIA
Baltic Sea
DENMARK
Copenhagen
Warsaw
POLAND
North Sea
Berlin
1942-43 Gestapo success
UNITED KINGDOM
NETH.
GERMANY
SLOVAKIA
ROMANIA
Shetland 'bus' route
Lysanders operating from south east England
Tempsford
Antwerp
BELG.
Budapest
HUNGARY
Bucharest
Black Sea
Tangmere
Beaulieu
Paris
SWITZ.
MONTENEGRO
SERBIA
BULGARIA
TURKEY
FRANCE
Lorient
St. Nazaire
Vichy
ALBANIA
GREECE
SYRIA
ITALY
Corsica
IRAQ
Bordeaux
Sardinia
Sicily
Gorgopotamos bridge blown up
Caique route
Mediterranean   Sea

ist zone in Yenan province, some 500 miles (800km) southwest of Peking (Beijing). It carried communist revolutionary ideas around China with it. Mao's metaphor of the guerrilla who moves among a supportive people as a fish moves in water now approaches proverbial status. His eventual success – he and his party controlled all China except Taiwan from 1949 – has inspired a myriad of revolutionaries elsewhere. It is worth recalling that he always held the role of guerrilla to be subsidiary; the Eighth Route Army maintained a serious, uniformed, regular fighting core.

Resisters provide tactical intelligence near Cherbourg (1944).

Polish underground resistance in World War II
Only the Poles, of the nations Germany was about to overrun, gave much thought in advance to sustaining an underground resistance to enemy occupation. They at least succeeded in hiding, or smuggling out of the country, all the dozen "Enigma" cipher machines they had made, and in hiding from the Germans the fact that they had been reading "Enigma" off and on since 1932. Still more important, the whole Polish population refused to play any part in the occupation governing system, although many Poles approved anti-semitism.

A few Polish communists were prepared to work with the Russians, who occupied eastern Poland in 1939. The course of the war here gave early warning of a problem that had already cropped up in China, and was to do so repeatedly again: wars are not necessarily only two-sided. Poland provided the battleground over which Germans and Russians fought each other; for most Poles, neither Germans nor Russians were welcome occupiers.

Yugoslavia in 1941–44 was the scene of a still more intricate polygonal war. Croat, Serb, Slovene and Montenegrin nationalists pursued divergent aims, often violently, some Croats atrociously (the fanatical nationalist Ustashe movement established the fascist "Independent Croatian State" in 1941); Roman Catholics, Orthodox and Muslims were at religious odds; there was a restive Albanian minority; the occupying forces themselves came from four powers with divergent interests, Germany, Italy, Hungary and Bulgaria. Moreover, local and regional groupings apart, there were two major rival resistance movements, one headed by General Mihailovich who looked to the royal government in exile overseas, the other by Broz under his alias of Tito. Tito, like Mao, had a peripatetic revolution, one he carried round the countryside with him. Although he attracted many German counteroffensives, he survived to bring Mihailovich to a show trial and to successfully create a communist federal Yugoslav republic.

SOE activity
Tito's task would have been even harder – probably, indeed, impossible – had he not had the support of Special Operations Executive (SOE), the British secret service that encouraged resistance and subversion in occupied territory; and later of the Royal Navy. SOE had originally supported Mihailovich, but switched support to Tito during the winter of 1942–43, in circumstances not yet clear in detail. Through SOE, air supply could be arranged for partisan units; and the Navy was able to ship out some 3,000 wounded whom Tito's partisan army had so far carried round the mountains with it, in the certain knowledge that any wounded who fell into enemy hands would be killed.

SOE arranged for some 17,000 tons of warlike stores to be flown into Yugoslavia; and that was far from its only field of activity. It worked also with success into Belgium, Burma, China, Denmark, Ethiopia, France, Greece, Italy, Malaya and Norway; its agents smuggled special steels out of Sweden; two men trained by SOE killed Heydrich in Czechoslovakia; nine men it trained foiled Hitler's plans to make an atomic bomb by dislocating Norwegian production of heavy water. SOE played a more doubtful role in Albania; most of the arms it sent there were used by the local communists to secure power, rather than to get rid of the Germans, who withdrew in their own time.

In Holland, SOE had a major disaster – the Abwehr and the *Sicherheitsdienst* (SD), the SS Security Service, working smoothly together, took over all its networks for 18 months. These were later retrieved and SOE sent in 50 more agents, few of whom were caught. Into Poland it would have worked much more effectively had the Russians ever allowed any RAF aircraft on clandestine duty to use Soviet airfields. Into Russia it did not try to work; and into Iberia and greater Germany its efforts were puny – in Iberia, for lack of much to do; in Germany, because the Gestapo on its home ground was too strong.

SOE helped underground warfare to develop in several ways. It provided a model for the Special Operations branch of OSS, which later grew into the CIA. It got some very senior commanders, notably Wavell and Eisenhower, used to the idea that clandestine operations might provide not only useful distractions, but also genuine economy of force. It was of incalculable but enormous moral worth to occupied nations. And on the purely technical front it made large advances. Plastic explosive was invented by one of its immediate secret service predecessors, and SOE developed many ways of applying it, such as the limpet mine or the "clam" (the Russians took over 1,000,000 of

SOE's "clams" for partisan use), and several ingenious booby-traps. It invented the "S-phone", later superseded by OSS's "Joan Eleanor" and by today's "walkie-talkie"; it developed a one-man submarine; and it invented the "Weasel", an efficient tractor for crossing snow.

On the Eastern Front in 1941–45, there was plenty of SOE-type activity, none of it inspired by SOE outside Poland (apart from a single man's brief excursus into Estonia, then still regarded by Britain as independent). Partisan war was waged behind the fronts of the Red Army's enemies under strict control by the Communist Party of the Soviet Union, laid down in detail by Beria, the head of Stalin's secret police. Partisans scored many substantial successes. The Poles, operating independently of the Russians, with the help of a little advice and a few parachuted stores from SOE, destroyed *inter alia* over 5,000 locomotives, thus severely disrupting the Germans' supply system, for which the Russians gave them no acknowledgment and no thanks. The even larger Russian effort gave the Germans a sense of lasting unease about their own rear areas, and thus severely hampered their fighting efficiency at the front.

A similar effect was secured at the other end of Europe, in the late summer of 1944, in France, into which SOE caused the RAF and USAAF to drop arms and sabotage equipment for about 500,000 men. As in Napoleon's Spain, in Pétain's France a single dispatch rider needed an escort 50-strong to be reasonably sure of surviving ambush. Here also the Germans' rear areas were made insecure, in an effort Eisenhower thought worth five or six extra divisions to him during the "Overlord" campaign.

The "Brandenburg" units
The Italians made no excursions into this field, unless one counts the work of their unusually brave "human torpedo" crews. The Germans, true to their pre-war extremist role, played with underground warfare, particularly through the "Brandenburg" units, which eventually expanded to divisional strength. These worked against the Russians with considerable effect, by dint of using captured Russian uniforms to penetrate the Red Army's lines and cause dislocation in rear areas; there is no adequate published account yet. Once, the same techniques were tried on the Western Front, during the Ardennes offensive of December 1944. Otto Skorzeny led a unit of picked men, dressed in American uniforms secured from prisoners of war, into the American lines. They caused a tremendous security flap, but secured few real tactical gains; mainly because no German could stand up to informal cross-questioning by American common soldiers on points known to every American boy but to very few Germans. The strategic significance of this attempt was nil.

A little more can be said for the other event for which Skorzeny is famous: his rescue of Mussolini from house arrest by light aircraft in Italy in the autumn of 1943; this gave the Duce a chance to run the Salo republic. Skorzeny is also said to have made arrangements for senior Nazis who wished to do so to escape to South America at the end of the war: a project so fabulous that fact and fiction are here unlikely ever to be disentangled.

A few general lessons for the future of underground warfare may be drawn from the experiences of 1936–45. The support of an external power is highly desirable for any body that proposes to put up any degree of organized resistance to the powers that be; without it, success can only come after a protracted struggle in hard terrain, that will tell more severely on more sophisticated and comfort-loving soldiers than on native forces. Air supply from that outside power is also highly desirable; land or sea supply will do instead, however, if geography and local tactics allow. A propaganda arm, as highly developed as possible, with access to the world's main news media, may well prove decisive.

During World War I, in occupied Belgium, there was a clandestine press of considerable influence, sustaining the morale of anti-German Belgians with reports on the course of the war that countered the German official propaganda with which the populace was saturated. Clandestine newspapers were much more widespread in German-occupied Europe during World War II; in several countries (e.g. Holland, Denmark) they provided for a long time the most conveniently available form of resistance activity. Large collections of these papers, and the pamphlets that often accompanied them, have now been made in many once-occupied countries, and they provide plenty of material for young historians' theses; but no one should think that the whole, or even a major part, of a resister's life can be reconstructed from them. They give a picture of life under occupation that is always interesting, but always partial, and need to be treated with an extra dose of historical scepticism.

As the shooting war turned into the "Cold War", in 1944–47, it became clear that underground struggles were by no means over: they were, in fact, usable by both leading powers in the Cold War, although the Russians were far more deft at handling them than the Americans. Even during the war against Hitler, Beria had managed to plant agents deep in the American and British civil services; their reports now began to be of importance.

Underground warfare since 1945
Most of the post-World War II underground campaigns have been waged by national groups seeking to rid themselves of some form of colonial occupying power; some have had covert support from the Soviet Union, some have been self-propelled. Of one attempt, made by the British and Americans, operating jointly, to destabilize Albania (supposedly the weakest link in the chain of Stalin-dominated states), the result can be given at once, and in a few words: it was betrayed, and failed.

The Israelis did better. Through the Haganah, they so organized the Jewish population of Palestine that they kept the Arabs at bay and at the same time made the country intolerably tiresome to hold down for the British; who announced, in 1948, that they would withdraw, leaving the Arabs and the Jews to fight it out between themselves. The Jews secured the new state of Israel. India by then had also become uninhabitable for the British. Wavell had almost succeeded in reconciling the Hindu and Muslim communities. Mountbatten, given full powers (which he drafted himself) before he left London, succeeded in convincing them that the British were actually going to leave, and left. From August 15 1947 a reduced India and a new state of Pakistan divided the subcontinent between them. Several hundred thousand deaths in the ensuing riots and tribulations hardly made this an advertisement for Mahatma Gandhi's principles of non-violence; and by a supreme irony Gandhi himself was assassinated by a fanatic only a few months later (January 30 1948).

More conventional underground pressure was put on the British by the Mau Mau movement in Kenya,

Clandestine newspapers?
Pamphlets and posters – here are a few examples, all from France – provided an important weapon in the struggle against Nazi occupation in Europe, 1940–1945. The Belgians had had plenty of practice in 1914–18. They could spread news where radio was prohibited; pass on advice from governments in exile; and above all sustain national morale. To be caught printing or distributing them involved the certainty of prison, the probability of deportation to Germany and the possibility of death. This poster, put out by the satellite Vichy regime, equates resisters with bandits; occasionally this equation was fair.

originally a tribal rising among the Kikuyu, which occupied a substantial number of British troops in 1952–56. The troops were unable adequately to detect and corner the subversives; again, the British finally went away. All the European powers with colonies in Africa divested themselves of them; the Belgians in such a hurry that a major civil war broke out in the former Belgian Congo as it became Zaire.

Wars by proxy, as fought by Russia against the USA in southeast Asia in the 1950s, do not count as underground wars. However, the war in Indochina smouldered on after the French withdrawal in 1955, and blazed up into a full-scale civil war in which the USA intervened directly. The US military authorities ignored the advice proffered by British security experts, who had recently wrestled with a similar challenge in Malaya, and insisted on treating the Viet Cong insurgents as full-scale opponents in formal warfare, save that they did not deploy nuclear weapons against them. The Viet Cong, with a devoutly Marxist leadership, the silent backing of Moscow and some practical support from Peking, infiltrated into the villages behind and between the US Army's outposts on Vietnamese soil, terrorizing villagers into providing food, lodging and secrecy for them. Major US air raids on Haiphong, the North Vietnamese capital, dislocated metropolitan life, caused many civilian casualties, yet were not strategically decisive. On the contrary, they stiffened North Vietnamese will to resist – just as German air raids on Barcelona had stiffened republican will to resist during the Spanish Civil War – and provided valuable anti-American propaganda. To the rest of the world, the USA began to appear as an ineffective bully. As soon as the Americans withdrew from southern Vietnam, the Viet Cong had their own way.

Cuba

A similar pattern has been perceptible in central America. In Cuba, a small body of disaffected Cubans was able in 1956–59 to secure the goodwill of the bulk of the populace and overthrow Batista's regime. Fidel Castro, their leader, was able to present himself as an opponent of a corrupt regime; he was widely supposed, therefore, to be a lover of liberty, and secured much well-meaning support from what used to be called world opinion: the intelligentsia of Britain, France and North America. Only gradually did it become clear how little appearance and reality here coincided: Castro was a Marxist, whose real aim was to make Cuba part of the world Soviet empire. How close he was in thought to Moscow became clear in 1962 at the time of the Cuban missile crisis.

His assistant, Ernesto ("Che") Guevara, who had fought alongside him in the mountain struggle, became a notable theoretician of guerrilla, and is said to have manifested a degree of personal ambition that made Cuba too small to hold both himself and Castro. He moved on to Bolivia, carrying with him his doctrines of revolutionary war but omitting the groundwork that such revolutionaries as Collins and Mao had shown to be essential. Theory alone provided an inadequate base; he was captured and killed by Bolivian troops in 1967.

The urban guerrilla

Crowding into large towns, one of the marks of society's growing complication over the past two centuries, has brought with it many more chances for urban guerrillas to make their mark on their neighbours' lives. Success at urban guerrilla depends partly on prearranged nets of safe houses, which seem to the passerby to be perfectly ordinary; partly on avoidance of the use of the telephone, which of course affords no sort of privacy and may give the other side useful information; partly on a careful study of traffic and the provision of getaway vehicles. That a lot can be done by urban guerrillas was proved as early as 1944 by the Belgian group which handed over Antwerp docks intact to the Allies, in spite of German plans to blow them up: a magnificent tactical coup, of which the value was much diminished by faulty Allied strategy.

The explosion of student discontent in the Western world's universities in 1968 had none of the discipline and none of the organization necessary for a successful urban guerrilla movement: it was long on enthusiasm, short on practical results. A few splinter groups of serious, humourless revolutionaries appeared all the same; such as the Baader-Meinhof gang in West Germany. Both Andreas Baader and Ulrike Meinhof had had their sleep as children much disturbed by RAF Bomber Command, on which a little of the blame for the damage they caused may be held to rest – but only a little. They had force enough between them for 20 ordinary people, power to organize, and readiness to ignore the sorrow they might cause to innocent bystanders: starting material enough for a major social blaze. Their essentially destructive effort did not come to much; nor did that of the parallel Red Brigades in Italy. Both at least achieved an enormous concentration of police effort against them. Like the Weathermen in the USA, they gave the impression of being spoiled children of a rich society rather than of cherishing useful plans for social reform.

Tribal motifs still seem among the strongest impulses towards irregular war. The Tamils in Sri Lanka have added force to the line in the hymn-book, "where only man is vile". Dissatisfied with their minority standing, they have developed numerous ambushes in attempts to detach their tribal community from the Sinhalese majority, while Tamil mercenaries spearheaded an abortive coup in the Maldives in November 1988. In this case, much publicity has so far generated small returns.

The analogy with Northern Ireland may not be at once apparent, at least to Ulstermen; but it exists. Since 1969 a savage minority among the Roman Catholic minority in the six counties of Northern Ireland has been trying to enforce its will on the Protestant majority, evidently in the hope that British mainland public opinion will weary of the Irish question, as it did in 1921, thus leading to the withdrawal of the British garrison. If it does so, a bigger bloodbath than ever can be foreseen: the Protestants have been there for more than three hundred years and have no intention whatsoever of being dominated by the Roman Catholics.

Atrocity means publicity; the extremist Irish seem at present to think that any publicity is better than none. The cost in Irish lives is high; but successful underground commanders have to be ready to accept severe casualties, in the hope of one day achieving their end.

As the Afghans have recently shown in their ten-year struggle to get a Russian invading force out of their country (1979–89), it is difficult to set bounds to the temper of a people that is wholly determined to see the withdrawal of an occupying power; but without some degree of outside support, some of it from "world opinion" and some of it from more substantial sources, would they ever have succeeded?

PD59. The Presidential Decision signed by President Carter, July 25 1980, that set out "a refinement, a codification of previous statements" of US nuclear strategy. The document developed earlier ideas of "limited" strategic war-fighting to give a greater emphasis to military and war-supporting industrial targets, finding and destroying new targets during a nuclear exchange and improving the command and control of American strategic forces.

"Peacekeeper" *see* MX MISSILE.

Peace Keeping Force. A multinational military force of the UN, generally armed only for self-defence and acting as "referee" of truce arrangements and the like.

Attack on "Battleship Row", Pearl Harbor

Pearl Harbor. American naval base, Oahu, Hawaii. As tension rose with Japan in 1940, the main US fleet was moved there as a deterrent. The reluctant Adm Yamamoto, C-in-C of Japan's Combined Fleet, saw an initial knock-out blow to the American fleet as Japan's only chance. Encouraged by the British success at Taranto, he decided to deliver that blow from his carriers. Torpedoes were modified to be dropped in shallow water and armour-piercing shells converted into bombs. The striking force of six carriers under Adm Nagumo sailed November 26 1941.

The Japanese intended to declare war just before the attack, but were prevented by accident. Breaking the Japanese codes made Washington aware of the declaration, but another series of accidents made the warning too late. The Japanese launched their 363 planes at dawn on December 7. The formations were detected by a new American radar, but the warning was ignored. The destroyer *Ward* sank a midget sub-

marine attempting to enter the harbour (four other such craft were lost in the attack – to no effect) but again the alert was not raised. Seven battleships were at their moorings, an eighth in dry dock, and all were caught there by the first wave of attackers.

Hardly any American fighters managed to get airborne. American aircraft were lined up at Hickam Field and elsewhere, easy targets for attack as the chief worry had been fear of sabotage by the large numbers of Japanese immigrants in Hawaii. All eight battleships were put out of action, *Arizona* and *Oklahoma* permanent losses. Two destroyers and a depot ship were also lost, three cruisers and a destroyer damaged. Adm Kidd and some 2,500 other Americans were killed. The Japanese lost 29 aircraft.

Nagumo, however, failed to launch a second strike to knock out the repair facilities and oil storage tanks which would be vital to the Americans' response, as were their three carriers (at sea on exercise). The local commanders, Adm Kimmel and Gen Short, were made scapegoats for lack of preparation – for which much of the blame lay in Washington. *DJL.*

Pebble Island. Off the north coast of West Falkland, its airstrip was the main base for Argentine Pucará ground-attack aircraft during the Falklands War of 1982. On the night of May 14, an SAS detachment destroyed every aircraft and cratered the runway, withdrawing under cover of naval gunfire.

Peenemünde, bombing of, (August 18 1943). The target was a series of small buildings housing V-weapons research and development. A total of 597 bombers were dispatched under the direct control of Gp Capt J H Searby of the Pathfinder Force. Target marking was aided for the first time by "Red Spot Fires" (marker bombs consisting of 250lb (114kg) cases packed with impregnated cotton wool which ignited at 3,000ft (915m) and then burnt vividly on the ground for up to ten minutes). The attack achieved important damage. The introduction of the V-2 was delayed by about two months. Forty bombers failed to return and 32 were damaged. *ANF.*

Peers, Lt Gen William R (b.1914). US. Headed the official inquiry into the My Lai Massacre of the Vietnam War, 1969–70. In his book, *The My Lai Inquiry*, Peers castigated the US Army for deficiencies in leadership and training. He also commanded, in Vietnam, the US 4th Infantry Division, January 1967–January 1968 and I Field Force, March 1968–March 1969.

Pegasus Bridge. At Bénouville, over canal midway between Caen and Ouistreham; first point in France liberated during "Overlord", captured by gliderborne infantry company of 6th Airborne Division at 0018 hours, June 6 1944.

"Pegasus" Operation. The US 1st Cavalry Division (Airmobile) and Marines came to the relief of the Khe Sanh combat base in Operation "Pegasus", April 1–15 1968. The Army of the Republic of Vietnam (ARVN) contributed four airborne battalions to this effort. The operation encountered sporadic resistance from withdrawing North Vietnamese troops; when it was completed the base was closed.

Pegu *see* BURMA CAMPAIGN (1941–45).

Peiper, Lt Col (*Obersturmbannführer*, SS) Joachim ("Jochen") (1915–76). Ger. In the Ardennes offensive, December 1944, Peiper commanded an armoured task group of 1st SS Panzer Division, briefly achieving deep penetration into Allied lines and massacring 86 US prisoners at Malmédy. Sentenced to death in 1946, Peiper was reprieved when a US Senate Committee found irregularities in trial procedures. He was released in 1957.

Peirse, Air Chief Marshal Sir Richard (1892–1970). Br. Deputy (latterly Vice) Chief of the Air Staff, 1937–40, AOC-in-C, Bomber Command, 1940–42, AOC-in-C, India 1942–43, Allied Air C-in-C, Southeast Asia, 1943–44. Succeeded Portal as C-in-C Bomber Command in a period in which the shortcomings of the force became apparent and in which new policies, new techniques and new equipment were shown to be neces-

P

sary. On the night of November 7–8 1941, Bomber Command lost 21 aircraft from a force of 169 dispatched to Berlin. Peirse's handling of the operation aroused criticism from Churchill and Portal. This led to a directive to conserve Bomber Command's strength until better equipped and, in effect, to Peirse's replacement by Harris, which followed early in 1942. Having thus, to a considerable extent, lost Portal's confidence in Europe, he also, in due time, forfeited that of Mountbatten in Southeast Asia. The brilliant prospects which seemed to await Peirse at the beginning of the war were not realized and degenerated into controversy and frustration. *ANF.*

Peleliu. As a preliminary to their invasion of the Philippines, the Americans assaulted the Palau Islands, 450 miles (725km) east of Mindanao, on September 15 1944. On Peleliu the US 1st Marine Division faced the precipitous Umurbrogol Ridge, where the Japanese had converted natural caves into a formidable series of interconnected strongpoints. The Marines and the US 81st Infantry Division, who relieved them, together lost nearly 2,000 killed before organized Japanese resistance ended on November 27.

Peltz, Maj Gen Dietrich (b.1914). A distinguished commander of "Stuka" units, Peltz was in 1943 appointed by Göring as *Angriffsführer England* (Assault Leader, England). Commanding *Fliegerkorps IX* (c550 bombers based in northern France and the Low Countries), he launched a generally unsuccessful series of "revenge" raids on British cities (the "Little Blitz") from January 1944.

Penang. Offshore island, northwest Malaya. Its air and naval facilities were captured near-intact by the Japanese, December 17 1941. Used as a base by Germany's Far East U-boat force, 1943–45.

Peng Teh-huai (Dehuai) Marshal (1900-1972). Chinese. Commanded the Chinese People's Volunteers during the Korean War. A participant in the "Long March" he had occupied a number of senior military positions during the Chinese Civil War, before being given the Korean assignment in October 1950. At first Peng achieved success against the Americans by surprise and encirclement, but his forces lacked the mobility to exploit their initial victories. Peng himself soon concluded that he could not drive the UN command from Korea. When truce talks began and the war entered its static phase, he built up a strong defence line. He was prepared to expend men recklessly in attacks on outposts in order to maintain the military initiative and put pressure on the UN side at Panmunjom. The year after the armistice he returned to China. *CM. See also* CHINESE FORCES IN KOREA.

Pennsylvania. US battleship. Launched 1915. Damaged in dry dock at Pearl Harbor, but repaired and saw extensive use in shore bombardment role at Aleutians, Gilberts, Marianas, Lingayen Gulf, and also fought at Leyte Gulf. Suffered kamikaze damage and nearly sunk by torpedo (1945). Expended in atomic tests at Bikini (1946) and as gunnery target (1948).

Pentagon. The US Department of Defense in Arlington near Washington, DC.

People's Army of Vietnam (PAVN). Grew out of the guerrilla movement organized by Vietnamese communists in the mountains near Vietnam's northern border in 1940–45. On December 22 1944, 34 men and women from this movement were commissioned the Vietnam Propaganda and Liberation Unit, the nucleus of a mobile force that was to become the PAVN. With additions from other guerrilla units and recruitment following the August Revolution, this force grew to nearly 100,000 combatants by December 1946, when war broke out with France. For officers the PAVN initially relied upon party members who had been involved in the guerrilla movement, few of whom had had much formal military training. After the August Revolution, rapid expansion created opportunities for educated middle class youths to become officers through short courses, but subsequent developments and political reforms in 1953 favoured the rural poor. By the war's end in 1954, the PAVN had six divisions and 160,000 regular troops supported by 70,000 regional forces and 100,000 local guerrillas. Weapons and equipment for the most part had been captured from the French or received, after 1950, from China.

In 1958, Soviet assistance helped the PAVN begin to modernize its force structure and professionalize its officer corps. Separate branches for navy, air, radar and other functions emerged. "People's War" remained the official doctrine, but officers began training to defend fixed positions by conventional means. When the party decided, in 1959, to support an armed struggle for reunification in the South, it was assumed the PAVN would provide only logistical support while defending the North. However, the inability of Southern revolutionary forces to prevail in the face of American intervention caused the party to commit PAVN regulars to combat. The first whole unit entered the South in December 1964. PAVN regulars increasingly filled the People's Liberation Armed Force (PLAF) and operated throughout the South. From 1968 to 1972, the number of PAVN troops in the South remained fairly stable at about 80,000 to 90,000, then rose to about 150,000 in 1974 (the PAVN total then was 570,000, organized into 18 infantry divisions, two training divisions and 10 regiments of artillery). With 900 Soviet-model T-34, T-54 and T-59 tanks and nearly 1,200 122mm and 130mm field guns, the PAVN, on the eve of the final offensive in 1975, was materially inferior to its adversary, the ARVN, but it enjoyed the crucial advantage of freedom to concentrate force at the time and place of its choice. In December 1978 the PAVN occupied Cambodia with 200,000 men (reduced to 100,000 in 1988), and it waged a short defensive action against a punitive attack by China in February–March 1979. At its peak of 1,000,000 men in the mid-1980s, the PAVN was the world's fourth largest army. *WST.*

People's Liberation Armed Force (PLAF). At its commissioning on February 15 1961, officially the armed wing of the National Liberation Front of South Vietnam. In fact, like the Front itself, the PLAF was directed by the communist party through the party's Central Office for South Vietnam (COSVN). It recruited troops from the Southern population and depended heavily for officers on Southerners, "regroupees", who had gone North in 1954, trained in the People's Army of Vietnam (PAVN), and infiltrated the South after 1959. From about 17,000 in 1962, the PLAF "main" or mobile force grew to an estimated 68,000 by mid-1966. Four PLAF divisions operated in the Mekong delta and populous central provinces. However, heavy casualties and recruitment difficulties after 1968 led to reinforcing PLAF units with Northern-born regulars. The PAVN absorbed the PLAF in 1976. *WST*.

Percival, Lt Gen Arthur Ernest (1887–1966). Br. Following his appointment in April 1941 as General Officer Commanding, Malaya, Percival recognized, but, himself being insufficiently forceful, largely failed to rectify, major shortcomings in the defences of Malaya and Singapore. In facing Yamashita's brilliant offensive (the Japanese, although better trained and equipped and with air superiority, were significantly inferior in numbers), he was ill-served by such subordinates as Bennett and Heath. On February 15 1942, he unconditionally surrendered Singapore. *RO'N*.

Pershing, Gen of the Armies John Joseph ("Black Jack") (1860–1948). US. A West Point graduate in 1886, Pershing saw action as a cavalry officer in frontier operations against Indians and also fought in the Spanish-American War and in the Philippines before becoming an observer in the Russo-Japanese War of 1904–05. On his return, Theodore Roosevelt raised him to brigadier general over the heads of 862 others, a promotion which caused considerable resentment. He led an inconclusive expedition into Mexico against Pancho Villa but, in May 1917, following the entry of the US into the war, he was given command of the American Expeditionary Force and sailed for France. The initial build-up of American troops in France was slow and on May 1 1918 the AEF still numbered

Gen Pershing (*left*) at Boulogne, 1917

only 429,659 officers and men. However, while Pershing made divisions available to free French units from quiet sectors during the German spring offensives of 1918, he strongly opposed additional attempts to incorporate American troops in Allied formations and insisted on maintaining the AEF's integrity until it could carry out an offensive as a national army with its own officers. After some wrangling with Foch in August 1918, Pershing consented to join in a general offensive provided that he could first proceed with his planned attack at St Mihiel. This operation, launched on September 12, eliminated the St Mihiel salient and netted 15,000 prisoners, even though the Germans were withdrawing at the time. As agreed, Pershing then rapidly switched 400,000 troops to the Argonne, ready to participate in the Allied offensive on September 26. The Meuse-Argonne attack proved a much more difficult undertaking for the Americans and Pershing must take some blame for the tactical errors and poor staff work which helped to inhibit American progress until November 1. Nevertheless, his very considerable achievement in creating and deploying a huge national army, almost from scratch, should not be underrated. He was honoured with the unique rank of "General of the Armies" in 1919 and retired in 1924. *PJS*.

Pershing missile. An American family of ballistic missiles that come into the category of intermediate nuclear forces. The first of 180 Pershing 1 missiles were deployed in West Germany in 1964, 108 launchers with the US Army and 72 with the Luftwaffe. These were upgraded to 1a stan-

dard in 1970-71. This missile has a range of up to 444 miles (740km) and delivers an American warhead with a yield of 60, 200 or 400 kilotons with a CEP of about 1,312ft (400m) at maximum range. The American missiles were replaced by the Pershing 2 from late 1983. This has doubled the range of the 1a and has radar terminal guidance to allow CEPs of about 147ft (45m). Pershing 2 is being destroyed under the INF Treaty and the Germans are also dismantling their 1a missiles. *EJG*.

Perth. Royal Australian Navy guided missile destroyer. She followed her sister ship *Hobart* into action off the coast of Vietnam during the Vietnam War. Under Australian command but US Navy operational control, *Perth* engaged in shore bombardment, picket duties and coastal patrolling.

Pétain on promotion to Marshal, 1918

Pétain, Marshal Henri Philippe (1856–1951). Fr. Pétain, who became an officer in the Chasseurs Alpins in 1878, saw no active service before 1914. His leadership of a brigade, then a division, in the early battles of 1914 earned him the command of XXXIII Corps in October that year. This was the only formation to make real progress in Artois in May 1915 and, soon afterwards, Pétain was placed at the head of the Second Army. He masterminded the defence of Verdun from February 1916, concentrating his artillery to increase German casualties, reorganizing the supply services and instituting the "noria" system whereby units were rapidly rotated in and out of the line. He was promoted to command the Central Army Group in April but his successor, Nivelle, won the glory for the effective French counterstrokes in the autumn, taking over as c-in-c in December 1916. However, when mutinies erupted following the 1917 spring offensive, Pétain was brought in on May 15 to replace Nivelle. By a mixture of discipline and reform Pétain restored French Army morale sufficiently to win victories in limited offensives at Verdun in August and the Chemin des Dames in October 1917. The wisdom of his advocacy of defence in depth was borne out during the German offensive in March 1918, yet his proposal to withdraw southwards – away from the British – led to the more optimistic Foch being appointed to coordinate Allied operations in France until World War I ended. Created a Marshal in December 1918, Pétain served briefly as War Minister in 1934 and on June 16 1940 he succeeded Reynaud as Prime Minister, quickly concluding an armistice with Germany. Titular head of the collaborationist Vichy regime from 1940 to 1944, he was sentenced to death for treason in 1945; this was commuted to life imprisonment on the Ile d'Yeu, where he died in 1951. *PJS*.

Petard *see* TANKS.

Petlyakov Pe-2 (USSR, WWII). Originally intended to be high-altitude interceptor, instead produced as dive bomber. Basic prototype flew May 7 1939, dive-bomber prototype December 22 1939. Deliveries began late 1940; large-scale production followed, eventual total 11,427. Operational units began to receive Pe-2s spring 1941; eventually equipped large majority Soviet bomber regiments, proving to be a potent weapon. Eight used operationally by Finnish air force: these were captured aircraft purchased by Finland from Germany. Two 1,100hp Klimov M-105RA engines; max. speed 335mph (539kph); up to 2,645lb (1,200kg) bombs, four machine guns.

Petrov, Gen Ivan. (1896–1958). Russian. Commanded the First Coastal Army in the defence of Odessa and Sevastopol, 1941–42. Later led the Fourth Ukrainian Front in the Soviet advance through the Carpathians but dismissed in March 1945 following a failed offensive.

Pfalz D III (German, WWI). Single-seat fighter. Prototype flew spring 1917; official acceptance test June 1917; by end 1917, 390 Pfalz D III/IIIa operational. Widely used; equipped, at least in part, 46 *Jastas*. Effective in competent hands, but opinion on its combat performance qualified. Production, approximately 1,000. One 160/180hp Mercedes D III/IIIa engine; max. speed 102.5mph (165kph); two 7.9mm machine guns.

Pham Van Dong (b.1906). Democratic Republic of Vietnam. A founding member of the Indochinese Communist Party, and close associate of Ho Chi Minh. He was Foreign Minister of the DRV, and leader of the DRV delegation to the Geneva peace talks in 1954. Served as Premier 1955–76. During the latter period he was also co-chair, with Vo Nguyen Giap, of the DRV's National Defence Council. As one of the "inner five" of the Political Bureau, Dong had a key role in policy making and spoke for the party in diplomatic initiatives. He continued as Premier of the Socialist Republic after reunification in 1976 and retired in 1986.

Pham Van Phu, Maj Gen (1929–75). Republic of Vietnam. Commander of ARVN II Corps in 1975, he deployed the bulk of his forces to protect Corps headquarters at Pleiku. This exposed Ban Me Thuot, which the PAVN attacked on March 10. Phu's precipitous implementation of an order to retreat from Pleiku and Kontum on the 15th, beginning with the evacuation of himself and his family, launched a chaotic flight of troops and civilians that left the PAVN in uncontested control of the central highlands (*see* BAN ME THUOT, BATTLE OF). When Saigon fell, Phu committed suicide.

Phan Huy Quat (1901–75). Republic of Vietnam. A reform-minded political rival of Ngo Dinh Diem in the 1950s. Prime Minister of South Vietnam, February 16–June 12 1965. A civilian, Quat became Prime Minister with the support of the military but was unable to stem the factional infighting. The military forced him to resign, and Air Vice Marshal Nguyen Cao Ky replaced him as prime minister under Nguyen Van Thieu.

Philby, Harold Adrian Russell ("Kim") (1912–88). Br. Spy, became communist at Cambridge; in SOE 1940–41; joined MI6 1941, head of anti-Russian section 1944, chief liaison man in Washington 1949–51; compromised by defection of his friends Burgess and Maclean; skipped to Russia from Lebanon 1963; senior post in KGB.

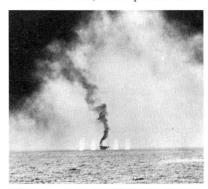
US carrier under fire, Philippine Sea

Philippine Sea, Battle of (June 19–21 1944). In June 1944, the Japanese were surprised by the American attack on the Marianas, but nevertheless committed their main naval strength against the invasion in the central Pacific in the hope of winning a decisive victory that would reverse the course of the war. The Japanese Mobile Fleet, which was divided into two groups, included five fleet and four light carriers, under the overall command of Vice Adm Ozawa, and was supported by a considerable number of land-based aircraft. Adm Spruance exercised overall command of the American Task Force 58, which included seven fleet and eight light carriers; tactical command was in the hands of Vice Adm Mitscher. Well informed of Japanese movements by intelligence, and charged with the task of protecting Marianas landings, Spruance remained in close proximity to the invasion forces, assuming a defensive posture.

On June 19, Japanese land-based aircraft were unsuccessful in their attacks on the American fleet and practically annihilated. From mid-morning to the late afternoon, the Japanese carriers launched a series of strikes, which inflicted insubstantial damage at a cost of three-quarters of the attacking aircraft. During this same period, American submarines torpedoed the *Taiho* and *Shokaku*, two of the largest Japanese fleet carriers, causing damage that resulted in their destruction. The next day the main elements of Task Force 58 set out in pursuit, but the failure to locate the Japanese fleet until late afternoon meant that the American carriers were able to launch only a single strike, carried out at sunset; it succeeded in sinking one fleet carrier and two oilers, and damaging several other major warships. Many American aircraft were lost in attempts to make night landings, although most of the air crews were picked up. The American pursuit was delayed by aircraft recovery and air crew rescue operations, which enabled what remained of the Mobile Fleet to escape.

The Japanese effort was undermined by the difficulty of coordinating land- and carrier-based aircraft operations, the inexperience and lack of training of Japanese air crew, and the Japanese qualitative and quantitative inferiority in ships and aircraft. The use of the American carriers with more understanding and aggression might have resulted in the sinking of a substantially greater proportion of the Japanese Mobile Fleet. Even so, Japan's losses in carriers, aircrew, and aircraft were so great that her carrier-borne naval airforce ceased to be a major threat to future American naval operations. *JTS.*

Philippines, fall of the (1941–42). Although the Philippines were put on a full war alert on November 27 1941, they were unprepared for the Japanese air raids launched on December 8 that all but completely destroyed the strong American Far Eastern Air Force based there. This effectively gave the Japanese control of the air during the campaign which, together with their naval superiority in the area, was to prove crucial. The commander of the United States Army Forces in the Far East, Gen MacArthur, had some 120,000 Philippine and American troops at his disposal but they were generally of a suspect quality. The first Japanese landings took place on Luzon on the 10th but the main assault of Lt Gen Homma's Fourteenth Army did not take place until December 22. From bridgeheads in the north and south of the island, the Japanese forced MacArthur's forces to withdraw to the Bataan Peninsula. On December 26 the capital, Manila, was declared an open city but the fighting continued on Bataan and it took Homma's forces more than three months to capture the peninsula, the defenders surrendering on April 9 1942. Resistance continued on the island of Corregidor, off Bataan, and also on Mindanao. On May 6 Maj Gen Wainwright, MacArthur's successor, ordered the surrender of the remaining American and Philippine units on the islands. *MS.*

Philippines, reconquest of the (1944). The Joint Chiefs of Staff and US commanders in the Pacific agreed in the autumn of 1944 that the recapture of the Philippines was to be a major strategic priority. On October 20 four divisions of Lt Gen Krueger's Sixth Army landed on Leyte Island, supported by the Seventh Fleet. Vital airfields were soon seized. Meanwhile, Japanese attempts to destroy the invasion fleet were thwarted in a series of naval engagements that marked the US Navy's domination of the Pacific. Bad weather and substantial reinforcement of the Japanese Thirty-fifth Army slowed Krueger's advance. Nevertheless, MacArthur felt able to announce on December 25 1944 that organized resistance on Leyte had ended. The now overwhelmingly superior American forces turned their attention to Luzon. On January 9 1945 the Sixth Army landed at Lingayen Gulf while other forces subsequently invaded at various points on the south of the island. Bataan and Corregidor proved to be as difficult to capture as they had been for the Japanese four years earlier and Manila was fiercely defended. Yamashita's forces resisted stubbornly and by the end of the campaign only 60,000 survived out of the original 250,000. American casualties were also high, with 10,000 killed and 30,000 wounded. While the bulk of the fighting took place on Luzon, Lt Gen Eichelberger's Eighth Army steadily cleared the smaller islands to the south-west. *MS.*

Phillips, Vice Adm Sir Tom S V (1888–1941). Br. Vice Chief of the Naval Staff in 1939. He proved unable to work well with Churchill, and as tension with Japan mounted in late 1941 took up his dormant appointment as c-in-c of the Eastern Fleet. He arrived in Singapore with *Prince of Wales* and *Repulse*, without air cover, just before the Japanese landed in Malaya. Land-based Japanese bombers struck as he was returning from an unsuccessful attempt to find and attack the landing force. He was lost with his two capital ships. *DJL.*

Phoenix (Phuong Hoang) Program. Launched in July 1968 to root out communist political organizations in South Vietnam by improving Saigon's police and intelligence services. The programme drew upon efforts by Robert Komer, director of CORDS, to coordinate US and South Vietnamese intelligence collection capabilities. Ideally it was to identify communist political operatives and arrest, try, or if necessary kill them. According to Komer's successor, William Colby, Phoenix resulted in the capture of 28,000 and the death of 20,000 communist organizers and so forth (85 percent in military actions) from 1968 to 1971, and since the war's end communist sources have attested to the inroads Phoenix made against local revolutionary organizations. However, corruption, quotas, and abuse of the programme by South Vietnamese officials resulted in uncounted false arrests and executions. The Easter offensive of 1972 forced Phoenix into suspension. *WST.*

"Phoney War". Slang for the inactive period in the West in World War II, from September 1939 to April 1940; sometimes called the "Sitzkrieg" (as opposed to "Blitzkrieg").

Phönix D I (Austro-Hungarian, WWI). Single-seat fighter. First deliveries to front-line *Fliegerkompagnien* February/March 1918. After modification, performed well in both army and naval units. Developed into D II by May 1918; D III too late for wartime use, but 17 to Sweden postwar. Production, over 300. One 200hp Hiero engine; max. speed 112mph (180kph); two 8mm machine guns.

Photographic Reconnaissance Unit (PRU). Nos 1, 2, 3 and 4 PRU, RAF carried out airborne photography respectively over Europe, the Middle East, India and North Africa during World War II.

Phoumi Nosavan, Gen (b.1920). Laotian. Chief of Staff of the Royal Lao Army in the 1950s. He headed the rightist forces that overthrew Laos's pro-Western neutralist government, with American encouragement, in December 1959. He served variously as deputy premier, minister of interior, minister of finance and minister of defence in subsequent governments. He owed his considerable political influence to the support of the US, which sought to steer Laos away from neutralism and communism. Once that support was withdrawn after cease-fire in 1973, his power waned and he fled abroad. *WST*.

Phuoc Binh. Capital of South Vietnam's Phuoc Long province, located in the foothills of the central highlands just west of major communist supply bases in Cambodia. It was so frequently the target of communist rocket attacks that American troops called it "rocket alley". In May 1965 communist forces routed a South Vietnamese Ranger Battalion and nearly overran the US Special Forces compound in Phuoc Binh. The city came under heavy direct attack again in the Tet offensive of 1968. From 1966 to early 1969, communist forces held the road to Phuoc Binh, which had to rely on resupply by air. It was the first province capital to fall in 1975. *WST*.

Phuoc Tuy Province. A coastal province located southeast of Saigon, and the site of an early important victory by communist forces in the Vietnam War (*see* BINH GIA, BATTLE OF). It was also the tactical area of operation, from April 1966, of the 1st Australian Task Force and the 161st Battery of New Zealand Artillery, headquartered near Ba Ria, the province capital. The special responsibilities of these forces were to secure Highway 15, which was threatened by the PLAF 274th Regiment based in the Hat Dich jungle, and to support operations in the eastern portion of the Rung Sat Special Zone.

Piave, Battle of the (1918) *see* ITALIAN CAMPAIGN, WORLD WAR I.

Picardy *see* SOMME, BATTLES OF THE.

Pieds-Noirs *see* ALGERIAN CAMPAIGN.

Pilckem Ridge *see* YPRES, THIRD BATTLE OF (1917).

Gen Pile: British anti-aircraft specialist

Pile, Gen Sir Frederick (1884–1976). Br. Served on the Western Front, World War I. After attending Staff College, he switched to the Royal Tank Corps in 1923, soon becoming recognized as a progressive officer who emphasized the potential importance of tanks in land operations. Pile commanded the 3rd Battalion RTC in the Experimental Mechanized Force in 1927–1928 and was then Assistant Director of Mechanization at the War Office until 1932. Having commanded Canal Infantry Brigade in Egypt, 1932–36, he took over the Territorial 1st Anti-Aircraft Division in 1937. This led directly to his appointment as GOC-in-C of Anti-Aircraft Command, a post which he held from July 1939 until April 1945. An outstanding organizer and leader, Pile strove throughout World War II to expand his Command and bring its weapons, ancillary equipment and training up to the standards of efficiency demanded in modern war. Relatively ineffective during the Blitz of 1940–41, Anti-Aircraft Command improved to such an extent that, in 1944, it was able to play a major part in defeating the German V-1 offensive. Pile's employment of ATS and Home Guard personnel on anti-aircraft duties also freed large numbers of regular gunners for service elsewhere. *PJS*.

Pill Box. Protected emplacement forming part of permanent defensive fieldworks.

Pilsudski, Marshal Józef (1867-1935). Polish. The creator of modern Poland. Pilsudski organized a "Polish Legion" in Austrian exile from c1906 and in 1914-16 led it under Austrian command against the Russians. Following the Russian Revolution, 1918, he led the forces of the newly proclaimed Polish Republic against the Red Army: his crushing defeat of Tukhachevsky at Warsaw, August 15-25 1920, and subsequent advance established the Polish-Russian border until 1939. From 1926 until his death, he was virtual dictator of Poland.

Plain of Jars. A grassy plateau in east central Laos; its three airfields and strategic location made it vital in both Indochina wars. Vietnamese communists tied down the French garrison on the plain (1953), the Laotian Civil War began there (May 1959) and the confrontation between US-supported rightists and neutralist and Pathet Lao forces was played out upon there in 1961. The plain subsequently changed hands several times and, when controlled by the Pathet Lao, was bombed heavily by the US. Mass evacuations reduced its population from 150,000 in 1960 to fewer than 9,000 a decade later. *WST*.

Plain of Reeds. Covers 2,600 sq miles (6,700 sq km) in the upper Mekong River delta of southern Vietnam. Remoteness, in combination with proximity to supply bases in Cambodia, made the plain an important base for communist forces in the Vietnam War. From it, they could mount operations into the populous, rice-rich delta and retreat either into the plain or across the border into Cambodia. US riverine operations extended to its fringes in the late 1960s.

Plan XVII. French plan adopted in 1913 to stem a German advance in war. It envisaged a French frontal attack on the German centre with the object of dominating her lines of communication and separating her wings. It was prepared by Joffre, by whom its execution was attempted in 1914.

Platoon. Part of a Company, consisting of about 30 men under the command of a subaltern officer.

Platt, Lt Gen Sir William (1885–1975). Br. British commander in the Sudan at the outbreak of World War II; invaded Italian Eritrea in January 1941, winning the Battle of Keren in March, taking Asmara and Massawa in April, and forcing the Duke of Aosta's capitulation at Amba Alagi in May 1941.

Plei Me, Battle of (1965). Plei Me was, in 1965, the site of a camp in South Vietnam's central highlands garrisoned by 12 US Special Forces 14 South Vietnamese Special Forces and 415 ethnic minority CIDG troops. Having recently decided to wage conventional war with regular units supported from the North, the communists threw three regiments against the camp on October 19. The communists did not anticipate the swift relief provided by the newly arrived US 1st Cavalry Division (Airmobile), and a South Vietnamese mechanized column reached Plei Me, despite heavy losses in an ambush on the way, on the 25th. The battle marked the beginning of "big unit" warfare in the highlands. *WST.*

Pleiku. Capital of South Vietnam's Pleiku province in the central highlands. Situated at the intersection of highways 14 and 19, the city was the hub of routes linking Kontum to the north, Ban Me Thuot to the south, and Qui Nhon on the coast. It was also the HQ of ARVN II Corps and various US units, 1965–70. US Special Forces trained CIDG units among the province's Jarai, Bahnar and Rhade ethnic groups.

The province sat astride infiltration routes from communist staging areas in Cambodia, which US and South Vietnamese forces sought to block. A communist attack on Camp Holloway and the Pleiku airfield on February 7 1965 was seized by President Johnson as a pretext to routinize the bombing of the North and to commit US ground units to combat in the South. The first major battle between American and whole units of the People's Army took place in November 1965 in the valley of the Ia Drang river in western Pleiku

province near the Cambodian border. Pleiku city was rocketed in 1967, and communist forces penetrated the city during the 1968 Tet offensive. In 1975, communist forces followed up their attack on Ban Me Thuot by isolating Pleiku, which fell on March 18. *WST.*

Plimsoll, Sir James (b.1917) Australian. *See* UNCURK.

Ploegsteert. ("Plugstreet"). Belgian village south of Messines and close to the French border. Occupied by the British Cavalry Corps and 4th Division in October 1914. For most of the war it was just inside the British lines. It was lost to the Germans on April 10 1918 but finally retaken by the British 29th Division on September 4 1918.

Polygon Wood *see* YPRES, THIRD BATTLE OF (1917).

Ploesti, bombing of (August 1 1943). Ploesti contained some of the most important oil installations in Europe. Some 40 miles (64km) north of Bucharest, it was beyond the range of bombers based in Britain. The raid was launched from Libyan bases after special planning and rehearsals. It was the first major attack at low level by American bombers and it was the longest range operation undertaken up to that time. Although many of the aircraft came from the Eighth Air Force, the operation was planned and executed by Gen Brereton, commander of the US Ninth Air Force. He dispatched 177 B-24s led by Brig Gen Uzal G Ent. The attack was delivered from below 500ft (150m). Bombers destroyed totalled 54, 40 of them in action. Five Congressional Medals of Honor were awarded. The attack achieved severe destruction but only a temporary interruption of supplies to Germany. *ANF.*

Plumer, Field Marshal Viscount (1857–1932). Br. As a lieutenant general, Plumer began a long association with the Ypres Salient early in 1915 when he took over the BEF's V Corps. He replaced Smith-Dorrien as commander, Second Army on May 6 1915, during the Second Battle of Ypres, but was himself near to dismissal when the St Eloi craters were lost in 1916. However, helped by an outstand-

ing chief of staff, Charles Harington, he won a lasting reputation with the brilliant capture of Messines Ridge in June 1917. Having reluctantly accepted the main role in the Ypres offensive towards the end of August, his methodical "step-by-step" tactics, based on thoroughly-planned set-piece assaults with limited objectives, were again successful in the subbattles of the Menin Road Ridge, Polygon Wood and Broodseinde in September and October. Soon after the capture of Passchendaele in November he was made commander of a British force sent to shore up the Italian front. He refused the post of CIGS when it was offered to him in February 1918 and returned to Flanders in time to conduct the defence of Ypres in April 1918. In the final Allied offensives of 1918, Plumer's Second Army, fighting alongside Belgian and French formations, advanced 51 miles (82km) between September 28 and November 11. *PJS.*

PLUTO. (Pipe Line Under The Ocean). The fuel pipeline laid between Britain and France in 1944.

Pocket battleship. Popular name for the three German *Panzerschiffe* (armoured ships) built in the early 1930s: *Deutschland* (later *Lützow*), *Admiral Scheer* and *Admiral Graf Spee*. Intended for long-range commerce raiding, they were basically armoured cruisers but with heavier guns (6 x 11in) than the usual 8in. The use of welding and diesel propulsion made for increased lightness and range. They caused a stir among other navies but were of greater tonnage, less range, and less well armoured than thought at the time. Perhaps a sensible answer to Germany's needs around 1930, they proved less than satisfactory, 11in guns being needlessly powerful for their main role. *DJL.*

Poincaré, Raymond (1860–1934). Fr. Prime Minister for five separate terms and President 1913–20. An energetic war leader. Following the peace negotiations, during which he clashed with Clemenceau, he became chairman of the commission of reparations, and later sanctioned the occupation of the Ruhr. He resigned from office in 1929. *SLB.*

Pokryshkin, Air Marshal Aleksandr Ivanovich (b.1913). Russian. Second-highest-scoring Soviet fighter pilot of World War II, with 59 "kills". Three times a Hero of the Soviet Union: the first citation gained at Rostov, November 1941, for a hazardous reconnaissance flight that revealed von Kleist's deployment and facilitated a successful counterattack. Postwar, a high-ranking staff officer.

German gunners in Danzig area, 1939

Poland, invasion of (1939). On September 1 1939, after staged border "incidents", Germany invaded Poland. In the north von Bock's Army Group North attacked Danzig and the Polish Corridor and struck south from East Prussia. Meanwhile von Rundstedt's Army Group South advanced from Silesia into central and southern Poland. The Polish forces, although numerically strong, were poorly coordinated and their plans were confused by Luftwaffe air strikes and the sheer speed of the German advance. By September 8 units of the German Tenth Army were in the outskirts of Warsaw and the Polish forces were encircled west of the rivers Vistula and Bug. On the 17th, two Soviet army groups invaded Poland, crossing the border to the north and south of the Pripet Marshes and destroying whatever last hopes still lingered of stemming the German attack. The next day the Polish government and Marshal Rydz-Smigly, the c-in-c of the Polish Army, crossed the border into Romania. A rare Polish counterattack at Kutno was crushed on the 19th. Desultory fighting continued, with Warsaw only being subdued on the 27th while the last of the Polish forces surrendered at Kock, October 5. Polish losses were 66,000 killed and nearly 700,000 taken prisoner; Germany suffered 14,000 killed or missing. *MS*.

Poland, reconquest of (1944–45). Advancing from the River Dneiper, the Red Army made rapid progress in the Ukraine in the early spring of 1944 and the Second Belorussian and First Ukrainian Fronts re-entered pre-war Polish territory. Von Manstein's Army Group South fought desperately to contain the assault but ultimately his failure resulted in his dismissal. A worse fate awaited Army Group Centre under Busch during the Soviet summer offensive. On June 23 Marshal Zhukov, in overall command of the First, Second and Third Belorussian Fronts, unleashed his armies, assisted by widespread partisan activity in the German rear. Brest-Litovsk, Bialystok and Lvov all fell by the end of July and Army Group Centre had been virtually destroyed. In spite of this success, Rokossovsky's First Belorussian Front failed to maintain its advance and halted before Warsaw. The Polish Home Army's uprising therefore received no support from the Red Army and was consequently crushed by German counter-insurgency forces in September. A renewed offensive in January at last brought about the liberation of Warsaw, achieved by the Fortyseventh Army on the 17th. Meanwhile a major drive north of the River Vistula by Rokossovsky cleared northern Poland and struck into East Prussia. The delay and caution of the previous autumn were replaced by a powerful push through German-occupied Poland as Zhukov bore down on Berlin. His First Belorussian Front, together with Koniev's First Ukrainian Front, raced westwards, overwhelming Harpe's Army Group A and Himmler's Army Group Vistula. *MS*.

Polaris. American solid-fuelled SLBM first deployed November 1960. Three versions were developed, A1 with a range of about 1,332 miles (2,220km), A2 with a range of 1,668 miles (2,780km) and A3 with a range of 2,780 miles (4,635km). A1 and A2 carried single warheads of 700-800 kilotons; A3 a 200 kiloton MRV triplet. CEP improved from one to about half a nautical mile. The US Navy commissioned 41 Polaris submarines; the Royal Navy acquired four. Polaris was replaced by Poseidon in 31 of the US Polaris submarines by 1978 and the last American Polaris patrol was completed on October 1 1981. Polaris remains in service in Britain in modified and remotored A3TK form with the Chevaline advanced MRV front end. *EJG*.

Polikarpov I-15 Chato (Snubnose) (USSR, WWII). Single-seat fighter. Prototype flew October 1933. Used operationally Spanish Civil War by Republicans; first action November 4 1936; established an excellent reputation. The I-152 development saw action in China against Japanese from November 1937; some went to Spain. Final development, I-153 *Chaika* (Gull) with retractable undercarriage, remained operational until 1943; a few in Finnish units serving into 1944. Production, about 6,580. One 700hp M-25 engine; max. speed 228mph (367kph); four 7.62mm machine guns, 220lb (100kg) bombs.

Polikarpov I-16 Mosca (Fly) (USSR, WWII). Single-seat fighter. Operationally contemporary Spain with I-15; advanced for its time. Later I-16 Type 10 had increased armament; further increases in later sub-types. I-16 remained a principal Soviet fighter until early 1943. Production, about 6,500. One 750hp M-25V, later 1,000hp Shvetsov M-62 engine; max. speed 273–326mph (439–525kph); two, later four, machine guns, finally two machine guns and two 20mm cannon; I-16 Type 24B had six rockets.

Polish Corridor. Poland's access between World War I and II to the free city of Danzig (Gdansk), a Baltic port on the Vistula, across German territory. A German pretext for war in 1939.

Polish Guarantee. Chamberlain's declaration of March 31 1939 that Britain and France would aid Poland if she was attacked.

Polish Parachute Brigade (First). Formed September 23 1941 and intended for use in Poland but it first saw action at Arnhem. Dropped to reinforce the 1st Airborne Division, it suffered heavy losses in the fighting. After the war it served in Germany until its disbandment in June 1947.

Pol Pot (neé Saloth Sar) (b.1928). Cambodian. Leader of the Cambodian Communists, (Khmers Rouges), during Cambodia's post-independence wars. Born into a prominent land owning family, he joined the Communist Party upon returning from study in France in 1953. He and other French-educated party members gained ascendancy when Pol Pot was confirmed as Party Secretary in 1963. Enjoying only tepid support from the Vietnamese, who restrained the Khmers Rouges in order not to jeopardize their relations with Prince Norodom Sihanouk, Pol Pot and his faction became increasingly populist and xenophobic in outlook. This orientation placed him at odds with Vietnamese-trained Khmers and with the Vietnamese themselves. Following the war in 1975 he exterminated his rivals, unleashed a reign of terror upon civilians who had not been on the revolutionary side, antagonized Vietnam by making claims on Vietnamese territory, and obtained support from China. Vietnam invaded to remove his regime by force in December 1978, and Pol Pot retreated to the jungle to wage a war of resistance from camps near the Thai border. *WST*.

Poperinghe. Town, 4 miles (7km) west of Ypres, which became an important recreation centre for British troops moving in and out of the Ypres Salient, 1914–18.

Po river, Battle of the (April 9–23 1945). The final Allied offensive of the Italian campaign, fought as a battle of annihilation by 15th Army Group (Clark) with Fifth Army (Truscott) and Eighth Army (McCreery) to destroy Army Group C (von Vietinghoff) south of the river.

Both Armies made their main thrusts directly towards Bologna, coupled with subsidiary flanking thrusts through difficult country. Eighth Army's flanking attack was through the narrow Argenta Gap between Lake Comacchio and German-created floods; Fifth Army's was through the higher Apennines, well to the west of its main thrust. Both flanking thrusts succeeded, leading to the encirclement and destruction of the Tenth and Fourteenth German Armies (Herr and Lemelsen).

Eighth Army attacked first on April 9 to draw German reserves away from Fifth Army's front. McCreery carried out his main thrust across the Senio, north of and parallel to the main Bologna road (Via Emilia). V Corps (Keightley) with four divisions and II Polish Corps (Bohusz-Szyszko) with two divisions, struck the boundary between LXXVI Panzer Corps (von Schwerin) and I Parachute Corps (Heidrich), and avoided the more heavily defended sector of the German line south of the road where Herr expected the main British effort. The attack was preceded by strategic bombers laying carpets of fragmentation bombs on the German defences and gun areas, and then by a novel "sandwich" of alternating artillery bombardments and air strikes by fighter-bombers, the last of which was a dummy attack as the assault troops crossed the Senio. Extensive use was also made of flame-throwing tanks.

Eighth Army's assault was successful and by the following evening both Corps were approaching the Santerno, which they had crossed by April 12. Meanwhile, the eastern side of the Argenta Gap had been secured by amphibious operations across Lake Comacchio. On April 13, McCreery directed Keightley's V Corps to thrust through the Argenta Gap, using a specially organized force of tanks and infantry in armoured personnel carriers, and with 6th Armoured Division held in reserve for the final breakthrough. The main thrust towards Bologna was to be continued by the Poles and XIII Corps (Harding), brought round from the quiet Apennine sector. By the time Fifth Army opened its offensive on April 14, Eighth Army was well into the Argenta Gap; and Hitler had refused a request by von Vietinghoff to take his last chance of saving Army Group C by withdrawing across the Po to the Alps.

Truscott's subsidiary attack, mounted by IV US Corps (Crittenberger), started first and tore open the front of LI Mountain Corps (Hauck), enabling him to start thrusting his way through the remaining mountains towards the Po Valley. The main Fifth Army attack by II US Corps (Keyes) opened next day, but made

slow progress against XIV Panzer Corps (von Senger), holding Bologna's well-prepared defences.

By April 19 Army Group C was nearing exhaustion: Eighth Army was almost through the Argenta Gap and Fifth Army was within a day of reaching the Po Valley west of Bologna. Von Vietinghoff decided to defy Hitler and ordered a withdrawal across the Po. He was too late. Allied Air Forces had already destroyed all the bridges and ferries. The two Allied armoured divisions leading the flanking thrusts – 6th South African under IV US Corps and 6th British under V Corps – joined hands at Finale nell'Emilia between Bologna and the Po on April 23. Most formations of Army Group C were destroyed by air action as they tried to reach the Po, or surrendered on its banks. *WGFJ*.

Po river, crossing of (April 23–26 1945). After the destruction of Army Group C south of the Po, engineering problems posed more difficulty than German opposition. Fifth Army (Truscott) started crossing the Po at San Benedetto on April 23, followed by Eighth Army (McCreery) between Ficarolo and Ferrara two days later. Fifth Army then advanced north and west to occupy Northwestern Italy, while Eighth Army swung eastwards towards Trieste, entered by Freyberg's New Zealanders on May 2 1945.

Pork Chop Hill. An outpost position in the I Corps sector during the Korean War which was the scene of heavy fighting in spring 1953. Judged to be too insignificant to justify the heavy casualties suffered by the US defenders, it was abandoned on July 10 1953.

Port Arthur, siege of (June 1 1904-January 2 1905). In the Russo-Japanese War, Port Arthur (Lushun), Russia's main Pacific naval base and the terminus of the Trans-Siberian Railway, was Japan's major strategic objective. Some 10,000 survivors of Stössel's 40,000-strong garrison surrendered. The Japanese lost heavily in infantry assaults until their heavy howitzers reduced the defences, suffering some 59,000 casualties, plus 33,000 sick.

P

Port Stanley. Capital of Falklands. Prior to the invasion of April 1982, a small Royal Marines garrison was based at Moody Brook, a few miles to the west. Stanley became the main Argentinian base, but although it was surrounded with minefields the Argentine garrison did not defend it once their troops were beaten.

Portal (*right*) with Air Marshal Peirse

Portal, Marshal of the RAF Lord (1893–1971). Br. Chief of the Air Staff 1940–45. Portal, who had a distinguished flying career in World War I, was noticed by Trenchard in the early years of the RAF. He was AOC-in-C Bomber Command from April to October 1940 and thereafter CAS for the rest of the war. Although a firm believer in the vital importance of air power and, in particular, of the strategic air offensive, he did not subscribe to the opinion that air power alone could determine the outcome of the war. Even so, he came into conflict with his naval and military colleagues on the Chiefs of Staff Committee, especially in the struggle for resources for the build-up of Bomber Command. He differed strongly from his American opposite number, Arnold, as to the latter's policy of daylight bombing, being a firm believer in the efficacy of night area bombing (although later in the war, he thought that daylight bombing could be used for selective purposes, especially the destruction of German oil production). This brought him into sharp disagreement with Harris whom, however, he decided not to remove from his command. There were some periods of tension between him and Churchill, for example, over the bombing of Dresden, which, though he had originally suggested it, Churchill sought to condemn. But overall, Portal achieved a standing unrivalled in the RAF during the war. *ANF.*

Poseidon. A MIRVed SLBM fitted in converted American Polaris submarines from 1970 onwards. Poseidon C-3 can carry up to 14 x 40 kiloton warheads about 2,400 miles (4,000km), but the normal loading is about 10 for a range of 3,120 miles (5,200km). The CEP was deliberately kept fairly large to emphasize the counter-value role of the weapon: 1,476ft (450m). Poseidon remains in service in 16 submarines.

Post-Boost Vehicle (PBV). The space vehicle or "bus" that carries the warheads in a MIRV system. The PBV has the capacity to manoeuvre into a number of different trajectories into each of which it releases a warhead. The Minuteman 3 PBV may take up to six minutes to complete this operation after a three-minute rocket burn by the booster.

***Potemkin* mutiny** (June 27 1905). The 750-strong crew of the Russian Black Sea Fleet battleship *Kniaz Potemkin Tavritchevski* mutinied, claiming that seamen had been threatened with execution for refusing tainted rations. Seven officers and one mutineer were killed: official reaction to the "lying-in-state" of the mutineer's corpse on the Odessa quayside provoked riots in which some 6,000 died. Failing to gain support from other Black Sea units, *Potemkin's* crew scuttled the battleship and surrendered to the authorities in Constanza, Romania.

Potez 63 Series (630.C3, 631.CN2, 633.B2, 63.11) (French, WWII). Heavy fighter/night fighter/light bomber/tactical reconnaissance; crew 3/2/2/3. Prototype flew April 25 1936. By outbreak of war 379 on French charge. Lack of spares critical; losses heavy; by June 25 1940 survivors totalled 1,049. Germans seized 134 Potez 63s (several sub-types). Production, over 1,350 (all variants). Two 700hp Gnome-Rhône 14 M4/M5 or M6/M7 engines; max. speed 275mph (443kph); armament (varied with function) two 20mm cannon, up to eight 7.5mm machine guns, 880lb (400kg) bombs.

Potsdam Conference ("Terminal"). Meetings between Stalin, Truman and first Churchill, then Attlee, held at Potsdam, near Berlin, July 17–August 2 1945. Discussions about Europe were concerned with the establishment of peacetime frontiers, areas of influence, the trial of war criminals and the division of spoils. Severe disagreements were exposed especially as regards Poland and the Balkans. The war against Japan was discussed and Truman revealed to Stalin that America had produced, and would shortly use, the atomic bomb.

POUM. *Partido Obrero de Unificación Marxista* – "Spanish workers' party of Marxist unification". Anti-Stalinist group splintered off from orthodox Spanish Communist Party in September 1935. Its main strength lay in Catalonia. Its doctrines were sharply revolutionary; its members took an active part early in the civil war. It was suppressed by Russian agents in Spain and their local helpers in June 1937, and its leader Andrés Nin was murdered.

Pound, Adm of the Fleet Sir Dudley (1877–1943). Br. First Sea Lord 1939–43. Highly respected by Churchill, but criticized on the ground that he interfered in too great detail with the actions of the commanders at sea. Such a view fails to recognize that the Admiralty was organized as an operational headquarters where, for example, the most important intelligence first arrived. Nevertheless, some of his decisions, particularly that regarding Convoy PQ 17 in 1942, proved unfortunate. Pound must also share with Churchill much of the blame for the extraordinarily muddled relationship between the naval and military commanders in the Norwegian campaign of April 1940. On the other hand, much of the credit for the preservation of Britain's most vital sea lanes in the darkest days of the war and for the turn of the tide in the war at sea which occurred in the spring and summer of 1943 is due to Pound. After the collapse of his health, he became decreasingly effective in the second half of 1943, but remained in office until within a few weeks of his death on October 1 1943. *ANF.*

Pozieres *see* SOMME, BATTLE OF THE.

Prasca, Gen Sebastiano Visconti. Italian c-in-c Albania, 1939–40: commanded Italian invasion of Greece, October 1940.

Precision bombing *see* BOMBING.

Precision Guided Munitions (PGM). General term for "smart" munitions that are terminally guided to their targets with a high degree of accuracy. These include bombs, shells and missiles that home on reflected laser energy and missiles, and bombs that home on a designated point on a television picture obtained by a camera in the nose of the weapon. The term also covers munitions, sometimes small submunitions carried in dispensers, that home on targets such as tanks by sensing their infrared emissions or by using millimetre wavelength radar.

Pre-emptive strike. A strike carried out by one side in anticipation of the other's launching an attack.

Pricolo, Gen Francesco. Italian. Chief of Air Staff when Italy declared war in 1940.

Pridham-Wippell, Adm Sir Henry (1885–1952). Br. Second-in-Command Mediterranean Fleet and Flag Officer Light Forces to May 1941; Flag Officer 1st Battle Squadron; temporarily c-in-c Mediterranean Fleet, April–May 1942.

Prien, Commander Günther (1908–41). Ger. Submarine commander. In *U-47*, penetrated the anchorage at Scapa Flow and sank the battleship *Royal Oak*, night of October 13–14 1939. Subsequently sank large total of merchant ships until killed when *U-47* was herself destroyed on March 8 1941 by HMS *Wolverine*.

Prince of Wales. British battleship. *King George V* class; completed 1941; 35,000 tons, 10 × 14in guns. Engaged *Bismarck* in the Denmark Straits, May 1941. Badly damaged, and with malfunctioning armament, she got an important hit in return before turning away. Sunk (with HMS *Repulse*) by Japanese air attack off Malaya, December 10 1941.

Princeton. US aircraft carrier. *Independence* class light carrier; completed 1943. During the Battle of Leyte Gulf, she was hit by a dive-bomber. Fires and explosions took control and sank this ship as well as badly damaging the cruiser *Birmingham* and killing 385 of her crew while she was alongside, helping to fight the fires.

Prinz Eugen. German heavy cruiser. Armament 8 × 8in guns. Saw great deal of service: sustained torpedo damage in Norwegian campaign (1940); survived *Bismarck's* Atlantic sortie (1941), escaping to Brest; in 1942 was in Channel Dash. Surrendered at Copenhagen (1945). Expended in atomic bomb test at Bikini (1947).

Prisoners of War (Korea). The POW issue proved the most contentious of the Korean War. Although neither the DPRK nor the US had ratified the Geneva Convention of 1949, both announced that they would apply its provisions. The Chinese did not accept the Geneva rules until July 1952. In fact neither side adhered strictly to the Convention and both treated POWs as political pawns. While the Chinese tried to re-educate their prisoners, the Americans attempted to win communist POWs for democracy. The POWs became an issue at the truce talks in 1952 when the UNC proposed the principle of non-forcible repatriation under which no POW would be compelled to return home. The communists insisted on Article 118 of the Geneva Convention which called for the automatic repatriation of all POWs at the end of hostilities. This question deadlocked the truce talks for over a year and was only finally resolved by handing over those POWs refusing repatriation to a Neutral Nations Repatriation Commission. *CM. See also* KOJE ISLAND PRISON CAMP; NEUTRAL NATIONS REPATRIATION COMMISSION.

Prittwitz, Gen Max von (1848–1917). Ger. A favourite of the Kaiser; appointed Commander of German Eighth Army (East Prussia) in 1914. Dismissed after ordering general withdrawal to line of Vistula after Battle of Gumbinnen. *See also* TANNENBERG AND THE MASURIAN LAKES, BATTLES OF.

Propaganda. An important arm of warfare, often neglected by commanders born into the old officer class, who affect to despise journalists and broadcasters. During this century, propaganda's main vehicles have been, in turn, newspapers, radio and television; books, pamphlets, leaflets, posters, plays, films, and megaphones for shouting slogans have also been useful from time to time. Propaganda has two main military objects: to maintain the morale of one's own side, and to sap that of enemies, actual or potental. It has no necessary connection with truth; save that, when it is known and provable to be truthful, it is all the more effective.

The build-up of the Dreadnought fleet, 1906–15, was much helped by newspaper propaganda, originally orchestrated by Fisher. One of the grounds of Anglo-German misunderstanding was that the German press was entirely under government control, and the Germans believed, wrongly, that the same was true of the press in England. Early in the 1914–18 war, newspaper reports – American as well as British and French – indicated that German troops advancing across Belgium had behaved with particular atrocity towards civilians; most of these stories turned out to be baseless on investigation, but they had tremendous effect in stiffening Allied will to fight. The Russian Bolsheviks, who siezed power in November 1917, relied largely on propaganda to secure their victory in the civil war that followed, and have conducted sustained campaigns against capitalism and imperialism ever since, with varying results. Both Mussolini's Italy and Hitler's Germany used propaganda extensively, in peace and in war, to assure their own citizens of their regimes' greatness and to intimidate their opponents. Goebbels showed particular skill at these tasks; his encouragement was as valuable as Himmler's policy of terror in holding Nazi Germany together for its last disastrous year. Churchill's wartime broadcasts did marvels for sustaining the British against Nazi attack, and encouraged the occupied peoples of Europe to hope; as did, in particular, Queen Wilhelmina's broadcasts to the Nether-

347

P

lands. In many German-occupied countries to possess a radio set was illegal; and many broadcasts suffered from jamming. During – even before – the war, rumours about Nazi concentration camps began to spread; most of them were shrugged off as propaganda. This made the truth, when it appeared in 1945, all the more horrifying.

Much of the Cold War has been fought by propaganda. Many apparently objective, quasi-historical studies of it and of the preceding world war are devised, from both sides, with propaganda motives. Once the Americans had dropped atom bombs in anger – in the belief that, by so doing, they were saving hundreds of thousands of lives; but this the propagandists decided to keep secret. The success of the campaign in Korea was attributed by millions of Chinese to germ warfare: long afterwards the truth was revealed.

Jamming of broadcasts has continued, on and off. No one has yet found a certain way of jamming a telecast. Widespread television coverage of life in the capitalist world may yet prove capitalism's most powerful weapon against a communist threat. Widespread television coverage of the war in Vietnam provided powerful propaganda for peace. *MF.*

Provence. French battleship. *Bretagne* class; completed 1915 and rebuilt in the 1930s. After being sunk at Mers-El-Kébir (1940), she was raised but then scuttled at Toulon (1942).

Provincial Mobile Forces (National Liberation Front of South Vietnam). One of three categories of troops nominally under NLF command during the Vietnam War (*see* PEOPLE'S LIBERATION ARMED FORCE). Known in Vietnamese as *Boi doi dia phuong*, or regional forces, they began as armed propaganda teams and later developed into platoons and companies, sometimes "independent" companies, capable of providing security for party organs, reconnaissance-in-force, and executing "tyrants". They were usually better armed and trained than local guerrillas, and unlike main forces they reported to district or provincial party committees rather than to a military command. *WST.*

Provisional Revolutionary Government of South Vietnam (PRG). In June 1969, the National Liberation Front of South Vietnam (NLF) and its allied organizations gave way to a Provisional Revolutionary Government (PRG). The PRG was created to represent the revolutionary side in negotiations and, it was hoped, to attract urban support. Front leaders, for the most part, became leaders of the PRG which remained, like the Front, subordinate to the Vietnam Lao Dong (Workers', or Vietnam Communist) Party. As befitted an organization created partly for reasons of diplomacy, its best known figure abroad was the Foreign Minister, Madame Nguyen Thi Binh. The PRG was one of four parties to the Paris Agreements of January 1973 and the ostensible government of South Vietnam from war's end in 1975 until formal reunification in 1976. *WST.*

Proximity fuse. A means of detonating an explosive by the closeness of the target as opposed to time expiry, altitude etc. A British invention revealed to the Americans in 1940 by Tizard, then mass-produced in the US. Vital in anti-aircraft gunnery against V-1s and kamikaze aircraft.

Pucará, FMA IA 58 (Argentine). Two-seat counterinsurgency aircraft. In service May 1976. About 60 in service at time of Falklands War, 1982; of about 40 committed, 25 lost. Two 1,022ehp Turboméca Astazou XVIG engines, four 7.62mm machine guns, 3,570lb (1,620kg) external ordnance.

Puller, Lt Gen Lewis B (1898–1971). US. Much-decorated Marine Corps officer who commanded the 1st Battalion of the 7th Marine Regiment on Guadalcanal in 1942 in the defence of the vital Henderson Field airstrip on October 24–25. He was executive officer of the 7th Marines in the Cape Gloucester campaign, December 1943–February 1944, and then led the 1st Marine Regiment in the difficult operations on Peleliu in September and October 1944. Puller commanded the 1st Marines again in the Korean War (where he won the Navy Cross for the fifth time), landing with them in Inchon in September 1950. *PJS.*

Punchbowl. Scene of the most bitter battles of the Korean War. It was a large volcanic crater 25 miles (40km) north of Inje and the same distance from the east coast on the sector of the front held by X Corps. In August-September 1951 the 1st US Marine Division, the US 2nd Division and ROK troops were involved in heavy fighting to clear the enemy from the ridges around the Punchbowl as part of Gen Van Fleet's autumn offensives to straighten his line and bring pressure to bear at the truce talks. *CM. See also* BLOODY RIDGE; HEARTBREAK RIDGE.

Pursuit aircraft *see* FIGHTER AIRCRAFT.

Pusan Perimeter campaign, the Korean War. After the fall of Taejon in mid-July 1950, the US Eighth Army fell back into the Pusan Perimeter, the last defensible position in South Korea. This was a line of outposts backed by mobile reserves along the Naktong river designed to hold the railway quadrilateral Taegu-Masan-Pusan-Kyongu and the port of Pusan whose docks were vital to the UN war effort. The American commander, Gen Walker, ordered a retreat behind the Naktong on August 1 1950. The perimeter was held by three US divisions and five ROK divisions, reinforced in the course of the battle by the 1st US Provisional Marine Brigade, the 27th British Infantry Brigade and various US units hastily sent to Korea. In defending the perimeter against the NKPA, Walker had the advantage of interior lines of communication and maximum support from the air and sea. Initially, there was a rough parity of ground forces, but by the end of August, Walker had a 2:1 superiority in men and 5:1 in tanks. Despite the changing military balance, the NKPA penetrated the perimeter at several points in its final offensive launched on August 31 and Walker considered withdrawal to the Davidson line, a final defence position around Pusan. By September 8, however, the attack had been halted. On September 16, the day after Inchon, Walker began a counteroffensive which broke out of the perimeter on September 23. *CM. See also* INCHON LANDING; WALKER, WALTON WARRIS, LT GEN.

Putnik, Marshal Radomir (1847–1917). Serbian. *Voivod* (c-in-c) of Serbian forces during the Balkan Wars, 1912–13, directing the successful defence-in-depth and subsequent counteroffensive against Bulgaria's pre-emptive strike of July 1913. During World War I he was *Voivod* in the Serbian campaign of 1914–15. Skilfully manoeuvring the three armies under his control against superior Austrian forces, he was victorious at the Jadar river, August 16–21 1914, but was forced by lack of ammunition to retire from the Rudnik Ridges, September 8–17, making a fighting retreat to Belgrade. Resupplied early in December, his counteroffensive drove the Austrians from Serbia. Outnumbered and defeated in October-November 1915 by August von Mackensen's German-Austrian-Bulgarian armies, Putnik, himself mortally ill, made an epic retreat with his surviving men through the mountains of Montenegro and Albania to the Adriatic. *RO'N.*

Pye, Vice Adm William Satterlee (1880–1959). US. Temporarily replaced Kimmel as commander, US Pacific Fleet after Pearl Harbor; much criticized, with Fletcher, for failing to relieve Wake Island.

Pyongyang. Capital of North Korea and one of the most heavily bombed targets of the Korean War. It was briefly occupied by UN forces in October 1950 but lost after China entered the war and reoccupied by the North Koreans on December 6 1950.

PZL P-11 and P-24 (Poland, WWII). Single-seat fighter. Prototype flew September 1931; first production deliveries (P-11a) 1934. September 1939, 128 P-11s in Polish squadrons; most soon lost. P-24 prototype flew May 1933; improved development of P-11c. Supplied to Turkey (40), Bulgaria (60), Greece (36), Romania (6). Impressive use by Greek air force from November 1940. Production: P-11, about 330; P-24, about 300. One 640hp PZL Mercury VI. 52 (P-24, 930/970hp Gnome-Rhône 14 KFs/NO7); max. speed 242/267mph (389/430kph); four 7.7mm/7.9mm machine guns (some P-24s two 20mm cannon, two machine guns), 220lb (100kg) bombs.

Q

Q-Ship. British ruse to draw U-boats into surface action against merchant ships with concealed armament.

Quebec Conferences. Meetings between Churchill and Roosevelt and their military advisers in Quebec, August 11-24 1943 and September 11-16 1944. The first ("Quadrant") took place in the aftermath of the successful operations in Sicily and Italy and with the prospect of the latter's imminent surrender. It was, therefore, primarily concerned with the exploitation of these advantages and, in particular, with the plans for the invasion of France both from the north and south. Some divergence of view between the British and the Americans arose as to the priority and timing of "Overlord". By the time of the second conference ("Octagon"), Rome had been captured, the Russians had made huge advances and Eisenhower's armies had come across France to the German frontiers. In the Pacific, the Americans had advanced to points from which they could mount a bombing offensive against Japan and in Burma the British were beginning to dominate the Japanese. The options which these successes offered were examined but the accords reached were somewhat vague. *ANF.*

Queen Elizabeth. British battleship. Launched 1913, completed 1915. Took part in the Dardanelles campaign; flagship of the Grand Fleet (Beatty), 1917–18, flagship of the Mediterranean Fleet (Cunningham), 1939–41. Served in the Pacific 1944–45.

Queen Elizabeth (RMS). Launched 1938; c83,000 tons gross. In World War II she transported more than 150,000 British and US troops all over the world.

Queen Mary (RMS). Cunard Liner launched 1934. Gross tonnage 81,000. As a troopship in World War II, she could carry a division in a single voyage relying upon speed, rather than convoy protection, for survival.

Quemoy-Matsu bombardments (1950-62). Withdrawing to Taiwan after the Chinese Civil War, 1949, Chiang Kai-shek's Nationalists retained and garrisoned the islands of Quemoy (some 10 miles/16km from the mainland) and Matsu. In October 1949, an amphibious assault on Quemoy by the 40,000-strong communist Third Field Army was repulsed with heavy communist losses (13,000 killed; 7,000 captured). Thereafter, Quemoy and Matsu were harassed by long-range artillery from the mainland, answered in kind – and with Quemoy-launched guerrilla raids – by the Nationalists. Heavy bombardments in August-December 1954 suggested imminent invasion: the US Seventh Fleet took up defensive positions and President Eisenhower signed a Mutual Security Pact with Taiwan. A determined attempt by communist artillery to blockade Quemoy in August-October 1958 was countered by the deployment of Seventh Fleet's ships and aircraft to escort supply vessels. US sea power deterred a further invasion threat in mid-1962 and thereafter bombardment declined. *RO'N.*

Quesada, Lt Gen Elwood R ("Pete") (b.1904). US. Began World War II as a combat flier with the rank of major. From early 1943 he led US 12th Fighter Command during the campaigns in Tunisia, Sicily and Italy, before taking command of 9th Fighter Command in Britain, October 1943. From early 1944, he was Commanding General of 9th Tactical Air Command, landing in Normandy on June 7 1944 to oversee air support for the Allied armies throughout Northwest Europe.

Quisling. A traitor or fifth columnist. The Norwegian ex-army officer and Minister of Defence Maj Vidkun Quisling (1887-1945) founded the Fascist *Nasjonal Samling* (National Union Party), 1933. He collaborated in the German invasion of Norway, 1940, and although not always fully trusted by the German occupation authorities, in spite of his staunch adherence Fascist doctrine, to served as pro-Axis Minister President 1942–45. Convicted of treason after Germany's defeat, he was executed on October 24 1945.

Rabaul campaign (1942–45). On January 23 1942 Japanese forces captured the port of Rabaul on the island of New Britain, Bismarck Sea. Building five airfields and exploiting the best natural harbour in the region, Japan dominated the skies and seas over New Guinea, the Solomons and the surrounding oceans. The capture or neutralization of Rabaul was a major priority for the Allies but it was anticipated that a direct amphibious attack held little chance of success. However, by October 1943 a strategy was agreed by which Rabaul would be isolated by the capture of the surrounding islands and the construction of air bases. This series of operations, the "Elkton" Plan, constituted an extended pincer movement. MacArthur's forces in the Southwest Pacific Area were to advance northwards through Papua and New Guinea while Adm Halsey's command, the South Pacific Area, was to deal with the Solomon Islands. On December 26 1943 American forces landed at Cape Gloucester on New Britain, allowing the construction of new air bases to strike at Rabaul. Meanwhile, on November 1, US Marines had assaulted Bougainville, the largest of the Solomon Islands. Now supported by their own powerful air forces, the landings continued in February and March 1944 and resulted in the capture of the northernmost islands in the Bismarck Archipelago, the St Matthias Group and the Admiralty Islands. Rabaul and its large garrison were now surrounded and were left to "wither on the vine." MS.

Raborn, Vice Adm William Francis (b.1905). US. From 1955, headed team that developed Polaris SSBM, deployed early 1960s; head of CIA, 1965–66.

Radar. Originally known as RDF (Radio Direction Finding), the system in which radio waves are broadcast and received back by echo to measure distance and bearing. Developed after 1940 as an aid to navigation, bomb aiming, submarine detection and air to air interception.

Radiation. Nuclear explosions normally emit 70-80 percent of their energy in electromagnetic radiation. The X-rays interact with the atmosphere to create the high-temperature fireball that itself emits "heat", i.e. radiation in the ultraviolet, visible and infrared spectrum. Gamma rays remain, and together with neutrons provide the initial "nuclear radiation" effects of the weapon, causing radiation sickness among those who have suffered heavy exposures. Small weapons under about 10 kilotons in yield use the latter effect as their primary kill mechanism. In addition, nuclear fallout emits radiation from decaying fission products in the form of alpha and beta particles and gamma rays. This can be lethal, depending on the dose received. *EJG.*

Radio Counter Measures (RCM) *see* ELECTRONIC WARFARE.

Rado, Sandor (1900–81). Hungarian Bolshevik, commissar under Bela Kun's brief dictatorship in Hungary, March–August 1919. After its overthrow, escaped to Switzerland; ran "Rote Drei" spy network for Comintern, 1938–43.

Raeder: C-in-C *Kriegsmarine*, 1935–43

Raeder, Grand Adm Erich (1876–1960). Ger. Served in *Lützow*, World War I, surviving her loss at Jutland. Promoted Adm in 1928, and became CNS at a time when the German navy was using great ingenuity to circumvent the Versailles Treaty, including the pocket battleship type and the secret development of submarine designs. Raeder was made C-in-C *Kriegsmarine*, 1935. He planned to build up a navy adequate to challenge Britain by about 1944 ("Z Plan") and was most upset by war breaking out in 1939. Despite its relative weakness, his navy performed well in the invasion of Norway but was left, crippled by losses, quite incapable of playing any serious part in an invasion of Britain. Raeder's main interest was in his larger ships, the submarines being largely left to Dönitz. Raiding into the Atlantic by the heavy ships ended with the loss of *Bismarck* and then the return of the ships at Brest to Germany. Thereafter they were moved to Norway to attack the Russian convoys. Hitler simultaneously insisted on extreme caution because of his fear of losses. Soon after the humiliation of the Battle of the Barents Sea in late 1942, Raeder resigned. At Nuremberg he was sentenced to life imprisonment but was released in 1955. *CJW/CD.*

Rafa, Battle of (1917). As Lt Gen Chetwode's Desert Column pushed the Turks back towards Palestine in late December 1916, they received reports that the enemy were preparing a substantial defensive position to the south of Rafa. Although concerned at operating with extended supply lines, it was decided to mount a raid with the Australian and New Zealand Mounted Division, together with support units. On January 9 1917, the Turkish positions grouped around a central redoubt were surrounded but heavy machine-gun fire at first slowed, and then halted the attack. Reports of approaching Turkish relief columns prompted Chetwode to order a withdrawal just as news arrived that New Zealand forces had captured the redoubt. The order was rescinded and victory was confirmed before the British troops disengaged, having taken 1,635 prisoners at a cost of 487 casualties. *MS.*

Railway gun. Artillery piece, usually a super-heavy siege weapon, mounted on a railway wagon. The largest was the 1,350-ton German 80cm "Gustav" Kanone, used at Sevastopol, 1942.

Ramcke, Lt Gen (*General der Fallschirmtruppen*) Hermann Bernhard (1889–1968). Ger. Commanding 2nd Paratroop Division in 1944, Ramcke, a dedicated Nazi, was personally ordered by Hitler to hold the port of Brest *à outrance*. In a siege beginning on

August 7, the port was almost completely destroyed before falling to US VIII Corps on September 18.

Ramillies. British battleship. "R" class; completed 1917. Grand Fleet, 1917-18; Mediterranean and at Cape Spartivento (1940); then convoy duty. In the Madagascar landings (1942), she was damaged by a Japanese midget submarine. Eastern Fleet (1943); Normandy and South of France landings and subsequent bombardments (1944).

Ramsay, Adm Sir Bertram Home (1883–1945). Br. Served in Dover Patrol, World War I: recalled from retirement in 1939 as Flag Officer, Dover. After successfully directing Dunkirk evacuation, he planned the North African landings, in which he was Deputy Commander of naval forces, 1942, and the Sicily landings, where he commanded Eastern Task Force. Naval c-in-c of the D-Day landings, whose success owed much to his planning ability and liaison skills. In January 1945, while organizing support for the advancing Allied armies, he was killed in an air crash.

Ramsden, Lt Gen W H C (1888–1969). Br. Commander 50th Division during the battles of Gazala and Mersa Matruh in June 1942; Commander XXX Corps on the El Alamein Line in July and at the Battle of Alam Halfa in August; replaced by Montgomery with Lt Gen Leese in August in preparation for the Battle of El Alamein.

Ram tank. Canadian-built medium tank based on M3 Grant design. Used, without turret, as APC in 1944–45. *See also* TANKS.

Rangers. US version of British Commandos; formed in 1942. First saw action at Dieppe and served in many US amphibious operations of World War II.

Rangoon (Burma campaign 1941–45). Capital of Burma, chief port and centre of rail connections. First Japanese air raids, December 23 and 25 1941. The only port of entry for reinforcements, including vital 7th Armoured Brigade from Western Desert. Evacuation of civilians, February 20–March 1 1942. Alexander arrived to take over command, March 5; next day,

he ordered a military evacuation. The exit was blocked by the Japanese, and efforts to break through proved unavailing; however, the roadblock was abandoned because the Japanese could not believe Rangoon would be surrendered without a struggle. During the next three years, numerous British and American air raids were made on the city, especially the dock area. March–May 1945, the British advance towards Rangoon was hazarded by fear of the monsoon halting movement. The Japanese abandoned the city on April 23. Because of the imminence of the monsoon, the decision was taken by Mountbatten to take the city from the sea (Operation "Dracula"). A parachute battalion was dropped at Elephant Point, May 1. Next day, landing craft brought in the first wave of XV Corps assault troops. On May 6, advance elements of IV Corps linked up with XV Corps, 27 miles (43km) north of the city. *HT.*

Rann of Kutch, India-Pakistan border. The Rann or marshland is a featureless waste where no clear international boundary was demarcated. Border skirmishes threatened to escalate into conflict early in 1965. The British prime minister urged that the question be referred to international arbitration. This proposal was accepted, the award favouring Pakistan; thus encouraging the Pakistan foreign minister to reactivate the question of the Indian occupation of Kashmir, leading to war later in 1965.

Rapallo Conference. At the Allied conference at Rapallo, Italy, in November 1917, Lloyd George and Painlevé successfully advocated the establishment of a Supreme War Council to provide a central direction and coordination of the Allied war effort. On November 7, the fifth session of the conference became the first session of the Supreme War Council. It was agreed that political representatives of the various governments would meet each month at Versailles, with a permanent body of military advisers. However, it proved difficult to prevent the various representatives from espousing the policies of their own nation's general staffs. *MS.*

Rapido (Gari), crossings of. The German Gustav Line at the southern end of the Liri Valley below Monte Cassino was based upon the small, fast-flowing Rapido, which was a tank obstacle. The Allies made two attempts to cross it. The first was on January 20 1944, when 36th US Division was disastrously defeated by 15th Panzer Grenadier Division, trying to cross at St Angelo. The failure led later to a Congressional inquiry.

The second attempt took place between May 11–14 1944. XIII Corps (Kirkman) crossed during the night of May 11–12 with 4th British and 8th Indian Divisions at the start of Alexander's "Diadem" offensive, opposed by LI Mountain Corps (Feuerstein). By midmorning of May 12, two bridges had been completed in 8th Indian Division's sector, the farthest from Monte Cassino, but 4th Division had none. During the following night the Engineers of 4th and 6th Armoured Divisions built "Amazon" bridge "regardless of cost", enabling the bridgehead to be expanded. By May 14, nine bridges had been built, and Eighth Army could start fighting its way up the Liri Valley. *WGFJ.*

Rapier missile. A British short-range air-defence missile, first deployed in 1967. Used by the army in towed and tracked versions and by the RAF for airfield defence. Rapier is automatically command-guided to the line of sight of the operator. Radar provides all-weather "blindfire" back-up to optical tracking in some systems, and infrared tracking is being developed. Maximum range about 4 miles (7km). Rapier shot down one Argentine Dagger attack aircraft in the Falklands War and contributed to the loss of a Skyhawk, and possibly other aircraft. A total of 25,000 has been built, and the system has been exported to 13 countries including Iran.

Rashid Ali *see* IRAQ, RASHID ALI REBELLION.

Ravenna, capture of (December 2–4 1944). I Canadian Corps (Foulkes) advanced north between the Montone and Lamone rivers, outflanking the defences of LXXVI Panzer Corps (Herr), and forcing Herr to abandon the city.

351

R

Rawalpindi. British armed merchant cruiser with 6in guns. Commanded by Capt E C Kennedy, she engaged *Scharnhorst* and *Gneisenau* in an unequal action, November 23 1939. She was sunk, but the German battlecruisers abandoned their sortie.

Sudan and Boer War veteran Rawlinson

Rawlinson, Gen Lord (1864–1925). Br. Rawlinson, who had served on Kitchener's staff in the Sudan and commanded a mobile column in the Second Boer War, was Director of Recruiting in August 1914, making a brief but important contribution to the expansion of the Army before taking over 4th Division on the Aisne and then being given command of the British force attempting to relieve Antwerp. This force became IV Corps in October 1914 and Rawlinson led it at First Ypres and, during 1915, at Neuve-Chapelle, Aubers Ridge, Festubert and Loos. In February 1916 he took command of the new Fourth Army, which had a leading role in the Somme offensive of that year. Rawlinson's planning for the initial assault on July 1 has been widely criticized although his attack near Longueval on July 14 showed considerable tactical ability. Early in 1918 he was British military representative on the Supreme War Council but was recalled to command a reconstituted Fourth Army in the defence of Amiens. Rawlinson soon demonstrated that he had absorbed the tactical lessons of the past three years and, from August 8 onwards, Fourth Army spearheaded the victorious British advance, breaking the Hindenburg Line and driving the Germans back over the Selle and the Sambre Canal. Rawlinson directed the withdrawal of Allied forces from North Russia in 1919 and was c-in-c, India, 1920–25. *PJS*.

RE8, Royal Aircraft Factory (Br, WWI). Two-seat reconnaissance bomber. First squadron (No. 52) to France, November 1916. Ordered in large numbers; never wholly satisfactory but in service throughout war. Operational RAF Middle East, Russia, 1919. Production, 4,282. One 140hp RAF 4a engine; max. speed 98mph (157kph); two, occasionally three, 0.303in machine guns, 224lb (102kg) bombs.

Redan Ridge. Strongly defended spur, north of Beaumont Hamel on the Somme battlefield, unsuccessfully attacked by the British 4th Division, July 1 1916. Even in November 1916 the 2nd Division secured only part of this feature.

Red Cross. Founded in Switzerland, 1864, as a voluntary aid organization to assist the victims of war. It initially provided for the treatment of the wounded and safeguarded the neutral status of those caring for them. Subsequent revisions to the original Geneva convention extended the Red Cross's assistance to the victims of the war at sea, prisoners of war and the suffering of civilians brought about by war and natural disaster. It operates as the Red Crescent in Muslim communities.

Reddersberg, Battle of *see* SANNA'S POST.

Red Orchestra (*Rote Kapelle*). Anti-Nazi communist spy network organized 1937–42 by Leopold Trepper (1904–82). His base was in Brussels; some of his informants were junior officers in German main HQ in Berlin. Allegedly, his group's information cost 200,000 German lives.

Red River delta campaign (1951). Vietnamese communist leaders were encouraged in 1950 by military assistance arriving from China and victory in the "Border War" to believe their forces were ready to attack entrenched French positions in the Red River delta. In what Vo Nguyen Giap billed as a general counteroffensive, the People's Army of Vietnam (PAVN) descended from the mountains in multidivision strength in January 1951. The attacks were unsuccessful, sometimes disastrous, as at Vinh Yen where a PAVN force of 20,000 men lost 6,000 dead and 8,000 wounded in assaults on 6,000 French. Closing the campaign in June 1951, PAVN commanders concluded that their forces simply could not prevail where the French were able to use artillery, aircraft and armour effectively. After this, the communists chose targets for frontal assault more carefully and bypassed strongpoints to operate behind French lines in the delta. The French lacked the manpower to exploit their victories. *WST*.

Red Three (*Rote Drei*). Anti-Nazi communist spy network organized from Switzerland, 1941–44, by Sandor Rado; provided USSR with vital information.

Regiment. 1) Administrative grouping of several battalions. 2) Battalion equivalent for Artillery, Armoured and other arms in the British Army. 3) In US and other armies, equivalent to the British Brigade.

Reichenau, Field Marshal Walther von (1884–1942). Ger. An ambitious officer who supported the Nazis to further his own career, von Reichenau was only prevented from becoming c-in-c of the Army in 1938 because of opposition from von Rundstedt and others. Though seen as a "political" general, he performed well in command of the German Tenth Army in Poland and also led this formation – redesignated as the Sixth Army – in the Low Countries and France. He was promoted to Field Marshal in July 1940 and stayed at the head of Sixth Army for the invasion of Russia, endorsing the SS massacre of Jews in Kiev in September 1941. He was chosen to replace von Rundstedt as commander of Army Group South on November 30 but had little chance to shine at this level, for he suffered a heart attack on January 12 1942 and died following an air crash while flying home for treatment five days later. *PJS*.

Reinhardt, Gen Georg-Hans (1887–1963). Ger. Commanded 4th Panzer Division in Poland in 1939 and XLI Panzer Corps in France in 1940. When Germany attacked Russia in 1941, XLI Panzer Corps formed part of Army Group North. Reinhardt's tanks reached the outskirts of Leningrad in mid-September but, the following month, he was made commander of the 3rd Panzer Group in Army Group Centre's late autumn advance towards Moscow. The formation became the Third Panzer Army in 1942 and Reinhardt remained with it on the Eastern Front. In August 1944 he was appointed commander of Army Group Centre and given the almost impossible task of stopping the Russian drive towards East Prussia. Outnumbered, and hampered by Hitler's refusal to permit sensible tactical withdrawals, Reinhardt fought ably but, after recommending the evacuation of East Prussia, was dismissed on January 26 1945. *PJS.*

Reitsch, Hanna (1912–79). Ger. A record-breaking civilian pilot; became a leading Luftwaffe test pilot, flying numerous experimental aircraft including jet- and rocket-powered prototypes.

Remagen Bridge *see* RHINE CROSSING (1945).

Remotely Piloted Vehicle (RPV). Small pilotless aircraft can be remotely guided to carry out various military missions. The Americans used RPVS carrying cameras and other intelligence-gathering equipment over North Vietnam and China in the 1960s. The Israelis used RPVS as decoys in the 1973 War and have developed very effective techniques of using them to help aircraft neutralize surface-to-air missile batteries. Their Mastiff and Scout mini-RPVS can be used for a wide range of reconnaissance, surveillance, artillery spotting, target designation, electronic warfare and communications relay missions. RPVS can carry laser target designators, television cameras or even weapons such as precision-guided munitions. Being pilotless, the RPV can be small, highly manoeuvrable and much more expendable than a manned aircraft and can be used with less political embarrassment. RPVS allow remote target acquisition and designation for long-range battlefield support systems such as MLRS. Pilotless aircraft that fly pre-programmed flight

paths are properly known as drones *EJG.*

Renault FT17 *see* TANKS.

Rennell Island, Battle of (January 29-30 1943). Final naval engagement of Guadalcanal campaign. Believing that Japanese activity presaged further reinforcement of Guadalcanal (in fact, the Japanese evacuated the island, February 2-9 1943) Halsey ordered Task Force 18 (Rear Adm Robert Giffen: six cruisers, eight destroyers, two escort carriers) to cover a US resupply convoy. Inexperienced in Pacific operations, Giffen left behind his carriers, relying for protection on anti-aircraft armament. On the evening of January 29, land-based torpedo-bombers severely damaged heavy cruiser *Chicago*; cruisers *Wichita* and *Louisville* being hit by torpedoes that failed to detonate. Taken in tow, *Chicago* was sunk next day by renewed torpedo-bomber attack; however, Japanese concentration on the Task Force allowed the US convoy to reach Guadalcanal without loss. *RO'N.*

Rennenkampf, Gen Pavel (Paul) Karlovich von (1853–1918). Russian. Commander of the Russian First Army in August-September 1914 during the Tannenberg and Masurian Lakes campaign. Served with distinction during the Boxer Rising; a cavalry divisional commander in Russo-Japanese War. It was here that the seed of the Russian defeat at Tannenberg was sown; Rennenkampf was publicly accused by a fellow general, Samsonov, of failing to support him adequately at the battles of Telissu and Liaoyang. The two generals came to blows on Mukden railway station, and only the personal intervention of the Tsar prevented a duel. Rennenkampf was unpopular at all levels in the Russian army, being arrogant, intolerant and out of personal touch with his juniors. His German-Balt ancestry made him suspect and, following the hesitant performance of his army in East Prussia after its initial success at Gumbinnen, it was widely said that he was disloyal. After his poor showing at Lodz in November 1914, he was replaced. He was shot by the Bolsheviks in 1918. *MH.*

Renown. British battlecruiser. Completed in 1916. She saw action against the *Scharnhorst* and *Gneisenau* in the Norwegian campaign, 1940, and later served in the Mediterranean and Home Fleets, 1940–43, and the Eastern Fleet, 1943–45.

Reparations. War indemnities imposed upon Germany by the Allies after World War I.

Republic of Korea (ROK) Army. Originated in the National Defence Forces created by the US Military Government in December 1945. When the ROK was established in August 1948, these became the nucleus of a national army. The ROK Army was trained by US military advisers and structured on the American model with a high proportion of manpower assigned to administrative units. It lacked heavy artillery or tanks, weapons withheld by the Americans to deter the ROK from attacking the north. When the Korean War broke out in June 1950, the ROK Army contained 98,000 men, 65,000 in eight infantry divisions and the remainder in non-combat roles. Four divisions were deployed in the area of the 38th Parallel. Inexperienced in anything but anti-guerrilla warfare and lacking heavy weapons, the ROK Army was rapidly driven back by the NKPA and many units disintegrated. Others joined the US Eighth Army and retreated into the Pusan Perimeter. In October 1950 ROK troops were the first to cross the 38th Parallel into North Korea, advancing to the Yalu at Chosan. Chinese intervention, however, shattered the ROK forces, which had to be rebuilt by the Americans after the truce talks began in July 1951. The new army was first tested against the NKPA in the bitter battles around the Punchbowl of August-September 1951 and was also involved in suppressing guerrillas. By the beginning of 1953 ROK strength had risen to 14 divisions and it held almost two-thirds of the front. Before the armistice, Washington authorized a further expansion to 20 divisions, or 655,000 men. ROK forces suffered heavily in the Battle of the Kumsong Bulge during the final Chinese offensive of July 1953. *CM.*

R

Republic of Vietnam (RVN). The RVN grew out of the State of Vietnam, an Associated State of the French Union created under French aegis in 1949. By agreement with France in June 1954, the State of Vietnam, its capital at Saigon, acquired full independence. Bao Dai appointed Ngo Dinh Diem as Premier. Many Vietnamese civil servants and military personnel who had served the French remained in office. With partition in 1954, the jurisdiction of this state was limited to Vietnam south of the 17th Parallel – hence the common appellation South Vietnam. Diem rigged a plebiscite to end the constitutional monarchy and establish a republic, and the Republic of Vietnam (RVN) was proclaimed with himself as first president on October 26 1955. Following Diem's assassination in 1963, a succession of military governments enjoyed American support until communist armed forces entered Saigon, bringing the RVN to an end, on April 30 1975. *WST.*

Repulse. British battlecruiser. *Renown* class; completed 1916. Grand Fleet; unsuccessful action with German light cruisers (1917). Major refit (1934–36). Troop convoys (1939). Norwegian operations (1940). Force Z at Singapore, sunk by Japanese air attack, December 10 1941.

Resistance movements. In World War I several groups of Belgians provided the Allies with intelligence on the German army's doings, ran a vigorous clandestine press, and helped Allied soldiers left behind to escape. These three tasks – intelligence, subversion and escape – were all taken up on a much wider scale by resistance movements in every Axis-occupied country during World War II. In Poland, Holland, Norway, resisters were active from the start; elsewhere, time was needed. Even before the war, Jews and socialists were being smuggled out of Germany and Austria; and in 1939–45 over 33,000 British, Commonwealth and US servicemen evaded capture or escaped from enemy hands. So efficient were the escape lines in France in mid-1944 that an unwounded shot-down Allied airman had an even chance of returning to his squadron.

About intelligence networks much less is known for certain. The decipher product of Bletchley Park was not distributed below army headquarters; a vast deal of more detailed information was provided, often at great risk, by devoted agents, usually amateurs.

In most occupied countries, the myth flourished that a national redoubt could be set up, perhaps with the help of Allied airborne troops: disaster came of this in premature risings in southern France and in Slovakia. Wilier resisters, such as the Poles and Norwegians, waited for the right moment. The Poles misjudged it at the Warsaw Rising; the Norwegians managed to seize all the main nodal points in Norway at the instant of the Germans' surrender.

Subversion was intensely political. The Poles who looked to their government in exile in London found themselves in competition with other Poles, of communist leanings, who looked to Moscow. In Yugoslavia there was a many-sided campaign, with Croat fascists, Serbian monarchists and south Slav communists fighting each other. Communist resisters in Greece used the arms dropped to them by SOE to attack non-communist resisters, rather than Germans. Communist resisters in France usually found themselves elbowed out of the way of arms supply; the Gaullists secured political power.

In the Far East, SOE was able to arm a substantial force of Karen hillmen, who inflicted important casualties on the retreating Japanese in 1945. SOE also persuaded the Japanese-run Burmese militia to change sides. *MF.*

Reuben James. US "flush decker" destroyer, completed 1920; first US warship lost in World War II. On October 31 1941, when USA was still officially neutral but aiding Britain, she was torpedoed and sunk (115 dead) by *U-562* while escorting an Atlantic convoy.

Revolutionary Development Program. A component of "pacification" in South Vietnam, the Revolutionary Development (also Rural Construction) Program was launched by the Saigon government in 1966. The programme

dispatched specially trained teams to live and work among the people at village level, in conscious imitation of communist techniques. A Revolutionary Development Training Centre at Vung Tau, headed by Col Nguyen Be, a former Viet Minh, trained the 59-man teams. The teams' lightly armed security sections performed police functions and trained People's Self-Defence Forces, while development sections helped with public works. When villages became secure and able to defend themselves, the teams moved on. In the peak year of 1969, the programme's 50,000 cadres were organized into smaller, 30-man teams and distributed among 1,400 villages. Effective despite shortcomings, the RD Program went into decline from 1970 when the US terminated funding. In 1971 the remaining RD cadres were dispersed among various ministries as civil servants. *WST.*

Reynaud, Paul (1878–1966). Fr. French Prime Minister, March–June 1940; forced to resign following pressure by politicians favouring an armistice with Germany.

Rhee, Syngman (1875-1965). Korean. President of the ROK during the Korean War. Rhee was jailed and tortured for anti-government activities in 1897 and on his release in 1904 went to the US where he studied at Harvard and Princeton. When he returned in 1910, Korea was a Japanese colony. He became involved in nationalist activity and, from 1912, spent many years in exile in the US lobbying for Korean independence. Rhee was smuggled back to Korea in October 1945 by the US occupation authorities in an attempt to contain the left. He was one of the few right wing leaders uncontaminated by collaboration with the Japanese and a militant anticommunist. Rhee opposed trusteeship and was prepared to head a separate right-wing regime in the south. He became president of the Republic of Korea when it was founded in 1948. Washington found Rhee a difficult ally during the Korean War. He opposed an outcome which left Korea divided and tried to sabotage the truce talks. In April 1960 Rhee was overthrown and retired to exile in Hawaii. *CM.*

Rhine crossing (1945). The difficulties encountered in reaching the River Rhine in the winter of 1944–45 led Allied commanders to anticipate major problems in forcing a crossing, it being certain that Germans would destroy all the bridges. But on March 7 1945 units of the US 9th Armoured Division found that the Ludendorff Bridge at Remagen was still intact and promptly seized it. A bridgehead was established and by the end of the day 8,000 American troops were on the east bank. Although the Germans tried to destroy the bridge with artillery, bombs, explosives and even V–2 rockets, it remained intact for ten crucial days. Meanwhile, to the south, Patton's Third Army had made plans for an assault crossing even if they failed to secure a bridge. On the night of March 22 two battalions of the US 5th Division slipped across the Rhine near Oppenheim and the next day engineers had constructed a temporary bridge and more troops expanded the bridgehead. These American coups pre-empted the main assault across the Rhine that had been assigned to Montgomery's 21st Army Group. The attack, Operation "Plunder", was to be made along a 22 mile (35km) front with units of the First Canadian Army, Second British Army and Ninth US Army taking part. After a fierce artillery bombardment, the first assault troops of 51st Highland Division began to cross the river at 2100 hours, followed by 1st Commando Brigade and the US 30th and 79th Divisions. The next day, Operation "Varsity" took place in which the British 1st and US 17th Airborne Divisions landed by glider and parachute to capture positions in advance of the bridgeheads. These airborne units suffered relatively high casualties in comparison to the cross-river assault but nevertheless captured their objectives. The overwhelming strength of the Allied forces, operating with extensive air support, proved too great for the overextended German defenders and by March 23 a bridgehead 35 miles (56km) wide and 12 miles (19km) deep had been built up. Further crossings continued to the south by the US Third and the French First Army and by the beginning of April seven Allied armies were on the east bank of the Rhine. *MS.*

Ribbentrop, Joachim von (1893–1946). Ger. Hitler's closest adviser on foreign affairs; Ambassador to Britain (1936–38); Foreign Minister (1938–45). Condemned to death at Nuremberg and hanged.

Richelieu. French battleship. Name ship of class. Eight 15in guns in two turrets forward; 47,550 tons full load; 95 percent complete at German invasion (1940). In British/Free French attack on Dakar; refitted USA (1943); British Eastern Fleet, then to Indochina (1944–45).

Richthofen, Capt (*Rittmeister***) Manfred Freiherr von ("Red Knight"; "Red Baron")** (1892–1918). Ger. Highest-scoring fight-

Air "ace" von Richthofen (*centre*)

er pilot of World War I, with 80 "kills" (most witnessed, since he rarely flew alone), Richthofen flew from September 1916 with Boelcke's *Jagdstaffel* II, and from July 1917 commanded *Jagdgeschwader* I (the "Flying Circus", so-called from its peripatetic role and multi-coloured aircraft). Some 60 of Richthofen's victories (including 21 "kills" during "Bloody April", 1917) were scored in an all-red Albatros DII/DV; the remainder in a Fokker DRI triplane. He was shot down and killed on April 21 1918: "officially" by the Canadian pilot Capt A Brown in a Sopwith Camel, but possibly by ground fire from Australian troops. *RO'N.*

Richthofen, Field Marshal Wolfram Freiherr von (1895–1945). Ger. Commissioned into a cavalry regiment in 1913, Wolfram von Richthofen transferred to the German Army Air Service in 1917. He scored 8 victories as a fighter pilot

and served with the *Jagdgeschwader Richthofen* (JG.1), led by and named after his legendary cousin Manfred. In the early 1920s he gained a doctorate in engineering before resuming his military career. With the birth of the Luftwaffe in 1933 he joined the new German Air Ministry, and during the Spanish Civil War he served as cos and, later, commander of the Condor Legion. It was in Spain that he became the leading German advocate of the use of dive-bombers in close air support of ground operations. As commander of *Fliegerkorps VIII* he employed these tactics with considerable success in Poland and France in 1939–40. Although his Stukas suffered heavy losses at the hands of the RAF's Spitfires and Hurricanes in the Battle of Britain, he won further laurels in the conquest of Yugoslavia and Crete in 1941 and subsequently in Russia, where he was appointed to command *Luftflotte 4* in July 1942. The following year Richthofen was promoted to Field Marshal and posted to Italy to command *Luftflotte 2* but, despite reorganization and reinforcements, he was unable to stem the tide of Allied air superiority in the Mediterranean. A brain tumour caused his retirement from active service in November 1944 and he died on July 12 1945. *PJS.*

Richthofen, Lt Lothar Freiherr von (1894–1922). Ger. Younger brother of Manfred, with 40 victories as a German fighter pilot on the Western Front, 1917–18.

Rickenbacker, Capt Edward V (1890–1973). US. Rickenbacker became the top-scoring American fighter pilot of World War I while serving with the 94th Aero Squadron in France in 1918. He is traditionally credited with 26 victories but recent research has amended this figure to 24.33, including four observation balloons.

Ridgway, Gen Matthew B (b.1895). US. Ridgway commanded 82nd Airborne Division (and then XVII Airborne Corps) in Europe during World War II, making a name as a fighting general. After 1945 he was groomed for high office at the Pentagon and was Deputy Chief of Staff for Operations when the Korean War began.

R

In December 1950 he assumed command of Eighth Army after the death of Walton Walker. Ridgway enjoyed the confidence of the Joint Chiefs of Staff and unlike MacArthur believed that the war must remain limited. As Washington's man, Ridgway refused to live in MacArthur's shadow and enjoyed an independence unknown to his predecessor. He arrived in Korea when the fortunes of Eighth Army were at a low ebb. He inherited a demoralized command which was in awe of the Chinese. Determined to attack, Ridgway fired incompetent officers and adopted new tactics, employing air power and artillery to wage a war of attrition. By March 1951 a revitalized army had halted the Chinese and driven them back across the 38th Parallel. In April 1951 Ridgway replaced MacArthur as c-in-c Far East and head of the UN Command. Unlike his predecessor he had no desire to extend the war to China, believing it would merely weaken the US by diverting resources from Europe, the vital strategic area. He was in full agreement with the decision to initiate truce talks in July 1950 although he sometimes favoured a tougher line in the negotiations than his superiors in Washington. On May 12 1952 Ridgway left Tokyo to assume command of NATO. He was COS, US Army, 1953-55. His successor as c-in-c Far East was Gen Mark W Clark. *CM*.

Riffian War (1919–26). Spain's enclaves in northern Morocco (*see* MOROCCAN WAR) were threatened in the west by the bandit chief Ahmed ibn-Muhammed Raisuli (1875–1925), and in the east by the Muslim Berber tribes of the Rif mountains under Abd el-Krim (1882–1963). Raisuli's revolt was quashed, 1920–21, by the Spanish Resident-General Dámaso Berenguer, while Gen Fernandez Silvestre moved against Abd el-Krim. On July 21 1921, at Anual, Silvestre's 20,000-strong force (12,000 killed) was surrounded and destroyed by the Rifs. With the modern equipment captured at Anual, the Rifs drove the Spanish from northeast Morocco, 1922–24. Proclaiming himself president of the "Riffian Republic", Abd el-Krim in April 1925 moved south with 20,000 men against the French,

breaking through their blockhouse line and threatening Fez. The French Resident-General Lyautey fought a skilful delaying action while Spanish and French expeditionary forces were prepared. From September 1925, a 50,000-strong Spanish force under Gen José Sanjurjo pressed south from the coast, while Pétain (Lyautey's successor), with 150,000 men, drove north. Surrounded at Targuist, Abd el-Krim surrendered on May 26 1926. *RO'N*.

Rifle. The breechloading, bolt-action rifle, magazine-fed with metallic cartridges employing smokeless propellant, was firmly established as the infantryman's principal weapon by the end of the 19th century and remained so, with exceptions noted below, until after World War II. Typical was the British Short Magazine Lee-Enfield: the Mark III of World War I, of 0.303in (7.7mm) calibre, fed by a 10-round box magazine and sighted to 2,000yd (1,829m), was near-identical with the Number 4 rifle of World War II.

With the bolt-action rifle, which must be cocked before each shot, 15 *aimed* rounds per minute (rpm) reflects a high standard of musketry. A much higher rate of fire is achieved with self-loading arms, in which the energy produced by the firing of a cartridge is utilized to eject the spent round and chamber and fire another. The first viable self-loaders, developed in the 1880s–1890s, were the recoil-operated Maxim machine gun and the gas-operated Colt-Browning machine gun. During World War I, the domination of infantry tactics by the machine gun led to the quest for greater fire power for the small unit (achieved via the light machine gun) and for the individual.

The latter need was answered by the sub-machine gun. The first in general production, to equip the German *stosstruppen* ("storm troops") of 1918, was the MP.18 ("Bergmann"), a compact weapon – 32in (81cm) long, as compared to *c*45–50in (114–127cm) for the average rifle – fed with 9mm pistol cartridges from a 32-round magazine (cyclic rate of fire: 400 rpm) and sighted to 200m (219yd). The sub-machine guns extensively used by the armies of World War II

did not differ significantly from this specification.

The sub-machine gun, with its low-powered pistol cartridge, was primarily a close-range weapon. A self-loading weapon equally effective at short and intermediate ranges – up to *c*400–600yd (360–550m) – was needed. Again, Germany led the field with the *Fallschirmjägergewehr 42* of 1942 and, notably, the 7.92mm *Maschinenpistole* MP.44 (called the *Sturmgewehr*, "assault rifle", and thus giving this type of arm the name it bears today), fed by a 30-round box magazine (500 rpm) and sighted to 800m (875yd). However, the bolt-action rifle still predominated, the only self-loading rifle in general issue being the American .30 calibre M1 (Garand) rifle (not to be confused with the .30 calibre M1 *carbine*, which, with its 15–30 round box magazine, represented a rifle/sub-machine hybrid).

In warfare since 1945, it has come to be accepted that the function of the rifle is to deliver a heavy volume of fire at ranges rarely exceeding *c*300yd (275m), in the hands of infantrymen operating from armoured personnel carriers. Thus, although the bolt-action rifle survives as a specialized snipers' weapon, assault rifles (compact, and adjustable for semi- or full-automatic fire) have become standard in most armies. Notable examples are the US 5.56mm AR-15 (M16) Armalite and the Soviet 7.62mm AK-47 (later model, AKM) "Kalashnikov", both fed by a 30-round magazine (600–900 rpm) and with an effective range of *c*330–440yd (300–400m). *RO'N*.

Rimini Line, breaching of (September 18–20 1944). Tenth Army (von Vietinghoff) tried to prevent Eighth Army (Leese) breaking out of the Apennine foothills into the Po Valley by holding a line running westwards from Rimini. Leese attacked with both his own corps: I Canadian Corps (Foulkes) cleared the San Fortunata ridge, and V Corps (Keightley) won the battles of Ceriano on the inland flank. Von Vietinghoff abandoned the line as the autumn weather broke, turning the supposedly good tank country into a morass for the winter.

Ritchie, Gen Sir Neil (1897–1985). Br. Took over command of Eighth Army from Cunningham when his health failed during the final offensive to relieve Tobruk in November 1941, and drove Rommel out of Cyrenaica. He was subsequently defeated by Rommel at Gazala in June 1942 and was superseded by Auchinleck on June 25 just before the Battle of Mersa Matruh. He commanded XII Corps in Northwest Europe, 1944–45, and became c-in-c Far East Land Forces, 1947–49.

River Assault Groups (RAGs). The twelve RAGS of the South Vietnamese Navy were originally organized and equipped by the French. Each group had about 20 boats for riverine troop lift, command and control, and patrol. Under American tutelage, the RAGS' mission shifted to close support of the South Vietnamese army, logistical support of outposts, and river patrols. The RAGS operated extensively in the Rung Sat swamp from 1962 to 1965, when increasing enemy use of heavy weapons made commanders prefer helicopters. The RAGS were subsequently used for escort in Mekong delta waterways.

Graf Spee, scuttled off Montevideo

River Plate, Battle of the (December 13 1939). Arose from the commerce-raiding activities of German pocket battleship *Admiral Graf Spee* (Capt Langsdorff) in the South Atlantic. Commodore Harwood, commanding the British Squadron on the South American Station, judged from reported sinkings that *Spee* was heading for the waters off the River Plate and took thither three cruisers, the most powerful the 8in *Exeter*. *Spee* had 11in guns but Harwood, in a skilful manoeuvre, neutralized this superiority by dividing the fire of his opponent. While *Spee* concentrated on the destruction of *Exeter*,

Harwood's two 6in cruisers, *Ajax* and *Achilles*, closed and inflicted enough damage to cause Langsdorff to put into the neutral port of Montevideo. The expected resumption of action did not occur for, believing he faced a far superior force, Langsdorff scuttled his ship and committed suicide. *ANF.*

Roatta, Lt Gen Mario (1887–1968). Italian. Roatta twice served as CGS of the Italian Army, 1941–42 and June to November 1943. In between, from January 1942 to February 1943, he commanded Italian occupation forces in the Balkans, rivalling the Nazis in his repression of partisans.

"Bobs" takes command, S Africa, 1900

Roberts, Field Marshal Earl ("Bobs") (1832–1914). In the later 19th century Roberts established himself as Britain's premier soldier, winning the VC during the Indian Mutiny (1858), achieving victory in the Second Afghan War after the famous Kabul-Kandahar march of 1880, and being promoted Field Marshal in 1895. Following British reverses early in the Second Boer War, he was appointed c-in-c, South Africa, with Kitchener as his COS. Arriving in January 1900, he remodelled the transport system, increased the number of mounted infantry, and conducted a campaign resulting in the occupation of Pretoria in June. In October 1900 Roberts returned to Britain to succeed Wolseley as c-in-c, British Army. Here, although he supported rearmament of the artillery and improved tactical training, particularly musketry, he came to be seen as an obstacle to War Office reform, and his post was abolished in 1904 as a consequence of the Esher Report. From 1905, as President of the National Service League, he advocated compulsory military serice. *PJS.*

Robertson, Field Marshal Sir William (1860–1933). Br. Robertson held the unique distinction of having risen from the rank of trooper to that of Field Marshal. He enlisted in the 16th Lancers in 1877, being recommended for a commission ten years later. He became, in 1896, the first ex-ranker to gain admission to the Staff College, and thereafter served principally in staff posts. He was Commandant of the Staff College 1910–13, and then Director of Military Training. In August 1914 he went to France as Quartermaster-General of the BEF. Fearing that the BEF's concentration area was too advanced, and displaying commendable foresight, he arranged for additional bases on the Atlantic coast, thus enabling supplies to be maintained throughout the retreat from Mons. In January 1915 he replaced Sir Archibald Murray as the BEF's COS and soon injected a brisker approach into the work of General Headquarters. His appointment as CIGS in December 1915 further weakened Kitchener's declining influence, for Robertson insisted, as a precondition of accepting the post, that the CIGS should henceforth be the Cabinet's only source of advice on military operations. Like Haig, the new British c-in-c in France, Robertson was firmly convinced that the war could only be won by defeating the German Army on the Western Front and his opposition to alternative strategic ideas brought him into increasing conflict with Lloyd George. On the other hand, Robertson shared the concern of politicians regarding Haig's profligacy with manpower, and recent scholarship suggests that it was Robertson, not Lloyd George, who held back reserves in Britain before the German March 1918 offensive. Robertson resigned as CIGS in February 1918 over Lloyd George's efforts to reduce his power by proposing Sir Henry Wilson as the British representative on an "Executive War Board" of the Supreme War Council. His last wartime posts were as GOC Eastern Command until June 1918 and then c-in-c, Home Forces. *PJS.*

Rocket Propelled Grenade (RPG). A family of Soviet infantry anti-tank weapons that fire

R

shaped-charge warhead rockets. The first RPG-2 was developed from the World War II German Panzerfaust and had a range of 492ft (150m). The more powerful RPG-7 replaced it from 1962. It is effective against a moving target at 985ft (300m) and a static target at 1,640ft (500m). Both weapons were also produced in China, and they have been widely distributed among guerrillas as well as regular armies. A more modern, smaller but longer-ranged RPG-16 is in service with Soviet forces and has been used by both sides in Afghanistan. The Soviets have copied the US Light Anti-Tank Weapon (LAW) as the RPG-18 and RPG-22. Unlike earlier RPGS, these have disposable launch tubes.

Rockpile. From July 1966, US Marines used the Rockpile, a 700-ft (215m) pinnacle 10 miles (16km) below the demilitarized zone in South Vietnam, as a lookout post and artillery base. It was about 15 miles (25km) west of the Marines' key base at Dong Ha, about half-a-mile off strategic Route 9, and near a fork in the Cam Lo river – the centre of an area where the Marines fought pitched battles with the People's Army of Vietnam (PAVN) in the late 1960s. In 1968, the 175mm guns at the Rockpile and at nearby Camp Carroll provided long-range fire support for troops besieged at Khe Sanh.

Rodney. British battleship. *Nelson*-class; 1927. Participated in sinking of *Bismarck*; landings in Sicily, Italy and Normandy.

Rojo Lluch, Gen Vicente (1894–1966) Spanish Republican. A career officer, Rojo remained loyal to the Republic in 1936. His rapid rise to General and COS began with his advisory role during the defence of Madrid and owed much to his cooperation with the communists. Unlike Rojo, the communist field commanders, Modesto and Líster, had had no officer training. Yet Rojo must share the blame for the inflexibility which led to such disastrous losses at Brunete, Teruel and the Ebro.

Rokossovsky, Marshal Konstantin (1896–1968). Russian. After service in the Imperial Russian Army during World War I, Rokos-

sovsky joined the Bolshevik forces during the Civil War. He rose to command of V Corps in Manchuria, but in August 1937, during Stalin's purge of the officer corps, he was arrested and charged with spying for Japan and Poland. He was imprisoned until March 1940. Reinstated in the army, he came to the attention of Zhukov with his skilful handling of IX Mechanized Corps during the German invasion of 1941. Given command of Sixteenth Army in July, he performed tenaciously during the defence of Moscow in November–December. In 1942 he led Don Front in the encirclement and destruction of Sixth German Army at Stalingrad. Established as a leading member of Zhukov's select band of trusted lieutenants, he commanded Central Front, holding the northern flank of the Soviet salient during the Battle of Kursk in July 1943. His forces participated in the subsequent counteroffensive and by the autumn had pushed the Germans back to the Pripet Marshes. In June 1944, Rokossovsky led First Belorussian Front, driving into Poland and to the outskirts of Warsaw, where his failure to aid the beleaguered Polish Home Army has provoked substantial criticism. In yet another reorganization of the Soviet command, in November, Rokossovsky was switched to Second Belorussian Front for the closing stages of the war, pushing north towards the Baltic while protecting the right flank of the Red Army's march on Berlin. Rokossovsky's career continued to flourish after the war, ironically with a period spent as Polish Minister of Defence. *MS.*

"Rolling Thunder" bombing campaign. Operation "Rolling Thunder", the sustained bombing of North Vietnam by the US Air Force and Navy, began in March 1965. Aircraft flew from bases in South Vietnam, Thailand and carriers in the South China Sea. Initially the campaign concentrated on transportation routes leading out of southern North Vietnam toward the Ho Chi Minh Trail. Later it expanded to include ammunition and fuel depots, then power and industrial installations, in all parts of the North. The number of annual sorties rose from 25,000 in 1965 to 79,000 in 1966

and 108,000 in 1967. The campaign dropped 643,000 tons of bombs on the North and lost 922 American aircraft before ending on November 1 1968.

In accordance with the doctrine of "phased escalation", the operation intensified in steps, punctuated by halts geared to diplomatic moves. The objectives shifted between deterrence, coercion, and interdiction. Although the campaign severely damaged the North's economy and left an estimated 52,000 civilian dead, it did not deter the North from supporting the war in the South and it only slowed the rate at which the North increased the flow of that support. *WST. See also* "LINEBACKER" OPERATIONS.

Roma. Italian battleship. Commissioned in June 1942 and carrying nine 15in guns, the *Roma* was the last Italian battleship to enter service. On September 9 1943, while en route to Malta to surrender to the Allies, she was sunk in the Gulf of Sardinia by German Dornier Do 217s using "Fritz X" radio-controlled bombs.

Romagna, river crossings (autumn 1944) by Eighth Army:
1) Marrechia; September 21.
2) Fiumecino; October 7–9.
3) Savio; October 19–23.
4) Ronco; October 31–November 7.
5) Montone; November 12.
6) Lamone; December 4–16
7) Senio; reached on December 16, but not crossed until the final offensive of the Italian campaign was launched on April 9 1945.

Romani, Battle of (1916) *see* EGYPT AND PALESTINE CAMPAIGN.

Romanian campaign (1916–18). Having remained aloof from the Great War until 1916, Romania's participation was brief and militarily disastrous. Her oil and grain reserves were valued by both sides and her position on the Black Sea flank of the Eastern Front was important. There was popular support for the Allied cause, for it was felt that here lay the best chance of recovering Transylvania from Austro-Hungarian rule, and as the Russians embarked on their series of victories in Galicia in 1916, nationalistic fervour and hopes of swift victory propelled Romania

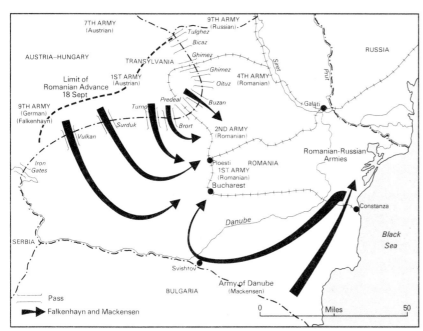

Romanian campaign, August 1916 – January 1917: victory for the Central Powers

into the Allied camp. If the decision had been made earlier in the summer, it is possible that Austria-Hungary would have been knocked out, for its German allies were heavily embroiled on the Western Front; but Prime Minister Ion Bratiano and his cabinet delayed to squeeze the best possible terms out of their prospective allies. Apart from more offensive action from the near-exhausted Russians, Bratiano called first for an offensive from the Anglo-French force at Salonika; second, for the deployment of three Russian divisions to guarantee sovereignty over Transylvania, Bukovina and other territories; and third, for 300 tons of munitions to be delivered daily at the port of Constanta. Agreement was not reached until late August. The Romanians mobilized on the 27th and declared war on the Central Powers. The Romanian army was 500,000 strong but was basically a militia army, lacking modern weaponry, particularly artillery and aircraft, and with only six weeks' war reserves. Its officer corps was largely weak and corrupt.

On August 28, the Romanians advanced through the high passes into Transylvania. Initially all went well and in three days advances of up to 45 miles (72km) had been made. It was then that the German General Staff showed

its mettle. Hindenburg and Ludendorff assumed supreme direction of operations in place of Gen von Falkenhayn who, following his forced resignation on August 28 and anxious to make good his military reputation, was appointed to command German Ninth Army in Transylvania. By mid-September he had stabilized the line, steadied Austrian First Army and was ready to counterattack. Meanwhile, on September 1, Bulgaria joined the war on the side of the Central Powers, adding her troops to Field Marshal August von Mackensen's German/Turkish Army of the Danube, which crossed into Southern Romania from Bulgaria on September 1 and made for the key port of Constanta. Although they cut the Constanta-Bucharest railway, vigorous counterattacks by Russian, Romanian and Serbian troops halted them and Mackensen, with most of his army, doubled back, crossed the Danube at Svishtov and made for Bucharest. On October 23, Mackensen's troops took Constanta, cutting off the meagre flow of Allied munitions.

Falkenhayn had now thrown the Romanians back through the passes and was ready to coordinate with Mackensen in a drive against Bucharest and the oil town of Ploesti. The Romanians tried desperately to prevent the junction of their opponents' armies, but

Bucharest fell on December 6 and on January 17 1917 the last Romanian divisions fell back behind the line of the River Siret, where they remained for the rest of the war. Well over 300,000 Romanian soldiers had become casualties and their country was effectively out of the war. The Central Powers now held the oilfields and the wheat and the Allies had experienced a major psychological defeat. *MH.*

Rome, capture of (1944) *see* ANZIO, ALLIED BREAKOUT FROM.

Rome, march on (1922). Italian political chaos in autumn 1922 led to fascist threats to seize power. On October 29 Mussolini was summoned to Rome and requested to form a government. His supporters' planned "march" on Rome never materialized; instead, 25,000 blackshirts arrived by train for a victory parade.

Rommel, Field Marshal Erwin (1891–1944). Ger. Came to Hitler's attention as Commander 7th Panzer Division in the invasion of France in June 1940; appointed to command the Afrika Korps, he landed at Tripoli in February 1941 with the task of stopping the British conquest of Libya. Despite High Command objections, he invaded Cyrenaica in April 1941, driving the British back.

He defeated two attempts to relieve Tobruk in the summer of 1941, but was himself defeated by Eighth Army during its "Crusader" offensive in November 1941, and was forced to raise the siege of Tobruk. He withdrew into Tripolitania to await tank replacements. Nevertheless, his operations in the Western Desert earned him the title of "the Desert Fox".

In January 1942, he counterattacked, driving Eighth Army back towards Tobruk. In the Battle of Gazala in June he won tank superiority, took Tobruk, and advanced to El Alamein. Promoted Field Marshal, he was then decisively defeated by Gen Montgomery at Alam Halfa and El Alamein that autumn, and was forced to withdraw to Tunisia. He was again defeated by Montgomery at Médenine, leaving Africa in March 1943 due to ill health and intrigue in the Axis High Command.

As Commander Army Group B,

R

Rommel directs operations, N Africa

he occupied Northern Italy when the Badoglio government capitulated in September 1943; and three months later was made responsible for the defence of the Channel coast in anticipation of the Allied invasion of Western Europe. He advocated a policy of forward defence because his experience in Africa persuaded him that it would be impracticable to move armoured formations in daylight under conditions of Allied air supremacy. Von Rundstedt and Guderian took the contrary view. In the event, the German panzer formations were committed piecemeal, and failed to destroy the Allies' beachhead in June 1944.

By the beginning of July, Rommel and von Rundstedt were trying to persuade Hitler to withdraw to the Seine. Rommel was seriously injured on July 15 when his car was attacked by Allied fighters just two days before the abortive attempt on Hitler's life. Implicated in the plot, he was forced to take his own life on October 14 1944. *WGFJ.*

Roosevelt, Eleanor (1884–1962). US. Wife of President F D Roosevelt; made morale-boosting visits to Britain (1942) and the Southwest Pacific (1943).

Roosevelt, Franklin Delano (1882–1945). US President, 1933–45. Assistant Secretary of the Navy, 1913–20; retired from public life, 1921–28, when stricken with poliomyelitis. Following landslide victory in Presidential election, 1932, implemented "New Deal" domestic policies; foreign policy increasingly influenced by Japanese expansion in Asia and, in 1939, outbreak of World War II.

Although restrained by the significant US isolationist lobby, Roosevelt gradually expanded American armed forces and, in 1940, adopted an increasingly helpful stance towards Britain. Anglo-American staff talks took place, the Lend-Lease Act was passed in May 1941, and in August 1941 Roosevelt and Churchill produced the Atlantic Charter. With America's entry into the war, Roosevelt, in spite of his physical disability, played a major part in the Allied conferences at Casablanca, Quebec, Cairo, Tehran and Yalta. He agreed to make the defeat of Germany the Allied priority, but opposed British proposals for Mediterranean and Balkan operations at the expense of an early cross-Channel invasion. Distrusting European, and particularly British, "colonialism", he yet proved more sanguine than Churchill regarding Soviet intentions in eastern Europe. He died on April 12 1945; succeeded as President by Harry S Truman. *MS.*

Root, Elihu (1845–1937). US Secretary of War, 1899–1904, initiating reforms similar to those of Haldane in Britain. His achievements included establishment of the Army War College in 1901 and creation, in 1903, of an efficient Army General Staff of the European model. As well as reforming the high command, he reorganized the reserve structure and encouraged weapons development programmes. Secretary of State under Theodore Roosevelt in 1905–09.

Rostov, Battle of (1941). In spite of the Red Army's staggering losses during the first months of the German invasion, on November 9 1941, Marshal Timoshenko, commander Southwestern Front, proposed a counteroffensive on his southern flank near Rostov. Ironically his attack on November 17 precisely coincided with a German offensive launched by von Kleist's First Panzer Army aimed not only at Rostov itself but also at access to the oilfields of the Caucasus and the Soviet supply route from Iran. On November 20 Rostov fell to von Mackensen's III Panzer Corps, but on the 27th, men of the 33rd Motorized Rifle Regiment of Gen Remezov's Fiftysixth Army attacked across the frozen River Don and

seized a bridgehead in the city. They were supported by two battalions of the Rostov militia who were joined by units of Gen Kharitonov's Ninth Army. Fearing encirclement, the German forces hastily abandoned the city and, by November 29, Soviet forces had reoccupied it. The German Army had thus sustained its first major reverse in operations against the Soviet Union. Furthermore, this setback on the southern flank resulted in the dispatch of reinforcements to the sector at the cost of weakening the central thrust against Moscow. *MS.*

Rostow, Walt W (b.1916). US. Adviser in the Kennedy and Johnson administrations. As chair of the State Department's Policy Planning Council and later as National Security Adviser, he advanced the "Rostow thesis". This held that externally supported insurgencies could be defeated only if military action terminated the support at its source. The "thesis" was influential in shaping American policy in the Vietnam War.

Rosyth, Firth of Forth, Scotland. World-War-I base of British battle cruisers; until 1938 intended Home Fleet base for war with Germany. Used thus, early World War II, while Scapa Flow defences were strengthened.

Rotterdam, bombing of (May 14 1940). The Luftwaffe planned to attack a number of Dutch centres of military resistance to the German capture of Rotterdam. The bombing was to start at 1500 hours. At 1415 hours a signal was received at *Luftflotte 2* HQ from the Germans in Rotterdam that the attack was to be postponed while negotiations for surrender proceeded. Already, however, 100 Heinkel He 111s of KG 54 led by Col Lackner were on their way to the target and they received no signal. Nor at first did they recognize red Very lights fired from the ground as instructions not to attack. At the last moment, about 40 bombers turned away but the remainder unloaded about 100 tons of HE bombs on the targets. Widespread damage was caused, mostly by fires that the Dutch were ill-equipped to control, and about 900 people were killed. *ANF.*

Rouen-Sotteville. French marshalling yards, the target of the US Eighth Air Force's first bombing mission, August 17 1942.

Royal Air Force (RAF). Formed on the basis of the Royal Naval Air Service and the Royal Flying Corps on April 1 1918. It was the world's first independent fighting air service.

Royal Armoured Corps (RAC), British Army. Formed shortly before World War II to rationalize manning and training of Royal Tank Regiment and of horsed cavalry regiments undergoing mechanization. US Army equivalent: Cavalry and Armor.

Royal Army Medical Corps (RAMC), British Army. Formed in 1898 to replace earlier (and often haphazard) systems of medical support in peace and war. Equivalents to be found in all armies.

Royal Army Ordnance Corps (RAOC), British Army. Historical roots in 15th century, when its HQ was in the Tower of London. Now responsible for Army's provisioning, including fuels and ammunition as well as all warlike and general stores.

Royal Army Service Corps (RASC), British Army. Responsible for supplies and transport and many ancillary tasks until rationalization of 1950s, when RAOC assumed task of supplying fuel, rations and ammunition. Transportation roles passed to new Royal Corps of Transport.

Royal Artillery (RA), British Army. Responsible for all types of indirect gun and missile fire support for the army. Organized in Regiments and Batteries. In US and most other armies, in battalions and companies.

Royal Corps of Signals, British Army. Evolved from branch of Royal Engineers which pioneered radio telephony in Army. US Army equivalent: Signal Corps.

Royal Corps of Transport (RCT). British Army. Assumed RASC and RE transportation roles in 1959. US equivalent is the Transportation Corps.

Royal Electrical and Mechanical Engineers (REME). British Army. Formed 1942 to rationalize field and base repairs of all types of military equipment.

Royal Engineers (RE). British Army. Supporting combat arm responsible for field and general engineering works, including bridges, airfield construction, demolitions, large-scale minelaying and minefield breaching.

Royal Flying Corps (RFC). Formed on the basis of the Air Battalion of the Royal Engineers on May 13 1912. It consisted of the Military Wing, administered by the War Office, the Naval Wing, administered by the Admiralty, and the Central Flying School, for which the responsibility was shared by the two departments. Its mechanical requirements were supplied by the Royal Aircraft Factory. The assumption that, although military and naval operational requirements would differ, the common interest of having an adequate supply of efficient flying men would best be met by a single force, failed to meet the conflicting views of the War Office and Admiralty. On the eve of the outbreak of war in 1914, the Naval Wing was rechristened the Royal Naval Air Service (RNAS) and the Military Wing assumed the title of the Royal Flying Corps. Thereafter, the RFC was predominantly engaged in the direct support of the Army in the field by reconnaissance and then bombing. Although increasing ranges led to some attempts at strategic bombing, this was a role in which the RNAS showed the greater interest. In 1917 Smuts recommended that the RFC and RNAS should be merged to form a new independent fighting service exclusively concerned with the air. This was done on April 1 1918 when the Royal Air Force came into being. *ANF*.

Royal Marines (RM). Britain's sea-soldiers. Their duties involved manning ships' guns and supplying landing forces. Having provided some commandos before 1945, they then took over the commando role entirely.

Royal Naval Air Service (RNAS) *see* ROYAL FLYING CORPS.

HMS *Royal Oak* fires a broadside

Royal Oak, British battleship, torpedoed and sunk (833 dead) while at anchor in Scapa Flow by *U-47* (Lt Commander Günther Prien), night of October 13–14 1939.

Royal Sovereign. British 'R'-class battleship, completed in 1916. She served in the Atlantic and with the Eastern Fleet in World War II before being transferred to the Russian Navy as the *Archangelsk*, 1944–49.

Royal Tank Regiment (RTR), British Army. Formerly Royal Tank Corps, formed 1923 specifically to man tanks and armoured cars. Became part of Royal Armoured Corps when cavalry mechanized.

Rozhdestvenski, Rear Adm Zinovi Petrovich (1848–1909). Russian. Few commanders have had a more difficult task than Rozhdestvenski, who, in 1904, was ordered to take the Russian Baltic Fleet to the Far East. His seamanship has been criticized, but it says much for his determination and organizational ability that he was able to shepherd some 45 ships of widely differing qualities in a 7-month voyage across 20,000 miles (32,000km) of oceans in which few bases were available for refuelling or repair. Tactical indecision contributed to his crushing defeat at Tsushima, but in a postwar court martial he was cleared of blame, having been severely wounded and unconscious when his deputy, Adm Nebogatov, surrendered. *RO'N*.

Rudnik Ridges, Battle of the *see* SERBIAN CAMPAIGN.

Ruge, Maj Gen Otto (1882–1961). Norwegian. C-in-C Norwegian Army, Norwegian campaign, 1940.

Ruhr, Battle of. British night bombing of Germany, March 5–

R

July 13 1943, when the Ruhr, and within it Essen, against which 2,070 sorties were dispatched in five major attacks, was the primary target. Other Ruhr towns heavily bombed included Duisburg, Krefeld, Düsseldorf, Dortmund, Gelsenkirchen, Wuppertal and Bochum. Numerous heavy attacks were also made on towns far beyond the Ruhr, including Berlin, Pilsen, Nuremberg, Munich and Frankfurt am Main, to keep the German defences spread. In all there were 43 major actions involving the dispatch of 18,506 sorties. A total of 872 bombers failed to return and 2,126 were damaged, some beyond repair and with the loss of their crews. The daily available strength of Bomber Command during the Battle varied from 593 to 787 aircraft with crews. The Battle was the first major test of heavy night attack led by the Pathfinder Force with the aid of Oboe and H2S. Oboe, which reached to the Ruhr but not much beyond it, proved to be more accurate than anything previously tried, and, by comparison, H2S was disappointing. For the first time in the war Bomber Command succeeded in inflicting major damage on the Ruhr towns. Goebbels and Speer, who were responsible respectively for morale and war production, both expressed anxiety because, although the German air defences destroyed more than the equivalent of the front line with which Bomber Command began the action, they failed, for the first time in the war, to prevent the constant repetition of severely devastating attacks. *ANF.*

Ruhr Pocket, Battle of (1945). The Ruhr, Germany's primary industrial centre, was a major objective for the Allied armies after their breakout from Normandy. Montgomery's attempt to make a rapid thrust into it had failed at Arnhem and it was not until the Allied armies had made crossings of the Rhine in March 1945 that the opportunity of an encirclement offered. In the south, VII Corps of First US Army pushed out of its bridgehead at Remagen with the 3rd Armoured Division's tanks speeding through the defences of Model's Army Group B. Meanwhile in the north, Ninth US

Army's 2nd Armoured Division pressed forward and on April 1 the US forces linked up at Lippstadt and the encirclement was complete. The Ruhr pocket was systematically reduced until, on April 17, all resistance was at an end and over 300,000 of its defenders taken prisoner. Model, judging himself disgraced, committed suicide on April 21. *MS.*

Rumpler C VII (German, WWI). Two-seat long-range reconnaissance. Late-1917 development of Rumpler C IV; both types noted for exceptional high-altitude performance. Almost identical Rubild (Rumpler C VI) photographic-reconnaissance type could operate at heights virtually unattainable by Allied fighters. One 240hp Maybach Mb IV engine; max. speed 109mph (174kph); two 7.9mm machine guns.

Field Marshal von Rundstedt

Rundstedt, Field Marshal Gerd von (1875–1953). Ger. During World War I, Rundstedt served on both the Eastern and Western fronts in staff and frontline posts. He remained in the army throughout the interwar years, developing a somewhat ambivalent attitude towards the Nazis. He approved of their strengthening of the armed forces but was openly critical of their ruthless treatment of his contemporaries, von Blomberg and von Fritsch. In 1938 he retired, but with the invasion of Poland returned to active service, helping prepare the attack and commanding Army Group South during the campaign. In 1940 his Army Group A delivered the unexpected blow in the Ardennes that turned the Battle of France; he was promoted Field Marshal in July 1940 and in 1941 was made c-in-c, Army Group South for "Barbarossa". Although doubting the wisdom of the attack, Rundstedt man-

aged to get the best out of a multinational force including Germans, Hungarians, Slovakians, Italians and Romanians. However, by winter he needed to withdraw some of his units but was refused permission by Hitler and relieved of his command on December 1 1941. In March 1942 he was appointed c-in-c, West with the task of securing Western Europe against Allied invasion. His clash with Rommel, his younger subordinate, over defensive strategy contributed to the poorly coordinated response to "Overlord". Rundstedt was once again relieved of his command, but was quickly recalled as c-in-c, West. Nominally he led the Ardennes offensive of December 1944, but although it was known at the time as the "Rundstedt offensive", it was Hitler's scheme and von Rundstedt had little faith in its success. The vindication of his doubts did not prevent him from a further dismissal and he held no further command. *MS.*

Rung Sat Special Zone. The Rung Sat, or "Forest of Assassins", straddles the narrow Long Tau river passage connecting Saigon with the South China Sea. During the Vietnam War, a communist sapper group based just north of the Rung Sat used its dense. mangrove swamp to plant mines and harass shipping in the channel. The Special Zone comprising this swamp was part of the Army of the Republic (ARVN) III Corps Tactical Zone. The US Navy, Marines and Army launched amphibious attacks into this stronghold beginning with Operation "Jackstay" in March-April 1966. By means of river patrols, minesweeping, hunts on land and drastic defoliation, US, South Vietnamese, Australian and Thai forces substantially cleared the zone, although sappers periodically returned to fire on ships in transit. *WST.*

Rupertus, Maj Gen William H (1889–1945). US. The Assistant Divisional Commander of the US 1st Marine Division in the Guadalcanal-Tulagi operations of 1942, Rupertus took overall command of the formation the following July, leading it in the assault on Cape Gloucester in December 1943 and on Peleliu in September 1944.

R

Rupprecht, Crown Prince of Bavaria (1869–1955). Ger. From August 9 1914, Rupprecht commanded both Sixth and Seventh (Gen von Heeringen) Armies in Alsace-Lorraine, on the extreme left of the German line of advance. Under the Schlieffen plan, his task was to tie up as many French troops as possible: thus, after taking Mulhouse on August 10, he fell back, a move intended by Moltke to draw the French right forward into a vulnerable salient. Following the French capture of Sarrebourg (August 18), however, Rupprecht urged a counterattack and Moltke – further watering-down the Schlieffen plan – agreed. In the Battle of Lorraine, August 20–24, Rupprecht drove back French First and Second Armies to Nancy, but, because of Moltke's reluctance to weaken the right further, failed too achieve a breakthrough.

A most able, if sometimes oversanguine leader, Rupprecht commanded with distinction throughout the war, notably at Messines and Third Ypres (Passchendaele), 1917, and in Ludendorff's final offensives of 1918, when he shared overall command of the German army groups with Crown Prince William of Germany. In September–October 1918, he struggled with some limited success to contain King Albert's Flanders' offensive, until the overall situation forced a general retreat. In November 1918, the outbreak of revolution in Bavaria deposed his house. *RO'N.*

Rusk, Dean (b.1909). US. As a colonel in the US War Department, assisted by Col Charles H Bonsteel, selected the 38th Parallel as the dividing line between the US and Soviet zones of occupation in Korea on the night of August 10-11 1945. In 1946 Rusk joined the State Department and was Assistant Secretary of State for Far Eastern Affairs when the Korean War broke out. From 1961–69 he was Secretary of State under the Kennedy and Johnson administrations and a leading spokesman on the Vietnam War policy.

Russia, invasion of and campaign in (1941–44). The Nazi–Soviet Pact of 1939 did not alter Hitler's intention to destroy the Soviet Union. His Directive No 21, December 18 1940, laid down invasion plans for Operation "Barbarossa", and from early 1941 there was an immense build-up of German forces along the frontier from the Baltic to the Black Sea. Anticipating speedy victory, the attack was launched on June 22 1941 by more than 3,000,000 men, 7,184 guns and more than 7,000 aircraft. Although Soviet ground forces were roughly comparable in number, the Germans were superior in armoured and air strength. Taken by surprise, with much of the Red Air Force destroyed on the ground at the outset, the Russians were initially out-generalled, out-manoeuvred and out-fought.

There were three major German thrusts. In the north, Army Group North (von Leeb) advanced rapidly through the Baltic states and, with the Finns advancing down the Karelian isthmus, converged on Leningrad by early September. Army Group Centre (von Bock) mounted the main thrust against Moscow. Here, Second and Third Panzer Groups executed rapid encirclements: 500,000 Russian prisoners were taken at Minsk in late June and a further 300,000 in the Smolensk pocket in mid-July. In the south, Army Group South (von Rundstedt) moved into the Ukraine and towards the Don basin. At Kiev, the panzer groups of Guderian and von Kleist effected a masterly envelopment, taking 665,000 prisoners.

Hitler's failure to define his ultimate strategic objectives and the consequent switching of units between commands tended to dissipate the initial German advantages. Diverting forces from Bock to Rundstedt resulted in major victory in the Ukraine but delayed the drive on Moscow which, in mud and snow, by December ground to a halt within sight of the Russian capital. In the north, the siege of Leningrad dragged on. Increasingly resolute Russian resistance, and the privations of an attritional winter campaign for which they were ill-prepared, blunted the German thrusts, and although they made better progress in the south, Soviet resistance continued at Sevastopol.

On December 6 1941, Zhukov launched a counteroffensive that removed the threat of encirclement from Moscow. In the south, the Germans were pushed back from Rostov, but a Soviet attempt to relieve Sevastopol failed and the city fell on July 2 1942. Hitler now gave priority to the southern flank, ordering Army Groups A and B to seize the Caucasus oilfields and capture Stalingrad. There, the besiegers were themselves trapped by a Russian offensive in November, surrendering soon after German withdrawal from the Caucasus was ordered in January 1943. By late February the Germans had been pushed back to a line running approximately from Leningrad to the Dnieper.

In mid-1943 the Germans planned to straighten their line, and inflict a crushing defeat on the Red Army, by eliminating the Soviet salient around Kursk, launching Operation "Citadel" on July 5. But they failed to achieve the all-important breakthrough and, in von Manstein's words, "initiative in the Eastern theatre... finally passed to the Russians". The Red Army advanced, recapturing Orel, Bryansk, Kharkov, Belgorod and, on November 6, Kiev. In winter 1943–spring 1944, the Germans were driven from the Ukraine and Crimea; in the north, the Soviets triumphed at Novgorod and relieved Leningrad.

In summer 1944, the Russians shattered Army Group Centre in Operation "Bagration", the Belorussian offensive, in which four Soviet Fronts, with massive armoured, artillery and air strength, attacked on June 22. Hitler forbade withdrawal and von Busch's command was crushed: only Soviet fatigue and the belated sanctioning of retreat restored a semblance of order to the German line. Driven from their eastern conquests, the Germans now had to defend their own homeland. *MS.*

Russian Revolution (1905, 1917 and 1918). By 1905 Russian autocratic rule was under threat from both radical and liberal demands for political change. Serious reverses in the Russo-Japanese War undermined the regime's credibility and on January 22 1905 troops opened fire on a workers' march in St Petersburg. Strikes and military mutinies proliferated and Tsar Nicholas II was finally obliged to issue the "October Manifesto" by

Russia, 1941–45: the vast area of the campaigns that followed the Axis invasion

which he offered a constitution, a legislative body (the Duma) and the appointment of a prime minister. This action appeased many of his critics and isolated revolutionaries who had established a workers' soviet. Fighting between the army and left-wing activists continued in Moscow until the New Year when order was restored.

By 1917 the unrelenting strains imposed by World War I precipitated another and more far reaching revolution. Economic chaos and the demoralizing effect of continuous military failure resulted in civilian unrest in Petrograd in March 1917. Army units ordered to quell the disturbances sided with the strikers and rioters, throwing into question the loyalty of the whole army. Lack of faith in Nicholas' ability to rule the nation led the Duma to form a provisional government while on the 15th, the Tsar's advisers persuaded him to abdicate. However the new government under Kerensky suffered from the same problems that had beset Nicholas and, in addition, the Bolsheviks continued to agitate for further political change. The provisional government's failure to unite the disparate political forces in Russia, solve the problems of food shortages and halt the disasters at the front resulted in a second revolution. Under Lenin's leadership the Bolsheviks mounted a coup in Petrograd on November 6–7, ousting Kerensky

and establishing a Soviet of peoples' Commissars. Their manifesto offered a promise of "Peace, land, bread" to the long suffering Russian masses and local soviets were quickly established throughout the country. A cease-fire was agreed with the Germans on December 15 and a final peace treaty was concluded at Brest–Litovsk on March 3 1918. The diversity of the Bolsheviks' enemies inhibited a concerted counter-revolution and although the "White" forces received help from the Allies they failed to defeat the Red Army and destroy the new communist state. *MS.*

Russian Civil War and foreign intervention (1917–22) *see* the essay underground warfare pp.324–326.

Russky, Gen Nikolai (1854–1913). Russian. Russky saw active service in the Imperial Russian Army before World War I, participating in the Turkish and Japanese wars. However, in spite of his experience, he showed a singular disinclination to cooperate with his fellow commanders. In September 1914 he failed to seize the clear opportunity of striking at the vulnerable flank of the Austrian armies as they attacked Gen Ivanov's forces to the north. Taking command of the Northwest Front in September, for a second time Russky neglected to come to the aid of his colleague when Ivanov

was heavily engaged in central Poland. However his performance improved during the Battle of Lodz in November when he reacted smartly to a German thrust against his Second Army. In March 1915 Russky left the Northwest Front and served as commander of the Sixth Army before taking command of the Northern Front in 1916. He was intimately involved in the Tsar's abdication with the crisis coming to a head at his headquarters at Pskov. Reports came in that Nicholas could no longer rely upon the support of his armies and, on March 15 1917, the Tsar signed his abdication, entrusting the document to Russky for safe keeping. Thereafter, Russky's influence upon events waned. The new regime removed him from command of the Northern Front and he was sent to the Caucasus. It was there that he was arrested by the Bolsheviks in the autumn of 1918 and was executed at Piatogorsk on October 19. *MS.*

Russo-Japanese War (1904–05). Russian intransigence, expressed in deliberately protracted negotiations, prevented Japan from exploiting the territorial gains she had made in Korea and Manchuria as a result of the Sino-Japanese War of 1894–95. In particular, Japan coveted Port Arthur (Lushun) on the Liaotung Peninsula, but Russia was determined to retain her only ice-free Pacific base, which was linked to Moscow by the 5,500-mile (8,850-km) Trans-Siberian Railway.

On February 8 1904, a Japanese squadron under Adm Togo made a pre-emptive strike on Port Arthur: a night attack by torpedo craft crippled two Russian battleships and a bombardment next morning inflicted further damage. Port Arthur was henceforth effectively neutralized by close blockade, preventing reinforcement of its squadron from Vladivostok, 1,000 miles (1,600km) to the north. On February 9, Adm Kamimura's cruiser squadron sank the two Russian cruisers that protected the Korean port of Chemulpo (Inchon), thus preparing the way for Japanese troop landings. War was declared on February 10.

Although Russia was considered a great power and Japan a minor one – the Russian army numbered more than 4,000,000 men, compared to Japan's full strength (including reservists) of around 680,000 – Russia had only about 130,000 troops in the Far East and could reinforce and supply them only via the single-track Trans-Siberian line (still incomplete, with a 100-mile/160-km hiatus at Lake Baikal). So long as she controlled the sea, Japan had no such logistical problems. Japan's soldiers were efficiently trained by German instructors and led by charismatic commanders; Russia's army suffered from a complex chain of command, arrogant and incompetent officers who relied on outdated techniques, and inefficient administrators. The Japanese navy, largely British-inspired, had six modern battleships and marked superiority in cruisers and torpedo craft; Russia's fifteen battleships were older and were manned mainly by unenthusiastic conscripts – and eight of them were deployed in the Baltic and Black Sea and could not be brought into action readily.

On February 17, Gen Kuroki's First Army landed at Chemulpo and marched northwards to the Manchurian border, where, on the Yalu river, Kuroki forced a crossing at Kiu-Lien-Cheng on May 1. Within a fortnight, the Japanese Second (Gen Oku) and Fourth (Gen Nodzu) Armies had landed on the Liaotung Peninsula, the former advancing southwest towards Port Arthur, the latter moving northwest towards Liaoyang, where the Russian c-in-c, Gen Kuropatkin, had concentrated his main force. Kuropatkin planned to delay the Japanese by a series of holding actions and gradual withdrawals, until reinforcements (at the rate of about 35,000 men per month by the railway) allowed him to mount a counteroffensive for the relief of Port Arthur. This sensible strategy was opposed by the egregious Adm Alexeiev, Viceroy of the Far East, and spoiled by subordinates who insisted on aggression against the "yellow monkeys".

The investment of Port Arthur was completed on May 25 by Oku's victory at Nanshan Hill, securing the port of Dalny (Dairen). Leaving Gen Nogi to conduct the land campaign against Port Arthur, Oku turned northward, frustrating a Russian thrust towards Port

Arthur at Telissu on June 14–15. Three days later, Kuroki drove Gen Keller's force from the Moteinlung river towards Liaoyang, on which three Japanese armies (Oku, Nodzu, Kuroki) now converged under the overall command of Field Marshal Iwao Oyama. In a ten-day battle at Liaoyang, ending on September 3, Oyama forced Kuropatkin's armies to retreat northwards again towards Mukden. Twice – on the Shaho river on October 5–17 and at Sandepu on January 26–27 1905 – Kuropatkin turned at bay, now having superiority in numbers (albeit many of his reinforcements were ill-trained reservists); on both occasions, Russian indecision in command was overcome by Japanese audacity. By February 1905, the Russians had been driven back to Mukden, where they entrenched.

Meanwhile, Nogi prosecuted the siege of Port Arthur with savage determination. While Togo maintained the blockade, defeating the one major Russian sortie in the Yellow Sea on August 10 1904, Nogi hurled his force of some 80,000 men against the 40,000-strong garrison. Although the Russian commander, Gen Stössel, was incompetent (if not actually a traitor, as was afterwards alleged), he had the advantage of three prepared defensive lines in which concrete forts and strongpoints fortified with barbed-wire entanglements and minefields had been efficiently combined. In frontal assaults in August, advancing in human waves against machine-gun positions, Nogi lost 15,000 men; further costly attacks in September gained ground but failed to take the vital 203 Metre Hill, commanding the harbour. However, the hard-won ground on the northern heights was to prove vital, for here, in October, Nogi sited some twenty 280mm howitzers, whose 700lb shells began to reduce the Russian fortifications. In his fifth and final major assault, November 27–December 5, Nogi carried 203 Metre Hill at the cost of some 11,000 Japanese dead. The surviving Russian warships now lay at the mercy of Nogi's guns, and on January 2 1905 Port Arthur surrendered. Nogi's victory obscured an important lesson: direct assault on positions pro-

tected by automatic weapons was now prohibitively expensive.

Nogi marched Third Army north to Mukden, and with this reinforcement giving him near-parity with Kuropatkin, Oyama attacked on February 21. Waged along a 47-mile (75km) front until March 10, Mukden was the largest land engagement to date. Although suffering heavy losses, Kuropatkin was able to avoid Oyama's attempted envelopment and retreat towards Harbin. The land campaign was now effectively over: the final act took place at sea, on May 27 1905, when the Russian 2nd Pacific Squadron ended its voyage from the Baltic in crushing defeat at Tsushima. Racked by revolutionary unrest at home and mutiny in her forces – the *Potemkin* mutiny erupted on June 27 – Russia needed peace if the Romanov dynasty was to be preserved.

Representatives of Russia and Japan met at Portsmouth, New Hampshire, under the auspices of President Theodore Roosevelt. Signed on September 5 1905, the peace treaty gave Japan the Liaotung Peninsula, protectorate powers in Korea and the southern half of Sakhalin Island. In the longer run, it confirmed Japan in the policy of Imperial expansion that would have its tragic climax in World War II. *RO'N.*

Ruweisat, First Battle of (July 14–16 1942). XIII Corps (Gott) launched a night attack on the Italian Brescia and Pavia Divisions with the New Zealand and 5th Indian Divisions. The Italians collapsed, but Afrika Korps (Nehring) counterattacked with tanks at first light and overran 4th New Zealand Brigade, retaking the Italian positions. Poor infantry/tank cooperation lay at the root of the British defeat.

Ruweisat, Second Battle of (July 21–23 1942). Almost a repeat of the First Battle, in that 5th Indian Division and 6th New Zealand Brigade carried their objectives with a night attack, but were overrun at dawn by Afrika Korps armour before the British tanks arrived in their support. A charge, reminiscent of Balaclava, by the latter, resulted in the loss of 89 tanks without reversing the British defeat.

S

SA. The *Sturmabteilung*, literally "Storm Detachment": first of the Nazi paramilitary organizations. Formed in 1921, the "Brownshirts" provided Hitler with violent support in his rise to power. By 1934 the SA threatened his long-term plans and he therefore neutralized its leadership in the "Night of the Long Knives".

Sabah *see* MALAYSIA-INDONESIA CONFRONTATION.

Sabotage. Briefly envisaged by British Chiefs of Staff in summer 1940 as best potential weapon for defeating Axis; SOE was created to foster it. Results were slight: a few coups mattered for a few weeks, e.g. destruction of bridges on main north-south railway across Greece on November 25–26 1942 and June 20–21 1943; in France, over 950 rail cuts on night of Normandy landings, June 5–6 1944. Industrial sabotage, though frequent, seldom caused important delays; only in Norway was it vital. Go-slow hindered German war effort more; e.g. making French railways all but unworkable except with German train crews. Retreating Russians made supply harder for Germans by destroying everything they could reach ("scorched earth"); and Polish resisters immobilized over 5,000 German locomotives. *MF*.

Sabre *see* F-86 SABRE.

SACEUR. NATO's Supreme Allied Commander Europe, responsible for the defence of Europe from the North Cape to the Eastern boundary of Turkey. Always an American general, he has his international HQ, Supreme Headquarters Allied Powers Europe (SHAPE), at Casteau, in Belgium. His command is split into three main areas, Northern, Central and Southern Europe, each under an Allied C-in-C. SACEUR has his own allocation of SLBMs, including the British Polaris force which is placed under his control "unless supreme national" issues are at stake.

Sagger. NATO code name for the Soviet 9M14 Malatyuka anti-tank missile used with great effect by the Egyptians in the 1973 Arab-Israeli War and still in widespread use with Warsaw Pact armies. A simple wire-guided weapon that must be "flown" by its operator all the way to the target, Sagger has a maximum range of 9,840ft (3,000m) and can penetrate 1.312ft (400mm) of armour with its 5.9lb (2.7kg) shaped-charge warhead. Later Sagger-C missiles mounted on vehicles have modified command-to-line-of-sight automatic guidance.

St Eloi. On a dominating spur at the southern neck of the Ypres Salient, St Eloi was the scene of extensive mining operations by both sides, 1915–17. A mine containing 95,600lb (43,350kg) of ammonal was blown here on June 7 1917; the largest single charge detonated before the British attack on Messines Ridge.

St Julien *see* YPRES, SECOND BATTLE OF (1915).

St Lô *see* NORMANDY, INVASION OF.

HMS *Campbeltown* at St Nazaire, 1942

St Nazaire raid (March 28 1942). St Nazaire, in the estuary of the Loire, in 1942 held the only dry dock big enough to take the German battleship *Tirpitz*. The Allies sought to destroy it to reduce the danger of the ship's raiding into the Atlantic. An old "lend-lease" US destroyer HMS *Campbeltown* had her bows loaded with three tons of explosive and was disguised as a German torpedo boat. She would ram the dock gates; commandos in 16 motor launches would land and demolish as much as they could, while an MTB fired delay-fused torpedoes into the gates. The naval commander, Commander Ryder (awarded the VC for this operation), successfully took his force up the estuary, re-

taining surprise for a vital couple of minutes by confusing signals. Despite intense fire, the gate was rammed and Commandos landed. Withdrawal was difficult – only 6 motor launches escaped and the Germans took most of the Commandos prisoner. Next day both the destroyer and the torpedoes exploded, killing many Germans and causing a panic outbreak of firing in which more Germans and some French were killed. The dock was wrecked in what was one of the most successful of all raids, despite the heavy losses. *DJL*.

St Vith *see* NORTHWEST EUROPEAN CAMPAIGN.

Saipan campaign (1944). The island of Saipan in the Marianas chain was selected by the US as a suitable base for air operations against the Philippines and Japan. Consequently, V Amphibious Corps was given the task of capturing the island. After a sustained bombardment, on June 15 1944 the 2nd and 4th Marine Divisions secured beachheads against fierce Japanese resistance. The 27th Infantry Division joined the Marines in beating off strong Japanese counterattacks before clearing the southern half of the island. The drive north proved more difficult especially as, with no hope of relief following the American victory at the Battle of the Philippine Sea, the Japanese garrison fought with fanatical ferocity. This was mirrored by Japanese civilians; many committed suicide rather than face capture. On July 9 the northern tip of Saipan was in American hands and the island was declared secure. *MS*.

Sakai, Lt (Navy) Saburo (b.1916). Jap. Highest-scoring Japanese fighter pilot to survive World War II (64 "kills"), Sakai scored his first victories in the Sino-Japanese War, and on December 10 1941, in a Mitsubishi A6M, was the first Japanese pilot to destroy a B-17 Flying Fortress. Over Guadalcanal, 1942, he lost an eye in a dogfight in which he destroyed three US fighters. Back in combat over Iwo Jima, 1944, he also flew kamikaze missions (although openly opposing suicide tactics), returning with honour after finding no suitable targets.

Salamaua. By early September 1943, this Japanese air and supply base on the Huon Gulf in northeast New Guinea had been encircled by the Allies. Under pressure from units of the Australian 3rd and 5th Divisions and the US 41st Division, the Japanese garrison evacuated the town on September 11.

Salan, Gen Raoul A L (1899–1984). Fr. Succeeded Marshal de Lattre as commander of French forces in Indochina in January 1952. His decision to withdraw from Hoa Binh left the highlands in communist hands. To recover the highlands, he proposed to fortify strongpoints at Na San, Lai Chau and "eventually Dien Bien Phu". That recommendation foretold the final battle, although Salan, departing in May 1953, did not participate in its planning. In April 1961 he led a mutiny in Algeria, for which he was sentenced to life imprisonment.

Armour at Salerno beachhead, 1943

Salerno, landings at and Battle of (September 9–17 1943). The Gulf of Salerno was chosen for the landing of Fifth Army (Clark) at the beginning of the Italian campaign, because it was the farthest north that Allied fighter cover could be provided from Sicily. The British X Corps (McCreery) with 7th Armoured, 46th and 56th Divisions landed on the northern half of the Gulf, and US VI Corps (Dawley) with 3rd, 34th, 36th and 45th US Divisions on the southern half. They were opposed initially by XIV Panzer Corps (Hube) with 15th Panzer Grenadier, the Hermann Göring Division, and 16th Panzer Division, which was responsible for the defence of both the Gulfs of Gaeta and Salerno.

The battles fell into three phases. The landings took place on September 9, and were an Allied success in that beachheads were established, although less easily than expected because the Ger-

mans disarmed their Italian colleagues quickly enough after the announcement of the Italian capitulation to be able to oppose the landings themselves, and to secure the high ground overlooking the beaches.

Forces were then built up between September 10–11, and in this the Germans had the upper hand because they could reinforce more quickly over land than the Allies could by sea. Von Vietinghoff, commanding Tenth Army in Southern Italy, concentrated XIV Panzer Corps (Hube) around the beachhead, while LXXVI Panzer Corps (Herr) was rushed back from Calabria with 29th Panzer Grenadier and 26th Panzer Divisions to mount a counteroffensive. 3rd Panzer Grenadier Division was also brought down from Rome when the capital was secured.

The German counteroffensive (September 12–17) was then carried out by LXXVI Panzer Corps down the Sele river into VI US Corps' sector. It almost reached the beaches, making the American position so precarious that HQ Fifth Army began making contingency plans for evacuation. These were stopped by Alexander, who arranged for the intervention of the Allied strategic bombers, the provision of naval gunfire support by the battleships *Warspite* and *Valiant*, and for the drop of part of 82nd US Airborne Division into the beachhead.

The weight of bombs dropped and naval broadsides fired during the 14th and 15th neutralized renewed German efforts to break through. Next day leading troops of Montgomery's Eighth Army reached the beachhead. Kesselring authorized a general withdrawal from September 18. *WGFJ*.

Salmson SAL. 2. A2 (French, WWI). Two-seat reconnaissance. Prototype flew spring 1917; by August 1 1917, 26 SAL. 2. A2s with front-line units. Sturdy and effective; used by at least 24 French *escadrilles* Western Front and Italy; 448 operational at October 1 1918. USAS acquired 705; from April 1918 equipped 11 American squadrons. Production, about 3,200. One 260hp Salmson (Canton-Unné) engine; max. speed 115.5mph (186kph); two/three 7.7mm machine guns.

Salmuth, Col Gen Hans von (1888–1962). Ger. Commander of Fifteenth Army, in Rommel's Army Group B, deployed east of the Normandy invasion area, June 1944. Although he advocated forward defence, Salmuth believed the major landings would be made in the Pas de Calais. Hitler, sharing this belief, refused to release any of Salmuth's 17 divisions to oppose the Allied build-up until late July.

Salonika campaign (1915–18). In return for guarantees of territorial gains in Serbian Macedonia, Bulgaria signed a military convention with the Central Powers on September 6 1915 and ordered general mobilization on September 23. This new threat led the Serbian government to make desperate appeals to Paris and London for military aid. At the same time, the Greek Prime Minister Venizelos, against the wishes of the pro-German King Constantine, also requested Allied assistance to enable Greece to fulfil treaty obligations to Serbia. To help the Serbs, Britain and France sent a combined expeditionary force to Salonika in Greek Macedonia, although Venizelos resigned on October 5, the very day on which the first Franco-British units disembarked at Salonika. Following the British and French declarations of war on Bulgaria on October 14–15, the small Allied force made a limited advance into Serbia but was unable to offer much real support. The Serbian Army, struck by the Germans and Austrians from the north and the Bulgarians from the east, had to retreat, under appalling conditions, through Albania to the Adriatic. From there Allied warships took around 100,000 survivors to Corfu early in 1916.

By then the Franco-British force, under the overall command of Gen Maurice Sarrail, had fallen back into a huge entrenched position around Salonika, which the Germans sarcastically called "the greatest internment camp in the world". After months on the defensive, the Allies moved up to the Serbian frontier in April 1916 and, during the latter half of the year, were joined by Serbian, Russian and Italian contingents. Venizelos established a provisional govern-

S

ment at Salonika in October and also provided some 23,000 Greek troops, bringing Sarrail's forces up to a strength of 350,000 men. An offensive planned for August was forestalled by a Bulgarian attack against the Serbs on the Allied left and had to be postponed until September 12. The only significant Allied success was the liberation of Monastir by the Serbs, with French and Russian support, on November 19. The Allied line now stretched from Monastir to the Gulf of Orfano, with the British Salonika Army, under Gen Milne, holding the right, overlooked by commanding heights, to the south of Lake Doiran and along the Struma Valley. Disease, especially malaria, ravaged the Allied units. In the British Salonika Army, non-battle casualties exceeded battle casualties by twenty to one.

Another Allied offensive in the spring of 1917 failed with heavy losses. King Constantine abdicated and Greece declared war on the Central Powers in June. Sarrail was replaced by Gen Guillaumat in December. Guillaumat boosted morale and restored unity among the Allied contingents. Under his successor, Gen Franchet d'Esperey, this theatre, so long considered a "sideshow" by the British and French, was suddenly transformed into the scene of spectacular triumphs. A major offensive, beginning on September 15, forced Bulgaria to surrender on September 29, the first of Germany's allies to drop out of the war. *PJS*.

Samar, Battle of *see* LEYTE GULF, BATTLE OF (1944).

Samoa (1914). The western islands of this South Pacific group, in German possession from 1899 (the remainder being US territory), included an important coaling-station at Apia. To deny this to von Spee's squadron and to commerce raiders, it was occupied by a New Zealand Expeditionary Force, escorted by Australian warships, on August 30 1914.

Samsonov, Gen Alexander Vasilievich (1859–1914). Russian. Commander of Russian Second Army in August 1914 at beginning of the Tannenberg campaign. His feud with Rennenkampf had be-

gun during the Russo-Japanese War (*see* RENNENKAMPF), and the decision to put both men into a campaign where success depended on their mutual trust and close cooperation was the first of many Russian errors. Like Rennenkampf, Samsonov tolerated the passing of vital intelligence and operational orders by unciphered radio telegraph, giving Col Hoffmann at German Eighth Army HQ a clear picture of Russian intentions. Samsonov compounded his problems through loose tactical handling and ambiguous instructions to subordinate HQs, resulting in the uncoordinated swing to the left carried out by his Army on crossing the East Prussian border, when, had it struck north and east against the German right flank, a decisive victory could have been won. When it became apparent that Second Army was on the verge of envelopment Samsonov, a brave and universally popular commander, rode forward in person to avert disaster, but committed suicide when it was clear that all was lost. *MH*.

San Bernadino Strait. Stretch of water between southeastern Luzon and northern Samar in the Philippine Islands. The Japanese Navy's Centre Force under Vice Adm Kurita passed through this channel on the night of October 24–25 1944 before its abortive attempt to destroy American amphibious units in Leyte Gulf.

San Carlos Bay. On northwest coast of East Falkland; chosen, in the Falklands War of 1982, as the best compromise landing place for 3rd Commando Brigade and 5th Infantry Brigade. Although the initial landings on May 21 were unopposed, naval vessels protecting anchorage in San Carlos Water suffered heavily from Argentine air attack, May 22–27, when HM ships *Ardent*, *Antelope* and *Coventry* were sunk and *Antrim*, *Argonaut* and *Broadsword* were severely damaged.

Sandepu (Heikoutai), Battle of (January 26–27 1905), Russo-Japanese War. In blinding snowstorms, Kuropatkin's attack with 300,000 men (losses 20,000) was repulsed by 220,000 Japanese (losses 9,000) under Oyama.

Sanders, Otto Liman von *see* LIMAN VON SANDERS.

Sangro river, Battle of (November 19–December 1 1943). Eighth Army (Montgomery) reached the Sangro on November 8, having fought its way over the Trigno by November 4. The Sangro was held by LXXVI Panzer Corps (Herr) with 65th, 1st Parachute and 16th Panzer Divisions. Montgomery planned to attack in the coastal sector with V Corps (Allfrey), using 78th and 8th Indian Divisions, while the New Zealand Division crossed farther inland. Preliminary operations started on November 19 with the river fordable, but heavy rain from the 20th to the 23rd flooded the valley. The delay gave Kesselring time to reinforce Herr with 126th Panzer and 90th Panzer Grenadier Divisions. When the attack was launched on November 28, V managed to establish a bridgehead, almost destroying 65th Division in the process, but Herr fell back to the embryo Gustav Line behind the Moro river with his front intact. Montgomery could not achieve the breakthrough that he needed for his advance on Rome. *WGFJ*.

Sanna's Post (Kornspruit), Battle of (March 31 1900), Second Boer War. De Wet, with c2,000 men and five guns, planned to capture the waterworks at Sanna's Post on the Modder river, 17 miles (27km) west of Bloemfontein. Learning of the approach of a large supply convoy escorted by c2,000 cavalry and two batteries (12 × 12-pounder guns) of Royal Horse Artillery, under Brig Broadwood, De Wet posted his guns, with 1,600 men, on high ground, while he himself, with 400 men, occupied ground commanding a gully. Fired on by the larger Boer force, the British column sought shelter in the gully, where De Wet sprang his ambush, capturing all the waggons and seven guns. Largely because of heroic resistance by the remaining RHA battery, during which four VCs were won, Broadwood was able to extricate his force, losing 155 killed or wounded and 426 captured; De Wet had only 8 casualties.

De Wet immediately rode south to deal with a garrison retreating from Dewetsdorp. The British, *c*500 men under Capt William M'Whinnie, were trapped on Mostert's Hoek ridge, about 5 miles (8km) northeast of Reddersberg, by *c*1,000 Boers with three Krupp guns. After a 24-hour bombardment, the waterless garrison surrendered (47 killed or wounded; 470 prisoners). *RO'N.*

Carrier USS *Hornet* afire at Santa Cruz

Santa Cruz, Battle of (October 26 1942). Naval battle fought by carrier aircraft off the Santa Cruz Islands, southwest Pacific. The Americans were defending Henderson Field, their foothold and air base on Guadalcanal. Both sides poured in reinforcements by sea and attempted to prevent the other doing so. The Japanese had an advanced force of one carrier, two battleships, five cruisers and 14 destroyers under Kondo, whilst the main force commanded by Nagumo had three carriers, two battleships, five cruisers and 15 destroyers. The US admirals, Kinkaid and Murray, had two carriers, one battleship, six cruisers and 12 destroyers, plus a further battleship with supporting ships having no direct part in the action. The Japanese hoped to recapture the airfield and fly in aircraft.

Initial contact was made and one American strike failed to find the enemy on October 25. The next day the Americans put carrier *Zuiho* out of action. Then, in simultaneous strikes which passed each other halfway, Japanese carrier *Shokaku* and USS *Hornet* were badly damaged, as was a cruiser on each side. Shortly afterwards, USS *Enterprise* was hit and *Hornet* further damaged – she had to be abandoned and was finally sunk by the Japanese. Although the Japanese drove the Americans off and inflicted more damage than they suffered, their success was marred by the loss of many irreplaceable aircrew, and they failed to take Henderson Field. *CJW/CD.*

Sarajevo, Bosnia-Herzegovina. Scene of the assassination on June 28 1914 of the heir to the Austro-Hungarian throne, Archduke Franz Ferdinand, precipitating World War I.

Saratoga. US aircraft carrier. *Lexington* class, converted from battlecruiser hull. Torpedoed January 1942 and missed Midway; torpedoed again at Guadalcanal; back in Solomons end of 1942; supporting Gilberts landings (1943). Marshalls, then operated with HMS *Illustrious* in East Indies (1944); operating night fighters at Iwo Jima, damaged by bombing (1945). Expended at Bikini (1946).

Sarikamis, Battle of (December 29 1914–January 3 1915). Following Russia's declaration of war on Turkey on November 4 1914, Enver Pasha, de facto Turkish C-in-C, ordered an offensive into the Caucasus. Some 95,000 men (Gen Achmet Izzet Pasha, under Enver's direction) advanced from Erzurum; from Kars, a Russian army some 60,000-strong (nominally under Gen Mishlayevski; in fact commanded by his COS, Gen Yudenich) marched to meet the Turks at Sarikamis, 33 miles (53km) southwest of Kars, on December 29. Although reduced to *c*80,000 men in their two-week advance through icy mountain passes, the Turks attempted an envelopment: the Russians, operating on shorter supply lines, were able to reinforce and hold the frontal attack, while deep snow prevented the deployment of Turkish artillery in the planned flank attacks. The Russian counterattack forced the surrender of one Turkish corps and shattered another: after losing some 30,000 men in the five-day battle, the Turks retreated in disorder, only *c*18,000 survivors reaching Erzurum. *RO'N.*

Sarrail, Gen Maurice (1856–1929). Fr. In an officer corps permeated with Catholic and monarchist sympathies, Sarrail, an infantryman who held strong Republican views, inevitably attracted attention. A supporter of Dreyfus in the 1890s, Sarrail subsequently served under the anticlerical Gen André in the French War Ministry and was Director of Infantry from 1907 to 1911. In

August 1914 he led the VI Corps at the Battle of Virton in the lower Ardennes before being appointed to replace the excitable Ruffey as commander of the Third Army at the end of the month. Sarrail's resolute defence of Verdun in early September provided an anchor for the Allied left wing and contributed to the Marne victory. He was now a popular hero and Joffre, seeing him as a potential rival, used the Third Army's reverses on the Argonne front in June-July 1915 as an excuse to remove him, thereby precipitating a political crisis. To placate his backers, Sarrail was given command of the French Army of the Orient sent to Salonika in October 1915. After consolidating their positions in Salonika, the Allied forces, under Sarrail's overall command, moved up to the Serbian frontier, liberating Monastir in November 1916. However, the failure of his 1917 spring offensive increased unrest among his allies, already alienated by his high-handedness and political meddling. When Clemenceau became the French premier in November 1917, even Sarrail's radical patrons at home could no longer shield him and he was relieved of command the following month. *PJS.*

Satellites. Satellites orbiting the Earth are used by both superpowers for military surveillance (including such tasks as photoreconnaissance, ocean surveillance, early warning, electronic intelligence-gathering and weather forecasting), communications and navigation. They play a vital part not only in military operations and planning but also as "national technical means of verification" for arms control. The American KH-11 reconnaissance satellite first launched in 1976 is almost 66ft (20m) long, weighs 29,700lb (13,500kg) and orbits at between 180 and 300 miles (300 and 500km) above the Earth for up to three years. It uses a powerful telescope and millions of picture elements recorded by "close-coupled devices" to receive electromagnetic radiation from the Earth by day and night. Daytime resolution is reportedly 8in (20cm). The data is then put into a digital and encrypted form for transmission to Earth. KH-11 can receive electro-

S

nic intelligence but the Americans also have specialized electronic "ferret" satellites in higher geosynchronous orbit for the latter work. An improved KH-12 with 4in (10cm) optical resolution and 20in (50cm) resolution imaging radar is due in 1989. Each satellite is intended to remain operational for 15 years. Soviet reconnaissance satellites tend to be smaller, currently 14,960lb (6,800kg), and shorter-lived. High-resolution satellites remain in orbit only for 6-8 weeks and use film capsules to get their information back to Earth, but area-surveillance satellites using digital readouts have been orbited since 1982 and remain operational for 180-200 days. *EJG*.

Saturation bombing *see* BOMBING.

Savoia-Marchetti SM 79 Sparviero (Sparrowhawk) (Italian, WWII). Bomber/torpedo-bomber. Flight testing military prototype began September 2 1935; production deliveries from October 1936. Used in Spanish Civil War from February 1937; by June 10 1940, of 694 *Sparvieri* on strength, 403 were fully operational; widely and successfully used. Production, at least 1,330. Three 780hp Alfa-Romeo 126 RC34 engines; max. speed 267mph (430kph); 2,756lb (1,250kg) bombs, three 12.7mm and one 7.7mm machine guns.

Savoia-Marchetti SM 81 Pipistrello (Bat) (Italian, WWII). Bomber/transport developed from SM 73 civil transport, 1935. Used in Abyssinian War, bombing, reconnaissance and air-supply missions; in Spanish Civil War operations of SM 81s started August 5 1936. June 1940 *Regia Aeronautica* had 304 serviceable; in use until 1944, serving Albania, Greece, Russia, Yugoslavia, Germany, Poland, Czechoslovakia, Austria and North Africa. Production, 584. Three radial engines: 670hp Piaggio PX, 580hp Alfa-Romeo 125, 900hp Alfa-Romeo 126, 680hp Piaggio PIX or 650hp Gnome-Rhône K14. Max. speed (with PX) 211mph (340kph); 4,410lb (2,000kg) bombs, five 7.7mm machine guns.

Savo Island, Battle of. Early on August 9 1942, the waters north of Guadalcanal became the scene of one of the US Navy's worst defeats of World War II when American and Australian warships patrolling around Savo Island were surprised by a Japanese cruiser force under Vice Adm Mikawa. As a result of this action, which lasted less than an hour, the US cruisers *Astoria, Quincy* and *Vincennes* and the Australian cruiser *Canberra* were sunk.

Sayn-Wittgenstein, Maj Prince Heinrich zu (1916–44). Ger. The Luftwaffe's third-ranking night-fighter pilot. After over 150 operations in bombers, he transferred to night fighters in 1941. Flying Ju 88s, he scored 83 victories, including 29 in Russia, before being shot down by an RAF Mosquito in January 1944.

Scapa Flow. British naval base in the Orkneys. Occupied in both world wars by, respectively, the Grand and the Home Fleets. Remote but convenient for blocking the exits into the Atlantic from the North Sea and Norway.

Scarborough, bombardment of (December 16 1914). Two German battlecruisers bombarded the British northeast coast harbour to little effect. No fleet action followed, but there was outrage in Britain, and the battlecruiser force was stationed at Rosyth as a precaution.

Scharnhorst* and *Gneisenau. (1) World War I, German armoured cruisers of *c*12,000 tons. In von Spee's East Asiatic Squadron, shared in victory at Coronel, November 1914; sunk at Battle of Falkland Islands, December 1914. (2) German battlecruisers, launched 1936; 32,000 tons standard; 9 × 11in guns. Sank carrier HMS *Glorious*, Norwegian campaign, 1940; sank 115,000 tons of shipping in North Atlantic, early 1941; broke out from Brest in "Channel Dash", February 1942. *Gneisenau* permanently disabled by bombing at Kiel, 1942. *Scharnhorst* bombarded Spitzbergen, with *Tirpitz*, September 1943; sunk at Battle of North Cape, December 1943.

Scheer, Adm Reinhard K F (1863–1928). Ger. A torpedo specialist, Scheer became COS, High Seas Fleet, in 1909; successively

Adm Scheer: bold manouevre at Jutland

commanded its 2nd and 3rd Battle Squadrons, 1914–15; and in January 1916 succeeded the ailing von Pohl as its C-in-C. Like his predecessor, but more aggressively, he sought to lure out and destroy units of the Grand Fleet. A sortie intended to lead British warships into a U-boat ambush, May 31 1916, resulted in the Battle of Jutland (called Skaggerak by the Germans), when Scheer's pursuit of British battlecruisers led him into action with the Grand Fleet. Scheer narrowly avoided Jellicoe's "crossing the T" by a bold manouevre, signalling "battle turn away together" to his major units and sending his torpedo flotillas in to attack. He escaped a second trap by launching his battlecruisers on a near-sacrificial "death ride". However, British mistakes and bad luck contributed substantially to Scheer's successful extrication of his fleet. Following Jutland, his sorties were cautious and generally ineffectual. In August 1918, Scheer moved to the Admiralty, while Hipper became C-in-C: neither was able to deal effectively with the Kiel mutiny. *CJW/CD*.

Schellenberg, Lt Gen (*Obergruppenführer* SS) Walter (1910–1952). Ger. A protégé of Heydrich; became head of Germany's combined military intelligence organizations in 1944 after the fall of Canaris. Self-serving and Machiavellian, he abetted Himmler's peace negotiations, 1945.

Schlemm, Lt Gen Alfred (1894–1986). Ger. Commander I Parachute Corps, Italian campaign, January-November 1944.

Schlesinger, James Rodney (b.1929). US. Director, CIA, January–July 1973; Secretary of Defense 1973–75.

Schlieffen plan. The war plan developed by Count Alfred von Schlieffen, Chief of the German General Staff from 1891 to 1905, was governed by the possibility that Germany might face a two-front war against France and Russia. Schlieffen envisaged that, by means of a wide sweep through neutral Belgium and the Dutch "Maastricht Appendix", with the German right-wing armies then wheeling west of Paris, France could be defeated in a lightning campaign before Russia's mobilization and deployment were complete. Schlieffen's successor, von Moltke, modified the plan, weakening the right wing and abandoning the proposed movement through Holland, while the stress of battle in August 1914 imposed further changes. It is doubtful, however, whether the plan would have succeeded even in its original form. It took too little account of human exhaustion, overextended supply lines and inadequate communication systems; it also underestimated the speed of Russian mobilization and the strength of Belgian resistance. *PJS*.

Schmid, Maj Gen Josef ("Beppo") (b.1901). Ger. As head of Luftwaffe intelligence 1939, advocated air-dominated strategy by Germany against England; as head of *Jagdkorps I* in 1943–45 in northwest Europe, failed sufficiently to check either USAF bomber attacks by day or RAF Bomber Command attacks by night on Germany.

Schmidt, Gen Harry (1886–1968). US. A Marine Corps officer since 1909, Schmidt commanded the 4th Marine Division in the assault on the Marshall Islands, and on Saipan, in 1944. Given command of V Amphibious Corps in July 1944, he led the formation in the operations on Tinian and Iwo Jima.

Schnaufer, Maj Heinz-Wolfgang (1922–50). Ger. The top-scoring German night-fighter pilot with 121 victories, mostly over RAF Halifaxes and Lancasters. Flying a Messerschmitt Bf 110, he destroyed 9 bombers in 24 hours on February 21 1945. He died after a motor accident in July 1950.

Schnee Eifel *see* ARDENNES OFFENSIVE.

Schräge Musik ("oblique music"). Slang term for effective German night fighter tactic in which the attack was made with a vertically upward-pointing gun from directly beneath the Lancaster or Halifax, which had no downward vision. The tactic was first used in the Peenemünde raid on the night of August 17–18 1943.

B-17 Flying Fortress of USAAF

Schweinfurt, bombing of (1943–44). On October 14 1943, 291 B-17 Flying Fortresses of the US Eighth Air Force undertook a daylight "precision" attack upon the ball-bearing plants in Schweinfurt. Sixty bombers were shot down over Europe, 17 returned irreparably damaged and over 100 with lesser damage. Destruction at the targets was considerable, but despite initial alarm in Germany, a way round the problems was soon found. Such a rate of casualties, if continued in the Eighth Air Force, would rapidly have exterminated it and therefore the Americans had either to abandon long-range daylight bombing or change its methods. The Schweinfurt raid prompted the latter course; most casualties were due to German fighters engaging the US bombers after they were out of the range of their own fighters. A solution was sought in a crash programme of long-range fighter production and a radical revision of day-bombing tactics.

The British Bomber Command night attack on April 26 1944, aimed at the town area associated with the ball-bearing plants, established another important point. Of the force dispatched, 9.3 percent failed to return and the Germans again quickly recovered. The policy of "selective area bombing", which the Air Staff had forced upon a reluctant Harris, was shown in this instance to have failed, a fact which strengthened the C-in-C's argument for "general area bombing". *ANF*.

Scirè. Italian submarine that launched human torpedo crews against shipping in the Bay of Gibraltar, 1940–41, sinking one merchant-man and damaging two. At Alexandria, December 1941, they disabled battleships *Queen Elizabeth* and *Valiant*. *Scirè* was sunk in August 1942 while attempting to launch human torpedoes off Haifa, Palestine.

Scobie, Lt Gen Sir Ronald (1893–1969). Br. Commander 70th Division, besieged in Tobruk, 1941; Commander Land Forces Greece during British re-occupation, October 1944, and Greek communist rebellion, December 1944–January 1945.

Scott, Adm Sir Percy Moreton (1853–1924). Br. One of the foremost gunnery experts in naval history. Commanding cruisers, he pioneered telescopic sighting and invented training devices – the "dotter", simulating the ship's roll; "loader", for loading practice; and "deflection teacher", simulating the horizontal movement of a target – that promoted "continuous aim" by keeping sights on target throughout the ship's roll. Using this system, Scott's gunners achieved around 80 percent hits to rounds fired, compared with a fleet average of about 30 percent, and almost doubled the rate of hits per heavy gun per minute. Appointed commander of gunnery school *Excellent*, 1903–05, and the Admiralty's first Director of Target Practice, 1905–07, Scott took advantage of advances in electronics and of the "fire control tables" developed by Adm Sir Frederick Dreyer (1878–1956), to evolve the "director sight": a command centre in the foretop of a dreadnought battleship from which a full broadside could be aimed and fired simultaneously. With the support of Fisher and Jellicoe, director firing was adopted by the Royal Navy from 1913. Retiring in 1913, Scott returned to active service in World War I, commanding London's AA defences during the Zeppelin raids of 1915–16. *RO'N*.

S

S

Scud missile. NATO code name for the Soviet nuclear capable short-range ballistic missile family also known in the West as SS-1. The first missiles, designated 8K11 in the East were deployed on tracked chassis in the mid-1950s. Maximum range was 90 miles (150km). An improved 8K17 Scud-B with a range of 168 miles (280km) was deployed in 1962 on a tracked chassis and from 1965 on a more reliable wheeled launcher. Scud-B is still in service with Warsaw Pact armies and has seen combat in Arab and Iranian hands. Versions have been produced in the Middle East (Egypt used Scud, to little result, in the Yom Kippur War of 1973) including longer-ranged derivatives.

Scutari, siege of (1912–13). Scutari (now Shkodër, Albania) resisted most strongly of all the Turkish positions attacked during the First Balkan War. Montenegrin forces had made no impression on Scutari's defences before the armistice of December 3 1912 and her Commandant refused to recognize it. In a series of assaults during February 7–9 1913, the Montenegrins succeeded in gaining a foothold within the eastern perimeter, but attacks by Montenegrins reinforced the Serbians on the southwestern side on March 31–April 1 failed. Quarrels caused the Serbians to leave on April 16 but Scutari surprisingly surrendered to the Montenegrins on April 22. The Great Powers had intended Scutari to belong to the new state of Albania, but it required intense international pressure to persuade the Montenegrins to give it up on May 6 1913. *SKF.*

SD (*Sicherheitsdienst*). The security service of the Nazi Party, founded under Heydrich 1931; staffed entirely by SS; notable for severity of its interrogations.

SE5a, Royal Aircraft Factory (Br, WWI). Single-seat fighter. First production aircraft completed March 1 1917; first squadron (No. 56) to France April 7; operational to end of war, with 18 squadrons. Production, 5,270. One 150/200hp Hispano-Suiza or 200hp Wolseley Viper engine; max. speed 126mph (202kph); two 0.303in machine guns, 100lb (45kg) bombs.

Seacat missile. The Royal Navy's first point defence surface to air missile which replaced the light gun armament of British warships in the 1960s. A simple command-guided weapon with a range of about 3 miles (5km), it is highly dependent on the skill of its operator, but the latter is helped in later installations by the use of television tracking. Seacat suffered from the problems of all first-generation SAM systems, but it probably contributed to some Argentine losses in the Falklands War and has been widely exported.

Sea Dart missile. The Royal Navy's area defence surface to air missile powered by a ram jet and with a range of over 39 miles (65km). Sea Dart uses semi-active radar homing and did well in the Falklands War, shooting down two helicopters, three Skyhawks, a Canberra and a Learjet reconnaissance aircraft. It is best against high-flying targets, but its capabilities against low-flying threats have been improved. It has a secondary surface to surface capability over reduced range.

Sea Fury, Hawker (Br, late- and post-WWII). Single-seat shipboard fighter. Prototype (F2/43) flew September 1 1944; Sea Fury prototype February 21 1945; first production September 30 1946. Deliveries to squadrons began August 1947. Saw much use Korean War. Used by RN, RAN, RCN. Production, 733 for RN, further production and conversions for foreign countries. One 2,480hp Bristol Centaurus 18 engine; max. speed 465mph (748kph); four 20mm cannon, 2,000lb (900kg) external ordnance.

Seaman, Lt Gen Jonathan (b.1911). US. Commander US 1st Infantry Division; promoted to head II Field Force, Vietnam, when it became operational at Long Binh on March 15 1966. Seaman launched Operation "Cedar Falls", the first corps-sized US mission and the first formally planned major combined operation of US and South Vietnamese forces in the Vietnam War.

"Search and destroy" operations. The US command in Vietnam adopted the term "search and destroy" in 1964 to describe multi-battalion operations designed to seek out, encircle and destroy large enemy units. Gen Westmoreland advocated the concept as an offensive alternative to the essentially defensive "enclave strategy". He applied it mainly against well-established base areas, which communist forces often fought vigorously to defend. Following the 1968 Tet offensive, "search and destroy" gave way to small unit patrolling. *See also* CORDON AND SEARCH OPERATIONS.

Sea Skua missile. A British semi-active homing air to surface missile designed to give the Lynx shipborne helicopter capability against small surface combatants. The missile has a range of over 9 miles (15km) and was rushed into service in the Falklands War, during which it seriously damaged at least one Argentine patrol vessel.

Seawolf missile. One of the most effective point defence surface to air systems in the world, Seawolf was designed to give British surface combatants protection from anti-ship missiles. Targets are tracked by radar and automatically engaged, the missiles being command guided to intercept. Television provides optical backup for low angle of sight and surface engagements. The maximum range of the system is about 3–4 miles (5–6km) and a vertically launched version will have longer reach. Seawolf, despite some software problems with crossing targets, distinguished itself in the Falklands, shooting down three Skyhawks on May 12. Later, the system destroyed a Dagger and contributed to the loss of at least one other Skyhawk. *EJG.*

Second Army (British). Formed in 1943 to be the British element of the Normandy invasion force. After D-Day, it held the Caen sector of the bridgehead before joining the breakout and liberating Brussels and Antwerp in September 1944. It took part in the operations in Holland and captured Hamburg on May 3 1945.

Second Front. Potential Anglo-American invasion of France from 1942 onwards i.e. second to Russian Front.

Second-strike capability. The capacity for a nuclear-armed state to strike back no matter what the enemy does by way of pre-emptive strike. Conferred by putting missiles into hardened silos or, better, by making them land- or sea-mobile. The second-strike system *par excellence* is the SLBM.

Secret services. Regarded as a necessity by all great powers, and many smaller ones. Two at least are normally required: one defensive, to handle security, which may include wireless and postal interception, and the planting of agents in suspect subversive bodies; and one offensive, to get information from abroad, which will certainly handle espionage and may also cover decipher, subversion, or sabotage. Rivalry between such services is normal, often intense.

In Germany in 1944, Himmler tried to bring all the secret services under his own wing, and absorbed the armed forces' Abwehr; but propaganda under Goebbels and two decipher staffs, one diplomatic under Göring and one naval under Dönitz, eluded his grasp. UK at the same time had at least eight separate secret services: MI5 for security; Radio Security Service for wireless interception; MI6 for intelligence; Government Code and Cipher School for decipher; MI9 for prisoners of war; SOE (Special Operations Executive) for subversion and sabotage; Political Warfare Executive for propaganda; and London Controlling Section for deception. How far these have been condensed since remains secret.

The Americans started late; the FBI goes back to 1907, but its deciphering service, started in 1915, was disbanded in 1929. The Office of War Information, founded in 1941, expanded into the OSS, 1942–45. Out of this the current CIA developed in 1947. The National Security Council, also founded in 1947, was expanded by Eisenhower in 1953 to supervise the whole field of national safety.

The Russians have two basic services, a large secret police force – currently called the KGB and supposed to be over a quarter of a million strong – and the GRU, responsible for collecting intelligence. *MF*.

Secret weapons. Intelligence and the diversity of scientific research have prevented most developments in weaponry from being truly secret. During World War I, new types of aircraft, tanks and poison gas perhaps surprised the soldier at the Front but were already known about by staff officers, scientists and designers. Rapid technological development led to an expansion in the number of "secret weapons" and in Germany during World War II their existence was flaunted to boost morale at home and to intimidate the enemy. But superior Intelligence permitted the Allies to see behind the bombast and analyse accurately many of the German developments in rocketry, jet propulsion, radar, aircraft design and atomic research. *MS*.

Security. A standing preoccupation for every commander: is his base secure, do his supply lines run freely, does the enemy know (or can he infer) his strength or his plans; is his own person safe against attack? A few high commanders, Stalin and Hitler in particular, lived in paranoiac fear of assassination, kept changing their arrangements, and always had armed bodyguards near them.

Busybodies who make it their business to know everything are a permanent threat to security; but in wartime can usually be barred off from dangerous knowledge by routine service precautions. Those who serve can be trained never to discuss plans, equipment or capacities outside service circles. For extra secret affairs, the "need to know" principle applies: nobody is to be told a secret if he does not need to know it in order to do his own work. Staff officers like to grade documents in ascending order of secrecy: restricted, confidential, secret, very (or most, or top) secret, ultra top secret, and so on. A safer precaution is to transmit highly secret documents only by hand of officer; or safer still, not to write anything down at all.

Messages and documents in transit are vulnerable. Nothing said by telephone, telegraph, fax or cable is in any way private. Devices for scrambling telephone conversations, invented *c*1940, did not become safe until the 1980s. Post can easily be intercepted, opened,

read, re-sealed and passed on. Cipher offers a substantial degree of security, if properly handled; though no cipher is utterly unbreakable, complicated ones may take years to break. Even if missives go by hand of officer, the officer may be robbed or suborned – or may secretly have gone over to the other side: a catastrophe against which it is hard to devise safeguards that will always work.

Security of buildings can be achieved by locks, bars, sentries, patrols and systems of passes; none of them quite impenetrable by lucky and resolute opponents. Equipment can usually be secured by keeping it out of sight, or – if it is too big to hide – by camouflage. Camouflage, in turn, can help with schemes of deception – feints to mislead the enemy about one's own intentions. It is a sound security precaution to train everybody to reveal only name, rank and number if captured; though enemy interrogators are certain to ask for much more.

Civil and military police can help to keep inquisitive passers-by away from service installations, fixed or temporary; again, a really resolute and determined spy, skilled in personal camouflage and in the use of binoculars, telescope and camera, can probably outwit them. Police are of more use in detecting and arresting deserters before they can go over to the enemy.

Most powers now employ a secret service devoted to security. This can grow, like the SS under Hitler or the KGB under Brezhnev, into a state-within-the-state of significant authority. The British and Americans believe that MI5 and FBI are under adequate, if remote, control by elected persons.

Security can be overdone, as the Nazis showed in occupied Europe. If you forbid people to own wireless sets, in case they listen to propaganda of which you disapprove; if you proliferate controls on movement; if you shoot when in doubt, and start asking questions later; if you execute a dozen hostages for each of your soldiers killed in a chance brawl; then you build a degree of opposition and resistance you may later regret. That generations of hostile security measures cannot cow the spirit of a nation for ever has been repeatedly demonstrated. *MF*.

Sedan, breakthrough at. In 1940 the French High Command considered that the Ardennes was impassable for German armour. However, on May 12 Guderian's XIX Panzer Corps captured Sedan, having passed through the forest in two days. The next day they forced crossings of the River Meuse and, having secured their bridgehead, broke through the flimsy French defences and advanced rapidly towards the Channel coast.

Seeckt, Gen Hans von (1866–1936). Ger. After service on the Western Front in 1914–15, appointed COS to von Mackensen's Eleventh Army in Galicia. Played a major role in summer offensive of 1915 and the drive into the Balkans. Postwar, his primary concern was revival of the German Army. Appointed C-in-C *Reichswehr*, he ensured that his small command was prepared for expansion, even arranging training facilities in the Soviet Union. A less than enthusiastic supporter of the Weimar Republic, he nevertheless used the army to restrain both right- and left-wing extremists. In October 1926, his autocratic behaviour resulted in dismissal. In 1934–35, military adviser to Chiang Kai-shek. *MS.*

Self-propelled guns. Artillery pieces mounted on tracked chassis (e.g. M109, Abbot), capable of good cross-country performance in support of mobile operations.

Senger und Etterlin, Lt Gen Fridolin von (1891–1971). Ger. Liaison Officer, Guzzoni's Sixth Army, Sicilian campaign; Commander of Corsica garrison, September 7 1943 until evacuated, October 3; Commander XIV Panzer Corps, Italian campaign.

Sense and Destroy Armour (SADARM). US sub-munition designed to be scattered over tanks and to home on them using millimetric wavelength radar. Sometimes known as "Skeets", they flutter down searching for targets, and, if they find one, fire a self-forging fragment at its lightly protected upper surfaces. If they do not immediately find a target, they can operate as effective mines. They can be dispensed by 155mm or 8in shells or MLRS rockets.

Seoul, Battle of (1950). When the NKPA began the Korean War on June 25 1950, the main thrust was directed towards Seoul, the ROK capital. It consisted of two infantry divisions supported by an armoured brigade. A ROK counterattack on June 26 failed and by evening the NKPA had taken Uijongbu, a key position on the road to the capital. The following day ROK units, lacking an adequate defence against tanks, began to disintegrate and the NKPA reached the outskirts of Seoul. A plan to hold the Han river line, south of Seoul, failed when engineer units panicked and blew the bridges prematurely in the early hours of June 28, forcing the ROK army to abandon much of its equipment. Later that day, Seoul fell. *CM.*

Serbian campaign (1914–15). Austria-Hungary declared war on Serbia, July 28 1914. The Austrian COS, Conrad von Hötzendorf, unwisely decided on a two-front offensive: against Russia in Galicia, to the north; and against Serbia to the south. Early in August, Austrian Second Army advanced across the Save river, on Serbia's northern border, while Austrian Fifth and Sixth Armies struck from Bosnia, in the west, across the Drina and Jadar rivers. The Austrian C-in-C, Gen Oskar Potiorek, deploying some 200,000 men in all, was opposed by three Serbian armies (about 190,000 men) under Marshal Putnik. Although better-equipped, the hastily-mobilized Austrian troops were inferior in both training and morale to the Serbian veterans of the Balkan Wars.

Keeping his forces concentrated, Putnik manouevred skilfully to defeat the independently-operating Austrian armies, holding Second Army in the north, while dividing Sixth and Fifth Armies, and severely mauling the latter, in a fierce counterattack (Battle of the Jadar river, August 16–21). Having lost some 40,000 men, Potiorek fell back across the Drina. Putnik, however, could not sustain a counteroffensive into Bosnia and, when Potiorek again attacked from the north and west on September 7, failed, after ten days' savage fighting (Battle of the Drina river, September 8–17) to eradicate the Austrian bridgeheads. With ammunition running low, Putnik gradually retreated southeastwards, withdrawing troops from Belgrade (occupied by the Austrians on December 2) and concentrating his armies in the central highlands around Mount Rudnik, where he was resupplied by the Allies via Salonika. Potiorek's advance from the north and west, October–November, overstretched the Austrian supply lines, and on December 3–9, at the Rudnik Ridges and the Kolubara river, a Serbian counter attack shattered Potiorek's armies, recapturing Belgrade (December 15) and driving the Austrians from Serbia. The campaign cost Potiorek some 227,000 casualties; Serbian losses were also great.

In September 1915, following Bulgaria's alliance with the Central Powers, Serbia faced invasion from north, west and east, with neutral Greece (resenting territory lost in the Balkan Wars) a potential danger to the south. On October 6, under the direction of Field Marshal August von Mackensen, German (Gen von Gallwitz) and Austrian (Gen Kövess von Kövesshàza) armies swept across Serbia's northern border, taking Belgrade (October 9), while two Bulgarian armies struck from the east, taking Vranje (October 19) and driving back the Serbs after a prolonged struggle for Veles (October 21–29). The Serbian stronghold of Mitrovitza fell to Kövess on November 23, while on the same day Gallwitz linked up with the Bulgarians at Pristina.

The Bulgarian offensive had blocked attempts to aid Putnik by the Anglo-French expeditionary force at Salonika (*see* SALONIKA CAMPAIGN): outnumbered nearly two-to-one and threatened with envelopment, Putnik withdrew his remaining forces, fighting a series of heroic rearguard actions, to the southwest. After a harrowing winter trek through the mountains of Montenegro (occupied by Austria, January 1916) and Albania, the Serbian survivors (some 100,000 Serbs out of about 180,000 engaged in the campaign became casualties) reached the Adriatic coast, whence they were evacuated by the Allies to Corfu. Re-equipped there, a 118,000-strong Serbian army returned to join the Allies at Salonika, July 1916. *RO'N.*

Serchio, German offensive (December 26–30 1944). LI Mountain Corps (Feuerstein) mounted a spoiling attack with one division against the 92nd US (Negro) Division, holding the Serchio Valley on the quiet Western sector of the Gothic Line. The 92nd Division collapsed. 15th Army Group (Clark), fearing a repetition of the Ardennes offensive, rushed troops over from the Bologna front. Having achieved his limited objectives, however, Feuerstein withdrew.

Seria *see* BRUNEI REVOLT.

Serre *see* SOMME, BATTLE OF THE (1916).

Sevastopol, Battle of (1942). The collapse of the Soviet defence lines on the Perekop isthmus in October 1941 allowed von Manstein's Eleventh Army to occupy the Crimea and lay siege to the naval base of Sevastopol. The strength of the defences precluded a rapid assault, but in December a German breakthrough was only averted by the deployment of Soviet reinforcements transported into Sevastopol by the Black Sea Fleet. By May 1942 the garrison had swollen to 106,000. To break into this heavily fortified position, Manstein employed a powerful siege. The final assault was launched on June 7 with the main attacks in the north by LII Corps and in the southeast by XXX Corps. Slowly the defensive perimeter was pushed back nearer Sevastopol itself and on the 26th the sea link with the outside was closed to supplies and reinforcements. On the 30th, Stavka's orders for the evacuation by air and submarine of key personnel were announced, but German control of sea and air made escape impossible for most of the garrison. When Sevastopol fell on July 3, the total of Soviet prisoners was some 120,000. *MS.*

Seventh Air Force (US). Originally called the Hawaiian Air Force, the US Seventh Air Force fought mainly in the Central and Western Pacific after mid-1943. Its B-24 and B-25 bombers supported the offensives in the Gilberts, Marshalls and Marianas and, by July 1945, were attacking the Japanese home islands from Okinawa.

Seventh Armoured Division (British). World-War-II nickname "the Desert Rats"; their divisional sign incorporated the jerboa, a North African rodent, perhaps reflecting the division's "darting and biting" tactics as part of O'Connor's Western Desert Force during the Libyan offensive of early 1941.

Seventh Fleet (US). New name, from February 1943, for South West Pacific Force, the forces involved in the amphibious campaign in that area. Postwar, this title has been used for the US fleet operating in the western Pacific.

Shaho river, Battle of (October 5–17 1904), Russo-Japanese War. Retreating north after the Battle of Liaoyang, Kuropatkin's 200,000 Russians (losses 40,000) turned to face Oyama's 170,000 Japanese (losses 20,000) along a 40-mile (64km) front. The battle was stalemated by severe weather.

SHAPE (Supreme Headquarters Allied Powers Europe). The HQ of SACEUR. Set up at Rocquencourt near Paris in 1951, it was transferred to Casteau near Mons in 1967. An international HQ with officers from the armed forces of every NATO country.

Shaposhnikov, Marshal of the Soviet Union Boris Mikhailovich (1882–1945). Russian. A noted strategist – CGS, 1928–31, 1937–40, 1941–42 – Shaposhnikov was one of the few senior Red Army commanders to survive the purges of 1937–38. His advocacy of defensive policies is believed to have considerably influenced Stalin until *c*1941.

Sharon, Gen Ariel ("Arik") (b.1928). Israeli soldier and politician. *See* ARAB-ISRAELI WARS.

Sharp, Adm Ulysses S Grant (b.1906). US. Promoted from C-in-C of the Pacific Fleet to C-in-C of the Pacific Command on June 30 1964. He was in charge of operations by the Seventh Fleet against North Vietnam and Laos and of the American build-up in the Vietnam War. A strong supporter of bombing the North, in 1967 he demanded an end to operational restrictions that required selection of

individual targets and application of steadily increasing pressures against target "systems".

Sheffield. British Type 42 destroyer of 4,100 tons full load. Hit by Exocet missile launched from Super Etendard on May 4 1982, during the Falklands War. At the time, *Sheffield* was on radar picket duty but not at full alert. Twenty-one of her crew were killed and many more injured. This was the first British warship lost to enemy action since 1945 and news of the ship's loss came as a grave shock to the British public.

Sherman (M4). American medium tank introduced 1942. 33 tons, 75mm gun. Firefly, a variant in British service, mounted a 17-pounder gun. *See also* TANKS.

Shinano. Japanese aircraft carrier. Laid down as a *Yamato*-class battleship; converted to an aircraft carrier while building; launched October 8 1944. Largest carrier of World War II: 70,755 tons fully loaded; 872ft (266m) overall length; 840-ft (256m) armoured flight deck. A "supply" carrier, possibly a mobile base for bombers carrying *ohka* piloted-bombs, she carried only 47 operational aircraft. On November 28 1944, with work on her watertight compartments and pumps incomplete, *Shinano* (Capt Toshiro Abe) began her maiden cruise from Tokyo Bay. At 0310 hours next day, she was badly holed by torpedoes from the submarine USS *Archerfish*. Abe attempted to hold his course, but his inexperienced crew was unable to control flooding and at 1055 hours she sank, killing Abe and 500 of his 1,400-strong crew. Her period of commission, some 17 hours, was the shortest of any major warship. *RO'N.*

Shinyo and Maru-ni. Japanese suicide weapons: one- or two-man explosive motorboats – typically *c*19ft (6m) long; *c*550lb (250kg) impact-fuzed warhead; maximum range *c*120 miles (190km) at 26kts – extensively deployed by Navy (*shinyo*) and Army (*maru-ni*) against US landing ships and escorts in the Philippines, Iwo Jima and Okinawa, 1944-45. They sank at least 10 minor warships and badly damaged several others.

Shoho. Japanese aircraft carrier. Converted from auxiliary in 1941; sunk at Coral Sea, 1942.

Short Seaplane, Admiralty Type 184 (Br, WWI). Two-seat maritime patrol. Prototype to RNAS April 21 1915. First wartime air-launched torpedo attack August 12 1915. Effectiveness improved by progressive engine changes; a few flown as single-seat bombers. Folding wings permitted operation from small seaplane carriers. A few operational in anti-Bolshevik operations 1919. Production, over 945. One 225/240/265hp Sunbeam or 240hp Renault engine; max. speed 85mph (137kph); one 0.303in machine gun, one 14in torpedo or 520lb (263kg) bombs.

Short Take-Off and Vertical Landing (STOVL). The normal form of operation of so-called V/STOL (Vertical/Short Take-Off and Landing) aircraft with vectored thrust jet engines. Such aircraft can only carry large loads of fuel and weapons if they use the lift of their wings as well as of their engines in take-off. A short take-off run is thus normally required, enhanced in ships by the use of a "ski-jump" ramp. Vertical landing is, however, normal. The only true STOVL aircraft currently operational is the Harrier, used by the British RAF and Royal Navy, the US Marine Corps, the Indian Navy and the Spanish Navy. The Soviet YAK-36 "Forger" naval fighter has separate lift engines and is more a Vertical Take-Off and Landing (VTOL) aircraft, but its successor, the YAK-41, will be capable of STOVL operation with ski-jump. The vectored thrust engines of the Harrier family give high manoeuvrability in dogfights, although the success of the Sea Harrier in the Falklands War was largely due to superior missiles. STOVL aircraft are currently all subsonic, as there are technical problems in combining vectored thrust with afterburning. *EJG.*

Short-Range Ballistic Missile (SRBM). A guided, ballistic missile with a range of less than about 500 miles (800km). Longer-ranged examples are now classed as short-ranged intermediate nuclear forces. "Battlefield" systems with ranges of less than 300 miles (500km) still deployable include the Western Lance and the Eastern SS-21 and Scud-B.

Shrapnel Corner. Frequently bombarded road junction near the Lille Gate, Ypres, 1914–18.

Shuri Castle and Shuri Line *see* OKINAWA CAMPAIGN.

Sibuyan Sea, Battle of *see* LEYTE GULF, BATTLE OF (1944).

Sicily, invasion of (July 10–August 17 1943). The first step towards the Allied invasion of Europe after the fall of Tunis.

Alexander's 15th Army Group

"Down ramps" on the Sicilian shore

comprised Eighth Army (Montgomery) with XIII Corps (Dempsey) and XXX Corps (Leese), and Seventh US Army (Patton) with II US Corps (Bradley). The Axis forces under Sixth Italian Army (Guzzoni) comprised XII Corps (Arisio), defending the west of the island, supported by 15th Panzer Grenadier Division, and XVI Corps (Rossi), defending the East, supported by the Hermann Göring Panzer Division.

Von Senger und Etterlin was the German Liaison Officer with Sixth Italian Army. He and Guzzoni wished to defend the coast lightly with their mobile divisions held well back for counterattack when the main Allied landings had been identified. Kesselring, c-in-c South, insisted on destroying the invaders on the beaches, because he doubted whether the mobile divisions would be able to move during daylight in the face of Allied air superiority. Kesselring had his way and the two German divisions were deployed at opposite ends of the island relatively close to the coast.

Operations fell into three phases. The landings took place between July 10–12. The invasion was preceded by airborne landings behind the beaches, which went awry due to high winds and inadequate air-crew training, but they confused Guzzoni. Montgomery landed on the southeast corner of the island, and took the port of Syracuse, vital for supply purposes, by evening. Patton met more resistance, particularly from Hermann Göring Division, whose counterattacks on July 11 were only repulsed with the help of naval gunfire. Allied bridgeheads were secure by the 12th.

The second phase (July 13–28) saw the Axis withdrawal to the Etna Line. Hitler had ordered the reinforcement of the island with 1st Parachute and 29th Panzer Grenadier Divisions, and with HQ XIV Panzer Corps (Hube) to take command of all German troops. By July 13 he had concluded that Italian resistance had collapsed, and that it was only practicable for Hube to hold a bridgehead in the northeast corner of the island. Hube withdrew as slowly as possible to allow time for the preparation of the bridgehead's defences – the Etna Line – running from coast to coast around the southern slopes of the volcano.

Patton advanced almost unopposed in the west, taking Palermo on July 22, and then turned east to advance on Messina along the north coast. Montgomery had to fight hard against stiffening German opposition as he thrust northwards up the east coast and through the central mountains. Both Armies were up against the Etna Line by July 23.

The Etna Line was breached and the Germans evacuated during the third phase (July 24–August 17). Bradley's II US Corps, using four divisions, broke through on August 6 in fierce fighting along the coast road and at Troina inland, and then advanced on Messina helped by a series of amphibious left hooks. Leese's XXX Corps with three divisions broke through in equally hard fighting through Agira, Centuripe and Regalbuto to Adrano on the western slopes of Etna which fell on August 3; and Dempsey's XIII Corps, held up on the east coast just south of Catania, found German opposition slackening by August 5. The fall of Mussolini on July 26 had resulted in a German decision to evacuate the island, starting on August 11. XIV Panzer Corps reached the mainland safely, despite Allied naval and air superiority. Bradley's troops entered Messina on August 16. *WGFJ.*

Sidewinder missile. Simple US infrared homing air to air missiles first deployed in 1956. They made their combat debut in Nationalist Chinese hands against the communists in 1958 and have seen much operational use. Originally designated AIM-9, the missile has been progressively improved and is now in its AIM-9M version. AIM-9L missiles, with their ability to be fired at relatively long range from a variety of angles, were the major factor in the victory of the Royal Navy's Sea Harriers in the Falklands War.

Sidi Barrani, Battle of (December 6–11 1940). The advance of Gen Berti's Italian Tenth Army into Egypt (September 13–18 1940), opposed only by light forces of British 7th Armoured Division's Support Group (Gott), halted at Sidi Barrani while Berti built up logistic resources. On the night of December 8–9, 4th Indian and 7th Armoured Divisions of British Western Desert Force (O'Connor), having advanced undetected from Mersa Matruh across 100 miles (160km) of desert, surprised Berti's fortified camps. Unnerved by O'Connor's apparently invulnerable "I" (Matilda) tanks, the Italians collapsed (33,000 prisoners) and Berti withdrew to Cyrenaica.

Sidi Bou Zid, Battle of (February 14–17 1943). Von Arnim mounted an offensive with 10th Panzer and 21st Panzer Divisions (Lt Gen Ziegler), to neutralize the threat posed by II US Corps (Fredendall) to Axis communications in southern Tunisia. Ziegler surprised 1st US Armoured Division and drove it out of Sidi Bou Zid. American counterattacks were repulsed with heavy losses, seriously undermining American morale just before Rommel attacked the nearby Kasserine Pass.

Sidi Rezegh, First Battle of (November 19–22 1941). Having taken Sidi Rezegh airfield, 7th Armoured Brigade hoped to link up with the Tobruk garrison, but

Rommel concentrated 21st Panzer and the Afrika Divisions to destroy the isolated British brigade. 7th Armoured Division's Support Group ("Jock" Campbell) reached the airfield just in time to help resist the German attacks. After two days of some of the fiercest fighting of the Desert War, in which Campbell won his VC, the survivors managed to withdraw as darkness fell on November 22.

Sidi Rezegh, Second Battle of (November 29–December 1 1941). While Rommel was making his dash to the Egyptian frontier, the New Zealand Division reoccupied Sidi Rezegh, hoping to link up the Tobruk garrison. Rommel returned to bring the whole weight of the tired but still battle-worthy Afrika Korps to bear on the New Zealanders. After three days' hard fighting, the New Zealanders withdrew, but they had brought Rommel to the point of acknowledging that he could no longer maintain the siege of Tobruk.

Siegfried Line. In autumn 1917 the Germans began the construction of a major defence line, the "Siegfried Stellung" (Siegfried Line), between Lens and Reims on the northern sector of the Western Front. In 1938, the name was applied to the extensive defence (officially the "West Wall") under construction along Germany's western frontiers, running approximately from east of Basel to Karlsruhe, west to Luxembourg, and east along the borders of Belgium and the Netherlands. Originally intended to defend the re-annexed Saar region in 1936, it was expanded to become a German counterpart to the Maginot Line. It primarily consisted of mines, tank traps and a thick band of pillboxes. Nazi propaganda elevated these fortifications, known to the Allies as the Siegfried Line, to an impregnable barrier. Left largely untouched during the "Phoney War", four years later it formed the last bastion of Germany against the Anglo-American armies. Although far weaker than both Hitler and the Allies believed, it was not fully breached until spring 1945. *MS.*

Sigint. Intelligence secured from signal activity through decipher or traffic analysis.

Sihanouk, Prince Norodom (b.1922). Cambodian. The French arranged for Prince Sihanouk to succeed his father's first cousin as King of Cambodia in 1941, believing him pliable. However, the young king became assertive, manoeuvred the French into granting Cambodia full independence in 1953, and abdicated in 1955 to become Premier of a constitutional monarchy. Brilliant, charming, vain, mercurial, Sihanouk continued to enjoy the charisma of kingship, ruling Cambodia in paternalistic, imperious fashion. His paramount diplomatic objective was to keep Cambodia out of the conflicts of its neighbours. This he sought to do by declaring Cambodia neutral and bending with the prevailing wind (*see* CAMBODIA, WARS SINCE INDEPENDENCE; SIHANOUK TRAIL). Overthrown on March 18 1970, he settled in China, joined forces with the Khmers Rouges, and returned to Phnom Penh in 1975. The Khmers Rouges kept him under virtual house arrest until the Vietnamese invasion of December 1978. Sihanouk subsequently headed the triparite Coalition Government of Democratic Kampuchea, which was opposed to the Vietnamese. *WST.*

Sihanouk Trail. In 1966, the Vietnamese communists began using the Cambodian port of Sihanoukville (Kompong Som), with Prince Norodom Sihanouk's consent, to supply their bases on Cambodia's border with South Vietnam. Chinese and Soviet bloc ships brought most of the supplies to the port, where the Royal Cambodian Army took charge of warehousing. Barges, sampans and the Hak Ly Trucking Company provided haulage to the Parrot's Beak for distribution to other bases and to units inside South Vietnam. By the late 1960s, the bulk of communist war material in lower South Vietnam was entering from Cambodia, mostly from Sihanoukville. US intelligence was slow to discover the "trail", and the US government, reluctant to exercise belligerent rights at sea in an undeclared limited war, eschewed blockade. Conservative elements in the Cambodian government forced Sihanouk to close the trail in April 1969. *WST.*

S

Sikorsky Il'ya Mouromets (Russian/USSR, WWI and after). Reconnaissance bomber; crew 4/5. Prototype flew January 1914. Adaptation for military purposes and development to meet operational requirements led to several variations in design, assortment of engines. First bombing raid February 15 1915. Production ended October 17 1917; total 80. A few taken over by Red Air Fleet; in service until 1924. Four Argus, Benz, MRB, RBVZ-6, Salmson or Sunbeam engines of 100–220hp each; max. speed 83mph (133kph); up to seven machine guns, 1,754lb (795kg) bombs.

Gen Sikorski: leader of "Free Poland"

Sikorski, Gen Wladyslaw (1881–1943). Polish. Commanded a division in Pilsudski's campaign against the Bolsheviks; retired 1926. In 1939, offer of his services was rejected by the Polish C-in-C, Smigly-Rydz, and on September 24 Sikorski arrived in Paris. The fall of Poland and the discrediting of the government and high command brought him to leadership of the Polish government-in-exile and C-in-C of the·Polish Army. With the defeat of France, Sikorski and most of his 100,000-strong force escaped to Britain where they made a valuable contribution to the Allied war effort. However, the Soviet Union's entry into the war in June 1941 created immense political difficulties. Sikorski and Maisky negotiated a recognition of Poland's pre-war frontiers, but the amnesty for Polish prisoners held in the Soviet Union had disappointing results: evidence of the Katyn massacre emerged in April 1943. The crisis was to a great extent defused, but the Polish cause was weakened by Sikorski's death in a plane crash at Gibraltar on July 4 1943. *MS.*

Silkworm missile. Chinese-made anti-ship missile emplaced by Iran to cover the Straits of Hormuz and in the Fao Peninsula in 1987. A number were subsequently fired, one damaging an American registered tanker and another Kuwait's main oil terminal. They seem to be unsophisticated weapons, near copies of the Soviet SS-N-2 "Styx", either the 57 miles (95km) range Hai Ying (Sea Eagle)-2 and/or the smaller Feilong (Flying Dragon)-2.

Silo. A concrete-protected hole in the ground in which a ballistic missile is stored and from which it is fired. Silos are hardened to resist the overpressures of a thermonuclear warhead bursting close by. Some Soviet ICBM silos are reportedly super-hardened to resist 6,000psi overpressures. Ignition of the missile in the silo is now being replaced by "cold launch", using gas generators: this allows a larger missile for a given silo.

Simpson, Gen William Hood ("Big Simp") (b.1888). US. From early September 1944, Simpson led US Ninth Army in the advance to the Siegfried Line, winning Eisenhower's high regard not least by his ability to cooperate with the British: Ninth Army serving under Montgomery during the Ardennes offensive. Early in April 1945, Ninth Army secured a bridgehead on the Elbe only 60 miles (96km) west of Berlin, and, if not ordered to halt on April 15, might have reached Berlin before the Soviets.

Sims, Vice Adm William Sowden (1858–1936). US. Leading figure in the improvement of the US Navy's gunnery from 1902, introducing techniques and training methods garnered from the British Adm Scott. On America's entry into World War I, April 1917, Sims became commander of all US Navy forces in European waters. He urged the Navy Department to commit all available resources to anti-submarine warfare and strongly supported Beatty and Lloyd George in advocating an improved convoy system.

Sinai campaigns (1956 and 1973) *see* SUEZ CRISIS; ARAB-ISRAELI WARS.

Singapore, fall of (1942) *see* MALAYA AND SINGAPORE.

Sino-Japanese War (1937–45). In September 1931, the Japanese Kwantung Army engineered the "Mukden Incident". Claiming that the Chinese had attempted to sabotage the Mukden-Port Arthur (Lushun) railway, the Japanese launched a campaign that drove all Chinese forces from Manchuria, which, in February 1932, was proclaimed an "independent" state (Manchukuo) under the puppet-Emperor Henry Pu-yi (1906–67). Further Japanese expansion into northern China and Inner Mongolia (the latter leading to border clashes with Soviet forces culminating at Nomonhan, 1939) followed in 1933–37. On July 7 1937, a supposed attack on Japanese troops at the Marco Polo Bridge, near Peking (Beijing), provided Japan with a pretext for the full-scale invasion of China, marking the beginning of the undeclared Sino-Japanese War.

The well-equipped Japanese expeditionary forces in China deployed some 300,000 regular troops (rising to *c*700,000 by 1945); the enormous Chinese armies (the National Government Army of Chiang Kai-shek, some 2,000,000-strong; some 150,000 troops, mostly guerrillas, of the communist People's Liberation Army under Chu Teh and Mao Tse-tung) were scantily-equipped and bedevilled by political rivalry (*see* CHINESE CIVIL WAR). Japanese air and naval superiority was absolute until later in World War II.

Japanese offensives quickly secured Peking and Tientsin (July 28-29 1937). An amphibious invasion (August 13), assisted by massive naval and air bombardments, resulted in the fall of Shanghai (November 11) after fierce Chinese resistance. Japanese troops marked the taking of Nanking (during which the gunboat USS *Panay* was sunk by Japanese bombers, December 12) on December 13 with several days' hideous atrocities, murdering some 50,000 civilians. Although a Chinese victory at Taierchwang, near Suchow, where *c*200,000 troops (Gen Li Tsung-jen) temporarily surrounded two Japanese divisions (*c*20,000 killed), raised morale, Japanese advances continued, securing Hankow (October 25 1938) and, in the south, Canton (October 21). Now controlling most of northern and central China and all major ports, Japan in 1939 settled down to exploit its conquests, establishing a puppet-government under Wang Ching-wei at Nanking, March 1940, and relying on attrition to wear away Chinese resistance (an estimated 800,000 Chinese troops had been killed since 1937; Japanese losses about 50,000).

During World War II in the Pacific, from December 1941, Chinese forces received increasing aid from the Allies. The most effective resistance to the Japanese in China itself came from the communist guerrilla forces. In April 1944, Japan's China Expeditionary Army (Gen Okamura) launched a major offensive (*Ichi-go*) to the east, aimed at seizing US Fourteenth Air Force's bases in the Kweilin-Liuchow area and thence assaulting Chungking. The air bases were secured by December, but speedy reinforcement and improved Chinese-US cooperation early in 1945 allowed Chinese forces to counterattack in both Honan and Hupeh (March-June), forcing Okamura to withdraw northwards. Japanese forces in China surrendered to Chiang Kai-shek in August 1945; the Kwantung Army surrendered to Soviet forces in Manchuria on September 2. The Sino-Japanese War is estimated to have cost China some 1,300,000 combat deaths, with around 1,880,000 wounded; civilian casualties were probably much higher. *RO'N*.

Sino-Vietnamese War (1979). On February 17 1979, 85,000 Chinese soldiers out of a total invasion force of 320,000 crossed the Vietnamese border. China justified its attack by alleging Vietnamese border violations, but in fact it was in retaliation for Vietnam's invasion of Cambodia and close alignment with the Soviet Union.

The invading troops, supported by armour and massive barrages of artillery and rockets, poured through five routes leading toward provincial capitals. Attacking in "human waves" not seen since the Korean War, seizing the major border towns one by one, they captured Lang Son on March 2.

This placed the Chinese at the gateway to the Red River delta, but on the 5th, Peking (Beijing) announced its intention to withdraw. During withdrawal, ending March 16, the Chinese dynamited many buildings in one of the few areas of Vietnam that US bombers had earlier left untouched.

Considering the scope and intensity of the attack, the Chinese advanced slowly. This was because the invasion routes led through narrow, densely wooded, steep-sided valleys in which the Vietnamese could fight from prepared positions on tactically advantageous ground. And although at first comprised mainly of local militia and regional forces, the defending force, which started with about 100,000 troops, included some regional units that were better equipped and trained than the Chinese. The attack revealed deficiencies in the Chinese army that stimulated demand for military modernization. *WST*.

Sirte, First Battle of (December 16–18 1941). 15th Cruiser Squadron (Vian), escorting the *Breconshire* to Malta, was intercepted by the Italian battle fleet (Iachino), covering a supply convoy for Rommel. The action was indecisive, but it led to the three cruisers of Force K from Malta running into a minefield off Tripoli with the loss of *Neptune* and damage to *Aurora* and *Penelope*.

Sirte, Second Battle of (March 22 1942). Vian's squadron of 4 light cruisers (15th) with destroyers, escorting a Malta convoy from Alexandria, fought off Italian battleship *Littorio*, two heavy cruisers and one light cruiser (Iachino) in a four-hour series of actions. The British force suffered damage but no losses. Two Italian destroyers sank in the subsequent storm.

Sittang river, Battle of (1942) *see* BURMA CAMPAIGN.

Sixth Army (US). Activated on January 25 1943, Sixth Army served in the Pacific Theatre. Commanded by Lt Gen Krueger, it fought with distinction in New Guinea, the islands of the Bismarck Sea and the Philippines and formed part of the Allied army of occupation of Japan.

Sixth Army Group (US). Commanded by Lt Gen Devers, this formation included Seventh US Army and First French Army and became operational in France on September 15 1944. It played an important part in the liberation of France and the subsequent drive into Germany.

Sixth Fleet (US). Postwar American Mediterranean fleet based at Naples and the core of US strength in that sea. Landings in Lebanon (1958). In the 1980s, it has been involved in bombardments in the Lebanon and incidents with Libya in the Gulf of Sirte.

Skorzeny, Col (*Standartenführer*, SS) Otto (1908-1975). Austrian. Invalided to Germany in December 1942 after service with the Waffen SS in France and Russia, Skorzeny took an intelligence post under Schellenberg and was ordered to train SS "commando" units. His rescue of Mussolini at the head of one such unit, September 1943, led to expansion of the programme: Skorzeny raised two SS Parachute Rifle battalions and a Special Services battalion and also directed the clandestine operations of the Luftwaffe's *Kampfgruppe 200*. Among the scar-faced giant's exploits were the kidnapping of the son of Adm Horthy (to prevent the Hungarian dictator from pursuing peace negotiations with Russia), October 1944, and the penetration of Allied lines in the Ardennes by SS troops in American uniforms, December 1944. Acquitted of war crimes in 1947, he escaped from internment and settled in Spain. *RO'N. See also* the essay UNDERGROUND WARFARE p.334.

Skyhawk, McDonnell-Douglas A-4 (US). Single-seat shipboard attack bomber. Prototype flew June 22 1954; first deliveries to US Navy October 1956, to US Marine Corps March 1960. Much operational use in Vietnam, Laos, Cambodia; with Israeli air force Middle East wars, and by Argentine air force Falklands. Production (several versions), 2,960. One 11,200lb (5,080kg) s.t. Pratt and Whitney J52-P-408A engine; max. speed 685mph (1,102kph); two 20mm cannon, up to 10,000lb (4,500kg) external ordnance.

S

SLAM ("seek, locate, annihilate, monitor"). The technique of coordinating heavy ground and naval artillery, tactical air support, and B-52 bombardment against enemy troop concentrations developed by USAF Force Gen Momyer during Vietnam War. B-52s struck first, then tactical air, naval gunfire, and finally ground artillery, creating waves of fire against small target areas. First applied in Operation "Neutralize" to relieve Con Thien in September-October 1967.

Slessor, Marshal of the RAF Sir John (1897–1979). Br. Director of Plans, Air Ministry 1937-41, Assistant Chief of the Air Staff (Policy) 1942–43, AOC-in-C, Coastal Command 1943–44, C-in-C, RAF Mediterranean and Middle East 1944–45. Slessor had a distinguished flying career in World War I. He became one of the most thoughtful and perceptive of the RAF's officers and, amongst them, probably exerted a greater influence on air policy in World War II than anyone other than Portal. He was chiefly responsible for the Western Air Plans before the war and later, as Assistant Chief of the Air Staff, played a critically important role in reconciling the severely different views of Portal and Arnold. As AOC-in-C, Coastal Command, in consort with naval colleagues, he virtually saw off the grave threat posed by U-boats operating in and near the Bay of Biscay. His diplomatic skill, however, did not avail when it came to dealing with the Russians on the question of helping the Poles in their rising against the Germans in 1944. *ANF.*

Gen Slim enters Mandalay, 1945

Slim, Field Marshal Lord (1891–1970). Br. Joined the army as a private in 1914. Fought in Gallipoli and Mesopotamia. He commanded 10th Indian Division against Vichy forces in Syria in 1941. Sent to Burma in March 1942, he took over the newly formed "Burcorps": virtually all units in Burma. His task was to hold the army together in its long retreat to India. In the following reorganization, he was given XV Corps, which included 14th and 26th Indian Divisions. His forces were involved in the first abortive advance into Arakan. A major reorganization followed and Slim took over the Fourteenth Army on October 15 1943. His first major test was the Japanese *U-Go* offensive, March-July 1944, which demanded nerve and stamina.

The next stage was complicated by the opposed objectives of Americans and British. The former wanted the route to China protected; the latter wanted to free Burma. Instructions issued from SEAC on September 16 1944 reflected these contradictions. British Indian forces were to clear Upper Burma from the Japanese, and, in a quite separate operation, there would be a seaborne assault on Rangoon. Operation "Capital", the plan to move into Upper Burma, was expanded by Slim in mid-December into "Extended Capital" to exploit opportunities for an advance into Lower Burma. One great hazard was the limited time available: only four months before the onset of the monsoon. Slim went confidently ahead, and his boldness succeeded: on May 6, Fourteenth Army linked up with the disembarking XV Corps at Hlegu. 18 miles (29km) from Rangoon.

Fourteenth Army was then to be switched to Malaya. Sir Oliver Leese informed Slim that planning for Malaya would be undertaken by the staff of Fourteenth Army and that mopping-up operations in Burma would be done by a newly formed Twelfth Army, which he, Slim, would take over. Slim refused and asked to be relieved. This bizarre situation was vigorously reversed by the CIGS in London, Brooke, who relieved Leese and designated Slim as his successor.

After the war he was Chief of Imperial General Staff, and later Governor-General of Australia (1953–60). *HT.*

Small arms. Light weapons carried by servicemen for their personal use. At the beginning of the century small arms were exclusively pistols and rifles; the term now embraces light and medium machine guns, submachine guns and automatic rifles.

Smart bombs (Razon/Tarazon). In late 1950 the USAF experimented with precision weapons against targets like Korean railway bridges. The first tests involved Razon bombs dropped from B-29 Superfortresses of the 19th Bombardment Group based on Okinawa. The Razon, developed during World War II, had remote controlled tail fins which allowed the bombardier to alter range and azimuth once the bomb had left the aircraft. Technical difficulties with the first batch of bombs were overcome and 15 bridges were eventually destroyed. Razon, however, was too light to damage large structures. In December 1950 the Tarazon was tested. This used the same guidance mechanism but weighed six tons. On January 13 1951 a B-29 destroyed two spans of the railway bridge at Kanggye with a Tarazon from a height of 15,000ft (4,500m). Tarazon, however, proved unreliable and was abandoned in March 1951. *CM.*

Smith, Lt Gen Holland McTyeire ("Howlin' Mad") (1882–1967). US. Senior US Marine Corps general of the Pacific war, an able, ruthless and undiplomatic commander, Smith exerted major influence on the development of amphibious warfare. As commanding general, Amphibious Force, Pacific Fleet (from September 1943, V Amphibious Corps) and, from August 1944, Fleet Marine Force, Pacific, he oversaw the recapture of the Aleutians and the invasions of the Gilberts and Marshalls. His dismissal of Maj Gen Ralph Smith, USA, for "poor performance" on Saipan provoked bitter argument between the US Navy/Marines and the Army: he was not given a major command postwar, retiring in 1946. *RO'N.*

Smith, Gen Walter Bedell (1895–1961). US. "Beetle" Smith fought in France as an infantry officer in World War I. In February 1942 he was appointed as the first US Secretary to the Combined Chiefs of Staff and in September went to England as Eisenhower's COS in the European Theatre of Operations. He remained with Eisenhower for the rest of the war, becoming COS at the Supreme Headquarters Allied Expeditionary Force (SHAEF) for the Normandy invasion and the Northwest European campaign. Pugnacious and quick-tempered, but also extremely efficient, he made a vital contribution to the Allied war effort. *PJS*.

Smith-Dorrien, Gen Sir Horace (1858–1930). Br. Smith-Dorrien, who was GOC Southern Command at the outbreak of World War I, took over II Corps of the BEF upon Sir James Grierson's death on August 17 1914. Less than a week later, on August 23, II Corps bore the major share of the fighting at the Battle of Mons. Having successfully disengaged, Smith-Dorrien decided, contrary to Sir John French's wishes, to make a stand at Le Cateau on August 26, feeling that his troops were too exhausted and the Germans were too close to risk further retreat that day. His decision was justified for, despite 7,812 casualties, the action at Le Cateau led to an easing of pressure on II Corps but, thereafter, relations between Smith-Dorrien and French steadily deteriorated. This was not immediately apparent as, following the operations on the Marne and Aisne and at Ypres, Smith-Dorrien became commander of the Second Army in the December reorganization of the BEF. However, he was blamed for the failure of a diversionary attack near Mount Kemmel in March 1915 and matters came to a head during the Second Battle of Ypres when Smith-Dorrien suggested falling back to a more tenable line close to Ypres itself. French refused and gave Second Army to Plumer, relieving Smith-Dorrien on May 6 1915. This was Smith-Dorrien's final field command and the BEF thereby lost the services of an able tactician. Ironically, Plumer's first task was to withdraw, just as his predecessor had proposed. *PJS*.

Smolensk, Battles of (1941 and 1943). Smolensk's central position on the main Moscow highway ensured that the city and the region around it were vital objectives during the German invasion of the Soviet Union in June 1941. Field Marshal von Bock's Army Group Centre advanced through Belorussia, bearing down upon Marshal Timoshenko's West Front. Vitebsk fell on July 9 and Guderian's Second and Hoth's Third Panzer Groups raced towards Smolensk, cutting off whole Soviet armies. In reply, Timoshenko mounted several counter attacks but, by the end of July, a large body of his command had been caught in a pocket around Smolensk. Soviet losses included 3,000 tanks and 300,000 men taken prisoner. The delay imposed upon the German advance was to prove crucial and Zhukov, the recently appointed commander of the Reserve Front, gained valuable time to prepare the defence of Moscow. Two years later the roles were reversed and Army Group Centre fought desperately to contain the 1943 Soviet summer offensive. Sokolovsky's Western Front began its attack on August 7 but even when joined by Yeremenko's Kalinin Front, the advance eventually stalled. Throughout the rest of the month, the Red Army battered its way through strong German defences until, on September 15, the battle reached its final phase and, on the 25th, the last German units were driven out of Smolensk. While the battle had proved to be costly for the Soviet forces, the Red Army could withstand such attritional tactics far better than the Germans with their limited resources of manpower. *MS*.

Smuts, Field Marshal Jan Christiaan (1870–1950). South African. A Cape Colony lawyer in 1899, Smuts sought to avert the Second Boer War by negotiation with the British. In 1900 he joined De La Rey on commando in the Transvaal, and in 1901–02 headed a guerrilla force in Cape Colony, skilfully evading British columns but failing to stir up general rebellion. As Botha's major supporter, he helped negotiate the peace treaty of Vereeniging, May 1902. With the establishment of the Union of South Africa, 1910, he became Premier Botha's Minister of De-

Jan Smuts: from guerrilla to PM

fence, laying the foundations of South Africa's armed forces.

In 1914 Smuts greatly assisted Botha in the suppression of the pro-German revolt led by De Wet. He was Botha's second-in-command in the German South West Africa campaign, 1915, and in 1916 was Imperial C-in-C during the East African campaign. In January 1917 he went to London as South African representative in the Imperial War Cabinet; co-opted into the British War Cabinet by Lloyd George, he produced the "Smuts Report", August 1917, influential in the foundation of the RAF as an independent service (*see* the essay THE EMERGENCE OF AIR POWER, pp.195-197). Postwar, he was a leader in the creation of the League of Nations.

Smuts succeeded Botha as Premier in 1919, but his advocacy (following Cecil Rhodes) of South Africa's expansion into a great multi-racial (albeit White-dominated) African state within the British empire alienated many Afrikaners, and in 1924 he was unseated by the Nationalist Party of Gen James Hertzog (1866-1942). Forming a coalition with Hertzog in 1933, Smuts became Deputy-Premier: in September 1939, when Hertzog favoured neutrality, Smuts won the crucial debate that regained him the Premiership and ensured South Africa's vital contribution (especially in the East and North African and Italian campaigns) to the Allied cause. During World War II, , Smuts (created Field Marshal, 1941) was a valued adviser to Churchill and the War Cabinet, attending the Cairo Conference, 1943. He assisted in the drafting of the United Nations Charter at the San Francisco Conference, April–June 1945. *RO'N*.

S

Snorkel. Tube by which diesel-electric submarines can proceed on diesels or use them to recharge batteries when submerged at periscope depth, thereby greatly increasing submerged speed and range. Dutch invention adopted first by Germans.

Solid fuel. The best way of fuelling a long-range ballistic missile is with solid mixtures of fuel and oxidant, e.g. polybutadiene acrylic acid, polyurethane or even nitrocellulose and nitroglycerine with ammonium perchlorate. This requires advanced explosive handling techniques and the Soviet Union has lagged behind the USA and France in deploying reliable solid-fuelled missiles. Solid-fuel missiles are easily stored in silos or on board submarines.

Flying Fortress over the Solomons, 1942

Solomon Islands campaign (1942–44). The twin chain of islands comprising the Solomons lies in the Southwest Pacific east of New Guinea, extending for *c*900 miles (1,450 km) from northwest to southeast. From early 1942, this British/Australian protectorate was occupied unopposed by the Japanese, to be used as bases for attacks on Australia and on the Allies' Pacific supply lanes. On August 7 1942, the invasion of Guadalcanal marked the opening of the first Allied offensive in the Pacific, beginning a drive towards the major Japanese base at Rabaul, New Britain. In an attritional campaign which, by early 1944, Japan proved unable to sustain, major air and sea battles were fought in the Solomons and some of the most bitter land combat of World War II was waged in their mountainous, malarial, jungle terrain; notably on Guadalcanal; Rendova and Vella Lavella in the New Georgia group (invaded

and secured in June–August 1943); and Bougainville and the Treasury Islands (invaded October–November 1943). *RO'N*.

Somaliland, British, Italian invasion of (August 3–18 1940). Italians troops under Lt Gen Nasi defeated the small British garrison at Tug Argan on August 11–12, and forced the territory's evacuation by the 18th. It was reoccupied by the British in March 1941.

Somaliland, Italian, British invasion of (February 1941). Gen Alan Cunningham advanced from Kenya with 1st South African Division directed on Moyale, and 12th African Division along the coast. The River Juba was crossed on February 19, and Mogadishu, the capital, fell on the 24th.

Somerville, Adm of the Fleet Sir James Fownes (1882–1949). Br. Invalided out of the navy early 1939. Volunteered to help Ramsay at Dover during the Dunkirk operation. Appointed Commander of Force H at Gibraltar, he immediately had the problem of dealing with the French fleet at Mers-El-Kébir. Negotiations failed and heavy damage was inflicted on the French. Force H then took the war to the Italians, fighting convoys through to Malta, repulsing a superior Italian force at Cape Spartivento and bombarding the Italian coast. Force H also took part in the abortive attempt at Dakar, and played a vital part in the *Bismarck* chase. In March 1942 Somerville was transferred to command the new Eastern Fleet in the Indian Ocean, and forced into the uncongenial task of keeping it in being by avoiding superior Japanese forces. In 1944 he went to Washington as head of the naval delegation. *DJL*.

Somme, Battles of the (1916 and 1918). In December 1915, it was agreed to mount a joint Franco-British offensive the following year. The decision to attack astride the Somme was made principally because that river marked the junction of the French and British armies on the Western Front, although there were no obvious strategic objectives immediately behind the German lines and the Germans here had built defences

Anglo-French force on Somme, 1918

of immense strength. When the Battle of Verdun began in February 1916, however, the Somme attack assumed a new importance as a means of relieving pressure on the French Army, another difference being that the British now had the main role in Picardy.

Haig, the British c-in-c, intended that, in the first stage of the offensive, Gen Rawlinson's Fourth Army should overrun the German front defences from Serre to Montauban, as well as their second position on the high ground between Ginchy, Pozières and the Ancre, and on the slopes before Miraumont. Once the third position in front of Flers and Le Sars was breached, Bapaume would be threatened and the path opened for Gough's Reserve Army to advance northward, rolling up the German lines towards Arras. Rawlinson, to whom Haig left the detailed planning and conduct of the attack, was more pessimistic about the prospects of a quick breakthrough, favouring a methodical "bite and hold" advance with the artillery preparing the way for each step. Rawlinson relied on a massive preliminary bombardment to ensure the success of the initial assault and, fearing that the inexperienced soldiers of the New Army divisions could not master subtle tactics, he not only allowed an over-rigid battle plan to be imposed in some corps sectors but also dictated that the infantry should go forward in long, close-formed lines.

The attack was launched at 0730 hours on July 1 1916 after a week-long artillery bombardment which largely failed to cut the German wire or harm the defenders in their dugouts. Consequently, in most places, the German machine-gunners were able to emerge from shelter in time to decimate the oncoming waves of British infantry. The only substantial British success on the first day was in the south where, helped by a creeping barrage and an advance on their right by the French – who employed more imaginative tactics – 18th and 30th Divisions took all their objectives, including Montauban, and 7th Division captured Mametz. The 36th (Ulster) Division, attacking with great dash and gallantry at Thiepval, actually seized the formidable Schwaben Redoubt but were forced to withdraw by nightfall because of lack of progress on their flanks. Similarly, 56th (London) Division penetrated the German defences in the diversionary attack at Gommecourt yet were compelled to retire when the neighbouring 46th Division was unable to make headway. The limited advance on the right – about a mile (1.5km) deep and 3.5 miles (5.5km) wide – was all that Haig and Rawlinson had to show for 57,470 casualties, the biggest losses ever suffered by the British army in a single day.

Nevertheless, the offensive continued until November 19 1916. In a dawn attack on July 14, men of the New Armies demonstrated their real abilities when, following a night assembly in No Man's Land, a 6,000-yd (5,500m) stretch of the German second position between Longueval and Bazentin le Petit was taken at one bound, but nearby Delville Wood was not finally cleared until August 27 and High Wood was secured as late as mid-September. Pozières, however, fell to the Australians late in July. By August the offensive had developed into a grim battle of attrition and it was only on September 15, when tanks were used for the first time, that British, Canadian and New Zealand units broke into the German third position at Flers-Courcelette. At the end of the offensive the British were still some 3 miles (5km) from Bapaume, and Serre – a first-day objective – remained in German hands. British and Imperial casualties on the Somme in 1916 totalled 419,654 while the French, to the south, lost 204,253. Estimates of German casualties vary between 450,000 and 680,000, although there is little doubt that 1916 seriously weakened the German forces in the west.

After manpower shortages and the adoption of a new flexible defence system had contributed to the German decision to retire to the Hindenburg Line in the early spring of 1917, relative peace descended on the Somme area for a year. Then, during their March 1918 offensive, the Germans swept back across the old battlefield, with British Third Army evacuating Bapaume on March 24 and Albert two days later, although a defensive line was established west of the latter town. On March 30 and April 4–5, German Second and Eighteenth Armies made a determined but unsuccessful bid to reach Amiens. Employing tanks themselves for the first time, the Germans came closest to Amiens on April 24 when they briefly held Villers-Bretonneux but, as a result of an Australian counterattack, they had been ejected by noon the next day. The opposing armies passed across the Somme battlefield once more between August 21 and September 3 1918 in the Battles of Albert and Bapaume. Having pierced German Second Army's front east of Amiens on August 8, the British Fourth Army, under Rawlinson, recaptured the ground won at such heavy cost two years before and then lost again earlier in 1918. Albert was taken on August 22, Pozières fell on August 24 and Bapaume was entered by the New Zealand Division on August 29. Thus in only one week the British had advanced further than they had in five months in 1916. The capture of Péronne and Mont St Quentin by the Australian Corps at the beginning of September 1918 heralded the end of the fighting in the Somme region during World War I. *PJS*.

Sonar. Sound detection of submerged submarines, either active (original British term ASDIC – Anglo/French invention 1918) or passive (hydrophones).

Sopwith F1 Camel (Br, WWI). Single-seat fighter; used by RFC and RNAS. First production deliveries May 1917. Production, 5,651. One 130/140hp Clerget, 110hp Le Rhône, 150hp BR1, 100hp Gnome Monosoupape engine; max. speed 113.5mph (183kph); two 0.303in machine guns, 100lb (45kg) bombs.

Sopwith 2F1 Camel (Br, WWI). Single-seat shipboard fighter. Prototype flew early 1917; generally similar to F1, but had detachable rear fuselage, redisposed guns. Allotted to warships, flying from tiny platforms. First carrier-borne strike in history, Tondern, July 19 1918; Zeppelin *L53* destroyed August 11 1918. Production, at least 275. One 150hp BR1 or 130hp Clerget engine; max. speed 121.5mph (196kph); two 0.303in machine guns, 100lb (45kg) bombs.

Sopwith 1½ Strutter (Br, WWI). Two-seat fighter-reconnaissance/single-seat bomber. Ordered for RNAS and RFC; deliveries spring 1916, many RNAS two-seaters transferred to RFC for Battle of Somme. Single-seat bomber version used operationally by RNAS only. Both versions extensively used France, Italy, Macedonia, Aegean, from ships. Used by French and US services. Production, Britain 1,294; France approx. 4,500. One 110/130hp Clerget or 110/135hp Le Rhône engine; max. speed 104mph (166kph); two 0.303in machine guns, 260lb (117kg) bombs (British) or 18 × 120mm bombs or equivalent (French).

Sopwith Pup (Br, WWI). Single-seat fighter. Production for RNAS and RFC; deliveries from September 1916. An aircraft of exceptional controllability. Pioneered practical deck flying; one flown from HMS *Yarmouth's* flight platform (15ft 6in [4.72m] long) shot down Zeppelin *L23*, August 21 1917. Production, 1,776. One 80hp Le Rhône, Gnome or Clerget, or 100hp Gnome Monosoupape engine; max. speed 111.5mph (179kph); one 0.303in machine gun, or eight Le Prieur rockets.

Sorge, Richard (1895–1944). Ger. Far Eastern correspondent of *Frankfurter Zeitung* in 1930s; a spy reporting to the German Embassy in Tokyo – but in reality a senior Soviet espionage officer. He is said to have given advance warning of "Barbarossa" and to have disclosed that Japan had no plans to strike into the USSR from Manchuria, but the influence upon Stalin remains debatable. Arrested in Tokyo, October 1941; executed, November 1944.

Souchez, Battle of (May 9 1915) *see* FESTUBERT, BATTLE OF.

Souphanouvong, Prince (b.1909). Laotian. The Vietnamese communists recruited Souphanouvong, a Lao engineer in Hanoi in 1945, to organize an anti-colonial movement in Laos beginning a long collaboration between Souphanouvong and the Vietnamese. In 1950 he broke with nationalists who accepted the limited independence conferred on Laos by France and proclaimed a resistance government headed by himself. He was a founding member of the Lao People's Revolutionary (Communist) Party and became head of the Lao Patriotic Front at its creation in 1956. Souphanouvong was the most visible Pathet Lao leader during the war years 1960–1973, nominally in charge of the Pathet Lao Army. He was chief spokesman for the Pathet Lao in negotiations with the Royal Lao government headed by his half-brother, Prince Souvanna Phouma. He became president of the Lao People's Democratic Republic upon its founding in December 1975. *WST*.

South Dakota. US battleship. Name ship of class of 16in battleships. Completed 1942. Suffered crippling power failure in action at Guadalcanal. Spent most of war in the Pacific.

South East Asia Command (SEAC). Formed after the Quebec conference ("Quadrant") in August 1943 with· Mountbatten as Supreme Commander, a US Deputy, and a substantial staff representing land, air and naval forces. HQ opened on November 1 1943 at Delhi and on April 15 1944 was transferred to Kandy, Ceylon: Mountbatten's critics emphasized its inordinate size. Originally it was expected that SEAC would mount combined operations to recover Japanese-occupied territories in Southeast Asia, but it soon became obvious that landing craft would not be supplied. The task would be mainly a land operation, predominantly British and Indian in personnel. During 1944, little advance was made, but early in 1945 SEAC became really operational. Mountbatten played a diplomatic and political role, with

Fourteenth Army as the fighting force. Among Mountbatten's personal decisions was one to recognize the Nationalist movement in Burma; his attempt to follow the same policy in Indonesia was blocked by Dutch intransigence. On August 15 1945 the boundaries of SEAC were extended to include the Dutch East Indies and French Indochina by order of MacArthur. Mountbatten handed over to Lt Gen Sir Montagu Stopford as Acting Supreme Commander, June 1946, and with the withdrawal of the British-Indian forces from Indonesia, SEAC ceased to exist on November 30 1946. *HT*.

South East Asia Lake Ocean River Delta Strategy (SEALORDS). Complemented Operation "Market Time", the blockade of the coast of South Vietnam during the Vietnam War, by attacking waterborne infiltration from Cambodia. This required intensive surveillance of the dense network of canals and rivers that criss-cross the Mekong delta from the Gulf of Siam to the outskirts of Saigon, in an attempt to blockade South Vietnam's land border. The strategy reorganized Operation "Game Warden", which had spread forces throughout the entire delta, by concentrating forces in a line against waterways in the border area. Beginning November 1968, SEALORDS deployed elements of three US Navy riverine assault forces and South Vietnamese naval craft along a 200-mile (325km) barrier. *WST*.

South East Asia Treaty Organization (SEATO). On September 8 1954, representatives of Australia, Britain, France, New Zealand, Pakistan, Philippines, Thailand and the USA signed a treaty at Manila, hoping to create a NATO-style organization. Their disparate interests resulted in SEATO's disbandment in the 1970s.

Southern France, Allied invasion of (1944) *see* FRANCE, SOUTHERN, ALLIED INVASION OF.

South Georgia, Argentine invasion of (1982) *see* GEORGIA, SOUTH.

Southwest Africa campaign *see* GERMAN SOUTHWEST AFRICA CAMPAIGN.

Souvanna Phouma, Prince (1901–1983). Laotian. Half-brother of Souphanouvong; intermittent terms as Premier after 1949. The centre of efforts to unite Laos through coalition government, 1960–73, but from 1964 accepted growing US presence and cooperated with military rightists. His Provisional Government of National Union collapsed in December 1975.

Soviet military assistance for North Korea. Some 250 advisers remained with the NKPA when Soviet troops withdrew, 1948, and Russia sold North Korea 150 T-34 tanks and 100 aircraft. The Russians re-equipped the NKPA after its defeats of 1950 and Soviets piloted MiGs against the Americans. According to US intelligence, there were 3,000 Soviet advisers with the communists in 1951.

Spaatz, Gen Carl ("Tooey") (1891–1974). US. Commander, US Strategic Air Forces, Europe 1944–45; Pacific 1945; perhaps, the greatest air commander of World War II. After command experience in North Africa and the Mediterranean, he succeeded Eaker as Commanding General, Eight Air Force, UK, following the Schweinfurt disaster. He maintained the daylight offensive, but not Eaker's tactics, seizing on the long-range fighter not merely as an escort to bombers but as an extension of their role, deploying the P-51 Mustang equipped with drop-tanks. He directed his bombers primarily to bring up enemy fighters, and his long-range fighters primarily to engage and destroy them, recognizing that the real target was the enemy air force in being and the essential prerequisite to victory its defeat in the air. It was mainly to him that the Germans owed their inability to control the daylight air at the time of the Normandy landings and afterwards.

Although Spaatz's Pacific command entailed responsibility for the atomic raids, Europe provided the greatest challenges to his original genius as a commander. He was appointed commander of the USAAF, February 1946, and in September 1947 became COS of the newly-formed USAF. *ANF*.

The nuclear stalemate

Lynn E Davis
Fellow, The Foreign Policy Institute
School of Advanced International Studies, Washington DC

In August 1945, the United States detonated atomic bombs on the cities of Hiroshima and Nagasaki with the military purpose of gaining the surrender of Japan. At that time the USA alone possessed nuclear weapons, and it used them, as it had its other weapons, to destroy the Japanese political will to fight. Whether or not the atomic bombs were decisive in ending the war is a matter of debate, but the tremendous shock of their advent changed the nature of warfare and the ways nations would henceforth undertake to assure peace.

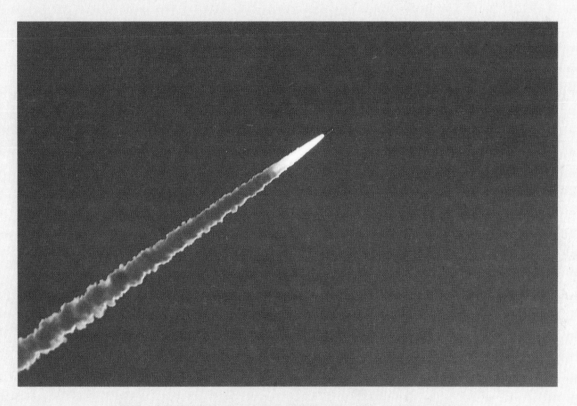

Wildcat missile test at Cape Kennedy, Florida (January 1987), a launch site most commonly associated with the space-bound rocket. Space travel and exploration were first made possible through military research into, and development of, this type of propulsion.

With the Baruch plan of the later 1940s, the USA briefly flirted with the idea of international control of atomic energy. But as East-West relations deteriorated, neither superpower was prepared to relinquish this new means of mass destruction. The Soviet Union vigorously pursued its own nuclear weapons programmes, and in August 1949 tested its first atomic bomb. Since the end of the American nuclear monopoly, American superiority in nuclear forces in the 1950s has been replaced by Soviet-American mutual vulnerability in the 1960s and by strategic parity in the 1970s. The 1980s saw the possibility that the build-up of nuclear weapons might end, and even offered visions of their ultimate elimination. Throughout these 40 years, nuclear weapons have been simultaneously the guarantor of each superpower's ultimate security, as well as the main threat to their security and to world peace.

The first nuclear weapons were atomic (fission) bombs, but in the 1950s both superpowers developed the more powerful hydrogen (fusion) bomb. While uncertainties exist as to the potential consequences of a nuclear war, estimates of the effects of a typical nuclear weapon – a one-megaton warhead, the equivalent of 1,000,000 tons of TNT – detonated on a major city in the USA are of about 250,000 immediate fatalities, up to 200,000 additional deaths from severe burns, and several hundreds of thousands injured. In the late 1980s, there were some 50,000 nuclear weapons in the arsenals of the USA, the USSR, Britain, France, and the People's Republic of China.

Nuclear weapons can be delivered with speed – a matter of minutes and hours – and can inflict their destruction on cities without the nation's military forces having been first defeated. They have accentuated the elements of surprise and terror in warfare, threatening to destroy not only military forces but also entire civilizations.

The unique characteristics of nuclear weapons required new thinking about the objectives they could serve and the means of avoiding their destructive powers. Strategies

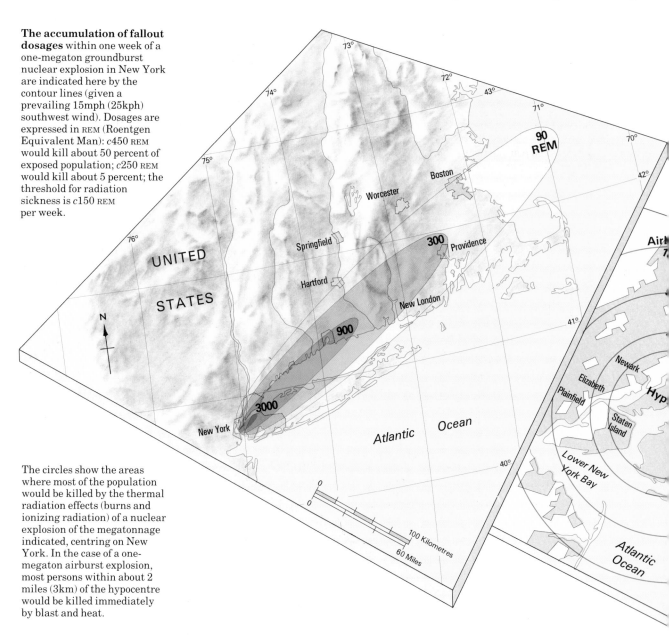

The accumulation of fallout dosages within one week of a one-megaton groundburst nuclear explosion in New York are indicated here by the contour lines (given a prevailing 15mph (25kph) southwest wind). Dosages are expressed in REM (Roentgen Equivalent Man): c450 REM would kill about 50 percent of exposed population; c250 REM would kill about 5 percent; the threshold for radiation sickness is c150 REM per week.

The circles show the areas where most of the population would be killed by the thermal radiation effects (burns and ionizing radiation) of a nuclear explosion of the megatonnage indicated, centring on New York. In the case of a one-megaton airburst explosion, most persons within about 2 miles (3km) of the hypocentre would be killed immediately by blast and heat.

had to be designed to prevent the use of these weapons against one's own territory, as well as one's friends and allies. The role of offensive and defensive nuclear forces had to be defined. Plans had to be devised for the use of nuclear weapons if war should occur, and for the structuring and targeting of nuclear forces.

Since the early 1950s, every new development in the nuclear technology and capabilities of each side has provoked a debate in the West over these issues. Fortunately the strategic theories have never been put to the test. The problem is that while it is not possible to have complete confidence in the success of one's nuclear strategy, the consequences of its failure would be catastrophic.

Strategic theories – the American approach

US nuclear strategy has been based upon the fundamental assumption that no political or military objective would be worth the devastation of a nuclear war, and that preventing nuclear war must be the highest priority of US national security policy.

Conceptually, four approaches exist to preventing nuclear war. First, rhetorically the USA and the Soviet Union call for a world without nuclear weapons – but political and ideological differences stand in the way. A second approach would be to have the capability to destroy by pre-emptive attack all the other side's nuclear weapons. However, given the destructive capability of only a few surviving weapons, it is extremely difficult to achieve such a dis-arming first strike, and the potential victim is unlikely to permit such a situation to develop.

A third approach – known as deterrence through denial – is through defences to prevent the other side from achieving any political or military objectives in a nuclear attack. Given the destructiveness of nuclear weapons, such an approach would require essentially perfect defences, which have, to date, proven technically impossible.

Thus, prevention of nuclear war has by default had to depend upon a fourth approach: deterrence through the threat of unacceptable punishment, or the strategy of nuclear retaliation. The USA threatens with its offensive forces that any use of nuclear weapons would result in costs far beyond any potential gains – costs in terms of the destruction not only of cities but also of the military forces and command structure of the Soviet Union. In *The Absolute Weapon* (1946), Bernard Brodie captured the essence of this deterrent strategy when he wrote:

Thus, the first and most vital step in any American security program for the age of atomic bombs is to take measures to guarantee to ourselves in the case of attack the possibility of retaliation in kind. The writer in making that statement is not for the moment concerned about who will *win* the next war in which atomic bombs have been used. Thus far the chief purpose of our military has been to win wars. From now on its chief purpose must be to avert them. It can have almost no other useful purpose.

Such a strategy must affect the perceptions of the enemy; and it assumes that he will act on the basis of rational calculation of costs and gains in using nuclear weapons. Some think that deterrence is assured simply by the existence of nuclear weapons, but most believe that

Atomic destruction at Hiroshima: a photograph dating from March 1946. "Little Boy", the atomic bomb detonated some 2,000ft (610m) above Hiroshima on August 6 1945, produced an explosion equivalent to 20,000 tons of TNT (trinitrotoluene), or an explosive yield of 20 kilotons (KT). Such an explosive yield would today – when the Soviet SS-18 intercontinental ballistic missile (ICBM) carries a 25-megaton (MT) warhead (i.e. with a yield equivalent to 25,000,000 tons of TNT) – class the Hiroshima bomb as a "small" weapon, but nevertheless its effect was devastating. The initial heat flash, some 10,000,000 degrees Fahrenheit at the core, and blast are believed to have killed more than 60,000 of some 320,000 persons in the city; most buildings within 4,000yd (3,550m) of the hypocentre were destroyed. "Fat Man", the 22KT atomic bomb dropped on Nagasaki on August 9, caused less widespread damage because of the city's hilly terrain, but still killed some 25,000 persons.

specific kinds of nuclear capabilities are necessary so as to be able to inflict the threatened punishment after surviving an enemy first strike. In addition, the threat to carry out the punishment must be credible.

To implement its strategy of retaliation, the USA has deployed a variety of nuclear weapon systems – long-range bombers and ballistic missiles capable of penetrating Soviet defences – and has assured their survivability by dispersing them on land and at sea. Because of uncertainties as to what is necessary to affect Soviet calculations, nuclear planners have tended to rely on worst-case scenarios and to hedge against technological surprises. As a result, the US strategic nuclear arsenal in the late 1980s included more than 10,000 strategic nuclear weapons deployed on a triad of nuclear forces: ICBMS, SLBMS and bombers. These strategic nuclear forces are capable of destroying not only soft targets such as cities and military forces, but also hardened targets such

A US Minuteman III ICBM rests on a shock-sprung mounting in its fully-hardened underground silo, at instant readiness for firing. Since Minuteman became operational in 1962, developments in missile accuracy have made such ICBM installations increasingly vulnerable to attack, and

methods of mobile deployment – firing from railway cars and from cross-country vehicles – are being adopted by both the USA and USSR.

Silo surveillance system: a two-acre fenced-off area around the silo has sensors to detect intrusion

Movable concrete lid – debris collection system ensures movement

Minuteman III silo

The concrete cover of the Minuteman silo is shown open in the illustration. Very little of the silo is visible from the surface: about the only notable above-ground feature is the "dish" of the silo surveillance system. These are the latest schemes for reducing vulnerability.

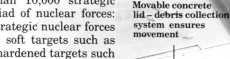

Warhead and guidance system maintenance area

as missile silos and command and control bunkers. To provide as capable and cost-effective a force as possible, the USA introduced in the 1970s land and sea-based missiles with multiple independently targeted warheads (MIRVS). To penetrate Soviet air defences, "stealth" or radar-evading technologies were developed for US bombers, as well as short-range attack missiles (SRAM) and air-launched cruise missiles (ALCMS). The USA has also deployed sea-launched cruise missiles (SLCMS) with nuclear warheads, and thousands of theatre nuclear weapons on land and in ships and aircraft worldwide.

The Soviet approach

In 1985, President Reagan and General Secretary Gorbachev agreed "that a nuclear war cannot be won and must never be fought". But not surprisingly, the Soviet approach to nuclear strategy differs from that of the USA, for it is influenced by Marxist-Leninist theory, Russian and Soviet history, and the geopolitical position of the Soviet Union on the Eurasian landmass. It places emphasis on pre-emption and strategic defences, as well as on retaliation with offensive forces.

Soviet nuclear strategy and planning proceeds from the conviction that the threat of nuclear war persists and that the Soviet Union must prepare for its eventuality. Soviet leaders, therefore, think about and plan to fight a nuclear war, believing such preparations are the best way to deter. Their stated objective in a nuclear war, following from their ideology, is to win – although they have given little indication of what would constitute victory. While consistently rejecting the concept of stability based on mutual

Side suspension buffers to protect missile from displacement

From the launch control centre (LCC) *lower right)*, two officers control 10 Minuteman silos. If a launch is ordered, they must open a safe, check the launch codes and each take a key. The keys must be turned within two seconds of each other and held for two more; if these orders are confirmed by a second LCC, the missile is launched.

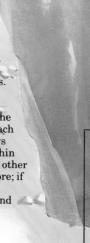

Shock isolated floor

Lower silo, 25 **deep**

A US Minuteman ICBM (*right*) is launched from its underground silo. Minuteman III, operational since 1970, carries three independently-targetable 350KT warheads (Mk-12A version). (*Below right*) Launch of a Trident SLBM, carried by US *Ohio*-class submarines.

Maintenance access hatch

The launch control centre, with its environmental stack visible above-ground, would be at least 3 miles (5km) from the silo.

Two-man Launch Control Centre (LCC) – 15m (50ft) underground

vulnerability, Soviet political and military leaders do, however, appear to recognize that situation as a reality – if not a particularly desirable one – given the destructiveness of nuclear weapons.

The Soviet Union prepares to destroy quickly the enemy's forces and war-making potential and to ensure the survival of its own structure of government and industrial base. Soviet doctrine is firmly rooted in the notion that the best defence is a good offence. The Soviet nuclear force posture emphasizes land-based ICBMS, but also includes sea-based missiles and long-range bombers. It incorporates the most modern technologies, including highly accurate MIRV warheads. In the late 1980s, deployed Soviet strategic nuclear warheads numbered more than 10,000. In planning for theatre conflicts, the Soviets, in their writings, manifest a distinct preference for non-nuclear contingencies. But they prepare for both an escalating nuclear conflict and the massive use of nuclear strikes at the outset of a war. In military exercises, they practise pre-emptive conventional and nuclear strikes upon warning of an imminent NATO conventional or nuclear attack.

The Soviets have also pursued a variety of defensive programmes to limit damage to the Soviet economy, population, war-making capability and leadership in the event of nuclear war. They have a nationwide civil defence programme and have deployed anti-ballistic missiles (ABMS) and extensive air defences around Moscow. However, in 1972 the Soviet Union signed the ABM Treaty which bans nationwide ballistic missile defences and, in a 1974 protocol to the treaty, limits deployment of ABMS to only one deployment area and 100 missiles. Why each side signed the ABM Treaty is a matter of debate, but the effect has been to ensure the mutual vulnerability of each to nuclear attack. As a result, the nuclear strategies of both superpowers have relied primarily on offensive nuclear forces. Each has the capability of inflicting massive damage on the other. The advent of nuclear weapons has thus given the offence a predominance unknown in the past history of warfare, and at the same time has had the effect of codifying the existence of the nuclear stalemate.

Evolution of the West's strategy

The fact of the nuclear stalemate has not, however, relieved the West of having to design specific strategies to deter various kinds of potential attacks, and to plan for the possibility that deterrence might fail. With each major improvement in Soviet nuclear capability, the West found itself debating anew how best to assure a credible deterrent. As a result, the West's strategy has been developed and refined in some significant, and at times controversial, ways.

American nuclear superiority

Superiority in nuclear weapons combined with an invulnerability to Soviet attack provided the basis in the 1950s for the US strategy of massive retaliation. For all possible attacks – nuclear or conventional, limited or large-scale – against the USA and its allies, the USA threatened all-out nuclear response. Alternative strategies were debated: for example, in 1950 a study by the National Security Council (NSC-68) recommended the deployment of "strong and ready" conventional forces around the periphery of the Soviet Union to support the policy of worldwide containment. But in the aftermath of the Korean War, with its frustrations in fighting a conventional war, and given the high costs of a conventional defence, the Eisenhower administration adopted the "New Look" strategy. Secretary of State John Foster Dulles announced in 1954 that the USA would "depend primarily upon a great capacity to retaliate instantly, by means and at places of our own choosing". In fact, in the early 1950s the USA had deployed some conventional forces to Europe and had developed shorter-range tactical nuclear weapons, thus gaining the capability to retaliate flexibly against a potential attack. But, rhetorically, US strategy was one of massive nuclear retaliation. Dulles also enunciated the fundamentals of a deterrent strategy: that a potential aggressor be left in no doubt that he would be certain to suffer damage outweighing any potential gain from aggression. Strategic bombing provided the means of carrying out this strategy.

American vulnerability
Developments in Soviet nuclear forces quickly provoked doubts about the credibility of the strategy of massive retaliation. In the late 1950s, the Soviets acquired a capability, through long-range bombers and ICBMS, to attack the USA. A strategy of massive nuclear retaliation still seemed adequate to deter such attacks, but the possibility of a surprise attack provoked concern over the survivability of US retaliatory forces. In "The Delicate Balance of Terror" (*Foreign Affairs*, 1959), Albert Wohlstetter suggested that serious problems existed for the US second-strike capability in surviving an enemy strike, in communicating the decision to retaliate, in penetrating enemy defences, and in destroying its targets. Americans also feared that the Soviets might achieve nuclear superiority following their launching of the "Sputnik" satellite and their first ICBM test. In response, the US undertook a major strategic modernization programme, involving the new Minuteman ICBMS and Polaris SLBMS, to ensure a survivable retaliatory capability as well as to prevent the Soviet Union from achieving any significant quantitative or qualitative advantages.

Concern also arose about the possibility of war as Soviet military power expanded and crises developed around the world, especially over the status of Berlin and the introduction of Soviet missiles into Cuba. Herman Kahn sought to get people "thinking about the unthinkable" of nuclear war, and in the early 1960s Secretary of Defense Robert McNamara concluded that the primary objective, if deterrence were to fail, would be to try to limit the damage inflicted upon the USA and its allies. He defined different ways this might be achieved: passive civil defence, active bomber and ballistic missile defence; and an offensive capability (counterforce) to destroy Soviet military forces remaining after a Soviet first strike. In his famous Ann Arbor speech in 1962, McNamara suggested that the principal military objective in the event of nuclear war should be the destruction of enemy military forces, not civilians, in the hope of deterring an attack upon civil society even in a war. But at the same time, to determine the number and kind of strategic nuclear forces the USA should acquire, McNamara called for an "Assured Destruction" capability – that is, the capability to ride out an enemy first strike and to respond by inflicting unacceptable damage (variously estimated as destruction of 20–33 percent of the enemy's civilian population and 50–75 percent of his industrial capacity).

Critics of McNamara's counterforce strategy argued that the capability to destroy Soviet nuclear forces

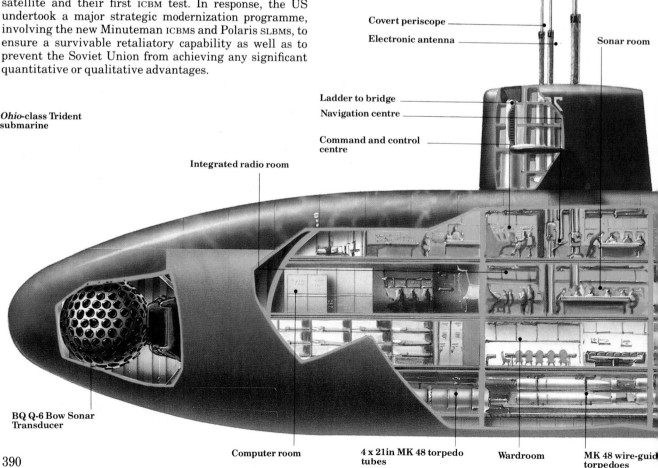

Ohio-class Trident submarine

Main observation periscope

Covert periscope

Electronic antenna

Sonar room

Ladder to bridge

Navigation centre

Command and control centre

Integrated radio room

BQ Q-6 Bow Sonar Transducer

Computer room

4 x 21in MK 48 torpedo tubes

Wardroom

MK 48 wire-guided torpedoes

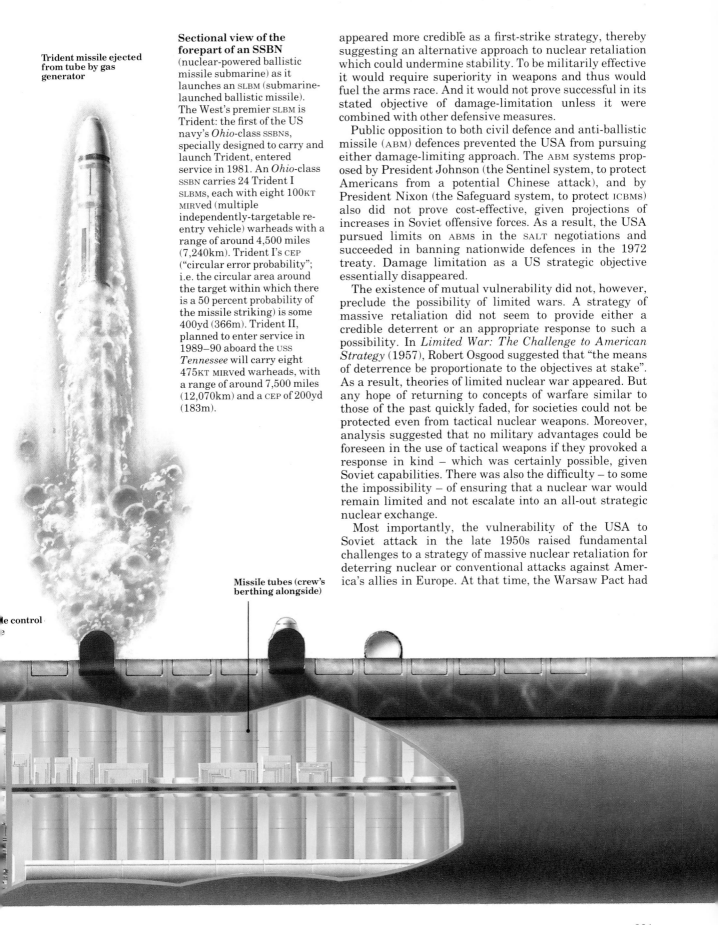

Trident missile ejected from tube by gas generator

Sectional view of the forepart of an SSBN (nuclear-powered ballistic missile submarine) as it launches an SLBM (submarine-launched ballistic missile). The West's premier SLBM is Trident: the first of the US navy's *Ohio*-class SSBNS, specially designed to carry and launch Trident, entered service in 1981. An *Ohio*-class SSBN carries 24 Trident I SLBMS, each with eight 100KT MIRved (multiple independently-targetable re-entry vehicle) warheads with a range of around 4,500 miles (7,240km). Trident I's CEP ("circular error probability"; i.e. the circular area around the target within which there is a 50 percent probability of the missile striking) is some 400yd (366m). Trident II, planned to enter service in 1989–90 aboard the USS *Tennessee* will carry eight 475KT MIRved warheads, with a range of around 7,500 miles (12,070km) and a CEP of 200yd (183m).

Missile tubes (crew's berthing alongside)

le control
e

appeared more credible as a first-strike strategy, thereby suggesting an alternative approach to nuclear retaliation which could undermine stability. To be militarily effective it would require superiority in weapons and thus would fuel the arms race. And it would not prove successful in its stated objective of damage-limitation unless it were combined with other defensive measures.

Public opposition to both civil defence and anti-ballistic missile (ABM) defences prevented the USA from pursuing either damage-limiting approach. The ABM systems proposed by President Johnson (the Sentinel system, to protect Americans from a potential Chinese attack), and by President Nixon (the Safeguard system, to protect ICBMS) also did not prove cost-effective, given projections of increases in Soviet offensive forces. As a result, the USA pursued limits on ABMS in the SALT negotiations and succeeded in banning nationwide defences in the 1972 treaty. Damage limitation as a US strategic objective essentially disappeared.

The existence of mutual vulnerability did not, however, preclude the possibility of limited wars. A strategy of massive retaliation did not seem to provide either a credible deterrent or an appropriate response to such a possibility. In *Limited War: The Challenge to American Strategy* (1957), Robert Osgood suggested that "the means of deterrence be proportionate to the objectives at stake". As a result, theories of limited nuclear war appeared. But any hope of returning to concepts of warfare similar to those of the past quickly faded, for societies could not be protected even from tactical nuclear weapons. Moreover, analysis suggested that no military advantages could be foreseen in the use of tactical weapons if they provoked a response in kind – which was certainly possible, given Soviet capabilities. There was also the difficulty – to some the impossibility – of ensuring that a nuclear war would remain limited and not escalate into an all-out strategic nuclear exchange.

Most importantly, the vulnerability of the USA to Soviet attack in the late 1950s raised fundamental challenges to a strategy of massive nuclear retaliation for deterring nuclear or conventional attacks against America's allies in Europe. At that time, the Warsaw Pact had superiority in conventional forces and was deploying new intermediate range missiles (IRBMS) which threatened Europe but not the USA. The burden of deterring an attack in Europe fell primarily upon US strategic nuclear forces, but serious doubts arose as to whether Americans would be prepared to risk the devastation of their cities in using these weapons to protect their allies.

The West's response was to introduce more flexibility and options into its strategy and nuclear forces. To deter a Soviet nuclear attack against Europe, the USA deployed thousands of tactical nuclear weapons there, so as to be able to respond in kind within the theatre. Given NATO's inferiority to the Warsaw Pact in conventional forces, the USA further raised the possibility that these tactical nuclear weapons would be used first if NATO were threatened by defeat in a conventional war. The resulting US superiority in theatre nuclear weapons made the threatened American response more credible and suggested that the Soviet Union could not gain a military advantage by using its tactical nuclear forces. At the same

time, to reduce the requirement for an early, and possibly first, use of nuclear weapons, the USA sought to build up NATO's conventional forces. After considerable controversy – and the withdrawal of France from the integrated military structure – NATO in 1967 adopted a strategy of flexible response (MC-14/3). This called for three types of response, as set out in the *1979 Defense White Paper*, Federal Republic of Germany.

Direct Defense with the intention of preventing an aggressor from reaching his objective, in fact at the level of military conflict chosen by him. Then either the aggression fails, or the aggressor is confronted with the risk of escalation. NATO does not preclude the use of nuclear weapons.
Deliberate Escalation is intended to repulse an attack by changing the quality of the defensive operations

European nuclear deployment. Western: 400 warheads on American SLBMS assigned to SACEUR; one of four British Polaris A3TK SSBNS on patrol with 16 missiles (32

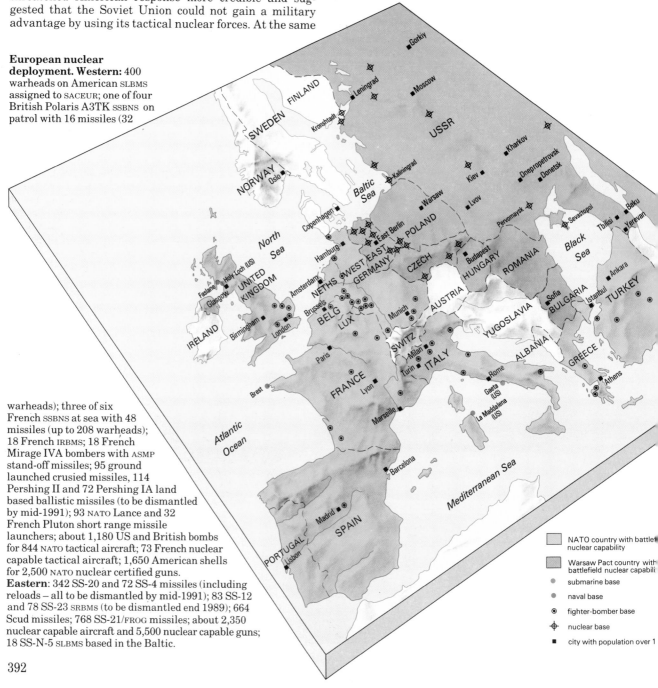

warheads); three of six French SSBNS at sea with 48 missiles (up to 208 warheads); 18 French IRBMS; 18 French Mirage IVA bombers with ASMP stand-off missiles; 95 ground launched crusied missiles, 114 Pershing II and 72 Pershing IA land based ballistic missiles (to be dismantled by mid-1991); 93 NATO Lance and 32 French Pluton short range missile launchers; about 1,180 US and British bombs for 844 NATO tactical aircraft; 73 French nuclear capable tactical aircraft; 1,650 American shells for 2,500 NATO nuclear certified guns.
Eastern: 342 SS-20 and 72 SS-4 missiles (including reloads – all to be dismantled by mid-1991); 83 SS-12 and 78 SS-23 SRBMS (to be dismantled end 1989); 664 Scud missiles; 768 SS-21/FROG missiles; about 2,350 nuclear capable aircraft and 5,500 nuclear capable guns; 18 SS-N-5 SLBMS based in the Baltic.

through the use of nuclear weapons or by expanding the regional scope of the conflict. The objective is to make the aggressor understand, through the politically-controlled selective use of nuclear weapons, that the prospects of success are no longer in proportion to the risk he incurs.

General Nuclear Response is directed mainly against the strategic potential of the aggressor and implies the employment of strategic nuclear weapons.

Having the flexibility to moderate and tailor its response would make more credible the West's threat of punishment in response to any conventional or nuclear attack in Europe. But the catastrophic consequences of a strategic nuclear response would be delayed, thereby raising another cause of concern among America's allies; namely, that a potential war and its devastation might be limited to Europe and US strategic nuclear forces "de-coupled" from Europe's defence. That concern led to a search for ways in which Europeans could participate in US decisions to use nuclear weapons, and also provide independently for their own security.

In 1962, the USA agreed in the Athens Guidelines to consult with its NATO allies on the use of nuclear weapons "time and circumstances permitting". Some US tactical nuclear weapons were deployed in Europe under bi-lateral Programs of Cooperation, whereby the host country owned and operated the delivery systems while the USA retained control over the weapons. The USA also sought to reassure Europeans through the Multilateral Force (MLF), which involved an internationally-manned surface and submarine fleet commanded by an American (Supreme Commander Atlantic) but operating under NATO Council guidance. The MLF proposal satisfied no one. West Germany remained concerned over the issue of nuclear control as the USA held a veto on its weapons. The French refused in principle to join any NATO nuclear force; the British were extremely reluctant to participate. The US

Congressional Joint Committee on Atomic Energy rejected the proposal because of uncertainties as to whether the USA could maintain effective control of its nuclear weapons. The Soviet Union also campaigned vigorously against the MLF, arguing that it represented a means of giving West Germany nuclear weapons. In its place, the USA agreed in 1966 to form the NATO Nuclear Planning Group for consultation and planning.

The nuclear weapons of Britain and France
Britain and France initially developed nuclear weapons in the late 1940s to enhance their own prestige and affirm their status as major powers. In the 1960s they deployed national nuclear forces to deter nuclear attacks against their own territories, as insurance against the unreliability of the American nuclear guarantee.

Britain began research on atomic weapons during World War II and participated, in a limited way, in the development of the American bomb. Collaboration was severely limited in the late 1940s when Congress prohibited the transfer of atomic secrets. The British government announced in 1948 its decision to develop its own nuclear weapons, and in the 1950s tested both atomic and hydrogen bombs. However, Britain became dependent upon the USA for nuclear delivery vehicles. Following the cancellation in 1962 of the Skybolt air-launched missile, the USA allowed Britain to purchase Polaris SLBMs: these, with long-range bombers, became the basis for the British independent nuclear deterrent. In 1980, Britain decided to modernize its submarine forces through the purchase of US Trident missiles, arguing, as it had in the past, that an independent nuclear force provides weapons of last resort and insures against the possibility of the Soviets doubting the credibility of the American nuclear guarantee. British nuclear submarines are assigned to SACEUR for planning and are targeted on Moscow and other Soviet cities.

The French independent nuclear deterrent (*force de frappe*) was a more direct response to concern over the

---

USA
640 SLBMs:
384 Trident C-4 and 256 Poseidon C-3, in 36 nuclear-powered ballistic missile submarines
5,632 warheads

1,000 ICBMs
450 Minuteman II, 511 Minuteman III, 39 Peacekeeper.
2,373 warheads

337 long-range bombers:
99 B-1 and 263 B-52, of which 158 B-52s carry air launched cruise missiles.
1,784

USSR
942 SLBMs
256 SS-N-6, 286 SS-N-8, 12 SS-N-17, 224 SS-N-18, 100 SS-N-20 and 64 SS-N-23 in 62 nuclear-powered ballistic missile submarines.
3,378 warheads.

1,386 ICBMs:
420 SS-11, 60 SS-13, 138 SS-17, 308 SS-18, 350 SS-19, 10 SS-24, 100 SS-25.
6,412 warheads

175 long-range bombers:
5 Bison and 170 Bears, of which 70 Bear-Hs carry AS-15 long-range cruise missiles.
805 warheads

Overall balance: USA – 2,002 launchers and 9,789 warheads
USSR – 2,503 launchers and 10,595 warheads

Comparative strategic nuclear strengths. Figures are for mid-1988 and based on those in *The Military Balance 1988–9* published by the International Institute For Strategic Studies. The warhead figures are based on American START counting rules. START will limit each side to 1,600 launchers and 6,000 warheads of which 4,900 may be on ballistic missiles. This will understate the actual numbers of nuclear warheads on each side as bombers can carry a number of free-fall bombs and short-range attack missiles. The current actual weapons delivery capabilities of the long-range bomber forces of both sides are almost 5,000 for the USA and only 800 for the USSR. Making up for this disadvantage is the Soviet medium bomber force targeted against Europe and Asia (1,020 aircraft), and the Soviet IRBM/MRBM force, now being dismantled but with 468 deployed SS-20 and SS-4 launchers (1,278 warheads) in mid-1988 The USA has 61 FB-111 medium-range bombers assigned to SAC; these are to be reassigned to Tactical Air Command which already operates 200 F-111s, 140 of which are based in Britain. Each side also deploys long-range sea launched cruise missiles (SLCMs). The USA has the TLAM-N Tomahawk on 46 submarines and 25 surface ships; the USSR has SS-N-21 missiles on about six submarines and a trials submarine with SS-N-24.

reliability of the American nuclear guarantee, although President de Gaulle in the 1960s also sought to reassert France's role in the world and leadership in Europe. According to General Pierre Gallois (*US Strategy and the Defense of Europe,* Orbis, 1963), "if resort to force no longer implies risking merely the loss of an expeditionary army, but hazards the very substance of national life, it is clear that such a risk can be taken only for oneself – and not for others, including even close allies."

In terms of deterring a potential Soviet attack, the French argued that an independent nuclear force creates uncertainty in the minds of enemy planners, increasing the possibility of a nuclear response by providing multiple centres of decision-making. The French theory of deterrence is based on threatening massive nuclear retaliation and rejects ideas of graduated nuclear escalation, like NATO's flexible response. French nuclear forces include long-range bombers, land- and sea-based strategic ballistic missiles and short-range tactical missiles. French targeting policy is uncertain (although probably similar to that of Britain), since the French eschew any consultation or coordination arrangements.

The USA objected to third-country nuclear forces, favouring defence expenditure on conventional forces and seeking to retain sole control over decisions to use nuclear weapons. McNamara argued that "limited nuclear capabilities, operating independently are dangerous, expensive, prone to obsolescence and lacking in credibility as a deterrent". But the USA had little choice in the 1960s but to accept the fact of the British and French national nuclear forces.

To discourage other independent nuclear forces and to prevent the further proliferation of nuclear weapons, for China had joined the nuclear club in 1964, the USA, Soviet Union and Britain pressed for the Non-Proliferation Treaty. Signed in 1968, this has been ratified by more than 130 countries. Under the treaty, the non-nuclear states pledge not to develop nuclear weapons, and accept safeguards monitored by the International Atomic Energy Agency (IAEA) on their nuclear installations. The safeguards involve reporting requirements, audits, and on-site inspections to verify that the nuclear facilities are not being used to support weapons programmes. In return, the nuclear powers agree to pursue negotiations in good faith to end the arms race and achieve nuclear disarmament under international control. The treaty has been a remarkable success, although Argentina, Brazil, India, Israel, Pakistan and South Africa have not joined and possess nuclear facilities which are not covered by IAEA safeguards.

The measures of the 1960s could not eliminate doubts about the credibility of the American nuclear guarantee. But the debate highlighted the different emphasis Europeans and Americans place on particular elements of a deterrent strategy. These differences, arising from the respective vulnerabilities of Americans and Europeans to a potential conventional or nuclear war, have not, to date, changed.

Europeans and Americans agree that deterrence depends upon the enemy's believing that he will suffer

This missile array illustrates the development of the ICBM from its beginnings in 1944, with the German V-2 (A-4) surface-to-surface tactical missile (**1**), to the monstrous Soviet SS-18 strategic missile (**16**) of the mid-1970s. The V-2 carried a warhead of 2,145lbs (975kg) of conventional explosive to a range of some 200 miles (320km), with a CEP of around 8,800yd (8,050m). The SS-18 has a 25MT warhead with an explosive yield some 25,000,000 times that of the V-2, or 1,250 times that of the Hiroshima atomic bomb, a range of around 7,500 miles (12,100km), and a CEP of some 380yd (350m).

3. SS-4 Sandal (USSR)

2. Redstone (USA)

1. V-2 (A-4) (Ger)

4. SS-6 Sapwood (USSR)

7. SS-7 Saddler (USSR)

6. Atlas D (USA)

5. Polaris A-1 (USA)

unacceptable damage if he invades Western Europe. Americans, however, emphasize the need to design rational strategies for the use of particular weapons systems if deterrence should fail. They consider that deterrence is inseparable from the capability to defend. The more certain, obvious and potentially punishing that capability, the less likely it is to be tested.

In contrast, Europeans emphasize the uncertainty which must exist in the mind of the enemy as to how particular weapons will be used. For them, nuclear weapons contribute to deterrence primarily by their existence, and it is the risk of their use, rather than the manner of it, that promotes deterrence. They focus on what they call the "political" dimension underlying deterrence. American interests must be inextricably bound to the interests of Europe, and the USA must be seen to be involved in Europe's political and military future. American conventional and nuclear forces stationed in Europe stake out the territory where superpower involvement in a conflict automatically begins; the existence of a capacity to escalate the war thus poses the risk that American strategic weapons would be unleashed to counter a loss at a lower level of military engagement. It is the risk of escalation that deters.

Loss of American superiority

In the 1970s, the Soviet Union achieved strategic nuclear parity with the USA. This was codified in the 1972 SALT I and 1979 SALT II treaties. As a result, the USA became concerned that a strategy of massive retaliation would not be an adequate deterrent against the full range of potential attacks against the USA itself. President Nixon asked in 1970:

Should a President, in the event of a nuclear attack, be left with the single option of ordering the mass

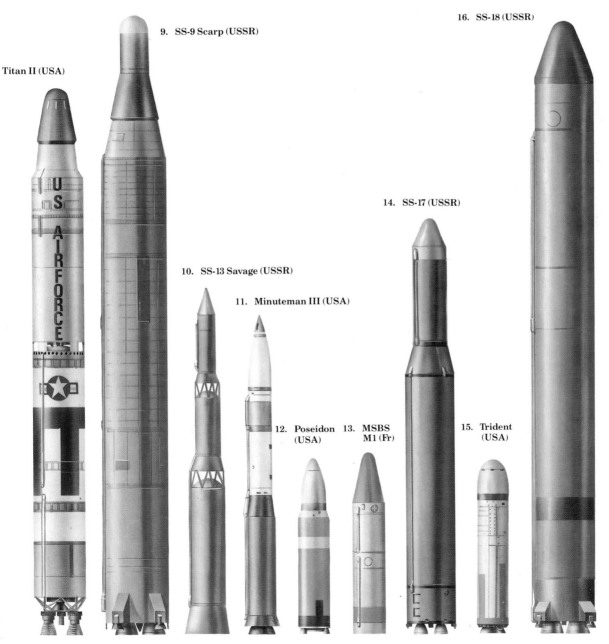

Titan II (USA)

9. SS-9 Scarp (USSR)

16. SS-18 (USSR)

14. SS-17 (USSR)

10. SS-13 Savage (USSR)

11. Minuteman III (USA)

12. Poseidon (USA)

13. MSBS M1 (Fr)

15. Trident (USA)

destruction of enemy civilians, in the face of the certainty that it would be followed by the mass slaughter of Americans? Should the concept of assured destruction be narrowly defined and should it be the only measure of our ability to deter the variety of threats we may face?

The American answer came in 1974 with the announcement of a new doctrine – National Security Decision Memorandum (NSDM)–242 – of limited nuclear options "to shore up deterrence across the entire spectrum of risk and to limit the chance of uncontrolled escalation if war occurred". This Schlesinger doctrine called for a "series of measured responses to aggression which bear some relation to the provocation, have prospects of terminating hostilities before general nuclear war breaks out, leaving some possibility for restoring deterrence".

In the light of the build-up of Soviet strategic forces, Americans feared that in a crisis the Soviet Union might fire, or threaten to fire, a limited number of nuclear weapons selectively against significant military targets while at the same time holding American cities hostage. If America's only choice was between responding massively against enemy cities or doing nothing, the enemy might threaten or carry out a limited use on the assumption that the USA would do nothing. If the USA had the capability and plans to react in a selective and controlled way against enemy military targets, the enemy's calculations would be altered, since his limited attacks would create a high risk of response in kind.

A second concern was the possibility that deterrence might fail through accident or miscalculation. In such circumstances, the American view was that the goal would be to limit damage to the USA and its allies by restricting the level and extent of violence. A selective and controlled use of nuclear weapons offered the prospect of terminating the nuclear conflict before nuclear weapons were unleashed on a large scale against populations and industry.

It was acknowledged that controlling escalation by the use of nuclear weapons did not confidently promise success. The US would need to tailor a restrained response which would give the enemy time to reconsider, but at the same time leave open the possibility of further destruction. Many had difficulty in accepting the idea that the limited use of nuclear weapons might terminate rather than escalate a war, particularly since Soviet theorists argue that restraint in a nuclear war makes no sense and suggest that strategies of flexible response and limited nuclear war are abstractions divorced from reality. But the Soviets appear to recognize the possibility that the homelands of the superpowers could be maintained as sanctuaries, and they also have the capability for limited nuclear attacks.

Critics of the Schlesinger doctrine had a more fundamental problem. They argued that plans for limited nuclear attacks undermined deterrence by making nuclear war more likely. Flexibility would tend to reduce inhibitions against the use of nuclear weapons by making nuclear war more thinkable, acceptable and respectable. They were also concerned that the new doctrine would generate requirements for new weapons and for improvements in American counterforce capabilities, for attacking hardened targets such as missile silos. Such counterforce capabilities were seen to be provocative and destabilizing, for they would indicate to the Soviet Union that the

USA was seeking a first-strike capability. Eventually, most concluded that flexibility was desirable, and that the question of acquiring counterforce capabilities should be decided separately.

In the late 1970s, concern arose over Soviet deployment of highly accurate ICBMs and the possibility that the Soviets might be preparing for a dis-arming first strike against US land-based missiles. Soviet writings also indicated that they were preparing to fight a protracted nuclear war in which victory might be possible. In response, the USA again refined its nuclear strategy, to "convince the Soviet leadership that no war and no course of aggression by them that led to the use of nuclear weapons – on any scale of attack and at any stage of conflict – could lead to victory, however they may define victory". To this end, the Carter administration's 1980 Presidential Directive (PD)–59 declared the intention to put at risk all that the Soviet leaders appear to value – political and military control structures, military forces both nuclear and conventional and the industrial capacity to sustain war. The Reagan administration accepted PD–59 and proceeded to implement this strategy with particular attention to improvements in command and control capabilities.

The loss of American superiority in strategic nuclear forces in the 1970s also raised fears in Europe for the continued credibility of the American nuclear guarantee. The issues left unresolved in the 1960s were exacerbated by Soviet deployment of the new SS–20 missiles – mobile, accurate, equipped with multiple warheads and targeted only on Western Europe. Chancellor Schmidt of West Germany was particularly concerned that the Americans were ignoring European interests in negotiating the SALT II treaty, which failed to limit the Soviet threat to Europe but banned for three years deployment of land and sea-based cruise missiles. As a result, NATO decided in 1979 to deploy new American land-based intermediate range nuclear missiles (INF) with the capability to strike the Soviet Union.

These missiles, like all US theatre nuclear weapons, provoked various interpretations of their contribution to deterrence. As the Soviet Union threatened to respond to any American attack on its homeland with an attack on the USA, NATO argued that the INF missiles made escalation of any nuclear war more likely, thereby enhancing deterrence. For others, the INF missiles undermined deterrence by permitting the USA to confine a war to Europe and to postpone or even avoid using its strategic nuclear weapons.

The West's response to the advent of strategic nuclear parity in the Schlesinger doctrine, President Carter's PD–59, and the NATO INF decision was to introduce even more options and flexibility into its nuclear strategy and forces. The NATO INF decision was, however, linked with an arms control approach, and in 1981 NATO called for the global elimination of all INF missiles. The INF Treaty in 1987 accomplished this, but the removal of the INF missiles had the effect of reducing NATO's flexibility and its options for deterring a Soviet attack in Europe. In the 1990s, the question of what kinds of American nuclear weapons in Europe will be necessary to maintain NATO's strategy of flexible response will again be raised.

New challenges of the 1980s

In the past, the West had difficulty in assuring a credible deterrent strategy because of developments in Soviet nuclear capabilities. In the 1980s challenges appeared which called the strategy itself into question. Western public opinion became opposed to the continuing build-up of nuclear weapons and to what appeared to be the West's nuclear war-fighting doctrines. The moral justification of strategies threatening nuclear retaliation was questioned. The Freeze Movement called for an end to nuclear testing and to the development of new weapons. The new MX missile came under attack because of what was viewed as its first-strike capability. In Europe, there were mass demonstrations against deployment of new American INF missiles. The political left in most European countries favoured unilateral nuclear disarmament. From East and West came proposals for nuclear-free zones and pledges of no first use of nuclear weapons.

The Reagan administration responded with calls for significant reductions in INF and strategic nuclear forces. In START, it sought to promote stability through constraints on the most threatening ballistic missiles and a restructuring of the force posture of the Soviet Union to reduce its significant advantages in heavy ICBMS and in missile throw weight. In 1986, General Secretary Gorbachev agreed in principle to the elimination of all INF, to a 50 percent reduction in strategic nuclear warheads, and to the main elements of the American START proposal. Arms control deflected public opposition to nuclear weapons and at the same time confirmed once again the existence of a nuclear stalemate, although this time with the possibility of substantially reduced levels of nuclear weapons.

The more important challenge to the nuclear strategies of the past – and perhaps even to the nuclear stalemate –

SDI developments. President Reagan announced the controversial Strategic Defense Initiative (SDI; popularly known as "Star Wars") in 1983. Although primarily concerned with ballistic missile defence, the programme has also covered other advanced, space-based surveillance systems like Teal Ruby, shown here. This experimental system uses mosaic infrared arrays to monitor air activity over potentially hostile territory. Its main targets are aircraft and cruise missiles but it could also be used to look for ships at sea. In the future, such space-based surveillance systems might be vulnerable to anti-satellite systems like the hypothetical enemy laser-armed satellite attacking Teal Ruby. The USSR is still many years away from developing such space-based directed energy weapons.

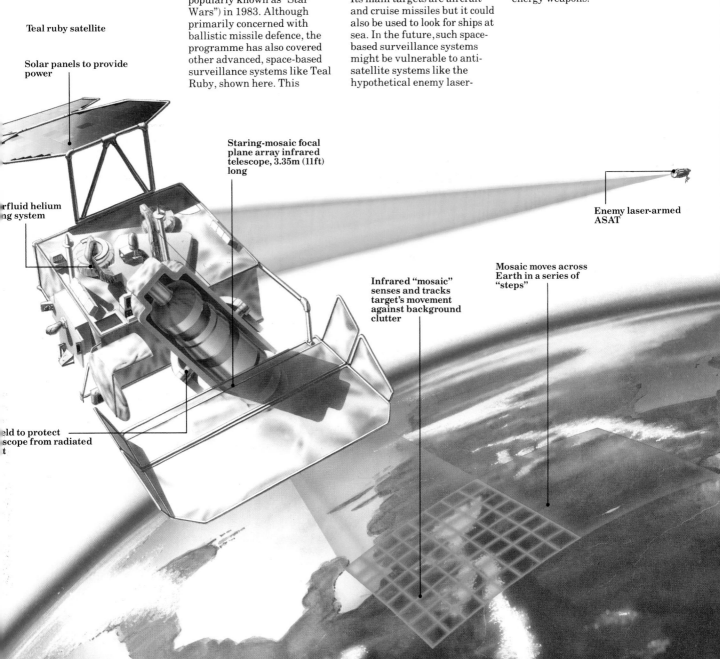

Teal ruby satellite

Solar panels to provide power

Staring-mosaic focal plane array infrared telescope, 3.35m (11ft) long

rfluid helium ng system

eld to protect scope from radiated t

Enemy laser-armed ASAT

Infrared "mosaic" senses and tracks target's movement against background clutter

Mosaic moves across Earth in a series of "steps"

was President Reagan's speech in 1983, announcing his Strategic Defense Initiative (SDI), popularly known as "Star Wars". Reagan asked:

> Would it not be better to save lives than to avenge them? Up until now we have increasingly based our strategy of deterrence upon the threat of retaliation. But what if free people could live secure in the knowledge that their security did not rest upon the threat of instant US retaliation to deter a Soviet attack; that we could intercept and destroy strategic ballistic missiles before they reached our own soil and that of our allies? ... is it not worth every investment necessary to free the world from the threat of nuclear war? We know it is!

He called for a long-term research and development programme "to give us the means of rendering these nuclear weapons impotent and obsolete". He hoped to replace the strategy of deterrence based upon the threat of retaliation by the development of new defensive technologies, thereby changing the past assumption that with nuclear weapons comes vulnerability to nuclear devastation. He called for deployment of nationwide defence if the new technologies proved cost-effective, and rejected the view, incorporated in the ABM Treaty of 1972, that extensive strategic defences are potentially destabilizing and could provoke a nuclear arms race. Given that the Soviet Union emphasizes strategic defences in its strategy, Reagan hoped for a jointly managed transition. Deterrence would be accomplished by denying the enemy the chance of gain from a nuclear attack.

SDI was motivated by doubts that Western publics would approve of the modernization of offensive nuclear forces and scepticism about the success of arms control in reducing the Soviet threat. The US administration also believed that the Soviets would reject mutual vulnerability and would deploy strategic defences once the required technologies were developed.

The effect of SDI has been to renew the debate over how best to assure peace in a world of nuclear weapons. It poses two competing strategic theories. One is that the ABM Treaty, in banning nationwide defences, provides each side with the *certainty* of devastating retaliation – and stability is thus imposed by the certainty that the cost of nuclear war would far exceed any potential gains. A ban on strategic defences has the effect of assuring confidence in one's retaliatory strategy, thus encouraging reductions in offensive forces.

The competing theory is that strategic defences create *uncertainty* in the mind of a Soviet planner as to his ability to carry out an effective attack. Lacking confidence in achieving his military objectives, he would be deterred from using his nuclear weapons. Strategic defences would make further deployments of offensive forces increasingly unattractive, and thus create the conditions for their progressive reduction.

Since 1983, the Soviet Union has called for a ban on space-based defences, arguing that such defences are destabilizing in that they are first-strike weapons. But the Soviets have deployed land-based strategic defences and have pursued research on defensive technologies.

"Exotic defensive technologies"

A choice as to the future of strategic defences cannot be made without knowing what kinds of defensive systems are technically feasible and what measures could be undertaken to defeat them. The SDI is a long-term research and development programme which seeks to develop what are called "exotic defensive technologies", such as lasers (X-ray, chemical, and free electron) and particle beams, as well as interceptor missiles, sensors and surveillance systems.

The SDI deployment concept involves multiple layers. A

The early warning command centre of North American Air Defense Command (NORAD), situated deep underground in the Cheyenne Mountain complex, Colorado. One of NORAD's vital tasks is the maintenance of the Distant Early Warning (DEW) line, the chain of optical and radar missile warning stations spanning the Alaskan and Canadian Arctic regions. NORAD also monitors the testing of Soviet anti-satellite (ASAT) devices and practises target tracking and discrimination techniques, activities that will make it an essential part of the projected Strategic Defense Initiative system.

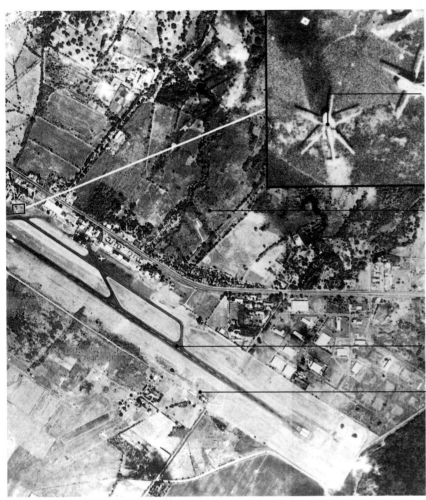

HIP
helicopters

Soviet anti-
aircraft guns

Runway length
7,940ft (2,420m)

Soviet anti-
aircraft guns

An aerial reconnaissance photograph (*above left*) of an airfield in Nicaragua, obtained by a Lockheed U-2 high-altitude "spy plane" of the US Air Force in January 1982, reveals the deployment of Soviet helicopters and anti-aircraft weapons. Because the American media cast doubt on reports of Soviet involvement in Nicaragua, the Reagan administration released a number of these previously-classified photographs to help justify its Central American policy. (*Below left*) Aerial reconnaissance photographs like this, obtained by a USAF U-2 and showing a Soviet missile site under construction in Cuba, October 1962, provided President Kennedy with the evidence he needed to take a hard line during the Cuban missiles crisis. The USSR had claimed that it was supplying only defensive weapons to Cuba: in fact, reconnaissance proved that SS-4 "Sandal" missiles, capable of reaching the southern USA with 1MT warheads, were being installed.

Missile erector

Cable

Missile shelter tent

Tracked prime movers

Fuel tank trailers

Oxidizer tank trailers

boost phase would be composed of space-based surveillance systems to detect Soviet missile launches and to alert the battle management stations in space. A mid-course phase would involve battle management systems transmitting target assignments to space-based interceptors, which would destroy missile boosters by extremely high-speed impact ("kinetic kill"). In this phase, tracking systems would also pick out the surviving warheads from any decoys in space. In the terminal phase, space- and ground-based interceptors would be assigned to destroy the remaining warheads as they entered the atmosphere.

The problem is that the initial defensive technologies can be expected to provide only a temporary shield, for countermeasures can be developed; for example, decoy warheads and faster-burning missiles. It is not certain that computer technology will be capable of processing the extraordinary amount of information necessary to track, discriminate between the warheads and intercept the missiles. Not until well into the 21st century will the more exotic defensive technologies be ready for testing.

The challenge of SDI is to decide which of the two competing theories of deterrence best promotes peace. The problem is that the activities of both the USA and the Soviet Union over the past five years have so undermined the ABM Treaty that its future viability is doubtful. The Soviets have exploited the Treaty's ambiguities in such a way as to lead the Reagan administration to claim that "the aggregate of the Soviet Union's ABM and ABM-related actions (e.g. radar construction, concurrent testing, SAM upgrade, ABM mobility and deployment of ABM components) suggests that the USSR may be preparing an ABM defense of its national territory".

To protect SDI, the Reagan administration rejected Soviet proposals for constraints on space-based research, and in addition chose not to negotiate constraints on the various Soviet activities which caused it concern. Instead, it pursued a vigorous research programme on land- and space-based systems and reinterpreted the ABM Treaty to permit the development and testing of space-based ABMs with exotic technologies. As a result, the two sides may, in practical terms, have given up the possibility of maintaining the strict limits of the ABM Treaty.

At the same time, defensive technologies cannot be expected to provide strategic defences sufficiently effective to replace a strategy based on offensive forces and nuclear retaliation. Technology does not, therefore, offer the opportunity of making nuclear weapons entirely impotent and obsolete.

So the strategic debate must consider what contribution, if any, limited defences could make in the future to a strategy based primarily on nuclear retaliation. Technologies will be available to serve a number of limited objectives: to create greater uncertainty for an attacker regarding the accomplishment of his objectives; to protect retaliatory forces; to insure against an accidental nuclear attack. Whether they should be deployed will depend on their costs, their effectiveness in the light of potential countermeasures, and their implications for arms control and the ABM Treaty. What the other side is doing with respect to offensive and defensive systems will be particularly important. Deployments of strategic defences by one side only could be destabilizing by giving an advantage to the side which strikes first, while potential countermeasures could negate their effectiveness. The development of the various defensive systems has not progressed to a point where choices can be made.

Prospects for the 1990s
The fundamental strategic issues will not change in the 1990s, but the political and military environment will be again in flux.

Eliminating nuclear weapons is widely favoured by Western public opinion and is supported rhetorically by both superpowers. Multilateral arms control has muted the calls for a nuclear freeze and for unilateral disarmament. But it will be difficult to gain public support in the USA and Europe for nuclear modernization programmes, especially since the USA and the USSR have agreed in principle to significant reductions in nuclear weapons.

Americans are increasingly anxious about the central role nuclear weapons play in NATO strategy. Both liberals, in calls for pledges of no first use, and conservatives, in proposals for new nuclear weapons capable of limited and discriminate attacks, are seriously looking for alternatives. Pressures are also increasing for reductions in American conventional forces around the world.

The INF Treaty has renewed European anxieties over the credibility of the American nuclear guarantee, as well as over the imbalance in conventional forces in Europe. Europeans are searching for ways to cooperate militarily as well as economically, to promote their security independently of the USA. The Western European Union has been revived and has called for a more cohesive European defence identity. One major difficulty is that West Europeans have no common view on the future role of nuclear weapons, and on whether their security is best promoted through nuclear modernization or arms control.

In the Soviet Union, President Gorbachev has undertaken radical reform of the economy. He has made a number of foreign policy and arms control initiatives, including the withdrawal of Soviet forces from Afghanistan. He has called for reasonable sufficiency in military forces and for an emphasis on defensive strategies. As a consequence, the West will almost certainly need to reassess the nature of the Soviet threat. As in the past, Soviet actions will be an important factor in how the West decides to define its strategic and arms control policies.

The problem is that while Americans and Europeans – and perhaps even the Soviets – are searching for new ways to promote peace and security, the West really has no alternative but to proceed on its current path. The West, like the Soviet Union and its allies, will continue to possess large numbers of nuclear and conventional weapons and will wish to have flexibility and options. America's interest in the security of its allies in Europe and Asia will remain vital, and these countries cannot alone provide for their own defence. Therefore, changes can only be made on the margins of the West's current nuclear and conventional strategies. Defensive systems may contribute to assuring a credible strategy of nuclear retaliation, but they will not provide an alternative to reliance upon offensive forces. Arms control may succeed in reducing nuclear and conventional weapons; there remain the problems of constraining new technologies, of placing limits on systems that carry both nuclear and conventional weapons, of designing global as well as regional ceilings, and of providing adequate verification. Visions of eliminating nuclear weapons are as unrealistic as efforts to achieve war-winning nuclear strategies.

In the 1990s, the West will almost certainly refine its nuclear strategy. But the existence of nuclear weapons condemns the world to a nuclear stalemate and it must be hoped this will maintain the peace as it has in the past.

S

Spad 7.C 1 (French, WWI). Single-seat fighter. Prototype flew April 1916; production deliveries to French *escadrilles* from August 1916. Also bought for RFC (later produced in Britain), but all deliveries initially slow. Sturdy and manoeuvrable; improved with more powerful engine. Used by Belgian, Italian, Russian and American units; some production Russia. Remained operational to war's end. Production, about 3,800. One 150/180hp Hispano-Suiza engine; max. speed 132mph (211kph); one rifle-calibre machine gun, 50lb (22.5kg) bombs.

Spad 13.C 1 (French, WWI). Single-seat fighter. Prototype flew April 4 1917; slow production (17 in French service by August 1 1917; deliveries to March 31 1918, 764). Developed from and more heavily armed than Spad 7; handicapped by engine troubles. Used by at least 74 French *escadrilles*, and by RFC, Belgian, Italian and US services. Production about 7,300. One 200/220hp Hispano-Suiza engine; max. speed 138mph (222kph); two 7.65mm/0.303in machine guns, 50lb (22.5kg) bombs.

Spandau. Nazi leaders convicted at Nuremberg were held in Spandau Prison, West Berlin; demolished in 1987 following the death of its last inmate, Hess.

Streetfighting in Toledo, Spain

Spanish Civil War (July 18 1936–March 31 1939). Of all civil wars, this "world war by proxy" was the most international. Its origins however, were entirely domestic. Long-standing rifts, authoritarian versus libertarian, centralist versus regionalist and right versus left, exploded with the attempted army coup of July 1936 which followed the Popular Front electoral victory in January.

Hitler and Mussolini helped Gen Franco from the beginning, first with aircraft, arms and advisers, then with combat formations like the Condor Legion. The Republicans' defence of Madrid accelerated the internationalization of the struggle, a development which Britain tried to curtail with the Non-Intervention Agreement. This soon became a monument to diplomatic hypocrisy as Axis aid to Franco went unchecked while the Republic was refused arms. It had no choice but to turn to the Soviet Union.

Soviet aid, purchased with the Spanish gold reserves, enabled the Republic to survive but not to win. Stalin, in the midst of purging the Red Army, was afraid of provoking Hitler. And Russian military advisers, influenced no doubt by the execution of Marshal Tukhachevsky, were numbingly unadventurous. Even aggressive young Spanish communist commanders showed no initiative. In one set-piece offensive after the other, Brunete, Teruel and the Ebro, they repeated the same mistakes. Propaganda considerations prevented retreat and their forces were left exposed to the enemy's superiority in artillery and airpower. With the Nationalist blockade, the loss of equipment was disastrous. At the Battle of the Ebro, the Republic's last hope of survival was destroyed just a year before the outbreak of World War II. Nationalist commanders in the field, on the other hand, made up for their early inferiority in numbers with daring and great initiative. The older generals like Franco and Mola were less impressive. Franco's obstinate refusal to allow the Reds to retake any territory led to as many unnecessary casualties. The greatest irony of his anti-communist crusade was that in the final stage, the communists, having aroused intense hatred in the Republican camp, were crushed by their former socialist, liberal and anarchist allies. *AB.*

Special Air Service Regiment (SAS). Formed as an elite force in 1942 for operations behind enemy lines in North Africa under the command of Capt (later Col) David Stirling, it had expanded to brigade strength by 1945, when it was disbanded. It was re-formed in Malaya in 1950 for special jungle operations as the Malayan Scouts, later renamed 22 SAS Regiment. The SAS has since been on active service in Borneo, South Arabia, Oman, the South Atlantic and Northern Ireland, and has been used worldwide in a number of specialist anti-terrorist activities. The SAS consists of one regular regiment (battalion) based at Hereford and two Territorial Army units. All ranks are volunteers and are selected only after arduous tests, based on mental as much as physical attributes. *MH.*

Special Boat Section. Offshoot of SAS, operated in the Aegean in 1942–44 and in the Adriatic in 1943–45, from caïques and other small craft, commanded by the second Lord Jellicoe (the admiral's son); numerous raiding coups.

Special Forces (ARVN). The Special Forces (*Luc luong dac biet*) of the Army of the Republic of Vietnam (ARVN) were trained by US Army Special Forces to carry out unconventional warfare operations behind enemy lines. Training began in 1957, with the creation of a 57-man nucleus of instructors and cadre. By early 1961, ARVN Special Forces were conducting long-range reconnaissance operations, commanding ethnic and sectarian irregulars, and gathering intelligence on the Laos and Cambodian borders. Reorganization in 1962 gave them their own command as a major subordinate element of the ARVN and assigned one detachment to each of the four ARVN corps tactical zones. Beginning in 1964, they contributed troops to Project Delta, a joint US/ARVN programme of long-range reconnaissance and intelligence gathering. ARVN Special Forces also had formal responsibility for the Civilian Irregular Defence Group programme, which in practice they abdicated to the Americans, until the "conversion" of CIDG troops to Rangers in 1970. *WST.*

Special Operations Executive (SOE). British secret service that ran subversion and sabotage, was launched in July 1940 and disbanded in January 1946. It countered the Axis powers with their own underhand methods. Its mainspring was (Sir) Colin Gubbins, its executive head from September 1943. It was formed by amalgamating an intelligence branch of the War Office, a branch of MI6, and a semi-secret propaganda branch of the Foreign Office. This last split away in August 1941 to become PWE; not before SOE, guided by (Sir) William Stephenson in New York, had helped persuade American news media that anti-Nazism was more constitutional than isolationism.

SOE operated the world over, except in the USSR; even there it had a small mission, kept under careful watch by the NKVD. In South America it countered Nazi influence unobtrusively, but effectively. In North America it ran a training camp near Toronto, valuable both for its own agents and for those of OSS; this provided a channel for extra secret Anglo-American exchanges by ciphered wireless messages.

In Yugoslavia SOE at first supported Mihailovich, then switched support to Tito's partisans, who were more vigorously anti-German. In Albania it could not prevent a communist seizure of power; in Greece, it just could. In northern Italy it sustained an all-party partisan effort in 1943–45; into France it helped the RAF and USAF drop arms for nearly half a million men, and so helped de Gaulle to power. In the Low Countries the Gestapo controlled too much of its work; but it helped resisters seize Antwerp docks intact. In Norway nine SOE agents, in two deft attacks, scotched German attempts to build an atomic bomb. SOE smuggled special steels out of Sweden, and helped to arm Danish as well as Norwegian resistance. Two Czechoslovaks trained by SOE killed Heydrich. Poland was almost out of range, as aircraft operating for SOE were forbidden the use of airfields under Russian control.

In the Far East, SOE could do little in Malaysia, though a tiny left-behind party accounted for over 1,000 Japanese, and a band of Australian heroes brought off one successful small boat raid against Singapore roads. Into the Dutch East Indies it was hardly able to penetrate; and Indochina was almost out of range. Siam (Thailand) was the scene of sharp rivalry with OSS. In Burma SOE scored

two main triumphs: it persuaded a large native security force to change sides and armed a rising of Karen hillmen that severely hindered the Japanese retreat.

Its strength was about 10,000 men and 3,000 women. Several women had distinguished careers as agents in France, but most were cipher clerks or radio operators inside the Allied lines. Traditionally it has been derided as "amateur", and it had indeed many defects arising from the tremendous hurry with which it was mounted under a cloak of secrecy; but it made a mark on the world war that any professional in the secret world might envy. *MF.*

Spee, Vice Adm Maximilian, Reichsgraf von (1861–1914). Ger. Spee became COS, North Sea Command, 1908, reaching flag rank in 1910. A gunnery expert, a brilliant tactician, and well-liked by all ranks in spite of his reputation as a fearsome disciplinarian, he was obviously marked for the highest command (had he lived, von Tirpitz may well have appointed him C-in-C, High Seas Fleet, in 1915); and in 1912 he took command of the elite East Asiatic Squadron.

On the outbreak of World War I, Spee intended to raid commerce in the China seas, but on Japan's entry into the war, August 23, and the blockade of Tsingtau, he decided that his force must be preserved so that its threat should tie up the largest possible number of British warships. Detaching the light cruiser *Emden* and two armed merchant cruisers to raid in the Indian Ocean, he steamed for the west coast of South America, with armoured cruisers *Scharnhorst* (flag) and *Gneisenau* and light cruisers *Leipzig*, *Nürnberg* and *Dresden*. Brushing aside Cradock's inferior force at Coronel, November 1, he rounded Cape Horn, intending to destroy the vital British coaling and communications base at Port Stanley, Falklands, before making a dash for Germany. But Sturdee's battlecruisers were waiting at the Falklands: on December 8, Spee's force was shattered – only *Dresden* escaped, to be sunk on March 14 1915 – and the admiral himself, and his two sons, died, along with some 1,800 seamen. *RO'N.*

Speer, Albert (1905–81). Ger. Attracted Hitler's attention as an architect capable of realizing his grandiose plans for the buildings of the "Thousand-Year Reich"; appointed Minister of Weapons and Munitions in 1941. Realistically appraising Germany's needs, Speer vigorously and ruthlessly reorganized labour and industry to combat the damage to production caused by Allied bombing. Mainly through his measures, including the deployment of slave labour (which contributed largely to his sentence at Nuremberg of 20 years' imprisonment), Germany was able to survive the ball-bearings crisis of October 1943 and greatly delay the impact of the oil crisis of May 1944 onward. Postwar, he claimed to have plotted against Hitler's life in 1945. *ANF.*

Speidel, Maj Gen Hans (1897–1984). Ger. Served on Western Front, World War I; Assistant Military Attaché, 1933–37; served Eastern Front, 1942–43. In April 1944 he was appointed Rommel's COS at Army Group B. Speidel was a leading member of the military conspiracy to remove Hitler and tried to enlist the support of Rommel and von Rundstedt. The failure of the assassination attempt of July 20 and the collapse of the army coups in Berlin and Paris cast suspicion upon Speidel. Although interrogated at great length, he survived, and postwar served with distinction in the Bundeswehr and NATO. *MS.*

Sperrle: senior Luftwaffe commander

Sperrle, Field Marshal Hugo (1885–1953). Ger. A brewer's son who was initially an officer in the Württemberg infantry, Sperrle ended World War I in charge of all flying units attached to the German Seventh Army on the Western Front. After holding various posts in the *Reichswehr*, he moved back to the air force in the 1930s and was the first commander of the Condor Legion in Spain in 1936–37, being rewarded with the rank of *General der Flieger*. In 1938 he was given command of *Luftwaffengruppe 3* at Munich. The formation was renamed *Luftflotte 3* in 1939 and Sperrle remained at its head for the next five years. In 1940 *Luftflotte 3* supported von Rundstedt's Army Group A with great success during the invasion of France, earning Sperrle promotion to Field Marshal. Based in Northwest France, with its HQ in Paris, *Luftflotte 3* was one of the two air fleets most heavily involved in the Battle of Britain. Despite its major reverses in that campaign it stayed behind in the west in 1941 to carry out sporadic operations against Britain and to defend the air space over France, Belgium and Holland. Denuded of aircraft for other fronts and weakened by combat losses, *Luftflotte 3's* efficiency gradually diminished, scarcely helped by the indolent Sperrle, whose taste for luxury rivalled that of Göring. On D-Day, *Luftflotte 3* could not even launch 100 sorties against the Allies, and Sperrle was removed from command. He was captured in May 1945 but acquitted of war crimes and freed in 1948. *PJS.*

Spion Kop, Battle of (January 22–24 1900), Second Boer War. In a second attempt to relieve Ladysmith, Buller crossed the Tugela with 20,000 men, driving back Botha's 5,000 Boers. In a night attack on January 22, 1,700 men under Brig Woodgate occupied Spion Kop: it had not been noticed that the hill's apparent summit was commanded by Boer positions on higher ground. The steepness of the slopes denied the brigade artillery support and during a day of fierce fighting it suffered around one-third casualties. With Woodgate dead, the survivors withdrew after dark, not realizing that the equally exhausted Boers were also abandoning the Kop. Next morning the Boers (losses: *c*150 dead; *c*150 wounded) swiftly reoccupied the heights, while Buller (losses: *c*380 dead; *c*1,050 wounded; *c*300 captured or missing) withdrew across the Tugela. *RO'N.*

Spitfire, Vickers-Supermarine (Br, WWII). Single-seat fighter. Prototype flew March 5 1936; first to squadron (No. 19) August 4 1938. Nine squadrons by outbreak of war; operational in many Marks beyond war's end. Griffon engine (from Mk XII) improved performance markedly. Widely used by many air services; 1,333 to Russia. Much use on photographic reconnaissance. Naval version Seafire. Production: 20,351 Spitfires, 2,408 Seafires. Spitfire F XIV had one 2,035hp Rolls-Royce Griffon 65 or 66; max. speed 448mph (721kph); two 20mm cannon, two 0.5in machine guns, 500lb (225kg) bombs or rocket projectiles.

Spruance, Adm Raymond Ames (1886–1969). US. Commanding a cruiser division at the outbreak of war, Spruance played a major part in the US victory at Midway, taking tactical command when Fletcher's *Yorktown* was damaged. After serving Nimitz's COS for operations in the Solomons and South Pacific, he took command of Fifth Fleet in 1943 for the "island hopping" campaign, triumphantly participating in operations at Tarawa, Kwajalein, Truk, Hollandia, Saipan, the Battle of the Philippine Sea and the Marianas. Alternating his attacks with those of Halsey's Third Fleet, he commanded at Iwo Jima and Okinawa. A brilliant, meticulous planner and an inspiring leader, he was hailed as beyond compare by the US Navy's historian. Postwar, he briefly commanded Pacific Fleet before becoming President of the Naval War College. *CJW/CD.*

Squadron. (1) Naval. A group of warships less than, or within, a fleet and under single command. (2) Military. Two Troops of a cavalry or tank regiment. (3) Air. Two Flights each of approximately eight aircraft.

SS. The *Schutzstaffel* (Guard Echelon-SS) was formed in 1925 to act as Hitler's bodyguard. Under Himmler's leadership, they implemented the "Final Solution" to the "Jewish problem" with hideous cruelty; controlled the police and intelligence organizations and, in October 1944, included 910,000 men in their military formation, the Waffen-SS.

SS1-25. The American code numbers for Soviet surface to surface ballistic missiles by which they are usually known; the alternative NATO code names are also given:

SS-1. A modified V-2 short-range ballistic missile (SRBM) first deployed in small quantities as "Scunner" in 1947 and developed into the "Scud" battlefield system in the 1950s.

SS-2 Sibling. A further developed SRBM with improved range and accuracy deployed in small numbers from 1950.

SS-3 Shyster. The first Soviet medium-range ballistic missile (MRBM) with a range of 720 miles (1,200km). Nuclear capable, it was deployed in service from 1955.

SS-4 Sandal. Entered service in 1958 as the definitive liquid-fuelled MRBM. With a range of 1,080 miles (1,800km), about 500 were deployed in both East and West, some of the latter until the INF Treaty of 1987.

SS-5 Skean. A liquid-fuelled IRBM with a range of 2,100 miles (3,500km) and a high-yield 5 megaton warhead. About 100 deployed from 1961; phased out of service in the 1980s.

SS-6 Sapwood. The world's first ICBM, tested in 1957 and used to put first Earth satellite into orbit. Missile took 12 hours to launch and only four were operationally deployed; rocket has been widely used as a space booster.

SS-7 Saddler. The USSR's first ICBM deployed in quantity, mostly in hardened silos, from 1962-63; 197 were deployed and were phased out in the late 1970s. A storable liquid fuel missile, its warhead yield was 3-6 megatons according to variant, with a CEP of about 6,560ft (2,000m).

SS-8 Sasin. A non-storable fuelled but smaller missile, to the same requirement as SS-7. Only 23 were deployed from 1963 and they were also phased out in the late 1970s.

SS-9 Scarp. A formidable heavy storable liquid-fuelled counterforce ICBM, 288 of which were deployed from 1964 onwards. It carried a 20 megaton warhead 6,300 miles (10,500km) with a CEP of about 3,280ft (1,000m) . It was used for MRV, ASAT and FOBS experiments and was replaced by the SS-18 in the late 1970s.

SS-10 Scrag. Although widely displayed in Moscow in the late

1960s, this was an unsuccessful non-storable fuelled competitor to SS-9 and was never deployed.

SS-11 Sego. Originally designed as a long-range anti-ship missile, the SS-11 became the first mass-production Soviet silo-based light ICBM. A storable liquid-fuelled weapon with a warhead of about 1 megaton and CEP of 4,592ft (1,400m), 1,030 were deployed from 1966, some alongside SS-4 as an IRBM to cover theatre targets in Europe. Two improved variants, one with greater accuracy (CEP 3,608ft/1,100m) and one with three MRVS appeared in 1973–75, and most of the 440 that remain are of these later versions.

SS-12 Scapegoat. A two-stage SRINF missile with a range of 480-540 miles (800-900km) carried on a mobile launcher; entered service in the late 1960s. It is being withdrawn under the INF Treaty.

SS-13 Savage. The Soviet Union's first solid-fuelled ICBM. A three-stage missile, it was not a successful design with a CEP of about 5,904ft (1,800m). It only entered service in limited numbers, 60 silos being deployed at Yoshkar Ola beginning in 1967.

SS-14 Scapegoat. An MRBM, based on the top two stages of SS-13 and carried in a tracked vehicle, the whole system being known as "Scamp". It was displayed in Moscow in the mid 1960s; briefly deployed in very limited quantities along the Chinese border.

SS-15 Scrooge. An experimental mobile IRBM displayed in Red Square in 1965. It was a member of the troubled SS-13 family, probably using the bottom two stages. Like SS-14 it may have seen very limited operational service along the Chinese border.

SS-16. This was a developed SS-13 for mobile deployment, first flight tested in 1972 but never deployed as a result of SALT-2.

SS-17 Spanker. A cold-launched, silo-based, storable liquid-fuelled, medium ICBM, developed by the same design bureau as the SS-9/18 heavy missiles. It was first deployed in 1972, carries four 500 kiloton MIRVS and has almost three times the throw-weight of the SS-11. Its CEP is 1,312ft (400m) and 150 are deployed.

SS-18 Satan. The current heavy counter-force missile. A throw-weight of over 15,950lb (7,250kg)

allows the storable liquid-fuelled missile to deliver ten half megaton MIRVS with a CEP of 820ft (250m). First in service in 1974 in single-warhead version (24 megatons) the first MIRVed variant followed in 1976; 308 are deployed deep inside the southern USSR.

SS-19 Stiletto. The follow-on to the SS-11, capable of delivering six 550 kiloton MIRVS with a CEP of 984ft (300m). It was first deployed in 1975. Some of the 360 in service are allocated to theatre targets. It is storable liquid-fuelled and hot-launched from its silo.

SS-20 Saber. The first descendent of the solid-fuelled SS-13 to be mass deployed. A mobile two-stage IRBM with three 150 kiloton MIRVS, it was used from 1977 to modernize and enlarge the USSR's long-range theatre striking forces. Its deployment led directly to the INF Treaty which provides for the destruction of all 441 deployed systems.

SS-21 Scarab. A 72-mile (120km) range battlefield SRBM which began to replace unguided FROG rockets in the late 1970s. Reported CEP varies from 164 to 984ft (50 to 300m) and nuclear (100 kiloton) and high-explosive submunition warheads are available. SS-21 is carried on a wheeled launcher.

SS-22. Used for a time for late model SS-12 SRINF missiles, sometimes known as SS-12M.

SS-23 Spider. A 300-mile (500km) range, more accurate (CEP 820-948ft/250-300m) follow-on SRBM to Scud, that has been sacrificed by the Soviets under the INF Treaty.

SS-24 Scalpel. A solid-fuelled medium ICBM with a throw-weight greater than SS-19, deployed on railway-mounted mobile launchers. It carries 8-10 100 kiloton MIRVS with a CEP of 656ft (200m).

SS-25 Sickle. The latest ICBM development of the SS-13 currently being deployed on mobile wheeled launchers. A single-warhead weapon of high accuracy (CEP 656ft/200m) its status as a "new" missile is a matter of some dispute between the USA and the USSR.

Stalin, Marshal Josef (1879–1953). Russian. Born in Georgia in southern Russia, Stalin was educated at a seminary before being expelled for revolutionary activities. This did not deter him from these pursuits and in 1902 he was

Caricaturist's view of the "man of steel"

arrested on the first of numerous occasions and exiled to Siberia. In the years before World War I, Stalin's reputation steadily rose in the Bolshevik party. He was active at Russian' and international conferences, was a prominent revolutionary journalist and became the party's spokesman on Nationalism and Marxism. Released from internal exile by the February 1917 revolution, he returned to Petrograd where he became temporary editor of Pravda and earned Lenin's ire by advocating support of the Provisional Government. During the Civil War he took part in the defence of Petrograd and Tsaritsyn, the latter being renamed Stalingrad in recognition of his efforts. Appointed Commissar for Nationalities, in 1922 he became Secretary General of the Communist Party and, with Lenin's health rapidly deteriorating, he entered the fray for the succession. In the struggle for political supremacy, Stalin formed an alliance to oust Trotsky and, once this had been achieved, turned on his erstwhile allies. He dominated the Party Congress of 1927 and thereafter increasingly exerted his control over all aspects of Soviet affairs. Stalin was ruthless in eliminating rivals from the ranks of the Party and the Red Army and throughout the 1930s millions of real and supposed enemies were tried, imprisoned and executed. He brought the same attitude to his diplomatic dealings and stunned the world in May 1939 by concluding a pact with Nazi Germany. This was followed by a period of territorial aggrandisement with part of Poland, the Baltic States and Finland coming under Soviet sway. But Stalin's actions had not removed the threat from Germany and he maintained a conciliatory attitude that contributed to Soviet unpreparedness for the eventual invasion. He exercised a close personal control of the conduct of the war and although his single-mindedness often reaped rewards, his interference with specific campaigns and battles was frequently counter-productive. Having begun the war relying upon generals who had been his associates during the Civil War, he had the sense to accept the counsels of younger, more versatile commanders such as Zhukov and Vasilevsky. Stalin also showed himself to be an astute and guileful negotiator at the many Allied conferences and succeeded in carving out of the post-war settlements a series of communist satellite states in eastern Europe. *MS.*

Stalingrad, Battle of (1942–43). In late June 1942, German Army Group South (von Bock) – from July 9 designated Army Group B (von Weichs) – began an offensive towards Stalingrad (Volgograd). Fourth Panzer Army (Hoth) reached the Don river at Voronezh, quelling opposition by the Russian Voronezh Front (Vatutin) on June 28–July 6, but was then briefly diverted to the Caucasus offensive. This slowed the progress of German Sixth Army (von Paulus), whose Don bridgehead around Kalach was only secured, after heavy fighting, on August 21. Now advancing rapidly, Paulus's XIV Panzer Corps reached the Volga river north of Stalingrad on Au-

gust 23, while Fourth Panzer Army returned to strike at the city from the southwest. Rather than complete the encirclement by flanking moves across the Volga to north and south, Hitler, concerned with the symbolic value of the city that bore Stalin's name as much as its strategic importance, ordered an all-out assault.

From September 12, when German troops reached the suburbs, Stalingrad's defenders – Sixty-second Army (Chuikov), with limited reinforcement and artillery support from Southeast (Stalingrad) Front (Yeremenko) east of the Volga – fought a heroic house-to-house battle, aided, ironically, by massive German bombardments that had reduced much of the city to rubble, providing excellent defensive positions. In October-November the Russian perimeter on the Volga's west bank was reduced to no more than 1,500yd (1,370m) depth in some places – but the determined defence had allowed Zhukov time to prepare a devastating counterattack. On November 19–20, Southwest Front (Vatutin) and Don Front (Rokossovsky) struck from the north and Yeremenko attacked from the southeast. The Russian pincers closed at Kalach, November 22–23, trapping Sixth Army and part of Fourth Panzer Army.

Paulus might have broken out, but Hitler, assured by Göring that the Luftwaffe could airlift 500 tons of supplies daily to Stalingrad (in

fact, air supply averaged only c80 tons per day), ordered him to hold "Fortress Stalingrad" until relieved. Attempting to relieve Paulus, Army Group Don (von Manstein) attacked Yeremenko from the south, advancing to within 30 miles (48km) of Stalingrad, December 12–23, but then retreating before the combined counteroffensive of Vatutin and Yeremenko. Paulus, his troops exhausted by combat, starving, sick and frostbitten, still refused to surrender, and on January 8 1943 Rokossovsky attacked. By January 21 all airfields had fallen to the Russians; Paulus surrendered at his HQ on January 31; a few Germans resisted a little longer. Some 140,000 Germans died at Stalingrad, and of approximately 91,000 taken prisoner there it is estimated that only about 6,000 survived captivity. *RO'N.*

Stand-Off bomb. An older name for air to surface missiles that allow their aircraft to "stand off" from their targets, thus avoiding terminal defences. A classic nuclear stand-off bomb, officially described as such, was the 192-mile (320km) range Blue Steel missile carried by British V-bombers from 1962 to 1975.

"S-Tank" (*Stridsvagn 103*) Swedish Main Battle Tank, introduced 1966. Dispensing with a conventional fully-traversing turret for its main armament (105mm gun), it carries it in the hull. The whole tank is traversed bodily on its tracks to shift target in azimuth and the suspension is adjusted for gun elevation. *See also* TANKS.

Star Wars *see* STRATEGIC DEFENSE INITIATIVE (SDI).

Stark, Adm Harold Raynsford ("Betty") (1880–1972). US. Chief of Naval Operations, 1939; in conjunction with Gen Marshall, prepared US strategy for the coming war. After Pearl Harbor, he was criticized for failing to keep Adm Kimmel fully informed of Japanese movements and was in effect replaced as head of the navy by King. Commander of US Naval Forces in Europe in 1942; spent the rest of the war as the chief liaison between the American and British navies.

German assault on Stalingrad, 1942: led to disaster, January 1943

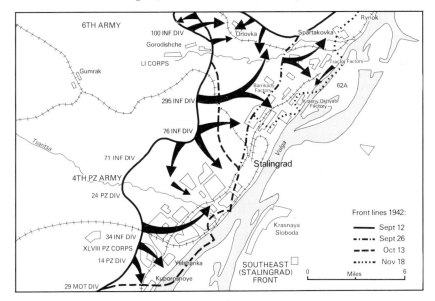

Stark **USS, incident** (1987). On May 17 1987 the frigate USS *Stark*, engaged in escorting Kuwaiti tankers in the Persian Gulf during the Iran–Iraq War, was attacked in international waters off Bahrain by an Iraqi Air Force jet. Two Exocet missiles badly damaged *Stark*, killing 37 crewmen and wounding 21. The USA accepted an Iraqi apology and offer of compensation for the "unintentional accident" – but censure of *Stark's* captain for being taken by surprise contributed to an incident in July 1988, when the cruiser USS *Vincennes* destroyed an Iranian airliner (290 killed) mistaken for an attacking aircraft.

Stavka. Term generally used to denote the high command and headquarters of the Imperial Russian, and later the Soviet, Army.

Stealth. Careful shaping to minimize reflective surfaces and use of non-reflective materials can greatly reduce the radar cross section of aircraft and cruise missiles, making detection difficult or impossible. The USA, sometimes in great secrecy, is developing "stealth" aircraft and missiles using these characteristics. These include a subsonic Lockheed strike fighter, now officially designated the F117, the B-2 strategic bomber; the Navy's Advanced Tactical Aircraft and the Advanced Cruise Missile.

Sten gun. The standard British sub-machine gun of World War II: robust, cheap and easily manufactured, and affectionately known to its users as the "tin tommy-gun". Its name derived from the initial letters of the surnames of its principal developers – Shepherd and Turpin of the Birmingham Small Arms Company (BSA) – and the first letters of the location of the Royal Small Arms Factory, Enfield. Many thousand Stens in a number of Marks were made; it was briefly produced in Australia (the "Austen") and was even copied by the Germans for use by the *Volkssturm* (home guard) in 1945. The Mark V Sten, which remained in British service until replaced by the Sterling in the mid-1950s, was of 9mm calibre, fed by a 32-round box magazine, with a cyclic rate of fire of 550rpm. Accurate only at short range, it had fixed sights.

Stephenson, Sir William (1896–1989). Br. Fighter pilot in France in World War I, commanded 1940–46 all British secret operations west of the Atlantic.

"Vinegar Joe" in the field, Burma, 1942

Stilwell, Gen Joseph Warren ("Vinegar Joe") (1883–1946). US. During World War I, Assistant Chief of Staff, 4th Army Corps in France. Following extensive Far East service, appointed COS to Chiang Kai-shek and commander of American forces in China-Burma-India Theatre, March 1942. On formation of SEAC, appointed Mountbatten's deputy, but was virtually independent in Northern Combat Area Command (NCAC) whose main task was to build the Ledo Road in order to boost support for China, limited to air supply over "The Hump". There were 40,000 US troops in India; the major combat unit, 5307 Composite Unit (Provisional) ("Merrill's Marauders"), made Chindit-style patrols, and on May 17 1944 took Myitkyina airfield. In October 1944, after repeated demands by Chiang Kai-shek, Stilwell was recalled to Washington. The CBI Theatre was split up with Lt Gen Dan Sultan taking over NCAC. In January 1945 the first convoy passed up the Ledo Road to the China border. Stilwell was sent to command US Tenth Army in Okinawa, where he took the Japanese surrender in August 1945. *HT*.

Stirling, Short S29 (Br, WWII). Heavy bomber. Prototype flew May 14 1939; first production May 7 1940. First squadron (No. 7) deliveries December 1940; first operation February 10/11 1941. Less successful than Halifax and Lancaster, but service as glider tug and transport to war's end. Production, 2,374 to November 1945.

Four 1,500hp Bristol Hercules XI engines; max. speed 260mph (418kph); 17,000lb (7,710kg) bombs, eight 0.303in machine guns.

Stirling, Col David (b.1915). Br. Responsible for initial formation of raiding and deep penetration force in North Africa, 1942, which grew into the SAS.

Stockwell, Gen Sir Hugh (1903–1987). Br. *See* SUEZ CRISIS.

Stopford, Lt Gen the Hon Sir Frederick (1854–1929). Br. Commander IX Corps in the landing at Suvla, 1915. *See* GALLIPOLI (1915–16).

Storable liquid fuel. In order to allow storage of ballistic missiles in an operational state, rapid-launch liquid fuels were developed that could be kept in missiles for extended periods. These have been particularly important in the Soviet Union which had problems developing reliable solid fuels. Typical storable fuels are forms of hydrazine (a compound of hydrogen and nitrogen) oxidized by dinitrogen tetroxide (N_2O_4). Even storable fuels are highly volatile, and the USSR has lost at least one submarine to missile explosion.

Storm troops. World War I name for élite German shock troops. (*Stosstruppen*). Specially trained in infiltration tactics, they sought out weak spots in opposing defences and then caused maximum confusion in the enemy rear by deep penetration and envelopment. They were employed with considerable success at Caporetto and Cambrai in 1917 and in the German 1918 offensives. *PJS*.

Stossel, Gen A M *see* RUSSO-JAPANESE WAR.

Strafe. World War I slang: a bombardment (from the German slogan *Gott strafe England!*: "God punish England!"). Later used mainly as a verb: to attack with an aircraft's machine guns or cannon.

"Strangle" Operation. Air interdiction operation against the North Korean transportation network begun in July 1951. The planners underestimated the capacity of the enemy to repair bomb damage and the attrition imposed by flak. The supply requirements of enemy divisions were low, so they could not be decisively weakened by bombing. By summer 1952, planners were looking for more effective ways to employ air power in Korea. *See also* AIR PRESSURE STRATEGY AND TARGETING SYSTEM.

Strategic Air Command (SAC). SAC was set up in 1946 to command all the USAAF's long-range striking forces designed to carry out direct attacks on the enemy's war industry, economy and population with both nuclear annd conventional weapons. SAC also carries out long-range reconnaissance and tanker missions. Originally equipped with bombers armed with free-fall bombs, SAC now operates intercontinental ballistic missiles and bombers equipped with a range of weapons including long-range cruise missiles. The most important SAC commander was Gen Curtis E Lemay who built the force up from 52,000 personnel and 837 aircraft in 1948 to 224,000 personnel and 2,711 aircraft in 1957. Since then SAC has had to share the strategic strike role with the US Navy and has come down in size to 104,000 personnel operating 1,000 ICBMS, 373 bombers, 93 reconnaissance and command aircraft and 696 tankers. *EJG.*

Strategic Arms Limitation Talks (SALT). In 1969 the USA and the Soviet Union began negotiations to agree on mutual limits on both sides' strategic nuclear forces, both offensive and defensive. It was decided to limit discussion of offensive forces to ICBMS and SLBMS, and in 1972, when a treaty was signed on ABM systems, a companion interim agreement was arrived at that created rough parity by balancing America's lead in MIRVed missiles against larger Soviet totals of missile launchers. The agreement also mandated that old ICBMS should be replaced by new SLBMS to enhance stability. The rapid development of Soviet MIRVed systems in the 1970s undermined the premises of SALT-1 and a new treaty was negotiated on the principle of parity in numbers and "no perceived advantage"; 2,400 strategic systems, including

long-range bombers, of which 1,320 could be MIRVed. A SALT-2 Treaty was signed in 1979 but never ratified by the US Congress. It thus never went completely into effect, but most of its provisions, notably the limits on MIRVS, were kept informally until the USA announced it would no longer be bound by them in 1986. *EJG.*

Strategic Arms Reduction Talks (START). US-Soviet talks on Strategic Arms Reduction began in 1982, but were broken off at the end of the following year. They were resumed along with the INF negotiations and the Defense and Space Talks at Geneva in 1985. Agreement has been reached on the principle of a 50 percent cut in strategic offensive arms and ceilings of 1,600 on strategic nuclear delivery vehicles and 6,000 warheads. There is still disagreement over sea-launched cruise missiles and linkage to an agreement on space weapons.

Strategic bombing offensive against Germany (1939-45). It was carried out by RAF Bomber Command 1939-45, US Eighth Air Force 1943-45 and US Fifteenth Air Force 1944-45. After the American intervention, it was generally known as the Combined Bomber Offensive. From Bomber Command's initial capacity of under 2,000 tons a month, the Combined Bomber Offensive built up to one of over 100,000 tons a month. At the beginning of the war, Bomber Command had under 300 bombers with crews available for operations. By the end, this had grown to more than 1,500 and, in the Eighth and Fifteenth Air Forces, more than 2,000. The campaign resulted in destruction in most of Germany's major cities and the deaths of between 750,000 and 1,000,000 of their inhabitants. It also culminated in the virtual elimination of oil production, the disruption of the transport system and severe damage to many other industries. It cost the lives of about 50,000 aircrew in Bomber Command, including more than 8,000 RCAF, over 3,400 RAAF and about 1,400 RNZAF. The American sacrifice, compressed into a shorter period, was approximately the same. Precise statistics are misleading due to the tactical opera-

tions which were also carried out by the crews taking part in the strategic air offensive.

In the first phase (September 1939–May 1940) the German bombing of Warsaw in September 1939 and Rotterdam in May 1940 was held to justify British attacks on German towns but the policy of Bomber Command was to avoid provocation until it was stronger. Little was therefore attempted beyond attacks on the German fleet and other undeniably "military" targets and the spreading of propaganda leaflets. The concept of daylight bombing was largely abandoned due to very heavy casualties incurred in attempts to carry it out.

In the second phase (May 1940-February 1942) Bomber Command gradually abandoned the plan of attacking precise targets, such as oil plants, at night due to the difficulty of hitting them. The policy of area attack upon the main cities was adopted as an indirect way of achieving the same aims.

In the third phase (February 1942–March 1944) Bomber Command mounted a sustained and increasingly destructive general area assault signalized by the Battles of the Ruhr, Hamburg and Berlin. A great expansion of the force in quantity and quality took place. Lancasters and Mosquitoes came into service, radar aids were introduced, the Pathfinder Force was created and bombing tactics were greatly improved. In addition, specialist squadrons achieved exceptions to the rule in such feats as the daylight attack on Augsburg and the Dams raid. From January 1943, the US Eighth Air Force joined in the attack on Germany with a policy of high-level daylight precision attack on key targets, but this had to be substantially broken off after the severe casualties incurred in the Schweinfurt raid on October 14 1943. Bomber Command's night casualties also became alarmingly high, especially in the Battle of Berlin which ended with the attack on Nuremberg on the night of March 30–31 1944. The main cause of these casualties was the German fighter force and in February 1944, in the "Big Week" operations, the Eighth Air Force took the offensive against this threat.

In the final phase (April 1944–

S

May 1945) the German fighter force was worn down and defeated in the air through the related use of bombers, to bring it up, and long-range fighters, to shoot it down. The destructive power of the British and American bombers was then released and the greater part of all the damage done to Germany throughout the war was achieved. Her cities were massively destroyed, especially Dresden, her oil production was virtually halted and her transport was rendered chaotic.

That the decisive effects of bombing were delayed until the last year of the war was due to the extraordinary resilience of the German people under a harsh regime, the ingenuity of Speer in organizing industry and the crippling effect upon the bombers of the German fighter force by day and night. Ultimately, however, the centre of the German war economy was decisively smashed but even then the Allied armies had to conquer the ground to enforce the surrender. *ANF.*

Strategic bombing offensive, Japan (1944–1945). The seizure of the Marianas Islands from mid-1944 provided bases within 1,500 miles (2,415km) of Japan from which a strategic bombing offensive could destroy military defences and industrial power in the Japanese home islands, preparatory to (or, possibly, even removing the need for) their invasion.

In late November 1944, B-29 Superfortresses from Saipan began to make high-altitude precision attacks against industrial targets in Japan. LeMay, who took command of XXI Bomber Command in January 1945, believed that area fire-bombing of major industrial cities would be more effective against Japan's many small, well-dispersed factories. The first major low-level incendiary attack was made on the night of March 9–10 1945, when 325 B-29s from Saipan, Tinian and Guam struck at Tokyo, creating a fire storm that burned out 15.8 sq miles (40.9 sq km) of the city, destroyed or damaged 23 key industrial targets, killed some 84,000 persons, injured c41,000 and left more than 1,000,000 homeless. In the following ten days, US bombers destroyed 31.81 sq miles (82.39 sq km)

of Japan's four major industrial cities: Nagoya, Osaka, Kobe and Tokyo. A shortage of incendiary ordnance, and the diversion of B-29s to aerial minelaying and tactical missions against kamikaze bases, subsequently forced LeMay to alternate urban area attacks with ordinary bombing of industrial and military targets.

Between April 1944–August 1945, XX and XXI Bomber Commands, Twentieth Air Force, flew more than 15,000 sorties (losing around 400 B-29s in combat) and dropped 104,000 tons of bombs, causing 806,000 casualties (including 330,000 dead) and destroying or damaging 169 sq miles (437.7 sq km) (42 percent of the total area) of the urban industrial area of 66 Japanese cities. However, enormous effort by ground and naval forces was required to position and maintain the bombers within striking distance, and their successes were achieved by massive and indiscriminate destruction rather than by the surgical strikes of precision bombing.

Strategic bombing had substantially destroyed Japan's industrial capabilities (although not, perhaps, weakening morale to the point where invasion became unnecessary) well before the atomic bomb attacks on Hiroshima and Nagasaki precipitated her surrender. However, its concentration on industrial and military targets was subsequently criticized by the United States Strategic Bombing Survey, Far East, which pointed out that submarine and air interdiction had already crippled Japan's industries by denying them access to raw materials, and that greater emphasis on aerial mining and the destruction of transportation facilities would have had more rapid and conclusive results. *CRS.*

Strategic Defense Initiative (SDI). In 1983 President Reagan announced a research programme into advanced anti-ballistic missile defences and a Strategic Defense Initiative office was set up in the Pentagon to supervise research into a range of suitable technologies. The main emphasis in SDI has been on the development of space-based weapons to destroy missiles during the boost phase of their flight before they can deploy

their warheads and "penetration aids" such as decoys. This gave the programme its nickname "Star Wars". SDI has been controversial, as it is seen by many to undermine the stability of nuclear deterrence. Its purpose has been confused; President Reagan expressed the hope that SDI would make nuclear weapons "impotent and obsolete" but the British Prime Minister obtained an assurance that it would instead help sustain deterrence. The SDI office themselves admit that they only conceive of a partial rather than a total defence. The exotic systems using directed energy technologies and electrically propelled railguns are no longer seen as near-term possibilities and instead, missile-based ABM "architectures", both ground- and space-based, are being concentrated upon. Congress has opposed too much emphasis on SDI research and has also opposed the "broad interpretation" of the ABM Treaty which the Administration claims allows testing of new ABM technologies. The Reagan administration's commitment to SDI has complicated the progress of negotiations to limit offensive arms. It remains to be seen how SDI will survive the departure of its main supporter, President Reagan. *EJG.*

Strategic Hamlet Program. Launched by President Ngo Dinh Diem of South Vietnam in March 1962 with the aim of severing the link between communist insurgents and the rural population. For design, the programme drew upon the failed "agrovilles" and the advice of British experts under Sir Robert Thompson who had run a successful counterinsurgency in Malaya. The idea was to gather the population into fortified communities, depriving the revolution of food, intelligence and recruits. Ignoring advice to restrict the scope, Diem set a goal of reorganizing virtually all of the South's hamlets. By forcing people to provide the free labour to build the hamlets, often far from their fields, the programme alienated rural support. Nor could it separate the revolutionaries from the population of which they were an integral part. Although the programme initially created some difficulties for the communists, in the long run it increased their popular support and was abandoned following Diem's overthrow. *WST*.

Strategic Rocket Forces (SRF). The senior service of the Soviet armed forces, set up in 1960 to control all land-based missile-forces with a range of over 600 miles (1,000km) and in addition the targeting of long-range air forces and SLBMs. The SRF consists of almost 300,000 personnel and is made up of six "Rocket Armies" organized in divisions, regiments, battalions and batteries. It now deploys over 1,400 ICBMs; its 553 IRBMS and MRBMS are currently being dismantled under the terms of the INF Treaty.

Stratemeyer, Lt Gen George E (1890–1969). US. Having graduated from West Point as an infantry officer, Stratemeyer began flying training in 1916 and transferred officially to the Air Corps four years later. By the time America entered World War II he had risen to the rank of brigadier general and was serving as Executive Officer to Gen Henry H Arnold, the Chief of the USAAF. In June 1942 he became CAS for Arnold and remained in this position until mid–1943 when he was posted to the China-Burma-India Theatre as air adviser to Gen Stilwell and as Commanding Gen of the India-Burma Sector. When Mountbatten reorganized the chain of command in Southeast Asia in December 1943, Stratemeyer was placed at the head of Eastern Air Command, which was formed to integrate the Allied air forces operating against the Japanese in Burma. He was promoted to Lt Gen in May 1945 and, shortly before the war ended, was chosen to command the USAAF in China. This was not to be his last combat command, however, for at the time of the communist invasion of South Korea in 1950 he was in Tokyo commanding the Far East Air Forces. His units at once provided the UN forces in Korea with vital air support, Stratemeyer's B-29 Superfortresses playing a major part in "Strangle" operations, but the strain of command took its toll and, in May 1951, Stratemeyer suffered a serious heart attack. He retired from the US Air Force the following January. *PJS*.

Strong, Maj Gen Kenneth William Dobson (1900–82). Br. Head of Intelligence to Eisenhower in Tunisia, and to Wilson and Alexander in Italy; negotiated the Italian capitulation in August 1943, and the surrender of German Army Group C in Northern Italy in May 1945.

Student, German paratroop commander

Student, Gen Kurt (1890–1978). Ger. A distinguished fighter pilot in World War I, who raised the first German experimental parachute force in 1936. He commanded 7th Parachute Division during the German invasion of Holland and Belgium in 1940. He took Fort Eban Emael by parachute and glider assault, and secured the crossings of the Meuse, being wounded himself.

In 1941, as Commander *Flieger-Korps XI*, composed of airborne units, he was ordered to capture Crete by airborne assault. He succeeded in forcing the British to evacuate the island, but his losses were so great that no further major German airborne operations were ever attempted.

Appointed Commander German Airborne Forces in 1942, he was forced to consent to their use as infantry divisions. Their recruiting was continued because of their high morale. In 1944, he became c-in-c First Parachute Army in Holland, successfully anticipating the Allies' airborne attack at Arnhem. *WGFJ*.

Stuka *see* JUNKERS JU-87.

Stumpff, Gen Hans Jürgen (1889–1968). Ger. Stumpff served as CGS of the Luftwaffe, June 1937–January 1939, and later commanded *Luftflotte 5* in Norway, May 1940–November 1943. In January 1944 he was made com-

mander of *Luftflotte Reich*, with responsibility for the air defence of Germany.

Sturdee, Adm of the Fleet Sir Frederick Charles Doveton (1859–1925). Br. Established reputation as torpedo specialist and tactician. Following a posting as Assistant Director, Naval Intelligence, 1900–02, and a cruiser command, 1903–05, he became COS to Adm Lord Charles Beresford (1846–1919), c-in-c Mediterranean and then Channel Fleet. Sturdee commanded 1st Battle Squadron, 1910, and in 1911 commanded all Home Fleet cruiser squadrons. By August 1914 he was Chief of Naval War Staff, but the appointment in October of Fisher – who regarded Sturdee as a leading supporter of his arch-enemy, Beresford – as First Sea Lord made his position untenable.

Thus, when Cradock's defeat at Coronel made it imperative to send a powerful force to the South Atlantic, Sturdee took command of the battlecruisers *Invincible* and *Inflexible*. Joined by five cruisers, he reached the Falklands on December 7 – only a few hours before von Spee's squadron was sighted, while Sturdee's ships were still coaling. Displaying admirable calm, Sturdee, in his own words "[gave] orders to raise steam at full speed and [went] down to a good breakfast". In the subsequent pursuit, he destroyed the German squadron. At Jutland, Sturdee commanded the 4th Battle Squadron, 1915–18. He later criticized Jellicoe's rigidity, and many believed that he, not Beatty, should have succeeded Jellicoe. *RO'N*.

Sub-machine gun *see* RIFLE.

Submarine-Launched Ballistic Missile (SLBM). Ballistic missiles launched from submarines have become increasingly important instruments of nuclear deterrence, being hard to find and destroy. The Soviet Union deployed short-range surface-launched SS-N-4 SLBMs on both conventionally and nuclear powered boats in the late 1950s, but the first SLBM with a range of over 1,000 miles (1,600km), capable of submerged launch and mounted in a nuclear-powered submarine, was the American Polaris of 1960. The Soviet Union

S

S

only matched Polaris capability with the SS-N-6 missile and the *Yankee*-class submarines of 1967. In the 1970s, the Americans concentrated on MIRVing their SLBM force with Poseidon and the Soviets on deploying long 4,800 mile (8,000km) range SS-N-8 SLBMs that could be fired from *Delta*-class submarines in defended "bastions" close to the Soviet Union; a MIRVed variant of the latter missile, the SS-N-18 appeared in 1977. In the 1980s the Americans have matched the Soviets in range with Trident and the Soviets have belatedly produced solid-fuelled SLBMs, the SS-N-20 mounted in the giant *Typhoon* submarines. Storable liquid-fuelled SLBMs remain in production in the USSR however in the shape of the SS-N-23 carried in the *Delta IV*. This has a higher payload than the SS-N-20, ten 100 kiloton MIRVs as opposed to six. Both France and China make and deploy their own SLBMs in submarines of their own design. *EJG*.

Submarines. As a practical weapon of war, the submarine is as old as the century. The French led the way, the Irish-American Holland close behind. The combination of internal combustion engines (the French were the first to use diesels, and also tried steam) for surface propulsion and battery-driven electric motors when submerged: the combined use of hydroplanes and ballast tanks for submerging and surfacing; all these were well established during the first decade of the century. In World War I the submarine established itself as the ideal commerce raider and a threat to all surfaced warships. Submarines grew in size (German "U-cruisers"), were shown to be ideal minelayers (Russia began this), the Italians built midgets and the British had anti-submarine submarines optimized for underwater performance.

The interwar years saw increasing reliability rather than innovation, and the submarines that fought World War II were mostly lineal developments of their predecessors (German Type VII and IX, British "S" and "T" classes, and the bigger American and Japanese submarines). British, Germans and Japanese built midget submarines (X-craft, Biber, Marder

etc.) for various purposes. The German submarine arm was the biggest innovator and paved the way for postwar developments by turning submersibles into true submarines by the use of snorkel, streamlining and increased battery power to produce the Type XXI and XXIII boats. The British carried on German experiments with turbines powered by hydrogen peroxide after the war, but it was the Americans, in developing nuclear-powered submarines, who took the process to its logical conclusion. By then putting intercontinental ballistic missiles in such craft, they produced what is so far the ultimate warship. *DJL*.

Subversion. A vital weapon of political warfare: sapping citizens' allegiance to their existing government in favour of another. SOE in its brief life, and the KGB over a much longer term, have recorded major successes in this field. The weapon is usually handled in such secrecy that those doing the bulk of the work – Lenin called them "useful fools" – are unaware of their task.

Sudetenland. The German-speaking part of Czechoslovakia which was ceded to Germany as a result of the Munich Agreement.

Suez Canal (Canal Zone). Following the defeat of Arabi Pasha at Tel-el-Kébir in 1882, Egypt became a de facto British Protectorate. Empire troops garrisoned the Canal Zone against Turkish incursions during World War I and British influence was consolidated by the Anglo-Egyptian Treaty of 1936. British strategic interests governed the use of the Canal throughout World War II and postwar British governments sought to retain this influence in the face of increasing Soviet interest in the Middle East.

Rising Arab nationalism in the early 1950s led to the fall of King Farouk and the declaration of an Egyptian Republic by President Neguib in 1953. Faced by mounting Arab pressures, Britain signed a new Treaty in 1954 agreeing to evacuate the Canal Zone. The British finally left Port Said on June 13 1956. Nasser, having supplanted Neguib as President in October 1954, now denied use of

the Canal to Israel and sought loans for building the High Dam at Aswan. Money was promised by the World Bank, Britain and the USA, but when the USSR offered to lend $1,200 million at low interest, the USA and Britain withdrew their offers. Nasser responded by nationalizing the Suez Canal on July 26 1956. *MH*.

Suez Canal, Turkish attack on (January 1915) *see* EGYPT AND PALESTINE CAMPAIGN.

Suez Crisis. Nasser's nationalization of the Suez Canal on July 26 1956 was accompanied by increased Egyptian hostility towards Israel, whose ships were banned from using the canal and denied use of their new port of Eilat by Egyptian batteries placed at the entrance to the Straits of Tiran. On July 29 the British, French and US governments conferred urgently. Anthony Eden, the British Prime Minister, obsessed with personal dislike of Nasser and apparently unaware of his newly found stature throughout the Arab world, pressed for military action to unseat the Egyptian government. In August the British government started to recall reservists and to prepare an expeditionary force. Following a conference of all interested parties in London (the Egyptians declined to attend), Australian Premier Sir Robert Menzies was sent to Cairo for abortive talks with Nasser. Tension increased throughout the Middle East, although the Egyptians soon showed that they were capable of running the Canal efficiently, even without many of the Canal Company's European pilots. After further military discussions, Britain and France announced a joint Task Force command structure in mid-August. The Supreme Allied commander was to be Gen Sir Charles Keightley (c-in-c British Middle East Land Forces). His Deputy was Vice Adm Barjot (c-in-c French Mediterranean Fleet). Lt Gen Sir Hugh Stockwell was appointed Commander Land Forces, with Gen Andre Beaufre as his deputy. Commander Allied Naval Forces was Vice Adm D F Durnford-Slater. Planning was hampered by enormous logistic and political problems, and France and Britain were simultaneously committed to internal security operations in Algeria and Cyprus. Port Said was selected as the target after Alexandria had been initially considered. Anglo-French forces earmarked for the operation, code-named "Musketeer", originally comprised 79,000 men, 21,000 vehicles, 500 aircraft and 130 warships, a force comparable to that landed at Anzio in 1944.

Whilst the allies prepared for war amidst rising domestic political discord, the Israelis attacked the Egyptians in the Sinai, launching their assault on October 29 as the Anglo-French forces embarked in Malta, Algiers and Cyprus, to be joined at sea by those dispatched from British and French ports. The US Sixth Fleet shadowed and at times hindered the Allied force as it headed towards the Eastern Mediterranean. Following warnings to the Egyptian civilian population, Anglo-French air attacks were launched against military targets from November 1, and within 48 hours the Egyptian Air Force had been driven off to friendly Arab states or destroyed on the ground. The air attacks, now augmented by carrier-borne aircraft, continued on November 3-4. At first light on November 5, British and French paratroops dropped on El Gamil airfield and Port Fouad. Early on November 6, the Allied fleet arrived off Port Said, and following a short bombardment launched the world's first helicopter-borne amphibious assault whilst landing craft went ashore with Commandos to take the town from the sea. As night fell, a cease-fire was negotiated, but not before elements of the British 16th Independent Parachute Brigade Group had rushed down the Canal towards Suez as far as El Kap, about 15 miles (24km) out of Port Said, where they dug in. The sea tail of the force began to arrive from England on November 10 in the form of part of 3rd Infantry Division, whose troops took over from the Commandos and Paras.

To a background of Security Council pressure at the United Nations and veiled threats of nuclear war from the USSR, the allies began to withdraw from Port Said on December 7 as the first units of a UN peacekeeping force arrived.

By December 22 the UN takeover was complete, the only remaining Anglo-French units being specialists who stayed behind for two months under UN auspices to help clear dozens of sunken blockships from the Canal. In the Sinai, a UN force replaced the Israelis, who withdrew back to their start lines in the north.

As the result of the operation, claimed as a triumph by the Egyptians, Anglo-French influence in the Middle East reached a nadir and that of the Soviet Union was now in the ascendant. It did not prove a great diplomatic success for the US, whose government under President Eisenhower and Secretary Dulles vainly sought to fill the vacuum left by the discomfiture of France and Britain. Anglo-American relations were for a time seriously eroded and the growing instability which has characterized the Middle East since 1956 began to be apparent. Eden's failing health, which throughout had seriously affected his political judgment, led to his resignation early in 1957. British casualties in "Musketeer" were negligible – 22 killed and fewer than 100 wounded. The French lost 10 men killed and 33 wounded. Ten allied aircraft were lost. Egyptian casualties in Port Said and Port Fouad amounted to about 750 killed and 2,400 wounded. *MH*.

Suffren (French battleship) *see* DARDANELLES (1915).

Sugiyama, Field Marshal Hajime (1880–1945). Jap. A leading advocate of war with the West and a "Strike South" policy, Sugiyama was Minister of War and chief director of the China campaign, 1937–38. CGS, 1940–44; Minister of War, succeeding Tojo, July 1944–April 1945. Then appointed Commander, First General Army, for "defence to the death" of Japan. Following the surrender, Sugiyama was influential in persuading the home forces to disarm peacefully, before committing suicide on September 12 1945.

Sukarno, Achmed (1897–1970). Indonesian. President of Indonesia (1949-67), when he was removed from power by Gen Suharto (b.1921). *See* MALAYSIA-INDONESIA CONFRONTATION (1963–66).

Sukhoi Su-7 "Fitter-A" (USSR). Single-seat strike fighter. Entered Russian service 1959; supplied to some 15 other air services. Used in combat in the India-Pakistan War 1971 and also in the Arab-Israeli War of October 1973. One 15,134lb (6,865kg) s.t. Lyulka AL-7F-1 engine; max. speed 1,056mph (1,699kph); two 30mm cannon, bombs and/or rockets.

Summerall, Gen Charles Pelot (1867–1955). US. A hero of the Boxer Rising, standing under fire while directing his gunners in the breaching of the Chi Hua Gate, Peking, August 1900. Summerall ended World War I in command of US V Corps at Meuse-Argonne Forest, 1918. At this time he began his development of fire direction centres for the central control of several batteries and for speedy and effective communication between advancing infantry and supporting artillery, providing the basis of US field artillery doctrine thereafter; also noteworthy was his successful advocacy of the 105mm howitzer as standard US divisional artillery. Summerall was US Army Chief of Staff, 1926–30. *RO'N*.

Sunda Straits, Battle of the *see* JAVA SEA, BATTLE OF THE.

Sunderland, Short S25 (Br, WWII and later). Reconnaissance/anti-submarine flying-boat; crew 10. Prototype flew October 16 1937; first production April 21 1938. Three squadrons operational by outbreak of war; remained in service until May 1958. Korean War; used Berlin airlift 1948. Development up to Mark V increased effectiveness. Postwar 19 to French *Aéronavale*, 16 to RNZAF. Production, 749. Four 1,010hp Bristol Pegasus XXII or 1,200hp Pratt and Whitney R-1830-90B/C/D engines; max. speed 213mph (343kph); up to ten 0.303in and two 0.5in machine guns, 4,960lb (2,250kg) bombs, mines and/or depth charges.

Superfortress *see* B-29 SUPERFORTRESS.

Supreme Headquarters Allied Expeditionary Force (SHAEF). The designation of Eisenhower's command of the Anglo-American

S

naval, military and air forces assigned to the operation codenamed "Overlord", the invasion of Europe, 1944.

Supreme War Council (1917–18 and 1939–40). Formed in November 1917 after the Italian collapse at Caporetto had made greater Allied coordination imperative. Its only substantial achievement was to create a general reserve of troops for the entire Western theatre. In 1939 Britain and France agreed to establish a Supreme War Council before the outbreak of war. This institution never acquired a permanent joint staff, but was otherwise reasonably successful in enabling the Allies to agree on broad plans for the conduct of operations in Western Europe and Scandinavia. Seventeen meetings were held between September 12 1939 and June 13 1940. *BB*.

Surface to Air Missile (SAM). Missiles designed to shoot down aircraft were first experimented with in World War II but did not enter service until Nike Ajax batteries began to be installed in the USA in 1953. Nike Ajax was succeeded by Nike Hercules, both of which used command guidance, as did the first generation Soviet SA-2 missiles used in large numbers in combat in Vietnam and the Middle East. The performance of Egyptian and Syrian air defences in 1973 equipped with Soviet SA-2, -3 and -6 missiles was a major factor in the Yom Kippur War. Although the Soviet Union still deploys over 9,000 SAMs for home defence, the USA now only fields SAMs for tactical defence on land and at sea. The US Army has Patriot and the Navy the Aegis system. Both use advanced radars to command the missiles to a point where semi-active homing takes over. The "Standard" missile used in Aegis is the descendant of the Terrier/Tartar/Standard continuously developed since the 1950s. SAMs come in three broad categories: area defence systems with ranges of over about 24 miles (40km); point defence systems that generally operate within a 6-mile (10km) range; and hand-held systems like Stinger and Blowpipe with ranges of less than 3 miles (5km). *EJG*.

Surface to Surface Missile (SSM). A missile designed to be fired from a land-based launcher or a ship at a surface target at land or sea. SSMs can be either ballistic or cruise in configuration and, if designed to engage precise targets such as ships, will be given some form of terminal homing using, for example, radar. The term SSM tends to be used for the shorter ranged tactical systems. Almost all SSMs rely on either an autopilot or an inertial navigation system for mid-course flight.

Surigao Strait, Battle of *see* LEYTE GULF, BATTLE OF (1944).

Surveillance *see* ELECTRONIC WARFARE; REMOTELY PILOTED VEHICLES; SATELLITES.

Sutherland, Lt Gen James W Jr (b.1918). US. Commander, US Army XXIV Corps in Vietnam, from June 1970 to June 1971. For part of that time he also served as the senior US Army adviser to the Army of the Republic of Vietnam (ARVN) I Corps Tactical Zone. He planned, coordinated and conducted American airmobile and aviation support of ARVN forces in Operation "Lam Son 719".

Suvla landings *see* GALLIPOLI.

Suzuki, Adm Kantaro (1867–1948). Jap. After a distinguished career in the Imperial Japanese Navy, Suzuki became Grand Chamberlain in 1929, thereafter acted as a moderating influence on national politics. In April 1945 he was made Prime Minister but failed to engineer peace until after the atomic raids.

Sweeney, Maj Charles W (b.1919). US. Pilot of the B-29 *Bock's Car* which dropped the atomic bomb on Nagasaki, August 9 1945.

Swimming tanks. Variant of Sherman medium tank, fitted with twin propellers ("Duplex Drive", or "DD") and collapsible immersion shield, and thus with a limited amphibious capability. *See also* TANKS.

Swinton, Col Sir Ernest (1868–1951). Br. Swinton may justly be called "the father of the tank". As an official war correspondent in

France in October 1914 he realized that an armoured vehicle might resolve the stalemate. It must be capable of destroying machine guns, crossing country and trenches, breaking through entanglements and climbing earthworks. He proposed that some Holt caterpillar tractors might be converted into fighting machines. The War Office was unenthusiastic, but Winston Churchill, then First Lord of the Admiralty, backed Swinton. The first naval experiments concerned cumbersome machines with large wheels and rollers in front designed to crush wire and cross trenches. Not until early 1915 was Swinton's idea of caterpillar tractors re-examined. At the first trials, September 1915, a model called "Big Willie" made a good impression. Soon afterwards, as camouflage, Swinton coined the generic name "tank".

Swinton was anxious that this new and potentially decisive machine should not be used prematurely with consequent loss of secrecy, but after the disastrous opening of the Somme campaign on July 1 1916 his protests were overruled. Some 50 tanks were sent over in August, but they were prone to mechanical breakdown and the crews were semi-trained and without tactical experience. First used on the southern sector on September 15, their surprise value was sacrificed without dramatic success. Only a handful of tanks reached the startline and apart from a much publicized advance through the ruined village of Flers, their performance was disappointing. Swinton's invention proved its worth at Cambrai in November 1917. In 1934 he became Colonel-Commandant of the Royal Tank Corps.*BB*.

Sword beach *see* NORMANDY, INVASION OF (1944).

Swordfish, Fairey (Br, WWII). Shipboard reconnaissance/torpedobomber; crew 2–3. Prototype flew April 17 1934; first production December 31 1935; first delivery February 19 1936. Thirteen squadrons by outbreak of war. Despite antiquated appearance and progressive increase in military load, proved remarkably effective and versatile, notably in Taranto operation, November 11 1940. Last operational flight June 28 1945. Production 2,393. One 690hp Bristol Pegasus IIIM3 engine; max. speed 139mph (224kph); two 0.303in machine guns, one 1,610lb (730kg) torpedo, one 1,500lb (675kg) mine, 1,500lb (675kg) bombs, or eight 60lb (27kg) rocket projectiles.

Sydney Harbour raid (May 31–June 1 1942). At dusk on May 31 1942, the Japanese submarines *I-22*, *I-24* and *I-27* each launched one Type A midget submarine *c*23 miles (37km) east of Sydney Harbour, NSW, Australia. Penetrating the naval base under cover of darkness (in what its participants accepted as a kamikaze mission) one midget was self-destructed when detected by patrol boats at the defence perimeter; the two-man crew of a second committed suicide when pursued by harbour defence craft. The third penetrated Man-of-War anchorage, surfaced to attack, but was sighted and forced down by gunfire from heavy cruiser USS *Chicago*. Surfacing again to locate a target, the midget was attacked by corvette HMAS *Geelong* but fired both its torpedoes, one narrowly missing *Chicago*, the other sinking barracks ship HMAS *Kuttabul* (19 dead; 10 wounded). The midget was scuttled by its crew: the "mother" submarines shelled the Sydney suburbs early next morning and escaped unscathed. Near-simultaneously (May 29–30), two Japanese submarines launched Type A midgets in a similar raid on Diégo Suarez, Madagascar, sinking tanker *British Loyalty* and severely damaging battleship *Ramillies*. *RO'N*.

Syria, British invasion of (June 8–July 14 1941). Carried out under Gen Wilson's command to prevent Syria becoming an Axis base in the Middle East by 7th Australian and 6th British Divisions, Free French forces under Gen Legentilhomme from Palestine, and "Habforce" from Iraq. The Vichy French under Gen Dentz resisted strongly on the Litani and Damour rivers. Damascus fell to Legentilhomme on June 20, and the Damour Line was breached on July 6, but Dentz did not finally ask for an armistice until July 11.

T-34. Russian main battle tank produced in enormous numbers during and after World War II. The first of a line of Soviet MBTs (T-54, 55, 62, 72 etc) all embodying the philosophy of high mobility, fire power, and small silhouette. *See also* TANKS.

T-80 Successor. Provisional name given to new Soviet main battle tank which is believed by Western intelligence experts to be of turretless configuration.

Tactical bombing *see* BOMBING.

Tactical nuclear weapons. Nuclear weapons designed for use in battlefield operations on land or at sea, including nuclear shells, warheads for surface to air or surface to surface missiles, bombs for tactical-strike aircraft and nuclear depth charges. The creation of the "intermediate nuclear forces" category has allowed a line to be drawn at 300 miles (500km) for the maximum range of land-based tactical missiles. These weapons are generally relatively low in yield in the kiloton range but there is considerable overlap in yield between them and "strategic" forces. Once thought of as a way of making up for deficiencies in conventional fire power and perhaps usable without the threat of escalation, tactical weapons are now thought of more as a way of communicating the threat of a full-scale nuclear exchange. *EJG*.

Taegu, southeast Korea. The HQ of US Eighth Army during the battle for the Pusan Perimeter, August–September 1950. There were fierce battles around the city as the NKPA attempted to break UN line and cut the road and rail links between Taegu and Pusan.

Taejon. Scene of the first major battle between the NKPA and the Americans during the Korean War. In July 1950, US 24th Infantry Division under Gen Dean attempted to hold the Kum river line in front of Taejon. On July 14 leading elements of the NKPA crossed the Kum and Dean ordered a

fall back on Taejon. The North Koreans attacked on July 19 and captured the city after heavy fighting. The 24th Division fought its way out but lost 30 percent of its men and much equipment. Gen Dean was captured after the battle, becoming the highest ranking US officer to fall into enemy hands. *CM*.

Taierchwang, Battle of (1938) *see* SINO-JAPANESE WAR.

Taku Forts, Battle of the (1900) *see* BOXER RISING.

Tanaka, Rear Adm Raizo (1892–1969). Jap. From the earliest days of the Pacific War, when he commanded invasion convoys in the Philippines and Dutch East Indies campaigns, Tanaka manifested the blend of skill and daring that places him among the finest destroyer flotilla commanders. Although he played an important part in the Japanese victory in the Java Sea, February 1942, his major fame was won in the naval campaign off Guadalcanal, August 1942–January 1943, where his high-speed "Tokyo Express" convoys were the mainstay of Japan's reinforcement efforts. In the naval battle off Guadalcanal, November 12–15 1942, Tanaka's supply convoy (11 transports with 13,000 men; 11 destroyers) was swamped by air attack: nevertheless, he successfully pushed through four transports (4,000 men) and rescued 5,000 survivors from his sunken ships during his withdrawal. His night-fighting expertise was best demonstrated in his defeat of a superior US force at Tassafaronga, December 1 1942.

Tanaka had, however, repeatedly criticized the Japanese high command's conduct of the Solomons campaign, in particular the failure to coordinate sea, air and land operations, and had advocated withdrawal from Guadalcanal. Early in 1943 he was removed from his command, never to receive another sea-going appointment. *RO'N*.

Tank destroyer. A high velocity direct-fire gun mounted on an armoured chassis (e.g. German *Jagdpanther* of World War II). Now largely replaced by guided weapons systems.

Tanks and Armoured Fighting Vehicles. Early in 1915 tactical deadlock had set in on the Western Front. The combatants were deeply entrenched behind barbed wire and the only solution lay in the ability of either side to effect and exploit a significant breakthrough. Artillery bombardment and infantry assault were not enough. A new weapon was needed and technology, in the form of the petrol engine and caterpillar track, was at hand. The first batch of machines was shipped to France from the UK in strictest secrecy as "water tanks", thus coining a name which stuck. These Mk I tanks, protected against shell splinters and small-arms fire, achieved a remarkable moral effect when first used against the Germans in September 1916, but it was not until the Battle of Cambrai (1917) that they were correctly used, in mass, to punch a hole in the main German line. The initial attack was successful but the horsed cavalry failed to exploit it and the Germans recovered. By 1918 the Allies had mustered a huge force of tanks, including faster and lighter models ("Whippets") capable of exploiting opportunities created by the more heavily armed machines; the new branch of the service featured prominently in Haig's decisive victories over the main German field army. Although the main thrust in tank design was initially British, the French Renault company began producing its FT17 light tank in 1917. With fully traversing turret and forward fighting compartment, it was the precursor of modern tank design.

After 1918, the British General Staff failed to develop the tank or its tactical handling; official policy discounted any Continental war, a view enshrined in the "Ten Year Rule". However, the writings of innovative British military thinkers such as Fuller, Hobart and Liddell Hart were closely studied in Germany and elsewhere. Theories of blitzkrieg owed much to Liddell Hart's thesis of the "Expanding Torrent" – armoured penetration exploited by highly mobile mechanized forces directed at the enemy's rear areas. In the USSR, as in Germany, development of new tanks went ahead. Anticipating a war of manoeuvre on the open plains, the Russians adapted the US Christie design into what eventually became the T-34.

The Germans had been steadily moving towards the concept of mechanized all-arms fighting formations led by universal "main battle" tanks. In France and Britain, tanks were considered to be subordinate to the cavalry and infantry. Their armies went to war in 1939 with slow, heavily armoured "infantry" tanks such as the French Char B and the British Matilda, for close support of dismounted infantry. In the traditional "cavalry" roles of reconnaissance and exploitation, the British used obsolescent Vickers light tanks and a family of "cruiser" tanks which, although fast, were outclassed by the German panzers in 1940 and again in the desert battles of 1941–42. Sensational initial successes against the Russians in the summer of 1941 confirmed the validity of German armoured doctrine when used in conjunction with a responsive tactical air force. However, the massive Soviet counteroffensivess of 1942–43 were headed by the new T-34 tank, which established itself as one of the outstanding fighting vehicles of World War II. The first true Main Battle Tank (MBT), its robust construction, simplicity of operation, the fire power of its 76mm gun and a good power-to-weight ratio for high mobility, enabled the Red Army to fight the German panzers on far better terms than could the Anglo-Americans. German tank design veered towards the defensive in the face of mounting Soviet armoured superiority, resulting in larger machines of which the 56-ton Tiger Mk I was a good example. Mounting the celebrated 88mm gun, it was heavily armoured, sacrificing mobility. The lighter (44-ton) Panther was more agile, with well-contoured armour conferring high levels of protection. Both tanks were superior to the American and British Shermans, Churchills and Cromwells pitted against them. Experiences of the 1944–45 campaign in Northwest Europe profoundly affected British tank design philosophy, with its stress on fire power and protection.

World War II's lessons were taken to heart by Soviet tank designers, and characteristics of the T-34 are still apparent in their latest models, designed for aggressive action, deep penetration and exploitation. They emphasize high mobility and fire power, relying on agility and compactness rather than heavy armour for protection. The Americans and British lay more stress on crew protection, resulting in heavily armoured vehicles which demand powerful engines, requiring bigger engine bays and more fuel; NATO's MBTs are now considerably larger than those used by the Warsaw Pact. Russian designers opted for automatic gun loading, giving a smaller fighting compartment for a three-man crew, lower silhouette, and lighter tank.

Even in World War I, it was apparent that tanks were vulnerable when unsupported; determined infantry with well-sited anti-tank weapons could stalk and destroy tanks which were not themselves closely protected by their own infantry. In Russia, early German successes of 1941–42 were achieved because Russian tanks were isolated from their infantry and artillery support, then destroyed in detail. In the North African campaign of 1941–42, the Germans aimed to destroy the British armour with skilfully handled anti-tank guns, keeping their small but well-trained tank force intact for decisive exploitation supported by motorized infantry, once the British tanks had been eliminated. Recognizing the need for "armoured infantry", the Allies used converted Canadian "Ram" tanks ("Kangaroos") as personnel carriers in the Northwest European campaign of 1944–45. In postwar campaigns, the same lessons have been re-learned. On the Golan Heights in 1973, the Syrians lacked close infantry support for their tanks and suffered appalling losses, whilst the Egyptians lured the unsupported tanks of an Israeli armoured brigade into a carefully prepared ambush of well-served anti-tank guided weapons and virtually destroyed it.

The range of armoured fighting vehicles with which the combatants ended the war was markedly different from that of 1939. The MBT was now recognized as the primary instrument of the offensive, and also, with the potent high-velocity guns now carried, as the key anti-armour weapon system in defence. To ensure its optimum deployment, a large family of supporting armour had been developed; this included self-propelled artillery, also armoured recovery vehicles capable of salvaging damaged MBTS on the actual battlefield. Special combat engineering vehicles were adapted from the tank chassis, including the Armoured Vehicle Royal Engineers (AVRE) based on the British "Churchill" tank body, carrying a heavy demolition mortar or Petard for the reduction of enemy fieldworks. There were other variants, widely known as "Funnies", developed by Maj Gen Hobart for his specialist 79th Armoured Division, tasked with breaching the German West Wall defences on the French coast. These included swimming tanks to lead the assault up the beaches, flamethrowers ("Crocodiles"), bridge and tracklayers, and flail tanks ("Crabs") for the detonation of minefields. Specialist vehicles continue to be an essential ingredient of all armoured forces and it is accepted that infantry working in conjunction with tanks now require fully protected vehicles capable of armed action when required. Thus the armoured personnel carrier (APC) has become the Mechanized Infantry Combat Vehicle (MICV).

The tank designer has to reconcile factors of mobility, fire power and protection; emphasis on these differs from nation to nation. High mobility and fire power have always been prime considerations for German and Russian designers but American and British tank design places a high premium on protection. The 63-ton British Challenger carries heavy armour protection for its four-man crew and mounts a 120mm gun. Israel's Merkava, designed for operations in the exposed conditions of the desert, is also heavily armoured, but for additional close protection carries a subsection of infantry within its 61-ton hull. The German Leopard is less heavily armoured but, like comparable Soviet tanks, has a power-to-weight ratio permitting good acceleration and high road and cross-country speeds.

There has been a move away

from the rifled gun as the tank's main armament. At present, only Britain appears to favour it and it will be carried by the improved Challenger which is to be the Royal Armoured Corps' future MBT. High-pressure smoothbore guns firing Armour Piercing Fin Stabilized Discarding Sabot (APFSDS) ammunition have been adopted by all other major powers. Fire control systems, computerized and capable of feeding in all required data necessary to give maximum chance of a first-round hit, are now essential, as are laser rangefinders and high-definition night vision equipment. These systems permit rapid engagement of successive targets and greatly relieve the crew workload in the 24-hour battle. Developments in power plants have resulted in higher power output for reduced bulk and a shift towards turbo-diesel engines. However, the American M1 Abrams MBT is powered by a gas turbine, whose compactness must be balanced against greatly increased fuel consumption and thus larger tankage under armour.

Developments in metallurgy have contributed to increased protection available to tank crews. One counter to the increasingly effective chemical energy (CE) warheads fitted to modern anti-tank guided weapons (ATGW) is the fitting of Explosive Reactive Armour (ERA) consisting of slabs of explosive which, detonating when hit by a CE warhead, diffuse the effect of the hit and prevent penetration of the main armour. Various forms of compound armour have also been developed against attack by Kinetic Energy (KE) ammunition. Although gun design has probably neared the limit of development, there is scope for improved CE warheads and fin-stabilized KE rounds fired from smoothbore high pressure tank guns.

The higher acceleration and running speeds of the newer tanks impose greater demands on their tracks and suspensions, and these too need to be developed to match the demands placed on them.

Future tanks could be markedly different in appearance if it is decided to do away with the turret and adopt the type of configuration already seen on the Swedish "S

tank" of the 1960s, whose low silhouette and three-man crew (as in current Soviet designs, using an autoloader) greatly reduces the target area whilst permitting a higher power-to-weight ratio and increased mobility both on and off the battlefield. There is evidence to show that the Russian T-80 Successor tank is turretless and mounts an extremely potent 135mm high-pressure gun. If so, it poses a serious threat to the present generation of NATO tanks. *MH.*

Tannenberg and the Masurian Lakes, Battles of (1914). Plans had long existed in Berlin and St Petersburg for the inevitable conflict between the Central Powers and Russia and France. Field Marshal von Moltke's concept of 1890 was to deal first with the Russian threat to East Prussia, holding the French on the Western Front until the full weight of the German war machine could be switched from the East, using the highly developed railway system carefully laid out with such strategic use in view. In 1891 the plan was recast by Schlieffen, the new German Chief of General Staff. On the assumption that Russian mobilization would take six weeks or more, he allotted only one army to cover the East whilst the master stroke was delivered against France. The armies would then be switched to defend East Prussia. Moltke's nephew, succeeding Schlieffen in 1906, assigned Prittwitz's Eighth Army to this task in 1914.

Russia was bound by treaty with France to put 800,000 men into the field 15 days after mobilization. This was asking a lot of the Russian military machine, especially the Imperial general staff. The French immediately found themselves in trouble on the Western Front and called for a Russian offensive in East Prussia to divert German forces. Although only partially mobilized, the Russians complied. Their western (Polish) province in 1914 was a salient pointing towards Berlin (only 180 miles/ 290km distant). This was threatened in turn by East Prussia from the north and the Austro-Hungarian province of Galicia to the south. The frontiers on both sides were guarded by numerous arsenal-fortresses around which great armies could pivot. Whilst it had long been Russia's policy to deprive her own frontier zones of good road/rail communications, East Prussia in particular was served by a carefully laid-out rail network tied into the German system; double-track lines ran East-West to permit rapid movement between fronts, and laterals allowed formations to be switched from flank to flank. To make matters worse for the invader, the gauge of the German system was narrower than the Russian.

The Russians deployed two armies against East Prussia; the First (Vilna), under Rennenkampf, was drawn up on the line of the Niemen, and the Second (Warsaw) under Samsonov was deployed to the south. Both were under overall command of the ineffective Zhilinsky in Warsaw. Rennenkampf was ordered to advance first, to draw the German Eighth Army forward; Samsonov would then attack from its southern flank.

On August 17, Rennenkampf crossed the frontier with six infantry and five cavalry divisions. Prittwitz met him in an encounter battle at Gumbinnen on August 20 where the Russians got the upper hand but failed to follow up. Prittwitz, hearing that Samsonov had now crossed the southern frontier, lost his nerve, ordered a general retreat to the line of the Vistula, and was promptly dismissed by Moltke, who recalled the respected Hindenburg from retirement to command Eighth Army, with Ludendorff as his COS. They arrived in East Prussia to find that Eighth Army's head of operations, the brilliant Col Max Hoffmann, had cancelled the withdrawal and drafted plans for a counterstroke which Ludendorff at once ratified (and for which he subsequently claimed the credit).

Samsonov continued to blunder forward, wheeling left and losing cohesion, whilst Rennenkampf, now held by only a screen of German cavalry, remained inert. Using the railway system, the Germans concentrated Eighth Army against Samsonov, now spread out over a 60-mile (96km) front with his right flank exposed. By August 27 the trap had been sprung: Russian Second Army disintegrated. Samsonov committed suicide; 92,000 Russian prisoners

were taken.

Hindenburg now turned to Rennenkampf, who had halted with his right flank on the Baltic shore and his left at the southern end of the Masurian Lakes. The Germans closed with Rennenkampf on September 9–10, ignoring the pleas of the Austro-Hungarians to go to their rescue in Galicia. Driving in the Russian left flank, Eighth Army began to roll up the enemy line. Rennenkampf managed to extricate most of the First Army by hard marching, but lost over 100,000 men. German casualties were 10,000. *MH.*

Taranto, air attack on, (1940). Taranto is the main naval base in the south of Italy. In 1940 the British Navy planned a carrier strike on the Italian fleet in harbour there. The attack was to be made using the two available carriers, *Illustrious* and *Eagle*, but the latter was unserviceable and some of her aircrew were transferred to the newer carrier. Operation "Judgment" was launched on the night of November 11 with 21 biplane Swordfish torpedo bombers, *Illustrious* having approached within 170 miles (270km) of Taranto. Those aircraft which carried torpedoes went in just above sea level, while bomb-carrying aircraft attacked from higher, as did those allocated to drop illuminating flares. The attack, mounted in two waves, was a complete success. Three Italian battleships were put out of action: *Cavour* (sunk although later raised), *Littorio* and *Duilio* (heavily damaged), plus damage to shore installations. Despite heavy flak, only two Swordfish were lost. This was the first great carrier victory, establishing British superiority in the Mediterranean for some time after – and providing some of the inspiration to the Japanese for the Pearl Harbor attack. *DJL.*

Taranto, landings at (September 9 1943). 1st British Airborne Division, carried in the ships of 12th Cruiser Squadron, seized the port before the Germans could react to the Italian capitulation. The landings were unopposed, and enabled V Corps (Allfrey) to advance rapidly north to seize Bari and Brindisi to which the Badoglio government had escaped from Rome.

US Marines at Tarawa

Tarawa campaign (November 1943). The first move in the Central Pacific campaign was Operation "Galvanic", the conquest of the Gilbert Islands, to provide air bases for the next "stepping-stone" in the Allied advance, the conquest of the Marshalls (*see* KWAJALEIN-ENIWETOK). "Galvanic's" major objectives were the atolls of Tarawa, Makin and Apamama.

Under the direction of the US Fifth Fleet (Vice Adm Spruance), Southern Attack Force (Rear Adm H W Hill) sailed for Tarawa with Marines of V Amphibious Corps (Maj Gen H M Smith), while Northern Attack Force (Rear Adm R K Turner) carried men of the 27th Infantry Division (Maj Gen R C Smith) to Makin. Apamama, virtually undefended, was secured by Marines of V Amphibious Corps Reconnaissance Company, landed by the submarine USS *Nautilus* on November 21.

The key to Tarawa atoll was Betio Island, strongly-fortified and defended by c2,800 naval troops (Rear Adm Keiji Shibasaki) and a 2,000-strong Korean labour battalion, well-equipped with coastal and field artillery and machine guns. Although the landings by 2nd Marine Division (Maj Gen J C Smith), beginning at 0900 hours on November 20, were preceded by massive air and naval bombardment, heavy losses were incurred: in the initial attacking waves, many armoured "amtracs" (tracked landing vehicles, able to negotiate the reef around the lagoon) were destroyed, and the heavily-laden Marines of the follow-up waves presented easy targets as they waded from reef to beach. Some 1,500 of the 5,000 Marines put ashore by nightfall became casualties. But bombardment had badly shaken the Japanese and destroyed their communications systems: Shibasaki could not launch a night counterattack that might have overwhelmed the beachhead. After 76 hours of savage close-quarter fighting, the Marines secured Betio on November 23, at a cost of just over 1,000 dead and 2,070 wounded; only 17 Japanese troops and 129 Koreans survived.

Meanwhile, some 105 miles (169km) to the north, the Japanese garrison on Makin – 400 naval troops (Lt Seizo Ishikawa) and 400 Koreans – fiercely opposed 165th Infantry Regimental Combat Team's invasion early on November 20. When Makin was secured, November 23, only one Japanese and 104 Koreans survived. US losses were 66 killed and 152 wounded – plus 644 naval personnel lost in the escort carrier *Liscombe Bay*, sunk off Makin by Japanese submarine *I-175* on November 24. *RO'N.*

Task force. American naval term for any group of ships assembled for a particular operation or purpose. Now more generally adopted.

Task Force 77. Carrier strike force of US Seventh Fleet that entered the Vietnam War during the Tonkin Gulf Incident, 1964. The Task Force initiated the 37-month bombing of North Vietnam in February 1965 and flew close-support missions over South Vietnam from April 1965. Carriers operating from "Yankee Station" in the Gulf of Tonkin flew "Rolling Thunder" missions against the North, while those at "Dixie Station" about 105 miles (170km) southeast of Cam Ranh Bay provided air support in the South.

Tassafaronga, Battle of (November 30–December 1 1942). Alerted by "Magic", US Task Force 67 (Rear Adm Carleton H Wright: four heavy cruisers; one light cruiser; six destroyers) intercepted Tanaka's "Tokyo Express" of eight destroyers (carrying supplies for Tassafaronga, northwest Guadalcanal), in Ironbottom Sound at *c*2300 hours on December 1 1942. Failing to exploit the tracking of the Japanese approach by his surface radar, Wright allowed Tanaka's force to pass, delaying his own

destroyers' attack until the Japanese warships were beyond effective US torpedo range. Alerted when the US cruisers opened fire, Tanaka detached four destroyers to drop supply containers off Tassafaronga and, although losing *Takanami* to US gunfire, counterattacked with Long Lance torpedoes, sinking heavy cruiser USS *Northampton* and so badly damaging heavy cruisers *New Orleans*, *Pensacola* and *Minneapolis* that they were out of action until late 1943. *RO'N.*

Taylor, Gen Maxwell (1901–87). US. A soldier with high academic qualifications, Taylor's career before World War II included service in Japan, China, South America and study at various US military establishments. In 1942 he was appointed Chief of Staff and artillery commander of the 82nd Airborne Division and took part in the campaigns in Sicily and Italy. Such was Taylor's aptitude that he was chosen to carry out a secret mission to Rome to try and negotiate arrangements for a seizure of the city by Allied airborne forces coincident with Italy's surrender. He subsequently commanded the 101st Airborne Division, leading it with distinction in Normandy, Operation "Market Garden" and the advance into Germany. His postwar career was equally varied. After a period as Superintendent of West Point, he commanded the US Eighth Army during the Korean War and served both as US Army Chief of Staff (1955–59) and Chairman of the Joint Chiefs of Staff (1962–64). A "political" general, Taylor had close associations with the White House and clashed with President Eisenhower over military policy. He developed a more harmonious relationship with President Kennedy, acting as his personal military adviser and, in 1961, was sent to report on the deteriorating situation in Vietnam. Taylor was influential in Kennedy's decision to increase the American commitment and continued as a military adviser to President Johnson. After a return to Saigon in 1964 as US Ambassador, Taylor was recalled to Washington in 1965 to serve as Chairman of the President's Foreign Intelligence Advisory Board. *MS.*

Tchepone (Sepone). Town located on Route 9 in the mountains of southern Laos. In 1961 Vietnamese communist forces helped the Pathet Lao carve out a liberated zone in the area in order to obtain unimpeded use of the Laotian panhandle for the Ho Chi Minh Trail. Because of its importance to North Vietnam's logistical effort, Tchepone was the objective of Operation "Lam Son 719" launched by the Army of the Republic (ARVN) in 1971.

Tedder: deputy for "Overlord"

Tedder, Marshal of the RAF Lord (1890–1967). Br. Air Commander in the Middle East and Mediterranean 1941–43, Deputy Supreme Commander (to Eisenhower) 1943–45. Regarded as one of the best brains in the RAF. In high command he showed outstanding qualities including a remarkable understanding of the American point of view and an instinctive ability to draw upon intellectual advice, notably from Professor Zuckerman. His experience in the Middle East and the Mediterranean theatre, where the principal uses of air power were to assist the conduct of Allied military operations, made him an admirable choice as Eisenhower's deputy for the invasion of Europe. The decisively important contribution of Anglo-American air power to the preparation and execution of "Overlord" was substantially due to Tedder's success in harnessing it to Eisenhower's purposes. Tedder developed a "common denominator" theory of air power which suggested that it should be employed on purposes which would benefit every aspect of the immediate general strategy. He thus advocated and, in large measure achieved, a priority in

417

T

bombing for transportation targets, which served the purpose of strategic attack upon Germany's industrial and adminstrative basis and also that of tactical attack upon her military lines of communication, which was required for the success of Allied military operations. Tedder's services were appreciated by Eisenhower but, perhaps because his position was ill-defined, not by many others, including Churchill, Montgomery and Harris. He became CAS after the war. *ANF.*

Tehran Conference 1943 *see* CAIRO AND TEHRAN CONFERENCES.

Telissu, Battle of (June 14–15 1904), Russo-Japanese War. A Russian force of 25,000 men (losses 3,500), moving to reinforce Port Arthur, was repulsed by the 35,000-strong (losses 1,200) Japanese Second Army.

Tell el Eisa, Battle of (July 10 1942). XXX Corps (Ramsden) attacked from the northern end of the El Alamein Line with 1st South African and 9th Australian Divisions. Both took their objectives, but Rommel succeeded in sealing off the penetration.

Tempest, Hawker (Br, WWII). Single-seat fighter. Prototype flew September 2 1942; first production June 21 1943; deliveries to squadrons April 1944. As a much-improved development of the Typhoon, the Tempest proved superior to Fw 190 and Bf 109; particularly successful against V-1s (destroyed 638). Tempest II (Centaurus engine) into service late 1945; this variant operational Malaya, anti-terrorist strikes. Production, 1,414. One 2,180/2,340hp Napier Sabre II/V, or 2,520hp Bristol Centaurus V or VI engine; max. speed 438mph (705kph); four 20mm cannon, 2,000lb (900kg) bombs or eight 3in rockets.

Templer, Field Marshal Sir Gerald (1898–1979). Br. As High Commissioner and Director of Operations Malaya (1952–54), Templer applied the resettlement policy of Gen Briggs, succeeding in isolating communist terrorists of the MRLA from people on whose support they relied. *See also* MALAYAN EMERGENCY (1948–60).

Tenaru river, Battle of the (August 21 1942). The first Japanese reinforcements to reach Guadalcanal, *c*800 men of 2nd Battalion, 28th Infantry (Col Kiyono Ichiki), landed from destroyers on August 18–19. Ichiki immediately moved to attack Henderson Field: from 0310 hours, August 21, Japanese troops attempted to storm the positions of 2nd Battalion, 1st Marine Division, at the mouth of the Tenaru (Ilu) river. The perimeter was held; meanwhile, 1st Battalion, 1st Marines, crossed the Tenaru upriver to cut off the Japanese retreat. By 1700 hours, after mopping-up by USMC tanks, 660 Japanese had been killed and 15 captured: Ichiki committed suicide. USMC losses were 35 dead, 75 wounded. *RO'N.*

Tennessee. US battleship. Name ship of class; sister-ship *California*. 32,600 tons standard; 12 x 14in guns. Completed 1920. Damaged at Pearl Harbor. Rebuilt and back in service 1943. Scrapped in 1959.

Tenth Air Force (US). Activated in US February 1942 and assigned to China-Burma-India Theatre. Provided tactical, strategic and logistic support for variety of operations, including Chindits.

Tenth Army (US). Although a new formation formed in June 1944, most of the Tenth Army's infantry and marine units were combat veterans. It took part in the invasion of the Ryukyu islands, losing its commander, Lt Gen Buckner, in the fierce fighting on Okinawa. His successor for the remainder of the campaign was Gen Joseph Stilwell.

Tenth Fleet (US). Set up May 1943 and ended June 1945. The shore-based command concerned with the US Navy's anti-submarine operations in the Atlantic.

Terauchi, Field Marshal Count Hisaichi (1879–1945). Jap. Minister of War, 1935; c-in-c Northern China, 1937. Terauchi was appointed c-in-c Southern Area Army in November 1941. A ruthless imperialist, he urged on the construction of the infamous Burma-Siam railway, 1942–43, and decreed the *defence à outrance* of Leyte, 1944–45.

Termoli, Battle for (October 3–6 1943). Montgomery landed the Special Service Brigade (Commandos) and two brigades of 78th Division just north of Termoli to hasten his advance up the Adriatic coast. LXXVI Panzer Corps (Herr) counterattacked with 16th Panzer Division and came near to defeating the landing force before British tanks could reach the beachhead from across the Biferno.

Territorial Forces Militia, Republic of Vietnam. At American insistence the ARVN neglected its militia auxiliaries in the 1950s in order to concentrate on meeting a conventional attack from the North. However, the initial threat came from insurgents within the South, and in 1964 the US helped to reorganize the Civil Guard and Self-Defence Corps as the Regional (RF) and Popular (PF) Forces. The RF consisted at first of rifle companies, which gradually developed into company groups, battalions, and finally mobile groups. From 888 companies in 1967, the RF grew to 1,810 companies (312,000 men) by 1974. PF units were never larger than platoons and fought in their own hamlets and villages. The PF in 1974 had 7,968 platoons and 220,800 troops. Together, the RF and PF from the mid-1960s onward comprised more than half of total ARVN strength; their casualties in 1968–72 were about twice those of the regular army.

While capable of manning outposts, conducting reconnaissance patrols, guarding bridges and defending hamlets against guerrillas, RF/PFS were never a match for communist main forces. Other RVN territorial forces included the Revolutionary Development (RD) cadres, the People's Self-Defence Forces (PSDF) instituted in the wake of the 1968 Tet offensive (numbering 1,000,000 members, half of them armed, by 1972), and the National Police. *WST.*

Territorials. Principal volunteer reserve component of British Army. Created before World War I under Haldane reforms which rationalized the many categories of reserve (militia, yeomanry, supplementary reserve etc.). Liable for service overseas once embodied by Queen's Order. Roughly equivalent to US National Guard.

Terror bombing *see* BOMBING.

Teruel, Battle of (December 1937–February 1938), Spanish Civil War. In late 1937 the Republican high command discovered that Franco was planning to attack Madrid again from the Guadalajara front. This sector was reinforced and an assault on the Nationalists' left flank hurriedly prepared. Teruel was attacked on December 15 with nearly 100,000 men including reserves, but soon suffered the fate of previous Republican offensives. After a rapid initial success, which in this case achieved the objective of spoiling Franco's plan, the Republic's ex-aggerated propaganda claims prevented withdrawal. The casualties sustained from heavy fighting and the appalling winter conditions led to the gradual disintegration of Republican units under the Nationalist counterattacks. A complete rout followed in mid-February after a surprise flank attack by Carlist and Legion formations near Alfambra prepared the ground for the Aragon offensive. *AB*.

Test Ban Treaty. In 1963 the USA, USSR and UK signed a treaty banning nuclear tests in the atmosphere, underwater and in outer space. This was one of the first steps to an improvement in superpower relations following the Cuban missile crisis, but the arms-control effect was limited. France and China did not sign, and continued for a time to test in the atmosphere while the signatories began to use underground tests not banned – because of verification problems. During the 1970s the superpowers agreed on a threshold test ban of 150 kilotons but this was never verified and talks on a comprehensive test ban also proved abortive. The Reagan administration regarded testing as an essential part of the maintenance of nuclear forces while the British argued that a comprehensive test ban was still unverifiable. The superpowers are currently discussing ways of implementing the threshold ban. *EJG*.

Tet offensive (1968). The turning point of the Vietnam War. Tet is the Vietnamese New Year, and over half of all South Vietnamese troops were on leave when communist forces, on January 30–31, launched a "general offensive and uprising" with attacks on 5 major cities, 36 province capitals and 64 district seats. Some 84,000 communist troops had assembled on city outskirts, yet the assault forces achieved almost complete surprise. Sappers penetrated the US embassy in Saigon and attacked the presidential palace and South Vietnamese general staff headquarters. In one blow the communists proved that they still held the strategic initiative and could strike at will in "secure" areas.

The offensive actually began not in the cities but with diversionary attacks in the highlands and at Khe Sanh. In the cities, South Vietnamese and US troops hastily regrouped to beat off the attacks in a few days. The popular uprisings anticipated by the communists mostly failed to materialize, as frightened civilians stayed indoors. The exception was at Hue, where the assault force, one of the few that consisted largely of North Vietnamese regulars, held out until February 24. Two more "violent surges", much weaker than the first, occurred in May and August.

Contrary to popular belief that the communists' aim was to affect American domestic opinion, their principal strategic aims were to improve their battlefield position and alter American leaders' assessments of the war's cost. With the war in stalemate, the communists sought to shatter American confidence by demonstrating their ability to attack when and where they pleased. At a maximum they hoped to so weaken South Vietnam's administration and army that a coalition including the National Liberation Front or its sympathizers could take its place. This new government, they calculated, would then sue for peace and demand American withdrawal. At a minimum they expected to jar the war into a new phase, leading to negotiations.

The attacks were extremely costly to the communists, who lost up to 40,000 dead, compared with 2,300 South Vietnamese and 1,100 Americans. The Americans and South Vietnamese used the opportunity to push "pacification" into areas long under communist control. However, in the US the offensive demolished the official optimism and strengthened opposition. The change persuaded President Johnson to announce he would not seek re-election and to call for peace talks. *WST*.

"Texas"/"Lien Kiet 28" Operation. An attack on March 19 1966 by the PLAF 1st Regiment on a South Vietnamese Regional Force outpost just south of the US Marine base at Chu Lai triggered Operation "Texas", or "Lien Kiet 28" to the Vietnamese. A joint Marine/South Vietnamese force relieved the outpost, then intercepted and inflicted over 600 casualties on the withdrawing PLAF.

Texas. US battleship. *New York*-class. Completed 1914, with Grand Fleet 1918. Bombardment duties at the "Torch", Normandy, South of France, Iwo Jima and Okinawa landings.

Theatre nuclear weapon. A non-strategic weapon designed for use in the context of military operations in a particular Eurasian theatre; the perspective of judgment is that of the superpowers. Theatre weapons cover both battlefield/tactical systems and intermediate forces. The dividing line with "strategic" forces is not rigid. The USA allocates some SLBMs to the theatre role, while the USSR does the same with both SLBMs and variable range ICBMs.

Thermonuclear weapon. A second-generation nuclear weapon, or "hydrogen bomb" in which a fission "primary" (often itself "boosted") provides the X-radiation to form a plasma which compresses a cylinder of thermonuclear material, usually a chemical compound of lithium and heavy hydrogen (deuterium). In the centre of the cylinder is a uranium "spark plug" that begins to fission due to radiation coupling with the primary. Neutrons from this reaction cause the lithium to transform into tritium, another isotope of hydrogen, which fuses with the deuterium at very high temperature, creating helium and enormous energy. The thermonuclear reaction provides the heat to sustain itself after being "ignited".

T

The casing of the cylinder is usually made of uranium-238 which fissions when bombarded by the high speed neutrons produced by fusion. The reaction can be passed on to another thermonuclear cylinder to increase the yield further. Enhanced radiation weapons employ an alternative design to optimize high-speed neutron production at very low yields. The yield of a normal fission-fusion-fission thermonuclear weapon is theoretically limitless; the largest test was a Soviet 57 megaton device but most modern weapons are in the high kiloton range. *EJG.*

Thetis. British warships. (1) Old *Apollo*-class second-class cruiser sunk as a blockship in the unsuccessful attempt to block Zeebrugge (April 23–24 1918). (2) T-class submarine lost on her trials in 1939, raised, renamed *Thunderbolt* and lost in action 1943.

Thiepval. Fortified village on a plateau at the northwestern end of the Pozières Ridge. Flanked by the Schwaben and Leipzig Redoubts, it was one of the strongest German defensive positions on the Somme in 1916. Fell to the British 18th Division on September 26 1916, although the Schwaben Redoubt was not finally cleared by the 39th Division until October 14.

Thiepval Wood. Front line and assembly area of 36th (Ulster) Division, Somme, July 1 1916.

Thieu, Gen Nguyen Van (b.1923). Republic of Vietnam. In 1945, Thieu entered the French-run military academy at Dalat, received further training in France, and emerged from the Indochina War a battalion commander. A convert to Catholicism under the Catholic regime of Ngo Dinh Diem, he commanded the troops that surrounded Diem's palace in November 1963. Adroit manoeuvring within the juntas that governed after Diem was ousted brought Thieu to the presidency in 1967.

Thieu consolidated personal power by manipulating the factional quarrels and corrupt practices of military and civilian officials alike. That ability earned him the support of the US, which prized political stability. However,

he was not a broadly popular figure. He instituted the Land-to-the-Tiller reform in 1970, partly to create a base of support for himself before the Americans withdrew. Torn between duty to country and dependency on the US, Thieu felt abandoned by the American failure to save his regime, resigned on April 25 1975, and exiled himself to Britain. *WST.*

Third Army (US). One of the follow-up units during the invasion of France. Commanded by Patton, it led the breakout from the Normandy bridgehead and rapidly swept through France. It further distinguished itself in the Ardennes and the advance into Germany and Czechoslovakia.

Third Fleet (US). Established March 1943, replacing the South Pacific Force. Later in the war, the designation of the main Pacific Fleet was the Third Fleet, when Adm Halsey commanded and Spruance was planning the next operation, and Fifth Fleet when the situation was reversed. Postwar, this is the number of the Eastern Pacific fleet.

Third Reich. Designation of Hitler's regime of 1933 – 45, succeeding Charlemagne's (first) and Bismarck's (second) empires.

Thirteenth Air Force (US). Activated in January 1943. Served in the South and Southwest Pacific, supporting the Allied advance from the Solomons to the Philippines. Its heavy and medium bombers also attacked Japanese installations at Truk, Formosa, French Indochina and Borneo.

Thirty-Eighth Parallel. Selected by Col Bonsteel and Col Rusk on the night of August 10–11 1945 as the dividing line between the Soviet and US zones of occupation in Korea. The choice was reached on the basis of a small-scale map and the Parallel was picked as the most obvious line of demarcation which would leave the Korean capital, Seoul, in US hands. The division was meant to be temporary but as the Cold War gathered momentum, it developed into a permanent dividing line. The 38th Parallel became the boundary between the opposing Korean states

founded in 1948 but was recognized by neither as an international frontier. It was the North Korean decision to cross the Parallel in June 1950 which provoked armed intervention by the UN. When truce talks began in July 1951, the communist side proposed the ending of hostilities on the basis of the 38th Parallel. The UN command insisted on the more. favourable line of military contact and the armistice was concluded on this basis. *CM.*

Von Thoma: armoured warfare expert

Thoma, Lt Gen (*General der Panzertruppen*) Wilhelm Ritter von (1891–1948). Ger. One of the architects of German armoured warfare doctrine in the 1930s. Thoma commanded the ground forces of the Condor Legion in Spain, 1936–39. He commanded a panzer brigade in Poland, 1939, and in 1940, after observing Graziani's preparations for the Cyrenaica offensive, submitted a prescient report on the difficulties inherent in a major German commitment in North Africa. Nevertheless, in September 1942, following a corps command in Russia, he succeeded Nehring as commander, Afrika Korps. On October 24 – 25 1942, at El Alamein, between Stumme's death and Rommel's hasty return from sick leave, Thoma was briefly c-in-c, Panzerarmee Afrika. When Rommel's withdrawal plan was overruled by Hitler, Thoma launched an abortive counterattack; he was captured on November 4 while attempting to stem the breakout by Montgomery's X Corps. *RO'N.*

Thompson, Sir Robert G K (b.1916). Br. Served in various capacities in Malaya, including Secretary for Defence, 1959–61, before heading a British advisory mission to South Vietnam, 1961–65. He advised the South Vietnamese and the Americans to apply the lessons from the successful British counterinsurgency in Malaya, of which the core concept was denial of enemy access to the people. While the Americans ignored Thompson's caution against excessive military force, the Vietnamese too eagerly applied his concept of strategic hamlets, in disregard of crucial differences between Malaya and Vietnam. *See also* STRATEGIC HAMLET PROGRAM.

"Thor" ("Karl"). German 60cm self-propelled howitzer, of the type used during the siege of Sevastopol, 1942. Only six of these weapons were built.

"Thousand-Bomber raid" *see* COLOGNE.

Throw-weight. This is the weight a ballistic missile can carry over its notional range in its normally planned trajectory. As well as the "payload" of warheads, it includes the post-boost vehicle and the inertial guidance package. Historically, Soviet ICBMS have had large throw-weights with "heavy" missiles like the SS-6, 9 and 18 in the 8,800-15,950lb (4,000-7,250kg) class and "medium" missiles like SS-17, 19 and 25 in the 6,600-7,700lb (3,000-3,500kg) class. The MX Peacekeeper is in the latter category, but the throw-weight of "lightweight" missiles like Minuteman is only 1,535-2,200lb (725-1,000kg). The higher the throw-weight, the larger the number and yield of the warheads and the greater the MIRV "footprint". A major aim of American arms control policy has been to even up the throw-weight balance. The higher the throw-weight the greater the counter-force potential. *EJG.*

Thunderbolt *see* P-47.

Tibbets, Col Paul W, Jr (b.1915). US. Pilot of the B-29 *Enola Gay* which dropped the first atomic bomb on the Japanese city of Hiroshima, August 6 1945.

Tiger. German PzKw VI (56 tons). Introduced 1942 as answer to Russian T-34 and the heavier JS and KV tanks. Improved version with contoured armour on turret, "King Tiger" (65 tons) introduced 1944. Both carried 88mm gun. *See also* TANKS.

"Tiger" convoy (May 5–12 1941). Ordered by Churchill to carry urgently needed tanks for Gen Wavell's offensive in the Western Desert. Run successfully through the Mediterranean with the loss of only one merchantman.

Tiger Moth, de Havilland DH. 82A (Br, pre-WWII and after). Two-seat elementary trainer. Prototype flew October 26 1931. Built in quantity and widely exported before World War II; production Canada began 1937, also built Norway, Sweden, Portugal. Many built during war, used British Commonwealth Air Training Plan; further production Australia, New Zealand, and DH82C Canada. After Dunkirk, some fitted with bomb racks for antisubmarine patrols. Production, 8,280. One 130hp de Havilland Gipsy Major engine; max. speed 104mph (166kph); 160lb (72kg) bombs.

Timoshenko: defended Moscow

Timoshenko, Marshal Semyon (1895–1970). Russian. Timoshenko served briefly in the Imperial Russian Cavalry during World War I before joining the Red Army in 1918. He fought throughout the Civil War and by the end of hostilities was in command of the Fourth Cavalry Division. An associate of Stalin's, he was untouched by the purges of the Red Army and, in September 1939 he was given the task of leading the forces of the Ukrainian Front against Poland's

unprotected eastern frontier. Later in the year, as commander of the Northwestern Front, Timoshenko tried to break the strong Finnish defences on the Karelian Pensinsula. Although ultimately victorious, the war against Finland had thrown up many glaring deficiencies in the Red Army and in May 1940 Timoshenko was appointed People's Commissar for Defence with orders to improve the situation. His reforms barely had time to show any effect before the German invasion of June 1941 put the Red Army to the test. On July 2 Timoshenko took command of the Western Front, which was, in effect, the centre of the Soviet line. In a long and costly battle centred on Smolensk, Timoshenko blocked the German advance on Moscow for two months. This relative success led to his being appointed commander of the Southwest Front in order to try and save something out of the disaster left by Budenny in Kiev. Timoshenko managed to achieve some stabilization of the front but his own offensive in May 1942 was soon checked and formed a prelude to a crushingly successful German advance. The penalty for his failure was dismissal and in July he was recalled to Moscow. He was given one more brief period of command with the Northwestern Front but his major contribution for the remainder of the war was staff and planning duties at Stavka. *MS.*

Tiran, Straits of *see* SUEZ CRISIS.

Tirpitz, Grand Adm Alfred von (1849–1930). Ger. Secretary of State of the German Imperial Navy 1897–1916. Throughout the years of the Anglo-German naval race and, in particular, after the British introduction of the *Dreadnought* class in 1906, Tirpitz was the dominant naval figure in Germany. His building of a first-class German fleet of modern ships, which by 1914 posed a serious threat to Britain's Grand Fleet, was an achievement without parallel in the history of naval construction and innovation. His political judgment that Britain, France and Russia would be unable to form an alliance proved for Germany to be disastrously wrong, nor does he seem to have anticipated the Anglo-Japanese alliance

T

which enabled Britain to concentrate the greater part of her naval strength in European waters. His frustration at the extent to which, after these developments, the Grand Fleet was able to neutralize the High Seas Fleet unhinged his strategic judgment. He resigned before the Battle of Jutland was joined and became an advocate of unrestricted submarine warfare. *ANF*.

Tirpitz. German battleship. Nearly 42,000 tons displacement increasing to over 52,000 when fuelled and armed. Eight 15in guns. Powerful secondary armament.

Fleet Air Arm bombers strike *Tirpitz*

Maximum speed 31 knots. Range 8,000 miles (13,000km). Mostly in port and only fired her main armament in anger once at Spitzbergen in September 1943. Nevertheless, her threat was a major factor in tying down Allied naval forces and absorbing air effort. The false rumour that she was putting to sea in July 1942 led to the disaster of convoy PQ 17. Repeatedly attacked by the British Fleet Air Arm, Bomber Command and Russian bombers. Seriously damaged by British midget submarines, for which Lt B C G Place and Lt D Cameron were awarded the VC. Direct hits from Lancasters of Bomber Command on November 12 1944 caused her to capsize and become a total wreck. Of her complement of 1,900, 1,000 were killed or injured. *ANF*.

Titan missile. Large American liquid-fuelled ICBM. Titan 1, in service 1962-66, had to be fuelled before launch and was deployed in silos from which it was hoisted to fire. The improved Titan 2, first deployed in 1963, had fully stor-

able propellant and was fired inside its silo. Fifty-four were retained into the 1980s to provide a high-yield strike capability. The missile could send a 9 megaton warhead 9,000 miles (15,000km) with a CEP of about 3,280ft (1,000m). The last were withdrawn in 1987.

Tito, President Josip (1892–1980). Yugoslavian. Born in Croatia, Josip Broz, later known as Tito, served in the Austro-Hungarian army during World War I. He was wounded and taken prisoner by the Russians in April 1915 but escaped from captivity in 1917 and took part in the Bolshevik seizure of power. After fighting against the White Russian forces he returned to Croatia in 1920 where he worked in an iron foundry while becoming increasingly involved in the illegal communist party. This led to his arrest and several years' imprisonment. On his release he made frequent trips to the Soviet Union and, in 1937, became General Secretary of the Yugoslav Communist Party. He denounced World War II as an "imperialist" struggle but with the German invasion of Yugoslavia in April 1941 and the subsequent attack on the Soviet Union, his attitude changed. Adopting the

Tito: Yugoslav partisan chief

nom de guerre of "Tito", he was sent to Belgrade by the Comintern to organize resistance and in August transferred his centre of operations to Serbia. He was soon in control of large areas of the region but his relations with Mihailovich, the other main Yugoslavian resistance leader was decidedly antagonistic. Negotiations between Tito's Partisans and Mihailovich's Chetniks soon broke down and armed clashes occurred between the two

groups. A German counteroffensive in December 1941 forced Tito to retreat into Bosnia and Montenegro but he was a master of guerrilla warfare and had sufficiently recovered his fortunes in November 1942 to capture Binac. Tito's standing with the Allies steadily increased and he received substantial supplies of arms and equipment, in addition to political recognition that led to summit talks with Churchill and Stalin. Surviving determined German anti-partisan operations in 1943–44, Tito's Partisans linked up with Soviet ground forces in October 1944 and made a substantial contribution to the liberation of their country. Tito's military, political and diplomatic skills ensured his ultimate victory both over the Axis and his own political opponents. In the postwar settlements he won important concessions for Yugoslavia and, significantly, managed to retain his independence from Stalin. In June 1953 Tito became President of Yugoslavia, a position he retained until his death in 1980. *MS*.

Tizard, Sir Henry Thomas (1885–1959). Br. Architect of the British radar defence system in the Battle of Britain. Tizard was conservative by nature and taste but radical in thought and action. As a physical chemist, he was employed on experimental flying in the RFC in World War I and then became, as he later put it himself, a scientist in and out of the civil service. After Hitler came to power and Britain gradually began to look to her defences, the most serious threat was from the revived Luftwaffe. No system of air defence would avail unless early warning of the approach of hostile bombers could be obtained. For a solution, the Air Ministry turned to Tizard. He recognized the relevance of Watson-Watt's radio echo system for tracking clouds. In the face of opposition and scepticism, Tizard drove this idea through as a means of detecting enemy bombers and obtained the resources for a chain of radar stations along the coasts of Britain. He won the confidence of the C-in-C, Fighter Command so that theoretical ideas could be tested and adapted to meet flying capacities. The result was that, when the Luftwaffe attack came in 1940, the

RAF had the most advanced air defence system in the world.

In September 1940 Tizard went to the USA to introduce Britain's principal military-scientific developments, including radar and the proximity fuse, to those whom it was hoped would one day be allies. Thereafter, due to tension with Cherwell, Tizard was relegated to the sidelines. After the war he became scientific adviser to the government. *ANF*.

Tizard: British wartime "boffin"

Tobruk, British capture of (January 5–22 1941). As soon as Bardia had fallen, Tobruk was invested by 6th Australian and 7th Armoured Divisions. The Australian assault on January 21 led to the surrender of the 25,000-strong garrison.

Tobruk, British reconnaissance in force towards (Operation "Brevity") May 15–17 1941. Made by Gott with 7th Armoured and 22nd Guards Brigade Groups. Only significant success was recapture of Halfaya Pass.

Tobruk, German siege of (April 11–December 10 1941). Rommel launched hastily organized attacks on the fortress perimeter on April 13, 16 and 30, all of which were thrown back by 9th Australian Division (Morshead). British reinforcement and supply by sea brought about a stalemate, which lasted until the successful British offensive to relieve Tobruk in November 1941. At the request of the Australian government, their troops were gradually replaced by 70th Division and 1st Polish Carpathian Brigade from August to October at considerable cost in air effort and in naval escort. Rommel lifted the siege on December 10 after his defeat at Bir el Gubi.

Tobruk, Rommel's capture of (June 20–21 1942). After Eighth Army's defeat at Gazala, Rommel once again invested Tobruk, garrisoned by the inexperienced 2nd South African Division (Klopper), reinforced with British infantry and tanks. Due to confusion in the British Command after Gazala, Tobruk was left inadequately supported, enabling Afrika Korps (Nehring) to breach the southeastern side of the defences in a blitzkrieg style assault, bringing about the collapse of resistance next day with the loss of 32,000 men.

Tobruk, second British offensive to relieve (Operation "Battleaxe") June 15–17 1941. The arrival of the "Tiger" convoy with replacement tanks enabled Wavell, against his better judgment, to carry out Churchill's instructions to mount an early attack on Rommel's forces investing Tobruk. The reconstituted Western Desert Force (Beresford-Peirse) – 7th Armoured and 4th Indian Divisions – attacked the fortified positions held by 15th Panzer Division on the Egyptian frontier on June 15 and was repulsed largely due to the Germans' novel use of 88mm Flak guns against tanks. Rommel used 5th Light Division to turn the British desert flank during the 16th, forcing them to break off the battle early next day. *WGFJ*.

Tobruk, third British offensive to relieve (Operation "Crusader") November–December 1941. Auchinleck attacked with the newly constituted Eighth Army (Cunningham), consisting of XIII Corps (Godwin-Austen) and XXX Corps (Norrie). XIII Corps, with the New Zealand and 4th Indian Divisions, was to pin down the Axis troops on the Egyptian Frontier, while XXX Corps with 7th Armoured and 1st South African Divisions made a wide turning movement through the desert along the Trigh el Abd towards Tobruk, seeking an armoured battle with the Afrika Korps (Cruewell). As XXX Corps approached Tobruk, the garrison was to break out to meet them.

The battle was fought in four phases. In the first phase, (November 18–21), XIII Corps advanced to within 10 miles (16km) of Tobruk with its northern flank threatened, first by 21st Panzer Division, and then by 15th Panzer Division, bringing on the tank battles of Gabr Saleh and Sidi Rezegh in which the Afrika Korps just gained the upper hand. The Tobruk garrison broke out on November 21, but did not manage to link up with 7th Armoured Division at Sidi Rezegh.

In the second phase (November 22–23), Cruewell concentrated his armour, overran 7th Armoured Division's positions in the First Battle of Sidi Rezegh on the 22nd, and the next day annihilated 5th South African Brigade in the Battle of Totensonntag. Rommel had by now won tank superiority.

During the third phase (November 24–December 1), Rommel personally led the Afrika Korps southeastwards in a dash to rescue his units on the Egyptian frontier, which were surrounded by XXX Corps. He scattered British headquarters and logistic units in his path, and entered Bardia, where he refuelled on the 26th. He fought his way back westwards and engaged New Zealanders in the Second Battle of Sidi Rezegh (November 292–December 1). Although he drove them away from Tobruk, his losses had been too great to maintain the siege.

Rommel made one last abortive effort in the final phase of the battle (December 2–January 6) by attacking XXX Corps at Bir el Gubi before accepting defeat. He lifted the siege of Tobruk on December 10, and withdrew into Tripolitania by January 6 1943 to await a re-supply of tanks.

During Operation "Crusader", Cunningham's health failed, and he was replaced in command of Eighth Army by Ritchie. British losses amounted to 15 percent of their forces engaged; the Germans 23 percent; and the Italians 44 percent. *WGFJ*.

TOC H. British Army signallers' version of the initials of Talbot House, a World-War-I rest house for all ranks at Poperinghe, near Ypres. Opened in December 1915 as a memorial to Lt Gilbert Talbot, who had been killed at Hooge in July that year. Later, Talbot House became the birthplace of a worldwide Christian movement, inspired and guided by one of its original founders, the Rev "Tubby" Clayton.

Todt Organization. Nazi agency under the leadership of Dr Fritz Todt. It was responsible for construction work e.g. the West Wall, U-boat shelters. It employed much slave labour.

Togo, Adm of the Fleet Marquis Heihachiro (1847–1934). Jap. c-in-c of the Japanese Grand Fleet during the Russo-Japanese War. Togo's strike at Port Arthur on February 8 1904 was, like Pearl Harbor in 1941, both pre-emptive and a partial failure. Concerned to keep his fleet in being to protect Japan's lines of communication, Togo did not press home an attack with his major units that might have shortened the war. However, he displayed great tenacity in maintaining his blockade and, when the Russian squadron at last made a sortie in force, mauled its ships severely in a hard-fought action in the Yellow Sea, August 10 1904, and drove them back to Port Arthur to be destroyed severally by land batteries.

Dour and taciturn, Togo was a cautious commander – but one who would take risks when the situation justified them. At Tsushima on May 27 1905, he turned his ships in succession, exposing each in turn to the fire of an opponent superior in heavy guns while masking his own supporting fire, in order to gain the tactical advantage that brought him the most emphatic naval victory since Trafalgar. The "Nelson of Japan" became a popular hero in Britain and the USA as well as at home, where his flagship at Tsushima, *Mikasa*, is preserved as a national monument. Like Nogi, Togo was hailed as the embodiment of the samurai virtues and subsequently became an icon of Japanese patriotism. *RO'N.*

Togoland (1914). In August 1914, a 160-strong French force from Dahomey and a 600-strong British force from the Gold Coast (native soldiers with European officers) invaded the German protectorate of Togoland, West Africa. Having succeeded in delaying the Allied advance through the bush until its objective, the wireless station at Atakpamé, 100 miles (160km) inland, had been destroyed, Togoland's 550-strong *Polizeitruppe* surrendered on August 26.

Japan's war leader: Gen Hideki Tojo

Tojo, Gen Hideki (1884–1948). Jap. A savagely efficient administrator as c-in-c, *Kempei-tai* (military police), Kwantung Army, 1935–36, and an effective field commander, as cos, Kwantung Army, 1937–40. A leading figure in the militarist "Control Group", he advocated aggression as Vice-Minister of War (1938) and War Minister (from July 1940), and was active in ousting both the more pacific Prince Fumimaro Konoye (1891–1945) and the anti-Axis Adm Mitsumasa Yonai (1880–1948) from the premiership, himself becoming Prime Minister in October 1941 and presiding over Japan's entry into World War II. Austere and eschewing rhetoric, Tojo was never the fearsome dictator that both Western propaganda and his personal appearance (almost a caricature of the "typical" militarist) suggested. However many offices he assumed, his power was always subject to that of the supreme command, who, in July 1944, forced his resignation as the scapegoat for Japan's reverses. Arrested by the US occupation forces in September 1945, Tojo survived a suicide attempt to be condemned to death for "war crimes" (like Yamashita and others, he attempted to shield Hirohito by accepting all blame). He was hanged on December 23 1948. *RO'N.*

Tokyo, bombing of (1942–45). The first Allied bombing raid on Tokyo took place on April 18 1942 when Lt Col Doolittle led sixteen B-25 bombers on an audacious carrier-borne operation. The raid did little damage but lifted American morale and shook Japanese feelings of impregnability. However, it was not until November 24 1944 that the new B-29 bombers

attacked Tokyo but these high altitude, precision raids proved ineffective. Gen LeMay, the commander of the US XXI Bomber Command, therefore changed the tactics to night-time bombing at low-level using incendiaries. The first raid took place on May 10 when over 300 B-29s created a firestorm that razed 15 sq miles (39 sq km) of Tokyo and inflicted 125,000 casualties. On May 26 464 bombers carried out the largest of the raids, releasing 2,200 tons of incendiaries and destroying another 19 sq miles (49 sq km) of the city. Devastating raids continued until the end of hostilities. *MS.*

"Tokyo Rose". Generic nickname given by US servicemen during World War II to several Nisei (US-born of Japanese parentage) girls who made pro-Japanese propaganda broadcasts from Tokyo. Best-known was Iva Ikuko Toguri d'Aquino (b.1916): sentenced to 10 years' imprisonment (served 6 years), she always maintained that she had acted under duress and was pardoned by President Ford in 1977.

Tolbukhin: liberator of the Crimea, 1944

Tolbukhin, Marshal Fedor (1894–1949). Russian. Tolbukhin. graduated from Frunze, 1934, and began World War II as cos of the Transcaucasus Military District and organized the occupation of northern Iran by Soviet forces in the autumn of 1941. However his attempt to relieve the pressure on Sevastopol by landing two armies on the Kerch Peninsula was a failure. He redeemed himself by commanding the Fifty-seventh Army in the withdrawal to the Volga in the summer of 1942 and in the Soviet counteroffensive at Stalingrad. Promotion followed and in April 1943 he was Col Gen in command of the South Front. After initial reverses against the German defence line along the River Mius, Tolbukhin's forces broke through in September and liberated the Donbass industrial area before freeing the Crimea in April 1944. The next month Tolbukhin was appointed commander of the Third Ukrainian Front and entered into a period of victories that was to last until the end of the war. Working in concert with Marshal Malinovsky's Second Ukrainian Front, he encircled five German corps at Jassy-Kishinev before his forces advanced into Romania and Bulgaria. He liberated three capital cities, Belgrade, Budapest and Vienna before the German surrender. *MS*.

Tompkins, Maj Gen Rathvon McCall (b.1912). US. Assumed command of the US Marine 3rd Division in December 1967 after the death of Gen Bruno Hochmuth. That change placed Tompkins in charge of forces, under Col David Lownds, defending Khe Sanh combat base in Vietnam just before the North Vietnamese besieged it. Tompkins subscribed to Gen Westmoreland's concept of using Khe Sanh as a bait to "lure the enemy to their deaths".

Tonkin Gulf incident (1964). Apparently in reaction to American and South Vietnamese activities along North Vietnam's coast, three North Vietnamese patrol boats intercepted the American destroyer *Maddox* outside the North's 12-mile (19km) limit on August 2 1964. The North Vietnamese fired two torpedoes at the *Maddox*, which returned fire, disabling one of the boats and damaging another. In bad weather on the evening of the 4th, the *Maddox*, joined by a second destroyer, the *C Turner Joy*, reported radar contact with five boats, called in air support and fired on unseen targets. Known collectively as the Tonkin Gulf Incident, these events supplied President Johnson with a pretext to extract the Southeast Asia Resolution from Congress, which gave him the authority to respond as he felt necessary, but avoided declaring outright war. It emerged that the attack on the 4th never took place. Congress revoked the resolution, May 1970.

Torgau. German town on Elbe; scene of link-up between US and Soviet units, April 25 1945.

Torpedoes. Around 1900, the introduction of gyroscopic control and of "steam heating" propulsion enabled torpedo performance to keep up with increase in fighting ranges. First successful use of aircraft torpedo 1915. Japanese adoption of large oxygen-driven "Long Lance" torpedoes with great performance – and also reloading arrangements – gave them an advantage in the Pacific War. Italians first to use "human torpedoes", copied by British for attacks on enemy harbours. Germans and Japanese used manned torpedoes at sea. Anglo-Americans and Germans both developed acoustic torpedoes, first used in 1943, which have led to true underwater-guided missiles like the modern British "Tigerfish". *DJL*.

Total war. A war in which all available resources, civil and military, of manpower, technology and wealth are committed to the achievement of a political end by military means (possibly including the limited use of nuclear weapons, as in World War II). *See also* ABSOLUTE WAR, LIMITED WAR.

Totensonntag (All Souls Day), Battle of (November 23 1941). The Afrika Korps overran 5th South African Brigade south of Sidi Rezegh. Losses were high on both sides, but those suffered by the Germans started the erosion of their forces, which led to Rommel raising the siege of Tobruk.

Tou Morong, Battle of (1966). The surrounding of a South Vietnamese Regional Force outpost at Tou Morong in Kontum province by the North Vietnamese 24th Regiment triggered Operation "Hawthorne"/"Dan Tang 61" in June 1966. The US First Brigade, 101st Airborne Division, and two ARVN battalions relieved the garrison on the 6th, but an attack on a detached American company resulted in heavy fighting with entrenched North Vietnamese. After 463 air strikes, 36 B-52 sorties and the dumping of 900 CS gas grenades, the North Vietnamese withdrew, having suffered 531 "known" casualties.

Toulon. Main French Mediterranean naval base. In 1942 most of the French fleet was assembled here. The Germans tried to take over on November 27; Adm Laborde's instructions were followed and 3 battleships, 7 cruisers and 32 destroyers were scuttled; a few lighter ships got away to join the Allies.

Tovey, Adm of the Fleet Sir John Cronyn (1886–1971). Br. After distinguished and extensive service in command of destroyers 1914–18, especially *Onslow* at Jutland, he reached flag rank in 1935; was made Rear Adm, destroyers then second in command of Mediterranean Fleet (1939). As c-in-c Home Fleet (October 1940– May 1943), his greatest single achievement was the hunting down and sinking of the *Bismarck*. Responsible for the Russian convoys, he protested against Admiralty interference which resulted in the PQ 17 disaster. He held the Nore command (1943–45) and assisted in the preparations for D-Day. *CJW/CD*.

TOW missile. American anti-tank missile automatically commanded to the line of sight of the aimer. The name stands for "Tube launched, Optically tracked, Wire guided". Maximum range is 12,300ft (3,750m); can be carried on vehicles or helicopters.

Townshend, Maj Gen Sir Charles (1861–1924). Br. *See* MESOPOTAMIAN CAMPAIGN (1914–18).

Toyoda, Adm Soemu (1885– 1957). Jap. Succeeded Koga as c-in-c, Combined Fleet, April 1944. Although a cautious strategist, Toyoda firmly espoused the "decisive battle" concept, presiding over the disastrous operations that led to the destruction of Japan's naval air power in the Philippine Sea and of her surviving naval strength at Leyte Gulf. In desperate attempts to retain Okinawa, April 1945, Toyoda ordered the *Yamato*'s "death ride" and the *kikusui* mass kamikaze attacks. Replaced as c-in-c by Ozawa, May 1945, he became Naval COS, opposing Japan's surrender but retaining office until accused of war crimes (tried and acquitted) in 1946. *RO'N*.

T

Tran Van Don, Gen (b.1917). Republic of Vietnam. Born in France, Tran Van Don served in the French Army in 1939 and returned to Vietnam after the fall of France to the Germans. He resumed a military career in 1945 by joining Gen LeClerc's headquarters staff, received further training in France, joined the newly created Vietnam National Army in 1950, and emerged from the war as COS. In 1955 he delivered the army's support to Ngo Dinh Diem, but in 1963 he organized the coup that overthrew him. Younger officers then nudged Don aside, and he shifted to civilian politics, serving at various times during the Vietnam War as senator and minister of defence.

Tran Van Tra, Lt Gen (b.1918). Democratic Republic of Vietnam. A Viet Minh officer who regrouped in the North following the Geneva Agreements in 1954 and re-infiltrated the South in 1963. In the interim he had become a deputy chief of staff of the PAVN. On returning to the South he took charge of the Central Military Committee of the Central Office for South Vietnam (COSVN) and headed the communists' military command for the lower half of South Vietnam (the "B-2 Front"). He had a major role in planning the Tet offensive and participated in the four-party commission that supervised cease-fire in 1973. In 1982 he published a book that questioned the war-time prescience of the high command in Hanoi and lost his seat on the party Central Committee. *WST*.

Trasimeno, Battle of Lake (June 20–28 1944). Kesselring made a major effort to check the Allied advance northwards from Rome on a line running east and west through Lake Trasimeno (the Albert Line). Fourteenth Army (Lemelsen) failed to impose much delay on Fifth Army (Clark) on the west coast, but Tenth Army (von Vietinghoff) was more successful in opposing Eighth Army (Leese) in the more defensible country around the lake. It took XIII Corps (Kirkman) with three divisions a week's hard fighting to unseat LXXVI Panzer Corps (Herr) and to force von Vietinghoff to continue his withdrawal towards Florence.

Treblinka Nazi extermination camp in Poland where 700,000 Jewish inmates were put to death.

Trenchard, Marshal of the RAF Lord (1873–1956). Br. General Officer Commanding the RFC in France 1915–18. Chief of the Air Staff (with a short gap) 1918–29. Trenchard was an enigmatic figure; not a good pilot, he became Assistant Commandant of the Central Flying School in 1913 and, in the course of 1915, he was promoted from Lt Col to Maj Gen.

The novelty of air power in 1914 and the rapid development in aircraft performance and fighting tactics which then followed made Trenchard's task as commander of the RFC a unique challenge. In many respects he met it with outstanding success and for much of the period of his command, although by no means all of it, the RFC had the upper hand in the control of the air over the battle lines. This enabled his aircraft to carry out numerous roles in support of the ground troops ranging from reconnaissance and artillery spotting to increasingly heavy bombing attacks upon what were considered to be key tactical points. For this work, Trenchard gained Haig's high opinion and he, in turn, showed a persistent loyalty to his C-in-C when the question of applying air power beyond the immediate battle zones arose. On these grounds he opposed the diversion of fighters from France to defend London against air attack and he also opposed the creation of the Royal Air Force as a separate service in the correct belief that this would diminish the direct support of the army in the field.

Once the RAF had been formed and Trenchard was installed as its chief, he became an equally dogged advocate of the independent use of air power and, in particular, of the strategic bombing role. He believed that air defence would be ineffective and that the decisive factor in air warfare would be the maintenance of the offensive. His view that civil morale would be rapidly vulnerable to bombing was the seed of the policy of area bombing of towns which Bomber Command later adopted. His doctrine was not successfully challenged until 1938, when, at political insistence, it was qualified by

the priority given to fighter production. The course of Bomber Command's wartime offensive showed numerous fallacies in the Trenchard doctrine, the chief of which were that civil morale proved highly resilient and fighters exercised a ceaseless superiority over bombers. *ANF*.

Trench mortars. Simple tubular projectors from which bombs are fired at high elevation, falling almost vertically on the target. High rate of fire compensates for relative inaccuracy.

Trench warfare. When tactical stalemate set in on the Western Front in autumn 1914, both sides resorted to elaborate trench systems stretching from the North Sea to the Swiss border. The front-line trenches lay behind fields of barbed wire and their garrisons spent most of the time in deep dugouts. Observation and listening posts in "no-man's-land" between the opposing trench lines were connected to the main system by "saps", and complex networks of communication trenches led far to the rear, housing command posts, first aid stations and ammunition reserves. It was in order to break this deadlock that the tank was secretly developed. *MH*.

Trentino, Battle of the (May 14–June 3 1916) *see* ITALIAN CAMPAIGN, WORLD WAR I.

Trepper, Leopold (1904–82). Polish. Convert to communism; headed Red Orchestra, the largest Soviet espionage organization in central and western Europe, 1940–44; on return to Russia, sent for 10 years to Siberia.

Triad. (a) the three complementary kinds of US strategic forces, land-based ICBMS, bombers and SLBMS (the "strategic triad"); (b) the three complementary kinds of forces maintained by NATO for Flexible Response, strategic nuclear, theatre nuclear and conventional (the "NATO triad").

Trident missile. Long-range American SLBM, the first to have the reach of an ICBM, 4,500 miles (7,500km). Trident C4 (Trident 1) has been deployed since 1979 on both converted Poseidon submarines and, since 1981, specially built giant *Ohio*-class submarines with 24 missile tubes. Each missile carries eight 100 kiloton MIRVS and stellar-aided inertial guidance gives a CEP of 1,640ft (500m). A larger Trident D-5 (Trident 2) is under development for the *Ohios* and the British, who will use it to replace Polaris in the 1990s, carried in four large *Vanguard*-class submarines. D-5 has greater payload and accuracy than C-4 and is a potential counter-force weapon. It is due in service in the USS *Tennessee* at the end of 1989. American missiles will carry eight 335 kiloton warheads and stellar- and satellite-assisted guidance will give a CEP of 3,936ft (120m). A total of twenty *Ohios* is planned; by 1998, 13 will be in service carrying 312 D-5s and C-4 will be phased out. *EJG.*

Trieste, capture of. Entered by the New Zealand Division (Freyberg) on May 2 1945. Already partially occupied by Yugoslav Partisans, who had set up a rudimentary administration and were intent on establishing Tito's claim to the whole of Venezia Giulia.

Tripoli. Main base for Rommel's Panzerarmee Afrika. The British planned to block the harbour entrance with the old battleship *Centurion*, but, when this proved impracticable, the RN bombarded the port, April 1941. Captured by Eighth Army, January 1943.

Tripoli, British advance to (November 12 1942–January 23 1943). Montgomery was determined not to be counterattacked and driven back by Rommel at the Tripolitanian frontier as had happened to his predecessors. He reached Rommel's position at El Agheila on November 23 and paused to bring forward fresh troops and build up logistic resources. He manoeuvred Rommel out of the El Agheila position on December 13, and did the same at Buerat, 150 miles (240km) farther west, on January 15, entering Tripoli eight days later.

Tripoli, bombing of (1986). Tension between the USA and Libya dated from the accession to power in 1969 of Col Muammar al-Qadhafi (Gaddafi) (b.1913). The

US, with evidence of Libyan backing for international terrorism, deployed Sixth Fleet off the Libyan coast, December 1985. On March 24 1986, after SAM-5 missiles were fired at US aircraft transgressing Gaddafi's unilaterally-proclaimed "line of death" in the Gulf of Sirte, US carrier aircraft sank two Libyan patrol boats and attacked missile sites (Operation "Prairie Fire"). The US claimed "irrefutable" evidence of Libyan involvement in terrorist attacks on a US airliner over Athens (4 dead), April 2, and a West Berlin nightclub (1 US soldier killed; *c*200 persons injured) April 5.

On the understanding that every effort would be made to avoid non-military targets, Mrs Thatcher agreed to the American use of British-based FB-111 bombers in a raid on Tripoli. On the evening of April 14, 24 FB-111s took off for the *c*2,800-mile (4,500km) flight (via Gibraltar to avoid French and Spanish air-space), with 28 KC-135 Stratotankers for in-flight refuelling. Early on April 15, the F-111s struck Tripoli in an 11-minute, low-level (*c*500ft/150m) attack, using infrared and laser equipment to aim 2,000lb bombs with near-surgical precision. Five aircraft, unable to "double lock" (with both radar and infrared sighting) on military targets, did not bomb; damage to civilian areas was probably caused by ordnance dislodged from the single F-111 lost to AA gun and missile fire. Missile sites, suspected terrorist barracks and the Sidi Bilal naval base were hit; Gaddafi himself narrowly escaped the destruction of his HQ at Bab-el-Azizia barracks. Air cover was provided by A-6 Intruders and F-14 Tomcats from the carriers USS *America* and *Coral Sea*. Carrier aircraft also made a simultaneous strike against missile sites at Benghazi, damaging the Benina military airfield with cluster bombs.

Although Western popular media, predicting terrorist reprisals throughout Europe, initially criticized the US action, the raids appeared at least to have discouraged Gaddafi's overt support for terrorism. *RO'N.*

Trones wood. Somme wood, taken by British 18th Division, July 14 1916 and August 27 1918.

Trotsky, Leon (1879–1940). Russian. Became Commissar for War, in March 1918, effectively creating the Red Army and organizing the defence of Bolshevism during the Civil War. Ousted from office and deported in 1929. He settled in Mexico where he was assassinated by a Soviet agent in 1940. *MS.*

Trott zu Solz, Adam von (1909–1944). Ger. Anti-Nazi diplomat; arrested, tortured and executed when July Plot failed.

Truk campaign (1944). Extending for more than 1,100 miles (1,770km) east-to-west in the central Pacific, the Caroline Islands formed a vital part of Japan's defensive perimeter. The key-point was Truk lagoon, eastern Carolines, a major Combined Fleet and air base from 1941. Following the conquest of the Gilbert Islands (*see* TARAWA), late 1943, Allied planners decided not to mount a potentially costly invasion of Truk, but to outflank it by securing the Marshall Islands (*see* KWAJALEIN), east of the Carolines, and, subsequently, the Palau Islands (*see* PELELIU), western Carolines.

The first and greatest attack on Truk was made by US Fifth Fleet on February 17–18, to cover the Eniwetok landings. Carrier aircraft of Mitscher's Task Force 58 struck the anchorages and airfields, while Spruance's battleships and cruisers deployed to intercept fleeing Japanese ships. Although Vice Adm Koga, suspecting imminent attack, had withdrawn major Japanese units a few days earlier, 2 light cruisers, 4 destroyers, 7 auxiliary warships and 24 merchant ships (totalling *c*200,000 tons, including 5 tankers) were sunk and some 270 Japanese aircraft destroyed for the loss of 25 US aircraft and damage to the carrier *Intrepid*.

Continued naval and air interdiction of Truk forced the withdrawal of the Combined Fleet to Yap, western Carolines. Yap, too, was isolated and left to "wither on the vine" when US forces, having secured a fleet anchorage at Ulithi, western Carolines, by unopposed landings on September 23 1944, completed the conquest of the Palaus by the capture of Angaur and Peleliu, September–November 1944. *RO'N.*

Truman doctrine. In a message to Congress on March 12 1947, referring mainly to the Greek Civil War, President Truman committed the USA to military and economic aid to "free peoples . . . resisting attempted subjugation by armed minorities or by outside pressure". This anti-communist statement marked an escalation of the Cold War.

President Truman faced a world of crises

T

Truman, President Harry (1884–1972). US. Born into a small farming community in Missouri, Truman had a variety of jobs before serving in the US Army during World War I when he saw action in France in 1918 as a captain in the artillery. On his return to civilian life, he became involved in Democratic Party politics and entered the US Senate in 1935. He first received real attention and acclaim as chairman of the Senate's Special Committee Investigating National Defence. By 1944 his reputation had grown to the extent that he was selected as President Roosevelt's running mate in that year's election and became Vice-President in January 1945. Although with a wide experience of domestic affairs, Truman was a novice at diplomacy and was therefore put under extreme pressure when Roosevelt died on April 12 1945. The new President was immediately faced with the leadership of America's war effort and unravelling the complexities of international affairs that included negotiating the postwar plans for Europe at the Potsdam Conference in July. Belatedly informed of the existence of the atomic bomb, it was Truman's decision that it was to be used against Japan in August 1945. His postwar career remained full of international crises largely engendered by the Cold War while

at home he had to deal with a hostile Congress. However he took a positive position on America's leadership of the West with the Marshall Plan, the Berlin airlift and the creation of NATO all becoming part of the "Truman Doctrine". It was also Truman's lot to have to deal with the Korean War that broke out in June 1950. Not only did he have to swing UN and American support behind intervention but he also had to check the overly assertive Gen MacArthur. Truman proved to be the equal of the war hero, although his stand resulted in his popularity plummeting. He retired from office in 1953. *MS*.

Truscott, Lt Gen Lucian King, Jr (1895–1965). US. Eisenhower's representative at his forward command post at Constantine during the Tunisian campaign; Commander 3rd US Division in Sicily, at Salerno and at Anzio; promoted to command VI US Corps on February 22 1944 at the height of the crisis at Anzio; commanded the break out from Anzio in May 1944; commanded VI US Corps (the assault corps) during the landings in Southern France, and during the advance up the Rhône Valley and in the Battle of Montélimar in August 1944; given command of Fifth Army in Italy when Clark was promoted to 15th Army Group on December 16 1944; led Fifth Army in the final battles of the Italian campaign.

Tsingtau, siege of (1914). Leased to Germany in 1898, Tsingtau, Kiaochow Bay, Shantung, north China, was by 1914 a heavily fortified naval base, the German Navy's major overseas outpost. To deny it to von Spee's East Asiatic Squadron, the Royal Navy mounted a blockade at the outbreak of World War I; Japan, seeking territorial gains in north China, demanded Germany's withdrawal and, this refused, declared war on August 23. Japanese warships, including the seaplane-carrier *Wakamiya*, joined an Allied force (battleship *Triumph*, one British and one French cruiser, five destroyers) in blockade and bombardment. On September 18, a 24,000-strong Japanese expeditionary force (total casualties during siege: *c*1,600), joined on

September 23 by 1,500 British and Indian troops (casualties: *c*75) landed north of Tsingtau and advanced on the base. Under constant naval and land bombardment (with "nuisance" bombing by Japanese aircraft) the *c*5,000-strong garrison (casualties: c700) held out until heavy siege artillery was brought up, surrendering on November 7. *RO'N.*

Tsushima, Battle of, Russo-Japanese War. Early on May 27 1905 the Russian 2nd Pacific Squadron under Rozhdestvenski, heading for Vladivostok, approached the 40-mile-wide (64km) strait lying between Japan and the island of Tsushima. The Japanese commander, Togo, held his main battle fleet at Masampo, southeast Korea, while his cruisers scouted Rozhdestvenski's course.

The Russian squadron was ill-balanced: four modern and four obsolescent battleships, nine cruisers of varying types, nine destroyers and eight auxiliaries. Its incompatibility limited Rozhdestvenski's speed to around nine knots. Although apparently outgunned by the Russian squadron, with 16 guns of 10in-12in compared to the Russians' 43, Togo's fleet of four modern battleships, eight cruisers and a strong torpedo flotilla was well-balanced and able to manoeuvre at up to 16 knots, enabling them to close the range in order to take advantage of a considerable superiority in 6in-8in armament. Togo made full use of wireless, here used in battle for the first time.

Togo's interception was made soon after 1300 hours on May 27. Using his superior speed, Togo "crossed the T", leading his ships across the Russian course at some 9,000yd (8,200m) range. Rozhdestvenski, meanwhile, had attempted a redeployment that succeeded only in throwing his battle line into confusion. First turning onto a course opposite and parallel to the Russians, Togo then audaciously turned his ships in succession: now, on a parallel course and slightly ahead, he was able to concentrate his full weight of fire on the leading Russian ships at a range of 3,000–5,000yd (2,700–4,500m).

Russian fire was at first accurate although ineffective. As the range closed, the Japanese gunners quickly reduced the Russian fleet to a shambles. By 1500 hours, Rozhdestvenski lay severely wounded in his sinking flagship, *Suvarov*, and *Oslyabya* had become the first ironclad battleship to be sunk by gunfire. As the Russian squadron, now commanded by Adm Nebogatov, attempted to continue to the north, Togo again "crossed the T" and engaged at short range, eventually sinking the battleships *Alexander III* and *Borodino*.

During the night, torpedo craft harassed and further dispersed the Russian ships and with the coming of day Togo committed his major units to mop up the stragglers. Resistance ended at 1130 hours on May 28. Only two destroyers and a light cruiser reached Vladivostok. Some 34 Russian ships were either sunk or captured, with 4,830 men killed and 5,917 wounded or made prisoner. The Japanese lost three torpedo boats only, with 117 killed and 583 wounded. *RO'N*.

Tuker, Lt Gen Sir Francis "Gerty" (1894–1967). Br. Commander 4th Indian Division from January 1942 during the Western Desert, Tunisian and Italian campaigns until February 1944. At Cassino, he requested the bombing of the monastery before his division attacked it in February 1944. He was taken ill at Cassino and returned to India. He then commanded IV Corps in the reconquest of Burma, and became c-in-c Eastern Command, India, during the postwar struggle for Indian independence, 1945–47.

Tukhachevsky, Marshal of the Soviet Union Mikhail Nikolaevich (1893–1937). Russian. An Imperial cavalry officer and fervent patriot, Tukhachevsky became disillusioned with Tsarism while a POW, 1915–17. Supporting the Bolsheviks after his release, he became a protégé of Trotsky, commanding in the successful western offensives against Kolchak and Wrangel during the Russian Civil War. Although severely defeated by Pilsudski at Warsaw and on the Niemen during the Polish campaign, 1920, he became COS, Red Army, in 1926. He was a major figure in its mechanization, reducing undue emphasis on armour's infantry support role by relating

traditional cavalry doctrines to tank employment, and in its development of airborne forces. Having worked closely with von Seeckt in the clandestine training of the German army, he advocated strategies against German aggression as early as 1936. The warning aroused Stalin's paranoiac ire: in June 1937, during the Red Army "purges", Tukhachevsky was arrested and executed. *RO'N*.

Tumbledown Mountain. The key Argentinian defence position before Stanley during the Falklands War of 1982. Resolutely defended by elite troops of the 5th Marine Regiment. The Scots Guards attacked on the night of June 12 in appalling weather and with little artillery support, and drove the defenders off, thus clearing the way for the final capture of Stanley.

Tunisian campaign (November 1942–May 1943). Hitler decided to forestall the eastward advance of Eisenhower's forces, which had landed in Algeria and Morocco, by occupying Tunis to protect the rear of Rommel's Panzerarmee Afrika, and to serve as the Axis supply base if Tripoli fell to Montgomery.

The Vichy Governor, Adm Esteva, welcomed the German intervention. In consequence, Kesselring, German c-in-c South, was able to rush troops and aircraft into Tunisia quicker over the short sea-crossing from Sicily than the Allies could do overland from Algeria and Morocco. By the time the leading elements of the British 78th Division were approaching Tunis in the last week of November, the improvised XC Corps (Nehring) was able to check them in the actions at Sedjenane, Tebourba, and Medjez el Bab, and to establish a bridgehead some 30 miles (48km) from the city.

A race then began to build up the opposing forces. Initially, the Axis commanders held the advantage, and were able to mount the first counteroffensives. Fifth Panzer Army (von Arnim), in the north, tried to relieve the pressure being exerted by the British First Army (Anderson) on Tunis with the offensive in January 1943, but it lacked the strength needed for decisive results.

Then in southern Tunisia, von

Arnim and Rommel each launched a highly successful spoiling offensive against the US II Corps (Fredendall). Von Arnim struck 1st US Armoured Division at Sidi Bou Zid on February 14, and Rommel initiated the Battle of the Kasserine Pass five days later. The Americans suffered demoralizing defeats in both battles, and left Rommel free to turn on Eighth Army (Montgomery), advancing from Tripolitania. He was, however, decisively beaten by Montgomery in the Battle of Médenine on March 6; and, thereafter, the Axis was thrown onto the defensive as the Allied build-up of troops and resources gained momentum.

Both sides reorganized their command structures in February. On the Allied side, 18th Army Group was formed under Alexander to coordinate the operations of the Allied forces already in Tunisia with those of Eighth Army. The Northwest African Tactical Air Force was formed at the same time under Coningham to coordinate the air support of the Army Group.

On the Axis side, Rommel returned to Germany in failing health on March 9 and was succeeded by the Italian Gen Messe. The Panzerarmee Afrika was retitled the First Italo-German Army. Von Vaerst took over Fifth Panzer Army in the north from von Arnim, who was made responsible for both Axis armies in Tunisia as commander Army Group, Africa.

Alexander's strategy was to stabilize the fronts of the inexperienced First British Army and II US Corps, while Montgomery's veteran Eighth Army drove Messe's Army northwards until the Axis forces were confined in their bridgehead around Tunis with no escape across the Sicilian Strait, which was dominated by Allied air and naval forces.

Montgomery defeated Messe in the battles of the Mareth Line (March 19-28) and Wadi Akarit (April 6) and drove him back northwards. The II US Corps (now under Patton) failed to cut him off with a thrust to the coast around Gabes; and the British IX Corps (Crocker) was equally unsuccessful with a flank attack at Fonduk. Messe fell back into the Axis bridgehead, where he defeated Montgomery's first attempts to break in at Enfidaville on April 19.

While Montgomery had been attacking Messe, von Arnim had mounted two diversionary but unsuccessful offensives against Anderson's First Army: in the centre at Medjez el Bab on March 5 and in the north at Sedjenane on March 19. By the beginning of April, von Arnim had lost the initiative, and Alexander was planning his final offensive to be launched on a wide front, for which II US Corps (now under Bradley) was moved to the northern flank to attack Bizerta, while V Corps (Allfrey), IX Corps (Crocker) and XIX French Corps (Koeltz) attacked towards Tunis.

Alexander's offensive, described contemptuously by Montgomery as a "partridge drive" because of its lack of concentration, started on April 22 and made disappointing progress. At Montgomery's prompting, Alexander decided to make a concentrated thrust down the Medjez el Bab-Tunis road on a narrow front. Gen Horrocks, Commander XIII Corps, who had gained valuable experience at Tebaga, was sent by Montgomery to take charge of the operation; and the veteran 7th Armoured and 4th Indian Divisions were transferred from Eighth Army in preparation.

The attack was launched in the early hours of May 6 with 4th Indian and 4th British Divisions attacking north and south of the road behind a moving curtain of artillery fire and air attacks. During the morning, 7th and 6th Armoured Divisions passed through, also north and south of the road, and by nightfall were some 8 miles (12km) inside the bridgehead. The next day, Axis resistance began to crumble as the two armoured divisions thrust their way into Tunis, which fell by mid-afternoon. In the north, Bradley's II US Corps was equally successful, entering Bizerta at about the same time. All Axis forces in Africa had surrendered by midday May 13 1943. *WGFJ.*

Tupolev SB-2 Katiuska (USSR, WWII). Bomber; crew 3. Prototype flew October 1934. Extensively used Spanish Civil War; first deliveries there October 15 1936; first sortie October 28. Operated Soviet-Finnish war 1939–40 and during German invasion of Russia. Finnish AF used captured Russian

SB-2s plus 16 from Germany. Also served with Chinese, Bulgarian air services. Production, 6,967. Two 960hp Klimov M-103 engines; max. speed 280mph (451kph); four 7.62mm machine guns, 2,422lb (1,100kg) bombs.

Tupolev Tu-2S (USSR, WWII). Bomber; crew 4. Prototype (ANT-58) flew January 1941; pre-production Tu-2s operational evaluation September 1942; quantity deliveries early 1944. Production version Tu-2S proved to be an exceptional aircraft. Production (total over 2,500) continued until 1948; deliveries to China, Bulgaria, Hungary and Poland; some participated in Korean War. Two 1,850hp Shvetsov M-82FN engines; max. speed 340mph (547kph); 6,614lb (3,000kg) bombs, two 20mm cannon, three 12.7mm machine guns.

Turing, Alan Mathison (1912–54). Br. Mathematician; recruited to Bletchley Park, where he played leading part in inventing world's first electronic computer and in breaking German "Enigma" ciphers; regarded as a security risk (he was a homosexual), therefore taken off secret work; at Manchester University, continued essential research on computers.

Tweebosch, Battle of *see* DE LA REY.

Twelfth Air Force (US). Activated in September 1942 to support "Torch" landings in North Africa, under Maj Gen Doolittle, hero of the Tokyo raid. After the North African campaign, 12th Air Force served in the Italian theatre and on the formation of 15th Air Force became the US Tactical Air Force for the Mediterranean Theatre of Operations, supporting landings in Southern France (Operation "Dragoon"), August 1944, then launching attacks deep into Austria and southern Germany.

Twelfth Army Group. Originally designated the 1st United States Army Group. Became operational on July 14 1944 under the command of Lt Gen Bradley. Its primary units during the liberation of France and the final Allied advance into Germany were the First and Third US Armies.

Twentieth (US) Air Force. Formed in 1944 to conduct a strategic bombing offensive against Japan using B-29 Superfortresses. It operated initially from advanced airfields in China and later from the Marianas. The early results achieved by high-altitude daylight attacks fell short of expectations. However, in March 1945, Maj Gen Curtis E LeMay switched the tactics to low-altitude night incendiary raids on Japanese cities. Thereafter the offensive became increasingly devastating in its effects, culminating in the dropping of the atomic bombs on Hiroshima on August 6 and Nagasaki on August 9 1945.

Twenty-First Army Group. Commanded by Gen Sir Bernard (later Field Marshal) Montgomery throughout the Northwest Europe campaign in 1944–45. This formation comprised the British Second Army and Canadian First Army. Until the US 12th Army Group became operational on August 1 1944, it also included the American ground forces in Normandy.

Twining, Gen Nathan Farragut (1897–1985). US. Commander Mediterranean Strategic Air Force and US Fifteenth Air Force during the Italian campaign from January 3 1944. COS, USAF, 1953–57; Chairman, JCS, 1957–60.

Tyne Cot. The largest Commonwealth war cemetery in the world, Tyne Cot, near Ypres, contains 11,908 graves. A memorial there also records the names of 34,888 men who went missing in the Ypres Salient after August 16 1917.

Typhoon, Hawker (Br, WWII). Single-seat fighter/fighter-bomber/ground attack. Prototype flew February 24 1940; first production May 27 1941; deliveries from September 1941. Aerodynamic, engine and structural difficulties hampered early operational use; most effective at low altitudes. After D-Day devastatingly employed as ground-attack fighter. Production 3,317. One 2,180hp Napier Sabre IIA engine; max. speed 405mph (652kph); four 20mm cannon, 2,000lb (900kg) bombs or eight 60lb (27kg) rocket projectiles.

U

U-boat *see* SUBMARINES.

Udet, Lt Gen Ernst (1896-1941). Ger. Second highest-scoring German fighter pilot of World War I (62 "kills"), when he flew with Manfred von Richthofen's *Jagdgeschwader* I. Udet rejoined the Luftwaffe in 1936: a protégé of Göring and Milch, he became its Chief of Supply and Head of Technical Office. Impressed by the dive-bombing potential of the American Curtiss Hawk, Udet shipped two examples to Germany and was thus instrumental in the development of the Junkers Ju 87. However his devotion to dive- and medium bombers and single-engined fighters, at the expense of heavy bombers, contributed largely to the Luftwaffe's failure to build an effective long-range bomber force. In November 1941; harassed by production difficulties with the Heinkel He 177, embittered by the recriminations of Göring and Milch, and disgusted by the reports of concentration camps, Udet committed suicide. *RO'N.*

Lt Gen Udet: "ace" pilot

Ugaki, Vice Adm Matome (1890–1945). Jap. As COS, Combined Fleet, 1941–43, Ugaki was concerned with Yamamoto in the planning of Japan's major naval operations. Surviving the "ambush" in which Yamamoto died on April 18 1943 – his own aircraft was shot down into the sea and he swam ashore – Ugaki took command of 1st Battleship Squadron (flagship *Yamato*), serving under Ozawa during the Battle of the Philippine Sea and under Kurita at Leyte Gulf. Early in 1945, he took command of the Kyushu-based 5th Air Fleet, his responsibilities including maintenance of the kamikaze offensive at Okinawa. On August 15 1945, following Hirohito's surrender broadcast, Ugaki flew with a sortie by 11 kamikaze dive-bombers against Allied warships off Okinawa. A final radio message announced that his force was "diving on the enemy" – but there are no Allied records that indicate any success by Ugaki's sortie, which was probably the Pacific War's last kamikaze mission. *RO'N.*

Ukrainian campaigns (1941 and 1943–44). Desire for the mineral and agricultural riches of the Ukraine was a major factor in Hitler's decision to invade the Soviet Union. On June 22 1941 it was attacked by units of von Rundstedt's Army Group South that made rapid progress. By July 11 von Reichenau's Sixth Army had come within 10 miles (16km) of Kiev with First Panzer Group and Seventeenth Army cooperating in a massive encirclement of over 100,000 Soviet troops around Uman. Operations benefited from Hitler's decision on August 21 to make the Ukraine, together with Leningrad, his major objective. Second Army and first Panzer Group were diverted to assist Army Group South and made a crucial contribution to the defeat of Budenny's Southwest Front. A total of 650,000 Soviet troops was taken.

The Soviet offensive to recapture the Ukraine formed part of the Red Army's winter offensive of 1943–44. On December 24 First and Second Ukrainian Fronts advanced from the Dnieper, trapping First Panzer Army at Korsun-Shevchenkosky. Von Manstein's counterattacks failed to liberate the beleaguered force but it managed a skilful breakout on its own. In the southern Ukraine, von Kleist's Army Group A was attacked by Second, Third and Fourth Ukrainian Fronts, forcing a German withdrawal to Odessa, in turn abandoned on April 10 1944. With the Germans pushed back to the Romanian border, the Ukraine was once more in Soviet hands. *MS.*

Soviet machine gun on Ukrainian front

"Ultra". Ultra secret information secured from breaking enemy codes at Bletchley Park, 1939–45, distributed to a closely limited circle of senior politicians, commanders and staff officers. MI6 controlled the flow of information tightly to ensure that the secret of the decipherers' success remained unbroken. Several thousand personnel were involved; all kept the secret until 1974.

UNC Allies. On July 7 1950, the UN Security Council authorized the establishment of a Unified Command, headed by the US, to control the operations of military forces supplied in response to the resolution of June 27 1950 calling on members of the UN to assist South Korea to repel aggression. During the Korean War, 16 members of the UN participated in the Unified Command (UNC), the US providing the majority of air, sea and ground forces. Other nations involved were Australia, Belgium, Canada, Colombia, Ethiopia, France, Britain, Greece, Holland, Luxembourg, New Zealand, the Philippines, South Africa, Thailand and Turkey. In July 1950 all Republic of Korea forces were placed under the Unified Command. Five countries, Denmark, India, Italy, Norway and Sweden, provided medical support. *CM.*

UNCOK (United Nations Commission on Korea). Established by the General Assembly of the UN on December 12 1948 to observe the withdrawal of occupation troops from Korea and facilitate Korean unification. The members of the commission were Australia, Nationalist China, El Salvador, France, India, Syria and the Philippines. On March 2 1950 it recommended the appointment of a military observer group to monitor the 38th Parallel. The Australians completed a survey of the Parallel on June 23 which reported that in the areas which they had visited, the ROK army was not deployed for an attack on the North. When the war began, UNCOK quickly concluded that South Korea was the victim of unprovoked aggression. *CM.*

UNCURK (United Nations Commission on the Unification and Rehabilitation of Korea). Created by the General Assembly on October 7 1950 to represent the UN in bringing about a free, democratic and unified Korea and to implement relief and rehabilitation policies. It replaced UNCOK and was formed by Australia, Chile, the Netherlands, Pakistan, the Philippines, Turkey and Thailand.

United Nations (UN). A term adopted by the Allies in January 1942; the UN became the successor to the League of Nations.

United Nations Command *see* UNC ALLIES.

United Nations General Assembly (Korean War). Since the Soviet Union had no veto in the General Assembly, it was to this body that the US turned when it first took the problem of Korea to the UN in October 1948, a move which resulted in the establishment of UNTCOK and the ultimate emergence of a separate South Korean state. The decisions which involved the UN in the Korean War were taken by the Security Council but with the return of the Soviet Union to that body in August 1950, action reverted to the General Assembly. As MacArthur's forces approached the 38th Parallel, a resolution drafted by the US and sponsored by Australia, Brazil, Britain, Cuba, the Netherlands, Norway,

Pakistan and the Philippines was presented to the Political Committee on September 30 1950. It called for actions to be taken, including elections held under UN auspices, and the economic rehabilitation of the country. It further pledged that UN forces would remain in Korea only until stability had been assured and a unified government established. UNCURK was to be established to oversee this process. The resolution was passed by the General Assembly on October 7. It fulfilled a UN commitment to Korean unification which had existed since 1948 and tacitly approved the crossing of the 38th Parallel by MacArthur's forces. *CM.*

United Nations Security Council (Korean War). In June 1950, the Security Council consisted of five permanent members, the US, Britain, China, France and the Soviet Union, plus Cuba, Norway, Ecuador, France, India, Yugoslavia and Egypt. The Soviet Union, however, was boycotting the Security Council over its failure to oust Nationalist China in favour of the People's Republic of China. The Security Council first considered the Korean crisis on June 25 1950 when it approved a US resolution calling for the immediate cessation of hostilities and the withdrawal of North Korean troops. A second US resolution, passed on June 27, called on UN members to "furnish such assistance to the Republic of Korea as may be necessary to repel armed attack and to restore international peace and security in the area". This resolution was passed 7:1. On July 7, a third resolution was passed establishing a Unified Military Command (UNC) under American control. The vote was 7:0. The return of the Russians to chair the Security Council in August 1950, restored the Soviet veto and paralysed any further action by the Security Council. *CM.*

United States Air Corps *see* UNITED STATES ARMY AIR FORCES.

United States Air Force. Brought into being in 1948 as the culmination of developments towards the creation of a separate US air service. Based upon the USAAF, formed in 1941 from the US Air

Corps. Naval air power remained under the USN and the Marines.

United States Air Force in Korea. Air power played an important role in the Korean War. It was, however, a frustrating war for the USAF. Strategic bombing was ruled out because the sources of communist industrial strength were in Russia and China and air power was largely employed in support of the ground forces. In the first two years of the war, the USAF found itself relegated to close support of troops or interdiction attacks on enemy lines of communication. The failure of interdiction to produce decisive results and a desire to assert a role independent of the army, led the USAF to develop the doctrine of air pressure in 1952, designed to bomb the enemy into compromise at the armistice talks. The doctrine was quickly taken up because it avoided the heavy casualties inherent in ground attacks. The USAF maintained air superiority throughout the war but lost 1,466 aircraft, mostly to ground fire. *CM. See also* AIR PRESSURE STRATEGY AND TARGETING SYSTEM; MIG ALLEY; "STRANGLE" OPERATION.

United States Army Air Forces (USAAF). Established 1941 from the US Air Corps to raise the status and unify the control of air power other than naval. Arnold, although still technically subordinate to Marshall, in effect became one of Joint Chiefs of Staff.

United States Forces in Vietnam. American military personnel in South Vietnam, rising from 875 in 1960 to 23,310 in 1964, were officially advisers until the first whole ground combat unit was introduced on March 9 1965. Total US troop strength grew to a peak of 543,000 in April 1969, then steadily decreased, to 45,600 in mid-1972, before the last US troops departed, March 29 1973.

The large majority of US forces in Vietnam were from the Army, which, during the course of the war, deployed seven infantry divisions, four independent infantry brigades and an armoured cavalry regiment. The Marine Corps provided a corps-level combat headquarters, two divisions, two regimental landing teams, a reinforced aircraft wing, and several battalion-size landing forces aboard ships of the Seventh Fleet. Elements of the Seventh Air Force deployed to Vietnam comprised, at their peak, about 60,000 men, 350 fighter-bombers, 100 C-130 transports and other craft. The Navy supplied three riverine assault forces and Seabees.

Forces stationed in South Vietnam were supplemented by others offshore, on Guam and Okinawa, and in neighbouring countries. Seventh Fleet deployed the carriers of Task Force 77 and patrolled the coast with help from US Coast Guard Squadron One. Thailand hosted eight Air Force wings and various Army support elements at the Korat, U Bon, U Dorn, Nakhon Phanom and U Tapao bases. B-52s of Strategic Air Command flew from Guam as well as Thailand, tankers from Okinawa. At the height of the war these additional forces totalled about 90,000 men. *WST*.

United States Marine Corps (USMC). Provided a division for France in 1917–18, spearheaded amphibious assault on Japan in the Central Pacific and played a major part in Korea and Vietnam. Amphibious specialists and highly trained assault troops, they are the largest force of "sea soldiers" in the world and have their own aviation and armour.

United States Navy in Korea. The USN supplied most sea power in the Korean War. It blockaded the North Korean coasts and provided air and artillery support for ground forces. Control of the sea gave UN Command a strategic flexibility denied to the enemy.

United States Strategic Air Forces In Europe (USSTAFE or USSTAF). Designation of Spaatz's overall command of the Eighth Air Force, based in Britain, and the Fifteenth, in Italy, 1944–45.

Unryu. Japanese aircraft carrier. Completed in 1944; soon sunk by US submarine *Redfish*.

Unsan, Battle of (1950), the Korean War. Unsan, northwest of the Chongchon river, was the scene of the first engagement between US troops and the Chinese People's

Volunteers on November 1-4 1950. In the last week of October, the Chinese attacked the ROK divisions on the flanks of Eighth Army as it advanced towards the Yalu. Gen Walker moved 1st Cavalry Division from Pyongyang to Unsan to bolster the South Koreans and on October 31 ordered US I Corps to halt its drive on Sinuiji and fall back to the Chongchon because of the threat on its flank. The wisdom of this decision was apparent on November 1 when the Chinese attacked and destroyed the 8th US Cavalry Regiment at Unsan. The battle showed the effectiveness of Chinese tactics against a US army which relied on the roads. *CM. See also* CHONGCHON RIVER; CHONGJU.

UNTCOK (United Nations Temporary Commission on Korea). Established by the UN General Assembly on November 14 1947 over Soviet opposition when it approved a resolution sponsored by the US. This called for elections by March 31 1948 to select a National Assembly for all Korea which would create a government and security forces. Foreign troops were to withdraw "at the earliest practicable date". The elections were to be supervised by a temporary commission, responsible to the General Assembly. UNTOK consisted of Australia, Canada, Nationalist China, El Salvador, France, India, Syria and the Philippines. The Ukraine was nominated but refused to serve. UNTCOK was refused entry into the north and found that all shades of opinion in the south except the far right opposed an election which would divide the nation and create a separate South Korean state. On February 9 UNTCOK voted to refer the problem back to the Interim Committee of the General Assembly which decided that it should observe the election "in such parts of Korea as are accessible . . .". A separate election was held in the south on May 10 1948. Although UNTCOK observed only two percent of the polling places, it pronounced the election valid. On this basis the General Assembly recognized the Republic of Korea (ROK) on December 12 1948 as a lawful government based on the will of the people and "the only such Government in Korea". *CM.*

Upham, Capt Charles VC and Bar (b.1911). New Zealand. The only man to win the VC twice in World War II and only the third ever to do so. He won the first in Crete in May 1941 and the second at Ruweisat Ridge in July 1942.

Urquhart, Maj Gen Robert (Roy) (1901–1988). Br. A brigade commander in Sicily and Italy, 1943, Urquhart was in 1944 appointed GOC, 1st Airborne Division for the Arnhem operation. He had no experience of airborne warfare, but his infantry experience proved invaluable once the paratroopers landed. His resolute leadership sustained his men in their nine-day fight against overwhelming odds, culminating in his extrication of some 2,000 survivors in a well-planned night crossing of the Rhine. He was GOC, Malaya, in 1950–52, at the height of the Malayan Emergency. *RO'N.*

Ushijima, Lt Gen Mitsuru (1887–1945). Jap. Commander of Thirty-second Army from August 1944, and entrusted with supreme command on Okinawa with orders to fight a defensive action to the last. He allowed US troops to land virtually unopposed on April 1 1945, having ordered the construction of inland defences – bunkers and caves, taking full advantage of the terrain and denying the invaders the full benefit of naval gunfire and air support – centring on his southern HQ at Shuri Castle. Ushijima's determined defence inflicted c50,000 casualties (the highest toll of the Pacific campaigns) on US forces before he conceded defeat by suicide on June 20. *RO'N.*

Ustashe. Croat fascist party, founded by Ante Pavelić 1929; came to power 1941 in puppet state of Croatia, Yugoslavia; behaved with utmost atrocity towards non-Catholic and non-Croat inhabitants; dispersed 1945.

Utah beach *see* NORMANDY, INVASION OF (1944).

Utah Line. Established in April 1951 during the Korean War north of the Kansas Line and designed to both threaten the base of the Iron Triangle (Chorwon, Kumwha, Pyongyang) and open the way for an advance to the Wyoming Line.

U

V/1500 *see* HANDLEY PAGE V/1500.

Vaagso raid. On December 27 1941 a British Combined Operations force raided the Norwegian islands of Vaagso and Maaloy. The German garrison in the town of South Vaagso offered stiff resistance to the Commando assault force but failed to prevent extensive damage to installations and shipping.

Vaal Kranz, Battle of (February 5–7 1900), Second Boer War. Following Spion Kop, Buller, with *c*20,000 men, again advanced across the Tugela. Planning to secure a gap in the hills surrounding Ladysmith, he feinted with one brigade at Brakfontein kopje, sufficiently distracting Botha's 4,000 Boers to enable a second brigade to take Vaal Kranz kopje. However, his failure to attack Doornkop, the other height commanding the gap, meant that the gain could not be exploited. For two days, the brigade on Vaal Kranz was left unsupported while Buller appealed to Roberts for advice. Buller withdrew, with 39 killed and 369 wounded; Boer casualties were negligible.

Vaerst, Lt Gen Gustav von (1894–1975). Ger. Commander 15th Panzer Division during the latter half of Operation "Crusader"; wounded at Gazala; given temporary command of the Afrika Korps when Nehring was wounded at Alam Halfa; Commander Fifth Panzer Army in Tunisia from March 1943; taken prisoner after the fall of Tunis in May 1943.

Valluy, Gen Jean Etienne (1899–1970). Fr. Gen Leclerc's replacement as commander in Indochina, Valluy ordered the occupation and bombardment of Haiphong that precipitated war in December 1946. After the failure of Operation "Lea", which he conceived, he was himself replaced. However, the Americans considered Valluy an effective commander, and in 1953 President Eisenhower urged the French government to reappoint him. The French appointed Gen Navarre instead.

Vandegrift, Gen Alexander Archer (1887–1973). US. Marine Corps officer whose combat experience dated back to the US interventions in Nicaragua (1912) and Haiti (1915) and the Veracruz landings, Mexico (1914). Appointed at short notice to prepare and command 1st Marine Division's landings in the Solomon Islands, 1942. After successfully initiating the Guadalcanal campaign, he commanded 1st Marine Amphibious Corps at Bougainville, November 1943. Commandant, USMC, 1944; in 1945, the first active-duty USMC officer to achieve four-star rank.

Vandenberg: eminent US air staff officer

Vandenberg, Gen Hoyt S (1899–1954). US. When America entered World War II, Vandenberg was Operations and Training Officer of the US Air Staff. In 1942, after participating in planning "Torch", he helped to organize the Twelfth Air Force and became its COS, playing a leading role in the direction of air operations during the final stages of the North African campaign. He returned to Washington in August 1943 as Deputy Chief of the Air Staff but by March 1944 he was in Europe as Deputy Air Commander of the Allied Expeditionary Force and Commanding Gen of the American Air Component. In this capacity he made an important contribution to the planning of the Normandy invasion before taking over the US Ninth Air Force in August 1944. His career reached its zenith when he succeeded Spaatz as COS of the USAF in 1948. *PJS*.

Van Fleet, Gen James Alward ("Big Jim") (b.1892). US. Commanded the US Eighth Army during the Korean War. Graduated from West Point in 1915 and served as a Corps commander during World War II. Head of the Joint Military Aid Group in Greece when he was ordered to Korea in April 1951. Under Van Fleet's command Eighth Army defeated the Chinese spring offensive and fought its way back over the 38th Parallel. When truce talks began in July 1951, he used the opportunity to rebuild the ROK Army and tackle the guerrilla problem behind the front. Van Fleet was frustrated by the continued military stalemate and favoured an advance to the Korean waist employing tactical atomic weapons. He retired in February 1953 and was succeeded by Gen Maxwell Taylor. *CM*.

Vang Pao, Maj Gen (b.1932). Laotian. Vang Pao, in 1960 a major in the Royal Lao Army and member of the Hmong minority, attracted attention by organizing resistance to neutralist and Pathet Lao forces in the Plain of Jars. American and Thai military advisers began secretly helping him to raise an army composed of his fellow Hmong in early 1961. This he did by doling out American aid to Hmong villages in return for recruits and permitting the US to bomb those that refused. His army reached a peak of 40,000 in 1967, and Vang Pao became the most powerful figure among the Hmong clans. As American aid dwindled in the early 1970s, so did Vang Pao's army. In May 1975, at the urging of Souvanna Phouma, he resigned his command and was evacuated to Thailand along with about 3,000 of his officers and their families. *WST*.

Vanguard. British battleships. (1) *St Vincent* class, completed 1910; served in the Grand Fleet at Jutland. Blew up when in harbour at Scapa Flow with 804 dead (July 9 1917). (2) The last British battleship. Early in World War II, it was seen that there was little chance of completing the 16in *Lion* class battleships only recently laid down. However, there were four spare twin 15in turrets available (removed from the large light cruisers *Courageous* and *Glorious* when they were converted to aircraft carriers), and these were used to produce a fast battleship for use in the Far East. The design was basically that of the *King George V*, but with improved seaworthiness from raised bow and transom

Vanguard: tragically destroyed, 1917

stern. An accident delayed her completion until 1946. She was broken up in 1960. Because the elderly 15in mounting was so good, the 51,420-ton *Vanguard* proved an excellent ship, although she never saw action. *DJL.*

Vann, Lt Col John Paul (1924–1972). US. Military adviser to the ARVN 7th Division when it performed with cowardice in its disastrous defeat at Ap Bac, January 1963. Unlike his superiors, who downplayed the ARVN's deficiencies, Vann openly complained about them. The dispute personified the tension between informed advisers in the field and the official optimism of senior officials. Vann questioned the ability of the Saigon regime to make necessary reforms and decried the use of heavy fire power in a war that called for discriminating, politically sensitive tactics.

After trying unsuccessfully to argue his case in Washington, Vann returned to Vietnam as a civilian official of the Agency for International Development, eventually becoming senior American adviser in ARVN II Corps in May 1971. He died in a helicopter crash, June 9 1972. *WST.*

Van Tien Dung, Senior General (b.1917). Democratic Republic of Vietnam. Without any formal military training, Dung organized and commanded the 320th Division of the People's Army of Vietnam (PAVN) in the war with France. In 1953 he became PAVN COS. After long service in the shadow of Vo Nguyen Giap, in 1980 he replaced Giap as Minister of National Defence and senior military member of the Communist Party Political Bureau.

Dung had a large hand in turning the PAVN into a modern conventional army during the Viet-

nam War, but he is best known for taking personal command of the offensive that brought the war to an end in 1975. For the opening attack on Ban Me Thuot, he chose the "blooming lotus tactic" of bypassing the city's defensive perimeters then exploding outwards, which he claimed to have pioneered in an attack on the town of Phat Diem in 1952. *WST.*

Van Tuong peninsula, Battle of (1965). US Marines chose the Van Tuong peninsula, located 15 miles (25km) south of their major base at Chu Lai, for the site of their first major operation in the Vietnam War. The peninsula contained three villages, one named Van Tuong, that had long concealed communist forces. In 1965, these forces consisted of the 2,000-man 1st Regiment of the PLAF, and it was to find and destroy this regiment that the Marines launched Operation "Starlight" on August 18. With 6,000 troops supported by air, artillery, armour and naval bombardment, the Marines pinned the PLAF against the sea. Bitter fighting left 45 Marines dead and 203 wounded along with 599 bodies (or 700 or 964, depending on the source) that the Marines claimed to be PLAF combatants. The success of "Starlight" led to other regimental amphibious-heliborne assaults, most notably Operation "Piranha" on the nearby Batangan peninsula. Communist forces, although weakened, continued to make use of both areas. *WST.*

Vasilevsky, Marshal Aleksandr (1895–1977). Russian. After service during World War I as an officer in the Imperial Russian Army, Vasilevsky joined the Red Army in 1919. Shortly after the launching of Operation "Barbarossa", he was made Deputy Chief of the General Staff and Chief of the Operations Section as Vatutin's replacement. This position brought him into regular contact with Stalin and their success in avoiding total catastrophe helped to establish Vasilevsky's career. In June 1942 he replaced Marshal Shaposhnikov as Chief of the General Staff, bringing a new purpose to the Stavka's conduct of the war. This was characterized by his policy of visiting commanders at

the front where he was able to help prepare and coordinate operations while acquiring an accurate appreciation of the fighting. However, by late 1944 Stalin and Zhukov desired to control the final phases of the war themselves and Vasilevsky's role diminished. In February 1945 he asked to be relieved as Chief of the General Staff in order to concentrate on coordinating the operations of First Belorussian and First Baltic Fronts. Following Chernyakhovsky's death he also assumed command of Third Belorussian Front and successfully continued the reduction of German resistance in East Prussia. Victory in Europe released Vasilevsky to take command of Soviet forces in the invasion and occupation of Japanese Manchuria in August 1945. *MS.*

Vatutin, Gen Nikolai (1901–1944). Russian. As Deputy Chief of the General Staff and head of the Operations Section, Vatutin helped Stalin prepare the initial response to the German attack of 1941. In July he was appointed COS of the Northwestern Front and in October helped to prevent a German breakthrough in the Kalinin sector. Vatutin briefly commanded Voronezh Front before taking over Southwestern Front. In November 1942 his forces formed the right wing of the encirclement of German forces around Stalingrad. Vatutin then returned to command Voronezh Front and helped prepare strategy for the defence of the Kursk salient. After holding the German offensive, his forces mounted a counterattack that resulted in the capture of Kharkov. Vatutin maintained the westward drive of his retitled First Ukrainian Front, taking Kiev in November. However, in February 1944 he was mortally wounded when ambushed by Ukrainian nationalist partisans. *MS.*

Vaux Fort *see* VERDUN, BATTLE OF.

V Bombers. Built to first RAF specifications for jet-propelled heavy bombers capable of delivering nuclear weapons. Three types: Vickers Valiant, Handley Page Victor, Avro Vulcan.

VE Day. "Victory in Europe" day, May 8 1945.

Vella Gulf, Battle of (August 6–7 1943). Around midnight, a force of six US destroyers (Commander Frederick Moosbrugger) intercepted a "Tokyo Express" of four Japanese destroyers (Capt Kaju Sugiura) carrying 900 men and 50 tons of materiel to reinforce the garrison on Kolombangara, Solomons. Deploying his ships in two columns, about 1,800yd (1,650m) apart, on a parallel reciprocating course with the Japanese, Moosbrugger was able to achieve complete surprise: radar-controlled torpedo salvoes fired by his first column from 4,000yd (3,600m) crippled three of the Japanese destroyers, which were swiftly finished off by gunfire and further torpedoes from the second column. The surviving destroyer escaped. *RO'N.*

Vella Lavella *see* SOLOMON ISLANDS.

Venizelos, Eleutherios (1864–1936). Greek. Became Prime Minister of Greece in October 1910 and led his country throughout the Balkan Wars. In 1914 he was faced with a diplomatic dilemma – King Constantine I favoured a pro-German position while Venizelos saw Greece's best interests lying with the Allies (especially after Turkey joined the Central Powers). He resigned in March 1915 after the King refused to assist the Allies' Dardanelles campaign, but returned to power in August. However, when an Allied force landed at Salonika in October, he was once more forced out. The conflicting policies of Venizelos and Constantine propelled the country to the brink of civil war. In June 1917 the politician emerged triumphant and Greece declared war on the Central Powers. Although Venizelos was to show diplomatic mastery at the peace conferences, his popularity at home suffered. He served several more terms as prime minister but died in exile in Paris. *MS.*

Verdun, Battle of (1916). When considering German strategy for 1916, Falkenhayn resolved to bleed the French Army to death. To achieve this he planned an offensive at Verdun on the Meuse, calculating that the French would feel compelled to defend this for-

Arms piled for a brief respite at Verdun

tress-city – a symbol of national pride – regardless of casualties, although it is not clear whether Falkenhayn himself actually intended the city to be captured. He did envisage, however, that the scale of German effort would be "limited", with the artillery doing the main work of execution as successive French reinforcements arrived. The attack, supported by over 1,220 guns, was launched on February 21 1916 by Crown Prince William's Fifth Army. On February 25, the day that the Germans took the important Fort Douaumont, Joffre's deputy, de Castelnau, decided that the right bank of the Meuse must be defended, just as Falkenhayn hoped. On the other hand, French tactical command at Verdun was now entrusted to Gen Pétain, who understood the nature of modern fire power and coordinated his artillery to inflict heavy losses on the Germans. He also ensured that supplies were maintained along the single secure road to the south, a route which became known as the *Voie Sacrée* ("Sacred Way"). On March 6 the Germans extended the offensive to the west, on the left bank of the Meuse, striving to secure the heights of Hill 304 and the aptly-named Mort Homme ("Dead Man"), both of which fell in May. By this time Verdun had become a slaughterhouse for both sides: the battle had developed its own momentum, totally overtaking Falkenhayn's plans for a "limited" offensive. Pétain's promotion to the Central Army Group in April and his replacement at Verdun by the aggressive Nivelle did nothing to ease the fury of the

struggle. Fort Vaux was captured by the Germans on June 7 but they were unable to take Fort Souville, the last major bastion northeast of Verdun, on July 11–12. Already short of manpower, Falkenhayn had been forced to switch reserves elsewhere by the Brusilov offensive in the East and the British attack on the Somme and, when he was removed from his post as Chief of the German General Staff in August, Hindenburg and Ludendorff ordered the cessation of all German attacks at Verdun. French counterstrokes between October and December, in which Nivelle employed the "creeping barrage" with great success, recaptured Forts Douaumont and Vaux, although Mort Homme stayed in German hands until August the following year. French casualties in this terrible attrition battle of 1916 were around 377,000, while the Germans lost some 337,000 men. Neither army fully recovered from the ordeal before the war ended. *PJS.*

Versailles, Treaty of. Ended the war between Germany and the Allies which had been suspended by the Armistice of November 11 1919. It was signed in the Palace of Versailles on June 28 1919. The Treaty established the League of Nations, to which Germany was admitted in 1926. Germany ceded territory in the west, north and east, including Alsace and Lorraine to France, the Saar to the League, northern Schleswig to Denmark and a considerable area of East Prussia to Poland. Her colonies were confiscated, the German army reduced to 100,000 men and her navy restricted to six old battleships, six cruisers, 12 destroyers and 12 torpedo boats. No submarines were allowed. There was to be no air force of any kind. The Kaiser and others were to be tried for war crimes. Severe reparations were imposed on Germany, ranging from payments in gold to the replacement of shipping destroyed in the war. The Rhineland was to be demilitarized and occupied by the Allies for 15 years.

Many of the clauses, including the trial of the Kaiser, were not carried out, the Germans evaded others, and some of them duly provided excellent propaganda targets for Hitler. *ANF.*

Adm Vian aboard *Cossack*

Vian, Adm of the Fleet Sir Philip (1894–1968). Br. Vian demonstrated outstanding flair, leadership and offensive spirit in successively larger commands. He won the DSO three times in 1940 and 1941. While commanding the destroyer *Cossack* in February 1940, he put a boarding party onto the German *Altmark* and rescued British prisoners. His flotilla launched the torpedo attacks on *Bismarck* which helped to slow her at a vital stage of the engagement and, in March 1942, commanding a weak cruiser squadron in the Mediterranean, he defeated an Italian squadron which included a major battleship and so preserved a Malta convoy. He commanded naval forces covering the landings in Italy and Normandy and then went to the Pacific in command of the carrier force. *ANF*.

Vichy France. Southern France left in the hands of a French government headed by Pétain and Laval from the armistice of 1940 until 1944, when Germany occupied it.

Vickers FB5 (Br, WWI). Two-seat fighter-reconnaissance. Prototype flew summer 1914; first deliveries September 1914; first to France February 1915 with RFC; a few to RNAS Dunkerque. No. 11 Squadron, RFC (first homogeneous fighter squadron ever formed), to France with FB5s, July 25 1915. Built in France and Denmark. Soon outclassed; succeeded by FB9 development. Production, at least 224. One 100hp Gnome Monosoupape engine; max. speed 70mph (112kph); one 0.303in machine gun, one 0.303in rifle (or occasionally a second machine gun).

Vickers gun (0.303in). Medium machine gun, introduced into British Army in 1912 to replace the Maxim of 1884, using similar principle of short recoil. Water-cooled and belt-fed, permitting sustained indirect predicted fire for harassment or direct support. The medium machine gun played a decisive role in the trench warfare of World War I and a special Machine Gun Corps was formed in the British Army to handle it. The Vickers gun was replaced during the 1970s by the General Purpose Machine Gun (GPMG). *MH*.

Vickers tank *see* TANKS.

Victor, Handley Page HP 80 (Br). Heavy bomber/photographic-reconnaissance/refuelling tanker; crew 5/6. Prototype flew December 24 1952; deliveries to service from November 28 1957. First squadron operational April 1958; equipped six bomber squadrons. Deliveries of conversions to in flight refuelling tankers began spring 1965; these played vital part Falklands war 1982. Production, 86. Four 11,000lb (4,990kg) s.t. Bristol-Siddeley Sapphire 202 or 17,250lb (7,825kg) s.t. Rolls-Royce Conway RCo11/Co17 engines; max. speed Mach 0.95; 35,000lb (15,880kg) bombs (load could include one Blue Steel air-launched missile).

Victor Emmanuel III, King of Italy (1869–1947; reigned 1900–46). Supported his country's entry into World War I on the side of the Allies and was frequently at the front throughout the hostilities, doing much to boost Italian morale in the face of military reverses. He displayed less effective qualities of leadership in the political strife of the 1920s and acquiesced in Mussolini's assumption of power. He subsequently offered scant opposition to Il Duce's policies and it was only when Italy faced total defeat that he acted to remove him. In September 1943 he agreed an armistice with the Allies and fled to their lines. He abdicated in favour of his son Umberto in May 1946. *MS*.

Victory ship. US war standard merchantman powered by turbines. A total of 531 victory ships – 414 cargo ships and 117 transports – were built from 1943.

Vietcong (a contraction of *Vietnam Cong-san*, or Vietnamese Communist). The term came into use during the regime of Ngo Dinh Diem, who used it in a derogatory sense, sometimes applying it to any of his political enemies. Americans used the term during the Vietnam War in reference, variously, to guerrilla forces of the NLF, the main forces of the PLAF, and all Southern revolutionary cadre as distinct from Northern personnel.

Viet Minh. The Indochinese (later Vietnam) Communist Party established a national united front known as the *Viet-nam Doc-lap Dong-minh* (Vietnam Independence League), or Viet Minh for short, in May 1941. Behind this front the communists began to organize a rural-based armed struggle, centred during 1941–45 in the mountains near Vietnam's border with China, against colonial rule. The communists sought to broaden support by creating a Popular National Front, the Lien Viet, in 1946, but the name Viet Minh remained the common term to describe all communist-led forces, including the People's Army of Vietnam (PAVN), throughout the war with France.

Vietinghoff, Col Gen Heinrich, von (1887–1952). Ger. Commander Tenth Army in the Italian campaign until Kesselring was injured in a car accident in October 1944; temporary C-in-C South West and Commander Army Group C until Kesselring's return in January 1945; then Commander Army Group Kurland until recalled to succeed Kesselring in March 1944 when the latter became C-in-C West; surrendered Army Group C to Alexander on May 2 1945.

Vietnam, Communist Popular and Regional Forces *see* LOCAL FORCES MILITIA NLF; LOCAL SELF-DEFENCE FORCES MILITIA DRV; PROVINCIAL MOBILE FORCES NLF.

Vietnam Main Forces *see* PEOPLE'S ARMY OF VIETNAM (PAVN); PEOPLE'S LIBERATION ARMED FORCE (PLAF); ARMY OF THE REPUBLIC OF VIETNAM (ARVN); SPECIAL FORCES (ARVN).

Vietnam, North *see* DEMOCRATIC REPUBLIC OF VIETNAM (DRV).

Vietnam, Second War (1960–1975). An extension of the struggle for independence that had left Vietnam divided in 1954 (*see* IN-DOCHINA-FRANCE WAR). By leaving the issue of reunification unresolved, that struggle laid the basis for renewed conflict among the Vietnamese. The introduction of American ground combat forces in 1965 internationalized and expanded the conflict into a major war.

Among the issues were the meaning and application of the Geneva Agreements of 1954. The Agreements, while affirming Vietnam's juridical unity, provided for the temporary partition of Vietnam between the North, governed by the communist Democratic Republic of Vietnam (DRV), and the South, governed by the anti-communist State (later Republic) of Vietnam (RVN), pending elections on reunification in 1956. The elections were never held because the government of Ngo Dinh Diem in Saigon, which had not signed the Agreements, refused to confer with Hanoi. Diem also suppressed the political rights of former communist cadres, contrary to provisions of the Agreement. These developments provided the communists with their pretext to seek reunification by means of a revolution in the South.

In fact, the communists had foreseen this eventuality and left behind in the South a nucleus of cadres, combatants and weapons when most of their forces had regrouped in the North. They also aided the Cao Dai and Hoa Hao religious sects in their confrontation with Diem, calculating that if Diem did not hold the elections, then his regime might be induced to collapse. As the date for elections passed, it was clear that this strategy had failed.

Under strong pressure from Southern party members, the Central Committee in Hanoi formally approved plans to prepare for armed struggle at its 15th Plenum in May 1959. The party's Third National Congress endorsed this decision in September 1960. The founding of the National Liberation Front of South Vietnam (NLF) on December 20 1960 and of the People's Liberation Armed Force (PLAF) on February 15 1961 were the direct results. While the com-

munists provided the organization, leadership and strategy, their success depended on sympathy for their aims in the South that was the result of Diem's autocratic rule, high rates of peasant tenancy and landlessness, and a repressive, corrupt bureaucracy. With considerable popular support, revolutionary organizations swiftly replaced Saigon's administration in much of the countryside.

American involvement had begun in the first war, and it had intensified in response to the Chinese Revolution and the Korean War. It was the American conviction that the US had a duty to halt advances by communism on behalf of the "free world". American policy was also influenced by a lingering sense of "manifest destiny" in Asia, a virulent anti-communism at home, and the strategy of "containment". To fill the vacuum left by France, the US organized the Southeast Asia Treaty Organization (SEATO) in September 1954 and began, in October, direct military assistance to the Saigon regime.

In 1956, the number of American military personnel assisting the Army of the Republic of Vietnam (ARVN) exceeded the limit of 350 placed on foreign military advisers set by the Geneva Agreements. Total American aid to South Vietnam that year was $270 million, third highest per capita after Laos and South Korea. American leaders came to believe the US could not withdraw without undermining America's credibility as an ally, and more aid followed. The US matched the quickening tempo of insurgency with increases in aid and military advice. From fewer than 800 in 1960, the number of American military advisers in South Vietnam grew to 3,000 in December 1961 and 11,000 in late 1962.

The communists formally commenced their armed struggle on January 26 1960 by overrunning an ARVN regimental headquarters in Tay Ninh province. From about 7,000 total combatants in 1960, the number of "regular" PLAF troops grew to 34,000 and guerrillas to an estimated 72,000, for a total of 106,000, by late 1964. These forces were recruited, trained, equipped and supplied largely from sources inside the

South. The first Soviet-design 7.62mm automatic weapons and RPG2 anti-tank grenade launchers to appear in the South were not captured until December 1964. However, Hanoi had set up two logistical "Groups" in 1959 to organize infiltration of men and supplies from the North, and from then until late 1964 an estimated 44,000 people, mostly Southerners who had regrouped in the North in 1954, returned to the South to provide a backbone of trained cadres and officers.

A key battle during this period took place near the hamlet of Ap Bac in My Tho province. There, in January 1963, PLAF troops soundly defeated a much larger ARVN force supported by air, helicopters, armed personnel carriers, and US advisers. The battle convinced American officials on the scene that direct US intervention was necessary. Another trouncing of the ARVN at Binh Gia in December 1964 drove the point home. Saigon's control was then limited to the chief towns and cities, while the communists roamed freely over 75 percent of the countryside.

But communist forces in the South were approaching the limits of their potential, while the United States, following the Tonkin Gulf incident, was stepping up its own involvement. Hanoi therefore began implementing an earlier decision to increase Northern support. The first whole unit of the People's Army of Vietnam (PAVN) comprising Northern-born regulars departed the North in August. By May 1965 the number of PAVN regulars in the South was estimated at 6,500, a figure that rose to 80,000 or 90,000 in the late 1960s. Parallel with and ostensibly in response to Hanoi's actions, the US in March 1965 began the sustained bombing of the North known as Operation "Rolling Thunder". A US Marine combat unit landed near Da Nang in June. By the year's end, the US had 184,000 men (rising to 543,000 in 1969) in Vietnam. South Korea, Thailand, Australia, New Zealand and the Philippines also sent troops. The conflict thus became an international war, although it retained civil and revolutionary dimensions. Just as the US took over much of the burden of combat and imposed its strategy upon the

ARVN, so did the PAVN, in part, displace the PLAF and local guerrilla forces.

Under Gen Westmoreland, commander of the Military Assistance Command, Vietnam (MACV), the US initially engaged North Vietnamese regular units in thinly populated areas, while the ARVN concentrated on "pacification" and security in the densely populated lowlands. American strategy was based on recognition that a ground offensive against the North was not politically feasible, and therefore sought by means of attrition to force the PAVN to retreat. Once that was accomplished, a strengthened ARVN was to take over all combat duties, permitting the Americans to withdraw.

Communist strategy sought to offset the US/ARVN manpower and material advantage by combining political and armed struggle. Political struggle was to weaken the Saigon regime while winning the popular support needed to build revolutionary armed forces locally. In this sense, political struggle had primacy. However, the mix of the two forms of struggle was to vary in the South's "three strategic zones". Combat by main forces was to be paramount in the mountains, political and armed struggle were to be balanced in the lowlands, and political struggle was to predominate in the cities. By thus operating in all three zones, the communists hoped to keep the enemy distracted, stretched thin, and worn down. At a suitable moment, a "general offensive and uprising", or simultaneous armed attacks and popular demonstrations in all three zones, was to stretch enemy resources beyond endurance. This strategy was one of attrition too, in the sense that it conceded inability to inflict outright defeat on the US and depended on denying the Americans victory to make them leave.

For a while the Americans could persuade themselves they were winning. They averted the ARVN's collapse, established vast logistical facilities, and launched "search and destroy" missions into many hitherto impregnable communist base areas. With unprecedented mobility and fire power, they inflicted heavy casualties, forced the communists to build sanctuaries in Cambodia, applied pressure

against the Ho Chi Minh Trail in Laos, and bombed North Vietnam. They also stabilized the Saigon regime and improved both the quantity and quality of Saigon's armed forces. However, the communist political apparatus in the South remained intact, and the PAVN as well as local guerrilla force levels actually increased. The communists remained able to choose the time and place of combat and thus to control their casualties and to go on fighting as long as they wished. Arms, ammunition and equipment in increasing quantities continued to flow down the Ho Chi Minh Trail. By late 1967 the Americans believed they had gained the upper hand, but in fact, considering that American endurance was limited, the war was in stalemate.

It was to destroy American confidence that the communists launched a "general offensive and uprising" during Tet, the Vietnamese New Year, in 1968. Even if this offensive did not sweep them to power, they reasoned, it would prove their ability to prolong the war. They also hoped to roll back US-Saigon gains in the countryside and, as the price for agreeing to negotiate, to end the bombing of the North. While communist forces suffered debilitating casualties, they achieved their strategic aims.

In the aftermath, while negotiations got underway, American and Saigon forces made considerable gains. This was due partly to communist exhaustion and partly to the effectiveness of such programmes as Accelerated Pacification, Revolutionary Development and Phoenix, which made inroads against the communists' political apparatus. The US also widened the war by bombing and invading communist sanctuaries in Cambodia and supporting Operation "Lam Son 719", a South Vietnamese "incursion" into southern Laos. The frequency of large-unit attacks by communist main forces declined. In response the Americans shifted emphasis from "search and destroy" to small unit patrolling. Claiming success for "Vietnamization", but mainly to satisfy American domestic opinion, the Nixon administration began withdrawing US troops.

The communists postponed plans for a major offensive to achieve

"decisive victory" from 1971 to 1972. By then Hanoi felt the need to force negotiations to a conclusion before US détente with the Soviet Union and China weakened international support. With Southern losses offset by increased infiltration from the North, the PAVN and PLAF struck on four fronts (see EASTER OFFENSIVE). The ARVN nearly collapsed at several points but for the timely support of American airpower. In retaliation, and as secret talks between Henry Kissinger and Le Duc Tho bogged down, the US bombed the North and mined its harbours. In the December "blitz" of Operation "Linebacker II", the US also made unprecedented use of B-52s. Further talks led to the signing of the Paris Agreement on January 27 1973, which provided for a ceasefire, withdrawal of remaining American troops by March 29, and consultations among the Vietnamese on the South's political future.

The cease-fire never really took hold, and open warfare resumed in 1974. Saigon then had more than 1,000,000 men in arms, 320,000 of them in ARVN main forces, lavishly supplied with new or discarded American equipment. Communist forces in the South totalled about 230,000 of which 150,000 were PAVN. The ARVN's advantage was offset, however, by orders to maximize territorial control. Holding widely scattered positions, it consumed vast quantities of declining American aid. Economic troubles and official corruption also sharpened opposition to Thieu's leadership.

The overrunning of Phuoc Long province by tank- and artillery-supported PAVN and PLAF units in January 1975, and American failure to respond, encouraged the communists to launch a massive campaign they hoped would bring victory in two years. In March, PAVN Gen Van Tien Dung concentrated force against Ban Me Thuot, which fell in a day. With other ARVN positions in the highlands now vulnerable, President Thieu ordered a retreat to the coast. But the retreat turned into a chaotic flight, sowing panic and confusion throughout the ARVN. Expecting American air support that did not come, many ARVN units disintegrated. The PAVN entered Hue on

March 26; Da Nang fell on the 28th. By mid-April, communist forces were poised for the assault on Saigon, dubbed the Ho Chi Minh campaign, which ended when Thieu's replacement, Gen Duong Van Minh, ordered the ARVN to surrender on the 30th.

The number of communist combatants killed in action from 1965 to 1974 was estimated by the American military at 950,765, a figure admittedly inflated by about 30 percent. ARVN killed-in-action during the same period were 220,357, perhaps 243,000 by the war's end. The US lost 58,718 dead, of which 10,298 were due to non-combatant causes. South Korean, Australian, New Zealand and Thai forces together lost 5,226 dead. South Vietnamese civilians suffered anywhere from 247,600 to 430,000 dead and 1,000,000 wounded, while an estimated 52,000 North Vietnamese civilians died in the bombing before 1972. *WST*.

Vietnam, South, *see* REPUBLIC OF VIETNAM (RVN).

Vietnam, South, Army of *see* ARMY OF THE REPUBLIC OF VIETNAM (ARVN).

Vietnam, South, Popular and Regional Forces *see* TERRITORIAL FORCES MILITIA RVN.

Vietnam, wars since reunification. The Vietnamese communists had hardly consolidated their 1975 victory in the war for reunification when they encountered difficulties in relations with both Cambodia and China. Their attention focused on the Khmers Rouges for, among other things, rebuffing their proffered "special relationship" and seeking help from Peking (Beijing). After obtaining Soviet assurance, the Vietnamese invaded Cambodia on December 25 1978 but could not completely exterminate the Khmers Rouges and other resistance forces. Their strategy of containing those forces along the Thai border while building a new Khmer regime under their protection proved costly, as it drained Vietnam's own meagre resources, although the Soviet Union supplied the bulk of arms, fuel and equipment. But the strategy was not entirely unsuccessful. In 1989,

Vietnam announced its intention to withdraw by September 30 1989, whether a political settlement was reached or not (*see* CAMBODIA, WARS SINCE INDEPENDENCE; POL POT).

Vietnam's distrust of China was exacerbated by Peking's rapprochement with the United States in 1971–72. The tension between them soon erupted in clashes between border guards and competing claims to islands in the South China Sea. Vietnam in turn antagonized China by joining the Soviet-led Council for Mutual Economic Exchange in June 1978 and signing a Treaty of Friendship and Cooperation with the Soviet Union in November. Vietnam's attack on Cambodia was the final provocation for China to launch a punitive strike across Vietnam's border from February 17 to March 16 1979. The Soviet Union supported Vietnam with intelligence gathered by Tu-95D "Bear" long-range reconnaissance planes, emergency shipments of arms and equipment and a 10-ship naval presence in the South and East China Seas, but it did not directly intervene. *WST*. *See also* SINO-VIETNAMESE WAR (1979).

Villers-Bocage *see* CAEN, BATTLE FOR (1944).

Vimy Ridge, Battle of (1917). In the plan for the British Arras offensive on April 9 1917, Horne's First Army was to protect the left flank of Allenby's Third Army by capturing Vimy Ridge, a chalk height overlooking the Douai plain. The actual task of storming the ridge was given to the four divisions of the Canadian Corps, under Lt Gen Byng. The British 13th Brigade would also participate. The thorough preparations for the assault included detailed

rehearsals for the infantry and other arms; the pinpointing of German batteries by sound-ranging and flash-spotting; and the completion of a series of subways enabling many of the Canadians to assemble under cover. At zero hour on April 9 the infantry attacked, in a snowstorm, behind a creeping barrage from the artillery. On the right the 1st and 2nd Canadian Divisions, with the British 13th Brigade, quickly took their principal objectives and, in the centre, the 3rd Division was similarly successful, although it experienced some trouble on its northern flank where the 4th Division was unable to secure Hill 145 – the ridge's highest point – until evening. Another feature on the left, known as the Pimple, fell on April 12. While helped by faulty German tactical deployment, the capture of Vimy Ridge, at a cost of over 11,000 Canadian casualties, was one of the outstanding operations of World War I, and it not only provided the British with a vital anchor point in the crisis of 1918, but also hastened Canada's emerging sense of nationhood. *PJS*.

Vindictive. British cruiser. Obsolete, *Arrogant* class. Used as the main assault ship on the mole at Zeebrugge (1918), carrying marines, flamethrowers, howitzers, mortars, machine guns and extra protection. Suffered heavy casualties and damage but successfully withdrawn. Used shortly afterwards as blockship on the second attempt to bottle up Ostend.

Vittorio Veneto. Italian battleship. *Littorio*-class. Completed 1940. Hit by aircraft torpedo at Matapan, later torpedoed by British submarine. Surrendered 1943. Scrapped in 1950s.

Allied troops move up as German prisoners are brought in; Vimy Ridge, April 1917

Vittorio Veneto, Battle of *see* ITA-LIAN CAMPAIGN, WORLD WAR I.

Vizcaya campaign, (spring 1937), Spanish Civil War. With stalemate round Madrid, the Nationalists set out to reduce the northern coast. The attack began from Villarreal in the southeast on March 31. The Nationalist army under Mola consisted of four strong Carlist brigades, Franco's finest Spanish troops, and an Italian division supported by the Italian Legionary Air Force and the Condor Legion. The Basque positions on mountain tops were easy targets for air attack. But to the Germans' exasperation, the over cautious Mola did not exploit the holes created for him. Although Nationalist attempts to blockade Bilbao were thwarted, a lack of supplies and demoralization from air attack (the Condor Legion's destruction of Guernica) contributed to the Basque retreat within the Iron Ring, Bilbao's optimistically named defence system. This was breached on June 12 and the Basque government ordered evacuation. The remaining troops retreated towards Santander and Gijón, and two subsequent campaigns that summer and autumn were followed by five months of intensive guerrilla warfare in the Asturias. This delayed Franco's achievement of numerical superiority on the other fronts until 1938. *AB.*

VJ Day. "Victory over Japan" day, August 15 1945.

Vlasov, Lt Gen Andrei, (1900–46). Russian. Commanding Second Shock Army, Vlasov was captured in June 1942 when encircled near Leningrad. He changed sides, broadcasting anti-Soviet propaganda and raising a "Russian Army of Liberation" (*Russkaya Osvoboditelnaya Armiya*; ROA) from Soviet POWs and forced labourers. This puppet force saw limited service on the East Front. In May 1945, Vlasov entered Prague with the 20,000-strong 1st ROA Division, securing the city against weak German resistance and attempting to surrender it to US Seventh Army. Constrained by Yalta, the Americans refused, handing over Vlasov to the Soviets, who executed him in 1946. *RO'N.*

Vo Nguyen Giap *see* GIAP, GEN VO NGUYEN.

Voie Sacrée see VERDUN (1916).

Voisin LA/LA S (French, WWI). Two-seat reconnaissance-bomber. Prototype (Voisin L) flew February 1914; two *escadrilles* equipped August 1914. Voisin LA introduced autumn 1914; on October 5 1914 France's first air-combat victory scored by an LA. Some LA. S had 37mm or 47mm cannon; first *Groupe de Bombardement* formed with Voisins November 1914. Supplied to RFC, RNAS and Russia; built in Italy for use by 5 *squadriglie*. One Salmson engine, either 130hp M9 or 140hp B9; max. speed 68.4mph (110kph); one rifle-calibre machine gun or 37mm cannon, 200lb (90kg) bombs.

Voisin 8 and 10 (French, WWI). Two-seat night-bomber; enlarged development of Voisin LA. Entered service late 1916; equipped at least 26 *escadrilles*; some remained in service until Armistice. Widely and successfully used as night-bomber, night-reconnaissance and in cannon-armed form. Load capacity increased in Voisin 10 with more powerful engine. Production, about 1,100 Voi8, 900 Voi10. One 220hp Peugeot (in Voi8), 300hp Renault (Voi10) engine; max. speed 75mph (120kph); two machine guns, one 37mm cannon, 650lb (295kg) bombs.

Volkssturm. A German Home Guard, established September 1944.

Volturno, crossing of the (October 12–14 1943). Fifth Army (Clark) attacked with X British Corps (McCreery) on the lower Volturno, and VI US Corps (Lucas) inland. The crossings were opposed by XIV Panzer Corps (Hube). The British were only partially successful in the coastal plain, but American successes in the hills turned the German line and persuaded Kesselring to authorize the continuation of the slow withdrawal to the Gustav Line.

Voluntary Aid Detachment (VAD). Formed in 1910, this nursing organization served the British armed forces in the 1914–18 and the 1939–45 wars.

Voormezeele. This village, which in 1917 was close behind the British lines near St Eloi, south of Ypres, was lost to the Germans during their April 1918 offensive but recaptured by the US 30th Division, attached to the British II Corps, on August 31 1918.

Voronezh, Battle of (1942) *see* STALINGRAD, BATTLE OF.

Voroshilov, Marshal Kliment (1881–1969). Russian. Played a leading role in the Bolshevik revolution in Petrograd and helped Dzershinsky to organize the Cheka to protect the new regime. In spite of his lack of military training, Voroshilov took command of Red Army units in the Ukraine, becoming commander of the Tenth Army in 1918. He fought throughout the Civil War, joining Budenny's First Cavalry Army in the campaigns against Denikin, the Poles and Wrangel. After the war, Voroshilov remained in the Red Army and, largely because of his close political ties with Stalin, became one of its leading figures. In 1935 he was appointed People's Commissar for Defence and created Marshal of the Soviet Union. But his position was dependent upon Stalin's favour and he failed to intervene in the latter's wholesale purges of the Red Army's officer corps in 1937. Voroshilov's influence on the development of the Red Army was often counterproductive and he was a fierce opponent of mechanization. Therefore, when the setbacks in the war against Finland showed up his and the army's shortcomings, Voroshilov was to all intents and purposes relieved of his command and effective control passed to Timoshenko. Nevertheless, in July 1941 Stalin recalled his crony to take command of the Northwest Front with orders to stem the German advance on Leningrad. This Voroshilov conspicuously failed to do and in September he was replaced by Zhukov. In spite of his lack of achievement, he retained his place on the Soviet State Defence Committee and acted as a Stavka representative at various front headquarters during the rest of the war. Furthermore, Stalin still had enough faith in Voroshilov to allow him to play a major role in negotiations at the Allied confer-

441

Veteran commander Voroshilov, 1936

ences at Moscow in 1942 and 1943. He was also a member of the Soviet delegation at the Tehran conference where, during the staff talks, he strongly pressed the Soviet demands for a Second Front. In 1953 he was elected Chairman of the Presidium of the Supreme Soviet. *MS.*

Vulcan, Avro 698 (Br). Heavy bomber; crew 5. Aerodynamic prototype (Avro 707 scale model) flew September 4 1949; first Vulcan prototype August 30 1952; first production February 4 1955. Vulcan was world's first operational delta-wing bomber. First deliveries to Service July 1956; first squadrons July-October 1957; nine had Vulcans. Enlarged and developed in service. Five air-refuelled missions to bomb Port Stanley airfield, Falkland Islands, May-June 1982: longest bombing missions ever flown. Production, 136. Four 17,000/20,000lb (7,710/9,070kg) s.t. Rolls-Royce (Bristol) Olympus 201/301 engines; max. speed Mach 0.98 (645mph (1,032kph) at 40,000ft (12,000m)); 21,000lb (9,525kg) bombs (could include a Blue Steel missile).

V-weapons. German, V for *Vergeltungswaffen* or "retaliation weapons". As the Allied invasion of Northern France approached and because of the overwhelming superiority of the Combined Bomber Offensive. Hitler placed great hopes on the introduction of V-weapons.

V-1 was a pilotless aircraft consisting of a 1,800lb (816kg) HE bomb with an Argus Tube pulse propulsion unit mounted above it. It was aimed at its target from a launching ramp; it flew at up to 400mph (640kph) generally at between 1,000 and 4,000ft (300–

1,200m). It was automatically controlled by magnetic means and its fuel was calculated to expire when the target range was exhausted. It was first used operationally against London on the night of June 12–13 1944. Subsequently some 8,564 were aimed at the same target. About 2,400 got through and killed 6,184 people. Later, more than 8,000 were aimed at Antwerp and over 3,000 at Liège. V-1 was vulnerable to the bombing of its launching sites and to anti-aircraft fire assisted by proximity fuses and fast interceptor fighters. Some were air launched.

V-2 (also known as A-4) was a rocket driven by liquid oxygen and alcohol. It rose to a height of 50 miles (80km), travelled at about 4,000mph (6,500kph) and had a range of about 200 miles (320km). Its nose consisted of a one ton HE bomb. Substantially the most advanced vehicle of World War II, there was no defence against it beyond the capture of its launching areas. It was first used operationally against London and Paris on September 8 1944. A total of 1,190 were subsequently aimed at London, killing 2,724 people.

V-3 referred to further projects under development but yet to be introduced at the end of the war. *ANF.*

German V-2 rocket, captured in 1945

Vyazma-Bryansk, Battle of (1941) *see* RUSSIA, INVASION OF.

Vyborg (Viipuri) *see* FINLAND, RUSSIAN INVASION OF.

Vyshinsky, Andrei (1883–1954). Russian. Deputy foreign minister of the USSR from 1940; exercised a major influence on Soviet foreign policy during World War II.

W

Waffen-SS. Fully militarized SS formations formed in 1939 and subsequently totalling some 40 divisions.

Wainwright, Gen Jonathan M (1883–1953). US. A forceful and popular US Army officer, Wainwright was posted to the Philippines as a major general in 1940. In March 1942, following the Japanese invasion, he took command of the US and Philippine forces when Gen MacArthur was ordered to Australia. With the fall of Bataan in April, Wainwright continued the fight from the island of Corregidor but, despite gallant resistance, he and the survivors of his command were compelled to capitulate on May 6 1942. He spent the next three years as a POW, experiencing considerable privations until he was freed on August 25 1945. He was present at the formal Japanese surrender aboard the USS *Missouri* in Tokyo Bay on September 2 1945 and was awarded the Congressional Medal of Honor on his return home. *PJS.*

Wake Island, Battle of. Construction of a US naval base at Wake atoll, *c*2,000 miles (3,200km) east of Hawaii, began in 1939. On December 7 1941, its *c*1,200 construction workers were protected by 450 men of 1st Defense Battalion, USMC (Maj James Devereux), 70 naval personnel (Commander Winfield Cunningham) and Marine Fighter Squadron 211 (12 Grumman F4F Wildcats). Within hours of the Pearl Harbor attack, Japanese aircraft from Kwajalein destroyed seven Wildcats on the ground. Daily raids followed, but early on December 11 an invasion force (Rear Adm Sadamichi Kajioka: 3 cruisers; 6 destroyers; 4 transports with 560 assault troops) was beaten off by Marine coastal batteries (6 x 5in; 12 x 3in AA) and the four surviving aircraft, losing two destroyers. On December 22, Kajioka returned with a stronger force, supported by carriers *Hiryu* and *Soryu*, and landed about 1,500 men of 2nd Maizuru Special Naval Landing Force. After a heroic fight, Devereux' garrison (50

Marines and 70 civilians killed) surrendered early on December 23. The ill-mounted Japanese invasions had cost them two destroyers and two transports sunk and around 1,150 killed or wounded. On the American side, Adm Pye's recall (possibly fearing an untimely fleet action) of Vice Adm Fletcher's task force sent from Pearl Harbor to relieve Wake – and Fletcher's dilatoriness in refuelling at sea, which contributed to Pye's decision – were subsequently much criticized. *RO'N.*

Wake Island (Truman-MacArthur meeting, October 15 1950), the Korean War. Occurred just after UN troops had crossed the 38th Parallel into North Korea. Truman proposed the meeting to associate himself with the victor of Inchon on the eve of congressional elections and to emphasize to MacArthur that the Far East was only a part of America's global responsibilities. MacArthur predicted an early end to the war and remarked that if the Chinese intervened they would be slaughtered by US air power. Eighth Army could begin redeploying to Japan by Christmas. Truman returned from Wake in an optimistic mood and expressed his full confidence in MacArthur. *CM.*

Walcheren. Although the port of Antwerp was captured almost intact by the British Second Army in September 1944, access to it was denied by the presence of strong German garrisons at the mouth of the Scheldt, on Walcheren and Beveland. The Canadian First Army was assigned to clearing these and reinforced with Royal Marines and Special Forces in order to overcome the strong West Wall fortifications. The RAF was called in to breach the dykes with heavy bomber attacks and this flooded the low-lying polderland. German resistance was fierce and casualties heavy. Even after the defence had been overcome, a 70-mile (112km) channel had to be swept of mines before the first ships were able to use the port of Antwerp on November 26. *MH.*

Waldau, Lt Gen Otto Hoffmann von (1898–1943). Ger. *Fliegerführer Afrika*, April–August 1942; then Commander *Fliegerkorps X.*

Walker, Capt Frederick J (1896–1944). Br. Greatest U-boat killer of World War II. Brilliant trainer of the 36th then 2nd Escort Groups which he commanded from *Stork.* The former fought a brilliant action around a Gibraltar convoy; the latter destroyed 16 U-boats. Walker developed the "creeping attack" – one escort guiding another into the attack. He died of a stroke brought on by overwork.

Walker, Gen Sir Walter Colyear (b.1912). Br. Walker's experience as an officer of Gurkhas in the Burma campaign, 1942–45, proved invaluable during the Malayan Emergency, 1948–60, when he headed a Jungle Warfare School. In December 1962, Walker, then commanding 17th Gurkha Division, was appointed Commander, British Forces, Borneo, and Director of Operations during the Malaysian-Indonesian Confrontation. His campaign along the Sabah-Sarawak border against raiders from Kalimantan, in which he made expert use of ambush by helicopter-borne troops, was especially successful when, from mid-1964, his forces were allowed to penetrate Kalimantan to a depth of about 11 miles (18km) in "Claret" raids. Walker's insistence on this politically-sensitive measure, together with his openly-expressed opposition to reduction in Gurkha strength, made him a somewhat controversial figure; however, he went on to serve as Deputy and Acting COS, Allied Forces Central Europe, 1965-67, C-in-C Northern Command, 1967-69, and C-in-C, Allied Forces Northern Europe, until his retirement in 1972. *RO'N.*

Walker, Lt Gen Walton Harris ("Johnny") (1889–1950). US. Served as one of Patton's corps commanders during World War II. In 1948 he took over the Eighth Army in Japan and became MacArthur's field commander in Korea on July 6 1950. His troops were poorly trained and rapidly driven back. On July 29 1950, as his command retreated into the Pusan Perimeter, Walker issued an order to "stand or die". Despite his dogged defence of the Perimeter in August 1950, he was blamed for the poor performance of his troops early in the fighting. In

October 1950 he captured the North Korean capital, Pyongyang, but Chinese intervention soon forced Eighth Army into headlong retreat and Walker was again criticized. On December 22 1950 he was killed in a jeep accident and replaced by Ridgway. *CM.*

Walrus, Supermarine (Br, WWII). Shipboard observation/air-sea rescue amphibian; crew 4. Prototype (Seagull V, for Australia) flew June 21 1933; ordered by RN as Walrus 1935. Operated from warships by catapulting, and from overseas bases; much varied wartime use; in service until 1946. Production, 25 Seagulls V, 746 Walrus. One 635hp Bristol Pegasus IIM2 or 750hp Pegasus VI engine; max. speed 135mph (216kph); two 0.303in machine guns, bombs and depth charges.

Walsh, Col Kenneth A (b.1916). US. Walsh won his wings as a USMC enlisted man, wa commissioned in 1942 and scored 21 aerial combat victories, mostly flying F4U Corsairs with VMF-124 in the Southwest Pacific.

Walt, Lt Gen Lewis W (b.1913). US. Assumed command of the US 3rd Marine Division, Vietnam, in June 1965. He served concurrently as commander of the III Marine Amphibious Force, which became a corps-level headquarters for all US Marine and Army units in I Corps Tactical Zone. Until his departure in 1967, he supervised the American build-up in the northern portion of South Vietnam.

Wanklyn, Lt Commander David (1911–42). Br. Successful submarine commander. Operating from Malta in *Upholder*, he won the VC, May 1941, for his attack on an Italian troop convoy. He also sank the 18,000-ton *Conte Rosso.* *Upholder* failed to return from patrol in April 1942.

Wallis, Sir Barnes Neville (1887–1979). Br. Designed the airship R 100 and from such work applied the principle of geodetic construction to aircraft, notably the Wellington. Invented the bouncing bomb used in the Dams raid and also the Tallboy and Grandslam penetrating bombs used by Bomber Command 1944–45.

W

War crimes. The desire to make the Nazi leaders and their more fanatical adherents accountable for instigating and prosecuting World War II led to the establishment of an Allied War Crimes Commission in October 1942. After the war Allied Military Tribunals at Nuremberg and Tokyo tried individuals indicted as war criminals.

Warlimont, Lt Gen (*General der Artillerie*) Walther (b.1894). Ger. The German Defence Ministry's representative at Franco's HQ during the early stages of the Spanish Civil War, Warlimont became Chief of the National Defence Section, OKW, in 1938 and in September 1939 was appointed Deputy-Chief, Armed Forces Operational Staff (*Wehrmachtsführungsstab*), OKW. As such, he was concerned in all major German military plans, but usually subjected his own judgment to Hitler's will. His major importance lies in the light that his postwar testimony sheds on Hitler's relationship with the high command. Although injured in the July Plot, 1944, Warlimont was immediately sent to Normandy as Hitler's personal representative to von Kluge, with orders to stiffen his resistance to the Allied advance. Possibly affected by his realization of the gravity of Germany's situation, Warlimont collapsed after reporting back to the *Führer*, remaining unfit for service until the war's end. *RO'N.*

Warsaw, Battle of (1914). Once the German General Staff realized the extent of the Austrian defeat in Galicia, they moved rapidly to forestall a Russian invasion of Silesia. The efficiency of their mobilization system permitted the immediate formation of a new Army, the Ninth, which deployed southwest of Warsaw under Hindenburg on September 28 and advanced at once. Progress was rapid and the line of the Vistula was reached on October 9. A week later, German patrols were only 12 miles (19km) from Warsaw. Grand Duke Nicholas, overall the Russian c-in-c, reacted decisively to this threat. In a brilliant feat of staff work and hard marching, he switched 12 corps from Galicia to a position north of Warsaw, threatening Hindenburg's left. Heavy rains now turned the primitive Polish roads into quagmires. The Germans retired and by November 1 were back on their start line of September 28. The withdrawal was covered by a skilful demolition programme which prevented the Russians from following up.

The Austrians, still smarting under their initial reverse in Galicia and German failure to go to their help, had declined to advance north to link up with Hindenburg, but did send their First Army across the Vistula towards Ivangorod, where it was defeated and forced back in disarray on Cracow. Elsewhere, they met with some success and relieved Przemysl, but were then held by the Russians, whose left (southern) flank remained secure.

On November 14 Hindenburg was appointed c-in-c of all German armies on the Eastern front. Handing over the Ninth Army to Mackensen, he prepared a new offensive on the northern flank of the Polish salient. He and Ludendorff believed that Russia could be knocked out by a single masterstroke, launched before the onset of winter with heavy reinforcements from the Western Front. Falkenhayn, at Supreme Headquarters, disagreed. He still had his eyes fixed on the Channel ports in France and when he eventually released formations for the East, it was too late.

Mackensen, with three-and-a-half corps and five cavalry divisions, moved them in 800 trainloads round to the north of the salient and advanced on Warsaw with his left flank on the Vistula, covering 50 miles (80km) in the first four days. Lodz fell on December 6, but only after stubborn resistance. Winter was now setting in and the Germans were still 35 miles (56km) short of Warsaw. The front stabilized and both sides dug in to await the spring.

On the Galician front, winter also put an end to manoeuvre after Conrad had attacked the Russian left flank from across the Carpathians, and the line stabilized on the River Dunajec. *MH. See also* EASTERN FRONT (1915); GORLICE-TARNOW OFFENSIVE.

Warsaw, fall of (1939). Poland's strategy in meeting the German invasion of September 1 1939 relied upon a concentration of forces on the frontier. However, the speed and dynamism of the German attack rendered this ineffective and by September von Reichenau's Tenth Army had reached the outskirts of Warsaw. The next day the 4th Panzer Division attacked from the southwest but was repulsed by Polish Army and civilian units. Although Hitler was consequently obliged to abandon hopes of a quick seizure of Warsaw, by the 16th the city was surrounded and the Germans laid siege to it. On the 24th over 1,000 German aircraft launched massed air raids against the city, followed on the 26th by a ground assault. With supplies of food and ammunition exhausted, the city was forced to capitulate the next day. Approximately 10,000 civilians and 2,000 Polish soldiers had been killed and 140,000 troops taken prisoner. *MS.*

Warsaw Pact (the East European Mutual Assistance Treaty). Signed on May 14 1955 for 20 years by Albania, Bulgaria, Czechoslovakia, East Germany, Hungary, Poland, Romania and the Soviet Union. The treaty was a direct response to the establishment of the Western European Union (WEU) and an agreement signed in Paris permitting West Germany to enter NATO. This was condemned by the eight powers in a declaration issued at the end of a conference held in Moscow in November/December 1954 as encouraging a revival of German militarism. By March 1955 agreement was reached as to the terms of a treaty of mutual assistance and the setting up of a unified command system (with a combined general staff based in Moscow). Within six days of West Germany acceding to NATO, the treaty was signed by the eight powers, though East German forces were not included in the military structure until January 1956. In September 1968, in protest against the Soviet invasion of Czechoslovakia, Albania withdrew from the Warsaw Pact. At the 1974 Warsaw Meeting, the Pact countries declared their willingness to disband if NATO did likewise, but so long as this existed and without "effective disarmament measures", it would continue. In May 1985 the Pact was renewed for a further 20 years. *BHR.*

Ruin in Warsaw after the rising of 1944

Warsaw rising (1944). By the end of July 1944 the Red Army was on the outskirts of Warsaw. In anticipation of their arrival, on August 1 Gen Bor-Komorowski, the commander of the Polish Home Army, ordered an uprising against the German garrison. Although they gained control of three-quarters of the city, events took a disastrous turn when the Soviet advance halted and the Germans reinforced the garrison. Stalin rejected all appeals for assistance and attempts to supply the uprising by air from the west proved costly and inadequate. Having endured two months of ferocious fighting and with his surviving units seeking the safety of the sewers, Bor-Komorowski was forced to surrender. When resistance ended on October 2 Warsaw lay devastated and some 200,000 of its inhabitants had become casualties. *MS.*

Warspite. One of the grandest British battleships of the 20th century. 15in guns. Served throughout both world wars including at Jutland, 1916, and at Narvik and in the Mediterranean in the second.

War Zone C. The scene of major search and destroy operations by US and South Vietnamese forces during the Vietnam War. Roughly triangular in shape, with the Cambodian border for its base, the zone extended through Tay Ninh, Binh Long and Binh Duong provinces to a point about 25 miles (40km) from Saigon. Proximity to supply bases in Cambodia made the zone a major staging area for communist forces. Operation "Attleboro" occurred in the zone during the autumn of 1966. *See also* JUNCTION CITY OPERATION (1967).

War Zone D. Just to the east of War Zone C in South Vietnam lay War Zone D, an area about 46 miles (75km) by 93 miles (150km) in size. The zone's jungled, hilly terrain provided excellent cover for communist forces moving against the Saigon-Bien Hoa area, and the US and South Vietnamese launched numerous operations to interdict them. War Zones C and D and the Iron Triangle met at a point in the town of Ben Cat about 25 miles (40km) northwest of Saigon.

Washington Conferences. Meetings between Churchill and Roosevelt and their military advisers in Washington December 22 1941–January 14 1942 ("Arcadia"), June 19–25 1942 and May 12–25 1943 ("Trident").

"Arcadia" took place at Churchill's initiative in the immediate wake of Pearl Harbor. Despite the Japanese threat it was agreed that a Germany-first policy would be pursued. Machinery to coordinate the work and views of the British Chiefs of Staff and the American Joint Chiefs of Staff was set up in the form of the Combined Chiefs of Staff.

June 1942 (not coded). It was decided to pool Anglo-American research on atomic energy with a view to the production of a bomb in America. There was also discussion of where and how to deploy Anglo-American armies into Europe which raised the issue of a Mediterranean versus a northern French strategy.

"Trident" continued this theme in the light of what should be done after the successful invasion of Sicily. The British wish to achieve the conquest of Italy was to some extent challenged by American anxiety about the need to build up for the invasion of northern France and to increase the pressure on Japan. *ANF.*

Washington. US battleship. *North Carolina* class. Completed 1942. Briefly in the Atlantic, then sank *Kirishima* at Guadalcanal. Remained in the Pacific for the rest of the war.

Wasp. US aircraft carriers. (1) Designed to use up the remaining treaty tonnage, therefore smaller than similar *Yorktown* class. Completed in 1942. Flew off Spitfires for Malta before going to the Pacific where sunk by submarine. (2) *Essex* class completed 1943. Served in the Pacific. Left service 1972.

Watson-Watt, Sir Robert (1892–1973). Br. A leading contributor to the application of radar to air defence. Somewhat by chance, Watson-Watt put it into the minds of the Tizard Committee that radio pulses, which he had been studying for meteorological purposes, might be used to detect the presence of aircraft.

Wavell, Field Marshal, the Earl (1883–1950). Br. C-in-C Middle East at the outbreak of World War II. He masterminded the Western Desert, East African, Greek, Iraq, and Syrian campaigns of 1940 and 1941, but he lost Churchill's confidence after the failure of the second offensive to relieve Tobruk, June 1941. Succeeded by Auchinleck on July 5 1941, and sent to replace him as C-in-C, India.

After Pearl Harbor, he was given the additional appointment of Supreme Commander of the American, British, Dutch and Australian (ABDA) forces in the Western Pacific with his headquarters in Java, but never had the resources with which to check the Japanese offensive. His command was disbanded in February 1942, and he returned to India to concentrate upon the defeat of the Japanese invasion of India from Burma. In June 1943 he succeeded Lord Linlithgow as Viceroy of India. He endeavoured to steer India to promised independence without jeopardizing its unity but, in the end, he did not manage to bridge the political gap between Hindu and Muslim aspirations. He was replaced by Mountbatten in March 1947. *WGFJ.*

Wedemeyer, Lt Gen Albert C (b.1897). US. An infantry officer by background, Wedemeyer joined the War Plans Division of the US War Department in 1941, working for a time under Eisenhower. In September 1943 he became Deputy COS of Southeast Asia Command, under Mountbatten, and remained in this post until October 1944 when he was chosen to command the US Forces in China and to serve as Chiang Kai-shek's COS.

W

445

Wehrmacht. The combined armed forces (army, navy and air force) of the Third Reich, created May 21 1935.

Wellington, Vickers (Br, WWII). Heavy bomber/reconnaissance torpedo-bomber; crew 5–7. Prototype flew June 15 1936; first production December 23 1937; quantity deliveries from October 1938. Nine squadrons by outbreak of war; operational from September 4 1939. Many variants evolved throughout war; design proved sturdy and versatile. Production until October 25 1945, total (all Marks), 11,461. Wellington III had two 1,535hp Bristol Hercules XI engines; max. speed 261mph (420kph); eight 0.303in machine guns, 4,500lb (2,040kg) bombs.

Welsh, Air Marshal Sir William (1891–1962). Br. Commander Eastern Air Command during "Torch" and the Tunisian campaign until February 1943.

Wepener, Battle of (April 9-25 1900), Second Boer War. Following victories at Sanna's Post and Reddersberg, De Wet moved south to attack the garrison at Wepener. Strongly entrenched on kopjes outside the town, 1,700 men of the Colonial Division (300 casualties) under Col E H Dalgety held off the 6,000-strong Boer force (23 casualties) for 17 days. De Wet withdrew on·the approach of relief columns. The siege had significantly delayed his campaign against British lines of communication: he had pressed it largely because of Boer hatred of the Cape Colony Afrikaners who formed a large part of Dalgety's force.

Werewolves. In spring 1945 Anglo-American staffs feared that the most fanatical Nazis would withdraw into Bavarian mountains, under codename "Werewolf" and leadership of Gen Walter Wenck, and make desperate trouble. So complete was the collapse of Nazism that·the idea turned out to be an illusion.

Western Air Plans. A series of carefully constructed plans for strategic bombing, framed by the British Air Staff in consultation with Bomber Command, 1936–40. They envisaged attacks upon German oil and aircraft production, the industrial concentration in the Ruhr and other industrial processes. They also provided for attacks upon the German fleet and to slow the advance of their armies.

Western Approaches. Atlantic approaches to the British Isles. The Battle of the Atlantic was controlled by this command, whose HQ moved from Plymouth to Liverpool in 1941.

Western Desert Air Force see MEDITERRANEAN, WAR IN THE AIR (1940–45).

Western Desert campaign (September 1940–January 1943). Operations ebbed and flowed across the deserts of Egypt and Cyrenaica for almost two-and-a-half years. The British were challenged and reposted three times.

The Italian challenge took place between September 13 1940 and February 7 1941. The Italians invaded Egypt on September 13, but a week later halted at Sidi Barrani for logistic reasons before reaching the main British defensive positions 60 miles (96km) farther east at Mersa Matruh. On December 9 they were surprised and defeated by the British Western Desert Force, and driven out of Egypt. British forces then invaded Cyrenaica, taking the fortified ports of Bardia, Tobruk and Benghazi. The withdrawal of the Italian Tenth Army into Tripolitania was intercepted by British armoured forces at Beda Fomm, just south of Benghazi, where it was forced to surrender on February 7 1941.

Rommel's first German challenge started in February 1941. The Afrika Korps landed at Tripoli during February, swept the British forces, weakened by withdrawals for Greece, out of Cyrenaica and laid siege to Tobruk; a succession of British counteroffensives led to the relief of Tobruk, and to Rommel's withdrawal to Tripolitania to await reinforcements, December 1941.

In his second German challenge (January 21 1942–January 23 1943), Rommel first counterattacked, driving the British, this time weakened by withdrawals to meet the Japanese threat in the Far East, back to the Gazala Line just west of Tobruk. There he destroyed the British armoured forces in the Battles of Gazala in June, opening the way to his objective, the Suez Canal. His advance into Egypt had lost its momentum through supply difficulties, British air attacks, and the exhaustion of his Panzerarmee Afrika by the time he reached El Alamein where he was stopped by Auchinleck. He was then decisively defeated by Montgomery at Alam Halfa in August, and in the Battle of El Alamein in October 1942, and was forced to withdraw to Tunisia. *WGFJ.*

Western Front. The entrenched battle lines between the Allies and Germany extending from Belgium to the Swiss frontier, World War I.

Westmoreland, Gen William C (b.1914). US. Became Commander, US Military Assistance Command, Vietnam (COMUSMACV), in June 1964. As chief tactical commander of American forces in Vietnam, his first task was to avert the almost certain collapse of the Saigon government. This he sought to do by building a logistical base for a large American force, then by searching out and destroying communist main force units in the highlands, helping the ARVN to "pacify" the lowlands, and preparing the ARVN to complete the task when the US withdrew. His strategy was essentially one of attrition, as it counted on the relentless grinding up of enemy troops to force the North's conventional army to retreat. For the purpose, Westmoreland emphasized "search and destroy" operations and heavy use of airmobility and fire power. Once the PAVN had withdrawn, he theorized, the ARVN would be able to cope with the local guerrillas that remained.

In November 1967, Westmoreland reported to the US Congress that victory was in sight. But the 1968 Tet offensive made that claim appear either ignorant or deceptive, and Westmoreland's request for 206,000 more troops provoked a public outcry. Although Westmoreland believed the offensive was the communists' "last throw of the dice", his strategy had not depleted their ranks at a rate greater than replacement, nor weakened Hanoi's resolve. The collateral damage caused by the operations his strategy required also

W

aroused civilian animosity and international indignation. In July 1968, he was succeeded as COM-USMACV by Gen Creighton Abrams. *WST*.

West Wall ("the Siegfried Line"). Fortifications along Germany's western frontiers begun in 1938. They were finally put to use in the defence of Germany in 1944–45.

Westphal, Lt Gen (*General der Kavallerie*) **Siegfried** (b.1901). Ger. A planner of genius, Westphal was Kesselring's COS, playing a major part in planning the defence of southern Italy, from mid-1943. In September 1944 he became COS to von Rundstedt (and then to Kesselring once more, from March 1945) on the Western Front.

Weyand, Gen Frederick C (b.1916). US. Beginning June 1972, Weyand was the last commander of the US Military Assistance Command, Vietnam (MACV). He had served previously in Vietnam as deputy commander of MACV (April 1970–May 1972), commander II Field Force (July 1967–July 1968), and commander 25th Infantry Division (January 1966–March 1967). He last visited Vietnam in March 1975 and reported, perhaps over-optimistically, to President Ford that emergency assistance of $722 million would be sufficient to prevent the defeat of Saigon's forces.

Weygand, Gen Maxime (1867–1965). Fr. Born in Brussels – some suggest as Leopold II's illegitimate son – Weygand became a French citizen and graduated from St Cyr in 1888 as a cavalry officer. For most of World War I he served with distinction as COS to Gen Foch, including the period from April 1918 onwards when the latter was C-in-C of the Allied Armies in France. In the early 1930s Weygand held the post of French CGS, supporting a moderate programme of modernization and the return of two-year service.

Having retired in 1935, he was recalled in 1939 to command the French forces in the Levant. On May 19 1940, with the Allied armies in France in disarray, he was summoned by PM Reynaud to succeed Gamelin as Allied C-in-C.

Despite his efforts to establish a new defensive front – the "Weygand Line" – behind the Somme and Aisne, the Germans broke through. By mid-June Weygand regarded the situation as hopeless and joined with Pétain in seeking an armistice. Between June and September 1940 he was Minister of War under the Vichy regime and was then Delegate Gen to French North Africa. His anti-Axis opinions led to his removal in November 1941 and to arrest and imprisonment by the Germans the following year. Released in 1945, he was re-arrested by the French and charged with treason. However, he was exonerated in 1948. *PJS*.

Wheeler, Gen Earle G (1908–1975). US. Served as chair of the US Joint Chiefs of Staff from 1964 to 1970. An administrative officer with limited combat experience, Wheeler was senior military adviser to the President during the period of the rapid American build-up in Vietnam. He strongly recommended direct intervention in 1965 and encouraged Gen Westmoreland in 1967 to make the request for additional troops and a call up of reserves that eventually persuaded President Johnson that the war involved costs he, and the US, were unwilling to pay.

Wheeler, Lt Gen Raymond A (1885–1974). US. Active service in Mexico, 1914, and in World War I. Sent to Burma during the British retreat early in 1942 to secure line of communication from Northern India to Gen Stilwell's Chinese troops in North Burma. This was achieved by building the Ledo Road. At Quebec Conference of August 1943, appointed as Principal Administrative Officer to Mountbatten's South East Asia Command. Responsible for the awesome task of coordinating all logistic support for SEAC's multi-national forces, integrating his staff with Mountbatten's. On the departure of Stilwell in 1944, Wheeler was made Deputy Supreme Commander.

White Rose (*Weisse Rose*). Small resistance group led in Munich University by Hans and Sophie Scholl, who thought Hitler was Antichrist. On February 19 1943 they distributed a printed leaflet,

saying so, and were arrested, tortured and killed.

White Russia. Following the Bolshevik Revolution of November 1917, conservative elements opposed to the new regime were generically termed "Whites". Although for the next three years White governments and armies often held vast areas of Russian territory, their inability to coordinate their political and military efforts ultimately doomed their cause to failure.

Whitley, Armstrong Whitworth AW 38 (Br, WWII). Heavy bomber/maritime reconnaissance; crew 5. Prototype flew March 17 1936; nine squadrons by outbreak of war. Deliveries of Merlin-powered Whitley V from August 1939. Considerable use Bomber Command; limited service with Coastal Command from September 1939. Later used as paratroop carrier and glider tug. Production, 1,812. Whitley V had two 1,145hp Rolls-Royce Merlin X engines; max. speed 230mph (370kph); five 0.303in machine guns, 7,000lb (3,150kg) bombs.

Whittle, Air Commodore Sir Frank (b.1907). Br. Invented, designed and tested the first British jet engine. The first jet-propelled aircraft came into operational service with the RAF in July 1944.

Whitworth, Vice Adm Sir William (1884–1973). Br. Flag Officer, Battlecruiser Squadron, during the Norwegian campaign of 1940; fought the Second Naval Battle of Narvik in *Warspite* on April 13 1940.

Wieltje. Village, about 2 miles northeast of Ypres. After the Second Battle of Ypres in 1915 it lay just inside British lines and was in the sector of the 55th (West Lancashire) Division on July 31 1917, opening of Third Battle of Ypres. Taken by the Germans in April 1918; regained during the Anglo-Belgian offensive on September 28 1918.

Wiese, Lt Gen Friedrich (1892–1975). Ger. Commander Nineteenth Army in Southern France during the Allies' landings in August 1944.

W

Wilde Sau ("Wild Boar"). German night fighter visual interception of bombers silhouetted by fires at the target.

Wilhelmina, Queen of the Netherlands (1880–1962). Reigned 1890-1948. During the German invasion of Holland in 1940 the Queen was transferred by a British warship to England, probably as a result of a misunderstanding. She then became the symbol of Dutch resistance and after the liberation of Holland was welcomed back to the throne with the utmost enthusiasm.

Wilhelmshaven. Chief German naval base on the North Sea. British planned a carrier strike on the German fleet there for 1919. The RAF launched unescorted bomber raids against ships there in 1939 which lost heavily. The town later suffered devastating raids.

William (Wilhelm), Crown Prince of Prussia and Germany (1882–1951). Ger. Born in Potsdam, the son of Prince William (later to be Kaiser William II). With the outbreak of World War I, the Crown Prince was given command of the Fifth Army. His lack of experience was plain, but he made a promising start, winning his first battle decorations after the Battle of Longwy. In early September 1914, Fifth Army retreated behind the Aisne, and the Prince set up headquarters at Stenay on the Marne, where he was to remain for two years.

In February 1916 he oversaw the German attack on Verdun, but he fell out with the COS von Knobelsdorf over the conduct of the assault, which was finally abandoned after the loss of 337,000 troops. With Falkenhayn's replacement by Hindenburg, the German Western Front was divided into two, the Prince taking command of the southern army group. In the spring of 1917 his troops fought defensive actions at Aisne, Champagne and Chemin des Dames, and in March 1918 achieved a breakthrough at St Quentin-la Fère. Following attacks at Chemin des Dames and Noyon by Seventh and Eighteenth Armies, he led an attack in the Marne Champagne sector, but with Foch's counterattack was forced to retreat. Battles followed against the French and the Americans in Champagne and on the Meuse.

With his father's abdication, the Prince was relieved of his military position and went into exile in Holland. He returned to his estate at Oels in 1923, living there as a private citizen during the Weimar Republic. His attitude to Hitler was ambivalent. Fearing the Russian advance in 1944 he left his estate for Bavaria, where he was captured by the French in May 1945. His last days were spent in obscurity in Hechingen. *SLB*.

William (Wilhelm) II Kaiser (1859–1941; reigned 1888–1918). Ger. Emperor and King of Prussia. William ascended the throne in 1888, and soon clashed with Bismarck, whom he dismissed in 1890. The Reinsurance Treaty with Russia was subsequently allowed to lapse, thus thwarting Bismarck's aim of keeping Russia and France from allying. The Kaiser's naval expansionism under von Tirpitz placed a severe strain on Anglo-German relations, as did a series of diplomatic blunders, such as the dispatch of a congratulatory telegram to Kruger after the Jameson Raid. With the assassination at Sarajevo, the Kaiser issued Austria the famous blank cheque for a confrontation with Serbia, but later tried to interpret Serbia's conciliatory reply as a "moral victory for Vienna". Within days these attempts to avert the crisis had failed.

The Kaiser spent most of the War at the Imperial Headquarters, but his leadership was by now merely nominal. He succeeded in keeping the German battlefleet from conflict in the North Sea until 1916, but displayed his customary vacillation over the U-boat question and in his failure to initiate peace talks with Russia.

With Germany's capitulation, the Kaiser tried desperately to save his throne, appointing Prince Max of Baden chancellor with the promise of constitutional reform. But with the outbreak of the German Revolution, the troops' disenchantment with the monarchy was made plain, and despite aggrieved protestations, the Kaiser was made to abdicate, to face 20 years of exile in Holland. *SLB*.

Wilson, Field Marshal Lord Henry Maitland ("Jumbo"), (1881–1964). Br. Commander British troops, Egypt, at the outbreak of war with Italy until February 1941; Commander of the British Expeditionary Force to Greece (Force W), February–April 1941; Commander Palestine and Transjordan from May 1941, responsible for the Anglo-French invasion of Syria in June–July 1941; C-in-C, Persia and Iraq Command from August 1942; C-in-C, Middle East Land Forces from March 1943, responsible for mounting the Eastern Task Force for the invasion of Sicily and for British operations in the Aegean; succeeded Eisenhower as Supreme Allied Commander, Mediterranean, in January 1944; handed over to Alexander in December 1944, succeeding the late Field Marshal Sir John Dill as British member of the Combined Chiefs of Staff and Head of the British Joint Staff Mission in Washington where he remained for the rest of the war. *WGFJ*.

Wilson, Field Marshal Sir Henry (1864–1922). Br. A Protestant from southern Ireland, Wilson served with the Rifle Brigade in India and Burma in 1885–87 yet most of his later career was as a staff officer. Articulate and imaginative, he was a successful Commandant of the Staff College from 1907 to 1910 and, as an ardent Francophile, forged a close bond with Foch, then his French counterpart. Between 1910 and 1914 Wilson was Director of Military Operations, preparing the detailed plans for the mobilization and deployment of the BEF in the event of war. However, his support for compulsory service and his involvement in the Curragh incident led to frequent contacts with opposition politicians and increased his reputation for intrigue. In August 1914 he went to France with the BEF as Sub-Chief of the General Staff, performing much of Sir Archibald Murray's work when the latter's health failed, but Robertson was preferred as Murray's replacement and, in January 1915, Wilson was appointed Chief Liaison Officer to the French General Headquarters. From December 1915 he spent an undistinguished year commanding IV Corps but maintained his political connections and impressed Lloyd George who succeeded Asquith as Prime Minister in December 1916 and found Wilson a useful ally in his efforts to reduce the influence of Haig and Robertson. Thus, after brief spells in a variety of posts in Russia, France and England, Wilson was chosen, in November 1917, as Britain's Permanent Military Representative on the Allied Supreme War Council at Versailles, a coordinating body of a type he had long advocated. Its acceptance of Wilson's proposal for an Allied general reserve, controlled from Versailles, precipitated Robertson's departure in February 1918 and Wilson succeeded him as CIGS. Manpower problems and the need to balance the demands of the various theatres were among his main concerns in the months before the Armistice. With the advent of peace his relationship with Lloyd George cooled, not least because of the Prime Minister's Irish policy. Wilson retired in February 1922 and was elected MP for North Down. Known as a strong Unionist sympathizer, he was killed by Irish republicans outside his London home on June 22 1922. *PJS*.

Wilson, President Woodrow (1856–1924). US. Although obliged to sanction military operations on the border with Mexico, Wilson's foreign policy was dominated by the maintenance of the United States' neutrality in World War I. He offered to mediate between the belligerents but his isolationist policies were paramount. However the US was inexorably drawn into the conflict. Germany's announcement in January 1917 of the resumption of unrestricted submarine warfare resulted in the severance of relations between the two countries. Matters further deteriorated in February with the disclosure of the contents of the Zimmermann telegram and public opinion now clearly swung in favour of the Allies. With American ships being sunk and the Allied cause taking on a less autocratic aspect with the abdication of the Tsar, Wilson decided on war. On April 6 1917 Congress approved his request for a declaration of war on Germany and Wilson threw himself wholeheartedly behind the war effort, building up the US military forces and war economy. In January 1918 he announced his blueprint for

Wilson: "Fourteen Points" for peace

peace, outlining Fourteen Points that he felt would resolve disputes between the warring nations and establish a stable base for future international relations. This was perhaps Wilson's apogee for, although he received popular acclaim on his visit to Europe at the end of hostilities, the pragmatic and nationalistic interests of other statesmen undermined his plans. He had little choice but to accept a series of compromise treaties at the Paris Peace Conferences, consoling himself that the formation of the League of Nations would remedy any faults. However, his hopes were dashed by the US Senate's refusal to ratify the Treaty of Versailles and therefore his country remained outside the League. A broken man, Wilson's health collapsed and he played little further part in political affairs. *MS*.

Window. Metalized strips of paper dropped from aircraft in massive quantities to swamp enemy radar. Known in Germany as "Angel's Hair". First used by Bomber Command in July 1943. *See also* CHAFF.

Wingate, Maj Gen Orde Charles (1903–44). Br. Devoted to the Old Testament of the Bible, his first independent command, Operation "Gideon", was in Palestine, 1936–39 when he led Jewish irregulars against Arab guerrillas. In 1941, as a Lt Col, he led Ethiopian guerrillas for Haile Selassie against the Italians, killing and capturing large numbers. He attracted Churchill's attention and was sent to India in 1942 as a brigadier to organize the force which became known as the Chindits. Wingate attracted great devotion and intense dislike, the latter

predominating. After the success of the first Chindit operation, a second on a wider scale with much improved support facilities was organized. Soon after it was launched in March 1944, Wingate (now Maj Gen) wanted to fly from Imphal to Comilla, the rear headquarters. He ignored a meteorological warning and took off: he was killed when his plane crashed in the jungle. *HT*.

Wireless Ridge. One of the Argentinian defence positions overlooking Port Stanley in the Falklands War of 1982. Defended by the 7th Marine Regiment, it was taken by 2 Para on the night of June 13.

Wisconsin. US battleship. *Iowa* class. Completed 1944, served in the Pacific and now back in service.

Wolff, Gen (*Oberstgruppenführer*, SS) Karl Friedrich Otto (1900–1984). Ger. SS and Police Commander in Italy, who negotiated the surrender of all German forces in Italy on May 2 1945.

Wolf packs. German term for coordinated attacks by groups of submarines, usually at night and on the surface. Developed by Dönitz and used with great success 1940–43. Also used by American submarines in the Pacific with smaller groups and great success.

Wolf's Lair (a loose translation of Wolfsschanze). Codename for Hitler's headquarters at Rastenburg in East Prussia from which he directed operations in the latter half of the war. Also the scene of the assassination attempt of July 20 1944.

"A wolf in his lair": Hitler at Rastenburg

Wolmi-Do. Small fortified island which controls the approaches to Inchon, Korea. During the Korean War, and prior to the Inchon landings, Wolmi was shelled and bombed for two days and secured on the morning of September 15 1950 by US Marines. Of the North Korean garrison, 136 were captured and an unknown number perished when they refused to surrender and were buried in their bunkers.

Women's services. In 1914, First Aid Nursing Yeomanry (FANYS), British veterans of the Boer War, crossed to France, since artillery warfare had increased the numbers of wounded and hence the need for nursing. British women staffed army canteens but were not allowed into uniform until 1917, with the formation of Queen Mary's Army Auxiliary Corps. By 1918 there were 11,000 women in Queen Alexandra's Imperial Military Nursing Service, The British Red Cross and the St John's Ambulance Brigade. QMAAC numbered 57,000; the Women's Royal Naval Service (WRNS) and the Women's Royal Air Force (WRAF) each numbered 5,000; all were employed in clerical, administrative and communications services.

In 1938 female volunteers formed the Auxiliary Territorial Service (ATS), and by 1939 20,000 women were trained to defend the nation in all three services. Women's war duties included fighter controllers and plotters, controlling barrage balloons, radar units, searchlights, anti-aircraft gun batteries, transport and signals. The Civil Defence Corps and Women's Volunteer Service (WVS) became auxiliary fire-fighters, rescue and demolition workers. In April 1941 female auxiliaries were given full military status; ATS were sent to the Middle East and WRNS to Singapore; all three services distinguished themselves as codebreakers at Bletchley; 1942 saw general female conscription to auxiliary services, Women's Land Army or munitions work. Despite outstanding achievements and acts of heroism, women were denied the VC on grounds that they were officially noncombatants; the civilian equivalent, the George Cross, was awarded to only four women.

The Commonwealth countries also developed their own equivalent services. By the end of World War II, a whole range were in existence – in Australia, the Australian Army Nursing Service, Australian Army Medical Women's Service, Women's Australian Auxiliary Air Force, Australian Women's Army Service, Women's Royal Australian Naval Service. Canadian women's services included the Royal Army Nursing Corps, Women's Royal Canadian Nursing Service, Canadian Women's Army Corps, Royal Canadian Air Force (Women's Division). Those of New Zealand included the New Zealand Army Nursing Service, Women's Royal New Zealand Naval Service, Women's War Service Auxilliary, Women's Army Auxiliary Corps, NZ Women's Auxiliary Air Force. And South African women's services included the South African Military Nursing Services, Women's Auxiliary Defence Corps, Women's Auxiliary Army Service, Women's Auxiliary Air Force, SA Women's Auxiliary Naval Service.

In the US, Congress limited female participation in World War I to minor clerical duties. In 1941 17,000 women formed the Women's League of Defence. Frustrated in their attempts to participate when the US joined the war, American women enlisted in the British Armed Forces. Congress authorized female conscription in 1942 and the Women's Auxiliary Army Corps (WAAC) was formed despite massive male resentment. The formation of WAVES and WAAF followed. In July 1943 women were granted full military status and WAAC became WAC (Women's Army Corps). At its peak WAC was 100,000 strong with units sent to Algiers (1942) and Italy (1943). By war's end there were 8,000 WACS on the Continent and MacArthur claimed that in the Pacific, WACS were his "best soldiers".

The USSR was exceptional in allowing women to join military combat. In World War II, the USSR had three all-female air regiments who showed great skill and daring. In 4,000 operational sorties they engaged in 125 aerial combats and scored 38 "kills". Vast losses on the ground also forced women into action as tank drivers.

In Germany Hitler decreed that no woman should bear arms; instead he encouraged *Helferinnen* – clerical helpers. Women grew more valuable as the war progressed: by 1945 250,000 women were assisting with signals and communications, and in manning anti-aircraft batteries. In March 1945 Hitler decided to let women bear arms, but rescinded the order a week later. Despite this some women took up arms in desperation in the last weeks of the war.

Wonju, east/central Korea, south of the 38th Parallel. In the heavy fighting which accompanied the Chinese offensive of February 1951, the French battalion attached to the US 2nd Division distinguished itself at the Battle of Chipyong-ni, northwest of Wonju. The communists suffered heavy casualties and withdrew.

Wonsan, landing at (the Korean War). A key element in MacArthur's plan for the advance into North Korea in October 1950. It called for X Corps under Gen Almond to leave the Seoul/Inchon area and sail to the east coast, landing at Wonsan to strike westwards across the peninsula towards Pyongyang, effecting a junction with Gen Walker's advancing Eighth Army. The outloading of X Corps took time and Wonsan had fallen to ROK troops before Almond's command could reach the east coast. The North Koreans had sown the harbour with over 3,000 mines and the 1st Marine Division was delayed for six days while they were cleared, until October 25 1950. Since Pyongyang had already fallen, X Corps was given a new mission to clear the northeast. *CM.*

Wonsan, siege of (the Korean War). Began in February 1951, when Vice Adm A E Smith, USN, seized several islands in the harbour. The operation, designed to impede the passage of supplies and pin down enemy troops, lasted for 861 days. The city was bombarded daily. The North Koreans responded by improving their coastal defences, releasing floating mines from sampans and raiding UN positions by night. Although supplies continued to move through Wonsan, 80,000 enemy troops were tied down in the area. *CM.*

Wood, Maj Gen John S (1888–1966). US. Commander of the US 4th Armoured Division which led the Allied breakout from Avranches, Normandy, July 1944.

Woodhouse, Col (Christopher) Montague, (b.1917). Br. Helped attack Gorgopotamos bridge 1942, head of SOE mission in Greece 1943–44; helped destabilize Mossadeq 1953.

Woodward, Rear Adm Sir John ("Sandy") (b.1932). Br. Commander of British naval task force during the Falklands War of 1982. Painfully aware of the threat posed by the formidable Argentine Air Force and his own shortage of air defence afloat, he had to balance the imperative of getting his land forces ashore against the prospect of losing one or both of his carriers and the large and vulnerable merchant ships like *Canberra*, to air or submarine attack. His decision to order the sinking of the *General Belgrano*, despite its being outside the TEZ, provoked a major political storm, but must be seen in retrospect as having been militarily sound. *MH.*

World War I (1914–18). The immediate cause of the war was the assassination of the heir to the Austro-Hungarian throne, Archduke Franz Ferdinand, at Sarajevo on June 28 1914. This led at the end of July to war between Austria and Serbia. Russia mobilized in Serbia's support, Germany in Austria's and France in Russia's. War between Germany and Russia began on August 1, between Germany and France on August 3 and between Germany and Britain on August 4, when German troops, as part of their plan to strike at France, crossed into Belgium, which had been guaranteed by Britain.

Military operations began with Russian advances into East Prussia, which for a time even threatened Berlin, and in Galicia in the general direction of Budapest and Vienna. The Germans advanced rapidly into France and threatened both Paris and the Channel ports. The possibility of the war being a short one was, however, extinguished when the Russians were halted and then thrown back both in East Prussia

at the Battle of Tannenberg and, although less disastrously, in Galicia and when, on the other hand, the Germans were halted short of Paris and the Channel along what became known as the Western Front. The campaign in the west bogged down into static trench warfare and, although that in the east was relatively one of movement, neither the Germans and Austrians nor the Russians showed the capacity to inflict outright defeat on each other. The Galician campaign continued with fluctuating fortunes until Russia collapsed in the revolution of 1917.

Both sides, the German-led Central Powers, and that of Russia, France, Britain and Japan, known as the Entente or the Allies, sought political and military solutions. Germany drew Turkey into the war on her side on November 1 1914, thus posing a threat to the Russian flank in the Caucasus and to the British position in the Near and Middle East. Italy declared war on Austria on May 23 1915 and, stimulated by the success of the Brusilov offensive in the Galician campaign, Romania declared war on Austria on August 27 1916. In addition to the massive battles on the western and eastern fronts, there were therefore now also severe campaigns in the Dardanelles and Gallipoli, Salonika and Mesopotamia, in Romania and on the Italian front. Moreover, principally because Germany was a challenging sea and imperial power, the war had spread far and wide. There were campaigns in East and West Africa and other parts of the British and German empires. Although Britain's ally Japan played only a minor role in the war, her naval strength in the Pacific enabled Britain to concentrate a Grand Fleet in the North Sea to meet the main German challenge which culminated at the Battle of Jutland on May 31 1916. Despite the arguments about who had won, this left the British with the command of the sea on the surface of it which meant that the Germans could not invade Britain nor prevent her continuing to dispatch and supply armies overseas. It also opened Germany to the threat, eventually an effective one, of blockade. It did not, however, deal with the action of German U-boats, which reached its peak in

1917. Although this threatened Britain with blockade, it also played a significant part in bringing the US into the war on the Allied side, an event which occurred on April 6 1917.

The collapse of the Russian war effort in the revolution of 1917 and the armistice which the Germans were able to impose on the Bolshevik government in March 1918 at Brest-Litovsk brought to a head the question of what to do on the Western Front. Germany, having now substantially escaped from the disaster of a major war on two fronts, could reinforce her position there and, in addition to that, despite the repeated efforts of the Allies in a series of costly offensives, she still occupied the tactically most favourable positions. The enormous cost of frontal attack in the West had been made fully apparent on the Somme, at Verdun, in the Nivelle offensive and at Passchendaele but the alternative strategies, such as those of the Gallipoli or Salonika campaigns, had proved no more successful and not much less costly. The French mutinies of 1917 had signalled the danger of a fatal collapse in the morale of the Allied armies and in Britain there were serious differences of opinion, notably between the Prime Minister, Lloyd George, and the C-in-C, Haig, as to what should be attempted. Despite a vast increase in artillery fire-power, the use of gas and the introduction of tanks, conditions still seemed to favour the defence and it seemed that the Germans, being in occupation, might well remain on the defensive. How then would the war be brought to a successful conclusion? In the Allied camp there was the hope that blockade would bring Germany to her knees and even the prospect that heavy bombing, which was to begin in 1919, when the new RAF's long-range machines were to come into service, would help the process. There was also the favourable prospect of a growing stream of American reinforcements which was at least some compensation for the loss of the Russian ally. Germany, however, despite her good fortune in the east, was now suffering a grave crisis. The blockade was indeed producing dire results, while in Austria there was serious starvation. Industrial unrest and even naval and military mutinies now began to emerge in Germany and the germs of Bolshevism were spreading westwards. The German High Command, so far from remaining defensively on their high ground, resolved upon a massive offensive which would terminate the war before the Americans could arrive in strength.

The attack began on March 21 1918 and was maintained until the middle of July. At first it had dramatic success and the breakthrough of Ludendorff's troops on the front held by the British Fifth Army suggested that the possibility of a war of movement had been resumed. Even so, the situation was eventually contained and the Allied Supreme Commander, Foch, was able to launch a counteroffensive which began on July 18. This was reinforced by Haig on August 8 when the British, supported by more than 400 tanks, began an advance which ceased only with the Armistice on November 11.

The Great War, as it came to be called, cost more than 10,000,000 dead in the armed forces of Germany, Austria-Hungary, Turkey, France, Britain, Russia, Italy and the US, but, having at its outset been nourished by the unresolved and combustible issues of the Balkan Wars, it created new and yet more combustible successors to these, which, in turn, nourished World War II. In terms of military science, however, it was more productive and the stalemate of the trenches was not to be repeated. *ANF*.

World War II (1939–45). Started by the German invasion of Poland on September 1 1939. Britain and France declared war on Germany two days later to honour the guarantee which they had given to Poland on the previous March 31. This guarantee was in response to the breach of the Munich Agreement of September 30 1938, which Hitler committed when he subsequently seized Czechoslovakia and Memel. The Guarantee, which also extended to Romania, did not, however, provide any military support for Poland, which was beyond the reach of Anglo-French forces. Nor were the latter willing to mount an offensive in the west to

relieve pressure on their ally. Under Gamelin's command, they took up defensive positions covered, as far as it ran, by the Maginot Line. As Germany and Russia had signed a non-aggression pact on August 21 1939, the Germans could now attack Poland without fear of interference. They quickly prevailed in the first act of what became famous as the blitzkrieg. To conclude the matter, the Russians attacked the Poles in their rear on September 17. This was their first move in the attempt to regain the territories they had lost at Brest-Litovsk in December 1917. Further moves in the same direction led the Russians to invade Finland on November 30. Due to the extraordinary resilience of the Finns under Mannerheim, the Russo-Finnish War lasted until March 13 1940 when the Finns capitulated. Partly as a counter to this and partly due to the fear that the British might occupy Norway, the Germans occupied Denmark and, on April 9 1940, invaded Norway. This was, perhaps, the most defensively inspired initiative Hitler ever took but it resulted in a brilliant success and showed how air power could be used to neutralize superior naval strength.

On May 10 1940 the "Phoney War" in France came to a sudden end at dawn when the German army swept into the Low Countries and France, drove the BEF, amounting to some 14 divisions, and portions of the French army into the sea at Dunkirk, took Paris and received the French capitulation on June 17. The success of the German tactics of coordinated air and land power and their vigorous exploitation of tank warfare astonished the world. Hitler now controlled the whole European littoral from the tip of Scandanavia to the Atlantic coast of France. He had thus achieved a golden opportunity for the immediate defeat of his last enemy, Britain, but there was no coherent plan for an invasion, since it was expected that she would soon sue for peace. Time and opportunities passed and then, instead of sealing their victory, the Germans suffered major defeat in what proved to be the first decisive battle of the war, the Battle of Britain. This took place between mid-July and mid-September

when, frustrated of their attempt to gain command of the air over Britain in daylight as a prelude to invasion, the Germans turned to the night bombing of British cities. The British, however, adopted the same policy, ultimately developing a strategic air offensive which was many times more effective than the German. Moreover, the German attack was drastically scaled down in the spring of 1941 when Hitler swung away from the West and struck first southwards against Yugoslavia and Greece, where his Italian ally had got into difficulties, and then, on June 22 1941, against Russia.

Although the Germans had also intervened in the Middle East, where the Italians had been heavily defeated by the British, and although Britain and Germany became locked in the Battle of the Atlantic, (a life-line for the former), the main scene of military action in Europe was henceforth to be in Russia until the Allied invasion of Normandy in June 1944. At first the effect of the German blitzkrieg in Russia was staggering; a rapid advance took place, huge numbers of Russian troops were captured and it seemed that Moscow would be taken before the end of the year. The Germans, however, missed this critical opportunity due to stiffening Russian resistance, which was brilliantly exploited by Gen Koniev, and to the southern diversion, which Hitler ordered, into the Caucasus. Also, as a result of their earlier operations in Yugoslavia and Greece, they were later on the scene than they had intended. Winter arrived to inflict dreadful deprivations upon the German army, and to give the Russians vital breathing space.

On December 7 1941, the Japanese launched a surprise attack by carrier-borne aircraft against the US Pacific Fleet at Pearl Harbor. Within two hours much of the American fleet lay crippled or sunk, but the American carriers happened to be at sea and so escaped the holocaust. This, in years to come, proved to be a decisive factor. In the immediate aftermath, the Japanese, swept rapidly across the Pacific area capturing Guam, the Philippines, Hong Kong, Singapore and Rangoon, brushing aside with surprising ease such resistance as the British and the Americans were able to offer. Pearl Harbor had, however, brought America into the war, all the more so since Hitler, in a singularly short-sighted act, declared war on the US and thus created the Grand Alliance of Britain, Russia and the US. This was a combination which had a greater war potential than Germany, Italy and Japan. The question remained as to whether the Grand Alliance would be able to mobilize and bring to bear its strength before victory was achieved by the Berlin-Rome-Tokyo Axis.

The year 1942 saw a continuing crisis in the Battle of the Atlantic, which governed Britain's existence and America's capacity to deploy into Europe; Rommel defeated the Eighth Army in the Western Desert and seemed near to throwing the British out of the Middle East; the Germans, having weathered the Russian counteroffensive, resumed their own and drew close to the capture of Leningrad and Stalingrad. The Japanese extended their conquests to a point which threatened both India and Australia. All this, however, proved to be the high tide of Axis prospects, for 1942 also saw a decisive turning of the tide. In the first days of June the Americans engaged and defeated the Japanese in the great naval Battle of Midway. This redressed the balance of sea power in the Pacific and gave Nimitz the chance, which he later seized, of gaining the upper hand. On October 23, Montgomery opened the second Battle of Alamein in which he crushed Rommel and began an advance to Tripoli and a junction with the Anglo-American force which had landed in November at the other end of the African littoral in Operation "Torch". On November 19 the Russians launched a massive counterattack which trapped the German Sixth Army in the outskirts of Stalingrad and within a few weeks led to its complete destruction or capture. Even the German homeland began to feel the weight of war for the first time; on the night of May 30 Harris launched a 1,000-bomber attack upon Cologne.

When, therefore, Roosevelt met Churchill at the Casablanca Conference in January 1943, despite the priority they still had to give to the defeat of German U-boats in the Battle of the Atlantic, they were primarily concerned with the architecture of victory and so too, although often from a different standpoint, was Stalin, who shortly was himself to begin to take part in these Allied conferences. In May 1943 Anglo-American forces invaded Sicily and then, in September, Italy; and although the Italian campaign proved to be prolonged, laborious and expensive, it opened a sore on Germany's southern flank which the Italians did not wish to heal and with which the Germans themselves had to deal. In Russia in July, the Germans' attempt at Kursk to revive the tactics of blitzkrieg produced a tremendous Russian victory in the greatest tank battle of the war. Although the American day bombing offensive was, for the time being, defeated in the action at Schweinfurt in October, the British night bombers drove a path of terrible devastation across Germany from the Ruhr to Berlin and the Battle of the Atlantic tipped decisively against the U-boats during the year. Many saw 1944 as the year in which Germany would be defeated, for this was when the Second Front, the Allied invasion of France, would be undertaken.

Long overdue in Stalin's view, Operation "Overlord" was launched on June 6 1944 when Anglo-American forces, under the supreme command of Eisenhower, landed on a series of beachheads in Normandy. On August 15, further landings were made in Southern France. At the end of August, after some unexpected delays, the Americans and British broke out of their Normandy lodgements and swept across France in a new version of the blitzkrieg. By the end of November the offensive had run out of steam, the Germans had reorganized and a stalemate had arisen far short of the Rhine. Moreover, this was broken, not by a resumption of the Allied advance, but by a German counterattack in the Ardennes in December. For a time, this even seemed to threaten a rerun of the German campaign of 1940, but it was soon contained. Even so, the Germans registered a sharp reminder of the fact that they were still far from accepting the inevitability of their ultimate defeat. The German re-

sistance movement, badly mauled after the July Plot fiasco, failed to raise its head and the Germans continued to follow Hitler's fanatical lead with stoic fortitude. The Combined Chiefs of Staff of Britain and the US concluded that the most immediate prospect of victory lay in the further advance of the Russian armies, a view which led to the bombing of Dresden in February 1945. No amount of fanaticism could stem the Russian advance towards Berlin and the Hungarian plain nor, eventually, the crossing of the Rhine by Eisenhower's armies and their subsequent progress until the Eastern and Western Allies met in the middle of Germany. Victory in Europe was proclaimed on May 8 1945.

The decision of the Allies to deal first with Germany had extended the Japanese lease of life, caused much frustration to those, such as the American Chief of Naval Staff, Adm King, who believed that Japan was the first enemy, and much resentment among the Allied troops such as the "forgotten" British Fourteenth Army in Burma. Nevertheless, by the time of Germany's downfall, Japan was well on the way to the same fate. In Burma the British had learnt to counter and then to develop their own version of Japanese jungle tactics and in the Pacific, under cover of growing command of the sea, the Americans, especially the Marines, had developed the power to seize island after island as stepping stones to Japan herself. These provided the forward bases from which the invasion of Japan could be mounted and they also provided runways which brought American B-29 bombers and long-range fighter protection within range of Japanese cities. The last of these steps was Iwo Jima, where the American landings began on February 19 1945, and Okinawa, where they began on March 26. The mounting strength of the bombing offensive by the B-29s began to eat the heart out of Japan where firestorms of terrifying proportions became more familiar than they had been even in Germany. The stranglehold of American sea power, crowned by the huge victory at Leyte Gulf in October 1944, not only provided the basic requirement of the American

W

island-hopping strategy, but it also imposed upon Japan an economic and military blockade which fatally undermined her strategic freedom of action. The remaining questions were whether the Japanese surrender could be secured without an American invasion and, if not, how many lives that invasion might cost. The matter was settled when, on August 6 1945, an American B-29 dropped the first atomic bomb on Hiroshima and the Russians declared war on Japan. On August 9 the second atomic bomb was dropped on Nagasaki. On August 10 the Japanese sued for peace.

World War II cost about 15,000,000 military dead and missing and, due to Nazi policies towards Jews, Slavs and the Russians, many more civilians. *ANF.*

Wrangel, Gen Baron Petr Nikolaevich (1878–1928). Russian. One of the ablest "White" commanders of the Russian Civil War, whose Caucasus Army defeated the Reds in January 1919 and swept on to Tsaritsyn (Stalingrad, now Volgograd). Supply problems enforced Wrangel's retreat but, replacing Denikin early in 1920, he launched an offensive from the Crimea, successful until the ending of Russo-Polish hostilities allowed Bolshevik reinforcement. Defeated at Perekop, November 1920, Wrangel's troops were evacuated by British ships.

Wright brothers. Wilbur (1867–1912), Orville (1871–1948). (US). Interested in flying from 1894, they built a kite in 1899, a manned glider in 1900, two further gliders 1901–02, and a powered biplane, which flew December 17 1903.

Würzburg. German ground-based radar for plotting aircraft. Introduced summer 1941.

Wyoming Line *see* KANSAS LINE.

Wytschaete. Village a few miles south of Ypres and one mile north of Messines, captured by the Germans in November 1914 and retaken on June 7 1917. The following April the British were forced to abandon the ruins but Wytschaete was regained during the Anglo-Belgian attack in Flanders on September 28 1918.

X

X-craft *see* SUBMARINES.

X-Gerät **and** ***Y-Gerät.*** German systems of beam navigation similar to but distinct from Knickebein.

Xuan Loc, Battle of (1975). Xuan Loc, 40 miles (65km) northwest of Saigon, was one place where the ARVN offered stiff resistance to the advancing People's Army (PAVN) in spring 1975. The PAVN opened its attack on March 17, and by April 9 three PAVN divisions supported by heavy artillery were involved. The exhausted ARVN 18th Division finally fell back on Bien Hoa on the 15th. The PAVN accepted heavy casualties at Xuan Loc in order that other units could manoeuvre into place for the assault on Saigon.

Xuan Thuy (1912–1985). Democratic Republic of Vietnam. Once Hanoi's Minister of Foreign Affairs, Xuan Thuy headed the North Vietnamese delegation to the Paris Peace Talks, May 1968. While remaining head of the delegation until agreement was reached (January 1973), Thuy was in fact supplanted as Hanoi's chief negotiator by Le Duc Tho when secret negotiations between Tho and Kissinger began in 1970.

Y

Yabasi *see* CAMEROONS (1914–16).

Yakovlev Yak-9 (USSR, WWII). Single-seat fighter (low-level and ground-attack), developed from Yak-7; introduced operationally late November 1942; improved version with increased range (Yak-9D) early summer 1943. Yak-9T had 37mm cannon for tank-attack work; other sub-types with armament and equipment changes were built; production until 1947, total 16,769. Outstandingly effective in combat. One 1,360hp Klimov M-105PF-3 engine; max. speed (Yak-9D) 374mph (602kph); one 20mm cannon, one 12.7mm machine gun.

The "Big Three" at the Yalta Conference

Yalta Conference ("Argonaut"). Meetings between Stalin, Roosevelt and Churchill in the Crimea, February 4–11 1945. Although there was some discussion over the plan to bomb Dresden, most of the negotiations regarding Europe were concerned with postwar arrangements. It was agreed that major German industry should be destroyed or brought under Allied control, that Germany should be divided into zones to be occupied by each of the main allies and that war criminals should be brought to trial. There was discussion of the liberated countries, including Poland and Romania, but the fact that they were occupied by the Red Army meant that Stalin was not inclined to listen to the Western allies' views. The future constitution of the United Nations was discussed and Russia undertook to enter the war against Japan shortly after the surrender of Germany. *ANF.*

Yalu, Battle of the *see* KIU-LIEN-CHENG.

Yalu river (the Amnok to the Koreans). Forms the border between North Korea and China.

Yamamoto, Fleet Adm Isoroku (1884-1943). Jap. Russo-Japanese War (1904); went to study in the USA (1919). He played a major part in the development of Japanese naval air power. Naval Attaché at Washington; Japanese negotiator at London naval conference (1934); deputy to the Navy Minister (1936-39). His opposition to proposals to attack America and Britain led to assassination threats by ultra-nationalist army officers. Partly to save him from these, he was posted as C-in-C of the Combined Fleet in 1939, a post he held till his death. The only course he saw was an initial knock-out blow to the US Pacific Fleet, a rapid offensive to seize as much territory as possible, then to sue for peace. It was not his fault that the American carriers happened to be at sea at the time of the attack. Apart from this his plan worked brilliantly in the first six months of the Pacific War – the Philippines, Malaya, Indonesia, Burma all fell, Force Z and the Allied fleet in Indonesia were destroyed. However, Yamamoto was forced to make another, probably over-complicated, plan for attacking the American fleet which met its nemesis at Midway. This was, in part, a victory obtained by American codebreakers. Early in 1943, these codebreakers found out that Yamamoto was on an inspection tour of the Solomon Islands. His "Betty" transport plane was ambushed and shot down by a force of American P-38 Lightning fighters. His body was found in the wreckage. *DJL.*

Yamamoto at London Naval Conference

Yamashiro. Japanese battleship. *Fuso* class. Completed 1917. Sunk in the Surigao Strait action 1944.

Yamashita, Gen Tomoyuki (1885–1946). Jap. Although, after heading a military mission to Berlin and Rome, Yamashita early in 1941 strongly opposed a declaration of war until the modernization of Japan's forces was complete, he was in December 1941 given command of Twentyfifth Army for the conquest of Malaya. Japan quickly established air and naval superiority, but on land Yamashita was outnumbered: for his initial landings on December 8 he deployed three divisions (about 62,000 men), opposed by Percival's c89,000 British and Commonwealth troops. His speedy advance down the Malayan peninsula, re-

lying on infiltration tactics (and facilitated by Allied weaknesses in command) forced Percival's withdrawal to Singapore Island by January 31 1942. Although now desperately short of materiel and outnumbered by more than two-to-one in men and artillery, Yamashita pressed his attack, forcing Percival's surrender.

From July 1942, largely because Tojo regarded the "Tiger of Malaya" as a rival, Yamashita was relegated to command of First Area Army in northern Manchuria. Following Tojo's fall in July 1944, he was appointed to command Fourteenth Area Army in the defence of the Philippines, taking up his post on October 5, only one week before the US invasion of Leyte. Hampered by divided command – he was subject to Terauchi's Southern Area Army, and had very little control over air and sea operations – Yamashita was forced to weaken the garrison of Luzon to reinforce what he recognized to be a hopeless attempt to hold Leyte (which fell in December). Following the US landings on Luzon, January 9 1945, he aimed to tie down as many US troops as possible for as long as he could, thus delaying the invasion of Japan itself. He ordered that Manila should not be defended – it was held *à outrance*, nevertheless, by Iwabuchi's Naval Defence Force – and retreated into the northern highlands, where, lacking all supplies, his men held out until the war's end.

Within a few weeks of his surrender, on September 2 1945, Yamashita was charged with "war crimes" (notably the atrocities committed by Iwabuchi's force), tried under MacArthur's auspices in Manila, and, in a process that many have subsequently acknowledged to have been unfair, condemned to death. He was hanged on February 23 1946. *RO'N.*

Yamato. Japanese battleship. Intended to counteract US numerical superiority in battleships by size and power, and built in great secrecy, she displaced more than 70,000 tons full load and was armed with 9×18.1in guns. With sister *Mushashi* the largest, most heavily armed battleship built. Sunk by overwhelming and repeated air attack.

Yannina, siege of (1912–13). Greece saw in the Balkan Wars the chance to enlarge her territories, not only by the acquisition of Crete, but also by the capture of land in Salonika and Epirus, with its great fortress of Yannina, still possessions of Turkey. She did not therefore join in the armistice signed by the other belligerents on December 3 1912. Greece had already begun a blockade of Yannina in November 1912 and during the winter she ferried troops around from Salonika by sea and began a general assault on March 5 1913. Yannina surrendered on March 6. *SKF.*

Yarmouth, raid on (November 3 1914). German battlecruisers *Moltke*, *Seydlitz* and *Von der Tann*, plus *Blücher* and three light cruisers, bombarded the English port of Yarmouth, opposed by light forces. The Harwich force attempted interception, but only the light cruiser *Undaunted* made contact although she was recalled as the German force escaped.

Yaunde *see* CAMEROONS (1914–16).

Yellow Sea, Battle of the (August 10 1904), Russo-Japanese War. A Russian squadron of 6 battleships, 4 cruisers and 8 destroyers, under Adm Vitgeft (killed in the action) sortied from Port Arthur in an attempt to join with the Vladivostok squadron. Intercepted by Togo's force of 4 battleships, 11 cruisers and 17 destroyers, the Russian squadron was severely mauled (one cruiser sunk) and dispersed, some ships regaining Port Arthur, others making neutral ports where they were interned.

Yeo-Thomas, Wg Commander Forest Frederic Edward ("Tommy") (1902–64). Br. Brought up at Dieppe, narrowly escaped death in Poland 1920; clerk in Paris; joined RAF 1939, commissioned 1941, joined SOE 1942. Two important missions into France to coordinate Gaullist resistance, 1943. Arrested in Paris 1944; escaped from Buchenwald.

Yeremenko, Marshal of the Soviet Union Andrei Ivanovich (1893-1970). Russian. A Red Army "work-horse", Yeremenko held di-

Y

visional commands in Poland, 1939, and the Far East, and army commands at Moscow, Stalingrad and Smolensk (1943). In April-May 1944 he commanded Independent Maritime Front in the successful conclusion, with Tolbukhin, of the Crimean campaign, then led 2nd Baltic Front in the Courland encirclement of German Army Group North. He commanded Fourth Ukrainian Front during the Czechoslovakian campaign, 1945.

Yezhovshchina. Severe purge of Russian armed forces organized for Stalin by Nikolai Ivanovitch Yezhov (1894–1939), head of his secret police. Every officer of the rank of major or above was imprisoned, briefly at least, with the exception of Stalin's brother-in-law Voroshilov.

Yom Kippur War (1983) *see* ARAB-ISRAELI WARS.

Yield. The total energy released by a nuclear weapon in its various forms, blast, heat and radiation. It is usually expressed in terms of the energy release of an equivalent tonnage of TNT, but this can be misleading, as the characteristics of a nuclear explosion are different from those of a chemical one. A fission weapon exploded in the air below about 33,360ft (12,000m) will only give 50 percent of its yield in blast; it is thus the equivalent in "bang" to only half the amount of high explosive. However, the latter does not have the added heat and prompt and delayed radiation effects, respectively 35, 10 and 5 percent of total yield. Moreover, the effectiveness of the weapon is not directly proportional to the yield. *EJG. See also* EQUIVALENT MEGATONNAGE.

Y-Gerät see X-GERÄT.

Young Turks. Political party formed in the last decades of the Ottoman empire aiming at reform by centralization of administration and Ottomanization. They were bitterly opposed in the provinces by Christian and Muslim minorities alike. Risings against Young Turk policies and the massacres that they provoked in Macedonia and Albania in part provoked the First Balkan War.

French (Earl of Ypres): C-in-C, BEF, 1914

Ypres, Field Marshal Earl of (Sir John French) (1852–1925). Br. During the Gordon Relief Expedition of 1884, French attracted the attention of Buller, who became his influential supporter, and by 1899, as an acting major general, he commanded 1st Cavalry Brigade. The Second Boer War made his reputation as a cavalry commander: he won a resounding victory at Elandslaagte (October 1899) and relieved Kimberley (February 1900) after a spectacular cavalry charge at Klip Drift, ending the war as a lieutenant general. In 1912 he was appointed CIGS (resigning after the Curragh Incident, 1914) and was promoted field marshal in 1913.

In August 1914 French was appointed C-in-C of the BEF. His task was made particularly difficult by the failure of the French plan and the exposed position of the BEF, but even so the Mons campaign did him little credit: he got on badly with Lanrezac, commanding the French Fifth Army on his right; quarrelled with Kitchener, Secretary of State for War; and relied too heavily on Henry Wilson, his headstrong Deputy-Chief of General Staff. Nevertheless, his personal bravery and charisma helped maintain his reputation within the army, while powerful political supporters opposed demands for his replacement. Certainly, despite his failings as a strategist, he held the BEF together in 1914 as no other general could have done.

Controversy again arose in March 1915, when French blamed his inability to break through at Neuve-Chapelle on the government's failure to provide sufficient shells, and in April, when he dismissed Smith-Dorrien for alleged failure at Second Ypres. Reluctantly agreeing to cooperate in Joffre's autumn offensive, he failed to commit the reserve corps in time at Loos, in September, and was replaced by Haig. He was C-in-C, Home Forces, until May 1918, and then became Lord Lieutenant (de facto military governor) of Ireland until 1921, a difficult task for which he lacked the necessary political acumen. Although undoubtedly temperamentally unsuited to high command, he has been fairly described as the most distinguished British cavalry leader since Cromwell. *RH.*

Ypres, First Battle of (1914). As a result of the "Race to the Sea" after the Battle of the Aisne, the BEF reached the area around Ypres, in Belgian Flanders, at the same time as the German Fourth Army, which contained four newly raised corps of young volunteers, and Sixth Army, transferred from Lorraine. The Germans were now making a belated attempt to secure the Channel Ports whereas the BEF hoped to turn the German right. When the opposing armies clashed on October 19–20 1914, the BEF at first held firm in the Ploegsteert-Messines sector to the south while Haig's I Corps, trying to advance in the north, near Langemarck, made little significant headway. On October 31 an attack by seven German divisions between Messines and Gheluvelt came near to success. A local counterattack by the 2nd Worcestershires forced the Germans out of Gheluvelt, in the centre, but Messines Ridge was lost by Allenby's Cavalry Corps. The arrival of increasing numbers of French troops on the BEF's flanks helped to stabilize the situation until November 11 when the Germans launched another onslaught. The Prussian Guard broke through north of the Menin Road, only to be driven off by a scratch force of cooks, engineers and batmen, joined by the 2nd Oxfordshire and Buckinghamshire Light Infantry. By the end of the battle, around November 22, the BEF was left in a dangerous salient at Ypres, with the Germans occupying the dominating ridges to the south and east. The old professional BEF, having suffered 58,000 casualties, was effectively destroyed. The Germans also had heavy losses, particularly among the young volunteers. *PJS.*

Y

Ypres, Second Battle of (1915). On April 22 1915, largely as an experiment but also to divert attention from preparations for their Gorlice-Tarnow offensive, the Germans employed poison gas on the Western Front for the first time, releasing chlorine gas from cylinders against Allied units on the northern flank of the Ypres Salient. The French 45th (Algerian) and 87th Territorial Divisions, between Langemarck and the Yser Canal, retreated in panic, leaving a 4.5 mile (7km) gap on the left of the 1st Canadian Division. However, the subsequent advance by the Germans was cautious and, lacking sufficient reserves to exploit the success, they wasted the opportunity to break through to Ypres itself. The British and Canadians managed to form a patchwork defensive line and despite being subjected to another gas attack near St Julien on April 24 the Canadians, using handkerchiefs soaked in urine or water as improvised respirators, prevented a fatal breach. Even so, starved of French support, British counterattacks failed to recover the lost ground. Smith-Dorrien, commanding the British Second Army, was dismissed after proposing a withdrawal to a shorter line but his successor, Plumer, was permitted to carry out such a movement early in May when it became obvious that substantial French reinforcements were not forthcoming. The Ypres Salient was now less than 3 miles (5km) deep. The Germans delivered further attacks on the Frezenberg and Bellewaarde Ridges during May with little additional gain. In all the BEF incurred some 58,000 casualties between April 22–May 31, German losses totalling nearly 35,000. *PJS.*

Ypres, Third Battle of (1917). Following the capture of Messines Ridge in June, Sir Douglas Haig, the British C-in-C, launched his long-planned Flanders offensive at Ypres on July 31 1917. The immediate objectives were to take the Passchendaele-Staden Ridge and the Gheluvelt plateau, as well as the Roulers-Thourout railway. It was hoped that, with the help of an amphibious landing, the Belgian coast could then be cleared and the Germans denied their U-boat bases at Zeebrugge and Ostend. The main attack was entrusted, not to Plumer's Second Army – which had taken Messines – but to Gough's Fifth Army, the change contributing to the delay of the offensive until July 31. Misled into believing that Haig envisaged a rapid breakthrough, Gough set overambitious targets for his units but, in the first three days, the Fifth Army advanced up to 3,000yd (2,750m) on the left, seizing much of Pilckem Ridge. However, August 1917 was unusually wet, and, with the local drainage destroyed by artillery bombardments, the battlefield swiftly turned into a morass. This, coupled with the flexible defence tactics of the Germans slowed the offensive to a crawl. Gough's failure to secure the Gheluvelt plateau prompted Haig, late in August, to transfer the leading role to Plumer, whose methodical assaults with limited objectives proved much more successful in the sub-battles of the Menin Road Ridge (September 20–25), Polygon Wood (September 26–October 3) and Broodseinde (October 4). The weather deteriorated again and both Plumer and Gough advised halting the offensive, although Haig persisted. On November 6

Desolation at Passchendaele, 1917

the Canadian Corps finally took the village of Passchendaele, a name often popularly applied to the whole battle, in which both sides incurred approximately 250,000 casualties. Despite advancing about 5 miles (8km), the British had achieved few of their original strategic objectives. The Third Battle of Ypres, during which men drowned in liquid mud, has since become symbolic of the horrors of World War I. *PJS.*

"Y" Ravine. Natural feature near Beaumont Hamel on the Somme. A British objective on July 1 1916, finally taken November 13 1916.

Yser, Battle of the. Following the fall of Antwerp on October 10 1914, the Belgian Army withdrew to the line of the River Yser from Dixmude to the coast north of Nieuport. The position was held by five Belgian divisions and a French Marine brigade. Declaring this to be the last line of Belgian resistance, King Albert refused to leave it to join the manoeuvres inland as both sides strove to outflank each other in the "Race to the Sea". Subsequent events justified his decision for, on October 18, Belgian outposts east of the Yser were driven back by elements of reconstituted German Fourth Army, commanded by Duke Albrecht of Württemberg. Aiming to break through to the Channel ports, the Germans continued to attack on October 19 and 20 but were repulsed at Dixmude and also at Nieuport, where they were heavily shelled by British and French warships. On October 21 Foch sent the French 42nd Division to reinforce the vital Nieuport sector, though the Germans secured a bridgehead across the Yser at Tervaete and, with the aid of 42cm howitzers, launched several more attacks on Dixmude, which was now in danger of being outflanked. By noon on October 30 the Germans had advanced south of Nieuport, taken Ramscapelle and gained a foothold in Pervyse. However, the Belgians opened sluice gates to flood the area east of the railway enbankment between Nieuport and Dixmude. This forced the Germans to halt their attacks and to concentrate instead on the sector around Ypres. *PJS.*

Y Service. Secret signals teams who listen to enemy wireless traffic, passing available data to relevant operational staffs, providing raw material for decipher and maintaining traffic analysis – observing location and activity of W/T and R/T stations.

Yugoslavia, German invasion of (April 6–17 1941). Carried out by Twelfth Army (List) to secure Hitler's southern flank before his invasion of Russia. Yugoslav resistance, although lasting only 11 days, imposed significant modifications to Hitler's plans for 1941.

Yugoslavia, British operations in (1943–1945). Initially, British missions worked with Mihailovich's Chetniks, and with Tito's Partisans. By the beginning of 1944, all support was withdrawn from the former, who had become more interested in attacking Tito's Communists than the Germans. Military support to the Partisans was provided by the British Balkans Air Force (Elliot), and by Land Forces Adriatic (Davy). Apart from continuous air support, supply dropping, casualty evacuation and coastal raiding, the major operations carried out were: i) (June–September 1944) raids on the German-held Dalmatian islands of Brac, Korcula and Solta; ii) (September 1944) concentrated air action against German withdrawal routes through Yugoslavia; iii) (October 1944–January 1945) "Floyd Force", composed of British artillery, engineers and commandos, sent to Dubrovnik to assist in trapping the isolated XXI German Mountain Corps withdrawing from Albania. Due to Partisan suspicion of British motives, the force's full potential was not exploited, and the Germans escaped, although sustaining heavy losses from British attacks. iv) (February 1945) establishment of an advanced air base at Zadar to support the final offensive by Fourth Yugoslav Army (Drapsin) towards Trieste in March–April 1945, and as an emergency airfield for strategic bombers attacking Central European targets. *WGFJ.*

Yugoslavia, German counter-Partisan operations in (November 1941–May 1944). Six offensives were launched by c-in-c South West (von Weichs) against Tito's Partisans: first, November 1941; second, April 1942; third, November 1942; fourth, January 1943; fifth, May 1943, during which Tito was wounded; and sixth, October 1943–January 1944. All failed to achieve decisive results.

With the capitulation of Italy in September 1943, Tito was able to arm his Partisans with equipment taken from the Italian divisions of the Axis occupation forces, creat-

Yugoslav partisan women fighters

ing the Yugoslav National Liberation Army. In May 1944, von Weichs mounted an operation using SS paratroopers to capture Tito in the caves at Drvar. Tito escaped with Allied assistance to the island of Vis, returning to the mainland three months later under Russian auspices as the Soviet armies approached Belgrade, which fell on October 20. Instead of mounting a seventh offensive against the Partisans, von Weichs had to use his resources to keep open routes for German forces in Greece and Albania, withdrawing northwards to avoid being cut off by the Russians. *WGFJ.*

Z

Zandvoorde. Village southeast of Ypres, lost to the Germans on October 30 1914, after a gallant defence by the British Household Cavalry. It was finally retaken by the British 35th Division on September 29 1918.

Zanussi, Brig Gen Giacomo (1894–1966). Italian. Emissary at negotiations for Italian capitulation, 1943.

Zeebrugge raid (1918). From early in World War I, German U-boats and destroyers from Zeebrugge and Ostend threatened Allied shipping in the Channel and North Sea. Their permanent base was some 7 miles (11km) inland at Bruges, connected to Zeebrugge and Ostend by canals. Plans for amphibious assaults on the Belgian ports, first suggested by Rear Adm Sir Reginald Tyrwhitt (1870–1951), were enthusiastically espoused by Vice Adm Roger Keyes, head of the Naval Plans Division, and Commander, Dover

Patrol, January 1918.

Keyes assembled and trained, in secrecy, a force of some 1,000 Royal Navy volunteers and 700 Royal Marines. Motorboats and launches would occupy the shore batteries with mock attacks and lay smokescreens around the harbour; a 900-strong landing and demolition force would storm the strongly-fortified Zeebrugge "mole" (the sickle-shaped pier protecting the harbour); three concrete-filled blockships (old light cruisers *Iphigenia, Intrepid* and *Thetis*) would be scuttled in the canal entrance. A simultaneous assault would be made at Ostend.

An initial attempt on the night of April 11–12 was abandoned when adverse winds dispersed the smokescreens. The second attempt was made on April 22–23. Under heavy fire from shore batteries, the old submarine *C.3* was detonated under the viaduct connecting the mole to the shore as landing parties from the cruiser *Vindictive* (specially fitted with landing ramps and with supporting armament including flame-throwers and mortars) and ferries *Iris* and *Daffodil* fought desperately with the mole's 1,000-strong garrison. The blockships' crews were taken off by launches after triggering delayed-action scuttling charges. Lasting for just over one hour, the raid cost 214 killed and 383 wounded.

The Germans opened channels around the blockships at Zeebrugge within a few days. Nor did a further operation at Ostend on May 9–10 seriously hamper German warships. As a morale-booster, the Zeebrugge-Ostend raids were a tremendous success, reflected in the award of 11 Victoria Crosses and 209 lesser decorations to those taking part. *RO'N.*

British blockships sunk at Zeebrugge

Zeitzler, Gen Kurt (1895–1963). Ger. Zeitzler came to prominence as COS of von Kleist's Panzer Group (later the First Panzer Army) during the campaigns in France, the Balkans and Russia in 1940–41. In September 1942 he was suddenly elevated, above many more senior generals, to succeed Halder as Army CGS. Zeitzler proved less subservient than Hitler expected and, although he argued in vain for an attempted breakout from Stalingrad, he *was* allowed to make vital defensive readjustments to the German positions in Russia early in 1943. However, in July, the failure of the Kursk offensive, which he had largely planned, exhausted the German armoured reserves and surrendered the strategic initiative to the Russians. Increasing ill-health and successive German reverses further weakened his influence. He was dismissed in July 1944, after the destruction of Army Group Centre and the bomb plot against Hitler. *PJS*.

Zemke, Col Hubert A (b.1914). US. Outstanding fighter leader and tactician who commanded the US 56th and 479th Fighter Groups in the European Theatre of Operations, 1943–44. Credited with 17.75 aerial combat victories, he became a POW when his P-51 broke up on October 30 1944. Zemke retired from the USAAF in 1967.

Zeppelin raids. The first Zeppelin attack on Britain was aimed at Yarmouth on the night of January 19–20 1915 and before the end of the year, five attacks were delivered against London. By the end of the war, 51 Zeppelin attacks had been made upon Britain, most of them in 1915 and 1916. Active defence against the Zeppelins seemed impossible owing to the relatively high altitudes at which they were able to operate, but methods of engaging them with anti-aircraft fire and fighter aircraft were evolved and the Zeppelins then began to suffer heavy casualties. In all, nearly 200 tons of bombs were dropped and 557 people were killed. Although the effects of these attacks were therefore, in the context of the war as a whole, of no great consequence, they did introduce a new element to warfare which, when it was

expressed by aeroplane attacks, became a much more serious issue. *ANF*. *See also* GOTHA BOMBERS.

Zeppelin-Staaken R VI (German, WWI). Heavy bomber; crew 7. Most numerous and best-known of all the *Riesenflugzeuge* (giant aeroplanes). Prototype completed late 1916; officially accepted June 6 1917; production by three additional contractors. Flown as night bombers mostly over Western Front and against England. Production, 18, of which at least 11 destroyed during World War I, plus one seaplane version to German Navy. Four 260hp Mercedes D IVa/D VIa or 245hp Mayback Mb IVa engines; max. speed 99.4mph (160kph); four-six 7.92mm machine guns, 4,409lb (2,000kg) bombs.

Zeppelin *see* AIRSHIP.

Zero fighter *see* MITSUBISHI A6M2 REISEN.

Zhukov, Marshal Georgi (1896–1974). Russian. A former NCO in the Imperial Russian cavalry, Zhukov joined the Red Army in August 1918. In June 1939 he joined First Army Group in Mongolia where Soviet clashes with the Japanese Kwantung Army were growing in intensity. With his defeat of the Japanese at Nomonhan, Zhukov's reputation soared and he was given command of the vital Kiev Military District. However, his relations with Stalin fluctuated and although he was made CGS in January 1941, he was dismissed in June for advocating Soviet withdrawal from Kiev early in the German invasion. Zhukov was sent to reorganize Leningrad's defences and, by a series of counterattacks, kept the Germans at bay. He performed a similar task at Moscow, holding the German thrusts from October to November then mounting his own offensive. Appointed Deputy Supreme Commander in August 1942, he ordered a resolute defence of Stalingrad while laying preparations for a major offensive to encircle the besieging Germans. His plan, Operation "Uranus", exacted a crushing defeat but Zhukov had meanwhile returned to Leningrad to oversee the breaking of the siege. Thereafter, he returned

south, coordinating the Battle of Kursk and, in June 1944, the Soviet destruction of Army Group Centre. From October, Zhukov was given First Belorussion Front in addition to his other duties. His attack on Berlin began on April 16 1945 and, in spite of fierce resistance and disagreements with other Soviet generals, the city fell on May 2. After the war Zhukov fell victim to Stalin's "purge of the heroes". He was rehabilitated after Stalin's death in 1953 but fell from grace again in 1957 and went into retirement. *MS*.

Zia-ur-Rahman, Gen (1935–81). Bengali. Regular officer in Pakistan army, commanded company of East Bengal Regiment in action in 1965 war. Led revolt among Bengali troops in 1971; seized Chittagong and proclaimed independence of Bangladesh, March 27. Led forces of Mukti Bahini. Appointed Chief of Army Staff after assassination of Sheikh Mujib-ur-Rahman. Arrested in counter-coup but released and appointed chief martial law administrator. President of Bangladesh 1978. Assassinated 1981.

Ziegler, Lt Gen (*General der Artillerie*) Heinz (1894–1964). Ger. Chief of Staff to von Arnim; commanded the offensive at Sidi Bou Zid, southern Tunisia.

Zimmermann Telegram. Fearing US entry into World War I, Germany hoped to conclude an alliance with Mexico. On January 19 1917, Arthur Zimmermann, the German foreign minister, sent a telegram from Berlin advocating a Mexican invasion of the US. Intercepted and decoded by British Naval Intelligence, the message was passed to the American authorities. It was influential in winning acceptance of American entry into the war.

Zuckerman, Professor Lord ("Solly") (b.1904). Br. Devised plan for the disruption of the Italian railway system before Alexander's "Diadem" offensive of May 1944.

Zuikaku. Japanese aircraft carrier. *Shokaku* class. Completed 1941 and took part in most of the Pacific battles until sunk at Leyte Gulf.

Acronyms/initialisms/ranks/ appointments

AA Anti-aircraft
AAA Anti-aircraft Artillery (US)
AAC Army Air Corps
AAM Air to Air Missile
ABDA Australian, British, Dutch, American Command
ABM Anti-Ballistic Missile
ACV Air Cushion Vehicle
Adm Admiral
ADM Atomic Demolition Munition
AEF American Expeditionary Force
AFB Air Force Base (US)
AFV Armoured Fighting Vehicle
AGM Air to Ground Missile
AI Air Interception
AIF Australian Imperial Force
AIM Air Intercept Missile (US; see also AAM)
ALBM Air Launched Ballistic Missile
ALCM Air Launched Cruise Missile
AMC Armed Merchant Cruiser
Amtrac Amphibious tractor (also called LVT)
ANZAC Australia and New Zealand Army Corps (WWI)
AOC-in-C Air Officer Commanding in Chief
APC Armoured Personnel Carrier
APDS Armour-Piercing Discarding Sabot
APFSDS Armour-Piercing Fin Stabilizing Discarding Sabot
ARM Anti-radiation missile
ARP Air Raid Precautions
ARV Armoured Recovery Vehicle
ARVN Army of the Republic of Vietnam
ASAT Anti-Satellite System
ASDIC Anti-Submarine Detection Investigation Committee
ASM Air to Surface Missile
ASV Air to Surface Vessel
ASW Anti-submarine warfare
ATACMS Army Tactical Missile
ATAF Allied Tactical Air Force
ATC Air Transport Command
ATGW Anti-Tank Guided Weapon
ATS Auxiliary Territorial Service
AVG American Volunteer Group ("Flying Tigers")
AVRE Armoured Vehicle, Royal Engineers
AWACS Airborne Warning and Control System

BAOR British Army of the Rhine
BCFK British Commonwealth Forces, Korea
BCOF British Commonwealth Occupation Force, Japan
BEF British Expeditionary Force
BMP (*Boyevaya Mashina Plavaushiy*) Soviet MICV, amphibious
Brig Brigadier
BVR Beyond Visual Range

CAM ship Catapult-Armed Merchant ship
CAP Combat Air Patrol
Capt Captain
CAS Chief of Air Staff
CB Construction Battalion (US Navy; "Seabees")
CBI China-Burma-India Theatre
CBW Chemical and Biological Warfare
CBO Combined Bomber Offensive
CCS Combined Chiefs of Staff
CDL Canal Defence Light
CE Chemical Energy
CEP Circular Error Probability
CGDK Coalition Government of Democratic Kampuchea
CGM Conspicuous Gallantry Medal
CGS Chief of the General Staff
CIA Central Intelligence Agency
CIDG Civilian Irregular Defence Group
CIGS Chief of the Imperial General Staff
C-in-C Commander-in-Chief
CINCMED Commander-in-Chief Mediterranean
CINCPAC Commander-in-Chief Pacific
CMP Counter Military Potential
CNO Chief of Naval Operations (US)
CNS Chief of Naval Staff
CO Commanding Officer
Col Colonel
COMINCH Commander-in-Chief, US Navy

ComSubPac Commander Submarines Pacific
COMUSMACV Commander of the US Military Assistance Command, Vietnam
CORDS Civil Operations and Rural Development Support
COS i) Chief of Staff (Chief Staff Officer of a Commander)
ii) Chiefs of Staff, British Chiefs of Naval, Imperial and Air Staffs
COSSAC Chief of Staff to Supreme Allied Commander
COSVN Central Office of South Vietnam
CP Command Post
CPC Communist Party of China
CPO Chief Petty Officer

DAK *Deutsches Afrika Korps*
DCM Distinguished Conduct Medal
DD Duplex Drive
DEMS Defensively Equipped Merchant Ships
DEW i) Directed Energy Weapon
ii) Distant Early Warning
DFC Distinguished Flying Cross
DFM Distinguished Flying Medal
DMZ De-Militarized Zone
DoD Department of Defense (US)
DPC Defence Planning Committee (NATO)
DPRK Democratic People's Republic of Korea
DRV Democratic Republic of Vietnam
DSC Distinguished Service Cross
DSM Distinguished Service Medal
DSO Distinguished Service Order
DUKW Amphibious Truck (from US Army vehicle designation codes: D = 1942; U = amphibian; K = all-wheel drive; W = dual rear axles)

E-boat German MTB (Allied term; see also S-boat)
ECCM Electronic Counter Counter Measures
ECM Electronic Counter Measures
Elint Electronic Intelligence
EMP Electromagnetic Pulse
EMT Equivalent Megatonnage
ENSA Entertainments National Service Association
EOKA *Ethniki Organosis Kuprion Agonistou* (National Organization of Cypriot Fighters)
ERA Explosive Reactive Armour
ERW Enhanced Radiation Weapon
ESM Electronic Support Measures
ETA Estimated Time of Arrival
ETO European Theatre of Operations
EW Electronic Warfare

FAA Fleet Air Arm
FANYS First Aid Nursing Yeomanry
FBI Federal Bureau of Investigation
FBS Forward Based Systems
FEBA Forward Edge of Battle Area
FF Free French (Fighting French)
FFI *Forces Françaises de l'Intérieur* ([Free] French Forces of the Interior)
FIDO Fog Investigation and Dispersal Operation
Flak *Fliegerabwehrkanone* (aviator defence gun)
Fl Lt Flight Lieutenant
FLN *Front de Libération National*
FLOT Forward Line of Own Troops
F/O Flying Officer
FOBS Fractional Orbit Bombardment System
FOFA Follow-on Forces Attack
FROG Free Rocket Over Ground
FSB Fire Support Base
FULRO *Front Unifié pour la Lutte des Races Opprimés*

GC George Cross
GEE (Grid) radar air-to-air navigation
Gen General
Gestapo *Geheime Staatspolizei* (Secret State Police)
GHQ General Headquarters
GI General Issue
GLCM Ground Launched Cruise Missile
GOC General Officer Commanding
GPMG General Purpose Machine Gun
Gr Capt Group Captain
GRU *Glavnoye Razvedyvatelnoye Upravleniye* (Chief Intelligence Directorate, Soviet General Staff)
GSFG Group Soviet Forces (Germany)

HE High Explosive
HEAT High Explosive Anti-Tank
HES Hamlet Evaluation Survey (Malaya)
HESH High Explosive Squash Head
HG Home Guard
HIJMS His Imperial Japanese Majesty's Ship
HMAS His (Her) Majesty's Australian Ship
HMCS His (Her) Majesty's Canadian Ship
HMNZS His (Her) Majesty's New Zealand Ship
HMS His (Her) Majesty's Ship
HQ Headquarters

ICBM Inter-Continental Ballistic Missile
IDF Israel Defence Force
IFF Identification, Friend or Foe
IJA Imperial Japanese Army
IJN Imperial Japanese Navy
INA Indian National Army
INF Intermediate Nuclear Forces
INLA Irish National Liberation Army
IRA Irish Republican Army
IRB Irish Republican Brotherhood
IRBM Intermediate Range Ballistic Missile
IZL *Irgun Zvai Leumi*

JCS Joint Chiefs of Staff
JG *Jagdgeschwader* (German fighter wing)
JSTARS Joint Surveillance and Target Attack Radar System
JTIDS Joint Tactical Information Distribution System

KE Kinetic Energy
KG *Kampfgeschwader* (German bomber wing)
KGB (*Komitat Gosudarstvennoi Bezopasnosti*) Soviet secret police
KGr *Kampfgruppe* (German bomber group)
KMT Kuomintang
KT Kiloton

LCA Landing Craft (Assault)
LCC Launch Control Centre
LCF Landing Craft (Flak)
LCI Landing Craft (Infantry)
LCS Landing Craft (Support)
LCSFA Limited Contingent of Soviet Forces
LCT Landing Craft (Tanks)
LDV Local Defence Volunteers
LORAN Long Range Navigation
LRBM Long Range Ballistic Missile
LRDG Long Range Desert Group
LRPG Long Range Penetration Group
LSD Landing Ship (Dock)
LSI Landing Ship (Infantry)
LSL Landing Ship (Logistic)
LST Landing Ship (Tank)
Lt Lieutenant
LVT Landing Vessel (Tracked)

MAAG Military Assistance Advisory Group
MAC Marine Amphibious Corps (US)
MAC ship Merchant Aircraft Carrier
MACV Military Assistance Command Vietnam
MAD Mutually Assured Destruction
Maj Major
MBT Main Battle Tank
MC Military Cross
MCP Malayan Communist Party
MEZ Maritime Exclusion Zone
MG Machine Gun
MGB Motor Gun Boat
MICV Mechanized Infantry Combat Vehicle
MIRV Multiple Independently Targetable Re-entry Vehicle
MLRS Multiple Launch Rocket System
MM Military Medal
MoD Ministry of Defence
MPAJA Malayan People's Anti-Japanese Army
MRBM Medium Range Ballistic Missile
MRLA Malayan Races' Liberation Army
MRV Multiple Re-entry Vehicle
MT i) Megaton
ii) Motor Transport
MTB Motor Torpedo Boat

NAAFI Navy, Army, Air Force Institute

NATO North Atlantic Treaty Organization
Nazi *Nationalsozialistische Deutsche Arbeiterpartei* (National Socialist German Workers' Party)
NCAC Northern Combat Area Command (Far East)
NEFA North East Frontier Agency
NEI Netherlands East Indies
NKPA North Korean People's Army
NKVD *Narodnyi Kommissariat Vnutrennykh Del* (People's Commissariat of Internal Affairs)
NLF National Liberation Front (Vietnam)
NNRC Neutral Nations Repatriation Commission
NNSC Neutral Nations Supervisory Commission
NORTHAG Northern Army Group (NATO)
NPT Non Proliferation Treaty
NVA North Vietnamese Army

OAS *Organisation de l'Armée Secrète*
OC Officer Commanding
OKH *Oberkommando des Heeres* (High Command of the German Army)
OKL *Oberkommando der Luftwaffe* (High Command of the German Air Force)
OKW *Oberkommando der Wehrmacht* (High Command of the German Armed Forces)
OSS Office of Strategic Services

Pak *Panzerabwehrkanone* (anti-tank gun; German)
PAVN People's Army of Vietnam
PBV Post-Boost Vehicle
PF Popular Forces (Vietnam)
PGM Precision Guided Munitions
PLA People's Liberation Army (China)
PLAF People's Liberation Armed Force
PLUTO Pipe Line Under the Ocean
POUM *Partido Obrero de Unificación Marxista* (Spanish Workers' Party of Marxist Unification)
POW Prisoner Of War
PPLI Princess Patricia's Light Infantry
PRC People's Republic of China
PRG Provisional Revolutionary Government
PRU Photo Reconnaissance Unit
PSDF People's Self-Defence Forces (Vietnam)
PT Patrol Torpedo Boat (US Navy MTB)
PWE Political Warfare Executive
Pz/PzKpfw/PzKw *Panzerkampwagen* (German AFV)

RA Royal Artillery
RAAF Royal Australian Air Force
RAC Royal Armoured Corps
RAF Royal Air Force
RAG River Assault Group
RAMC Royal Army Medical Corps
RAN Royal Australian Navy
RAOC Royal Army Ordnance Corps
RAR Royal Australian Regiment
RASC Royal Army Service Corps
RCAF Royal Canadian Air Force
RCM Radio Counter Measures
RCN Royal Canadian Navy
RCT i) (US) Regimental Combat Team
ii) Royal Corps Transport
RE Royal Engineers
REME Royal Electrical and Mechanical Engineers
RFC Royal Flying Corps
RHA Royal Horse Artillery
RM Royal Marines
RN Royal Navy
RNAS Royal Naval Air Service
RNZAF Royal New Zealand Air Force
ROA *Russkaya Osvoboditelnaya Armiya* (Russian Liberation Army)
ROC Republic of China (Taiwan)
ROK Republic of Korea
RPG Rocket Propelled Grenade
RPV Remotely Piloted Vehicle
RTC Royal Tank Corps
RTR Royal Tank Regiment
RVN Republic of Vietnam

SA *Sturmabteilung* (Storm Detachment)
SAAF South African Air Force
SAC Strategic Air Command
SACEUR Supreme Allied Commander Europe
SADARM Sense and Destroy Armour

SALT Strategic Arms Limitation Talks
SAM Surface to Air Missile
SAS Special Air Service
SBA Sovereign Base Area
S-Boat *Schnellboot* (Fast Boat) (German MTB; *see also* E-boat)
SCAEF Supreme Commander, Allied Expeditionary Force
SCAP Supreme Commander, Allied Powers
SD *Sicherheitsdienst RFSS* (Security Service, *Reichsführer SS*)
SDI Strategic Defense Initiative
SEAC South East Asia Command
SEALORDS South East Asia Lake Ocean River Delta Strategy
SEATO South East Asia Treaty Organization
SHAEF Supreme HQ Allied Expeditionary Force
SHAPE Supreme Headquarters Allied Powers Europe
SLAM Seek, Locate, Annihilate and Monitor
SLBM Submarine Launched Ballistic Missile
SLCM Surface Launched Cruise Missile
SLU Special Liaison Unit
SOE Special Operations Executive
SP/SPG Self-Propelled Gun
SRBM Short-Range Ballistic Missile
SRF Strategic Rocket Forces
SRINF Short Range Intermediate Nuclear Forces
SRV Socialist Republic of Vietnam
SS *Schutzstaffel* (Protection Patrol)
SSM Surface to Surface Missile
s.t. Static thrust
St G *Stukageschwader* (German dive-bomber wing)
START Strategic Arms Reduction Talks
Stavka *Stavka Glavnovo Komandovaniya Vooruzhennykh SSSR* (GHQ of the Armed Forces of the USSR)
STOVL Short Take-Off and Vertical Landing
Stuka *Sturzkampfflugzeug* (German dive-bomber)

TAC Tactical Air Command (USAF)
TAF Tactical Air Force
TEZ Total Exclusion Zone
TF Task Force (naval)
TG Task Group (naval)
TMT Paramilitary Turkish-Cypriot movement
TNT Trinitrotoluene
TNKU *Tentera Nasional Kalimantan Utara* (North Kalimantan National Army
TOW Tube launched, Optically tracked, Wire guided missile

UAR United Arab Republic
U-boat *Unterseeboot* (German submarine)
UHF Ultra-high Frequency
UN United Nations
UNC Unified Command (Korea)
UNCOK United Nations Commission on Korea
UNCURK United Nations Commission on the Unification and Rehabilitation of Korea
UNTCOK United Nations Temporary Commission on Korea
USAAC United States Army Air Corps
USAAF United States Army Air Force
USAF United States Air Force
USARV United States Army Vietnam
USMC United States Marine Corps
USN United States Navy
USS United States Ship
USSTAF United States Strategic Air Force

VAD Voluntary Aid Detachment
VC Victoria Cross
VF Fighter Squadron (US Navy)
VHF Very High Frequency
VMA Tactical Attack Squadron (USMC)
VMF Fighter Squadron (USMC)
V/STOL Vertical/Short Take-Off and Landing
VTOL Vertical Take-Off and Landing

WAAC Women's Auxiliary Army Corps (US)
WAAF Women's Auxiliary Air Force
WAVES Women Accepted for Voluntary Emergency Service (US Navy)

Wg Commander Wing Commander
WRAF Women's Royal Air Force
WRNS Women's Royal Naval Service

Codewords

Adlertag (Eagle Day, Aug 13 1940) German start of Battle of Britain
A-Go (June 1944) Japanese plan for decisive battle east of Philippines (Battle of Philippine Sea)
Anvil *see* ""*Dragoon*"
Arcadia (Dec 1941) Allied conference in Washington
Argument ("Big Week", 1944) US air operation against the Luftwaffe
Avalanche (Sept 1943) Allied assault on Salerno
Barbarossa (June 1941) German invasion of Russia
Barrel Roll (Dec 1963) US air support to the Royal Lao Army
Battleaxe (Nov 1941) Second British operation to relieve Tobruk
Blücher (1918) German attack along the Chemin des Dames
Bodyguard (1944) Various Allied stratagems to disguise the precise timing and location of "Overlord".
Brevity (May 1941) First British operation to relieve Tobruk
Capital (1944) Recapture of northern Burma – "Extended Capital" also included Meiktila
Cartwheel (1943) Allied operations in the Solomon area
Case White (*Fall Weiss*, 1939) German invasion of Poland
Case Yellow (*Fall Gelb*, 1939) German invasion of France and the Low Countries
Catchpole (Feb 1944) US assault on Eniwetok
Cedar Falls (Vietnam, 1967) US search and destroy operation in the Iron Triangle
Cerberus (Feb 1942) German plans for "Channel Dash"
Charnwood (July 8 1944) British offensive near Caen, Normandy
Chromite (Korea, 1950) MacArthur's plan for the landings at Inchon in conjunction with a counteroffensive by Eighth Army
Circus (from June 1941) RAF fighter sweeps aimed to draw Luftwaffe into action within range of superior numbers of Spitfires
Citadel (*Zitadelle*, July 1943) German attack on Kursk salient
Cobra (July 25 1944) US breakout from Normandy bridgehead
Cockade (1943) Aspect of Allied activities (overall codename "Jael") intended to convince Germans that cross-Channel invasion would be made in 1943
Coronet (March 1946) Planned Allied invasion of Honshu, Japan
Crusader (Nov-Dec 1941) Third British operation to relieve Tobruk
Diadem (1944) Allied operation to capture Rome
Dracula (May 1945) Allied attack on Rangoon from the sea
Dragoon (earlier "Anvil", 1944) Allied landings in Southern France
Dynamo (May-June 1940) Allied evacuation from Dunkirk
Enosis Union between Greece and Cyprus
Epsom (July 18 1944) British offensive near Caen, Normandy
Eureka (Nov-Dec 1943) Allied conference in Tehran
Excess (Jan 1941) First Allied convoy to Malta
Fairfax (Vietnam, 1966–67) First large-scale attempt to train South Vietnamese by pairing them with American units
Felix (1940) German plan to capture Gibraltar
Flaming Dart I and II (Vietnam, Feb 1965) First routine US air strikes against North Vietnam from carriers in Tonkin Gulf
Flintlock (Jan-Feb 1944) US invasion of Marshall Islands
Fortitude (1944) Allied deception plans preceding "Overlord"

Galvanic (Nov 1943) US assault on Gilbert Islands
Georgette (1918) German attack on British front on both sides of River Lys, between Armentières and the La Bassée Canal
Goodwood (July 1944) British offensive east of Caen, Normandy
Halberd (Sept 1941) Fourth Malta convoy
Harpoon (June 1942) Sixth Malta convoy
Hudson Harbour (Korea) US experiments for the use of tactical atomic weapons
Husky (July 3 1943) Allied invasion of Sicily
Iceberg (1945) Allied offensives to capture Okinawa
Ichi Go (1944) Japanese offensive against US air bases in China
I Go (1943) Japanese Rabaul-based offensive in Solomons/Papua area
Jackstay (Vietnam, 1966) First US attack into Rung Sat Special Zone
Jubilee (Aug 19 1942) Raid on Dieppe
Judgment (1940) Allied air attack on Taranto
Junction City (Vietnam, 1967) US search and destroy operation into area known as War Zone C
Lam Son 719 (Vietnam, 1971) ARVN attempt to cut Ho Chi Minh Trail
Lea (Vietnam,1947) French attack on communist headquarters in conjunction with attempted envelopment of enemy units
Linebacker I (Vietnam,1972) US bombing in response to communists' Easter offensive
Linebacker II (Vietnam,1972) US 11-day "Christmas bombing"
Lorraine (Vietnam, 1952) French attempt to sever communist communication and supply lines along the Red River
Manhattan (1942–45) Allied atomic programme (*see also* "Tube Alloys")
March (March 1942) Fifth Malta convoy
Marita (1941) German attack in the Balkans
Market Garden (1944) Allied operations to seize bridges in occupied Holland
Market Time (Vietnam, 1965) US and South Vietnamese efforts to interdict seaborne infiltration of arms and supplies from North Vietnam to the South
Mars (1918) German attack at Arras as part of Ludendorff's March offensive
Matador (1942) Proposed British advance into Thailand
Menace (Sept 1940) Anglo-Free French Dakar expedition
Menu (Vietnam, from 1969) US attacks against communist base areas in Cambodia
Mercury (*Merkur*, May 1941) German assault on Crete
Michael (1918) First attack of German March offensive
MiG (Korea, July 1951) Seizure of crashed MiG by US for intelligence evaluation purposes
Mincemeat (1943) Operation to distract German attention from Allied preparations for invasion of Sicily
Moolah (Korea, 1953) US reward scheme to entice MiG pilots to defect
Musketeer (1956) Anglo-French operation against Egypt
Neptune (1944) Naval aspect of "Overlord"
Neutralize (Vietnam, 1967) US operation to relieve Con Thien
Octagon (Sept 1944) Allied conference at Quebec
Orange (pre –1941) US plans for war with Japan
Overlord (1944) Allied invasion of Normandy
Oyster (1942) Allied daylight air attack on Philips factory in Eindhoven
Pedestal (Aug 1942) Malta convoy
Pegasus (Vietnam, 1968) US and South Vietnamese offensive to relieve Khe Sanh combat base
Piranha (Vietnam, 1965) US search and destroy operation on Batangan Peninsula
Portcullis (Dec 1942) Tenth Malta convoy

Quadrant (Aug 1943) Allied conference at Quebec
Rainbow (1939–41) US plans for anti-Axis warfare
Rolling Thunder (1965–68) US air operations against North Vietnam
Sea Lion (*Seelöwe*, 1940) Planned German invasion of England
Sextant (Nov 1943) Allied conference at Cairo
Sho-go (Oct 1944) Japanese plans for Battle of Leyte Gulf
Starlight (Vietnam, 1965) US search and destroy operation on the Van Tuong Peninsula
Steel Tiger (Laos, from April 1965) US bombing of Ho Chi Minh Trail
Stonehenge (Nov 1942) Ninth Malta convoy
Strangle (Korea, from July 1951) Air operation against North Korean transportation network
Style (July-Aug 1941) Third Malta convoy
Substance (July 1941) Second Malta convoy
Symbol (Jan 1942) Allied conference at Casablanca
Terminal (July-Aug 1945) Allied conference at Potsdam
Texas (Vietnam, 1966) Joint US/South Vietnamese operation (also codenamed "Lien Ket 28") to relieve An Hoa.
Thayer II/Pershing (Vietnam, 1967) South Vietnamese operation in the An Lao Valley
Thunderclap (Feb 1945) Allied air operations against Dresden
Thursday (1944) Second Chindit operation in Burma
Totalize (Aug 8 1944) Allied attack towards Falaise, Normandy
Torch (Nov 1942) Allied invasion of North Africa
Tractable (Aug 14 1944) Second Allied attack towards Falaise, Normandy
Trident (May 1943) Allied conference at Washington
Tube Alloys (1942–45) British atomic programme
U-Go (1944) Japanese Imphal offensive
Varsity (March 1945) Allied airborne operation during Rhine crossing
Veritable (Feb 1945) Allied operation to clear Rhine approaches
Vigorous (June 1942) Malta convoy
White Wing (Vietnam,1966) US operation in the An Lao valley
Winter Storm (*Wintergewitter*, Dec 1942) German attempt to relieve Stalingrad
Zipper (1945) Projected Allied invasion of Malaya

General

Stephen E Ambrose *Rise to Globalism* (London 1985; 4th ed, New York NY 1985)
Christopher Andrew *Secret Service* (Heinemann 1985)
Robert B Asprey *War in the Shadows* (1973)
Brian Bond *War and Society in Europe, 1870-1970* (London 1986; New York NY 1984)
Bernard Brodie *Sea Power in the Machine Age* (2nd ed, London 1969; Westpoint CT 1969)
George Bruce (ed) *Harbottle's Dictionary of Battles* (3rd rev edn, London 1986)
Raymond Carr *Spain; 1808-1975* (2nd rev ed, Oxford 1982; New York NY 1982)
Aileen Clayton *The Enemy is Listening* (London 1980; New York NY (1982)
J R Colville *Man of Valour: F M Lord Gort VC* (London)
George C Constantinides (ed) *Intelligence and Espionage: An Analytical Bibliography* (Boulder CO 1983)
Conway Maritime Press *Conway's All the World's Fighting Ships* (Many vols, Annapolis MD 1979-83)
Robin Corbett *Guerrilla Warfare; From 1939 to the Present Day* (London 1986; Philadelphia PA 1986)
James E Dorman and Nigel de Lee *The Chinese War Machine* (London 1979)
R Ernest Dupuy and Trevor N Dupuy (eds) *The Encyclopaedia of Military History from 3500BC to the Present* (Rev ed, London 1986; New York NY 1986)
Edward M Earle (ed) *Makers of Modern Strategy: Military Thought from Machiavelli to Hitler* (Princeton NJ)
David Eggenberger (ed) *An Encyclopedia of Battles: Accounts of Over 1,560 Battles from 1479BC to the Present* (New York NY 1985)
Christopher F Foss (et al) *Encyclopaedia of the World's Tanks and Fighting Vehicles* (London 1977)
Noble Frankland and Christopher Dowling (eds) *Decisive Battles of the 20th Century* (London 1976)
Norman Friedman *US Carriers: An Illustrated Design History* and *US Battleships: An Illustrated Design History* (London 1985; Annapolis MD 1985)
John Gooch *Armies in Europe: Military Organisation and Society 1789-1945* (London 1980; New York NY 1980)
Richard Holmes *The World Atlas of Warfare* (London 1988)
Michael Howard *War in European History* (Oxford 1976; New York NY)
Stephen Howarth *Morning Glory: A History of the Imperial Japanese Navy* (London 1983)
Robert J Icks *Famous Tank Battles* (Windsor 1972)
Robert L Jackson *The Red Falcons: The Soviet Air Force in Action, 1919-1969* (London 1970)
H Jentschura and Dieter Jung *Warships of the Imperial Japanese Navy, 1809-1945* (London 1977; Annapolis MD 1976)
John Keegan and Andrew Wheatcroft (eds) *Who's Who in Military History* (London 1987)
Peter K Kemp (ed) *The Oxford Companion to Ships & the Sea* (Oxford 1988)
Paul M Kennedy *The Rise and Fall of British Naval Mastery* (2nd edn, London 1983; Melbourne FL 1982)
George C Kohn *Dictionary of Wars* (Oxford 1987; New York NY 1987)
Jeremy Mackenzie and Brian Holden Reid (eds) *The British Army and the Operational Art of War* (London 1988)
Arthur J Marder *From the Dreadnought to Scapa Flow* (5 vols, Oxford 1961-78)
Willian H McNeill *The Pursuit of Power: Technology, Armed Force and Society Since 1000AD* (Oxford 1983; Chicago Il 1982)
Frederick Myatt *Modern Small Arms* (London 1978)
Edgar O'Ballance *The Red Army of China* (London 1962; New York NY 1962)
Peter Padfield *Guns at Sea* (London 1973)
Alan Palmer (ed) *The Penguin Dictionary of Twentieth Century History, 1900-1978* (2nd rev edn, London 1983; New York NY 1984)
Peter Paret et al (ed) *Makers of Modern Strategy from Machiavelli to the Nuclear Age* (Oxford 1986; Princeton NJ 1986)
O Parkes *British Battleships*
Roger Parkinson *Encyclopaedia of Modern War* (London 1979)
Edward H Sims *The Fighter Pilots* (London 1967; 2nd edn, Blue Ridge Summit PA 1980)
Sir John Slessor *The Central Blue* (London)
Hew Strachan *European Armies and the Conduct of War* (London 1983; New York NY 1984)
John W R Taylor *A History of Aerial Warfare* (London 1974)
Barbara W Tuchman *Sand Against the Wind: Stilwell and the American Experience in China, 1911-45* (London 1981)
Martin Windrow and Francis K Mason *A Concise Dictionary of Military Biography* (London 1975; New York NY)
Peter Young *A Dictionary of Battles 1816-1976* (London 1977)

Up to and including World War I

James P Baxter *The Introduction of the Ironclad Warship* (2nd edn, Hamden CT 1968)
Geoffrey Bennett *Naval Battles of the First World War* (London 1974)
Geoffrey Bennett *Coronel and the Falklands* (London 1962)
Geoffrey Best *War and Society in Revolutionary Europe, 1770-1870* (London 1982; New York NY 1986)
J Corbett and H Newbolt *Naval Operations* (5 vols, London)
Virginia Cowles *The Kaiser* (London 1963)
Sir James Edmonds *British Official History of the Great War: Military Operations, Italy, 1915-1919* (London 1949)
Sir Geoffrey Evans *Tannenberg 1410-1914* (London 1970)
Byron Farwell *The Great Boer War* (London 1978)
Byron Farwell *The Great War in Africa, 1914-18* (London 1987; New York NY 1987)
John F C Fuller *The Decisive Battles of the Western World* Vol 3 (London 1956)
Thomas E Griess *The Great War* (Garden City Park NY 1987)
Reginald Hargreaves *Red Sun Rising: The Siege of Port Arthur* (London 1962)
Holger H Herwig *Luxury Fleet: The Imperial German Navy 1888-1918* (2nd rev edn, London 1987; Atlantic Highlands NY 1987)
Edgar Holt *Protest in Arms: The Irish Troubles 1916-1923* (London 1960)
Rayne Kruger *Goodbye, Dolly Gray: A History of the Boer War* (London 1974)
Andrew Lambert *Battleships in Transition: The Creation of the Steam Battlefleet, 1815-60* (London 1984; Annapolis MD 1985)
T E Lawrence *Seven Pillars of Wisdom* (London 1986; New York NY 1976)
Alexander McKee *The Friendless Sky* (London 1962; Chicago Il 1984)
Thomas Pakenham *The Boer War* (New edn, London 1982; New York NY 1979)
Barrie Pitt *1918: The Last Act* (London 1984)
Sir Walter Raleigh and H A Jones *The War in the Air* (6 vols, Oxford 1922-37)
Theodore Ropp *The Development of a Modern Navy: French Naval Policy, 1871-1904* (Annapolis MD 1987)
John Silverlight *The Victors' Dilemma: Allied Intervention in the Russian Civil War* (London 1970)
Edward H Sims *Fighter Tactics and Strategy 1914-1970* (London 1972)
Norman Stone *The Eastern Front 1914-1917* (London 1985)
A J P Taylor *The First World War* (London 1970)
John Terraine *Mons* (London 1960)
John Terraine *The Western Front 1914-1918* (London 1964)
Barbara W Tuchman *August 1914* (London 1980)
David Walder *The Short Victorious War* (London 1973)
Sir Archibald P Wavell *The Palestine Campaigns* (London 1928)
Leon Wolff *In Flanders Fields* (London 1979; New York NY 1983)
David Woodward *Armies of the World 1854-1914* (London 1978)

Interwar years

Antony Beevor *The Spanish Civil War* (London 1982; New York NY 1983)
Burnett Bolloten *The Spanish Revolution: The Left and the Struggle for Power During the Civil War* (London 1979; Chapel Hill NC 1982)
Brian Brud *Britain, France and Belgian 1939-1940* (Brassey's)
Robert Colodny *The Struggle for Madrid* (New York 1959)
Ronald Fraser *The Blood of Spain: An Oral History of the Spanish Civil War* (London 1979; New York NY 1980)
Gabriel Jackson *The Spanish Republic and the Civil War 1931-39* (Princeton NJ 1965)
Stephen W Roskill *Naval Policy Between the Wars, 1919-1939* (London 1968-76)
Hugh Thomas *The Spanish Civil War* (London 1977; Rev edn, New York NY 1977)

World War II

Louis Allen *The End of the War in Asia* (London 1976; Woodstock NY 1976)
Louis Allen *Burma: The Longest War, 1941-45* (London 1986; New York NY 1985)
R E Appleman et al *US Army in World War II: War in the Pacific, Okinawa, the Last Battle* (Washington DC 1948)
Christopher Argyle *Chronology of World War II* (London 1980)
Bernard Ash *Norway 1940* (London 1964)
Hanson W Baldwin *Battles Lost and Won: Great Campaigns of World War II* (London 1967)
Clay Blair, Jr *Silent Victory: The US Submarine War Against Japan* (New York 1975)
John Costello *The Pacific War* (London 1985; New York NY 1982)
W F Craven and L J Cate (eds) *The Army Air Forces in World War II* (7 vols, Chicago 1949-51)
T K Derry *The Campaign in Norway* (British Official History of the Second World War, London)
Paul S Dull *A Battle History of the Imperial Japanese Navy: 1941-45* (Annapolis MD 1978)
L F Ellis *Victory in the West: The Battle of Normandy* (London 1962)
John Erickson *The Road to Berlin: Continuing the History of Stalin's War with Germany* (London 1983; Boulder CO 1983)
John Erickson *The Road to Stalingrad* (London 1975; Boulder CO 1975)
M R D Foot *Resistance: European Resistance to Nazism 1940-45* (London 1977; New York NY 1977)
M R D Foot *SOE in France* (Frederic MD 1984)
Benis M Frank *Okinawa: Touchstone to Victory* (London 1970)
Roger Freeman *The US Strategic Bomber* (London 1975)
Brian Garfield *The Thousand-Mile War: Alaska and the Aleutians* (New York NY 1975)
G H Gill *Royal Australian Navy 1942-1945* (Canberra 1968)
Heinz Guderian *Panzer Leader* (Costa Mesa CA 1988)
Max Hastings *Overlord: D-Day and the Battle for Normandy* (London 1984; New York NY 1984)
Saburo Hayashi and Alvin D Coox *Kogun: The Japanese Army in the Pacific War* (London 1978; Westpoint CT 1978)
F H Hinsly et al *British Intelligence in the Second World War* 4 vols (HMSO 1978-88)
Alistair Horne *To Lose a Battle: France, 1940* (New edn, London 1979; New York NY 1979)
Richard Humble *Hitler's Generals* (London 1973; New York NY 1981)
W G F Jackson *The Battle for Italy* (London 1967)
W G F Jackson *The North African Campaigns, 1940-1943* (London 1976)
R V Jones *Most Secret War* (London 1978); *The Wizard War* (New York NY 1978)
John Keegan *Six Armies in Normandy: From D-Day to the Liberation of Paris* (London 1982; New York NY 1982)
Paul Kennedy *Pacific Onslaught: 7th Dec 1941/7th Feb 1943* (New York 1972)
James Ladd *Commandos and Rangers of World War II* (London 1978)
Ronald Lewin *The American Magic: Codes, Ciphers and the Defeat of Japan* (New York NY 1982)
Ronald Lewin *Ultra goes to War: The Secret Story* (London 1988)
Donald Macintyre *Leyte Gulf* (London 1970)
Sir J C Masterman *The Double-Cross System* (New York NY 1982)
S E Morison *The Two-Ocean War: A Short History of the United States Navy in the Second World War* (Boston 1963)
S E Morisson *Victory at Sea*
Williamson Murray *Luftwaffe Strategy for Defeat* (London)
Masatake Okumiya et al *Zero: The Air War in the Pacific in World War II, from the Japanese Viewpoint* (Washington DC 1956)
Richard O'Neill *Suicide Squads: Axis and Allied Special Attack Weapons of World War II* (London 1981; New York NY 1982)
Thomas Parrish (ed) *The Encyclopaedia of World War II* (London 1978)
Barrie Pitt (ed) *Military History of World War II* (London 1987)
Alfred J Price *Luftwaffe Handbook* (London 1986; New York NY 1977)
Alan Raven and John Roberts *British Cruisers of World War II* (London 1980; Annapolis MD 1980)
William Richardson and Seymour Freidin (eds) *The Fatal Decisions* (London 1956)
J Rohwer and G Hummelchen *Chronology of the War at Sea 1939-1945* (2 vols, London 1972)
Stephen W Roskill *The War at Sea, 1939-45* (Vol 1, London 1954-61)
Stephen W Roskill *The Navy at War, 1939-1945* (London 1960): *White Ensign: The British Navy at War, 1939-1945* (Annapolis MD 1960)
Albert Seaton *The Russo-German War, 1941-45* (London 1971)
Henry L Shaw Jr *Tarawa: a legend is born* (New York 1969)
John Strawson *The Battle for North Africa* (London 1969)
John Strawson *The Italian Campaign* (London 1987; New York NY 1988)
W H Tantum and E J Hoffschmidt *The Rise and Fall of the German Air Force* (CT 1969)
Christopher Tunney *A Biographical Dictionary of World War II* (London 1972)
Warren Tute *D-Day* (London 1974)
United States Naval History Division *Naval Chronology,*

World War II (Washington DC 1955)
Sir Charles Webster and Noble Frankland *The Strategic Air Offensive against Germany, 1939-1945* (4 vols, London 1961)
H P Willmott *Empires in the Balance: Japanese and Allied Pacific Strategies to April 1942* (London 1982; Annapolis MD 1982)
Chester Wilmot *The Struggle for Europe* (London 1952; New York NY 1986)
S Woodburn-Kirby *The War Against Japan* (5 vols, London 1957-1969)
Peter Young (ed) *The Almanac of World War II* (London 1981)
Peter Young (ed) *Atlas of the Second World War* (London 1973)

Postwar years

Ashley Brown *Modern Warfare* (London 1985; New York NY 1985)
Michael Carver *War Since 1945* (London 1980; new edn, Ashfield Pr 1989)
Golam W Choudhury *The Last Days of United Pakistan* (London 1974)
Richard Clutterbuck *The Long Long War: The Emergency in Malaya 1948-1960* (London 1967)
James Cotton and Ian Neary (eds) *The Korean War in History* (Manchester 1989; Atlantic Highlands NY 1989)
Bruce Cumings *The Origins of The Korean War; Liberation and the Emergence of Separate Regimes* (Princeton NJ 1981)
Ashley Cunningham-Boothe and Peter Farrar (eds) *British Forces In the Korean War* (London 1988)
Bernhard Dahm *Sukarno and the Struggle for Indonesian Independence* (Ithaca, NY 1966)
William J Duiker *The Communist Road to Power in Vietnam* (Boulder CO 1982)
Van Tien Dung *Our Great Spring Victory: An Account of the Liberation of South Vietnam* (New York NY 1977)
Geoffrey Fairbairn *Revolutionary Guerrilla Warfare* (London 1974)
Bernard B Fall *Street Without Joy: Insurgency in Indochina 1946-63* (London 1964; New York NY 1976)
Herbert Feldman *From Crisis to Crisis, Pakistan in 1962-9* (London 1973)
Stanley Karnow *Vietnam: A History* (London 1985; New York NY 1984)
Burton I Kaufman *The Korean War: Challenges In Crisis, Credibility and Command* (New York 1986)
Robert F Kennedy *The Thirteen Days: A Memoir of the Cuban Missile Crisis* (New York NY 1988)
Gabriel Kolko *Vietnam: Anatomy of a War, 1940-75* (London 1986); *Anatomy of a War: Vietnam, the United States and the Modern Historical Experience* (New York NY 1986)
Robert W Komer *Bureaucracy at War: US Performance in the Vietnam Conflict* (Boulder CO 1986)
Andrew F Krepinevich Jr *The Army and Vietnam* (Baltimore MD 1986)
Peter Lowe *The Origins of the Korean War* (London 1986; White Plains NY 1986)
Callum A MacDonald *Korea: The War Before Vietnam* (London 1986; New York NY 1987)
Neville Maxwell *India's China War* (London 1970)
Hubert Moineville *Naval Warfare Today and Tomorrow* (Oxford 1983; New York NY 1984)
Anthony Nutting *No End of a Lesson: Story of Suez* (London 1967)
Robert Osgood *Limited War: The Challenge to American Strategy* (Chicago 1957)
Jeffrey Race *War Comes to Long An: Revolutionary Conflict in a Vietnamese Province* (Berkeley CA 1972)
David Rees *Korea: The Limited War* (London 1964)
Arthur M Schlesinger Jr *One Thousand Days: John F Kennedy in the White House* (London 1965)
William Shawcross *Sideshow: Kissinger, Nixon and the Destruction of Cambodia* (London 1986; New York NY 1987)
Anthony Short *The Communist Insurrection in Malaya 1948-60* (London 1975; New York NY 1974)
William W Stueck Jr *The Road to Confrontation: American Policy Toward China and Korea, 1947-1950* (Chapel Hill NC 1981)
Robert Thompson *Defeating Communist Insurgency* (London 1966)
Sir Robert Thompson and John Keegan (eds) *War in Peace: An Analysis of Warfare from 1945 to the Present Day* (3rd ed, London 1985; New York NY 1985)
W Scott Thompson and Donaldson D Frizell (eds) *The Lessons of Vietnam* (New York NY 1977)
Gregory F Treverton *Covert Action: The Limits of American Intervention in the Post-War World* (London 1988; New York NY 1989)
William S Turley *The Second Indo-China War: A Short Political and Military History, 1954-75* (Aldershot 1986; Boulder CO 1986)
Mark Urban *War in Afghanistan* (London 1987; New York NY 1988)
Bruce W Watson and Peter M Dunn *Military Lessons of the Falklands Islands War* (Boulder, CO 1984)

World War I

Aachen, Battle of; Aisne, Battle of the (1917); Aisne, Battle of the; American Expeditionary Force; Amiens 1918; Ancre, Battle of 1917; Arab Revolt; Armentiéres; Arras, Battle of April 1917; Asiago, Battle of 1918; Aubers Ridge; Bapaume; Bazentin le Grand and Bazentin le Petit (Somme); Beaumont Hamel; Belgium, invasion of 1914; Bernafay Wood (Somme); Big Bertha; Black Day (of the German army) 1918; Bloody April 1917, air battles (Western Front); Brest-Litovsk, Treaty of; Broodseinde; Brusilov offensives (July 1 1916 and July 2 1917; Bull Ring (Etaples); Bullecourt; Butte de Warlencourt; Cambrai, Battle of 1917; Cameroons 1914-16; Canadian Expeditionary Force 1914-18; Canal du Nord; Caporetto, Battle of 1917; Champagne, First Battle of (Feb 1915); Champagne, Second Battle of (Sept-Nov 1915); Chantilly HQ; Charleroi, Battle of 1914; Chemin des Dames; Coronel, Battle of 1914; Cuxhaven, Raid on; Damascus; Dardanelles 1915; Darfur; Delville Wood; Dogger Bank, Battle of 1915; Drocourt-Quéant Line; East African campaign 1914-18; Egypt and Palestine campaign; Emden; Etaples mutiny; Falklands, Battle of the 1914; Festubert, Battle of May 1915; Flers, Battle of; Flesquières; Fort Douaumont; Fort Vaux; French Army mutinies 1917; Fromelles; Frontiers, Battle of the; Galician campaign 1914-17; Gallipoli 1915-16; Gaza, First, Second and Third Battles of (March-Nov 1917); German Southwest Africa campaign 1915; Givenchy; Gorlice-Tarnow campaign 1915; Gotha bombers, attacks by 1917; Gumbinnen, Battle of 1914; Haifa, Battle of 1918; Hartlepool, bombardment of; Harwich Force; Hébuterne; Hejaz; Hejaz railway; Heligoland Bight, Battle of 1914; Hell Fire Corner; High Wood; Hill 70 (Lens); Hindenburg Line; Huj, Battle of 1917; Isonzo, Battles of 1915-17; Italian campaign; Jerusalem, capture of; Jutland, Battle of; Kiel mutiny 1918; La Boisselle; Le Cateau, Battle of 1914; Lens; Liège, Battle of 1914; Loos, Battle of; Lorraine, Battle of 1914; Louvain; Lusitania, sinking of 1915; Madras, bombardment of 1914; March offensive, German 1918 (to July); Margate, destroyer raid on; Maricourt; Marne, Battles of the 1914/1918 (1918 Champ-Marne Jly Aisne-Mar Aug); Mediterranean Expeditionary Force; Menin Gate; Menin Road/Ridge; Mesopotamian campaign 1914-18; Messines, Battle of 1917; Meuse-Argonne Forest, Battle of 1918; Middle East campaign 1916-18; Montreuil; Mulhouse, Battle of 1914; Namur, Battle of 1914; Néry, Battle of; Neuve-Chapelle, Battle of March 1915; New Armies; Notre Dame de Lorette; Oppy Wood; Ostend raid 1918; Paris gun; Piave river, Battle of the 1918; Ploegsteert (Plug Street); Poperinghe; Rafa, Battle of 1917; Redan Ridge; Romanian campaign 1916-18; Salonika campaign 1915-18; Samoa 1914; Sarikamis, Battle of 1914-15; Scarborough, bombardment of; Schlieffen plan; Serbian campaign 1914-15; Shrapnel Corner; Somme, First and Second Battles of 1916 and 1918; Souchez, Battle of; St Eloi; Storm troops; Tannenberg and the Masurian Lakes, Battles of; Thiepval (Somme); Thiepval Wood; Toc H; Togoland 1914; Trentino, Battle of; Trones Wood (Somme); Tsingtau, siege of 1914; Tyne Cot; Verdun; Vimy Ridge, Battle of 1917; Vittorio Veneto, Battle of 1918; Voormezele; Warsaw, Battle of 1914; Wieltje; World War I; Wytschaete; Y Ravine; Yarmouth, raid on; Ypres, First Battle of (Oct 1 1914); Ypres, Second Battle of (April 2 1915); Ypres, Third Battle of (Aug 3 1917); Yser, Battle of the; Zandvoorde; Zeebrugge raid 1918; Zeppelin raids; Zimmermann telegram.

World War II

Aarhus; ABDA Command; Admiralty Islands; Alam Halfa; Albania, Italian invasion of 1939; Aleutian Islands (1942-43); Altmark incident 1940; landings at; Anzio, Allied landings; Anzio, Allied breakout from; Anzio, German counteroffensives; Ardennes (1940, 1944-45); Armistice negotiations, German in Italy; Armistice negotiations, Italian; Arnhem, Battle of; Arras, Battle of 1940; Atlantic, Battle of; Atlantic wall; Avranches, Battle of; Babi Yar; Balkans, German campaign in 1941; Banzai charge; Bardia, Battle of 1941; Barents Sea, Battle of Dec 1942; Bataan-Corregidor campaign 1942; Beda Fomm, Battle of 1941; Berlin, Battle for 1945 (Land); Berlin, Battle of 1943-44 (Air); Big Week 1944; Bir el Gubi; Bismarck Sea, Battle of 1943; Bizerta; Bletchley Park; Bloody Ridge, Battle of 1942; Bodyguard (deception plans); Bologna, Allied autumn offensives towards; Bougainville campaign 1943-44; Brandenburg Unit; Britain, Battle of; Britain, planned invasion of 1940; Broad front strategy; Bruneval raid 1942; Budapest, Battle for 1944-45; Buerat, Battle of; Burma campaign 1942-45; Caen, Battle for 1944; Cairo and Tehran conferences 1943; Calabria, naval action off; Camino Monte, Battles of; Cape Bon, naval action off; Cape Esperance, Battle of 1942 (Guadalcanal); Cape Gloucester (New Britain); Cape Spada, naval action off; Cape Spartivento, naval action off; Cape St George (Pacific); Casablanca Conference 1943; Cassino, Battles of 1944; Cassino, bombing of the monastery; Ceylon, Battle of 1942; Chain Home; Channel Dash 1942; Channel Islands, occupation of; Chengtu (B-29 base); Cherbourg, capture of 1944; China-Burma-India theatre; Chindit Operations; Clark Field (Manila); Coast Watchers; Colditz; Colmar pocket; Cologne, thousand bomber raid on 1942; Coral Sea, Battle of 1942; Corregidor operations 1942 and 1945; Cos and Leros; Coventry, bombing of 1940; Crete, German invasion of; Crimean campaign 1941-44; Cyrenaica, Rommel's first offensive into; Cyrenaica, Rommel's second offensive into; Dakar 1940; Dams raid 1943; Darwin, Battle of 1942; Dieppe raid 1942; Dnieper, Battle of the 1943; Donets, Battle of 1943; Dresden, bombing of; Duisburg convoy; Dunkirk 1940; Dutch East Indies campaign 1942; East Prussian offensive 1944-45; Eastern Solomons, Battle of the 1942; Eben Emael fort, capture of 1940; Eindhoven; El Agheila, Battle of; El Alamein Line, British withdrawal to; El Alamein, Battle of; El Alamein Line, defence of; El Alamein, pursuit from; Elba, capture of; Enfidaville, Battle of; Eritrea, British campaign in; Ethiopia, British campaign in; Etna Line; Falaise Gap, Battle 1944; Felix (German plan); FIDO (Fog dispersal); Final Solution; Finland, Russian invasion of 1939-40; Florence, Battle for; Flying Tigers (American volunteer group); Force H; Force K; Force Z; France, Battle of 1940; France, capitulation in the Mediterranean; France Southern, Allied invasion of 1944; Free French; Garigliano river, crossing of; Gazala, Battle of; Genghis Khan Line; Gideon Force; Gothic Line; Gothic Line, breaching of; Greater East Asia Co-prosperity Sphere; Greece, first Italian invasion of; Greece, second Italian invasion of; Greece, German invasion of; Greece, liberation of; Greer USS (incident Sept 1941); Guadalcanal campaign 1942-43; Guadalcanal, naval battles off; Gustav Line; Gustav Line, breaching of; Hamburg, Battle of 1943; Hiroshima, atomic attack on; Hitler Line; Hollandia campaign 1944; Holocaust 1933-45; Home Guard; Hongkong, fall of 1941; Hürtgen forest, Battle of 1944-45; Indianapolis USS, sinking of; Iraq, Rashid Ali rebellion; Italian campaign 1943-45; Italy, German occupation of; Iwo Jima, Battle of 1945; Japan, plan to invade 1945; Java sea, Battle of the 1942; July Plot 1944; Kaiten; Kamikaze; Kasserine Pass, Battle of 1943; Katyn Wood massacre 1940; Kerch Peninsula, Battle of 1941-42; Keren, Battle of 1941; Kharkov, Battles of 1942 and 1943; Kiev, Battle of 1941; Kohima, the struggle for; Kolombangara, Battle of 1943; Komandorski Islands, Battle of the 1943; Kula Gulf, Battle of 1943; Kursk, Battle of 1943; Kwajalein-Eniwetok, Battle of 1944; Leckwitz (meeting of US and Red Armies 1945); Ledo Road; Lend Lease; Leningrad, siege of 1941-44; Leyte campaign 1944-45; Leyte Gulf, Battle of 1944 (sea); Lidice; Lingayen Gulf; Long Range Desert Group; Low Countries, invasion of 1940; Lübeck, bombing of 1942; Lüneburg Heath; Luzon campaign 1945; Maastricht; Madagascar campaign 1942; MAGIC; Majo Monte, Battle for; Makassar Strait, Battle of; Malaya and Singapore 1941-42; Malmédy massacre; Malta convoys; Malta, siege of; Manchurian campaign 1945 (Soviet-Japanese); Mannheim, bombing of 1940; Maquis; Mareth line, Battle of; Mariana Islands campaign 1944; Matapan, Battle of 1941; Médenine, Battle of 1943; Mediterranean campaigns 1939-45; Mediterranean, war in the air; Mediterranean, war at sea; Mers-el-Kébir, bombardment of; Mersa Matruh, Battle of 1942; Messina, crossings of the Straits of; Metz, Battle of 1944; Midway, Battle of 1942; Mindanao; Minsk; Morrison shelter; Moscow, Battle of 1941; Moscow Conference; Nagasaki, atomic attack on; Namsos, landings at; Narvik, Battles for; Nazi-Soviet Pact 1939; New Guinea campaign; Nijmegen; Normandy, invasion of 1944; North African landings; North Cape, Battle of the 1943; Northwest European campaign 1944-45; Norway, German invasion of; Norwegian campaign 1940; Nuremberg, bombing of 1944; Nuremberg Trials; Okinawa campaign 1945; Oradour-sur-Glane; Orel, Battle of 1943; Ormoc; Orne river; Orsogna, Battles of; Ortona, Battle of; Osaka, bombing and mining of; Pantellaria; Paris, liberation of 1944; Pearl Harbor; Peenemünde; Pegasus Bridge; Peleliu; Penang; Philippine Sea, Battle of 1944; Philippines, fall of the 1941-42; Philippines, reconquest of the 1944; Ploesti, bombing of 1943; PLUTO; Po river, crossing of the; Po river, Battle of the; Poland, invasion of 1939; Poland, reconquest of 1944-45; Potsdam Conference; Quebec conferences 1943-44; Quisling; Rabaul campaign 1942-45; Rangoon campaign 1942-45; Rapido river campaign 1944 (Italy); Ravenna, capture of; Rennell Island, Battle of 1943; Reuben James USS (Sunk 31.10.41); Rhine crossing 1945; Rimini Line, breaching of; River Plate, Battle of the; Romagna river crossings; Rostov, Battle of 1941; Rotterdam, bombing of 1940; Ruhr, Battle of the 1943; Ruhr Pocket, Battle of the 1945;

Russia, invasion of 1941; Russian campaign 1941-44; Ruweisat, First Battle of; Ruweisat, Second Battle of; St Nazaire raid 1942; Saipan campaign 1944; Salamaua; Salerno, landings at and Battle of; San Bernadino Strait; Sangro river, Battle of; Santa Cruz, Battle of 1942; Savo Island, Battle of 1942; Schweinfurt, bombing of 1943-44; Sedan, German breakthrough at; Serchio, German offensive; Sevastopol, Battle of 1942; Shinano (Jap warship Nov 1944); Shinyo; Sicily, invasion of 1943; Sidi Barrani, Italian advance to; Sidi Barrani, Battle of 1940; Sidi Bou Zid; Sidi Rezegh, First Battle of; Sidi Rezegh, Second Battle of; Siegfried Line; Sino-Japanese War 1937-45; Sirte, First Battle of; Sirte, Second Battle of; Smolensk, Battles of 1941 and 1943; Solomon Islands campaign 1942-44; Somaliland, British; Somaliland, Italian; South East Asia Command (SEAC); Stalingrad, Battle of 1942-43; Strategic bombing offensive (Germany); Strategic bombing offensive (Japan); Sudan, Italian invasion of; Sydney Harbour, raid on 1942; Syria, British invasion of; Taranto, air attack on 1940; Taranto, landings at; Tarawa campaign 1943; Tassafaronga, Battle of 1942 (Sea); Tell el Eisa; Tenaru river, Battle of the 1942; Termoli, Battle for; Tiger convoy; Tobruk, British capture of 1941; Tobruk, British reconnaissance in force towards ("Brevity"); Tobruk, German siege of; Tobruk, Rommel's capture of; Tobruk, second British offensive to relieve ("Battleaxe"); Tobruk, third British offensive to relieve ("Crusader"); Tokyo, bombing of 1942-45; Torgau (US Russian meeting Elbe 1945); Totensonntag, Battle of; Trasimeno, Battle of Lake; Treblinka; Trieste, capture of; Tripoli; Tripoli, British advance to; Truk campaign 1944; Tunisian campaign; Ukraine campaigns 1941 and 1943-44; ULTRA; Vaagso raid; Vella Gulf, Battle of 1943 (sea); Volkssturm; Volturno; Waffen SS; Wake Island, Battle of 1941; Walcheren; Warsaw, fall of 1939; Warsaw rising 1944; Washington Conference; Werewolves; West wall; Western Desert campaign; World War II; Yalta Conference 1945; Yugoslavia, British operations in; Yugoslavia, German invasion of; Yugoslavia, German counter-partisan operations in.

Korea

Air Pressure Strategy and Targeting System; Australian forces in Korea; Bloody Ridge, Battle of 1951; British forces in Korea; British Commonwealth Occupation Force, Japan (BCOF); Canadian forces in Korea; Chinese forces in Korea; Chongchon river, Battle of the; Chongju; Chosin reservoir; Commonwealth Division; Demilitarized Zone (DMZ); Eighth Army (US-Korea); French forces in Korea; Geneva conference on peace settlement in Korea 1954; Heartbreak ridge, Battle of 1951; Helicopter medical evacuation; Hook The, Battles of; Imjin river, Battle of the 1951; Inchon landings 1950; Indian army in Korea; Jamestown Line; Japan bases for UN Command and forces; Japan, logistic support by; Kaesong; Kansas Line; Kapyong river, Battle of the; Koje Island, prison camp; Korea, Democratic People's Republic of, state and govt (North); Korea, Republic of, state and govt (South); Korean War 1950-53; Little Gibraltar (Hill 355); Manchuria; MiG Alley; MiG Operation; Military Armistice Commission; "Moolah" Operation; Namsi, Battle of 1951 (air); Neutral Nations Repatriation Commission; Neutral Nations Supervisory Commission; New Zealand forces in Korea; North Korean People's Army; Osan, Battle of; Pakchon, Battle of; Panmunjom, armistice negotiations; Pork Chop Hill, Battle of 1953; Prisoners of war; Punchbowl; Pusan Perimeter campaign 1950; Pyongyang; Republic of Korea (ROK) Army; Seoul, Battle of 1950; Smart bombs; Soviet military assistance for North Korea; "Strangle" Operation; Taegu; Taejon; Thirty-eighth Parallel; UNC Allies; UNCOK; UNCURK; United States Navy in Korea; United Nations Security Council; United Nations General Assembly; United States Air Force in Korea; UNKRA; Unsan, Battle of; UNTCOK; Utah Line; Wake Island (Truman-MacArthur meeting); Wolmi-do; Wonju; Wonsan, siege of; Wonsan landing; Yalu river.

Vietnam

A Shau, Battle of; Agroville Program; Allied Forces, Vietnam; An Loc, siege of; An Lao Valley, Battle of 1966; Ap Bac, Battle of; Army of the Republic of Vietnam (ARVN); B-2 Front; Ban Me Thuot, Battle of 1975; Bien Hoa; Binh Xuyen; Binh Gia; Border War 1950; Cam Ranh Bay; Cambodia (wars since Independence); Cao Bang 1950; Cao Dai religious sect; "Cedar falls" Operation (1967); Chieu Hoi; City Bunker complex, Cambodia; Civil Operations and Rural Development Support (CORDS); Civilian Irregular Defense Group (CIDG); Con Thien, Battle for; Cordon and search operations; COSVN; Dak To, Battle of (1967); Da Nang;

De Lattre Line; Democratic Republic of Vietnam (DRV); Dien Bien Phu; Easter offensive (1972); "Fairfax" Operation; Fire Support Base (FSB); Fishhook; "Flaming Dart" Operations I and II; Fontainebleau Conference; FULRO; Geneva agreements 1954; Green Berets (US Special Forces); Haiphong; Hamlet Evaluation Survey; Hanoi; Hill fights, Vietnam War 1967; Ho Chi Minh Trail; Ho Chi Minh campaign 1975; Hoa Hao religious sect; Hoa Binh, Battle of 1951-52; Hobart HMAS; Hue, Battle of 1968; Ia Drang river, Battle of the (1965); Indochina, French reoccupation of; Indochina, Japanese invasion of; Indochina-French War 1946-54; Iron Triangle; "Junction City" Operation 1967; Khe Sanh, siege of 1968; Khmers Rouges; Kontum; "Lam Son 719" Operation 1971; Land reform; Lang Son, Battle of 1979; Laos (wars since Independence); "Lea" Operation; "Linebacker" Operations 1972 (air); Loc Ninh, Battle 1967; Local Self-defense Forces Militia RVN; Local Forces Militia NFL; "Lorraine" Operation 1952; "Market Time" Operation; McNamara wall; Mekong river; "Menu" Operations; Military Assistance Command Vietnam (MACV); Montagnards; My Lai massacre 1968; Na San, Battle of 1952; Nam Dong, Battle of 1964; National Liberation Front of South Vietnam (NLF); "Neutralize" Operation; New Jersey USS; Nghia Lo Ridge campaign 1952; Pacification Programs; Paris peace talks; Parrot's Beak; Pathet Lao; "Pegasus" Operation; People's Liberation Armed Force (PLAF); People's Army of Vietnam (PAVN); Perth HMAS; Phoenix Program; Phuoc Tuy Province; Phuoc Binh; Plain of Reeds; Plain of Jars; Plei Me, Battle of 1965; Pleiku; Provincial Mobile Forces NFL; Provisional Revolutionary Government of South Vietnam (PRG); Red River delta campaign 1951; Republic of Vietnam (South) (RVN); Revolutionary Development Program; River Assault Groups (RAGS); Rockpile, Battle of the; "Rolling Thunder" bombing campaign; Rung Sat Special Zone; Search and destroy operations; Sihanouk Trail; Sino-Vietnamese War 1979; SLAM; South East Asia Lake Ocean River Delta Strategy (SEALORDS); Special Forces (ARVN); Strategic Hamlet Program; Task Force 77; Tchepone (Sepone); Territorial Forces Militia RVN; Tet offensive 1968; "Texas" Operation (Lien Ket); Tonkin Gulf incident 1964 (sea); Tou Morong, Battle of 1966; United States forces in Vietnam; Van Tuong Peninsula, Battle of 1965; Viet Minh; Viet Cong; Vietnam, wars since unification; Vietnam, Second War 1965-75 (Japanese occupation to date); War Zone D; War Zone C; Xuan Loc, Battle of.

Acknowledgments

Abbreviations used are: T, top; B, bottom; L, left; R, right; C, centre; TL, top left; TR, top right; CR, centre right; BL, bottom left; BR, bottom right; IWM – Imperial War Museum; MARS – Military Archive and Research Services, Lincs.

p.1, Robert Hunt Library; 2, Signal/Robert Hunt Library; 4B, Paul Wilkinson Archive; 4T, Paul Wilkinson Archive; 6, Signal/Paul Wilkinson Archive; 8, National Maritime Museum/ET Archive; 9, Nelson Museum, Monmouth/ET Archive; 12-13, Bundesarchiv, Koblenz; 13TL, Bundesarchiv, Koblenz; 13TR, Peter Newark's Military Pictures; 16, IWM; 17T, Roger Viollet/ET Archive; 18-19, Jessica Johnson; 18-19C, Bundesarchiv, Koblenz; 21B, IWM; 23, Gamma /Frank Spooner; 26, ECPA; 27, IWM; 28, IWM; 30, IWM; 32, Popperfoto; 34, Popperfoto; 36, Gamma/Frank Spooner; 39, Bundesarchiv, Koblenz; 42, IWM; 45, Hulton Deutsch Picture Company; 47, IWM/Taylor Photo Library; 48, Robert Hunt Library; 49, IWM; 50, Popperfoto; 51, Bundesarchiv, Koblenz; 52, Gamma/ Frank Spooner; 53, IWM; 54, IWM; 56, Bundesarchiv, Koblenz; 58, Canadian Short Film and Video Centre; 60, IWM; 61, IWM; 62, Popperfoto; 63, IWM; 65, Bruno Barbey/Magnum; 66L, IWM; 66R, Peter Newark's Military Pictures; 67B, Jessica Johnson; 67C, Jessica Johnson; 67T, Jessica Johnson; 68L, Paul Wilkinson Archive; 70, IWM/Robert Hunt Library; 71, IWM/Robert Hunt Library; 74, IWM; 75, IWM/ Robert Hunt Library; 79B, Rene Burri/Magnum; 79T, Bell Helicopter; 81, Hulton Deutsch Picture Company; 86, Popperfoto; 87, Popperfoto; 90, Popperfoto; 91, IWM; 92, Popperfoto; 94, IWM; 96, IWM; 97, Popperfoto; 99B, Popperfoto; 99T, Novosti; 101, Bibliothèque Mational Paris/ET Archive; 102, Robert Hunt Library; 103, Robert Hunt Library; 104, Popperfoto; 105, IWM; 107, IWM; 109, Popperfoto; 110, Bundesarchiv, Koblenz; 113, IWM; 117, IWM; 119, IWM; 120L, ECPA; 120R, IWM; 121, IWM; 122, IWM;

123T, Robert Hunt Library; 123B, Popperfoto; 124, IWM; 125, IWM; 126, IWM; 128, IWM; 130-1, Paul Wilkinson Archive; 135, Robert Hunt Library; 137CR, Robert Hunt Library; 137T, IWM; 141CR, Hulton Deutsch Picture Company; 141TR, Hulton Deutsch Picture Company; 145, Bundesarchiv, Koblenz; 147, IWM; 149, Hulton Deutsch Picture Company; 152, IWM; 153, IWM; 154, Hulton Deutsch Picture Company; 157, IWM; 159, Robert Hunt Library; 160, ECPA; 163, Popperfoto; 164, Robert Hunt Library; 166, Bundesarchiv, Koblenz; 167, IWM; 168, Popperfoto; 169, IWM; 170, IWM; 171, Tirage Archives/Magnum; 172, Bundesarchiv, Koblenz; 173, Bundesarchiv, Koblenz; 177, Bundesarchiv, Koblenz; 178, IWM; 179, Robert Hunt Library; 183, Robert Hunt Library; 184, IWM; 186L, IWM; 186R, IWM; 188, Gamma/Frank Spooner; 189, Robert Hunt Library; 190, IWM; 191, IWM; 192, Bundesarchiv, Koblenz; 193, Taylor Photo Library; 197, Robert Hunt Library; 199, RAF Museum, Hendon; 208, MARS; 209, Robert Hunt Library; 210, IWM; 211, IWM; 213, Robert Hunt Library; 214, Robert Hunt Library; 219, Hulton Deutsch Picture Company; 223, IWM; 225L, IWM; 225R, Ullstein Bilderdienst; 226, Popperfoto; 230L, Popperfoto; 230R, Bundesarchiv, Koblenz; 234, IWM; 237, IWM; 238, P Jones Griffiths/John Hillelson/Magnum; 242, IWM; 244, ECPA; 246, Robert Hunt Library; 248, Novosti; 251, Robert Hunt Library; 253, IWM; 254, Popperfoto; 255, Bundesarchiv, Koblenz; 256B, Robert Hunt Library; 256T, Ullstein Bilderdienst; 257, Don McCullin/ Magnum; 258, Hulton Deutsch Picture Company; 260, Popperfoto; 262, ET Archive; 263, Popperfoto; 264B, Robert Hunt Library; 264T, Robert Hunt Library; 265, ET Archive; 270, Don McCullin/Magnum; 271, Don McCullin/Magnum; 273, Robert Hunt Library; 274, Bundesarchiv, Koblenz; 275, ECPA; 278, Novosti; 280, Bundesarchiv, Koblenz; 282, Robert Hunt Library; 284, Robert Hunt Library; 287, IWM; 289, IWM; 292, Bundesarchiv, Koblenz; 295, Bundesarchiv, Koblenz;

296, Popperfoto; 297, Popperfoto; 298, Novosti; 299, Popperfoto; 301, Robert Hunt Library; 306, IWM; 307, IWM; 308, Paul Wilkinson Archive; 313B, Popperfoto; 313T, IWM; 315, IWM; 316, IWM; 317, Robert Hunt Library; 319, Popperfoto; 321T, Adam Winkler/Gamma/ Frank Spooner; 323B, Robert Hunt Library; 323C, Gamma/Frank Spooner; 324, Popperfoto; 326, Popperfoto; 327, Popperfoto; 328, MARS; 329, Robert Hunt Library; 330B, Robert Capa/Magnum; 330-331, Robert Capa/Magnum; 331, David "Chim" Seymour/ Magnum; 333, Popperfoto; 335B, ET Archive; 335TL, ET Archive; 335TR, JC Charmet/ET Archive; 337, Popperfoto; 339B, IWM; 339T, IWM; 340, Robert Hunt Library; 342, IWM; 344, Bundesarchiv, Koblenz; 346, IWM; 350, Robert Hunt Library; 352, IWM; 355, Bundesarchiv, Koblenz; 357B, IWM; 357T, Popperfoto; 360, Bundesarchiv, Koblenz; 361, IWM; 363, Bundesarchiv, Koblenz; 366, Popperfoto; 367, IWM/ Robert Hunt Library; 369, Robert Hunt Library; 370, IWM; 371, Explorer Archive; 376, IWM; 378, IWM; 380, IWM; 381, IWM; 382B, Robert Hunt Library; 382T, IWM; 385, Sipa Press/Rex Features; 387, US Air Force/ ET Archive; 389B, Rex Features; 389T, Rex Features; 398, Rex Features; 399B, Popperfoto; 399T, US Dept of Defense/MARS; 401, Robert Hunt Library; 402, Popperfoto; 404, Popperfoto; 406, Robert Hunt Library; 408, Robert Hunt Library; 410, Robert Hunt Library; 416, Robert Hunt Library; 417, IWM; 420, Ullstein Bilderdienst; 421, Novosti; 422, Popperfoto; 423, Popperfoto; 424B, Novosti; 424T, Robert Hunt Library; 428, Popperfoto; 431B, Robert Hunt Library; 431T, Novosti; 434, IWM; 435, IWM; 436, ECPA; 437, IWM; 440, IWM; 442T, Novosti; 442B, Robert Hunt Library; 445, Bundesarchiv, Koblenz; 449B, Bundesarchiv, Koblenz; 449T, Popperfoto; 454, Popperfoto; 455, Bettman News Photo/Hulton Deutsch Picture; 456, Popperfoto; 457, IWM; 458B, IWM; 458T, Robert Hunt Library.